SOCIAL PSYCHOLOGY

SOCIAL PSYCHOLOGY
THIRD EDITION

ROBERT S. FELDMAN

University of Massachusetts at Amherst

Prentice
Hall

Upper Saddle River, New Jersey 07458

Library of Congress Cataloging-in-Publication Data

Feldman, Robert S. (Robert Stephen),
    Social psychology: Robert S. Feldman.—3rd ed.
    p.cm.
    Includes bibliographical references and index.
    ISBN 0-13-027479-8 (alk. paper)
    1. Social psychology. I. Title.
HM1033 .F4 2001
302—dc21   00-033992

VP/Editorial Director: Laura Pearson
Executive Editor: Bill Webber
Development Editor: Barbara Muller
AVP and Director of Production and Manufacturing:
    Barbara Kittle
Managing Editor: Mary Rottino
Project Manager: Lisa M. Guidone
Prepress and Manufacturing Manager: Nick Sklitsis
Prepress and Manufacturing Buyer: Tricia Kenny
Creative Design Director: Leslie Osher
Art Director/Interior Designer: Anne Bonanno Nieglos
Cover Design: Thomas Nery

Chapter Opener Art Creation: Bruce Killmer
Art Manager: Guy Ruggiero
Line Art Coordinator: Mirella Signoretto
Photo Research: Linda Sykes
Image Specialist: Beth Boyd
Manager, Rights and Permission: Kay Dellosa
Director, Image Resource Center: Melinda Reo
Director of Marketing: Beth Gillett
Marketing Manager: Sharon Cosgrove
Copyeditor: Kathy Pruno
Proofreader: Rainbow Graphics
Indexer: Niels Buessem, Andover Publishing Services

Acknowledgments for copyrighted material may be found beginning on
p. 587, which constitutes an extension of this copyright page.

Cover art © Julia Lapine. Represented by Carolyn Potts and Associates, Inc.

This book was set in 10.5/12 Garamond by Lithokraft II and was printed
by Von Hoffman Press. The cover was printed by The Lehigh Press, Inc.

© 2001, 1998, 1995 by Prentice-Hall, Inc.
A Division of Pearson Education
Upper Saddle River, New Jersey 07458

Printed in the United States of America
10 9 8 7 6 5 4 3 2

ISBN 0-13-027479-8

Prentice-Hall International (UK) Limited, *London*
Prentice-Hall of Australia Pty. Limited, *Sydney*
Prentice-Hall Canada Inc., *Toronto*
Prentice-Hall Hispanoamericana, S.A., *Mexico*
Prentice-Hall of India Private Limited, *New Delhi*
Prentice-Hall of Japan, Inc., *Tokyo*
Pearson Education Asia Pte. Ltd., *Singapore*
Editoria Prentice-Hall do Brasil, Ltda., *Rio de Janeiro*

To Kathy, my love.

BRIEF CONTENTS

CONTENTS

ix

CHAPTER 13 | Law and Order

Applying Social Psychology in the Legal and Political Arenas   422

CHAPTER 14 | Groups

Joining with Others   458

SPECIAL FEATURES

PREFACE

A glance at any daily newspaper illustrates the extremes of human social behavior. We see violence, heroics, war, political scandal, terrorism, bravery, and a multitude of other manifestations of the extraordinary range of social conduct. At the same time, our own personal lives—involving friends, family, neighbors, lovers, acquaintances, and even chance encounters with total strangers—reflect the stuff of social behavior.

Each of our experiences with our social environment raises a host of questions. What are the sources and consequences of kindness and cruelty? Why and how are people susceptible to the influence of others? How do we develop and maintain our relationships with other individuals? How do people come to grips with the meaning of their social environment? How does our culture influence our behavior?

The discipline of social psychology addresses such questions. Embracing a vast range of human behavior, the field seeks to answer the fundamental issues that underlie our social world. It is a discipline that holds the promise of providing real improvements in the human condition.

The central challenge in writing an introduction to social psychology is to capture the essence of a dynamic, ever-changing discipline. Social psychology must be presented in a way that fosters readers' intrinsic interest in social psychological phenomenon, doing so with scientific integrity and accuracy.

THE GOALS OF THIS BOOK

To meet this challenge, the third edition of *Social Psychology* has been written keeping in mind three major goals. First and foremost, it provides a broad, balanced overview of social psychology. It introduces readers to the theories, research, and applications that constitute the discipline, examining both the traditional areas of the field as well as more recent innovations. The book pays particular attention to the applications developed by social psychologists. While not slighting theoretical material, the text emphasizes what social psychologists know and how this knowledge may be applied to real-world problems. In fact, the very structure of the book is designed to make the applied material as prominent as the theoretical material by integrating more applied chapters throughout the text, rather than relegating them to the end of the book.

The second major goal of the text is to explicitly tie social psychology to students' lives. The findings of social psychologists have a significant degree of relevance to students, and this text illustrates how these findings can be applied in a meaningful, practical sense. For instance, applications are presented within a contemporaneous framework. The book includes current news items, timely world events, and contemporary uses of social psychology that are designed to draw readers into the field. Numerous descriptive scenarios and vignettes reflect everyday situations in students' lives, explaining how they relate to social psychology. For example, each chapter begins with an opening prologue that provides a real-life situation relating to the chapter subject area. This scenario is reconsidered at the end of the chapter, where integrative, critical-thinking questions tie the prologue to the chapter content. Furthermore, all chapters also have The Informed Consumer of Social Psychology section, which explicitly suggests ways to apply social psychological findings to students' experiences. Each chapter also includes a feature called Applying Social Psychology that discusses ways social psychology research is being used to answer problems of an applied nature.

Finally, the third goal of the text is to make the field of social psychology engaging, accessible, and interesting to students. The book is user friendly and written in a direct, conversational voice, meant to replicate as much as possible a dialogue between author and student.

Social Psychology, third edition, is a text that students can understand and master on their own, without the intervention of an instructor. To that end, it includes a variety of pedagogical features. Each chapter contains a Looking Ahead overview that sets the stage for the chapter, a running glossary, a numbered summary, a list of key terms and concepts, and an epilogue. In addition, each chapter has three Review and Rethink sections that provide enumeration of the key concepts and questions that promote and test critical thinking.

In short, *Social Psychology* seeks to blend and integrate theory, research, and applications. Rather than concentrating on a few isolated areas and presenting them in great depth, the emphasis is on illustrating the breadth of social psychology. Concentrating on the scope of the field permits the examination of a variety of evolving and nontraditional areas of social psychology. Finally, the text seeks to illustrate social psychology as it now stands and is evolving, rather than providing a detailed historical record of the development of social psychology. While covering the classic studies, the decided emphasis is on the field in its current state.

Ultimately, this text seeks to provide a broad-based overview of social psychology, emphasizing its theories, research, and applications. It is meant to show the relevance of social psychology to students' lives while acquainting them with the scientific basis of the discipline. It is designed to be a user-friendly text, one that captures the excitement—and promise—of a growing, developing scientific field.

SPECIFIC FEATURES

CHAPTER-OPENING PROLOGUES
Each chapter begins with a short vignette that describes an individual or situation that is representative of basic social psychological phenomena. For instance, chapter prologues tie descriptions of ethnic cleansing, James Byrd Jr.'s murder at the hands of white extremists, and a couple falling in love to social psychological principles presented in their respective chapters.

PROLOGUE
A Fatal Ride

James Byrd Jr.'s torso was found first. When police in Jasper, Texas, went out to Huff Creek Road . . . to check out reports of a dead body, they turned up the badly mutilated remains of the 49-year-old black man—and a trail of blood. Deputies followed the dark red stains for a mile and found Byrd's head. Then his right arm. Another mile, and they found tennis shoes, a wallet, even his dentures. And then the trail ended, at a churned-up patch of grass strewn with empty beer bottles, a lighter bearing white supremacist symbols and a wrench set inscribed

APPLYING SOCIAL PSYCHOLOGY
This feature, found in every chapter, describes current social psychological research or research issues applied to everyday problems. They include descriptions of ambivalent stereotyping, the slime effect (explaining why we dislike likeable behavior), and attitude change over the course of the life span.

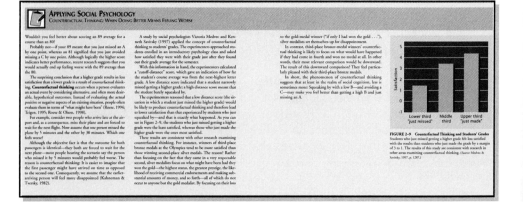

SPEAKING OF SOCIAL PSYCHOLOGY

Gloria Balague
Sport Team Specialist
Year of Birth: 1941
Education: Five-year degree in Psychology, University
of Barcelona, Spain; M.A., Psychology,
University of Illinois at Chicago; Ph.D.,
Clinical and Social Psychology, University
of Illinois at Chicago
Home: Chicago, Illinois

"One of the best skills a team can have is the ability to communicate with each other openly and effectively."

Although teamwork is a foundation for any successful endeavor involving a group of people pursuing a single goal, in the highly competitive area of sports, teamwork makes or breaks the success of the group.

Sports psychologist Gloria Balague, who has worked closely with the 1992 U.S. Olympic track and field team and the 1992 and 1996 U.S. Olympic gymnastics teams, notes that a sports team's success is affected by several factors relating to group performance.

"Spectators can have a major impact on the performance of a team. It often raises the level of motivation, but it also raises the level of anxiety. Depending on the level of the team's experience, this anxiety can affect the outcome," she said.

"For an experienced team, it enhances performance, and consequently the increase in anxiety can increase the intensity of play, which is good," Balague added. "With an inexperienced team, it tends to interfere. Moreover, for those teams that require a lot of precision—such as basketball—the skills are less likely to tolerate anxiety."

According to Balague, pressure becomes exceptionally high when one individual on a team is more clearly defined as responsible, such as goalie in hockey or soccer, a kicker in football, or a basketball player shooting a foul shot.

Two other areas of importance that can affect teamwork are communications and coaching. "One of the best skills a team can have is the ability to communicate with each other openly and effectively," Balague said. "As soon as the lines of communication break down, a team can start to lose effectiveness, and it can happen quickly.

"Ultimately, it is very important to a team's success to have a mixture of skills, ranging from physical to social."

"For instance, if one of the team members gets anxious and makes a mistake, and another team member makes a face, a third member can interpret this as anger. As play continues, communication becomes unchecked," she explained. "Performance can be affected dramatically and confidence is also affected. If they think a particular team member will not pull his or her weight, then they won't pass the ball to that person."

Coaching is also a major factor in determining the success of a team. According to Balague, one of the most common mistakes a coach can make is being too negative when interacting with team members.

"Coaches have a tendency to tell athletes what they do wrong, and that's relatively negative and often not very helpful," said Balague. "What the athletes need to be told is how to do something right. If they are only told what they are doing wrong, you can see the morale of the team sinking. They need to know what they can do right to build confidence."

Finally, players on the bench—teammates who are not actually participating in the competition—can strongly influence a team's performance.

"When the team becomes demoralized and the bench becomes quiet, and they hang their heads, it transmits the sense of loss. Players on the field pick up on that. It does have an impact," she said.

"Ultimately, it is very important to a team's success to have a mixture of athletes with a variety of skills, ranging from physical to social."

SPEAKING OF SOCIAL PSYCHOLOGY
These boxes report interviews that were conducted with people who use the findings of social psychology, either explicitly or implicitly, in their work. For the most part, interviewees are not social psychologists but rather people whose professions employ social psychological findings. For example, interviewees include a newspaper reporter (social cognition), an advertising executive who uses celebrity endorsements (interpersonal attraction), and a trial consultant (law and politics).

SOCIAL.WEB
FINDING LOVE IN CYBERSPACE

Josh Marquis and Cindy Price seemed all wrong for each other. She had just left a job as a foreign-policy analyst at a conservative think tank. He, a district attorney in Astoria, Oregon, was a Democrat who thought Ronald Reagan was, he says, "the Antichrist." But they agreed on one issue: the guilt of O. J. Simpson.

Marquis, now 46, and Price, 44, met in 1995 on a Court TV-sponsored AOL message board devoted to the raging Simpson trial. Neither was seeking love—"just good conversation," says Price, then living in Sherman Oaks, California. They and other prosecution advocates split off into a private 3-mail group. The two admired each other's writing—then hit it off when about 50 group members met at California's Beverly Hills Tennis Club to commiserate over Simpson's acquittal. Back home, their e-mail turned romantic. "This is what they call falling in love," the never-wed Marquis wrote Price, who had been briefly married. She flew to Oregon for their first date and

without cues about their physical appearance. Because physical attractiveness is such a powerful determinant of initial liking, it consequently biases the way that people are perceived. Cyberspace interactions, however, permit people to present themselves as they want to be viewed—in terms of their interests, attitudes, and personalities, devoid of the physical attractiveness factor.

Furthermore, Internet communications permit self-disclosure at an early stage of acquaintanceship. And because many people initially communicate anonymously, the Internet permits them to divulge personal information with less risk than if they were self-disclosing to another person face-to-face (McKenna & Bargh, 1998).

Internet communication has another advantage, particularly for those who are shy and find traditional dating difficult: It allows one to "lurk," the term for someone who simply reads material posted by others. Lurking permits a hesitant observer

SOCIAL.WEB
Four essays describing the impact of technology and the World Wide Web are interspersed throughout the book. These include discussions of the impact of violent video games, finding love in cyberspace, use of e-mail, and social stigmas.

EXPLORING DIVERSITY

CULTURE AND CONFORMITY

Mahatma Gandhi urged his fellow citizens of India to engage in passive resistance to secure their independence.

When Mahatma Gandhi exhorted citizens of India to conform to his then-radical views of passive resistance, he did so by making an emotional appeal based on the right to "manufacture salt" and "weave one's own cloth" (Sinha, 1990, cited in Moghaddam, Taylor, & Wright, 1993). Although such encouragement sounds rather odd to the ear of residents of North America at the beginning of the 21st century, in fact it was quite effective in rallying supporters to Gandhi's cause.

Clearly, conformity to social norms depends on the content of those norms. Moreover, the degree to which conformity is typical and valued varies from one culture to another. Consider, for instance, one of the primary dimensions on which cultures differ: individualism versus collectivism (Triandis, 1990, 1994). Societies reflecting **individualism** hold that the personal identity, uniqueness, freedom, and worth of the individual person are central. People in individualistic societies emphasize that their own goals should hold greater weight than the goals of the groups

EXPLORING DIVERSITY
These sections, integrated within every chapter, highlight issues relevant to the multicultural society in which we live. They illustrate social psychological issues relevant to race, ethnicity, and culture. For example, various Exploring Diversity sections examine cultural influences in attribution, cultural determinations of health, ethnic differences regarding the stigma of obesity, relationships among gay and lesbian couples, and gender and cultural patterns of leadership.

THE INFORMED CONSUMER OF SOCIAL PSYCHOLOGY
Every chapter includes information on specific uses that can be derived from research conducted by social psychologists. For example, various chapters discuss how to draw appropriate conclusions from others' behavior, overcome stereotypes, deal with anger, and resist persuasion.

REVIEW AND RETHINK
Interspersed throughout each chapter are three short recaps of the chapters' main points, followed by questions designed to provoke critical thinking.

SOCIAL LINKS COMPANION WEBSITE (CW)
These marginal icons indicate that relevant material can be found on the World Wide Web by going to the Feldman Social Psychology Website (*http://www.prenhall.com/feldman*). By referring to the specific book page where the Social Link is found, readers will find a link to a relevant Web page.

END-OF-CHAPTER MATERIAL
Each chapter ends with a numbered summary (Looking Back), list of key terms and concepts, and an epilogue containing critical-thinking questions about the chapter-opening vignette.

DEALING WITH ANGER

When angry, count ten before you speak; if very angry, a hundred.
—Thomas Jefferson

When angry, count four; when very angry, swear.
—Mark Twain

Whether you count to 10, 100, or 4 (or swear, for that matter), anger is a psychological state with which most people have to deal. Indeed, most adults experience the emotion of anger considerably more often than they express overt aggression (Tangney et al., 1996).

Although you may suspect that the best response to anger is to ignore it, a considerable amount of data suggests otherwise. As we discussed in Chapter 5, people who consistently suppress their anger may develop a variety of adverse reactions, including physical illness, self-condemnation, and psychological dysfunction (Julius, 1990; Pennebaker, 1990; Mills & Dimsdale, 1993; Redmond & Redmond, 1994).

If unexpressed anger has such negative consequences, what is the best way to deal with the emotion effectively? According to psychologists who have studied the issue, several

THE INFORMED CONSUMER OF SOCIAL PSYCHOLOGY

REVIEW AND RETHINK

Review
- Organizations are groups of people working together to attain common goals.
- The four basic models of organizations are the bureaucratic, human relations, contingency, and Japanese models.
- Organizations have cultures, which are patterns of assumptions, perceptions, thoughts, feelings, and attitudes shared by their members. Some organizations also harbor subcultures.

Rethink
- Compare the Japanese model of organizations with the three Western models. What cultural factors might work for and against the implementation of the Japanese model in Western society—and vice versa?
- How does organizational "culture" differ from organizational "climate"? What does the "strength" of the culture within an organization refer to?

LOOKING BACK

What is aggression?
1. Defining aggression precisely and universally is a difficult matter. Although some experts reject a definition based on intention, most social psychologists view aggression as intentional injury or harm to another individual. (p. 297)

What are the roots of aggressive behavior?
2. Several approaches have sought to identify the roots of aggression. For example, Freud and Lorenz saw aggression as instinctual. The most recent advocates of instinctual views of aggression are evolutionary psychologists, who examine the biological roots of aggression. (p. 300)
3. In contrast to proponents of biological approaches, social learning theorists suggest that aggression is largely learned through the observation and imitation of

WHAT'S NEW IN THIS EDITION?

A considerable number of new topics and areas have been added to the third edition. For instance, advances in such areas as culture, emotions, close relationships, psychophysiology, and evolutionary approaches to social phenomenon receive expanded and new coverage.

In addition, a wealth of contemporary research is cited in this edition. Hundreds of new research citations have been added, most from the last few years. A sampling of topics either newly included in this edition or expanded also illustrates the scope of the revision; they include new material on behavioral genetics, counterfactual thinking, paternalistic and envious prejudice, relationship harmony, resiliency, the slime effect, mandatory volunteerism and helping, exposure to gratuitous violence, the disrupt-then-frame approach to persuasion, and antinormative behavior and deindividuation.

Furthermore, several entirely new features have been added to the third edition. As mentioned earlier, each chapter now includes Social Links, marginal icons linking the textbook to the book's Companion Website on the World Wide Web. In addition, several boxes, titled Social.Web, are interspersed throughout the book. Social.Webs discuss social psychological issues related to technology and the use of the Internet and the Web. Finally, every chapter ends with an Epilogue that asks critical-thinking questions about the chapter-opening prologue.

TEACHING SUPPORTS THAT ACCOMPANY THE BOOK

SUPPLEMENTS FOR INSTRUCTORS

Instructor's Resource Manual with Tests by Diana Punzo and Bill Webb. This manual provides the instructor with resources and test questions in one single volume. The instructor's resource section includes complete lecture outlines, learning objectives, lecture and discussion ideas, projects and activities, and audiovisual suggestions for each chapter. It also contains a new section devoted to showing how information from the Web can be integrated into the classroom or assigned as homework. The test bank provides over 1,000 questions allowing instructors to develop any number and variety of tests covering key terms, concepts, and applications from the textbook. Conceptual, applied, and factual questions are available in multiple choice, true/false, short answer, and essay forms.

PH Custom Tests (Windows, DOS, and Macintosh Formats). This computerized form of the test bank section of the Instructor's Resource Manual with Tests allows instructors to quickly and easily generate their own tests. This testing system provides two-track design for constructing tests—FastTests for novice users and FullTest for more advanced users. PH Custom Test offers a rich selection of features such as OnLine Testing and an Electronic Gradebook.

800-Number Telephone Test Preparation Service. Instructors can call a special toll-free number and select up to 200 questions from the test bank section of the Instructor's Resource Manual with Tests. The test (with an alternate version, if requested) and answer key are mailed within 48 hours, ready for duplication!

ABC News/Prentice Hall Video Library for *Social Psychology.* This customized video library features segments from a variety of award-winning ABC News programs and provides a contemporary look at such topics as cultural diversity, gender, prejudice, and relationships.

ABCNEWS

SUPPLEMENTS FOR STUDENTS

Classic and Contemporary Readings in Social Psychology, **third edition,** compiled and edited by Erik Coats and Robert S. Feldman. This reader is designed to accompany *Social Psychology,* third edition. Each of the fifteen chapters contains two readings—one classic from a primary source, and the other from a contemporary secondary source. Critical thinking questions, focused on metholodology and ethics, conclude each selection. (ISBN: 0-13-087366-7)

Practice Test and Review Manual by Pamela C. Regan. In addition to providing chapter reviews, summaries, and practice tests, this study guide provides five cases per chapter to show social psychological principles in action. Each case describes a typical social interaction, such as buying a used car. After reading the vignette, students are asked a series of questions in which they must analyze what transpired from a social psychological perspective.

Companion Website™. A free Companion Website™ is available at http://www.prenhall.com/feldman. This Website provides learning objectives, practice tests, lists of key terms, related Web links, message boards, and chat rooms for each chapter. Students are given instant feedback on their practice tests along with page references where they can review the correct answers.

***The New York Times* Program.** *The New York Times* and Prentice Hall are sponsoring a *Themes of the Times Program* designed to enhance student access to current information in the classroom. Through this program, the text is supplemented by a collection of time-sensitive articles from one of the world's most distinguished newspapers, *The New York Times.* These articles demonstrate the vital, ongoing connection between what is learned in the classroom and what is happening in the world around us. To enjoy the wealth of information of *The New York Times,* daily, a reduced subscription rate is available in deliverable areas. For information, call 1-800-631-1222.

REVIEWERS

I am grateful to the following reviewers, who provided a wealth of comments, criticism, and encouragement: Ronald Keith Barrett, Loyola Marymount University; William Calhoun, University of Tennessee at Knoxville; Erik Coats, Vassar College; Eric Cooley, Western Oregon State University; Kellina M. Craig, California State University at Long Beach; David Gersch, Houston Community College; Joe Ferrari, Depaul University; Kenneth Foster, Hunter College; Eugene Indebaum, The State University of New York at Farmingdale; Robert Levine, California State University at Fresno; Helen Linkey, Marshall University; Diane Mello-Goldner, Pine Manor College; Carol Milstone, University of Ottawa; Jamie Newton, San Francisco State University; Miles Patterson, University of Missouri at St. Louis; Chia Rosina, East Carolina University; Wesley Schultz, The University of California at San Marcos; Mark Stewart, American River College; and Alan Swinkels, St. Edwards University.

ACKNOWLEDGMENTS

Many people contributed to this book, and in many different ways. Karl Scheibe introduced me to social psychology at Wesleyan University, and his example of teacher–scholar remains an inspiration. My graduate work was done at the University of Wisconsin, where the late Vernon Allen honed my appreciation for the discipline. I could not have asked for a finer education.

My colleagues at the University of Massachusetts provide an atmosphere in which all types of intellectual endeavors are nurtured and supported, and I am grateful to them for making the University a terrific place to work. I have also been continually inspired and challenged by our graduate students, who have been helpful in many ways.

Bill Webber has been a superb editor, and I have enjoyed his savvy and enthusiasm. Barbara Muller, developmental editor on the book, provided thoughtful and sound advice, prompting me to produce a manuscript several magnitudes better than would have been possible without her efforts. I'm also grateful to Sharon Cosgrove, who I'm sure will work her marketing magic. My production manager, Lisa M. Guidone, turned the business of production into an art. Finally, my thanks go to Nancy Roberts, Laura Pearson, and Phil

Miller, who, hovering in the background, unceasingly pushed for excellence. I'm proud to be part of this world-class team.

In addition, I thank Chris Rogers, who long ago started me thinking about doing a book of this sort, and Rhona Robbin, who continues to teach me so much about writing. I also thank Jim Anker and Susan Brennan, who steered me to Prentice Hall.

Finally, I am very grateful to John Graiff, who was involved at every critical juncture in the writing and production of the book. John does a terrific job, and I, as well as readers of this book, are in his debt. I also am very grateful to Dan Hrubes and Chris Poirier, who helped in a number of ways, and with whom I enjoy working immensely. Finally, I thank Erik Coats, who, despite his departure from the University of Massachusetts, still remains eager to provide unsolicited criticism and suggestions.

Ultimately, I thank my family, to whom I owe most everything.

Robert S. Feldman

ABOUT THE AUTHOR

Robert S. Feldman is professor of psychology at the University of Massachusetts, where he is Director of Undergraduate Studies, former head of the Personality and Social Psychology Division, and winner of the College Distinguished Teacher Award. He was educated as an undergraduate at Wesleyan University, where he graduated with High Honors, and at the University of Wisconsin in Madison, from which he earned a Masters and Ph.D.

Author of more than 100 books, chapters, and articles, his books include the edited volumes *Applications of Nonverbal Behavioral Theory and Research* (Erlbaum), *Fundamentals of Nonverbal Behavior* (Cambridge University Press, with Bernard Rimé), and *Social Aspects of Nonverbal Behavior* (Cambridge University Press, with Pierre Philippot and Erik Coats). He is a recipient of grants from the National Institute of Mental Health and the National Institute of the Disabilities and Rehabilitation Research, which have supported his research on nonverbal behavior and emotional development. He is also a former Fulbright lecturer and research scholar.

During the course of his two decades as a college teacher, he has taught social psychology numerous times at a wide range of institutions, including Mount Holyoke College, Wesleyan University, and Virginia Commonwealth University. An excellent cook, a passionate music lover, but a lapsed pianist, he lives with his wife and three children in Amherst, Massachusetts, overlooking the Holyoke mountain range.

SOCIAL PSYCHOLOGY

CHAPTER 1

AN INTRODUCTION TO SOCIAL PSYCHOLOGY

PROLOGUE

Putting a Face on Ethnic Cleansing

In contrast to the inhumanity suffered by hundreds of thousands in the Balkans, there was also a generous outpouring of help from all over the world.

The term *ethnic cleansing,* has an air of sterility about it. But to ethnic Albanians of Yugoslavia, whose lives were torn apart by an "ethnic cleansing" campaign by Serbia, it was anything but sterile.

The stories were grim, yet oddly familiar: a family, forced to flee with only the clothes on their backs as neighbors taunted them . . . hundreds of people, lined up together, shot in cold blood only because they were Albanians living in Serbia . . . a panicked mother who literally lost her infant during the confusion of a forced march into a refugee camp. It was a frenzy of brutality directed at people whose only crime was belonging to a particular ethnic group.

Yet at the same time that the horrific became commonplace, acts of astonishing humanity occurred. People risked their lives to help potential victims escape the savageness, relief workers spent every waking moment tending to the needy, and individuals took families they never met before into their homes. It was as if the worst of human behavior also gave rise to the best. ◼

LOOKING AHEAD

The troubling events in Yugoslavia, which mirror those in other times and places, raise a range of perplexing issues—many of which are central to social psychology. For instance, consider the various perspectives that social psychologists would bring in an effort to understand the situation:

- ◆ Social psychologists who study prejudice and discrimination would seek to understand the roots of the hatred between the different ethnic groups.

- ◆ Social psychologists who study aggression might ask what led the violence in the region to boil over into war.

- ◆ Social psychologists who seek to understand helping and altruism would ask why some people were so generous in what they did for others.

- ◆ Social psychologists who focus on the self might examine how members of the groups changed their views of themselves as a result of being the target—or perpetrator—of ethnic cleansing.

- ◆ Those social psychologists who study relationships might seek to examine how the stresses of war affect friendships and family unity.

- ◆ Social psychologists who study groups might ask about how one ethnic group perceives other ethnic groups.

- ◆ Finally, social psychologists who study attitudes would be interested in how people developed opinions about whether military intervention on the part of non-Yugoslavian countries was warranted.

Although each of these perspectives considers different aspects of ethnic cleansing, they all derive from the same discipline: social psychology. As we will see, the scope of social psychology is wide and in some ways is as varied as the range of human behavior that we find in different social situations.

In this chapter, we orient ourselves to the field of social psychology. After defining the field, we consider the general topics it covers and the boundaries of the discipline. We also discuss the demographics and history of the field, examining how social psychology has evolved over the last hundred years and speculating on the future of the discipline.

Next, we turn to the research techniques used in social psychology. We explore how social psychologists construct and refine specific research questions, and we discuss the various ways that they carry out research. Finally, we consider some threats to the accuracy and validity of research findings, threats that make research on social psychological topics particularly challenging.

In sum, after reading this chapter, you'll be able to answer these questions:

- ◆ What is the scope of social psychology?

- ◆ What are the major milestones and trends in the development of the field, and what is the future likely to hold?

- ◆ How do experimental and correlational research differ, and what are the major types of studies that social psychologists carry out?

- ◆ What are the major threats to the validity of research findings?

ORIENTATION TO SOCIAL PSYCHOLOGY

Each of us is a novice social psychologist. For instance, if you've ever wondered why you've been persuaded to buy a coat that cost more than you intended to spend, you've asked the same question that a social psychologist would ask. If you've watched as a friend unsuccessfully tried to strike up a romantic liaison at a party, you've made the same kind of observation that a social psychologist might make. And if you were part of a group project in a class and tried to figure out why some of the people did more work than others, you were raising the same sort of query that a social psychologist would consider.

Social psychology is the scientific study of how people's thoughts, feelings, and actions are affected by others. Social psychologists seek to investigate and understand the nature and causes of people's behavior in social situations.

In some ways, the definition of social psychology is disarmingly simple. However, in a field that covers as much territory as social psychology, it is necessary to probe behind the

social psychology: The scientific study of how people's thoughts, feelings, and actions are affected by others.

definition. In fact, it is useful to consider separately the implications of each of the parts of the definition.

♦ Social psychology is a *scientific* discipline. Social psychologists do not rely on abstract, untested theories. Instead, as we'll see in the latter part of this chapter, they use precise, methodical, and systematic means of investigation in order to understand phenomena. This does not mean that social psychologists do not develop theories. They do. However, they don't conclude with a theory, but rather use scientific procedures to test the adequacy of the theory.

♦ Social psychology focuses on *people*. Although some research focuses on the social lives of nonhumans, the vast majority of research conducted by social psychologists studies humans. Social psychologists seek to identify the broad, universal principles that underlie all social behavior, while also considering the consequences of membership in particular ethnic groups and cultures.

♦ Social psychology considers people's *thoughts*. Much of contemporary social psychology is devoted to a cognitive approach that scrutinizes the thinking processes of individuals in order to understand social behavior. Social psychologists largely reject the view, advocated by some behavioral psychologists, that we should concentrate solely on observable behavior. Instead, they suggest that thinking processes are a central component of social behavior.

♦ The *feelings* that people experience are a central part of social psychology. Our likes and dislikes and emotions are investigated by social psychologists, who use a variety of means to measure our feelings about social stimuli. In fact, some social psychologists study physiological reactions, such as heart rate and brain wave patterns, as a means of assessing how people feel in a given situation.

♦ Finally, social psychologists study people's *actions*. By examining behavior—ranging from whom we choose as romantic partners to what brand of soft drink we purchase—social psychologists come to understand how the social world in which we live affects our behavior.

Given the broad definition of social psychology, the field clearly covers a great deal of territory. As a consequence, many diverse areas of study fit comfortably within the discipline (see Table 1–1).

For example, one major focus of social psychologists is on the *consequences of social influences on individuals and the way they understand the world.* Even when we are alone, the way

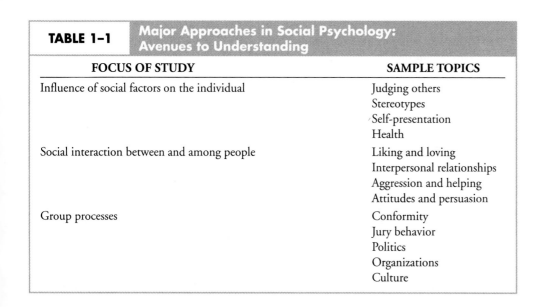

TABLE 1–1	**Major Approaches in Social Psychology: Avenues to Understanding**
FOCUS OF STUDY	**SAMPLE TOPICS**
Influence of social factors on the individual	Judging others Stereotypes Self-presentation Health
Social interaction between and among people	Liking and loving Interpersonal relationships Aggression and helping Attitudes and persuasion
Group processes	Conformity Jury behavior Politics Organizations Culture

The field of social psychology examines the behavior of people when they are in groups, with another person, or even when they are alone.

we think and behave is affected by others. And the influence of others on our behavior is even more profound when they are physically present.

Accordingly, social psychologists interested in the individual person study such basic processes as perception, learning, and the ways information is acquired and processed. More specifically, social psychologists concerned with individual processes might examine how people make judgments about others, how people learn attitudes, and how jurors determine whether a defendant is guilty or innocent.

Social interaction between and among people is a second principal focus of social psychologists. Those who take this approach are interested in the unique characteristics of social behavior when two or more people are talking, working, bargaining, planning, or engaging in any of the myriad activities that people do together. For example, these social psychologists investigate how one person can influence another, why we begin to like someone and fall in love, and why people are aggressive or helpful toward others.

The third primary focus of social psychologists is on *group processes*. Those taking this approach study the properties that groups exhibit, such as roles, status, group pressure, and communication patterns. On a broader stage, social psychologists study organizations, societal institutions such as political and legal systems, and culture. Questions about how to maintain our independence in group situations, how to promote the effective functioning of organizations, and how culture influences our views of the world illustrate the range of the group processes focus.

THE BOUNDARIES OF SOCIAL PSYCHOLOGY: DIFFERENTIATING THE FIELD

Our discussion of the wide sweep of social psychology may leave you wondering if the field excludes anything. In fact, the field does have boundaries, although, as we'll discuss later, they are not rigid. As you can see in Figure 1–1, social psychology is part of the broader field of psychology, which itself is situated in the general realm of social sciences. Although members of related disciplines may address issues that are similar to those addressed by social psychologists, they adopt special—and different—perspectives according to their particular discipline.

Within the field of psychology, social psychology is most closely related to personality psychology. Personality psychology focuses on the identification of individual characteristics or traits that differentiate one person from others and the processes that explain the consistencies within an individual's behavior. Like social psychologists, personality psychologists

FIGURE 1–1   **Situating Social Psychology**   Social psychology is allied with several other disciplines outside the field and is also related to several subareas within psychology.

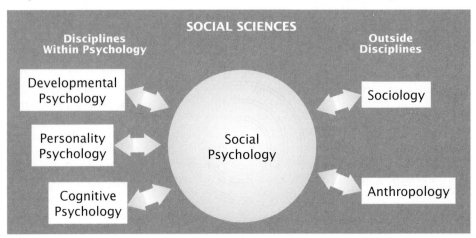

focus on the individual. However, personality psychologists look primarily at what makes individuals different from one another, whereas social psychologists seek to determine the similarities that join us as individuals and explain our behavior in general. A personality psychologist would ask, for example, why some people are more prejudiced than others. A social psychologist would consider how prejudice arises in general and how to diminish its damaging consequences.

Outside the field of psychology, social psychology's nearest cousins are sociology and anthropology, two disciplines that have related but distinct vantage points. Sociology is the science of society and social institutions. It focuses on how members of groups are subject to culturally universal influences that determine how the group as a whole performs. When sociologists consider group behavior, they are apt to concentrate on the behavior of the group as a whole. In contrast, when social psychologists look at a group, their focus will be centered on the individual members of the group.

Let's suppose we are interested in how the racial makeup of a school affects the school's educational effectiveness. A sociologist would be most apt to compare the overall success of school graduates, as a group, in different types of schools. In contrast, a social psychologist might approach the issue by looking at individual students in the context of a particular school, perhaps probing how socioeconomic background might affect particular students' performance.

Anthropology, the study of the consequences of culture on human behavior, is another discipline closely related to social psychology. Anthropology takes a broad approach to social phenomena, concentrating on the universals in a given culture and placing only minor emphasis on the individual. For instance, anthropologists might examine how family structure is related to economic productivity in different cultures. In contrast, social psychologists, taking their more individualistic approach, might investigate whether certain child-rearing practices lead individual children to higher levels of motivation to achieve.

Areas of interest are not the only factors that differentiate social psychology from other disciplines: The methods used by social psychologists to investigate problems are also distinctive. Sociologists and anthropologists are most likely to examine existing situations, assessing them as they naturally occur. For example, a sociologist interested in relationships might examine marriage and divorce statistics, attempting to derive an understanding of the phenomenon by looking at statistical trends.

In contrast, social psychologists rely most heavily on experimental methods: They actively make changes in a situation, which permits them to examine the consequences of that change. To study relationships, then, a social psychologist might set up an experiment to learn the conditions under which people are attracted to one another.

THE DEMOGRAPHICS OF SOCIAL PSYCHOLOGY: THE CHANGING FACE OF THE DISCIPLINE

EXPLORING DIVERSITY

Wanted: Social psychologist to teach at a large urban university. The successful applicant will be expected to teach classes in basic and advanced social psychology, social influence, and attitudes. Duties include carrying out research in a specialty area and advising student interns.
Wanted: Advertising firm seeks social psychologist to conduct survey research on consumer buying habits. Must be willing to travel and consult with clients nationally and internationally. Strong background in basic social psychology and statistics necessary.
Wanted: U.S. government seeks a staff social psychologist to work on an AIDS prevention program. Candidates must have experience in developing health education programs and in reaching economically deprived populations.

Many social psychologists apply their knowledge in areas outside of a laboratory setting including human services agencies.

As these want ads indicate, the range of jobs performed by social psychologists is wide. The majority of social psychologists are employed by colleges and universities, but many also work in business and industry, for state and federal governments, and in human service agencies. Furthermore, as we'll see throughout the book in the Speaking of Social Psychology interviews, social psychology is part of many people's everyday jobs, even if they have not received doctorates in the discipline.

Social psychologists tend to have fairly uniform educational backgrounds. Almost all have a master's degree (either an M.A. or an M.S.) and a doctorate (Ph.D.) in psychology, although some individuals who identify with the discipline have degrees in sociology. The Ph.D. is a research degree, meaning that all social psychologists are trained in research methods. A typical Ph.D. program takes 4 to 5 years to complete, and study toward the degree includes conducting original research in the form of a dissertation.

Once on the job, social psychologists tend to be productive researchers. Although less than 3% of all psychologists who belong to the American Psychological Association (APA) identify themselves as social psychologists, the topics of more than 10% of the articles indexed in the leading register of psychological publications pertain to social processes, social issues, and experimental social psychology (PsychINFO, 1998).

Who are social psychologists? Of the approximately 2,106 members of the American Psychological Association who identify themselves as social psychologists, most are male, and most are white. Like other areas of psychology (as well as other scientific fields), social psychology has been traditionally dominated by white men.

However, the discipline is changing. The major shift has been in the number of women entering the field. In recent years, significantly more women have received graduate degrees in social psychology, considerably expanding the proportion of women making up the field (see Figure 1–2). In fact, recent figures show that more women than men are enrolled in graduate social psychology programs, and since 1984 more women than men received doctoral degrees in social psychology. These figures suggest that eventually women may constitute the majority of social psychology practitioners. Furthermore, even though significant numbers of women have only recently entered the field, women have already made important contributions to the discipline. For example, 8 of the 50 most frequently cited authors in social psychology texts are women (Gordon & Vicari, 1992; American Psychological Association [APA], 1996).

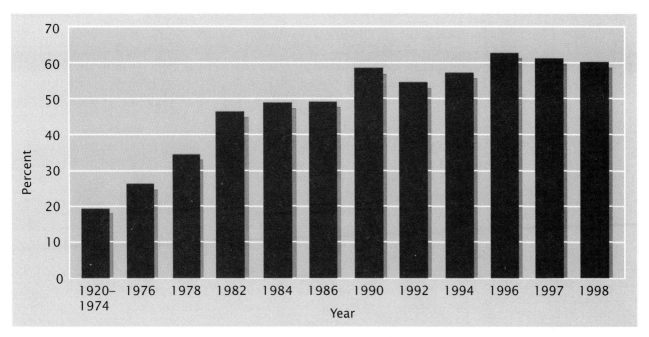

FIGURE 1–2   Proportion of Ph.D.s in Social Psychology Awarded to Women The proportion of women who received Ph.D.s in social psychology was small until the 1980s; since then it has increased dramatically. In fact, since 1984, more women than men have received doctorates in the field. (*Source:* APA, Research Office, 1999).

The numbers of racial minorities within the field are also increasing, although at a far lower rate than those for women. For example, just 6% of all social psychologists who identify their racial background on surveys are members of minority groups. However, minority representation is likely to increase, because 13% of the recent graduates of social psychology doctoral programs are members of ethnic minorities (APA, 1996).

The lack of minority representation in social psychology represents a serious problem for several reasons. First, the discipline may be impaired by an absence of minority perspectives, with important questions going unasked. In addition, minority social psychologists act as role models for younger minority students. Consequently, unless the numbers of minority social psychologists are enlarged, the field will be hampered by a lack of minority representation.

THE ROOTS OF SOCIAL PSYCHOLOGY: A BRIEF HISTORY

Pinpointing the birth of a discipline that covers as much territory as social psychology is largely impossible and, in some ways, not terribly productive. Although such philosophers as Plato and Aristotle wrote about social behavior centuries ago, no individual can be singled out as the founder of social psychology. Scientific disciplines develop slowly, coming to life typically not in sudden revolutionary intellectual leaps forward but as a consequence of evolutionary changes in approaches, perspectives, and interests (Jones, 1998).

The field in its infancy.   Two dates stand out if we are to seek the birth of the field: 1897 and 1908. In 1897, Norman Triplett carried out what has come to be considered the first experiment in social psychology. Triplett, as we'll discuss in Chapter 14, was interested in the effects of competition on performance, and he conducted an experiment to compare the performance of participants who were alone with that of participants in groups (Triplett, 1897). Triplett's study remains a notable moment in the evolution of the field. Although contemporary scientists can criticize various aspects of Triplett's methods, his research was the first experiment in which social psychological issues were studied. Triplett was also asking a question that has endured: What are the effects of other people's presence on an individual's behavior?

Another way of establishing the beginning of the field of social psychology is to consider the earliest publication of textbooks on the discipline. This happened in the first decade of the twentieth century, when two books with "social psychology" in their titles were published. One was written by American Edward Ross (1908) and the other by English psychologist William McDougall (1908).

The publication of these textbooks was unmistakable testimony that a new discipline had emerged, one with a distinct perspective and orientation. For instance, McDougall argued that social behavior was produced largely by instincts. Today, almost all social psychologists would reject such a perspective. However, McDougall's view was influential for several years in the early development of the field and was seen as evidence that social behavior could be studied in a systematic, methodical manner.

Still, not until the 1920s can social psychology be said to have outgrown its infancy. In 1924, a third book with "social psychology" central to its title was published, this one written by Floyd Allport. The approach and emphasis of Allport's book in some ways are remarkably similar to those of contemporary social psychologists. For instance, Allport wrote about such topics as the comprehension of emotions via facial expressions and the consequences of an audience on performance—two areas that are widely researched even today.

Social psychology's adolescence.   Allport's text gave impetus to the growing field of social psychology, and the field entered an adolescence marked by rapid spurts forward. For example, in the 1930s, Muzafer Sherif began a series of pioneering studies on *social norms,* the shared rules that influence our behavior (Sherif, 1935, 1936). In systematically studying these norms, Sherif laid the groundwork for subsequent research on conformity and other forms of social influence.

During the same period, one of social psychology's towering figures emerged: Kurt Lewin. Lewin, a German social psychologist who immigrated to the United States when the Nazis came to power, developed a theory to explain how the interaction between people's environment and their personal characteristics combined to produce social behavior (Lewin, 1931, 1935, 1936). Lewin's contribution went well beyond the theoretical; his research vividly illustrated how theoretical concepts could shed light on solutions to the most practical, everyday problems. His research also illustrates how the impetus for research may come from the basic values that social psychologists hold.

Lewin—who was deeply affected by the ravages of World War II—attempted to contribute to the war effort in several ways. For example, he studied ways of convincing people to make dietary changes, persuading them to eat less-preferred, but more readily available, foods during the war (Lewin, 1943). Similarly, he examined different styles of leadership, attempting to demonstrate the benefits of democratic government over more authoritarian and laissez-faire doctrines (Lewin, Lippitt, & White, 1939). Lewin's work provided the foundations of contemporary research on attitude change, persuasion, and political psychology (discussed in Chapters 11 and 13).

The field enters adulthood.   Following the end of World War II, social psychology entered into a golden period in which unabashed confidence reigned. Social psychologists believed the solutions to significant social problems were within their grasp. The government agreed, generously funding social psychological research. Much of the research focused on groups and group behavior, examining ways of making groups more productive, seeking methods for improving interactions among group members, and investigating how groups influence the attitudes of their members. The 1950s, in fact, can be considered "the decade of the group" in social psychology.

The emphasis on groups did not last, however. In the late 1950s, Leon Festinger published a book that was to influence a generation of social psychologists: *A Theory of Cognitive Dissonance* (Festinger, 1957). As we discuss in Chapter 10, Festinger introduced the concept of *cognitive dissonance,* which states that when people hold opposing attitudes within themselves they experience unpleasant feelings, which they are motivated to reduce. This simple principle led to some surprising findings. For instance, social psychologists learned that people sometimes grow to like the things for which they suffer most (Aronson & Mills, 1959), and that receiving a small reward for saying things we don't believe is more effective in producing attitude change than receiving a large reward (Festinger & Carlsmith, 1959).

The theory of cognitive dissonance led not only to a large number of studies designed to test the theory, but also to other research that focused more on people's personal thoughts, or cognitions, and less on the social processes among individuals. In addition, the norm for social psychological experiments became studies that included elaborate deceptions, motivated by social psychologists' desire to involve experimental participants in engaging, dramatic situations. Furthermore, experimental results that were counterintuitive, yielding findings that common sense would be unable to predict, became prized within the field. For instance, social psychologists discovered that the likelihood of someone receiving aid in an emergency situation is greater if only a few potential helpers are present than if there are many—a phenomenon we'll discuss further later in the chapter.

Crisis!   During the 1960s and 1970s, the number of social psychologists and the range of topics they studied increased substantially. At this same time, though, the field entered a period of crisis. Social psychologists began to express self-doubt about the utility and value of their science. These doubts took several forms.

Some social psychologists complained that the field was merely the study of social practices at a given moment and that social psychology was unable to identify universal, fundamental social principles that spanned multiple historical eras and cultural backgrounds (Gergen, 1967, 1973; Wallach & Wallach, 1994). Other social psychologists argued that the dominant form of data collection in the field—the laboratory experiment—was severely limited. As we'll discuss later in this chapter, critics suggested that laboratory experiments, especially those that use college students as participants, are not representative of the world outside the laboratory. In addition, the extensive use of experiments that deceived participants about their true purpose raised concerns regarding the ethics and validity of the discipline (Kelman, 1967, 1968; Stracker, Messick, & Jackson, 1969; Forward, Canter, & Krisch, 1976).

Although the crisis in social psychology was real, it did not diminish the output of theory or research. In fact, the 1970s saw the emergence of several major areas of research that have had lasting influence. For instance, social psychologists began to focus on *attribution,* the processes by which we seek to determine the reasons behind behavior (Jones & Harris, 1967). Furthermore, gender became an established area of study, as social psychologists grappled with the factors that lead to differences in the behavior of men and women (Maccoby & Jacklin, 1974).

Ironically, the crisis in social psychology, which proved to be temporary, strengthened the field of psychology. Social psychologists focused increasing attention on historical and cultural factors, taking them into account in the development of theory and the choice of experimental procedures. Moreover, ethical concerns led to the development of alternatives to the traditional laboratory experiment, especially experiments that involve deception. We will discuss these alternatives later in the chapter.

Current developments.   Today, social psychology is a mature, multifaceted discipline. As we've already seen, the scope of the field is broad. Social psychologists' interests range from the most individualistic aspects of social life to sweeping questions about society and culture.

The dawn of the 21st century is bringing new emphasis on multiculturalism and the role of culture in people's social worlds.

Two major trends mark contemporary social psychology. One is an increased emphasis on how *cognitive* factors—our thoughts, beliefs, attitudes, and general understanding of the world—influence social behavior. In an approach that has been imitated by other disciplines in the broader field of psychology, many social psychologists have embraced the belief that cognitions are a primary aspect of social behavior.

Consequently, social psychologists who specialize in cognitive factors have argued, quite convincingly, that our understanding of social behavior is not complete without the knowledge of how people understand the world around them. For instance, cognitive approaches lead researchers to explore the ways in which people act as "naive scientists," seeking to uncover the causes of their own and other people's behavior; the errors and biases that distort our perceptions of others; and the ways our goals and motivation affect the strategies we adopt for understanding the world (Fiske & Taylor, 1991; Sherman et al., 1999).

A second major trend in the field is the increasing application of knowledge derived by social psychologists in settings outside the laboratory. Of course, social psychology has always had an interest in applying its findings, as illustrated by Kurt Lewin's early work on changing dietary preferences during World War II. However, the most recent decades have seen the emergence of several subdisciplines within social psychology that are centered on particular social issues.

For instance, the social psychology of well-being and health (which we discuss in Chapter 5), of law (Chapter 13), and of industrial and business settings (Chapter 15) have developed as major topical areas in the field. Social psychologists focusing on these areas might ask questions such as, "How do the interpersonal skills of physicians affect patient recovery rates?"; "How do juries reach decisions?"; and "How do pay scales affect worker performance?" In each case, social psychology theory and research have been applied in an effort to solve vexing social problems.

SOCIAL PSYCHOLOGY IN THE NEW MILLENNIUM

As the world starts a new century, social psychology begins its second century as a discipline. Where is the field headed? Although even the most scientific of crystal balls is clouded, we can make a few predictions with some confidence about where social psychology is headed.

Among the most important trends: (1) There will be an increasing emphasis on multiculturalism in social psychology; (2) new approaches, particularly those involving biology and evolutionary approaches to social phenomenon, will have an increasing impact on the field; and (3) the traditional boundaries that have differentiated social psychology from other areas are likely to become less distinct.

Developing a culturally diverse discipline.   An examination of simple demographic patterns in the United States is sufficient to point to the need for greater understanding of the role of culture in people's social worlds. For example, the proportion of people of Hispanic background is expected to more than double by the year 2050, and the proportion of non-Hispanic whites will decline from the current 74% to 53%. College enrollments are expected to reflect this trend; the number of minority students is expected to mirror the rise in the general population. As minority populations continue to grow at a rapid pace, social psychologists have begun to recognize the need for taking cultural factors into account (Klineberg, 1990; U.S. Bureau of the Census, 1996; see Figure 1–3).

How does a concern with culture correspond to the explicit desire of social psychologists to identify universal principles of social behavior? The answer is that general principles can be identified only if social psychology takes into account people's cultural backgrounds. For instance, social psychologists will never know just how general their findings relating to social behavior are unless they include research participants from a variety of backgrounds. Furthermore, because the very questions that social psychologists ask are a consequence of a particular cultural context, cultural factors must be taken into account (Segall, Lonner, & Berry, 1998).

In fact, social psychology is already taking issues of cultural diversity into account. For example, as we discuss in Chapter 7, researchers examining close relationships have attempted to identify the factors that result in the choice of a marriage partner. By addressing the question cross-culturally, they have been able to identify some universal principles that guide the

FIGURE 1–3   State-by-State College Enrollment by Racial and Ethnic Group   Social psychologists are beginning to recognize the need for taking cultural factors into account as the minority population in the United States grows at a rapid rate. The percentages refer to the proportion of minority population in each state. (*Source: Chronicle of Higher Education,* 1999.)

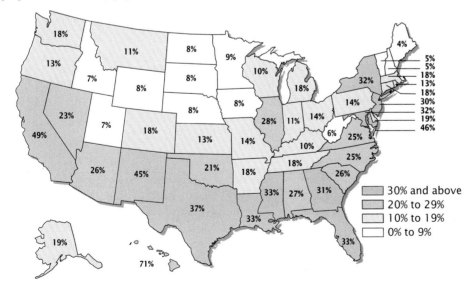

kinds of choices that are made—principles that never would have been identified unless research was conducted in several very different types of cultures (Buss et al., 1990).

Similarly, researchers looking at the development of relationships have traditionally focused on heterosexual couples and have largely ignored homosexual relationships. Today, however, social psychologists have come to recognize that a full understanding of liking and loving (as well as other social psychological phenomena) must consider gays and lesbians along with other groups. Consequently, increasing numbers of studies seek to identify the factors that lead to the development, maintenance, and deterioration of gay and lesbian relationships (Herek et al., 1991; Kurdek, 1991; Patterson, 1994).

Another factor that has led to blossoming interest in multiculturalism within the discipline is the increasing presence of social psychologists living and working outside the United States. Although the bulk of social psychological research and theory building is done in the United States, social psychologists are active in every part of the globe. Furthermore, the easy availability of communication via e-mail and the World Wide Web increasingly has encouraged collaboration by social psychologists in different parts of the globe. This intellectual exchange of ideas clearly will promote substantial advances in the discipline (Hewston et al., 1988).

The growth of biological and evolutionary approaches.   Advances in our understanding of genetics and the biology that lies behind behavior lead to a second prediction about social psychology's future: that increasing attention will be paid to the biological and evolutionary underpinnings of social behavior.

Behavioral genetics studies the effects of heredity on behavior. Growing out of classic research that examined stable characteristics such as hair and eye color, behavioral genetics considers how our social behavior is affected by genetic factors. For example, behavioral geneticists examine such questions as whether risk taking is an inherited trait—it does, at least in part, seem to be!—and whether aggressive tendencies are inherited.

A related area of study, *evolutionary psychology,* applies the laws of evolution to behavior. For example, social psychologists who take an evolutionary stance argue that when it comes to the development of close relationships, women are naturally attracted to high-status men (because they are potentially better providers), while men are most attracted to younger, more attractive women (who are potentially better at producing children). The argument goes even further, stating that these preferences were developed hundreds of thousands of years ago as part of the evolution of the species (Buss & Kenrick, 1998; Geary, 1998).

Both behavioral genetics and evolutionary psychology are highly controversial areas, producing much contentiousness among proponents of alternate explanations for social behavior. In particular, critics of the two approaches object to explanations that suggest that behavior is "hard-wired" into the species and unfolds automatically (Eagly & Wood, 1999). Evolutionary psychology, in particular, has been a lightening rod of criticism, because it seems to suggest that status differences between men and women are inevitable results of evolutionary forces. The disputes between proponents and critics of evolutionary psychology have led to lively arguments among social psychologists holding different positions, and the differing perspectives promise to enliven the field in the new century.

A blurring of boundaries.   Our third prediction about the future of social psychology is that the traditional boundaries among different disciplines are likely to become less distinct. For example, the point at which social psychology leaves off and other disciplines begin is likely to become more ambiguous. Social psychological findings have been used with increasing frequency by people in other fields. Hence, educators interested in cooperative learning draw on the social psychological literature on groups; business executives consider the work of social psychologists in designing advertising campaigns; politicians look to social psychological findings to lure votes; and safer-sex advocates use persuasive techniques designed by social psychologists (e.g., Feldman, 1990, 1992; Miller, 1995; van Wel & Knobbout, 1998;

Houston, Doan, & Roskos-Ewoldsen, 1999; Vakratsas & Ambler, 1999). As we will see throughout this book, the work of social psychologists has had significant implications for a variety of areas.

Moreover, the relationship between social psychology and other disciplines is not a one-way street. Social psychologists have also embraced, and profited from, work going on in other disciplines—a tendency that will likely grow. For example, social psychology has benefited from findings in allied disciplines such as clinical psychology, industrial-organizational psychology, sociology, and anthropology (e.g., Jahoda, 1986; Fiske, 1991a). As the lines between disciplines become increasingly blurred, traditional distinctions among various types of research are likely to grow less distinct. In particular, social psychologists have traditionally distinguished between purely *theoretical research,* designed specifically to test some explanation of social behavior, and *applied research,* meant to provide practical solutions to immediate problems.

As social psychology develops further, the distinction between theoretical and applied research may well diminish. Even the most applied research has relevance to theory-building efforts, for results of applied studies are invariably used not only for their immediate applications to the problem at hand but also for their implications for theory. Furthermore, work in applied areas can illuminate where gaps exist in theoretical formulations. For instance, programs that are designed to increase interracial interaction in schools have helped social psychologists hone theories of prejudice (Hedrick, Bickman, & Rog, 1993; Semin & Fiedler, 1996).

At the same time, theory can lead to solutions to applied problems that might otherwise be overlooked. Theories are able to suggest new approaches and strategies for dealing with the problems facing society. For example, theories of group processes have led to the use of work groups in industry and cooperative learning in educational settings.

In sum, social psychologists are increasingly recognizing that both theoretical and applied research have similar underlying goals. Whether explicit or implicit, social psychologists have a fundamental commitment to building knowledge, a concern regarding the quality of life, and an interest in how knowledge of social psychology is ultimately utilized and employed (Mayo & LaFrance, 1978; Smith, 1990). Although the paths to these goals may differ, depending on the orientation of a particular social psychologist, the interaction between theory and applied research in the quest for improving the human condition has become increasingly accepted in the field (Snyder, 1993).

In its continuing emphasis on finding solutions to social problems, the discipline is echoing earlier calls for melding theoretical and applied research. As Kurt Lewin wrote several decades ago:

> Many psychologists working today in an applied field are keenly aware of the need for close cooperation between theoretical and applied psychology. This can be accomplished in psychology . . . if the theorist does not look toward applied problems with high-brow aversion or with a fear of social problems, and if the applied psychologist realizes that there is nothing so practical as a good theory. (Lewin, 1951, p. 169)

Lewin's dictum that there is "nothing so practical as a good theory" captures a central characteristic of social psychology—the interactive relationship that exists between theories and applications. For example, examine the work of Ann McLendon discussed in the accompanying Speaking of Social Psychology interview.

In considering the kinds of questions social psychologists have asked, we have been introduced to the basic subject matter of the discipline, but our introduction to the discipline is incomplete. Social psychologists don't just raise questions; they answer them. Before beginning our journey through the field of social psychology, then, we need to consider how social psychologists find answers to the questions they ask. In the next section, we discuss the paths followed by social psychologists to conduct research.

REVIEW AND RETHINK

Review

- Social psychology is the scientific study of how people's thoughts, feelings, and actions are affected by others.

- Although the roots of the discipline can be traced to Plato and Aristotle, the field has been a scientific discipline for less than 100 years.

- Major recent trends include an increased emphasis on cognitive factors and the application of knowledge outside the laboratory.

- In the future, it is likely that there will be increasing emphasis on multiculturalism in social psychology and that the traditional boundaries that have differentiated social psychology from other areas are likely to become increasingly blurred.

SPEAKING OF SOCIAL PSYCHOLOGY

Ann McLendon

AIDS Educator

Year of Birth: 1949

Education: B.A., Education, Howard University; M.Ed., University of Hartford; doctoral work in education; University of Connecticut; doctorate in ministry, Aspen Christian College

Home: Hartford, Connecticut

"It is important that the norms of the broader community in which they live be influenced in ways that encourage the desired behavior. "

The war against AIDS, one of the most pressing social issues of the 20th century, is being waged on numerous fronts all over the world. In the state of Connecticut, Ann McLendon, AIDS education chief for the state Department of Public Health, is using education and grass-roots community-level intervention as weapons to confront the deadly disease.

"While individual and group-level interventions play significant roles in achieving change in a person's health-related behavior," McLendon says, "any resolutions or promises to change behavior that result from such interventions are doomed to be short-lived without support from one's primary social network in the community. Without equally effective community-level initiatives to complement the individual and group strategies, long-term success is questionable."

A pilot program based on the community approach was launched in Hartford's Par-South Green neighborhood in the mid-1990s.

"We began by developing a neighborhood-specific campaign, which involved in this case having young artists from the neighborhood paint a large mural on a prominent building in the community," McLendon says. "We then arranged a special event to unveil the mural, with the support of local celebrities.

Rethink

- Many of the concerns of contemporary social psychologists were also the concerns of philosophers more than 2,000 years ago. If the topics of interest were the same for both of these groups, why aren't these ancient thinkers considered "psychologists"? What distinguishes contemporary social psychology from early philosophy?

- Most social psychologists believe that their research will yield knowledge that could be used to improve the lives of others and the world in which they live. What dangers exist for a discipline with such aspirations?

- Using the definition of social psychology provided in this chapter, discuss the field's movement into such areas as health, business, and law.

- What are some questions that a social psychologist might ask that relate to advertising? schooling? sports? politics?

"With the mural image in place and the memory of the community event in people's minds, we next had outreach workers go door-to-door in the neighborhood and attend tenants' association meetings. We also contacted local churches and merchants and committed ourselves to working at every level to expand neighborhood awareness of AIDS and HIV."

"Even if we disappear as an agency, the impact will continue because the awareness now belongs to the community."

A follow-up survey conducted in the community found that the results of the community intervention were quite positive, McLendon notes.

"One area that people really identified with was the wide-openness that the mural and our outreach activities brought to the issue. People reported being better able to address the issue of AIDS/HIV in their families and with their children, and having more knowledge about the disease as an epidemic.

"To promote true, long-term HIV prevention and risk reduction behavior in individuals and in target population groups, it is important that the norms of the broader community in which they live be influenced in ways that encourage the desired behavior. This means designing interventions for specific populations within the community, such as religious institutions, parents' groups, school systems, civic groups, and businesses."

The success of the Hartford program led to the development of a similar program in New Haven as well as plans for at least six more community interventions in key Connecticut neighborhoods over the following 18 months.

"As community members take more and more ownership, they make sure that the effort will continue," McLendon says. "Even if we disappear as an agency, the impact will continue because the awareness now belongs to the community."

RESEARCH IN SOCIAL PSYCHOLOGY

It was one of the most graphic examples of human indifference. Kitty Genovese, a young woman living in New York, was savagely attacked by a mugger. During her 30-minute ordeal, Genovese was repeatedly pursued and stabbed. Despite loudly screaming for help, not one person came to her aid—although approximately 40 people heard her cries.

Why didn't anyone come to Kitty Genovese's rescue? The many neighbors who admitted hearing her screams had a similar excuse for not intervening: they believed that because so many people were present in neighboring apartments, someone else would help her.

The disheartening behavior of the bystanders who passively witnessed Genovese's attack ultimately led to one of the most enduring (and surprising) principles of social psychology: The more bystanders present in an emergency situation, the less likely that a given individual will intervene. The way social psychologists reached this conclusion illustrates the paths taken in conducting research.

THEORIES AND HYPOTHESES: FRAMING THE QUESTION

At the heart of all research lies a question that can be addressed scientifically: Why do we conform to group pressure? How do we encourage people to help one another? How does a defendant's appearance affect a jury's deliberations?

Developing theories.   Typically, social psychologists' questions come from *theories,* broad explanations and predictions of phenomena of interest. All of us develop theories of social behavior (Sternberg, 1985; Anderson & Lindsay, 1998). For instance, we may assume that people follow certain standards of dress and behavior because they wish to be popular. Whenever we develop such an explanation, we are actually building our own theories. However, our personal theories usually rest on unverified observations, developed in an unsystematic manner—hardly the stuff from which a science is developed. In contrast, the theories of social psychologists are more formal, based on a systematic and orderly integration of prior social psychological findings and theorizing. Such theories summarize and organize prior observations and permit social psychologists to move beyond observations and make deductions that are not readily apparent from the individual pieces of data that already exist. Consequently, theories provide a guide to the future collection of observations and suggest the direction in which research should move.

Suppose, for example, you were interested in developing an explanation for why bystanders are reluctant to intervene in emergency situations—an issue that social psychologists Bibb Latané and John Darley tackled. The impetus for Latané and Darley's theorizing: the murder of Kitty Genovese, where no bystanders helped.

In their quest to explain why no one helped Genovese, Latané and Darley developed the theory of *diffusion of responsibility* (Latané & Darley, 1970). Their theory suggested that the greater the number of bystanders or witnesses to an event that requires help, the more the responsibility for helping is perceived to be shared by the bystanders. Because of this sense of shared responsibility, then, the more people present in an emergency situation, the less personally responsible each person feels, and the less likely it is that any single person will provide help (Darley & Latané, 1968).

Formulating hypotheses.   Although Latané and Darley's theory makes sense, it was merely the first in a series of stages. The next challenge they faced was to formulate a hypothesis. A **hypothesis** is a prediction stated in a way that permits the prediction to be tested. Hypotheses must be drawn from theories. Theories provide a background and basis for producing reasonable hypotheses, which can fit together with other known explanations of social phenomena. In this way, we can build a body of information from which to determine the validity of the explanation.

hypothesis: A prediction stated in a way that permits it to be tested.

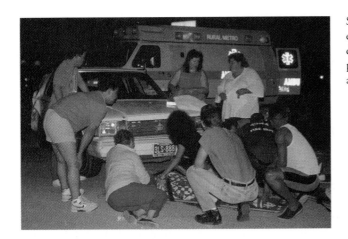

Social psychologists have utilized experimental research to determine how the number of people present at an accident affects helping.

Of course, social psychologists develop hypotheses from sources other than theories. They may have hunches and intuitions like anyone else, but without a valid theoretical underpinning, a hypothesis will do little to explain human social behavior in a larger sense, and consequently it will not advance our understanding of social behavior very far.

Based on their general diffusion of responsibility theory, Latané and Darley derived a straightforward hypothesis: The more people who witness an emergency, the less likely it is that a bystander will provide help (Latané & Darley, 1968). This is just one of several hypotheses that could be derived from their theory. For instance, the researchers might have formulated the hypothesis that if a victim's emergency was likely to affect a bystander in the future, a bystander would be more likely to help. (In fact, this derivation was tested in a later study; Aronson, 1988). But first it seemed most reasonable to test what seemed to be the most basic hypothesis, relating number of bystanders and helping.

Choosing a research strategy.   After developing a hypothesis, researchers must devise a strategy to test its validity. There are two major classes of research to choose from: experimental research and correlational research. **Experimental research** is designed to discover causal relationships between various factors. In experimental research, the researcher deliberately introduces a change in a situation in order to observe the effect that change has on the situation. For instance, experimental research has the potential to determine whether the presence of more people in an emergency situation *causes* less helping.

In contrast, **correlational research** seeks to identify whether an association or relationship between two factors exists. Correlational research cannot be used to determine whether one factor causes changes in the other. For example, correlational research could tell us whether the presence of more people in an emergency is *related* or *associated* with less helping—but not whether their presence *causes* less helping.

Because experimental research can identify cause–effect relationships, it represents the first-choice strategy of most social psychologists. However, correlational research also provides invaluable information, particularly in situations in which it is impossible to carry out experiments due to ethical or logistical constraints. And, as we'll see, both types of research offer significant benefits—and some pitfalls, as well. (Table 1–2 outlines the two classes of research.)

EXPERIMENTAL RESEARCH: ESTABLISHING CAUSE–EFFECT RELATIONSHIPS

To run an **experiment** to test a hypothesis, a researcher must first devise at least two different experiences, or treatments. A **treatment** is the procedure provided by an investigator. One group of participants receives one of the treatments, while other groups of participants receive either no treatment or alternative treatments. The group receiving the treatment is known as the **treatment group**, whereas the no-treatment or alternative-treatment group is called the **control group**. The differing treatments that are given to the two groups are called the experimental **conditions**. (A medical analogy is helpful here: in an experiment to test the

experimental research: Research designed to discover causal relationships between various factors, in which the researcher deliberately introduces a change in a situation in order to observe the effect that change has on the situation.

correlational research: Research that seeks to identify whether an association or relationship between two factors exists, regardless of whether one factor produces changes in the other.

experiment: Procedure to test a hypothesis.

treatment: The procedure in an experiment provided by an investigator.

treatment group: The group that receives the treatment in an experiment.

control group: The no-treatment or alternative-treatment group in an experiment.

conditions: The differing treatments that are given to the different groups in an experiment.

TABLE 1–2	Research Strategies	
	EXPERIMENTAL RESEARCH	**CORRELATIONAL RESEARCH**
Process	Researcher manipulates a situation in order to observe the outcome of the manipulation	Researcher examines previously existing situations
Desired outcome	Information regarding how one factor causes changes in another	Identification of associates between factors
Types	Field experiments Laboratory experiments	Naturalistic observation Archival research Survey research Evaluation research

effectiveness of a drug in *treating* a disease, one group of participants would receive the drug—that is, would be part of the *treatment* group. In contrast, another group of participants would not receive the drug *treatment;* they would be part of the no-treatment *control* group. This example has two conditions: the treatment condition and the control condition.)

The central feature of an experiment, then, is the comparison of the effects of different treatments on different groups of participants. The use of both treatment and control groups permits researchers to rule out the possibility that something other than the experimental manipulation produced the results found in the experiment. For example, if no control group was used, experimenters couldn't be certain that some other factor—such as the temperature of the room, the time of day the study was being conducted, or even the mere passage of time—produced the changes observed. By employing a control group, experimenters can isolate the true cause of their results and can thereby draw inferences about the cause–effect relationship.

Before experimenters can actually develop an experiment, they must make a decision regarding operationalization of the hypothesis. **Operationalization** is the process of translating a hypothesis into specific testable procedures that can be measured and observed. For instance, if we were interested in investigating how the number of bystanders affects helping in an emergency situation, we could operationalize "number of people" as two, three, ten, *or* any other number; "helping" as the number of minutes that pass before participants call the police *or* directly intervene *or* avert their eyes *or* do something else; and the "emergency situation" as one in which someone breaks a leg *or* has a seizure *or* experiences some other type of emergency.

There are many ways of operationalizing a hypothesis. Logic and ethical constraints dictate what choice an experimenter will make. Obviously, the way a hypothesis is operationalized is crucial in determining the kinds of conclusions that may be drawn from a study.

In choosing the operationalization to be used in an experiment, researchers are guided by the variables of interest. *Variables* are behaviors, events, or other characteristics that can change, or vary, in some way. Researchers employ two kinds of variables in experiments: the independent variable and dependent variable. The **independent variable** is the variable that is manipulated in the experiment by the researchers. In contrast, the **dependent variable** is the variable that is measured in an experiment and is expected to change as a result of the experimental manipulation. (A straightforward way of remembering this: A hypothesis predicts how a dependent variable *depends* on the manipulation of the independent variable.)

For instance, let's return to Latané and Darley's hypothesis: The more people who witness an emergency, the less likely it is that help will be provided. To test this hypothesis, Latané and Darley decided to manipulate the number of people present during an emergency situation in order to determine how the number of people present affected their level of helping (Darley & Latané, 1968). Consequently, the independent variable was the number

operationalization: The process of translating a hypothesis into specific testable procedures that can be measured and observed.

independent variable: The variable that is manipulated in the experiment by the researchers.

dependent variable: The variable that is measured in an experiment and is expected to change as a result of the experimental manipulation.

of people present, and the dependent variable was the level of helping displayed by participants in the study.

Once they had identified the independent and dependent variables, Latané and Darley had to determine what operationalization they should use. They could have chosen any one of several paths. For instance, they could have decided to operationalize the "number of people present" (their independent variable) as groups of one, two, three, or even six individuals exposed to an emergency situation. They could have operationalized the emergency situation itself by placing participants in an increasingly smoky room, by having them hear a woman fall and apparently break an ankle, or by having them listen to someone having an epileptic seizure in an adjoining room. Finally, they could have determined that the measure of helping—the dependent variable—should be how quickly a participant responded to the emergency or simply whether the participant responded at all. (In fact, Latané and Darley [1970] used each of these operationalizations in a series of several experiments designed to test the hypothesis.)

Choosing a research setting.   In determining the operationalizations to employ in their research, Latané and Darley also had to choose a setting for the study. Their choices centered on two basic alternatives: the laboratory or the field. A **laboratory study** is a research investigation conducted in a controlled setting explicitly designed to hold events constant. A laboratory may be a room or building designed for research, such as a room in a university's psychology department. In contrast, a **field study** is a research investigation carried out in a naturally occurring setting. An example of a field study is research conducted on a street corner, aboard a bus, or in a classroom.

Both laboratory and field studies carry advantages and drawbacks. In laboratory studies, the environment can be controlled to the smallest detail, permitting an investigator to create a world that involves and engages participants. The laboratory setting protects the study from unexpected and inadvertent intrusions, which may often occur in field settings.

On the other hand, laboratory studies may appear artificial and contrived. Participants in laboratory research certainly are aware that they are in a study, and their behavior (as we discuss more completely later in the chapter) can reflect this recognition. If this occurs, there may be a problem with *generalization,* the application of the results of a study to other settings and populations beyond those immediately employed in the experiment.

Although the laboratory study presents potential problems of generalization, it remains the dominant research technique used by social psychologists. The reason is that the drawbacks of laboratory research can, to a large extent, be overcome through the use of a well-designed study. In laboratory research, it is not necessary, or even appropriate, to re-create a situation exactly as it appears outside the laboratory in order to understand a naturally occurring phenomenon. For example, if we're interested in re-creating an emergency situation in the laboratory, we don't need to include every component of an actual emergency in the real world, such as a dirty street, cars parked along the road, a parent passing by pushing a baby carriage, and so forth.

Instead, a laboratory study attempts to isolate the component parts of a phenomenon in order to capture its essence. Furthermore, because events in a well-designed laboratory study can be controlled in a way that typically is impossible in the field, more accurate inferences about cause–effect relationships often can be made.

In short, effectively designed laboratory studies are high in *experimental realism,* which is the degree to which an experiment is involving and believable and affects a participant. Studies high in experimental realism may or may not also be high in *mundane realism,* the degree to which a study mimics the real world. Even though field studies are high in mundane realism, they do not necessarily provide better information about human behavior: Many real-world settings are simply boring or uninfluential (Aronson et al., 1990; Aronson, Wilson, & Brewer, 1998).

Consequently, we shouldn't be fooled into thinking that either laboratory or field research is inherently better than the other. Instead, the choice depends on the question being asked by the investigators and the type of operationalization of independent and dependent variables

laboratory study: A research investigation conducted in a controlled setting explicitly designed to hold events constant.

field study: A research investigation carried out in a naturally occurring setting.

random assignment: In an experiment, the method of assigning subjects to particular groups on the basis of chance.

control: The degree to which an experimenter is able to limit and restrict events within the experiment to those that are intended.

that the investigator chooses to study. Both the laboratory and the field can provide answers to the kinds of questions social psychologists ask.

Random assignment of participants to conditions.   The final key to the successful design of an experiment involves the assignment of *participants,* as the individuals being studied in experiments are known, to treatment and control groups. In **random assignment**, participants are assigned to a different experimental group or condition on the basis of chance and chance alone. The statistical laws of probability ensure that particular participant characteristics—such as intelligence, motivation levels, sex, and height—will be represented in approximately equal numbers in each condition, as long as participants are assigned on a completely random basis. Random assignment is a simple yet elegant procedure that safeguards researchers' ability to make appropriate interpretations of experimental results.

The virtue of random assignment becomes apparent when we consider alternatives. Suppose, for example, we assigned the first 20 volunteers for a study to the treatment condition, and the second 20 volunteers to a control condition. It is possible that those who volunteer earliest might have different personality characteristics than those who volunteer later. Perhaps, for example, the early volunteers are more motivated, greater risk takers, or smarter than the late-volunteering participants. If the experimental results subsequently show a difference between those participants in the treatment condition and those in the control condition, we would then be unable to attribute the difference to the experimental manipulation alone: It is possible that differences in participant characteristics produced the results.

In contrast, random assignment would assign participants to conditions entirely on the basis of chance. If there were two conditions, each participant would have a 50-50 chance of being in either condition. Consequently, every highly intelligent participant would have a 50-50 chance of being assigned to a particular condition, every risk taker would have a 50-50 chance of being assigned to a condition, and so forth for every participant characteristic. The outcome of such a procedure is that there will be roughly the same number of highly intelligent participants, risk-taking participants, and participants with other characteristics in each condition.

Random assignment enables researchers to avoid *confounding* results: instances in which factors other than the independent variable are allowed to vary. If confounding occurs, a researcher cannot determine whether changes in the dependent variable are due to the manipulation of the independent variable or to the other, confounding factors. For instance, if in one condition of an experiment all the participants are highly intelligent, and in the other condition all the participants are not terribly smart, we would say that confounding had occurred. We would not be able to separate the effects of participant intelligence from the effects due to the experimental manipulations. Random assignment helps ensure that any potential confounding factors are distributed equally across the various experimental conditions, allowing researchers to interpret results with more certainty.

The use of random assignment is one more way in which experimenters seek to maintain control in experiments. **Control** is the degree to which an experimenter is able to limit and restrict events within the experiment to those that are intended. The greater the control over an experimental situation, the greater the confidence an experimenter can have that the results of a study reflect just the experimental manipulations and not any extraneous factors. In contrast, the less control that exists within an experiment, the higher the probability that the experimental results are confounded by unintended factors.

The essentials of an experiment.   We've now considered the key elements of experimental research. To review, experiments comprise the following:

- A hypothesis, a prediction stated in a way that permits it to be tested.

- An independent variable, the variable that the researcher manipulates in the experiment.

- A dependent variable, the variable that is measured in an experiment and that is expected to change as a result of the experimental manipulation.

Experiments, such as these listed on a college's psychology department bulletin board recruiting participants, permit researchers to determine cause-and-effect relationships.

◆ An experimental procedure in which participants are randomly assigned to different experimental groups or conditions of the independent variable.

Only when every one of these elements is present can researchers be assured that they have created a true experiment, one that will allow them to determine cause–effect relationships.

Experimental research in action.   Let's return to Latané and Darley's hypothesis for a moment and consider how it was tested in an actual experiment. In a classic study, Bibb Latané and colleague Judith Rodin (1969) invited participants to engage in a survey of game and puzzle preferences. This was not the true purpose of the study, but the experimenters surmised they had to disguise the actual purpose in order to get a true assessment of participants' behavior in emergency situations. (How could they announce an emergency in advance?)

Upon arrival, an attractive woman led the participants to the testing room and gave them a series of questionnaires to complete. The woman then moved to a different part of the room, separated by a room-dividing curtain. A few minutes later, while participants were filling out the questionnaire, they heard a loud crash and scream that sounded like the chair had collapsed and the woman had crashed to the ground. The participants heard a woman moan, "Oh, my God, my foot . . . I . . . I . . . can't move . . . it. Oh . . . my ankle . . . I . . . can't get this . . . thing . . . off me." She cried and moaned for about a minute longer, but the cries eventually faded away. Eventually, she mumbled something about going outside and was heard knocking over a chair and closing the door behind her. (In actuality, the "emergency" was a tape recording, repeated in every experimental session.) The "emergency" took just over 2 minutes.

The primary independent variable of the study was whether participants were (1) alone or (2) with another participant while they filled out the questionnaires. Participants were assigned randomly to one of these two conditions.

The major dependent measure was whether participants offered aid to the supposed victim. We might expect a fairly high level of helping, because the costs of offering assistance were so low—getting up from a table and entering another part of the room. In fact, a clear majority—70% of the participants—did help, but only when they were in the condition in which they were alone. When participants were in the condition in which they were working in the same room with another participant, only 40% of them helped—a substantial difference.

The findings are surprising only to those who are unaware of Latané and Darley's original hypothesis. Recall that they predicted, based on the concept of diffusion of responsibility, that the more people who witness an emergency, the less likely it is that help will be

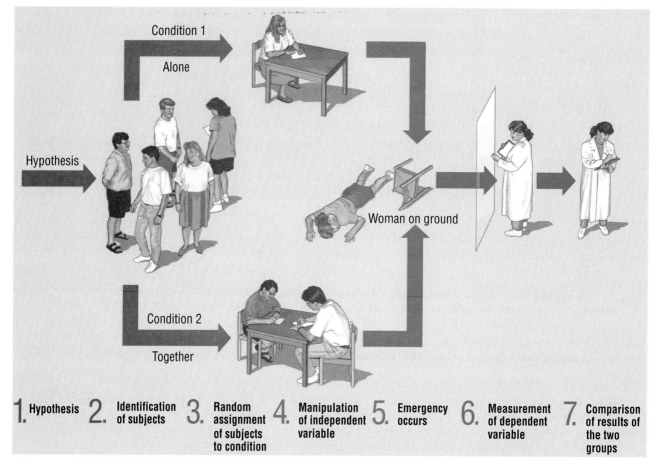

FIGURE 1–4   The Ingredients of an Experiment This experiment tests the diffusion-of-responsibility hypothesis. Beginning with a hypothesis, the researcher identified subjects and then randomly assigned them to one or two conditions: (**1**) working alone, or (**2**) working with others. Consequently, the independent variable was the presence or absence of others. The dependent variable—what was measured in the experiment—was how long it took subjects to help in the emergency. The final step was to analyze results statistically by comparing differences between conditions.

provided. And this is exactly what occurred: Less help was offered in the condition when two people were present than in the condition when one was present.

One last step remained for the researchers: To make sure that the difference in helping between the two conditions was a real one, they had to conduct several statistical tests. These tests established that the difference was large enough to warrant the conclusion that it was statistically meaningful and not merely the result of chance. In the vocabulary of research methods, Latané and Rodin could state that the differences found in the experiment were large enough to reach statistical significance. *Statistical significance* is said to characterize an outcome that would be expected to occur by chance less than 5 times out of 100. In other words, a significant difference is one in which there is a 95% or better probability that the difference an experimenter finds is due to real differences between two groups rather than to chance.

Latané and Rodin's experiment had all the ingredients of a true experiment. As you can see in Figure 1–4, they started with a hypothesis. Their independent variable was whether participants were alone or together with another person, and their dependent variable was whether participants helped. They randomly assigned participants to one of the two experimental conditions.

Although the results of this study confirmed the hypothesis, one study cannot unequivocally confirm a theory. Before accepting experimental results, social psychologists demand *replication,* in which experiments are repeated to verify the original results. Sometimes replications are exactly the same as in an original experiment in order to corroborate the initial results, but more frequently they represent conceptual replications. In a conceptual replication, most features of the original experiment are kept intact, but some components are modified in order to build on and extend the original results.

Latané and Darley carried out several different conceptual replications to establish the diffusion-of-responsibility principle (Darley & Latané, 1968). They were joined by other researchers interested in the same issues (Bickman, 1971). By using a variety of approaches and techniques, different social psychologists were able to establish the viability of the theory. In fact, some 50 studies were carried out in the decade following the publication of the initial experiments, which together supported the concept of diffusion of responsibility (Latané and Nida, 1981). In sum, we can say with confidence that, at least in emergency situations, more is less: The greater the number of bystanders or witnesses to an event that requires help, the less likely it is that any single person will offer help.

But what if the research had not been so consistent? Is there a way to combine the results of many different studies, some of them contradictory? The answer is yes. In the last decade, social psychologists routinely have begun to employ a technique called *meta-analysis,* a procedure in which the outcomes of different studies are quantified so that they may be compared and summarized. By statistically combining the direction and strength of the findings from a series of studies, researchers can come to an overall conclusion regarding a theory or phenomenon. For instance, meta-analyses have been used to combine the results of dozens of investigations to determine gender differences in group performance—as we'll discuss in Chapter 14.

REVIEW AND RETHINK

Review

- The two major classes of research are experimental research, which can establish cause–effect relationships, and correlational research, which identifies whether an association or relationship exists between two factors.

- Theories are broad explanations and predictions of phenomena of interest, and hypotheses are predictions, derived from theories, stated in a way that permits them to be tested.

- The essentials of an experiment include a hypothesis, independent and dependent variables, and a procedure in which participants are randomly assigned to experimental groups or conditions.

- Random assignment helps ensure that potential confounding factors are distributed across experimental conditions and are unlikely to interfere with researchers' interpretations of results.

Rethink

- Why is it important for social psychologists to derive hypotheses that they use to test theories? Explain whether it is possible to form theories from hypotheses.

- What is the function of control groups in psychological experiments? Imagine a study in which college students took a math test before and after a training program designed to improve math skills. Would a control group be necessary in this study? Why or why not?

- Why is it important to assign participants to conditions in a random fashion? What confounding factors can be controlled by using random assignment? Name confounding factors that would not be controlled by using random assignment.

- What are some advantages and drawbacks of laboratory studies compared with field studies?

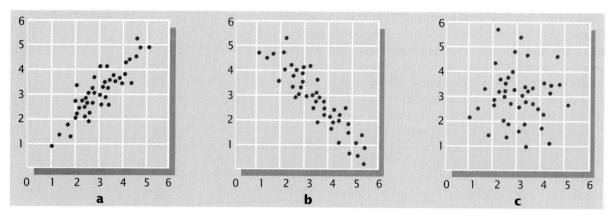

FIGURE 1–5   Types of Correlations These graphs indicate three types of possible relationships between variables. In (**a**), we find a positive correlation between the amount of helping and the number of people present (as values of one variable rise, so do the values of the other variable). In (**b**), as the number of people increases, the amount of helping declines (as values of one variable fall, values of the other variable rise). Finally in (**c**), we see no relationship between the two variables: they are uncorrelated.

CORRELATIONAL RESEARCH: ESTABLISHING ASSOCIATIONS BETWEEN VARIABLES

No matter how ingenious a researcher, there is no way to study participants' reactions to the stress of a natural disaster by manipulating their exposure to an earthquake. Similarly, researchers cannot experimentally manipulate the sex of participants in order to study whether male and female students are treated differently by their employers. Nor can we cut off participants' hands in one treatment condition in order to study people's reactions to being physically handicapped. In each of these cases, practical, ethical, and moral constraints prevent us from manipulating variables that are necessary to conduct a true experiment.

However, there is an alternative class of research: correlational research. As we discussed earlier, correlational research examines the relationship between two (or more) variables to determine whether they are associated or "correlated." Correlational research basically has three possible outcomes:

◆ When values of one variable are high, values of the second are also high, and when values of the first variable are low, values of the second are also low. This situation produces a *positive correlation*. For example, if we assumed that *more* people present in an emergency situation would result in *more* helping (a prediction contrary to that made by Latané and Darley), we would expect to find a positive correlation between number of people and helping (see Figure 1–5a).

◆ Second, when values of one variable are high, values of the second are low, and when values of the first variable are low, values of the second are high. This produces a *negative correlation*. For instance, if Latané and Darley's hypothesis is correct in predicting that as *more* people are present, *less* helping will occur, we would expect to find a negative correlation (see Figure 1–5b).

◆ Finally, no relationship may exist between the two variables. This yields a finding of "no correlation." If, for example, the number of bystanders present was unrelated to helping, no correlation would be present (see Figure 1–5c).

The strength of a correlation is represented by a mathematical score ranging from +1.0 to −1.0. The closer a correlation comes to positive or negative 1.00, the stronger the relationship between the two variables. Hence, a strong positive correlation would be close to +1.00, and a strong negative correlation would be close to −1.00. Conversely, weak or no relationships result in a correlation that will hover around 0.00.

The most critical point about correlations is that no matter how strongly two variables are correlated with each other, there is no implication that one of the variables *causes* the other. The finding of a correlation means only that the variables are associated with one another. Although changes in one variable may cause the changes in the other, it is equally plausible that they do not. It is even possible that some third, unmeasured—and previously unconsidered—variable is causing both variables to increase or decrease simultaneously.

Let's take a concrete example. Suppose you were a social psychologist who hypothesized that long-term exposure to violence on television produced aggression in children. Because controlling everything children watch on television during their entire childhood is not possible, experimental research on the long-term effects of viewing is simply not practical. Consequently, you would be compelled to use correlational research.

Stated in correlational terms, your hypothesis would be that there is a positive correlation between the amount of aggressive television programs children view and the aggressive behavior they display. Now suppose you conduct an experiment and find that the results support your hypothesis: Children who are exposed to the most televised aggression are the most apt to show high aggression, and those exposed to lower amounts of television aggression tend to show lower aggression. Does such a result mean that exposure to televised aggression causes actual aggression in children?

The answer is no. Although drawing such a conclusion would be tempting, it would be inappropriate and quite possibly inaccurate. Consider, for instance, some of the alternative explanations illustrated in Figure 1–6. For example, children who exhibit high aggression may prefer to watch shows that are high in aggressive content because of their own aggressive tendencies.

FIGURE 1–6   The Causal Possibilities: The Relationship Between Exposure to Television Violence and Aggressive Behavior At least three possible causal paths underlie a positive correlation between televised violence and aggression: (**a**) watching shows with aggressive content leads to viewer aggression; (**b**) children who act aggressively choose to watch shows containing violence; and (**c**) a third factor—neglectful parents—leads to both watching aggression on television and acting aggressive.

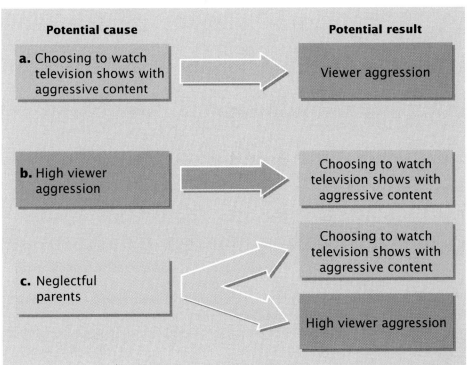

Children who are exposed to the most aggression on television are also most apt to show high aggression themselves. Does this mean that observation of a violent TV show actually causes aggression?

Similarly, some third factor may produce both actual aggression and the tendency to watch highly aggressive television shows. For example, neglectful parents may tolerate both high levels of television viewing and high levels of aggression in their children. Their lack of discipline may produce unrestrained, uncontrollable children who do whatever they desire, including watching large amounts of television and behaving aggressively. In such a case, no causal links would exist between televised aggression and aggressive behavior.

Despite their inability to draw causal connections from correlational research, social psychologists regularly carry out research of this nature because it enables them to study areas that could not be examined in a laboratory. Conclusions from such research have illuminated important issues and have led to significant advances in the field. In fact, social psychologists have developed an inventory of several correlational procedures that illustrate a range of possibilities in the collection of data (see Table 1–2 on page 20). We'll discuss some of the major ones: naturalistic observation, archival research, survey research, and evaluation research.

Naturalistic observation.   Every day of our lives, we engage in naturalistic observation. As we walk down college corridors, stand on street corners, or grab breakfast at a restaurant, most of us are taking mental note of what people around us are doing.

Social psychologists make the same kinds of observations, although in a considerably more systematic manner. In **naturalistic observation**, investigators simply observe some naturally occurring behavior and do not intervene and make changes in the situation. For instance, a social psychologist interested in the size of naturally occurring groups may examine various locations (parks, streets, restaurants) to determine how many people are generally found together. The critical point is that researchers using naturalistic observation do not intervene and modify the situation as they might if they were carrying out an experiment. Instead, they seek to record what they find in as careful and unbiased a manner as possible.

There are actually two sorts of naturalistic observation: nonparticipant and participant observation. In **nonparticipant observation**, the researcher records people's behavior in a given setting but does not actually enter into it. For example, an experimenter interested in understanding how often people obey traffic regulations could secretly record the number of times drivers pass through a stop sign without fully stopping.

Similarly, nonparticipant observation can take the form of indirect, unobtrusive measures. For instance, one ingenious study using nonparticipant observation determined which of several exhibits in a children's museum was the most popular by examining the rate at which the floor tiles in front of the different exhibits had to be replaced (Webb et al., 1966). (For the record, the hatching chicks exhibit was the favorite!)

naturalistic observation: A process in which investigators observe some naturally occurring behavior but do not intervene in the situation.

nonparticipant observation: The type of naturalistic observation in which the researcher records people's behavior in a given setting but does not actually enter into it.

One of the newest examples of nonparticipant observation can be seen in the observation of consumer habits.

In contrast to nonparticipant observation, **participant observation** occurs when an observer actually engages in the activities of the people being observed. In one classic study, for example, an investigator interested in the behavior of friendship patterns among neighborhood residents actually moved into the community and participated in various leisure-time activities. In this way, the researcher was able to examine, first-hand, the relationships among people living in the area (Whyte, 1981).

Both nonparticipant and participant observation have assets and drawbacks. Participant observers are able to get close to the people being studied and may be in a better position to understand fully what is actually occurring in a field setting. On the other hand, a participant observer runs the risk of inadvertently influencing the activities of the people being studied. If that occurs, the observed behavior may not reflect what participants would have done had the observer not been involved in their activities.

When participants in field studies are mindful that they are being observed, they may show reactivity. *Reactivity* is behavior that occurs as a result of participants' awareness that they are being studied. Although reactivity typically declines over time, as participants become acclimated to being studied, it can be a serious problem in short-term observational studies (Velicer et al., 1992).

Archival research.   Suppose a friend commented that the phases of the moon affected people's behavior, making them act "crazy." What might you do to verify or refute the accuracy of your friend's claim?

One approach would be to employ archival research. In **archival research**, researchers analyze existing records or documents in an attempt to confirm a hypothesis. For example, in this case you might consult the *Farmer's Almanac* for a 5-year period to document when changes in the moon's phases occurred. By examining records of admissions to mental hospitals and correlating them with the moon's phases, you might be able to confirm—or refute—such a hypothesis.

Archival research has the advantage of being completely nonreactive: Participants do not know they are being observed, and their behavior will be uninfluenced by the observation. Even more important, researchers can test hypotheses that span vast periods of time, history, and cultures. Consequently, archival research can confirm the validity of principles developed in the present from data that has been collected in the past.

However, archival research does have disadvantages. Sometimes the data needed to confirm a hypothesis simply do not exist or are unavailable or incomplete. Even when such data can be collected, the sheer mass may be so great that it is hard to tell what is and is not important. Finally, the researcher is at the mercy of the original collectors of the material. If they have done a poor job, the results of archival research will be inconclusive at best, and misleading at worst (Jones, 1985; Stewart & Kamins, 1993).

Survey research.   Are you a Democrat, a Republican, an independent, or none of the above? Should women have the right to obtain an abortion? Do you believe that homosexuality should be grounds for discharge from the military?

Questions like these are typical of those asked in surveys, one of the most direct techniques for determining how people think and feel about a topic. In **survey research**, a *sample* of people is chosen to represent some larger group of interest—called the *population;* these people then answer a series of questions about their behavior, thoughts, or attitudes. If the sample of people surveyed has been scientifically selected, researchers are able to draw quite accurate inferences about the larger population. For example, the outcome of presidential elections usually can be predicted within one or two percentage points if a sample of just a few thousand voters is surveyed, provided the sample is painstakingly identified (Fowler, 1993; Rogelberg & Luong, 1998).

Although survey research is a proven technique for learning about people's behaviors and attitudes, survey responses cannot always be taken at face value. For one thing, people do not

participant observation: The type of naturalistic observation in which the researcher actually engages in the activities of the people being observed.

archival research: Research in which an investigator analyzes existing records or documents in an effort to confirm a hypothesis.

survey research: Research in which an investigator chooses people to represent some larger population and asks them a series of questions about their behavior, thoughts, or attitudes.

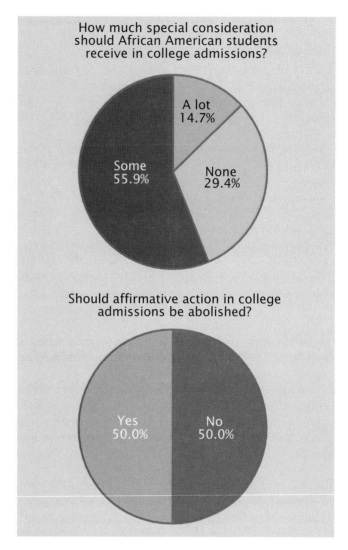

FIGURE 1–7 Our responses to questions are influenced by the specific way in which the questions are worded. For instance, when a sample of first-year college students were asked whether African American students should receive special consideration in college admissions, more than 70% thought they should receive "some" or "a lot." But when an equivalent sample of students were asked whether affirmative action in college admissions should be abolished, 50% agreed. (*Source:* Higher Education Research Institute, 1996.)

always respond accurately. They may not precisely remember their own past behavior; they may not wish to reveal information about themselves; or they may not even know how they feel and may answer without giving the issue full consideration. Because people may try to present themselves favorably, their answers may not be fully honest. Consequently, one important drawback of survey research is that the researcher is not able to directly observe behaviors in question but instead relies on the accuracy of those who are surveyed (Weisberg, Krosnick, & Bowen, 1996).

The conclusions that can be drawn from a survey are further affected by the way that questions are phrased. For example, surveys that asked for people's opinion of President Bill Clinton at the height of the Monica Lewinsky controversy found favorability ratings 20 percentage points lower if they asked for opinions of Clinton "as a person," compared with surveys that omitted the "as a person" phrase. Similarly, if survey researchers ask the question "How much special consideration should African American students receive in college admissions?" the majority of college students respond either "some" or "a lot." In contrast, if the question is phrased "Should affirmative action in college admissions be abolished?" some 50 percent agree; see Figure 1–7 (Higher Education Research Institute, 1996; Witt, 1999). (Also see the Applying Social Psychology box.)

APPLYING SOCIAL PSYCHOLOGY
HOW DO YOU COUNT?: CHOOSING THE BEST SURVEY TECHNIQUE FOR THE U.S. CENSUS

They've gone over the river and through the woods. They've walked through nude beaches and across mountaintops, all with one goal in mind: getting a count of every single individual who inhabits the United States.

Mandated by the Constitution to conduct a complete census every 10 years, the U.S. government periodically conducts the largest of all surveys. The goal is to create not only a specific number representing the total U.S. population, but to draw a statistical portrait of the country. The year 2000 census is no

The care with which surveys are carried out varies considerably. For instance, telephone surveys do not include people who do not have phones, thereby omitting individuals who are particularly disadvantages. In contrast, the U.S. Census attempts to contact every household in the United States.

exception, as census takers fan out across the country seeking to enumerate every man, woman, and child.

What is different about the 2000 census is that a curious mix of science and politics has had an impact on the way in which the count is conducted. The issue was whether scientific sampling, long a staple of most surveys, could be used in the official census count.

The Census Bureau initially planned to use a sampling procedure to make inferences about the larger population, which is a common approach in most surveys. Specifically, some 10% of the population would not have been directly contacted. Rather, by using sophisticated sampling techniques, the characteristics of that segment of the population would have been estimated, based on survey sampling techniques. This procedure was designed to overcome a problem that has plagued the Census Bureau in the past: dealing with people who do not respond to repeated requests to provide data or who cannot be found.

Although the Census Bureau had elaborate plans, which were endorsed by leading survey experts, politics intruded. The Republican-led Congress, which felt that such procedures might lead to a large population increase in poorer—and traditionally Democratic—areas, argued that the Constitution mandated an exact count, not one based on sampling. The issue was brought before the Supreme Court, which ruled in favor of the nonsampling position. Consequently, the 2000 census ended up making use of traditional means of counting (Wright, 1999).

Most social psychologists, along with experts from several other disciplines, argue that the approach mandated by the Supreme Court will yield a count that is less than fully accurate. But the controversy also reveals an important fact: the work done by social psychologists has important practical implications—implications that can affect all our lives.

Evaluation research.   In recent years, the U.S. government has invested millions of dollars to encourage the public to use safer-sex practices in order to prevent the spread of AIDS. How successful have these efforts been?

To answer this question, social psychologists would turn to evaluation research. **Evaluation research** is a technique designed to determine whether a program is meeting its goals and to contribute information to help improve the program in the future. The program in question can be a small, local one ("Is the college's new program to reduce freshman student dropouts effective?") or a large-scale assessment of the effectiveness of a national program ("Is Head Start successful in increasing student scholastic achievement?").

evaluation research: A technique designed to determine the effects of a research program—specifically, whether it is meeting its goals—and to contribute information to help improve the program in the future.

demand characteristics: The cues that participants receive in an experiment that provide information regarding expected or appropriate behavior.

confederates: Employees or colleagues of the experimenter who pose as participants in an experiment and who may be used to produce a scene that has impact on subjects, engaging and involving them.

The outcome of evaluation research is often controversial and can be related to politics. Consider, for instance, the Head Start program. Although the program has been in place for several decades, evidence concerning its success in improving student performance is still not definitive. In fact, the evidence is quite contradictory, with some studies showing positive gains for the program and others yielding little or even contrary evidence for its effectiveness. Because such a mixture of results is amenable to alternative interpretations, it is not surprising that the way the results are interpreted may be influenced by political considerations (DeParle, 1993).

As a consequence, social psychologists may be the targets of political pressure, particularly by program advocates and administrators who feel threatened by a negative evaluation. Although such real-world pressures can make the program evaluator's job a difficult one, program evaluation is an activity in which social psychologists increasingly are involved (Archer, Pettigrew, & Aronson, 1992; Aronson, Wilson, & Brewer, 1998).

THREATS TO RESEARCH VALIDITY: ON THE SOCIAL PSYCHOLOGY OF DOING RESEARCH

So far, we've been discussing research as if participants were fairly passive responders to stimuli, reacting to events in experiments with little awareness or concern that they are, in fact, participating in an experiment. However, those of us who have been participants in a study know that nothing could be further from the truth. Participants constantly wonder about questions such as these: What is happening? What does this mean? Why am I being told this? What is the experimenter trying to prove? In an attempt to answer questions such as these, participants may pose some serious threats to the validity of any findings the experiment produces.

Demand characteristics.   If a stranger came up to you on the street and asked you to answer 20 pages of math problems, you would probably refuse. But if an experimenter asked you to do the same thing in the course of an experiment, you would probably be considerably more agreeable. The reason? You would likely assume that the task had some meaning, particularly in the light of the presumed expertise and authority of the experimenter.

Participants who volunteer for an experiment make interpretations about what the experimenter is looking for. Moreover—and even worse in terms of the validity of the results—they may act on their interpretations. They may try to "help" experimenters by conforming to their guess of the hypothesis; or, if so inclined, they may try to disprove the hypothesis. In either case, their behavior in experiments is not necessarily a valid representation of real-life behavior; rather, it is an indication of how participants feel they ought to behave.

Demand characteristics are the cues that participants receive in an experiment that provide information regarding expected or appropriate behavior (Heiman, 1999). These cues may include the location of the experimental laboratory, the demeanor of the experimenter, or the kind of equipment involved in the study. Any of these factors might be sufficient to lead participants to develop their own notion about what kind of behavior the experimenter is looking for.

The most common way to prevent demand characteristics from biasing the results of an experiment is the use of deception. When social psychologists use the term *deception,* they mean research methods that disguise or mislead participants regarding the actual purpose of a study. If participants then attempt to change their behavior to support (or refute) the fake hypothesis that they have devised, their behavior is presumably unlikely to affect responses relevant to the true question of interest.

In many cases, social psychologists employ elaborate deceptive scenarios to disguise the true purpose of an experiment. They not only conceal the hypothesis, they also use **confederates**—employees or colleagues of the experimenter who pose as participants—in an attempt to produce a scene that has a certain impact on participants, engaging and involving them to create the needed experimental conditions (Suls & Rosnow, 1988; Heiman, 1999).

The frequent use of deception in social psychological experiments raises concerns of both a methodological and an ethical nature. For instance, some critics argue that the use of deception will ultimately lead to a scarcity of untainted, "naive" participants (participants who are taken in by the experimental deception). They suggest that the problem will grow as social psychologists' routine use of deception becomes increasingly well known by the general population, and particularly among college students who, as we mentioned earlier, serve as the discipline's most frequent participants (Kelman, 1967; Greenberg & Folger, 1988).

However, at least some research on the use of deception in experiments suggests otherwise. For example, survey data collected over the last 2 decades show little change in college students' attitudes toward research. Participants have apparently not become more suspicious or distrustful of psychologists (Sharpe, Adair, & Roese, 1992; Epley & Huff, 1998).

Other critics of social psychology's use of deception raise ethical concerns. They suggest that there is something inherently contradictory about a discipline that calls itself a science—a term that implies an open and public quest for knowledge—and yet uses deception as a major research tool. Furthermore, the use of deception raises several related ethical dilemmas, including such issues as whether people should be studied without their knowledge, whether the true purpose of experiments should be revealed to participants, whether research procedures place people under stress, whether participants should be actively deceived, and whether research should induce participants to engage in behaviors that they otherwise would be unlikely to carry out (Greenberg & Folger, 1988; Aronson et al., 1990; Stanley et al., 1996).

To deal with such ethical issues, social psychologists adhere to a strict set of ethical guidelines that protect the rights of participants. These ethical principles require that participants be told enough about the experiment to give their *informed consent,* that is, that they agree to proceed as participants after the possible risks and benefits have been fully disclosed and explained. The only time informed consent is not required is when the risks to participants are minimal, as when a study using naturalistic observation is conducted in a public setting such as a street corner or shopping mall (American Psychological Association, 1990, 1996).

Furthermore, the ethical principles state that deception should be used only if no other techniques are available; that participants should not be harmed or placed in discomfort; and that the benefits of participation should outweigh the risks for participants. Furthermore, immediately following the completion of a study, researchers must provide a complete **debriefing,** a full, careful explanation of the procedures used in the study. A debriefing must include the study's rationale, as well as full disclosure of any deception that was employed and the reasons for its use. Institutions in which research is conducted must have review boards, composed of professionals not involved in the research, who evaluate every experiment before it is run to ensure that the methods employed strictly follow ethical guidelines (Chastain & Landrum, 1999).

Experimenter expectations.   In most studies, the experimenter plays a central role in the proceedings. Consequently, it seems reasonable to suppose that the experimenter's behavior, personal qualities, and expectations can affect participants' behaviors.

If an experimenter treats all participants the same way, there is no problem, because experimenter effects will be roughly the same for all participants. However, experimenter behavior and characteristics that affect some participants in one way and others in a different way create a problem. If, for instance, an experimenter treats attractive participants differently from unattractive participants, the outcome of the experiment clearly can be affected.

The most scientifically threatening experimenter effects take the form of *experimenter expectations,* in which an experimenter unintentionally communicates cues to participants about the way they are expected to behave in a given experimental condition (Rosenthal, 1976; Sieber, 1996). For example, an experimenter who hypothesizes that participants will act aggressively in one condition and passively in another may relate to participants in a way that evokes from them aggression in the first condition and passivity in the second. Experimenters may not be aware of their behavior, but they may communicate their expectations inadvertently through the things they say and do.

debriefing: A full, careful explanation of the procedures used in the study.

convenience samples: Samples chosen more because participants are easily available than for their representativeness.

Although experimenter expectations can never be completely eliminated, several techniques can reduce their likelihood. For instance, if the people who carry out the experiment are unaware of the experimental hypotheses that are being tested, they obviously will be unable to communicate accurate expectations to participants. In addition, experimenters may employ "expectation-free" substitutes for themselves, such as tape-recorded instructions. The difficulty with this solution, however, is that it raises problems of its own, because it may produce an experiment that is uninvolving and sterile.

Research participants: Choosing the ideal representative.   If a goal of social psychology is to discover principles that apply to people in general, it would seem logical to use research participants who somehow represent "people in general."

Obviously, even the most ingenious experimenter is unable to find participants that are fully representative of everyone. In fact, social psychology has been criticized for its reliance on **convenience samples**, participants chosen more because they are easily available than because they are representative. In particular, the frequent use of college students as participants is problematic. As with other fields within psychology, critics have noted that the discipline is developing a science of "the behavior of the college sophomore" (Rubenstein, 1982).

If college students were representative of the population at large, their frequent use would not be problematic. However, college students generally are younger and better educated and have a higher socioeconomic status than the rest of the population of the United States. They may also differ on important social psychological dimensions. For instance, their attitudes may be less established than those of older adults, and consequently they may be more susceptible to social influence (Sears, 1986).

The participants in social psychological experiments also tend to be disproportionately white. Remarkably, the percentage of research studies on African Americans has declined

FIGURE 1–8   Number of Articles on Decline   Underrepresentation of African Americans at some colleges and concerns associated with conducting socially sensitive research have contributed to the decline in the use of African Americans as participants in research studies. (*Source:* Graham, 1992.)

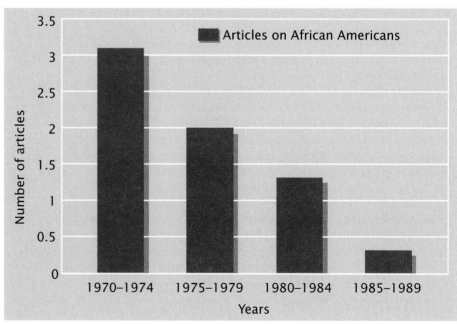

from the early 1970s to the late 1980s, even as awareness and sensitivity about minority inclusion have risen. For instance, Figure 1–8 illustrates the decline over this period in the number of publications involving African Americans in the *Journal of Personality and Social Psychology,* the major journal of social psychology (Graham, 1992).

The decline in the use of African Americans as participants stems from several potential causes. For one thing, fears associated with conducting socially sensitive research have led some researchers to shy away from involving minorities for fear of politicizing their research. Furthermore, the fact that African American students are underrepresented at some colleges often prevents researchers from finding sufficient numbers of African American participants for their studies.

Whatever the reasons, the lack of research involving African Americans is troubling. As one consequence, government agencies that fund research now ask researchers to indicate when they submit research proposals how they plan to include underrepresented populations (Graham, 1992; National Institute of Mental Health [NIMH], 1993).

THINKING CRITICALLY ABOUT SOCIAL PSYCHOLOGY

THE INFORMED CONSUMER OF SOCIAL PSYCHOLOGY

"The Ten Best Ways to Build a Relationship!"

"How to Read Another Person Like a Book"

"Rescuing Your Child from a Cult"

We encounter information relevant to social psychology not only in textbooks, but also in the daily newspaper, on the 6 o'clock news, or in a shopping mall bookstore. We are constantly confronted—even bombarded—with apparent wisdom pertaining to people's social lives, as exemplified in the titles cited above.

We face a formidable challenge when we attempt to sort through this information and separate appropriate claims from inappropriate ones. Several principles, derived from the strategies used by social psychologists in their exploration of the underpinnings of social behavior, can aid in evaluating such material (Coats, Feldman, & Schwartzberg, 1994):

◆ *Identify and challenge assumptions.* Every statement has multiple underlying assumptions. For instance, a person who claims that allowing gays and lesbians in the military will reduce unit cohesion may hold any one of several underlying assumptions: (1) all homosexuals behave in similar ways; (2) unit cohesion is critical to the military's effectiveness; (3) unit cohesion is affected by the sexual orientation of those in the unit; (4) homosexuals are not already serving in the military. Regardless of whether one agrees or disagrees with such underlying assumptions, the point is that these assumptions must be considered before the original statement can be rejected or accepted.

◆ *Consider factual accuracy and logical consistency.* In critically evaluating the claims that people make, always consider the validity of the evidence on which a claim is staked. Claims must be substantiated, and the source of the information must be verified. The mere fact that something is printed in a magazine or newspaper—or even a textbook!—does not guarantee that it is correct; writers are human, and they make human errors. Furthermore, consider the logic behind an argument's conclusions. For instance, hearing that "no other toothpaste is recommended more than Toothwasher" doesn't mean that Toothwasher is the toothpaste most often recommended—just that nothing else is recommended more. In fact, such a statement suggests that other toothpastes may be just as good as Toothwasher.

◆ *Consider context.* An assertion may be valid in some contexts but not in others. In fact, very few claims are universally applicable. Consider, for instance, the old proverb, "Two heads are better than one." If we interpret this to mean that two people working on a problem are more likely to come to an accurate solution than one person, then social psychological research is supportive, as we'll see in Chapter 14. But if we consider the proverb in the context of whether two people working on a problem are more efficient than one person, the answer is just the opposite. According to the same body of research, groups are less efficient than individuals working alone.

Context is also crucial in taking account of cultural factors. Although we tend to be embedded in our own culture, keep in mind that people from different cultures may respond in diverse ways. Just as social psychologists struggle with the challenge of determining the degree to which principles are universal, all of us need to keep in mind the potential limitations of broad claims.

◆ Imagine and explore alternatives. Evaluating the claims of others consists of more than just poking holes in their arguments. It is also useful to generate new ideas and alternative explanations. For instance, one approach is to assume that an assertion is wrong, and to think of arguments for its opposite. If we can develop plausible alternative explanations, the shortcomings of the original claims may become apparent.

By adhering to these guidelines, you can become more astute in your evaluations of the claims that you encounter in the popular press, as well as those espoused by friends, teachers, and other acquaintances. Furthermore, the same criteria can be used to appraise the theories and research carried out by social psychologists. By applying a critical eye to the assertions you encounter, you'll be better able to appreciate the very real advances in our understanding of behavior that social psychologists have made.

REVIEW AND RETHINK

Review

- Correlational research examines the relationship between two (or more) variables to determine whether they are associated.

- The major types of correlational research are naturalistic observation, archival research, survey research, and evaluation research.

- Threats to the validity of experiments include demand characteristics, experimenter expectations, and the characteristics of the participants used in the study.

Rethink

- What benefits are provided by an experimental design in which the experimenter is "blind" to the hypotheses being tested? Are there any costs involved in keeping experimenters blind? Explain.

- What type of correlation would you expect to find between height and weight? How might this correlation affect the results of a study that demonstrates a positive association between height and a tolerance for alcohol?

- Consider these four types of research studies: an experiment conducted in the field, an experimental study conducted in a laboratory, a correlational study using naturalistic observation, and a correlational study using archival research methods. Which would you use to test the following hypotheses?

    a. Are elementary school teachers more nonverbally supportive of their younger pupils than their older pupils?

    b. Does nonverbal support from a classroom teacher help children learn more effectively?

    c. Does the presence of a full moon produce a change in normal behavior?

d. Will rewarding people for doing something that they always enjoyed reduce their inherent pleasure in performing the task?

e. Will watching 1 hour of violent television programming increase aggressive behavior?

• What benefits does correlational research have over experimental research? Are experimental designs always preferable when feasible? Why or why not?

L O O K I N G   B A C K

What is the scope of social psychology?

1. Social psychology is the scientific study of how people's thoughts, feelings, and actions are affected by others. Social psychologists focus on the consequences of social influences on individuals and the ways they understand the world; social interaction between and among people; and group processes. (p. 4)

2. Within the broader field of psychology, social psychology's closest companion is the subdiscipline of personality psychology. Outside psychology, sociology and anthropology are closely related to social psychology. (p. 6)

3. Although the field of social psychology is made up primarily of white males, demographic trends are changing, as increasing numbers of women get degrees in the area. However, the record on minority representation is less positive: Only 6 percent of social psychologists are members of minority groups. (p. 8)

What are the major milestones and trends in the development of the field, and what is the future likely to hold?

4. Although the roots of social psychology were foreshadowed by Plato and Aristotle, the scientific discipline of social psychology can be traced to 1897, when the first social psychological experiment was conducted, and to 1908, when two social psychology texts were published. However, it was not until the 1920s that social psychology became an established, independent discipline. The 1930s saw the emergence of such pioneers as Muzafer Sherif, who studied social norms, and Kurt Lewin, who made both theoretical and applied contributions. (p. 9)

5. Following World War II, social psychology flourished. Group behavior was a central topic at that time, a trend that continued well into the 1950s. By the 1960s, however, another shift occurred, and the emphasis turned to within-individual social processes, compared to the earlier emphasis on between-individual processes. Attribution theory, which focuses on the processes by which people determine the reasons behind behavior, and gender studies, which focus on male–female differences, became established and influential areas of research. (p. 10)

6. Despite the rapid expansion of the field in the 1960s and 1970s, some social psychologists argued that it was in crisis because it was unable to identify universal, fundamental principles that spanned historical eras and cultural differences. Ultimately, concerns about the crisis in the field led to a strengthening of the discipline. (p. 11)

7. Over the last decade, the field has focused on the role of cognitive factors in social behavior. Applications of social psychological theory and research have also grown. Although it is difficult to forecast the future, three trends are likely: There will be an increasing emphasis on multiculturalism in social psychology; behavioral genetics

and evolutionary psychology will play an increasing role in the field; and the traditional boundaries that have differentiated the field of social psychology from other areas are likely to become less distinct. (p. 12)

How do experimental and correlational research differ, and what are the major types of studies that social psychologists carry out?

8. Research, which may be experimental or correlational, begins with questions derived from theories, which are broad explanations and predictions about phenomena of interest. The questions researchers ask are put in the form of hypotheses, predictions stated in a way that permits them to be tested. (p. 18)

9. Experimental research is designed to discover causal relationships between various factors. In contrast, correlational research seeks to identify whether an association or relationship exists between two factors—regardless of whether one factor actually produces changes in the other. (p. 19)

10. Experimental research includes at least two conditions: a treatment group and a control group. In an experiment, the independent variable is the variable that is manipulated, while the dependent variable is the variable that is measured and expected to change as a result of the manipulation of the independent variable. (p. 19)

11. Operationalization is the process of translating a hypothesis into specific testable procedures that can be measured and observed. (p. 20)

12. Research takes place either in the laboratory (a controlled setting explicitly designed to hold events constant) or in the field (a naturally occurring setting). Whatever the location of the study, participants in true experiments must be assigned to conditions using random assignment, through which they are placed in groups on the basis of chance. Random assignment avoids confounding, in which factors other than the independent variable are allowed to vary. (p. 21)

13. Although correlational research cannot determine causality, several significant types of research are correlational. Among the most frequently used are naturalistic observation (including participant and nonparticipant observation), archival research, survey research, and evaluation research. (p. 27)

What are the major threats to the validity of research findings?

14. Several situations threaten the validity of research findings. They include demand characteristics, experimenter expectations, and the use of inappropriate participants. (p. 32)

15. Among the strategies for evaluating material relevant to social psychology are identifying and challenging assumptions, considering factual accuracy and logical consistency, considering context, and imagining and exploring alternatives. (p. 35)

EPILOGUE

As our introduction to the discipline has indicated, the scope of social psychology is broad. We've traced it from its early beginning to its present status, and we've discussed the research procedures that social psychologists use to answer the questions they ask.

Before turning to the specific topics covered in the remainder of the book, return for the moment to the opening prologue of the chapter. In the light of what you now know about the discipline, consider the following questions about the ethnic cleansing that took place in Yugoslavia:

1. The prologue describes the events in terms of characteristics that might interest a social psychologist. Suggest a theory that explains one aspect of the situation.

2. What hypotheses (predictions that can be tested) can you frame that relate to your theory?

3. Try to design an *experimental* study to test one of your hypotheses that predicts a cause–effect relationship. Describe the elements of the experiment (conditions, operationalization, variables, research setting, etc.).

4. Try to design a *correlational* study to test another of your hypotheses. What correlational method(s) would you use (e.g., naturalistic observation, archival research, survey research)? What advantages and drawbacks are there in this study as compared with an experimental study?

——— KEY TERMS AND CONCEPTS ———

archival research (p. 29)

conditions (p. 19)

confederates (p. 32)

control (p. 22)

control group (p. 19)

convenience samples (p. 34)

correlational research (p. 19)

debriefing (p. 33)

demand characteristics (p. 32)

dependent variable (p. 20)

evaluation research (p. 31)

experiment (p. 19)

experimental research (p. 19)

field study (p. 21)

hypothesis (p. 18)

independent variable (p. 20)

laboratory study (p. 21)

naturalistic observation (p. 28)

nonparticipant observation (p. 28)

operationalization (p. 20)

participant observation (p. 29)

random assignment (p. 22)

social psychology (p. 4)

survey research (p. 29)

treatment (p. 19)

treatment group (p. 19)

CHAPTER 2

SOCIAL COGNITION

Perceiving and Understanding People

PROLOGUE

Murderer or Savior?

Dr. Jack Kevorkian.

The act itself was never in doubt. As captured on a videotape that was shown on the television show *60 Minutes,* Dr. Jack Kevorkian administered a deadly combination of drugs to Thomas Youk, who suffered from amyotrophic lateral sclerosis, commonly known as Lou Gehrig's disease. The videotape showed Youk, whose body was contorted and whose speech was labored, asking Kevorkian to kill him, and Kevorkian complying.

Supporters of Kevorkian argued that physicians have the right—and perhaps even a duty—to help patients with terminal diseases avoid a painful, lingering death. To them, Kevorkian was a savior who ended Youk's misery by complying with his personal request to terminate his suffering.

But to Michigan prosecutors, Kevorkian was nothing more than a murderer. They argued that regardless of whether Youk had asked to die, Kevorkian had taken matters into his own hands and had killed him as surely as if he had put a gun to Youk's head. Described by the prosecutors as a "medical hit man," Kevorkian was labeled a zealot and publicity hound who took the law into his own hands.

A jury apparently agreed with the prosecutors: Kevorkian was found guilty of second-degree murder and sentenced to decades of prison. ■

LOOKING AHEAD

You be the judge: Was Kevorkian acting as Thomas Youk's murderer or savior?

The stark divergence of the differing explanations of Kevorkian's actions illustrates a problem that all of us continually face: figuring out the causes that lie behind others' behavior. In contrast to the perception of inanimate objects, making sense of people—a process known as **social perception**—is a far more complicated task. How do we determine what motivates others' behavior? What does a given act represent? How can we form an overall impression of people from their individual traits? In short, how do we make the leap from what we see of people's appearance and behavior to what lies beneath the surface?

social perception: The task of making sense of people by going beyond appearance and behavior to what lies beneath the surface.

social cognition: The study of how people understand and make sense of others and themselves.

person perception approaches: Approaches to social cognition that consider the ways people assess and combine the traits of other persons to form overall impressions.

In this chapter, we examine social cognition as a way of investigating how social psychologists have answered these questions. *Social cognition* is the area of social psychology that seeks to explain the processes people employ to understand others and themselves. We start by considering how people perceive others, investigating how they form impressions of others based on the particular combination of traits they encounter. Next, we examine how people draw conclusions regarding the causes of others' behavior. We'll consider how observers try to analyze how much of another person's behavior is caused by personality traits and how much is due to characteristics of the situation.

Finally, we look at how people organize and store in memory information about others and how this process affects their views of others. We'll also consider the biases that cloud our ability to view others accurately and some ways to view others with greater clarity.

In sum, after reading this chapter, you'll be able to answer these questions:

♦ How do we combine people's individual personality traits into an overall impression?

♦ How do we make judgments about the causes of others' behavior?

♦ To what kinds of systematic errors are we vulnerable when we consider others' behavior?

♦ How do we organize and remember information about social stimuli, and how does this process affect our social judgment?

SOCIAL COGNITION: AN ORIENTATION

To his friends and neighbors, Ted Bundy seemed personable and humane. Yet there was another side to him: Bundy brutalized and murdered dozens of women and is now remembered as one of the world's most notorious serial killers. When he was brought to trial, he was suspected of killing more than 100 people. But even after he was convicted and executed, many of his acquaintances still could not believe he was capable of such crimes.

How could so many people have misjudged Bundy so fundamentally?

We humans are not always accurate in discerning what others are like, explaining their actions, and predicting their future behavior. And yet at times we seem to be remarkably talented in understanding others and judging and forecasting their behavior. Like social psychological versions of Sherlock Holmes, we can look at just a small snippet of people's behavior and construct elaborate—and sometimes quite accurate—profiles about their underlying characteristics, and we can often make precise predictions about their future behavior.

Social cognition is the study of how people understand and make sense of others and themselves. Research on social cognition covers a wide territory, encompassing many of the central areas of social psychology. For instance, social cognitive approaches can be found in such diverse topics as the study of attitudes (Chapter 10; Chaiken, 1980; Petty & Cacioppo, 1986a; McCann, Higgins, & Fondacaro, 1991; Eagly & Chaiken, 1993), groups (Chapter 14; Mullen, Johnson, & Anthony, 1994; Nye & Brower, 1996; Thompson, 1998), and prejudice and stereotyping (Chapters 2, 3, and 4; Devine & Sherman, 1992; Fiske, 1992a, 1993; Macrae, Stangor, & Milne, 1994; Deaux, 1995; Greenwald & Banaji, 1995; Yzerbyt, Leyens, & Schadron, 1997). The central theme of this research is the pursuit of an understanding of how people mentally represent and think about others, as well as the exploration of mental strategies people use to make sense of their social worlds.

In their study of social cognition, social psychologists have followed three major avenues (summarized in Table 2–1). The first approach, which was the historical forerunner of a good deal of current work in social cognition, focuses on the perception of others, or person perception. **Person perception approaches** consider the ways we assess and combine the traits of other persons to form overall impressions. These approaches are based on the view that

TABLE 2–1	**Major Approaches to Social Cognition**	
APPROACH	**MAJOR QUESTION ADDRESSED BY PERCEIVER**	**MAJOR GUIDING PRINCIPLE USED BY PERCEIVER**
Person perception approaches	How are traits combined to form an overall impression?	Rational combining of trait information
Attribution approaches	What are the causes of behavior?	Naive scientist model
Schema approaches	How is the meaning of behavior and traits interpreted?	Cognitive miser or motivated tactician models

people are thoughtful and fairly rational perceivers of others, who notice others' traits and pull them together into a consistent framework (Kelley, 1950; Heider, 1958; Kenny, 1994).

Other work in social cognition focuses less on how we form impressions of others' personal traits and more on how we interpret the *causes* of others' behavior. **Attribution approaches** seek to identify how we understand what brings about the behavior—our own and others'—that we observe. According to attribution theorists, we act as "naive scientists," rationally weighing and combining different sources of information. By deliberating about the relative influence of people's actions, on the one hand, and the situation in which they are behaving, on the other, we make systematic judgments about the reasons behind their behavior (Jones & Davis, 1965; Kelley, 1967; Zelen, 1991).

Finally, the third approach to social cognition focuses on how we interpret the *meaning* of others' behavior and traits. **Schema approaches** consider how we organize information and store it in memory, and how we use this information to understand behavior.

Schema approaches hold a view of information processing different from that of attribution approaches. Instead of seeing us as the "naive scientists" of the attribution approach, schema approaches view us in one of two ways. One school of thought views people as Scrooge-like cognitive misers (e.g., Stroh, 1995). This *cognitive miser model* suggests that because of limited information-processing capabilities, we expend no more than the minimum effort necessary to solve a social problem or answer a social question. To save ourselves from the task of constantly gauging our impressions of others, then, we do what we can to minimize the expenditure of cognitive effort. In sum, rather than acting as diligent and industrious naive scientists, cognitive misers seek efficiency in the ways they make judgments about others.

On the other hand, research has found that we don't invariably act as cognitive misers. Proponents of the schema approach suggest that an alternative model is needed to provide a full explanation of how we interpret the meaning of behavior and traits. This alternative, the *motivated tactician model,* focuses on the ways that goals, motivations, and needs affect how we view the world. In this model, there are instances in which efficiency is relatively unimportant and other goals—such as accuracy—are more critical. In such cases, the motivated tactician model provides a more precise account of social cognition than the cognitive miser model (Fiske & Taylor, 1991; Fiske, 1992).

As we'll see throughout this chapter, each of the three perspectives on social cognition—the person perception, attribution, and schema approaches—has yielded significant information about the ways we come to understand others, as well as ourselves. These approaches, which we'll discuss in turn, supplement one another and are not necessarily contradictory. As they focus on different kinds of information and different questions that we ask about human behavior, these approaches provide us with a palette we can use to paint a full portrait of the people we encounter in our social world.

attribution approaches: Approaches to social cognition that seek to identify how we understand what brings about the behavior—our own and others'—that we observe.

schema approaches: Approaches to social cognition that consider how people organize information and store it in memory, and how this information is used to understand behavior.

PERSON PERCEPTION: FORMING IMPRESSIONS OF OTHERS

Warm. Industrious. Critical. Practical. Determined.

If you were told that someone embodied this list of traits, you probably would quickly form an impression that was fairly positive. However, suppose the list contained these traits:

Cold. Industrious. Critical. Practical. Determined.

Although only one trait is different (the substitution of "cold" for "warm"), your assessment would probably be quite different—and considerably more negative. The reasons for this difference in overall impression are explored in research work on person perception, which considers the way people assess and integrate others' traits and characteristics to form an overall impression.

FIRST IMPRESSIONS: USING PEOPLE'S OUTWARD APPEARANCE AND BEHAVIOR TO DRAW INFERENCES

Do blondes have more fun? Are fat people jolly? Do people with glasses study more? Most people seem to think so.

Physical appearance.   Although we're taught that appearances can be deceiving, we often act as if we've never heard that advice. Study after study has shown that people use superficial clues, such as clothing, eyeglasses, and jewelry, to form judgments about what others are like (Alley, 1988; Bull & Rumsey, 1988; Berry, 1990; Marino et al., 1991; Workman & Johnson, 1991; Aune, 1999; Kaiser, 1999). Although people make such judgments every day, they often have no evidence to support those judgments.

Physical attractiveness also contributes powerfully to people's judgments of others (Romano & Bordieri, 1989; Ritts, Patterson, & Tubbs, 1992; Wilson & Nias, 1999). As we'll discuss more in Chapter 6, physical attractiveness plays a significant role in determining how much we like people (e.g., Hatfield & Sprecher, 1986; Feingold, 1992a). Even the configuration of a person's face affects the judgments that others make. For example, "baby-faced" physical characteristics—relatively large eyes and small noses—are viewed as signs of powerlessness, submissiveness, and social incompetence (Cunningham, Barbee, & Pike 1990; Zebrowitz, 1997).

Nonverbal behavior.   In addition to physical appearance, we also use people's **nonverbal behavior**—that is, actions separate from speech—as an indication of their inner feelings. A large body of research suggests that people can accurately identify from facial expressions at least the basic emotions of happiness, surprise, sadness, anger, disgust, and fear. Furthermore, the display of these emotions is universal across cultures, and observers who live in very different cultures identify them with high degrees of accuracy (Ekman & O'Sullivan, 1991; Philippot, Feldman, & Coats, 1999; see Figure 2–1).

On the other hand, people do not invariably show what they are feeling. For instance, if you have ever traveled to an Asian country, you may have noticed that people tend to be more restrained in their facial display of emotions than people in Western cultures. Similarly, some research indicates that, in the United States, Caucasians show more restrained emotionality than African Americans, and people living in southern climates are viewed as more emotionally expressive than those living in northern climates (Hanna, 1984; Manstead, 1991; Pennebaker, Rimé, & Blankenship, 1996).

nonverbal behavior: People's actions separate from speech that are used as indications of their inner feelings.

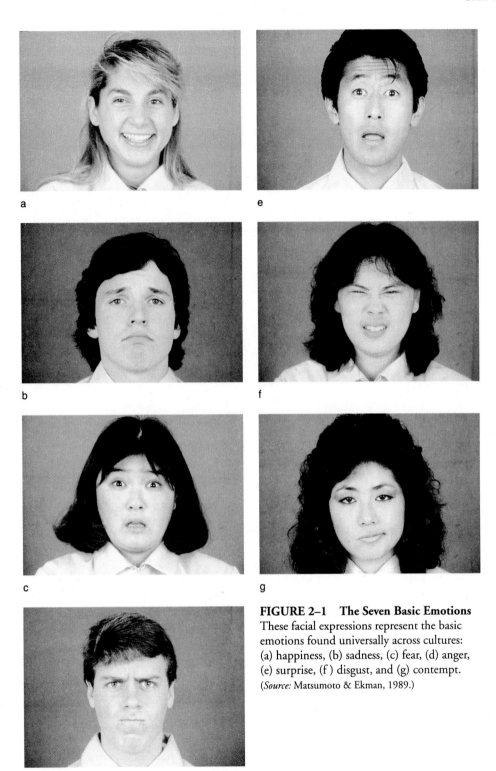

FIGURE 2–1   The Seven Basic Emotions
These facial expressions represent the basic emotions found universally across cultures: (a) happiness, (b) sadness, (c) fear, (d) anger, (e) surprise, (f) disgust, and (g) contempt. (*Source:* Matsumoto & Ekman, 1989.)

The reason for these differences is that members of various cultural, racial, and ethnic groups hold different **display rules**, guidelines that govern the appropriateness of nonverbal shows of emotion. Learned during childhood from parents, peers, and the media, display rules may minimize, exaggerate, or mask emotional expressions (Feldman, 1982, 1992; Matsumoto, 1993, 1996; Philippot, Feldman, & Coats, 1999).

display rules: Guidelines that govern the appropriateness of nonverbal shows of emotion.

FIGURE 2–2 What Does This Mean? Your understanding of the meaning of this gesture depends on your cultural origin. In North America, people interpret it as meaning "everything's great." In contrast, in many other cultures, the gesture represents the female sexual anatomy.

Although they may reduce our accuracy in interpreting the true meaning of others' non-verbal behavior, display rules greatly facilitate social interaction. For instance, by learning not to display our actual emotions upon receiving disappointing gifts, we avoid insulting gift givers and thereby preserve our relationships with them.

However, people are not invariably able to mask their true feelings, and they may emit subtle, and sometimes perceptible, indications that give their actual emotions away—a process called *leakage*. For instance, there is a slight difference in the specific muscles that are employed to display true and sham smiles, and observers are sometimes able to discern from facial expressions when others are being truthful or deceptive (Ekman, 1997; Frank, Ekman, & Friesen, 1997; Miller & Stiff, 1992).

In addition to facial expressions, other kinds of nonverbal behavior are sources of information about others. For example, body language, and in particular the gestures that accompany speech, provide data that we use to develop inferences about others (Ekman & Friesen, 1999; Rimé & Schiaratura, 1991).

Unlike the basic facial expressions, which observers interpret in fairly similar ways across cultures, gestures have quite different meanings from one culture to another. For example, in North America people interpret the "A-OK" gesture (see Figure 2–2) in very positive terms, meaning "everything's great." In contrast, in many other cultures the gesture represents the female sexual anatomy. In Greece, for instance, if a male uses the sign when interacting with a female, it is viewed as a sexual proposition. If he gestures in the same way during a conversation with another male, it is considered an insult to the recipient's masculinity. Clearly, the meaning of gestures can differ significantly across cultures (Ricci Bitti & Poggi, 1991).

COGNITIVE MATH: 1 + 1 DOESN'T ALWAYS EQUAL 2

Although such features as appearance and nonverbal behavior provide clues regarding the personality and character of others, the bits of information are like pieces of an incomplete puzzle, randomly strewn about a table top. How do people take these individual pieces and combine them into a full, complete picture? How, in other words, do we form an overall impression of others based on the bits and pieces of cognitive data that we are able to collect?

This question has been asked throughout the history of social psychology, and it has received many different answers. One of the first responses came over 50 years ago, when social psychologist Solomon Asch argued that certain personal attributes, which he termed central traits, played an unusually influential role in determining a general impression (Asch, 1946; Asch & Zukier, 1984; Watkins & Peynircioglu, 1984). **Central traits** are characteristics that serve to organize an impression of another person and provide a framework for interpreting other information about that person.

Asch's proposition received support in a classic study by social psychologist Harold Kelley (1950) that examined students' impressions of a professor. In the experiment, students were given one of two descriptions of a lecturer whom they had never met. Then they took part in a discussion led by the lecturer. One group of students was told that the lecturer had the five traits listed earlier—that he was "a rather warm person, industrious, critical, practical, and determined." In contrast, the second group of students was told that the same lecturer was "a rather cold person, industrious, critical, practical, and determined."

As you might guess, the replacement of the word *cold* for *warm* in the second description made a dramatic change in the way the lecturer was perceived in the two conditions. Although the lecturer's behavior did not vary between the two groups, students who were told that the lecturer was cold rated him far less positively after the discussion than those who were told he was warm.

Asch's interpretation of these findings was that the presence of a central trait altered the meaning of additional descriptive traits. Consequently, in the context of the description of

central traits: Characteristics that serve to organize an impression of another person and provide a framework for interpreting other information about that person.

an individual, the word *determined* takes on a very different meaning depending on whether it is preceded by the central trait of *warm* or *cold*.

The notion of central traits was not to go unchallenged as the field of social psychology developed. The most immediate disagreement resulted from what has been called the **cognitive algebra approach**, which argues that perceivers consider each individual trait; evaluate each trait individually, in isolation from the others; and then combine their evaluations into an overall judgment (Anderson, 1965, 1981). In this procedure, the meaning of the individual traits is relatively fixed and does not change in response to any other traits that are present.

For instance, suppose we encounter a person who appears adventurous and bold, but unintelligent. If we assign values to each trait, we simply combine those values together to form an overall judgment. The positive traits—*adventurous* and *bold*—add to the final impression; the negative trait—*unintelligent*—subtracts from it. However, the value of each trait doesn't change as a result of the presence (or absence) of others.

The relative merits of the cognitive algebra and central trait views were hotly debated by social psychologists, and the two approaches became increasingly refined. For instance, cognitive algebra theorists found that our impressions of others are more accurate when we consider the importance of each piece of information (Kaplan, 1975). Furthermore, negative information is usually weighted more heavily than positive information. Consequently, a supposedly "balanced" letter of recommendation that contains equal amounts of positive and negative information about a graduate school applicant is likely to produce an overall negative impression of the applicant (Skowronski & Carlston, 1989; Klein, 1991; Vonk, 1993).

However, neither the cognitive algebra view nor the central trait view emerged as predominant, as it became increasingly clear that neither approach provided a complete account of impression formation. Still, these two approaches generated a considerable amount of research. For instance, as we see next, they helped explain the puzzling phenomenon that the order in which we receive information about a person influences our ultimate overall impression.

cognitive algebra approach: An explanation for impression formation that suggests that perceivers consider each individual trait; evaluate each trait individually, in isolation from the others; and then combine the evaluations into an overall judgment.

ORDER EFFECTS IN PERSON PERCEPTION: THE FIRST SHALL BE LAST?

Does it matter whether we initially learn that another person is "intelligent, industrious, impulsive, critical, stubborn, and envious," or learn the same information but in the reverse order?

Although logically it shouldn't matter, the reality is different. According to an early study by Asch, people who hear the list with the more positive attributes first form a more positive impression than those who hear it in the reverse order (Asch, 1946). This finding is consistent with subsequent research, which has shown that there is a strong and pervasive primacy effect in the influence that information has on the recipient (McKelvie, 1990; Titus, 1991; Betz, Gannon, & Skowronski, 1992). A *primacy effect* occurs when early information has a stronger impact than later information.

Primacy effects are found not only in the realm of traits, but even when a single dimension of behavior varies over time. For instance, consider school performance. Which ultimately leaves a better impression: doing better initially in class and then declining, or starting off poorly and improving?

Experimental results are clear in illustrating a primacy effect: The earliest information plays the dominant role in determining the ultimate evaluation. For example, in one study, early performance on a 30-item test was considered more indicative of a person's true ability than later performance on the same test—even if the person showed a substantial improvement or decline (Jones & Goethals, 1972).

On the other hand, *recency effects,* in which later information is given more weight than earlier information, occasionally occur. For example, people who are strongly motivated to pay attention to incoming information are likely to weight later information more heavily. Similarly, if the time span between the receipt of initial and later information is great enough, primacy effects are reduced and recency effects occur (Stewart, 1965; Kruglanski & Freund, 1983).

Why are we susceptible to primacy and recency effects? One answer is that we often pay less attention to information as time goes on. Consequently, as the amount of information we have available increases, we focus on it less closely, even if it contradicts earlier information (Belmore, 1987). In addition, primacy effects are consistent with Asch's speculation that information received earlier influences our perception of the meaning of additional information. For example, when we first learn that a person is envious, and hear only later that she is intelligent, the information takes on a less positive meaning than if we had initially learned about her intelligence (Asch & Zukier, 1984).

The existence of both primacy and recency effects suggests that the cognitive algebra approach does not provide a complete account of social cognition. Clearly, if perceivers were simply weighing individual traits and combining them in a mathematical fashion, the order in which the traits were presented would make no difference. Furthermore, neither the central trait nor the cognitive algebra approach fully considers how people uncover the causes of others' behavior, nor how they categorize and organize traits in their own minds. These shortcomings within the person perception model led to the development of two additional approaches to social cognition: the attributional approach (which we discuss next) and the schema approach. (Also see Speaking of Social Psychology.)

SPEAKING OF SOCIAL PSYCHOLOGY

Scott Canon

Newspaper Reporter

Education: B.A., Journalism, Southern Illinois University at Carbondale; M.A., Public Affairs Reporting, University of Illinois at Springfield

Year of Birth: 1960

Home: Kansas City, Missouri

"You need a balance between research and what you go into the interview with."

Most of us base our views of newsworthy people on the reporting that we read, hear, and see in the media. Is a world figure competent? Smart? Kind? Funny?

The precision of our impressions is based on the ability of reporters to form and convey accurate assessments of people in the news. According to Scott Canon, a reporter with the *Kansas City Star* in Kansas City, Missouri, this is no easy task.

For Canon, capturing an individual in an interview involves doing a lot of work and asking many questions. "It is customary to do some background research initially on the individual," he said. "How you go about it also depends on whether you are writing about someone running for the U.S. Senate or an individual who did a good deed in their neighborhood.

REVIEW AND RETHINK

Review

- Social cognition is the study of how people understand and make sense of others and themselves.

- The three major approaches to social cognition are the person perception, attribution, and schema approaches.

- Person perception approaches consider the way an individual's traits are assessed and combined to form an overall impression.

- Both central trait and cognitive algebra approaches are aspects of the person perception approach that have been employed to understand how information is integrated when people form impressions of others.

- Primacy and recency effects influence person perception, a fact that reveals the inadequacy of the cognitive algebra approach.

Rethink

- What are broad similarities and differences in the three major approaches to social cognition? Could they all, in part, be accurate? Explain.

"You first want to talk to people who know the individual to get some sense of who they are," Canon added. "You need a balance between research and what you go into the interview with to give the source a sense that what you do is serious."

One cannot know every detail about an individual's life, according to Canon. He notes that at times doing too much research actually may be detrimental to forming an accurate impression.

"The more experienced I become, the more cautious I get about coming to a conclusion about someone's personality."

"You don't need to know every last thing about a person," he said. "Too much research before you interview someone may incline you to prejudice yourself. It also may make you fall into the trap of writing the same story everyone else has." Canon pointed to Ted Kaczyinski, the alleged Unabomber, as an example of how the news media examined his background to come up with similar profiles of the individual.

Canon also suggested that, with experience, a reporter develops the ability to detect whether a subject is being truthful.

"One thing that sets me off is if someone speaks with great confidence about something he or she would not know about first hand," he noted, "or if they are very quick to pass on information as solid, when they can only have gotten it second hand.

"Other behavior that suggests interviewees are lying are if interviewees are too glib about something, answers come too quickly or too colorfully, or they are quick with clever phrases," Canon added. "A reporter is keenly aware of these things, not because we are great talents at reading others, but because we are required to be cautious.

"The more experienced I become, the more cautious I get about coming to a conclusion about someone's personality," he said.

- What are the two major explanations for the primacy effect phenomenon? Can the logic of these explanations be reconciled with the existence of recency effects?

- What are central traits, and how do they differ from primacy effects? Why or why not?

- What basic difference separates cognitive algebra theorists from central trait theorists? What would each have to say about the importance of first impressions and the potential for changing them?

ATTRIBUTION: EXPLAINING THE CAUSES OF BEHAVIOR

Over the course of the semester, Kate has come to have great respect for her history professor, Professor Kirk. Even though she isn't doing all that well in class, she likes his effusive, outgoing lecture style and the way he makes ancient history entertaining and provocative. Near the end of the term, she sees Professor Kirk in the campus center coffee bar and decides to tell him how much she likes his class. Expecting a cordial response, she is startled by his cool and indifferent reaction. She leaves feeling confused and a little foolish and wondering why he reacted the way he did.

Kate's attempt to understand the professor's reaction illustrates several central issues in **attribution**, the process by which people attempt to identify the causes of others' (as well as their own) behavior. In this case, Professor Kirk's behavior can be explained by considering the central attributional dilemma he faces: whether to attribute Kate's compliment to situational or dispositional causes.

SITUATION OR DISPOSITION? A CENTRAL ATTRIBUTIONAL DILEMMA

In seeking to explain another person's behavior, people rely on two general categories of causes: situation and disposition. **Situational causes** are reasons for behavior that rest on the demands or constraints of a given social setting. Most situations call for certain kinds of behavior. For instance, people in a lecture class basically sit, take notes, and ask or answer questions. They don't stand up in the middle of the class and express their personal opinions. Likewise, if the setting is a baseball game on a miserably hot day and the home team is behind by six runs, the manager's temper tantrum when a runner is called out is probably due to the situation and not to the manager's temperament. Certain circumstances, then, produce particular kinds of behavior.

In contrast, in some situations, behavior is produced by **dispositional causes**—reasons for behavior that rest on the personality traits and characteristics of the individual carrying out the behavior. Some people are habitually friendly, or hostile, or energetic, regardless of the particular situation in which they find themselves. Consequently, when they act friendly, hostile, or energetic, respectively, the cause of their behavior is most likely their disposition.

In the case of Professor Kirk, Kate's compliment placed him in a quandary over interpreting her behavior. Is Kate's compliment due to her disposition ("She really seems nice and friendly and sincere, and she must genuinely like the course")? Or is her compliment due to situational constraints ("She must be saying that to raise her grade; students always tell me they like my class—just before the end of the term")?

In this case, the professor is unlikely to make a dispositional attribution, for two reasons. First, Professor Kirk doesn't know Kate, and therefore he has no information about how friendly she is. Second, and even more important, situational constraints against saying anything *except* what Kate did are extremely strong. (Would you go up to a professor and tell him how much you hated his class?) Consequently, given that he doesn't know Kate and can't easily attribute her behavior to dispositional causes, Professor Kirk is most likely to attribute her remarks to situational (and less flattering) motives.

But what of Kate? Like Professor Kirk, she is faced with the attributional puzzle of determining the causes of another's behavior—in this case, Professor Kirk's. If she looks to

attribution: The process by which people attempt to identify the causes of others' and their own behavior.

situational causes: Reasons for behavior that rest on the demands or constraints of a given social setting; most situations call for certain kinds of behavior.

dispositional causes: Reasons for behavior that rest on the personality traits and characteristics of the individual carrying out the behavior.

dispositional causes, she's faced with an inconsistency, because Kirk would then seem warm and outgoing in class but cold in person. A more likely conclusion is that his cool behavior toward Kate was due not to dispositional factors but to situational causes. Kate sadly concludes that Professor Kirk reacted to her specifically (a situational stimulus) and that he really doesn't like her that much.

Such reasoning illustrates a general principle about attributions: Behavior will be attributed to a situational cause when external reasons are more likely or plausible than dispositional causes. Conversely, behavior will be attributed to dispositional factors when external causes are unlikely (Hilton et al., 1990). This point was demonstrated in an experiment in which participants were asked to rate the personality of a job applicant. To some participants the applicant presented himself as having the characteristics that were prerequisites for the job; to other participants he presented himself as not having those characteristics (Jones, Gergen, & Davis, 1961).

When the applicant indicated that he had traits that were necessary for the job, participants were not terribly confident about their ratings of the candidate—they thought he might be trying to make a good impression just to get the job. In other words, he seemed to be responding to the situational requirements of the job interview. But when the candidate indicated that he had traits that were contrary to ones related to the job requirements, participants were considerably more confident about their ratings. In this case, his behavior was viewed as a reflection of his disposition.

We can see the operation of this principle in politics. When a Democratic senator follows a Democratic president's wishes and votes in favor of a bill, the most likely attribution is a situational one: The senator is voting for the bill because of pressure to remain loyal to the president. But if the senator votes against the president's position, we are much more likely to make a dispositional attribution (for instance, that the senator truly believes the bill is unwise), because the senator is acting contrary to the external pressures of the situation.

Attribution approaches assume that people make their attributions on the basis of mini-experiments that they carry out in their minds. Implicitly using the principles that underlie experimentation, discussed in Chapter 1, people seek to identify the "Why?" behind the behavior of others. However, because the process of forming attributions is not immune to biases and error, such people are considered "naive scientists" by social psychologists (Harvey, 1989; White, 1992). Like trained scientists, laypeople attempt to make systematic use of the social data at hand; like naive scientists, though, they are not always exact in the methods they use to interpret information.

As we discuss next, two major theories of attribution seek to explain the systematic processes people use in forming attributions: Jones and Davis's theory of correspondent inferences, which considers the ways in which we infer intentions, traits, and dispositions; and Kelley's model of causal attribution, which focuses on how we consolidate different sorts of information to make attributions.

Jones and Davis's correspondent inference theory: From acts to dispositions.   Consider the following situation:

Dan is alone in his dorm room, working on a term paper. There is a knock at the door, but Dan ignores it. The knock becomes louder and a voice outside the door says, "C'mon, Dan. I know you're in there. I just want to talk to you for a minute about catching a quick movie." Dan answers the door, talks to the visitor for half an hour, and finally decides to go to the movie.

As an observer of this scene, what kind of judgment would you make about the motives behind Dan's behavior? Social psychologists Edward Jones and Keith Davis (1965; Jones, 1979, 1990) developed a theory of attribution that helps us understand how an observer would answer this question. Further, the theory covers the more general case of how we use a person's behavior to make inferences about enduring personality traits and motivations.

correspondent inferences: Observers' notions of how closely an overt behavior or action represents a specific underlying intention, trait, or disposition.

The Jones and Davis theory examines **correspondent inferences**, observers' notions of how closely an overt behavior or action represents a specific underlying intention, trait, or disposition. The more a behavior appears to reflect the underlying disposition, the greater the correspondence between these two factors (Jones, 1990).

According to Jones and Davis, we learn most from behaviors of others that lead to unique or *noncommon effects.* The theory assumes that any behavior leads to a particular set of consequences. However, the behaviors that are most helpful in forming correspondent inferences are those that result in consequences that other, alternative behaviors would not have produced.

For example, if we knew that Dan could work on his term paper equally well whether he was alone or chatting with a visitor, we would know little about the extent of his motivation for completing the paper because there would be a lack of noncommon effects. That is, whether he chose to chat or to remain alone, the effect on the paper would be the same. However, this is not the case in the above scenario: It is clear that if Dan chats with the visitor, he will be unable to continue writing; whereas if he does not answer the door and chat, he can continue to write. We can say, then, that the two alternative behaviors (chatting versus not answering the door) have noncommon effects. Dan's choice of behavior—to talk to the visitor—is informative, then, in that it suggests that Dan's motivation to write his term paper is not particularly high.

One additional factor that colors our attributions is the *social desirability* of a behavior—the degree to which society encourages and values a behavior. The greater the social desirability of a behavior, the more difficult it is to draw a correspondent inference between the act and a disposition. For example, because the visitor knew that Dan was in his room, it would have been an outright insult for Dan to refuse to open the door. Because Dan's behavior—inviting the visitor inside his room—has an element of social desirability, it is relatively uninformative about what it represents. In contrast, if Dan had refused to answer the door, even in the face of repeated requests, his behavior would clearly be low in social desirability. As a result, it would tell more about Dan's motivations and disposition, suggesting that Dan was strongly committed to completing his term paper.

Another basis for making attributions relates to the degree of *choice* an individual is seen to have in carrying out a behavior. For instance, if you are assigned by a teacher to argue in favor of capital punishment in a debate, it is unlikely that your classmates will assume that you necessarily believe what you were saying. In contrast, if you choose on your own to argue that side of the issue, then it is a fair assumption that you believe what you are arguing. Similarly, if Dan chooses to invite a visitor into his room, his behavior is more informative than if the visitor barges in without an invitation.

Jones and Davis's theory of correspondent inferences considers how observers take a small part of a person's behavior and use it to determine how representative that sample is of the person's underlying traits and other characteristics. But that is only one aspect of the attribution process. Another approach to attribution, which we discuss next, focuses on how we determine whether a behavior is caused primarily by situational forces or personal factors.

Kelley's model of causal attribution: Searching for consensus, consistency, and distinctiveness.   Consider the following situation: You're at a party. You suddenly see your classmate Mia get angry with another classmate, Josh, and begin to yell at him. What psychological processes operate as you figure out why Mia yelled at Josh?

Several possibilities come to mind. For instance, Mia's behavior might have been caused by something about Mia herself (who, in social psychological terms, is the "actor" in this context). Perhaps she has a bad temper and is easily angered. That's one possibility: Mia is yelling at Josh because she has a quick temper.

Another possibility is that the fight was caused by something about Josh (the target of the behavior), who may be the kind of person who often angers others by his blunt remarks. In other words, Mia is yelling at Josh because he said something inflammatory.

Still another possibility is that the fight was caused by the specific situation—something that happened at the party. Perhaps Mia was particularly volatile because she had begun to

For a Catholic mother, taking a pro-choice position on abortion may well be lower in social desirability than taking an anti-abortion stance. Because it is low in social desirability, though, her behavior allows observers to be more confident in drawing correspondent inferences between the behavior and the underlying disposition.

feel ill. Consequently, Mia is yelling because she was feeling sick and lost control during a minor disagreement.

Social psychologist Harold Kelley suggests that, in attempting to choose among these potential causes, people consider three different kinds of information (Kelley, 1972; Kelley & Michela, 1980). First, they use consensus information. *Consensus information* is data regarding the degree to which other people react similarly in the same situation. For example, if others frequently get angry with Josh at parties, there would be high consensus; if it is rare for others to get angry with him at parties, there would be low consensus.

In addition to consensus information, observers use a second category of data, called consistency information. *Consistency information* is knowledge regarding the degree to which people react in the same way in a variety of situations. If Mia's behavior is highly consistent (she often gets angry at Josh and frequently fights with him), there is high consistency. If she seldom gets angry with Josh at parties, her behavior is of low consistency. Information that is low in consistency is not very informative in terms of making dispositional attributions.

Finally, the third category of data available to an observer is distinctiveness information. *Distinctiveness information* refers to the extent to which the same behavior occurs in relation to other people or stimuli. For example, if Mia gets angry only with Josh and doesn't get angry with anyone else, getting angry is high in distinctiveness for Mia. But if she frequently gets angry at her dates and reacts by fighting with them, the behavior of getting angry is low in distinctiveness.

Taking into account information about consensus, consistency, and distinctiveness allows people to attribute a certain behavior either to dispositional factors (something about the actor) or to situational factors (something about the target person or the particular circumstances). More precisely, when consensus and distinctiveness are low and consistency is high, people tend to make dispositional attributions (see Figure 2–3). On the other hand, when consensus, consistency, and distinctiveness are all high, people tend to make attributions to external, situational factors (Reynolds & West, 1989; Iacobucci & McGill, 1990).

More concretely, if others don't get angry with Josh (low consensus); Mia often gets angry with Josh (high consistency); and Mia gets angry with most of her dates (low distinctiveness), an observer would likely conclude that something about Mia led to her anger. In contrast, if people in general and Mia in particular frequently get angry with Josh (high consensus and high consistency), and Mia gets angry only with Josh but not with other dates (high distinctiveness), then the source of Mia's anger will most likely be attributed to Josh.

Subsequent research has lent support to Kelley's attribution model. In a typical study, researchers provide participants with differing kinds of information and then trace the kinds of attributions they make (McArthur, 1972; Harvey & Weary, 1984; Försterling, 1989; Cheng & Novick, 1990). Furthermore, even when some of the three sources of information are absent, people still make causal inferences similar to the ones predicted by the model. For instance, simply knowing that a behavior is of low distinctiveness can lead observers to attribute its cause to internal (dispositional) factors. Learning that there is high consensus associated with a particular behavior is sufficient to lead an observer to attribute the cause to external (situational) factors, even without any other information (Orvis, Cunningham, & Kelley, 1975).

However, Kelley's model has certain limitations (Cheng & Novick, 1990). Although the theory works well when people have concrete, explicit information regarding consensus, distinctiveness, and consistency, it does not work quite so well when people must seek, find, or recognize the information on their own. For example, reading in a consumer testing magazine about the high reliability of Toyota automobiles theoretically should provide a powerful, objective source of consensus information. However, such information may have less impact on a person's attributions than the complaints of a next-door neighbor about the unreliability of her particular Toyota, even though consensus in such a case is limited (Nisbett & Ross, 1980; Davidson & Hirtle, 1990; Heller, Saltzstein, & Caspe, 1992).

In sum, although the general principles of Kelley's theory appear to be valid, the theory is most accurate in describing how people make attributions when they have clear and unambiguous information on which to base the attributions. It also is most accurate when people

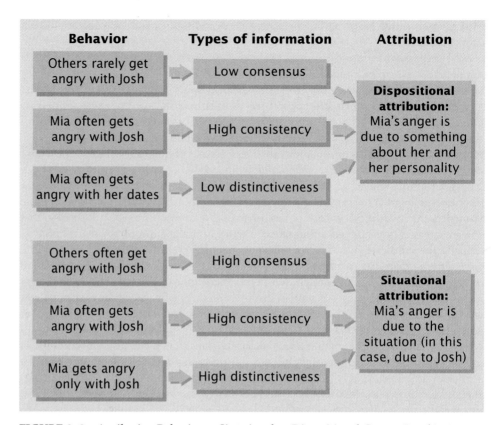

FIGURE 2–3   Attributing Behavior to Situational or Dispositional Causes By taking information about consensus, consistency, and distinctiveness into account, people attribute behavior either to dispositional factors (something about the person) or to situational factors (something about the target person or the particular circumstances). Specifically, when consensus and distinctiveness are low and consistency is high, people make dispositional attributions. In contrast, when consensus, consistency, and distinctiveness are all high, people make attributions to external, situational factors.

encounter unexpected events, which they are unable to explain in terms of what they already know about the person or situation (Nisbett & Ross, 1980; Bohner et al., 1988).

BIASES IN ATTRIBUTION: THE FALLIBILITY OF THE NAIVE SCIENTIST

Let's face it: We don't always have the ability, the motivation, or simply the time to sort through behavior and come up with an accurate accounting of the motives behind it. Consequently, people are not always as rational in making attributions as the various attributional theories might suggest. The naive scientist within us sometimes falls prey to a variety of biases and errors (Vorauer & Ross, 1993; Piattelli-Palmarini, 1994). We turn now to some of the most frequent pitfalls.

The fundamental attribution error: What you see is not (necessarily) what you get.   As we discussed at the beginning of the chapter, at the same time that some observers concluded that Dr. Jack Kevorkian's behavior was produced by psychological character flaws, Kevorkian's supporters claimed that he was simply reacting to the circumstances in which he found himself and following Thomas Youk's pleas to die.

Although the particulars of the Kevorkian case were more extreme than most everyday occurrences, they reflect social psychological processes that are hardly unique. In fact, the assumption that other people's behavior represents some inner trait underlies one of the most common and powerful attributional biases: the fundamental attribution error. The

fundamental attribution error is the tendency to overattribute others' behavior to dispositional causes and the corresponding failure to recognize the importance of situational causes (Ross, 1977; Ross & Nisbett, 1991).

The fundamental attribution error is pervasive. For instance, letters to advice columns such as Ann Landers or "Dear Abby" provide a good illustration of the phenomenon. When social psychologists Thomas Schoeneman and Daniel Rubanowitz analyzed the letters (1985; Fischer, Schoeneman, & Rubanowitz, 1987), they found that *writers* tended to attribute the causes of their circumstances to the situation when describing their problems ("I'm always late to work because the bus doesn't run on time," or "We're having marital problems because my wife won't sleep with me any more"). On the other hand, *readers* of the letters were more apt to see the problem in terms of the characteristics of the person writing the letter ("She's too lazy to take an earlier bus" or "He should take a bath more often").

Why should the tendency to view others' personality characteristics as the cause of their behavior be so strong? One reason is merely perceptual. When we view the behavior of other people, the information that is most conspicuous is that which comes from the individual. Typically, the environment appears relatively static and unchanging, while the individual moves about and reacts—making the person the target of attention. Consequently, we focus on the person and his and her disposition.

Furthermore, we may simply be unaware or lack knowledge of situational constraints that are affecting another's behavior. And even when we know something about the situation, we may misinterpret what we know, and our misinterpretation may lead us to inflate the degree to which a behavior is produced by dispositional causes. In short, we may overemphasize the role of dispositional factors in causing a behavior either because we know little or nothing about the situation, or because what we do know leads us to interpret behavior erroneously as being caused by dispositional factors (Gilbert & Malone, 1995; Gilbert, Miller, & Ross, 1998).

Another reason for the fundamental attribution error rests on the presumed basic process observers follow when they make an attribution. Specifically, social psychologist Daniel Gilbert has speculated that the attribution process actually consists of two sequential stages (Gilbert, Krull, & Pelham, 1988; Gilbert, 1989; Gilbert et al., 1992; Gilbert, Miller, & Ross, 1998). Gilbert argues that the first step people take is to make a fast, automatic dispositional attribution, inferring that personal characteristics explain the behavior. However, once they make this quick initial determination, people then correct or adjust it by taking into account situational constraints that may have produced the behavior. This follow-up correction is more thoughtful and occurs at a relatively slower, more leisurely pace.

Because the situational correction is sluggish, the process is relatively easy to disrupt. For example, if people are distracted by some outside diversion or do not pay attention closely, they are apt to make do with their initial—dispositional—judgment. Hence, people are likely to overemphasize dispositional judgments not because they carefully weigh the possible situational or dispositional causes of a person's behavior and then attribute the behavior to dispositional factors. Instead, they often stop at the first stage of the attributional process, considering only their initial dispositional judgment and not sufficiently correcting it with additional data that may be available (Gilbert & Osborne, 1989; see Figure 2–4).

To test this reasoning, Gilbert devised an experiment in which participants were led to be "cognitively busy" in some conditions (Gilbert, Krull, & Pelham, 1988). In the study, all participants watched a silent videotape of a woman who appeared to be extremely anxious, biting her nails, twirling her hair, tapping her fingers, and shifting in her chair. However, some participants were told that the woman was discussing such anxiety-provoking subjects as her sexual fantasies, whereas other participants were told that she had been taped while discussing bland topics, such as world travel. Participants were then asked to characterize how anxious the woman typically was. In other words, they had to indicate how *dispositionally* anxious she was.

Clearly, a typical person might reasonably appear nervous while discussing anxiety-producing topics. Hence, although observers might first make a dispositional attribution (she is a nervous person), they should subsequently correct it with a situational attribution (she acts

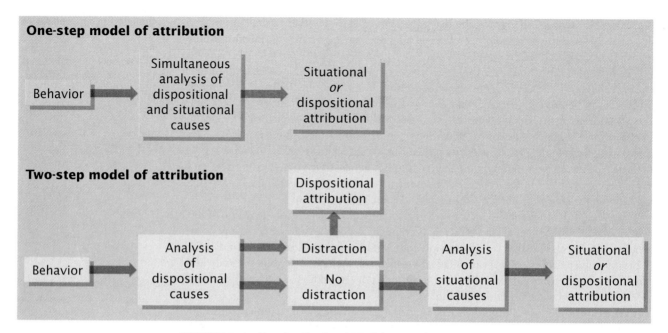

FIGURE 2–4   **Two Attributional Models**   According to the one-step model of attribution, people simultaneously analyze whether a behavior is due to dispositional or situational causes. In contrast, the two-step model suggests that they first analyze dispositional causes and then consider situational possibilities.

nervous because of the anxiety-producing topic she is discussing). On the other hand, observers who are distracted might never get to the second stage, and they would likely stick with their uncorrected dispositional attribution.

In the experiment, half of the participants were distracted as they watched the woman on the tape by being asked to memorize the list of topics the woman was supposedly discussing. The remaining participants watched the tape without such distraction. The prediction, then, was that those who were cognitively busy would be prone to make dispositional attributions, regardless of topic, whereas those who were undistracted would make attributions that were less dispositional when supposedly anxiety-producing topics were being discussed on the tape.

As you can see in Figure 2–5, the predictions received clear support. Cognitively, the attributions made by busy participants were unaffected by the topics supposedly under discussion. In contrast, those participants who were not distracted took the supposed topics into account, making attributions that were more dispositional when the woman's nervousness appeared during discussions of bland topics.

In sum, the two-stage account of attribution seems accurate: We first make dispositional characterizations, and then, if we're not otherwise cognitively busy, we take situational information into account. As Gilbert has observed, "Perceivers do not ponder, 'Did Arthur take the money because he is dishonest [dispositional causation] or because his friends pressured him to do so [situational causation]?' Rather, perceivers of such behavior first draw a dispositional inference ('Arthur is dishonest') and then correct this inference with information about the situational constraints on the actor ('But given that his friends pressured him to take the money, I guess he isn't *really* dishonest')" (Gilbert, 1989, p. 193).

The person positivity bias: Looking for the bright side of others.   Like Pollyanna, the heroine of Eleanor Porter's 1913 novel, who could see no evil in the world, many of us have a blind optimism about others. This tendency to see the world (and other people) in positive terms is referred to as the **person positivity bias**, or "Pollyanna effect" (Sears, 1982; Miller & Felicio, 1990; Singh et al., 1997).

person positivity bias ("Pollyanna effect"): The tendency to see the world (and other people) in positive terms.

The person positivity bias operates in several domains. For example, when participants are asked during an experiment to rate people they have just met, they tend to judge them positively. Similarly, people's evaluations of important historical and public figures—such as presidents—tend to be generally positive.

There are exceptions to the person positivity bias, however. For instance, people tend to rate positively their own representative to the U.S. Congress but hold negative attitudes toward Congress as an entity. Although humorist Will Rogers may have never met a person he didn't like (to paraphrase his famous quote), not all of us would agree.

Motivational biases: Wanting to look good at the cost of accuracy.

Have you ever had the opportunity to teach or tutor someone? If your student later did well on a test, how did you explain the success? If you're like most people, you probably gave yourself a bit of credit. But suppose the student did poorly. Were you equally ready to claim responsibility for your student's failure?

Probably not. The reason stems from several biases that fall into the collective category of **motivational biases**: sources of error that stem from a need to present oneself well, either to impress others or to maintain one's self-esteem. Unlike the more cognitively oriented attributional biases that we've considered up to now, motivational biases don't originate from failures or inadequacies in examining and drawing conclusions from received information. Instead, they result from the desire to achieve some goal, such as making oneself look good (Agnostinelli et al., 1992; Forsyth & Kelley, 1996).

The operation of motivational biases in attribution was demonstrated in a classic study in which experienced teachers taught a lesson to pupils, whose performance—in terms of both level and progression—was manipulated by the experimenters (Beckman, 1970). When the pupils' performances improved, the instructors tended to attribute the improvement to their abilities as teachers. But when the pupils' performances declined, the instructors attributed the failure to the students.

In contrast, a group of uninvolved observers who had no responsibility for the students' performance attributed good performance to the students and bad performance to the teachers—exactly the opposite pattern from that of the instructors' attributions. Clearly, the kind of involvement a person has in a situation has a powerful effect on the person's causal attributions.

In fact, a general attributional bias, known as the self-serving bias, sometimes occurs when people feel they may be responsible for others' behavior. The **self-serving bias** is a general tendency to attribute personal success to internal factors—skill, ability, or effort—and to attribute failure to external factors, such as chance or a particular situation. For instance, coaches may feel their teams' successes are due to their coaching, while a poor record is due to the poor skills of their players. Movie directors may assume that good reviews are brought

motivational biases: Sources of error that stem from a need to present oneself well, either to impress others or to maintain one's self-esteem.

self-serving bias: A general tendency to attribute one's own success to internal factors—skill, ability, or effort—and to attribute failure to external factors, such as chance or a particular situation.

FIGURE 2–5 Cognitively Busy and Undistracted Participants' Attributions
Undistracted participants made stronger dispositional attributions when the woman on the tape was thought to be discussing bland topics than when she was supposedly discussing anxiety-producing topics. In contrast, participants who were cognitively busy never corrected their initial dispositional attribution, regardless of the topic. (*Source:* Adapted from Gilbert, Krull, & Pelham, 1988, p. 735.)

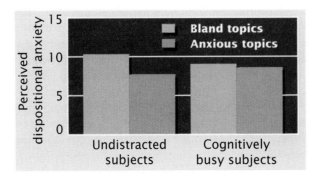

Belief in a just world can lead a gambler to feel that she deserves to win, if she has suffered in other areas of her life.

about by their accomplished directing but poor reviews are due to a lousy script. Authors may surmise that the success of a book is attributable to their writing skills but that failure is caused by poor editing and marketing (Schlenker, Weigold, & Hallam, 1990; Tandon, Ansari, & Kapoor, 1991; Schlenker & Weigold, 1992; De Michele, Gansneder, & Solomon, 1998; Campbell & Sedikides, 1999).

In some cases, motivational biases take a particularly cruel twist, when observers, in order to maintain their view of the world, hold victims of disaster responsible for their own misfortune. This misattribution may stem from the fact that most of us hold a *belief in a just world,* the notion that people get out of life what they deserve. Such a belief often leads to the related belief that people tend to deserve what happens to them (Lerner, 1980; Janoff-Bulman, 1992).

Although the just-world belief results in positive evaluations of others who have good things happen to them, because the judgment is generally that people deserve their good fortune, it can produce unwarranted negative impressions when disaster strikes. For instance, robbery and assault victims may be perceived as having done something to invite the crime, such as leaving their doors unlocked or carelessly wandering into unsafe areas. Rape victims are often asked what they did to bring on the misfortune. People with AIDS may be thought to have acquired the disease through their own moral failings; battered wives may be suspected of having acted in ways that provoked their beatings (Kristiansen & Giulietti, 1990; McCaul et al., 1990; Hunter & Ross, 1991; Anderson, 1992; Best, Dansky, & Kilpatrick, 1992; Bell, Kuriloff, & Lottes, 1994; Heaven, Connors, & Pretorius, 1998).

Such blame-the-victim attributions are **defensive attributions** that enable observers to deal with perceived inequities in others' lives and to maintain the belief that the world is just. Presumably, blaming the victim permits observers to distance themselves from the misfortune of others. To admit that negative events might happen just on the basis of chance is highly threatening. People tend to view negative outcomes as being deserved, in order to protect themselves against this reality. By making such attributions, people are able to convince themselves that they are less likely to suffer adversity (e.g., Thornton et al., 1986; Thornton, 1992).

Of course, people are likely to make defensive attributions only to the extent that they feel threatened by the misfortunes of others. In particular, people who live in cultures with high levels of *fatalism*—the acceptance of events as inevitable—may be less susceptible to just-world beliefs than those in less fatalistic societies. For instance, evidence shows that people living in many Asian cultures, which are particularly fatalistic, may be less prone to defensive attributions than those in Western cultures (Yang & Ho, 1988).

The lower Asian susceptibility to defensive attributions raises broader questions about the universality of the attributional processes that we have been considering. In fact, as we discuss in the Exploring Diversity section, even the most basic attributional processes seem to be influenced by cultural factors.

defensive attributions: Attributions that enable observers to deal with perceived inequities in others' lives and to maintain the belief that the world is just.

CULTURAL INFLUENCES ON ATTRIBUTION: CULTURE AND CAUSE

The evidence could not be more compelling: By the time the average student in Japan has reached the upper grades of public school, he or she is doing better than the average U.S. student. The situation doesn't start this way: In first grade there is relatively little difference in mathematics performance between Japanese and U.S. students. By fifth grade, however, Japanese students consistently outperform American students on standardized tests of math achievement. Results on reading tests are similar: Although U.S. students actually outperform Japanese students in reading scores in the first grade, by fifth grade the Japanese children have caught up with the Americans (Stevenson & Lee, 1990). Why do Japanese students end up outperforming those in the United States?

Although several reasons for the difference have been suggested—ranging from the fact that Japanese students spend many more days in school to the presence of greater cultural pressure on Japanese students to excel scholastically—one of the most compelling explanations rests on differences in the attributions made in the two cultures about the causes of academic performance. According to work by educational psychologist Harold Stevenson and his colleagues, people in Western and Asian societies hold very different attributions about the underlying causes of academic performance. Specifically, Westerners are more likely to point to stable, internal causes for a student's performance (such as a student's native level of intelligence), whereas Asians are more apt to see temporary, situational factors (such as effort) as being responsible for the performance.

The Asian view is derived in part from Confucian writings about the important role of effort in achieving success. Asian society minimizes individual differences in achievement across all domains and accentuates the role of hard work and perseverance. In contrast, Americans are more likely to emphasize the importance of innate ability in making causal attributions for a person's performance. If a student does not do well, Western cultures may assume he or she lacks the intellectual abilities necessary for good performance, whereas Asian cultures may assume he or she is not working hard enough.

Such attributions regarding the causes of academic performance influence people's reactions to poor performance. For Japanese and Taiwanese students, poor performance is seen as a temporary state, one that hard work will remedy. For U.S. students, however, poor performance is an indication of lack of ability, which may lead to discouragement and withdrawal from academic endeavors rather than diligence and perseverance to overcome initial difficulty.

The differences between Western and Asian approaches to academic success reflect differences between collectivistic and individualistic cultures. **Collectivistic cultures** emphasize membership in groups and the group's well-being, whereas **individualistic cultures** emphasize personal identity, individual uniqueness, and individual freedom. In collectivistic cultures, people are identified more as group members than as individuals, and groups have a powerful influence on the individual. In contrast, members of individualistic

Culture can be a powerful lens for perceiving others' behavior. Members of individualistic societies tend to attribute the behavior of others to personal, internal factors. On the other hand, members of collectivistic societies are more likely to hold the view that social behavior is shaped by relationships and situational factors.

collectivistic culture: A culture that emphasizes membership in groups and the group's well-being.

individualistic culture: A culture that emphasizes personal identity, individual uniqueness, and individual freedom.

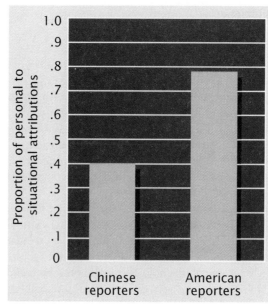

FIGURE 2–6 Chinese and American Reporters' Susceptibility to the Fundamental Attribution Error In the more collectivistic Chinese culture, reporters were more likely to emphasize situational factors as the cause of behavior, whereas American reporters, reflecting the more individualistic Western culture, emphasized personal factors in their accounts of a murder. These data suggest, then, that the Chinese reporters were less susceptible to the fundamental attribution error than American reporters. (Higher figures indicate more personal than situational attributions.)
(*Source:* Morris & Peng, 1994.)

cultures are identified primarily as individuals rather than group members, and their behavior tends to reflect personal preferences more than the desire to do what is good for the group.

Social psychologists Michael Morris and Kaiping Peng (1994) argue that the collectivistic or individualistic tendencies of a culture play a fundamental role in determining the way causal attributions for behavior are made. They suggest that members of individualistic cultures tend to hold implicit theories of social behavior in which the causes of events are due to general, stable internal dispositions. In contrast, people in collectivistic cultures are more likely to hold the view that social behavior is shaped by relationships and situational pressures.

We might expect that these fundamental differences in viewing causality in the social world would produce differences in susceptibility to the fundamental attribution error—and they do. For example, Morris and Peng examined the attributions made by U.S. and Chinese reporters in newspaper accounts of two murders, one committed by an American and one by a Chinese perpetrator. Regardless of whether the perpetrator was American or Chinese, the articles by American reporters tended to emphasize personal traits (the murderer had a "very bad temper" or was "mentally unstable"), whereas the Chinese reporters emphasized situational factors (the murder was due to the easy availability of guns, or reflected societal pressures, with the murderer being "a victim" of the competitiveness of society). Overall, the proportion of personal attributions was far greater for American reporters, illustrating that the Chinese reporters were less susceptible to the fundamental attribution error (see Figure 2–6).

Other facets of culture, such as language, also may promote the use of situational, over dispositional, attributions. For instance, people who use English might say, "I am late," suggesting a dispositional cause ("I tend to be a tardy person.") In contrast, when users of the Spanish language report the same occurrence, their language expresses it as "The clock caused me to be late," suggesting a situational cause for their tardiness (Zebrowitz-McArthur, 1988; Holtgraves, 1997).

Clearly, then, the cultural lens through which people view the world influences how they attribute the causes of others' behavior. Furthermore, cross-cultural research has clearly shown that the biases that social psychologists once thought to be fundamental may not be so fundamental after all (Krull & Erickson, 1995; Lee, McCauley, & Draguns, 1999; Choi, Nisbett, & Norenzayan, 1999).

REVIEW AND RETHINK

Review

- The two major categories of causes to which people attribute behavior are situational causes and dispositional causes.

- The Jones and Davis attribution theory focuses on correspondent inferences—observers' notions of how closely an overt behavior or action represents a specific underlying intention, trait, or disposition.

- Kelley's model of causal attribution considers causes of behavior in terms of consensus, consistency, and distinctiveness information.

- Among typical attribution biases are the fundamental attribution error, the person positivity bias, and motivational biases, including defensive attributions.

- Attributions of behavior appear to be subject to distinct cultural influences.

Rethink

- According to Kelley's attribution theory, what three questions do observers ask themselves when trying to make sense of another's behavior?

- How does the Jones and Davis attribution theory differ from Kelley's model?

- Identify the attributional bias in each of the following sentences.

    a. In general, people hate Congress but love their congressional representatives.

    b. Alex Trebek (the host of the TV game show "Jeopardy") is one of the smartest people I have ever known.

    c. I know that the lottery is a long shot, but I can't help but think that I'll win because I need the money so badly.

    d. I did all I could to study for that exam, but fate was against me. The instructor managed to ask only questions I was unsure about.

- What is the explanation for the fundamental attribution error?

SCHEMAS: ORGANIZING IMPRESSIONS

Consider what it would be like if each time you encountered an individual, you had to make a novel, unique judgment about that person. And think how difficult and time consuming it would be if each time you encountered that person in the future, you had to revise your impression to incorporate information about his or her particular behavior newly gathered on that occasion.

The primary way we simplify and organize impressions of others is through schemas. **Schemas** are organized bodies of information stored in memory. The information in a schema provides us with a representation of the way the social world operates, and it enables us to categorize and interpret new information related to the schema (Fiske & Taylor, 1991; Smith, 1998).

We all hold schemas relating to everyday objects in our environment. Most of us, for instance, hold a schema for automobiles. We have an idea of what automobiles look like, how they are used, what they can do for us, and how to differentiate them from other vehicles such as trucks or wagons or bicycles. More importantly, from a social psychological point of view, we hold schemas for particular people (our mothers, girlfriends, boyfriends, brothers, and sisters) and for classes of people playing particular roles (mail carriers, teachers, librarians). Each of these schemas provides a way of organizing behavior into meaningful wholes.

schemas: Organized bodies of information stored in memory.

FIGURE 2–7   The Prototype of the "Committed Person" The prototype of the "committed person" can be divided into different levels of a hierarchy, ranging from the more general to the more specific. (*Source:* Adopted from Cantor & Mischel, 1979.)

The personality types that we assemble and use when perceiving others are organized into schemas known as prototypes. *Prototypes* are schemas that organize a group of traits into meaningful personality categories. Prototypes represent the typical or average example of a category. We can think of a prototype, then, as the schema of a particular personality type.

For example, consider the prototype of "committed person," an individual who is concerned about, involved with, and dedicated to a particular cause (Cantor & Mischel, 1979). As you can see in Figure 2–7, this prototype can be divided into different levels of a hierarchy that relate to different levels of specificity. For instance, at the most specific level, called the subordinate level, the prototype consists of different types of committed individuals, such as monks, nuns, and activists for a particular cause. The middle level is represented by general classes of people: the religious devotee or social activist. Finally, the subordinate and middle levels of specificity are subsumed under the broader superordinate level, which encompasses as a whole the prototype of a committed person.

Just as we have mental prototypes to represent particular types or classes of people, we have mental scripts to represent particular situations. A *script* is the organized knowledge people hold regarding a particular situation and the way events in that situation unfold (Abelson, 1981). For instance, most of us have a script for "classroom behavior." It includes walking into a class, finding a seat, taking out pen and paper for taking notes, and listening as the professor lectures. Like the script of a play, the script for a social scenario describes a sequence of actions (sitting down, taking out a pen), props (pen, notebook), roles (student, professor), and sequence rules (sitting down before taking notes).

The components of scripts are mentally organized into hierarchies, similar to the hierarchical arrangement of prototypes. For instance, exam-taking behavior and review session behavior are subordinate to general classroom behavior. In turn, classroom behavior may be subordinate to college behavior in general (Price & Goodman, 1990).

THE VALUE OF SCHEMAS: FURNISHING A SOCIAL FRAMEWORK FOR OLD AND NEW INFORMATION

Schemas, prototypes, and scripts are important to our social lives for several reasons. For one thing, they influence the ways we understand and interpret information about the social world.

Further, they help determine how we remember material to which we have been exposed previously. Finally, they influence the inferences we draw regarding incomplete information.

The utility of schemas: Recalling and interpreting the world.   To illustrate the utility of schemas in organizing our understanding of social events, social psychologists Susan Fiske and Shelley Taylor (1991) provide an example based on an ancient Native American folktale. In the folktale, the hero participates with several companions in a battle and is shot by an arrow, but he feels no pain. When he returns to his home and recounts the story, something black emerges from his mouth, and he dies the next morning.

For those of us unschooled in this particular Native American culture, the story makes little sense, and so we omit, add, change, or interpret aspects of it to fit in with our schemas. However, for someone familiar with the culture in question, the story is easily understood. For example, the hero doesn't feel pain because his companions are ghosts, and the "black thing" coming from his mouth is his departing soul. The point is that previous experiences, and more broadly our cultures, provide us with schemas that allow us to understand and interpret the meaning of the social world around us. When we do not have such a schema, our comprehension is reduced.

One central way that schemas aid people's comprehension of the behavior of others and of themselves is through their influence on memory. Schemas affect both how information is initially stored and how well it can later be recalled (Cohen, Stanhope, & Conway, 1992; Cowan, 1992; Greenberg, Westcott, & Bailey, 1998; Smith, 1998).

What we remember about others reflects the schemas that we see as relevant in a social setting. In particular, we tend to recall material that is relevant and consistent with a schema and forget information that is irrelevant and inconsistent (Laszlo, 1986; Hansen, 1989). For instance, we tend to remember pieces of information that fit with our notion of the ways people representing certain schemas behave, and at the same time ignore or forget data that do not seem to fit (Van Manen & Pietromonaco, 1994).

In an experiment illustrating this point, participants watched a videotape of a woman celebrating her birthday with her husband (Cohen, 1981). In one condition, the participants were told that she was a librarian, whereas in another they were told that she was a waitress. If the participants thought she was a librarian, they recalled her as having glasses and enjoying classical music. On the other hand, participants who thought she was a waitress reported that she drank beer and owned a television. Obviously, what was remembered was based on which particular schema was aroused by the occupational information provided.

Furthermore, our memories do not just consist of dry, factual information about people; they also harbor emotional content. For example, a woman who has been raped may recall and reexperience the terror she suffered when she finds herself in a location or under circumstances that remind her of where and when she was raped. It is not surprising, then, that when people encounter a person or situation relevant to a schema, the emotion attached

What is your schema of "older person"?

priming: The process by which recent exposure to stimuli such as people, ideas, or even mere words influences the interpretation of new information.

to the schema may be triggered. For instance, if we confront a member of the clergy, our "clergy" schema may be aroused, and we may experience whatever emotions are attached to that schema. Similarly, if a person meets a woman who reminds him of his mother, the emotions associated with his relationship to his mother may be aroused (Fiske & Pavelchak, 1986; Fiske & Neuberg, 1990).

Furthermore, obvious physical characteristics, such as age, sex, and race, are used to place others into relevant schemas at the very first moments of perception. This initial influence of schemas occurs with great speed and seemingly automatically, without the involvement of critical thinking (Gilbert & Hixon, 1991; Bargh et al., 1995).

Because they are so readily noticed, overt physical characteristics may be represented in primary, universal schemas. Such schemas may be so powerful that they decrease awareness of other, potentially more pertinent, social information relating to the person's specific characteristics (Brewer, 1988; Brewer & Lui, 1989; Brewer, Weber, & Carini, 1995). For example, once someone is categorized as an "old woman," the schema relevant to such a category may overwhelm other types of information. (What comes to mind when you think of the old woman category?) As we will see in Chapter 3 when we discuss prejudice and stereotyping, schemas may be so powerful that they prevent people from noting and remembering other, potentially more relevant information. When this happens, people may be in danger of viewing others from the perspective of their connection to a schema, rather than in terms of more personal, individualistic information.

Priming: Planting ideas in people's minds.   So far, we have discussed how schemas affect our recall and interpretation of people and events. However, schemas play another role: They prepare us for the future receipt of information through the phenomenon of priming.

Priming is the process by which recent exposure to stimuli such as people, ideas, or even mere words influences the interpretation of new information. Priming readies people to respond in a particular manner when relevant information is brought to mind (Bower, 1986; Tulving & Schacter, 1990; Smith, 1998).

Suppose, for instance, that you watch *Cujo*, the horror movie about a vicious dog with rabies who tries to murder its owner. If you encounter a dog soon after viewing the film, it would not be too surprising if even its most innocent behavior appeared to be menacing. Similarly, a physician who attends a lecture on the prevalence of child sexual abuse may be primed to identify cases of abuse in the next patient she treats.

Priming has been demonstrated in a variety of circumstances and contexts (e.g., Bargh, 1989; Philippot et al., 1991; Dovidio, Kawakami et al., 1997). Some of the earliest research focused on the way that mere exposure to a list of words predisposed people to judge another person in a way that was consistent with the list of words. For instance, in one of the original priming experiments, participants heard one of two lists of words during what they thought was a memory experiment (Higgins, Rholes, & Jones, 1977). In one condition, the words had positive connotations, such as brave, independent, and adventurous; in the other, they were less positive, such as reckless, foolish, and careless. Later, in what these same participants thought was another study, participants were asked to make judgments about a man who engaged in such activities as navigating a sailboat across the Atlantic and participating in a car demolition derby.

The findings were clear. Participants with previous exposure to the more positive words rated the man more favorably than those with previous exposure to the negative words. In sum, the initial words seem to have activated the equivalent of either "adventurous" or "foolhardy" schemas, and these schemas created either a positive or a negative mind-set in the participants.

Priming effects occur even when people are not consciously aware that they have been exposed to relevant prior information (Higgins & Brendl, 1995). For example, in some experiments, stimulus words are presented so quickly that participants report having no conscious awareness of being exposed to them. Even under such conditions, the words affect later judgments and evaluations. Obviously, exposure to the words—even though it occurs without conscious knowledge—acts as a prime (Bargh & Pietromonaco, 1982; Niedenthal & Cantor, 1986; Bargh, 1989).

Priming does more than just affect people's judgments of others. It also can have important consequences in the ways we treat them. For instance, in one experiment participants were primed through exposure to categories of people who, at the time, were viewed as hostile and competitive (such as rock star Alice Cooper and Indiana University basketball coach Bobby Knight). After such exposure, participants were placed in a situation in which they interacted with partners. The primes had their expected effect: Participants who had been primed acted toward their partners in a more hostile, competitive way than participants who had not been primed (Herr, 1986). Obviously, priming can be a potent phenomenon.

THE BIASES OF SCHEMAS: THE FALLIBILITIES OF THE COGNITIVE MISER

Although schemas play a central role in the ways we organize our social world, they have their drawbacks. Earlier in the chapter we mentioned how people may act like "cognitive misers" due to restrictions in their information-processing capabilities. As cognitive misers, they take shortcuts in considering information and may unwittingly value efficiency over accuracy in the ways they come to judgments.

Consider, for instance, an experiment in which participants were exposed to a conversation between two business executives (Holtgraves, Srull, & Socall, 1989). In some conditions they were led to believe that Robert was the boss of a company and Michael was his subordinate. In other conditions, though, Robert and Michael were presented as having equal status. Two days later, participants were asked to remember what Robert had said in the conversation.

As Figure 2–8 shows, the recollections depended on how the two people had been described earlier. When Robert was presented as the boss, he was recalled as acting in a considerably more assertive manner than when he was initially presented as having an equal status with Michael. The participants' "boss" schema, which presumably had been activated in the first condition, biased their recollections of how Robert had behaved.

Clearly, reliance on schemas may lead people to view the social world in an inaccurate and biased manner. Several other factors related to schemas can also lead to errors in our perception of others.

The representativeness heuristic: Considering mental matches. Suppose you meet a student named Nick at a party. Nick seems highly intelligent, neat, and orderly but a bit dull. Although he has a strong sense of morality, he seems to be self-centered, lacking feelings and sympathy for others. Assume you find out that he is a writer (although someone mentions that his writing is fairly dull) and that he occasionally makes corny puns and has flashes of a science fiction imagination.

When you talk about Nick to a friend the next day, you pause when the friend asks what Nick's major is. For some reason, you never found out. But you're willing to take a guess, because most of the people at the party were either humanities majors or computer science majors. You guess and say that he seems like the kind of guy who is involved in computer science.

FIGURE 2–8   Recall Is Consistent with One's Schema Participants' recollections of an earlier conversation depended on whether they thought one of the conversants was a boss or both were of equal status. (*Source:* Adapted from Holtgraves, Srull, & Socall, 1989, p. 155, Table 3.)

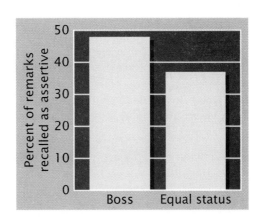

representativeness heuristic: The rule that is applied when judging people by the degree to which they represent a certain category.

base-rate fallacy: The tendency to underemphasize base-rate data because of the influence of more prominent, although ultimately less meaningful, information.

How do you come to such a conclusion? The most likely process involves mentally comparing Nick with your perception of what humanities majors and computer science majors are like. Because he fits fairly well with your schema of a computer science enthusiast, you come up with the theory that he is most likely a computer science major.

If this scenario sounds plausible to you, it is because of your use of a *heuristic*. Heuristics are a rule of thumb or mental shortcut that we employ to make decisions and solve problems. Although heuristics can sometimes be useful, they can also lead us astray. Consider, for instance, the **representativeness heuristic**, a rule we apply when we judge people by the degree to which they represent a certain category. Although the representativeness heuristic can often be helpful in guiding our judgments of others, it can lead us to ignore other information that might help us make accurate judgments.

For instance, suppose you learned that 80 percent of the people at the party were humanities majors and 20 percent were computer science majors. Would such additional information change your guess of Nick's major?

If you are like the participants in a classic experiment carried out by psychologists Daniel Kahneman and Amos Tversky (1973), the answer is no. When confronted with such a situation, participants generally stuck with their original judgment. Unfortunately, such judgments are not necessarily correct. If one were to follow strictly the laws of logic and probability, the answer should be revised. After all, given that it is considerably more likely that any single individual at the party is a humanities major, the most logical guess would be that Nick is a humanities major.

Base-rate fallacy: Ignoring the data.   The reason that most people make the wrong choice is that they ignore base-rate information. *Base-rate information* is data regarding the frequency with which some event occurs in the general population. Although the use of base-rate information should increase judgmental accuracy, people often ignore it. Disregarding base-rate data is a result of a bias known as the base-rate fallacy. The **base-rate fallacy** is the tendency to underemphasize base-rate data because of the influence of more prominent, although ultimately less meaningful, information (Bar-Hillel, 1980; Taylor & Thompson, 1982; Tindale, 1993).

An illustration of the base-rate fallacy is provided by an experiment in which participants read a vivid, lively description of a Puerto Rican woman who lived on welfare for many years (Hamill, Wilson, & Nisbett, 1980). According to the description, the woman led a comfortable, contented life with her many children. In one condition, participants were provided base-rate information that people on welfare tend to stay on welfare for long periods of time—information that was consistent with the scenario. In the other condition, participants received base-rate information that was contradictory to the scenario. This information (which was factual, by the way) suggested that most welfare recipients are on welfare for only a relatively short time.

When participants were asked to respond to the scenario, the base-rate information was largely disregarded, having little impact on participants' attitudes regarding welfare. Even when participants received base-rate information that contradicted the scenario, participants focused on the more colorful and involving scenario, ignoring the base-rate data. Plainly, the base-rate fallacy is a powerful bias.

Base-rate information, then, can help us make more accurate conclusions. This is not true, however, if the information is inaccurate. For instance, popular television programs portray a level of violence that far exceeds what is found in the real world. Not surprisingly, heavy television viewers, who use what they see on television as base-rate information, tend to overestimate substantially the amount of real violence in the world. In turn, this leads heavy viewers to be more fearful and anxious about violence than the facts warrant (Liebert & Sprafkin, 1988).

Because airplane crashes receive more publicity than auto crashes, the availability heuristic leads people to recall plane crashes more readily. This leads them to the erroneous conclusion that airplanes are less safe than automobiles.

Availability heuristic: Using what pops into your head.   Quick. Which do you think are more prevalent in the English language, words beginning with the letter *r*, or words that have *r* as the third letter? Most people guess that words beginning with *r* are more common. But they're wrong. The letter *r* occurs considerably more often as the third letter of English words than the first.

Why do so many people make this mistake? The answer is the **availability heuristic**, a rule we apply in judging the likelihood of an event by considering the ease with which it can be recalled from memory (Dawes, 1998). Thus, because words that start with *r* are relatively easy to recall, we assume they are more prevalent. Similarly, many more people are fearful when they take an airplane flight than when they go for a car ride—despite statistics showing that airplanes are much safer than cars. One reason is that airplane crashes are much more widely publicized than auto crashes and therefore much more easily retrievable from memory. The availability heuristic, then, leads people to assume that they are more likely to crash in a plane than in a car (Slovic, Fischhoff, & Lichtenstein, 1976; Schwarz et al., 1991).

The availability heuristic can easily skew our perception of what others believe. For instance, college students attending a liberal college may assume that because most of their acquaintances share their liberal views on abortion, the general population also shares those views. However, once they leave campus and interact with a broader cross-section of the population, these students may be surprised to learn the degree of variability in viewpoints.

Indeed, the tendency to believe that others share our views, spawned from the availability heuristic, is so powerful that it can produce another bias: the false consensus effect. The **false consensus effect** is the tendency to overestimate the degree of agreement for our own opinions, beliefs, and attributes (Ross, Greene, & House, 1977; Marks & Miller, 1987; Ross & Nisbett, 1991; Krueger & Clement, 1994; Yinon, Mayraz, & Fox, 1994; Higgins, 1997; Bosveld, Koomen, & Vogelaar, 1997).

For instance, if we think that strict environmental laws should be passed, we assume that other people believe the same thing. By the same token, if we believe in the death penalty, we think that others hold the same view. If we smoke, we think that many others smoke.

availability heuristic: A rule applied in judging the likelihood of an event by considering the ease with which it can be recalled from memory.

false consensus effect: The tendency to overestimate the degree of agreement for our own opinions, beliefs, and attributes.

APPLYING SOCIAL PSYCHOLOGY
COUNTERFACTUAL THINKING: WHEN DOING BETTER MEANS FEELING WORSE

Wouldn't you feel better about scoring an 89 average for a course than an 80?

Probably not—if your 89 meant that you just missed an A by one point, whereas an 81 signified that you just avoided missing a C by one point. Although logically the higher score indicates better performance, recent research suggests that you would actually end up feeling worse with the 89 average than the 80.

As a result of counterfactual thinking, a third-place bronze-medal winner may be more satisfied than a second-place silver-medal winner.

The surprising conclusion that a higher grade results in less satisfaction than a lower grade is a result of counterfactual thinking. **Counterfactual thinking** occurs when a person evaluates an actual event by considering alternative, and often more desirable, hypothetical outcomes. Instead of evaluating the actual positive or negative aspects of an existing situation, people often evaluate them in terms of "what might have been" (Roese, 1994; Teigen, 1995; Roese & Olson, 1998).

For example, consider two people who arrive late at the airport and, as a consequence, miss their plane and are forced to wait for the next flight. Now assume that one person missed the plane by 5 minutes and the other by 30 minutes. Which one feels worse?

Although the objective fact is that the outcome for both passengers is identical—they both are forced to wait for the next plane—most people hearing the scenario say the person who missed it by 5 minutes would probably feel worse. The reason is counterfactual thinking: It is easier to imagine that the first passenger might have arrived on time as opposed to the second one. Consequently, we assume that the earlier-arriving person will feel more disappointed (Kahneman & Tversky, 1982).

A study by social psychologists Victoria Medvec and Kenneth Savitsky (1997) applied the concept of counterfactual thinking to students' grades. The experimenters approached students enrolled in an introductory psychology class and asked how satisfied they were with their grade just after they found out their grade average for the semester.

With this information in hand, the experimenters calculated a "cutoff-distance" score, which gave an indication of how far the student's course average was from the next-highest letter

Across a variety of issues, people consistently exaggerate the number of individuals who agree with their position (Granberg, l987; Marks & Miller, 1987).

Why does this occur? One reason may be that people want to believe others agree with them, because this belief provides evidence that their own behavior or choices are reasonable (Marks & Miller, 1987). But there are additional reasons for the effect. For instance, we often remember examples of people who agree with us more readily than examples of people who disagree. Because instances of agreement are easier to recall, we are misled into thinking that more people hold our position than is actually the case.

Finally, as we will discuss more in Chapter 6, we choose our friends on the basis of similarity of attitudes, beliefs, and values. As a result, we're exposed more often to instances of agreement with our positions than with instances of disagreement (Wetzel & Walton, 1985). Consequently, we overestimate the degree of agreement in the general population with our particular position—leading to the false consensus effect.

counterfactual thinking: Thinking that evaluates an actual event by considering alternative, and often more desirable, hypothetical outcomes.

grade. A low distance score indicated that a student narrowly missed getting a higher grade; a high distance score meant that the student barely squeaked by.

The experimenters reasoned that a low distance score (the situation in which a student just missed the higher grade) would be likely to produce counterfactual thinking and therefore lead to lower satisfaction than that experienced by students who just squeaked by—and that is exactly what happened. As you can see in Figure 2–9, the students who just missed getting a higher grade were the least satisfied, whereas those who just made the higher grade were the ones most satisfied.

These results are consistent with other research examining counterfactual thinking. For instance, winners of third-place bronze medals at the Olympics tend to be more satisfied than those winning second-place silver medals. The reason? Rather than focusing on the fact that they came in a very respectable second, silver medalists focus on what might have been had they won the gold—the highest status, the greatest prestige, the likelihood of receiving commercial endorsements and making substantial amounts of money, and so forth—all of which do not occur to anyone but the gold medalist. By focusing on their loss to the gold-medal winner ("if only I had won the gold . . ."), silver medalists set themselves up for disappointment.

In contrast, third-place bronze-medal winners' counterfactual thinking is likely to focus on what would have happened if they had come in fourth and won no medal at all. In other words, their most relevant comparison would be downward. The result of this downward comparison? They feel particularly pleased with their third-place bronze medals.

In short, the phenomenon of counterfactual thinking suggests that at least in the realm of social cognition, less is

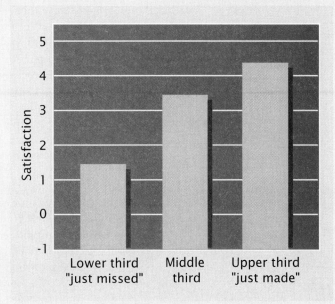

FIGURE 2–9   Counterfactual Thinking and Students' Grades
Students who just missed getting a higher grade felt less satisfied with the results than students who just made the grade by a margin of 3 to 1. The results of this study are consistent with research in other areas examining counterfactual thinking. (*Source:* Medvec & Savitsky, 1997, p. 1287.)

sometimes more: Squeaking by with a low B—and avoiding a C—may make you feel better than getting a high B and just missing an A.

A variety of additional biases cloud our views of the social world. For instance, we sometimes view our successes and failures in the social world not just in terms of their current consequences, but in relation to alternative scenarios that might have occurred had events been different. As we discuss in the Applying Social Psychology box, these alternative, hypothetical scenarios may lead us to be unhappy with events that are, objectively, quite positive.

THE MOTIVATED TACTICIAN:
AN ALTERNATIVE TO THE COGNITIVE MISER MODEL

So far, our discussion of the schema approach to social cognition has taken the cognitive miser model at face value. From this perspective, people are relatively limited in their abilities to process complex information. To maximize their success in judging the social

motivated tactician model: The approach to social cognition in which the way people view the world depends on their goals, motivations, and needs.

automaticity: The processing of social information that requires little or no effort, is routine, and often occurs outside awareness.

confirmation biases: The tendency to seek out, interpret, or formulate information that is consistent with one's current beliefs.

situations they constantly encounter, they hoard their cognitive resources. People employing the cognitive miser model, then, seek the most efficient solution to questions about why people behave the way they do.

Newer approaches to social cognition have moved in a somewhat different direction, however. In the **motivated tactician model**, the way people view the world depends on their goals, motivations, and needs (Fiske, 1992). According to this approach, people are flexible in their cognitive labors, choosing among various strategies to find the ones that are most appropriate for a given situation.

For instance, if accuracy in understanding others is the predominant goal, the motivated tactician may sacrifice speed in order to come up with an accurate understanding of a social situation (Thompson et al., 1994). If accuracy is relatively unimportant, however, the goal of making a rapid decision may prevail—and people may fall back on their more miserly ways. In either case, the motivated tactician model assumes that perceivers hold particular goals and that these goals influence the kind of social cognition perceivers employ in social situations (Fiske & Neuberg, 1990; Hilton & Darley, 1991; Snyder, 1992; Moskowitz, 1993).

But aren't some goals—such as accuracy—always important? Why are there ever instances in which accuracy in perceiving others is inconsequential? The answer is that in some ways absolute accuracy isn't always necessary for smooth social functioning. Routine judgments, made with little thought, are perfectly adequate in some cases. For instance, our processing of social information can occur at several levels of **automaticity**, a term that refers to processing that requires little or no effort, is routine, and often occurs outside awareness. When a situation requires little thought, such as determining why a cashier at a movie theater is asking us to buy tickets, automatic processing works perfectly adequately (Bargh, 1989; Uleman & Moskowitz, 1994; Wegner & Bargh, 1998).

In other cases, we construct our own social realities and are motivated to confirm and act on those realities. In fact, as we see next, people making social judgments are less concerned with accuracy than with verifying and supporting their existing views of the world.

CONFIRMATION BIASES: MAKING SOCIAL JUDGMENTS REAL

If you met someone for the first time who you had been told was a terrific student but not much of an athlete, what might you choose to talk about? Many of us would probably decide to talk about our classes and skirt around issues having to do with sports. And when this new acquaintance began to talk about his studies, we'd probably feel that our prior information about him was correct, thereby confirming our beliefs.

Not so fast. The responses we're hearing might reflect more the questions we chose to ask than the person's true nature. In fact, if we had instead asked about sports, we might have received an impression of the person entirely at odds with our earlier information.

Our tendency to ask questions designed to confirm our beliefs, rather than contradict them, is an example of the confirmation bias. **Confirmation biases** reflect the tendency to seek out, interpret, or formulate information that is consistent with one's current beliefs. As we'll see, confirmation biases not only color our judgments of the world, but also can actually produce behavior in others that reflects those judgments.

Confirmatory hypothesis testing: Detecting what we think we ought to detect.   An early experiment by social psychologists Mark Snyder and Nancy Cantor (1979) illustrates how we often let our hypotheses about what people are like bias our views of them. In the study, participants read an account of a woman named Jane who in some situations was outgoing (she often spoke to strangers when she was out jogging), but in others was timid and shy (such as at the supermarket). Several days later, participants were asked to provide evidence that Jane was suited for the job of either real estate salesperson (a job associated with extroversion) or research librarian (a job associated with introversion).

Participants who thought Jane was being considered for a real estate job were apt to recall qualities relating to her extroversion, whereas those who thought she was being considered for a library position recalled evidence of her introversion. In short, they focused on confirmatory information and were insensitive to information that disconfirmed their expectations.

Other research went a step further, showing that once we form expectations about what other people are like, our expectations influence the kinds of interactions we subsequently have with them. For instance, in an experiment that was to become a classic, Snyder and Swann (1978) led participants to believe that a student they were about to interview was either introverted or extroverted. They were then given a list of questions that they might ask the student during the interview. As expected, participants chose a disproportionate number of questions that elicited information that was consistent with the specific expectation that they had been given. When they thought a participant was extroverted, they chose to ask such questions as, "What would you do if you wanted to liven things up at a party?" When their expectation was that the participant was introverted, they asked questions such as, "What factors make it really hard for you to open up to people?" Clearly, they appeared to seek confirmation for the validity of their prior impressions.

More striking were the results that the choice of questions brought about. According to impartial judges, who heard tapes of the interviews, students who were asked more questions about their supposed extroversion came across as more extroverted, whereas those who were asked questions about their ostensible introversion appeared more introverted.

More contemporary research supports these early findings (Zuckerman et al., 1995). In fact, confirmatory hypothesis testing is prevalent, even among those trained to avoid it. For instance, trained psychotherapists choose questions to ask their patients that tend to evoke confirmation of their own hypotheses (Haverkamp, 1993). On the other hand, sometimes people are sufficiently motivated to be accurate that they overcome their tendencies to seek confirmatory evidence and instead seek information that is more reliable (Kruglanski, 1990). Still, people's initial hypotheses about what another person is like can frequently lead them to erroneous conclusions (Zuckerman et al., 1995).

In some cases, confirmation biases are so strong that perceivers are not the only victims. Specifically, in certain cases, the perception of reality that we construct takes on a life of its own, as our expectations about the world are transmitted to others and affect their behavior.

The self-fulfilling prophecy: Turning cognition into reality.   Suppose you were a teacher who received the following information at the start of the school year:

All children show hills, plateaus, and valleys in their scholastic progress. A study being conducted at Harvard with the support of the National Science Foundation is interested in those children who show an unusual forward spurt of academic progress. . . . As part of our study we are further validating a test that predicts the likelihood that a child will show an inflection point or "spurt" within the near future. This test, which will be administered in your school, will allow us to predict which youngsters are most likely to show an academic spurt. . . . The development of the test for predicting inflections or "spurts" is not yet such that every one of the top 10 percent will show the spurt or "blooming" effect. But the top 20 percent of the children will show a more significant inflection or spurt in their learning within the next year or less than will the remaining 80 percent of the children. (Rosenthal & Jacobson, 1968, p. 66)

How would you react to such information? Would you treat your students differently, according to the kind of information you received about them?

Although most of us would want to think that we would treat people in an unbiased, equitable manner, the information that we have discussed throughout this chapter might lead you to suspect that this is not the case. As active social perceivers, we tend to use the information at hand to help us form impressions of our students. As a result, we would potentially treat students differently on the basis of our newly formed impressions. This inclination to act as if our expectations were true is reflected in the self-fulfilling prophecy.

self-fulfilling prophecy: The
tendency for people to act in a way
that is consistent with their
expectation, belief, or cognition about
an event or behavior, thereby
increasing the likelihood that the
event or behavior will occur

A **self-fulfilling prophecy** is the tendency for people to act in a way that is consistent with their expectations, beliefs, or cognitions about an event or behavior, thereby increasing the likelihood that the event or behavior will occur (Snyder, 1974). Self-fulfilling prophecies operate in a variety of contexts. For instance, patients who, on the advice of their physicians, take biologically ineffective medications (placebos) may feel better simply because they expect to feel better. Similarly, the experimenter expectancy effect that we discussed in Chapter 1—in which experimenters' hypotheses lead to behavior that ultimately brings about the expected behavior in participants—is another example of a self-fulfilling prophecy.

Might teacher expectations produce academic performance consistent with their expectations? To answer that question, social psychologists Robert Rosenthal and Lenore Jacobson (1968) told a school's teachers that five students who would be in their classes during the upcoming school year were likely, according to test results, to "bloom." In reality each of the students was chosen at random from the class list. Despite the fact that the information was bogus, a year later, when all children in the school took a battery of tests, many of the students designated as "bloomers" showed significantly greater academic gains than students about whom teachers had received no information.

How did the teachers confirm their expectations? According to subsequent research, teachers who expect a student to perform well behave in ways that elicit the expected behavior. They create a more positive social climate, reacting more positively to students' answers and comments and behaving in a more encouraging way. They also furnish more precise feedback, and allow more opportunities to perform well for students they expect to do well than for those for whom they hold lower expectations (Kolb & Jussim, 1994). In turn, students flourish in such an environment and, as can be seen in Figure 2–10, actually begin to behave consistently with the expectation (Harris, 1991; Rosenthal, 1991).

By the way, just as teachers communicate their expectations to students, students can communicate their expectations to the teacher and thus affect the teacher's behavior. For instance, when students in an experiment were led to believe that their teachers were particularly good or bad, they behaved in ways that actually elicited the expected behavior from the teachers. Teachers whose students expected them to do a good job actually did a more effective job in teaching the material; those whose students expected them to do poorly did worse. In sum, our teachers' behavior may be at least partially a consequence of the way we treat them (Feldman & Theiss, 1982; Jamieson et al., 1987; Jussim & Eccles, 1992).

The results of this study and subsequent research are clear in demonstrating the power of our expectations to bring about behavior that confirms them (Eden, 1990; Jenner, 1990; Harris et al., 1992; Eden & Zuk, 1995). These results also accentuate the importance of developing accurate impressions and attributions in the first place. Our expectations about

FIGURE 2–10   Teacher Expectations Can Affect Student Performance Holding a positive or negative expectation about a student can actually bring about student behavior consistent with the expectation.

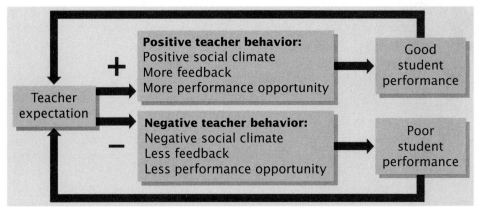

Expecting certain students to do well may lead teachers to behave more positively towards those students thereby eliciting positive performance. Similarly, students who have high expectations of teachers' abilities tend to elicit better teaching from their teachers.

others not only affect our behavior but also induce others to act in a way that is consistent with those expectancies. Clearly, then, we need to be cautious in the kinds of conclusions we draw about others (Snyder, Campbell, & Preston, 1982; Slowiaczek et al., 1989; Snyder, 1992).

Fortunately, we are not destined to make constant errors in the way we view others. As we consider in the Informed Consumer of Social Psychology section, we can increase the accuracy of our impressions in several ways.

DRAWING THE APPROPRIATE CONCLUSIONS FROM OTHERS' BEHAVIOR

Social psychologist Susan Fiske argues that people are "good-enough perceivers" (Fiske, 1993). What she means is that, generally speaking, people are sufficiently accurate in their perceptions of others to ensure their reasonably successful navigation through social seas. But is it possible for people to change from just "good-enough" to "excellent"? Social psychologists have discovered several means of increasing the validity of one's interpretations of others and their behavior (Funder, 1987; Darley et al., 1988; Neuberg, 1989; Colvin & Funder, 1991; Sanitioso & Kunda, 1991). Among them:

THE INFORMED
CONSUMER
OF SOCIAL
PSYCHOLOGY

◆ Make accuracy a goal. Simply keeping in mind the objective of discovering people's true characteristics will help you to be more accurate in your impressions and will decrease the impulsiveness with which you make some judgments (Kruglanski, 1989).

◆ Keep in mind the biases that distort attributions. For instance, your awareness that people tend to overemphasize the dispositional determinants behind behavior that they observe— the fundamental attribution error—should lead you to ask yourself what situational constraints may be at work as you observe another person's behavior.

◆ Be alert for inconsistent and negative information. Even after you've made up your mind about someone's motivations in a given situation, stay alert for new data that may lead to a midcourse correction.

◆ Avoid a rush to judgment. Although people are sometimes quite accurate in inferences based on brief slices of behavior (Ambady & Rosenthal, 1992, 1993), the more information you can garner about people, across very different kinds of situations, the more accurate your judgments will be.

◆ If all else fails, keep in mind that bias does not equal error. The fact that judgments may deviate from formal rules of logic does not mean they are wrong. For example, sometimes dispositional factors do adequately explain the causes of people's behavior, and in such cases the fundamental attribution error will only act to increase the accuracy of judgments.

REVIEW AND RETHINK

Review

- Schemas are organized bodies of information stored in memory.

- Priming is the process by which recent exposure to stimuli such as people, ideas, or even words influences the interpretation of new information.

- Among the biases related to the use of schemas are the representativeness heuristic, the base-rate fallacy, the availability heuristic, and the false consensus effect.

- Confirmation biases reflect the tendency to seek out and detect information that is consistent with one's beliefs and expectations, and to ignore information that contradicts those beliefs and expectations.

- Acting on expectations can lead to the operation of self-fulfilling prophecies.

Rethink

- What is a prototype, and how are prototypes related to schemas?

- In what ways do scripts differ from schemas? Describe a possible script and a possible schema for how to behave when meeting new people.

- What is the availability heuristic, and can this heuristic help explain the priming effect?

- What is the false consensus effect, and how is it related to the person positivity bias discussed earlier in the chapter?

- What is the sequence of events involved in the self-fulfilling prophecy? Give an example.

L O O K I N G   B A C K

How do we combine people's individual personality traits into an overall impression?

1. Social cognition is the study of how people understand and make sense of others and themselves. Three main approaches characterize this area of social psychology. (p. 42)

2. Person perception approaches consider how an individual assesses and combines the traits of others to form overall impressions. Attribution approaches seek to identify how people understand the causes of others' and their own behavior; according to attribution theorists, people act as "naive scientists," rationally weighing and combining different sources of information. Schema approaches consider how people organize and store information in memory, and how they use this information as a framework to understand others' and their own behavior. (p. 42)

3. Although sometimes our impressions are based on outward, surface features, we often combine various traits to form an overall impression. The central traits theory suggests that certain characteristics serve to organize an impression and provide a framework for interpreting subsequent information; in this way central traits have the major influence on a person's final judgment of another person. (p. 46)

4. In contrast, the cognitive algebra approach suggests that perceivers consider each individual trait, evaluate each trait individually, and then combine the evaluations into an overall judgment. No approach has been fully successful in explaining the judgment process, in part because of such phenomena as primacy and recency effects. (p. 47)

How do we make judgments about the causes of others' behavior?

5. Attribution studies consider how people understand the causes of others' and their own behavior. Attribution theories seek to explain how people, acting like "naive scientists," look for situational and dispositional causes behind behavior. (p. 50)

6. Jones and Davis's correspondent inference theory of attribution focuses on correspondent inferences, observers' notions of how closely an overt behavior or action represents a specific underlying intention, trait, or disposition. To make their judgments, observers focus on unique or noncommon effects of behaviors. (p. 52)

7. Kelley's model of causal attribution focuses on the role of three different kinds of information. Consensus information concerns the degree to which other people react similarly in the same situation. Consistency information concerns the degree to which people react in the same way in different situations. Distinctiveness information concerns the extent to which the same behavior occurs in relation to other people or stimuli. (p. 53)

8. According to Kelley's model, when behavior exhibits low consensus and distinctiveness and high consistency, people tend to make dispositional attributions; when behavior exhibits high consensus, consistency, and distinctiveness, people tend to attribute the behavior to external, situational factors. (p. 53)

To what kinds of systematic errors are we vulnerable when we consider others' behavior?

9. The fundamental attribution error, which is pervasive and powerful, is the tendency to overattribute others' behavior to dispositional causes and to underemphasize the role of situational causes. Other biases include the person positivity bias, which is sometimes called the Pollyanna effect, and motivational biases, which are due to a desire to present oneself well. (p. 55)

10. One motivational bias is the self-serving bias, which is a general tendency to attribute one's success to internal factors (skill, ability, or effort) and failure to external factors (chance or something about the situation). Another motivational bias is the belief in a just world, the notion that people get out of life what they deserve and that people deserve what happens to them. (p. 57)

How do we organize and remember information about social stimuli, and how does this process affect our social judgment?

11. Schemas are organized bodies of information stored in memory. They provide a representation of the way the social world operates, and they enable us to categorize and interpret new information related to the schema. Two major types of schemas are prototypes (for personality information) and scripts (for information regarding situations). (p. 61)

12. Priming is the process by which recent exposure to stimuli—such as people, ideas, or even mere words—influences the interpretation of new information. Priming prepares people to respond in a particular manner when relevant information is brought to mind. (p. 64)

13. The use of schemas may lead to mistakes in social judgment. There are four major sources of such errors. The representativeness heuristic occurs when people are judged by the degree to which they represent a certain category. The base-rate fallacy is the tendency to underemphasize base-rate data because of the influence of more prominent, although ultimately less meaningful, information. The availability heuristic occurs when the likelihood of an event is judged by considering the ease with which it can be recalled from memory. The false consensus effect is the

tendency to overestimate the degree of agreement with our own opinions, beliefs, and attributes. (p. 65)

14. Confirmation biases reflect the tendency to seek, detect, interpret, and process information that is consistent with one's current beliefs and expectations. Confirmation biases can lead to self-fulfilling prophecies. (p. 70)

15. A self-fulfilling prophecy is the tendency for people to act in ways that are consistent with their expectations, beliefs, or cognitions about an event or behavior, thereby increasing the likelihood that the event or behavior will occur. Self-fulfilling prophecies lead people to act in ways that make their social judgments become reality. (p. 72)

16. To avoid making errors in social judgment, people can employ several strategies. These include making accuracy an explicit goal, being aware of potential biases, being alert for inconsistent and negative information, avoiding rushed judgments, and recalling that bias does not always lead to error. (p. 73)

EPILOGUE

As we have seen, social cognition is a wide-ranging and important aspect of social psychology. By focusing on the ways we form impressions of others, make personality and character judgments, understand motivations, and even influence behavior through our expectancies, social cognition reveals sources of error and bias and suggests approaches to achieving greater accuracy in our understanding of other individuals.

Before turning to the next chapter, review once again the prologue that opened this chapter. In the light of what you now know about social cognition, consider the following questions about the conviction of Dr. Jack Kevorkian.

1. Based on the fundamental attribution error, how do you think Dr. Kevorkian views the reasons for his actions? How are others likely to view his behavior?

2. If you first met Dr. Kevorkian, and knew nothing about him, would your initial impression likely be positive or negative? Explain your answer, referring to one of the biases discussed in the chapter.

3. Suppose, upon hearing of Dr. Kevorkian's conviction, someone says, "I'm sure he deserved being found guilty; he's probably not a nice person." How might the concept of defensive attributions explain the comment?

4. Newspaper accounts of trials such as that of Dr. Kevorkian often focus on descriptions of the defendant's eyes, hands, posture, and movements. From a social cognition perspective, what information are the reporters attempting to convey? To what sorts of biases are they (and their readers) likely to be subject?

KEY TERMS AND CONCEPTS

attribution (p. 50)

attribution approaches (p. 43)

automaticity (p. 70)

availability heuristic (p. 67)

base-rate fallacy (p. 66)

central traits (p. 46)

cognitive algebra approach (p. 47)

collectivistic culture (p. 59)

CHAPTER 3

PREJUDICE, DISCRIMINATION, AND STEREOTYPES

PROLOGUE

A Fatal Ride

James Byrd, Jr.

J ames Byrd Jr.'s torso was found first. When police in Jasper, Texas, went out to Huff Creek Road . . . to check out reports of a dead body, they turned up the badly mutilated remains of the 49-year-old black man—and a trail of blood. Deputies followed the dark red stains for a mile and found Byrd's head. Then his right arm. Another mile, and they found tennis shoes, a wallet, even his dentures. And then the trail ended, at a churned-up patch of grass strewn with empty beer bottles, a lighter bearing white supremacist symbols and a wrench set inscribed with the name "Berry" (Van Boven & Gesalman, 1998, p. 33) ■

LOOKING AHEAD

In a crime that is nothing short of horrific, James Byrd had been chained to the back of a pickup truck by white supremacists and dragged for miles. Pathologists would later report that Byrd may well have been conscious up until the time his head was ripped from his body.

Although the horrific crime against James Byrd was exceptional, the attitudes that motivated the attack are not. Unfortunately, many people face prejudice, discrimination, and stereotyping on a daily basis. A Latino who receives poor service in a store because of his ethnic background, an elderly patient who is addressed by a physician in baby talk, and a woman who is passed over for a promotion because of her gender are all the victims of prejudice.

In this chapter, we consider the roots of prejudice and discrimination. We begin by differentiating three fundamental concepts used to explain why people demonstrate bias and bigotry toward others: prejudice, discrimination, and stereotypes. We discuss the psychological definition of a minority group, and we learn that a numerical advantage does not necessarily make a group a majority. We also examine what lies behind prejudice and discrimination, how any group that is different from our own may be subject to prejudice and discrimination, and why group membership is often a source of self-esteem.

Finally, we focus on the two most frequent manifestations of bias: gender prejudice and race prejudice. We consider how these prejudices affect the way people view others, and we discuss the damaging consequences of discrimination. We end on a positive note, discussing ways to reduce prejudice and discrimination.

In sum, after reading this chapter, you'll be able to answer these questions:

- ◆ What differentiates prejudice, discrimination, and stereotyping?
- ◆ How is prejudice learned and maintained?
- ◆ How do stereotypes provide the cognitive foundations for prejudice and discrimination?
- ◆ How prevalent is racism, and is it inevitable?
- ◆ Why does sexism occur, and what are the roots of gender stereotyping?
- ◆ What are some ways social psychologists have devised to reduce prejudice and discrimination?

PREJUDICE, STEREOTYPES, AND DISCRIMINATION: EXPLAINING INTOLERANCE

Resettled Cambodian, Vietnamese, and Laotian refugees have faced a rash of physical assaults, including beatings, rock throwing, vandalism, arson, intimidation, and racial slurs.

***

A Jewish student was shot five times with a BB gun on a large state college campus. As the attacker fired, he shouted "Heil Hitler" and other anti-Semitic epithets. An underground campus newspaper hailed the assailant as a hero and suggested that next time he use a flamethrower on the victim.

***

Five white cadets at a military academy, wearing masks and white sheets, entered the room of an African American cadet. While shouting obscenities, they threw a burned paper cross onto the floor.

These incidents illustrate that ethnic and racial hate is alive and well in U.S. society. But it is not only in such obvious physical and verbal attacks that we find hostility and rancor. When people presume that someone is likely to behave in a certain way because she is a woman, or an African American, or a lesbian, the assumption springs from the same foundations as more visible and overt forms of prejudice and discrimination (U.S. Commission on Civil Rights, 1990).

To understand such acts and assumptions, social psychologists first have sought to delineate and clarify the basic concepts of prejudice, stereotypes, and discrimination.

PREJUDICE, STEREOTYPES, AND DISCRIMINATION: THE FOUNDATIONS OF HATE

Prejudice refers to the negative (or positive) evaluations or judgments of members of a group that are based primarily on membership in the group and not necessarily on the particular characteristics of individuals. For example, gender prejudice occurs when a person is evaluated on the basis of being a male or female and not because of his or her own specific characteristics or abilities.

Although prejudice is generally thought of as a negative evaluation of group members, it can also be positive: As we'll see, at the same time people dislike members of other groups, they may also positively evaluate members of their own group. In both cases, the assessment is unrelated to qualities of particular individuals; rather, it is due simply to membership in the specific group to which the individuals belong.

prejudice: The negative (or positive) evaluations or judgments of members of a group that are based primarily on membership in the group and not necessarily on the particular characteristics of individuals.

The cognitive framework that maintains prejudice is a stereotype. A **stereotype** is a set of beliefs and expectations about members of a group that are held simply because of their membership in the group. Stereotypes are oversimplifications that we employ in an effort to make sense of the complex social environment in which we live.

Stereotypes can be thought of as particular kinds of schemas, those cognitive bodies of information we discussed in Chapter 2. Social psychologist Gordon Allport (1954) described stereotyping as operating under the "law of least effort," consistent with the cognitive miser model of social cognition we discussed in Chapter 2. Schemas relating to stereotypes organize information and provide a framework for prejudiced individuals to view others' behavior. Such schemas distort people's perception so that they view others through the lens of prejudice (Rojahn & Pettigrew, 1992; Jussim et al., 1995; Leichtman & Ceci, 1995).

Stereotypes, like all schemas, support cognitive processes through which information consistent with the schema is more conspicuous and remembered more easily than other information. Consequently, information inconsistent with the stereotype is ignored and is readily forgotten. In addition, stereotypes determine how information is interpreted, so that even when people are exposed to data contrary to their stereotypes, they may interpret the information in a way that supports their prejudice (Wyer, 1988; Fiske & Neuberg, 1990; Hamilton, Sherman, & Ruvolo, 1990; Biernat, Manis, & Nelson, 1991).

Ultimately, stereotypes increase the chance that discrimination will occur. **Discrimination**, the behavioral manifestation of stereotypes and prejudice, refers to negative (or sometimes positive) actions taken toward members of a particular group because of their membership in the group. Although prejudice and discrimination often go hand in hand, one may be present without the other. A person who harbors prejudice may not necessarily engage in overt discrimination, because the target of his or her prejudice may not be present. For example, someone may dislike Turks without ever having had an opportunity to interact with one. Furthermore, laws against discrimination, as well as strong social norms or standards, may prevent overt discrimination, although subtle forms of discrimination still may occur. Hence, the presence of prejudice does not always lead directly to discrimination (Pfeifer, 1992; Lott & Maluso, 1995).

In contrast, the presence of discrimination is a fairly good indication that prejudice also exists. But not always. For instance, the white president of a company, who is not herself prejudiced, may impede the hiring of a Korean American executive because she thinks that person would have difficulty dealing with the business's prejudiced customers. This would be a case of discrimination without prejudice.

MINORITY GROUPS: THE NUMBERS OF SUBORDINATION

To whom are prejudice, stereotyping, and discrimination directed? In most cases, they are directed toward minority groups. Of the concepts we've discussed, the term *minority group* seems to be the easiest to understand. However, minority groups are not just groups that are numerically smaller than larger, majority groups.

For instance, in some parts of the southern United States, African Americans far outnumber whites; in South Africa, whites make up only a small percentage of the population; and in the United States there are slightly more females than males. In each of these three examples, however, we can argue that those in the numerical minority should actually be considered the majority, because they have had considerably more power, control, and influence than the numerical majority. From a social psychological point of view, then, a **minority group** is a group whose members have significantly less power, control, and influence over their own lives than do members of a dominant group (Simpson & Yinger, 1985; Schaefer & Lamm, 1992).

Social psychologists consider the psychological, as opposed to strictly numerical, characteristics of minority groups. Specifically, minorities make up subordinate parts of a society, have physical or cultural characteristics that are held in relatively low esteem by dominant groups, and are aware of their minority status. Furthermore, minority membership is passed on through norms that encourage affiliation and marriage with other minority group

stereotype: A set of beliefs and expectations about members of a group that are held simply because of their membership in the group.

discrimination: Negative (or sometimes positive) actions taken toward members of a particular group because of their membership in the group.

minority group: A group whose members have significantly less power, control, and influence over their own lives than do members of a dominant group.

Children learn the prejudices of their parents through social learning processes. These young children were not born discriminating against gays and lesbians, but were taught their prejudice.

members. In some ways, then, being a minority or majority group member is something that is socially defined, regardless of what the absolute numbers imply.

To further complicate matters, categorizations such as "race" and "ethnic group" are often vague and indistinct. *Race* is a biological concept referring to classifications based on physical characteristics, and *ethnic group* relates to cultural background, nationality, religion, and language. However, neither term is precise. For example, race is commonly used as a description ranging from skin color to religion to culture. Depending on how it is defined, there are between 3 and 300 races, and certainly there is no such thing as a biologically pure race (Betancourt & Lopez, 1993).

Furthermore, disagreement exists over the names of various groups. Is "African American," which has geographic and cultural implications, preferable to "black," which focuses on skin color? Is "Native American" preferable to "Indian"? And is "Hispanic" a better choice than "Latino"? The answers to these questions are not trivial, because they have important implications both for a group's sense of its own identity and in determining the precision of research that is conducted to understand prejudice and discrimination (Jones, 1994; Evinger, 1996).

THE ROOTS OF PREJUDICE

Female. African American. Islamic fundamentalist. Gay.

Quick: What images first come to mind when you read or hear each of these words? For most people, encountering a description of a person that includes such a label is enough to summon up a rich network of impressions, memories, and probably even predictions of how that person will behave in a given situation. The presence of such connections suggests that we are all susceptible to prejudice.

But where does prejudice originate? Social psychologists have considered several answers, ranging from early learning to basic cognitive processing (Duckitt, 1994a; Gaines & Reed, 1995; Fiske, 1997).

SOCIAL LEARNING EXPLANATIONS: THE SCHOOL OF STEREOTYPING

We are not born feeling prejudice and showing discrimination to members of different religions, ethnic groups, or races. It is something that is taught to us, in much the same way that we learn that $2 + 2 = 4$.

The *social learning view* suggests that people develop prejudice and stereotypes about members of various groups in the same way they learn other attitudes, beliefs, and values (as we'll discuss more in Chapter 10). For instance, one important source of information for children regarding stereotypes and prejudice is the behavior and teaching of parents, other adults, and peers (Zinberg, 1976; Kryzanowski & Stewin, 1985). Through direct reinforcement, and through observation of the reinforcement given to others, people learn about members of other groups. Such learning begins at an early age: By the age of 3 or 4, children are able to distinguish between African Americans and whites, and even at that age they can possess preferential feelings for members of their own group over others (Katz, 1976).

Children are not the only ones who learn stereotypes and prejudice from others. Although significant improvements have been made in the past decade, television and other media often portray minority group members in shallow, stereotyped ways. For instance, portrayals of African Americans perpetuate some of society's most distasteful stereotypes, with many African American males being portrayed as sexually obsessed and shiftless who speak primarily in jive. Other groups are stereotyped in the media in equally derogatory ways: Godfather-like Italian mobsters, greedy Jewish bankers, and Hispanics in criminal or menial jobs (Jussim, Milburn, & Nelson, 1991; Wahl, 1995; Gow, 1996; Mok, 1998; Ono, 1998).

Women, too, are portrayed in stereotypical ways in the media (Chrisler & Levy, 1990). For instance, women are less likely than men to be shown as employed, and they are more

TABLE 3-1	Portrayal of Men's and Women's Occupation in Oscar-Winning Roles					
MEN (BEST AND SUPPORTING)			**WOMEN (BEST AND SUPPORTING)**			
Occupation	N	Percent	Occupation	N	Percent	
Soldier	15	13.8	Actress	16	14.7	
Sheriff	9	8.3	Prostitute	13	11.9	
Criminal	9	8.3	Heiress	4	3.7	
Politician	7	6.4	Teacher	4	3.7	
Actor	7	6.4	Artist	4	3.7	
Writer	7	6.4	Hotel proprietress	4	3.7	
Laborer	7	6.4	Farmer's wife	4	3.7	
Businessman	6	5.5	Secretary	4	3.7	
Lawyer	5	4.5	Businesswoman	3	2.7	
Journalist	5	4.5	Queen	3	2.7	
Prizefighter	4	3.7	Politician	3	2.7	
Priest	3	2.8	Nurse	2	1.8	
Teacher	3	2.8	Seamstress	2	1.8	
Scientist	2	1.8	Maid	2	1.8	
King	1	0.9				
Other	15	13.8	Other	4	3.7	
No gainful work	4	3.7	No gainful work	37	34.0	
Total	109	100.0	Total	109	100.0	

Source: Levy, 1990.

apt to be seen as involved with family and home. An analysis of Oscar-winning film roles of men and women confirmed that men were most likely to be soldiers, whereas women were most apt to be unemployed (see Table 3–1). Even the print media portray men and women differently. For example, an analysis of almost 2,000 magazine photos showed that the face was more prominent (relative to other elements in the photo) when the subject of the photo was a man than when it was a woman—a phenomenon called *face-ism* (Archer et al., 1983; Levy, 1990).

Repeatedly observing such differential portrayals of women and men characters takes a toll. For people whose exposure to minority group members is limited to what they see in the media, such portrayals cultivate and maintain undesirable and inaccurate views of minority groups (Hammer, 1992; Evans, 1993).

The situation is not entirely bleak. The different media have recently shown increased sensitivity to how they portray minority group members. The number of positive portrayals of minorities shown on television, in particular, has grown dramatically. For instance, television programs such as "Law and Order" show Latino men as strong and responsible characters. If we expect that negative media portrayals perpetuate stereotypes and ultimately prejudice—as social learning theory suggests—it also stands to reason that positive media portrayals should help reduce stereotyping and prejudice (Evuleocha & Ugbah, 1989; Donovan & Leivers, 1993).

Similarly, even advertisers are seeking to provide more sensitive portrayals of characters in ads. For example, the fictitious Betty Crocker underwent a facelift by General Mills, who has used Crocker in ads for the past 75 years. Using a computer, artists combined the features of dozens of women from a variety of ethnic and racial backgrounds, hoping to create a face that reflects greater diversity (Quick, 1995).

MOTIVATIONAL APPROACHES TO PREJUDICE: THE AUTHORITARIAN PERSONALITY

Instead of focusing on the ways people acquire their prejudices through social learning, motivational approaches contend that prejudice is the outcome of motivational conflicts of which a person is unaware. Building on Sigmund Freud's *psychodynamic model* of personality and the unconscious, such approaches attempt to identify the psychological conflicts and maladjustments that underlie a person's displays of prejudice.

The most influential use of psychodynamic theory is found in a classic book, *The Authoritarian Personality* (Adorno et al., 1950). Based on the results of hundreds of interviews and batteries of personality assessments, the theory reported in the book suggests that prejudice stems from a particular set of characteristics shared by people with what is called an authoritarian personality.

The term *authoritarian personality* refers to individuals who believe uncritically that authorities always act legitimately, and they show prejudice as a consequence of unconscious hostility toward rigid and demanding parents. Authoritarians typically are raised in environments in which parents are sharply critical and difficult to satisfy. However, because of a strong belief that authority is always right, authoritarians are unable to direct toward their parents the hostility they develop. Instead, they displace their hostility toward groups that they perceive as weak or unconventional—most typically, toward members of minority groups. Authoritarians also tend to be politically and socially conservative, and they view the world in rigid categories in which the weak are expected to be dutifully obedient to the powerful.

To test their theory, Adorno and his colleagues devised a personality scale to measure authoritarianism. During extensive interviewing, they found that people high in authoritarianism were unusually prejudiced and had parents with traits similar to those predicted by the theory. Using their data, the authors suggested that authoritarian personalities were responsible for the German Holocaust, in which millions of Jews and other ethnic group members were murdered.

Later researchers, however, have found several inconsistencies with this early work. Most important is the finding that not all prejudiced people have had harsh, demanding parents. Furthermore, even people who are low in authoritarianism may be quite prejudiced.

Still, recent work continues to indicate the importance of the concept of authoritarianism. For instance, research has found that people high in authoritarianism tend to have harsh attitudes toward those with AIDS, think that homeless people are lazy, react with disfavor to laws that protect the environment, and oppose the right to choose an abortion. Clearly, authoritarianism is related to a broad, consistent outlook on life (Peterson, Doty, & Winter, 1993; Duckitt, 1993, 1994a; Rickert, 1998; Rousseau & de Man, 1998; Lavine et al., 1999).

REALISTIC CONFLICT: THE CLASH OF COMPETITION

Put two rodents who are unfamiliar with each other into a small cage, and they are likely to fight over the limited amount of space available. Does prejudice begin in the same way, when two groups compete over scarce resources?

According to realistic conflict theory, the answer is yes. **Realistic conflict theory** argues that prejudice is the outcome of direct competition over valued, but limited, resources (Brown & Williams, 1984; Hilton, Potvin, & Sachdev, 1989; Duckitt, 1992; Nagel, 1995; Duckitt & Mphuthing, 1998). In this view, the things we value most in life—a good job, a safe and comfortable environment, and a high standard of living—are limited, and people must compete with others to obtain what they consider their fair share. If they perceive that members of minority groups prevent their attaining a fair share, they will view those minorities in an increasingly hostile manner. Consequently, prejudice develops, fueled by the competition for desired resources (Langford & Ponting, 1992; Huddy & Sears, 1995; see Figure 3–1).

For example, consider a dirty, unsafe, and impersonal environment in a noisy, crowded city. If majority group residents blame the difficulties of urban life on the presence of a particular minority group, they may act in a hostile and antagonistic manner toward the members of that

realistic conflict theory: The theory that argues that prejudice is the outcome of direct competition over valued, but limited, resources.

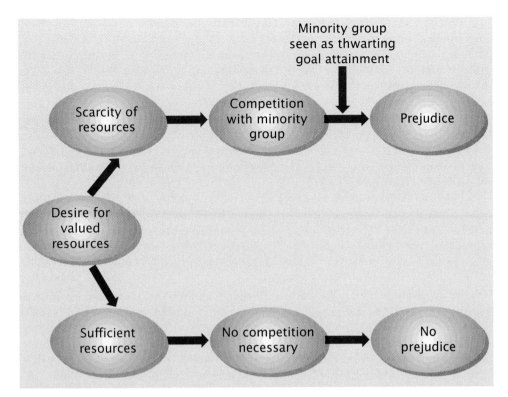

FIGURE 3–1   Realistic Conflict Theory According to realistic conflict theory, prejudice is the outcome of direct competition over limited resources. If resources are insufficient, prejudice will occur, but if the resources are adequate, prejudice will be avoided.

minority group. Similarly, in times of high unemployment and intense competition for a handful of jobs, prejudice may be directed toward members of minority groups if they are regarded as "taking jobs away" from majority group members (Rickert, 1998).

Competition at Robber's Cave.   Experimental evidence as well as historical evidence supports the argument that competition leads to stereotyping, prejudice, and ultimately conflict. For example, social psychologist Muzafer Sherif (1966) conducted a classic field study at a boys' summer camp called Robber's Cave. Two groups of middle-class 11- and 12-year-olds—who did not know they were in an experiment—were settled on opposite sides of the camp. Initially, each group was unaware of the other's existence. Then, after the two groups had been established, the researchers devised a tournament of games in which the two groups competed for a series of attractive prizes that only one group could win. According to realistic conflict theory, the conditions were ripe for stereotyping and prejudice to develop: The two groups were in a position of competition over scarce resources.

The results were more than the researchers bargained for. Not only did the groups compete vigorously during the games, but the competition soon went well beyond the tournament. The groups picked fights, raided each other's campsites, and generally behaved in an angry and combative manner. According to the researchers, an outside observer would characterize the children as "wicked, disturbed, and vicious bunches of youngsters" (Sherif, 1966, p. 58). In just 2 short weeks, the groups had developed a deep-seated malice toward each other.

Although it was easy to foster antagonism between the two groups, taming it proved to be considerably more difficult, and the researchers' first efforts were inadequate. For instance, members of the two groups were brought together to share pleasant experiences, such as watching movies. However, as soon as the lights were dimmed, fights broke out. Moral exhortations also proved useless. Even the introduction of a third group, which was supposed to act as a kind of common enemy, was ineffective in reducing hostility.

Researchers have found that working cooperatively toward a common goal can contribute to the reduction of group hostility.

Fortunately, though, one procedure did work: the introduction of *superordinate goals,* goals simultaneously shared by members of conflicting groups that can be achieved only when members of different groups jointly contribute resources or work together. Reasoning that common goals led to the formation of the groups initially, the researchers calculated that the introduction of goals that were common to both groups—superordinate goals—might be effective in uniting them.

They were right. The researchers arranged for a series of apparent emergencies. For instance, the water supply broke down, and the boys were forced to work jointly if they wanted water to drink. After a number of such events, group hostility was reduced, friendships developed across group lines, and the superordinate goals became effective in unifying the previously hostile groups.

Subsequent work has suggested that it was probably not only the jointly held goals that reduced group hostility. An additional process may have been at work: a cognitive recategorization in which members of the two separate groups came to see one another as members of a single group (Gaertner et al., 1989; Gaertner et al., 1994; Dovidio et al., 1995).

Relative deprivation. Does the study at Robber's Cave present us with a microcosm of society? Do stereotypes and prejudice develop merely as a result of competition between groups sparring over scarce resources?

Although the results of the study clearly support realistic conflict theory, they do not represent the total picture. Some research suggests that competition, by itself, is not enough to bring about stereotyping and prejudice. For instance, whites who reluctantly comply with school busing plans to promote the desegregation of their local schools often show no more prejudice toward African Americans than those who are not personally involved (Sears & Kinder, 1985; Sears & Funk, 1991). Such findings suggest that prejudice involving competition is not just the result of the absolute level of resources that people feel they lack. Instead, it is the feeling of relative deprivation that is crucial.

Relative deprivation is the sense that one lacks a desired resource in comparison to another group, which is perceived to have more. Relative deprivation may arise as people measure themselves against the world around them, particularly as it is mirrored on television and film. For instance, in the 1960s, minority group members saw that the economy was prospering for most people—except for members of minority groups, who lagged well behind the majority. The perception that for them the "American Dream" was going unfulfilled led to violence and rioting in some urban areas of the United States (Sears & McConahay, 1981; Gonzalez-Intal, 1991).

Similarly, majority group members may perceive that members of minority groups are succeeding at a more rapid pace than members of the majority group, leading to prejudice against minorities (Ellemers & Bos, 1998; Mummendey et al., 1999). For instance, consider anti-affirmative action views that grew to become a political issue in the late 1990s. In part, these views were based on majority group members' perception that affirmative action programs permitted minority groups to achieve success more rapidly than the majority (Danziger & Wheeler, 1975; Brown et al., 1986; Olson, Herman, & Zanna, 1986; Bobocel et al., 1998; Collins, 1998).

However, neither realistic conflict theory nor relative deprivation approaches to stereotyping and prejudice provide the full story. For example, even though past research had seemed to suggest that more lynchings occurred in the South during times of economic downturns—in support of realistic conflict theory—a more careful analysis recently found that no such relationship existed. In fact, evidence that a relationship exists between economic conditions and the incidence of hate crimes in general is lacking (Green, Glaser, & Rich, 1998).

Furthermore, in most cases, minority group members represent no credible threat. In fact, members of minorities are rarely in a position to threaten the well-being of majority group members, and in the struggle for scarce resources, minority group members are most often at a distinct disadvantage. Stereotyping and prejudice, then, are produced by factors

relative deprivation: The sense that one lacks a desired resource in comparison to another group, which is perceived to have more.

beyond realistic conflict. One possibility: the role that membership in racial, religious, ethnic, and gender groups plays in people's identity.

social identity theory: The theory that suggests people use group membership as a source of pride and self-worth.

SOCIAL IDENTITY THEORY: THE SELF-ESTEEM OF GROUP MEMBERSHIP

Think about your ethnic or religious identity for a moment. Are you proud of it? Does it make you feel good to be part of the group? Would you feel threatened if your group were criticized or attacked?

According to social psychologists Henri Tajfel (1982) and John Turner (1987), the groups to which we belong play a crucial role in maintaining our personal self-esteem. Their **social identity theory** suggests that we use group membership as a source of pride and self-worth. However, to feel such pride, we must assume that our group is, in fact, superior to others. As a result, our quest for a positive social identity leads us to inflate the positive aspects of groups to which we belong and belittle groups to which we do not belong (Tajfel & Turner, 1986; Turner et al., 1992; Abrams & Hogg, 1999; Turner & Onorato, 1999).

Certainly, ample evidence exists that members of various cultural groups tend to see their own groups in more positive terms than others. For instance, one cross-cultural investigation that examined 17 different societies found that, universally, people rated the group to which they belonged as more peace-loving, virtuous, and obedient than other groups (LeVine & Campbell, 1972). Even countries in which national pride is relatively lower than that of other countries still are viewed quite positively by their citizens (see Table 3–2).

TABLE 3–2	National Pride by Countries				
NATIONAL PRIDE IN SPECIFIC ACHIEVEMENTS			**GENERAL NATIONAL PRIDE**		
Rank	Country	Score	Rank	Country	Score
1	Ireland	39.3	1	Austria	17.6
2	United States	38.5	2	United States	17.2
3	Canada	37.5	3	Bulgaria	17.0
4	Austria	36.5	4	Hungary	16.7
5	New Zealand	36.4	5	Canada	16.6
6	Norway	35.2	6	The Philippines	16.5
7	Great Britain	34.7	7	New Zealand	16.4
8	The Netherlands	34.6	8	Japan	16.4
9	Japan	34.5	9	Ireland	16.3
10	Spain	33.1	10	Spain	16.0
11	The Philippines	32.4	11	Slovenia	16.0
12	Germany (West)	32.2	12	Norway	15.8
13	Sweden	31.6	13	Poland	15.8
14	Bulgaria	31.4	14	Great Britain	15.4
15	Germany (East)	31.0	15	Russia	15.3
16	Slovenia	30.9	16	The Netherlands	14.5
17	Italy	30.5	17	Sweden	14.4
18	Czech Republic	29.5	18	Czech Republic	14.3
19	Hungary	28.4	19	Italy	14.1
20	Slovakia	28.2	20	Latvia	13.9
21	Poland	28.2	21	Germany (West)	13.7
22	Russia	28.0	22	Germany (East)	13.6
23	Latvia	27.8	23	Slovakia	13.5

Source: GSS News, 1998.

Even in cases in which objective behavior displayed by different groups is similar, people interpret the behavior quite differently (Bagby & Rector, 1992; Schruijer et al., 1994). Hence, groups to which we belong are described as generous; the same sort of behavior, when practiced by a member of a minority group, is viewed as wasteful and extravagant. Members of our own group are seen as devoted; members of other groups are cliquish.

Of course, not all groups allow us to achieve the same sense of self-worth as others. Groups must be small enough so that people can feel somewhat unique and special. In fact, minority group membership sometimes produces stronger feelings of social identity than majority group membership (Verkuyten, 1995). Minority group leaders of the past who used slogans such as "Black is Beautiful" and "Gay Pride" reflected an awareness of the importance of instilling group pride. Research has supported this strategy: Ethnic group membership can be an important source of psychological support, particularly for minority group members (Ethier & Deaux, 1994; Sellers et al., 1997; Swan & Wyer, 1997).

On the other hand, favoritism toward groups to which we belong is reduced when we perform well while our group is less successful. In such cases we may look less favorably on our group. However, this is largely a Western cultural phenomenon: In more collective Eastern societies, individual success leads to greater favoritism for one's own group, even if the group is not succeeding (Chen, Brockner, & Katz, 1998).

Overall, membership in a group provides people with a sense of personal identity and self-esteem. When a group is successful, self-esteem can rise; and, conversely, when self-esteem is threatened, people feel enhanced attraction to their own group and increased hostility toward members of other groups (Swan & Wyer, 1997; Branscombe et al., 1999).

REVIEW AND RETHINK

Review

- Stereotypes, discrimination, and minority groups are primary concepts in the study of prejudice.

- Among the explanations for prejudice are social learning approaches, motivational approaches, and realistic conflict theory.

- Social identity theory suggests that people derive a sense of pride from group membership, which leads to exaggeration of both their own group's positive aspects and other groups' negative aspects.

Rethink

- What is prejudice, and how does it differ from stereotypes and discrimination?

- How do social psychologists define a minority group? In what way is being a minority group member a state of mind?

- According to the realistic conflict and relative deprivation theories, how does prejudice arise? How do these theories explain anti-affirmative action attitudes?

- According to studies of relative deprivation, are people who are financially well-off more likely or less likely to feel prejudice toward poor people than those who are less well-off?

- According to social identity theory, how would people feel about themselves after being given a chance to discriminate against members of a group to which they do not belong? After a basketball game, would the winning or losing team be more likely to exhibit discriminatory behavior? Explain.

THE COGNITIVE FOUNDATIONS OF PREJUDICE: VIEWING THE WORLD THROUGH STEREOTYPES

We all have a natural tendency to categorize, to sort objects into groups. If you are asked what kinds of dishes you have in your kitchen cupboard, for instance, you are unlikely to reply with a list of each individual plate ("Let's see, plate number one is blue and has a chip; number two is also blue and . . ."). Instead, you'll probably say that you have eight dinner plates, eight salad plates, five bowls, and so forth.

In the same way, we use **social categorization**, the process of classifying people according to particular social characteristics, to sort out the world of people around us. In particular, we are influenced by such visually conspicuous physical features as race, sex, and age to categorize and form schemas about members of different groups. Consequently, even when we meet a person for the first time, social categorization processes provide us with a rich—although not necessarily accurate—set of expectations about what this new acquaintance is like (Brewer & Lui, 1989; Zarate & Smith, 1990; Lee, Jussim, & McCauley, 1995; Banks & Eberhardt, 1998; Marques et al., 1998; Wittenbrink, Hilton, & Gist, 1998).

Cognitive approaches to prejudice suggest that such social categorization processes lie at the heart of prejudice. Rather than forming individuated views of others, based on their specific attributes or characteristics, people use stereotypes—beliefs and expectations about members of a group that are held solely on the basis of their membership in the group. Stereotypes are based on the categories to which a person belongs.

Stereotypes contain both descriptive and prescriptive beliefs about others (Terborg, 1977; Fiske, 1993). *Descriptive stereotypes* provide information about the ways that most people in a group supposedly behave, their preferences, and their particular competencies. According to common descriptive stereotypes, as we'll see later in the chapter, women may be good secretaries, but men make good engineers.

But stereotypes may also contain other elements: They may be prescriptive. *Prescriptive stereotypes* suggest how members of groups *ought* to think, feel, and behave (Deaux & LaFrance, 1998). According to prescriptive stereotypes, for instance, women should be polite and nice, and boys should be good at athletics. If members of categories do not conform to such stereotypes (an abrasive women, or an uncoordinated, unathletic boy), they may be penalized (Eagly, Makhijani, & Klonsky, 1992).

In addition to provoking stereotypes, social categorization plays other roles in determining how we view others. For example, once we sort people into social categories, they seem to us more like other members of those categories than is actually the case. As a result, people often assert that members of a particular group "all act the same" or "all look alike," believing that there is less variability among members of a group than there really is. In this way, social categorization leads people to minimize the differences between individuals in the same classification and—at the same time—overestimate the degree of difference that exists among individuals in different social categories (Wilder, 1986; Urban & Miller, 1998).

One fundamental way that people are categorized is on the basis of ingroup and outgroup membership. An **ingroup** is a group to which a person feels that he or she belongs; an **outgroup** is a group to which a person feels that he or she does not belong. For instance, a white male may perceive that he is part of the ingroup of white males; nonwhite, nonmales would be thought of as outgroup members. The categorization of people into ingroups and outgroups results in several biases.

Ingroup–outgroup bias: The us-versus-them mentality.   Suppose you were part of a group of 10 people that was randomly divided into two groups. How would you react toward the members of your own team, and would you favor them over the members of the other team?

social categorization: The process of classifying people according to particular social characteristics.

ingroup: A group to which a person feels that he or she belongs.

outgroup: A group to which a person feels that he or she does not belong.

The people in this auditorium would begin to develop an ingroup–outgroup bias if each side of the aisle were simply designated a separate team.

A good deal of research suggests that just on the basis of a random assignment to two teams, most people would come to value their own team and discriminate in favor of its members (Vanbeselaere, 1993). The reason is the **ingroup–outgroup bias**, the tendency to hold less favorable views about groups to which we do not belong, while holding more favorable opinions about groups to which we do belong (Wilder, 1986, 1990; Mullen, Brown, & Smith, 1992; Flippen et al., 1996; Harmon-Jones et al., 1996; Reichl, 1997).

In a typical experiment examining ingroup–outgroup biases—known as the *minimal group* procedure—participants are divided into two groups, supposedly on the basis of their preference for one of two artist's paintings. In reality, each person is assigned randomly to one of the two groups, producing an ingroup, to which the person belongs, and an outgroup. Later in the experiment, participants are asked to distribute money to a member of their own group and a member of the outgroup, using one of several distribution rules. One method follows an equality rule, in which each person receives a similar amount. A second approach that participants can follow is to maximize the outcome so that the total amount awarded is highest, without regard to group membership. Finally, a third potential strategy is to show bias in favor of the ingroup.

Results of studies using this basic procedure identify a consistent pattern: Not only do participants tend to reward members of their own group at the expense of members of other groups, but they do so in a way that magnifies the differences in reward between the two groups (e.g., Tajfel, 1982; Wilder, 1990; Hartstone & Augoustinos, 1995).

What is particularly striking about these results is that the ingroups and outgroups are so minimally differentiated from each other. There is no direct, face-to-face interaction among participants, either within their own group or with members of the other group. The participants are anonymous, and the categorization is based on a criterion unrelated to participants' earlier behavior. In sum, membership in the groups is totally arbitrary. Given that discriminatory behavior toward outgroups occurs in such a situation, it is hardly surprising that bias against the outgroup would be even stronger when outgroup members differ in obvious and salient ways from ingroup members.

The ingroup–outgroup bias is consistent with the self-serving bias that we discussed in Chapter 2. People see the success of their group as a manifestation of their own group's abilities, whereas they see their group's failures as due to circumstance. In contrast, people attribute outgroup success to luck or extraordinary, atypical hard work, whereas they believe outgroup failure illustrates ineptness (Brewer & Kramer, 1985; Hamilton & Trolier, 1986).

ingroup–outgroup bias:
The tendency to hold less favorable views about groups to which we do not belong, while holding more favorable opinions about groups to which we do belong.

The bias against outgroup members and in favor of ingroup members may have its roots in basic perceptual phenomena (Turner, 1987). For instance, categorization leads to perceptual distortion, in which objects in the same category (e.g., the ingroup) appear more similar to one another, and more different from objects in different categories (e.g., outgroups), than if they had not been categorized (Wilder, 1986; Herringer & Garza, 1987; Turner, 1987).

As a consequence, characteristics (such as race, facial configuration, and dialect or accent) that differentiate minority group members from majority group members may be particularly conspicuous. And majority group members will use these perceived differences to infer that other differentiations exist. Ultimately—to people in both the majority and the minority—outgroup members are viewed more negatively and ingroup members more positively. In summary, then, stereotypes about outgroup members may develop through our habit of categorizing people as we seek to understand and simplify our own social environment.

More recent research has sought to identify the circumstances under which we are most prone to discriminate against an outgroup. One important factor is a person's mood. For instance, when the relevance of their group membership is high, people who are in a bad mood (e.g., sad) are more apt to favor their own group at the expense of the outgroup. They are also more likely to make harsh, stereotypical judgments about outgroup members (Esses & Zanna, 1995; Forgas & Fiedler, 1996).

outgroup homogeneity bias: The perception that there is less variability among the members of outgroups than within one's own ingroup.

Outgroup homogeneity bias.   Sorting people into categories produces several kinds of biases in social perception that lead to stereotyping. First, the **outgroup homogeneity bias** is the perception that there is less variability among the members of outgroups than within one's own ingroup. We assume that members of other groups are similar to one another, whereas we are keenly aware of the differences among members of our own group (Lorenzi-Cioldi, 1993; Haslam, Oakes, & Turner, 1996; Linville, Fischer, & Yoon, 1996; Linville & Fischer, 1998).

Why do people assume that the outgroup is so homogeneous? One reason is that they have less complex conceptualizations of outgroup members. Whites asked to describe African Americans tend to use fewer descriptive dimensions, just as young people have more general and incomplete views of older people. In contrast, people tend to have considerably more strongly differentiated views of members of their own group. If you are Latino, all Latinos don't seem similar; if you're white, all whites don't appear to act alike (Linville, 1982; Fiske & Taylor, 1991; Judd, Ryan, & Park, 1991).

Furthermore, people may process information about ingroup and outgroup members differently. According to Thomas Ostrom and colleagues (Ostrom et al., 1993), we are more apt to consider information about outgroup members in terms of *attribute categories.* In other words, we might describe outgroup members in terms of attributes such as general personality traits, broad interests, and activities that they are prone to carry out ("They are industrious" or "They are good athletes"). These attributes are viewed in relatively abstract terms, applying more to the group and less to individuals. In contrast, ingroup information is more likely to be processed in terms of *person categories.* Because we are more familiar with and more likely to differentiate and individualize ingroup members, we process information on the basis of personal data ("Dan is a go-getter" or "Erik is a great teacher").

Another reason for the outgroup homogeneity bias is a lack of contact with outgroup members. If people rarely interact with members of outgroups, they are unlikely to view them as individuals with differing opinions, beliefs, values, and traits (Linville & Fischer, 1993). Even when they do interact, the circumstances may be limited, thereby preventing the development of more complex, heterogeneous views of outgroup members (Quattrone, 1986; Judd & Park, 1988).

illusory correlation: The result of people overestimating the strength of a relationship between two distinctive or unusual events.

Illusory correlation: The fictitious missing link.   In our search for order in the world, we sometimes mistakenly perceive that a relationship exists between two variables—even when, in reality, there may be little or no relationship at all. **Illusory correlation** occurs when people overestimate the strength of a relationship between two distinctive or unusual events. Illusory correlation is at work when two events that may be only minimally related to one another—or not related at all—are perceived as being closely associated.

Illusory correlation helps explain why stereotypes develop and survive, even when supportive evidence is lacking (Mullen & Johnson, 1995; Kubota, 1997; McConnell, Leibold, & Sherman, 1997). Illusory correlation operates, for example, when people overestimate how often members of minority groups engage in negative or unpleasant behaviors. Social psychologist David Hamilton (1979; Hamilton & Gifford, 1976) observes that members of a majority group tend to have relatively few interactions with members of minority groups. For instance, for many white people, meeting an African American is a relatively rare event, making it a distinctive interaction. Furthermore, for most of us, encounters with others are mostly positive and pleasant; negative, unpleasant interactions are relatively rare—and therefore distinctive.

In short, because interactions with minority group members *and* unpleasant, negative encounters are both relatively rare events, they are highly distinctive—and memorable— when they do occur. As a result, the ingredients for illusory correlation are present: Two rare, distinctive factors that may actually be only minimally associated with one another are assumed to be strongly correlated (Schaller, 1991; Johnson & Mullen, 1994). Furthermore, distinctiveness may lead us to recall such events more readily, making us overestimate the number of times they have actually occurred in conjunction (McConnell, Sherman, & Hamilton, 1994).

How likely is such a scenario? Quite plausible, actually. For instance, newspapers may report the racial identity of minority group members who commit crimes, but fail to state the racial identity of majority group members who commit the same type of offense. In the minds of the public, then, crimes (relatively unusual, rare events) get linked with minority group members. The end result, through the workings of the illusory correlation bias, is the development and reinforcement of a stereotype about minority group members.

The illusory correlation bias also may promote the *confirmation biases* that we considered in Chapter 2. Remember that confirmation biases lead us to seek out, interpret, or formulate information that is consistent with our current beliefs. Consequently, if illusory correlation leads us (erroneously) to leap to the conclusion that, say, members of a particular minority group are likely to be involved in crimes, we are apt to focus on and even seek out information that confirms our beliefs. Confirmation biases, then, are apt to strengthen stereotypes and make them enduring.

In the most extreme case, people's biases lead them to engage in self-fulfilling prophecies. As we discussed in Chapter 2, *self-fulfilling prophecies* reflect the tendency of people to act in ways that are consistent with their expectations, beliefs, or cognitions about an event or behavior, thereby increasing the likelihood that the event or behavior will occur. Consequently, if people think that members of a certain group are lazy, they may act in a way that actually elicits laziness from the members of that group.

The treacherous consequences of self-fulfilling prophecies were illustrated in a classic study carried out by Carl Word and colleagues (Word, Zanna, & Cooper, 1974). They found that when white interviewers questioned African American interviewees for a job, they tended to sit further away, make more speech errors, and interview for a shorter time than when they questioned white interviewees. In turn, they found, this nonverbal behavior led interviewees to perform less well than their white counterparts—thereby fulfilling the original expectations of the interviewers.

Such behavior is hardly of merely theoretical importance. Rather, it suggests that members of minority groups, who may trigger the prejudices of interviewers in the job market, may face a difficult time. It is not easy to put one's best foot forward when one is the recipient of negative treatment.

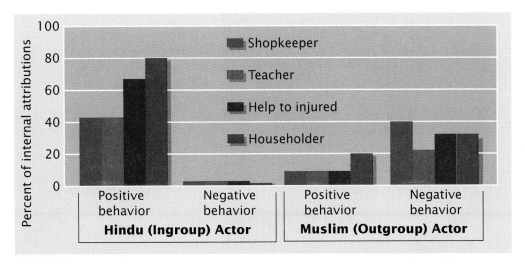

FIGURE 3–2   The Ultimate Attribution Error When Hindu participants read about positive behavior on the part of an ingroup (Hindu) actor, they made internal attributions, whereas negative behaviors were not seen as indicative of internal characteristics. In contrast, attributions were made in the opposite direction when the actor was an outgroup member. Percentages refer to percentage of participants making internal attributions. (*Source:* Adapted from Taylor & Jaggi, 1974, Table 2.)

The ultimate attribution error: Heads I win, tails you lose.   If you've ever tried to argue with someone who is prejudiced, you know that logic doesn't easily prevail. Social psychologist Gordon Allport (1954) captured this fact perfectly in his classic book *The Nature of Prejudice*:

> *Mr. X:* The trouble with the Jews is that they only take care of their own group.
>
> *Mr. Y:* But the record of the Community chest campaign shows that they gave more generously, in proportion to their numbers, to the general charities of the community than did non-Jews.
>
> *Mr. X:* That shows they are always trying to buy favor and intrude into Christian affairs. They think of nothing but money; that is why there are so many Jewish bankers.
>
> *Mr. Y:* But a recent study shows that the percentage of Jews in the banking business is negligible, far smaller than the percentage of non-Jews.
>
> *Mr. X:* That's just it: they don't go in for respectable business; they are only in the movie business or run night clubs. (Allport, 1954, pp. 13–14)

One reason for the difficulty in using logical argument to counteract stereotyping is that people tend to make inaccurate attributions regarding the causes of both minority and majority group members' behavior. More specifically, social psychologist Thomas Pettigrew (1979; Jemmott, Pettigrew, & Johnson, 1983) suggests that people who hold stereotypes are prone to the ultimate attribution error, which is an extension of the fundamental attribution error that we discussed in Chapter 2. You will recall that the fundamental attribution error is the tendency of observers to attribute others' behavior to stable traits and dispositions, but their own behavior to situational factors.

The **ultimate attribution error** goes several steps further. It suggests that when people who hold strong stereotypes see a minority group member engaging in negative behavior, they will attribute the behavior to dispositional characteristics; but when they see a minority group member engaging in positive behavior, they will attribute it to situational factors (see Figure 3–2).

Hence, when a minority group member acts in an undesirable way, the attribution is something on the order of "That's the way those people are" or "They're born like that." But the view is different when a minority group member is observed engaging in desirable

ultimate attribution error: The tendency among people holding strong stereotypes to attribute negative behavior on the part of a minority group member to dispositional characteristics, and correspondingly, to attribute positive behavior on the part of a minority group member to situational factors.

The ultimate attribution error might lead a prejudiced person to see opera star Jessye Norman's success as due to special advantage or luck, but not due to her positive qualities.

behavior. To be consistent with their negative stereotypes, the observers go through some cognitive acrobatics to find an attribution that fits. It's not all that hard, it turns out: There are at least four ways that a person who holds stereotypes can approach the problem (Pettigrew, 1979; Jemmott, Pettigrew, & Johnson, 1983; Rothbart & John, 1985):

1. *The exceptional case.* First, the positive act can be viewed as an exceptional case, and the person can be strongly differentiated from other members of the minority group ("He's the exception that proves the rule," or "She's so different from most other African Americans"). In fact, the perceiver might even view the positive behavior as deviant in some way.

2. *Special advantage or luck.* A second way in which a person holding a negative stereotype can explain positive minority group behavior is by deciding that the behavior is due to some kind of special advantage or simply to luck ("She must have gotten into medical school because of affirmative action" or "What a lucky person to get that job").

3. *The situational context.* There is a third way in which a person holding negative stereotypes can explain positive acts on the part of minority group members: The actions are caused by situational factors outside the control of the individual, rather than by some personality or dispositional factor ("Anyone in that position would have done well"). In other words, the minority person's membership in the minority group is overlooked as a causal explanation; the particular role or position that the person occupies is assumed to be the explanation for his or her behavior.

4. *Extraordinary motivation and effort.* Finally, an observer may assume that a successful minority group member has shown disproportionately high, even excessive, motivation to succeed and overcome minority group membership. In this view, the underlying negative characteristics of the minority group are still present, but exceptional motivation has enabled one particular individual to overcome his or her "true" state.

Curiously, though, the very success of minority group members that people who hold stereotypes attempt to explain away allows them to deny that prejudice and discrimination have negative consequences for the targets of prejudice. After all, they observe, some people do manage to be successful.

These four attributions for desirable minority group member behavior clearly represent a damned-if-you-do, damned-if-you-don't, no-win situation. If minority group members engage in negative acts, their behavior is seen as confirmation of an underlying flaw shared by all members of the group. If the behavior is positive, any one of the four unflattering explanations discussed above will be used to avoid acknowledging the value of the individual and his or her behavior.

THE DIVERSE APPROACHES TO PREJUDICE: WHERE DO WE STAND?

We've seen a variety of approaches taken by social psychologists in their efforts to explain prejudice. The diversity of theories spans a wide path, ranging from the level of the individual to broad, societal-level factors.

It is tempting to ask which of the approaches provides the most convincing explanation for prejudice. Yet such a question is largely unanswerable. The phenomenon of prejudice is so intricate and complex that no single explanation is likely to suffice. Such a knotty and enduring problem can be explained only through a variety of interrelated approaches, each of which informs the others.

In a way, the multiplicity of approaches provides us with an opportunity, for each of them suggests different avenues for seeking to reduce and overcome this most intractable of social problems. In fact, the work done by social psychologists suggests some very practical approaches for reducing various aspects of prejudice, discrimination, and stereotyping. For a look at one area—overcoming stereotypes—see the Informed Consumer of Social Psychology section.

OVERCOMING STEREOTYPES

We've seen how pervasive—and enduring—stereotypes can be. Are there any reliable means of overcoming their influence as we judge others?

According to research on stereotyping, there are several ways that you can judge people in a more individuated manner and avoid drawing conclusions in terms of the groups they represent. Among them:

◆ Seek out information about people's personal characteristics and behavior. The more you know about people, the more successful you can be at making judgments based on their individuality instead of their membership in a group. Consider their behavior across a range of situations, their prior experience, and the expectations held by others that might be motivating their behavior.

◆ Similarly, it is always important to recognize that people's behavior is not just driven by their personal characteristics and their group membership, but by the situation in which they find themselves. In other words, avoid becoming susceptible to the fundamental attribution error that we discussed in the previous chapter, in which people tend to overattribute others' behavior to dispositional causes and fail to recognize the importance of situational factors.

◆ Be motivated to be accurate. Study after study shows that if people are not strongly motivated to be accurate, they tend to rely on judgments that are based more on the groups to which people belong than on personal considerations. Furthermore, people who are distracted, in a hurry, or otherwise cognitively busy make less individualized judgments. Hasty, unthoughtful decisions are apt to be based on stereotypes, not on an individual's characteristics (Pratto & Bargh, 1991; Anastasio et al., 1997; Spears & Haslam, 1997).

THE INFORMED
CONSUMER
OF SOCIAL
PSYCHOLOGY

REVIEW AND RETHINK

Review

- Cognitive approaches to prejudice suggest that social categorization processes lead to stereotypes.

- One primary categorization is the distinction between ingroups and outgroups.

- Among the cognitive biases relating to prejudice are the ingroup–outgroup bias, the outgroup homogeneity bias, illusory correlation, and the ultimate attribution error.

Rethink

- What characteristics does U.S. culture commonly use to form ingroups and outgroups? Are these the only characteristics that logically can be used to form such groups? Explain why or why not.

- What is the outgroup homogeneity bias? Is it possible that such a bias could be used to reduce prejudice? Explain why or why not?

- What is the ultimate attribution error, and how does it differ from the fundamental attribution error?

- How might illusory correlation affect attitudes toward women in contemporary culture?

RACISM AND SEXISM: THE CONSEQUENCES OF PREJUDICE

When Philip McAdoo, a 22-year-old senior at the University of North Carolina, stopped one day to see a friend who worked on his college campus, a receptionist asked if he would autograph a basketball for her son. Because he was African American and tall, "she just assumed that I was on the basketball team," recounted McAdoo.

Jasme Kelly, an African American sophomore at the same college, had a similar story to tell. When she went to see a friend at a fraternity house, the student who answered the door asked if she was there to apply for the job of cook.

White students, too, find racial relations difficult and in some ways forbidding. For instance, Jenny Johnson, a white 20-year-old junior, finds even the most basic conversation with African American classmates difficult. She describes a conversation in which African American friends "jump at my throat because I used the word 'black' instead of African American. There is just such a huge barrier that it's really hard . . . to have a normal discussion." (Sanoff & Miner-brook, 1993, p. 58)

The consequences of prejudice can be seen not only in the blaring headlines about conspicuous, flagrant racial incidents, but also in the stuff of daily life for memb   .oups that are the victims of prejudice. And majority group members, too, are affecte   a world afflicted with prejudice and discrimination.

We turn now to a discussion of two of the major manifestations of prejudice: racism and sexism. **Racism** is prejudice directed at people because of their race; **sexism** is prejudice directed at women or men because of their gender. Although, lamentably, we could consider many other types of "isms," such as ageism (prejudice against the elderly), racial and sexual prejudice have been most often and most thoroughly addressed by social psychologists.

To make matters worse, the problems of racism and sexism are not likely to go away—although the targets of prejudice may ultimately shift in the future as the population distribution undergoes major changes. For instance, current projections of the population makeup of the United States suggest that by the year 2050, the non-Hispanic white population will decline to less than 53 percent of the total population of the United States (see Figure 3–3).

racism: Prejudice directed at people because of their race.

sexism: Prejudice directed at women or men because of their gender.

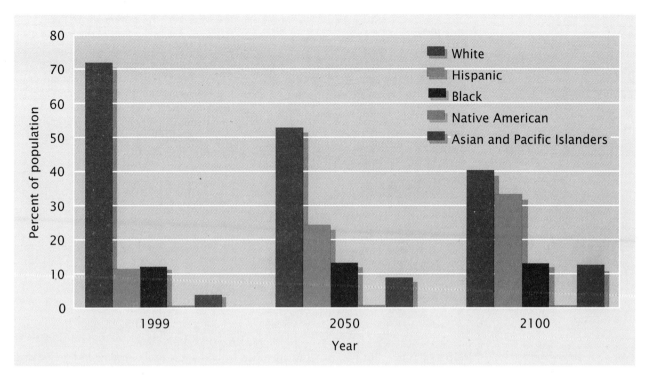

FIGURE 3–3   U.S. Racial and Ethnic Population Projections Projections of the population makeup of the United States show that the proportion of non-Hispanic whites will decline as the proportion of minority group members increases over this century. (*Source:* U.S. Bureau of Census, 1999.)

RACISM: HATRED IN COLOR

In his classic novel, *Invisible Man,* Ralph Ellison, an African American, wrote, "I am an invisible man. I am a man of substance, of flesh and bone, fiber and liquids—and I might even be said to possess a mind. I am invisible, understand, simply because people refuse to see me" (Ellison, 1952, p. 3).

Five decades later, Ellison's words, unfortunately, still ring true. Despite enormous strides in the civil rights arena, including the end to legal segregation in the United States, African Americans still fall behind whites on many crucial measures of economic and social success. The proportion of African Americans who have completed college is half that of whites; the African American unemployment rate is more than double that of whites; and the proportion of African Americans who live below poverty levels is three times greater than that of whites (U.S. Bureau of the Census, 1999).

Curiously, such grim social and economic facts fly in the face of data regarding white society's stated views about African Americans, which, at least on the surface, have become considerably more positive over the years. For example, studies of stereotypes begun in the 1930s and followed up through subsequent decades show that many of the more blatant negative views about African Americans, which people admitted freely in the first half of this century, have been moderated. In general, when directly asked, fewer people feel that African Americans as a group harbor such negative traits as "laziness" or "ignorance"— stereotypes that were believed and openly acknowledged as recently as the 1950s (Katz & Braly, 1933; Karlins, Coffman, & Walters, 1969; Dovidio & Gaertner, 1986). Furthermore, whites feel that relations between whites and African Americans have been improving—a view not shared by African Americans, who tend to think just the opposite, as indicated in Figure 3–4 (McQueen, 1991).

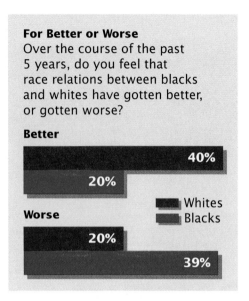

For Better or Worse
Over the course of the past 5 years, do you feel that race relations between blacks and whites have gotten better, or gotten worse?

Better

40% Whites

20% Blacks

Worse

20%

39%

Whites
Blacks

FIGURE 3–4   Improvements in Race Relations Are in the Eyes of the Beholder
The views of whites and African Americans are almost the mirror image of one another. Whites tend to believe that race relations between whites and African Americans have been improving, whereas African Americans tend to think they have become worse.
(*Source: The Wall Street Journal*/NBC News Poll, reported in McQueen, 1991.)

Modern racism.   But has the white majority, by and large, really become less prejudiced? Some social psychologists suggest that despite the apparent reduction of visible stereotyping of African Americans and other racial minorities, a new kind of racism has taken its place. According to social psychologists Samuel Gaertner and John Dovidio, overt racism has been replaced by modern racism. **Modern racism** is a subtle form of prejudice in which people appear, on the surface, not to harbor prejudice, but they actually do hold racist attitudes. According to this view, if we scratch the apparently nonracist surface of many people, we will find bigotry lurking beneath (Gaertner & Dovidio, 1986; McConahay, 1986; Dovidio & Gaertner, 1991).

Modern racism arises because people often embrace competing beliefs and values. They want to see themselves as part of the mainstream of society and as fair, humanitarian, and egalitarian individuals (Katz & Hass, 1988). At the same time, though, they may still hold somewhat negative views of members of groups other than their own (Biernat et al., 1996). In most cases, they keep their prejudice under wraps, but when placed in situations in which they are given social support for racism, they are willing to express, and sometimes act on, their unfavorable opinions (Schnake & Ruscher, 1998).

For instance, most people avoid publicly endorsing overtly racist statements because of social pressures against such behavior. But when more subtle measurement techniques are used, it becomes clear that many negative stereotypes of African Americans and members of other racial groups remain in force (McConahay, Hardee, & Batts, 1981; Pettigrew, 1989; Pfeifer & Ogloff, 1991; Fazio et al., 1995).

Consider, for example, the results of a large-scale survey conducted in 300 U.S. communities (Smith, 1990). To measure prejudice, the study employed a novel technique that circumvented people's reluctance to appear prejudiced. In the survey, participants were asked to indicate whether people in each of several racial groups were closer to one or the other end of a series of seven-point scales. For instance, survey respondents were asked whether members of a racial group were closer to scale end points marked "hardworking" (at one end of the scale) or "lazy" (at the opposite end of the scale). By comparing the ratings given to the various racial groups, the researchers were able to determine which racial groups were the targets of the greatest stereotyping.

The results were disheartening. As shown in Figure 3–5, compared with their beliefs about whites, survey respondents held considerably more negative stereotypes about members of each of the three racial groups studied (African Americans, Asians, and Hispanics). For instance, 77 percent of respondents thought that African Americans were more likely than whites to "prefer to live off welfare." Overall, African Americans, Asians, and Hispanics were

modern racism: A subtle form of prejudice in which people appear, on the surface, not to harbor prejudice, but actually do hold racist attitudes.

According to the theory of modern racism, prejudice is subtle. Although we may denounce discrimination, our evaluations of people of different backgrounds can still reflect prejudice and discrimination.

seen as lazier, more prone to violence, less intelligent, and less patriotic than whites. In sum, when their underlying beliefs were tapped through somewhat indirect questions, people expressed negative stereotypes about members of minority groups—an example of modern racism.

Other studies of stereotyping support these findings. When an ethnically diverse group of college students in one study were asked to list the first 10 adjectives that came to mind when they thought of members of various racial and ethnic groups, the lists reflected traditional stereotypes. For instance, African American males were seen as "antagonistic" and "athletic," whereas Mexican American males were seen as "lower class." In contrast, Anglo-American and Asian American males were viewed more positively, although no group was viewed as possessing uniformly positive traits (Niemann et al., 1994).

Even relatively positive stereotypes about members of particular groups may have negative consequences. As we discuss in the Applying Social Psychology box, views of minorities that on the surface are benign actually can be just as damaging as more blatantly hostile prejudice.

Is racism inevitable? A less pessimistic view.   Although both modern racism and ambivalent stereotyping approaches to prejudice suggest that racism is nearly inevitable, some social psychologists think this view may be overly pessimistic. For instance, social psychologist Patricia Devine suggests that the fact that people sometimes experience prejudiced thoughts should not automatically lead us to assume they are racists. Instead, she suggests that even

FIGURE 3–5   Prejudice: Alive and Well in the United States   Compared with their beliefs about whites, survey respondents viewed minorities more negatively on each of the characteristics illustrated in the figure. The higher the percentage, the more respondents who felt the characterization (such as "poor," "lazy," and so forth) was more appropriate for minority group members than for whites (*Source:* Smith, 1990.)

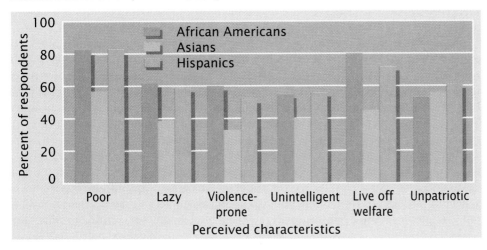

APPLYING SOCIAL PSYCHOLOGY
WHEN BEING NICE IS NOT SO NICE

According to football player Reggie White, "blacks are gifted at worship and celebration" and Native Americans are "spiritual," and Hispanics are "gifted in family structure" because they "put 20 or 30 people in one home." On the other hand, whites are especially proficient at "structure and organization," permitting them to "do a good job at building businesses," and Asians are "inventive" and "can turn a television into a watch." (Reggie White's address, 1998)

In the view of social psychologists Peter Glick and Susan Fiske, White's views—offered during an address to the Wisconsin State Assembly—represent a form of stereotyping that is no less harmful than more blatant, completely hostile forms. In their view, White is guilty of **ambivalent stereotyping**—stereotyping combining both hostile and favorable beliefs about outgroup members. Ambivalent stereotyping results in outgroups being seen as either competent *or* as likeable, but not both. As a result, ambivalent stereotyping is reflected in two kinds of prejudice: paternalistic prejudice or envious prejudice (Fiske et al., 1998; Glick & Fiske, 1999).

Paternalistic prejudice is directed at socioeconomically unsuccessful outgroups seen as likeable, but not competent. According to Glick and Fiske's research, targets of paternalistic prejudice include such groups as African Americans, Latinos, disabled individuals, retarded people, welfare recipients, and housewives. In contrast, *envious prejudice* is directed toward groups that are competent, but not likeable. Examples of groups that research shows falls into this category are Asians, Jews, rich people, and feminists—groups that are viewed as successful economically, academically, or on some other important dimension.

Because both paternalistic and envious prejudice contain some positive components, they may seem relatively harmless at first. However, both forms of ambivalent prejudice can have negative consequences for the targets. For instance, an employer harboring paternalistic prejudice may offer to give a disabled person an easy job so he won't have to work so hard. Although the employer may feel that she is merely being thoughtful, in fact she may be making the disabled person feel that he is not taken seriously and may undermine his view of his competence.

Envious prejudice may lead members of targeted groups to be distrusted in business dealings or to be seen as conspiring to wrest control from majority groups. Although their success is admired, they are viewed as potentially powerful and even dangerous, and they are both envied and feared.

Why does ambivalent stereotyping occur? One reason is that it allows prejudiced individuals to maintain an image of themselves as unprejudiced. Because they are not showing pure hostility to the group in question, people who use ambivalent stereotyping can maintain a positive self-image, seeing themselves as egalitarian and unprejudiced.

The reality is that ambivalent stereotyping can be just as harmful as direct, hostile stereotyping. In fact, paternalistic and envious prejudice may be even more harmful than hostile prejudice, in part because ambivalent stereotyping is, on the surface, often apparently benign. Clearly, we need to be vigilant for all the varieties of stereotyping and prejudice, whether blatant or more subtle.

---

those who completely reject prejudice may sometimes experience unintentional prejudice-like thoughts or feelings due to prior learning (Devine, 1989; Devine et al., 1991).

In this view, then, racism is akin to a lingering bad habit that surfaces despite people's best efforts to avoid it. This view is based on a critical distinction between *automatic information processing* and *controlled information processing* (Shiffrin & Schneider, 1977; Shiffrin & Dumais, 1981; Wegner & Bargh, 1998). Automatic information processing is largely involuntary; it involves the unintentional activation of well-learned responses found in memory. Such processing occurs in spite of voluntary efforts to suppress or circumvent it. In contrast, controlled information processing involves voluntary, intentional processes and relates to decision making and problem solving (Banaji & Hardin, 1996; Blair & Banaji, 1996).

ambivalent stereotyping:
Stereotyping combining both hostile and favorable beliefs about outgroup members.

Automatic and controlled processing can operate independently of each other (e.g., Logan & Cowan, 1984; Bargh, 1989b; Wegner & Bargh, 1998). Consequently, in the presence of a member of a minority group, a person may automatically activate racist stereotypes about minority groups, learned through society's stereotypical vision of minorities. Furthermore, because racial stereotypes are so pervasive, they can be activated automatically in both high- and low-prejudiced people. For example, automatic processing may activate thoughts in a person that minorities are often involved in criminal activities—a frequent societal stereotype—regardless of whether the person is prejudiced (Logan & Cowan, 1984; Bargh, 1989b; Lepore & Brown, 1999).

At the same time, though, more controlled processes will likely produce different behavioral consequences for high- and low-prejudiced individuals (see Figure 3–6). High-prejudiced people are likely to hold strong beliefs that are consistent with the cultural stereotypes, leading them to show biased behavior even when controlled processing subsequently kicks in. For instance, because they hold beliefs consistent with the societal stereotype that minorities are often involved in crime, they are likely to show biased behavior, such as becoming defensive or appearing threatened, even under the influence of controlled processing.

In contrast, low-prejudiced individuals are likely to hold beliefs that reject the stereotype. When controlled processing occurs for low-prejudiced individuals, then, a conflict will occur between automatic and controlled processing, with controlled processing emerging the winner.

How is this conflict manifested in behavior? When unprejudiced people are permitted the luxury of time and can give attention to their thoughts, they are apt to use more controlled cognitive processes. Ultimately, the use of controlled processing allows those who are relatively unprejudiced to react with little or no racism to situations involving minority group members. In contrast, in situations in which controlled, thoughtful processing is obstructed or impeded (such as when people are preoccupied with some involving task or activity), or where people are just not terribly attentive, the underlying automatic processing may produce prejudiced behavior. Furthermore, such prejudice may emerge even in relatively unprejudiced individuals (Devine, 1989; Macrae, Hewstone, & Griffiths, 1993).

FIGURE 3–6   Prejudice and Automatic and Controlled Processing According to Patricia Devine, both high- and low-prejudiced people engage in automatic information processing that makes them susceptible to societal stereotypes. However, when a low-prejudiced person engages in controlled processing, unbiased behavior is the consequence. (*Source:* Based on Devine, 1989; Devine et al., 1991.)

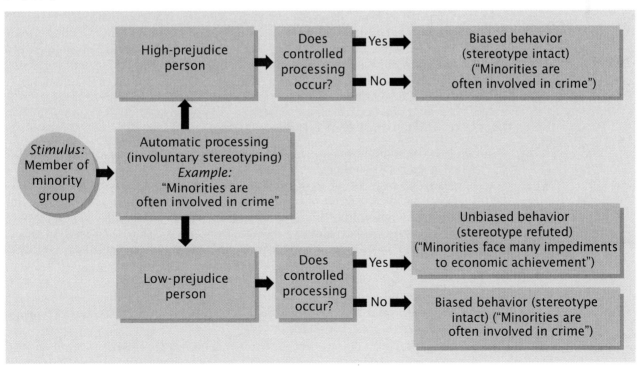

The type of clothing used to dress boys and girls differs significantly, starting from the moment of birth and continuing throughout childhood.

This view of prejudice does not regard racism as inevitable in our society. Instead, it suggests that when people are more attentive and thoughtful, they can overcome any underlying negative stereotypes they may have learned. This view also raises the possibility that even underlying, automatic processes are subject to change over time. If society as a whole is able to transmit a more positive message about race, the production of negative stereotypes may not be an automatic cognitive reaction.

This view of prejudice has other implications. For instance, it implies that even when low-prejudiced people consciously try to behave in a nonprejudiced manner and convey their nonprejudiced attitudes in intergroup situations, the result is not always positive. Specifically, low-prejudiced people may experience doubt and uncertainty in intergroup situations as they "try to do the right thing." In fact, the high motivation of low-prejudiced individuals to respond without prejudice may actually interfere with their attempts to convey their lack of prejudice. They may become anxious and awkward, leading to nonverbal behaviors that signify anxiety. Unfortunately, this behavior may be interpreted by others as a manifestation not of anxiety but of prejudice or dislike. Ironically, then, the efforts of low-prejudiced individuals to behave in a nonprejudiced manner may actually sabotage their intentions (Devine, 1996).

SEXISM: PREJUDICE AND GENDER

You hear that someone has had a baby. What's the first question you're likely to ask? For almost everyone, it's "Boy or girl?"

In fact, "It's a boy" or "It's a girl" are almost always the initial words spoken in the delivery room upon the emergence of an infant into the world. And as soon as the gender of the child becomes known, other things quickly unfold: Girls are wrapped in pink, boys in blue; girls and boys are dressed in different styles of clothing; and different toys are given to boys and girls. From the moment of birth, boys and girls are treated quite differently (Malatesta & Lamb, 1987; Fogel, Toda, & Kawai, 1988; Grieshaber, 1998).

Gender roles and stereotypes.   The difference in the way boys and girls are treated is a result of **gender roles**, the set of expectations, defined by society, that indicate what is appropriate behavior for males and females.

If the gender roles for men and women were similar, they would have only a minimal impact on males' and females' lives. However, the contrary is true: The expectations for males

gender roles: The set of expectations, defined by society, that indicate what is appropriate behavior for males and females.

and females are so different that they often lead to bias and stereotyping. Such stereotypes produce sexism, negative attitudes and behavior toward people based on their sex (Bem, 1984, 1993; Raag & Rackliff, 1998; Swann, Langlois, & Gilbert, 1999).

In our society, stereotypes about males and females fall into consistent, well-established patterns. For instance, a classic study in the 1970s identified several traditional stereotypes for males and females. In the study, a group of male and female college students were given a list of traits and were asked to indicate which were more appropriate for the typical male and the typical female (Broverman et al., 1972). Results showed that the traits fell into two clusters, one relating to competence and one relating to warmth and expressiveness. The students judged traits relating to warmth and expressivity as most appropriate for females and competency traits as most appropriate for males. Because Western societies traditionally hold competence in higher esteem than warmth and expressivity, such differences in perception favor males over females.

Subsequent research has shown the resiliency of gender role stereotyping. Although we might expect that the growth of the women's movement and feminism would blunt the edge of stereotyping, this has not happened. Differences in what is expected of men and women remain (Swim, 1993; Sims, 1994; Durkin & Nugent, 1998; Kulik, 1998; Eccles, Barber, & Jozefowicz, 1999).

For instance, despite the fact that the degree of negative stereotyping of women has declined slightly, the decline has not produced overall feelings of equality. For example, although men and women now tend to be characterized as having equally positive traits, this does not translate into the view that men and women are equals. In numerous studies, men continue to be held in higher esteem than women (Eagly & Mladinic, 1989; Williams & Best, 1990). For instance, one 25-nation study found that certain adjectives used to describe men and women were similar across cultures: Women were seen as sentimental, submissive, and superstitious, whereas men were viewed as adventurous, forceful, and independent (see Table 3–3).

However, there also were differences based on the dominant religion of the country. In predominantly Catholic countries, women were seen more favorably, whereas in Muslim countries women were perceived in a more negative light. In every country studied, gender stereotypes emerged early, in most cases before the age of 5, and tended to be fully developed by the time children began adolescence (Williams & Best, 1990).

Gender stereotyping is also mirrored in people's perceptions of which occupations are most appropriate for people of each sex. For example, even though women are present in increasing numbers throughout the workforce, they still are perceived as best suited for jobs traditionally filled by women: secretary, teacher, cashier, and librarian. Men, in contrast, are viewed as better suited for such professions as physician, police officer, and construction worker (Bridges, 1988; McLean & Kalin, 1994; St. Pierre et al., 1994; Truss, Goffee, & Jones, 1995). According to social psychologists Alice Eagly and Valerie Steffen (1984), women are seen as most appropriately filling professions that are **communal**, that is, professions associated with relationships. In contrast, men are perceived as best suited for **agentic** professions, which are associated with getting things accomplished. Traditionally, professions relating to communal concerns are of lower prestige and are lower paying than are agentically oriented professions (Eagly & Steffen, 1984, 1986a).

Society's messages are heard by men and women. For instance, when first-year college students are asked to indicate their likely career choices, women are unlikely to say they will enter traditionally male-dominated careers, such as engineering or computer programming. Furthermore, when asked to guess their entering and peak salaries, women expect to be paid less than men (Glick, Zion, & Nelson, 1988; Martin, 1989; CIRE, 1990). Such expectations are not unwarranted: Although the gap between men's and women's salaries is declining, on average, women still earn only 74 cents for every dollar that men earn (see Figure 3–7). Furthermore, women who are minority group members fare even worse: African American women earn 62 cents for every dollar men make, and for Hispanic women, the figure is just 54 cents (U.S. Department of Labor, 1999).

Sources of gender stereotypes.   Those blue and pink baby blankets that male and female babies are wrapped in at birth are only the beginning of a lifetime of different treatment

communal: Professions associated with relationships.

agentic: Professions associated with getting things accomplished.

TABLE 3-3	Descriptive Adjectives for Men and Women in At Least 20 of 25 Countries

The following items represent adjectives that were found to apply most to men or to women, respectively, in at least 20 of the 25 countries examined in the Williams and Best (1990) study:

ITEMS ASSOCIATED WITH MALES		ITEMS ASSOCIATED WITH FEMALES	
Active	Initiative	Affected	Gentle
Adventurous	Inventive	Affectionate	Mild
Aggressive	Lazy	Attractive	Sensitive
Ambitious	Logical	Charming	Sentimental
Arrogant	Loud	Curious	Sexy
Assertive	Masculine	Dependent	Softhearted
Autocratic	Opportunistic	Dreamy	Submissive
Clear-thinking	Progressive	Emotional	Superstitious
Coarse	Rational	Fearful	Talkative
Courageous	Realistic	Feminine	Weak
Cruel	Reckless		
Daring	Robust		
Determined	Rude		
Disorderly	Self-confident		
Dominant	Serious		
Egotistical	Severe		
Energetic	Stern		
Enterprising	Stolid		
Forceful	Strong		
Hardheaded	Unemotional		
Hard-hearted	Wise		
Independent			

Source: Adapted from Table 3.5, page 77, in Williams and Best, 1990.

because of sex (Pomerleau et al., 1990; Grieshaber, 1998). For instance, middle-class mothers speak more to their female children than to their male children, and fathers play more roughly with their infant sons than with their daughters. Even though the extent of behavioral differences in parental treatment of sons and daughters may not be great, there is little doubt that adults, and especially fathers, treat male and female babies and children differently (Houston, 1983; Eccles, Jacobs, & Harold, 1990; Lytton & Romney, 1991).

Such differences in treatment are also translated into differential gender schemas. According to social psychologist Sandra Bem (1987), a **gender schema** is the cognitive framework that organizes information relevant to gender. Gender schemas are particularly powerful, as sex represents one of the most salient and potent social categories that people employ (Stangor et al., 1992).

Bem suggests that gender schemas are learned early in life, and like the other schemas that we discussed in Chapter 2, provide a lens through which people view the world. She also suggests that there are individual differences in how widely gender schemas are applied. For some people, gender schemas are relatively less developed, and these individuals are more apt to apply non-gender-related schemas to social settings. Others, though, use gender schemas far more readily (Bem, 1982, 1983, 1993). One experiment, conducted by Deborrah Frable and Sandra Bem (1985), clearly illustrates differences in people's use of gender schemas. In the study, participants were first categorized into two groups: those with strong, well-developed gender schemas and those with relatively weak, circumscribed gender schemas.

gender schema: The cognitive framework that organizes information relevant to gender.

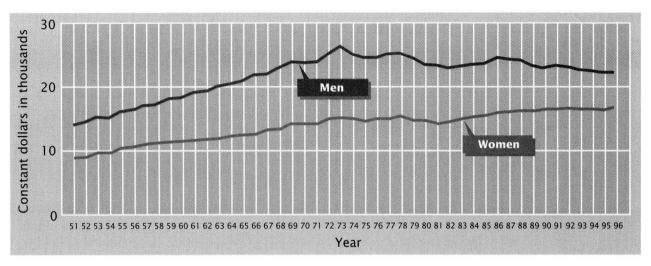

FIGURE 3–7   Women's Wages: Still Lower than Men's The annual pay gap between men and women has persisted for the past 45 years, and although closing slightly over the past 20 years, still remains large. In 1996, the most recent year for which data on annual earnings are available, the earnings gap was 26.2 percent. (*Source:* U.S. Department of Labor, 1999.)

Next, all participants listened to a group discussion. When later asked to recall who said what in the discussion, the participants with the strongest gender schemas were apt to confuse people of the same sex with one another (see Figure 3–8). In contrast, participants with less pronounced gender schemas demonstrated no propensity to mix up people of the same sex. Apparently, people with extremely strong gender schemas were categorizing group discussion members on the basis of sex and to the exclusion of other factors that would have permitted them to see the group discussion members as individuals.

How do we discourage people from evaluating others according to gender schemas? According to Sandra Bem, one way is to encourage children to be **androgynous**, a state in which gender roles encompass characteristics thought typical of both sexes (Bem, 1998). For instance, androgynous males may sometimes be assertive and pushy (typically thought of as male-appropriate traits), but they may also behave with warmth and tenderness (typically seen as female-appropriate traits).

androgynous: A state in which gender roles encompass characteristics thought typical of both sexes.

FIGURE 3–8   Does the Other Sex All Look Alike? It Depends on Who's Looking When participants with strong gender schemas were asked to recall who said what in a discussion they had viewed, they were more likely to confuse members of the other sex than those of the same sex—suggesting that members of the other sex "all looked alike" to them. In contrast, those with weak gender schemas were no more likely to confuse members of the same sex than those of the other sex. (*Source:* Based on Frable & Bem, 1985.)

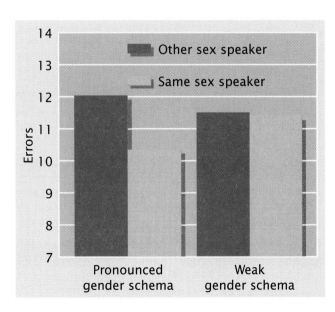

Similarly, androgynous females may behave with empathy and tenderness but also may be competitive, aggressive, and independent. The key point is that androgynous people do not react to individual situations on the basis of traditional expectations about what constitutes masculine or feminine behavior. Instead, they draw on both sets of characteristics, behaving in ways that are appropriate for given situations (Bem, 1993).

The idea of the androgynous man and woman does not mean that men and women should be expected to behave in exactly the same way, or that the differences between men and women, of which there are many, should be altogether minimized or ignored. Similarly, it does not imply that the use of gender schemas necessarily leads to sexism. What the concept does suggest is that rather than acting in ways that society deems appropriate for men and women, people should behave in a human way, based on freely made choices.

EXPLORING DIVERSITY

REDUCING PREJUDICE AND DISCRIMINATION

Are prejudice and discrimination destined to color our interactions with others, or are there ways we can reduce them? Social psychologists have devised several means of reducing prejudice and discrimination against minority groups in society. As we come to the end of the chapter, we consider several of the major approaches.

Contact.   No strategy for reducing prejudice has received greater attention than creating opportunities for contact between members of majority and minority groups. The idea is that contact between prejudiced persons and the targets of their prejudice will lead to more favorable attitudes (Allport, 1954; Miller & Brewer, 1984; Stephan, 1985). For instance, one rationale for school desegregation is that majority–minority contact in schools will reduce prejudice.

It turns out, though, that not just any contact will do. For instance, school desegregation has not always reduced prejudice. In fact, when emotions run high, such as has been the case in some instances of court-ordered desegregation, prejudice can actually increase (Stephan, 1986; Gerard, 1988).

Does this mean we should give up on our attempts to produce more integrated schools and to increase the incidence of contact between people of different races? Not at all. According to the **contact hypothesis**, direct contact between hostile groups will reduce prejudice only under certain conditions (Brewer, 1996; Dovidio, Gaertner, & Validzic, 1998). Decades of research have identified what such "certain conditions" include. Among the most significant are the following:

◆ Contact must occur between people who have relatively equal status, at least in the situation in which they find themselves. No matter how frequently a white employer interacts with her African American employee, the status differential built into the employer–employee relationship will not be helpful in reducing either party's prejudice.

◆ Contact must be close and personal to be successful. Sitting next to someone of a different race on a daily bus ride will not ensure a reduction in prejudice unless an act with some degree of psychological intimacy, such as holding a conversation and sharing personal information, occurs.

◆ People need to cooperate with one another, seeking to achieve similar goals. For example, a prejudiced white women who hires a Latino maid is unlikely to surrender her prejudices on the basis of such contact. In contrast, a prejudiced white women who works with a Latino woman on a committee to improve children's schools is considerably more likely to experience a reduction in prejudice.

contact hypothesis: The hypothesis is that direct contact between hostile groups that will reduce prejudice only under certain conditions.

Why can contact be effective? The answer is in the changes that can be effected in schemas regarding stereotyped groups. As the degree of contact increases, schemas become more detailed, accurate, and individualized (Desforges et al., 1991; Pettigrew, 1997; Dovidio, Gaertner, & Validzic, 1998; Gaertner et al., 1999).

The jigsaw technique.   The jigsaw technique is a classroom procedure for increasing inter-group interaction. Using a process based on the way one constructs a jigsaw puzzle by taking small pieces and placing them together, students who participate in the **jigsaw technique** are each given a small amount of information, which they are then required to teach to a set of partners in a group. When the information from all the students is put together, it forms a meaningful whole, enabling the group to understand the entire lesson. Several studies have shown that the jigsaw technique not only results in effective learning, but it also promotes self-esteem, interpersonal interaction, and empathy for members of different ethnic and racial groups (Aronson et al., 1978; Aronson, 1988; Singh, 1991; Walker & Crogan, 1998).

Making humanitarian values more conspicuous.   Rather than hoping contact will bring about changes in stereotypes and schemas indirectly, there is a more direct approach—illustrating how the values of equality and fair treatment conflict with negative stereotyping. For example, in some experimental studies, people are forced to confront the fact that the positive values they hold about equality and freedom are inconsistent with their negative perceptions of minority group members (e.g., Rokeach, 1971). When such inconsistencies are pointed out to people, by showing them their incompatible responses on questionnaires, their prejudice is often reduced.

Similarly, when people overhear others strongly condemning racism, they are considerably more apt to make strong statements themselves against prejudice. Apparently, situations in which public standards, or norms, against racism are more prominent—such as public condemnations of discriminatory behavior—can reduce its occurrence. Making the voice of equality heard, then, is an important means of combating prejudice, stereotyping, and discrimination (Blanchard, Lilly, & Vaughn, 1991; Fiske & Von Hendy, 1992). (Also see the Speaking of Social Psychology interview).

jigsaw technique: A classroom procedure for increasing intergroup interaction based on the way one constructs a jigsaw puzzle.

REVIEW AND RETHINK

Review

- Racism is prejudice directed at people because of their race. Although overt indications of racism have declined, modern racism may be no less strong, although more subtle.

- Sexism—prejudice directed at people because of their gender—arises from strong endorsement of gender roles.

- Sexism may be hostile or benevolent, but both forms result in discriminatory treatment and harm their targets.

- Among the means of reducing prejudice and discrimination are increasing contact between majority and minority group members, using the jigsaw technique, and making humanitarian values more salient.

Rethink

- Does the existence of modern racism suggest that there has been little progress in the reduction of prejudice toward minority group members?

- Why might the projected increase in the proportion of minority group members among the U.S. population have implications for the amount of prejudice in U.S. society?

- Are the ways of reducing prejudice that have been discussed equally applicable to combating racism *and* sexism, or is there something unique about one or the other type of prejudice? Why?

SPEAKING OF SOCIAL PSYCHOLOGY

Deborah Terry-Hays

Antiprejudice Workshop Coordinator

Year of Birth: 1952

Education: B.A., Educational Psychology, Western Washington University, Bellingham, Washington

Home: Seattle, Washington

"We conduct workshops that are built around a series of experiential exercises."

Prejudice and discrimination have long been obstacles to the advancement of many minority groups in the United States. Although progress in correcting these problems has been slow, people such as Deborah Terry-Hays are working energetically to end the mistreatment of groups that fall victim to prejudice and discrimination.

Terry-Hays is director of the Seattle chapter of the National Coalition Building Institute. In her position, she conducts workshops designed to sensitize participants to the prevalence and experience of prejudice and discrimination.

"We conduct workshops that are built around a series of experiential exercises. They are meant to help people better understand stereotypes and oppression," said Terry-Hays.

LOOKING BACK

What differentiates prejudice, discrimination, and stereotyping?

1. Prejudice refers to negative or positive evaluations or judgments of members of a group that are based primarily on membership in the group. A stereotype is a set of beliefs and expectations about members of a group that are held solely because of their membership in the group. Discrimination is the behavioral manifestation of stereotypes and prejudice. (p. 80)
2. Prejudice is often targeted at minority groups, which are groups whose members have significantly less power, control, and influence over their own lives than do members of a dominant majority. (p. 81)

How is prejudice learned and maintained?

3. Social learning explanations of prejudice suggest that people develop prejudice and stereotypes about members of various groups through direct reinforcement and teaching. (p. 82)
4. Motivational approaches to prejudice suggest that conflicts within the individual stemming from characteristics associated with the authoritarian personality produce

The day-long workshops serve between 25 and 40 individuals and are offered to groups such as schools, civic organizations, police, churches, and communities at large.

"We look at all the different kinds of diversity relating to those attending a workshop," she added. "People generally think of prejudice and discrimination in terms of race and gender, but not beyond to areas such as age, family order, and even where you were born— all of which represent potential areas of discrimination.

Started 12 years ago in Boston, the National Coalition Building Institute is dedicated to ending mistreatment of all groups, whether it stems from nationality, race, class, gender, religion, sexual orientation, age, physical ability, job or life circumstance, according to Terry-Hays.

"Furthermore, we hold the philosophy that every issue counts."

"In our workshops, we start by looking at stereotypes. We ask people to pick a group to which they do not belong and to then note what their first thoughts are about that group," she explained. "We also ask them about groups to which they belong, and ask what they are and are not proud of as members of that group. All those areas in which they feel less proud are places where prejudices can slip out."

One group that receives particular attention in workshops is gays and lesbians. "The area of gays and lesbians is a place where people tend to feel okay about their prejudices, because expressions of hate for this group are backed up by some major institutions such as religious groups.

"Furthermore, we hold the philosophy that every issue counts. We even look at white men as an object of prejudice, considering changes in their culture," she added.

"In the workshops we pick particular groups to focus on and ask people to share personal experiences," Terry-Hays said. "You cannot only change participants' minds, but you have to change their hearts as well."

prejudicial attitudes toward groups perceived to be relatively powerless and in the minority. (p. 84)

5. Realistic conflict theory suggests that prejudice is the outcome of direct competition between members of different groups over valued, but limited, resources. Competition alone, though, does not always produce prejudice; the presence of relative deprivation, the sense that one lacks a desired resource in comparison to another group, may be crucial. (p. 84)

6. Social identity theory holds that people use group membership as a source of pride and self-worth, which leads them to inflate the positive aspects of their group and belittle groups to which they do not belong. (p. 87)

How do stereotypes provide the cognitive foundations for prejudice and discrimination?

7. Cognitive approaches to prejudice suggest that social categorization processes lead to stereotypes. One primary categorization is in terms of ingroups (groups to which people feel they belong) and outgroups (groups to which people feel they do not belong). (p. 89)

8. Among the biases that lead to stereotyping is the ingroup–outgroup bias, the tendency to hold less favorable views about groups to which we do not belong, while holding more favorable opinions about groups to which we do belong. (p. 89)

9. Similarly, the outgroup homogeneity bias is the perception that there is less variability among the members of outgroups than there is within one's own ingroup. (p. 91)

10. Illusory correlation occurs when a perceiver overestimates the strength of a relationship between two variables. (p. 92)

11. The ultimate attribution error suggests that when people holding strong stereotypes view negative behavior on the part of a minority group member, they attribute it to dispositional characteristics; but when they see a minority group member engaging in positive behavior, they attribute the behavior to situational factors. (p. 93)

How prevalent is racism, and is it inevitable?

12. Racism is prejudice directed at people because of their race. Although on the surface, overt manifestations of racism have declined, modern racism, in which people hold underlying racist attitudes, still exists. (p. 96)

13. Even relatively unprejudiced people may experience unintentional negative thoughts and feelings due to prior learning. These negative reactions reflect the distinction between automatic versus controlled information processing. (p. 100)

Why does sexism occur, and what are the roots of gender stereotyping?

14. Sexism is prejudice directed at females or males on the basis of their gender. Sexism arises out of strong societal gender roles, the set of expectations that indicate what behavior is appropriate for males and females. (p. 102)

15. As a consequence of gender stereotyping, women are seen as most appropriately filling communal professions (which emphasize relationships), whereas men are perceived as best at agentic professions (in which the emphasis is on getting things done). One source of stereotyping lies in gender schemas, the cognitive framework that organizes information relevant to gender. (p. 103)

What are some ways social psychologists have devised to reduce prejudice and discrimination?

16. Among the ways to reduce prejudice and discrimination are creating opportunities for contact between members of majority and minority groups, using the jigsaw technique, and making humanitarian values more conspicuous. (p. 106)

EPILOGUE

In this chapter, we've considered how people are perceived on the basis of their membership in particular groups. Powerful social psychological forces often lead people to make judgments based primarily on group membership, and prejudice, stereotyping, and discrimination remain among the most stubborn and enduring social issues of our time.

Yet, the problems are not insurmountable. As we discussed in both this chapter and Chapter 2, in which we considered how people develop an understanding of other individuals, our social cognitive capabilities provide at least the potential for accurate and discerning judgments of others. Certainly, the theory and research discussed in these two chapters paves the way for a more precise understanding of what others are like and the causes of their behavior. Even more important, the material contributes to efforts to diminish the corrosive consequences of prejudice, stereotyping, and discrimination.

Before proceeding to the next chapter, return to the prologue of this one, about the horrific death of James Byrd Jr., who was chained to a pickup truck and dragged to his death. Consider the following questions:

1. How might realistic conflict theory explain the attack made on Byrd?

2. Assume that you overheard Byrd's assailants discussing minorities in a positive way several days before the attack. How could such comments be consistent with their later behavior?

3. According to the outgroup homogeneity bias, to what degree do you think Byrd's assailants differentiated him from other African Americans?

4. If you were asked to devise ways to reduce prejudice and discrimination of the sort displayed by Byrd's attackers, what approaches might you try?

KEY TERMS AND CONCEPTS

agentic (p. 103)

ambivalent stereotyping (p. 100)

androgynous (p. 105)

communal (p. 103)

contact hypothesis (p. 106)

discrimination (p. 81)

gender roles (p. 102)

gender schema (p. 104)

illusory correlation (p. 92)

ingroup (p. 89)

ingroup–outgroup bias (p. 90)

jigsaw technique (p. 107)

minority group (p. 81)

modern racism (p. 98)

outgroup (p. 89)

outgroup homogeneity bias (p. 91)

prejudice (p. 80)

racism (p. 96)

realistic conflict theory (p. 84)

relative deprivation (p. 86)

sexism (p. 96)

social categorization (p. 89)

social identity theory (p. 87)

stereotype (p. 81)

ultimate attribution error (p. 93)

CHAPTER 4

THE SELF

Perceiving and Understanding Oneself

PROLOGUE

The Many Bill Clintons

As a skillful politician, Bill Clinton knew how to keep his inner self private.

When Bill Clinton looks in the mirror, who does he see?

Is it the man who became President of the United States, commander-in-chief, leader of the free world?

Does he see a loving father and husband, a man who gives speeches on the importance of the family and of loving relationships?

Does he view himself as a lawyer and defender of the Constitution, an idealist who seeks to make the world a better place?

Or, on the other hand, does he see a man who had a sexual relationship with a woman his daughter's age that nearly led to the undoing of his presidency? A person whose lack of judgment brought him to an impeachment trial in the Senate? An individual who was not truthful giving sworn testimony before a court?

What does Clinton see in the mirror? The answer may well be "none of the above." As a skillful politician who is a master of self-presentation, Clinton keeps private his inner self. ■

LOOKING AHEAD

Although Bill Clinton's multiple—and sometimes contradictory—identities may be extreme, he spotlights a fundamental question that all of us ask: Who am I?

In the last decade, social psychologists have come to see the study of the self as central to their field. It has become increasingly clear that the way people view their own inner selves has important implications for how they interact with others—a fact that makes the self an important social topic.

We begin this chapter with a discussion of the structure of the self and how people perceive the components of the self. We also examine how people use others to understand their own abilities, emotions, and attitudes.

We then turn to the ways in which people evaluate themselves, considering issues related to the emotional response associated with the self. We also look at the systematic biases that affect the way we view the self.

Finally, the chapter considers how people present themselves to others. We discuss how people monitor their behavior to manage the impressions they give. We consider both verbal and nonverbal strategies for self-presentation, and we end by discussing effective strategies for impression management.

In sum, after reading this chapter, you'll be able to answer these questions:

◆ What are the components of the self?

◆ How do people use others' (and their own) behavior to assess their abilities, emotions, and attitudes?

◆ How do self-esteem and self-awareness affect people's interactions with others?

◆ What biases exist in the ways people view themselves?

◆ What self-presentation strategies do people employ, and which are most effective?

DEFINING THE SELF

If you've ever had dogs or cats as pets, perhaps you've seen them the first time they catch a glimpse of themselves in a mirror. Although they may appear to be interested or startled by the image they behold, their reaction is not due to their understanding that they are encountering an image of themselves. Far from it: Except for certain apes and possibly some species of dolphin, animals other than humans do not recognize likenesses of themselves, and they do not appear to have a sense of themselves as individuals (Tanner & Byrne, 1993; Gallup, 1977, 1995; Marten & Psarakos, 1995; Parker, 1996).

People, however, begin to develop a sense of themselves at an early age. Even infants as young as 12 months appear to recognize themselves: They are startled when they see in a mirror that a spot of red rouge has been dabbed on their noses, as researchers have done in studies of self-awareness (Lewis & Brooks-Gunn, 1979; Liu, Zhang, & Tang, 1993; Asendorpf, Warkentin, & Baudonniere, 1996).

The knowledge that we exist as individuals, separate from everyone else, emerges by the age of 18 months. Before then, according to child development experts, children feel totally merged with their caregivers, unable to distinguish themselves from these caregivers and other people (Mahler, Pine, & Bergman, 1975). As they get older, though, children soon develop a sense of themselves as separate individuals, ultimately forming a self-concept.

FORMING A SELF-CONCEPT: WHO AM I?

Our **self-concept** comprises our sense of identity, the set of beliefs we hold about what we are like as individuals (Baumeister, 1998). When we think of ourselves as sociable, energetic, outgoing, a little chubby, and temperamental, we're describing aspects of our self-concept. (Before continuing, consider the ingredients of your own self-concept; most people have well-defined, explicit, and fairly precise knowledge about what they are like.)

Self-schema: Organizing a self-concept.   Although a person's self-concept is made up of a variety of attributes, the "glue" that holds these impressions together is known as a self-schema. A concept derived from the work on social cognition that we discussed in Chapter 2, a **self-schema** is the organized body of information that relates to a person's self. According to social psychologist Hazel Markus, self-schemas, like other schemas, are based on prior experience, and they guide both people's understanding of what is currently happening and their expectations about what to anticipate in the future (Markus, 1977; Pace, 1988; Baumeister, 1998).

Unlike the broader notion of self-concept, which includes the entire sum of a person's impressions about himself or herself, self-schemas are more specific and relate to particular personality dimensions (see Figure 4–1). For example, some people may be particularly concerned with the domain of independence and may have an especially well-developed sense of their independence (or lack of it). They would be said to have a self-schema relating to independence. To others, the domain of independence might be of little concern; they would be seen as lacking a self-schema for independence. Similarly, some people might have a self-schema for gender, whereas others, to whom gender is less relevant, would be seen as

self-concept: An individual's sense of identity; the set of beliefs he or she is like as an individual.

self-schema: The organized body of information that relates to a person's self.

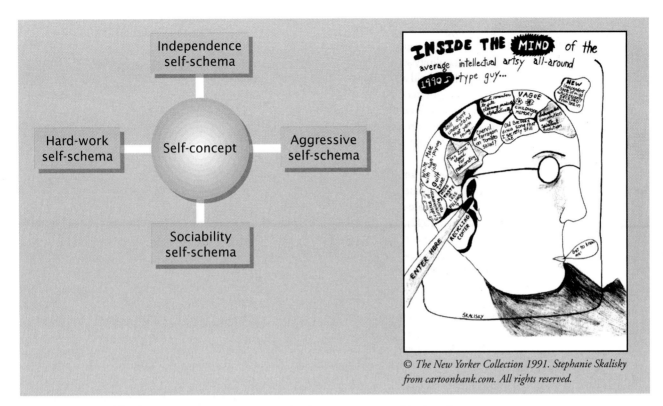

FIGURE 4–1   Self-Schemas Each person has a set of self-schemas, organized bodies of information that relate to a person's self. In this example of one individual's self-schema, the major components relate to the concepts of independence, hard work, aggression, and sociability.

lacking a self-schema for gender (Markus & Nurius, 1986; Fiske & Taylor, 1991; Cross & Markus, 1994).

Self-schemas serve several functions. They help people sift and filter information relevant to the self-schema. People also become more aware of, and quicker to respond to, information that is consistent with the schema than information that is not consistent (Markus & Sentis, 1982; Worth, Smith, & Mackie, 1992; Neubauer & Malle, 1997). Moreover, self-schemas help people remember information related to the schema. For instance, a person who holds an independence self-schema is more likely to notice behavior in other people that is indicative of independence (Hochwaelder, 1996). In addition, the person will be more likely to recall times when he or she has acted independently in the past, in comparison with someone who does not hold such a self-schema (Pietromonaco & Markus, 1985; Forsyth & Wibberly, 1993; Rudolph, 1993; Udo, 1993).

The ability to remember information more readily when it is related to self-schemas is an example of the self-reference effect. The **self-reference effect** is the phenomenon in which information is recalled better when it is related to the self. For instance, we're more apt to remember the name of an obscure food that we've had the opportunity to eat than one that we've never eaten but only read about. Similarly, we can remember best the details of places we've personally visited and can relate to our self-schemas, rather than ones that we've seen photos of in the *National Geographic* (Klein & Loftus, 1988; Klein, Loftus, & Burton, 1989; Conway & Dewhurst, 1995; Symons & Johnson, 1997).

Self-schemas also affect the way people perceive information and integrate it into meaningful units. Just as a computer programming expert can scan a multipage printout of computer codes and perceive its broad, underlying patterns, people who hold self-schemas in a given domain consider social information in broader groupings, or "chunks," of information than those who don't hold such self-schemas.

self-reference effect: The phenomenon in which information is recalled better when it is related to the self.

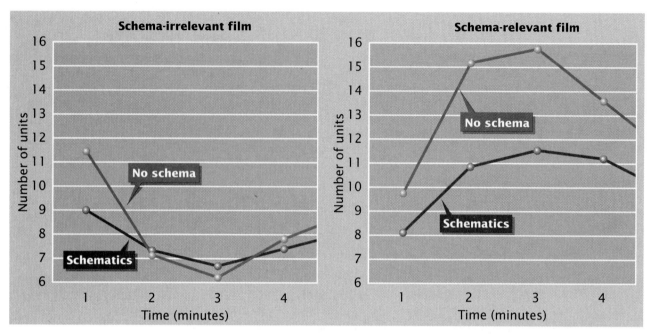

FIGURE 4–2   Self-Schemas and People's Perception of Information Relevant or Irrelevant to the Self-Schema Regardless of whether or not they held a masculinity self-concept, participants who watched a film showing men involved in activities unrelated to a masculinity self-schema perceived a similar number of units or chunks of information (as illustrated in the first graph). In contrast, when the film was relevant to the masculinity self-schema, people who held that self-schema employed larger chunks than those who did not have a masculinity self-schema (as illustrated in the second graph). In both graphs, smaller numbers indicate larger units (*Source:* Markus, Smith, & Moreland, 1985, p. 1499.)

To illustrate this phenomenon, Hazel Markus and colleagues conducted a study with men who either had or lacked a well-defined self-schema related to masculinity (Markus, Smith, & Moreland, 1985). In the experiment, the participants were shown two films. In one film, they viewed men who were involved in stereotypically masculine activities, such as weight lifting or watching a baseball game. In the other film, the activities portrayed were irrelevant to masculine stereotypes, such as playing records or eating apples. While the men were watching each film, they were asked to signal when they thought a "meaningful" grouping, or "chunk," of behavior had occurred.

The results were clear. When the film was relevant to the masculinity stereotypes, the men with masculinity self-schemas perceived the film as having larger groupings, or chunks, than those who did not hold a masculinity self-schema (see Figure 4–2). In contrast, when the film had nothing to do with masculinity-relevant information, the size of the chunks did not vary between those who did and those who did not have a masculinity self-schema. The data supported the notion that the men with masculinity self-schemas functioned like "masculinity experts" and viewed masculinity-relevant information as a specialist would—in broad, meaning-filled units.

Possible selves and identity.   In addition to helping guide our current behavior, self-schemas aid in our consideration of what we might become in the future. A portion of the self is composed of **possible selves**, those aspects of the self that relate to the future (Niedenthal, Setterlund, & Wherry, 1992; Shepard & Marshall, 1999). Possible selves reflect our aspirations, our concerns, and our views of what is likely to happen to us. For instance, a law student may hold several possible selves about her future, seeing herself as a corporate lawyer, a prosecuting attorney, or a Supreme Court justice. However, not every possible self is

possible selves: Those aspects of the self that relate to the future.

necessarily positive: Our possible selves may include a view of being extremely overweight, as developing a brain tumor, or as becoming homeless.

Obviously, such alternative possible selves represent only possibilities, but they influence our current behavior and the choices we make. They may act as incentives (such as studying hard in order to be successful in the future) or as barriers (as when we avoid overeating in order to prevent gaining weight). In fact, people make use of possible selves to consider their future throughout life, even into old age (Markus & Nurius, 1986; Ruvolo & Markus, 1992; Bakhurst & Sypnowich, 1995; Hooker & Kaus, 1995; Oyserman, Grant, & Ager, 1995; Shepard & Marshall, 1999).

In addition to considering the self in terms of self-concept and self-schemas, some social psychologists have focused on the notion of identity. **Identity** reflects the roles and group categories to which a person belongs, along with the set of personal meanings and experiences related to those roles and categories. In other words, identity is a combination of social identity (roles or group membership categories to which a person belongs) and personal identity (traits and behaviors that people find descriptive of themselves and that are linked to social identity categories) (Deaux et al., 1995; Michael, 1996; Stevens, 1996; Deaux & Ethier, 1998; Deaux et al., 1999).

According to social psychologist Kay Deaux (1993), each of us "packages" our own identity, in terms of both the categories that are important to us and the meaning that we attach to the categories. For example, when several Hispanic first-year college students were asked to list their identities and the characteristics associated with each identity, they came up with very different representations of the same identity. As you can see in Table 4–1, a comparison of two of the participants' reports reveals very different patterns of responses (Ethier & Deaux, 1990).

Furthermore, people arrange their identities in hierarchies, clustering together similar identities and attributes relating to particular identities. As we can see in Figure 4–3, one individual's identities of wife and mother, which share similar attributes, are viewed in terms of being accepting, reliable, and understanding. The related identity of friend is characterized by the attributes of happy, peaceful, and appreciative (Deaux, 1992).

The view of identity depicted in Figure 4–3 is unique, produced from the responses of a single participant. Other individuals would characterize their identities in their own, unique

Possible selves reflect our aspirations, our concerns, and our views of what is likely to happen to us.

identity: The combination of roles and group categories to which a person belongs, along with the set of personal meanings and experiences related to the roles and categories.

	CHARACTERISTICS	
Identity	**Subject 1**	**Subject 2**
Hispanic	Confused	Proud
	Proud	Loyal
	On guard	Happy
	Representative	Part of a big family
	Questioning	Lucky
	Aware	Cared for
	Token	Stand out in good and bad ways
	Excluded	Social
		Religious
Student	Conscientious	Hard
	Flexible	Big change
	Self-sacrificing	Pressure
	Curious	Freedom
	Assertive	Responsibilities
	Demanding	New environment

TABLE 4–1   Self-Identities of Two Hispanic Students

Source: Ethier & Deaux, 1990.

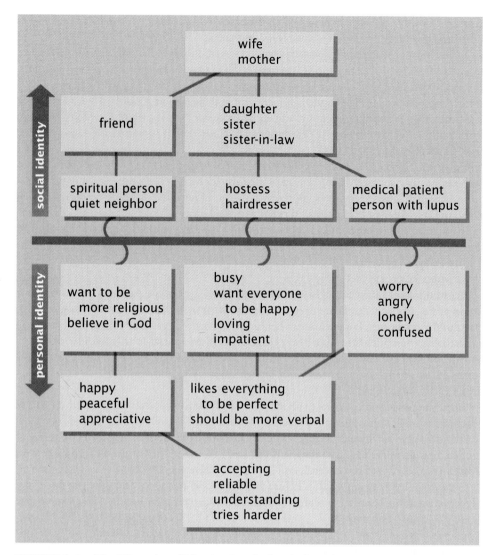

FIGURE 4–3   The Hierarchy of Identity People classify their identity into hierarchies. The levels of identity at the top relate to the social aspects of identity, whereas those in the bottom half of the figure are aspects of identity pertaining to personal characteristics. (*Source:* Deaux, 1992.)

manner. But where do such hierarchies come from? More broadly, how do we develop a sense of ourselves as singular, unique individuals?

Ironically, our view of ourselves is built largely on our experience with other people. From the beginnings of both psychology and sociology, theorists have argued that without the presence of others, we would be unable to develop a sense of who or what we are (Fiske et al., 1998; Oyserman & Markus, 1998).

For instance, William James, one of the founders of the discipline of psychology, suggested that one's personal identity could not exist without feedback and judgments from others (James, 1890). Sociologist Charles Horton Cooley (1902) referred to the "looking-glass self" as a means of explaining how we use others as mirrors to perceive ourselves. He suggested that other people provide us with the data that we use to formulate the core of our self-concepts.

More recent work has supported these speculations (McNulty & Swann, 1994; Brooks et al., 1995; Oyserman & Markus, 1998). For instance, as we see next, people use others to hone their views of their own skills and capabilities. Indeed, even when we consider the realm of emotions and feelings, people sometimes rely on others to define what they are experiencing at a given moment.

SOCIAL COMPARISON: USING OTHERS TO CLARIFY WHERE WE STAND

Ed Koch, a former mayor of New York City, became famous for the question he asked his constituents as he traveled around the city: "How'm I doing?" In fact, all of us may ask this same question to determine how we compare to others.

The need for social comparison.   According to a theory developed by social psychologist Leon Festinger (1954), people have a need to evaluate their opinions and abilities—leading to a desire for **social comparison**. In many cases, the answers come easily; objective, physical evidence provides the answer. For instance, if a student thinks her route from home to campus is shorter than the route a friend takes, she can objectively determine whether her opinion is correct by using her car odometer to measure the mileage of the two routes.

But suppose she wants to know how good a tennis player she is. Here, objective means are lacking. According to Festinger, in this case she will turn to social reality to satisfy her needs for evaluating her ability. *Social reality* refers to understanding that is derived from considering how other people act, think, feel, and view the world.

For instance, the college student who wishes to determine how well she plays tennis will compare her abilities with other tennis players. But who is the most useful comparison person? Unless the student is a top-ranked pro, she already knows she doesn't play as well as Steffi Graf or Monica Seles, but she also knows that she plays better than someone who has just taken up the game. Consequently, the most likely candidates for comparison are people who are at a level fairly similar to her own.

This example illustrates a general rule: People determine their abilities by comparing themselves to others who are similar to themselves along relevant dimensions. Consequently, when we cannot objectively evaluate our abilities, we look to others who are similar (Goethals & Darley, 1977; Suls & Wills, 1991; Albright et al., 1993; Foddy & Crundall, 1993; Gibbons, Benbow, & Gerrard, 1994).

On the other hand, we don't always use similar others as guides to our abilities. If we are motivated to make ourselves look good, we may employ *downward social comparison,* in which we compare ourselves to others who are inferior to us or worse off than we are. By comparing ourselves to those who are less fortunate, we obviously make ourselves look better in comparison (Van Vugt, Howard, & Moss, 1998; Blanton et al., 1999; Stanton et al., 1999).

In other cases, we use *upward social comparison,* in which we compare ourselves to people who are significantly better at something than we are. By exaggerating our perceptions of the ability of people who perform better than we do, we are able to deflect threats to our own view of our abilities (Wills, 1981; Alicke et al., 1998; Blanton et al., 1999).

The two-factor theory of emotions: Determining how we feel.   Perhaps it is not surprising that we use others to develop a self-schema regarding our abilities. But some social psychologists have taken this notion a step beyond the domain of abilities. If we use information from others to determine something as stable as our own abilities, they ask, might not information from others also be used to determine what we are emotionally experiencing at any given moment?

According to social psychologists Stanley Schachter and Jerome Singer, the answer is an emphatic yes (Schachter & Singer, 1962). In what has become a classic experiment, the two researchers demonstrated that the labels people assign to their emotional experiences may be due in large measure to the information that others provide and the situation in which they find themselves.

In the study, two groups of participants were told that they would be given injections of a "vitamin" called Suproxin. In reality, they were given epinephrine, a drug that induces physiological arousal, such as an increased heart rate and flushing of the face—responses

two-factor theory of emotion: The theory that states that emotions are a joint result of (1) nonspecific physiological arousal and (2) the interpretation of the arousal.

self-perception theory: The theory that suggests that people come to be aware of their own dispositions, emotions, attitudes, and other internal states in the same way they learn about other people—through observation of behavior.

that occur during natural emotional experiences. One group of participants was informed of the drug's effects, and the other was not.

Participants were then asked to complete a series of questionnaires. In both groups a confederate acted either very joyful and exhilarated—lobbing papers into a wastebasket and throwing paper airplanes—or quite angry. Participants then were asked to describe their own emotional states. Those who had been informed of the effects of the epinephrine were generally unaffected by the confederate's behavior; they attributed their physiological arousal to the drug and thus were not faced with the need to find an explanation for it.

In contrast, participants who were uninformed of the drug's effects on them were affected by the confederate's behavior: When the confederate acted euphoric, they reported feeling happy, but when he acted angry, they reported feeling angry. Basically, participants who experienced unexplained physiological arousal functioned as problem solvers. In attempting to explain their arousal, they turned to the environment and used external cues, in the form of others' behavior, to label their own emotional state.

In sum, the Schachter and Singer experiment pointed to a **two-factor theory of emotion**, in which emotions are a joint result of (1) nonspecific physiological arousal and (2) the interpretation of the arousal. Unfortunately, the validity of the theory remains far from certain. The methods and theoretical arguments of the original experiment have been criticized, and attempts to replicate the findings have not been consistently successful (e.g., Marshall & Zimbardo, 1979; Reisenzein, 1983; Chwalisz, Diener, & Gallagher, 1988). Still, one basic premise of the original study has remained supported: When people are unsure about how they feel, they may infer their emotional states by observing the behavior of others and the situations in which they find themselves.

DEFINING OURSELVES THROUGH OUR BEHAVIOR

The two-factor theory of emotions suggests that we may use a combination of internal arousal and situational cues to make inferences about our emotional states. What other sources of information might we employ to increase our understanding of our inner selves?

One likely candidate is our own behavior. According to social psychologist Daryl Bem, people sometimes make attributions regarding the causes of their own behavior in the same way they make attributions regarding the causes of others' behavior (Bem & McConnell, 1970; Bem, 1972).

Self-perception theory.   Building on the work on social cognition that we discussed in Chapter 2, Bem's **self-perception theory** suggests that people come to be aware of their own dispositions, emotions, attitudes, and other internal states in the same way they learn about other people—through observation of behavior. To the extent that situational cues or past experience are irrelevant, weak, or ambiguous, the theory suggests that people use the basic principles of impression formation to identify the causes of the behavior they observe in themselves. Moreover, they use the same principles to assess their own inner states that they employ to consider the inner states of others.

A few examples help clarify Bem's theory. If you see someone patiently helping an elderly woman cross a busy street, you can reasonably infer that the helper is altruistic or perhaps is favorably disposed toward the elderly. But suppose that person is you, and you find yourself helping the woman cross the road. When you look back to analyze your own behavior, Bem's theory suggests that you would make the same kind of attributions about your own behavior that you would make about another person's behavior: that you have an altruistic streak and hold positive attitudes toward the elderly. (We'll discuss the role of self-perception in the domain of attitudes in Chapter 10.)

Consider another example: As part of an experiment, you are looking at a group of attractive nudes, all of which are sexually appealing. When you see some of them, though, your heart rate (which is being monitored and amplified through a speaker) speeds up or slows down, while with others it stays the same. You're then asked which ones you liked best.

If you're like the real participants in this study, which was actually carried out, you'll probably choose the ones for which your heart rate changed rather than the ones for which it remained stable (Valins, 1966). What is particularly intriguing about these results is that in the experiment, the heart-rate changes that the participants heard were false: The experimenter used bogus tape recordings of accelerating, decelerating, and steady heartbeats to lead participants to believe there had been actual variations in their own heartbeats.

In sum, Bem's theory of self-perception indicates that people will apply the same principles of attribution to their own behavior that they use with others. Through this process, they are able to understand and infer their own attitudes and make attributions regarding why they have engaged in certain behavior. Furthermore, the motivation behind their choice of particular tasks and how much they ultimately enjoy them may be affected by self-perception processes, as we consider next (Sanbonmatsu et al., 1994; Anderson & Cychosz, 1995; Kwok, 1995).

Action identification theory suggests that this person could see himself as simply reading a book or cramming for an exam, depending on the level of interpretation being employed.

Overjustification: Turning play into work.   Consider this situation: Bob's son, Jonathan, is 8 years old and loves to use machinery of any kind. Each week he begs Bob for permission to use the power lawn mower. Despite some qualms about safety, Bob usually agrees, because Jonathan does an excellent job. In fact, he does such a good job that Bob is considering paying Jonathan so that he'll continue to mow the lawn enthusiastically. Should Bob pay him?

In the light of self-perception theory, the answer is clearly no. Here's why: According to a derivative of self-perception theory, rewarding Jonathan will make him lose his **intrinsic motivation**, motivation that causes people to participate in activities for their own enjoyment, not for the reward the activities bring them. Instead of being intrinsically motivated, Jonathan will be subject to **extrinsic motivation**, motivation that causes people to participate in activities for tangible rewards.

The phenomenon in which intrinsic motivation is replaced with extrinsic motivation is known as overjustification. **Overjustification** occurs when incentives are used to bring about behavior that would have been done voluntarily, without any incentive (Lepper, 1983; Deci & Ryan, 1985; Tang & Hall, 1995; Lepper, Greene, & Nisbett, 1996).

When people are rewarded for something they have done, two explanations for their behavior are possible—their own interest in the task (intrinsic motivation) and the external reward (extrinsic motivation). If the reinforcement is clear and unambiguous, then external reward provides the most reasonable cause of the behavior. But if no external reinforcement is present, the person's own interests, dispositions, or motivations provide the most reasonable explanation for the behavior.

In the example of Bob and Jonathan, giving Jonathan a financial reward for mowing the lawn provides him with clear, external reinforcement. As a result, Jonathan may begin to view his own behavior in terms of the external reward rather than in terms of his internal motivation. The result: He'll be less apt to view mowing as an enjoyable, intrinsically motivated behavior. Clearly, Bob's notion of paying Jonathan would be a strategic error.

Overjustification effects have been demonstrated in many contexts (Tang & Hall, 1995). For example, in one experiment, a group of nursery school children were promised a reward for drawing with colored markers—a pastime for which they had previously shown great enthusiasm (Lepper & Greene, 1978). However, once the reward was promised, their enthusiasm for the task dropped, and they showed considerably less zeal for drawing. Apparently, the promise of a reward undermined their intrinsic motivation for the task.

This phenomenon occurs with adults as well: People rewarded for tasks they already like not only begin to enjoy the tasks less, but the quality and creativity of their work also decline (e.g., Amabile, 1983; Amabile, Hennessey, & Grossman, 1986; Seta & Seta, 1987). Through overjustification, then, play can clearly be turned into work.

Action identification: Levels of doing.   What are you doing at this moment? The most obvious answer is "reading a book." But consider some alternative responses you might have made: "looking at a string of letters on a page" or "learning social psychology" or

intrinsic motivation: Motivation that causes people to participate in activities for their own enjoyment, not for the reward the activities bring them.

extrinsic motivation: Motivation that causes people to participate in activities for tangible rewards.

overjustification: A phenomenon that occurs when incentives are used to bring about behavior that would have been done voluntarily, without any incentive.

action identification theory: The theory that suggests that people's interpretation of their own behavior varies in terms of whether the behavior is seen at a high or low level.

"desperately trying to finish a chapter before a test" or "becoming a better human being." All may be equally valid, but they vary in terms of the level of abstraction with which they seek to respond to the question.

According to action identification theory, proposed by Robin Vallacher and Daniel Wegner (1985, 1989), the kind of answer that you give has important implications. **Action identification theory** suggests that people's interpretation of their own behavior varies in terms of whether the behavior is seen at a high or low level. High-level interpretation looks at the broad scenario, taking an abstract approach. In contrast, low-level interpretation looks at the details of behavior, breaking behavior down into its parts.

Action identification theory suggests that the level at which people typically view their current actions has implications for future behavior. For example, identification of actions at higher levels leads to greater stability in future behavior. Consequently, people who tend to view their actions at higher levels find it more difficult to modify subsequent behavior.

More specifically, high-level action identification may make it harder to change maladaptive behaviors. For instance, alcoholics who identify their drinking behavior at high levels ("drinking helps me to relax in social situations") may find it more difficult to break the drinking habit than those who identify their drinking behavior in terms of its lower-level components ("beer quenches my thirst"). In sum, the level at which we perceive our own actions affects the stability of our behavior and its susceptibility to change (Wegner, Vallacher, & Dizadji, 1989; Dickerson, 1995).

EXPLORING DIVERSITY

THE SELF IN A CULTURAL CONTEXT: SQUEAKY WHEEL OR POUNDED NAIL?

In Western cultures, the "squeaky wheel gets the grease." In Asian cultures, "the nail that stands out gets pounded down."

These two maxims represent quite different views of the world. The Western saying suggests that to get the attention one deserves, one should strive to be special and different and to make one's concerns known to others. The Asian perspective is quite the opposite, suggesting that one ought to try to blend in with others in society and refrain from making waves or being noticed.

The two maxims, and the reasoning that lies behind them, illustrate profound cultural differences in the view of the self. According to Hazel Markus and Shonobu Kitayama (1991, 1994, 1998), people in most Asian societies have an interdependent view of themselves. They see themselves as part of a larger social network in which they work with others to maintain social harmony. Individuals in interdependent societies strive to behave in accordance with the ways that others think, feel, and behave.

People living in many Western countries, in contrast, have an independent perspective on the self. They tend to see themselves as self-contained and autonomous, competing with others to better their own lot in life. Individuals in independent societies strive to behave in ways that express their uniqueness. They consider that their behavior is brought about by their own special configuration of personal characteristics (see Figure 4–4).

This difference between Asian and Western views of the self has several consequences. For instance, Markus and Kitayama report that students in India see themselves as more similar to one another than do American college students. While American students emphasize qualities that they feel differentiate themselves from others, Indian students emphasize qualities that they share with others.

Furthermore, Westerners are more apt to experience emotions that are related to their view of themselves as independent, unconnected individuals—emotions such as jealousy and anger. In contrast, people living in Japan are more likely to experience "other-focused" emotions, which are related to cooperation with others. Specifically, the Japanese language describes emotions that are not even present in the English vocabulary, such as feeling "oime," which refers to being indebted to another.

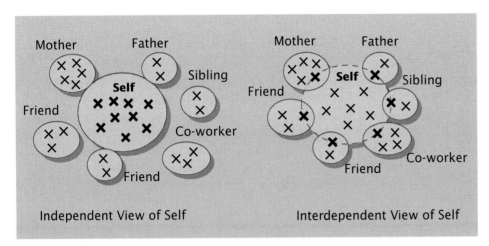

FIGURE 4–4.   Representations of the Self in Two Cultures   In a typically American view of the self, people see themselves as independent, self-contained, and autonomous. In an Asian view of the self, people see themselves as interdependent, related to a large social network with others. (*Source:* Markus & Kitayama, 1991, p. 227.)

Finally, people living in independent cultures see achievement in terms of personal gains, viewing themselves as better or worse achievers than others. They compare their salaries and their grades with those of their peers, and they seek and receive individual rewards for good performance. The self-concepts of people in independent cultures, then, are based on personal, individual successes and failures.

The perspective of those in interdependent cultures is different. In these cultures, people are rewarded on the basis of their contributions to group achievement. For example, an employee's contribution to a company might be evaluated in terms of its effects on the company's overall success. If the company does well, all workers receive benefits; if the company does not do well, everyone suffers. It is as if students in a class received grades based not just on their own performance but on the performance of their classmates, as a whole, on the final exam (Oyserman, 1993; Guisinger & Blatt, 1994; Markus & Kitayama, 1994; Singelis, 1994; Fiske et al., 1998).

REVIEW AND RETHINK

Review

- Self-concept is the sense of identity, the set of beliefs a person holds about what he or she is like as an individual.

- Self-schemas organize information relating to a person's self. In addition to descriptive self-schemas, people have possible selves, which relate to aspirations, concerns, and views about the future.

- Identity reflects the roles and group categories to which people belong, as well as their personal traits and behaviors.

- People use social comparison to clarify their abilities and, according to the one theory, use others even to interpret their emotions.

- Self-perception theory explains how people come to understand their own internal states by acting as observers of their own behavior.

- The level at which people interpret their actions, according to action identification theory, helps to determine the stability of their future behavior and the difficulty they will experience in changing it.

Rethink

- What is a self-schema? Describe the relationship of self-schema and self-concept.

- What are possible selves? How can possible selves help us attain future goals?

- What two types of identity do people have? Which of these is more important for most Americans, and which is more important for most Asians?

- Without comparing yourself to anyone else, try to answer the questions, "How good a tennis player am I?" and "How outgoing am I?"

- Compare self-perception theory with the two-factor theory of emotion. How does each theory explain how people know they are experiencing an emotion? How does each theory explain how people know which emotion they are experiencing?

EVALUATING AND PROTECTING THE SELF

If you're like most people, you see yourself not as just a student, but as a good, bad, or indifferent one. You don't consider yourself as having simply a face and a body, but as having an attractive or an unattractive face and body. You probably don't think of your personality as composed of just a neutral set of characteristics, but as having traits that you like or dislike.

When it comes to the self, we are not neutral, unbiased observers. Instead, we evaluate the self, considering its positive and negative dimensions. Moreover, we try to protect our view of self, reacting to threats by attempting to change either the situation or the way in which we view it. As we will see, these self-protective efforts sometimes color both our behavior and the way we view the world.

SELF-ESTEEM: RATING THE SELF

Self-esteem is the affective component of self, a person's general and specific positive and negative self-evaluations. In contrast to self-concept, which reflects our beliefs and cognitions regarding the self, self-esteem is more emotionally oriented (Baumeister, 1993, 1998).

Just as the self is composed of multiple self-schemas, self-esteem is not one-dimensional. Instead, we may view particular parts of the self in more positive or less positive ways. For instance, a person may hold his academic self-schemas in high regard but consider his weight and body-type self-schema negatively (Marsh, 1986; Pelham & Swann, 1989; Moretti & Higgins, 1990; Baumeister, 1998).

Furthermore, self-esteem varies over time: Depending on the situation, sometimes we feel quite good about ourselves, and other times quite bad. For instance, transitions between different schools often result in lower self-esteem; when students leave elementary school and enter middle school, their self-esteem often drops but then gradually rises again. Self-esteem even rises and falls over shorter periods: We may feel better about ourselves after learning we did particularly well on a test, and worse after learning we failed (Eccles et al., 1989; Heatherton & Polivy, 1991).

The constituents of self-esteem vary according to cultural factors. For example, having high *relationship harmony*—a sense of success in forming strong bonds with others—is more important to self-esteem in collectivistic Asian culture than in more individualistic Western society (Kwan, Bond, & Singelis, 1997).

Although everyone occasionally goes through times of low self-esteem, such as after an undeniable failure, some people are chronically low in self-esteem, and for them, life can be painful. For instance, those with low self-esteem respond more negatively to failure than people with high self-esteem, in part because those with low self-esteem focus on their shortcomings following failure. In contrast, people with high self-esteem focus on their strengths following failure. In short, the consequences of chronic low self-esteem can be

self-esteem: The affective component of self, a person's general and specific positive and negative self-evaluations.

profound, including physical illness, psychological disturbance, or—as we'll discuss in the next chapter—a general inability to cope with stress (Baumeister, 1993; Dodgson & Wood, 1998).

One reason that low self-esteem is so damaging is that it becomes part of a cycle of failure that is difficult to break—a self-fulfilling prophecy of the kind we discussed in Chapter 2. For example, consider students with low self-esteem who are facing an upcoming test. As a result of their low self-esteem they expect to do poorly. In turn, this expectation produces high anxiety and may lead them to reduce the amount of effort they apply to studying. After all, why should people who expect to do badly bother to work very hard? Ultimately, of course, the high anxiety and lack of effort produce just what was expected—failure on the test. Unfortunately, as seen in Figure 4–5, the failure simply reinforces the low self-esteem, and the cycle continues.

On the other hand, high self-esteem is not invariably positive, as we discuss in the accompanying Applying Social Psychology box.

SELF-EFFICACY: EXPECTATIONS FOR SUCCESS

The cycle of failure brought about by low self-esteem is not unalterable. In fact, psychologist Albert Bandura suggests that such self-defeating behavior can be overcome by increasing a person's sense of self-efficacy. **Self-efficacy** refers to learned expectations that one is capable of carrying out a behavior or producing a desired outcome in a particular situation (Schunk, 1991; Bandura, 1982, 1993, 1995; Pajares & Miller, 1995).

People who expect to be successful tend to exert greater effort and show greater persistence when faced with challenging tasks—thereby increasing their likelihood of success (George, 1994; Eden & Zuk, 1995; Orpen, 1995). This is particularly true in both the academic and professional realms. People high in self-efficacy regarding their scholastic ability are successful—a finding that holds true for both students and college professors—and high self-efficacy is also associated with better performance at work (Scheier & Carver, 1992; Mone, Baker, & Jeffries, 1995; Stajkovic & Luthans, 1998).

How do we develop a sense of self-efficacy? There are several ways. One is to observe our prior successes and failures at a task. If people try roller-blading and have little success, they will be less likely to attempt it again. If their initial attempts were promising, however, they'll be more likely to try it again in the future. Self-efficacy also comes from direct reinforcement

self-efficacy: Learned expectations that one is capable of carrying out a behavior or producing a desired outcome in a particular situation.

FIGURE 4–5   The Cycle of Low Self-Esteem People with low self-esteem who expect to do poorly on a test will likely experience high anxiety and therefore will not work as hard. As a result, they actually fail, which in turn confirms their negative view of themselves.

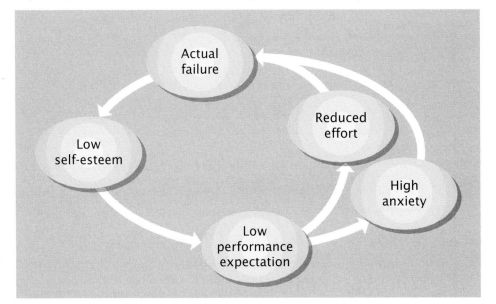

APPLYING SOCIAL PSYCHOLOGY
THE DOWN SIDE OF HIGH SELF-ESTEEM:
WHEN LOVE OF SELF LEADS TO HATE OF OTHERS

High self-esteem is good. Low self-esteem is bad.

Increasing evidence suggests that such everyday wisdom is not, after all, so wise. In fact, it may be that high self-esteem, if it is unwarranted, may actually result in violence toward others.

According to Brad Bushman and Roy Baumeister (1998), perpetrators of violence not only frequently see themselves in a favorable light, but in fact have an inflated view of themselves. Even in the face of contrary evidence such as school failure, the inability to get along with peers, and family strife, some individuals hold surprisingly positive views of themselves, and in fact it is these positive views that lead to violence.

According to this argument, when individuals with high, but unjustified, self-esteem—an attitude known as *narcissistic*—are challenged, they vigorously seek to maintain their view of themselves as superior, often through violent means. In contrast, people with justified self-esteem can brush off such challenges. Similarly, those with lower self-esteem are less prone to lash out at others when attacked or challenged, because such threats to their self-worth are in keeping with their negative view of themselves.

To test this view, Bushman and Baumeister conducted an experiment in which participants wrote an essay that later received praise ("No suggestions, great essay!") or criticism ("This is one of the worst essays I have read!"). The participants, who varied in terms of whether their self-esteem was narcissistic or justified, then were able to play a game against an opponent who had supposedly written the critique. When participants beat the opponent in the rigged game, they had the opportunity to vary the intensity and duration of a blast of loud noise they delivered to their opponent.

The results were clear. The greater the narcissism of the participant, the greater the aggression after being criticized (see Figure 4–6). These findings clearly support the view that people with unwarranted self-esteem are motivated to maintain their high level of self-regard. When challenged by others or by various circumstances, they direct their anger toward others or

toward the situation. In turn, this tactic allows them to avoid revising their view of themselves in a negative direction.

The results suggest that feel-good messages ("Everyone is special" and "We applaud ourselves!") that emphasize the importance of high self-esteem may be misdirected. Instead of suggesting that everyone should have high esteem, regardless of whether it is warranted, parents, schools, and other societal institutions should concentrate on providing a means for people to earn self-esteem through their accomplishments (Begley, 1998).

FIGURE 4–6 Narcissism and Aggression Current studies have found that the greater the narcissism, high but unjustified self-esteem, the greater the aggression after being criticized. (*Source:* Bushman & Baumeister, 1998.)

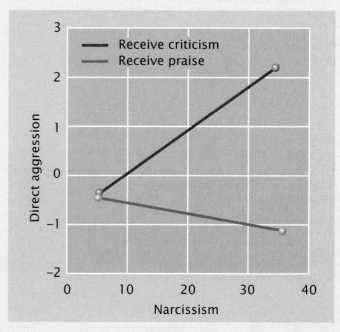

and encouragement from others (Bandura, 1988; George, 1994; Mone, Baker, & Jeffries, 1995; Jenkins & Gortner, 1998).

SELF-EVALUATION MAINTENANCE: WHEN OTHERS' SUCCESS HURTS

Did you ever wonder what it would be like to be the brother or sister of a U.S. president? Despite the ability to hang out at the White House, the experience might not be all that good for your self-esteem—at least according to self-evaluation maintenance theory.

In the view of social psychologist Abraham Tessor, **self-evaluation maintenance theory** predicts that people will react to the accomplishments of important people in their lives by showing either jealousy or pride (Tesser, 1988; Achee, Tesser, & Pilkington, 1994; Beach et al., 1998). What determines which of the two reactions will occur?

The critical factor is the relevance of the other person's success to one's self. For instance, someone who has political aspirations of his or her own or who wants to be in the limelight might experience jealousy when a sibling becomes president or experiences other political success. On the other hand, if the success is not central to one's view of oneself and poses no threat, then the sibling's success will be a source of pride and positive emotions (Pilkington, Tesser, & Stephens, 1991; Beach & Tesser, 1993; Beach et al., 1998).

STEREOTYPE VULNERABILITY: ERECTING RACIAL BARRIERS FOR ONESELF

If you felt that—because of your race—you might never do all that well in school, would this feeling affect your efforts to succeed academically?

According to social psychologist Claude Steele, the answer is most certainly yes. In his eyes, the relatively high scholastic failure and dropout rates of African American students, compared with those of whites, arise in part from **stereotype vulnerability**, obstacles to performance that come from awareness of the stereotypes held by society about minority student performance. For instance, African Americans faced with teachers who doubt their competence, schools that routinely develop remedial programs for minorities, and a society that assumes that African Americans are at risk for failure may themselves buy into society's stereotyped views, feeling particularly susceptible to failure (Steele, 1992; Steele & Aronson, 1998).

In Steele's view, the awareness of such stereotypes has grave consequences for the performances of minority students. He suggests that whenever African American students are faced with an academic task, they feel vulnerable to the possibility of confirming society's worst stereotypes. Such a mind-set at best hinders their performance and at worst leads to a change in self-concept, in which scholastic endeavors are no longer regarded as an important component of self-esteem. Minority students may even decide that failure in academic tasks, because it would confirm societal stereotypes, is so risky that the struggle to succeed is not worth the effort. Instead, they may not try particularly hard to succeed and, ironically, perform poorly—thereby confirming the stereotype.

In time, African Americans may "disidentify" with academic success by putting forth less effort on academic tasks and generally downgrading the importance of academic achievement. Ultimately, such disidentification may act as a self-fulfilling prophecy, increasing their chances of academic failure (Osborne, 1995; Steele & Aronson, 1995).

To test his theory, Steele and colleagues conducted an experiment in which two groups of African American and white students were given identical tests composed of difficult verbal-skills items from the Graduate Record Exam. However, the stated purpose of the test was varied across participant groups. Some participants were told that the test measured "psychological factors involved in solving verbal problems"—information that presumably had little to do with underlying ability. It was stressed that the test would not evaluate their ability. In contrast, other participants were told that the test was concerned with various "personal factors involved in performance on problems requiring reading and verbal reasoning abilities," and that the test would be helpful in identifying their personal strengths and weaknesses.

The results provided clear evidence for the stereotype vulnerability hypothesis. African American participants who thought the test measured psychological factors performed as well as white participants. But African American participants who thought the test measured core abilities and limitations scored significantly lower than the white participants. In contrast, white participants scored equally well, regardless of the test description (see Figure 4–7). Clearly, having to contend with the stereotype resulted in poorer performance (Steele & Aronson, 1995).

These results help explain the puzzling finding that led Steele to his hypothesis in the first place. While a professor at the University of Michigan, Steele found that no matter

self-evaluation maintenance theory: The theory that people will react to the accomplishments of important people in their lives by showing either jealousy or pride.

stereotype vulnerability: Obstacles to performance that come from awareness of the stereotypes held by society about minority student performance.

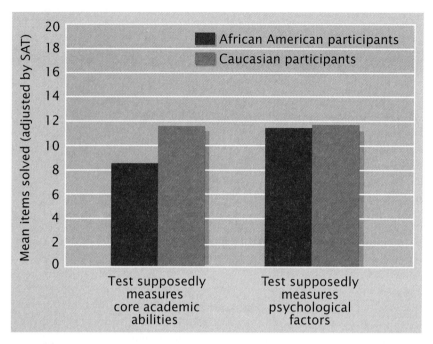

FIGURE 4–7   Mean Test Performance When a test was described as measuring core academic abilities, African American participants scored lower than when they thought the test measured psychological factors relating to verbal abilities. However, white participants did not differ according to the description of the test. (*Source:* Adapted from Steele & Aronson, 1995, p. 800.)

how well qualified African American students were, they fell behind similarly qualified white students as they progressed through their college careers. Even African American students who had entered with stellar SAT scores were ending up with low college grades (Steele, 1992).

Happily, Steele's findings leave room for optimism. They show that even relatively subtle changes in a situation—such as the way a test is described—can reduce vulnerability to stereotyping. Ultimately, intervention programs designed to inform members of minority groups about their susceptibility to society's negative stereotypes may provide a means of reducing to some extent the otherwise discouraging consequences of those stereotypes.

SELF-AWARENESS: FOCUSING ON THE ME

Most of us cannot resist taking a peek at ourselves as we pass by a mirror or a reflecting store window. And once we've seen that image, we generally engage in a bit of self-reflection.

At least that's what research on self-awareness suggests. **Self-awareness** is a state in which attention is focused on the self. According to social psychologist Robert Wicklund and colleagues, certain situations make people more conscious of themselves. For instance, seeing oneself in a mirror, having one's picture taken, or giving a talk in front of an audience all lead to an increase in self-awareness (Wicklund, 1975; Wicklund & Frey, 1980; Duval, Duval, & Mulilis, 1992; Ferrari & Sternberg, 1998).

Wicklund argues that being in a state of self-awareness leads to a particular consequence: People begin to focus on how their actual self compares to ideal standards they hold for themselves. Typically, the result is an unpleasant affective state—as people find their actual selves less than ideal—followed by a temporary loss of self-esteem.

Once people become aware of the discrepancies between their actual and ideal selves, they have two main ways of resolving the situation. One is simply to flee: moving away from a mirror or refusing to have a picture taken, for instance. A second strategy is to attempt to decrease the discrepancy between their actual and ideal selves. To that end, people who are

self-awareness: A state in which attention is focused on the self.

highly self-aware tend to behave in accordance with their ideal selves. For instance, people placed in a self-aware state are more helpful to others, are more resistant to change in personally important attitudes, work harder, and are more honest than those who are not self-aware (Gibbons & Wicklund, 1982; Gibbons & Wright, 1983; Gibbons, 1990; Hutton & Baumeister, 1992).

Clearly, self-awareness may lead to positive outcomes. But what if people choose the other option: to escape the situation? Although in many instances self-awareness can be readily avoided, in some cases it is inescapable. (Consider a professor, who must repeatedly appear in public to give lectures, or a trial lawyer, who must argue cases in court.) In such situations, the aversive consequences of self-awareness may become so unpleasant that people will engage in self-injurious behavior, including drunkenness, masochism, and even—in the most extreme cases—suicide (Baumeister, 1991, 1997a, 1997b).

Are there different forms of self-awareness? According to social psychologist Allan Fenigstein, self-awareness can be broken down into two categories—private self-consciousness and public self-consciousness. **Private self-consciousness** refers to awareness of inner thoughts, feelings, and self-evaluations. **Public self-consciousness** consists of a focus on one's outward behavior and on appearances that are visible to others (Fenigstein, Scheier, & Buss, 1975; Teixeira & Gomes, 1995; Ruganci, 1995; Nasby, 1996).

People tend to vary in the nature of self-consciousness that they are most apt to experience. Some people are chronically high in private self-consciousness; they are most concerned with how they measure up to their own personal standards (Davies, 1994b, 1997). In contrast, other people are chronically high in public self-consciousness; they are more concerned with behaving in accordance with societal norms. Researchers have devised a personality scale to distinguish the two types of people; some of the items on the scale are shown in Table 4–2.

People high in public self-consciousness are particularly attuned to the impressions their behavior makes on others. For this reason they are more easily persuaded by other people's arguments, and they are more likely to see themselves as the focus of other people's attention. In contrast, people higher in private self-consciousness are more resistant to persuasion and less easily influenced by pressure from others (Hutton & Baumeister, 1992; Davies, 1997).

MISPERCEPTIONS OF THE SELF: TO THINE OWN SELF BE FALSE

Most of the evidence about the self that we've discussed so far suggests that people are pretty good perceivers of themselves and their own behavior. In fact, we might conclude that people look at themselves almost as dispassionately as they look at strangers, and that they apply to themselves the principles of social cognition we first discussed in Chapter 2.

As you might suspect, however, this conclusion is far from being universally true. In fact, people actively seek to protect themselves from damaging, hurtful information, often by interpreting it in a way that maintains their positive view of themselves. Furthermore, even when they are not protecting themselves, individuals may view and interpret what is happening to

private self-consciousness: One's awareness of inner thoughts, feelings, and self-evaluations.

public self-consciousness: A focus on one's outward behavior and on appearances that are visible to others.

Looking in a mirror can help bring on a state of self-awareness.

TABLE 4-2	Sample Items From the Self-Consciousness Scale

Items Relating to Public Self-Consciousness
   I'm concerned about what other people think of me.
   I'm concerned about the way I present myself.
   I usually worry about making a good impression.
   One of the last things I do before leaving my house is look in the mirror.

Items Relating to Private Self-Consciousness
   I'm always trying to figure myself out.
   I'm alert to changes in my mood.
   I'm aware of the way my mind works when I work on a problem.
   I'm constantly examining my motives.

Source: Fenigstein, Scheier, & Buss, 1975.

them in ways that are very different from how others see the same situation. Two of the biases that occur regularly when we analyze our own behavior are the actor–observer bias and self-handicapping.

The actor–observer bias: You say I'm an angry person, I say you make me angry.   Suppose you've waited in a long line at a bank, becoming increasingly annoyed. When you finally reach the teller, your anger spills out, and you act hostile and resentful. The teller thinks, "What a mean person!" Would you agree?

Most likely not. To you, your behavior is simply a reaction to the situation, and it has little to do with your own personality. You were simply in a bad mood after waiting so long.

Your reliance on situational factors to explain your behavior, and the teller's reliance on dispositional factors, is an example of the actor–observer bias (Jones & Nisbett, 1972). The **actor–observer bias** is the tendency of people to attribute their behavior to situational factors, whereas people observing the behavior tend to attribute it to the actor's stable, unchanging dispositions.

The actor–observer bias is closely related to the *fundamental attribution error* that we discussed in Chapter 2. You'll recall that the fundamental attribution error is the tendency to overattribute others' behaviors to dispositional causes, and the corresponding failure to recognize the importance of situational factors in their behavior. In both the actor–observer bias and the fundamental attribution error, then, outside observers overemphasize dispositional causes of behavior while neglecting the importance of the situation as a determinant of behavior.

Why does the actor–observer bias lead actors to emphasize situational explanations of their own behavior and observers to focus on the characteristics of the actors? One reason is perceptual (Storms, 1973; Taylor & Fiske, 1978). When people are involved as actors in social interactions, they are looking, listening, and responding to what is happening in the environment around them. Thus, their focus is on the external world. In contrast, observers are apt to focus more on the behavior of actors—because it is so striking and vivid—than on the relatively inanimate, lifeless situation. In part, then, the bias is due to a difference in focus or perspective.

There's another reason, though, for the actor–observer bias: Actors have more information than observers. Actors know where they were yesterday, last night, and this morning; they know that in each situation they behaved differently, and they understand the reasons for their behavior. Because actors have seen themselves behave very differently in various situations, they are more likely than an observer to look to the situation for an explanation.

For instance, a student knows that an impending paper made her spend yesterday in the library; that the party she attended last night gave her the opportunity to dance for hours; and that the upcoming visit of her parents made her scrub her bathroom this morning. In

actor–observer bias: The tendency of people to attribute their behavior to situational factors, whereas people observing the behavior tend to attribute it to the actors' stable, unchanging dispositions.

contrast, an observer viewing her behavior may know much less. Depending on which situation the observer happened upon, he or she might conclude that the student is extremely studious, or a real party animal, or obsessed with cleanliness.

Although the actor–observer bias is very common, it has its limits. For instance, as we first discussed in Chapter 2, people sometimes fall prey to the *self-serving bias,* the tendency to attribute personal success to internal factors (such as skill, ability, or effort), while attributing failure to external factors (such as bad luck or something about the situation). In short, anytime we're motivated to protect our self-concepts, the actor–observer bias will be overridden in our favor (Gioia & Sims, 1985; Green et al., 1985; Osberg & Shrauger, 1986; Gifford & Hine, 1997). In fact, in some cases the desire to protect our self-concepts is so great that it goes beyond coloring our perceptions and actually affects our performance—and not always in a positive way, as we see next.

Self-handicapping: Erecting hurdles for ourselves.   From time to time, most of us experience anxiety and insecurity about the extent of our own abilities. Are we smart enough to succeed in school? Will we do well enough on the job? Will we make the grade?

Unfortunately, the strategy that some people use to deal with this problem actually interferes with their own performance. According to social psychologists Stephen Berglas and Edward Jones, who first described the phenomenon, **self-handicapping** is a tactic in which people set up circumstances that allow them to avoid attributing poor future performance to low ability, and instead permit them to attribute future failure to less threatening causes (Berglas & Jones, 1978; Higgins, Snyder, & Berglas, 1990).

Consider, for example, a student who goes to a bar the night before a test, and the next day says, "I don't think I'm going to do very well on today's test: I was up late drinking and didn't get a chance to study." If, in fact, the student ends up not doing well on the test, he has an obvious excuse—being drunk. Because being drunk is a temporary, external factor that doesn't relate to a lack of academic competence, it is presumably less threatening to self-esteem than if the student were forced to attribute his failure to a lack of ability (Feick & Rhodewalt, 1997; Arkin et al., 1998).

Several types of behavior can be used to shift attributional attention away from personal abilities. For example, research has shown a rich variety of self-handicapping strategies—feeling anxiety, being in a bad mood, acting shy, becoming depressed, creating distracting work conditions, reducing effort, choosing a difficult task, and procrastinating (Baumgardner, Lake, & Arkin, 1985; Schouten & Handelsman, 1987; Shepperd & Arkin, 1989a; Baumgardner, 1991; Matsuo, 1994).

In a broader sense, self-handicapping strategies vary along two dimensions—internal versus external, and acquired versus claimed (Arkin & Baumgardner, 1985). The internal–external dimension relates to whether the excuse pertains to oneself (internal) or to the situation (external). The acquired–claimed dimension relates to whether the handicapping behavior is actually performed (acquired) or is merely claimed, but not necessarily true (claimed).

These two dimensions, when considered jointly, delineate four types of self-handicaps (Leary & Shepperd, 1986). As shown in Figure 4–8, self-handicaps may be internal acquired (such as drug use), internal claimed (as when a person asserts that tests always make him anxious), external acquired (choosing overly difficult goals), or external claimed (as when one claims that a particular test is too hard) (Arkin & Baumgardner, 1985; Leary & Shepperd, 1986; Hirt, Deppe, & Gordon, 1991).

In some instances, self-handicapping may become habitual, as in the case of a person who consistently drinks too much and whose performance in many areas of life suffers. Alcohol provides a ready excuse for explaining failures that might otherwise have to be attributed to internal factors. Similarly, students who habitually employ self-handicapping develop poor study habits and perform less well academically (Zuckerman, Kieffer, & Knee, 1998).

Interestingly, there are gender differences in self-handicapping. Males are more likely to self-handicap than females. Men and women may also differ in the ways they self-handicap.

self-handicapping: A tactic in which people set up circumstances that allow them to avoid attributing poor performance to low ability and instead permit them to attribute failure to less threatening causes.

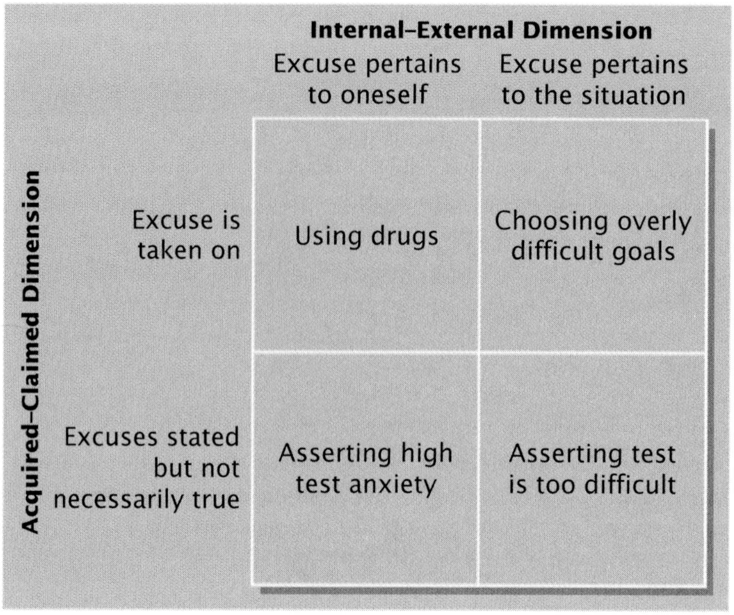

FIGURE 4–8 **Self-Handicapping Strategies** Self-handicapping strategies vary along two dimensions: whether they are internal–external or acquired–claimed. The internal–external dimension relates to whether the excuse pertains to oneself (internal) or to the situation (external). The acquired–claimed dimension relates to whether the handicapping behavior is actually performed (acquired) or is merely claimed but not necessarily true (claimed). (*Source:* Based on Arkin & Baumgardner, 1985.)

Men tend to use more alcohol and drugs, and women are more likely to claim stress or physical illness (Shepperd & Arkin, 1989b; Hirt, Deppe, & Gordon, 1991; Arkin et al., 1998).

Individuals who are high in public self-consciousness are also more apt to use self-handicapping than people high in private self-consciousness (Ferrari, 1991b). For example, one study found that when a task was presented as an important one, participants high in public self-consciousness (who are, by definition, concerned with public performance) showed a heightened tendency to self-handicap, compared with those low in public self-consciousness. On the other hand, when the experimenter suggested that the task was not all that important, participants—whether high or low in public self-consciousness—showed little difference in the tendency to self-handicap (Shepperd & Arkin, 1989b).

Why do people self-handicap? The most obvious reason is to protect their self-esteem (Nurmi, 1993; Feick & Rhodewalt, 1997; Arkin et al., 1998). People who adopt a self-handicapping strategy are not responsible for their failure—at least in their own eyes—and this allows them to maintain a positive view of themselves (Jones & Berglas, 1978; Ferrari, 1991a; Tice, 1991).

However, self-handicapping also helps protect one's public image. Hence, by self-handicapping, people provide not only to themselves but also to observers a reasonable excuse for failure (Snyder & Higgins, 1988; Luginbuhl & Palmer, 1991; Arkin et al., 1998). Of course, this strategy doesn't always work. Observers sometimes don't buy into self-handicapping, seeing it simply as making excuses (Rhodewalt et al., 1995). In other cases, though, the benefits derived by the self-handicapper from making excuses may outweigh the costs that come from others' disapproval, as we discuss next.

Excuses, excuses: It's not my fault. "The dog ate my homework." "The water pipe broke in the dorm, and I had to evacuate." "My grandmother died."

Conventional wisdom advises that we shouldn't make excuses for our behavior, but instead should own up to our failures and accept the consequences. Recent research, however, suggests otherwise.

According to social psychologists C. R. Snyder and Raymond Higgins of the University of Kansas, excuses are not all bad (Snyder & Higgins, 1988; Higgins & Snyder, 1989). In fact, people who make excuses may have higher self-esteem, do better on tests of performance, and even have better physical health than those who refuse to make excuses for their own performance.

Snyder and Higgins consider excuse making as a process in which people shift attributions for negative events away from causes that are relatively central to their sense of self and toward causes that are less pivotal. By focusing on less important causes, people are able to improve their image of themselves and their sense of control.

More specifically, Snyder and Higgins argue that successful excuses begin when some negative outcome threatens people's positive views of themselves and their sense of control (see Figure 4–9). Excuse makers develop external attributions for the behavior that led to the negative outcome, making potential threats to self-esteem less potent. This process leads them to focus less on themselves and more on the situation. Ultimately, this outward focus benefits self-esteem, emotion, health, and even future performance (Doherty & Schlenker, 1995). Moreover, it can help the person maintain both a positive self-image and a sense of control over outside events.

In contrast, when people don't make excuses in the face of some negative outcome, their attributions for the cause of the unpleasant event can turn inward. In this case, they maximize their self-focus and concentrate on internal attributions. By not making excuses, they may thereby suffer from a loss of esteem, and as a consequence, may experience negative emotions, poorer health, and impaired future performance. Eventually, such outcomes can lead to a deflated self-image and loss of the sense of control.

FIGURE 4–9   Making Excuses Depending on how one attributes a negative outcome, excuses can be beneficial. (*Source:* Adapted from Snyder & Higgins, 1988, p. 30.)

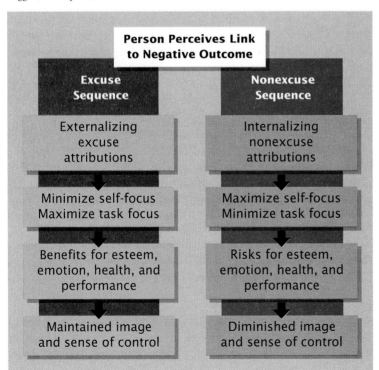

The way we explain our behavior to ourselves, including the kind of excuses we make, can affect our self-esteem. Although it is useful to avoid blaming others for our mistakes, seeing mistakes as something to be avoided at all costs is not beneficial to our self-esteem.

Clearly, excuses can be helpful. But not all kinds of excuses are equally effective. The most effective excuses emphasize how the circumstance being excused was unintentional and could not be foreseen or controlled. In addition, excuses that are ambiguous as to their true purpose work better than excuses that appear to others to be clear-cut, obvious attempts to justify unpleasant occurrences (Higgins & Snyder, 1989; Higgins, Snyder, & Berglas, 1990).

Effective excuse makers also try to use excuses that prevent others from labeling their behavior as chronic and habitual (Gonzales, 1992). For instance, consider the student who excuses his lack of academic success on tests by explaining that he was out celebrating the night before and had too much to drink. If he continually uses the same excuse, he runs the risk of being labeled an alcoholic—not a particularly prudent strategy.

In sum, the right kind of excuse can be a boon to one's self-image. Consequently, if someone complains that you're just making excuses, don't take her criticism too hard: You may be doing yourself a favor. (For some of the best—and worst—kinds of excuses, see the The Informed Consumer of Social Psychology section.)

THE INFORMED CONSUMER OF SOCIAL PSYCHOLOGY

MAKING EXCUSES: GOOD AND BAD

There are good excuses and bad ones. The following are guidelines for making excuses, based on the work of C. R. Snyder (Slade, 1995):

Good excuse makers . . .

- use excuses in moderation.
- don't spend a lot of time distancing themselves from performances that didn't meet their standards.
- expect to make mistakes, but see mistakes as a means to achieve a positive goal.
- avoid blaming others, especially people with whom they must work.
- do not excuse their actions in front of experts who know better.
- acknowledge their own link to failure by admitting that they did something that did not lead to the desired outcome.
- attribute the failure to something other than personal qualities, like talent or intelligence; they might say, for example, that they used the wrong strategy.
- indicate that they learned from the mistake and that, thanks to this lesson, they can search for new strategies that will achieve what they and others want.
- **Best excuse:** an apology, since it acknowledges some responsibility for a mistake, asks forgiveness, and suggests that an effort will now be made to make things better.

Bad excuse makers . . .

◆ use excuses often and in ways that are disproportionate to the transgression.

◆ concentrate on cutting losses and distancing themselves from the mistake to the point that they cannot move on.

◆ see mistakes as negative outcomes only, to be avoided at all costs.

◆ blame others, even people with whom they must work.

◆ excuse their actions in front of experts who know better.

◆ give excuses that relieve them of any accountability, which makes the excuses less credible.

◆ attribute failure to inadequacies in others.

◆ do not see mistakes as lessons in what works and doesn't work; do not fashion strategies for going beyond the mistake.

◆ **Worst excuse:** "I didn't do it; she did"—since this acknowledges no responsibility for a bad decision or poor judgment (which seems incredible) while blaming someone else (which seems dishonorable). Children generally offer this excuse for bad behavior.

REVIEW AND RETHINK

Review

• Self-esteem, the affective component of self, is multidimensional and may change over time.

• Self-awareness leads to a focus on how the actual self compares to ideal standards, and consequently can induce an unpleasant affective state.

• Self-awareness may be broken into two categories: private self-consciousness (awareness of inner thoughts, feelings, and evaluations) and public self-consciousness (a focus on outer behavior and appearances).

• The actor–observer bias and self-handicapping are two forms of bias in self-perception.

• Excuse making is a way to maintain self-esteem. In moderation, appropriate excuse making can be beneficial.

Rethink

• How do the concepts of self-esteem and self-concept differ? Which is more variable over time and across situations?

• What is private self-awareness, and how does it differ from public self-awareness? Which is more likely to be brought on by seeing oneself in a mirror? By having to give a speech in front of a large group?

• How might a person explain his or her behavior in the following two situations: (1) hiding under the bed covers during an evening thunderstorm; (2) doing well on an exam? How might an impartial observer explain these behaviors?

• Briefly describe four types of self-handicapping, and describe a situation in which each would be most effective.

PRESENTING ONE'S SELF TO THE WORLD

When the late entertainer Sammy Davis Jr. said, "As soon as I go out of the front door of my house in the morning, I'm on, . . . I'm on," he was merely reflecting what William Shakespeare had written, somewhat more elegantly, over three centuries earlier. In Shakespeare's

self-presentation: The process by which people attempt to create specific, generally positive impressions regarding themselves.

self-monitoring: The regulation of one's behavior to meet the demands of a situation or the expectations of others.

comedy *As You Like It,* the character of Jacques suggests that "All the world's a stage, and all the men and women merely players."

Most social psychologists would be tempted to agree. People don't just passively react to social stimuli. Instead, they attempt to regulate and control the information they present to others. Although they may not be fully aware of it, people have agendas that they wish to accomplish during social interactions, and they engage in self-presentation. **Self-presentation**, or *impression management,* is the process by which people attempt to create specific, generally positive impressions regarding themselves (Tice et al., 1995; Robinson, Johnson, & Shields, 1995; Baumeister, 1998). One way they do this is through self-monitoring.

SELF-MONITORING: KEEPING TABS ON ONE'S BEHAVIOR

Most of us have acquaintances who appear at ease in almost any social situation, comfortably fitting in with others. And most of us also know people who seem oblivious of social norms, acting as if driven by an inner compass that does not vary from one situation to another.

The differences between the two types of people reflect differences in self-monitoring (Snyder, 1974a, 1987, 1995). **Self-monitoring** describes the regulation of one's behavior to meet the demands of a situation or the expectations of others. Although related to public self-consciousness, self-monitoring involves more extensive behavioral adjustments to the perceived expectations of others. Self-monitoring focuses on behavior—how one presents oneself—whereas self-consciousness emphasizes attention and where it is focused.

People who are chronically high in self-monitoring lead very different lives from those who are characteristically lower on the trait (Kilduff & Day, 1994). As indicated in the sample items from a scale that measures self-monitoring, presented in Table 4–3, high self-monitors are social chameleons, changing their colors according to the requirements of the situation (Snyder, 1974a; Snyder & Gangestad, 1986). They are attentive to how others expect them to behave, concerned about the appropriateness of their behavior, and adept at changing their behavior to match their understanding of the social situation (Anderson & Randlet, 1994; Graziano & Bryant, 1998; Guarino, Michael, & Hocevar, 1998).

In contrast, low self-monitors are relatively insensitive to the social demands of a given situation. As a consequence, their behavior is more consistent across situations (Ajzen, Timko, & White, 1982; Shaffer, Smith, & Tomarelli, 1982; Prislin, Akrap, & Sprah, 1987; Lippa & Donaldson, 1990; DeBono & Ormoto, 1993). In addition, low self-monitors seem to have a clearer sense of themselves. They see themselves as having a "principled self," based on their own philosophy of behavior, as opposed to the "pragmatic self" of the high self-monitor (Snyder, 1987; Fine & Schumann, 1992; Leone & Corte, 1994).

A good deal of research has illustrated stark differences between high and low self-monitors in a variety of domains. For example, high self-monitors seek out information about other people and remember it better (Snyder, 1987). They make more accurate

TABLE 4–3	*Sample Items from the Self-Monitoring Scale*

Items Relating to High Self-Monitoring
  I would probably make a good actor.
  I may deceive people by being friendly when I really dislike them.
  I can make impromptu speeches on topics about which I have almost no information.
  In different situations and with different people, I often act like very different persons.

Items Relating to Low Self-Monitoring
  I find it hard to imitate the behavior of other people.
  In a group of people, I am rarely the center of attention.
  I can only argue for ideas which I already believe.
  I feel a bit awkward in company and do not show up quite as well as I should.

Source: Snyder & Gangestad, 1986.

courtroom eyewitnesses than low self-monitors: They are so keenly aware of the happenings in their social environment that they pay more attention to what is happening—even in the midst of a crime (Hosch & Platz, 1984). On the other hand, high self-monitors do not make perfect witnesses; they are likely to be tripped up by leading questions (Lassiter, Stone, & Weigold, 1988). High and low self-monitors also differ in their personal relationships. High self-monitors remember more about others, and to observers they appear more friendly and less anxious (Berscheid et al., 1976; Lippa, 1976). Furthermore, the kinds of relationships they have with others are qualitatively different from those of low self-monitors. High self-monitors are more likely to choose their friends on the basis of the particular activity in which they are interested and less on the friend's personal qualities, such as attitude similarity. Thus, if high self-monitors want to play tennis, they'll choose a partner on the basis of tennis ability; low self-monitors, in contrast, will be more apt to choose on the basis of friendship (Snyder, Gangestad, & Simpson, 1983). Dating behavior shows a similar pattern: Low self-monitors choose dates more or less independently of the specific activity that they will engage in on the date, and high self-monitors are more influenced by the planned activity (Snyder & Simpson, 1984; Jones, 1993).

In sum, high self-monitors place a premium on responding effectively to the demands of a social situation. They make shrewd and accurate assessments of the behaviors that are best suited to a given social situation, and they attempt to carry out those behaviors. Does this mean that it is better to be a "pragmatic" high self-monitor than a "principled" low self-monitor?

The answer depends on one's values. On the one hand, an observer might label the behavior of high self-monitors as superficial, transitory, equivocating, and lacking in underlying integrity. (Think of politicians who make promises based on whatever they think their particular audience wishes to hear.) On the other hand, behavior of a low self-monitor might be viewed as rigid, insensitive, and thoughtless. A skeptic might view low self-monitors as people who are socially incompetent, are unheeding of others, or simply don't care about the social niceties that keep the engine of social relations running smoothly.

The truth, no doubt, lies somewhere in between. Both low and high self-monitors can lead effective social lives. Both low and high self-monitoring strategies permit people to present themselves in ways that balance their desire to expedite social interactions with their need to maintain their own sense of themselves. Furthermore, it appears that the tendency to self-monitor decreases with age. For example, one study that looked at a sample of people ranging in age from adolescence to old age found that self-monitoring scores declined with age (Reifman, Klein, & Murphy, 1989). Apparently, as people become older, they feel more comfortable "letting it all hang out."

SELF-PRESENTATION: SELLING OURSELVES TO OTHERS

If "all the world's a stage," as Shakespeare wrote, a good deal of time is spent working out roles to play and developing scripts. No one wants to look foolish, or ignorant, or inept; people want to be seen in the best possible light. To this end, people try to present themselves in positive ways.

Why do we try to present ourselves well? According to social psychologist Roy Baumeister, two main motives fuel self-presentation (Baumeister & Hutton, 1987; Baumeister, 1998). The first is audience pleasing. **Audience pleasing** is behavior designed to make an audience feel good. As a rule, people want others to experience a positive reaction to them, either because they generally want to please others or because they want to manipulate others' behavior in particular ways. People may also want to prevent others from holding them responsible for undesirable consequences of their behavior (Baumeister, 1982; Schlenker, 1982; Baumeister, Hutton, & Tice, 1989).

Another reason that people are motivated to make good impressions has to do with self-construction. **Self-construction** is self-presentation meant to corroborate our own view of ourselves. We try to make our behavior match our "ideal self," supporting the view we have of ourselves. Moreover, we self-present in order to "audition" different selves, with the goal

audience pleasing: Behavior designed to make an audience feel good.

self-construction: Self-presentation meant to corroborate our own view of ourselves.

ingratiation: A deliberate effort to make a favorable impression.

of choosing identities that might eventually be incorporated into our central identity. A relatively introverted person might, for instance, try to act particularly outgoing at a social occasion to see how others react. In sum, other people are not the only audience of our self-presentations; sometimes we want to see for our own benefit the impact of our behavior.

In addition to the audience-pleasing and self-construction motives for seeking to present ourselves well, social psychologist Edward Jones suggests an additional motive—the attainment of power during social interaction (Jones & Pittman, 1982; Jones, 1990). Jones argues that people attempt to maintain and augment their social power through self-presentation in order to achieve their own social goals. To Jones, self-presentation involves several strategies, including ingratiation, self-promotion, intimidation, exemplification, and supplication. These are summarized in Table 4–4.

Ingratiation: The art of self-presentation. One key strategy for effective self-presentation is ingratiation (Orpen, 1996). **Ingratiation** is a deliberate effort to make a favorable impression. Through the use of various ingratiation strategies, people seek to make themselves more likable. For instance, people can ingratiate themselves by agreeing with others' opinions. Other ingratiation approaches include doing favors for others and praising another person's achievements, conduct, or personality (Jones, 1990; Deluga & Perry, 1994).

Ingratiation does not always proceed along a smooth path. In fact, if it is not done with subtlety and finesse, ingratiation can backfire if the recipient realizes the ingratiator's true motivations. In fact, there is something of a Catch-22 in ingratiation: The less power a person has in a particular situation, the more apt he or she is to try to use ingratiation tactics. At the same time, though, ingratiation from a person with lower power is more likely to be seen for what it is and consequently is generally less effective. For example, when a store employee effusively praises her boss, the boss may suspect that the flattery is an attempt to get a raise (Vonk, 1996).

Sometimes, though, ingratiators have little to worry about, because both ingratiators and the targets of their ingratiation engage in a kind of conspiracy. Both ingratiators and their targets are motivated not to expose ingratiation—ingratiators because they don't want to see

TABLE 4–4	Self-Presentational Strategies			
	ATTRIBUTIONS SOUGHT	NEGATIVE ATTRIBUTIONS RISKED	EMOTION TO BE AROUSED	PROTOTYPICAL ACTIONS
1. Ingratiation	Likeable	Sycophant Conformist Obsequious	Affection	Positive self-characterization Opinion conformity Other enhancement Favors
2. Self-promotion	Competent (effective, "a winner")	Fraudulent Conceited Defensive	Respect (awe, deference)	Performance claims Performance accounts Performances
3. Intimidation	Dangerous (ruthless, volatile)	Blusterer Ineffectual	Fear	Threats Potential anger
4. Exemplification	Worth (suffers, dedicated)	Hypocrite Sanctimonious Exploitative	Guilt (shame, emulation)	Self-denial Helping Militancy for a cause
5. Supplication	Helpless (handicapped, unfortunate)	Stigmatized Lazy Demanding	Nurturance (obligation)	Self-deprecation Entreaties for help

Source: Adapted from Jones, 1990, p. 198.

The use of ingratiation strategies is common to those seeking to make themselves more likable. If not done with subtlety and care, though, it can backfire, revealing the ingratiator's true motivations.

themselves as manipulative, and targets because they actually want to believe the flattery they receive. Consequently, mutual self-deception promotes positive feelings for both parties in the interaction.

Self-promotion: Creating the impression of competence.   While ingratiation focuses on making a person seem more likable, **self-promotion** is designed to make a person seem more competent. For instance, in job interviews self-presentation efforts will focus more on cultivating an air of competence than likability. In such cases, a person may use self-promotion techniques (Stevens & Kristof, 1995; Bornstein et al., 1996).

Self-promotion can be carried out in several ways. For example, people may flaunt or boast about their prior successes and minimize their previous failures. They also may admit a minor weakness, which is clearly secondary to the ability of primary concern (Baumeister & Jones, 1978). By admitting to a weakness, self-promoters hope to show that, although they have both strong and weak points, in general they are confident about their overall abilities. In addition, admitting to a weakness helps disguise the fact that they are self-promoting.

Of course, the use of self-promotion, like ingratiation, carries several risks. For instance, self-promoters gamble that they will not be seen as conceited or defensive. Furthermore, if their ability turns out to be less than they claimed, they may appear fraudulent. Still, self-promotion remains one of the most common self-presentational strategies (Giacalone & Rosenfeld, 1986; Gardner, 1992; Orpen, 1996).

Intimidation and exemplification.   Some self-presentation strategies are more blatant than ingratiation and self-promotion. For instance, **intimidation** occurs when people communicate their ability and willingness to produce negative outcomes for other people. For instance, a high-level employee who implies that a low-level worker will be dismissed if the low-level worker doesn't provide a particular favor is using intimidation.

Although intimidation certainly lacks refinement and subtlety, it may be useful in bringing about desired outcomes. However, intimidators may, in the process, end up being disliked. Consequently, intimidation is often reserved for social situations in which relationships are involuntary, such as a college classroom in which a disagreeable and tough college professor uses intimidation to motivate his or her students.

The self-presentational tactic that is in some ways the polar opposite of intimidation is **exemplification**, a technique in which people attempt to create the impression of moral superiority and integrity. Rather than seeking to control a situation through fear, as with intimidation, people using exemplification try to present themselves in such a virtuous light that they create an atmosphere of control. The danger with exemplification is that people who

self-promotion: An action designed to make a person seem more competent.

intimidation: A self-presentation strategy in which people communicate an ability and inclination to produce negative outcomes for other people.

exemplification: A technique in which people attempt to create the impression of moral superiority and integrity.

supplication: A means of self-presentation which consists of creating the impression that one is needy, weak, and dependent.

power semantic: The power or status level that a conversant holds.

solidarity semantic: The degree of shared social experience that exists between two people.

use it may be seen as hypocritical or sanctimonious, such as rich people who brag about the amount of money they give to the needy.

Supplication: Power through neediness.   A final means of self-presentation is **supplication**, in which a person creates the impression that he or she is needy, weak, and dependent. For instance, panhandlers may justify their requests for spare change by saying they are hungry or homeless, or students may beg professors for higher grades in class because they are on academic probation and will be thrown out of school if they don't get a certain grade. By creating an aura of neediness, supplication is intended to make others feel responsible for our needs. Consequently, others may decide to help. Supplication is usually the self-presentation technique of last resort, used by people with little power.

THE LANGUAGE OF SELF-PRESENTATION: MAINTAINING SOCIAL CONTROL THROUGH WORDS AND ACTIONS

Perhaps you've been surprised, and even slightly annoyed, by a telephone salesperson who calls you at home and uses your first name as if you were longtime friends. Or perhaps you've overheard a conversation between a young physician and an elderly patient in which the physician uses the patient's first name, while the patient addresses the physician with the formal title "Doctor."

The spoken word and self-presentation.   As these two examples illustrate, the spoken language that people employ has important self-presentational consequences (Levinson, 1980; Clark, 1985). The choice of language helps to maintain and direct the social relationship between two speakers. For instance, a difference in status between two speakers is often represented in the way the two people address each other (Duranti, 1992). People use first names when addressing close friends, and they use formal titles (Dr., Congressman, Ms.) and last names when addressing someone of higher status. Within a status level, there is a fairly strong tendency to reciprocate the level of formality in address.

When two people at different status levels have been addressing each other at different levels of intimacy, such as Mr. Coats (the boss), who addresses his employee as "Erik," the form of address may eventually change as the level of intimacy evolves. However, such changes usually occur only at the behest of the higher-status person. For instance, it is likely that Mr. Coats would have to ask Erik to address him more informally before Erik would do so.

According to social psychologist Roger Brown and colleagues, choices of personal address are based on the power semantic and the solidarity semantic (Brown & Gilman, 1960; Brown, 1996). The **power semantic** is the power or status level that a conversant holds, whereas the **solidarity semantic** refers to the degree of shared social experience that exists between two people. The power semantic suggests that people of greater power or status ought to be addressed with great formality, whereas the solidarity semantic operates to allow greater familiarly between people in situations of social closeness, for example, between close neighbors, friends, or classmates (Ng & Bradac, 1993).

In many languages other than English, the existence of distinct forms of the word *you* allows for power and solidarity semantics to be reflected in the form that a speaker chooses—the formal or informal. In French, a speaker must choose between *tu* (familiar) and *vous* (formal); in German, the choice is between *du* (familiar) and *Sie* (formal). Each culture has its own set of rules. For example, the French use *tu* for intimate friends, family, and children, and *vous* for nonfamilial adults. And children use *vous* for all adults except their closest family members.

Some shifts have occurred in the use of the formal and informal *you* that seem to reflect historical and cultural changes in society. In societies that have moved toward greater egalitarianism, the trend has been toward less of a distinction in use between the formal and informal *you*. In modern France, for example, more people are addressed by the informal *tu* than ever before. And at one time, English speakers had a choice between the formal *you* and the informal *thou,* a distinction that has long since disappeared from everyday conversation.

In addition to conveying the nature of intimacy between conversants, the language one employs also helps create impressions regarding one's political leanings. Thus, people who consistently address women as "Ms." rather than "Miss" or "Mrs." may be making a political statement regarding their views of feminism (Tannen, 1991, 1993).

Finally, as we consider in the Social Web box, language is an important component—and, in some cases, the *only* component—of self-presentation on the World Wide Web.

Nonverbal behavior and self-presentation: Making use of display rules. When people receive gifts that turn out to be disappointing, they rarely frown, pout, or otherwise outwardly display signs of unhappiness. Instead, people in this situation are likely to smile and proclaim how pleased they are to have received, for instance, a package of socks and underwear. What prevents these people from revealing how they actually feel is the existence of social norms that define appropriate behavior. Social norms are learned early in life and tell us, among other things, that gift givers should be thanked and made to feel that their gifts are appreciated. Such norms influence not only verbal behavior, but nonverbal behavior as well.

SOCIAL.WEB
PRESENTING YOURSELF ON THE INTERNET: LANGUAGE CHANGES FOR :-) AND :-(

OFF CPRING: Wuzup?
PRETYFLI5: n2m
OFF CPRING: well g/g c ya

Loose translation: Not too much is up with Prettyfli5, and Off Cpring has got to go and will see Prettyfli5 later. (Harmon, 1999, p. B7)

If all this seems like Greek to you, you haven't been spending much time using the Internet. The newest forms of communication—e-mail and online chat groups—are spawning a language all their own, changing the way in which people present themselves through their use of written language.

One of the earliest Internet developments in terms of self-presentation was the use of *smileys,* the combination of letters and symbols designed to communicate emotion. Meant to overcome the loss of verbal nuances in written communication, smileys range from the straightforward, such as :-) (good/pleased/happy) and :-((bad/displeased/sad) to the more unusual, such as :-! (foot in mouth) and @@@@:-) (Marge Simpson). Some e-mailers took particular pleasure in devising exotic smileys in an effort to demonstrate their sophistication with the medium. More recently, the visually oriented smileys have been replaced with a more direct written description of the sentiment behind the smiley, such as (grin) or (shrug), as well as the widespread use of abbreviations.

In addition to smileys and abbreviations, the Internet has spawned a vocabulary of its own, particularly in terms of negative labels applied to others' e-mail, behavior, and personal characteristics. For example, *spam* (junk e-mail) and *flame* (a nasty or insulting critical message) are two common words with special Internet meanings. More exotic labels include *Cancel-Bunny* (a person who deletes others' messages) and *spod* (a computer geek without any redeeming qualities).

The speed and ease with which e-mail can be created facilitates communication. And, according to Larry Friedlander, a professor at Stanford University, it helps in the development of new skills, including the ability to formulate ideas quickly. In the end, he says, "Language is a tool. It's a tool with which we bring things together and create intimacy in our lives" (Harmon, 1999, A17).

On the other hand, sometimes the intimacy is more apparent than real. It is not rare for people to misrepresent their age, occupation, and gender when they use online chat groups. Furthermore, it is easier to be critical or negative toward another person when one is communicating anonymously. In fact, some researchers argue that the anonymity of some forms of Internet communication can lead to more antisocial behavior than one would find in face-to-face interaction, although the evidence is mixed. What is clear is that the way in which people present themselves on the Internet continues to evolve at a rapid pace (Kiesler, Siegel, & McGuire, 1984; Turkle, 1997; McKenna & Bargh, 1998).

self-verification: The desire to be perceived by others in a way that is consistent with our self-concept.

The guidelines that govern what society sees as appropriate nonverbal behavior are known as display rules (Ekman & Friesen, 1975; Ekman & O'Sullivan, 1991; Andersen & Guerrero, 1998). *Display rules* (as we discussed briefly in Chapter 2) are the implicit rules that define what type of nonverbal behavior is appropriate for a given situation or interpersonal relationship, and what type is not. Display rules are learned during childhood as children's cognitive abilities and control of facial muscles increase (Feldman, 1982; Feldman & Rimé, 1991; Halberstadt, 1991; Halberstadt et al., 1992; Banerjee, 1997).

There are at least four strategies through which display rules can modify the expression of emotion: *intensifying, deintensifying, neutralizing,* and *masking an emotion* (Ekman, Friesen, & Ellsworth, 1972). In intensification, a person exaggerates an expression, such as a smile, in order to convey the appearance of a stronger emotion than he or she is actually feeling. In deintensification, the opposite occurs: The communication of a felt emotion is minimized. For example, when we have bested someone in a business negotiation, we may try not to show how happy we are; rather, we may try to minimize our true delight.

When people neutralize an expression, they attempt to withhold any indication of how they actually feel. The term *poker face* characterizes a person's attempt to show no emotion of any sort. This is accomplished by neutralizing the nonverbal expressions representative of emotions that are actually being experienced.

The most extreme form of modification of nonverbal behavior occurs when someone masks one expression with another. For instance, you might mask your glee at the funeral of an old and hated rival with appropriate expressions of grief, or you might smile and congratulate the winner of a race for which you had trained extensively. In both examples, the expression being displayed is precisely the opposite of the feeling being experienced.

How successful are people at self-presentation through the modification of facial expressions? Although the research evidence is not entirely consistent, in many cases people are able to manage and disguise their nonverbal behavior successfully (DePaulo, 1991; Miller & Stiff, 1992; Ekman, 1997). However, no matter how much effort they employ, there are always visible differences between true and feigned emotional displays.

For instance, psychologist Paul Ekman and colleagues have found differences between true smiles of enjoyment and smiles produced to conceal negative emotions (Ekman, Friesen, & O'Sullivan, 1988; Frank, Ekman, & Friesen, 1997). True smiles, known as "Duchenne smiles," involve a unique pattern of facial muscles that does not appear in false smiles (see Figure 4–10, which illustrates the subtle difference between feigned and Duchenne smiles).

Given that display rules are socialized during childhood, it should not be surprising that the rules vary greatly across cultures and ethnicity (Matsumoto, 1992). For instance, in Asian cultures it is generally considered inappropriate to display emotions, whereas in Mediterranean and Latin cultures volatile nonverbal displays are expected in social interactions.

In addition to general differences in nonverbal expressiveness, research has found that cultures sometimes differ in the display of a particular emotion. For example, one study found that the Japanese, who place a strong emphasis on group harmony and cohesion within their own ingroup, felt that nonverbal displays of anger and disgust were more appropriately shown to outgroup members than to ingroup members. In contrast, people in the United States, a more individualistic culture, felt that displays of anger, disgust, and sadness were more permissible toward members of ingroups than outgroups (Matsumoto, 1990; Lee et al., 1992).

(For an applied view on the topic of self-presentation, see the accompanying Speaking of Social Psychology interview with political consultant Tobe Berkovitz.)

SELF-VERIFICATION: SEE ME AS I VIEW MYSELF

We're not always out to make ourselves look good. In fact, under some circumstances, we strive to make others see us as we really are.

According to William Swann (1987, 1992, 1997), people wish to be seen in a way that matches their view of themselves. **Self-verification** is the desire to be perceived by others in

a   b

c

FIGURE 4–10   Which Is the True Smile? The smile in (a) is a Duchenne (true) smile, whereas those in (b) and (c) are false, masking smiles. (*Source:* Ekman, Friesen, & O'Sullivan, 1988.)

a way that is consistent with our self-concept. For instance, if I see myself as a good student, I will be motivated to receive feedback from others that will confirm that I am academically capable. If I see myself as warm, friendly, and sociable, I will endeavor to find situations that make others see me as socially skilled.

But what if I view myself in negative terms? If I view myself as a lackluster student or as socially inept, will I really be motivated to verify my shortcomings? Swann and colleagues argue that the answer is yes. According to their research, in some cases our motivation to present ourselves well takes a backseat to our desire for self-verification.

For example, one study found that people prefer friends who view them as they perceive themselves, even if their self-perception is negative. Similarly, participants in an experiment who held a positive self-concept were most likely to choose to interact with someone who they thought had evaluated them favorably. In contrast, participants with negative self-concepts were more likely to want to interact with a person who held an unfavorable view of them. Even married couples illustrate the phenomenon: People with positive self-concepts are more committed to their marriages when their spouses hold positive views of them, whereas those with negative self-concepts are more committed to spouses who see them more unfavorably (Swann, Stein-Seroussi, & Giesler, 1992; Swann, Hixon, & DeLaRonde, 1992; Ritts & Stein, 1995).

In short, we may seek out and prefer others who confirm our self-concepts—whether our self-concepts are good or bad. Sometimes, then, having others look at us favorably is less important than having them look at us accurately.

THE INFORMED CONSUMER OF SOCIAL PSYCHOLOGY

MAKING A GOOD IMPRESSION

Regardless of whether we are high or low self-monitors, all of us are concerned to some degree with presenting ourselves well—as much of the material in this chapter has illustrated. As it turns out, research conducted by social psychologists suggests several effective strategies for making a positive impression. In addition to the specific self-presentation techniques we have already discussed (such as ingratiation, self-promotion, intimidation, exemplification, and supplication), several broad principles underlie successful self-presentation (Snyder, 1977; Schlenker, 1980; Kleinke, 1986; Fiske & Taylor, 1991):

◆ *Conform to the social norms of a given situation.* Every social situation has particular norms that govern appropriate behavior. At a dance, it is permissible to dance with a friend's date, but asking for too many dances might be frowned upon. When we attend funerals, society suggests that we should wear dark colors and say only nice things about the recently departed, no matter how much we disliked him or her. Keeping situational norms in mind is central to creating a good impression (Sagatun & Knudsen, 1982).

◆ *Use behavioral matching.* Another way to produce a good impression is to try to match the behavior of others. Research indicates that people in successful interactions coordinate and synchronize their interpersonal interactions, on both a verbal and nonverbal level (Bernieri & Rosenthal, 1991).

SPEAKING OF SOCIAL PSYCHOLOGY

Tobe Berkovitz

Political Consultant

Year of Birth: 1949

Education: B.F.A., Theater, University of Connecticut; M.A., Dramatic Arts, University of Connecticut; Ph.D., Mass Communications, Wayne State University, Detroit, Michigan

Home: Brookline, Massachusetts

The communications theorist Marshall McLuhan once observed that "Politics will eventually be replaced by imagery. The politician will be only too happy to abdicate in favor of his image, because the image will be much more powerful than he could ever be."

McLuhan's prediction may well have come true, partially due to the explosion of electronic media, and partially through the efforts of political consultants used by politicians to create an image for themselves and increase their chances of being elected to office.

Tobe Berkovitz has been a political consultant for numerous congressional candidates over the past 20 years. He concurs with McLuhan, adding that an important attribute for today's politicians is their ability to present themselves with confidence.

"A lot of a candidate's self-presentation has to do with inner confidence. Candidates have to have self-assurance both in their personal character and politics," he said. "They have to be confident and sure of themselves as individuals, and at the same time be secure in their understanding of their ideology, political beliefs, and positions."

"A lot of a candidate's self-presentation has to do with inner confidence."

◆ *Use verbal immediacy in your conversations.* "Immediacy" refers to the directness and intensity of verbal communications. For example, saying "I'd like to go with you to the lecture" is more immediate than saying "I guess I'll go to the lecture." Qualifications such as "maybe," "I suppose," "kind of," and "I think" make communications less immediate, and they are seen by others as being less personal. Consequently, more immediate communications make a more positive impression.

◆ *Keep verbal and nonverbal behavior consistent with each another.* To be perceived as genuine and trustworthy, you must ensure that verbal and nonverbal messages match. If you're trying to convey the message that you are pleased, make sure that your nonverbal behavior matches what you are saying. Otherwise, you may come across as counterfeit and deceptive (Feldman, 1992).

◆ *Don't overstate your accomplishments—but don't understate them, either.* Honesty *is* the best policy when it comes to discussing your positive assets. If you exaggerate your accomplishments, you'll be seen as a braggart. If you minimize your assets, you're not putting your best foot forward, and you may be seen as lacking confidence. Presenting yourself effectively, then, is in part a matter of presenting yourself honestly.

Is likeability as critical as competence in a political candidate? According to Berkovitz, likeability is a crucial factor.

"In fact, likeability may be more important than competence," he noted. "This is a result of the age of television. We are living in a video environment, and likeability has become more and more important. It can be demonstrated by the warmth and charm that a candidate exudes in his or her communications style. But it has to be inherent and part of the candidate's human nature. It's difficult to pour on the charm and warmth if it's not part of you."

> *"In fact, likeability may be more important than competence."*

Leadership, intelligence, and character also are important attributes that most voters seek in their elected officials, and Berkovitz notes that the candidate must be strong in all three areas.

"To show leadership, you have to be confident and decisive," he said. "You can't appear to waver. Intelligence is being able to articulate your position, and character is about the moral courage to take a stand and demonstrate that your values are unshakable."

Because of the intensity of the media and television in particular, today's political candidates can readily use self-promotion techniques, sometimes without even appearing to do so.

"This is the duality of the media age," Berkovitz explained. "It works on the conscious and subconscious level at the same time. You as a voter are aware of being manipulated, but you're also not protected by that knowledge."

And what advice does Berkovitz have for those who wish to go into the field of political consulting?

"The first thing to do is get involved in politics and political campaigns. Campaigns live by volunteers and interns, and they are everywhere," he said. "And second, follow the news. You have to be a constant communications grazer, understanding the issues and what goes on in the world."

REVIEW AND RETHINK

Review

- People differ widely in their levels of self-monitoring, through which they regulate their behavior to meet the demands of a situation or the expectations of others.

- Self-presentation, the result of audience-pleasing and self-construction motivations, occurs through both verbal and nonverbal behavior.

- Several strategies underlie self-presentation, including ingratiation, self-promotion, intimidation, exemplification, and supplication.

- Both spoken language and nonverbal behavior convey important self-presentation messages.

- Despite the desire to present a favorable image, people also strive for self-verification, the desire to be perceived in ways that are consistent with their self-concepts.

Rethink

- Discuss three possible reasons that people actively use self-presentation techniques.

- High and low self-monitors often choose different self-presentational techniques. Discuss the types of self-presentation, focusing on which group would be likely to prefer each one.

- Using the notions of power semantic and solidarity semantic, explain how an employee might begin referring to his supervisor by first name instead of Mr. Y or Ms. Z.

- Explain how different norms regarding nonverbal display might contribute to stereotypes about "inscrutable Asians." What corresponding stereotypes might Asians hold about Americans?

LOOKING BACK

What are the components of the self?

1. Self-concept is a person's sense of identity, the set of beliefs about what he or she is like as an individual. (p. 114)

2. Cognitions about identity compose the self-schema, an organized body of information that relates to a person's self and pertains to specific domains, such as dependence or femininity. In addition to self-schemas, part of the self is composed of possible selves, those aspects of self that relate to the future. (p. 114)

3. The concept of identity reflects roles and group categories to which a person belongs (the social identity), along with the set of personal meanings and experiences related to those roles and categories (the personal identity). (p. 117)

How do people use others' (and their own) behavior to assess their abilities, emotions, and attitudes?

4. Because people have a need to evaluate their opinions and abilities—a need for social comparison—they compare themselves to others who are similar along relevant dimensions. (p. 119)

5. The two-factor theory of emotions suggests that when people are unsure about how they feel, they may infer their emotional state by observing the behavior of others and the nature of the situation in which they find themselves. (p. 120)

6. Self-perception theory suggests that, to the extent that situational cues or past experience are irrelevant, weak, or ambiguous, people become aware of their own dispositions, emotions, attitudes, and other internal states through observation of their own behavior. One derivative of the theory is the concept of overjustification, which may occur when external incentives replace intrinsic motivation. (p. 120)

7. Action identification theory suggests that people's interpretation of their own behavior varies in terms of whether the behavior is seen at a high (abstract) or low (more concrete) level. According to the theory, the level at which people typically view their current actions affects the stability of their behavior and has implications for their ability to change their behavior. (p. 122)

8. One cultural difference in the view of self is exemplified in Western and Asian cultures. Asian societies tend to have a more interdependent view of the self, whereas people living in Western countries tend to view the self more independently. (p. 122)

How do self-esteem and self-awareness affect people's interactions with others?

9. Self-esteem is the affective component of self, consisting of a person's general and specific positive and negative self-evaluations. Low self-esteem may lead to a cycle of failure, although the cycle may be overcome by increasing a person's sense of self-efficacy—learned expectations that one is capable of carrying out a behavior or producing a desired outcome in a particular situation. (p. 124)

10. Self-evaluation maintenance theory predicts that people will react to the accomplishments of important people in their lives by showing either jealousy (if the other person's success is in an area that is central to one's view of oneself) or pride (if the success is in an area that is not central). (p. 127)

11. Self-awareness involves focusing attention on the self. Increased self-awareness can lead people to compare their actual selves to the ideal standards they hold for themselves, a process that typically results in an unpleasant affective state. (p. 128)

12. The two types of self-awareness are private self-consciousness and public self-consciousness. People vary in the type of self-consciousness that they typically experience. (p. 129)

What biases exist in the ways people view themselves?

13. The actor–observer bias is the tendency for actors (the individuals involved in a situation) to attribute their behavior to situational requirements, whereas observers tend to attribute the same behaviors to stable dispositions. Perceptual and informational reasons have been suggested to explain the phenomenon. (p. 130)

14. Self-handicapping is a tactic by which people set up circumstances that allow them to avoid attributing poor performance to low ability and enable them to attribute it instead to less threatening causes. (p. 131)

15. Self-handicapping strategies fall along two dimensions—internal versus external, and acquired versus claimed. Not all self-handicapping is strategically wrong; the use of excuses, for instance, can have benefits for self-esteem and achievement. (p. 131)

What self-presentation strategies do people employ, and which are most effective?

16. Self-presentation, or impression management, is the process by which people attempt to create specific, generally positive impressions regarding themselves. People differ in their typical level of self-monitoring, which consists of regulating one's behavior to meet the demands of a situation or the expectations of others. (p. 136)

17. Two main motives lie behind self-monitoring efforts—audience pleasing (focused on pleasing others) and self-construction (meant to confirm one's view of oneself). (p. 137)

18. Among the self-presentational strategies that people employ are ingratiation, self-promotion, intimidation, exemplification, and supplication. Language and nonverbal behavior also support self-presentation, the latter through culturally appropriate display rules. (p. 138)

19. Self-verification is the desire to be perceived by others in ways that are consistent with one's self-concept, whether positive or negative. (p. 142)

20. Ways that people can make a favorable impression on others include conforming to the social norms of a given situation, using behavioral matching, using verbal immediacy in conversation, maintaining congruence between verbal and nonverbal behavior, and stating one's accomplishments accurately. (p. 144)

EPILOGUE

In our consideration of the self, we've focused on how people view and evaluate themselves, and their strategies for presenting themselves effectively to the world. Put another way, we've examined the self in term of its cognitive, affective, and behavioral components. As we'll see in Chapters 10 and 11, such a three-part consideration of self mirrors the view, held by many theorists, that attitudes are composed of cognitive, affective, and behavioral components.

What we haven't yet discussed, though, is how our sense of self relates to our general well-being, on both a psychological and a physical level. In the next chapter we turn to this issue, considering how social psychological factors underlie both our physical and our mental health.

To round out our consideration of the self, then, we consider such topics as how our sense of well-being is affected by the kinds of illusions we hold about ourselves and the world, how we cope with stress, and how major health problems have social psychological components. In our discussion of these topics, we'll discover how the understanding of the self that we arrived at in this chapter leads to concrete suggestions regarding how to better people's physical and mental resiliency and coping capabilities.

Before we proceed to the next chapter, turn back to the prologue and read again about President Clinton. Consider the following questions:

1. Identity is often said to be an especially complex issue for public "personalities." What conflicts might Clinton experience between his social identity and his personal identity?

2. Would you suppose that Clinton is high in public self-consciousness or private self-consciousness, or perhaps both? Why?

3. Do you think Clinton is a high or low self-monitor? Why?

4. What strategies of self-presentation (ingratiation, self-promotion, intimidation, exemplification, or supplication) do you think Clinton uses? Why? Can you think of public people who use different strategies?

KEY TERMS AND CONCEPTS

action identification theory (p. 122)

actor–observer bias (p. 130)

audience pleasing (p. 137)

exemplification (p. 139)

extrinsic motivation (p. 121)

identity (p. 117)

ingratiation (p. 138)

intimidation (p. 139)

intrinsic motivation (p. 121)

overjustification (p. 121)

possible selves (p. 116)

power semantic (p. 140)

private self-consciousness (p. 129)

public self-consciousness (p. 129)

self-awareness (p. 128)

self-concept (p. 114)

self-construction (p. 137)

self-efficacy (p. 125)

self-esteem (p. 124)

self-evaluation maintenance theory (p. 127)

self-handicapping (p. 131)

self-monitoring (p. 136)

self-perception theory (p. 120)

self-presentation (p. 136)

self-promotion (p. 139)

self-reference effect (p. 115)

self-schema (p. 114)

self-verification (p. 142)

social comparison (p. 119)

solidarity semantic (p. 140)

stereotype vulnerability (p. 127)

supplication (p. 140)

two-factor theory of emotion (p. 120)

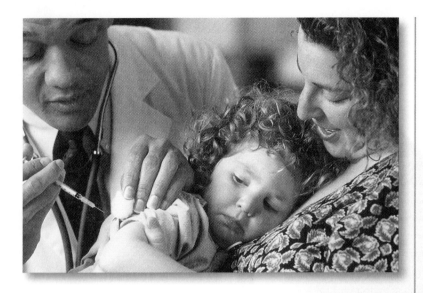

CHAPTER 5

WELL-BEING
AND THE SELF

Applying Social
Psychology to Health
and Wellness

PROLOGUE

Do It, and Do It Now

Elizabeth Oettinger's day sometimes seems like an endless to-do list.

Here's a typical day in the life of Elizabeth Oettinger, minister and single mother, with two daughters, Jessie, 16, and Sarah, 14, living in Corvallis, Oregon:

5:30 A.M.   Elizabeth wakes to the sound of Jessie's alarm clock, but stays in bed for 15 minutes to "work things out."

5:48 A.M.   Feeds the dog and four cats. Puts in a load of laundry.

6:55 A.M.   Drives Sarah (and her cello) to orchestra practice.

7:40 A.M.   Arrives back home, showers, then checks her e-mail to see if her friend from Idaho will visit today. No word.

8:10 A.M.   Does another load of laundry, cleans the kitchen.

8:25 A.M.   Drives to church, stopping at the Starbucks downtown for a tall latte: 2% and sweetner.

8:59 A.M.   Gets fitted for a silk-and-cotton stole for her vestments, by a congregant who is a fiber artist.

10:02 A.M.   Dashes home for the spanakopita she baked for the ministers' 11 o'clock meeting. Reads Corvallis Gazette-Times' obituaries, then the local news. Checks e-mail: still no word from Idaho friend.

10:40 A.M.   Drives to Sarah's school to drop off her lunch, which she forgot. Leaves her car with her "whatever he is, soon-to-be-ex-husband," whose own ride is in the shop.

11:00 A.M.   Back at the monthly clergy meeting, she finds her friend from Idaho in attendance. Under discussion: the role of female pastors.

2:30 P.M.   Speaks with a new parishioner about the congregation. Assures her that the church has an "open and affirming" attitude toward lesbians and gay men.

3:45 P.M.   Catches a lift home. Talks with Jessie about her lesson and her physics class, where she was disappointed to receive her first B. Leaves, in Jessie's car, to visit a sick parishioner.

4:47 P.M.   Drives home, praying on the way. "One of these days I'm going to write a book about car prayer. Travel time is the time that I have to be reflective."

5:02 P.M.   Checks on Sarah's homework progress and returns phone calls.

5:21 P.M.   Leaves for her first session with her therapist, to whom the church referred her after her separation. "They just wanted to make sure I had a place to take my stuff."

6:31 P.M.   Returns home and heats up a quick dinner of beef-and-vegetable soup. The girls say grace: "Thank you, God, for the food. Amen."

7:31 P.M.   Leaves for a meeting of the Corvallis Youth symphony, for which she's arranging a fund-raiser.

9:15 P.M.   Back home, helps Jessie with a speech she's writing for school, then watches the last half of "E.R."

11:04 P.M.   Tucks the girls in.

11:16 P.M.   Gets into bed. Prays. "There are people I promise to pray for during the day. This is when I get to do it." Sleeps. (D'Antoni, 1999, p. 26) ■

LOOKING AHEAD

For many people, this is the age of the endless to-do list. Whether it's picking up a quick dinner at McDonald's, writing a paper, getting to a job on time, doing the laundry, planning a party, or applying to graduate school—every item takes up that most precious of commodities: time. But this constant busyness does something else. It produces stress, which in turn requires continual coping efforts. And ultimately, if attempts at coping fail, stress leads to a number of consequences—none of them good—that affect people's sense of well-being and health.

In this chapter, we continue our focus on the self by considering social psychological issues relating to *well-being,* the sense of psychological and physical robustness, and **health psychology**, which focuses on physical health, illness, and wellness. Issues of well-being and health have become a central part of the discipline, and many social psychologists now concentrate on wellness and the prevention and treatment of medical problems.

We begin our discussion by focusing on psychological well-being and mental health. We'll consider how our view of the self influences our perception of well-being, how a sense of helplessness may lead to depression, and how attributional patterns affect psychological health. We also discuss how certain kinds of illusions we mistakenly hold may ultimately produce a sense of well-being.

Next, we consider stress and coping. We examine the causes of stress, its short- and long-term consequences, and the strategies that have been developed to deal with stress. We then turn to a discussion of three major health issues: coronary heart disease, cancer, and AIDS. We'll look in particular at the social psychological aspects of these illnesses, including the effects of social factors on the course of the diseases.

Finally, we discuss physician–patient interactions. We'll see that the way physicians and other health care workers communicate with patients has important implications for the

health psychology: The specialty area that focuses on physical health, illness, and wellness.

success of treatment, and we'll discuss how patient compliance with medical recommendations can be increased.

In sum, after reading this chapter, you'll be able to answer these questions:

◆ What are the ingredients of a sense of well-being?

◆ What are the determinants and consequences of stress, and what are some strategies for coping with it?

◆ What are the social psychological components of coronary heart disease, cancer, and AIDS?

◆ How do patients' interactions with their physicians affect their health and their compliance with medical treatment?

WELL-BEING

How are you?

If you're like most people, the answer you give will depend on a constellation of factors. Before you reply, you'll perhaps think about the bruise on your knee, or the headache you've had since you woke up, or the itching patch of poison ivy on your arm. However, you won't stop there: How you assess your well-being depends on psychological factors as well. Your mood, your emotional state, your level of anxiety—all will enter into your response to the question.

In sum, our overall sense of well-being is influenced as much by our everyday state of mind as it is by physiological factors. Building on theory and research on the self that we discussed in Chapter 4, social psychologists have examined the social psychological components that determine people's sense of well-being.

SELF-COMPLEXITY AND WELL-BEING: THE BENEFITS OF MULTIPLE SELVES

Do you see yourself as primarily a woman or man, a student, or a son or daughter? Or is your view of yourself more multifaceted, made up of a complex mixture of roles and attributes? Although all of us hold various self-schemas of the sort we spoke about in Chapter 4, some people's views of themselves are more complex than other people's. According to social psychologist Patricia Linville (1987; Linville & Carlston, 1994), **self-complexity** is the phenomenon of viewing oneself as having many distinct facets.

Self-complexity functions as a barrier against illness and depression: People with higher self-complexity show greater resistance to depression brought about by stress, and their rate of physical stress-related illness is lower (Kalthoff & Neimeyer, 1993; Smith & Cohen, 1993; Evans, 1994; Tennen & Affleck, 1998).

How does self-complexity produce its benefits? The answer lies in the multiple roles that self-complexity encompasses. When a person with high self-complexity has difficulties on the job, for instance, she can turn for psychological compensation to successes that she is experiencing in other domains of her life. In contrast, when a woman with low self-complexity, who defines herself primarily in terms of her career performance, has problems on the job, the story is very different. Because she does not have as many alternative selves to turn to, the consequences of her job problems are more profound.

The findings relating to self-complexity help explain an otherwise puzzling phenomenon: Women who juggle jobs and family obligations often report a higher degree of mastery, pride, and competence than women who stay at home to raise their children (Hoffman, 1989; Crosby, 1991). Although they report high levels of stress (Beena & Poduval, 1992; Duxbury, Higgins, & Lee, 1994) and typically do a greater percentage of the housework than their husbands (Googans & Burden, 1987; Biernat & Wortman, 1991; Duxbury & Higgins, 1991), women who both work and raise children still end up with a greater sense of psychological well-being than women who don't have jobs outside the home.

self-complexity: The phenomenon of viewing oneself as having many distinct facets.

One explanation is that the self-complexity of working mothers increases, providing them with a buffer against stress and stress-related illness (Rosenbaum & Cohen, 1999). When they experience problems in one domain, women who work and raise a family can turn to the positive aspects of their other roles. Ironically, then, the stress of having more than enough to do may sometimes help as much as it hurts.

SELF-DISCREPANCY THEORY: MATCHING REAL AND IDEAL

Who we are is not always who we would like to be. Despite our desire to be brilliant, likable, and terrific-looking, the truth is that many of us see ourselves as quite different from our ideal.

According to social psychologist E. Tory Higgins's self-discrepancy theory, people compare their self-view to internalized standards called *self-guides*. **Self-discrepancy theory** argues that the discrepancy between self-concept and self-guides leads to negative emotions and ultimately to lower psychological well-being (Higgins, 1989).

What are the self-guides to which the theory refers? Self-guides are the standards that people strive to attain. There are actually several types of self-guides, including the ideal self and the ought self. The *ideal self* is made up of the hopes and aspirations that either the person or others feel are important. For instance, your ideal self might consist of being a successful athlete and being likable and popular. In contrast, the *ought self* is composed of what people feel they ought to do—the obligations they place on themselves and on others. For example, your ought self might consist of devoting yourself to academics and doing community service.

In short, the ideal self is what people want to be, and the ought self is what people feel they should be. What happens when there is a discrepancy between our ideal or ought selves, on the one hand, and the reality of who we are? Failure to match our internal standards may have a negative impact on our sense of who we are (Polasky & Holahan, 1998). For instance, discrepancies between our ought self and our actual behavior may result in guilt, shame, and fear, while discrepancies between our ideal self and our actual self can produce disappointment, sadness, and dissatisfaction. Ultimately, such emotions can lead to depression and reduced self-esteem. Furthermore, such self-discrepancies can produce a chronic sense of indecision and confusion about one's identity (Alexander & Higgins, 1993; Scott & O'Hara, 1993; Kikendall, 1994).

At the same time, minor inconsistencies between actual self and self-guides can be helpful in sparking efforts to reduce the discrepancy (Higgins, Strauman, & Klein, 1986; Duval, Duval, & Mulilis, 1992). In such cases, incongruities between actual self and self-guides promote psychological well-being if people feel a sense of progress in reducing the gap between their various selves.

SELF-DISCLOSURE AND WELL-BEING: CONFESSION MAY BE GOOD FOR THE SOUL

How open are you with others?

In certain ways, according to some social psychologists, the more you disclose about yourself the better. According to this reasoning, **self-disclosure**, in which information about the self is exchanged with others, holds several advantages.

For example, as we'll discuss further in Chapter 7, one important consequence of self-disclosure is an increase in the level of intimacy in social interactions. This increased intimacy may in turn provide social support that can help reduce stress. Self-disclosure also may promote more honest responses from others, who may then become more useful sounding boards. In this situation, others ultimately may provide worthwhile feedback that can reduce stress (Derlega et al., 1993; Johnson, Hobfoll, & Zalcberg-Linetzy, 1993; Emmons & Colby, 1995).

Furthermore, according to the research of social psychologist James Pennebaker, self-disclosure may be good not only for the soul, but also for the mind and the body. Pennebaker and colleagues have found that giving people the opportunity to air their most personal and

self-discrepancy theory: The theory that states that the discrepancy between self-concept and self-guides leads to negative emotions and ultimately to lower psychological well-being.

self-disclosure: A situation in which information about the self is exchanged with others.

"I'm only a <u>good</u> dane."

disturbing experiences, which they typically have kept hidden, produces clear health benefits (Pennebaker, 1990; Davison & Pennebaker, 1997; Petrie, Booth, & Pennebaker, 1998).

In a series of experiments, Pennebaker explored the effects of revealing information that people usually keep to themselves. For example, in one study, groups of healthy undergraduates were asked to write over a 4-day period a series of anonymous essays about the most traumatic, emotionally upsetting, and stressful events they had experienced during their lifetimes. One group was told only to describe the events factually; members of a second group were instructed not to write about the facts, but only about their feelings regarding the facts; and a third group wrote about both the facts *and* their feelings concerning the events. There was also a control group that wrote about insignificant topics for the 4-day period (Pennebaker & Beall, 1986).

The nature of participants' confessions had important, long-lasting consequences. Participants who wrote about the emotions connected with past traumatic events, or about combined facts and emotions, reported feeling the most upset directly after their participation in the study. However, the long-term outcomes for one of these groups were more positive. Six months after the study, participants who had written about the facts *and* their emotions reported feeling healthier and experiencing fewer illnesses, as well as fewer days of restricted activity due to illness, than participants in the other groups.

In short, although initially upsetting to the participants, the disclosure of traumatic information proved to have lasting benefits (Petrie et al., 1995). But why should confession be so worthwhile? One reason is that inhibiting or restraining traumatic information requires both a physical and a mental effort. This effort results in heightened stress that ultimately produces physical symptoms and stress-related illness. Conversely, disclosing hidden traumas, even if only during the course of a psychological experiment, provides a temporary respite in the effort required to suppress the information. Ultimately, this results in reduced stress and an enhanced sense of well-being.

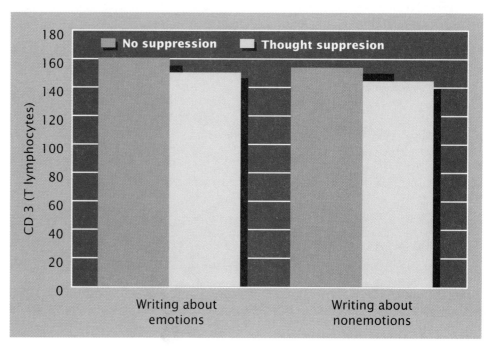

FIGURE 5–1   The Value of Confession Participants in an experiment who were told to suppress their thoughts by putting them "out of their mind" showed a decrease in cells involved in the functioning of the immune system. (*Source:* Petrie, Booth, & Pennebaker, 1998, p. 1269.)

Direct support for this reasoning comes from a recent study in which participants were asked to suppress their thoughts, being told to concentrate on putting thoughts "out of their minds" about descriptions they wrote of either important emotional events or nonemotional events. Compared with participants who were encouraged to think about what they had written, blood samples showed that thought suppressors showed an immediate decrease in CD3 (T lymphocyte) cells, cells which are involved in the operation of the immune system (see Figure 5–1). Other research concurs: The conditions of patients with chronic asthma or rheumatoid arthritis improved after being given the opportunity to write about emotion-laden experiences in their lives (Petrie, Booth, & Pennebaker, 1998; Smyth et al., 1999).

There's another reason confession is worthwhile: When we reveal past traumatic events, either aloud or in writing, we are forced to translate the occurrence into linguistic terms, thereby confronting the event in a way that may be novel to us. In fact, the use of language may transform unpleasant events into information that is more coherent and understandable. Ultimately, this translation makes it possible to cope with stress more readily (Pennebaker, 1990, 1993, 1998; Mancuso & Pennebaker, 1994).

SELF-REGULATION FAILURE: WHEN WE CAN'T CONTROL OURSELVES

Crime. Teen pregnancy. Drug abuse. Gambling.

If people could only control themselves better, such problems might well disappear. At least that's the idea behind work on **self-regulation failure**, inadequacies in the control of one's behavior. Self-regulation failures are seen in the actions of a dieter who goes on an eating binge, a person on a tight budget who goes on a spending spree, or a recovering alcoholic who goes on a "bender" (Baumeister & Heatherton, 1996; Heatherton & Baumeister, 1996; Baumeister et al., 1998).

According to social psychologists Roy Baumeister and Todd Heatherton, self-regulation failures actually take two forms: underregulation and misregulation. In *underregulation,* people are unable to exert self-control. People who crave cocaine and can't stop themselves from indulging in it and dieters who can't stay away from hot fudge sundaes exemplify

self-regulation failure: Inadequacies in the control of one's behavior.

underregulation. In contrast, *misregulation* is the attempt to exert control over oneself, but in ways that are either misguided or counterproductive; the result is another kind of self-regulation failure. For example, a student who seeks to do well at his studies may set unrealistically high goals for himself, enrolling only in difficult, time-consuming honors courses. Ironically, because his goals are unreasonably high, his efforts to succeed actually make him fail in a way that would not have occurred if he hadn't attempted self-regulation (Baumeister, Heatherton, & Tice, 1993, 1994).

Baumeister and Heatherton (1996) suggest that some forms of misregulation occur when people try to control things that simply cannot be easily controlled. For instance, people who try to control their moods directly are likely to be unsuccessful, since it is quite difficult to exert direct control over one's emotions. Not understanding this, they may end up feeling like failures—and, as a result, they may find themselves feeling worse than they did initially. Similarly, the attempt to drive unwanted thoughts from one's mind is doomed to failure (Wegner & Erber, 1992; Gold & Wegner, 1995; Lane & Wegner, 1995). For example, efforts to suppress thoughts of hunger ("I just won't think about how hungry I am on this diet") are likely to lead only to *more* thoughts of food and to emphasize how desperately hungry one is (Wegner, 1994).

In short, self-regulation failure is attributable to several causes. In summarizing their findings, Baumeister and Heatherton (1996) suggest that underregulation occurs because people

- lack stable, clear, consistent standards
- fail to monitor their actions sufficiently
- lack the strength to override the responses they wish to control

In contrast, misregulation occurs because people

- hold false assumptions about themselves and the world
- try to control things that can't be directly controlled
- focus on emotions, neglecting more basic problems

ATTRIBUTIONAL STYLE AND DEPRESSION: LEARNING TO BE DEPRESSED

Have you ever heard someone say, "No matter how hard I try, I'll never do better in math" or "I could rehearse until doomsday, but I know I'll never learn my lines"? To psychologist Martin Seligman, such statements would probably represent instances of learned helplessness. **Learned helplessness** is the belief that one can exert no control over one's environment. When people hold such a belief, they feel unable to escape their environment and may simply give up—leading, in some cases, to profound feelings of depression (Seligman, 1975).

Seligman first demonstrated learned helplessness in experiments with animals. In one experiment he exposed dogs to a series of moderately painful shocks that were not physically damaging but could not be avoided. Although at first the dogs anxiously tried to escape the shocks, they ultimately realized that escape was impossible and came to accept them with seeming resignation. It was their subsequent behavior that proved most puzzling: When the same dogs were later placed in a cage in which they *could* avoid the shocks simply by jumping over a short barrier, they did not. Instead, they passively accepted the shocks despite the opportunity to escape them. In contrast, a control group of animals, who had not been earlier exposed to the inescapable shocks, readily jumped over the barrier to avoid the shocks.

The results of the experiment convinced Seligman that the dogs had learned to be helpless. He argued that the animals that had earlier been exposed to the unavoidable shock had been taught a harsh, although erroneous, lesson—that there was no way to escape from the unpleasant experience, and the only way to deal with it was passive acceptance.

A series of later experiments convincingly demonstrated that not only animals, but humans, too, experienced the phenomenon. For instance, college students who were not permitted to escape a shrill tone early in an experiment later made fewer attempts to escape the tone than experimental participants who had not been exposed earlier to the tone—even

Learned helplessness, the belief that no control can be exerted over one's environment, may prevent battered spouses and children from seeking help.

when the opportunity to escape was available (Hiroto & Seligman, 1975; Mineka & Hendersen, 1985).

Learned helplessness has proved to be a durable concept, relevant to both physical health and general psychological well-being (e.g., McKean, 1994). For example, battered children and spouses sometimes do not seek help even when given the opportunity; they come to accept passively what is happening to them and feel that there is no way out. Similarly, learned helplessness provides an explanation for severe depression, in which people come to feel that they are the victims of a hostile world that is beyond their control. Specifically, clinical psychologist Lynn Abramson and colleagues suggest that depression may be the result of hopelessness, a combination of learned helplessness and an expectation that negative outcomes in one's life are inevitable (Abramson, Metalsky, & Alloy, 1989; Abramson, Alloy, & Metalsky, 1995; Showers, Abramson, & Hogan, 1998).

Abramson suggests that depression is related to three major types of attributions: stable versus unstable, internal versus external, and global versus specific. The stable–unstable dimension refers to whether the cause of an event is seen as enduring across time (stable) or temporary (unstable). The internal–external dimension refers to whether the cause is seen as due to personal characteristics and behavior (internal) or to the situation (external). And the global–specific dimension relates to whether the cause is seen as affecting many different aspects of life (global) or as being restricted to a particular domain (specific).

Those most prone to depression caused by learned helplessness tend to have a particular **attributional style**, a tendency to make certain kinds of causal attributions across different situations (see Figure 5–2; Alloy, Lipman, & Abramson, 1992; Joiner, Metalsky, & Wonderlich, 1995; Haack et al., 1996). According to this view, people at risk for depression habitually attribute *positive* events in their lives to external, unstable, and situation-specific causes (Gladstone & Kaslow, 1995). For instance, a person with such an attributional style would attribute getting a good job to causes that are external ("The employer was desperate to hire"), unstable ("It was just luck"), and situation-specific ("It probably won't happen again").

At the same time, people prone to depression attribute *negative* events to internal, stable, and global causes (Gladstone & Kaslow, 1995; Rodriguez & Pehi, 1998; Dill & Anderson, 1999). For instance, losing a job would be attributed to causes that are internal ("I'm no good"), stable ("I'll never be any better"), and global ("No matter what I do, I fail"). When individuals who characteristically make such attributions for positive and negative events encounter a situation in which they lack control or efficacy (Houston, 1995), they are apt to experience depression—as well as several other types of health difficulties (Robins, 1988; Burn, 1992; Pinto & Francis, 1993; Hilsman & Garber, 1995).

Although learned helplessness provides an explanation for severe depression, it is not the only cause. For example, genetic and biological factors may predispose people to the ups and downs of depression and related mental health disorders (Egeland et al., 1987; Roy, 1993; Grigoroiu-Serbanescu, 1994; Parker, 1994; Staner, Linkowski, & Mendlewicz, 1994; Syvalahti, 1994; Rossen & Buschmann, 1995). In addition, some psychologists argue that depression is the result of maladaptive cognitions (Kwon & Oei, 1994). For instance, clinical psychologist Aaron Beck has proposed that depressed people consider themselves to be life's losers, blaming themselves whenever anything goes wrong (Beck et al., 1979; Beck, 1991). Because they focus on the negative side of life, they feel incompetent and unable to make constructive changes.

However, depression is far from the norm. On the contrary, happiness seems to be the norm—as we consider in the Applying Social Psychology box.

Attribution training: Overhauling faulty attributions.   The fact that certain psychological disorders are the result of maladaptive attribution styles suggests a way of restoring psychological well-being: change people's attributional styles (Veeninga & Kraaimaat, 1995). In fact, social psychologists have developed several forms of **attribution training**, in which inaccurate, harmful attributions are replaced with more accurate, and beneficial, ones.

In attribution training, social psychologists attempt to alleviate psychological distress and anxiety by replacing internal attributions with external ones. Specifically, they may teach

attributional style: A tendency to make certain kinds of causal attributions across different situations.

attribution training: The approach in which inaccurate, harmful attributions are replaced with more accurate, and beneficial, ones.

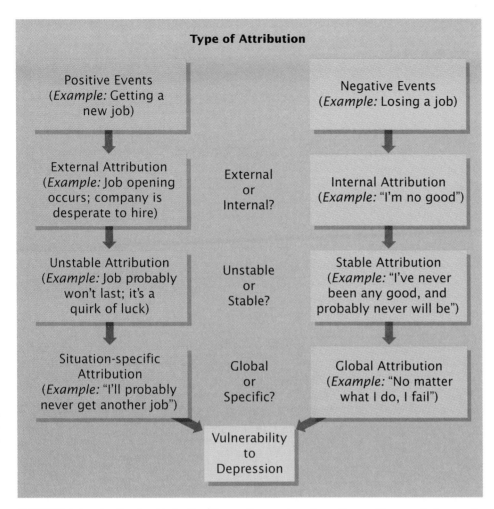

Type of Attribution

FIGURE 5–2   Attribution Styles Leading to Depression According to Abramson's theory of depression, people at risk for depression habitually view positive events as due to external, unstable, and specific causes. At the same time, they view negative events as produced by stable, internal, and global causes. Both patterns lead to depression. (*Source:* Based on Abramson, Metalsky, & Alloy, 1989.)

people to attribute negative events to some nonthreatening source outside themselves instead of to their own supposed failings.

Consider, for instance, the plight in which many first-year college students find themselves. If you think back to your own experience, you probably felt some trepidation about your academic performance, were unsure about how well you compared with your fellow classmates, and worried about whether you were doing as well as you could. If you initially performed poorly, you may have seen this as confirmation of your greatest fears, and perhaps you assumed that you just weren't cut out to make the grade—an attribution based on stable, internal causes.

If you felt this way, you weren't alone: Most first-year college students make similar attributions (Peterson & Barrett, 1987). However, research by social psychologists Timothy Wilson and Patricia Linville (1982, 1985) suggests a way, based on attribution retraining, to break this attributional pattern. They devised a program designed to change first-year students' attributions from stable to unstable causes. Basically, students were exposed to information that led them to attribute their problems to temporary factors that were amenable to change, instead of to permanent, unchangeable causes.

To test their reasoning, the experimenters exposed a group of first-year students at Duke University, who had expressed concern over their first-term performance, to statistical

Applying Social Psychology
Happiness: You Can't Buy It, But You Probably Already Have It

If you won the lottery, you'd be a lot happier. Right?

Wrong. According to a growing body of research, although your spirits might rise for a while, by a year later, you would most likely return to your previous level of happiness. In fact, even people who suffer spinal cord injuries reestablish previous levels of happiness after time has gone by (Diener et al., 1999).

The reason behind these phenomena may in part be genetic. Studies of twins suggest that people have a *set point* for happiness, a genetically determined characteristic level of mood. Although circumstances can temporarily elevate or depress mood, people ultimately return to their general level of happiness (Diener & Diener, 1996; Lykken & Tellegen, 1996).

In twins research, investigators found that identical twins who were raised apart showed little difference in their ratings of their own happiness, even though their circumstances in life varied widely. Salary, marital status, and education were related to happiness to only a minor degree (Lykken & Tellegen, 1996).

Of course, people do vary in their happiness depending on life events. A death in the family or the loss of a job is going to temporarily depress an individual's mood, just as getting married or a new job will elevate a person's mood. However, the set point theory suggests that both the depression and elevation in mood will be temporary, and that people ultimately will return to their general level of happiness.

Interestingly, most people have happiness set points that are relatively high. For instance, surveys show that 3 out of 10 U.S. citizens say they are "very happy," and only 1 in 10 say that they are "not too happy." Most admit to being "pretty happy." Furthermore, there is no difference between men and women in their views of how happy they are, and ethnicity, culture, and geography play only a small role. For instance, African Americans are only slightly less likely than European Americans to rate themselves as "very happy" (Myers & Diener, 1996; Mroczek & Kolarz, 1998; Schkade & Kahneman, 1998; Staudinger, Fleeson, & Baltes, 1999).

Long-term trends in level of happiness show little change. As can be seen in Figure 5–3, despite substantial increases in levels of disposable income, even after controlling for inflation and taxes, the level of happiness stayed remarkably stable over a 40-year period in the United States (Diener et al., 1999).

In short, people, in general, tend to be happy. And—according to set point theory—even when bad things happen to them, they are apt to eventually return to their happy state. The down side of this set point view of well-being: That glow people feel following a great accomplishment is also likely to fade, as they eventually return to their characteristic level of happiness.

---

information demonstrating that college students typically improve their grades over the course of their college careers. In addition, the participants watched videotapes of juniors and seniors discussing how their grades had improved since their freshman year.

In comparison to members of a control group, who received no treatment, the students who had experienced the attribution training showed improved grades in the semester following the study, and their dropout rate was significantly lower. Remarkably, one-time exposure to information suggesting that poor first-semester performance was due to unstable rather than stable causes was sufficient to bring about changes in the students' performance.

Other research has shown that retraining attributions from internal causes to external ones can alleviate poor performance, psychological distress, and other symptoms (Fulk, 1996; Yasutake, Bryan, & Dohrn, 1996; Orbach, Singer, & Murphey, 1997). In sum, attribution training, in which inaccurate attributions are replaced with more accurate ones, shows considerable promise (Försterling, 1985).

Misattribution training: Replacing accurate attributions with inaccurate ones. In some cases, it is not the inaccuracy of people's attributions that leads to detrimental consequences. In fact, sometimes attributions are all too accurate, producing dysfunctional consequences. In such cases, social psychologists have devised another intervention strategy: misattribution training. In *misattribution training,* people are led to replace their accurate, but harmful, attributions with inaccurate, but more beneficial, attributions.

Consider, for instance, people who have chronic insomnia. For them, going to bed each night is a tension-filled experience: They anticipate having difficulty sleeping, and they lie

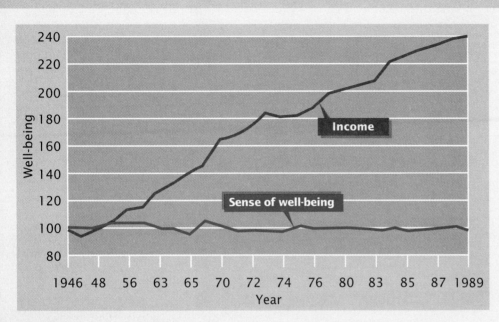

FIGURE 5–3   Money Can't Buy You Happiness The level of happiness in the general U.S. population has remained surprisingly stable over a 40-year period even though disposable income has increased substantially. (*Source:* Diener et al., 1999, p. 288.)

awake first worrying about their problems and then experiencing anxiety because they are not sleeping. Typically, such insomniacs attribute their inability to sleep to anxiety, to problems in general, or to a host of personality factors. Such internal attributions make it difficult for them to sleep.

Suppose, however, that people with insomnia were told that their inability to get to sleep was due not to anxiety or to other internal factors, but to some factor that was essentially beyond their control. It is conceivable that they might fall asleep more quickly than usual, since the usual source of worry—themselves—could not be blamed.

Using this reasoning, Michael Storms and Richard Nisbett (1970) conducted a classic experiment in which they told one group of insomniacs that they would be taking a pill that would relax them and allow them to sleep more easily. In contrast, another group of insomniacs was told that the pill would keep them awake. In reality, the pills given to both groups were inert sugar pills that had no real physiological effects.

The results of the study supported the researchers' prior reasoning. Participants who were told that they would be able to get to sleep more easily actually took about 15 minutes *longer* to fall asleep than they usually did. In contrast, those who could attribute their initial sleeplessness to the side effects of the pill actually took *less* time to fall asleep than they usually did. Apparently, the fact that these latter participants could attribute their potential insomnia to an external factor, outside their own control, provided them with the "excuse" to fall asleep easily.

Later research has supported the benefits of replacing accurate attributions with inaccurate ones (e.g., Storms & McCaul, 1976; Olson & Ross, 1988). However, misattribution

Looking at the world with a clear, honest vision may not be as emotionally healthy as we might at first assume. For instance, it may be beneficial to one's mental health to have an unrealistically high opinion of oneself.

training does not work for all people. Such training seems most effective for relatively introspective and thoughtful individuals (Brockner & Swap, 1983). Still, misattribution training offers a promising route for promoting better health and psychological well-being.

THE BENEFITS OF ILLUSIONS: WHERE WRONG IS RIGHT

Most of us would probably endorse the notion that one of the hallmarks of good mental health is holding a clear, accurate view of both ourselves and the world, and that distorted and inaccurate perceptions are a sign of psychological disorder.

However, not everyone would agree. According to social psychologists Shelley Taylor and Jonathan Brown, looking at things with a clear, honest eye may not be entirely beneficial for one's mental health (Taylor & Brown, 1988; Taylor & Armor, 1996). For instance, victims of depression and people low in self-esteem often see themselves clearly and accurately—warts and all. They make the same sorts of attributions regarding the causes of their misfortunes that neutral, objective observers do, and they are less apt to exaggerate their sense of control over events that are not easily controlled (Haaga & Beck, 1995). It would seem that perhaps sometimes holding accurate self-perceptions, then, is not always associated with positive psychological outcomes (Taylor & Brown, 1994; Brown & Dutton, 1995).

In fact, the peril of having an accurate view of the world and of oneself seems so pronounced that Taylor and Brown argue that certain types of inaccuracies about oneself and others may actually promote mental health (Taylor & Brown, 1988; Aspinwall & Taylor, 1992). Specifically, they suggest that three basic illusions are associated with better psychological functioning: holding unrealistically positive evaluations of oneself, having an exaggerated sense of control over occurrences in one's life, and being unrealistically optimistic. These positive illusions are related to happiness and contentment, productivity and creativity, and the ability to care about others.

Obviously, there are limits to how far people can twist reality, and sometimes it is clearly maladaptive to ignore objective threats and to assume that one can always exert control over any situation. Furthermore, some social psychologists argue that the preponderance of evidence suggests that in most cases, positive illusions are unrelated to mental health. In fact, they suggest that holding overly positive illusions may well produce poor, biased decisions and inappropriate behavior based on erroneous assumptions. Although Taylor and Brown's critics acknowledge that positive illusions may help regulate moods and may make people feel better in the short term, they argue that, over the long run, distortions about the world become maladaptive (Colvin & Block, 1994; Colvin, Block, & Funder, 1995).

Although the issue is far from settled, it is clear that, at least in some situations, certain sorts of biased self-perceptions are beneficial (Taylor et al., 1992). The questions that are yet to be answered pertain to the extent to which such illusions are beneficial, when they are most likely to occur, and what their full, long-term consequences are (Taylor & Brown, 1994; Salovey, Rothman, & Rodin, 1998).

The findings regarding the value of inaccuracies in one's view of the world raise another question: How do we define what is normal and what is disordered when it comes to mental and physical health? Surprisingly, it turns out that the answer differs considerably across different cultures.

CULTURAL INTERPRETATIONS OF MENTAL AND PHYSICAL HEALTH: HOW DO WE DETERMINE WHAT IS HEALTHY AND WHAT IS NOT?

EXPLORING DIVERSITY

Hearing the voices of your ancestors speaking to you from the afterlife is hardly noteworthy. At least if you are a member of one Plains Indian group that regards hearing from the dead as nothing out of the ordinary. On the other hand, members of many other cultures would find such a situation far from routine. According to Western health-related disciplines, for instance, hearing voices is a symptom of certain severe psychological disorders.

The difference between the two perspectives illustrates the central role that culture plays in determining what is healthy, and unhealthy, behavior. In fact, most of the disorders seen today as signs of psychological disorder are found only in North America and Western Europe. Only four—schizophrenia, bipolar disorder, major depression, and anxiety disorders—are seen in all cultures (Kleinman, 1991).

For example, consider the Western view that dissociate identity disorder, or multiple personalities, represents a severe mental health problem. Labeling the condition a disorder is reasonable only in a culture in which the sense of self is concrete and stable. In some societies, including many cultures in India, the self is based less on internal factors than on external attributes that are relatively independent of the individual. Consequently, when a person shows symptoms of what Westerners would label multiple personalities, the attributions are very different. For instance, the cause of the behavior may be assumed to be possession by demons, which is regarded as a malady, or possession by gods—which is not seen as a problem.

Other disorders are found only in certain cultures. For example, *koro* is the sense of panic felt by men in Southeast Asia that the penis is about to retract permanently into their bodies. In Malaya, people demonstrate *amok,* wild outbursts in which a typically quiet and shy individual severely injures or kills others. And people in rural Japan sometimes are susceptible to *kitsunetsuki,* a belief that they have been possessed by a fox. As a consequence, they show facial expressions that make them look like that animal (Carson, Butcher, & Coleman, 1992).

In addition, various cultures have very different definitions of appropriate behavior related to health issues. For instance, in many cultures people routinely undergo procedures that physically alter their bodies. Male circumcision, the removal of the foreskin of the penis, is a practice that has deep cultural and religious roots. Furthermore, in many African cultures a woman's clitoris is routinely removed during childhood. This practice, which prevents women from ever experiencing sexual pleasure, is seen as enhancing a girl's attractiveness, and thereby making her more socially acceptable and marriageable. It is estimated that, worldwide, the operation has been performed on 100 million girls (Crossette, 1995).

In short, cultural views of what is healthy and normal, and what is unhealthy and abnormal, color people's understanding of themselves and others. We cannot fully understand an individual's sense of well-being and health without taking into account the culture in which he or she lives (Javier, Herron, & Bergman, 1995).

REVIEW AND RETHINK

Review

- Self-complexity is the phenomenon of viewing oneself as having many distinct facets; it is helpful in combating stress and depression.

- Self-discrepancy theory suggests that the discrepancy between one's self-concept and self-guides leads to negative emotions and ultimately has psychological costs.

- Self-disclosure, in which information about oneself is exchanged with others, can have positive health effects.

- Self-regulation failures, which are inadequacies in the control of one's behavior, take two forms: underregulation and misregulation.

- Learned helplessness has been linked to depression and to particular attributional styles.

- Attribution training and misattribution training both aim to change the types of attributions people make.

Rethink

- According to Higgins's self-discrepancy theory, what emotions would a person experience who felt that his or her hopes and aspirations were largely going unfulfilled? How would a person's level of self-complexity influence these emotions?

- Some research suggests that thinking about a past negative event may be psychologically harmful, but writing about it may be beneficial. Use Pennebaker's work to explain why this might be true.

- What role do cognitive thought processes play in the phenomenon of learned helplessness?

- Based on the findings of Taylor and Brown, what might be the role of accuracy in attribution training?

STRESS AND DISEASE

It was only 10:34 A.M., and already Jennifer Jackson had put in what seemed like a full day. After getting up at 6:30 A.M., she studied a bit for an American History exam scheduled later in the afternoon. She gulped down breakfast as she studied and then headed off to the campus bookstore, where she works part-time.

Her car was in the shop with some undiagnosed ailment, so she had to take the bus. The bus was late, so Jennifer didn't have time to stop off at the library before work to pick up the reserve book she needed. Making a mental note to try to get the book at lunchtime (although she thought it probably wouldn't be available by then), she sprinted from the bus to the store, arriving a few minutes late. Although her supervisor didn't say anything, she looked irritated as Jennifer explained why she was late. Feeling that she needed to make amends, Jennifer volunteered to sort invoices—a task that she, and everyone else, hated. As she sorted the invoices, she also answered the phone and jumped up to serve a steady stream of customers who were placing special orders. When the phone rang at 10:34 A.M., it was her garage mechanic telling her that the car repair would cost several hundred dollars—a sum she did not have.

If you were to monitor Jennifer Jackson's heart rate and blood pressure, you wouldn't be shocked to find that both were higher than normal. You also wouldn't be surprised if she reported feeling stress.

Most of us are well acquainted with **stress**, the response to events that threaten or challenge us. Everyday life is filled with **stressors**, circumstances that produce threats to our well-being. And it is not just unpleasant events, such as tests or job demands, that produce stress; even happy circumstances, such as getting prepared for a week's vacation or winning an election, can produce stress (Brown & McGill, 1989; Lazarus, 1999).

STRESS AND COPING: REACTIONS TO THREAT

How do circumstances become stressful? According to psychologists Richard Lazarus and Susan Folkman, people who confront a new or shifting environment move through a series of stages (see Figure 5–4). The first step is *primary appraisal,* the assessment of an event to determine whether its implications are positive, neutral, or negative. If people determine that the implications are negative, they appraise the event in terms of how harmful it has been in the past, how threatening it appears to the future, and how likely it is that the challenge can be addressed successfully (Lazarus & Folkman, 1984; Lazarus, 1993, 1999).

The next step is secondary appraisal. *Secondary appraisal* is the assessment of whether one's coping abilities and resources are adequate to overcome the harm, threat, or challenge posed by the potential stressor. During this stage, people seek to determine whether their personal resources are sufficient to meet the dangers posed by the situation.

According to Lazarus and Folkman, the experience of stress is the outcome of both primary and secondary appraisal. When the potential harm, threat, and challenge produced by circumstances are high, and coping abilities are limited, people will experience stress (Anderson, E.H., 1995; Florian, Mikulincer, & Taubman, 1995; Chang, 1998; Mishra & Spreitzer, 1998).

For example, consider a student who receives a lengthy reading list at the beginning of a term. First, she engages in primary appraisal, analyzing the implications of the list in terms

stress: The response to events that threaten or challenge us.

stressors: Circumstances that produce threats to our well-being.

CW

FIGURE 5–4   Appraisal Leading to the Perception of Stress According to the Lazarus and Folkman model, potential stressors are assessed using primary and secondary appraisal. If primary appraisal indicates that a potential stressor represents a challenge, and secondary appraisal suggests that the resources available to cope with the potential stressor are inadequate, then the perception of stress will occur. (*Source:* Adapted from Kaplan, Sallis, & Patterson, 1993, p. 123, based on Lazarus & Folkman, 1984.)

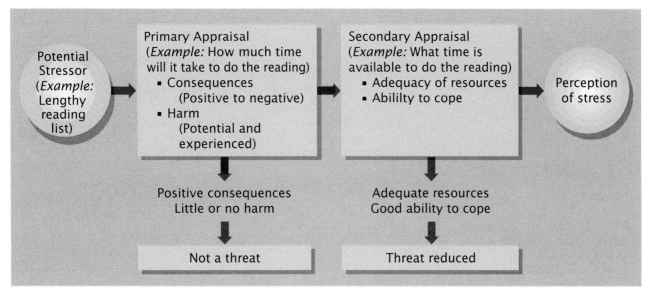

Appraisal determines whether circumstances are seen as stressful. For some people rock climbing produces no stress, whereas for others, it is highly stressful.

of the time it will take to do the reading and assessing how threatening the task appears. Next, she engages in secondary appraisal, considering whether she has sufficient time to complete the reading. If the answer is yes, then the threat is reduced. But if she decides that time will be an issue because she faces numerous other time demands during the term, her secondary appraisal will result in the perception of stress.

STRESSORS: WHAT'S PLEASURE FOR YOU IS STRESS FOR ME

As the Lazarus and Folkman model suggests, stress is a very personal thing (Bodenmann, 1995). For some of us, bungee jumping and deep-sea diving would produce high degrees of stress; for others, they are simply recreational activities that, because of the distractions they present, may ultimately *reduce* stress.

Certain kinds of circumstances, however, produce stress in almost everyone. For instance, some professions, such as firefighter (Murphy et al., 1994; Corneil et al., 1999), surgeon, and pilot, consistently produce high levels of stress (see Table 5–1 for a list of the most stressful jobs).

In other cases, specific events or circumstances bring stress. Social psychologists have identified three main types: cataclysmic events, personal stressors, and daily hassles (Lazarus & Cohen, 1977; Gatchel & Baum, 1983).

Cataclysmic events are strong stressors that occur suddenly and affect many people simultaneously. Disasters such as tornadoes, hurricanes, and floods are examples of cataclysmic events that affect literally hundreds of thousands of people at once.

Although cataclysmic events affect many people at the same time, the stress that they produce is often less intense than events that initially are less dramatic. This is because cataclysmic incidents usually have a clear end point, after which the danger has passed. (One exception: the 1993 Mississippi River flooding, which continued to threaten residents for months.) In addition, the stress of cataclysmic events is lessened because it is shared with many other people. Consequently, no individual feels personally singled out and others are available to provide social support to those affected (Cummings, 1987; Bell, 1995; Granot, 1995; Kaniasty & Norris, 1995; Winge & Ulvik, 1995; Williams, Zinner, & Ellis, 1999).

Still, people who experience cataclysmic events are at risk for posttraumatic stress disorder (Keane et al., 1994; Lundin, 1995). *Posttraumatic stress disorder* is a phenomenon in which victims of major incidents reexperience in flashbacks or dreams the original stress-producing event and associated feelings (Wilson & Raphael, 1993; Freedy & Hobfoll, 1995; Brewin, 1998; David et al., 1999). According to some estimates, as many as 60 percent of all Vietnam War veterans may suffer from the condition, although other estimates are much lower (Hobfoll et al., 1991; Solomon, 1993; Everly & Lating, 1995). Even soldiers who fought in the Persian Gulf War show signs of the syndrome, such as sleep problems, drug

cataclysmic events: Strong stressors that occur suddenly and affect many people simultaneously.

and alcohol abuse, and high rates of suicide. Why should the Gulf War, which actually produced few U.S. casualties, be so stressful? The answer is that stress is brought about by the *perception* of threat or challenge, and even a war that produces few casualties is bound to trigger substantial stress in front-line troops (Solomon, 1994).

Personal stressors are a second major type of stressor—major life events that have immediate negative consequences. The death of a loved one, the termination of an important relationship, or a major school or job failure might all be considered personal stressors. Although the immediate impact of personal stressors can be profound, with time the consequences often taper off as people learn to adapt. In some cases, however, such as the occurrence of a violent physical assault, people may experience posttraumatic stress disorder (Foa & Riggs, 1995).

Finally, there is a third type of stressor, one with which we are all familiar—background stressors or, more informally, daily hassles. **Daily hassles** or **background stressors** are the minor irritants of life that produce minor stress. Although the circumstances that produce daily hassles are not, by themselves, all that aversive, the negative consequences of daily hassles add up and can ultimately produce even more stress than a single, initially more extreme event (Fernandez & Sheffield, 1996; Nyklicek et al., 1998; van Eck, Nicolson, & Berkhof, 1998).

Daily hassles have positive counterparts—uplifts. **Uplifts** are those minor positive events that make people feel good, even if only temporarily. Uplifts range from having a pleasant experience with others, to feeling healthy, to eating out at a favorite restaurant. Uplifts may help to counteract the negative consequences of daily hassles and aid in fending off the stress they cause (Kanner et al., 1981; Hart, Wearing, & Headey, 1994). In fact, some research suggests that the effects of uplifts may last longer than those of hassles. For example, one study found that although the negative consequences of hassles lasted for one day, uplifts still had lingering effects three days later (Stone et al., 1994). (The most common daily hassles and uplifts are shown in Figure 5–5.)

personal stressors: Major life events that have immediate negative consequences.

daily hassles (or background stressors): The minor irritants of life that produce minor stress.

uplifts: Minor positive events that make people feel good, even if only temporarily.

TABLE 5–1   The Most Stressful Jobs

HOW SELECTED OCCUPATIONS RANKED IN AN EVALUATION OF 250 COMMON JOBS

Rank	Stress Score	Rank	Stress Score
1. President of the United States	176.6	103. Market-research analyst	42.1
2. Firefighter	110.9	104. Personnel recruiter	41.8
3. Senior executive	108.6	113. Hospital administrator	39.6
6. Surgeon	99.5	119. Economist	38.7
10. Air-traffic controller	83.1	122. Mechanical engineer	38.3
12. Public-relations executive	78.5	124. Chiropractor	37.9
17. Real-estate agent	73.1	144. Bank officer	35.4
20. Stockbroker	71.7	149. Retail salesperson	34.9
22. Pilot	68.7	150. Tax examiner/collector	34.8
25. Architect	66.9	154. Aerospace engineer	34.6
31. Lawyer	64.3	173. Accountant	31.1
33. Physician (general practitioner)	64.0	193. Purchasing agent	28.9
35. Insurance agent	63.3	194. Insurance underwriter	28.5
47. Auto salesperson	56.3	212. Computer programmer	26.5
50. College professor	54.2	216. Financial planner	26.3
60. School principal	51.7	229. Broadcast technician	24.2
67. Psychologist	50.0	241. Bookkeeper	21.5

Source: Murphy et al., 1994.

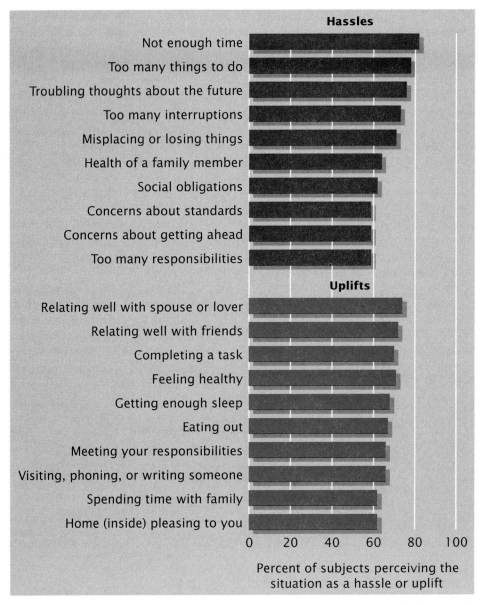

FIGURE 5–5 Everyday Hassles and Uplifts These are the most common everyday hassles and uplifts. (*Sources:* Hassles—Chamberlain & Zika, 1990; Uplifts—Kanner et al., 1981.)

Although the nature of specific stressors varies from one person to another, several broad principles explain which events are appraised as stressful. According to social psychologist Shelley Taylor, these principles include the following (Taylor, 1995):

◆ *Occurrences that evoke negative emotions are more apt to produce stress than positive occurrences.* For most people, then, planning a wedding is less stressful than planning a funeral.

◆ *Events that are uncontrollable or unpredictable are more stressful than those that can be controlled or predicted.* For example, people living near airports, who hear airplane takeoffs and landings at seemingly random intervals, report high levels of stress. In comparison, for people who feel they have enough control to stop or influence an unpleasant event, stress is likely to be lower (Evans, Hygge, & Bullinger, 1995).

◆ *Circumstances that are unclear and ambiguous typically produce more stress than those that are unambiguous and precise.* If an event is not easily understood, people must struggle to comprehend it, rather than dealing with it directly.

◆ *Situations in which a person faces multiple tasks that strain resources are more apt to produce stress than those in which people have fewer things to do.* A person whose to-do list contains many things that need to be accomplished in the same time frame is a prime candidate for stress.

The costs of stress.   When people appraise an experience as stressful, they experience both physical and psychological consequences. Immediate reactions may include a rise in heart rate and blood pressure, an increase in skin conductance due to sweating, and the secretion of certain hormones by the adrenal glands. In the short term, these reactions may be beneficial, because they produce a burst of energy that may help a person cope with the immediate threat that the stressor poses. For instance, because of immediate physical reactions to stress, a woman may outrun a thief who is attempting to steal her purse (Selye, 1976; Cacioppo, 1994; Cacioppo et al., 1995).

In the long run, however, the physical changes brought on by stress can be harmful. The ongoing secretion of stress-related hormones may cause important body tissues, such as the blood vessels and the heart, to deteriorate. Furthermore, ongoing stress can impede the functioning of the *immune system,* the systems of organs, glands, and cells that make up the body's defense against disease (Gavrilova & Shabanova, 1998; Miller, 1998; Segerstrom et al., 1998). In fact, increasing evidence shows conclusively that stress reduces the body's ability to ward off germs, making people more susceptible to disease. For instance, people exposed to stress often experience such common ailments as headaches, backaches, skin rashes, indigestion, and chronic fatigue. Even the common cold is associated with stress (Cohen, Tyrrell, & Smith, 1993; Rawson, Bloomer, & Kendall, 1994; Cohen, 1996).

In addition, stress is linked to **psychophysiological conditions**, medical problems related to the interaction of psychological, emotional, and physical difficulties (Gavrilova & Shabanova, 1998; Gruzelier et al., 1998). Ulcers, asthma, arthritis, and high blood pressure are common examples of conditions that are sometimes triggered or made worse by stress. Psychophysiological conditions were previously called "psychosomatic disorders," but that term has been discarded because of the implication it carried that the physical symptoms were somehow unreal. This is not the case: Psychophysiological conditions have a clear biological basis. What distinguishes them from other diseases is that they are affected by stress.

Stress has even been linked to severe, life-threatening illnesses. According to some studies, the greater the number of stressful events that a person experiences over the course of the year, the more likely the person is to have a major illness (see Table 5–2). Although such research is hardly definitive (not everyone who experiences high stress is destined to become ill), it does suggest the magnitude of the physiological reactions produced by stress.

In short, stress produces three main sorts of outcomes, summarized in Figure 5–6. First, there are direct physiological effects, such as elevated blood pressure, a decrease in the functioning of the immune system, and increased hormonal activity (Uchino et al., 1995). Second, stress leads people to engage in behaviors that harm their health, including increased smoking and use of alcohol, decreased nutrition and sleep, and increased drug use. Finally, stress produces indirect consequences that affect health-related behaviors, including decreased compliance with medical advice, increased delays in seeking medical care, and a diminished likelihood of seeking care in the first place (Baum, 1994).

Of course, not everyone reacts to stressors identically. For example, men and women appear to respond in different ways to certain kinds of stressors (Gadzella, 1994; Murphy et al., 1994; Hammelman, 1995; Lash, Eisler, & Southard, 1995). Psychologist Janice Kiecolt-Glaser found that when newlyweds engaged in a 30-minute discussion, women responded more strongly on a physiological level than men at points when their spouse acted negative or hostile (Kiecolt-Glaser et al., 1998).

Other research, however, finds that although men and women may report different levels of stress from similar stressors, their physiological reactions may be similar. For instance, male victims of Hurricane Andrew in Florida reported more stress than female victims—although careful physiological measurements showed little difference in hormonal levels (Ironson, 1993).

psychophysiological conditions: Medical problems related to the interaction of psychological, emotional, and physical difficulties.

TABLE 5-2	Will Stress in Your Life Produce Illness?

Using the following scale, you can assess the degree of stress in your life (Rahe & Arthur, 1978). To do this, take the stressor value given beside each event you have experienced and multiply it by the number of occurrences over the past year (up to a maximum of four), then add up the scores.

87	Experienced the death of a spouse	49	Had a major change in amount of independence and responsibility
77	Getting married	47	Had a major change in responsibilities at work
77	Experienced the death of a close family member	46	Experienced a major change in use of alcohol
76	Getting divorced	45	Revised personal habits
74	Experienced a marital separation from mate	44	Had trouble with school administration
68	Experienced the death of a close friend	43	Held a job while attending school
68	Experienced pregnancy or fathered a pregnancy	43	Had a major change in social activities
65	Had a major personal injury or illness	42	Had trouble with in-laws
62	Were fired from work	42	Had a major change in working hours or conditions
60	Ended a marital engagement or a steady relationship	42	Changed residence or living conditions
58	Had sexual difficulties	41	Had your spouse begin or cease work outside the home
58	Experienced a marital reconciliation with your mate	41	Changed your choice of major field of study
57	Had a major change in self-concept or self-awareness	41	Changed dating habits
56	Experienced a major change in the health or behavior of a family member	40	Had an outstanding personal achievement
54	Became engaged to be married	38	Had trouble with your boss
53	Had a major change in financial status	38	Had a major change in amount of participation in school activities
52	Took on a mortgage or loan of less than $10,000	37	Had a major change in type and/or amount of recreation
52	Had a major change in use of drugs	36	Had a major change in church activities
50	Had a major conflict or change in values	34	Had a major change of sleeping habits
50	Had a major change in the number of arguments with your spouse	33	Took a trip or vacation
50	Gained a new family member	30	Had a major change in eating habits
50	Entered college	26	Had a major change in the number of family get-togethers
50	Changed to a new school	22	Were found guilty of minor violations of the law
50	Changed to a different line of work		

If your total score is above 1,435, you are in a high-stress category. According to Marx, Garrity, and Bowers (1975), a high score increases the chances of experiencing a future stress-related illness. However, a high score in no way guarantees that you will suffer from a future illness. Because the research on stress and illness is correlational, major stressful events cannot be viewed as necessarily causing illness (Dohrenwend et al., 1984; Lakey & Heller, 1985). Furthermore, other research suggests that future illness is predicted better by daily ongoing hassles, rather than by the major events depicted in the questionnaire (Lazarus et al., 1985). In fact, some research has questioned whether the particular values for each event are always appropriate (Birnbaum & Sotoodeh, 1991). On the other hand, too much stress is clearly undesirable, and thus it is reasonable to reduce it where feasible (Marx et al., 1975, p. 97; Maddie, Barone, & Puccetti, 1987).

Stress reactions also vary across cultures. One of the most extreme examples of this phenomenon is the sudden death disorder that afflicts male Southeast Asian refugees in the United States. Although the incidence has been low, the consistency—and mystery—of the circumstances under which the deaths have occurred has been puzzling.

In the disorder, apparently healthy males die in their sleep without warning (Lemoine & Mougne, 1983). Victims make gurgling noises, thrash about in bed, and die. Although no cause has been found, one hypothesis is that a combination of physical, psychological, and cultural factors produces death.

One theory proposes that an inherited heart defect puts potential victims at risk. When stress is high—due to the pressures of multiple jobs, family arguments, academic concerns,

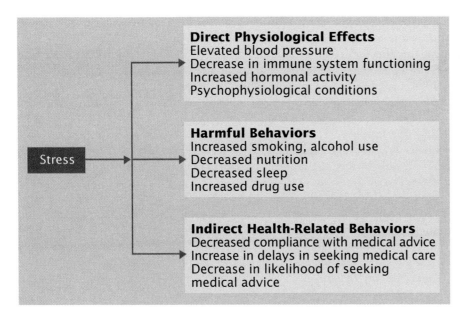

Direct Physiological Effects
Elevated blood pressure
Decrease in immune system functioning
Increased hormonal activity
Psychophysiological conditions

Harmful Behaviors
Increased smoking, alcohol use
Decreased nutrition
Decreased sleep
Increased drug use

Indirect Health-Related Behaviors
Decreased compliance with medical advice
Increase in delays in seeking medical care
Decrease in likelihood of seeking
medical advice

Stress

FIGURE 5–6   The Major Outcomes of Stress   Stress produces three types of consequences: direct physiological effects, harmful behaviors, and indirect health-related behaviors. (*Source:* Adapted from Baum, 1994.)

or other factors—extremely vivid unpleasant dreams may trigger the inherited flaw and lead to death. For instance, not long before they died some victims reported dreams foretelling their deaths. Because the Hmong, a Cambodian ethnic group to which most of the victims have belonged, place great credence in their dreams, dreams foretelling death could have produced extremely high levels of stress—leading to the fatal consequence.

Coping with stress.   When faced with potential stressors, some people manage much better than others. We all know some people who withdraw and retreat when confronted with even the most minor stressor, and others who appear to thrive under stress, becoming energized and working tirelessly to overcome any challenge. The difference lies in their coping skills.

Coping is the effort to control, reduce, or learn to tolerate the threats that lead to stress. All of us use habitual coping responses to help deal with stress, although we're not always aware of our responses. For instance, some people use **defense mechanisms**, unconscious reactions to threats that reduce anxiety by distorting or denying the true nature of the situation (Norem, 1998). One study examined how students living in a dormitory that was considered vulnerable to earthquakes rated their susceptibility to a future tremor (Lehman & Taylor, 1988). Compared with students living in a safer dormitory, those who resided in the unsafe one rated their personal danger as lower!

But not all coping mechanisms occur unconsciously. People also make conscious efforts to cope with stress, with varying degrees of success. Some social psychologists suggest that people use one of two alternative coping strategies: problem-focused coping and emotion-focused coping (Folkman & Lazarus, 1988; Norman et al., 1995). In *problem-focused coping,* people attempt to manage a stressful problem or situation by directly changing the situation to one that produces less stress. They may try to make the people who generate the stress change their behavior, or they may leave the situation altogether. A student who tries to talk a teacher into extending the due date of a paper, or who decides to drop a stress-inducing class, is using problem-focused coping.

In contrast, in *emotion-focused coping,* people try to deal with stress by consciously regulating their emotions. For instance, people who tell themselves they should look at the bright side of a situation, or who try to cheer themselves up by accepting sympathy from others, are using emotion-focused coping.

coping: The effort to control, reduce, or learn to tolerate the threats that lead to stress.

defense mechanisms: Unconscious reactions to threats that reduce anxiety by distorting or denying the true nature of the situation.

The social support offered to this California woman, who had just lost her home of 42 years to a fire, is likely to help her cope with the disaster.

social support: Assistance and comfort supplied by a network of caring, interested people, which is a boon to people living under stressful circumstances.

Does one type of coping work better than the other? Most research suggests that neither emotion-focused nor problem-focused coping is invariably effective, and that their success may depend on the particular situation (Lazarus & Folkman, 1984). Furthermore, problem-focused and emotion-focused coping can often be used together (Broadstock & Borland, 1998; Ingledew & McDonagh, 1998). For instance, a person who loses his job may profitably employ both problem-focused coping ("I'll study the want ads to try to find another job") and emotion-focused coping ("I'll try not to make myself feel worse about this by taking it personally").

Gender differences exist in coping strategies. Women seem to use emotion-focused coping more than men, whereas men use problem-focused coping more than women (Zeidner & Ben-Zur, 1993; Ptacek, Smith, & Dodge, 1994).

Another way of coping with stress is to turn to others for support. **Social support**, assistance and comfort supplied by a network of caring, interested people, is a boon to those living under stressful circumstances. People can provide both emotional support—such as listening sympathetically—and concrete support—such as tutoring for a student who is struggling academically. The awareness that you are part of a network of relationships can ease the burden of stress (Pierce, Sarason, & Sarason, 1996; Zaleski et al., 1998; Ystgaard et al., 1999).

TABLE 5-3 How Resilient Are You?

Rate how much each of the following applies to you on a scale from 1 to 5, with 1 = very little and 5 = very much.

1 2 3 4 5 Curious, ask questions, want to know how things work, experiment.

1 2 3 4 5 Constantly learn from your experience and the experiences of others.

1 2 3 4 5 Need and expect to have things work well for yourself and others. Take good care of yourself.

1 2 3 4 5 Play with new developments, find the humor, laugh at self, chuckle.

1 2 3 4 5 Highly flexible, adapt quickly to change.

1 2 3 4 5 Feel comfortable with paradoxical qualities.

1 2 3 4 5 Anticipate problems and avoid difficulties.

1 2 3 4 5 Develop better self-esteem and self-confidence with the passage of time. Develop a conscious self-concept of professionalism.

1 2 3 4 5 Listen well. Read others, including difficult people, with empathy.

1 2 3 4 5 Think up creative solutions to challenges, invent ways to solve problems. Trust intuition and hunches.

1 2 3 4 5 Manage the emotional side of recovery from trauma; let go of the past.

1 2 3 4 5 Expect tough situations to work out well, keep on going. Help others, bring stability to times of uncertainty and turmoil.

1 2 3 4 5 Find the good in accidents and bad experiences.

1 2 3 4 5 Convert misfortune into good fortune.

Scoring

Add up the numbers you circled, and use the following scale as a rough guide to your level of resilience:

60–70: highly resilient

50–60: above-average resiliency

40–50: average resiliency

30–40: below-average resiliency

below 30: unusually low resiliency

Source: Adapted from Siebert, 1998.

Coping success also varies as a result of the kind of "coping style" we have, our general tendency to deal with stress in a particular way. For example, people with a "hardy" coping style are especially successful in dealing with stress. **Hardiness** is a personality characteristic associated with a lower rate of stress-related illness.

Hardy individuals are take-charge people who revel in life's challenges. It is not surprising, then, that people who are high in hardiness are more resistant to stress-related illness than those who show less hardiness. Hardy people react to potentially threatening stressors with optimism, feeling that they can respond effectively. By turning threatening situations into challenging ones, they are less apt to experience high levels of stress (Wiebe & Williams, 1992; Nathawat & Joshi, 1997; Horner, 1998).

For people who face the most profound of life's difficulties—such as the death of a loved one or a permanent injury such as a spinal cord injury—a key factor in their reactions is their level of resilience. *Resilience* is the ability to withstand, overcome, and actually thrive following profound adversity (Werner, 1995; Siebert, 1998).

Resilient individuals tend to be easygoing, be good-natured, and have good social and communication skills. They are independent, feeling that they can shape their own fate and are not dependent on others or luck. In short, they work with what they have and make the best of whatever situation they find themselves in (Werner, 1993, 1995; Eisenberg et al., 1997; Staudinger et al., 1999).

You can get a sense of your own level of resiliency by completing the questionnaire in Table 5–3.

hardiness: A personality characteristic associated with a lower rate of stress-related illness.

COPING WITH STRESS

Stress is part of everyone's life. However, although the phenomenon is universal, there are no universal formulas for coping with stress. This is primarily because stress depends on an individual appraisal of how threatening and challenging particular situations are. Still, several general approaches have proved effective in coping with stress (Holahan & Moos, 1987, 1990; Kaplan, Sallis, & Patterson, 1993; Sacks, 1993; Conduit, 1995). Among them are the following:

THE INFORMED CONSUMER OF SOCIAL PSYCHOLOGY

- ◆ *Attempt to exert control over the situation.* As we've noted, controllable events produce less stress than those that cannot be controlled. One coping strategy, then, is to try to maintain a sense of control. By attempting to exercise control over a situation, one can induce a sense of mastery over the situation and reduce the experience of stress (e.g., Taylor et al., 1991; Burger, 1992). For instance, if a paper deadline is looming and causing high stress, it may make sense to negotiate a later due date with the professor. Not only would such a strategy reduce the immediate stress, but it would provide more time to do a better job.

- ◆ *Reappraise threats as challenges.* If a stressor cannot be controlled, at least it can be appraised in a different, less threatening manner. The old truism, "Every cloud has a silver lining," reflects the social psychological finding that people who can discover something positive in otherwise negative situations show less distress and are better able to cope than those who are unable to do so (Silver & Wortman, 1980; Smith & Ellsworth, 1987; Bowman & Stern, 1995).

- ◆ *Seek out social support.* As we've discussed, support from other people can provide relief and comfort when we are confronting stress. Consequently, asking for assistance can be a means of reducing stress. Friends, family, and even telephone hotlines staffed by peer counselors can provide significant support. (For help in identifying appropriate hotlines, the U.S. Public Health Service maintains a "master" toll-free number that can provide telephone numbers and addresses of many national groups. Call 800-336-4797.)

- ◆ *Use relaxation techniques.* If stress produces chronic physiological arousal, it follows that procedures that reduce such arousal might reduce the harmful consequences of physiological wear-and-tear. Several techniques have been developed, including transcendental meditation, Zen and yoga, progressive muscle relaxation, and even hypnosis. One procedure that is simple and effective is relaxation training, which includes the basic components of several other techniques. What stress expert Herbert Benson calls the "relaxation response" is

TABLE 5–4	**How to Elicit the Relaxation Response**

Some general advice on regular practice of the relaxation response

- Try to find 10 or 20 minutes in your daily routine; before breakfast is a good time.
- Sit comfortably.
- For the period you will practice, try to arrange your life so you won't have distractions. Put the phone on the answering machine, and ask someone else to watch the kids.
- Time yourself by glancing periodically at a clock or watch (but don't set an alarm). Commit yourself to a specific length of practice, and try to stick to it.

There are several approaches to eliciting the relaxation response. Here is one standard set of instructions used at the Mind/Body Medical Institute:

Step 1. Pick a focus word or short phrase that's firmly rooted in your personal belief system. For example, a nonreligious individual might choose a neutral word like *one* or *peace* or *love*. A Christian person desiring to use a prayer could pick the opening words of Psalm 23, *The Lord is my shepherd;* Jewish person could choose *Shalom.*

Step 2. Sit quietly in a comfortable position.

Step 3. Close your eyes.

Step 4. Relax your muscles.

Step 5. Breathe slowly and naturally, repeating your focus word or phrase silently as you exhale.

Step 6. Throughout, assume a passive attitude. Don't worry about how well you're doing. When other thoughts come to mind, simply say to yourself, "Oh, well," and gently return to the repetition.

Step 7. Continue for 10 to 20 minutes. You may open your eyes to check the time, but do not use an alarm. When you finish, sit quietly for a minute or so, at first with your eyes closed and later with your eyes open. Then do not stand for one or two minutes.

Step 8. Practice the technique once or twice a day.

Source: Benson, 1993, p. 240.

effective in reducing stress and can be elicited by following the instructions shown in Table 5–4 (Benson, 1993; also see the Speaking of Social Psychology interview with Benson).

- *Exercise.* Ironically, exercise—which leads to temporary physiological arousal—may ultimately reduce stress. The reason is that regular exercise, once the exercise session is completed, reduces heart rate, respiration rate, and blood pressure. In addition, exercise provides time off from the circumstances that may be producing stress in the first place (Brown, 1991; Aldana et al., 1996).

SOCIAL PSYCHOLOGICAL COMPONENTS OF MAJOR ILLNESS

Just two decades ago, most physicians would have scoffed at the notion that social psychological factors were related to major illness. To them, heart disease was solely the result of a temporary loss of oxygen-rich blood to the heart, and cancer was the result of unrestrained multiplication of cells in a tumor.

Today, however, physicians acknowledge that social psychological factors play a role in several kinds of major physical illness. As we'll see, social psychological factors are related both to the causes of major diseases and to their successful treatment (Stein & Baum, 1995).

Type A's, Type B's, and coronary heart disease.   Do you churn when you're forced to wait in a long, slow-moving line at a bank? Do you seethe when a slow-moving vehicle prevents you from driving as fast as you'd like? Are you quick to anger when the book you're looking for in the library is not on the shelves? If you answer yes to questions such as these, you may have a set of personality characteristics known as the Type A behavior pattern. The **Type A behavior pattern** is characterized by competitiveness, impatience, and a tendency toward frustration and hostility. Type A people appear driven, habitually trying to do better than others, and they are verbally and nonverbally hostile if they are prevented from reaching a goal.

The Type B behavior pattern is essentially the opposite of the Type A behavior pattern. The **Type B behavior pattern** is characterized by noncompetitiveness, patience, and a lack of aggression. Unlike Type A's, Type B's don't have a sense of time urgency, and they are rarely hostile. Although most people are neither purely Type A nor Type B, they usually can be placed into one of the two categories on the basis of predominant characteristics (Rosenman, 1990; Strube, 1990).

The distinction between these two behavior patterns is important because a good deal of research evidence suggests that they are related to the incidence of coronary heart disease. For instance, some studies have found that men characterized as Type A's have double the rate of coronary heart disease, suffer significantly more fatal heart attacks, and have five times as many heart problems as Type B's (Rosenman et al., 1976). Even when other, potentially confounding factors are experimentally controlled, such as age, blood pressure, smoking behavior, and cholesterol levels, Type A behavior is clearly linked to coronary heart disease (Williams et al., 1988; Shapiro, 1996).

What is it about Type A behavior that increases the risk of heart problems? One suggestion is that when Type A's are in stressful situations, they become excessively aroused physiologically. As a consequence, they experience an increase in heart rate, blood pressure, and production of the hormones epinephrine and norepinephrine, which causes inordinate wear-and-tear on the circulatory system—and ultimately leads to coronary heart disease (Matthews, 1982; Lyness, 1993; Palmero, Codina, & Rosel, 1993).

Although most research has found a link between the Type A behavior pattern and coronary heart disease, there are exceptions. For instance, one study found that the risk for later heart attacks following an initial attack may be greater for Type B's than Type A's (Fischman, 1987; Ragland & Brand, 1988).

The contradictions in the research are puzzling. Because of the inconsistencies, recent research has tended to focus on the specific components of the Type A behavior pattern that may lead to heart disease. One emerging answer seems to be that hostility and negative emotions—regardless of whether they are manifested through aggressive competitiveness, frustration, anger, or depression—may be the underlying link to coronary heart disease. People who are chronically angry and hostile, then, are at greater risk for coronary heart disease than those who are more emotionally placid (Miller et al., 1996; Shapiro, 1996; Grunbaum, Vernon, & Clasen, 1997; Siegman et al., 1998).

If you habitually exhibit behavior associated with the Type A behavior pattern or are often hostile, are you clearly destined to suffer from coronary heart disease? Not at all. For one thing, people can be trained to reduce such behavior. Through such training, people learn to be more

Type A behavior pattern:
Behavior that is characterized by competitiveness, impatience, and a tendency toward frustration and hostility.

Type B behavior pattern:
Behavior that is characterized by noncompetitiveness, patience, and a lack of aggression.

Type A individuals who are competitive, impatient, and have a tendency toward frustration and hostility may also be more prone to coronary heart disease and fatal heart attacks than Type B individuals.

SPEAKING OF SOCIAL PSYCHOLOGY

Herbert Benson

Stress Specialist

Year of Birth: 1935

Education: B.S., Biology and Chemistry, Wesleyan University; M.D., Behavioral Medicine, Harvard University

Home: Boston, Massachusetts

"Our personal powers and potential for well-being are shaped by the negative or positive ways we think."

As the world prepares to enter the twenty-first century, many people worry that everything is happening too fast. Technology is advancing with lightning speed, and although it hopefully will make life easier, it also brings stress. Over the years people have found many ways to deal with stress. However, according to Dr. Herbert Benson, a leading proponent of relaxation techniques, the best way has been around for a long time.

"Our personal powers and potential for well-being are shaped by the negative or positive ways we think," he says, "and we've known this for quite some time. The first-century Roman philosopher Epictetus recognized this fact, observing: 'Man is disturbed not by things, but by his opinion of things.' What we're learning to do now is a bit like using our minds to take control of our opinions of things."

Meditation, prayer, and personal beliefs have long been recognized as ways to alleviate stress, notes Benson, who has developed a stress-reduction technique known as the *relaxation response.*

patient, to reduce their competitiveness, and in general to slow down their pace. Research suggests that such training can reduce the risk of coronary heart disease (Williams, 1993; Orth-Gomer & Schneiderman, 1996).

Furthermore, the trends might not apply to females. The incidence of coronary heart disease is much higher for males than females, and with a few exceptions, almost all the results linking Type A behaviors with heart disease have been found in studies using men as participants. Until more studies are done with women as participants, then, the role that the Type A behavior pattern plays in women's heart disease remains uncertain (Thoresen & Low, 1990; Orth-Gomer & Schneiderman, 1995; Orth-Gomer, Chesney, & Wenger, 1996).

Cancer: The role of emotions and attitudes.   If you're like most people, you probably fear cancer more than any other disease. A diagnosis of cancer is often seen as a sentence to a painful death, preceded by long periods of suffering. Fortunately, the reality is less grim. Many forms of cancer respond to medical therapy, and scientists' understanding of the disease and the range of treatment approaches available are rapidly expanding.

Although it is still highly tentative, one of the most intriguing approaches to the study of cancer suggests that social psychological factors, and emotions and attitudes in particular, affect the course of the disease. For example, one study examined how the type of emotional response cancer patients displayed toward their disease affected their recovery.

"The relaxation response refers to the inborn capacity of the body to enter a special state characterized by a lower heart rate, a decreased rate of breathing, lower blood pressure, slower brain waves, and an overall reduction in the speed of metabolism," he explains. "In addition, the changes produced by the relaxation response counteract the harmful effects and uncomfortable feelings of stress."

"The changes produced by the relaxation response counteract the harmful effects and uncomfortable feelings of stress."

Benson notes that stress evokes the fight-or-flight response seen in nonhumans, in which the reaction to a specific threat by another animal is either to flee the scene or to engage in combat. Stress also is related directly to a number of diseases, including hypertension, depression, anxiety, cardiac arrhythmia, and many forms of chronic pain.

"The relaxation response is the way to deal with some of these things. The physiological response that we teach is the very opposite of the fight-or-flight response. It is a fundamental bodily response," he says, "that we learn to activate."

But he also adds a caution.

"The relaxation response is not a blueprint to turn us into supermen or superwomen. Each of us is mortal and must operate within certain genetic limitations," he points out. "This means that we all have set ceilings on how far our minds and bodies will take us. The relaxation response is not all-powerful. Furthermore, the technique should be used only in conjunction with modern medicine. It should be an *addition* to the awesome cures that the medical profession can now effect, not a *substitute* for accepted medical care.

"As we attempt to learn the full role the brain plays in alleviating or aggravating symptoms and diseases, we now recognize that the power of the mind must never be dismissed. For example, we now know that any treatment is more likely to be successful if the patient has faith in his or her physician," says Benson. "The relaxation response is a further manifestation of the power of the mind to affect the body."

In the research, a group of women who had had a breast removed due to breast cancer were categorized according to their attitudes—those who felt their situation was hopeless; those who stoically accepted their cancer, trying not to complain; those who had a "fighting spirit," asserting that they would lick the disease; and those who (mistakenly) denied the cancer. Ten years later, when the researchers examined death rates among the women in the study, they found that initial attitude was related to survival. There was a significantly higher death rate among the women who 10 years earlier had stoically accepted their cancer or who had felt hopeless. On the other hand, the death rate was considerably lower for those who had a "fighting spirit" or who had denied the disease (Pettingale et al., 1985; see Figure 5–7).

Psychologist Sandra Levy and colleagues have also found evidence for a link between a positive mental state and survival (Levy et al., 1988; Levy & Roberts, 1992). In Levy's research, mental resilience and vigor, a set of emotions and attitudes she labeled collectively as "joy," were the best predictor of survival time for a group of patients with recurrent breast cancer. Related studies showed that cancer patients who were characteristically optimistic reported less psychological and physical distress than those who were lower in optimism (Carver & Scheier, 1993; Carver et al., 1993; Post-White, 1998; Watson & Greer, 1998).

Results of studies such as these suggest that emotional outlook and attitudes may be related to survival rate. But why might this be true? One possibility, of course, is that cancer

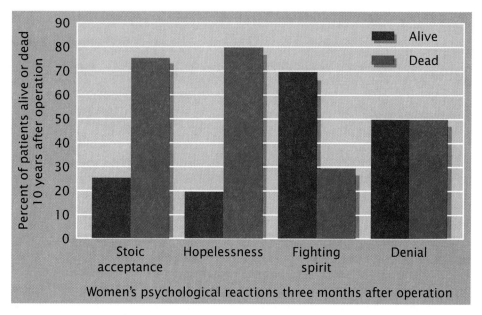

FIGURE 5–7 **Attitudes and Survival in Cancer Patients** Women's attitudes about their cancer close to the time of their initial diagnosis were related to the probability that they were alive 10 years later. (*Source:* Pettingale et al., 1985.)

patients who have positive emotions and attitudes simply are more likely to adhere to the complex, involved medical treatment required by their illness than those who are more negative (Friedman et al., 1992). As a consequence, the patients who carefully follow their treatment regimens may have better medical outcomes (Holland & Lewis, 1993).

Something more may be at work, however. For instance, some health psychologists argue that positive emotions and attitudes benefit the body's immune system, the natural line of defense against disease. In this view, the immune system is bolstered by a positive emotional outlook and is thereby stimulated in the production of natural killer cells that can attack cancerous cells. Conversely, negative emotions and attitudes may impair the ability of natural killer cells to fight cancer (Glaser et al., 1986; Kiecolt-Glaser & Glaser, 1991, 1993, 1995; Seligman, 1995; Kiecolt-Glaser et al., 1998).

Our growing knowledge of the links among emotions, stress, and illness has led to the development of a rapidly expanding subspecialty called **psychoneuroimmunology**, or **PNI**, which is the study of the relationship between psychological factors and the immune system. Scientists studying PNI have accumulated increasing evidence of links between our attitudes and emotions and our susceptibility to a variety of illnesses. In addition, psychological factors affect our ability to recover from surgery and disease and to withstand pain (Kiecolt-Glaser et al., 1998; Marucha, Kiecolt-Glaser, & Favagehi, 1998).

AIDS: The 20th-century plague. It was only in the early 1980s that the first handful of cases of AIDS were reported. Today, AIDS has grown into one of our major health problems. AIDS is now the leading cause of death among men 25 to 44 years of age in the United States, and the third leading cause of death among women in that age range. Some 16 million people have already died from the disease worldwide, and 34 million people are carrying the AIDS virus. Many, if not most, of these people will eventually die from complications related to AIDS unless a cure is found.

Acquired immunodeficiency syndrome, or **AIDS**, is a fatal disease caused by a virus that destroys the body's immune system. It has no known cure. The most typical route of transmission is through sexual activity, but AIDS also is spread through blood transfusions

psychoneuroimmunology (PNI): The study of the relationship between psychological factors and the immune system.

acquired immunodeficiency syndrome (AIDS): A fatal disease caused by a virus that destroys the body's immune system and has no known cure.

TABLE 5-5	Safer Sex: Preventing the Transmissions of AIDS

Health psychologists and educators have devised several guidelines to help prevent the spread of AIDS. Among them are the following:

- **Use condoms.** The use of condoms greatly reduces the risk of transmission of the virus that produces AIDS, which occurs through exposure to bodily fluids such as semen and blood.
- **Avoid high-risk behaviors.** Such practices as unprotected anal intercourse or the exchange of needles among drug users greatly increase the risk of AIDS.
- **Know your partner's sexual history.** Knowing your sexual partner and his or her sexual history can help you evaluate the risks of sexual contact.
- **Consider abstinence.** Although often not a practical alternative, refraining from sexual activity prevents the spread of AIDS from one's partner.

and the use of shared needles during intravenous drug injection. Although initially the casualties of AIDS in the United States were primarily homosexuals, today the incidence of new cases of AIDS is growing more rapidly among heterosexuals. Members of minority groups have been particularly hard hit: African Americans and Hispanics account for 40 percent of the cases of AIDS, although they make up only 18 percent of the U.S. population.

Reducing the spread of AIDS has proved to be a major challenge. However, because AIDS is communicated through specific types of high-risk behavior, it is possible to prevent its spread—if people change their behavior. For instance, health educators have developed inventories of "safer-sex practices"—behaviors that reduce the risk of contracting AIDS during sex (see Table 5–5). In addition, in some urban areas, intravenous drug users are provided with sterile needles, thereby reducing the chances that they will share used, contaminated needles (Compton et al., 1992; Guydish et al., 1995).

Unfortunately, efforts to decrease risky behavior and increase safer practices have met with only scattered success (Colon et al., 1995). For instance, although reductions in risky behavior have occurred in some groups, such as gay men, in other groups little or no change has occurred. Programs that are effective emphasize knowledge about specific behaviors and social interaction, rather than information about the threat of infection (Kalichman et al., 1996; Sheeran, Abraham, & Orbell, 1999).

Of course, in some cases AIDS prevention is too late, and people develop the disease. How do people cope with AIDS? The question is a difficult one, because the course of the disease varies significantly from one person to another. For instance, some people may carry the HIV for years without showing symptoms, whereas others quickly become ill.

Although there have been only a few studies of how people cope with AIDS, the existing research consistently finds that **active behavioral coping**, in which people mobilize to fight the illness directly, results in higher self-esteem, better mood, and increases in the belief that one is receiving significant social support. In contrast, people who use avoidant coping do not fare as well (Fleishman & Fogel, 1994; Clement & Schoennesson, 1998). In **avoidant coping**, people refuse to think about their illness, and they evade or postpone acting in ways that deal directly with the disease. Avoidant coping leads to depression, anxiety, lower self-esteem, and a weaker sense of social support (Commerford et al., 1994; Stein & Nyamathi, 1999). Similarly, people with AIDS who have a greater sense of control over their disease and its treatment show better coping than those who have a lower sense of control (Nicholson & Long, 1990; Wolf et al., 1991; Taylor et al., 1993).

AIDS presents other social psychological issues. Should people at risk for AIDS be tested to determine whether they carry the virus that produces the disease? How do we reduce the anxiety of people whose contacts with AIDS patients are casual and whose fears of catching the disease are therefore groundless? How do people negotiate safer-sex practices with their partners? At what point should sex education that stresses the use of condoms to prevent the spread of AIDS begin? Does the distribution of condoms and sterile needles promote sexual behavior and drug use?

active behavioral coping: A behavioral approach in which people mobilize to fight the illness directly, resulting in higher self-esteem, better mood, and increases in perceived social support.

avoidant coping: Behavior in which people refuse to think about their illness, and they evade or postpone acting in ways that deal directly with the disease.

Until a cure is found for the disease, each of these questions—and many more—must be answered if we are to deal effectively with the health crisis brought on by AIDS.

REVIEW AND RETHINK

Review

- Stress is the response to events, known as stressors, that threaten or challenge a person. Stress can have negative health consequences.

- The three major types of stressors are cataclysmic events, personal stressors, and daily hassles.

- People use problem-focused coping, emotion-focused coping, and social support to deal with stress.

- Coronary heart disease, cancer, and AIDS all raise important social psychological issues.

Rethink

- Why might flooding of your entire neighborhood be less stressful than flooding that affects only your house? Is the difference due to primary or secondary appraisal?

- Think of a cultural explanation for the sudden death syndrome of the Cambodian Hmong. Then think of a biological explanation. Could both explanations be correct? Explain.

- Separate the methods for reducing stress described in this chapter according to whether they are problem-focused coping strategies or emotion-focused strategies.

PHYSICIANS AND PATIENTS

Patient: I can hardly drink water.
Physician: Uh-huh.
Patient: Remember when it started? . . . It was pains in my head. It must have been then.
Physician: Uh-huh.
Patient: I don't know what it is. The doctor looked at it . . . said something about glands.
Physician: OK. Aside from this, how have you been feeling?
Patient: Terrible.
Physician: Uh-huh.
Patient: Tired . . . there's pains . . . I don't know what it is.
Physician: OK. . . . Fevers or chills?
Patient: No.
Physician: OK. . . . Have you been sick to your stomach or anything?
Patient: (Sniffles, crying) I don't know what's going on. I get up in the morning tired. The only time I feel good . . . maybe like around suppertime . . . and everything (crying) and still the same thing.
Physician: Uh-huh. You're getting the nausea before you eat or after? (Goleman, 1988, p. B16)

How would you feel if you were the patient in this scenario? What would you think of the physician, and how likely would you be to follow the suggestions you received?

No matter how good the technical advice provided by such a doctor, it would be difficult to walk away from such an exchange (which is an excerpt from an actual case study used to train physicians at Harvard Medical School) feeling that our medical concerns had been properly heard and acknowledged. In fact, when a Harris poll questioned people as to why they had changed from one physician to another, most answers involved issues of communication (see Figure 5–8, Ferguson, 1993; Plichta, Duncan, & Plichta, 1996).

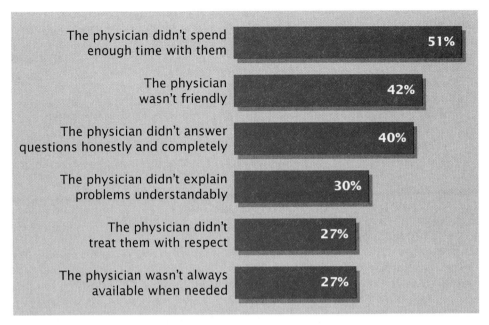

FIGURE 5–8   Reasons for Changing Physicians These are the major reasons that patients cited as causing them to change their physician.

Clearly, factors other than pure medical competence are required for a successful medical practice. In fact, as we'll see, several social psychological factors play an important role in the success of medical treatment. We'll begin by looking at communication between physicians and patients.

PATIENT–PHYSICIAN COMMUNICATION

To follow a physician's recommendations, we need to understand exactly what the physician wants us to do. Frequently, however, physicians miscommunicate (Parrott, 1994), and patients misinterpret advice and recommendations.

One important source of miscommunication is the language used by physicians to present information to their patients (Hadlow & Pitts, 1991). For instance, when a physician has a druggist indicate on a prescription label that a tablet should be "taken with meals," the instructions may be translated in a variety of ways: Should the pill be taken before the meal, during the meal, or after the meal? Furthermore, since mealtimes may vary a great deal from patient to patient, the schedule on which the drug is administered may vary significantly from one patient to the next, depending on the patient's individualistic interpretation of the instructions (Ley, 1982; Morris & Chenail, 1995).

If the written instructions on medicine containers sometimes prove ambiguous, we might expect that recommendations delivered orally by physicians might occasionally be even less clear to patients—and this seems to be the case. For instance, some 60% of patients in one study misunderstood their physician's oral directions regarding how they should take their medication (Boyd et al., 1974).

The use of medical jargon and scientific terms by physicians tends to decrease the likelihood that patients will successfully adhere to medical treatments. For example, instead of telling a patient he is "hypertensive" and needs to reduce his "sodium intake," a physician might consider informing the patient that he has high blood pressure and needs to reduce the amount of salt in his diet (DiMatteo & DiNicola, 1982).

Of course, physicians must walk a fine line between communications that are too technical and those that are overly simplistic. Medical practitioners often underestimate their patients' understanding of their medical conditions (McKinlay, 1975; Waitzkin, 1985). Some even use baby talk or exhibit condescending attitudes toward their patients, resulting in

The manner in which physicians communicate with their patients plays an important role in treatment success.

patient anger and reduced attention to medical advice. For example, a physician who said, "Nurse, would you just pop off her things for me? I want to examine her," elicited the following comments from a patient:

> In the hospital, everything is "popped" on or off, "slipped" in or out. I don't think I met a single doctor who, in dealing with patients, didn't resort to this sort of nursery talk. I once heard one saying to a patient, an elderly man, "We're just going to pop you into the operating theater to have a little peep into your tummy." (Toynbee, 1977)

Cultural factors are related to the success with which information is successfully communicated to patients. For instance, to patients for whom English is not the first language, receiving medical recommendations in English may be problematic. Similarly, certain groups are more apt, in general, to act on physicians' recommendations. Male patients and younger patients are less likely to follow health recommendations than female and elderly patients (Samora, Saunders, & Larson, 1961; Bush & Osterweis, 1978).

In addition, status differences often exist between physicians and patients, with patients perceiving physicians as having a higher status than themselves. Certainly, if income level is the main determinant of status, this perception is often accurate.

Because they attribute higher status to their physicians, some patients may credit them with other abilities. For example, they may believe that their physicians are so adept at making diagnoses that they can recognize patients' problem on the basis of a physical examination alone—in the same way that a good auto mechanic can identify a problem by examining a car by touch, sight, and sound (Leigh & Reiser, 1980; Mentzer & Snyder, 1982). If patients feel that the success of their medical care is the sole responsibility of a high-status, remarkably skilled physician, they may become more passive and less attentive to their health, and less compliant with medical advice.

The manner in which physicians communicate information—sometimes called their bedside manner—may be as important as its content. For instance, physicians who are perceived as being aloof, antagonistic, or insensitive to patients' needs generally have lower rates of compliance than physicians who are viewed as being interested in their patients' psychological well-being as well as their physical health (Davis, 1968; Lepper, Martin, & DiMatteo, 1995; Rodriguez et al., 1998).

On the other hand, in some cases physicians who communicate anger and anxiety in their voices produce greater compliance in their patients. It is possible that signals of tension and anger may emphasize the seriousness of a medical condition, thereby motivating patients to be more compliant to the physician's recommendations (Hall, Roter, & Rand, 1981; Buller & Street, 1992).

COMPLIANCE WITH MEDICAL REGIMENS:
FOLLOWING DOCTORS' ORDERS

After a full physical examination of her patient, the physician makes her diagnosis: The patient's symptoms could be significantly relieved by weight loss of at least 20 pounds. The patient nods, agreeing that he understands the problem and that he will go on a diet immediately. He leaves the physician's office, relieved that the problem isn't more serious. On the way home, by way of a little celebration, he stops at a newsstand and picks up a couple of candy bars. "After all," he says to himself, "I can start to diet tomorrow."

Perhaps you've found yourself in similar circumstances: A physician gives you advice, and—despite your best intentions—you neglect to follow it. Certainly, most of us have been in situations in which we agree wholeheartedly with certain advice and yet are unable to make ourselves comply.

Failure to comply with medical advice represents a major health problem—one that has long been recognized. Even before modern times the problem of noncompliance with health care regimens was recognized. For instance, in the 1600s, the playwright Molière explained his physician's job to the king in this way: "Sire, we converse. He gives me advice which I do not follow and I get better" (Treue, 1958, p. 41, cited in Taylor, 1991).

Not everyone gets better, however. Nonadherence to medical regimens may cause an illness to become more severe. In the most extreme cases, it can result in death. Furthermore, a physician may not be aware of the degree to which a patient has been noncompliant. As a result, the physician may reach a faulty conclusion about the success or failure of a particular treatment or medicine because of the patient's failure to follow directions.

Noncompliance is widespread. Estimates range from as little as 15% to as much as 93%. For example, some estimates suggest that of the 750 million prescriptions for medicine written each year, close to 70 percent are not taken as prescribed (Alpert, 1964; Stone, 1979; Rapoff & Christophersen, 1982; Gatchel & Baum, 1983; Becker, 1985; Buckalew & Sallis, 1986; Kaplan, Sallis, & Patterson, 1993; Buckalew & Buckalew, 1995).

Noncompliance can take many forms: Patients may not take medicine at scheduled times or may discontinue its use prematurely. In some cases, they may not even fill a prescription.

Furthermore, patients are even less prone to follow medical advice that calls for deprivation of some sort or requires a major investment of time. Consequently, physicians' recommendations that require participation in an exercise program or adherence to a strict diet are particularly apt to be ignored. In fact, some studies show that when health recommendations involve changes in personal habits such as eating or smoking, adherence ranges from only 20% to 50% (DiMatteo & DiNicola, 1982).

In some cases, nonadherence to medical regimes takes a creative turn. Suppose, for example, you regularly took a drug for a particular medical condition. If you believed that you were the person most knowledgeable about your own body's reaction to the drug, wouldn't you be tempted to take matters into your own hands and adjust the dosage of the drug yourself? Many patients modify prescription dosage, figuring that they are more sensitive than anyone else to the way drugs affect them. Such nonadherence to medical regimens has been termed creative nonadherence. In **creative nonadherence**, patients adjust or augment a treatment prescribed by a physician, relying on their own medical judgment and experience (Weintraub, 1976; Taylor, 1995).

Creative nonadherence may occasionally work just fine. Frequently, patients are, in fact, more successful in determining reactions to their medication than others. Diabetics taking insulin can often detect minute reactions to the drug, and they can modify their intake on an ongoing basis. Furthermore, one study of children with asthma found that parental modification of the prescribed treatment produced better results than strict adherence to physicians' instructions. For instance, parents were more sensitive to their children's specific symptoms and could take into account seasonal changes in allergies (Deaton, 1985).

Unfortunately, creative noncompliance is sometimes detrimental to a patient's health. Patients may misjudge the effects of medication modification or lack critical knowledge

creative nonadherence: A situation in which patients adjust or augment a treatment prescribed by a physician, relying on their own medical judgment and experience.

reactance: A disagreeable emotional and cognitive reaction that results from the restriction of one's freedom that can be associated with medical regimens.

about drug effects. Moreover, extraneous factors may influence decisions about medication use. For example, low-income patients may sometimes ration their drug usage, apportioning only a fraction of the prescribed dosage in order to make an expensive drug last longer.

In other cases, patients develop inaccurate theories of disease and symptomology. Such noncompliance with prescribed regimens can be injurious (Leventhal, Nerenz, & Leventhal, 1985). For example, a patient with high blood pressure may assume—erroneously—that headaches are a symptom of the disease. Because of this faulty assumption, the patient may conclude that it is necessary to take medication for the condition only when he has a headache, regardless of a physician's prescription to take the medicine daily. The patient's mistaken medical theory may be reinforced if he measures his blood pressure only on days when he has a headache—and finds that his blood pressure is high. Obviously, if he had taken his blood pressure at other times, he probably would have found it to be high as well, thereby making the inaccuracy of his theory evident. Unfortunately, though, he is less likely to measure his blood pressure at times when he is, in his opinion, free of symptoms, and thus his inaccurate theory is likely to persevere.

In some cases, noncompliance is due to psychological reactance. **Reactance** is a disagreeable emotional and cognitive reaction that results from the restriction of one's freedom (Brehm & Brehm, 1981). When people experience reactance, they feel hostility and anger, and as a result, they seek to restore their freedom. Ironically, reactance often motivates people to pursue the restricted behavior with renewed vigor.

Particularly complex, involved medical regimens may unwittingly set the stage for patient reactance. For example, physicians who order patients to make major lifestyle changes may virtually guarantee that the resentment characteristic of reactance will emerge. Similarly, a major illness, by itself, can cause reactance, if patients feel that their lives are unduly restricted by their medical condition.

How do patients deal with psychological reactance? One means is to seek out ways to restore lost freedom. Consequently, patients may choose to behave in a noncompliant fashion. Rather than following physicians' advice, then, patients may act in quite the opposite manner. Obviously, such behavior is self-destructive, but it does help to diminish the unpleasant feeling of reactance.

INCREASING COMPLIANCE WITH MEDICAL REGIMENS

We've seen the various types of social psychological forces that can reduce compliance with medical regimens. Even when patients know that a course of action is in their best interests, they may be unable or—in the case of reactance—unwilling to follow a treatment prescription.

However, several approaches exist for reducing the level of patient noncompliance that occurs (DiMatteo, Reiter, & Gambone, 1994; Cramer, 1995; Murdaugh, 1998). According to social psychologist Shelley Taylor (1995), several strategies have proved successful in increasing compliance.

◆ *Changing medical practices: Institutional reform.* The increasing use of prepaid medical insurance, which covers all medical expenses, has sometimes led to the depersonalization of medical treatment. Rather than having a particular physician with whom patients develop a personal relationship, they may receive medical care from whichever physician happens to be available at a given time. When physicians are seen as interchangeable, patients may feel that they are viewed in the same way, and hence that the health care provider they see is less committed personally to their well-being. Furthermore, patients may have to wait for long periods of time before they can see a physician, which may discourage them from seeking treatment for certain minor ailments. Such depersonalization may reduce compliance with the advice of a physician who is a virtual stranger.

To reduce feelings of depersonalization, medical organizations have tried several approaches. One is to permit each member of a health care organization to choose a primary care physician. Consequently, rather than being assigned to providers on a first-come, first-served basis, patients make appointments with the physician of their choice. In addition, improved scheduling procedures can reduce the waiting time for appointments. Finally, some health care organizations place a special focus on preventive measures. By dealing with patients when they are healthy, they establish an atmosphere of caring that may enhance compliance with medical regimens if and when their patients become ill.

◆ *Changing how health care providers impart medical information: Cognitive factors.* One reason patients do not comply with medical regimens is that they simply do not understand them. As a result, one approach to increasing compliance with treatment suggestions involves attempting to maximize patients' ability to understand complex medical information (Lin et al., 1995).

For instance, if patients become confused by intricate treatment instructions that a health care provider delivers orally, it may be useful to provide the information in written form. When patients have written descriptions of the medications prescribed to them, including possible side effects and dosage levels, they are considerably more compliant (Peck & King, 1982).

Furthermore, patients can be quizzed on their understanding of medical information and their ability to remember its content. The goal is not to turn doctors into teachers, but to ensure that patients fully understand and recall the content of their treatment regimens.

◆ *Improving the communication skills of physicians: Emotional issues.* When communicating with patients, health care providers must take into account the delicate emotional balance that exists between providers and patients (Buller & Street, 1992). Because of the importance of communication skills in promoting proper compliance, providers need training in ways to interact with patients.

For example, physicians often provide only meager amounts of information to their patients—although they often think otherwise. One study found that while physicians estimated that they spent nearly half of the average 20-minute office visit providing suggestions and recommendations to their patients, the actual figure was about 1 minute (Waitzkin & Stoeckle, 1976). Another study found that most physicians interrupted their patients during the first 18 seconds of their encounter, when the patients were attempting to explain their problems (Beckman & Frankel, 1984).

Naturally, the quality of communications, as well as the quantity of time that physicians spend communicating with their patients, is important. Even rudimentary improvements in physician–patient communication may lead to the enhancement of patients' sense of well-being. For instance, physicians who are explicitly taught to be courteous—saying hello, addressing patients by their names, and saying goodbye at the end of a clinical interview—are thought of as warmer and more supportive than physicians who do not follow such basic procedures (DiMatteo & DiNicola, 1982; Thompson, 1988; Thompson, Nanni, & Schwankovsky, 1990).

◆ *Using social support to promote adherence.* As we noted earlier in the chapter when we discussed ways of coping with stress, social support can have powerful effects on stress reduction. Just as social support can help an individual withstand pressure and stress, it can also enhance people's ability to follow a treatment regimen. Social support from friends and family can help people adhere to medical advice, as well as help them cope with the stress brought about by illness (Dunkel-Schetter, Folkman, & Lazarus, 1987; Taylor, Buunk, & Aspinwall, 1990; Croyle & Hunt, 1991; Belgrave & Lewis, 1994).

When family members participate in the medical regimens of patients, compliance increases. Participation can range from simply helping patients remember when to take their medicine to actually administering certain kinds of medical treatment or procedures. Social support can also help patients avoid certain behaviors. For instance, refraining from serving a rich dessert to a dieter helps ensure that the dieter will succeed. In contrast, urging a dieter to sample a piece of cake because it tastes so good just makes it more likely that the dieter will ultimately fail.

The social support of concerned family and friends can also help prevent the patient from relapsing to unhealthy habits once the health problem has been overcome. For instance,

TABLE 5–6	**Improving Compliance with Medical Treatment**

After surveying the research on patient compliance, social psychologist Shelley Taylor of the University of California, Los Angeles, generated the following lists of behaviors that lead to increased adherence to treatment:

1. Listen to the patient.
2. Ask the patient to repeat what has to be done.
3. Keep the prescription as simple as possible.
4. Give clear instructions on the exact treatment regimen, preferably in writing.
5. Make use of special reminder pill containers and calendars.
6. Call the patient if an appointment is missed.
7. Prescribe a self-care regimen in concert with the patient's daily schedule.
8. Emphasize the importance of adherence at each visit.
9. Gear the frequency of visits to adherence needs.
10. Acknowledge the patient's efforts to adhere to the regimen at each visit.
11. Involve the patient's spouse or other partner.
12. Whenever possible, provide patients with instructions and advice at the start of the information to be presented.
13. When providing patients with instructions and advice, stress how important they are.
14. Use short words and short sentences.
15. Use explicit categorization where possible. (For example, divide information clearly into categories of causes, treatment, or likely outcomes.)
16. Repeat things where feasible.
17. When giving advice, make it as specific, detailed, and concrete as possible.
18. Find out what the patient's worries are. Do not confine yourself merely to gathering objective medical information.
19. Find out what the patient's expectations are. If they cannot be met, explain why.
20. Provide information about the diagnosis and the cause of the illness.
21. Adopt a friendly rather than a businesslike attitude.
22. Avoid medical jargon.
23. Spend some time in conversation about nonmedical topics.

Source: Adapted from Taylor, 1995, p. 368; based on Haynes, Wang, & da-Mota-Gomes, 1987; and Ley, 1977.

people who have overcome drug abuse can be helped to avoid lapses through the encouragement and reinforcement of others.

In short, providing social support, as well as promoting institutional reform and taking cognitive and emotional factors into account, can increase compliance with medical regimens. By using these techniques, summarized in Table 5–6, patients are more likely to follow the recommendations made by those to whom they have entrusted their care.

REVIEW AND RETHINK

Review

- Physician–patient communication relies on both the language and the manner of physicians, and it can affect patient compliance.

- Nonadherence to medical regimens is widespread and takes many forms, including creative noncompliance and reactance.

- Compliance can be increased through changing medical practices, improving the quality and presentation of medical information, and using social support.

Rethink

- In recent years the status of physicians has declined somewhat. How might this change affect physician–patient interactions?

- Why is "bedside manner" an important factor in patient compliance?

- Which methods of increasing compliance with medical regimens focus on the physician end of the physician–patient relationship? Which focus on the patient end? Which might be most relevant for convincing a patient to quit smoking?

L O O K I N G   B A C K

What are the ingredients of a sense of well-being?

1. Self-complexity, viewing oneself as having many distinct facets, is linked to a positive sense of well-being. (p. 153)

2. Self-discrepancy theory argues that the discrepancy between people's self-concept and their self-guides leads to negative emotions and ultimately to lower psychological well-being. (p. 154)

3. Self-disclosure, in which information about the self is exchanged with others, holds several advantages. In fact, confession of past disturbing experiences can reduce stress and produce clear health benefits. (p. 154)

4. Learned helplessness, the belief that one can exercise no control over one's environment, can cause people to give up and potentially develop deep feelings of depression. (p. 157)

5. People most prone to depression habitually view positive events in their lives as due to external, unstable, and specific causes. At the same time, they attribute negative events to internal, stable, and global causes. (p. 158)

6. Attribution training replaces inaccurate, harmful attributions with more accurate and beneficial ones. In contrast, through misattribution training people are led to replace their accurate, but harmful, attributions with inaccurate, but more beneficial, attributions. (p. 158)

7. Research on illusions has shown that a clear and accurate sense of the world is not always beneficial. Among the most beneficial illusions are holding unrealistically positive evaluations of self, having an exaggerated sense of control over occurrences in one's life, and being unrealistically optimistic. (p. 162)

What are the determinants and consequences of stress, and what are some strategies for coping with it?

8. Stress is the response to events (known as stressors) that threaten or challenge a person. Circumstances become stressful following primary appraisal (the assessment of an event to determine whether its implications are positive, neutral, or negative) and secondary appraisal (the assessment of the adequacy of one's coping abilities and

resources to overcome the harm, threat, or challenge posed by the potential stressor). (p. 165)

9. There are three basic categories of stressors: cataclysmic events, personal stressors, and daily hassles. People who experience cataclysmic events may develop post-traumatic stress disorder. Stress can be reduced by uplifts, minor positive events that make people feel temporarily good. (p. 166)

10. Events that are negative, uncontrollable or unpredictable, unclear or ambiguous, and that contain multiple tasks that strain resources are most likely to produce stress. (p. 168)

11. The immediate reaction to stress is physiological arousal, which may be beneficial in the short term. In the long run, however, such arousal may damage the body and lead to psychophysiological disorders. (p. 169)

12. Coping is the effort to control, reduce, or learn to tolerate the threats that lead to stress. Coping may include the use of defense mechanisms, or may involve problem-focused and emotion-focused coping. Coping success also may vary according to a general coping style such as hardiness. (p. 171)

13. Among the means of dealing with stress are attempting to exert control, reappraising threatening events, seeking social support, using relaxation techniques, and exercising. (p. 172)

What are the social psychological components of coronary heart disease, cancer, and AIDS?

14. The Type A behavior pattern is characterized by competitiveness, impatience, a tendency toward frustration, and hostility. In contrast, the Type B behavior pattern is characterized by noncompetitiveness, patience, and a lack of aggression. The Type A behavior pattern has been linked to an increased likelihood of coronary heart disease, although certain components of the pattern are likely most important. For instance, the presence of hostility and negative emotions may be the underlying link to coronary heart disease. (p. 175)

15. The course of cancer has been linked to attitudes and emotions. One reason for the relationship may be that the immune system, the body's natural line of defense against disease, may be bolstered by a positive emotional outlook. (p. 176)

16. Acquired immunodeficiency syndrome, or AIDS, is transmitted by certain risky practices. Successful reduction of unsafe behavior is the result of three factors: information, motivation, and behavioral skill. (p. 178)

How do patients' interactions with their physicians affect their health and their compliance with medical treatment?

17. Physicians may miscommunicate through their oral language and nonverbal manner, leading to patient dissatisfaction and ambiguities in treatment recommendations. Noncompliance with health care regimens is widespread, with some estimates as high as 93%. Noncompliance can take several forms, including creative nonadherence, in which patients adjust or augment a treatment based on their own medical judgment and experience. Reactance can also lead to noncompliance. (p. 181)

18. Among the ways to increase compliance are introducing reforms in the practice of medicine, changing the ways medical information is imparted, improving the communication skills of physicians, and using social support. (p. 184)

EPILOGUE

In this chapter and the previous one, we've considered what social psychologists know about the self. In Chapter 4, we saw how we develop and maintain a general sense of the self. We considered how people's evaluation of themselves is formed, and how they attempt to present themselves to the world.

In this chapter, we built on our earlier view of the self, taking a more applied approach. Here, we've considered some of the ways that social psychological factors relate to well-being and psychological and physical health. We've looked at the components of well-being, considering the links between people's view of the self and their general perception of wellness. We then examined how people cope with stress and how ailments once considered purely physical have significant psychological components. We've also investigated how patients' relationships with their physicians affect the success of their treatment.

The material we discussed in this chapter moved us from psychological domains into the physical realm of illness and disease. However, what should be apparent from our discussions in this and the previous chapter is how closely linked the two worlds are. Our understanding of how people perceive themselves is enhanced by examining both the psychological and physical aspects of the self and of well-being. The mind and body work interdependently, jointly creating our experience as humans.

Before we turn to the next few chapters, which deal with relationships, reread the prologue of this chapter, about the busy life of Elizabeth Oettinger. Consider these questions:

1. How does the phenomenon of self-complexity relate to Oettinger's life? Would she be likely to say that her life is stressful? Is she more likely to report satisfaction or dissatisfaction with her life? Why?

2. How do busy people like Oettinger respond to an unexpected, potentially stressful event, such as the sudden illness of one of her children that would keep her home from work?

3. Can you describe the appraisal processes Oettinger might go through in assessing the degree of stress she experiences from an unexpected event that prevented her from working?

4. How might Oettinger apply problem-focused coping and emotion-focused coping to the problem of a sick child?

KEY TERMS AND CONCEPTS

acquired immunodeficiency syndrome (AIDS) (p. 178)

active behavioral coping (p. 179)

attribution training (p. 158)

attributional style (p. 158)

avoidant coping (p. 179)

cataclysmic events (p. 166)

coping (p. 171)

creative nonadherence (p. 183)

daily hassles (or background stressors) (p. 167)

defense mechanisms (p. 171)

hardiness (p. 173)

health psychology (p. 152)

learned helplessness (p. 157)

personal stressors (p. 167)

psychoneuroimmunology (PNI) (p. 178)

psychophysiological conditions (p. 169)

reactance (p. 184)

self-complexity (p. 153)

self-disclosure (p. 154)

self-discrepancy theory (p. 154)

self-regulation failure (p. 156)

social support (p. 172)

stress (p. 165)

stressors (p. 165)

Type A behavior pattern (p. 175)

Type B behavior pattern (p. 175)

uplifts (p. 167)

INTERPERSONAL ATTRACTION

Developing Liking

CHAPTER 6

PROLOGUE
Friends for Life

Many close and lasting friendships begin at a very young age. Social psychologists continually examine how such friendships evolve and strengthen through time.

For two years after I changed schools in the second grade, Peggy was just another classmate, someone I said hello to, but didn't save a seat for at lunch. Then, halfway through fourth grade, Peggy came to class clutching a Raggedy Ann doll. By chance, that same day, I had brought my Raggedy Andy, then at the top of my list of favorite things.

We discussed the relative merits of our dolls, including the rumor that they had real candy hearts, and agreed they were much superior to Barbie, the rage with the rest of our classmates. I knew I had found a kindred spirit. . . .

I spent the majority of my weekends for the next five years at Peggy's house, weekends which stretched into weeks in the summer. Happy to be doing just about anything in each other's company, we overcame the challenges of preadolescence together. . . .

When Peggy went away to school in the ninth grade, I was very upset, surmising, correctly, that our time of being together had ended. What I didn't realize then was that it would do nothing to change our friendship. Ever since, we have lived no closer to each other than a six-hour drive. . . .

It doesn't matter. When we do talk, it is as if we talk every day, as if our last conversation ended just minutes ago. I tell Peggy the stuff I don't tell anyone else, heartaches and dreams. She tells me what I need to hear in such a way that I accept it and I try to do the same for her.

As she has since she first became my friend, Peggy remains the only person who consistently makes me laugh until tears run down my cheeks. (Mitchell, 1997, p. 11) ■

LOOKING AHEAD

interpersonal attraction: The degree of liking that people have for one another.

For most of us, friendships are a central component of our lives. But how do we make the transition from stranger to friend and build meaningful and lasting friendships? In this chapter, we'll answer that question as we consider the forces that lead to **interpersonal attraction**, the degree of liking that people have for one another.

We begin by examining the roots of attraction: our need for affiliation and our desire to be in the presence of others. We also consider the factors that produce loneliness and identify the differences between loneliness and being alone.

Next, we turn to some of the specific factors that underlie our liking for others. We look first at situational factors, such as our proximity to specific individuals, as well as how we may grow to like people merely because they become more familiar. And finally, we consider how people's personal characteristics—including their personal qualities, physical attractiveness, and similarity to us—lead to liking.

In sum, after reading this chapter, you'll be able to answer these questions:

◆ What are the origins of interpersonal attraction?

◆ How do situational factors such as proximity and familiarity lead to liking?

◆ What are the primary personal qualities that lead people to be liked by others?

◆ What strategies for making friends do the principles of interpersonal attraction suggest?

AFFILIATION: THE ORIGINS OF ATTRACTION

When Terry Anderson, who spent years as a hostage of captivity in Lebanon, looked back at his life in captivity, the companionship of others was one of the few bright spots during seven years of imprisonment. As he wrote when he was freed:

> All of the nine men I shared cells with at various times helped me, and I hope I helped them. We talked, endlessly and about everything. We played chess, and cards. (Secretly at first with homemade decks—cards are forbidden by the strict fundamentalists who held us. Later, they conceded us the privilege.) We made a Monopoly set, and a Scrabble game. We taught each other things—agriculture, economics, education, journalism, literature. Mostly, we depended on each other. (Anderson, 1992, p. A10)

You don't need to be held hostage to realize the importance of others in your life. Humans are social animals, and most people find companionship to be a central and essential component of life. In fact, people forced to live alone—such as prisoners in isolated confinement—typically begin to feel extreme apathy and a sense of withdrawal, not unlike what people with schizophrenia report experiencing. The longer their isolation, the more they think and even dream about other people (Brodsky & Scogin, 1988; Thompson & Heller, 1990; Palinkas & Browner, 1995).

Why is physical isolation from others so unpleasant? Social psychologists suggest that there is a fundamental need that the presence of others fulfills: the need for affiliation.

THE NEED FOR AFFILIATION: REDUCING FEAR AND ISOLATION

Suppose you had agreed to be a participant in an experiment, and these were the instructions that you received from experimenter "Dr. Gregor Zilstein":

> What we will ask each of you to do is simple. We would like to give each of [you] a series of electric shocks. Now, I feel I must be completely honest with you and tell you exactly what

Terry Anderson, who was held hostage in Lebanon for almost 7 years, experienced the extremes of isolation.

you are in for. These shocks will hurt; they will be painful. As you can guess, if in research of this sort we're to learn anything at all that will really help humanity, it is necessary for our shocks to be intense. (Schachter, 1959, p. 13)

Suppose, further, that Dr. Zilstein, who also had provided you with a brief lecture on the importance of research on electric shock, then asked where you wished to wait for the procedure to begin. Given the choice of waiting alone or waiting in the presence of other participants who were also waiting their turn to be shocked, which would you choose?

If you are like most of the actual participants, you'd be certain to choose to wait with others. In the original, now classic study, carried out by social psychologist Stanley Schachter (1959), most participants who were in this high-fear situation chose to wait with others. In contrast, in a control condition in which participants were threatened with a mild, relatively painless shock, most participants chose to wait by themselves.

To Schachter, the results of his study suggested that affiliation needs could be aroused by fear. This might be the case for at least two reasons. For one thing, participants expecting a strong shock may have anticipated that the presence of other people could directly reduce their anxiety by offering comfort, consolation, and reassurance.

A second factor, however, relates to social comparison processes. As we first considered in Chapter 4, *social comparison* is the need to evaluate one's own behavior, abilities, expertise, and opinions by comparing them with those of other people. According to social comparison theory, people are dependent on others for information about the world around them, and they use the behavior and views of others to evaluate their own. People need to do this, the theory suggests, because the objective reality of a situation is often ambiguous or simply unknowable.

For Schachter's experimental participants, social comparison processes may have led fearful participants to attempt to understand and control their own emotions by comparing themselves with others in the same situation. By seeking out the company of others, participants may have tried to understand more fully the meaning of their emotions and feelings (Morris et al., 1976; Wills, 1981).

Regardless of the specific reason for participants' preference to be with others when they were afraid, Schachter argued that the results of his study illustrated the need for affiliation. The **need for affiliation** is the desire to seek relationships with other people. Although the strength of this need varies from one person to the next and from one situation to another, everyone holds to some degree a basic desire to forge associations with others.

However, people don't indiscriminately pursue relationships with others. For instance, Schachter's later research showed that individuals fearful of receiving shocks in his experiments didn't just seek out *any* company. Instead, they pursued the presence of others who were in a position similar to their own. Specifically, participants who thought that they would receive a severe shock were likely to choose to affiliate with others, but only if they knew the others were also expecting to be shocked. Apparently, people who were not going to receive a shock provided none of the solace offered by those who were similarly afflicted. According to Schachter, then, misery does not love just any company; it loves only miserable company.

However, Schachter was only partially correct. Subsequent research demonstrates that it is not critical for others to be equally miserable for their presence to be comforting. Instead, what counts is that other people face similar circumstances, not necessarily that they feel exactly the same way about those circumstances. Hence, it is the similarity of the situation that makes their presence desirable (Kulik, Mahler, & Moore, 1996; Kulik & Mahler, 1997).

People seek out others who are in a similar situation because others help clarify the situation they face. In turn, the others provide a clearer definition of the situation and more information that may be useful in reducing anxiety. In simple terms, the presence of others provides information about what to expect, and others do not always have to feel miserable themselves to provide useful information (Buunk, Schaufeli, & Ybema, 1994; Kulik, Mahler, & Earnest, 1994; Buunk, 1995; Gump & Kulik, 1997). In some instances, however, the level of misery is so strong that people avoid the presence of others. When circumstances provoke very strong negative emotions, people avoid others. For example, when President John

need for affiliation: The desire to seek relationships with other people.

social anxiety: The experience of negative emotions revolving around interactions with others.

need for belongingness: The need to establish and maintain at least a minimum number of interpersonal relationships.

attachment: The positive emotional bond that develops between a child and a particular individual.

Kennedy was assassinated in 1963, people who felt the most upset by his death typically wanted to be alone (Sheatsley & Feldman, 1964).

It may be that when people are deeply distressed, they fear that exposure to the unhappiness or depression of others will increase their own unhappiness. Moreover, when emotions are so strong as to be unambiguous, there is little need to obtain additional information about the situation (Wheeler, 1974). Consequently, at times of deep emotional turmoil, people may forgo contact with others.

People also may avoid contact with others because of their **social anxiety**, the experience of negative emotions revolving around interactions with others. Individuals who experience social anxiety are so fearful of the possible consequences of being with people, such as rejection, that they sometimes avoid contact with others. Ironically, in such cases, their avoidance of social contact may cause them to be seen by other people as aloof, unpleasant, and socially inept—and others actually begin to reject them (Meleshko & Alden, 1993; Smari, Bjarnadottir, & Bragadottir, 1998; Papsdorf & Alden, 1998).

Despite instances of individuals avoiding others, in most cases people seek out the presence of others and find it desirable. In fact, as we see next, some researchers suggest that people have a fundamental need to maintain relationships with others.

THE NEED TO BELONG: SEEKING RELATIONSHIPS

Some social psychologists suggest that the need for affiliation is part of a broader human motivation: the need for belongingness. According to Roy Baumeister and Mark Leary (1995; Baumeister & Dori, 1998), the **need for belongingness** is the need to establish and maintain at least a minimum number of interpersonal relationships.

Arguing that a universal desire exists among humans to seek out belongingness, Baumeister and Leary suggest that people are naturally driven toward forming and preserving relationships that allow them to experience a sense of belonging (Manstead, 1997; Rice, 1999). Unlike the more limited need for affiliation, which suggests only that under certain conditions people will seek out the company of others, the need for belongingness broadens the concept, suggesting that people are motivated to maintain a minimum *quantity* of ongoing relationships.

The need for belongingness has two essential components. First, to experience belongingness, people require relatively frequent interactions and personal contacts with other individuals. We can't feel much in the way of belongingness if we don't have periodic contact with others.

Second, a sense of belongingness occurs when relationships are stable, when they are likely to continue into the future, and when the parties involved genuinely like one another. We seek to maintain our relationships with others, and to end stressful relationships, a phenomenon that persists across the lifetime and universally across different cultures (Hazan & Shaver, 1994).

The importance of belongingness is illustrated by the consequences that befall those who are deprived of stable, positive relationships. People who lack belongingness suffer from a higher incidence of both physical and mental disorders, experiencing problems that range from poorer health and adjustment to a higher rate of criminal activity to suicide. Conversely, belongingness is associated with better physical and psychological health and, overall, better adjustment (e.g., Sampson & Laub, 1993; Baumeister & Leary, 1995; Baumeister & Dori, 1998).

ATTACHMENT: THE ROOTS OF AFFILIATION AND BELONGINGNESS

The importance of others in our lives begins at the moment of birth. Anyone who has seen children smiling at the sight of their mothers or fathers has seen graphic evidence of the importance of the early affiliative bonds that exist between children and their caregivers.

Attachment is the positive emotional bond that develops between a child and a particular individual (Ainsworth et al., 1978; Bretherton, 1992). According to social psychologist Phillip Shaver and colleagues, attachment serves two primary functions. First, attachment provides children with a sense of security based on the presence of the person with whom they are attached. When faced with an anxiety-producing situation, children can turn to this individual for support and comfort. Second, the attached person can provide information about the situation. In an unfamiliar situation, the child can look to this person for hints about how to respond (Shaver & Klinnert, 1982).

Three major styles of attachment have been found in infants. **Secure attachment** characterizes a positive, healthy relationship between a child and an adult, based primarily on trust in the adult's comfort and love. In contrast, **avoidant attachment** characterizes relationships in which the child appears relatively indifferent to caregivers and avoids interactions with them. Finally, **anxious–ambivalent attachment** is seen in children who show great distress when separated from their caregivers, but who appear angry on their return (Bowlby, 1969; Ainsworth, 1979, 1985; Koski & Shaver, 1997).

The specific person to whom infants become attached is not always the same. Initially, researchers speculated that the bond between mother and infant was the most critical. However, more recent research shows that children can be simultaneously attached to both mother and father, although the nature of attachment to the two parents is not always identical. For instance, a child can be securely attached to the mother and insecurely attached to the father (Lamb, 1982; Belsky, Garduque, & Hrncir, 1984).

The type of attachment style that people develop during infancy may well determine their behavior with others for the rest of their lives (e.g., Hazan & Shaver, 1994; Mikulincer & Florian, 1996; Koski & Shaver, 1997; Fraley & Shaver, 1998). Adults can be classified into attachment categories on the basis of their responses to the questions shown in Table 6–1, and the category into which they fall characterizes their adult relationships.

Typically, just over half of all adults agree with the first statement, which suggests that they are securely attached. A further one-quarter say that the second statement is the most appropriate description, suggesting an avoidant attachment style. Finally, approximately 20 percent fall into the third category, which describes an anxious–ambivalent attachment style.

LONELINESS: ALONE IN A SOCIAL WORLD

If you have ever felt lonely, you are not alone: One survey found that more than one-quarter of people polled in a national survey stated that they had felt "very lonely or remote" from others during the prior few weeks. In fact, if you are an adolescent or an adult in your early twenties, you are within the age segment of society that reports being the loneliest of

Attachment, the positive emotional bond that develops between child and adult, provides children with a sense of security and can provide information about the world.

secure attachment: The style of attachment that characterizes a positive, healthy relationship between a child and an adult, based primarily on trust in the adult's comfort and love.

avoidant attachment: The style of attachment that characterizes relationships in which the child appears relatively indifferent to caregivers and avoids interactions with them.

anxious–ambivalent attachment: The style of attachment that is seen in children who show great distress when separated from their caregivers, but who appear angry on their return.

TABLE 6–1　**What Is Your Attachment Style?**
Which of these three statements best describes you?
1. I find it relatively easy to get close to others and am comfortable depending on them and having them depend on me. I don't often worry about being abandoned or about someone getting too close to me.
2. I am somewhat uncomfortable being close to others; I find it difficult to trust them completely, difficult to allow myself to depend on them. I am nervous when anyone gets too close, and often love partners want me to be more intimate than I feel comfortable being.
3. I find that others are reluctant to get as close as I would like. I often worry that my partner doesn't really love me or won't want to stay with me. I want to merge completely with another person, and this desire sometimes scares people away.
The choice you make suggests where you fit into one of three types of attachment styles. A choice of statement 1 suggests a secure attachment style; a choice of statement 2 suggests an avoidant attachment style; and a choice of statement 3 is considered anxious–ambivalent attachment. However, keep in mind that such a minimal, one-time assessment is inexact and should not be taken as unerring or infallible.

Source: Shaver, Hazan, & Bradshaw, 1988.

all. In spite of the conventional wisdom that elderly people are most apt to be lonely, loneliness actually declines with increasing age—at least until someone's activities must be restricted due to health or other problems (Weiss, 1973; Peplau & Perlman, 1982; Schultz & Moore, 1984; Wagner, Schuetze, & Lang, 1999).

Loneliness is the inability to maintain the level of affiliation one desires. It is a subjective state: A person can be alone and not feel lonely, or be in a crowd and feel lonely (Andersson, 1998). The partners in a long marriage can experience loneliness, whereas a recently widowed person may not feel lonely (Tornstam, 1992). Loneliness occurs only when the actual level of affiliation does not correspond to the desired level.

Loneliness comes in two forms (Peplau & Perlman, 1982; Clinton & Anderson, 1999). In **emotional isolation** a person feels a lack of deep emotional attachment to one specific person. By contrast, people who experience **social isolation** suffer from a lack of friends, associates, or relatives (Dugan & Kivett, 1994; Clinton & Anderson, 1999).

The two types of loneliness often do not go hand in hand. For example, an individual may have many friends and acquaintances and a large, extended family, yet lack any single person with whom to share a deep relationship. Similarly, people who frequently attend parties or eat in crowded cafeterias with many others may still experience a sense of loneliness if they feel emotionally detached from the people who surround them. Although they might not feel socially isolated in such cases as these, they may experience emotional isolation (Russell et al., 1984; Bell, 1993).

Of course, being alone is not invariably bad. Many people crave time by themselves. What is critical in producing loneliness, then, are the attributions we make regarding the experience of being alone (Archibald, Bartholomew, & Marx, 1995; Dykstra, 1995).

Those who view isolation as largely attributable to unstable, controllable factors ("We are all studying hard this semester and don't have much time to socialize") are unlikely to experience loneliness. On the other hand, people who attribute isolation to their own stable, uncontrollable personal shortcomings ("I'm by myself because I'm not very likable or interesting") are much more likely to experience loneliness (Cutrona, 1982; Peplau, Micelli, & Morasch, 1982; Laine, 1998; Tur-Kaspa, Weisel, & Seger, 1998). Finally, as might be expected, a combination of controllable and stable causes—or uncontrollable but unstable, temporary causes—produces an intermediate degree of loneliness (see Figure 6–1).

SITUATIONAL INFLUENCES ON ATTRACTION

If people were concerned only with fulfilling their general needs for affiliation, it probably wouldn't matter much who fulfilled those needs. We know, however, that people are considerably more discriminating than that. Some people become friends and lovers, and others develop into enemies and antagonists. We will now examine the factors that underlie attraction to specific individuals, considering what makes individuals like (and dislike) particular people.

PROXIMITY: THE ARCHITECTURE OF ATTRACTION

Circumstances of geography determine friendships. Consider, for example, who your closest friends were when you were growing up. In most cases, they were probably children who lived close to you. The reason: *proximity,* the degree to which people are geographically close to one another, plays a central role in determining who we like.

The importance of proximity is often seen in college dorms: Students are often friendliest with people whose rooms are nearby, and least friendly with those who are assigned to rooms farthest away (Newcomb, 1961; Hays, 1985). Perhaps more surprisingly, a similar situation occurs with more intimate relationships, such as marriage. For example, one study of marriage license applications in a city during the 1930s showed that one-third of the couples were

loneliness: The inability to maintain the level of affiliation one desires.

emotional isolation: A form of loneliness in which a person feels a lack of deep emotional attachment to one specific person.

social isolation: A form of loneliness in which people suffer from a lack of friends, associates, or relatives.

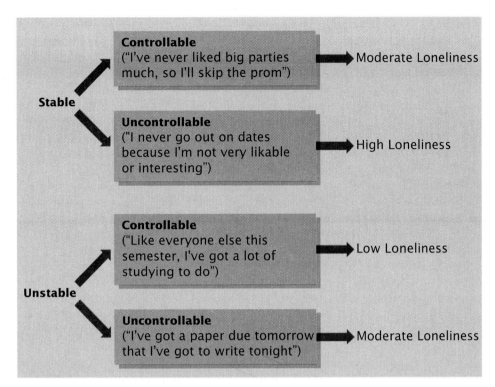

Stable

Controllable
("I've never liked big parties much, so I'll skip the prom")

→ Moderate Loneliness

Uncontrollable
("I never go out on dates because I'm not very likable or interesting")

→ High Loneliness

Unstable

Controllable
("Like everyone else this semester, I've got a lot of studying to do")

→ Low Loneliness

Uncontrollable
("I've got a paper due tomorrow that I've got to write tonight")

→ Moderate Loneliness

FIGURE 6–1   Attributions Leading to the Experience of Loneliness

people who lived within five blocks of each other, and that the number of licenses declined as geographical distance increased. And these findings do not include the 12% who shared the same address before they were married (Bossard, 1932; Whitbeck & Hoyt, 1994).

One of the classic studies in interpersonal attraction highlighted the influence of the architectural configuration of buildings in determining friendships. Social psychologists Leon Festinger, Stanley Schachter, and Kurt Back (1950) carefully scrutinized friendships in a housing complex for married college students. They found that particular architectural features of the buildings in the complex—each of which contained 10 apartments—affected the development of friendships.

For example, they found a close association between friendships and the proximity of apartments to one another. Couples who lived one door apart were more likely to be friends than those living two doors apart; those living two doors apart were more likely to be friends than those living three doors apart; and so on. In addition, people who lived near mailboxes or stairways had more friends in the building than those who lived farther from such architectural features. In fact, any architectural feature that generated heavy traffic made those living nearby more popular.

We might wonder, of course, whether the fact that proximity is related to attraction results from the fact that people who like one another may choose to live close to one another; in other words, instead of proximity leading to attraction, attraction might lead to proximity. However, this does not seem to be the case. In fact, people who are assigned to living quarters instead of choosing them are subject to the same relationship between proximity and liking. For instance, a study in which police trainees were assigned classroom seats and rooms alphabetically according to last name found a clear proximity pattern: The closer together in the alphabet were two trainees' last names, the more likely they were to become close friends (Segal, 1974).

How close we live to each other can play a major role in determining who we like. On the other hand, proximity does not ensure that a friendship will develop.

Of course, proximity does not guarantee that people will grow to like each other. Crime statistics show that victims of robberies often are either acquainted with or related to the robbers. Similalry, one-third of all homicides occur during family quarrels. Research also finds that although most of our closest friends may be physically proximate, the same is also true of the people we grow to dislike the most (Ebbesen, Kjos, & Konecni, 1976).

Clearly, proximity provides the opportunity for friendship to develop, but does not ensure that it will. Why should proximity so often be a forerunner of liking? One explanation is that people can obtain social rewards—such as companionship, social approval, and help—at relatively little cost from those who are nearby. Conversely, the costs involved in building and maintaining a friendship with someone physically distant may be considerably higher. Consequently, people are more apt to develop and maintain friendships with those with whom friendship is relatively more rewarding and less costly—those who are in close physical proximity.

FAMILIARITY: FAMILIARITY BREEDS CONTENT

When students in social psychologist Rick Crandall's classes arrived each day, they glimpsed at a few strange, non-English words written in the corner of the chalkboard. Although these words were clearly not part of the lesson at hand, they became an accepted, unremarkable part of the backdrop of the class.

What was not obvious to the class was that the words were varied in a systematic way over the course of the term, some words appearing only once and others appearing as many as 25 times. At the end of the term, students in the class were surprised to be given a questionnaire to assess their favorability ratings for a list of words. Embedded among the list were all the words that had appeared on the chalkboard at one time or another during the term.

When the ratings were tabulated, the results were clear: The more frequently a word had appeared on the chalkboard, the higher its favorability rating. Increasing exposure to the words generated more positive feelings toward them (Crandall, 1972).

The study conducted in Crandall's class demonstrated what became a well-established finding, called the mere exposure effect. The **mere exposure effect** states that repeated exposure to any stimulus increases the positivity of its evaluation. Contrary to conventional wisdom that "familiarity breeds contempt," experimental evidence suggests that the more often people are exposed to something, the more likely they are to like it (Zajonc, 1968; Bornstein, 1989).

mere exposure effect: The phenomenon that repeated exposure to any stimulus increases the positivity of its evaluation.

The mere exposure effect applies not only to words but also to all kinds of stimuli. For instance, people tend to enjoy musical passages and pieces of art as they become increasingly familiar. Similarly, they like politicians the more they are exposed to them (Zajonc, 1968; Harrison, 1977; Grush, 1980; Bornstein & D'Agostino, 1992; Young & French, 1998).

Furthermore, humans are not the only species vulnerable to the mere exposure effect. Even rats exposed to pieces of music enjoy them more if they have had prior experience with them. In one study, for example, experimenters exposed rats to selections written either by the 18th-century composer Mozart or by the contemporary composer Schoenberg (Cross, Halcomb, & Matter, 1967). The rats heard selections by the same composer for 12 hours a day over a 2-month period. Then, after a 15-day period of silence, the rats' musical preferences were tested by allowing them to activate a switch to play music of either Mozart or Schoenberg.

The newly cultured rats were clear in their choices: They preferred the music with which they were familiar. And we should note that the specific musical selections played during the testing period were not the same as the ones played during the 2-month exposure period. Hence, the animals' preferences involved not specific familiar pieces but styles of music— pretty impressive, considering that we are talking about rats.

Not surprisingly, the mere exposure phenomenon also operates in interpersonal attraction. The more we are exposed to another person, the greater the attraction to that person—all other factors being equal. The phenomenon occurs when we see photographs of a person, when we are simply exposed to a person's name, and—most important—when we actually meet the person (Moreland & Beach, 1992).

Like other things in life, however, there can be too much of a good thing. For instance, repeated exposure to the same commercial can become increasingly irritating, as can hearing the same song over and over. Clearly then, increased exposure does not bring about increased attractiveness indefinitely. In fact, after some optimal level of exposure is reached, liking can decline with repetition (Hill, 1978). Further, *sexual* attraction does not increase with familiarity. Research carried out on both humans and animals suggests that as familiarity between sex partners grows, sexual attraction declines (Dewsbury, 1981; Rosenblatt & Anderson, 1981).

Despite these exceptions, increasing exposure to other people most often causes them to become increasingly attractive. Although social psychologists agree on this principle, they cannot explain why it occurs. Several factors may be at work. For one thing, simply encountering a familiar stimulus may be pleasurable, as anyone who has caught sight of a familiar face in a crowd of strangers at a party knows. It is possible, then, that the process of recognizing a previously encountered stimulus may produce positive feelings. These positive feelings may subsequently become associated with the stimulus itself, causing increased attraction (Birnbaum & Mellers, 1979).

Another possibility is that the more people are exposed to a stimulus, the more they learn about it and about any interesting or novel aspects it possesses (Berlyne, 1970; Stang, 1973). Because learning is a positive experience, increased exposure leads to increased positive feelings. This also explains why attraction may decrease after too much exposure: After overexposure to a stimulus, the stimulus no longer presents any novel aspects. Learning grinds to a halt, boredom sets in, and feelings toward the stimulus become less positive.

Finally, the mere exposure phenomenon may have its roots in evolution. Preference for familiar—and, in all likelihood, safer—stimuli may have permitted our prehistoric human ancestors to live longer than those who preferred stimuli that were strange and unfamiliar (and perhaps more dangerous). As a result, those preferring the familiar were more likely to reproduce and to pass on this adaptive trait. Although speculative, such an evolutionary argument does help account for the mere exposure phenomenon (Bornstein, 1989).

Social psychologists are still not certain what underlies the mere exposure phenomenon. What is clear is that repeated exposure, in and of itself, generally results in enhanced attraction. If you are trying to decide whether your absence or your presence will make the heart of your desired grow fonder, you had best opt for your continuing—and repeated—presence. (For a look at how familiarity and liking are related to the world of advertising, see the accompanying Speaking of Social Psychology interview.)

SPEAKING OF SOCIAL PSYCHOLOGY

Steven Levitt

Marketing Executive

Year of Birth: 1940

Education: B.A., Marketing, Hofstra University; M.A., Marketing, C.W. Post, Division of Long Island University

Home: Oyster Bay Cove, Long Island, New York

"Angela Lansbury was rated high because people perceived her to be sincere and trustworthy."

In the competitive world of marketing, it is not enough to have someone who is well known to advertise your product. He or she must be likable as well. This explains in part why we frequently see Bill Cosby and Michael Jordan in advertisements, but not Michael Jackson or Madonna. But how does an advertiser determine who is likable? Many call on the services of Steven Levitt.

Levitt is president of Marketing Evaluations, a marketing research firm. Levitt utilizes a mathematical concept widely used by advertisers known as a Q-Rating (Q is for "quotient," as in I.Q.) that measures familiarity and popularity.

"The rating is simply a mathematical representation of two factors," Levitt explains. "One is the degree to which somebody is familiar to an audience or market, and two, the overall appeal that the person generates. If you put 100 people in a room and ask them if they are familiar with me, let's assume that 25 of the 100 would say they know me. Consequently, the level of familiarity is 25%.

"If they then are asked to rate me on what kind of person I am, let's say that 12 of those 25 think I'm their favorite person. We then take the 12, and divide it by the 25% of the

REVIEW AND RETHINK

Review

- The mere presence of others is rewarding for several reasons, including the desire for social comparison and the need for affiliation.

- The need for belongingness is the need to establish and maintain at least a minimum quantity of interpersonal relationships.

- Attachment in infancy displays several distinct styles and has lasting effects throughout people's lives.

- Loneliness, as distinct from being alone, is the inability to maintain a desired level of affiliation.

- Proximity and familiarity, which is related to the mere exposure effect, lead to liking.

Rethink

- Why might the presence of others be important for humans?

people who know me. The result would be a Q-Rating of 48," he said, "which would be a high rating."

However, Levitt points out that despite his high Q-Rating, advertisers would make a big mistake in hiring him, because the demographics of the specific groups for whom he would be popular would be severely limited.

"In short, the Q-Rating helps us understand the strength of appeal among people who know the performer."

To obtain the Q-Rating of potential advertising spokespersons, each personality is rated by 1,800 people representing a cross section of the U.S. population based on Census Bureau statistics. Of this group, 10% are children, 10% are teenagers, and the rest are younger and older adults.

In other studies, Marketing Evaluations has looked at personality traits and characteristics to see which celebrities are perceived to be most appropriate and believable. Two who scored similarly, but with significant personality differences, were actresses Angela Lansbury and Helen Hunt.

"Angela Lansbury was rated high because people perceived her to be sincere and trustworthy, while Helen Hunt scored high because she was perceived as being a fun person, someone who you'd want as a friend," said Levitt.

To show how popularity and likability change over time, Levitt noted the ratings of two well-known celebrities. "Bruce Jenner, who was an extraordinary athlete and very popular at one time, comes out low on positive dimensions and high on negative dimensions each time he's rated, because he's yesterday's news. By contrast, Tom Hanks is rated very high these days. The reason is that recently he's had some tremendous roles and given wonderful performances, so people have gotten to know more about him," Levitt noted. "They see him as sincere, a gifted and talented actor, not on his seventh wife, his ego is still in the back seat, and someone who has good values."

"In short, the Q-Rating helps us understand the strength of appeal among people who know the performer," he added. "It helps us to determine who we should be using in advertisements."

---

* Compare the mere exposure effect to the need for affiliation phenomenon. How can the mere exposure effect account for the pleasure associated with being socially active?

* What are the three primary parent–child attachment styles? What becomes of these interaction styles as people grow older?

* What age group suffers the most from loneliness? Is this the age group that is most often alone? Can you explain the discrepancy?

* "Absence makes the heart grow fonder" but "out of sight, out of mind." How would a social psychologist evaluate these two opposing sayings?

OTHER PEOPLE'S PERSONAL CHARACTERISTICS

As Darius met his new roommate for the first time, he began peppering him with the most obvious questions: Where did he come from? Was it a small or big town? What did he plan to major in?

But as Darius heard the answers to his first questions, his anxiety level—already soaring—rose even further. His roommate could hardly have been more different. Darius, an African American midwesterner who had lived on a farm all his life, would be living with a Hispanic American raised in downtown New York City. Darius had gone to a high school with just 60 kids in his graduating class; his roommate had gone to a huge urban high school 10 times the size.

After a while, though, Darius began to feel a little better. He and his roommate shared several significant similarities: a passion for Italian food, rap music, and film. They even expected to have the same major. As they discovered more and more commonalities, Darius began to feel better. They were going to get along just fine, he decided.

Why did Darius end up feeling positively about his new roommate? Although it is unlikely that any single factor accounted for his conclusion, his discovery that he did in fact share several important similarities with his roommate was probably no small consideration. We turn now to a discussion of similarity and its effects on liking, along with several other ingredients of interpersonal attraction.

SIMILARITY: DO BIRDS OF A FEATHER FLOCK TOGETHER?

If we used folk wisdom as a guideline for determining whether similarity is associated with liking, we'd be faced with mixed messages. We are told not only that birds of a feather flock together, but, in addition, that opposites attract.

Social psychologists have been able to make a clear choice between these two conflicting proverbs: With only a few exceptions, people like others who are similar to them. Regardless of whether attitudes, values, or personality traits are the consideration, similarity between two people can kindle interpersonal attraction. And similarity is important even from afar: For instance, we like politicians who hold attitudes similar to our own more than ones with dissimilar attitudes (McCaul et al., 1995).

Attitude and value similarity. Probably the clearest examples of the relationship between similarity and interpersonal attraction are attitude and value similarity. Since the early 1900s, researchers have found that people who like one another tend to share similar attitudes (Schuster & Eldeston, 1907). The more challenging issue for researchers became the chicken-and-egg question: Does discovering shared attitudes with another person lead to a liking of that person, or does attraction to another person influence the development of similar attitudes? (To complicate matters further, there's yet another possibility: that some additional factor leads to both the attraction *and* the attitude similarity.)

By experimentally manipulating the perceived degree of agreement between two people, researchers discovered that similarity of attitudes can, in fact, produce interpersonal attraction. In the prototypical experiment used to demonstrate this principle, participants are asked to respond to a series of questions regarding their attitudes toward various topics, such as school and politics. The experimenter then collects the results, and under the guise of ascertaining participants' impressions of a stranger, provides information regarding the "stranger's" supposed responses. The responses, which are actually bogus and contrived by the experimenter, are manipulated to produce various degrees of agreement with the participant's own attitudes. In the last step in the study, the experimenter assesses the participant's attraction to the confederate "stranger" (Smith et al., 1993; Shaikh & Kanekar, 1994; Pilkington & Lydon, 1997).

Although quite simple and straightforward, this experimental paradigm allows for some elegant hypothesis testing. For instance, experimenters can vary the absolute number of perceived agreements and disagreements (e.g., comparing the effects of agreement on 8 versus 5 versus 3 statements). On the other hand, an experimenter can vary the proportion of agreement and disagreement (e.g., 30 percent versus 50 percent versus 70 percent agreement). In addition, the experimenter can also vary the specific attitudes under consideration.

Results of a long line of studies indicate that one of the most critical factors underlying the relationship between attitude similarity and attraction is the proportion of agreements, not the absolute number of agreements. For instance, one would tend to like a person more who was thought to agree on three out of four attitudes (75%) than a person who was similar on 5 out of 10 attitudes (50%), even though the absolute number of agreements is greater in the second case. In fact, if we were to summarize graphically the results derived from many studies of the relationship between attraction and the proportion of similar attitudes, we would find a remarkably consistent result: As the proportion of similar attitudes rises, so does attraction (Byrne, 1971; see Figure 6–2).

Although attitude similarity seems to clearly lead to attraction, social psychologist Milton Rosenbaum has raised a plausible alternative hypothesis (Rosenbaum, 1986). Rejecting the view that similarity leads to attraction, he suggests instead that attitudinal *dis*similarity leads to interpersonal repulsion. **Interpersonal repulsion** is the desire to escape from another's presence; it is the opposite of interpersonal attraction.

According to Rosenbaum, attitude similarity is not particularly important or even noticed when people interact. Instead, they focus on dissimilarities, which are considerably more interesting psychologically because they are surprising and unexpected. The more dissimilarities people find, the more apt they are to avoid an individual, because they assume that interacting with that person will be unpleasant. Whether people tend to focus on attitudinal similarity (which then leads to interpersonal attraction) or on attitudinal dissimilarity (which produces interpersonal repulsion) is not certain. However, both explanations make the same prediction—that a positive relationship exists between attitude similarity and attraction. It is only the underlying explanation that is in dispute (Smeaton, Byrne, & Murnen, 1989).

Social psychologist Donn Byrne and colleagues suggest that both processes may be at work, although occurring at different stages in the course of developing attraction to another person (Byrne, Clore, & Smeaton, 1986). In their view, when we make new acquaintances we do an initial screening in which we check out how dissimilar they are from us. If they are too different, we avoid them altogether. But if they pass this initial test, we then take into account attitude similarity, liking best those whose attitudes are most similar to ours. In this way, both attitude similarity *and* attitude dissimilarity are considered in determining how attracted we are to other individuals (see Figure 6–3).

Because similarity of *attitudes* leads so clearly to interpersonal attraction, it should come as no surprise that similarity of *values* is also associated with liking. For instance, college

interpersonal repulsion: The desire to escape from another's presence; it is the opposite of interpersonal attraction.

FIGURE 6–2   Attraction and Attitude Similarity As this summary of several studies indicates, as the proportion of similar attitudes increases, so does our attraction for the other person. (*Source:* Byrne & Clore, 1966.)

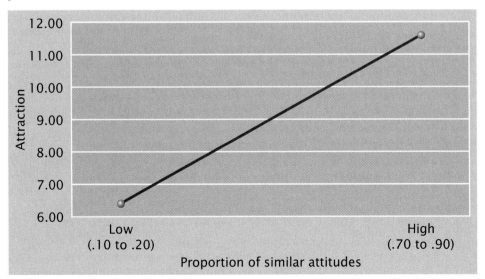

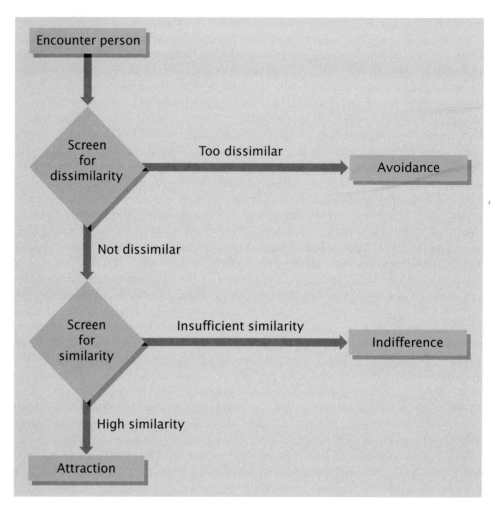

FIGURE 6–3   How Attitude Similarity and Dissimilarity Produce Attraction According to a model of interpersonal attraction proposed by Byrne, Clore, and Smeaton (1986), we first screen others to determine their attitudinal dissimilarity and then consider their similarity.

roommates who choose to live together exhibit significantly greater similarity of fundamental values regarding such subjects as religion and politics than those who have been assigned to be roommates (Hill & Stull, 1981). In addition, the greater the degree of value similarity measured at the start of the fall term, the greater the likelihood that the pair would remain roommates in the spring term, a finding that suggests that value similarity enhances liking.

Similarity of personality traits.   If you are introverted, low in sociability, and timid, you'll probably be attracted to people who are . . . introverted, low in sociability, and timid.

At least that's the conclusion from research suggesting that people like others who have personalities relatively similar to their own. However, although the relationship between personality similarity and liking is generally positive, it is considerably less strong than the relationship between attitude similarity and attraction. The reason for the difference is that almost everyone finds certain personality traits attractive—such as warmth and intelligence—whether or not they have those traits themselves (Neimeyer & Mitchell, 1988; Krueger & Caspi, 1993; Burleson, Kunkel, & Szolwinski, 1997).

We might also assume that in certain cases, *dissimilarity* of personality may lead to increased interpersonal attraction—if the differences allow one person to fulfill more effectively the needs of another. Such reasoning reflects the **need complementarity hypothesis**—the notion

need complementarity hypothesis:
The notion that individuals are attracted to others who have significantly different personalities, but whose needs complement their own.

that individuals are attracted to others who have significantly different personalities, but whose needs complement their own.

The need complementarity hypothesis has been applied primarily to marriage partners, who in some cases appear to have radically different personalities. The hypothesis argues that husbands and wives are most compatible when the needs of one spouse are fulfilled through the needs of the other (Winch, 1958). For instance, a dominant wife may get along best with a submissive husband; or a husband and wife may differ in the degree to which they hold the same personality traits (a high-dominant husband with a low-dominant wife). In either instance, the needs of each fit together in the total context of the relationship.

The need complementarity hypothesis makes intuitive sense, reflecting the folk wisdom of a statement like this one, cited in a book on marriage: "I've known a lot of couples where the rocks in *her* head seemed to fit the holes in *his*." Folk wisdom aside, however, the research on the need complementarity hypothesis has not been especially successful in garnering experimental support. Despite some early research that found that married partners did demonstrate complementary needs (Kerckhoff & Davis, 1962), later research has been largely unable to support the concept (e.g., Levinger, Senn, & Jorgensen, 1970; Meyer & Pepper, 1977; Aron et al., 1989). Instead, as is the case in other relationships, married partners tend to be attracted to one another on the basis of similarity more than difference.

Why similarity leads to attraction.   Whether on the basis of attitudes, values, or personality, similarity consistently relates to interpersonal attraction. But why?

Four possibilities help explain the relationship. First, similarity may be directly reinforcing. For example, individuals may have learned through prior experience to associate people with attitudes similar to their own with rewarding circumstances or situations. Second, the fact that another person has attitudes or qualities similar to one's own may confirm one's views of the world. For example, if you believe that global warming should be prevented by controls on industrial production, you may be particularly attracted to a person who shares your view, because—in a very real sense—that person's agreement validates your opinion. Moreover, as we noted earlier in our discussion of social comparison, people who are similar to us or in similar situations help us to evaluate our abilities and opinions more readily than dissimilar others or those who are in dissimilar situations (Hendrick & Seyfried, 1974; Burleson & Samter, 1996).

The third explanation for the relationship between similarity and liking is that learning the attitudes and values of another person helps us form a more complete impression of that person. We are apt to form positive impressions of similar people, because their similarity means they share traits with us that we value. According to this view, then, we like people who are similar because we infer that they have positive traits, and not directly because of similarity per se (Ajzen & Fishbein, 1980).

Finally, people may like similar others because they assume that *they* will be liked by those others. As we'll see next, knowing that someone likes you generally attracts you to that

Similarity consistently leads to interpersonal attraction.

TABLE 6–2	Similarity and Interpersonal Attraction: Four Explanations
Similarity is directly reinforcing.	We learn through prior experience that people with similarities are associated with rewarding circumstances or situations.
Similarity confirms our worldview.	People who are similar validate our understanding of the world and are useful for purposes of social comparison.
Similarity provides knowledge of others' traits.	Learning that others hold similar, positive traits gives information about others' personality, which leads to liking.
Similarity leads to inferences that others will like us.	We assume that similar others are going to like us in return, making them more attractive.

person. Hence, similarity may lead to an inference that the other person is attracted to you, and consequently, your level of attraction may increase.

Keep in mind that none of these explanations (summarized in Table 6–2) is sufficient by itself to explain the similarity–attraction relationship (Huston & Levinger, 1978; Berscheid, 1985). In addition, at times we like dissimilar others just as much as those who are similar. For example, you may find that someone dissimilar can teach you something important, and this discovery may lead you to be attracted to that person (Kruglanski & Mayseless, 1987). Nonetheless, more often than not, perceived similarity will lead to greater interpersonal attraction.

RECIPROCITY OF LIKING: I LIKE YOU BECAUSE YOU LIKE ME

It doesn't much matter how we find out. Whether it is demonstrated by subtle glances, shown by deeds, or spoken directly, when we learn that another person likes us, we tend to like that person in return. One of the most powerful and consistent social psychological findings is that of **reciprocity of liking**, which states that you like those who like you. And the phenomenon goes even further: When you like someone, you tend to assume that they like you in return (Metee & Aronson, 1974; Condon & Crano, 1988).

The consequences of learning that someone likes you are immediate and striking. For example, in one experiment, participants overheard confederates, with whom they had just spoken, telling an experimenter that they either liked or disliked the participants. When the confederates and participants were then required to work together, the participants' nonverbal facial expressions differed according to what they had overheard. Participants who had heard that the confederates liked them were more nonverbally positive than those who had heard that the confederates disliked them. Further, subsequent written ratings showed that liked participants were much more attracted to the confederates than those who thought they were disliked. Other research demonstrates similar findings: People act more positively, and hold more positive attitudes, toward those whom they think like them (Feldman, 1976; Curtis & Miller, 1986).

The reciprocity-of-liking phenomenon would come as no surprise to Dale Carnegie, who long ago noted in his famous book, *How to Win Friends and Influence People,* that the best way for people to acquire friendship was to be "hearty in their approbation and lavish in their praise." However, before we rush to lavish praise of others in order to win their friendship, we should consider situations in which expressions of friendship may not invariably result in liking.

One exception to the reciprocity-of-liking scenario occurs for people with exceptionally low self-esteem (Shrauger, 1975). For people in this category, who don't much like themselves, finding that someone likes them is at odds with their own self-concept. In such a case, they may consider a person who likes them as insensitive or undiscerning, and they may actually dislike that person as a consequence. It is also possible that the inconsistency between

reciprocity of liking: The social psychological finding which states that you like those who like you.

their own view of themselves and the view of them held by another person is unpleasant or uncontrollable.

Another exception to the reciprocity-of-liking rule occurs when people suspect that others are saying positive things in order to ingratiate themselves. As we first discussed in Chapter 4, *ingratiation* is a deliberate effort to make a favorable impression, often through flattery (Jones, 1964; Jones & Pittman, 1982). For instance, a student who tells his social psychology professor how much he likes her and enjoys her class risks being viewed as having an ulterior motive. As a consequence, the professor may end up with an unfavorable impression of the student—representative of a phenomenon called the *slime effect*, described in the accompanying Applying Social Psychology box.

PERSONAL QUALITIES: WHOM DO YOU LIKE?

Not surprisingly, people with positive qualities are liked more than those with disagreeable qualities. For example, a survey of some 40,000 individuals found that such qualities as warmth and affection, the ability to keep confidences, loyalty, and supportiveness were most valued in people identified as friends (Parlee, 1979; Aron et al., 1989; Fehr, 1995; see Figure 6–4).

But the sheer number of positive qualities is not the whole story. Sometimes people prefer those who display positive qualities that are a bit tarnished by negative qualities over those who are seemingly flawless. An example of this phenomenon was produced by an experiment in which either a very competent person or an average person clumsily spilled a cup of coffee (Aronson, Willerman, & Floyd, 1966). After the mishap, liking for the competent person

APPLYING SOCIAL PSYCHOLOGY
THE SLIME EFFECT: WHY WE DISLIKE LIKABLE BEHAVIOR TOWARD SUPERIORS

An employee laughs uproariously at a boss's joke, telling the boss how funny she is . . . an army private tells his platoon leader that he's really grateful to be in his platoon . . . the Secretary of Defense tells the President what an excellent job the President is doing.

What's the reaction of the higher-status person to such likable behavior? In each case, rather than reacting favorably to the praise, the higher-status person may come to dislike the bearer of good tidings. The reason for such a reaction is a phenomenon called the *slime effect* by social psychologist Roos Vonk (1998).

The *slime effect* refers to the negative reaction to those who show likable behavior toward superiors while engaging in unpleasant behavior toward those who are subordinates. In a series of experiments examining the slime effect, Vonk found that participants who read about a person who displayed a combination of likable behavior toward a supervisor, in conjunction with unpleasant behavior toward those of lower status, resulted in lower ratings of liking—and higher ratings on a "sliminess" scale.

For example, one person was portrayed as doing likable things, such as getting coffee, for a superior while refusing to help someone with a problem who was a subordinate. The greater the number of positive behaviors displayed toward a superior and the greater the negative behaviors displayed toward subordinates, the slimier the person was believed to be.

The results suggest the existence of a "slime schema" that contains knowledge of a personality type in which people attempt to ingratiate themselves toward those of higher status while treating people in subordinate positions with contempt. The schema is activated when we encounter someone who is likable toward superiors, and it is confirmed if we learn that the person acts unpleasantly to those who are of lower status. On the other hand, if the person acts likable toward both superiors and subordinates, then the slime schema is disconfirmed, and the person displaying the indiscriminant likable behavior will be seen as likable.

The results suggest that real-world ingratiators need to be careful in the strategies they use to gain favor from their superiors. For example, social psychologist Edward Jones (1990) suggests that effective ingratiators hide their motives by disagreeing with superiors on trivial matters, saving their agreement on more important issues. Whether such a tactic is more or less slimy in the eyes of observers is a matter of future research.

increased, whereas attraction toward the average individual fell. Hence, very competent people who commit blunders become more human and approachable—and consequently more attractive. On the other hand, average people gain little from social blunders; they are already seen as human enough.

In addition to personality characteristics, interpersonal attraction is associated with gender and racial factors. For example, women and men show different kinds of friendship patterns. Although close to 80% of all men say that they have casual friendships with other males, just 20% report that they have close relationships with other men (Rubin, 1985; Ickes, 1993; Kenrick et al., 1993; Canary & Dindia, 1998).

In contrast, women are more likely to report having close friends and being able to confide in them, perhaps due to their higher rates of self-disclosure (as we'll discuss in Chapter 7) and their greater willingness to provide emotional support. Furthermore, women tend to have a wider network of people they call friends than men do (Trobst, Collins, & Embree, 1994; Olson & Shultz, 1994; Coates, 1997).

Ethnicity, too, plays a role in interpersonal attraction (Chambers et al., 1994). For example, African American and white adolescents tend to select friends of the same race. Even when they report having close friends of the other race at school, they are not likely to socialize with such friends outside of school (Hallinan & Williams, 1989; DuBois & Hirsch, 1990; Clark & Ayers, 1992; Fishbein & Imai, 1993).

FIGURE 6–4 What Makes a Friend? According to a survey of some 40,000 people, these are the primary qualities in a friend. (*Source:* Parlee, 1979.)

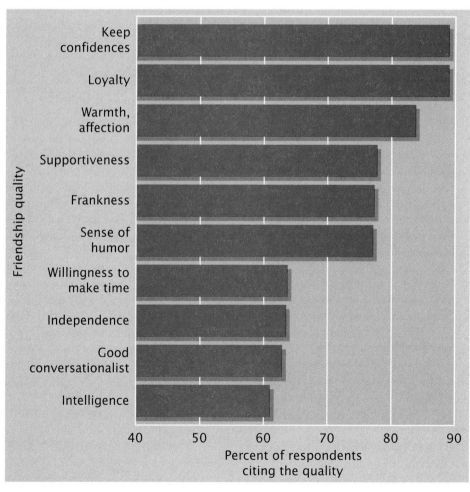

In contrast to women, men have casual friendships with other males, and are less likely to report having a close relationship with a same-sex friend.

REVIEW AND RETHINK

Review

- Similarity of attitudes, values, and personality traits is related to interpersonal attraction.

- The reciprocity-of-liking phenomenon suggests that people like those who like them.

- Personal qualities relating to personality characteristics, gender, and race are associated with interpersonal attraction.

Rethink

- Is the similarity–attraction relationship stronger in the domain of attitudes or personality traits? Why might this be the case?

- How does Rosenbaum's interpersonal repulsion hypothesis differ from the traditional similarity–attraction hypothesis? If the repulsion hypothesis is correct, what strategies would you suggest to someone attempting to make a good impression?

- Describe two notable exceptions to the general tendency for people to reciprocate interpersonal attraction.

- How might the tendency to like people who have positive qualities explain the similarity–attraction relationship?

PHYSICAL ATTRACTIVENESS AND LIKING: BEAUTY BEATS THE BEAST

If Sharon Stone and Tom Cruise were ugly, would we still like them?

In our supposedly egalitarian and democratic society, most of us would maintain that people should be judged for what they are and what they do, rather than what they look like. Yet, despite general agreement with the old adage, "Beauty is only skin deep," most people act as though physical attractiveness were a good measure of likability. However unwarranted such a bias may be, physical appearance is in fact an important determinant of how people view others.

With startling consistency, people who are physically attractive are liked more than unattractive people, beginning with nursery school and continuing into old age. In addition, a physically attractive individual's behavior is interpreted more positively than the behavior of physically unattractive people (Hatfield & Sprecher, 1986; Agnew & Thompson, 1994; Zuckerman, Miyake, & Elkin, 1995; VanWinkle et al., 1998).

For example, social psychologist Karen Dion (1972) presented adults with descriptions of mild or severe misbehavior by a 7-year-old child and asked them to judge the typicality of the child's behavior. Included with the descriptions were photos of either an attractive or unattractive child. When the misbehavior was mild, no effects due to the appearance of the child were detected. But when the misbehavior was severe, the physical attractiveness of the child determined how the behavior was interpreted. Participants viewed attractive children's misbehavior as a temporary, atypical incident, unlikely to be repeated. One participant described in this way an attractive girl who threw a rock at a sleeping dog:

> She appears to be a perfectly charming little girl, well-mannered, basically unselfish. It seems that she can adapt well among children her age and make a good impression. . . . She plays well with everyone, but like anyone else, a bad day can occur. Her cruelty need not be taken seriously.

In contrast, similar incidents committed by unattractive children were judged considerably more harshly as examples of chronic misbehavior, symptomatic of an underlying behavior problem. For instance, one unattractive girl who threw a rock at a sleeping dog was perceived like this:

> I think the child would be quite bratty and would be a problem to teachers. . . . She would probably try to pick a fight with other children her own age. . . . She would be a brat at home—all in all, she would be a problem.

Obviously, the same behavior was judged in very different ways, depending on the physical attractiveness of the transgressor.

Even parents are affected by their children's attractiveness. For instance, mothers of more attractive infants show them more affection and are more playful with them than mothers of less attractive infants, both soon after birth and at 3 months of age. At the same time, mothers of less attractive children are more apt to pay greater attention to people other than their infants and to engage in routine, perfunctory caregiving, than mothers of more attractive children (Langlois et al., 1995; see Figure 6–5).

The consequences of physical attractiveness persist well beyond childhood. Numerous experiments in the 1960s and 1970s used the guise of "computer dating," a craze in which people completed questionnaires that were then fed into computers. The computers were programmed to identify a person's "ideal" date.

In a series of experiments, researchers altered the computer programs and matched dates on a completely random basis. By then looking at the success of the matches, they were able to determine what personal factors were most important. In study after study, the most influential factor in determining attraction was the physical attractiveness of one's date. In fact, physical attractiveness was more important in determining liking than attitudes, values, personality traits, or intelligence (e.g., Walster et al., 1966; Tesser & Brodie, 1971).

Why was physical attractiveness so important in these situations? One answer is that most of the dating experiments involved only the initial encounters between a man and woman. In such a situation, we would expect that societal expectations about personal attractiveness would be particularly pronounced. In fact, one of the most widely held societal stereotypes is relevant to dating: the "beautiful-is-good" stereotype.

The beautiful-is-good stereotype.　Society in general holds a widespread beautiful-is-good stereotype regarding physical attractiveness. According to the **beautiful-is-good stereotype**, physically attractive people possess a wide range of positive characteristics. Research on the stereotype finds that these perceived traits include higher sociability, greater dominance, and better social skills. In addition, physically attractive people are thought to be more intelligent, sexually warmer, and in better mental health than less physically attractive people (Feingold, 1992b; Locher et al., 1993; Larose, Tracy, & McKelvie, 1993; Kalick et al., 1998).

beautiful-is-good stereotype: The belief that physically attractive people possess a wide range of positive characteristics.

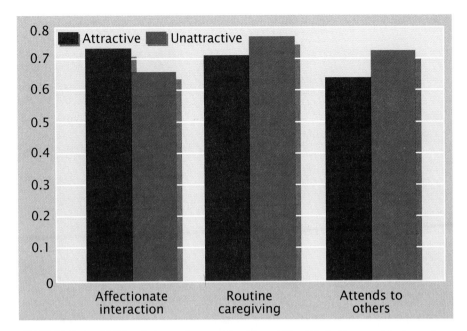

FIGURE 6–5   Children's Attractiveness Can Even Affect Their Parents Mothers of more attractive infants show them more affection and are more playful with them, whereas mothers of less attractive children are more likely to pay greater attention to people other than their infants. (*Source:* Langlois et al., 1995.)

How accurate is the beautiful-is-good stereotype? Although the physically attractive do have better social lives, better social skills, and more sexual experiences, they do not differ from the less attractive in basic personality dimensions, such as emotional stability, self-esteem, and dominance (Feingold, 1992b; Kalick et al., 1998). Further, intelligence and academic ability show no relationship to attractiveness (thereby putting the lie to the myth of the "dumb blonde"; attractive people are neither more nor less intelligent that unattractive people).

Furthermore, the content of the beautiful-is-good stereotype differs from one culture to another. For example, although they still assume that attractive people are better people, Asians rate attractive people as higher in integrity and in concern for others than do Westerners. The reason: The collectivistic culture of Asians stress harmonious relationships, and integrity and concern for others are more important traits than in Western cultures (Wheeler & Kim, 1997).

Obviously, the beautiful-is-good stereotype has its limitations, especially given that attractive and unattractive people differ relatively little in terms of basic personality traits. Why, then, is the stereotype so pervasive? Several reasons may explain it (Feingold, 1992a).

For one thing, the entertainment media, particularly television and film, portray a world in which the key players are exceptionally attractive. Both male and female leading actors are unusually handsome or beautiful, and they are also charming and sensual. In addition, other actors surrounding the stars are often relatively unattractive, and they frequently play bumbling, socially inept roles. (The television show *Seinfeld* is a good example of this phenomenon.) Based on what the media present, it is little wonder that society expects physically attractive people to have exceptionally good personalities as well.

The fundamental attribution error, which we first discussed in Chapter 2, provides another explanation for the pervasiveness of the beautiful-is-good stereotype. Although the primary reason attractive people receive preferential treatment may initially be the beautiful-is-good stereotype, this special treatment may be perpetuated by the fundamental attribution error.

Specifically, when observers see physically attractive people receiving preferential treatment, the fundamental attribution error may lead them to overemphasize dispositional factors in attributing the causes of the special treatment. Thus, the observers conclude that dispositional

Who we consider to be physically attractive, and the qualities that we attach to such attractiveness, vary across different cultures.

factors—such as the "wonderful personalities" of attractive people—are responsible for the special treatment. At the same time, the fundamental attribution error leads observers to underestimate the contribution of situational factors (the behavior of others in the situation) to the preferential treatment that attractive people receive.

Finally, emerging evidence suggests that the beautiful-is-good stereotype in part may be the result of inborn, genetic factors. Although most researchers have traditionally assumed that standards of beauty are established within a society, recent evidence suggests that this conclusion may not be entirely accurate. For example, in one study psychologist Judy Langlois and colleagues showed 6- to 8-month-old infants pairs of photos—one of a woman judged attractive by adults and the other of a woman judged unattractive (Langlois et al., 1987). The infants spent a significantly greater amount of time looking at the attractive face than the unattractive one—suggesting that attractive faces were of greater interest.

Other research concludes that infants show greater social responsiveness to the physically attractive. In one study, 1-year-olds interacted with a stranger who wore a mask that was professionally constructed to simulate either an attractive or an unattractive face. When the stranger wore an attractive mask, the infants showed more positive emotions and played more than when the stranger wore an unattractive mask. Furthermore, other studies show that infants play more with dolls that have attractive faces than with dolls that have unattractive faces (Langlois, Roggman, & Rieser-Danner, 1990).

The babies in these studies are unlikely to have already learned societal standards for attractiveness (Adams & Crane, 1980). Instead, the results argue that there is some genetic predisposition toward a certain kind of beauty, and that faces of particular dimensions and conformations provide socially useful information that enhanced our ancient ancestors' adaptive value.

The proportions of beauty.   Have you ever encountered people who look as though they need to be nurtured and taken care of? If you look more closely, you might find that they have relatively large eyes and small noses—characteristics that can be labeled "babyishness." According to social psychologists Michael Cunningham and Leslie Zebrowitz, babyishness plays an important role in determining our reactions to others. The more that people have facial features similar to those of a baby, the greater the impression of childlike innocence

(Berry, 1991). At the same time, if these characteristics are not offset by more mature features, such as large cheekbones and a strong chin, they may also convey powerlessness, submissiveness, and social incompetence. The impact of babyishness is so strong that it is found across different cultures, throughout the lifespan, and even in different species (Keating, 1985; McArthur & Berry, 1987; Zebrowitz & Montepare, 1990; Zebrowitz, Brownlow, & Olson, 1992; Collins & Zebrowitz, 1995).

In research conducted by Cunningham and colleagues that supports these conclusions, groups of adult men and women indicated their attraction to men's faces. In the research, participants were shown photos of men's faces and were asked to judge how attractive they were on an 8-point scale ranging from extremely unattractive to extremely attractive. Each of the photos was then carefully examined to determine both the absolute size of the facial features and the relationships among the various features (Cunningham, Barbee, & Pike, 1990).

Using the ratings and the measurements, researchers could then determine the characteristics of the preferred male face. For example, judges preferred prominent cheekbones and a large chin, considered to be indications of maturity. But they also preferred large eye height and width and a small nose, associated with a baby face. Hence, preferred faces seemed to contain a combination of mature and babylike features, conveying a combination of ruggedness and cuteness. Cunningham speculates that such features elicit from observers a combination of respect and nurturing tenderness.

Such findings are consistent with what could be called the "Leonardo DiCaprio" effect: People of both sexes prefer feminine-looking male faces over rugged, macho-looking men. Researchers have found that the Scottish, the Japanese, and hunter-gatherers in the Amazon all prefer feminine-looking male faces over more masculine ones (Perrett et al., 1998).

FIGURE 6–6   Facial Proportions That Relate to Liking Ratings of preferred female faces show surprising uniformity in the ratios of the various measures of facial configuration shown here. For instance, preferred faces had a chin length that was one-fifth the height of the face. (*Source:* Cunningham, 1986.)

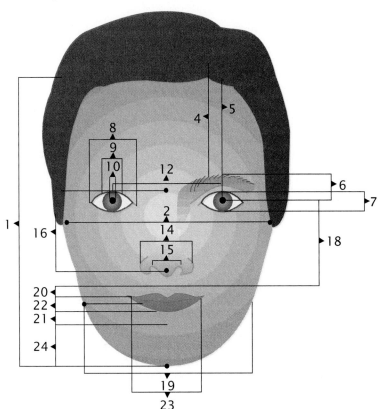

Another facial preference is based on being average. When computers make composites of many faces to form an "average face," the resulting photos are preferred over the individual faces that go into the composite. Why? The answer may be that average faces are more representative of our face schema, and therefore are more familiar to us. And, because familiarity breeds liking, we're therefore drawn to the average. Furthermore, composite average faces are more symmetrical—and we tend to prefer symmetry in faces, which evolutionary psychologists suggest are associated with health and potential reproductive fitness (Rhodes, Sumich, & Byatt, 1999).

Female faces and bodies.   It's not only men's faces that evoke preferences: Clear, consistent preferences exist for women's faces as well (Cunningham, 1986). Research has found that the preferred female face has large eyes, a small nose, high cheekbones, and narrow cheeks. In addition, calculations of the precise configuration of facial features, using the different measures illustrated in Figure 6–6, reveal great uniformity in judgments. For instance, the preferred face has an eye width (#12 in the figure) three-tenths the width of the face at the level of the eyes (#2). Similarly, the preferred distance from the center of the eye to the top of the eyebrow (#6) is one-tenth the height of the face (#1).

Keep in mind that these proportions represent composite preferences and not the particular dimensions found in any single person (Alley & Cunningham, 1991). (In other words, don't start measuring how far your eye is from your eyebrow in order to assess your own attractiveness.) Facial configuration is but one of the factors that enters into judgments of physical attractiveness, and attractiveness is only one of several aspects of interpersonal attraction.

Furthermore, some of society's standards of beauty vary from one culture to another. For instance, compared with white Americans, Asians are more accepting of women with lower cheekbones and wide cheeks, and less favorably inclined toward women with wide chins. On the other hand, Asian, Hispanic, and white Americans all prefer females with faces that include

FIGURE 6–7   Historical Changes in Preferred Female Body Types   During the course of the 20th century, norms regarding women's body types have changed significantly. This graph shows the mean "bust-to-waist" ration, a measure of full-figuredness, of models appearing in *Vogue* and *Ladies' Home Journal* during the 20th century. (Smaller ratios indicate greater overall slenderness.) As depicted in women's magazines, slenderness has been in style in only two periods: the mid-1920s and in recent decades. In other times, societal standards supported relatively full figures. (*Source:* Silverstein et al., 1986.)

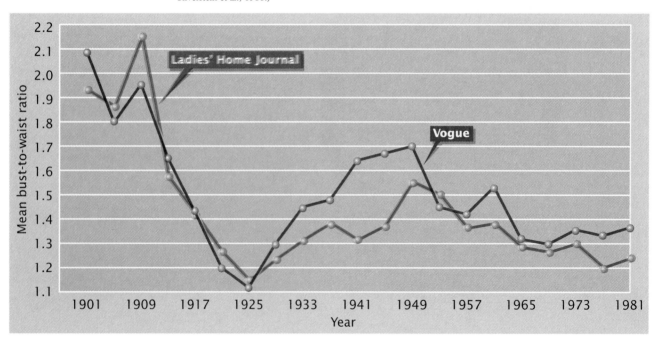

such features as large eyes, greater distance between the eyes, small noses, narrower faces with small chins, expressive, higher eyebrows, and well-groomed, full hair (Cunningham et al., 1995).

Standards relating to the ideal body size also have varied significantly over time. For example, in 19th-century Hawaii the women who were considered the most attractive were also the most overweight. Similarly, even within U.S. society, there have been significant shifts in society's view of the "ideal" weight. For instance, one survey of the exemplary figure, as depicted in models in fashion magazines, reveals that the standard of slenderness in vogue today is matched historically in only one other period: the mid-1920s. As illustrated in Figure 6–7, for most of the rest of the century, the ideal female figure was relatively full (Silverstein et al., 1986; Stice & Shaw, 1994; Thompson et al., 1999).

We also need to remember that these historical changes primarily relate to the majority white culture in the United States. As we consider next, minority groups may hold different standards of physical attractiveness.

THE STIGMA OF OBESITY: DIFFERENCES IN BLACK AND WHITE

EXPLORING
DIVERSITY

> "She's big, but she's solid. And she looks nice in her clothes. As long as she looks nice and can find pretty clothes, I'm not so worried about her weight." (An African American mother's statement about her 198-pound daughter, quoted in Wadden et al., 1990, p. 350.)

The pursuit of slenderness is often assumed to be a universal obsession of U.S. society, and Americans actually spend more money on weight reduction than they invest in education (Brownell, 1991). However, increasing evidence suggests that this obsession is restricted largely to *white* Americans. African Americans may have weight-related standards that are quite different from those of whites (Cunningham et al., 1995; Parker et al., 1995; Ofosu et al., 1998).

According to studies conducted by social psychologist Todd Heatherton and colleagues, African Americans generally judge heavier women more positively than whites do. In the research, a group of black and white participants rated photographs of thin, average, and large black and white women. Regardless of whether the women in the photos were college students or professional models, there was little difference in the general findings: White judges generally rated the large women in the photos, and particularly the large white women, as lower in attractiveness, intelligence, job and relationship success, happiness, and popularity than the average-weight or thin women.

In contrast, the black judges rated both white and black large women more favorably. Large black women, in particular, were judged no less positively than average-weight and thin women. In sum, the standards of attractiveness for African American and white judges differed significantly, with the white judges viewing heavy women far more negatively than the African Americans (Heatherton, Kiwan, & Hebl, 1995; Hebl & Heatherton, 1998).

The differing standards of attractiveness between whites and blacks raise some difficult issues. Because the idealized image of female beauty presented in advertising is almost always a white one, African Americans clearly receive mixed messages, having to choose between their own cultural standards or those of the dominant culture. To make matters more complicated, even the few advertisements that include African American models typically portray women who are light-skinned, slender, and young—similar in most ways to the white ideal portrayed by the media.

Furthermore, although there have been efforts to promote the message that "black is beautiful," African American women sometimes report being rejected by African American men because of their dark skin. A similar situation, in which white standards of beauty are forced on women without regard for cultural differences, is found in some Asian countries, where some women have surgery on their eyelids to look more Westernized. In short, the beautiful-is-good stereotype presents an even more troubling message for members of minority groups than for those in the majority (Chapkis, 1986; Freedman, 1986; Unger & Crawford, 1996).

matching hypothesis: The theory that suggests that people are attracted to those whose level of physical attractiveness is similar to their own.

The matching hypothesis: Equating looks in long-term relationships.   Despite its importance, physical attractiveness is hardly the full story in determining interpersonal attraction. For instance, although physical attractiveness may be preferred in the abstract and during initial encounters, evidence indicates that people tend to use a somewhat different standard in longer-term relationships. For example, the **matching hypothesis** suggests that people are attracted to those whose level of physical attractiveness is similar to their own (Berscheid & Walster, 1974; Feingold, 1988; Forgas, 1993).

A good deal of evidence supports the matching hypothesis: During courtship and marriage, the level of physical attractiveness of couples tends to correspond fairly closely. And, as we discussed earlier, there is even some evidence that married couples come to look more alike the longer they live together (Zajonc et al., 1987).

It's not just romantically linked couples that show attractiveness matching. Friends tend to have corresponding levels of physical attractiveness. There is a also a gender difference, with pairs of male friends corresponding more closely than pairs of female friends (McKillip & Riedel, 1983; Feingold, 1988). Consequently, rather than turning to a mirror to get a sense of how physically attractive you are, you might just take a look at your friends!

The downside of physical attractiveness.   After an exhaustive job search, the final two candidates for the executive position have been identified. Both candidates have equally strong backgrounds, and both were highly successful in their previous positions. Both even look good and present themselves well in person: One is a good-looking man, the other an equally attractive woman. Who gets the job?

The answer is not so pretty: the attractive man. The reason is that attractive women are viewed as gentle, soft, and indecisive, whereas attractive men are considered to be tough, competent, and decisive (Schellhardt, 1991).

 According to the bulk of research findings, most people would wish to be physically attractive, if they had the choice. Certainly, given the amount of money and time spent on clothing, makeup, physical fitness, and plastic surgery, physical attractiveness seems a goal to which many aspire.

Yet, physical attractiveness has its downside, and some research suggests that the expected social rewards of beauty can be illusory, particularly for women. For example, beauty can produce less positive impressions of women in work-related situations. One common, although totally unfounded, stereotype holds that successful, attractive women have attained their positions as a result of their looks rather than their abilities (Heilman & Stopeck, 1985; Schellhardt, 1991).

Similarly, other research shows that physical attractiveness may be overrated. For instance, consider the results of one study that examined the relationship between women's physical attractiveness in college and their adjustment and happiness 20 years later (Berscheid, Walster, & Campbell, 1974). The results showed that, contrary to what might be expected, women who were attractive in college tended to be *less* happy and *less* well-adjusted in their later lives than those who had been relatively unattractive in college. It may be that the normal process of aging is more devastating to someone who was initially very attractive than to someone less attractive early in life.

Similarly, research refutes the stereotype that attractive people experience a greater sense of well-being than those who are less attractive. Although some modest correlations do exist between physical attractiveness and subjective well-being, the relationship is generally quite small. Being physically attractive, then, does not necessarily lead to satisfaction with one's life (Diener, Wolsic, & Fujita, 1995).

Findings such as these reinforce an important point: Although the significance of physical attractiveness is undeniable, many other factors help determine interpersonal attraction. For example, a pleasant facial expression evokes higher ratings of physical attractiveness than an unpleasant or neutral expression. One experiment found that people who were smiling were not only thought to be more attractive than people in an unsmiling control group, but also were considered to be more sincere, sociable, and competent (Reis et al., 1990).

Two attractive people, equally qualified, apply for a job. One is male, the other female. Who gets the job?

THEORIES OF ATTRACTION

Why do such factors as similarity, reciprocity of liking, and physical attractiveness lead to liking? Researchers' explanations belong to two main theoretical families: learning theory approaches and cognitive theory approaches.

Learning approaches.   You are more apt to like someone who provides you with rewards; and you are more apt to dislike someone who provides punishments. Such straightforward propositions grow out of one of the most basic approaches to interpersonal attraction— *learning theory* (Byrne & Clore, 1970; Byrne & Murnen, 1988; Tzeng & Gomez, 1992). According to the **reinforcement-affect model**, for instance, liking follows the basic principles of learning embodied in classical and operant conditioning. This model suggests that the positive emotions people experience in the presence of someone who is rewarding lead to attraction, whereas negative emotions lead to reductions in attraction.

For instance, consider the classical conditioning of Pavlov's dogs, which you may remember from your introduction to psychology. In Pavlov's experiments, dogs learned to salivate when they heard the sound of a bell, because the bell had become associated with food. Similarly, classical conditioning may occur in humans when other people's presence becomes associated with either rewarding or punishing circumstances. Subsequently, individuals transfer feelings about the circumstances they have experienced to the people themselves (Lott & Lott, 1974).

Furthermore, operant conditioning may account for attraction. For instance, pigeons may be trained, via operant conditioning, to peck a key in order to produce the reinforcer of food. In the same way, we humans may come to learn that specific aspects of other people are reinforcing—such as their rewarding behavior toward us, their rewarding traits, or the access they provide to particular rewards.

Cognitive approaches.   *Cognitive approaches* to interpersonal attraction focus on people's perceptions of relationships they hold with others. Unlike learning theories, which examine the absolute degree of rewards and punishments provided by others, cognitive approaches consider how people's thoughts, beliefs, attitudes, and perceptions determine their liking for others.

For instance, **comparison level theories** suggest that attraction to others is based on comparison of a relationship to some hypothetical baseline (Thibaut & Kelley, 1959). This baseline, known as a *comparison level,* is a kind of summary of the past outcomes that have

reinforcement-affect model: The theory that liking follows the basic principles of learning embodied in classical and operant conditioning.

comparison level theories: Theories that suggest that attraction to others is based on comparison of a relationship to some hypothetical baseline.

equity theory: The theory that suggests that people take into account not only their own outcomes, but also the outcomes that are perceived to be attained by others.

balance theory: The approach in which people strive for consistency, or balance, in their likes and dislikes.

been experienced or that are prominent in a given situation. If the rewards received from the relationship are above the person's comparison level, the person will be satisfied with the relationship; if the rewards fall below it, the person will be dissatisfied. However, the availability of alternatives also determines whether an individual will seek to maintain a relationship. For instance, one may choose to maintain an unsatisfactory relationship with someone if no better alternatives are available (Black et al., 1991; Floyd & Wasner, 1994; Morrow & O'Sullivan, 1998; Rusbult et al., 1998).

Equity theory takes comparison level theory a step further, suggesting that people take into account not only their own outcomes, but also the outcomes that are perceived to be attained by others (Walster, Walster, & Berscheid, 1978; Walster, Walster, & Traupmann, 1978). According to this view, people try to maintain a balance between the rewards and costs they experience themselves and those experienced by a friend or partner in a relationship (Sprecher, 1992; Kollock, Blumstein, & Schwartz, 1994).

For instance, if you perceive that a friend is receiving more (or less) than his or her due from a relationship, you may experience distress and try to restore equity. You could do this by modifying your perception of what you are getting out of the relationship—or by modifying your feelings for your partner. Consequently, if you feel that you are putting an undue amount of effort into a friendship (perhaps by always being the one to arrange for various social activities), you may experience feelings of inequity and reevaluate your liking for the friend.

However, the desire to maintain equity is not a universal phenomenon; rather, it is based on particular societal standards. For instance, in cultures that highly value interdependence and reliance on others, efforts to maintain equity are less pronounced. In contrast, in the United States, where independence is highly valued, people strive harder to ensure that equity is preserved (Fiske, 1991b; Van Yperen & Buunk, 1991).

One final cognitive approach to interpersonal attraction is represented by balance theory. According to **balance theory**, people strive for consistency, or balance, in their likes and dislikes (Heider, 1958). Balance theory suggests that when we like another person, we are in a state of balance when the other person likes the same things we do. Furthermore, we are attracted to others who hold attitudes similar to our own and who like the same things and people that we do. Similarly, when we dislike someone, we are in a state of balance if that person *dislikes* the things we like. Moreover, we are predisposed to dislike those who hold dissimilar attitudes and who like things and people we don't like (Chapdelaine, Kenny, & LaFontana, 1994).

The two approaches in perspective. As is often the case in social psychology, neither learning approaches nor cognitive approaches alone provide a full explanation of interpersonal attraction. Similarly, no single factor related to attraction—similarity, reciprocity of liking, physical attractiveness, or any of the other components of liking—is sufficient to explain attraction.

On the contrary, a complex web of ingredients determines whether an initial encounter between two people will result in interpersonal attraction. And, as we'll see in Chapter 7, an even more intricate web of social psychological forces determines whether such attraction will blossom and grow into a deeper relationship.

THE INFORMED CONSUMER OF SOCIAL PSYCHOLOGY

MAKING FRIENDS

A quick glance at the self-help section of any bookstore suggests that many of us consider the ability to make friends to be highly important, sometimes to the point of anxiety. Even if we don't seek out self-help books on the topic, making friends is one of our most basic and common concerns.

Although no simple formula exists for making friends, the work of social psychologists points to several approaches worth considering. Among them are the following:

◆ *Let other people know that you like them.* As we've seen, reciprocity of liking is one of the most powerful phenomena in the area of interpersonal attraction. We like those who like us.

Consequently, if you want someone to like you, show that you like him or her. Although such honesty can produce feelings of vulnerability—with good reason—it also may pay to take the risk of demonstrating your liking for another.

◆ *Reveal yourself.* It is hard for people to feel they are similar to you if they know little about you. For many of the factors that have been discussed in this chapter to be effective (such as similarity of values and attitudes), others need to know where you stand. Don't assume that they will somehow know or guess what you think about things; let them know how you feel. Also, self-disclosure, in itself, can produce interpersonal attraction, as we discussed in Chapter 5. When you honestly communicate your own ideas and feelings, others can learn what they have in common with you. Of course, there can be too much disclosure: Revealing significant, personal facts about yourself too early in a relationship can actually impede its progress (Collins & Miller, 1994).

◆ *Take part in shared activities.* The research showing the close correlation between proximity and friendship suggests another strategy for making friends: Take part in shared activities. As we'll see in the next chapter, relationships evolve over time, and engaging in mutual activities may set the stage for the development of lasting friendships.

REVIEW AND RETHINK

Review

- Physical attractiveness is an important determinant of liking and also influences people's interpretations and judgments of actions.
- The beautiful-is-good stereotype suggests that physically attractive people have other positive qualities.
- Learning and cognitive approaches have both been used to explain interpersonal attraction.

Rethink

- List some of the more common stereotypes that our society holds about attractive people. Do any of these stereotypes have a basis in truth? Explain.
- What evidence suggests that attraction to people with certain physical features is innate?
- What disadvantages may result from physical attractiveness? What would the matching hypothesis suggest about the dating success of extremely attractive individuals?
- Describe and differentiate the two main approaches to explaining the interpersonal attraction literature.

LOOKING BACK

What are the origins of interpersonal attraction?

1. We seek out the companionship of others for several reasons. The presence of others can reduce anxiety and permit social comparison, allowing us to evaluate our own abilities, expertise, and opinions by comparing them with others. (p. 193)
2. We also have a need for affiliation, the desire to establish and maintain relationships with other people, which some social psychologists believe is part of our need for belongingness. (p. 193)

3. The roots of affiliation can be found in attachment, the positive emotional bond that develops between a child and a particular individual. Attachment provides children with a sense of security and with information about a given situation. (p. 194)

4. There are three major attachment styles: secure attachment, avoidant attachment, and anxious–ambivalent attachment. The attachment style formed in infancy can have lasting effects on relationship formation throughout life. (p. 195)

5. Loneliness is the inability to maintain the level of affiliation we desire. Among the types of loneliness are emotional isolation, in which we feel a lack of deep emotional attachment to one specific person, and social isolation, in which we lack friends, associates, or relatives. (p. 196)

How do situational factors such as proximity and familiarity lead to liking?

6. Proximity is a powerful factor in producing interpersonal attraction. Proximity permits us to obtain the rewards of friendships—companionship, social approval, and help—at relatively little cost. (p. 196)

7. The mere exposure effect is the phenomenon that repeated exposure to any stimulus increases the positivity of its evaluation. One explanation for this effect is that our positive feelings of recognition when we encounter a frequently experienced stimulus transfer to the stimulus itself. Another possibility is that the more we are exposed to a stimulus, the more we learn about its interesting, novel aspects. Finally, the mere exposure phenomenon may have its roots in evolutionary factors. (p. 198)

What are the primary personal qualities that lead people to be liked by others?

8. We are attracted to those who are similar to us. Among the types of similarity that produce liking are attitude similarity, value similarity, and similarity of personality traits. (p. 202)

9. Similarity may lead to attraction because it is directly reinforcing, it confirms our views of the world, it permits us to form an impression of others' traits, and it allows us to assume that the similarity will produce liking in return. (p. 205)

10. Reciprocity of liking is a strong determinant of interpersonal attraction: We like those who like us. However, exceptions occur in the case of ingratiation and for people with exceptionally low self-esteem. (p. 206)

11. In addition, we like others who have positive qualities, although sometimes we prefer people who have at least a few negative qualities to those who are seemingly flawless. Gender and race are also factors in attraction. (p. 207)

12. People who are physically attractive are liked more—and more consistently—than unattractive people. One reason is the beautiful-is-good stereotype, which suggests that physically attractive people hold a range of other positive characteristics. However, the stereotype is not entirely accurate. (p. 209)

13. Physical attractiveness is most important during initial encounters. The matching hypothesis suggests that we are ultimately attracted to others whose level of physical attractiveness is similar to our own. (p. 216)

14. The two main families of explanations for interpersonal attraction are learning approaches and cognitive approaches. Learning approaches maintain that liking follows the basic principles of classical and operant conditioning. Cognitive approaches focus on the ways in which people's thoughts, beliefs, attitudes, and perceptions determine their liking. Comparison level theory, equity theory, and balance theory are examples of cognitive approaches. (p. 217)

What strategies for making friends do the principles of interpersonal attraction suggest?

15. Among promising strategies for making friends are letting others know that you like them, revealing yourself to others, and taking part in shared activities. (p. 218)

EPILOGUE

We've traced the development of liking in this chapter, discussing why people seek out others and how the roots of attraction develop. In looking at attraction, we've concentrated on the forces that bring people together in the first place, such as situational factors and personal characteristics.

What we haven't done, however, is to look at the way initial attraction leads to close, long-term relationships. In Chapter 7, we take this leap, moving from the origins and first stirrings of liking to the development of full-blown close relationships. We'll see how people form and maintain associations with one another and consider why some relationships falter and sometimes end entirely. As we discuss love, marriage, and several other varieties of enduring relationships, we'll see how the work that we examined in this chapter has paved the way for our understanding of close relationships.

Before we go on, however, return to the description of the friendship in the prologue of this chapter. Consider these questions:

1. Based on evidence in the prologue, what do you think are some of the reasons that the two women developed a personal attraction? What kind of similarity might have been most important?

2. In what ways might similarity have played a role in this friendship?

3. Explain how someone using a learning theory approach (including principles of classical and operant conditioning) might hypothetically trace the development of the friendship between the two girls.

4. Do the same from the point of view of cognitive approaches, including comparison level theory, equity theory, and balance theory.

KEY TERMS AND CONCEPTS

anxious–ambivalent attachment (p. 195)
attachment (p. 194)
avoidant attachment (p. 195)
balance theory (p. 218)
beautiful-is-good stereotype (p. 210)
comparison level theories (p. 217)
emotional isolation (p. 196)
equity theory (p. 218)
interpersonal attraction (p. 192)
interpersonal repulsion (p. 203)
loneliness (p. 196)
matching hypothesis (p. 216)
mere exposure effect (p. 198)
need complementarity hypothesis (p. 204)
need for affiliation (p. 193)
need for belongingness (p. 194)
reciprocity of liking (p. 206)
reinforcement-affect model (p. 217)
secure attachment (p. 195)
social anxiety (p. 194)
social isolation (p. 196)

CHAPTER 7

CLOSE RELATIONSHIPS

Developing Connections with Others

PROLOGUE

Drive-by Romance

As a result of a casual meeting, many people build relationships with others and develop increasing degrees of interdependence and intimacy as a result.

Jessica Casey was on her way home from classes at Greenfield Community College in 1993 with a friend and had picked up some French fries at McDonald's. As they drove over the Sunderland bridge, which was under repair at the time, the friend recognized the police officer who was directing traffic there, Christopher Mattson.

"We pulled over and asked, 'Do you want some French fries?'" Jessica recalls. She handed him the bag—and Chris Mattson tossed it right back at her. "He didn't think there were any fries in the bag, so he threw them back," Jessica says.

That little display didn't prevent Jessica and her friend from trying again the next day. Soon they were bringing Chris lunch every day. Jessica's friend had a reason for the meals-on-wheels service. She didn't care for Jessica's boyfriend at the time, and thought Chris would be a far better match.

The friend was so intent on fixing up Jessica and Chris that she finally dragged him over to Jessica's house—despite the fact that Chris referred to her as "the girl who lied about the French fries." (Cleary, 1999, p. 10)

LOOKING AHEAD

Five years later, Chris and Jessica still argue about the French fries. But they do so as husband and wife: They were married in 1997 and have two children.

How did Chris and Jessica's relationship progress from mere acquaintances to marriage partners, and how does it continue to evolve? Questions such as these underlie the study of close relationships, which we consider in this chapter. Building on the work discussed in the previous chapter on the initial determinants of attraction, we consider the types and characteristics of close relationships. We examine how people build relationships with others and develop increasing degrees of interdependence and intimacy.

We then consider love, a characteristic of our most important relationships, and one of the most difficult subjects to study scientifically. We examine several approaches to the phenomenon of love, including systems for categorizing the different types of love.

We next turn to several varieties of close relationships. Although we focus in particular on marriage, we also consider less traditional alternatives, including staying single and gay and lesbian relationships. We discuss the qualities that people seek out in potential partners, as well as the sources of satisfaction and discontent. We also look at a bleaker side of relationships, discussing family violence and rape.

Finally, we look at the breakdown and ending of relationships, discussing the decline of relationships and considering the phases through which relationships pass on the road to termination.

In sum, after reading this chapter, you'll be able to answer these questions:

- ◆ What factors lead to the development of close relationships, how do these relationships evolve, and what roles do intimacy, self-disclosure, and sexuality play?

- ◆ What are the different categorizations of love?

- ◆ What are the varieties of relationships?

- ◆ What factors lead to the decline of close relationships?

BUILDING RELATIONSHIPS

Acquaintance. Associate. Friend. Relative. Partner. Intimate. Lover.

Each of these labels represents a very different sort of relationship. But what specifically determines whether a relationship can be considered close? According to social psychologist Sharon Brehm (1992), **close relationships** (which she refers to as "intimate relationships") are characterized by at least one of three factors: emotional attachment, need fulfillment, and interdependence. Emotional attachment relates to typically positive (although sometimes negative) feelings for another person. Need fulfillment suggests that partners help fulfill significant psychological or physical needs. Finally, the interdependence criterion presumes that people involved in a close relationship have an impact on each other.

Clearly, such a formulation of close relationships is broad, encompassing a wide variety of different sorts of relationships, both traditional and unconventional. For instance, it covers such common relationships as marriages and engagements. But it also includes less traditional relationships, such as the unions of committed heterosexual couples who live together without marriage and gay and lesbian relationships.

One of the key factors that distinguishes close relationships from others is the degree of interdependence between the two individuals in the relationship. **Interdependence** is the degree of influence two people have over each other and the quantity of activities in which they jointly engage. If two individuals' behaviors, emotions, and thoughts are mutually interconnected, they are interdependent and have a relationship (Kelley et al., 1983; Laursen & Williams, 1997; Agnew et al., 1998; Berscheid & Reis, 1998).

To measure the strength of relationships objectively, social psychologist Ellen Berscheid and colleagues developed the **Relationship Closeness Inventory** (Berscheid, Snyder, & Omoto, 1989a, 1989b). As you can see from the sample items presented in Table 7–1, the questionnaire investigates the nature of interactions between two particular individuals. Specifically, it asks how long the two were together and what they have been doing. In addition, the inventory examines the kind of influence the individuals have over one another's emotions, thinking, and behavior in areas such as social life, financial decisions, and educational choices.

Using the Relationship Closeness Inventory, social psychologists have found that people are remarkably similar in their perceptions of close relationships (Berscheid, Snyder, &

close relationships: A relationship characterized by at least one of three factors: emotional attachment, need fulfillment, and interdependence.

interdependence: The degree of influence two people have over each other and the quantity of activities in which they jointly engage.

Relationship Closeness Inventory: A method used to measure the strength of relationships objectively.

TABLE 7–1   Relationship Closeness Inventory

What kind of relationship do you have with a particular person? The following sample items, drawn from the Relationship Closeness Inventory (Berscheid, Snyder, & Omoto, 1989a), provide examples of the kinds of questions you might ask yourself in order to assess the closeness of your relationship.

For the following items, indicate which activities you did *alone* with the particular individual:

_____ did laundry

_____ prepared a meal

_____ watched TV

_____ went to an auction/antique show

_____ went to a restaurant

_____ went to a grocery store

_____ went for a walk/drive

_____ discussed things of a personal nature

_____ attended class

_____ went on a trip (e.g., vacation or weekend)

For each of the following items, indicate the amount of influence the same individual, labeled "X" here, has on your thoughts, feelings, and behavior. Use a 7-point scale, with 1 = I strongly disagree and 7 = I strongly agree.

1. _____ X will influence my future financial security.
2. _____ X does *not* influence everyday things in my life.*
3. _____ X influences important things in my life.
4. _____ X influences which parties and other social events I attend.
5. _____ X influences the extent to which I accept responsibilities in our relationship.
6. _____ X does *not* influence how much time I spend doing household work.*
7. _____ X does *not* influence how I choose to spend my money.*
8. _____ X influences the way I feel about myself.
9. _____ X does *not* influence my moods.*
10. _____ X influences the basic values that I hold.

(*Items with asterisks are reverse-scored—a 1 is considered 7, 2 becomes 6, 3 becomes 4, and so on.)

Finally, indicate the degree to which your future plans and goals are affected by X. Use a 7-point scale, with 1 = not at all and 7 = a great extent.

1. _____ my vacation plans
2. _____ my marriage plans
3. _____ my plans to have children
4. _____ my plans to make *major* investments
5. _____ my plans to join a club, social organization, church, etc.
6. _____ my school-related plans
7. _____ my plans for achieving a particular financial standard of living

Because these are sample items, it is not possible to obtain a fully accurate score. However, in general, the higher your score, the closer the relationship.

Omoto, 1989b). For example, men and women express the same degree of closeness in their relationships; they also view romantic relationships as closer than relationships with family and friends. In fact, when asked to indicate the one person with whom they felt closest, 47% chose a romantic partner, whereas 36% chose a friend. Only 14% named a family member, and the remaining 3% identified someone else altogether.

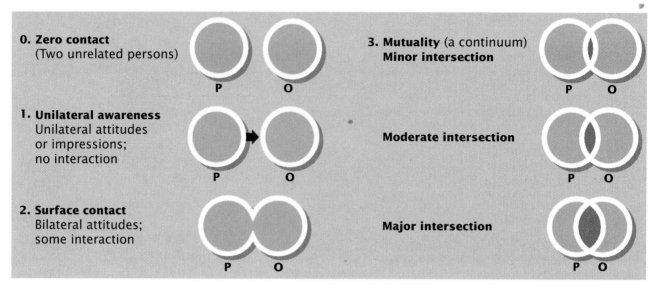

FIGURE 7–1   Levels of Relatedness George Levinger suggests that there are three basic levels of relatedness between two individuals (here labeled "P" and "O"). (*Source:* Levinger, 1974.)

The Relationship Closeness Inventory also provides information about how various kinds of relationships develop. For instance, the road of romantic relationships is the most likely to be seen as having twists and bends and—sometimes—dead ends. People believe that romantic liaisons can end abruptly and permanently in ways that friendships and family relationships cannot. In contrast, they perceive relationships among friends and family members as continuing, even when little actual contact occurs among the individuals. When relationships among friends and family members begin to deteriorate, they are more likely to end with a whimper than a bang (Aron et al., 1989; Berscheid, Snyder, & Omoto, 1989b; Fehr, 1995).

LEVELS OF RELATEDNESS

According to social psychologist George Levinger, relationships should be considered not only in terms of specific types (such as relationships between friends, lovers, and relatives) but also in terms of their underlying level of relatedness. He suggests that there are three basic levels of relatedness: unilateral awareness, surface contact, and mutuality (Borden & Levinger, 1991; see Figure 7–1).

Unilateral awareness is the level at which individuals view the outward characteristics of others. Those who are perceived at this level are not even aware that they are being observed or judged. For instance, although you may remember the checkout staff at the grocery store at which you shop, to them you might be just one of hundreds of customers they see each day. Most of our relationships occur at such levels of unilateral awareness.

With *surface contact,* the second level of pair relatedness, both people are aware of each other. Each forms attitudes and impressions of the other, as well as beliefs and emotions regarding the relationship itself. Most daily interactions with others fall into this category. Even though we frequently see the same people—grocery clerk, bus driver, building custodian, or bank teller—the depth and closeness of our relationships with them are relatively minor.

When relationships reach the third stage, that of mutuality, they become truly personal. In *mutuality,* the individuals in a relationship share knowledge of each other, experience a sense of responsibility for each other, and develop a set of personal norms that informally regulate their relationship. At the mutuality stage, interactions are no longer merely transitory or fixed within a restricted role relationship (such as in a clerk–customer interaction).

unilateral awareness: The level at which individuals view the outward characteristics of others.

The mutuality stage of relationships is itself subdivided into three stages. During the early stages of mutuality, referred to as *minor intersection* in Figure 7–1, people are hesitant to disclose information about themselves. The degree of self-disclosure increases as the relationship progresses to the level of *moderate intersection,* an intermediate stage of relationship development, and then to *major intersection,* a strong, binding relationship. The partners increasingly reveal intimate and important attitudes and feelings about themselves. Further, each partner learns the sources of the other person's happiness and satisfaction, and each begins to behave in ways that make the relationship rewarding to the other person. Such behavior maintains and strengthens the relationship.

One of the transformations that can occur during the course of relationships is a change from exchange relationships to communal relationships. According to social psychologist Margaret Clark, **exchange relationships** are associations based on an economic model of interaction, in which people seek to maximize their benefits and minimize their costs (Clark & Mills, 1979, 1993; Clark & Reis, 1988; Clark, Mills, & Corcoran, 1989). Exchange relationships are characterized by reciprocity: If a person provides something positive to a partner within an exchange relationship, then he or she expects a return benefit. Thus, people who give presents to mail carriers or trash collectors during the December holidays typically do so to receive the benefit of good service during the following year—not because they hope to establish a close friendship. In sum, they expect that any costs will be compensated by future benefits. We tend to have exchange relationships with first-time acquaintances and business people.

Communal relationships are a different story. In a **communal relationship**, the participants feel mutual responsibility, and each provides benefits according to the other's needs or to exhibit concern for the other person. For example, we might take flowers from our garden to a neighbor, not because we expect a gift in return, but because we value the friendship and like the recipient. Unlike exchange relationships, communal relationships occur most often with romantic partners, family members, and friends (Williamson & Clark, 1996; Grote & Clark, 1998).

The behaviors involved in exchange and communal relationships are dramatically different. For example, in exchange relationships, people keep careful track of their input, and they expect

exchange relationships: Associations based on an economic model of interaction, in which people seek to maximize their benefits and minimize their costs.

communal relationship: A relationship where the participants feel mutual responsibility, and each provides benefits according to the other's needs or to exhibit concern for the other person.

In a communal relationship, such as that shared by these Amish men working to raise a barn, participants feel mutual responsibility and provide benefits according to the needs of others.

that a favor will be repaid fairly quickly. However, in communal relationships people may view rapid repayment of a favor negatively, interpreting it as an indication that the partner views the relationship in exchange terms, rather than in the more desirable communal terms.

Even when they know that they are not likely to receive specific reimbursement, people in communal relationships provide aid based on the needs of the other person. Their goal, then, is not to be directly compensated for their efforts but to provide benefits to a partner for the sake of the continuing relationship and without thought of future reward (Clark & Mills, 1979, 1993; Clark, 1984; Lahno, 1995; Williamson & Schulz, 1995).

Of course, one could argue that although people in communal relationships do not keep a running psychological balance sheet, carefully tallying the costs and benefits on an ongoing basis, they still have an ultimately self-serving goal in mind: the long-term maintenance of the relationship. After all, we would not expect a relationship to last over the long term if one partner consistently provided benefits and the other never reciprocated. Consequently, although people in communal relationships forgo an accounting of rewards and benefits in the short run, their expectation is that rewards and costs will be balanced over the long term. This issue is a thorny one, and we will return to it in Chapter 8, when we discuss whether truly altruistic helping behavior exists (Batson, 1993).

INTIMACY: OPENING UP TO OTHERS

One of the key factors that differentiates various types of relationships is intimacy. In a social psychological sense, **intimacy** is the status in which a person communicates important feelings and information to another through a process of self-disclosure (Prager, 1995; Berscheid & Reis, 1998).

We discussed self-disclosure earlier in Chapter 5, in terms of its benefits to the person revealing the information. However, self-disclosure provides another advantage: It enhances the sense of intimacy in a relationship. As a result of self-disclosure, people come to feel understood, cared for, and validated by the partner in a relationship (Waring, Schaefer, & Fry, 1994; Ben-Ari, 1995; Dolgin & Minowa, 1997).

There are many varieties of self-disclosure, of course; revealing your student identification number is quite different from discussing your sexual fantasies. One of the key distinctions in self-disclosure, then, is the distinction between descriptive self-disclosure and evaluative self-disclosure (e.g., Morton, 1978). In **descriptive self-disclosure**, people share *facts* about their lives. Revealing your place of birth and your parents' professions are examples of descriptive self-disclosure. In contrast, **evaluative self-disclosure** communicates information about personal *feelings*. Expressing shame—an emotion—over a past misdeed is an illustration of evaluative self-disclosure (Laurenceau, Barrett, & Pietromonaco, 1998).

The two types of self-disclosure occur in different contexts and result in different degrees of intimacy. For example, in one study participants were told in one condition to seek out accurate information about a partner during a discussion; in another condition, participants were told to create a favorable impression during a discussion (Berg & Archer, 1982). In the information-seeking condition, the rate of descriptive self-disclosure and the rate of evaluative self-disclosure on the part of participants were about equal. On the other hand, when participants were trying to make a good impression on a partner, they used significantly more evaluative self-disclosure.

Further, people sometimes tentatively offer limited amounts of information about themselves to test the reaction of their partners. For example, a student may make a joking comment about the difficulty of an upcoming exam to judge the listener's reaction. If the comment is met with sympathy, the student may then make a fuller disclosure regarding the strong anxiety that actually underlies his anticipation of the exam. Conversely, if no sympathy or reciprocal self-disclosure is forthcoming, the student may drop the topic (Miell & Duck, 1986; Duck, 1988).

According to social psychologists Irving Altman and Dalmas Taylor (1973), self-disclosure, in general, increases as partners become better acquainted. In their **theory of social penetration**, they suggest that relationships gradually progress through increasingly deeper

intimacy: The status in which a person communicates important feelings and information to another through a process of self-disclosure.

descriptive self-disclosure: Self-disclosure in which people share facts about their lives.

evaluative self-disclosure: Self-disclosure in which people communicate information about personal feelings.

theory of social penetration: The theory that suggests that relationships gradually progress through increasingly deeper intimacy.

intimacy. Initially, people reveal relatively little about themselves, providing partners with superficial information through descriptive self-disclosure. However, as the relation becomes more intimate, both the level and the degree of disclosure increase. The inf tion becomes broader, encompassing more areas of a person's life; and it becomes d embodying more delicate, hidden material that is revealed through evaluative self-disc (Hornstein & Truesdell, 1988; Cooper & Sportolari, 1997).

Although self-disclosure continues to be an important factor throughout the life o tionship, it may reach its highest level as soon as 6 weeks into the development o relationship (Hays, 1984, 1985). After that point the rate of disclosure tends to lev

Although self-disclosure generally yields positive results and leads to increased i in some cases it has negative consequences. If people disclose that they actually don' other person much, then self-disclosure may be harmful. For example, reports u₁ u.. disclosure in faltering marital relationships show that the depth of self-disclosure actually increases in couples under these circumstances. Unfortunately, what is revealed is displeasure over the relationship. Although the depth of disclosure increases, the breadth of disclosure declines, as partners focus on communicating their discontent (Tolstedt & Stokes, 1984).

RECIPROCITY OF SELF-DISCLOSURE

Altman and Taylor's theory of social penetration also suggests that as each partner discloses more intimate information, the other partner responds in kind. This phenomenon is known as the **reciprocity of self-disclosure**. Within Western cultures, norms of reciprocity lead people to attempt to match the level of self-disclosure provided by new acquaintances. As relationships progress, that norm continues to operate—but only up to a point. In well-established relationships, precise reciprocity is less likely to occur (e.g., Laurenceau et al., 1998).

One of the puzzling questions regarding reciprocity of self-disclosure concerns the issue of cause and effect. Do people show reciprocity within relationships because individuals who usually disclose equivalent amounts of information tend to prefer one another? Or, alternatively, do people show reciprocity because of the nature of their own particular relationships?

The answer seems to be that reciprocity of self-disclosure has its roots in the particular kind of relationship that develops between two individuals (Miller & Kenny, 1986; Miller, 1990). People don't seek out others who are similar in their levels of self-disclosure in order to form relationships. Instead, people within relationships jointly determine their own specific level of reciprocal self-disclosure.

One major focus of research on close relationships is the association between self-disclosure and gender. Theoreticians have traditionally argued that norms regarding masculine behavior inhibit self-disclosure in men, because society encourages males to be objective and unemotional and discourages self-awareness and insight (e.g., Jourard, 1971; Dolgin, Meyer, & Schwartz, 1991; Shaffer, Pegalis, & Cornell, 1991, 1992). Most research has supported this hypothesis. Overall, women tend to self-disclose slightly more than men, although the differences are relatively small (Rotenberg & Chase, 1992; Clark & Ayers, 1993; Derlega et al., 1993; Stein & Brodksy, 1995). In addition, the nature of the material men and women disclose varies. For example, one study found that women were more apt to disclose information about feelings and negative emotions, whereas men disclosed more factual and more emotionally positive information (Rubin et al., 1980; see Table 7–2).

Gender differences in disclosure are more pronounced in same-sex heterosexual interactions than in mixed-sex interactions. Relationships between two women have the highest degree of self-disclosure, and relationships between two men have the lowest. The reciprocity principle helps explain these findings: Because of women's inclination to disclose more than men, their high self-disclosure may induce their partners to self-disclose even more. On the other hand, because men disclose less than women, their low rate of self-disclosure may discourage their partners' self-disclosure (Dindia & Allen, 1992; Dolgin & Kim, 1994).

TABLE 7–2	Sex Differences in Self-Disclosure

Female students self-disclose more information than men about:

    Feelings toward parents

    Feelings toward closest friends

    Feelings toward classes

    The things in life they are most afraid of

    Their accomplishments

Male students self-disclose more information than women about:

    Their political views

    The things about themselves that they are most proud of

    The things they like most about their partners

Source: Rubin, Hill, Peplau, & Dunkel-Schetter, 1980.

Regardless of gender differences in self-disclosure, one thing is certain: Disclosure of important information leads the partners in a relationship toward greater levels of intimacy (Derlega, 1988; Camarena, Sarigiani, & Petersen, 1990; Jones, 1991; Laurenceau et al., 1998). In some cases, this intimacy steers people into deeper and deeper relationships.

STAGES OF RELATIONSHIPS

We've examined several of the building blocks of relationships, such as interdependence, intimacy, levels of relatedness, and self-disclosure. Yet relationships are hardly static. As two people become increasingly involved with each other, their feelings, thoughts, and behavior evolves, and their interactions change.

Do relationships develop in particular patterns? According to some researchers, relationships pass through a series of stages. For instance, the following general patterns can be seen in relationships as people become increasingly attached to each other (Berscheid, 1985; Love & Brown, 1999).

- The partners interact with each other more frequently and for longer periods of time in an increasing variety of settings.

- The two individuals increasingly seek out each other's company.

- They open up to each other more and more, disclosing secrets and sharing physical intimacies. They are more willing to share both positive and negative feelings, and they are more apt to offer criticism as well as praise.

- Their goals for the relationship become compatible, and they show greater similarity in their reactions to situations.

- They begin to sense that their own psychological well-being is tied to the success of the relationship, viewing it as unique, precious, and irreplaceable.

- They begin to act as a couple, rather than as two separate individuals.

Social psychologist Bernard Murstein views these developments through the lens of what he calls **stimulus-value-role (SVR) theory** (Murstein, 1976, 1986, 1987). According to this theory, relationships proceed in a fixed order through a series of three stages. In the first phase, the stimulus stage, relationships are built on external characteristics such as physical qualities. Typically, this represents just the first encounter.

The second step, the value stage, often occurs from the second to seventh contact. In the value period, the focus in the relationship changes to similarity of values and beliefs. Finally, during the third and last period, dubbed the role stage, the relationship is based on specific roles played by the participants, such as boyfriend–girlfriend or husband–wife.

stimulus-value-role (SVR) theory: The theory that relationships proceed in a fixed order through a series of three stages: stimulus stage, value stage, and role stage.

Self-disclosure, through opening up and sharing secrets, is one of the patterns found in close relationships. Such disclosure allows people to air negative feelings and provides the opportunity to offer criticism as well as praise.

Although stimulus, value, and role factors predominate at particular points in the relationship, they may be at least somewhat influential at other junctures. The relationship between the three factors is illustrated in Figure 7–2.

Not everyone agrees with stage approaches. For example, although SVR theory suggests that the stages in a relationship occur in a fixed, invariant sequence, it is not entirely clear that this is logically true. Why couldn't a relationship be initiated on the basis of similarity of values, and then develop in terms of stimulus attributes? Moreover, in some cultures, such as those in which marriages are arranged, relationships begin with role considerations (Gupta & Singh, 1982; Sternberg, 1986). Stimulus attributes and values come into play only at some later point, contrary to SVR theory.

FIGURE 7–2   Stages of Relationships According to Stimulus-Value-Role Theory Depending on the stage of the relationship, stimulus, value, or role factors predominate. (*Source:* Murstein, 1987.)

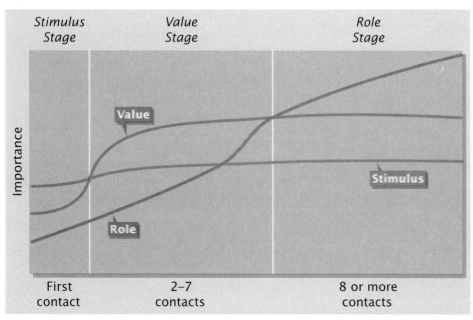

double standard: The view that premarital sex is permissible for men but not for women.

permissiveness with affection standard: The view that premarital intercourse is permissible for both men and women if it occurs within a long-term, committed, or loving relationship.

In short, stage theories do not always accurately describe or explain the development of any one particular relationship. They also do not address a central aspect of relationships to which we turn next: the role of sexuality.

SEXUALITY AND RELATIONSHIPS

Until the 1960s, societal standards provided clear standards for heterosexual couples. According to the traditional view, sexual intercourse was not to occur until marriage—a dictum that has traditionally been more rigid for women than men. Women were warned that "nice girls don't do it," whereas men were allowed to "sow their wild oats." The view that premarital sex was permissible for men but not for women came to be known as the **double standard** (Gentry, 1998).

In the last few decades, however, societal views have undergone a dramatic shift. As you can see in Figure 7–3, the percentage of people who feel that sexual intercourse prior to marriage is not wrong at all has increased significantly. On the other hand, the number of people who believe that sex before marriage is always wrong has increased, too, although not as dramatically (Stapinski, 1999).

As societal standards became more permissive, the actual rate of heterosexual premarital intercourse has risen. For example, three-quarters of 18- to 24-year-olds say they have been sexually active (Stapinski, 1999).

The end of the double standard?   Do these figures suggest that the double standard has disappeared? Most experts agree that it has, although it has been replaced with a new standard: permissiveness with affection. According to psychologist Janet Hyde (1990), the **permissiveness with affection standard** represents the view that premarital intercourse is permissible for both men and women if it occurs within a long-term, committed, or loving relationship (Reiss, 1960; Hyde, 1994; O'Sullivan, 1995).

FIGURE 7–3   Attitudes Toward Premarital Sexual Intercourse Although the percentage of younger adults who think it is always wrong to have sex before marriage has increased over the past 25 years, the number of older adults who find premarital sex permissible has risen dramatically over the same period. (*Source:* Gallup Poll News Service, 1998.)

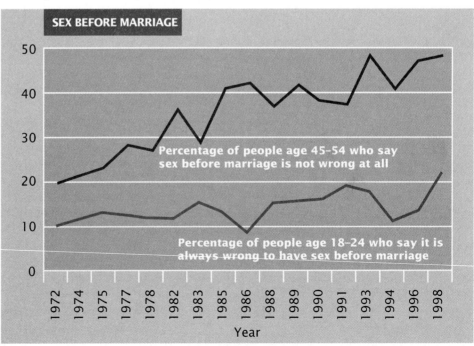

At the same time, remnants of the double standard remain, with women frequently being held to stricter sexual standards than men (Oliver & Hyde, 1993; Sprecher & Hatfield, 1996; Sheeran et al., 1996). For instance, surveys of college students suggest that men's behavior and women's behavior are held to different standards. Men who were involved in considerable sexual activity were seen as more attractive than men who engaged in little activity, whereas the opposite was true for women (Moffat, 1989; Breay & Gentry, 1990). (Interestingly, the same attitudinal double standard holds for married men and women. Surveys have found that men consider it more permissible for a man to engage in extramarital affairs than for a woman to do so [Margolin, 1989].)

Substantial cultural differences exist in the incidence and timing of premarital sexual intercourse. In Japan, for example, both men and women are much less likely to engage in premarital sex than men and women in the United States. Rates of intercourse in Mexico are much lower for females than for males, in contrast to the United States, where the gender gap is much smaller. Even in the United States, subcultural differences are found. For instance, on average, African American males are likely to have sexual intercourse some 2 years earlier than their white counterparts (Liskin, 1985; Moore & Erickson, 1985; Gage & Meekers, 1994).

Does the higher incidence of premarital sexual intercourse lead to happier relationships? Most evidence suggests that sexual behavior, per se, is not crucial in determining the long-term success of a relationship. For instance, one study found that heterosexual college students who had sexual relationships were more apt to be dating 3 months after they were first contacted than those who didn't have sexual relationships (Simpson, 1987). However, the long-term effects of premarital sex appear to be either neutral or slightly negative (Bentler & Newcomb, 1978; Markman, 1981; Glenn, 1990).

In contrast, among married couples, sex is positively related to overall satisfaction with the relationship. Significantly, marital happiness does not depend on the frequency of sexual intercourse. At least among married couples, quality of sex apparently is more important than quantity (Song, Bergen, & Schumm, 1995; Kurdek, 1998; Young et al., 1998).

RELATIONSHIPS AMONG GAY AND LESBIAN COUPLES

EXPLORING DIVERSITY

> We try not to make arguments a matter of who wins. I don't have any notches in my belt, and he doesn't have any notches in his belt that I'm aware of. I don't think we keep track, and I don't think it's important.
>
> We talk things out better than we used to. We confront things better. In years past we might have harbored resentments; we don't any longer. We have a lot of "I" dialogues. For example, "I feel down" or "I feel wonderful," and then, of course, the other person is supposed to say, "Why?" and that helps things get talked about on the right basis. . . . Perhaps sometimes we don't share enough, but that is because of the closeness, of the number of years we've been together, of that whole osmosis thing; we assume that our partner sometimes knows more than he does. (Blumstein & Schwartz, 1983, pp. 542–543)

The speaker: a 47-year-old gay man named Joel, who has been in a relationship for 15 years with his partner, Gary. Both Joel and Gary expect their relationship to continue for the rest of their lives.

Although most studies on relationships have examined heterosexual couples, an increasing amount of research has focused on gay and lesbian couples. This research has taken on new urgency as political questions regarding gay and lesbian marriages have become increasingly prominent.

Most research suggests that the similarities between heterosexual and homosexual couples are greater than the differences. For example, gay males describe successful relationships in ways similar to those of heterosexuals. For instance, good relationships involve appreciation of the partner and of the couple as a unit, minimal conflict, and positive feelings toward the concept of love (Jones & Bates, 1978). Similarly, lesbian women value attachment, caring, intimacy, affection, and respect (Caldwell & Peplau, 1984; Peplau & Cochran, 1990). One survey showed that 82% of lesbians questioned were currently involved in a relationship, and the majority of women said that having a permanent relationship was either very important or the most important thing in their lives—responses similar to those provided by heterosexuals (Peplau, Padesky, & Hamilton, 1982; Brehm, 1992).

However, gay men and lesbians do not place equal value on all aspects of relationships. For instance, lesbian couples place greater emphasis than gay men on the importance of equality in their ideal relationships (Kurdek, 1994, 1995).

Furthermore, studies comparing gay men, lesbians, and heterosexual couples find that labor is divided more evenly in homosexual households than in heterosexual households. Gay and lesbian couples place greater emphasis on an egalitarian allocation of household chores than heterosexual couples, and each partner in a homosexual relationship is more likely to carry out similar numbers of chores than partners in heterosexual couples. Although gay and lesbian couples who adopt children become more specialized in their household chores, with a less egalitarian arrangement, the same shift typically occurs in heterosexual couples upon the arrival of children (Patterson, 1992, 1994; Deutsch, Lussier, & Servis, 1993; Kurdek, 1993; Flaks et al., 1995).

In short, most evidence suggests that both male and female homosexual relationships may be more like than unlike heterosexual relationships. Like their heterosexual counterparts, most gays and lesbians seek loving, long-term, and meaningful relationships (Caldwell & Peplau, 1984; Peplau & Cochran, 1990; Kurdek, 1991, 1992).

REVIEW AND RETHINK

Review

- Three key elements in close relationships are emotional attachment, need fulfillment, and interdependence.
- People may be involved in exchange relationships, which focus on an economic model of costs and benefits, or communal relationships, characterized by mutual responsibility.
- Intimacy is the process in which a person communicates important feelings and information to another through self-disclosure.
- According to one theory, relationships proceed through stimulus, value, and role stages.
- Sexual behavior may be an important component of relationships.
- Gay and lesbian relationships are similar in many ways to heterosexual relationships.

Rethink

- How do exchange relationships differ from communal relationships? What type of relationship is likely to operate in each of Levinger's three levels of relatedness?
- Explain how norms of reciprocity affect the level of intimacy in female–female, male–male, and female–male interactions. Would norms of reciprocity of self-disclosure be stronger in exchange or communal relationships?
- How would you characterize the type of self-disclosure that predominates at the beginning of a relationship? How does this type of disclosure differ from the self-disclosure of healthy and unhealthy long-term relationships?

LOVE

For something that "makes the world go 'round," as the old song goes, love is one of the most elusive phenomena in our everyday lives. We aspire to love, we are overjoyed to be in love, and we seek to establish permanent relationships with those we love, but understanding love has proved to be a daunting task.

Love plays a central role in intimate relationships. Given its influence on marriage and divorce, love is of crucial concern to society.

Love has always seemed a difficult topic to understand. For instance, social philosopher H. T. Finck said in 1902, "Love is such a tissue of paradoxes, and exists in such an endless variety of forms and shades, that you may say almost anything about it that you please, and it is likely to be correct" (p. 224). More recently, one U.S. senator argued that research on love was unnecessary: "I believe that 200 million other Americans want to leave some things in life a mystery, and right at the top of the things we don't want to know is why a man falls in love with a woman and vice versa" (Proxmire, 1975).

Until the 1970s, many social psychologists would have agreed that love was an inappropriate topic of study, although for different reasons (Rubin, 1988). The study of romantic love was considered to be unscientific, primarily because the phenomenon was so difficult to observe in a systematic way. More recently, however, social psychologists have modified this stance, and they have offered a number of significant theories to explain love (Hendrick & Hendrick, 1986, 1997; Beall & Sternberg, 1995; Berscheid & Reis, 1998). Given the importance love plays in people's most intimate relationships, as well as its influence on marriage and divorce, understanding love better may prove to be of crucial concern to society.

PASSIONATE AND COMPANIONATE LOVE: TWO TERMS OF ENDEARMENT

When social psychologists first sought to understand love, they attempted to identify the factors that distinguish loving from mere liking (Sternberg, 1987). Taking this approach, they argued that love is not simply liking in a greater quantity, but a qualitatively different psychological state (Walster & Walster, 1978; Lamm & Wiesmann, 1997; Berscheid & Reis, 1998). For instance, love—at least in its early stages—includes a relatively intense physiological arousal, an all-encompassing interest in another person, recurring fantasies about the other person, and relatively rapid swings of emotion. In contrast to liking, love includes elements of intimacy, passion, captivation, and exclusivity (Hendrick & Hendrick, 1989).

Of course, not all love is the same. There is a difference in the way one loves a spouse, a girlfriend or boyfriend, a clandestine lover, a sibling, a best friend, a parent. Consequently, we can distinguish between two main types of love: passionate love and companionate love

(Singelis, Choo, & Hatfield, 1995; Barnes & Sternberg, 1997; Hendrick & Hendrick, 1997). **Passionate (or romantic) love** is a state of intense absorption in someone. It includes intense physiological arousal, psychological interest, and caring for the needs of another. In comparison, **companionate love** is the strong affection that we have for those with whom our lives are deeply involved. Although passionate love may evolve, over time, into companionate love, the two differ in fundamental ways (Hatfield, 1988).

Passionate love.   When poets and lyricists sing the praises of love, they are usually referring to passionate love. Societal norms are rather specific in their definitions of love; most people feel that if they are truly in love, their hearts ought to beat faster at the sight of their loved one, they should experience intense desire for each other, and they must forgive each other's shortcomings and focus on their strong points.

Actually, such a view is not all that far removed from what people actually report they feel during the early stages of a romantic relationship. People who are in love don't just *think* about their partners; they physically *experience* intense passion. In contrast to simple liking, which develops more gradually, passionate love often has a swift onset. It can also be more volatile: Love's greater intensity may lead to a roller-coaster pattern of ups and downs. Finally, passionate love involves an exclusivity that may preclude interest in other people (Walster & Walster, 1978).

Although experts generally agree on the characteristics that distinguish deeper passionate love from more superficial attraction, loving and liking remain somewhat difficult to quantify and specify in scientific terms. One approach to differentiate the two emotions is a questionnaire devised by social psychologist Zick Rubin (1973), which uses two independent scales to measure liking and loving. Each scale consists of a series of items in which the respondent fills in the name of someone to whom he or she is attracted and then indicates agreement with each statement on a 9-point scale. For instance, the love scale items include the following:

- I feel that I can confide in _____ about virtually everything.
- I would do almost anything for _____.
- I feel responsible for _____'s well-being.

The more you can agree with each item, the greater the love you are experiencing. In contrast, consider the following questions, also drawn from Rubin's scale:

- I think that _____ is unusually well adjusted.
- I think that _____ is one of those people who quickly wins respect.
- _____ is one of the most likable people I know.

Items such as these tap liking, not love. The more you agree with them, the more you like the individual you have in mind when answering.

As we would expect, couples who score high on the love scale differ substantially from those with lower scores. For instance, high scorers gaze at each other more, and their relationships are more apt to be intact 6 months after completing the questionnaire than those who score lower (Rubin, 1973).

Although the scale helps distinguish between loving and liking, it does not explain why passionate love is so different from liking. Moreover, it does little to explain why people fall in love.

According to one theory that seeks to address such issues, negative emotional responses such as jealousy, anger, and a fear of rejection by another person may help convince people that they are in love. In social psychologists Elaine Hatfield and Ellen Berscheid's **labeling theory of passionate love**, people experience romantic love when two events occur together: intense physiological arousal and situational cues that indicate that "love" is the appropriate label for the feelings they are experiencing (Berscheid & Walster, 1974). Building on Schachter's theory of emotion labeling, which we first discussed as the two-factor theory of emotion in Chapter 4, the labeling theory of passionate love suggests that when

passionate (or romantic) love: A state of intense absorption in someone.

companionate love: The strong affection that we have for those with whom our lives are deeply involved.

labeling theory of passionate love: The theory that suggests that people experience romantic love when intense physiological arousal and situational cues occur together.

physiological arousal is labeled as being due to "falling in love" or "she's so wonderful" or "he's just right for me," the experience can be labeled "romantic love." The source of the physiological arousal can be sexual arousal, excitement, or even negative emotions such as fear, jealousy, and anger.

The labeling theory of passionate love is particularly useful because it explains why a person who keeps being hurt or rejected by someone else can still feel love for that person. Such negative emotions can produce strong physiological arousal. If an individual labels that arousal as love-related, attraction to the other person will be maintained and perhaps even heightened by these circumstances.

Several experiments support this two-factor theory of love (Walsh, Meister, & Kleinke, 1977). However, most of the evidence has been indirect, focusing on the notion that arousal of any sort can lead to the intensification of attraction. For example, in one intriguing study, social psychologists Donald Dutton and Arthur Aron stationed an attractive, college-age woman at the end of a dangerous, swaying, 450-foot suspension bridge that spanned a deep, rocky canyon (Dutton & Aron, 1974). The woman supposedly was conducting a survey, and she asked men who had just managed to make it across the bridge a series of questions. She then offered to give the participants more information about her survey if they desired, and wrote her telephone number on a small piece of paper so they could get in touch later. In a control condition, the same female was at the end of a safe and sturdy bridge only 10 feet off the ground.

The experimenters reasoned that the danger of the suspension bridge would lead to physiological arousal, and that participants would interpret this arousal as attraction in the presence of the attractive woman. As predicted, of the participants who contacted the woman later, many more had crossed the dangerous bridge than the safe one. The results supported the notion that participants associated the increased physiological arousal they likely experienced when they crossed the dangerous bridge with attraction to the woman. Their fear, then, had led to attraction.

The labeling theory of passionate love suggests an explanation for what has been called the "Romeo and Juliet effect" (Driscoll, Davis, & Lipitz, 1972). The **Romeo and Juliet effect** is the phenomenon in which couples who experience strong parental interference in their relationships report greater love for one another than those who receive little interference. Consistent with the two-factor theory, parental interference may raise the general level of arousal between two lovers. They may interpret their heightened physiological arousal as enhanced passion for each other.

However, what the labeling theory of passionate love does not do is explain *why* people come to interpret physiological arousal as love. One explanation comes from our cultural norms about love. For us to label arousal as passionate love, we must live in a culture that communicates the concept of passionate love. We need to know that passionate love is a possible, acceptable, and desirable response—something our culture understands, appreciates, and does with gusto (Dion & Dion, 1988, 1996).

In our society, no one can dispute that passionate love is portrayed as a worthy state, and not only in TV soap operas, love ballads, and romance novels. In many ways, and through diverse kinds of messages, we are told that love leads to happiness, companionship, and sexual fulfillment. Our culture places love on a pedestal, suggesting that a lack of passionate love in one's life has catastrophic implications.

Interestingly, not all cultures hold such a view of passionate love (Hendrick & Hendrick, 1997; Jankowiak & Fischer, 1998). In several cultures, for instance, love is not a particularly important concept. Even today in many parts of the world, marriages are arranged by parents on an economic basis or for reasons relating to politics and status (Xiaohe & Whyte, 1990; Rockman, 1994). In fact, even within Western cultures, the notion of love is a relatively recent phenomenon. For instance, before the Middle Ages, love in its current form did not exist. The ancient Greeks, for example, saw love as a form of madness. When our current conception of love as a feeling that leads to marriage was originally put forward by social thinkers in the Middle Ages, it was meant to serve as a more desirable alternative to raw sexual desire (Lewis, 1958).

Romeo and Juliet effect: The phenomenon in which couples who experience strong parental interference in their relationships report greater love for one another than those who receive little interference.

Josh Marquis and Cindy Price seemed all wrong for each other. She had just left a job as a foreign-policy analyst at a conservative think tank. He, a district attorney in Astoria, Oregon, was a Democrat who thought Ronald Reagan was, he says, "the Antichrist." But they agreed on one issue: the guilt of O. J. Simpson.

Marquis, now 46, and Price, 44, met in 1995 on a Court TV-sponsored AOL message board devoted to the raging Simpson trial. Neither was seeking love—"just good conversation," says Price, then living in Sherman Oaks, California. They and other prosecution advocates split off into a private 3-mail group. The two admired each other's writing—then hit it off when about 50 group members met at California's Beverly Hills Tennis Club to commiserate over Simpson's acquittal. Back home, their e-mail turned romantic. "This is what they call falling in love," the never-wed Marquis wrote Price, who had been briefly married. She flew to Oregon for their first date and stayed (she now hosts a local cultural-affairs radio show). They wed in March 1996. Their plans? Says Marquis: "Live happily ever after." (People Weekly, 1999, p. 50)

For many people, the Internet is more than a communications link: It's the newest love connection. America Online claims that over 1,200 weddings have had their origins from chats on their dating bulletin board area, and the number of cyberspace romances sparked by e-mail is many times higher.

Why does romance thrive on the Internet? One reason is that it offers people the chance to present themselves initially without cues about their physical appearance. Because physical attractiveness is such a powerful determinant of initial liking, it consequently biases the way that people are perceived. Cyberspace interactions, however, permit people to present themselves as they want to be viewed—in terms of their interests, attitudes, and personalities, devoid of the physical attractiveness factor.

Furthermore, Internet communications permit self-disclosure at an early stage of acquaintanceship. And because many people initially communicate anonymously, the Internet permits them to divulge personal information with less risk than if they were self-disclosing to another person face-to-face (McKenna & Bargh, 1998).

Internet communication has another advantage, particularly for those who are shy and find traditional dating difficult: It allows one to "lurk," the term for someone who simply reads material posted by others. Lurking permits a hesitant observer to learn about a specific individual by reading his or her postings before making initial contact, thereby ensuring that a commonality of interests and attitudes exists.

On the other hand, there is a downside to building relationships in cyberspace. Because it is unnecessary to deal with anything negative—simply by turning off the computer—one may not learn how to connect effectively with others. Furthermore, there may be aspects of people that you can't know by simply reading messages from them, no matter how revealing they may be. Ultimately, face-to-face contact is necessary for a relationship to fully develop (Sleek, 1998).

Still, passionate love is a widespread phenomenon. For instance, in one study, researchers looking at 166 cultures found at least some form of passionate love in almost 90% of them (Jankowiak & Fischer, 1992, 1998). Certainly, passionate love is seen as the cornerstone of long-term relationships within Western cultures today. This cultural notion of love allows us to interpret (or, in some cases, misinterpret) physiological arousal as love.

Companionate love. Although love in its passionate form probably comes closest to societal ideals about love, in reality companionate love is the more frequent and steadfast type. Most people don't experience the ups and downs of passionate love in their feelings for parents, siblings, other relatives, and best friends. Instead, companionate love is relatively stable and invariant (Brehm, 1988).

Perhaps because it is less electrifying than passionate love, companionate love has received somewhat less attention from social psychologists. Yet, companionate love lies at the heart of people's most treasured relationships. The partners in such relationships care deeply for each another, and their own happiness depends in part on the happiness of their partners.

Companionate love, then, is decidedly a communal, rather than an exchange, relationship (Hecht, Marston, & Larkey, 1994).

The partners in a companionate relationship hold a high degree of trust in each other. Such trust is actually of two types: reliability and emotional trust (Johnson-George & Swap, 1982). Reliability is the expectation that partners will do what they have said they will do. Emotional trust exists when people feel that their partner is tied to them emotionally and that the emotional outcomes for both partners are linked (Hatfield, 1988).

In some circumstances, companionate love can develop into passionate love, as when a long-standing friendship turns into passionate love. Likewise, passionate love can shift to companionate love, as when a love relationship breaks up and the two parties remain confidants. (Think of the characters of Jerry and Elaine on the television show *Seinfeld.*) The shift from passionate love to companionate love is eased if the people held companionate love for one another before entering the passionate love relationship (Metts, Cupach, & Bejlovec, 1989).

The newest medium through which relationships develop is through the Internet. As we consider in the Social Web box, love in cyberspace has its own set of rules.

STERNBERG'S LOVE TRIANGLE: THE EIGHT FACES OF LOVE

For psychologist Robert Sternberg, two-sided love is not enough. Sternberg argues that the traditional apportionment of love into companionate and passionate love misses the mark. Instead, he suggests that love is actually composed of three components: intimacy, passion, and decision/commitment (Sternberg, 1988, 1997). The *intimacy component* encompasses feelings of closeness, affection, and connectedness. The *passion component* is made up of the motivational drives relating to sex, physical closeness, and romance. This factor is exemplified by intense, physiologically arousing feelings of attraction. Finally, the third aspect of love, the *decision/commitment component,* embodies both the initial cognition that one loves another person and the longer-term determination to maintain that love (see Figure 7–4).

Overall, according to Sternberg, eight types of love can be formed from different combinations of these components. One kind of love is *nonlove,* which includes relationships with

FIGURE 7–4   The Kinds of Love Sternberg argues that love is composed of three components: intimacy, passion, and decision/commitment. Various types of love can be formed by different combinations of these components. Nonlove contains none of the components.

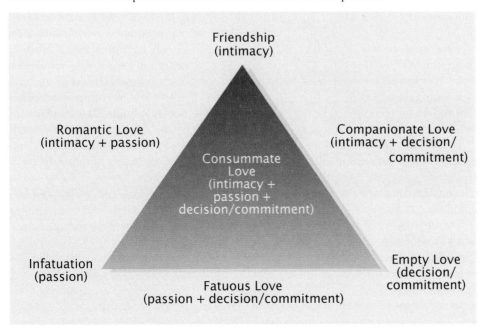

According to Sternberg, infatuation—such as what one might feel for a very attractive star—is a kind of love in which attraction exists without intimacy or commitment.

people with whom we have only casual interactions during the course of our lives. *Friend-ships* form the second type of love, in which only the intimacy component of love is present. This type of love is actually closer to liking than to love.

A third kind of love is *infatuation,* in which passion exists without intimacy or decision/commitment. "Love at first sight" falls into this category. The fourth type of love, called *empty love,* has only the decision/commitment component and lacks intimacy and passion. Long-term relationships that have grown stagnant and lack zest are representative of empty love.

Romantic love contains both intimacy and passion, but it is lacking in decision/commitment. Couples who are romantically in love are drawn together physically and emotionally, but they do not necessarily see their relationship as continuing over the long term.

Companionate love, according to Sternberg, is the result of intimacy and decision/commitment without passion. Companionate love can be seen in long-lasting marriages in which physical passion has ceased, but the bonds between the partners remain strong, or in long-lasting close friendships. In contrast, *fatuous,* or mindless, love has components of passion and decision/commitment but lacks intimacy. Relationships built on fatuous love may not be lasting because no emotional bond between the partners is present.

Finally, the eighth kind of love is *consummate love.* In consummate love, all three components of love are present. Although we may be tempted to consider consummate love as representing the ideal love, such a view is not necessarily accurate. Many gratifying, lasting relationships are maintained with one or even two components only minimally present or not present at all.

The importance of each of the three components tends to vary over the course of a relationship, with each component following a specific trajectory (see Figure 7–5). For instance, in strong, loving relationships the level of commitment peaks and then remains stable. Passion, on the other hand, peaks quickly, and then declines and levels off comparatively early in a relationship.

In Sternberg's view, then, love is a dynamic, changing process rather than a static, invariant state. Over time, the various components may change in intensity and in their relationships to one another. As circumstances and people change, so do the underlying ingredients of love. (For another approach to love, see the Speaking of Social Psychology interview.)

THE RAINBOW OF LOVE

If Sternberg's three-component, eight-type classification of love strikes you as too paltry to delineate the full range of love, you may be attracted to—and perhaps even love—psychologist John Lee's (1977) multifaceted view of love. According to Lee, love should be thought of as the colors on a painter's palette. Three basic kinds of love are analogous to the primary colors; these are used to form secondary types of love, just as combinations of colors can be formed from the primary colors. Beyond these primary and secondary types of love, still other kinds of love exist—just as more and more combinations of colors can be derived from mixtures of only a few basic colors.

What are the primary types of love? Lee suggests three main kinds, based on Greek terminology: eros, ludos, and storge. *Eros* is intense, emotional, and passionate love. In contrast, *ludos* is playful love, in which the partners view the relationship as a kind of game-playing situation. Finally, *storge* is love in which friendship and companionship prevail (Lee, 1974, 1977).

Similarly, Lee identifies three secondary categories of love (with similarly peculiar names): mania, agape, and pragma. In *mania,* love is possessive and demanding, and jealousy is common. *Agape* is selfless love, in which partners put their lover's welfare over their own. Finally, in *pragma,* practical concerns underlie love. Lovers seek out partners who meet the "right" criteria according to age, religion, and other pragmatic concerns (Rotenberg & Korol, 1995; Yancey & Eastman, 1995; Hahn & Blass, 1997).

Other types of love can be derived from these six. With so many possible varieties of love, relationships can easily become complex, because the two partners may have differing goals and aspirations for the relationship. Further, the intensity of love, the commitment of the partners, and their expectancies about the relationship may vary drastically, further complicating loving partnerships (Borrello & Thompson, 1990; Cho & Cross, 1995; Morrow, Clark, & Brock, 1995).

PROTOTYPES: UNDERSTANDING THE CONCEPT OF LOVE

Quick: When you hear the word *love,* what examples come to mind?

Your responses to this question provide important insights into the way you understand the concept of love, according to one relatively new approach to the study of love. In the view of several contemporary researchers, one of the most fruitful ways of understanding love is

FIGURE 7–5   The Changing Ingredients of Love The three components of love vary in strength over the course of a relationship. (*Source:* Sternberg, 1986.)

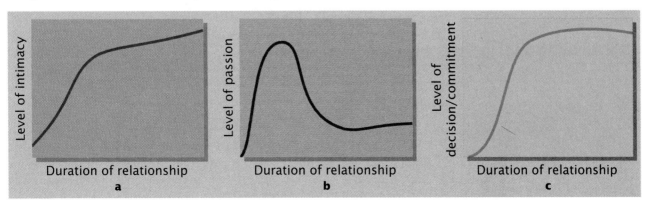

SPEAKING OF SOCIAL PSYCHOLOGY

Scott Thompson

Social Psychologist

Year of Birth:	1953
Education:	B.A., Psychology, University of North Carolina at Asheville; Ph.D., University of Maine at Orono
Home:	Shirley, Massachusetts

"We tend to see the object of our attention and love in an extreme way. Their positive qualities get exaggerated, while their negative attributes get ignored."

Love at first sight. It is a phrase regularly used to describe our feelings when we are overwhelmed by an attraction to another person. But can infatuation be studied scientifically?

According to Scott Thompson, one of a handful of researchers who are studying infatuation in the laboratory, the answer is yes.

by considering how people naturally describe, think about, and categorize the concept of love (Russell, 1992; Taraban & Hendrick, 1995; deMunck, 1998; Regan, Kocan, & Whitlock, 1998).

Thus, rather than identifying two, eight, or more kinds of love, or the characteristics that differentiate love from other forms of interpersonal attraction, some researchers are seeking to identify how people commonly conceptualize and define love. This approach grows out of the work on prototypes and social cognition that we first discussed in Chapter 2 (Fitness & Fletcher, 1993; Fehr, 1994).

For example, psychologists Beverley Fehr and James Russell sought to understand love from the perspective of prototypes, asking participants which of 20 types of love were the most representative of the general concept of love. The results, shown in Table 7–3, formed a pattern that was in some ways surprising. In contrast to approaches to love that emphasize its passionate aspects, participants considered that the best examples of love were *not* romantic in nature. Instead, the most typical concepts of love related to familial love and friends, with maternal love, parental love, and friendship topping the list (Fehr & Russell, 1991; Fehr, 1994).

In fact, the idea of love seemed to be formed from several major prototypes. These include love of a parent for a child, love between romantic partners, love between old friends, and love between siblings. The layperson's conception of love, then, is a broad one, encompassing a variety of types of love on which more traditional approaches do not focus.

More recent work suggests that people in ongoing romantic relationships believe that their love, commitment, and satisfaction increase over time, feeling that each passing year brings them to greater heights of love for their partner. There's just one hitch to these perceptions: They don't match the absolute ratings the same people make when they are asked to give specific ratings to their feelings. For people with intact relationships, the absolute level of emotion changes relatively little, at least according to the results of a three-year study of dating couples at one university (Sprecher, 1999).

"In the past decade, theorists have argued that infatuation is characterized by a process referred to as idealization," Thompson explains. "We tend to see the object of our attention and love in an extreme way. Their positive qualities get exaggerated, while their negative attributes get ignored."

"Almost everyone involved in examining infatuation agrees that it is doomed to end."

Thompson noted that biases in the way we look at objects of our infatuation are so strong that we can see their beautiful eyes, while overlooking the wart on their nose.

When one is infatuated, does the rest of the world look equally wonderful? Not necessarily, according to Thompson's research.

"Infatuation is related to intense physiological arousal, and we know that arousal narrows attention. Consequently, only the person you're in love with is the object of the attention," Thompson explains. "In our studies, infatuated people judge strangers in the same way as if they were in a noninfatuated state."

Although noninfatuated love can be nurtured and grows, infatuation is more fleeting, according to Thompson.

"Almost everyone involved in examining infatuation agrees that it is doomed to end. It can arise almost instantaneously and can disintegrate just as quickly," he said. "The relationship either ends, or it evolves into another type of relationship."

TABLE 7–3	Prototypicality Ratings for 20 Types of Love
TYPE OF LOVE	**PROTOTYPICALITY**
Maternal love	5.39
Parental love	5.22
Friendship	4.96
Sisterly love	4.84
Romantic love	4.76
Brotherly love	4.74
Familial love	4.74
Sibling love	4.73
Affection	4.60
Committed love	4.47
Love for humanity	4.42
Spiritual love	4.27
Passionate love	4.00
Platonic love	3.98
Self-love	3.79
Sexual love	3.76
Patriotic love	3.21
Love of work	3.14
Puppy love	2.98
Infatuation	2.42

Prototypicality ratings were based on a scale ranging from 1 (extremely poor example of love) to 6 (extremely good example of love.) Source: Adapted from Fehr & Russell, 1991.

The advantage of such descriptive analyses of the way in which people understand love is that they permit us to conceptualize how love regulates people's understanding of events. For example, the way judges comprehend the concept of love may guide their decisions about whether a father or mother should have custody of children in divorce proceedings. Similarly, a mother's concerns about whether she provides sufficient love for her child, and questions about whether one is really in love, can be addressed, in part, by considering the prototype of love. Thus, prototypic analysis of love provides an alternative to approaches that categorize love into various types.

REVIEW AND RETHINK

Review

- Love can be divided into two broad types: passionate (or romantic) and companionate.
- Sternberg's categorizations of love suggests that it has three basic components: intimacy, passion, and decision/commitment.
- The prototype approach to love considers love in terms of ordinary people's cognitions about the concept.

Rethink

- Is love qualitatively different from liking or merely quantitatively different? How would Rubin answer this question? How would Sternberg answer?
- Given that cultures differ in their views of what love is or ought to be, is it possible that individuals within a culture may differ with respect to their views of love? Is there any evidence that males and females hold differing concepts of love? Explain.
- Discuss how each of the following approaches to understanding love would address cultural differences in views of love: Rubin's loving versus liking, Hatfield and Berscheid's labeling theory, Sternberg's triangle theory, and Fehr and Russell's prototype theory.
- Even psychologists who study love admit that it is not an easy phenomenon to understand. Why do you think love is such a difficult subject to study? Is it an appropriate topic for scientific investigation? Explain.

VARIETIES OF RELATIONSHIPS

On Monday, Corporal Floyd Johnson, 23, and Mary Ellen Skinner, 19, total strangers, boarded a train at San Francisco and sat down across the aisle from each other. Johnson didn't cross the aisle until Wednesday, but Skinner later said, "I'd already made up my mind to say yes if he asked me to marry him." Thursday the couple got off the train in Omaha with plans to be married. Because they would need the consent of the bride's parents if they were married in Nebraska, they crossed the river to Council Bluffs, Iowa, where they were married Friday. (San Francisco Chronicle, cited by Burgess & Wallin, 1953, p. 151)

Talk about whirlwind courtships: from stranger to spouse over the course of 5 days.

For most of us, the transition across different types of relationships takes considerably longer and presumably involves more deliberation and analysis than in this example. But, in fact, how do people come to view particular relationships as exclusive and as so important that they feel compelled to celebrate them in public ceremonies?

In contrast to social psychologists who study the development and typologies of love (a state that cuts across different types of relationships), some researchers have chosen to focus on specific, important types of relationships (Buss et al., 1990; Smadi, 1991; Johnson et al., 1992). We'll consider several varieties, including marriage and cohabitation.

SELECTING A SPOUSE: SIFTING THROUGH THE POSSIBILITIES

How does a person choose a spouse from among the many potential candidates? One answer comes from a filtering model developed by Louis H. Janda and Karen E. Klenke-Hamel (1980). They suggest that people seeking a mate screen potential candidates through successively finer-grained filters, just as we sift flour to remove objectionable material.

As you can see from the model displayed in Figure 7–6, an individual first filters for factors relating to the broad determinants of interpersonal attraction, such as proximity and similarity. Once a potential partner has passed these early screens, more refined criteria are employed, such as those related to the level of physical attractiveness. The final filters relate to compatibility of expectations and a concept of the roles a potential partner will play in a relationship. Obviously, as each successive screen is applied, fewer and fewer people make it through.

The filtering process takes place in the context of several roadblocks created by society that constrain the choice of a potential spouse. One is the principle of homogamy. **Homogamy** is the tendency to marry someone who is similar in age, race, education, religion, and other basic demographic characteristics. Homogamy is a primary standard in most marriages in the United States (Kalmijn, 1991; Surra, 1991; Qian & Preston, 1993; Blackwell, 1998; Kalmijn, 1998).

The marriage gradient is another societal standard that determines who marries whom. The **marriage gradient** is the tendency for men to marry women who are slightly younger,

homogamy: The tendency to marry someone who is similar in age, race, education, religion, and other basic demographic characteristics.

marriage gradient: The tendency for men to marry women who are slightly younger, smaller, and lower in status, and women to marry men who are slightly older, larger, and higher in status.

FIGURE 7–6   The Filtering Model of Partner Selection According to this model, potential marriage candidates are screened through a series of successively finer-grained filters. (*Source:* Janda & Klenke-Hamel, 1980.)

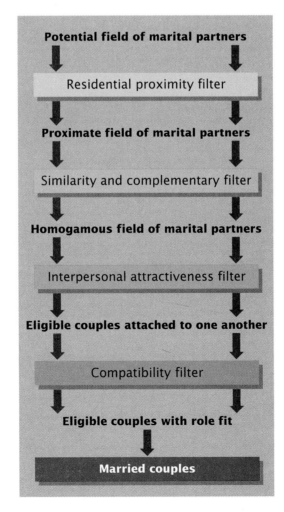

smaller, and lower in status, and women to marry men who are slightly older, larger, and higher in status (Bernard, 1982).

The marriage gradient, which is a powerful standard applied to marriage in the United States, has important, and sometimes hidden, effects on partner choice. First, it limits the number of potential mates for women, especially as they get older. At the same time, it allows men a wider choice.

In addition, the marriage gradient prevents some men from marrying, either because they can't find women of low-enough status to meet the demands of the gradient, or because they can't find women of the same or higher status who are willing to accept them as mates. Such men are, in the words of sociologist Jessie Bernard (1982), "bottom of the barrel" men. In contrast, some women do not marry because they are higher in status than anyone in the available pool of men—"cream of the crop" women, in Bernard's words.

The marriage gradient makes finding a spouse particularly difficult for well-educated African American women. Fewer African American men attend college than African American women, making the potential pool of men who are suitable—as defined by society's marriage gradient—relatively small. Consequently, compared with women of other races, African American women are more apt to marry men who are less educated than they are (Taylor et al., 1991; Tucker & Mitchell-Kernan, 1995).

You may be complaining to yourself at this point that social psychology paints a decidedly unromantic view of the choice of a marriage partner. Doesn't love play a role? As we discuss next, the answer is yes—at least in Western societies. In other cultures, love plays a much more modest role.

EXPLORING DIVERSITY

Is Love a Necessary Ingredient of Marriage?

The characteristics one finds most desirable in a mate vary considerably between men and women and among cultures.

Yuri Uemura sat on the straw tatami mat of her living room and chatted cheerfully about her 40-year-old marriage to a man whom, she mused, she never particularly liked.

"There was never any love between me and my husband," she said blithely, recalling how he used to beat her. "But, well, we survived." (Kristof, 1996, p. A1)

Is love a necessary ingredient of marriage?

To most people in the United States, the answer is yes. National surveys invariably place love at the top of any list of reasons why people choose a particular spouse.

But if you live in a host of other cultures, love, it turns out, is not quite so important. For instance, consider the results of a cross-cultural survey in which college students were asked if they would marry someone they did not love. As you can see in Figure 7–7, if you lived in the United States, you'd be unlikely to agree to such a marriage. Residents of Pakistan and India, however, might consider it (Levine, 1993).

Similar results emerged from research conducted by psychologist David Buss, who conducted a survey of close to 10,000 people from around the world. The survey found that the characteristics sought in a mate differed considerably from country to country (see Table 7–4). Whereas people in the United States said that love and mutual attraction were the primary characteristics, in China men ranked good health as most important, and women rated emotional stability and maturity highest. In contrast, men in Zulu South Africa ranked emotional stability first, and women considered dependable character to be of highest concern (Buss et al., 1990).

Despite such cross-cultural variations in desired qualities, commonalities did occur. For example, love and mutual attraction, although not at the top of the list in many cultures, were valued by almost all people. Also highly valued were such traits as dependability, emotional stability, kindness, understanding, and intelligence.

Commonalities were also seen across cultures in the differences that existed between what men and women sought in a potential spouse. For example, men, more than women, preferred mates who were physically attractive. Women, more than men, preferred marriage partners who showed ambition and industriousness and other indications of earning potential. Furthermore, these gender differences held true not only across cultures, but within subcultural groups in the United States (Sprecher, Sullivan, & Hatfield, 1994; Singh, 1995).

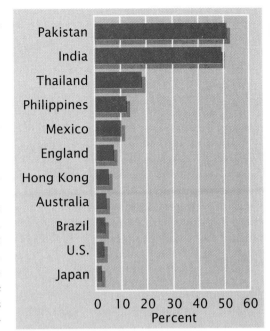

FIGURE 7–7   Choosing a Partner
Do love and marriage go together like a horse and carriage? Not everywhere, as this graph indicates. It shows the percent of students in various countries who say they would marry someone they did not love. (*Source:* Adapted from Levine, 1993.)

TABLE 7–4	Most Desired Characteristics in a Spouse					
	CHINA		**SOUTH AFRICAN (ZULU)**		**UNITED STATES**	
	Males	Females	Males	Females	Males	Females
Mutual attraction—love	4	8	10	5	1	1
Emotional stability and maturity	5	1	1	2	2	2
Dependable character	6	7	3	1	3	3
Pleasing disposition	13	16	4	3	4	4
Education and intelligence	8	4	6	6	5	5
Good health	1	3	5	4	6	9
Sociability	12	9	11	8	8	8
Desire for home and children	2	2	9	9	9	7
Refinement, neatness	7	10	7	10	10	12
Ambition and industriousness	10	5	8	7	11	6
Good looks	11	15	14	16	7	13
Similar education	15	12	12	12	12	10
Good financial prospects	16	14	18	13	16	11
Good cook and housekeeper	9	11	2	15	13	16
Favorable social status or rating	14	13	17	14	14	14
Similar religious background	18	18	16	11	15	15
Chastity (no prior sexual intercourse)	3	6	13	18	17	18
Similar political background	17	17	15	17	18	17

Source: Buss et al., 1990.

Buss interprets these results in evolutionary terms. He argues that the similarities across different cultures suggest that human beings, as a species, seek out specific characteristics that will strengthen the overall quality of the gene pool. Males, in particular, are genetically programmed to seek mates that have traits potentially indicative of high reproductive capacity. Thus, they view physically attractive, younger women as having higher reproductive potential, because they are seen as more capable of having children.

In contrast, females are more apt to value characteristics that signal the potential to acquire scarce resources to help ensure the survival of their offspring. Thus, they seek out partners who are most likely to demonstrate high economic capabilities and potential (Kenrick & Keefe, 1992; Hayes, 1995; Fletcher et al., 1999).

Although Buss's evolutionary hypothesis is intriguing, it is equally plausible that the cultural similarities found in men's and women's preferences merely reflect commonalities in social learning across cultures and have nothing to do with evolution. Furthermore, the differences in valued characteristics between cultures—such as the emphasis U.S. males place on good looks—clearly suggest that individual cultures socialize specific values.

THE MARRIED LIFE: STAYING THE COURSE

After they are married, couples enter into what both they and society expect to be a lifelong enterprise. Yet most marriages usually follow not a straight, unvarying path, but a twisting, sometimes bumpy route.

For example, one of the first transitions that often occurs is that romanticized, idealized images of one's partner are replaced with more realistic views. Prior to marriage, people focus on the positive, seeing primarily their partner's good qualities and minimizing or ignoring any negative ones. The relationship is seen in such positive terms that it encourages *sentiment override,* in which negative aspects are ignored or disregarded (Murray, Holmes, & Griffin, 1996; Murray & Holmes, 1997; Peven & Shulman, 1999).

However, sentiment override declines after marriage. One factor responsible for this change is the fact that, whereas during courtship people try to make positive impressions, as time goes by they are more likely to permit their true nature to emerge. Such changes in behavior may produce eye-opening transformations. This is probably a major reason why, 2 years after being married, couples are usually less satisfied (and less affectionate) than they were as newlyweds (MacDermid, Huston, & McHale, 1990; Peven & Shulman, 1999).

Furthermore, research by social psychologists Ted Huston and Anita Vangelisti suggests that expressions of negativity are related to declines in marital satisfaction (Huston & Vangelisti, 1991; Carstensen, Gottman, & Levenson, 1995). According to this research, husbands and wives differ significantly in their reactions to expressions of negativity. Whether communicated by the husband or the wife, negativity was related to declines in wives' marital satisfaction, but not to declines in husbands' satisfaction. The explanation for the difference may be that husbands tend to react to expressions of negativity by psychologically "turning off" and withdrawing from the relationship. Wives, in contrast, react to negativity by remaining psychologically engaged and involved in the relationship; but they find their experience within the marriage to be less satisfying.

Over time, marital satisfaction for many couples falls and rises in a U-shaped configuration. As you can see in Figure 7–8, marital satisfaction begins to decline after the wedding, and it continues to fall until it reaches its lowest ebb following the births of the couple's children. Satisfaction doesn't begin to increase until the youngest child leaves home (Figley,

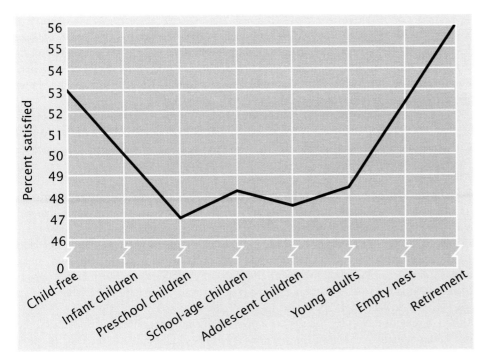

FIGURE 7–8   The Course of Marital Satisfaction over Family Life Cycle Stages
Marital satisfaction for many couples falls and rises in a U-shaped pattern over the life of the marriage, ending with a degree of satisfaction almost equal to that when the couple first married. (*Source:* Adapted from Rollins & Cannon, 1974.)

1973; Noller, Feeney, & Ward, 1997). Eventually, though, satisfaction reaches the same level that it held at the start of the marriage.

Does this finding mean that children lie at the heart of marital dissatisfaction? Probably not, because most couples state that they want children, enjoy their children, and are glad that they had children (Luckey & Bain, 1970). The finding does suggest, however, that no matter how welcome children are, they are a source of stress for husbands and wives. Moreover, this increased stress is likely to diminish marital satisfaction (Steinberg & Silverberg, 1987; Glenn, 1990, 1991; Lavee, Sharlin, & Katz, 1996).

Changes in marital satisfaction do not occur in the same way for all couples. The overall decline in marital satisfaction during child-rearing years tends to be moderate for most couples. In fact, some couples report increased satisfaction during these years. This is particularly true of couples who hold realistic expectations regarding the extent of the child-rearing and household responsibilities they will face upon the arrival of children (Cowan & Cowan, 1988; Belsky, Rovine, & Fish, 1989; Hackel & Ruble, 1992).

COHABITATION: THE ABCS OF POSSLQS

Although surveys show that most heterosexuals prefer marriage to being single, a significant number of couples choose to live in unwedded bliss, in a state known as **cohabitation**. The U.S. Bureau of the Census calls them **POSSLQs**—"persons of the opposite sex sharing living quarters."

cohabitation: The state in which an unmarried couple choose to live together.

POSSLQs: Persons of the opposite sex sharing living quarters—the term given by the U.S. Department of the Census to couples who cohabitate.

The number of people cohabiting has increased dramatically since 1960 (U.S. Bureau of the Census, 1998; see Figure 7–9). Most people who cohabitate are young; almost 40% are under the age of 25. Surveys show that 25% of undergraduate college students have cohabited, and an additional 50% say that under certain circumstances they would do so. There are also subcultural differences, with African Americans more likely to cohabitate than whites (Bianchi & Spain, 1986; Spanier, 1983).

Couples offer several reasons for cohabiting. Some couples are practicing for marriage. Others are not ready to make a lifelong commitment, and they see cohabitation as a prelude to a possibly longer relationship. This view is reflected in the later age at which people are marrying: The average time of first marriage is 25 years for women and 26.8 years for men (Phillips, 1999).

In some cases, people view marriage negatively, believing that they will be happier staying unmarried than married. Such a belief may be grounded in reality: Although married people still report a level of happiness higher than unmarried people, married individuals are less happy than they once were. This change is especially true for women, whose increased economic opportunities permit greater independence from their spouses and may make them more willing to admit discontent with unsatisfactory relationships. Furthermore, never-married individuals, particularly men, report being relatively more happy than they were in the past (Glenn & Weaver, 1988; Nock, 1995).

Although the number of POSSLQs has grown significantly over the last few decades, the United States actually has a lower proportion—just 4% of all couples—than many other countries. For instance, in Sweden, about 25% of all couples cohabitate, and cohabitation is almost as respected a social institution as marriage (Popenoe, 1987).

Marriage remains a more popular choice than cohabitation in U.S. society for several reasons. For one thing, most people still view marriage as the culmination of a loving relationship, the end point in a series of steps that lead to fuller closeness and intimacy (MacLean & Peters, 1995). Furthermore, for some people, marriage formalizes the several roles that spouses can fulfill (Nass, 1978). For example, spouses play a therapeutic role, in which they provide advice or act as sounding boards for each other. In their recreational role, spouses share

Some research suggests that marital satisfaction reaches its lowest point following the birth of a couple's children and doesn't begin to increase until the last child has left home.

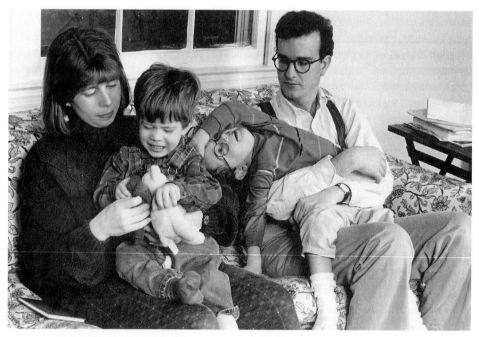

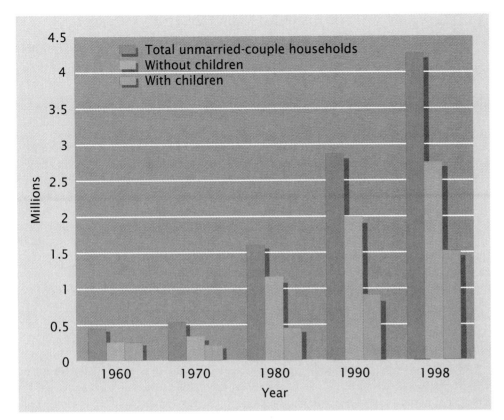

FIGURE 7–9 Cohabitation in the United States Since the 1960s there has been a dramatic rise in the number of individuals classified as "POSSLQs" by the U.S. Census Bureau.

pastimes and engage in leisure activities, and in their economic role, they may provide economic security and contribute to the couple's financial well-being.

Husbands and wives also play a sexual role. For those who view marriage as the only morally acceptable avenue for sexual activities, a spouse provides the only means of obtaining sexual fulfillment. And even for people who approve of premarital sex, marriage can still provide a frequency of sexual activity that may be less likely in nonmarital situations.

Finally, marriage partners play a child-rearing role. Even today, when attitudes toward childbearing out of wedlock are substantially more relaxed than in previous periods, marriage still provides the most socially acceptable environment for having and raising children.

In sum, marriage has several important attributes that for some make it preferable to cohabitation. Still, for many people, cohabitation offers distinct advantages.

STAYING SINGLE: I WANT TO BE ALONE

For some people, neither marriage nor cohabitation is the preferred option. To them, living alone represents a good path, consciously chosen, through life.

People who choose not to marry or live with a partner give several reasons for their decision. One is that they view marriage negatively. Rather than seeing marriage in the idealized terms presented in the media of the 1950s (the families in *Leave It to Beaver* or *Ozzie and Harriet,* for instance), they focus more on high divorce rates and marital strife. Ultimately, they conclude that the risks of forming a lifetime union may be too high.

Others view marriage as too restrictive. These individuals place great value on personal change and growth, which would be impeded by the stable, long-term commitment implied by marriage. Finally, some people simply do not encounter anyone with whom they wish to spend the remainder of their lives. Instead, they value their independence, autonomy, and freedom (Urbanska, 1992; Bird & Melville, 1994).

A BLEAKER SIDE OF RELATIONSHIPS: FAMILY VIOLENCE AND RAPE

She was a competent, articulate professional. A lawyer, she was known for the brilliant, vigorous arguments she made on behalf of her clients. Yet a few things were amiss: she wore long-sleeved, high-collared clothing in even the hottest weather. She also claimed to be unusually accident-prone, reporting that she sometimes tripped and bumped into doors and walls, bruising or scraping her face. Her apparent clumsiness became something of an office joke.

The truth, however, was no laughing matter. The lawyer was a victim of spousal abuse. She was terrorized by her husband, who, when drunk, lashed out at her brutally. She rationalized his behavior, saying that she loved him, and he was perfectly well behaved most of the time. She blamed his aggression on his drinking and on her inability to meet his exacting standards. If only she could be a better wife, he wouldn't hit her so often.

One of the ugliest truths about family life is the prevalence of domestic violence. As many as two-thirds of high school and college students report that they have been the victims of some form of violence (Gelles & Cornell, 1990). The particular form of violence they have experienced runs the gamut from childhood sexual abuse to parental beatings to rape. No one is safe from abuse within the family—men and women, young and old, wives and husbands, children and parents.

Spousal abuse.   Violence occurs in about 25% of all marriages, and between 20% and 30% of women who require emergency surgical interventions need it because of violence sustained at home. Severe, continuing violence occurs in about 15% of all marriages in the United States. Furthermore, although in most cases of abuse a husband batters a wife, in around 8% of the cases wives physically abuse their husbands (Straus & Gelles, 1990; Browne & Williams, 1993; Cook, 1997; Van Hightower & Gorton, 1998).

Spousal abuse occurs throughout all segments of society, across all social classes, races, ethnic groups, and religions. Certain factors, however, increase the likelihood of abuse. Lower socioeconomic status, a high level of verbal aggression, large family size, economic worries, and having grown up in a violent family are all associated with an increased risk of spousal violence (Straus & Gelles, 1990).

The cycle of violence.   Does violence breed violence? Quite often, the answer is yes. Spouse abusers have often themselves suffered from abuse as children, leading to the notion that a cycle of violence exists. The *cycle of violence hypothesis* suggests that children who suffer abuse and neglect are predisposed as adults to abuse and neglect members of their family (Dodge, Bates, & Pettit, 1990; Harway & Evans, 1996; Holden, Geffner, & Jouriles, 1998).

Spousal abuse directed toward wives usually occurs in three stages (Walker, 1984, 1989). The first stage is *tension building,* in which a batterer becomes angered for some reason and initially is verbally abusive. He may also show his anger through pushing or shoving. Although a wife may attempt to calm her spouse or to withdraw, this behavior often results merely in enraging the husband.

Subsequently, the violence escalates into the next stage, the *acute battering incident.* Lasting from a few minutes to several hours, it may take the form of shoving a wife against a wall or a hot stove, pinching, choking, slapping, or punching. Wives may be thrown down stairs or burned with cigarettes. In about 25% of the cases, the incident includes forced sexual activities.

Finally, the incident sometimes (but not always) may move into the *loving contrition* stage, in which the abuser expresses his remorse over his behavior. He begs for forgiveness and apologizes for his actions. He may even tend to the wounds that he has inflicted on his wife, promising that he will never be abusive again.

The loving contrition stage explains why some wives remain in relationships with abusive husbands. Desperately wishing to believe their husbands, or seeing no good alternatives, they stick with the husband. Other wives remain with their husbands due to fear, because the husband promises to hunt them down and punish them if they dare to leave. Finally, some wives remain in such relationships because, as children, they were abused by a parent. In such cases, abuse is a seemingly normal part of family life.

As the cycle of violence hypothesis would suggest, husbands and wives who abuse their spouses often have been raised in homes in which physical abuse occurred. However, being abused as a child does not inevitably lead adults to abuse their family members (Holden et al., 1998). In fact, statistics show that only about one-third of those people who were abused or neglected as children abuse their spouse or their own children; the remaining two-thirds of people abused as children do not become abusers. Clearly, then, additional factors, beyond a history of abuse, account for spouses' violence to their mates (Kaufman & Zigler, 1987).

Rape.   If you assume that rape is a rare crime or is most often committed by strangers, think again. **Rape**, which occurs when one person forces another to submit to sexual activity, happens fairly often, and statistically it is more likely to be committed by acquaintances than by strangers.

Often, those acquaintances are involved in the early stages of a relationship with their victim. For example, in one national survey conducted at 35 universities, one out of eight women reported having been raped. Of that group, about half said the rapists were first dates, casual dates, or romantic acquaintances—something that has come to be known as *date rape* (Sweet, 1985; Koss et al., 1988). Overall, a woman has a 26% chance of being raped sometime during her lifetime (Russell & Howell, 1983).

Furthermore, a survey of close to 3,000 college men found that more than 4% admitted to behaviors that fit the legal criteria of rape, 3.3% said they had attempted rape, 7.7% said they had sexually coerced a women, and more than 10% said they had forced or coerced sexual contact. Overall, some 25% of college men acknowledged that they had engaged in some form of sexual aggression (Koss et al., 1988).

Women in certain segments of society appear to be more at risk for rape than others. For instance, in one survey, 25% of the African American women reported being the victim of sexual assault at least once, compared to 20% of white women (Wyatt, 1992). Other ethnic groups also experience sexual assault at differing incidence levels, probably in part because of differences in cultural views of women and different definitions of what constitutes permissible sexual conduct (Sorenson & Siegel, 1992).

What are the underlying causes of rape? Surprisingly, rape is often motivated not by sexual needs, but by the need to demonstrate power and control over a victim. In other cases, the primary motivation is anger, often directed at women in general (Lisak & Roth, 1988; Gelman, 1990).

Rape is also motivated by the myth that it is both appropriate and desirable for men to seek out sex, and that sexual aggression is acceptable behavior. In this view, sex is a battle, with winners and losers, and violence and intimidation are one way to attain sex (Mosher & Anderson, 1986; Hamilton & Yee, 1990; Drieschner & Lange, 1999).

The view that sexual coercion is acceptable is completely groundless, although it is surprisingly widespread. For instance, in one study, high school students were given a list of circumstances and asked whether it was acceptable, under those conditions, for a man to hold a woman down and force sexual intercourse. Just 44% of the females and 24% of the males considered that no situation warranted forced sex; the remainder felt that under some conditions rape was acceptable (Mahoney, 1983; White & Humphrey, 1991).

Misattributions can also explain some instances of rape, particularly in dating situations. For instance, the erroneous and harmful societal belief that a woman who says no to sex really doesn't mean it may result in misinterpretations that ultimately lead to rape (Muehlenhard & Hollabaugh, 1988; Drieschner & Lange, 1999).

For example, consider these two perspectives on a case of date rape reflecting very different explanations for the events:

> **Bob:** Patty and I were in the same statistics class together. She usually sat near me and was always very friendly. I liked her and thought maybe she liked me, too. Last Thursday I decided to find out. After class I suggested that she come to my place to study for midterms

rape: The act of one person forcing another to submit to sexual activity.

One survey of college men found that 4% admitted to behaviors that fit the legal criteria of rape. Avoiding drinking to excess and assertiveness training can help reduce the likelihood of date rape.

together. She agreed immediately, which was a good sign. That night everything seemed to go perfectly. We studied for a while and then took a break. I could tell that she liked me, and I was attracted to her. I was getting excited. I started kissing her. I could tell that she really liked it. We started touching each other and it felt really good. All of a sudden she pulled away and said "Stop." I figured she didn't want me to think that she was "easy" or "loose." A lot of girls think they have to say "no" at first. I knew once I showed her what a good time she could have, and that I would respect her in the morning, it would be OK. I just ignored her protests and eventually she stopped struggling. I think she liked it but afterwards she acted bummed out and cold. Who knows what her problem was?

Patty: I knew Bob from my statistics class. He's cute and we are both good at statistics, so when a tough midterm was scheduled, I was glad that he suggested we study together. It never occurred to me that it was anything except a study date. That night everything went fine at first, we got a lot of studying done in a short amount of time, so when he suggested we take a break I thought we deserved it. Well, all of a sudden he started acting really romantic and started kissing me. I liked the kissing but then he started touching me below the waist. I pulled away and tried to stop him but he didn't listen. After a while I stopped struggling; he was hurting me and I was scared. He was so much bigger and stronger than me. I couldn't believe it was happening to me. I didn't know what to do. He actually forced me to have sex with him. I guess looking back on it I should have screamed or done something besides trying to reason with him but it was so unexpected. I couldn't believe it was happening. I still can't believe it did. (Hughes & Sandler, 1987, p. 1)

Clearly, the two explanations reflect significant misinterpretations of the meaning behind the other person's behavior—with disastrous consequences. However, as we discuss next, there are several ways of reducing the risk of date rape.

Reducing the risk of date rape.   Several guidelines, developed by university counseling centers, health services, and women's and men's groups, suggest ways in which men and women can form more accurate impressions and make more appropriate attributions about their dates' behavior (Hughes & Sandler, 1987; Warshaw, 1988; American College Health Association, 1989; Goleman, 1989; Unger & Crawford, 1992). They include the following:

- Set clear sexual limits. You should clearly articulate what your sexual limits are, and you should do so early on.
- Don't give mixed messages. Don't say no when you don't mean no. Say yes if you mean yes.
- Be assertive if someone is pressuring you. Don't worry about politeness. Remember that passivity may be taken for a sign of assent to further sexual activity.
- Be aware of risky situations. Remember that others may make unwarranted interpretations regarding your form of dress or behavior. Never assume that everyone holds the same sexual standards that you do.
- Remember that alcohol and drugs are often associated with date rape.
- Trust your feelings. If a situation seems dangerous or risky, or if you feel that you are being pressured, leave the situation or confront your date.

ENDING RELATIONSHIPS

"Al, I don't love you any more. I want a divorce."

I couldn't believe my ears. A divorce! . . . My mind was spinning. Everything was a jumble, fragmentary images of what we were and what Jean was saying. This couldn't be. This couldn't be the same Jean, the Jean I had known and loved all those years. I couldn't find words to answer immediately. My mind and my voice were in two different places. Finally, I half cried and half choked, "You can't mean that. Why? What for? What about us? What about the kids?" (Martin, 1975, pp. 5–7)

In fairy tales, after the beautiful maiden is swept off her feet by the handsome prince, they go off into the sunset and live happily ever after. However, if fairy tales were given a contemporary twist, the couple might ultimately separate and divorce, going their separate ways.

THE ROOTS OF DIVORCE

Statistics tell the story: There is nearly one divorce for every two marriages, and 40% of children will experience the breakup of their parents' marriage before they are 18 years old.

Overall, more than 1 million marriages end in divorce each year, a rate of 4.6 divorces per 1,000 individuals. Although the rate of divorce is actually lower than 20 years ago, and the median duration of marriages ending in divorce has increased (from 6.7 years in 1970 to 7.2 years in 1990), the rate of divorce is still high. Moreover, divorce is not just a problem in the United States. As can be seen in Figure 7–10, the divorce rate is high throughout the world, although it is particularly high in the United States (Scott, 1990; Cherlin et al., 1991; Edwards, 1995; Phillips, 1999).

Why are divorce rates so high? There is no single trigger that leads to divorce; instead, the disintegration of a marriage represents the culmination of a complex process that may begin in the very earliest stages of a relationship (Kalb, 1983). Several demographic factors are related to a higher probability of divorce. For example, marriages are more likely to end in divorce when the partners are younger, they have had a child prior to marrying, they have previous marriages, they have stepchildren. Economic difficulties can also lead to distress in relationships, as does the birth of a first child. Finally, people of different races or ethnic backgrounds

FIGURE 7–10   Breaking Family Ties Around the World Increases in divorce rates are not just a U.S. phenomenon: Data from other countries also show significant increases. (*Source:* Population Council, 1995.)

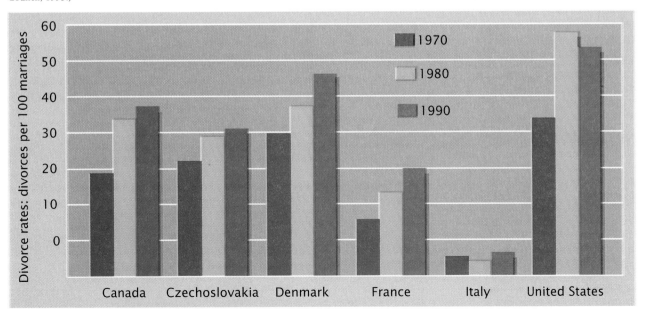

have a higher probability of divorce, although different religious backgrounds do not increase the chances of divorce much (Bumpass, Martin, & Sweet, 1991; Bird & Melville, 1994; Esterberg, Moen, & Dempster-McCain, 1994; Conger, Rueter, & Elder, 1999).

Although demographic factors are helpful in describing general trends, they do not fully explain why people divorce. One promising approach is discussed in Applying Social Psychology.

ATTRIBUTIONAL AND COMMUNICATION PROBLEMS LEADING TO DIVORCE

Do marriages falter because of the impaired attributions of husbands and wives? The answer is that a clear difference exists in the kinds of attributions made by partners in distressed, as compared with successful, relationships. Spouses in distressed marriages attribute negative

APPLYING SOCIAL PSYCHOLOGY
THE SCIENCE OF A GOOD MARRIAGE

Walking into this laboratory is anything but romantic. It is filled with electronic gear, ranging from videotape recorders to instruments that monitor respiration rate and sweating to motion detectors that measure fidgeting.

But the Family Research Laboratory at the University of Washington in Seattle has provided groundbreaking information on what keeps a marriage from unraveling. According to psychologist John Gottman, who directs the lab, his research on marriage allows him to predict, with 90% accuracy, which married couples are likely to enjoy a stable relationship and which are headed for divorce court (Carrere & Gottman, 1999; Gottman & Silver, 1999).

Gottman's work is based on a careful reading of the verbal and nonverbal behavior of married couples. Analysis of just 15 minutes of a couple holding a conversation about a topic on which they disagree and an oral history questionnaire makes it possible to identify the degree of marital problems. The key factors that predict divorce are the frequency of criticism, contempt, defensiveness, and stonewalling. Contempt, signaled by such nonverbal behavior as the rolling of a partner's eyes, is often one of the most important signals of serious marital problems, particularly if it is accompanied by insults or sarcasm.

Gottman's work debunks several common myths about the factors that lead to divorce. For example, although it is often assumed that having an affair is an important cause of divorce, this is not the case. Furthermore, couples who engage in screaming matches aren't necessarily distressed, and it isn't necessary to resolve every problem; many couples live for years without talking through all their differences.

Marriages are particularly vulnerable at certain points. The first 7 years are the most perilous, with divorces peaking at

around 5 years. But a second danger point comes around 16 to 20 years into a marriage. For this group, the average time of divorces is 16.4 years.

What distinguishes marriages that are in trouble from those that aren't? Several kinds of questions were most helpful in identifying distressed couples (see Table 7–5). Among the most critical dimensions were the following:

- Affection displayed toward the spouse
- Amount of negativity communicated to the spouse
- Expansiveness or expressivity in communicating information about the relationship
- A sense of "we-ness," or perceiving oneself as part of an interdependent couple, rather than as one of two separate, independent individuals
- Tradition in sex roles
- Volatility and intensity of feelings in conflict situations
- A sense of control over one's life, as opposed to feelings of chaos
- Pride in successfully getting through previous difficulties in the relationship
- Disappointment and disenchantment with the marriage

When divorce was likely, husbands tended to be low in fondness, "we-ness," and expansiveness, while high in negativity and disappointment. For wives, the best predictors of divorce were low "we-ness" and high disappointment scores. Overall, the very best single predictor of divorce was the degree of disappointment the husband felt about the marriage.

events to their partners. When bad or unpleasant things happen, then, these things are seen as the spouse's fault and as due to qualities in the spouse that are relatively enduring and unchangeable. For example, if a wife fails to give her husband an important message, the husband might attribute that failure to the irresponsibility of his wife—viewed as an enduring, relatively unvarying trait (Bradbury & Fincham, 1992; Fincham & Bradbury, 1992).

In solid marriages, however, negative events are explained by causes that minimize the spouse's responsibility. The causes are viewed as situational and attributable to a particular set of circumstances. In the same example, for instance, the wife's failure to pass on the message might be seen as the result of temporary forgetfulness due, perhaps, to her unusually busy schedule (Bradbury & Fincham, 1990).

Although it is clear that more negative attributions are made in distressed marriages than in satisfactory ones, it is not clear whether such negative attributions are the cause or the result

---

TABLE 7-5   Know Your Spouse

Test the strength of your marriage in this relationship quiz.

	TRUE	FALSE			TRUE	FALSE
1. I can name my partner's best friends	☐	☐	13. My partner appreciates the things I do in this relationship		☐	☐
2. I can tell you what stresses my partner is currently facing	☐	☐	14. My partner generally likes my personality		☐	☐
3. I know the names of some of the people who have been irritating my partner lately	☐	☐	15. Our sex life is mostly satisfying		☐	☐
4. I can tell you some of my partner's life dreams	☐	☐	16. At the end of the day my partner is glad to see me		☐	☐
5. I can tell you about my partner's basic philosophy of life	☐	☐	17. My partner is one of my best friends		☐	☐
6. I can list the relatives my partner likes the least	☐	☐	18. We just love talking to each other		☐	☐
7. I feel that my partner knows me pretty well	☐	☐	19. There is lots of give and take (both people have influence) in our discussions		☐	☐
8. When we are apart, I often think fondly of my partner	☐	☐	20. My partner listens respectfully, even when we disagree		☐	☐
9. I often touch or kiss my partner affectionately	☐	☐	21. My partner is usually a great help as a problem solver		☐	☐
10. My partner really respects me	☐	☐	22. We generally mesh well on basic values and goals in life		☐	☐
11. There is fire and passion in this relationship	☐	☐				
12. Romance is definitely still a part of our relationship	☐	☐				

Scoring: Give yourself one point for each "True" answer. Above 12: You have a lot of strength in your relationship. Below 12: Your relationship could stand some improvement and could probably benefit from some work on the basics, such as improving communication.

Source: Gottman, 1999.

of the distress (Bradbury & Fincham, 1992). It may be that negative attributions simply reflect the reality of a spouse's unpleasant personality and behavior. Some husbands and wives do, in fact, have negative personality characteristics that make them difficult to live with (Kelly & Conley, 1987; Buss, 1991).

It is also possible, however, that spouses who characteristically make negative attributions do so even with respect to the most benign and innocent behavior on the part of their partners. Such an unforgiving attributional style may actually be the cause of marital distress. After all, if you had a spouse who tended to consider your personality flaws as the source of many of life's disagreeable events, you might well react negatively—thereby increasing marital distress for both yourself and your partner. In sum, consistent negative misattributions tend to cause resentment that grows with each occurrence and gradually poisons the relationship (Bradbury et al., 1996).

Other aspects of communication between partners hold important keys to understanding marital discord (Parker & Drummond-Reeves, 1993). Distressed and successful marriages differ in both verbal and nonverbal communications. For example, although people in unhappy marriages often misinterpret the meaning of their partners' nonverbal behavior, they are unaware of their misinterpretation. In fact, they are often overconfident that they have correctly perceived nonverbal emotional messages from their spouses, and in addition they feel certain that any messages that they intended to convey have been communicated effectively—even if they have not (Noller, 1992; Noller & Feeney, 1998).

Similar patterns of miscommunication characterize verbal messages. Distressed couples often show patterns of negativity, in which one partner complains about the other's failings, triggering an attack by the other partner. At the same time, the underlying concerns that led to the initial complaint are never addressed (Duck, 1988; Canary & Stafford, 1994; Duck & Wood, 1995).

As miscommunication in a relationship escalates, judgments about the meaning of a partner's behavior undergo a shift. For example, behavior that was once seen as "charming forgetfulness" becomes "uncaring indifference," and the partner becomes less valued as a result (Levinger, 1983). Ultimately, a person may begin to solicit criticism of a partner from individuals outside the relationship and to look to others for the fulfillment of needs that were once met by the partner.

Social psychologist Steven Duck suggests that a deteriorating relationship proceeds through a series of stages, in much the same way that developing relationships tend to follow a general pattern (Duck, 1982, 1988; Vanzetti & Duck, 1996; see Figure 7–11). In his view, the first phase occurs when a threshold is reached in which a partner feels he or she can no longer tolerate participation in the relationship. This feeling results in an *intrapsychic phase* in which the partner privately considers whether to withdraw from the relationship.

If another threshold is reached in which the partner feels justified in leaving the relationship, the intrapsychic phase is followed by a *dyadic phase,* in which the partner confronts the other person and negotiates the fate of the relationship. If these negotiations do not produce a reconciliation, and a decision to terminate the relationship is reached, the person moves into the *social phase.* In the social phase, public acknowledgment is made that the relationship is being dissolved, as friends and family are informed. A public accounting is made regarding the events that led to the termination of the relationship.

Finally, the last stage is a *grave-dressing* phase, in which the major task is to terminate the relationship physically and psychologically. The partners may reconsider the entire relationship, rewriting its history and making what occurred appear reasonable and consistent with their perceptions of the breakup.

Although declining marital relationships often cycle downward in a seemingly irreversible pattern through the stages described by Duck, not all do. In some cases, people can repair relationship difficulties. For example, people can be taught to make different types of attributions about their partners' behavior, or they can learn to act more responsively to their spouses (Reis & Shaver, 1988; Holmes & Boon, 1990; Duck & Wood, 1995). In other cases, as we discuss next, they can learn to handle discord in a manner that ultimately strengthens their relationship.

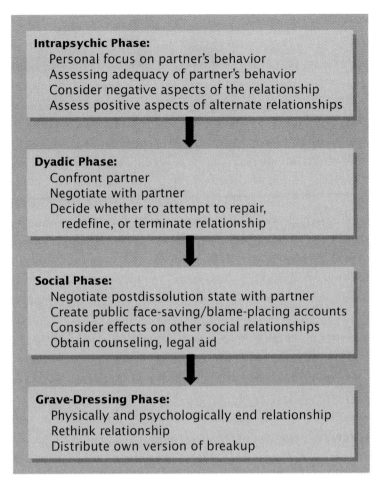

Intrapsychic Phase:
   Personal focus on partner's behavior
   Assessing adequacy of partner's behavior
   Consider negative aspects of the relationship
   Assess positive aspects of alternate relationships

Dyadic Phase:
   Confront partner
   Negotiate with partner
   Decide whether to attempt to repair,
      redefine, or terminate relationship

Social Phase:
   Negotiate postdissolution state with partner
   Create public face-saving/blame-placing accounts
   Consider effects on other social relationships
   Obtain counseling, legal aid

Grave-Dressing Phase:
   Physically and psychologically end relationship
   Rethink relationship
   Distribute own version of breakup

FIGURE 7–11   The Stages of Relationship Dissolution
(*Source:* Based on Duck, 1984, p. 16.)

FIGHTING THE GOOD FIGHT

Frequent arguments and fights are a sure sign of a declining relationship.

Although such a statement might represent common sense, in fact it is wrong. According to a growing body of research, the number of arguments is less important than the nature of their content in determining whether a marriage will decline or flourish. Such findings contradict conventional wisdom, which has traditionally suggested that couples who were more likely to fight with each other were the least satisfied with their marriages (Canary, Weger, & Stafford, 1991; Canary, Cupach, & Messman, 1995; Fehr et al., 1999).

Instead, it turns out that certain types of arguments actually can improve certain relationships. The kinds of arguments in which partners are free to express their anger, while keeping a rein on the intensity of their feelings, are the most likely to solve problems and to improve relationships. In contrast, fights in which partners become defensive or stubborn, whine, or repress their anger are more likely to be detrimental to the health of the relationship. The most destructive behavior of partners is making excuses for their behavior, rather than taking responsibility for it. In addition, acting stubborn, insulting the partner, whining and complaining, or focusing on what the partner should stop doing rather than what he or she should do more of, are among the behaviors during arguments that were found to be least constructive (Gottman & Krokoff, 1989; Siegert & Stamp, 1994).

What makes for a good fight? Experts suggest several strategies for maximizing the positive outcomes from an argument, including the following (Goleman, 1989; Gottman & Silver, 1999):

**THE INFORMED
CONSUMER
OF SOCIAL
PSYCHOLOGY**

◆ Make explicit complaints, avoiding vague generalities. Charging a partner with being "a slob" not only conveys the information that you are upset, but it sends a threatening message as well. A better strategy is to say, "It would help me feel that the housecleaning is not just my responsibility if you rinsed your dishes after you have a snack." Instead of blaming the problem on your partner's personality, suggest that your concern is over a changeable behavior.

Arguing may not necessarily be a sign of problems in a relationship, according to a growing body of research. The number of arguments a couple has is less important than the nature of those arguments.

◆ Don't state your disagreement with something your partner has said by accusations such as, "You are completely wrong." Instead, paraphrase what you hear your partner saying, and try to find a solution. Saying "I'm hearing you criticizing my neatness, and it makes me feel bad" is better than the accusatory "Why are you saying I'm sloppy?"

◆ Show that you are listening to your partner. Say, for instance, "I hear your concern about helping with the garden, and I know that we should talk about it." Acknowledge that your partner may have a point, or at least that the issue is worthy of discussion. Don't fire back with a countercharge every time your partner makes a new complaint.

◆ Acknowledge that you are angry, if that is what you are feeling. You can say, "I'm getting pretty angry about this issue." Don't pretend that something doesn't bother you if it really does. Ultimately, relationships in which the partners gloss over their anger may be at greater risk than those in which partners air their problems and feelings.

Although strategies such as these aren't guaranteed to take the sting out of arguments, they can go a long way in helping to prevent some of the most destructive consequences of arguing.

REVIEW AND RETHINK

Review

• The filtering model and the principles of homogamy and the marriage gradient have been used to explain the process of selecting a spouse.

• In choosing marriage partners, people across many disparate cultures value love and mutual attraction.

• Marriages typically cycle through several transitions, including the replacement of idealized views of the spouse with more realistic ones.

• Alternatives to marriage include cohabitation and living alone.

• Domestic violence tends to pass through three stages: the tension-building stage, an acute battering incident, and the loving contrition stage.

• Rape most often involves acquaintances.

• Marital relationships decline and may end in divorce, in part because of faulty attributional patterns and misunderstood verbal and nonverbal behavior.

Rethink

• What is the relationship between sexual satisfaction and marital satisfaction? Explain this relationship.

- Describe the general relationship between marital satisfaction and child rearing. Considering the exceptions to the general rule, what factors do you think are responsible for this relationship?

- Consider the negative correlation between negative attributions and marital satisfaction. Give three possible explanations for this observed correlation.

- According to Duck, what stages does a deteriorating relationship pass through as it declines? Recall the triangle theory of love proposed by Sternberg. How might the eight types of love differ with respect to the path that their breakup takes?

LOOKING BACK

What factors lead to the development of close relationships, how do these relationships evolve, and what roles do intimacy, self-disclosure, and sexuality play?

1. Close relationships are characterized by emotional attachment, need fulfillment, and interdependence. The three basic levels of relatedness are unilateral awareness, bilateral surface contact, and mutuality. The mutuality stage of relationships may itself be subdivided into three stages. (p. 224)

2. Exchange relationships are associations based on an economic model of interaction, in which people seek to maximize their benefits and minimize their costs. In contrast, in a communal relationship, the participants feel mutual responsibility for each other, and each provides benefits according to the other's needs or to exhibit concern for the other person. Exchange relationships occur most often with first-time acquaintances and in business relationships; communal relationships occur most often with romantic partners, family members, and friends. (p. 227)

3. Intimacy is the status in which a person communicates important feelings and information to another through self-disclosure. As a consequence of self-disclosure, the person comes to feel understood, cared for, and validated by the partner in the relationship. Self-disclosure can either be descriptive or evaluative in nature. (p. 228)

4. According to the theory of social penetration, relationships gradually progress through increasingly deeper intimacy. This increasing intimacy leads to reciprocity of self-disclosure, in which people who are the recipients of intimate information respond with increasing disclosure. (p. 228)

5. Research suggests that relationships may pass through a series of stages. For example, stimulus-value-role (SVR) theory suggests that relationships proceed in a fixed order through three stages: the stimulus stage, the value stage, and the role stage. (p. 230)

6. Sexuality is a key issue in many close relationships. Although the double standard long suggested that premarital sex was permissible for men but not for women, in recent years it has been supplanted by the permissiveness with affection standard. Still, attitudes regarding sex remain more liberal for men than women. In addition, there are cultural and subcultural differences in sexual patterns, although heterosexual and homosexual relationships are more similar than different. (p. 232)

What are the different categorizations of love?

7. One model of love suggests that there are two types. Passionate (or romantic) love represents a state of intense absorption in another person, including intense physiological interest and arousal and caring for the needs of the other. In comparison, companionate love is the strong affection that individuals have for those with whom their lives are deeply involved. (p. 235)

8. According to the labeling theory of passionate love, people experience romantic love when two events occur together: intense physiological arousal and situational cues that indicate "love" is the appropriate label for the feelings they are experiencing. (p. 236)

9. According to Sternberg's model, love consists of three components: intimacy, passion, and decision/commitment. The various combinations of these components produce eight different types of love. (p. 239)

10. Lee suggests that love is analogous to the primary colors on a painter's palette, which can then be combined into other types. The three primary types of love are eros, ludos, and storge. (p. 241)

11. According to prototype approaches, love should be considered in terms of how people naturally describe, think about, and categorize the concept. Among the major prototypes of love are love of a parent for a child, love between romantic partners, love between old friends, and love between siblings. (p. 242)

What are the varieties of relationships?

12. Although there is considerable variation across cultures in desired qualities in marriage partners, cross-cultural commonalities exist as well, including love and mutual attraction. There are also consistent gender differences in desired qualities for husbands and wives, suggesting the possibility that certain traits are important in evolutionary terms. (p. 248)

13. In long-term relationships such as marriage, several transitions occur over time. For example, romanticized, idealized images of one's partner are replaced by more realistic views. (p. 248)

14. In cohabitation, unmarried persons of the opposite sex live together. Although there has been a large increase in the number of people cohabiting in the last 30 years, the actual proportion of people doing so is relatively small. (p. 249)

15. Other people choose to remain single instead of either marrying or cohabiting, and, despite stereotypes to the contrary, lead full lives. (p. 251)

16. Some form of violence occurs in a quarter of all marriages. Violence crosses lines of socioeconomic status, race, ethnicity, and religion, although the likelihood of violence is higher in families that are subject to economic or emotional stresses. (p. 252)

17. Rape, which occurs when one person forces another to submit to sexual activity, is surprisingly common: As many as one of eight college women say they have been raped. Rape is often motivated not by sexual desire but by power and control needs, anger, or the myth that it is acceptable to be sexually aggressive. (p. 253)

What factors lead to the decline of close relationships?

18. In some cases, long-term relationships decline. Among the factors related to declines are changes in expressions of affection and negativity on the part of spouses. Although some research suggests that marital satisfaction follows a U-shaped pattern, being highest during the early and late years and lowest during the child-rearing years, some couples find their greatest satisfaction while they are raising their children. (p. 255)

19. There is nearly one divorce for every two marriages, and 40% of all children will experience the breakup of their parents' marriage before they are 18 years old. (p. 255)

20. In addition to certain demographic factors related to divorce, there are also significant psychological processes. For example, the nature of partners' attributions and their verbal and nonverbal communication are related to divorce. In addition, relationship dissolution passes through a series of stages. (p. 258)

21. The types of fights and arguments that couples have are related to the ultimate success or failure of a relationship. Among the strategies for fighting in a way that can improve a relationship are making explicit complaints, stating disagreements constructively, showing that you are listening, and acknowledging anger. (p. 259)

EPILOGUE

In this chapter and the previous one, we've sought to answer the question of how people develop and maintain their relationships with others. We began in Chapter 6 by considering the roots of interpersonal attraction, considering how particular characteristics and traits—both our own and those of other people—lead us to be drawn to particular people. In this chapter, we continued the discussion by looking at deeper sorts of relationships. We examined how people build relationships, move from liking to loving, and ultimately undertake the processes involved in forming lasting relationships.

Although it may seem that these two chapters ended on a pessimistic note, as we considered the decline and failure of relationships, in fact most of the work done by social psychologists has an optimistic foundation. By seeking to understand the dynamics that lie behind interpersonal attraction and relationships, social psychologists look toward a future in which people are better able to get along with one another and form deeper, more meaningful relationships that can raise the quality of life.

Before we turn to an examination of helping in the next chapter, turn back to the prologue of this chapter, concerning the relationship between Jessica Casey and Chris Mattson. Consider these questions:

1. How might you apply SVR theory to the Casey–Mattson relationship?

2. Speculate on the Casey–Mattson relationship in terms of the theory of social penetration. How do you think it changed over time?

3. Can you describe the Casey–Mattson relationship in terms of Sternberg's three components and eight types of love? How would you guess the relationship would evolve in terms of the three components as the length of their marriage increased?

4. If theirs is a typical relationship, how did the birth of their two children following their marriage change the kind of relationship Casey and Mattson had?

KEY TERMS AND CONCEPTS

close relationships (p. 224)

cohabitation (p. 249)

communal relationship (p. 227)

companionate love (p. 236)

descriptive self-disclosure (p. 228)

double standard (p. 232)

evaluative self-disclosure (p. 228)

exchange relationships (p. 227)

homogamy (p. 245)

interdependence (p. 224)

intimacy (p. 228)

labeling theory of passionate love (p. 236)

marriage gradient (p. 245)

passionate (or romantic) love (p. 236)

permissiveness with affection standard (p. 232)

POSSLQs (p. 249)

rape (p. 253)

reciprocity of self-disclosure (p. 229)

Relationship Closeness Inventory (p. 224)

Romeo and Juliet effect (p. 237)

stimulus-value-role (SVR) theory (p. 230)

theory of social penetration (p. 228)

unilateral awareness (p. 226)

CHAPTER 8

HELPING

Origins and Consequences of Prosocial Behavior

PROLOGUE

A Lesson in Helping

Jake Geller and Jack Buchholz are an inseparable pair.

Jake Geller will leave his Medway [Massachusetts] home this morning in a lift-equipped van that will take him and his parents to Phoenix, where he will be a freshman at Arizona State University.

The trip will be one of the longest and most difficult of his life. Geller, 19, has muscular dystrophy, which makes any type of travel an elaborate effort.

But after Geller's parents drop him off on August 17, he will not be alone. His lifelong friend, Jack Buchholz, will be his roommate and serve as his personal care attendant.

While many people have been amazed by Buchholz's dedication to his friend, Buchholz himself is unfazed.

"It's not that big a deal," he insisted. "Waking up a half hour earlier in the morning is not that difficult."

Buchholz will get Geller, who uses a wheelchair, out of bed every morning, dress him, and help him shave and shower. At night, he will undress him, help him with such routine bathroom chores as brushing his teeth, and put him into bed. . . .

Geller says he is grateful to Buccholz for the sacrifices he has made, and Geller hopes to hire a personal care attendant in the next few months to help him at school and take the burden off his friend.

But do not expect them to be spending any less time together.

"As a pair, they're inseparable," said George Murphy, the director of the computer camp where the two have spent the last few summers. "Their personalities mesh together so well that they're a great team. I think of them as a pair of super-heroes, each with his own strength." (Kiehl, 1998, p. C1) ■

LOOKING AHEAD

In an era in which the news is often bad, Jack Buchholz's willingness to sacrifice his energies and time for Jake Geller stands out. People like him, and others who make exceptional sacrifices, seem unusual. Yet, such behavior is an essential—and not, it turns out, altogether rare—part of human behavior, and social psychologists have sought to answer the questions of why, and under what circumstances, we help our fellow humans.

In this chapter, we examine prosocial behavior. **Prosocial behavior** is helping behavior that benefits others. The help may be trivial, such as picking up a dropped piece of paper for a stranger, or extraordinary, such as rescuing a child who has fallen through the ice in a partly frozen pond. It may be premeditated and thoughtful, as when volunteers collect money for

prosocial behavior: Helping behavior that benefits others.

charity, or impulsive, as when a person rushes heroically into a burning car to save a trapped mother and child. The common thread tying together prosocial behaviors is the benefit that flows to others from an individual's helping actions.

We first consider the roots of helping behavior. We begin by examining prosocial behavior in emergencies, detailing the forces that lead people to intervene—or not to intervene—in a crisis. We then turn to altruistic behavior, helping that requires self-sacrifice. After examining whether any helping behavior can be entirely altruistic, we question whether such behavior may be genetically programmed. We also consider how empathy, attributions, and emotions relate to helping, and we examine societal norms, or standards, that promote helping.

Finally, we consider practices that are designed to increase prosocial behavior. We discuss how rewards and helpful models bring about increased prosocial behavior. We also speculate on the adequacy of methods for directly teaching moral behavior and moral reasoning.

In sum, after reading this chapter, you'll be able to answer these questions:

- ◆ What is prosocial behavior, and how is it exhibited in emergencies?
- ◆ What is altruism, and does it have genetic roots?
- ◆ How do emotions and attributions affect helping?
- ◆ What societal norms, or standards, promote helping?
- ◆ How can we increase prosocial behavior?

PROSOCIAL BEHAVIOR AND ALTRUISM

- ◆ Miep Gies, a resident of Holland, risked her life every day for more than 2 years to feed and provide a place to hide Anne Frank and her family during the Nazi Holocaust.
- ◆ Lenny Skutnik repeatedly jumped into the freezing Potomac River to rescue victims of a plane crash. "I just did what I had to do," explained Skutnik later.
- ◆ Hundreds of people of all ages rushed to help residents of Oklahoma after a devasting series of tornadoes leveled whole towns and killed over 50 people. Although their own homes were safe, many felt compelled to help strangers who lived hundreds of miles away.

What makes people like these so helpful? Social psychologists have long pondered the question, and they have come up with a variety of answers. We'll investigate the major considerations that go into helping, beginning with the way in which people react during emergency situations.

DEALING WITH EMERGENCIES: WHEN WOULD YOU HELP A STRANGER IN DISTRESS?

Suppose you were in an experiment, talking to a small group of students over an intercom, and you suddenly heard one of them say the following:

> I-er-um-I think I-I need-er-if-if- could-er-er-somebody er-er-er-er-er-er-er give me a little-er give me a little help here because-er-I-er-I'm-er-er-h-h-having a-a-a real problem-er-right now and I-er-if somebody could help me out it would-it-would-er-er s-s-sure be-sure be good . . . because-er-there-er-er-a cause I-er-I-uh-I've got a-a one of the-er-sei-er-er-things coming on and-and- and I could really-er-use some help so if somebody would-er-give me a little h- help-uh-er-er-er-er-er c-could somebody-er-er-help-er-us-us-us [choking sounds]. . . . I'm gonna die-er-er-I'm . . . gonna die-er-help-er-er-seizure-er- [choking sounds, then silence]. (Latané and Darley, 1970, p. 379)

Most of us probably assume that if we were in such a situation, we'd rush into action, trying to see how we could help the victim.

Unfortunately, most of us would be wrong. According to the results of a landmark study carried out by social psychologists Bibb Latané and John Darley—first mentioned in Chapter 1—and a series of experiments that followed, the poor victim would probably have been better off with just a single companion, rather than with a group.

Diffusion of responsibility: Where more is less.   Latané and Darley's research confirmed that the *greater* the number of people present in a situation in which help is required, the *less* likely it is that any one person will provide it—a phenomenon they labeled diffusion of responsibility. **Diffusion of responsibility** is the tendency for people to feel that responsibility for acting is shared, or diffused, among those present. The more people that are present in an emergency, then, the lower is any one individual's sense of responsibility—and the less likely it is that a person will feel obligated to help. In contrast, with fewer people present to share the responsibility for helping, the more likely it is that help will be provided (Darley & Latané, 1968; Latané & Darley, 1970; Latané & Nida, 1981; Kalafat, Elias, & Gara, 1993; Swim & Hyers, 1999).

Such reasoning has been proved sound in literally hundreds of experiments. For example, in the experiment using the seizure "emergency" described above—which was, in reality, staged by the experimenters to test the theory—Latané and Darley found clear evidence for the diffusion-of-responsibility phenomenon. In the study, participants, placed in groups of either two, three, or six people, heard the faked seizure over the intercom. As predicted, the more people who supposedly could overhear the seizure, the less likely it was that any one person would provide help. Specifically, when just two people were present (the bystander and victim), 85% of the participants helped. In contrast, when two bystanders and the victim were present, 62% provided aid; and when five bystanders and the victim were present, only 31% helped (Darley & Latané, 1968).

The concept of diffusion of responsibility helps to explain—although not pardon—a considerable number of everyday incidents that exemplify "Bad Samaritanism." For instance, perhaps you recall the true events depicted in the Jodie Foster movie *The Accused,* in which a New England woman was savagely raped on a pool table in a bar as dozens of onlookers stood idly by. Police accounts describe her crying and begging for help, and yet not one person came to her aid. While she was being repeatedly raped by several men, one customer did try to call the police, but he dialed a wrong number and gave up. Finally, the woman broke away from the rapists and fled the bar, dazed and half-naked. A passing motorist stopped and drove her to a telephone, where she called for help.

The concept of diffusion of responsibility allows us to speculate on the social psychological situation that permitted the rape to proceed without intervention. Because the bar was crowded, each of the patrons could feel little individual responsibility for helping the victim. Instead, the obligation for helping was shared among the many people present, a diffusion that lowered the likelihood that any one person would be sufficiently moved by the victim's plight to help her. Ironically, if fewer people had been in the bar, the victim's pleas might well have been answered.

Help in emergencies: A model.   Although the diffusion-of-responsibility phenomenon explains part of what goes into making the decision to help, it is just one of the factors that accounts for helping in emergency situations. As illustrated in Figure 8–1, several distinct decision-making points must be traversed to determine whether helping will occur. Specifically, they include:

◆ *Noticing a person, event, or situation that potentially may require help.* For even the potential for helping to exist, an individual must notice the circumstances that may require assistance of some sort.

◆ *Interpreting the event as one that requires help.* Simply noticing an event is no guarantee that someone will provide help. If the event is ambiguous enough, onlookers may decide that it really is not an emergency at all (Shotland, 1985; Bickman, 1994).

diffusion of responsibility: The tendency for people to feel that responsibility for acting is shared, or diffused, among those present.

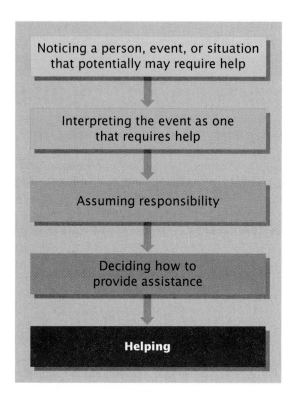

FIGURE 8–1 Latané and Darley's Model of Helping in an Emergency According to the research, the decision to help is made in several steps. (*Source:* Latané & Darley, 1970.)

People are often motivated to decide that a situation is not an emergency. Defining the situation as a routine, nonemergency event means that no further psychological (and physical) effort is required. We may thus be primed to discount information that would lead us to conclude that a situation is an emergency, and conversely, especially attentive to information suggesting that there is no emergency (Wilson & Petruska, 1984).

Similarly, viewing other bystanders who are not themselves intervening may help bolster the interpretation that the event is not an emergency (Harrison & Wells, 1991). We may convince ourselves that if the situation really were an emergency, then others would be jumping in to help. Such a mind-set is due to **pluralistic ignorance**, a phenomenon in which bystanders in an emergency or ambiguous situation use the behavior of others to determine whether help is actually required (Taylor, 1982; Miller & McFarland, 1987; Miller & Prentice, 1994; Schroeder & Prentice, 1998). Each person in the situation mistakenly assumes, based on the behavior of the others, that help is unnecessary. As a result, no one intervenes.

Unfortunately, in such situations the reality may be quite different. Like us, the other people present may feel uncertain about what to do, and they may be looking to others to figure out the appropriate course of action. But when all the people in a situation see no one responding, they make the same, erroneous attribution, and everyone becomes immobilized. If people are able to move beyond pluralistic ignorance and understand the true motivation behind the collective inactivity of the onlookers, they are more likely to intervene. Obviously, in an ambiguous situation, communication with others helps to end the state of pluralistic ignorance.

◆ *Assuming responsibility.* If people notice an event and determine that it is an emergency, they have reached a major decision point. At this point, they ask themselves whether they should take responsibility for helping. This is the point at which diffusion of responsibility may occur: If many others are present, the burden of helping is seen to be shared, and helping by any one person is less likely to occur.

Of course, diffusion of responsibility is not the only reason that people may not be helpful in an emergency. Sometimes people take no responsibility because they don't know what they ought to do and they lack the expertise to intervene effectively. For instance, if someone

pluralistic ignorance: A state that occurs when bystanders in an emergency or ambiguous situation use the behavior of others to determine whether help is actually required.

with apparent medical expertise is present when a medical emergency occurs, it is unlikely that a person without medical training will feel compelled to offer aid; more likely the inexpert person will defer to the specialist.

One study, conducted on the subways of New York, illustrated this point nicely. In the experiment, researchers arranged for a bogus crisis to occur, in which a passenger appeared to collapse, with blood trickling out the corner of his mouth. Other passengers were considerably less likely to intervene when an apparent medical school "intern" was present than when no such person was present. Not unreasonably, those without medical training readily deferred to the supposed expertise of the intern (Piliavin & Piliavin, 1972).

Ironically, fear of unwanted legal ramifications may prevent experts from becoming involved in providing emergency medical assistance. For example, physicians have been successfully sued for intervening unsuccessfully in emergency situations. In response, many states have passed "Good Samaritan" laws, which prevent medical and other professionals from being sued for providing unsuccessful assistance in emergencies (Northrop, 1990; Taylor, 1990; Rosenberg, 1992).

Moreover, people who furnish emergency help are sometimes viewed suspiciously by onlookers. A person who is providing aid may be seen by late-arriving onlookers as the possible source of the harm that befell the victim—a phenomenon dubbed **confusion of responsibility** (Cacioppo, Petty, & Losch, 1986). Awareness of the confusion-of-responsibility phenomenon may in fact suppress a person's willingness to provide aid during an emergency.

◆ *Deciding how to provide assistance.* If people reach this step in the sequence, they must choose from a variety of potential forms of assistance. Should they call the police? Provide medical assistance? Ask another bystander to get help?

Because the potential choices for helping vary so widely, helpers must weigh the costs and benefits of each potential action, employing a kind of psychological calculus. In an emergency, people quickly tally both the actual and psychological costs of providing particular kinds of aid. For instance, indirect forms of aid, such as getting others to help, are less costly than direct aid. At the same time, various types of help bring different kinds of rewards. You can expect to receive more gratitude and approval when you leap into a pond to save a drowning child than when you merely call the child's plight to the attention of a nearby police officer.

Many experiments have confirmed that as the costs of helping increase, relative to the rewards, helping is less likely to occur (Bell et al., 1995; Yee & Greenberg, 1998). One example comes from a classic study involving theology students who were on their way to give a talk either on the Good Samaritan parable—which emphasizes the importance of helping—or on a subject having nothing to do with helping (Darley & Batson, 1973). To control the cost of helping, the researchers manipulated the degree to which the students were late in arriving to give their talk.

On the way to give their talk, participants passed a confederate, planted by the experimenters, who was slumped on the ground in an alley, coughing and groaning. Would the theology students help?

confusion of responsibility: A state in which observers assume that a person who is actually aiding a victim is in some way responsible for the emergency situation.

Whether you decide to help this person depends on a number of factors, such as whether you think he needs help, whether you perceive it is an emergency situation, and how many others are present.

"Look, Joanna, I've told you over and over -- I don't have time for sharing and caring when I'm moving and shaking."

The answer depended on whether the participants were late. Participants who were late (which corresponded to a greater cost for helping) were less likely to provide help than participants who had ample time. Ironically, the topic of their talk had no effect on their helping behavior; participants about to speak on the virtues of helping were no more likely to provide help than those who had rehearsed a speech on another subject.

We should not sink into despair over the unwillingness of the tardy theology students to help the confederate. Subsequent research suggests that their lack of help may have been induced by their perception that the "greater good" would be fulfilled by their arriving at the talk on time, thereby helping a larger number of people, than by their stopping to help a lone person in need (Batson et al., 1978).

Clearly, then, the kind of assistance to be offered in an emergency situation is selected in part by an assessment of the personal rewards and costs of helping. Tallying the rewards and costs of various types of helping, people make a decision about what kind of assistance they will provide.

◆ *Helping in the emergency—the final step.* After weighing the rewards and costs of intervening in an emergency situation, people finally reach the stage of action. However, their intention to help does not guarantee that their help will be effective. For instance, if bystanders decide to phone the police for help, they may find that route blocked: They might not be able to find a phone, or the phone may be broken. Even if they decide to intervene directly, they may be frozen with fear and unable to act. The decision to help, then, does not guarantee that those in need will receive the aid they require.

ALTRUISM: DISREGARDING THE REWARDS AND COSTS OF HELPING

Latané and Darley's model emphasizes the rational weighing of the rewards and costs of helping. However, in some cases a logical analysis of the benefits and expenses of helping does not satisfactorily explain why helping occurred. For example, a cost–reward analysis does not convincingly explain why a medic would risk his own life during fierce combat just to retrieve the body of a dead soldier so that it can be sent back to the soldier's family.

To explain such situations, some social psychologists have proposed the concept of **altruism**: helping behavior that is beneficial to others but requires clear self-sacrifice. In altruism, helpers have no expectation of receiving rewards, and they expect no condemnation from others if they do not provide help (Eisenberg, 1986; Batson, 1990b, 1991; Batson et al., 1999).

Many forms of helping can be considered altruistic: running into a burning house to rescue a stranger, sheltering Jews in Nazi-occupied countries during World War II, adopting a baby born with AIDS. In each of these cases, the costs (or potential costs) to the helper are significant, far outweighing possible rewards.

Some experts have criticized the notion of altruistic behavior. They argue that if we analyze various helping situations closely, we can often identify potential rewards even in behavior that at first seems completely altruistic. For instance, a helper may gain greater self-esteem, may receive praise from others, or may be the recipient of enormous gratitude and a sense of obligation on the part of the victim. Hence, psychological rewards may lie behind seemingly altruistic behavior (Batson, 1990a; Anderson, 1993; Serow, 1993; J. Baron, 1997).

A number of social psychological studies have examined altruism and the question of whether a behavior can be totally altruistic (Shapiro & Gabbard, 1994). For instance, some investigators have focused on altruism, and helping in general, as a type of personality trait. The concept of an **altruistic personality** suggests that certain individuals have enduring personality characteristics that consistently lead them to help (Bierhoff, Klein, & Kramp, 1991; Ashton et al., 1998).

Despite the appeal of the notion that some people are consistently helpful, evidence for the existence of a consistently altruistic personality type has not been found. Most research suggests that people are not invariably helpful or, for that matter, unhelpful. Instead, whether particular individuals act in a prosocial manner depends on their personality *and* the specifics of the situation. Furthermore, no single pattern of specific, individual personality traits determines prosocial behavior. Rather, the way that specific personality factors fit together, as well as the demands of the particular situation, determines whether a person will help (Carlo et al., 1991; Knight et al., 1994).

Research has shown, however, that some groups of people are more helpful than others. For instance, some studies have suggested that men exhibit slightly higher levels of helpfulness, in general, than women (Eagly, 1987). However, the greater helpfulness of men may be more apparent than real and may depend largely on the type of situation in which it has been studied. For instance, men show particularly high levels of helping when they are being observed by others and when the victim is a woman (Eagly & Crowley, 1986). Such results suggest that men may be motivated as much by their desire to exhibit strength and mastery as by altruistic intentions (Erdle et al., 1992).

In contrast, the type of help offered by women may be more nurturing than the help offered by men (George et al., 1998). For instance, one study found that women were more likely than men to say they would help a friend in need (Belansky & Boggiano, 1994).

altruism: Helping behavior that is beneficial to others but requires clear self-sacrifice.

altruistic personality: A concept suggesting that certain individuals have enduring personality characteristics that consistently lead them to help.

EVOLUTIONARY EXPLANATIONS FOR HELPING: IS HELPING IN OUR GENES?

When an elephant is injured and falls to the ground, other elephants will try to help it get up again. When a mother grouse's chicks are threatened by a predator, she will pretend to have a broken wing—calling attention to her presence—in order to divert the predator's attention from the chicks. When a bee hive is threatened, bees will seek to protect the hive by stinging the intruder. The act of stinging, however, results in certain death to the bee. (Sikes, 1971; Trivers, 1971; Wilson, 1975)

In an extraordinary case of primate help-giving, this female gorilla (shown with her baby, named Koola) went to the aid of a boy who fell into her habitat at a zoo in Illinois.

Such seemingly altruistic behavior seems to fly in the face of Darwin's notion of natural selection, or "survival of the fittest." The theory of evolution stresses that organisms are genetically programmed to behave in ways that enable them to survive long enough to pass on their genes to future generations. Therefore, we would not expect animals to engage in behavior that has no benefit to themselves and actually can threaten their existence. Helping other members of the species, particularly when it incurs costs to themselves, seems to be unusual behavior for animals that are instinctually programmed toward self-preservation.

One explanation for the phenomenon of animal helping comes from evolutionary psychology, which considers the biological roots of behavior. Focusing on how organisms pass on their genes to future generations, evolutionary approaches suggest that helping actually advances the goal of strengthening the species as a whole (Paris, 1994; Sober & Wilson, 1998).

How does this happen? Proponents of evolutionary approaches argue that natural selection occurs at the level of genes, not individuals. Rather than seeking to preserve themselves, then, organisms have as their goal the preservation of their genes. What this implies is that individuals who share one's genes—one's kin—are likely to help the general goals of natural selection (Barber, 1994). For instance, when a mother aids her child at the expense of her own well-being, the mother is actually ensuring the continuation of her gene pool, because the child has a relatively high percentage of similar genes.

But what of nonkin, who do not share similar genes? Why should they be the recipients of seemingly altruistic behavior? The answer is *reciprocity,* the notion that we help other members of the species because we (or our kin) will receive help from others in the future. Consequently, helping increases the probability that our genes will be protected for future reproduction (Nowak, May, & Sigmund, 1995; Sigmund, 1995).

In some ways, evolutionary explanations make sense. They certainly help explain such phenomena as why we are more likely to run into a burning house to save our own children than the children of our neighbors (Burnstein, Crandall, & Kitayama, 1994; Wilson & Sober, 1994; Reeve, 1998). Yet, evolutionary approaches have many critics. Because evolutionary explanations are based more on nonhuman species than on human behavior, they do not take into account the higher cognitive abilities of humans. In addition, they do not provide much in the way of specific predictions about the conditions under which people will be helpful. Furthermore, they do not explain why different cultures vary so much in terms of their helpfulness, as we see next. Still, because no evidence convincingly rules out evolutionary approaches as an explanation for altruism, they remain viable, although quite speculative.

TABLE 8–1	Helping in Different Cultures

The number of helpful acts that occur during children's play varies according to culture. In a 1975 survey, children in the Philippines, Kenya, and Mexico showed higher levels of helpfulness than children in Japan, the United States, and India.

COUNTRY	NUMBER OF HELPFUL ACTS
Philippines	280
Kenya	156
Mexico	148
Japan	97
United States	86
India	60

Source: Whiting & Whiting, 1975.

EXPLORING
DIVERSITY

CULTURAL DIFFERENCES IN HELPING

Does culture affect helping behavior? The clear answer is yes. For instance, people living on Israeli kibbutzim, or collective farms, tend to show greater helpfulness and even different reasoning about morality than members of the dominant culture in the United States (Mann, 1980; Fuchs et al., 1986).

Differences in altruistic behavior are linked to the way in which a culture's children are raised. For instance, one cross-cultural study found that children's helping behavior, as judged from observations made while they were playing, varied substantially in different cultures (see Table 8–1). Children in the Philippines, Kenya, and Mexico were most altruistic, whereas children in the United States scored among the lowest. These differences appeared to be related to the degree of children's involvement with family obligations. In those cultures in which children had to cooperate with other family members to do chores or to help in the upbringing of younger children, altruism was greatest. In contrast, when a culture promoted competition—such as in the United States—altruism was lowest (Whiting & Whiting, 1975; Whiting & Edwards, 1988).

Similarly, different cultures vary in the ways they view reciprocity, the notion that we help because we expect to receive help from others in the future. Yet, significant differences exist in views of reciprocity across various cultures. For example, Hindu Indians see reciprocity as a moral obligation, whereas college students in the United States consider reciprocity as more of a personal choice (Moghaddam, Taylor, & Wright, 1993; Miller & Bersoff, 1994; Miller, 1997).

EMPATHY: THE HEART OF ALTRUISM

Despite the evidence against the existence of consistent altruistic behavior, not all investigators have abandoned the issue. For instance, according to C. Daniel Batson and colleagues, at least some helping behavior is motivated solely by the goal of benefiting someone else and thus represents what could be described as altruistic behavior. But he argues that our altruism is limited to certain cases: It occurs only when we experience empathy for the person in need (Batson, 1990a; Batson, 1998).

Empathy is an emotional response corresponding to the feelings of another person. When people see a person in distress, they feel that person's suffering; when they encounter a person

empathy: An emotional response corresponding to the feelings of another person.

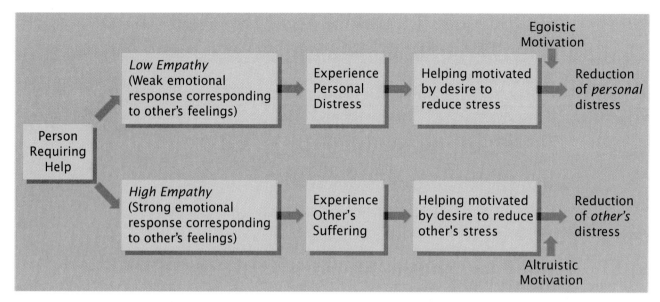

FIGURE 8–2   The Empathy–Altruism Hypothesis According to Batson's empathy–altruism hypothesis, experiencing empathy motivates people to reduce others' distress. In contrast, egoistic motivation leads to helping due to a desire to reduce one's own personal distress. (*Source:* Batson, 1991.)

who is sad, they experience the person's sadness. According to Batson's **empathy–altruism hypothesis**, empathy lies at the heart of altruistic behavior. As can be seen in the bottom half of Figure 8–2, experiencing true empathy motivates people to reduce other people's distress.

In contrast, people may help only because helping reduces their own personal distress or produces pleasure at meeting another's needs. In this case (illustrated in the top half of Figure 8–2), they are acting with **egoism**, behavior motivated by self-benefit (Batson & Oleson, 1991; Batson, 1991).

Finding support for the empathy–altruism hypothesis is difficult, because to distinguish altruistic from other motivations we must assess underlying motives that can be inferred only indirectly from behavior. However, researchers have come up with some ingenious experimental solutions to this problem (Batson, 1991; Davis, 1994; Davis, Luce, & Kraus, 1994; Batson & Weeks, 1996; Batson et al., 1999).

For example, support for Batson's reasoning comes from a study that directly compared the empathy–altruism hypothesis with the negative state relief model, which—as we'll consider later in the chapter—suggests that helping is based on an effort to end unpleasant emotions that come from observing a victim's plight. In the experiment, participants listened to an account of a female college student who was having difficulty completing an important assignment because of illness and then were given the opportunity to help (Dovidio, Allen, & Schroeder, 1990).

The experimenters manipulated the degree of empathy for the woman by telling participants either that they should imagine how the woman felt, thereby inducing high empathy, or that they should simply observe the circumstances being described, inducing low empathy. In addition, participants were given the opportunity to help the woman either on the specific problem that they heard about or on a different problem.

The researchers reasoned that if empathy were the source of helping, participants would be motivated to relieve the student's immediate, particular problem—not to solve her problems in general. Consequently, if the empathy–altruism hypothesis were valid, participants in the high-empathy ("imagine") condition would show high levels of helping on the same problem and low levels of helping on a different problem. Conversely, if the negative state relief model were valid, helping should occur regardless of whether the problem were the same or different, because the goal of the egoistic motivation would be to reduce the helper's negative emotions, which could be accomplished by helping on any task.

empathy–altruism hypothesis: The theory that empathy lies at the heart of altruistic behavior.

egoism: Behavior motivated by self-benefit.

FIGURE 8–3   Empathy Leads to Helping Supporting the empathy–altruism hypothesis, the results of the Dovidio, Allen, and Schroeder (1990) study showed that the degree of helping varied according to whether participants could help solve a current problem or a different one. When helping was possible on the current problem, participants who were asked to identify with the woman's feelings—the high-empathy condition—were more apt to help than those who had been asked merely to observe. Conversely, helping did not differ significantly between high- and low-empathy conditions when a different problem was involved. (*Source:* Dovidio, Allen, & Schroeder, 1990.)

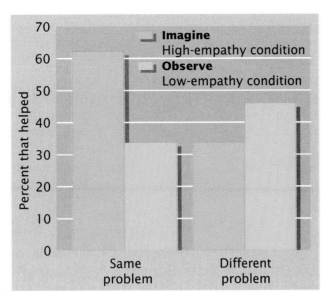

As you can see from Figure 8–3, the experiment supported the empathy–altruism prediction. Helping levels varied according to whether participants could help on the same or a different problem. When helping was possible on the same problem, participants who were asked to identify with the woman's feelings were more likely to volunteer than were those who had been asked merely to observe. Conversely, when helping was possible for a different problem, the difference in helping between high- and low-empathy conditions was not significant.

Findings from other research also support the empathy–altruism hypothesis (Shaw, Batson, & Todd, 1994; Batson et al., 1995; Sibicky, Schroeder, & Dovidio, 1995). For instance, in one recent study participants identified as high or low in empathy were led to be successful on a task meant to help another person, but they failed to relieve the other person's need through no fault of their own. Although low-empathy participants showed little mood change as a result of their failure, the mood of high-empathy participants declined substantially (Batson & Weeks, 1996).

Even though many studies support the empathy–altruism hypothesis, no final word can be said on the ultimate validity of the hypothesis. Plausible alternatives to the hypothesis abound. For instance, one suggestion is that helping is motivated not by selfless altruism but by the potential "empathic joy" an individual experiences when helping others (Smith, Keating, & Stotland, 1989; Cialdini, 1991; Warren & Walker, 1991; Roberts & Strayer, 1996; Cialdini et al., 1997; Neuberg et al., 1997).

Although a plausible hypothesis, the empathic joy explanation remains only one of several reasonable hypotheses. To date, no experiment has unequivocally supported any of the alternatives.

Furthermore, even if helping behavior is motivated by empathy-induced altruistic behavior, such help is not without cost. For instance, although altruism may benefit a particular individual, it may come at the expense of the larger group. For example, a business executive may keep an ineffective employee employed out of concern for the employee's welfare, but the company and customers may suffer. Similarly, sheepherders may overgraze their fields not out of selfishness but to feed their families (an altruistic motive). The problem in both cases is that the altruism results in a cost to the greater good. Even altruism, then, can have its downside (Batson et al., 1999).

TABLE 8–2	Major Motivational Principles That Underlie Helping Behavior
PRINCIPLE	**CHARACTERISTICS**
Egoism	Behavior motivated by self-benefit
Altruism	Helping behavior that is beneficial to others but requires clear self-sacrifice
Prosocial collectivism	Helping behavior whose goal is to increase the welfare of a group or collective
Prosocial principlism	Helping behavior with the goal of upholding some broad moral principle

PROSOCIAL COLLECTIVISM AND PRINCIPLISM: IS THERE MORE THAN EGOISM AND ALTRUISM?

According to Daniel Batson, the debate between egoism and altruism has contributed to a lack of attention to two other, potentially important, forms of motivation that may underlie prosocial behavior: collectivism and principlism (Batson, 1994). **Prosocial collectivism** is motivation with the goal of increasing the welfare of a group or collective, whereas **prosocial principlism** is motivation with the goal of upholding some moral principle.

Prosocial collectivism can be seen in efforts to help members of various groups, even if one does not belong to the group. For instance, we may wish to support members of various racial or ethnic groups, the homeless, or gays and lesbians, although we ourselves are not members of such groups. Although collectivism sounds in some ways similar to altruism—acting for the benefit for others—it is different: Altruism focuses on the welfare of another, single individual, whereas collectivism targets members of a group. The group may be small (marriage partners or a couple), or it may be large (members of a race or religion), but it is a group of some sort. In the words of Robyn Dawes and colleagues, the concern is "not me or thee but we" (Dawes, van de Kragt, & Orbell, 1988).

In contrast, prosocial principlism has a more abstract goal: the support of some broad moral principle such as justice or equality. Supporters of principlism reject the existence of altruism, because altruism is too often based on empathy. Similarly, they disavow collectivism, because it singles out particular groups of individuals to the exclusion of others. Instead, proponents of principlism suggest that adherence to broad principles, such as "love thy neighbor as thyself," can produce prosocial behavior.

More than likely, all four major forms of motivation—egoism, altruism, prosocial collectivism, and prosocial principlism (summarized in Table 8–2)—underlie helping at different times, depending on the circumstances, who is doing the helping, and the type of help required. One challenge for social psychology is to sort out these different motivations to learn the best ways of improving people's helpfulness.

REVIEW AND RETHINK

Review

- According to the phenomenon of diffusion of responsibility, the greater the number of people present in an emergency, the lower the likelihood that any one person will provide help.

- According to one model of helping behavior, a person must pass through several decision points before determining to offer help.

- The question of whether truly altruistic behavior exists is a difficult one, confounded by many possibly self-serving motivations.

prosocial collectivism: Motivation with the goal of increasing the welfare of a group or collective.

prosocial principlism: Motivation with the goal of upholding some moral principle.

- Prosocial behavior varies across the genders and across cultures.

- According to Batson, empathy, rather than egoism, lies at the heart of altruistic behavior. Also important are prosocial collectivism and principlism.

Rethink

- What is the relationship between the number of bystanders present during an emergency and (a) the odds that any single, particular bystander will provide aid, and (b) the odds that *someone* will provide aid?

- How does pluralistic ignorance affect the likelihood that a situation will be interpreted as an emergency? What factors might motivate a person to misinterpret emergency situations?

- Does the principle of reciprocity—that we help others in the hope of receiving help in the future for ourselves or our kin—operate among strangers? If so, how?

- Why might U.S. children have scored low on a cross-cultural measure of altruism? Can this be changed? Should it?

- How might an evolutionary approach explain prosocial collectivism and principlism?

attributional model of helping and emotions: A model suggesting that the nature of an attribution for a request for help determines a person's emotional response and the help provided.

EMOTIONS AND NORMS

You're walking down a busy city street, and an unshaven, disheveled man, wearing dirty clothes and carrying a sign that says, "I'm homeless," comes up to you. In a loud voice, he asks for some spare change to buy some food.

How do you respond? The way in which you interpret the man's request, your mood, and the standards for helping that you employ may well influence your response to the man's request. We turn now to the role played by attributions, emotions, and norms in determining helping behaviors.

EMOTIONS AND ATTRIBUTIONS: THE FEELINGS OF HELPING

According to the **attributional model of helping and emotions**, you may experience any one of a number of emotions at the moment you're approached by a man asking for help: sadness over his plight, annoyance at being accosted on the street, disgust that the government has not been able to solve the problem of homelessness, happiness that you have a job and do not have to beg for food, fear that the man may be deranged and is about to rob you. The specific emotion you experience may well determine whether you'll agree to his request or refuse it.

The attributional model suggests that when you initially are approached by the stranger, your general physiological arousal increases due to the uncertainty of the situation. To understand and label the arousal, you initiate an attributional assessment process in which you analyze the cause underlying the person's need for help. If you attribute his need to internal, controllable causes—he's lazy or he's a drunk—the emotion will likely be a negative one. Conversely, if you attribute his need to external causes that the victim is unable to control—he's been trying to find a job for months and hasn't been able to find one because the economy is bad—your emotions will be more sympathetic and positive (Meyer & Mulherin, 1980; Weiner, 1980, 1996; Menec & Perry, 1998; see Figure 8–4).

Ultimately, the emotions you experience help determine whether you will provide help (Dooley, 1995). According to the attributional model, if the emotions the person evokes are positive, you'll be more apt to help. A negative emotional response will probably discourage you from providing aid.

Mood and helping. The attributional model just examined assumes that we approach helping situations in an emotional state that is not already positive or negative. But suppose it's been a great day and you feel on top of the world. Are you more likely to help than you would be at the end of a long, upsetting day, when you are in an awful mood?

When confronted with a request for help, we are likely to experience a range of emotions. Whether we help or not is determined by the particular nature of the emotions aroused by the request.

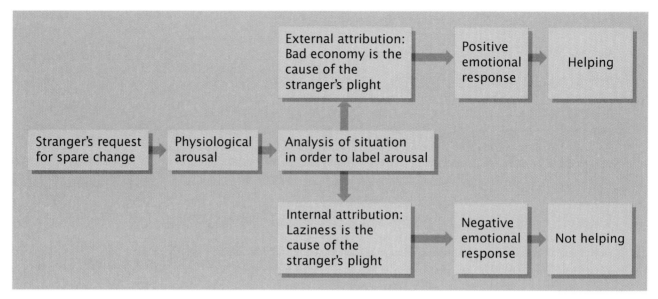

FIGURE 8–4   An Attributional Analysis of Helping   The attributional model of helping suggests that the way in which people attribute their physiological arousal determines whether they will provide help. (*Source:* Based on Weiner, 1980, and Meyer & Mulherin, 1980.)

The answer is a definite yes. People who are in a good mood are considerably more apt to help than those who are not (Carlson, Charlin, & Miller, 1988; Eisenberg, 1991; R. A. Baron, 1997). And it does not take much to bring on a good mood: Something as simple as finding a dime in a pay phone or smelling coffee and cookies in a mall is enough to make a person more likely to help others in need (Isen & Levin, 1972; R. A. Baron, 1997).

Of course, if you plan to use these findings to choose a good-mood moment to ask your boss for a raise, you'd better move quickly. Good moods do not last too long, and helpfulness drops off after only a few minutes (Isen, Clark, & Schwartz, 1976).

A person in a good mood is more likely to help for several possible reasons. For one thing, the circumstances that put people in a good mood may lead them to focus their attention on themselves. Because of this, they may be reminded of the societal standards that they learned as children about the importance of helping, and their thought processes may lead to greater helpfulness. Similarly, the good mood may activate a whole network of positive memories, leading to recollections of previous favorable experiences in which helping occurred. Finally, people may want to maintain their good mood, and acting helpfully toward another person may help them sustain their good feelings (Salovey & Rodin, 1985; Carlson, Charlin, & Miller, 1988; Salovey & Rosenhan, 1989; Carlson, Charlin, & Miller, 1994; Wegener & Petty, 1994).

If good moods lead people to behave more prosocially, does it follow that being in a bad mood will lead to a lower likelihood of helping? In this case the answer is: It depends.

Bad moods often foster lower levels of helping than neutral moods. However, they also sometimes lead to more helping, and in other cases make no difference at all (Cialdini, Kenrick, & Baumann, 1982; Feldt, Jagodzinski, & McKinley, 1997). One explanation for this confusing state of affairs is provided by the negative state relief model proposed by social psychologist Robert Cialdini (Cialdini et al., 1987; Cialdini & Fultz, 1990).

The **negative state relief (NSR) model** seeks to explain the relationship between bad mood and helping behavior by focusing on the consequences of prosocial behavior for the help *provider*. The model suggests that people in a bad mood will be helpful if they think their own mood will be improved by helping. For instance, we might help a fellow student study

negative state relief (NSR) model: The model that seeks to explain the relationship between bad mood and helping behavior by focusing on the consequences of prosocial behavior for the help *provider*.

for an exam if we think that our own bad mood might thereby be improved (Manucia, Baumann, & Cialdini, 1984; Schaller & Cialdini, 1990).

On the other hand, if people perceive that helping will do nothing to benefit their mood—or, even worse, if helping will make them feel bad—they will do nothing to provide aid. In support of such reasoning, studies show that younger children, who have not yet learned the rewards of helping, are less apt than adults to be helpful if they're in a blue mood (Cialdini & Kenrick, 1976).

Others argue that the NSR model does not tell the full story regarding the relationship between negative mood and helping. One alternative explanation suggests that negative mood influences what people think about, which in turn influences the tendency to be helpful. If their mood arouses inward-focused thoughts, such as despair, helplessness, and thoughts of personal inadequacy, people are unlikely to help others. In contrast, if their mood leads them to look outward, such as to the unfortunate plight of the person who needs help, a negative mood can increase the incidence of helping (Rogers et al., 1982; Pyszczynski & Greenberg, 1987; Wood, Saltzberg, & Goldsamt, 1990; Salovey, Mayer, & Rosenhan, 1991).

It is also possible that a negative mood changes the feelings of responsibility that people have for the welfare of others (Gibbons & Wicklund, 1982; Aderman & Berkowitz, 1983). If a bad mood leads people to feel less responsibility for others, then helping will be inhibited. Conversely, if an unpleasant mood increases people's sense of responsibility—perhaps because it raises their level of guilt—then the mood will be associated with more helpfulness.

Does helping improve one's mood?   The relationship between mood and helping is not a one-way street. Although we've been considering how good and bad moods affect helping, we can also examine how helping affects mood.

According to social psychologist Peter Salovey, people may provide help for others precisely in order to regulate their moods over the long term. Helping may do more than give them a momentary emotional boost: It also may bolster their spirits over long periods of time. People's awareness that they have been helpful in the past may permit them to view themselves more positively in the future. Ultimately, their self-concept may rise due to their prior helpfulness (Salovey, Mayer, & Rosenhan, 1991).

Considering the long-term benefits that helping brings to mood provides a way of at least partially understanding some of the more extraordinary instances of helping, in which the immediate consequences are quite negative. For example, Christians who helped Jews escape from Nazis during World War II put themselves at substantial risk, while probably feeling little immediate satisfaction from their actions. In the long run, however, they could look back on their behavior with pride, thereby uplifting their mood. In fact, interviews with rescuers and their relatives show that they experienced pleasure from their actions long after the war had ended (Oliner & Oliner, 1988).

OVERHELPING: KILLING WITH KINDNESS

> There are different ways of assassinating a man—by pistol, sword, poison, or moral assassination. They are the same in their results except that the last is more cruel.
> —Napoleon I, *Maxims* (1804–1815)

According to social psychologists Daniel Gilbert and David Silvera, Napoleon had it right: The way to injure a fellow person most grievously is not through physical means, but by injuring his or her character. And one of the best ways to accomplish such injury is by offering help in a way that makes the recipient seem incapable, inept, and generally incompetent—a process that Gilbert calls **overhelping** (Gilbert & Silvera, 1996).

Gilbert suggests that overhelping occurs when an individual tries to damage an observer's impression of a person by offering help in achieving a goal in such a way that the person's success is viewed as due to the help and not to the person's efforts or characteristics. Consequently, rather than being viewed positively, as a sign of hard work or superior ability, the

overhelping: The offering of help in a way that makes the recipient seem incapable, inept, and generally incompetent.

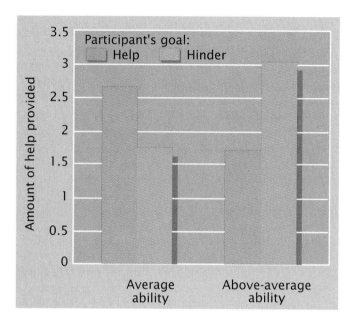

FIGURE 8–5
Overhelping When a job candidate supposedly had only average ability, participants in a study who were asked to help the job seeker provided a relatively high amount of aid, whereas participants motivated to hinder the average-ability job applicant provided relatively little help. However, when the job candidate was supposedly above average in ability and participants' goal was to help the job seeker, participants actually provided relatively little help. In contrast, participants who were seeking to hinder a high-ability job candidate provided *more* help to the candidate—a case of overhelping. (*Source:* Adapted from Gilbert & Silvera, 1996.)

person's success is attributed to the efforts of the helper or to sheer luck. In addition, over-helping can actually prevent success, inducing the recipient of the aid to fail.

For instance, consider a manager at a cookie factory, whose rival at work is asked by the company president to complete a complex, difficult report on the amount of peanuts being consumed in the production of peanut butter cookies. One way for the manager to sabotage the rival is to schedule a long meeting, during which the manager provides an overwhelming amount of data on peanuts—current peanut farm production figures in Georgia, the latest weather in Georgia, the amount of peanuts that are used in peanut butter, and so forth.

If the amount of data is simply overwhelming, the rival may spend hours sifting through it. As a consequence, the report is delayed and the reputation of the rival suffers. At the same time, the manager looks good, because he is viewed as having helpfully provided the information needed to produce the report. Another scenario is possible, however. Suppose the rival produces an excellent report. Here, the president of the company may attribute the success of the report to the data supplied by the manager. In either case, the "helping" provided by the manager has made the recipient look bad—a clear-cut case of overhelping.

Gilbert and Silvera found support for the occurrence of overhelping in a series of experiments. For instance, participants in one study were told their goal was either to help or hinder (depending on condition) a job applicant who was trying to solve word problems in order to get the job. When the job candidate supposedly had only average ability, participants trying to help the job seeker provided relatively substantial aid. On the other hand, participants motivated to hinder the average-ability job applicant provided relatively little help—a case of underhelping.

The story was very different when the job candidate supposedly had far-above-average ability. In this case, participants whose goal was to help the job seeker actually provided relatively little help. In contrast, participants who were seeking to hinder the high-ability job candidate provided *more* help to the candidate, making it appear that the candidate could succeed only because of the help—a clear case of overhelping (see Figure 8–5).

Of course, overhelping works only under certain conditions. People are most likely to overhelp when they think that they are actually providing insufficient help, but that the help will be considered effective by observers. If they are wrong, overhelping may backfire. For instance, sometimes help will be so effective that the person actually succeeds. If observers attribute the person's success to his or her own efforts or abilities, then overhelping will have failed (from the overhelper's point of view, at least).

At the same time, overhelping can be an effective sabotage strategy, particularly in cases in which the help actually worsens a person's performance but is thought (mistakenly) by observers to improve it. People can—and sometimes do—kill by kindness, providing useless aid to those they wish to see fail. Not all helping, then, is helpful.

NORMS AND HELPING: STANDARDS OF AID

The United Way, the largest charity in the United States, frequently employs a formula to suggest how much money people should contribute on a regular basis. Called the "Fair Share," it implies that people ought to donate a fixed percentage of their income in order to shoulder their part of the burden of caring for the needy.

The ability of the Fair Share concept to produce large donations—which, it turns out, it does quite impressively for the United Way—rests on societal norms about helping. **Norms** are general standards or expectations regarding appropriate behavior. When people are taught, "Do unto others as you would have them do unto you," "Kindness is its own reward," and "He who helps others helps himself," they are learning the norms that society holds dear.

Norms of social responsibility.   One of the most fundamental societal norms that encourage helping behavior is the norm of social responsibility. The **norm of social responsibility** suggests that people should respond to the reasonable needs of others, and that all people have a societal obligation to aid those in need (Rutkowski, Gruder, & Romer, 1983; Bornstein, 1994; Unger & Thumuluri, 1997). The norm of social responsibility is particularly influential when those requiring help are seen to be dependent or lacking the capacity to help. Thus, obligations to children, who are clearly dependent, are felt especially keenly themselves (Berkowitz, 1972; Harrell, 1994).

At the same time, the norm of social responsibility is so broad that it sometimes can be interpreted in ways that permit people to *sidestep* helping others. Thus, people might justify not giving change to a panhandler by the rationalization that true social responsibility lies in discouraging begging. Furthermore, norms that encourage helping must be experienced internally; it's not possible to force people to help and expect them to become more helpful in the future, as we discuss in the Applying Social Psychology box.

Norms of reciprocity.   If you agree with the sayings "What goes around, comes around," "tit for tat," or "an eye for an eye," then you probably adhere to the norm of reciprocity. The **norm of reciprocity** asserts that we should help others because they have helped us in the past or may help us in the future.

Norms of reciprocity are found in almost every culture. We see them manifested when a student lends his car to his roommate with the expectation that the roommate will let him borrow his compact disc player at some point in the future. Similarly, people may donate to charity with the understanding that if they ever lose their jobs and need help, they will have the right to ask for charity because of their prior contributions (Gouldner, 1960; Miller & Bersoff, 1994; Uehara, 1995; Burger et al., 1997).

The norm of reciprocity is powerful. Indeed, people who have been helped not only reciprocate help to the specific individuals who have helped in the past, but also are more likely to help other people. However, their help may not be as generous to others as it would be to the specific person who initially provided them help (Lerner & Meindl, 1981).

norms: General standards or expectations regarding appropriate behavior.

norm of social responsibility: The norm suggesting that people should respond to the reasonable needs of others, and that all people have a societal obligation to aid those in need.

norm of reciprocity: The norm asserting that we should help others because they have helped us in the past or may help us in the future.

APPLYING SOCIAL PSYCHOLOGY
MANDATORY VOLUNTEERISM: A CONTRADICTION IN TERMS?

By the end of their senior year, all students must have engaged in some form of community service of at least 5 hours a week over the course of a term. Examples of community service include working at a shelter for the homeless or soup kitchen, tutoring, holding an internship in a human service agency, or working with children in an after-school program.

Sound like a good idea for a school requirement? It does to many high schools and colleges, which have instituted required community service programs to encourage students to become involved in their community. One reason for such requirements is to increase the probability that people will volunteer in the future, resulting in an increase in community volunteers.

There's a hitch, though: According to a study by social psychologists Arthur Stukas, Mark Snyder, and E. Gil Clary (1999), such programs may have unintended consequences. In fact, they found that those who felt forced into volunteering due to a requirement ended up saying they were *less* likely to volunteer in the future.

In the first of two studies, the researchers surveyed a group of students required to enroll in a college service-learning course. They found that students who had prior volunteer experience, but who saw themselves as required to participate in the service-learning course, had *lowered* intentions to volunteer in the future. Participation in the course, then, had the ironic effect of reducing their interest in future volunteer work.

In the subsequent study, the results of the survey were supported. In the experiment, a group of participants were required to carry out a "volunteer" activity—reading to the blind. For participants who prior to the experiment said they were unlikely to volunteer in the future, being forced to volunteer in the study led to lower intentions to volunteer. On the other hand, for those who prior to the experiment felt that they would have volunteered even if they weren't required to, being forced to volunteer had little effect on their willingness to participate in the future.

Why would requiring volunteer work make participants less likely to volunteer in the future? One explanation is that community service requirements may alter people's perceptions of why they help. Instead of seeing themselves as willing volunteers, their forced participation may lead to the view that the sole reason they are helping is to fulfill a requirement. Consequently, they are unable to view themselves as volunteers doing good deeds, and they may be less eager to volunteer in the future. Furthermore, as we first discussed in Chapter 5, forced participation in any activity may lead to *reactance,* hostility and anger that results from the restriction of one's freedom (Brehm & Brehm, 1981). If people experience reactance as a result of being required to volunteer, they may seek to reestablish their sense of freedom by downgrading volunteerism.

The results of the studies suggest that "mandatory volunteerism" may have a downside. Rather than producing a corps of willing volunteers, community service requirements may lead to volunteers who are actually less likely to volunteer in the future. To be successful, then, community service programs must make people volunteer in as uncoercive a manner as possible.

Personal norms.   Sometimes the most potent norms are not the general ones handed down to us by society. Instead, they are our **personal norms**, our own personal sense of obligation to help a specific person in a specific situation.

Consider, for example, a girl whose parents die in an auto crash and who is subsequently raised by an elderly uncle. When she is older, her sense of obligation to help her uncle may be profound—but it is not necessarily accompanied by a sense of responsibility toward the elderly in general. Indeed, it may be that the woman expends most of her resources on her uncle and has little sense of obligation to society as a whole.

Personal norms also help explain devotion to particular political causes. For instance, in the 1960s, strongly committed civil rights workers often displayed an unusually strong sense of identification with their parents, whom they viewed as holding high moral standards. In raising their children, these parents taught a philosophy that included an emphasis on the rights of others and the obligation to help others. Rather than adhering only to broad,

personal norms: Our own personal sense of obligation to help a specific person in a specific situation.

general societal norms, then, the civil rights workers viewed themselves as following a set of more personal standards based on their parents' standards (Rosenhan, 1970).

Norms deterring helping.   Perhaps you've seen photos of people carefully avoiding a person sprawled face-down on the sidewalk of a city. This lack of care for someone so obviously in need reflects what has been called a **norm of noninvolvement**, a standard of behavior that causes people to avoid becoming psychologically (and physically) entangled with others.

The norm of noninvolvement is sometimes adopted by urban dwellers, who face so much stimulation that they may attempt to distance themselves from nonacquaintances (Milgram, 1977a). Furthermore, people in cities may experience insecurity about contact with individuals very different from themselves. Adopting a norm of noninvolvement permits them to remain detached from the needs of these others (Fischer, 1976; Matsui, 1981).

Norms acting to deter helping provide an understanding of one of the nagging problems found in our cities: the reluctance of people to act prosocially. Consistent with the stereotype of the cold-hearted, unfriendly city dweller, people living in urban areas are less prone to help others than people living in rural areas—whether the help required is direct or indirect, whether bystanders are present or not, and regardless of the age or gender of the victim. Furthermore, the higher the population density and the greater the cost of living in a city, the lower the level of helping behavior. Table 8–3 shows the top 20 cities ranked in one study in terms of overall helpfulness (Hedge & Yousif, 1992; Levine et al., 1994; Bridges & Coady, 1996).

Intriguingly, it is not true that people raised in rural areas are inherently more helpful; when living in a city they too begin to act less helpfully. City life seems to bring out the worst in people—at least when it comes to the likelihood of behaving prosocially.

RECEIVING HELP: IS IT BETTER TO GIVE THAN TO RECEIVE?

A classmate, who has finished her classroom project early, turns to you and offers to help you finish what you are doing. Instead of reacting with gratitude, you feel a combination of anger, embarrassment, and annoyance. You reject her help, with a cold "No thanks."

norm of noninvolvement: A standard of behavior that causes people to avoid becoming psychologically (and physically) entangled with others.

The norm of noninvolvement, the standard that allows us to avoid becoming psychologically and physically entangled with others, permits people to remain detached from the very real needs of others.

TABLE 8–3	Raw Scores and Ranks on Helping Measures by City			
CITY	**REGION**[a]	**POPULATION**[b]	**SCORE**[c]	**RANK**
Rochester, NY	NE	M	10.81	1
Houston, TX	S	L	10.74	2
Nashville, TN	S	M	10.69	3
Memphis, TN	S	M	10.66	4
Knoxville, TN	S	S	10.62	5
Louisville, KY	S	S	10.58	6
St. Louis, MO	NC	L	10.58	7
Detroit, MI	NC	L	10.55	8
E. Lansing, MI	NC	S	10.54	9
Chattanooga, TN	S	S	10.54	10
Indianapolis, IN	NC	M	10.46	11
Columbus, OH	NC	M	10.42	12
Canton, OH	NC	S	10.35	13
Kansas City, MO	NC	M	10.33	14
Worcester, MA	NE	S	10.24	15
Santa Barbara, CA	W	S	10.17	16
Dallas, TX	S	L	10.13	17
San Jose, CA	W	M	10.11	18
San Diego, CA	W	L	10.05	19
Springfield, MA	NE	S	9.92	20

[a]*NE = northeast, S = south, NC = north central, and W = west.* [b]*S = small (350,000–650,000), M = medium (950,000–1,450,000), L = large (>2,000,000). Based on estimates for metropolitan or primary statistical area for 1989.* [c]*Average of standardized scores (M = 10, SD = 1.0) for the six measures.*

Source: Levine et al., 1994.

Does this sound familiar? It might, because such a reaction is common. Recipients of help are not always so grateful for the help that they are offered. In fact, some research suggests that recipients of aid may be psychologically worse off than before they receive any help. In fact, in many cases, the self-esteem of recipients drops after receiving help from others.

According to the **threat to self-esteem model**, the way in which help is offered influences whether the help is viewed as positive or negative (Fisher, Nadler, & Whitcher-Alagna, 1982; Fisher, Nadler, & DePaulo, 1983). Several factors produce negative consequences for recipients' self-esteem. For example, help that emphasizes the higher ability or status of a donor is likely to produce threats to the recipient's self-esteem. Furthermore, help that prevents a recipient from reciprocating (and thereby fulfilling societal norms of reciprocity) is likely to be seen as threatening. Help that is given grudgingly or out of guilt is also viewed as threatening. Finally, people with high self-esteem typically react more negatively to help than those with low self-esteem.

Fortunately, help can be provided in several ways that do not threaten self-esteem. Among the most nonthreatening kinds of aid are the following (Fisher et al., 1982; Searcy & Eisenberg, 1992; Shell & Eisenberg, 1992, 1996):

◆ Aid from donors with positive characteristics and motivation

◆ Aid from siblings and older relatives

◆ Aid that can be reciprocated by the recipient

threat to self-esteem model:
The model that argues that the way in which help is offered influences whether the help is viewed as positive or negative.

◆ Aid that does not threaten the recipient's autonomy and sense of control

◆ Aid that is offered, rather than asked for

◆ Aid that comes from donors with relatively low resources or expertise

The most effective aid, then, occurs when recipients feel that the donor likes and is interested in them and views them as independent and autonomous. Furthermore, a person most readily accepts help when it is clear that it will increase the recipient's likelihood of future success.

REVIEW AND RETHINK

Review

- According to the attributional model of helping and emotions, people in a potential helping situation attribute causes to a person's need for help, and they either help or don't help depending on their attributions.

- People's moods affect their helping behavior, with good moods generally contributing to a higher incidence of helping and bad moods having mixed effects.

- The negative state relief model suggests that even bad moods can induce people to be helpful if the people believe that helping will improve their moods.

- Helping affects people's moods positively, sometimes for a long time.

- Individual helping behavior is influenced by both societal norms and personal norms.

Rethink

- Would the attributional model of helping predict that a well-employed veteran would be more or less likely than a nonveteran to help a man holding an "Unemployed Vietnam Veteran" sign? Why or why not?

- How does helping affect a person's mood? Can this phenomenon explain altruistic behavior? What aspects of a helping situation affect whether a person in a bad mood will help?

- Does a charity that offers benefits to poor children in another country depend on different societal norms than a charity that focuses on curing a disease, such as cancer or heart disease, that potential givers may one day contract? What norms do the two charities depend on? Why?

- How do personal norms and societal norms differ? How might they clash or complement each other?

- Is the norm of noninvolvement related to the principle of diffusion of responsibility? How do they differ?

INCREASING PROSOCIAL BEHAVIOR

You realize you left your wallet on the bus, and you give up hope of ever seeing it again. But someone calls that evening asking how to return the wallet to you.

***

Two toddlers are roughhousing when one suddenly begins to cry. The other child rushes to fetch his own security blanket and offers it to his playmate.

***

Driving on a lonely country road, you see a car stopped on the shoulder, smoke pouring from the hood. The driver waves to you frantically, and instinctively you pull over to help, putting aside thoughts of your appointments as well as your personal safety. (Kohn, 1988, p. 34)

Although the acts of violence, terrorism, crime, and war that dominate the headlines may lead us at times to think otherwise, helping is a central aspect of human behavior. Indeed, instances of prosocial behavior are part of most people's everyday lives—acts as simple as holding the door for a stranger or picking up and replacing a package that has toppled from a grocery store shelf. In the remainder of this chapter, we consider some social psychological findings that suggest ways of increasing helping behavior.

REWARDING PROSOCIAL BEHAVIOR

If you've ever received a reward for good conduct, you know the potency of reinforcement. We learn at an early age that acting prosocially brings rewards. At the most basic level, for example, parents reward children for sharing and behaving generously and punish them for selfishness. But, as social learning theory suggests, we also learn to be helpful by observing the behavior of others, vicariously experiencing the rewards and punishments that others receive. Ultimately, we model the behavior of those who have been rewarded (Bandura, 1974, 1977, 1978).

At first, prosocial behavior is guided through direct reward and punishment. One early experiment showed that when candy was provided to 4-year-old children who shared a marble, their sharing behavior increased (Fischer, 1963). But as children become older, verbal reinforcement becomes equally effective. In another study, 12-year-old children's donations to charity increased following verbal approval (Midlarsky, Bryan, & Brickman, 1973).

Just as positive reinforcement can promote increases in helping, negative reinforcement and punishment diminish the likelihood of future helping behavior. For instance, in one study, a confederate on a street corner in Ohio asked participants for directions (Moss & Page, 1972). To some participants, she offered thanks for the help she received, whereas to others she said, "I cannot understand what you're saying. Never mind, I'll ask someone else."

Further down the street, participants encountered a second confederate, who dropped a small bag but continued walking, pretending not to notice the dropped bag. Participants who had received the verbal punishment from the ungrateful confederate were less likely to provide help to the second confederate than those who had received thanks earlier. The moral: Verbal gratitude for helpful deeds is apt to increase helping, whereas verbal punishment is likely to discourage helping behavior.

MODELING AND HELPING

Just as Columbia University was about to begin a major fund-raising drive, it announced a gift of $25 million by John W. Kluge, a 1937 graduate of Columbia and chairman of the Metromedia Company.

The announcement was no coincidence. It reflected the belief—well supported by a wealth of social psychological research—that the example of a generous model can nurture the generosity of others. In both adults and children, the observation of someone behaving prosocially leads to increased prosocial behavior on the part of the observer. The reverse holds true as well: If a model behaves selfishly, observers tend to act more selfishly themselves (e.g., Spivey & Prentice-Dunn, 1990; Grusec, 1991; Janoski & Wilson, 1995).

Social psychologists James Bryan and Mary Ann Test demonstrated the importance of a helpful model in a classic study (Bryan & Test, 1967). In the field experiment, people driving along a busy Los Angeles highway passed a woman whose car seemed to have a flat tire but who was receiving help in changing it from an apparent passerby. Coincidentally, a quarter mile down the road, another woman seemingly had a flat tire.

In actuality, the entire scene was an elaborate set-up, designed to determine how many people driving by would stop and help the (second) woman in distress. The rate at which people stopped was compared with another condition in which passersby did not first see a helpful model. The results were clear. In the no-model condition, just 35 out of 4,000 passersby stopped, whereas in the helpful-model condition, more than twice as many people (98) stopped to offer aid. (We might note, of course, that in neither condition was the incidence of helping terribly impressive.)

Not only do people sometimes report that helping and volunteering provides a sort of physical "high," but also that the feelings linger beyond the actual act of helping. Many people said they experience positive feelings simply by recalling instances in which they helped.

Later research confirms that the consequences of viewing a helpful model are powerful and lasting (Grusec, 1982, 1991; Grusec & Kuczynski, 1997). But why do helpful models lead to greater prosocial behavior on the part of observers? There are several reasons. For one thing, if we see models being rewarded for their helpfulness, we learn through the basic processes of social learning that prosocial behavior is desirable. In addition, though, models act as salient reminders of society's norms about the importance of helpfulness. They show us, in a concrete way, how socially desirable behavior may be enacted in a particular situation, thereby paving the way for our own prosocial behavior. In other words, they make it easier to do what we know we should do (Hensel, 1991).

Thus, modeling goes beyond simply mimicking the behavior of others, and it plays a particularly significant developmental role as we move through childhood into adulthood. As we get older, we build general rules and principles in a process called *abstract modeling*. Rather than always modeling others' specific behaviors, we begin to draw generalized principles that underlie the behaviors we have observed. Hence, after observing several instances in which a model is rewarded for acting in a prosocial manner, we initiate a process in which we infer and learn the meaning of such acts, and we build and internalize our own model of behaving in an altruistic fashion.

EXPERIENCING A HELPER'S HIGH: THE REWARDS OF HELPING

If you are a long-distance runner, you may experience a physical "high" during or after your run. Such a runner's high typically consists of feelings of well-being, calmness, and sometimes euphoria.

Surprisingly, some research suggests that similar physical responses may occur as a result of something much less exhausting—helping other people. According to the results of a large-scale survey of women who had helped others in some way, the majority reported feeling an actual pleasant physical sensation while they were helping (Luks, 1988). In fact, those who engaged both in helping and physical exercise frequently reported that the positive sensations were quite similar.

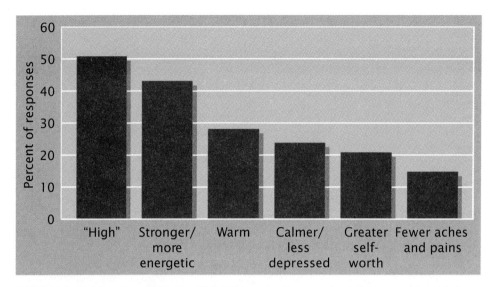

FIGURE 8–6   How Does It Feel to Help? Most people report that helping provides a kind of physical "high." (*Source:* Luks, 1988.)

As you can see in Figure 8–6, the actual response to helping differed among respondents. Approximately half reported feeling "high" in some way, and more than two-fifths said that helping made them feel stronger or more energetic. A significant proportion said they felt "warm" or "calmer and less depressed," and almost one-fifth said they felt greater self-worth and experienced fewer aches and pains due to their prosocial behavior.

The positive feelings that arose from helping also lingered beyond the actual period of helping behavior. Most respondents said they experienced positive feelings whenever they remembered their helping activities.

These findings are consistent with intriguing research that has been done on reactions to donating blood. According to the research of social psychologist Jane Piliavin and collaborators, people who habitually give blood may experience increasingly positive reactions following each donation. The positive emotional response leads habitual givers to become, in a very real sense, psychologically addicted to the donation process, and it increases the frequency with which they will give blood in the future (Piliavin, Evans, & Callero, 1984; Piliavin & Callero, 1991).

In sum, prosocial behavior may bring its own special reward—a helper's high. (For another perspective on the benefits of helping, see the accompanying Speaking of Social Psychology box.

TEACHING MORAL BEHAVIOR: DO AS I SAY, NOT (NECESSARILY) AS I DO

Despite emphatic intentions to avoid it, more than one parent has fallen back on the adage "Do as I say, not as I do." The old dictum tends to emerge when a child points out some inconsistency between the parent's prior behavior and what the parent is now telling the child to do.

When such an admonition occurs, parents are engaging in a fundamental form of moral education. People often use moral exhortations and preaching in an effort to promote altruistic and prosocial behavior. It turns out, though, that such an approach is not terribly effective. For example, in comparison with models who *act* generously, a model who *preaches* generosity is considerably less effective in eliciting donations (e.g., Grusec & Skubiski, 1970).

Of course, not all exhortations to behave in a prosocial manner are doomed to failure. One key to the success of moral prompts is the attribution made by the targets of these prompts if they do behave in a prosocial manner. Specifically, the effectiveness of preaching depends on the degree to which the preaching suggests that the enactment of moral behavior is related to someone's moral character, instead of simply representing a reaction to external pressure. For example, exhorting people to do good because of their underlying positive qualities ("underneath we're all good") is more effective than telling people to help in order to receive an external reward ("other people will owe you a debt of thanks").

Consequently, when people are led to believe that moral behavior demonstrates that they have high personal moral standards, they will be more likely to behave altruistically in the future. Conversely, to the extent that they are led to attribute their altruistic actions to external, situational pressures, they will be less apt to behave helpfully in the future (Lepper, 1983; Grusec & Dix, 1986; Grusec, 1991; Grusec, Rudy, & Martini, 1997).

Attributional approaches suggest that steering people toward the development of internal attributions for their prosocial behavior is an effective means of promoting more helping in the future. It is quite consistent with techniques used by charitable organizations, which sometimes engineer future large donations by attempting to obtain only tiny ones at first.

For instance, one successful slogan is "even a dollar will help." The motto represents a double-barreled strategy. First, once we have given even a small amount, we are likely to experience the positive reinforcements that a charity dispenses to any giver—a thank-you note, a membership card, and an explanation of how useful the contribution will be to the cause.

Second, the donation of even a small amount of money may be sufficient to allow us to modify our attributions about ourselves. Once we've given a donation in the past, we may come to see ourselves as donors motivated by an internal trait of generosity, as opposed to being motivated by external prompts. For both reasons, then, when asked for donations in the future, we may increase the size of our gifts (Dillard, 1991; Gorassini & Olson, 1995).

VALUES CLARIFICATION AND MORAL REASONING: INSTRUCTION IN MORALITY

When the United States initiated formal schooling in the 19th century, one of the primary goals was to provide education in moral values. Slowly, however, educational objectives changed, and today the teaching of moral values occurs only rarely. In fact, the teaching of values is a highly politically charged notion, associated with particular political ideologies.

At the same time, certain basic prosocial values are universal, regardless of people's political orientation. For example, few people would dispute the general importance of helping others. To instill the value of prosocial behavior, educators have developed several approaches (Damon, 1989). Among the primary methods they have identified are values clarification techniques and the teaching of moral reasoning.

Values clarification is a procedure in which students are encouraged to become aware of their current values, to consider how their values were formed, and how their values may differ from those of others. Although there are several values clarification techniques, one of the most prevalent is "Either-Or Forced Choice" (Simon, Howe, & Kirschenbaum, 1972). In this procedure, teachers ask questions that raise two conflicting underlying values, such as "Do you identify more with a Honda Civic or a Mercedes?" Forced to choose and explain one of the two alternatives, students find that their underlying values come to the surface. In addition, by producing cognitive conflict between particular values, the technique may provide insight into the assumptions about prosocial behavior that students hold.

Of course, the values clarification method does have potential drawbacks. For one thing, although it makes people aware of their values, it does not provide them a means to resolve underlying conflicts. Furthermore, it really isn't designed to teach new values; it only provides a framework for understanding existing ones.

A more direct means for promoting prosocial values in schools is an attempt to increase the level of sophistication of people's moral reasoning. The underlying assumption here is that by improving people's reasoning powers, we can ultimately induce them to behave in more prosocial ways.

SPEAKING OF SOCIAL PSYCHOLOGY

Gerard A. Jacobs

Red Cross Volunteer

Year of Birth: 1952

Education: B.A., Classical Languages, Xavier University; M.A., Clinical Psychology, Xavier University; Ph.D., Clinical/Community Psychology, University of South Florida

Home: Vermillion, South Dakota

"In a disaster, the first priority for services goes to the disaster relief personnel. "

The Red Cross, through its tireless efforts to provide humanitarian care in times of war and peace, has come to symbolize prosocial and altruistic behavior. Whether at the front lines of a major international conflict or on the front lawn of a burning single-family home, the Red Cross is there to provide comfort and aid. Established by Clara Barton in 1881, the Red Cross involves more than 1 million active volunteers. Among them is Gerard Jacobs, National Consultant for Disaster Mental Health, who was on alert as Hurricane Bertha headed toward the United States in July 1996.

"In every one of the states that the hurricane was expected to hit, disaster services were busy getting teams together and preparing to feed and house people evacuated from their homes," he reports. "Disaster health services bring in health nurses to take care of physical needs, and disaster mental health services are put in place to meet the emotional and psychological needs of the people affected."

Within 1 day of receiving notice, Red Cross volunteers are in place and ready to provide aid, according to Jacobs. Of the thousands of people who work with the Red Cross, about 95% are, like Jacobs, unpaid volunteers.

One procedure for increasing the sophistication of moral reasoning involves the discussion of moral dilemmas. Students who are forced to articulate their moral reasoning and to hear the conclusions reached by others are better able to come to grips with the complexity of the issues entailed by moral dilemmas. Furthermore, the cognitive conflict created by class discussion can lead students to a better understanding of other students' logic and perspectives. Through the process of discussion, then, students' reasoning abilities may increase to higher, more sophisticated levels (Reimer, Paolitto, & Hersch, 1983).

Assuming that these techniques are successful in raising the level of moral thinking, does elevated moral thinking translate into behavior that is more socially responsible? The answer is mixed. Some research finds that moral judgments are related to prosocial behavior (Candee & Kohlberg, 1987; Janssens & Dekovic, 1997). In contrast, other studies suggest that the relationship between moral judgments and moral behavior is more tenuous. Understanding the difference between right and wrong does not invariably lead people to behave in a moral fashion (Darley & Schultz, 1990).

We should not think, then, that the values inherent in prosocial behavior are easy to convey in the classroom. But the possibility exists that people can be taught to appreciate the merits of helping others, and that their own conduct will improve as a consequence.

"In a disaster, the first priority for services goes to the disaster relief personnel. It is essential to keep them healthy and functional so they can help others. Then we provide services to the people affected by the disaster," he says.

Although the Red Cross has always provided traditional disaster services, emergency services to military personnel, and the most advanced blood program in the world, the organization has moved only recently into the area of mental health services, assuming a formal role in that area in 1991, according to Jacobs.

"The reason I volunteered is that I could see the needs of people, and I wanted to help."

Relief efforts are shared between local emergency workers and Red Cross people. The idea is for the Red Cross to supplement and complement local efforts, not to supplant them. For instance, Jacobs notes, when Flight 427 crashed in Pennsylvania in September 1994, a local mental health team had already jumped into action while Red Cross mental health disaster volunteers were being brought in.

"The local people were well trained and in place," he says. "We provided some support in areas that they were less strong in, and we did some outreach work. The job of the Red Cross is to augment the local disaster plan and to try to respond to the specific needs of the local workers. Basically, we get there as quickly as we can and try to fill whatever gaps exist.

"Our role differs in each community. What we do depends on the resources of the community and the disaster plan that is in effect. In a disaster like a hurricane, services are typically provided at a Red Cross facility to anyone who comes seeking the service," Jacobs says.

What motivated Jacobs to become one of millions of people who contribute their time and expertise to the Red Cross?

"The reason I volunteered is that I could see the needs of people, and I wanted to help," Jacobs said. "I noted that the need for disaster mental health helpers was going unmet, and I volunteered to try and change that.

"For me it is a sense of knowing that I am one small piece of a puzzle that must be completed in order to meet people's needs."

INCREASING HELPFULNESS

THE INFORMED CONSUMER OF SOCIAL PSYCHOLOGY

Throughout this chapter we have considered a variety of techniques for increasing prosocial behavior. Let's summarize some of the main strategies that can be derived from our discussion:

◆ If you need help, be explicit and personal. In an emergency situation, explicitly ask for the kind of help that is required. Don't just say, "Help!" Instead, say, "I've fallen and hurt my leg—call an ambulance." A victim should try to make eye contact with a passerby and direct the call for help to him or her, thereby personalizing the situation and reducing the possibility of diffusion of responsibility. Do anything that can reduce the ambiguity of the situation.

◆ Activate norms appropriate for helping. If you are raising funds for a charity, make use of the powerful norms of society that support helping behavior. Remind people that there is a duty to help those less fortunate (norm of social responsibility), or that donations of blood permit them to be recipients of blood themselves later on (norm of reciprocity). Former students can be reminded that they received scholarships when they were in college and they now have a chance to help others by contributing to their alma mater (personal norms).

◆ Act as a helpful model. If you wish others to contribute to a worthy cause, make sure they know that you have already made your own contribution.

◆ Personalize help. Because we are more apt to help those for whom we feel empathy, efforts should be made to show the human side of those in need. It is relatively easy to refuse to help the abstract stereotype of "people on welfare." It is far more difficult to refuse help to a particular single mother who has just given birth and who is on welfare because her husband has deserted her.

Use of these strategies should increase the probability that help will be provided. Of course, no approach works every time; there are no guarantees that people will show the care for others that represents the best side of humanity. Still, as social psychologists—along with other students of human behavior—clarify and refine their understanding of prosocial behavior, the promise exists of a betterment of the human condition that will help us all.

REVIEW AND RETHINK

Review

* Positive reinforcement and observation of helpful models are effective in increasing helping behavior.

* In some ways, helping is its own reward, producing a "helper's high" that tends to increase the incidence of future prosocial behaviors.

* In teaching moral behavior, practice is more effective than preaching, but appeals to people's underlying moral character can also be effective.

* Two techniques for moral instruction that have been used in the United States are values clarification and practice in moral reasoning. However, the link between moral thinking and moral behavior is tenuous.

Rethink

* What is abstract modeling, and how does it relate to prosocial behavior?

* Compare the effectiveness of moral exhortations with modeling in increasing prosocial behavior.

* Describe the values clarification approach to increasing prosocial behavior. Under what conditions would such an approach be most successful?

* Identify some common fund-raising techniques that rely on the principles of encouraging prosocial behavior discussed in this chapter. Do advertisers of commercial products use similar techniques?

LOOKING BACK

What is prosocial behavior, and how is it exhibited in emergencies?

1. Prosocial behavior is helping behavior that benefits others. Its roots and motivations are the subject of study by social psychologists. (p. 265)

2. Diffusion of responsibility—the tendency for people to feel that responsibility for acting is shared among those present—discourages helping. The more people present at an emergency, the less likely it is that any individual will take responsibility for helping. (p. 267)

3. According to one model of helping, among the steps that a person takes in emergencies are noticing a person, event, or situation that potentially may require help; interpreting the event as one that requires help; assuming responsibility; deciding how to provide assistance; and actually helping. (p. 267)

What is altruism, and does it have genetic roots?

4. One source of debate among social psychologists is whether altruism—helping behavior that is beneficial to others but requires self-sacrifice—actually exists. Rewards–costs analyses of helping suggest that some reward is always inherent in any act of helping. (p. 271)

5. The question of whether some people have an altruistic personality—a set of dispositional characteristics that consistently lead them to act helpfully—is also open. However, most research suggests that people do not invariably behave altruistically, and there are gender and cross-cultural differences in helping behavior. (p. 271)

6. According to evolutionary approaches, there may be genetic roots to helping behavior, with individuals working together to preserve their genes and the genes of their close relatives. The principle of reciprocity—the notion that we help others because we expect to receive from others future help for ourselves or our kin—is used to support evolutionary explanations. (p. 272)

How do emotions and attributions affect helping?

7. Although some researchers suggest that people are largely egoistic, or motivated by self-benefit, others suggest that altruism can occur when people experience empathy for needy persons. Empathy is an emotional response corresponding to the current emotions of another person. According to the empathy–altruism hypothesis, it is empathy that motivates us to help, rather than the desire to reduce our own unpleasant reactions to victims' needs. (p. 273)

8. Two other forms of motivation that may underlie prosocial behavior are prosocial collectivism—the desire to increase the welfare of a group—and prosocial principlism—the desire to uphold moral principles. (p. 276)

9. The attributional model of helping and emotions suggests that uncertainty related to a person in need leads to an increase in arousal. When people attribute the need for help to internal, controllable causes, they feel negative emotions; when they attribute the need to external, uncontrollable causes, their emotions are positive. Negative emotions discourage helping, whereas positive ones increase the likelihood of helping. (p. 277)

10. People in good moods are more likely to help than those in neutral moods. On the other hand, being in a bad mood does not invariably produce a decrease in helping. According to the negative state relief model, people in a bad mood may be helpful if they think that their mood will be improved by helping. In contrast, if they perceive that helping will not improve their mood, they will be unmotivated to help. (p. 278)

What societal norms, or standards, promote helping?

11. Underlying helping behavior are several norms—societal standards or expectations regarding appropriate behavior. The norm of social responsibility suggests that people should respond to the reasonable needs of others. The norm of reciprocity states that we should help others because they have helped us in the past or may help us in the future. Finally, individuals have personal norms, their own sense of obligation to help a specific person in a specific situation. On the other hand, some norms deter helping, such as the norm of noninvolvement. (p. 281)

12. The threat to self-esteem model suggests that the way in which help is offered influences whether the help is viewed as positive or negative. Help that emphasizes the donor's higher ability or status, prevents the recipient from reciprocating, and is given grudgingly or out of guilt is likely to produce negative reactions from recipients. (p. 284)

How can we increase prosocial behavior?

13. One means of increasing prosocial behavior is to provide direct positive reinforcement, or reward, for instances of helping behavior. Another technique involves observation of helpful models, because the observation of someone behaving prosocially leads to increased prosocial behavior on the part of the observer. The reverse also holds true: If a model behaves selfishly, observers tend to act more selfishly themselves. (p. 286)

14. There is evidence that helping provides its own rewards, producing a sort of "helper's high" that can lead to a higher incidence of helping in the future. (p. 287)

15. Another technique to encourage helpful behavior is to use moral admonitions, urging people to behave prosocially. However, in comparison with models who act helpfully, a model who preaches helpfulness is considerably less effective. (p. 288)

16. Attributional approaches suggest that steering people toward the development of internal attributions for their prosocial behavior is an effective means of promoting more helping behavior in the future. (p. 289)

17. Other techniques have been used to produce increased prosocial behavior. One is values clarification, a procedure in which people are encouraged to examine their values. The notion behind the technique is that students will become aware of their current values and perhaps reexamine them. (p. 289)

18. In addition, attempts have been made to increase the sophistication of moral reasoning through the discussion of moral dilemmas. However, it is not clear that changes in reasoning capabilities about moral issues result in increased helping behavior. (p. 290)

EPILOGUE

As we've seen, the roots of helping are multifaceted. In considering the variety of complex explanations for prosocial behavior, we come to the understanding that helping is brought about not just by one simple cause but by a variety of factors operating jointly.

Before we proceed to our examination in Chapter 9 of aggression, the opposite side of the coin from the helping behavior we discussed in this chapter, return to the prologue of this chapter, about the help that Jack Buchholz provides to Jake Geller, who suffers from muscular dystrophy. Consider these questions:

1. What do you think is the primary motivation behind Jack Buchholz's willingness to help Jake Geller?

2. Discuss Buchholz's helping in terms of at least three different explanations of helping that were considered in this chapter (e.g., altruism, egoism, evolutionary explanations, the helper's high, empathy, societal norms, etc.).

3. Discuss evidence that supports and refutes the idea that Buchholz's helping is truly altruistic. What are possible benefits that Buchholz receives from acting as Geller's helper?

4. Based on the research on personality and helping, do you think that Buchholz is, in general, a particularly helpful individual? Why?

5. How do you think Geller feels in terms of being the recipient of help, particularly in the light of the research on self-esteem?

——— KEY TERMS AND CONCEPTS ———

altruism (p. 271)

altruistic personality (p. 271)

attributional model of helping and emotions (p. 277)

confusion of responsibility (p. 269)

diffusion of responsibility (p. 267)

egoism (p. 274)

empathy (p. 273)

empathy–altruism hypothesis (p. 274)

negative state relief (NSR) model (p. 278)

norm of noninvolvement (p. 283)

norm of reciprocity (p. 281)

norm of social responsibility (p. 281)

norms (p. 281)

overhelping (p. 279)

personal norms (p. 282)

pluralistic ignorance (p. 268)

prosocial behavior (p. 265)

prosocial collectivism (p. 276)

prosocial principlism (p. 276)

threat to self-esteem model (p. 284)

CHAPTER 9

AGGRESSION

Origins and Consequences of Violence and Hostility

PROLOGUE

High School Terror

The mass shootings at Columbine High School in Littleton, Colorado, were a tragic reminder that few places in the world are safe from violence and aggression.

For most Littleton, Colorado, high school students, April 20, 1999, started like any other day. There were the usual complaints about upcoming tests and papers due and talk of senior pranks and graduation.

But the day ended like no other. Two students went on a carefully planned rampage, gunning down fellow classmates and a teacher after rigging dozens of bombs around the school.

In the end, after murdering 13 people, the two killers took their own lives. They left behind a record of pro-Nazi hate literature, diaries that described a killing plan that had been hatched a year earlier, and a Web site that contained rantings foreshadowing their killing spree. ■

LOOKING AHEAD

The Littleton attack was a fearful reminder that schools—although still among the safest of society's institutions—are not immune from large-scale violence. The killings, and the subsequent extensive media coverage, also brought forth a wave of copycat threats, in which hundreds of schools received bomb threats, and several bombs and guns were actually found (see Figure 9–1).

What explains such aggression? We address this question in this chapter as we look at aggression, the opposite side of the coin from our focus on helping behavior, discussed in Chapter 8. *Aggression,* which refers to intentional injury or harm to another person, may be as commonplace as a parent's swatting a child's hand or as extreme as a murder spree. As with prosocial behavior, aggression may be thoroughly calculated, as when a mobster hires a hit man to kill a rival, or entirely spontaneous, as when a child flies into a violent rage at his sister's merciless teasing. The common link: behaviors whose purpose is the intentional hurting of another individual.

In this chapter, we first discuss the difficulty of developing a satisfactory definition of aggression. We then consider different theories that seek to explain why people are aggressive,

FIGURE 9–1   Copycat Threats Following the shootings in Littleton, Colorado, hundreds of threats were reported across the United States. (*Source:* Kay, 1999.)

ranging from biological to social explanations. We examine the link between frustration and aggression, and look at some social factors that lead to aggression. We discuss the effects of exposure to media violence, examining the extraordinary amounts of aggression to which most people are routinely exposed. Finally, we discuss how aggression and its consequences can be reduced and potentially eliminated.

In sum, after reading this chapter, you'll be able to answer these questions:

◆ What is aggression?

◆ What are the roots of aggressive behavior?

◆ What social and situational factors lead to aggression?

◆ Does exposure to media violence and pornography produce aggression in viewers?

◆ How can we reduce aggressive behavior?

THE ROOTS OF AGGRESSION

In many ways, it represented a collective nightmare of New York City life: a woman found in Central Park, brutally beaten. Because she was initially unidentified, the quest for her name became front-page news, as this Everywoman came to represent the fears of aggression that residents of the city always, at some psychological level, seemed to harbor. (Perez-Pena, 1996)

This attack is an example of only one form of extreme, unacceptable aggression that people may encounter. The print and electronic media report one form of physical aggression after another, from wars to murders to muggings. Parents and—in some states—teachers use physical punishment to induce good behavior. Moreover, aggression is not only physical. Many of us frequently confront verbal aggression and anger, whose sting may be as hurtful as physical pain.

DEFINING AGGRESSION: CHARACTERIZING AN ELUSIVE CONCEPT

The fact that aggression is so common and widespread does not make it easy to define (Mak & de Koning, 1995). Why is this so? Consider the following circumstances:

- A soldier bayonets an enemy soldier, causing horrible pain and eventual death.

- A physician carries out an emergency operation on a choking woman in a restaurant, cutting a hole in her throat to allow her to breathe. The emergency action causes excruciating pain, but it saves the woman's life.

- A police officer tortures a person to extract information about terrorist plans to ignite a bomb in a religious shrine, which if undetected would kill hundreds of innocent people.

- A mother slaps her child's face after he purposely knocks down his younger sister.

- In a fit of anger, a father tells his child that she is a failure and that it would have been better if she had never been born.

Although each of these incidents involves inflicting a degree of injury on another person, most of us would probably agree that they do not all represent aggressive behavior. For example, even though a physician may cause as much pain as a torturer, most people would be unwilling to label the physician's behavior aggressive. However, some social psychologists disagree, arguing that it is ultimately impossible to make fine distinctions between various types of injury. Consequently, social psychologist Arnold Buss (1961) suggests that aggression is any behavior that harms or hurts someone else. Using this definitional approach makes it simple to identify which of the five incidents described above are aggressive: According to Buss, all are expressions of aggression.

However, most experts pursue a different path in defining aggression. They suggest that the *intent* of a person's behavior must be considered in determining whether a given action is aggressive (Linneweber et al., 1984; Carlson, Marcus-Newhall, & Miller, 1989; Lysak, Rule, & Dobbs, 1989; Lovas, 1997; Braun et al.,1998).

A definition in which "intent" plays a central role certainly has a drawback. How can anyone clearly establish a person's "intention," which is an unobservable, hypothetical state that can be guessed at only indirectly from the person's overt behavior. How can we ever be certain that an observer's inference about intent is the appropriate one? Further, if we wish to construct a broad definition of aggression that applies to both humans and other species, intention is not a very practical concept, given the difficulty of establishing—and verifying—intent from the actions of animals.

Despite such conceptual difficulties, the notion of intent remains central to most contemporary definitions of aggression. Consequently, we'll consider **aggression** as intentional injury or harm to another person. According to this definition, the injury or harm can be either physical or psychological. Aggression contrasts with **violence**, which is a deliberate attempt to carry out serious physical—but not psychological—injury (Berkowitz, 1974, 1993; Carlson et al., 1989; Baron & Richardson, 1994; Kunkel et al., 1995; Bushman & Anderson, 1998).

Some social psychologists divide aggression into two types: instrumental and emotional. **Instrumental aggression** is injury or harm in which the goal is to obtain something of value. For instance, a man who murders a relative to obtain an inheritance would be guilty of instrumental aggression. In contrast, **emotional aggression** is injury or harm that is carried out for the explicit goal of hurting someone—harm inflicted for its own sake. A brawl erupting in a bar or a husband battering his wife in the heat of an argument are both examples of emotional aggression.

Both instrumental and emotional aggression are intentional. Using a definition of aggression that emphasizes intent unravels several knotty questions. Is a physician who causes

aggression: Intentional injury or harm to another person.

violence: A deliberate attempt to carry out serious physical—but not psychological—injury.

instrumental aggression: Aggression in which the goal is to obtain something of value.

emotional aggression: Aggression with the explicit goal of hurting a victim.

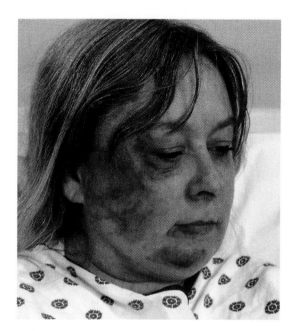

Injury or harm that is carried out for the sole purpose of hurting someone is an example of emotional aggression.

untold pain to save someone's life aggressive? The answer is no; a physician hardly wishes to hurt the patient. Is a soldier whose goal is to kill an enemy acting aggressively? The answer is yes, because his intention is to hurt the enemy. Is a parent whose anger leads him to want to wound his children with his words behaving aggressively? Yes, because his intention is to hurt his children.

Relying on the concept of intention does not solve all our definitional problems, however. For example, a person who tortures a terrorist is aggressive—the torturer intends to inflict pain—although in some ways the ultimate goal of saving many lives is a noble one. Clearly, aggression, as a label applied to specific acts, can sometimes reside in the eyes of the beholder.

Even the best of definitions doesn't explain the causes of aggression. Given the widespread existence of belligerence and combativeness, probably even in your own life (see Table 9–1), we need to consider how aggression comes to play such a prominent role in the social world.

AGGRESSION AS INSTINCT: INSTINCTUAL AND EVOLUTIONARY PERSPECTIVES

The fact that aggression is so common in both the human and animal worlds suggests that its roots can be found in the same primeval chemical stew that brought forth life itself. Emphasizing the "nature" side of the proverbial nature–nurture issue that provokes continuing debate within psychology, the notion that aggression is a universal inheritance has been proposed for centuries in the essays of philosophers and other observers of human nature. For instance, philosopher Thomas Hobbes, writing in the 1600s, called the human species *Homo lupus,* or "human wolf," due to his view that people were little more than savage animals, restrained only by a veneer of civilization.

Hobbes's view was mirrored by Sigmund Freud, who, when he surveyed the world in the second decade of the 1900s, found battlefields on which hundreds of thousands of soldiers had been killed. World War I had come and gone, and to Freud the war proved that people were instinctively prone to aggressive behavior.

Instinct approaches.   Freud's view, which grew out of his psychoanalytic theory, was that humans have a primitive instinct he called *thanatos,* or a death drive (Freud, 1920). Freud thought that the energy of thanatos drove people toward aggression and hostility, most often channeled toward others.

TABLE 9–1	Are You Aggressive?

To learn how your level of personal aggression stacks up against that of others, answer the following questions:

1. Once in a while I cannot control my urge to harm others. Yes ____ No ____
2. I can think of no good reason for ever hitting anyone. Yes ____ No ____
3. If somebody hits me first, I let him have it. Yes ____ No ____
4. Whoever insults me or my family is asking for it. Yes ____ No ____
5. People who continually pester you are asking for a punch in the nose. Yes ____ No ____
6. I seldom strike back, even if someone hits me first. Yes ____ No ____
7. When I really lose my temper, I am capable of slapping someone. Yes ____ No ____
8. I get into fights about as often as the next person. Yes ____ No ____
9. If I have to resort to physical violence to defend my rights, I will. Yes ____ No ____
10. I have known people who pushed me so far that we came to blows. Yes ____ No ____
11. When I disapprove of my friends' behavior, I let them know it. Yes ____ No ____
12. I often find myself disagreeing with people. Yes ____ No ____
13. I can't help getting into arguments when people disagree with me. Yes ____ No ____
14. I demand that people respect my rights. Yes ____ No ____
15. Even when my anger is aroused, I don't use strong language. Yes ____ No ____
16. If somebody annoys me, I am apt to tell him what I think of him. Yes ____ No ____
17. When people yell at me, I yell back. Yes ____ No ____
18. When I get mad, I say nasty things. Yes ____ No ____
19. I could not put someone in his place, even if he needed it. Yes ____ No ____
20. I often make threats I don't really mean to carry out. Yes ____ No ____
21. When arguing, I tend to raise my voice. Yes ____ No ____
22. I generally cover up my poor opinion of others. Yes ____ No ____
23. I would rather concede a point than get into an argument about it. Yes ____ No ____

To determine your score for physical aggression, give yourself one point for each of the following questions to which you responded with a "yes": 1, 3, 4, 5, 7, 8, 9, and 10. To find your score for verbal aggression, give yourself one point for each of the following questions to which you responded with a "yes": 11, 12, 13, 14, 16, 17, 18, 20, and 21. To compare yourself with others, look at how close you are to the average scores for men and women listed below:

Physical aggression: Men's average = 5.1, women's average = 3.3
Verbal aggression: Men's average = 7.2, women's average = 6.8

Keep in mind that these averages were determined several decades ago and might well be somewhat different if measured today. Still, your answers give you a chance to contemplate how aggressive you might be in a variety of situations.

Source: Buss & Durkee, 1957.

Freud's gloomy view of aggression was shared in important respects by a second major advocate of the aggression-as-instinct model, Konrad Lorenz. However, Lorenz approached the problem from a different orientation. As an ethologist, an expert on animal behavior, Lorenz argued that aggression is adaptive, in contrast to Freud's view of aggression as representative of basically destructive impulses.

Lorenz (1966, 1974) believed that animals—including humans—share a fighting instinct that serves a number of critical functions. For one, aggression allows animals to preserve their own territories, thereby ensuring a steady supply of food. Aggression also serves to weed out weaker animals, allowing only the strongest and most fit to live and reproduce. Aggression, then, provides long-term evolutionary benefits to the species.

Konrad Lorenz argued that people, as well as nonhumans, have an instinct to behave aggressively.

Although Lorenz's research focused on animals, he extended his theorizing to include human behavior. This extension created considerable controversy. He suggested that humans, unlike almost all other species, kill each other because of a breakdown in the primeval "fight-or-flight" reaction to danger. He noted that animals who have relatively little natural means of defending themselves (humans being a prime example) tend to flee at the sign of danger. Other species, which are better able to defend themselves, are more apt to fight it out when threatened.

At the same time, animals who usually flee at the sign of danger have few inhibitions regarding the use of aggression, because aggression against members of one's own species will be relatively ineffective. In humans, however, the pattern has gone awry. Because humans originally reacted to danger with flight, they are in the class of animals whose innate inhibitions against aggression are relatively weak. But because their superior brain power has permitted them to develop weapons of great destruction, humans have become a unique hybrid: animals uninhibited in their use of aggression within their own species, but with effective aggressive weapons.

Lorenz coupled his ideas about the readiness of humans to act aggressively with an even more controversial notion: Aggressive energy is built up continually within people until it is finally discharged in a process called **catharsis**. The longer the energy is bottled up, the greater will be the magnitude of aggression when it is finally discharged. Lorenz suggested that society, to protect itself, should encourage participation in acceptable forms of aggression, such as sports and games. These means would allow people to discharge their pent-up aggression.

Evolutionary perspectives on aggression.   The most recent advocates of instinctual explanations of aggression place their arguments within the context of evolutionary psychology, the field that considers the biological roots of behavior. As we discussed in Chapter 8, evolutionary approaches seek to identify how behavior might aid the goal of perpetuating the species as a whole. In the evolutionary view, the ultimate goal of aggression is not personal survival, but survival of one's genes to pass on to future generations (McKenna, 1983; Reiss, 1984; Buss & Shackelford, 1997).

The evolutionary point of view helps explain why aggression is not a consistent pattern of behavior; after all, no species can afford to act aggressively all the time. Instead, humans and other species take time for care of their young and for courtship, and they engage in organized, cooperative activities. To the evolutionary psychologist, then, a species must regulate aggressive behavior in order to achieve the ultimate goal of transmitting its genes to future generations.

catharsis: The process of discharging aggressive energy that is continually built up within people.

Although the theories of Freud, Lorenz, and the evolutionary approach make intuitive sense, most social psychologists feel that they are all incomplete. For one thing, they are based more on animal behavior than human behavior, and they ignore the higher cognitive abilities of human beings. Furthermore, instinct theories provide little specific guidance about when and how people will act aggressively, other than contending that aggression is an inevitable part of human behavior. The presence of cultural differences in aggression—which we'll discuss later in this chapter—makes the broad, universal claims of the evolutionary approach suspect (Ruback & Weiner, 1995).

The most glaring weakness of instinctual explanations of aggression, however, is the lack of experimental support. In some cases, such support is impossible to obtain (how, for instance, does one measure the energy produced by the hypothetical drive of thanatos?), and in other cases, the research evidence is clearly not supportive, as we will see later. Finally, instincts do not provide scientific explanations that are completely satisfying: "People aggress because they have an aggressive instinct, which we know because they act aggressively." Clearly, such a circular analysis of aggression does not take us very far in understanding *why* people behave aggressively.

Social psychologists, then, have largely focused on other approaches. Still, the notion that aggressive behavior is produced by instinctual and biological factors should not be dismissed entirely. For instance, increasing evidence suggests a link between hormones and aggression (Archer, 1994; Tremblay et al., 1997). In fact, some scientists suggest that specific genes may be associated with aggression (Morell, 1993; Maxson, 1998).

AGGRESSION AS A CONSEQUENCE OF LEARNING: THE NURTURE SIDE OF THE NATURE–NURTURE ISSUE

Nine-year-old Billy watches a cartoon in which G.I. Joe shoots at an enemy with his rifle and then whirls around and swings his gun at another enemy soldier who is about to sneak up on him from behind. The next day, Billy picks up a stick, pretends to shoot his younger sister, and then swings the stick at her.

Is there a connection between the two events? Your answer will be yes if you believe that aggression is largely a learned behavior. **Learning approaches to aggression** suggest that aggression is based on prior learning. To understand aggressive behavior, then, we should look at the rewards and punishments found in an individual's environment.

Learning approaches to aggression reflect an explanation of aggression first put forward by the 17th-century philosopher John Locke. He argued that we enter the world as a *tabula rasa,* or "blank slate." To Locke, people were taught aggressive behavior by the individuals and environment they encountered as they grew up. In this view learning and experience are at the heart of aggression. Furthermore—as we'll discuss later in the chapter—people can be taught to be less aggressive.

Social learning theory.   A modern-day representation of Locke's view is the **social learning theory**, which emphasizes how social and environmental conditions teach individuals to be aggressive (Fry, 1992; MacEwen, 1994; Muller, Hunter, & Stollak, 1995). The theory suggests that the primary mechanism for learning aggressive behavior is direct reinforcement and punishment. Children learn that they can play with the most desirable toys in preschool if they respond aggressively to classmates' requests for sharing. And hit men know that they get paid only if they successfully murder their victims.

But reinforcement for aggression also comes in indirect ways. Social psychologist Albert Bandura is one of the strongest advocates of social learning explanations of aggression. He suggests that a primary means of learning aggressive behavior is through observation of models (Bandura, 1973, 1983). **Models** are people whose behavior can be imitated and who provide a guide to appropriate behavior.

A long roster of experiments has demonstrated that exposure to an aggressive model leads observers to exhibit heightened aggression, especially if the observers are angered, insulted,

learning approaches to aggression: The theory suggesting that aggression is based on prior learning.

social learning theory: The theory that emphasizes how social and environmental conditions teach individuals to be aggressive.

models: People whose behavior can be imitated and who provide a guide to appropriate behavior.

or frustrated. For instance, Bandura demonstrated the power of models in a classic study of nursery-school-age children (Bandura, Ross, & Ross, 1963). One group of children watched an adult play violently and aggressively with a Bobo doll (a large, inflatable plastic dummy that always returns to an upright position after being pushed down). In contrast, children in another condition watched an adult play sedately with a set of Tinker Toys.

Later, the children were permitted to play with a number of toys, which included both the Bobo doll and Tinker Toys. But first the children were made to feel frustrated by being refused the opportunity to play with a favorite toy. As social learning theory would predict, the children modeled the behavior of the adult. Those who had seen the violent model playing with the Bobo doll were considerably more aggressive than those who had watched the placid model playing with Tinker Toys.

Subsequent research has shown that people are most likely to imitate aggression when models are seen to be rewarded for their aggressive behavior (Bandura, 1973). And even if people do not immediately exhibit the same aggressive behavior they just observed, they learn something about the permissibility of violence in society (Donnerstein & Donnerstein, 1978). Consequently, as we'll discuss in detail later in the chapter, media portrayals of violence, whether actual or fictionalized, can have a powerful impact on the subsequent behavior of viewers of aggression (Liebert, 1975; Wood, Wong, & Chachere, 1991; Molitor & Hirsch, 1994; Smith & Donnerstein, 1998).

The upside of the social learning approach to aggression is that observation of *non-aggressive* models can *reduce* aggression. We learn from others not only how to be aggressive, but also how to avoid confrontations. Similarly, we can directly teach nonviolence. Hence, just as social learning theories of aggression suggest that rewards and punishments are at the heart of aggressive behavior, they also suggest that these same factors are central to nonaggression.

Rejecting the nature–nurture dichotomy. Attributing the causes of aggression to either nature or nurture is tempting; but it is also wrong.

Just as it is overly simplistic to suggest that aggression stems solely from an instinct to behave aggressively, it is also unlikely that all aggressive behavior is learned. Instead, the truth lies somewhere in between. Inborn, genetic factors—nature—certainly may lead us toward an impulse to behave aggressively in certain situations. Whether we actually do so, though, depends in part on what we have learned about the appropriateness of aggressive displays within a given context—nurture. Further, society teaches us how to restrain our aggression. The degree to which we've learned such lessons factors into whether we'll act aggressively in a particular situation. In sum, nature and nurture interact to determine aggressive behavior.

REVIEW AND RETHINK

Review

- Aggression is a difficult concept to define in a universally acceptable way, but most social psychological definitions include the notion of intent.
- Instinctual and evolutionary approaches to aggression consider aggression to have innate components.
- Social learning approaches suggest that aggression is learned through the observation of models.

Rethink

- Consider a parent who strikes a child painfully. Describe circumstances in which this act would and would not be an example of aggression. Why would it be difficult to reach a consensus with your classmates on a definition of parental aggression?

- Why is the notion of intent important for definitions of aggression? What difficulties does the notion of intent pose for research psychologists?

- How might philosopher John Locke explain an observed relationship between hormones and aggression? How would Thomas Hobbes explain this relationship?

- Many theories of aggression are based in part on the behavior of animals other than humans. What dangers does this methodology carry? On the other hand, why is this type of research necessary?

- In what ways is the nature–nurture dichotomy in the study of aggression misleading? How might consideration of the nature–nurture issue still be useful in examining causes of aggressive behavior?

frustration–aggression hypothesis: The theory that frustration always leads to aggression of some sort, and that aggression is *always* the result of some form of frustration.

frustration: The thwarting or blocking of some ongoing behavior directed toward a desired goal.

SOCIAL DETERMINANTS OF AGGRESSION

You've stopped at a traffic light that seems interminable. The day is beastly hot, without a sign of a breeze at all, and the trip home, which is supposed to take 10 minutes, has turned into a 45-minute struggle in stop-and-go traffic. Finally the light turns green, and as you're about to proceed through the intersection, another car cuts you off. You slam on your brakes, and the car behind you nearly smashes into you. As you inch forward, the light turns red again, and you have to wait for the light all over again. You reach the breaking point, and start swearing. You turn on your radio so hard that the knob comes off. That's it: You take the knob and throw it out of the car window as hard as you can.

If you have ever been in this kind of situation, there is little need to explain what you feel: extreme frustration. And it is also not hard to guess how close to physical violence such frustration brings you.

We turn now to several explanations for aggression related to social factors in particular situations. These factors—such as frustration—lead directly to aggression, produce a greater likelihood that it will occur, or increase its strength.

THE FRUSTRATION–AGGRESSION LINK

According to one of the most influential and durable explanations for human aggression, frustration and aggression are closely linked. As initially formulated, the **frustration–aggression hypothesis** stated that frustration always leads to aggression of some sort, and that aggression is *always* the result of some form of frustration (Dollard et al., 1939). In this context, **frustration** refers to the thwarting or blocking of some ongoing behavior directed toward a desired goal.

The frustration–aggression hypothesis has largely stood the test of time, although—as you'd expect with a formulation more than 50 years old—it has undergone considerable

Frustration is the thwarting or blocking of some ongoing behavior directed toward a desired goal. Imagine how frustrated—and possibly aggressive—you might feel if you were stuck in a massive traffic jam.

aggressive cues: Learned stimuli that have previously been associated with aggression.

cognitive neoassociationistic model: Berkowitz's theory that aversive circumstances produce negative affect, in the form of anger, hostility, or irritation.

revision. Most importantly, we now know that the links between frustration and aggression are much weaker than originally proposed. Frustration does not inevitably produce aggression, and aggression is not invariably preceded by frustration (Berkowitz, 1989).

Aggressive cues and aggression.   What frustration does lead to is a readiness to act aggressively, due to the presence of anger that frustration produces. Whether an individual responds aggressively rests on the presence, or absence, of aggressive cues that trigger actual aggressive behavior. **Aggressive cues** are learned stimuli that have previously been associated with aggression (Berkowitz, 1984; Carlson, Marcus-Newhall, & Miller, 1990).

How might aggressive cues lead to aggression? One answer comes from a clever study in which participants met a confederate who in one condition deliberately angered them or in another condition acted neutrally toward them (Berkowitz & Geen, 1966). Participants then watched an excerpt from the movie *The Champion,* a violent boxing film starring Kirk Douglas. Following this interlude, the participants were led to believe that they could give varying numbers of shocks to the confederate, as part of a procedure designed to study learning processes.

The major experimental manipulation was the confederate's supposed name: In one condition, he was named "Bob," whereas in the other he was called "Kirk." These names were not chosen at random. Instead, the name Kirk was meant to act as an aggressive cue due to its association with Kirk Douglas, the boxer in the film. "Bob," on the other hand, was designed to be a neutral cue, unrelated to the aggression in the film.

If the modified frustration–aggression hypothesis were correct, we would first expect to see a difference in aggression displayed toward the confederate based on whether the confederate had first angered the participant, and this was the case. Participants who had been angered by the confederate gave him considerably more shocks than those who had not been angered.

But a second finding helped clarify that aggressive cues can be crucial in bringing about aggression: When the confederate was named Kirk, he acted as a lightning rod for aggression, receiving significantly more shocks than when he was named Bob. (Kirks of the world, beware.)

More vivid reminders of aggression than merely hearing a name associated with prior aggressive behavior may be significantly more potent aggressive cues. For instance, the mere sight of weapons may function as an aggressive cue (Berkowitz & LePage, 1967; daGloria et al., 1989; Bettencourt & Kernahan, 1997). Research supports the hypothesis that people become more aggressive after viewing a gun, even if the gun is simply sitting on a shelf, unused. Furthermore, studies have shown that even the anger produced by viewing a sports team losing an important game is enough to produce aggression. Homicides rise abruptly and disproportionately in cities whose professional football team has lost a playoff game. The apparent reason: The loss of the game produces frustration, which leads to a readiness to aggress. Because urban environments contain abundant aggressive cues, the readiness to aggress boils over into actual aggression of the most deadly variety (White, 1989).

Cognitive associations: The thoughts behind aggression.   The most recent reinterpretation of the frustration–aggression model suggests that frustration produces aggression only to the extent that it brings negative feelings, or affect. According to Leonard Berkowitz, it is not frustration *per se* that leads to aggression; instead, it is the negative affect that the frustration evokes (Berkowitz, 1990, 1993, 1998).

In his **cognitive neoassociationistic model**, Berkowitz argues that aversive circumstances produce negative affect in the form of anger, hostility, or irritation. These feelings then activate particular patterns of cognitions or memories related to prior experiences with aggression, as well as the physiological reactions associated with them.

What is the result of all this cognitive activity? The answer is that it depends on several conditions within the situation. If environmental cues are present that support aggressive action—such as the presence of weapons or of other people who are acting aggressively—

thoughts and memories conducive to aggression may be brought to mind, and aggression may result. In contrast, if environmental cues of a different nature are available—such as the presence of people who are acting peacefully—a network of thoughts may be aroused that is inconsistent with aggression. In such a case, the result can be a reduction in aggression.

THE SOCIAL ENVIRONMENT AND AGGRESSION

If you've ever seen the movie *Body Heat,* you know that a central theme of that evocative film is the murderous aggression that lies just beneath the surface of the suffocatingly hot Florida climate. Do high temperatures, in fact, lead to aggression? And do other factors in the environment, both physical and social, result in aggression? We'll consider several possibilities.

Physical arousal and aggression: Does sweat lead to swat?   What do exercise, sexual arousal, anger, and fear have in common? Under the right circumstances, each of them can lead to aggression, for the same reason: physical arousal. According to the **excitation transfer model**, physiological arousal acts to intensify subsequent emotional experiences, even if these experiences are unrelated to the initial arousal (see Figure 9–2). Thus, if people are angered or frustrated while they are in a state of physiological arousal, they are more apt to lash out with higher levels of aggression than if they are not in a state of arousal. However, their arousal will intensify aggression only to the extent that it is attributed to the angering or frustrating experience. If the arousal is attributed to an initial, neutral source, then aggression is unlikely (Zillman, Hoyt, & Day, 1974; Zillman, 1983, 1988, 1994).

Consider the consequences of exercise, for instance. After exercising, people experience a number of dramatic physiological changes: Their heartbeats rise, their respiration rates increase, and they sweat more. Although these physiological responses begin to calm once exercising is completed, they do not disappear immediately. Instead, a residue of arousal remains, which may last for many minutes before the body returns to its prearousal state.

It is during this period of mild arousal that people are susceptible to aggression. For instance, if a person frustrates or angers them and they attribute their arousal to that person, they will be predisposed to act aggressively. However, if they attribute the arousal to its true source—the earlier exercise—they will be unlikely to behave aggressively. Moreover, if they are not angered in the first place, the arousal will simply dissipate, and no aggression will occur (Zillman, Katcher, & Milavsky, 1972; Zillman, 1988).

For example, suppose you've just completed a rigorous exercise routine at the health club and are now dressing in the locker room. Someone clumsily knocks your clothes on the floor and into a puddle of water. Your heightened physiological arousal due to the exercise you have just undergone may well turn your anger into aggression, but only if you attribute the arousal to the clumsy person. If you are aware that your heightened arousal is due to exercising, you'll be less apt to act aggressively.

Provocation as a source of aggression: Hurt me, and I'll hurt you.   During an NBA basketball game, former Chicago Bulls star Dennis Rodman deliberately butted his head against a referee. Although the reason for Rodman's behavior remained something of a puzzle, we can guess the feelings of the ref at the receiving end of the aggression: an urge to strike back at Rodman. (The ref did retaliate, at least symbolically, by throwing Rodman out of the game.)

Indeed, physical aggression often begets a physical response. When people are in physical pain, they respond with aggression toward the source of the pain. Further, as social learning theory predicts, they tend to match their level of retaliatory aggression to the level of pain they have received (Taylor & Pisano, 1971; Jaffe & Yinon, 1979). The same kind of norm of reciprocity that we discussed earlier in reference to helping behavior may be operating here: People seem to feel that it is permissible to reciprocate aggression that is directed toward them (Dengerink & Covey, 1983).

excitation transfer model: The theory that states that physiological arousal acts to intensify subsequent emotional experiences, even if they are unrelated to the initial arousal.

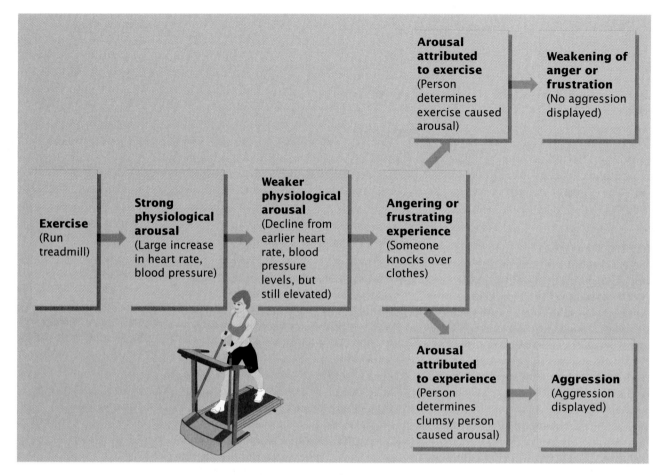

FIGURE 9–2   Excitation Transfer Model According to the excitation transfer model, physiological arousal acts to intensify subsequent emotional experiences. However, the extent to which the arousal will lead to aggression depends on what the arousal is attributed to. (*Source:* Based on Zillman, 1983.)

In some cases, people even carry out anticipatory aggression if they believe that someone is planning to be aggressive toward them at some future time (Greenwell & Dengerink, 1973; Donnerstein & Donnerstein, 1977). This makes it clear that aggression is not just an automatic, unthinking response to the provocation of others. Instead, a person may think through and carefully engineer his or her aggression in advance. Clearly, members of our society take seriously the Biblical dictum, "an eye for an eye, a tooth for a tooth"—even if the eye and the tooth have not yet been harmed.

Environmental stress: The heat of aggression.   The phrases "boiling mad," "hot under the collar," and "in the heat of anger" reflect the widely held belief that high temperatures are related to the display of aggression. Is this notion well founded? The answer is, only partially (Vrij, van der Steen, & Koppelaar, 1994).

According to social psychologist Robert Baron's **negative affect model of aggression**, high temperatures, as well as other aversive stimuli in the physical environment, can lead to higher aggression—but only to a point. When the weather gets too hot, people either

negative affect model of aggression: The theory that high temperatures, as well as other aversive stimuli in the physical environment, can lead to higher aggression—but only to a point.

become immobilized or flee to cooler surroundings, and aggression becomes too costly to pursue (Baron & Ransberger, 1978; Bell, 1992).

Although appealing as a theory, Baron's model has not been entirely supported by experimental research. For instance, one field study that investigated the incidence of aggressive crimes such as rape and murder over a 2-year period in Houston, Texas, found that the higher the temperature, the more crime occurred (Anderson & Anderson, 1984; Anderson, 1989). There was no hint of a decline in aggression when it became intolerably hot (and the Houston climate provides quite a few instances of extremely hot weather). Similarly, another field study showed that during major league baseball games the number of baseball players hit by pitches—an indication of aggression—increased as temperatures rose, with no sign of a decline in even the hottest weather (see Figure 9–3; Reifman, Larrick, & Fein, 1991).

Despite the mixed experimental support for Baron's negative affect model, it does seem reasonable that eventually the temperature will rise so high that aggression—or any other behavior involving physical activity—is unlikely. In sum, we have not heard the last word on the relationship between heat and aggression (Anderson & DeNeve, 1992; Bell, 1992; Anderson, Deuser, & DeNeve, 1995).

Other environmental factors have been implicated in aggression. Crowding produces higher levels of aggression in both humans and animals (Fisher, Bell, & Baum, 1984; Edwards, Fuller, Vorakitphokatorn, & Sermsri, 1994). Similarly, subtle changes in air quality, such as the level of negative ions in the air, can promote the display of aggressive behavior (Baron, Russell, & Arms, 1984). In fact, air pollution in general produces a rise in aggression (Rotton & Frey, 1985).

Although the evidence is clear that a relationship exists between air temperature and aggression, several alternative explanations have been proposed for this phenomenon. Consider, for instance, the finding that regions of the country with warmer climates have higher murder rates. Although the most obvious explanation is that the greater aggression is due to the greater heat, as the negative affect model of aggression suggests, at least one alternative explanation is drawing increasing attention. Specifically, some researchers suggest that the higher level of violence in some locations is due to cultural values, as we consider next (Rotton, 1993).

As temperatures rise so do incidents of baseball players at bat being hit by pitchers—an indication of aggression.

FIGURE 9–3   The Heat of Aggression As temperatures rose, so did aggression in the two contexts illustrated by these figures. In (**a**), the mean number of baseball players hit by a pitch (HBPs) increases as the temperature increases. In (**b**), the number of violent crimes is shown to increase as it becomes hotter. (*Sources:* (a) Reifman, Larrick, & Fein, 1991; (b) Anderson & Anderson, 1984.)

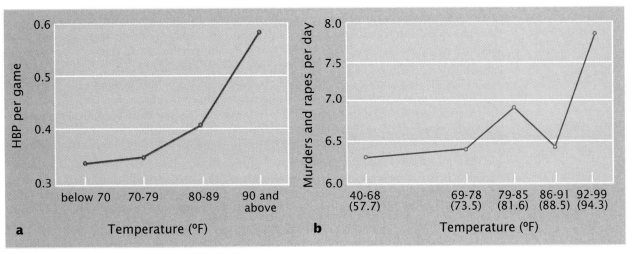

EXPLORING DIVERSITY

DOES A "CULTURE OF HONOR" LEAD TO AGGRESSION?

When Rhett Butler uttered his famous words, "Frankly, my dear, I don't give a damn" as he left an unloving Scarlett O'Hara in *Gone with the Wind,* was he actually articulating a philosophy that at times has characterized southern regions of the United States?

Although we cannot be sure, the words certainly are reflective of a philosophy that has come to be labeled the "culture of honor." According to social psychologists Richard Nisbett and Dov Cohen, the culture of honor, most prevalent in southern portions of the United States, reflects the view that a man's reputation is central to his economic survival. Nisbett and Cohen argue that in regions in which herding was the primary form of economic activity, males had to be strongly protective of their animals, because they were readily stolen. Because the stakes were high, the most successful men were those who were most willing to take high risks and to protect their herds—and their honor—the most vigorously (Cohen & Nisbett, 1994; Nisbett & Cohen, 1996).

In short, successful males (the argument says nothing about females) were the ones who were most apt to support the notion of "honor." And even though the economy changed, and herding became less important, cultural norms continued to support the culture-of-honor philosophy. In fact, the cultural norms are so strong, Nisbett and Cohen argue, that they may account for persistent differences in violence between the present-day North and South. Specifically, white male homicide rates in the South (and areas of the western United States initially settled by southerners) are significantly higher than those of the North. However, the numbers are higher in the South only for killings related to arguments or conflicts. When other types of homicides are considered, such as those related to robbery or burglary, there is no difference in rates between different geographical regions. Furthermore, although southerners show no generally higher approval of violence than northerners, they are more likely to support the use of violence for protection and as a response to insults (Nisbett, 1993; Cohen et al., 1996; Cohen & Nisbett, 1997).

Clearly, the culture-of-honor argument is built on a number of assumptions, and critics have pointed out several alternative explanations for the higher homicide rate in the South. For one thing, the legacy of slavery may produce a greater readiness to act aggressively. Similarly, other social factors that differentiate northern and southern regions of the country—such as population density, wealth disparities, or other socioeconomic factors—might result in differences in aggression. Most obviously, the hotter climate of the South might be expected to produce greater levels of aggression, regardless of cultural norms (Anderson & Anderson, 1996).

Some critics also object to the basic underlying suppositions of the theory, which rely largely on evolutionary considerations. As is the case with other evolutionary approaches, it is difficult, if not impossible, to devise a research-based test that can unequivocally confirm or refute the theory. Furthermore, the prevalence of the "culture of honor" among southern men is far from clear. Certainly, not all men in the South—and perhaps not even most men in the South—are likely to adhere to such cultural norms; and certainly some men in other areas of the United States may support culture-of-honor norms.

Nevertheless, researchers have demonstrated that the culture of honor may in fact be somewhat more prevalent among southern males than northern males, even if the culture has not been linked directly to violence. For example, in one series of studies, participants were insulted by a confederate, who bumped into them and called them an offensive name. In comparison to northern male participants, southern male participants became more physiologically aroused and were more primed for aggression, as evidenced by the fact that their testosterone levels increased (see Figure 9–4). In addition, they were more likely to engage in actual aggression, and they tried to exhibit greater dominance (Cohen et al., 1996).

The fact that southerners behave in ways more in keeping with the culture-of-honor hypothesis hardly proves that cultural norms underlie the higher rates of violence found in southern portions of the United States. But it does at least support the notion that cultural norms may underlie differences in aggressive behavior found in various regions of the United

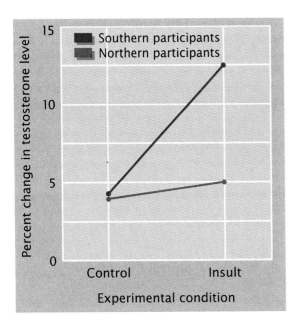

FIGURE 9–4   Aggression in Northern Males Versus Southern Males In an experiment in which male participants were called an insulting name, southern participants showed a greater rise in testosterone than northern participants. In contrast, there was no difference in northern and southern participants in a control condition, in which there was no insult. (*Source:* Cohen et al., 1996, p. 952.)

States. And, as we'll consider later in the chapter, it suggests an explanation for the higher rates of aggression found in the United States as a whole compared with rates in other developed countries.

MEDIA AGGRESSION: VISIONS OF VIOLENCE

At 8:00 P.M. on a typical Tuesday in a typical U.S. city, a person who wants to watch a movie on TV can choose from the following selection:

8 P.M. (WFXT) *Bad Boys.* A scar-faced street fighter becomes king of reform school and spots the guy who assaulted his girlfriend.

8 P.M. (WHLL) *The Contender.* A small-town Oregonian quits college to become a boxer.

8 P.M. (WNDS) *Sword of Gideon.* Five commandos avenge the massacre of Israeli athletes by terrorists at the 1972 Munich Olympics.

8 P.M. (WGOT) *Charley Hannah.* A Florida policeman befriends a wayward runaway boy while tracking down a band of killer teens. (*TV Week,* 1992)

This sampling offers a telling commentary about the state of the airwaves in the United States. It is hard for people to insulate themselves from aggression, whether real or fictitious. As we'll discuss, whether aggression is viewed through the lens of the media or is observed in real-life situations (as in cases of family violence), exposure to aggression has a profound impact on people's lives, as social learning theory suggests.

By the time the average child in the United States finishes elementary school, he or she will have viewed more than 8,000 murders and over 100,000 additional acts of violence. Almost two-thirds of prime-time fictional dramas involve violence. Even Saturday morning cartoon shows, designed specifically for children, contain lengthy sequences of aggression (Huston et al., 1992; Fabrikant, 1996).

In fact, one study of children's television found that children's programs contained an average of 32 violent acts per hour, and 74% of the characters on these programs were victims of violence (see Figure 9–5). Although there is some indication that the amount of violence on television has declined from earlier levels, the absolute level remains extraordinarily high (Gerbner, Morgan, & Signorelli, 1993; Waters, 1993; Oliver, 1994).

What are the consequences of viewing such heavy doses of violence? The answer is not simple because of several complicating factors. For one thing, it is nearly impossible to design an experiment that would accurately determine the consequences of watching the massive amounts of media aggression to which children are exposed. Ideally, an experimenter would seek to compare children who are placed in a condition in which they watch large amounts of violence over a long period with children in a control condition who are led to watch media violence in smaller doses. Obviously, though, such an experiment is both impractical and unethical, particularly if the hypothesis underlying the research is that exposure to media violence yields aggression.

Given the difficulties involved in conducting an actual experiment, investigators have turned to correlational studies, in which they assess and compare both television viewing and aggressive behavior. Such studies are able to determine whether a relationship exists between viewing violent shows and subsequent aggression. However, like all correlational research, these studies cannot show that media violence *causes* aggression. Alternative explanations are equally plausible; for example, that both a person's interest in aggressive media and the person's subsequent aggressive behavior are caused by some other factor, such as educational level or socioeconomic status. Furthermore, the relationship between viewing media depictions of violence and performing acts of aggression may be circular, with observation of violence affecting subsequent aggression, and aggressive individuals increasingly choosing to watch aggressive television shows and movies (Huesmann, Lagerspetz, & Eron, 1984; Bushman, 1995; also see the accompanying Speaking of Social Psychology interview).

SPEAKING OF SOCIAL PSYCHOLOGY

John P. Murray

Media Researcher

Year of Birth:	1943
Education:	B.A. Psychology, John Carroll University, Cleveland, Ohio; M.A., Ph.D., Psychology, Catholic University of America, Washington, DC
Home:	Manhattan, Kansas

"Exposure to violence makes people more aggressive, and they develop more of a propensity to be violent. "

John Murray's interest in aggression and televised violence took shape during his years as a graduate student when he was looking at imitation and preschool children.

"I was studying how children's cognitive development was influenced by their social environment, and the question of whether violence on television influenced viewers' aggression was a burgeoning issue," he said. "The U.S. Surgeon General began a study of television violence and children, and I joined in on the research and spent the next several decades studying the issue."

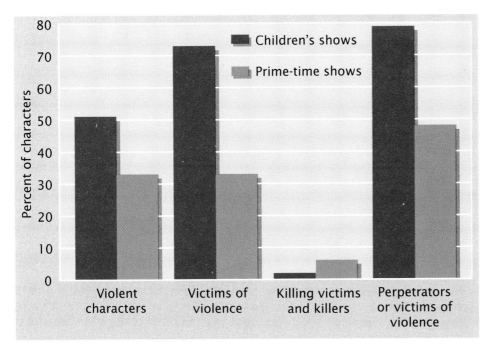

FIGURE 9–5   Violence on Television In television programs targeted for both children and adults, violence occurs at high levels. (*Source:* Gerbner, 1996.)

Murray is currently exploring how the human brain reacts to exposure to televised violence. His work suggests that such exposure results in several consequences.

"First, exposure to violence makes people more aggressive, and they develop more of a propensity to be violent. The second effect is that people become less sensitive to violence; it makes less of an impact on them. The third consequence of exposure to aggression, which is demonstrated primarily in adults, is that heavy viewers of television begin to believe that they themselves will become victims of violence. These individuals become more suspicious of the world and are more likely to take defensive action."

"In fact, video games are probably more worrisome," said Murray, "because they are the vehicle by which you teach desensitization."

Furthermore, observation of aggression stimulates the amygdala, which is part of the brain's limbic system. "The amygdala has a connection to the prefrontal cortex, an area that is directly involved in the control of emotion," Murray added. "This process affects long-term memory storage, and it tags perceptions in memory and makes them easier to recall. Consequently, we remember things that are shocking, and that may make the use of violence more likely."

While previously the greatest emphasis has been on the impact of aggression viewed on television, more recently video games have come under scrutiny. "In fact, video games are probably more worrisome," said Murray, "because they are the vehicle by which you teach desensitization. With a video game in which you are rewarded for brutalizing others, you are invited to take action, whereas with television you are invited to view."

Despite their inability to demonstrate unequivocally that viewing media depictions of aggression produces subsequent aggressive behavior, correlational studies clearly establish a significant link between observation of violence and later aggression (Paik & Comstock, 1994; Lazar, 1994). For example, one long-term project (dubbed the "Rip Van Winkle" study) extended for more than 2 decades. The study found that children who had watched more televised violence in their grade school years showed relatively higher levels of aggression in adulthood than children who had been exposed to lower levels of televised aggression (Eron et al., 1972; Eron & Huesmann, 1984; Huesmann et al., 1996).

However, the findings were far from universal. For some adults, aggression was unrelated to their early viewing patterns; and the findings were more accurate in predicting for males than for females. In addition, other researchers have found contradictory results, suggesting to some social psychologists that exposure to aggression is unrelated to later aggression (Freedman, 1996). Overall, however, the correlational work, coupled with the experimental research on social learning of aggression conducted in laboratory settings, leads to the logical—but still controversial—conclusion that a causal relationship exists between exposure to media violence and later aggression (Eron, Gentry, & Schlegel, 1994; Huesmann & Moise, 1996; Bushman, 1998).

Because of the difficulty of establishing causal relationships from correlational studies, researchers have begun to turn their experimental spotlights toward more focused questions. Rather than asking whether viewing violence leads to aggression, they have been attempting to discover the circumstances under which media violence is translated into actual aggression and the specific causes that might produce a link between the observation of aggression and the enactment of aggression.

Why does observation of aggression produce aggression?   What has become increasingly clear is that aggression following media exposure is not just a matter of simple imitation of aggressive acts or social learning. Rather, several mechanisms may be involved. For example, a *normative approach to media aggression* suggests that viewing media depictions of aggression can lead people to assume that aggression is a socially acceptable behavior. In some cases, observing aggression may actually teach people how to be aggressive in a particular manner. In one dismaying case, for instance, a group of men raped a young girl with a soda bottle, apparently in imitation of a similar incident in a television movie that had aired a few days earlier. It seems unlikely that the perpetrators would have attempted such an unusual and specific act without having seen the movie (Phillips, 1982; Gunter, 1988).

The normative approach suggests that people learn "scripts" for aggressive behavior. After a script has been learned—presumably through exposure to media violence—it may be recalled in some future situation, providing a guide for behavior. Individuals, then, may come to see aggression as a legitimate response within the context of a particular situation (Huesmann, 1986).

Why are aggressive scripts triggered in particular situations? Leonard Berkowitz's cognitive neoassociationistic model, discussed earlier, suggests an explanation. You will recall that this model proposes that aggressive stimuli may prime, or bring to mind, other thoughts and emotions that are linked to aggression. In turn, these aggressive cognitive and emotional reactions to observed violence may ultimately lead to increased aggression on the part of the viewer (Bushman & Geen, 1990; Berkowitz, 1993; Bushman, 1998).

One example of this is the finding that even socially sanctioned violence—in this case, observation of prize fights—may lead to increased aggression of other sorts. Specifically, one analysis of national homicide statistics found that during the period immediately following nationally televised championship prize fights, the homicide rate rose slightly. (Nationally, about 12 more homicides occurred following each bout.) Although several explanations are possible, the results are consistent with the suggestion that observation of the fight led to thoughts and emotions related to violence, making viewers more prone to subsequent aggression (Phillips, 1986). Similarly, as we consider in the Applying Social Psychology box, observation of unnecessary violence produces increases in subsequent aggressive behavior on the part of viewers.

APPLYING SOCIAL PSYCHOLOGY
GETTING BACK: VIEWING NEEDLESS VIOLENCE LEADS TO HOSTILITY AND RETALIATION

By the time the average American has reached the age of 18, he or she has watched some 200,000 violent acts on television. Even worse, much of the violence is needless and unnecessary to the plot line of the show.

Does the observation of such violence lead to future violence? According to a recent study by social psychologists Dolf Zillmann and James Weaver (1999), the answer is yes.

In their study, undergraduates watched a feature film each day for four consecutive days, supposedly to provide ratings of the entertainment value of the films. Half saw films that contained needless violence (for example, *Death Warrant*). The other participants in the study watched nonviolent films. On the fifth day, all participants returned, supposedly to participate in an entirely different study on emotion recognition. During the course of the study, a research assistant either behaved abusively or neutrally toward the participants. Later, they were given the (supposed) opportunity to harm the research assistant.

The participants were more apt to try to harm the research assistant who had been abusive to them. Even more important, exposure to the needless violence produced significantly greater efforts to harm the research assistant, regardless of whether the research assistant had behaved abusively or neutrally. Furthermore, the results held for both men and women: Regardless of gender, even unprovoked people who watched films containing needless violence were much more likely to exhibit hostile behavior.

Weaver and Zillman concluded that prolonged exposure to needless violence in the media can indeed change people's behavior for the worse. Perhaps even more worrisome than the effect on young adults is the impact such films could have on children, who are less able to distinguish between fact and fantasy.

In addition to fostering societal norms about displays of aggression, observation of aggression may also produce another result: an inaccurate view of the world and a consequent rise in concern about one's personal safety. For instance, the high incidence of violence on television and in the movies may convince people that their environment is more violent than it actually is. Indeed, children who watch higher-than-average levels of television tend to overestimate the number of violent crimes that actually occur (Morgan, 1983; Gerbner, 1996).

Another explanation for the effects of observing media violence is attributional. The *attributional approach* to media aggression suggests that the conditions to which people attribute the aggression they observe have a significant effect on their subsequent aggression. If people believe that a particular instance of observed aggression is justified, they are more likely to act aggressively than if they assume the aggressive act is unjustified or random (Berkowitz & Powers, 1979). For instance, in one experiment, participants were shown actual news footage of a North Vietnamese soldier being stabbed to death by South Vietnamese soldiers (Meyer, 1972). Researchers varied the context of the killing: Some participants were told that the killing represented retaliation for the victim's earlier atrocities against innocent civilians, whereas others were told that it was a cold-blooded killing of a prisoner of war. Participants were subsequently given the opportunity to behave aggressively. Those who thought the aggression represented legitimate retaliation were more aggressive than those who viewed it as unjustified.

Another explanation for the consequences of media aggression relies on the phenomenon of disinhibition. According to the *disinhibition hypothesis,* exposure to media violence reduces people's normal inhibitions against behaving aggressively (Drabman & Thomas, 1974). For instance, having previously viewed a film in which a mother slaps her child, a mother may feel less inhibited to acting out her own aggressive impulses when her child has frustrated and angered her. If she had not viewed the film, the typical societal restraints that work to inhibit the enactment of violence may have been sufficiently strong to prevent her aggressive behavior.

Disinhibition is eased by the apparent lack of consequences that often are the outcome of media aggression. Most violent acts shown on television portray no painful consequences, and in almost half, the harm befalling victims is not illustrated. And most acts of violence go unpunished (Seppa, 1996; Kunkel et al., 1995).

Finally, frequent exposure to media violence can produce *desensitization,* a reduction in the negative reaction to aggressive stimuli. After people consume a steady diet of brutality, the kind of stimuli that earlier might have repelled or disgusted them (and thereby diminished the likelihood of their acting aggressively) may eventually come to produce little or no reaction (Mullin & Linz, 1995; Smith & Donnerstein, 1998; Wilson & Smith, 1998).

One classic experiment confirmed the process of desensitization: Viewers of a series of graphic puberty rites carried out in a different culture showed a marked decrease in stress by the time they viewed the fourth cut in a young boy's genitals (Lazarus & Abramovitz, 1962). In the same way, soldiers often become accustomed to the death and injury they encounter during the heat of battle; the violence eventually produces little reaction. As people become less sensitive to the meaning and consequences of aggression, they may feel more free to act aggressively themselves.

In sum, several explanations support the conclusion that observation of media violence is linked to subsequent aggression (Kunkel et al., 1995; summarized in Table 9–2). However, regardless of the reason—and it is likely that multiple causes are at work—a steady diet of observed aggression clearly has potentially severe consequences.

SEX AND AGGRESSION:
THE CONSEQUENCES OF VIEWING VIOLENT PORNOGRAPHY

Each week, people purchase approximately two million tickets to X- or XXX-rated videos. Moreover, movies are just one source of pornographic images: Sexually explicit magazines, books, and images are widely distributed throughout the world and are easily accessible over the World Wide Web.

The omnipresence of media depictions of sexual activity in our society raises several important issues. What are the results of exposure to pornographic material? Can viewing pornography result in aggression? Does the specific content of sexually explicit material lead to particular kinds of outcomes?

To judge the issue ourselves, consider the research. Recall, as we discussed earlier, that viewing some types of sexually arousing material has been linked to increases in aggression

TABLE 9–2	**Explanations for the Links Between Observation of Media Violence and Subsequent Aggression**

Social Learning

Aggressive behavior is imitated because of rewards the model receives.

Normative Approach

Viewing media depictions of aggression leads to the assumption that violence is socially acceptable.

Attributional Approach

The attributions regarding the reasons behind observed aggression are crucial. If aggression is seen as justified, it is more likely to be modeled.

Disinhibition

Exposure to media violence reduces people's normal inhibitions against behaving aggressively.

Desensitization

Observing aggression diminishes the negative reaction to aggressive stimuli.

The negative consequences of viewing sexual violence may be greater from viewing R-rated films than X-rated movies, given that R-rated films contain higher levels of violence toward women.

(Allen, D'Alessio, & Brezgel, 1995). The excitation transfer model suggests that heightened physiological arousal can lead to higher levels of aggression. Because pornography can lead to physiological arousal, sexually explicit pornographic materials can induce heightened aggression, depending on the level of arousal that the material produces (Zillman, 1984).

However, it turns out that a more critical factor in determining whether pornography produces aggression is whether the pornography links sex with violence. The evidence clearly suggests that pornographic depictions of violence against women lead to increased aggression (Boeringer, 1994; Allen, D'Alessio, & Brezgel, 1995; Donnerstein & Linz, 1998; Malamuth, 1998).

Other research shows that long-term exposure to violent and sexually degrading depictions of women leads to emotional and physiological desensitization. For instance, people who were shown a series of R-rated violent "slasher" movies later showed less anxiety and depression when exposed to depictions of violence against women, and demonstrated less sympathy toward victims of rape, than people who saw a series of nonviolent films (Linz, Donnerstein, & Adams, 1989; Donnerstein & Malamuth, 1997).

Similarly, viewing films containing sexual violence against women leads to inaccurate attitudes and beliefs about rape. For instance, men exposed to violent pornography are more apt to subscribe to the dangerous (and completely misguided) myth that women enjoy being the victims of violent sexual assault (Malamuth & Check, 1985; Allen et al., 1995).

The data are clear in suggesting, then, that observing pornography that includes violent content can increase the likelihood of actual aggression on the part of viewers. Furthermore, exposure to such material produces beliefs and attitudes that support the concept that sexual violence against women is permissible.

Do the links between pornography and aggression argue in favor of banning erotic material? The answer is complex, because it involves constitutional rights of free speech. One obstacle to finding a reasonable answer is the difficulty of defining what constitutes pornography and obscenity, a problem that has confounded lawmakers and courts for decades. Another complication is the issue of who will be the judge of the vast array of sexually explicit material that is produced each year.

REVIEW AND RETHINK

Review

- The frustration–aggression hypothesis suggests that frustration leads to a readiness to act aggressively, especially in the presence of aggressive cues.

- According to the cognitive neoassociationistic view, negative affect can result in aggression by activating cognitive patterns related to prior experiences with aggression.
- The excitation transfer model argues that aggression may be heightened by physical arousal.
- A substantial link exists between observation of violence in the media and later aggression.
- Explanations for media effects on aggression include social learning, normative, attribution, disinhibition, and desensitization approaches.

Rethink

- Describe the relationship between anger and aggression, and between frustration and anger.
- Explain the frustration–aggression hypothesis as originally developed some 50 years ago. Compare this hypothesis with the cognitive neoassociationistic theory.
- What is the relationship between viewing televised violence and behaving aggressively? How can this relationship be explained?
- Why aren't social psychologists more certain about the long-term consequences of watching television and movie violence? What methodological difficulties do they face? What political difficulties do they face?
- Briefly describe the attributional, normative, and desensitization approaches to understanding the effects of being exposed to media portrayals of violence. Are any of these views mutually exclusive?
- Why might R-rated movies be potentially more hazardous than X-rated movies? Do you think our society is prepared to condemn R-rated movies as readily as X-rated movies? Why or why not?

REDUCING AGGRESSION

It had not been an easy day for high school student Darryl Johnson. He had done poorly on his history midterm—much worse than he expected—and the girl he liked told him she would rather go shopping this weekend than attend the football game with him. To top it off, Johnson's boss at his part-time job had given him a harsh dressing-down the day before, telling him if he was late one more time, he'd be out of a job.

Consequently, when Jack Bobbin bumped into him in the hall—it was not clear whether it was on purpose or a mistake—Darryl was primed to retaliate. Unthinkingly, he turned on Jack and punched him in the stomach. As Jack fell to the ground in pain, a teacher grabbed Darryl by the shoulder and took him to the principal, who promptly called his parents. "This isn't the first time Darryl's hit another student," the principal said. "Somehow, we've got to get his aggression under control."

Similar scenes take place every day in schools throughout the United States. Dealing with aggression effectively is one of the major challenges facing not only educational institutions but society at large.

CATHARSIS AND PUNISHMENT

Although no single means of controlling aggression has proved invariably effective, the various explanations of aggression that we discussed earlier in this chapter suggest some solutions to Darryl's aggression. Consider, for instance, an approach based on the notion of catharsis. As we noted in our discussion of Freud and Lorenz, the notion of catharsis proposes that people experience a continual buildup of aggressive energy. If this pent-up energy is not discharged through some socially acceptable means—such as physical exercise—it can manifest itself in episodes of aggression (Baron, 1983).

In theory, catharsis can occur in several ways. Some theorists, taking a psychoanalytic approach, suggest that hitting others with foam-covered bats, which actually produce no pain or injury to the victim, may have therapeutic results. The assumption (largely unproved) underlying this therapy is that, following such a session, the tendency toward actual aggression will be reduced (Bach & Wyden, 1968; Feshbach, 1984; Tachibana, Ohgishi, & Monden, 1984).

Following the catharsis approach, we might suggest that Darryl participate in some sports activity that involves a good deal of violence, such as football or hockey. Additionally, we might recommend that Darryl be encouraged to watch violent films, which potentially could release his pent-up aggression in a more acceptable manner.

The idea of catharsis is appealing, because it suggests that permitting people to "let off steam" can reduce their subsequent violence. Despite its appeal, though, results of experiments investigating catharsis do little to buttress the claims of theorists (Warren & Kurlychek, 1981; Griffiths, 1997; Bushman, Baumeister, & Stack, 1999). For example, studies have shown that high school football players are *more* aggressive after the football season than before it. Similarly, observation of sporting events is no guarantee of reduced aggression: One study of Canadian and American spectators of hockey, football, and wrestling matches found that people showed more hostility after viewing a contest than before it (Arms, Russell, & Sandiland, 1979; Russell, 1983, 1985; Coons, Howard-Hamilton, & Waryold, 1995). In sum, little evidence exists to support the catharsis notion.

Of course, social psychologists have identified other tactics that may be employed to control aggression. Consider, for example, the use of punishment. Punishment is actually one of society's favorite means for controlling aggression: Convictions for assaults, muggings, and rape lead to long prison terms, and in most parts of the world murder is punishable by death. On a lesser scale, it was not long ago that corporal (physical) punishment was common in U.S. schools, and it is still legal in some jurisdictions. Spanking by parents remains an established, and largely socially acceptable, child-rearing practice (Graziano et al., 1992; Holden, Coleman, & Schmidt, 1995; Holden & Miller, 1999).

Although punishment is widely used as a deterrent to aggression, its long-term effectiveness is highly questionable (Mathis & Lampe, 1991; Strassberg et al., 1994; Deater-Deckard & Dodge, 1997). For one thing, physical punishments are likely to arouse anger in the recipient, and such anger is often itself a cause of aggression. In addition, the people who mete out the punishment might be perceived as aggressive models themselves and thereby could increase the likelihood that witnesses will behave aggressively in the future.

Furthermore, those who administer punishment may regard it as having positive results because it usually leads to at least a temporary cessation of the aggression being punished. Consequently, people administering punishment may become more likely to act aggressively themselves in the future—in effect punishing without true need, and thereby escalating the climate of violence. Finally, the consequences of punishment are typically transitory. Although punishment may temporarily reduce future violence, the decrease usually does not last (Sulzer-Azaroff & Mayer, 1991; Sanson et al., 1996).

SOCIAL LEARNING APPROACHES TO CONTROLLING AGGRESSION

If viewing aggressive models can lead observers to act aggressively, can observing nonaggressive models reduce aggression? A host of laboratory studies have in fact demonstrated that when people have seen a model act nonaggressively, they are subsequently less aggressive than if they have seen a model act aggressively (Baron & Kepner, 1970; Donnerstein & Donnerstein, 1977).

Although these findings sound very promising, the unfortunate reality is that the number of nonaggressive models is often minimal in situations in which aggression is likely. Furthermore, the actions of aggressive models are considerably more conspicuous than the nonactions of passive, nonviolent models. Because their behavior is relatively restrained and subdued, people who are behaving in nonaggressive ways are less likely to be prominent and to attract attention. Thus, the likelihood is greater that the focus of attention will be on the aggressive models (Gunter & Furnham, 1986).

In spite of the obstacles that prevent nonaggressive models from producing much social learning themselves, this theoretical approach has spawned several powerful byproducts with a potential for reducing the impact of aggression (Hoberman, 1990). One of the most promising has been a program developed by social psychologists Rowell Huesmann and Leon Eron (Huesmann et al., 1983). Their basic strategy for reducing the influence of aggressive models is to modify how observers perceive and interpret aggressive acts.

Their procedure is straightforward and ingenious. Rather than being concerned with whether a model is behaving aggressively or nonaggressively, they teach observers that media violence represents an unrealistic portrayal of life. They also teach that aggressive behaviors do not have the same degree of acceptability in the real world that they have on television and in movies. Finally, they inform viewers that modeling the aggressive behavior demonstrated by television and film characters is not an appropriate response to grievances. In sum, the clear, unmistakable message is that violence is an unsatisfactory way of behaving.

Is this message actually conveyed? According to results of several studies, observers of media violence who have been trained in this procedure do, in fact, come to modify their attitudes regarding aggression. For example, one experiment studied a group of first- and third-grade children who reported viewing high amounts of televised aggression (Huesmann et al., 1983). In the initial phase of the study, the children attended three training sessions designed to teach that the behavior of the characters on violent shows does not represent the behavior of most people, that camera techniques and special effects provide only the illusion that aggression is occurring, and that most people use alternatives to aggression to solve their problems.

SOCIAL.WEB
DOES PLAYING VIOLENT COMPUTER GAMES LEAD TO ACTUAL VIOLENCE?

Fresh corpses litter the ground. Blood is everywhere. Victims moan and beg for mercy. Others scream for help. (Gahr, 1999, p. W13)

Although this may sound like a scene from a mass murder, in fact it's just part of the game Postal. In the game, sharpshooters, playing the role of Postal Dude, run amok, shooting at everyone in their path. Some victims catch fire, and all eventually are mowed down and fall to the ground.

Postal Dude is hardly the only game of its sort. Doom, a favorite of one of the Littleton, Colorado, killers discussed in the beginning of this chapter, features aliens whose guts splatter on the walls and floors when they're killed. Players get their choice of handguns, rifles, rocket launchers, or chainsaws.

Do such graphic, participatory renderings of aggression spill over into the real world? The answer is that no one knows for sure. Like the research on the consequences of viewing media violence, there is no definitive way to tie the playing of violent video games to subsequent real-world aggression. Although some evidence from laboratory studies shows that levels of

aggression are higher for those who have played an aggressive video game, compared with those who played a video game

Although no solid evidence demonstrates that playing violent video games causes actual aggression, such games do contribute to honing the skills used with actual weapons.

Nine months later, the children attended an additional training session. In this part of the study, they were explicitly taught that watching television violence was undesirable. The experimenters emphasized the importance of avoiding imitation of the aggression.

The experimental program was a great success. Compared with a control group of children who received training on issues unrelated to aggression, those participants taught to reinterpret the meaning of aggression were rated by their classmates as showing significantly lower aggression. In addition, participants' attitudes regarding televised aggression became decidedly more negative.

In sum, altering people's interpretation of the meaning of observed aggression, and their attitudes toward it, is an effective way to offset the consequences of exposure to violence (Sinclair, Lee, & Johnson, 1995; Huesmann, 1998). Still, social learning theory suggests an even more direct way to reduce aggression: limiting exposure to aggressive models. If television and other media were to reduce the violent content of programming, it seems reasonable that aggression on the part of viewers could be reduced.

Similarly, some observers believe that reducing opportunities to model aggression in computer video games might also reduce aggression in observers. Are they right? For a discussion, see the Social Web box.

COMPETITION AND AGGRESSION: A UNIQUELY AMERICAN WAY OF LIFE?

No one can deny the high level of aggression and violence in U.S. society. Tales of murder, rape, mugging, and other violent crimes fill our daily papers. And it is no mere misperception that violence is "as American as apple pie," as one observer put it (Berkowitz, 1993). The

with little violence, it is not clear that playing games over longer periods translates into aggression outside the laboratory (Cooper & Mackie, 1986; Cohn, 1996; Griffiths, 1997).

Still, the same theoretical reasons that suggest a relationship exists between viewing media violence and actual violence also suggest that an association between violent video games and subsequent aggression would also exist. In fact, video games teach something that the mere observation of violence does not do: the motor skills involved in aggression. By practicing firing weapons at people and objects appearing on the screen, game players presumably hone the skills that would make them more effective in using actual weapons. Furthermore, game players are likely to become desensitized to violence, potentially leading to a smaller reaction in the face of actual violence.

Still, despite the theoretical reasons suggesting that violent video games and actual aggression are linked, no solid research evidence exists. Furthermore, cross-cultural findings do not support a link between observation of violent video games and aggression. For example, use of violent video games by

children and adolescents in Japan is as widespread as in the United States, and yet the rate of violence in Japan is far lower than in the United States. In fact, the number of deaths from guns is almost 700 times greater in the United States than in Japan. On the other hand, Japan is not free of violence: The crime rate among juveniles in Japan is growing, and student violence against teachers doubled between 1993 and 1998 (Zielenziger, 1998).

Clearly, there is no definitive answer to whether the use of violent computer video games leads to actual aggression. This hasn't stopped the question from becoming a political issue. For instance, after legislators held hearings on games in 1993, the software industry adopted a voluntary rating system that alerts purchasers to the degree of violence in a game. More recently, the Minnesota legislature considered a ban on the purchase of violent video games by those under 18. Without solid scientific evidence, it is hard to know whether such bans would make a difference.

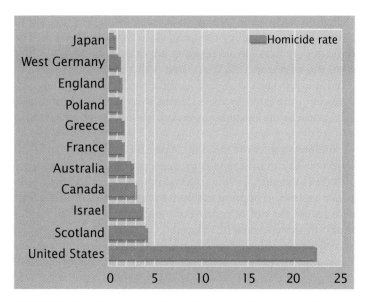

FIGURE 9–6 Comparative Homicide Rates This chart, which illustrates the number of killings per 100,000 men between the ages of 15 and 24 years old, shows that the homicide rate in the United States is much higher than in other industrial nations. (*Source:* Fingerhut & Kleinman, 1990.)

facts support such a contention. For example, the number of murders of men 15 to 24 years of age is higher in the United States than in any other developed country (see Figure 9–6).

Other indicators of aggression suggest that the amounts and kinds of aggression displayed across various cultures are substantially different. Before considering such data, however, keep in mind that it is quite difficult to study aggression in different cultural contexts, and even more difficult to make valid cross-cultural comparisons.

To understand why this is true, recall the difficulty we had in initially coming up with a precise definition of *aggression* in Western cultures. As we discussed earlier, most researchers believe that aggression must involve intentional injury or harm to another individual. But how do we assess intention in a culture very different from our own? For instance, painful rites of passage or initiation ceremonies are found in some cultures. Should practices that inflict pain as part of such ceremonies be considered aggression? Furthermore, even more basically, how do we adequately assess the concept of "harm"? For example, children in a schoolyard may be observed shoving and hitting one another. But is such behavior aggressive? It may merely represent play and have little to do with actual aggression.

Despite these difficulties, researchers have carried out several large-scale, comprehensive studies of aggression that have provided clear evidence of cross-cultural differences in aggression. In one of the most meaningful studies, cross-cultural psychologist William Lambert examined aggression in Kenya, India, Mexico, Okinawa, the Philippines, and the United States (Lambert, 1971).

The study began with an inquiry into how mothers (the primary caregivers in each of the six cultures) reacted to their own children's displays of aggression toward other children. It turned out that Mexican parents were most strict, whereas U.S. mothers showed the greatest tolerance for aggressive behavior in their children. In contrast, for aggression against an adult, the children who lived in Kenya, the Philippines, and Mexico received the greatest punishment, whereas children in India received the least punishment. Children living in the United States and Okinawa received a moderate degree of punishment.

These differences in parental reactions to aggression are associated with differences in the overall amounts of aggression in the different societies, although the relationships are neither simple nor obvious. For example, children with the greatest level of social activity and interaction (the ones that have the most opportunity to behave aggressively) differ from those with lower levels of social activity in the amount of aggression they show. Furthermore, the most active children appear to have learned most effectively the social values of their culture regarding aggression. Hence, the active children in Mexico are less aggressive, because their mothers react to their aggression strongly, whereas the more active children in the United States tend to be more aggressive (the lesson they learn from their parents' lack of strong reactions). In contrast, relatively inactive children, who have had fewer opportunities to acquire the social values of their society, show differing patterns of aggression than their more active counterparts.

Although this complex account of the origin of differences in aggression among various cultures seems reasonable, it does not explain why cultures have different norms to begin with. Cultures produce a specific set of socialization pressures that lead to different degrees of aggressive behavior.

Although there are many differences among various cultures in levels of aggression, there are also some commonalities. Perhaps the most universal theme is that aggressive behavior is committed more by males than females. There is no known culture in which males are less aggressive than females. Regardless of whether we look at children or adults, the gender difference holds (Gladue & Bailey, 1995; Knight, Fabes, & Higgins, 1996; Halloran et al., 1999).

Although men clearly act more aggressively than women, a definitive explanation for this phenomenon remains elusive. An explanation based on innate, biological factors seems most obvious, but this is not the only possibility. For example, parents and society in general hold different expectations about aggression for male and female children, who are subjected to different socialization pressures. Consistent with such a notion, some research indicates that in a variety of cultures boys are explicitly urged and taught to behave aggressively, whereas aggression in girls is discouraged. Furthermore, some studies find that women behave as aggressively as men in situations in which aggression is seen as appropriate and permissible (Barry et al., 1976; Eagly & Steffen, 1986b; Lightdale & Prentice, 1994; Bettencourt & Miller, 1996).

Another theory meant to explain the higher aggressiveness of males relates to child-rearing practices (Whiting, 1965). Because males in almost all societies are reared by women, males engage in aggressive behavior as part of an effort to differentiate and distinguish themselves from their female caregivers. To establish their masculine identity, then, male children adopt what they see as a dominant behavioral pattern of adult males—acting aggressively.

Ultimately, there is no definitive explanation for the higher levels of male aggression found around the world, or for the general pervasiveness of aggressive behavior. Given the disparities in displays of aggressive behavior across cultures, high levels of aggression must not be a necessary feature of the human condition, despite the prevalence of aggression in certain cultures.

DEALING WITH ANGER

> When angry, count ten before you speak; if very angry, a hundred.
> —Thomas Jefferson

> When angry, count four; when very angry, swear.
> —Mark Twain

THE INFORMED CONSUMER OF SOCIAL PSYCHOLOGY

Whether you count to 10, 100, or 4 (or swear, for that matter), anger is a psychological state with which most people have to deal. Indeed, most adults experience the emotion of anger considerably more often than they express overt aggression (Tangney et al., 1996).

Although you may suspect that the best response to anger is to ignore it, a considerable amount of data suggests otherwise. As we discussed in Chapter 5, people who consistently suppress their anger may develop a variety of adverse reactions, including physical illness, self-condemnation, and psychological dysfunction (Julius, 1990; Pennebaker, 1990; Mills & Dimsdale, 1993; Redmond & Redmond, 1994).

If unexpressed anger has such negative consequences, what is the best way to deal with the emotion effectively? According to psychologists who have studied the issue, several approaches are useful (Pennebaker, 1990; Redmond & Redmond, 1994; Bass, 1996). These are among the strategies that you can follow:

◆ *Fantasize.* One safety valve is to act out your hostilities toward others in your mind. By thinking through what you might do, you at least are able to experience cognitively the satisfaction you might feel if you were to let yourself go and show your true feelings.

◆ *Empathize with the people who are producing the anger.* By trying to see a situation from their point of view, you may come to understand their behavior better, thereby dissipating your anger (Richardson et al., 1994).

◆ *Use diversionary tactics.* Instead of expressing your anger at the time you first experience it, take a few deep breaths and try to do something else for a while. This tactic will buy you time to react in a more rational manner.

◆ *Diminish the importance of the situation.* Anger often occurs when you overrate how vital a situation is. Does it really matter that someone cut in front of you in a line or took a parking place for which you were waiting? By placing a situation into perspective, you may reduce the anger you experience.

◆ *Write about your feelings.* People who write about unexpressed negative emotions such as anger avoid the unpleasant outcomes of emotional repression. Keeping a journal, in which you describe your feelings of anger, may be helpful in preventing some of the negative consequences of anger.

◆ *Express your anger—appropriately.* Although screaming at the source of your anger may make you feel better temporarily, such a display of anger rarely has lasting effects. Instead, a better strategy is to use constructive anger, in which you express anger in a way that takes into account the self-respect of the person provoking you. By calmly informing others in a nonthreatening manner that their actions make you feel angry, you stand a chance of changing their behavior—and reducing your own anger at the same time.

REVIEW AND RETHINK

Review

• The theory that catharsis—the release of pent-up tension—can rechannel and reduce aggression has not found experimental support. Similarly, the use of punishment to reduce future aggression has been largely ineffective.

• Exposure to nonaggressive models and altering interpretations of, and attitudes toward, observed aggression (especially in the media) have proved useful in discouraging aggressive behavior.

• Researchers have found significant cross-cultural differences in the amount and types of aggression in various societies, with a probable relationship to child-rearing practices and parental reactions to aggression.

• Successful tactics for dealing with anger include fantasizing, empathizing, using diversionary tactics, diminishing the importance of the situation, writing about one's feelings, and expressing anger appropriately.

Rethink

- Explain how the concept of catharsis has been used in an attempt to reduce violent behavior. According to social learning theorists, why might catharsis-based techniques generally be unsuccessful?

- What are some reasons why punishment does not prove to be an effective deterrent to aggression? Might punishment be more effective in some cultures than in others? Why?

- Give an example of a situation in which a nonaggressive model is less conspicuous and instructive than an aggressive model.

- How do you think the level of aggression in Japan might compare with that in the United States? Why? What new societal developments might change this situation over time?

L O O K I N G   B A C K

What is aggression?

1. Defining aggression precisely and universally is a difficult matter. Although some experts reject a definition based on intention, most social psychologists view aggression as intentional injury or harm to another individual. (p. 297)

What are the roots of aggressive behavior?

2. Several approaches have sought to identify the roots of aggression. For example, Freud and Lorenz saw aggression as instinctual. The most recent advocates of instinctual views of aggression are evolutionary psychologists, who examine the biological roots of aggression. (p. 300)

3. In contrast to proponents of biological approaches, social learning theorists suggest that aggression is largely learned through the observation and imitation of aggressive models. However, most experts on aggression reject the either-or view of the nature–nurture argument, suggesting that both factors work together to produce aggression. (p. 303)

What social and situational factors lead to aggression?

4. One of the most enduring explanations of aggression is the frustration–aggression hypothesis. Originally, it suggested that frustration always leads to aggression of some sort, and that aggression is always the consequence of frustration. More recent formulations suggest that frustration leads to a readiness to act aggressively; if aggressive cues are present, actual aggression is more likely to occur. (p. 305)

5. The cognitive neoassociationistic view suggests that frustration produces negative feelings that activate patterns of thought related to prior experiences with aggression. If these thought patterns are activated in the presence of aggressive environmental cues, actual aggression may result. (p. 306)

6. According to the excitation transfer model, physical arousal may intensify later emotional experiences. Consequently, if people are angered or frustrated while in a state of physiological arousal, aggression may be higher due to the earlier arousal. (p. 307)

7. A norm of reciprocity operates in aggression, inducing the recipients of physical aggression to act aggressively in turn. In some cases, people carry out anticipatory aggression in advance of a supposed physical provocation. (p. 307)

8. The negative affect model of aggression suggests that high temperatures (as well as other unpleasant features of the environment) can lead to aggression, at least up to a point. However, if conditions become too extreme, aggression becomes too costly a behavior in which to engage. Although the experimental support for the model is mixed, other environmental factors, such as crowding, air quality, and noise, foster the display of aggression. (p. 308)

9. Some social psychologists believe that a "culture of honor" influences some groups, particularly white males in the southern regions of the United States, to meet perceived threats to their honor with physical aggression. (p. 310)

Does exposure to media violence and pornography produce aggression in viewers?

10. Given the high level of exposure to media depictions of aggression by the average person, the question of whether observation of violence leads to subsequent aggression is an important one. Correlational studies clearly show a significant link between the observation of violence and later aggression, although they have been unable to demonstrate unequivocally that viewing media depictions of aggression produces the subsequent aggressive behavior. (p. 312)

11. Several approaches seek to explain the link between the observation of media aggression and later violence. Social learning theory suggests that the observation of models who act aggressively teaches aggressive behavior. The normative approach suggests that viewing media depictions of aggression leads people to assume that aggression is socially acceptable. The attributional approach suggests that the nature of viewers' attributions regarding the causes of viewed aggression determines whether they will behave aggressively. Disinhibition approaches suggest that exposure to media violence reduces people's normal inhibitions against behaving violently. Finally, frequent exposure to media violence can produce desensitization, a reduction in the negative reaction to aggressive stimuli. (p. 314)

12. Observing pornography that includes violent content results in an increased likelihood of actual aggression on the part of viewers. In addition, exposure to such material produces beliefs and attitudes that sexual violence against women is permissible. (p. 317)

How can we reduce aggressive behavior?

13. Approaches to reducing aggression through catharsis and punishment have been suggested, but little evidence demonstrates that either technique is effective. (p. 319)

14. In contrast, exposure to nonaggressive models—a procedure suggested by social learning theory—is a promising approach. Furthermore, altering people's interpretation of, and attitudes toward, observed aggression can decrease the consequences of exposure to violence. (p. 319)

15. Aggression is not unique to any one culture, but the characteristic level of aggression varies considerably from one culture to another. In fact, the United States is revealed by cross-cultural studies to have a fairly high level of aggression. Cultural differences may be traced in part to child-rearing practices. (p. 322)

16. There are also commonalities across cultures. For example, males universally display higher levels of aggression than females. (p. 323)

EPILOGUE

In this chapter and the previous one, we've considered the positive and negative sides of human behavior: helping behavior and aggression. In our travels through these areas, you may have noted that we have not addressed a larger issue about helping and aggression: the question of whether human behavior is basically good or bad.

This has not been an oversight. Instead, it reflects the orientation of social psychology and, to a large extent, the field of psychology as a whole. Most social psychologists argue that such a question is best answered by other disciplines, such as theology and philosophy. Still, scratch the surface of almost any social psychologist and you will find an optimist regarding the existence of at least the potential for human goodness. For in exploring the kinds of issues that their discipline addresses, social psychologists find it nearly impossible to avoid the practical implications of their research. Hence, even the most theoretical explanations of helping and aggression have, in some ways, provided hints and suggestions about ways of improving the human propensity for caring, socially responsible behavior—an admirable, albeit ambitious, goal.

In the meantime, let's return to our opening prologue, which discusses the case of the Littleton, Colorado, shooting incident in which 13 high school students and a teacher were killed by two rampaging high school students. Consider these questions:

1. How might Thomas Hobbes view the situation at Littleton? How might Konrad Lorenz interpret the situation?

2. If you were a social learning theorist, what sorts of experiences would you expect to find in the killers' background that might have led to their aggression?

3. Based on your reading of this chapter, what do you think is the best explanation of the violence shown by the killers in Littleton?

4. Would you have been more or less surprised about the Littleton situation of the killers had been girls, rather than boys? Why?

5. What steps would you take to prevent such violence among adolescents?

KEY TERMS AND CONCEPTS
---

aggression (p. 299)

aggressive cues (p. 306)

catharsis (p. 302)

cognitive neoassociationistic model (p. 306)

emotional aggression (p. 299)

excitation transfer model (p. 307)

frustration (p. 305)

frustration–aggression hypothesis (p. 305)

instrumental aggression (p. 299)

learning approaches to aggression (p. 303)

models (p. 303)

negative affect model of aggression (p. 308)

social learning theory (p. 303)

violence (p. 299)

ATTITUDES

Evaluating
the Social World

CHAPTER 10

PROLOGUE

Death of a Doctor

Dr. Barnett Slepian was killed because of his stance on abortion.

A long with others who shared his pro-choice views on the abortion issue, Dr. Barnett Slepian held deeply felt attitudes about the right of women to have abortions. He knew, though, that his attitudes were hardly shared by everyone: As one of several health care providers at an abortion clinic outside of Buffalo, New York, Slepian was used to being the target of antiabortion protestors, who felt that abortion was morally wrong and should be stopped.

The two sets of opposing attitudes about abortion converged in tragedy one cold October night in 1998. As Slepian stood in the kitchen of his suburban home, talking with his wife and four children, a single shot rang out, and Slepian died immediately.

The slaying came several days after police had issued a warning to abortion providers throughout the United States and Canada to be on guard against violent attacks. Based on threats issued by antiabortion groups who held extreme attitudes, authorities counseled abortion providers to stay away from windows and to be on guard for suspicious activity at their clinics. In the light of the threats, police had little doubt that Slepian's killing was a reaction to his abortion activities. ■

LOOKING AHEAD

Few people hold attitudes so extreme that they result in murder. Still, abortion remains an emotional and divisive moral and political issue, and attitudes regarding abortion tend to raise strong feelings in almost everyone.

To social psychologists, attitudes—which we examine in this chapter—are among the primary ingredients in people's social worlds, and we must take them into account if we are ever to understand human behavior fully. In our discussion of attitudes, we first consider the various approaches that social psychologists take to define the concept. Despite (or perhaps because of) the fact that attitudes play such an important role in our everyday lives, there is little agreement regarding how best to formulate the concept. We explore how attitudes are formed and examine several of the major vantage points from which to view them. We also examine the origins of attitudes and the various functions they serve, and the ways in which they can be measured.

Finally, we consider how attitudes are related to behavior. We discuss how people strive for consistency among attitudes and how they resolve inconsistencies. We conclude by exploring some strategies for evaluating reports of public polls about attitudes.

In sum, after reading this chapter, you'll be able to answer these questions:

◆ What is an attitude?

◆ How are attitudes formed, and what functions do they serve?

◆ Are our attitudes internally consistent, and how do we strive to maintain consistency?

◆ How is behavior related to attitudes?

◆ What factors should we consider in evaluating the results of attitude surveys?

THE ABCs OF ATTITUDES

Japan. Welfare. The president of the United States. Smoking. The economy. Your social psychology instructor.

It's unlikely that you are completely neutral about anything on this list. Instead, as you read through these items, each one probably rings at least one mental bell of recognition.

The very mention of the word *abortion,* for instance, may conjure up your thoughts and beliefs about the topic, your opinion about whether it should be legal, and perhaps the recollection of participating in a demonstration about abortion in the past or the anticipation of engaging in some activity relating to abortion in the future. Your response to the mention of abortion, then, stems from the attitudes that you hold about it.

DEFINING ATTITUDES: FORMULATING AN APPROACH

Although attitudes are a central concept in social psychology—or perhaps because they are so pivotal—social psychologists have not reached agreement on a single definition. We'll consider the three primary approaches: attitudes as evaluations, attitudes as memories, and the three-component model of attitudes.

Attitudes as evaluations. According to the attitudes-as-evaluations approach, **attitudes** are learned predispositions to respond in a favorable or unfavorable manner to a particular person, object, or idea. According to this definition, attitudes represent primarily a positive or negative evaluation of an individual, behavior, belief, or thing (e.g., Eagly & Chaiken, 1993; Cacioppo & Berntson, 1994; Chaiken, Wood, & Eagly, 1996; see the top panel of Figure 10–1).

Although most social psychologists agree that evaluations lie at the core of attitudes, several other definitions of the term have evolved that reflect different emphases and theoretical issues. These alternatives stress the relationship of evaluations to other aspects of an attitude, such as relevant cognitions and behaviors. For instance, one alternative approach emphasizes the way that attitudes are stored in memory.

Attitudes as memories.   Focusing on cognitive aspects of attitudes, some researchers regard attitudes as a set of memories that link cognitions regarding the topic about which the attitude is held to evaluations of that topic (e.g., Fazio, 1990; Bassili & Roy, 1998; Eagly et al., 1999; see the second panel of Figure 10–1).

According to this view, an attitude is a set of interrelated memories about a particular person, object, or idea. The memories are about different kinds of information—some about beliefs, others about feelings, and still others about behavior concerning the object of the attitude. When a stimulus in the environment triggers one of these memories, it activates an entire mental network of related memories having to do with the object of the attitude.

attitudes: Learned predispositions to respond in a favorable or unfavorable manner to a particular person, object, or idea.

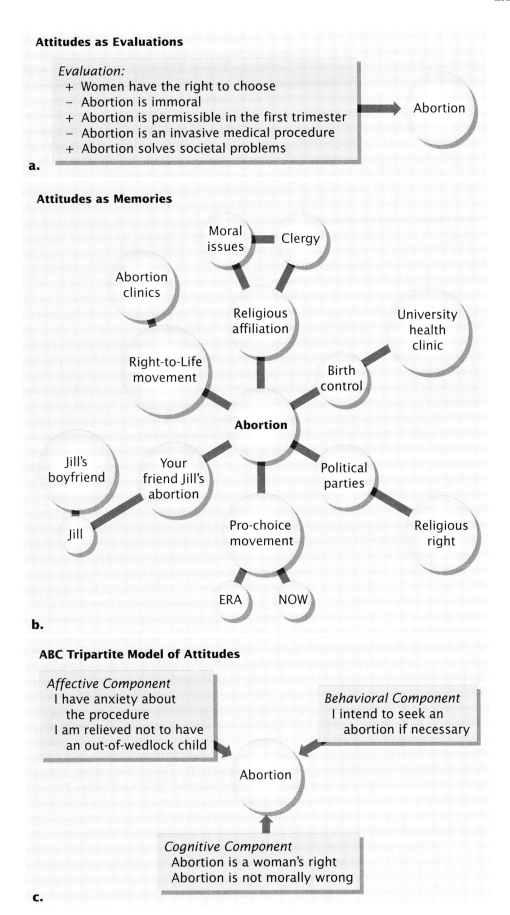

Attitudes as Evaluations

Evaluation:
+ Women have the right to choose
– Abortion is immoral
+ Abortion is permissible in the first trimester
– Abortion is an invasive medical procedure
+ Abortion solves societal problems

a.

Attitudes as Memories

b.

ABC Tripartite Model of Attitudes

Affective Component
I have anxiety about the procedure
I am relieved not to have an out-of-wedlock child

Behavioral Component
I intend to seek an abortion if necessary

Cognitive Component
Abortion is a woman's right
Abortion is not morally wrong

c.

FIGURE 10–1   **Attitudes Toward Abortion: Three Approaches**

ABC tripartite model: The notion that attitudes are composed of three components: an affective component, a behavioral component, and a cognitive component.

The ABC tripartite model.   A third approach to attitudes focuses on their underlying structure. According to the **ABC tripartite model**, attitudes have three components: an affective component, a behavioral component, and a cognitive component (Breckler, 1984; Fabrigar & Petty, 1999; see the third panel of Figure 10–1). The affective component encompasses emotional reactions—positive and negative. As we saw in the chapter prologue, people harbor strong positive or negative emotions regarding abortion.

The behavioral component of the attitude consists of a predisposition or intention to act in a way that reflects the attitude. For example, this part of the attitude would include your intention to participate in a proabortion or antiabortion rally, or your consideration of whether you might ever have an abortion.

Finally, the cognitive component of an attitude refers to beliefs and thoughts about the object of the attitude. In reference to abortion, we might hold strong moral or religious beliefs that shape our views of the legitimacy of the practice.

Of course, no one of these components is entirely independent of the others; rather, all three are interrelated. Our emotional reactions are likely to affect our behavioral intentions, just as our beliefs will influence our emotions. For example, if a woman believes that abortion is immoral (the cognitive component), and if the thought of abortion produces a strong negative reaction (the affective component), she is unlikely to form the intention of seeking an abortion (the behavioral component).

On the other hand, if the woman believes that abortion is an appropriate moral option and considers the decision to be a woman's choice (the cognitive component), and if she reacts favorably to abortion as an option (the affective component), she is considerably more likely to intend to participate in a pro-choice rally or even to seek an abortion herself (the behavioral component).

In short, the A, B, and C of the tripartite model often are consistent with one another—but not always. For instance, a woman might believe that abortion is an appropriate moral option and consider the decision to be a woman's choice (cognition), and she may react positively to abortion as an option (affect), but she might not consider abortion as an option for herself (behavior).

RECONCILING THE APPROACHES

We've encountered three approaches to attitudes: Of these three approaches to attitudes, one focuses on evaluative aspects, a second concentrates on the basis of attitudes in memory, and a third emphasizes the three interrelated components of attitudes. Which of these three approaches provides the most accurate description?

Actually, the three approaches are less contradictory than they may seem at first: To a large extent, they represent not different views but different areas of focus. The evaluative approach concentrates on likes and dislikes; the view of attitudes as memories embraces the notion that memories can represent affect, cognition, and behavioral intentions; and the ABC tripartite model concentrates on several aspects of an attitude, including likes and dislikes. Hence, the three approaches share many common elements.

Although these different emphases direct researchers to different theoretical and research paths, all three approaches assume that there is a structure to attitudes and that attitudes cannot be considered in isolation from one another. Finally—and perhaps most important—all three agree on the fundamental importance of attitudes in shaping human behavior.

THE ORIGINS AND FUNCTIONS OF ATTITUDES

We are not born adoring 'N Sync, loathing Brussels sprouts, or feeling so-so about Ivory soap. Somewhere in our past, we developed an attitude about each of them. Where did we acquire these attitudes?

From the day you were born, you were bombarded with stimuli that generate attitudes. Parents, friends, the media, teachers—anyone or anything can provide information that may lead to attitude formation. Whether this information is translated into an attitude depends, to a large extent, on the basic principles of learning.

CLASSICAL CONDITIONING OF ATTITUDES: FORMING ATTITUDES TOWARD A MODERN-DAY HITLER

Each time you eat broccoli you get sick to your stomach—apparently a result of an allergic reaction. Is it any surprise that you grow to hate the vegetable?

The process that led you to develop your negative attitude toward broccoli is *classical conditioning*. In previous psychology courses you probably learned about Pavlov's experiments concerning conditioning in dogs. Pavlov discovered that when he paired two stimuli, such as the sound of a bell and the sight of meat, hungry dogs learned to respond—in this case salivate—not only when the bell sound occurred in conjunction with the meat, but eventually when the bell was sounded alone (Pavlov, 1927).

The key to Pavlov's process was stimulus substitution, by which a stimulus that evoked a definite response (the meat) was paired with a previously neutral stimulus that did not naturally bring about a response (the bell). When the two stimuli were repeatedly presented together, the second stimulus eventually took on the properties of the first. In effect, the second stimulus was substituted for the first. This very elementary type of learning is what psychologists refer to as classical conditioning.

Attitudes can be learned in the same fashion (Cacioppo et al., 1992; Grossman & Till, 1998; Kim, Lim, & Bhargava, 1998). In the case of aversion to broccoli, the repeated pairing of broccoli with an upset stomach eventually might produce a strong negative affective reaction to the broccoli alone—one that will occur without your having to go through the trouble (and consequences) of eating it. This negative reaction, according to learning theory, constitutes an attitude.

Phenomena other than unpleasant physical reactions can produce the kind of experiences that result in classical conditioning. For example, supporters of U.S. involvement in the Persian Gulf War in 1991 repeatedly equated the Iraqi leader Saddam Hussein with Adolf Hitler. Hussein was frequently referred to as a modern-day Hitler, and U.S. citizens were told of routine torture and executions at Hussein's behest (*U.S. News & World Report,* 1991). It is no surprise that the label stuck: Ultimately people's attitudes about Saddam Hussein took on the same negative qualities as those they held toward Hitler.

Classical conditioning of a more covert nature helps explain, at least in part, the origins of prejudice, in the form of negative attitudes toward members of particular racial, religious, ethnic, and gender groups. For example, consider children who repeatedly overhear their parents discussing members of particular groups in negative terms ("the Irish drink too much, Turks are cruel, Arabs are devious, women are overly emotional"). These children clearly are at risk for learning from their parents to associate these groups with the negative evaluations inherent in the characterizations of drunkenness, cruelty, deviousness, and emotionality—regardless of their own experiences with members of these groups (Staats & Staats, 1958; Riordan & Tedeschi, 1983; Domjan, 1998).

OPERANT CONDITIONING: IN PRAISE OF ATTITUDES

Great idea. Perfect. You're right.

Forget it. That's the dumbest opinion I ever heard. Not on your life.

If you've ever been in the position of hearing such replies to a comment of yours, you know the power of both praise and condemnation. In fact, one of the central ways our attitudes are formed and shaped is through our receiving the compliments and critiques of others (Guerin, 1994).

Once again, basic learning theory provides an explanation for this form of attitude formation. In this case, however, the specific process is *operant conditioning,* a concept that grew

Social learning theory explains how children learn their attitudes through the observation and imitation of the behavior of others. In this case, a girl watches as her father gives a Nazi salute at a Ku Klux Klan rally in the early 1990s.

out of the work of B. F. Skinner (1957, 1983). According to operant conditioning approaches, when we are rewarded, or reinforced, for expressing certain attitudes, we are more likely to voice similar attitudes in the future. Conversely, when we are punished for expressing a particular view, we are less likely to state that view in the future (Insko, 1965; Pierce & Epling, 1999).

For example, one early demonstration of the power of reinforcement comes from a study in which participants held a conversation with an experimenter. In one condition, the experimenter expressed agreement; in another condition, disagreement. As the conversation progressed, participants made an increasing number of statements of opinion when the experimenter expressed agreement. Conversely, in conditions in which the experimenter expressed disagreement, the number of opinion statements declined (Verplanck, 1955).

It is not just pleasant or unpleasant verbal responses that lead us to develop positive or negative attitudes toward particular objects. We also respond to the deeds of others. A professor who gives you an A in a course is providing the kind of reinforcement that may well lead you to develop positive attitudes about the course and the subject matter.

Social learning theory (or *observational learning*), a derivative of operant conditioning, also helps explain attitude acquisition. As we saw in the previous chapter, social learning theorists maintain that people learn attitudes by observing and imitating the behavior of others. Children who observe others acting aggressively and being rewarded for their aggression are apt to imitate that aggression if they are placed in similar circumstances. Furthermore, they learn the lesson—and come to hold the attitude—that aggression is a permissible behavior (Bandura, 1977; Erdley & Asher, 1998). Social learning is one of the central reasons for concern over the high levels of aggression depicted in the media (Liebert & Sprafkin, 1988; Smith & Donnerstein, 1998; Carll, 1999).

At the same time, people can also learn positive behaviors through observation. For example, in one experiment children whose attitudes toward dogs were extremely unfavorable, amounting to strong fear, were divided into groups. One group watched a model (dubbed the "Fearless Peer") happily playing with a dog; the other group did not see the model. The fearful children who had seen the model were much more likely to play with a strange dog than those who hadn't been exposed to the model (Bandura, Grusec, & Menlove, 1967).

GENETIC FACTORS: ARE WE BORN WITH ATTITUDES?

Although the vast majority of social psychologists would agree that attitudes are acquired through experience, a small body of research suggests that genetic factors may also contribute to attitude formation. Specifically, studies suggest that genetically identical twins hold attitudes that are more similar to each other than do genetically nonidentical (fraternal) twins. Furthermore, the attitudes of twins who were separated early in life and raised in different households are also more similar to each other than are those of nontwin siblings and unrelated persons (Waller et al., 1990). These studies demonstrate that greater genetic similarity is associated with greater similarity of attitudes (Tesser, 1993).

Why should this be the case? Surely, people are not born having specific positive attitudes about Mother Teresa or The Backstreet Boys and specific negative attitudes about Adolph Hitler or Demi Moore movies. Instead, genetics provides people with a certain temperament, patterns of arousal and emotionality, and certain kinds of abilities. For instance, some of us are genetically predisposed to be more active, more irritable, or more distractible than others. Because of such predispositions, our behavior influences our caretakers and may create a particular environment for ourselves, as we focus on those aspects of our environment that are most consistent with our genetically determined temperament and abilities. For instance, our attitude toward playing basketball may be determined, in part, by our genetically determined activity level and our natural abilities (Scarr, 1992, 1993).

Despite the possibility that genetic factors play at least some role in determining our attitudes, most social psychologists place far greater weight on environmental factors. Certainly, specific attitudes are learned, not inherited from our ancestors.

ATTITUDE ACQUISITION: WHY BOTHER?

Could we lead our lives without attitudes?

Although the work on attitude acquisition that we have discussed shows how learning processes help explain *how* we acquire attitudes, we have not yet addressed what is perhaps a more fundamental question: *Why* do we develop attitudes in the first place?

The question is not a trivial one. One could argue, for instance, that society would be considerably better off if we were not predisposed to like or dislike particular individuals or objects on the basis of previously acquired attitudes. We might wish instead that people would make judgments on a case-by-case, moment-by-moment basis, and not by relying on a set of evaluations that color the way they view the world.

It turns out, however, that attitudes play several critical psychological roles. The two main roles have been called knowledge functions and self functions (Pratkanis & Greenwald, 1989; Fazio, 1995; Eagley & Chaiken, 1998).

The **knowledge function of attitudes** refers to those aspects of attitudes that permit us to organize and make sense of the world. They provide clues about why people behave as they do, and they allow us to summarize our understanding of people and events in the world and to cope with those events. They also help us organize and recall new information to which we are exposed. For example, people holding strongly positive attitudes toward sports often possess a wide array of detailed information about particular athletes and games. Their positive attitude toward sports helps them learn and remember information on athletic topics.

In addition to knowledge functions, attitudes also serve self functions. The **self function of attitudes** rests on the desire to create and maintain a positive sense of oneself. For instance, by holding attitudes that are shared by people who are important to us, we may hope to gain their esteem and liking, which will lead us to feel more positively about ourselves.

knowledge function of attitudes: The aspect of attitudes that permits us to organize and make sense of the world.

self function of attitudes: The aspect of attitudes that enables people to create and maintain a positive sense of oneself.

Similarly, we may gain self-esteem by embracing (and expressing) a particular set of attitudes. Hence, a person who values freedom of choice may gain self-esteem by participating in a demonstration in favor of abortion rights for women.

One further self function of attitudes relates to their ability to permit us to identify with social institutions that are important to us, such as religious organizations or professional groups. Specifically, by holding attitudes that support such groups, we may experience a greater sense of belonging.

In short, we form attitudes for two basic reasons. First, they serve a knowledge function by helping us summarize and cognitively package the world around us. They also play another role: In their self function, attitudes help us maintain our self-esteem and foster a positive sense of ourselves as individuals.

TAKING THE MEASURE OF ATTITUDES

Although we're all acquainted with the concept of attitudes, none of us has actually ever seen or heard one. The reason is that attitudes are **hypothetical constructs**, abstract concepts that cannot be directly observed. This creates a dilemma for social psychologists who wish to study attitudes: What is the best way to approach something that cannot be directly observed? To solve this dilemma, social psychologists use both direct and covert approaches.

DIRECT MEASUREMENT OF ATTITUDES

If you want to know someone's attitudes toward the use of drugs, just ask.

At least that's the theory behind direct attitude measurement techniques, in which people are asked straightforwardly to identify their attitudes about a particular person or issue (Schuman & Presser, 1995). Typically, direct measurement involves translating an abstract attitude into some sort of numerical scale (see Table 10–1 for examples of different kinds of scales; O'Neal & Chissom, 1994).

The Likert scale.   Probably the most direct and simplest way to measure attitudes is through a Likert scale, named after the person who originated it, Rensis Likert (Likert, 1932). In a **Likert scale**, a researcher presents a rater with a statement about the object of an attitude, together with a numbered evaluative response scale to indicate the extent of agreement or disagreement with the statement. Suppose, for example, you wish to know people's attitudes toward sexual harassment. Using the Likert technique, you might present a statement such as "Sexual harassment usually is primarily a woman's issue." To respond, raters indicate their level of agreement with that statement, using a 7-point scale such as the one shown in Table 10–1.

By having raters respond to a series of such statements, researchers can obtain a summary score for a general attitude. Researchers can also vary the number of categories; there are 5-category Likert scales, which provide general information, and there are 100-category Likert scales, which potentially provide more refined information.

Semantic differential measure of attitudes.   Another way to approach the study of attitudes is to assess specific aspects of attitudes. For example, we might want to target directly the evaluative aspect of an attitude. To do this, researchers often employ a semantic differential measure (Osgood, Suci, & Tannenbaum, 1957). In the **semantic differential**, an object is rated on a pair of adjectives, which are opposites. For instance, a researcher might ask people to rate "welfare" along such dimensions as good–bad, valuable–worthless, and fair–unfair.

The advantage of the semantic differential is that it allows researchers to target the evaluative component of the attitude. In addition, it permits researchers to assess attitudes toward general, broad concepts, rather than very specific ones.

Guttman scales.   If you know how to figure out that $(15/3) \times 5 = 25$, you're sure to know that $5 \times 5 = 25$. That's the logic behind a Guttman scale of attitude measurement.

hypothetical constructs: Abstract concepts that cannot be directly observed.

Likert scale: An approach to the measurement of attitudes in which objects are rated on the basis of a numbered evaluative response scale.

semantic differential: An approach to the measurement of attitudes in which objects are rated on the basis of a pair of adjectives that are opposites, such as, good–bad, attractive–unattractive.

TABLE 10-1   Examples of Direct Measures of Attitudes

LIKERT SCALE
Some Items from the Short Form of the Attitudes Toward Women Scale

1. Swearing and obscenity are more repulsive in the speech of a woman than of a man.

   DISAGREE   1   2   3   4   5   6   7   AGREE

2. Women should take increasing responsibility for leadership in solving the intellectual and social problems of the day.

   DISAGREE   1   2   3   4   5   6   7   AGREE

3. Both husband and wife should be allowed the same grounds for divorce.

   DISAGREE   1   2   3   4   5   6   7   AGREE

4. Intoxication among women is worse than intoxication among men.

   DISAGREE   1   2   3   4   5   6   7   AGREE

5. Under modern economic conditions with women being active outside the home, men should share in household tasks such as washing dishes and doing the laundry.

   DISAGREE   1   2   3   4   5   6   7   AGREE

6. There should be a strict merit system in job appointment and promotion without regard to sex.

   DISAGREE   1   2   3   4   5   6   7   AGREE

7. Women should worry less about their rights and more about becoming good wives and mothers.

   DISAGREE   1   2   3   4   5   6   7   AGREE

8. Women earning as much as their dates should bear equally the expense when they go out together.

   DISAGREE   1   2   3   4   5   6   7   AGREE

SEMANTIC DIFFERENTIAL MEASURE

Welfare

Good	_ : _ : _ : _ : _ : _ : _	Bad
Unattractive	_ : _ : _ : _ : _ : _ : _	Attractive
Valuable	_ : _ : _ : _ : _ : _ : _	Worthless
Ugly	_ : _ : _ : _ : _ : _ : _	Beautiful
Fair	_ : _ : _ : _ : _ : _ : _	Unfair
Wise	_ : _ : _ : _ : _ : _ : _	Foolish

GUTTMAN SCALE
Items from a Guttman Scale of Attitudes Toward Handgun Control

1. Institute a waiting period before a handgun can be purchased, to allow for a criminal records check.

2. Require all persons to obtain a police permit before being allowed to purchase a handgun.

3. Require a license for all persons carrying a handgun outside their homes or places of business (except for law enforcement agents).

4. Require a mandatory fine for all persons carrying a handgun outside their homes or places of business without a license.

5. Require a mandatory jail term for all persons carrying a handgun outside their homes or places of business without a license.

6. Ban the future manufacturing and sale of non-sporting-type handguns.

7. Ban the future manufacturing and sale of all handguns.

8. Use public funds to buy back and destroy existing handguns on a voluntary basis.

9. Use funds to buy back and destroy existing handguns on a mandatory basis.

Source: Adapted from Spence, Helmreich, & Stapp (1973, pp. 219–220), Teske & Hazlett (1985, p. 375), and reprinted in Eagly & Chaiken (1993).

Guttman scales: A measurement that presents a gradation of attitudes, ranging from the least extreme to the most extreme.

Guttman scales present a gradation of attitudes, ranging from the least extreme to the most extreme (refer back to Table 10–1). The scale assumes that people will be able to endorse all the items up to a certain degree of extremity, but beyond that they will no longer be able to endorse the rest (Guttman, 1944).

In the example depicted in the last part of Table 10–1, for instance, people who agree that public funds should be used to buy back and destroy exiting handguns on a voluntary basis (Item 8) would surely agree with the earlier notion that all persons should obtain a police permit before being allowed to purchase a handgun (Item 2). Conversely, if they do not agree with Item 8, they wouldn't be expected to agree with the more extreme Item 9 relating to the use of public funds to buy back and destroy existing handguns on a *mandatory* basis.

All three types of direct measures of attitudes—Likert scales, semantic differential measures, and Guttman scales—are used not only by social psychologists involved in research, but also by professionals who poll the public on current issues. For a discussion of some of the issues survey researchers face, see the accompanying Speaking of Social Psychology interview.

SPEAKING OF SOCIAL PSYCHOLOGY

Lydia K. Saad

Pollster

Year of Birth: 1963

Education: B.A., Political Science, Villanova University; M.A., Political Science (with Survey Research concentraton), University of Connecticut

Home: Princeton, New Jersey

"Question wording is probably the greatest source of bias and error in the data, followed in significance by question order."

During the 1936 presidential campaign, George Gallup accurately predicted the outcome of the upcoming election using scientific polling methods. From that moment, Gallup polls have been relied on to provide an accurate assessment of people's attitudes, beliefs, and values.

Today, Gallup polls are used to examine a large range of topics. Methods for gathering and interpreting polling data have become refined and quite specialized. Nevertheless, Lydia Saad, a senior research analyst with the Gallup organization, notes that surveys still are prone to error. As a result, she argues, it is very important that anyone doing a survey be on the lookout for bias and error.

"There is a litany of standard caveats to observe when interpreting any poll results," Saad noted. "Primary among these are issues related to question wording, order, the sample population, the random selection technique used in creating the sampling frame, and whether the method of interviewing is done in person, by telephone, or by mail.

"The technical aspects of data collection are critically important. If such factors as appropriate sampling are not carried out properly, they can reduce the reliability of even a perfectly worded question," she added. "However, when it comes to modern-day attitude surveys conducted by most of the major national polling organizations, question wording is

COVERT MEASURES OF ATTITUDES

Although the Likert scale, semantic differential, and Guttman scale enable us to assess attitudes directly, they suffer from the same drawback: They are susceptible to participant self-presentational motives (Iedema & Poppe, 1994; Antonak & Livneh, 1995; Krysan, 1998). Even the most prejudiced college students would likely pause before admitting their prejudice on a questionnaire; even they are likely to be aware of the range of socially acceptable responses on a college campus and to be reluctant to admit that they hold views that are not "politically correct."

Similarly, although exit polls in 1990 showed that African American Douglas Wilder would beat his white opponent by a wide margin in a Virginia election for governor, he actually won by only the slimmest of margins. The reason for the discrepancy: White voters apparently were reluctant to admit that they would actually be voting against Wilder for fear of being thought of as racially prejudiced (Traugott & Price, 1991).

probably the greatest source of bias and error in the data, followed in significance by question order."

In some cases there is no way around the fact that wording will affect results, according to Saad. This was evident when the public was polled on U.S. involvement in Bosnia.

"Is the United States 'sending' or 'contributing' troops to the UN peacekeeping force in Bosnia? While neither phrase is more correct, comparison of results among several major polls in 1995 suggested that the difference in the interpretation of these two words resulted in figures relating to support of the mission that differed by as much as 15 percent," Saad explained. "Rather than viewing one result as correct, and the other as incorrect, the difference provides important insights into the nature of American opinion toward the mission."

"Public opinion on a given topic cannot be understood in a single poll question asked a single time."

In addition to taking extreme care in developing the wording of questions, Gallup is also careful in the interpretation of the results.

"We tend to be extremely cautious in drawing conclusions from trends when the differences from one poll to the next are relatively small, even if they are within the margin or error," said Saad.

"An example of this is measuring the importance of religion. Approximately four times each year, Gallup asks respondents to rate the importance of religion in their lives. Over the last half century, Gallup has observed considerable volatility in respondents' answers based on the time of year (Christmas-time versus summer, for example), and some sensitivity based on the questions which precede it in the survey.

"Despite the best efforts to control these variables when asking the question, Gallup is still cautious about reporting shifts in the importance of religion until they can be replicated in subsequent polling," she added.

"To summarize, public opinion on a given topic cannot be understood in a single poll question asked a single time," Saad explained. "It is necessary to measure attitudes along several different dimensions, to review attitudes based on a variety of different wordings, to verify findings on the basis of multiple inquiries, and to be conservative about reporting changes over time."

covert measure of attitude: An approach to measuring behavior in which the measurement technique is disguised in some way.

The problem of self-presentation becomes particularly acute when comparing responses on attitude scales across different cultures. For example, consider people living in cultures in which the expression of negative attitudes against outgroup members is not seen as particularly socially undesirable. In such cultures, people are more likely to express more extreme, negative attitudes toward outgroup members than people in cultures in which there are stronger norms against appearing prejudiced (Moghaddam, Taylor, & Wright, 1993; Romero & Roberts, 1998).

Because people are sensitive to social desirability in their questionnaire responses, social psychologists have turned to covert measures of attitude. In a **covert measure of attitude**, the measurement technique is disguised in some way. For example, researchers may assess subtle, nonverbal measures of attitudes. Specifically, as we discussed in Chapter 4, facial expressions reflect emotional response, and some researchers have inferred attitudes on the basis of facial expression (e.g., Feldman & Rimé, 1991; Pizzagalli et al., 1998).

However, people can manipulate facial expressions to conceal their feelings and attitudes (as any of us know who have smiled as we opened a disappointing gift in front of the giver). Consequently, researchers have devised subtler physiologically based measures to assess attitudes. For example, different patterns of changes in certain facial muscles seem to differentiate both positive and negative attitudes, as well as the intensity of these attitudes (Cacioppo, Berntson, & Crites, 1996; Dimberg, 1997; Dimberg & Karlsson, 1997).

Another covert approach to the measurement of attitudes is the examination of brain wave patterns that reflect electrical activity in the brain (Cacioppo et al., 1993; Crites et al., 1995; Pizzagalli et al., 1998). Advertising agencies, which have more than a passing interest in ensuring that consumers react positively to their advertisements, have begun to investigate whether the right or left hemisphere of the brain is more involved in processing information.

One such study found that commercials appealing primarily to logic are processed largely by the left hemisphere of the brain. In contrast, commercials with an emotional message are processed primarily by the right hemisphere. Such results suggest that the type of initial cognitive processing people engage in may influence the attitudes that they ultimately develop. In turn, this knowledge may permit advertisers to craft ads that evoke the desired attitude. Although this approach to measuring attitudes has not been sufficiently validated, it does suggest a promising avenue of research (Cacioppo et al., 1993; Ito et al., 1998; Cacioppo & Gardner, 1999).

EXPLORING DIVERSITY

HOW ETHNICITY SHAPES ATTITUDES

The reactions of these college students to the jury's verdict of not guilty of the charge of murder in the first O. J. Simpson trial were divided along racial lines.

Was O. J. Simpson guilty of murdering his ex-wife?

One of the best predictors of people's answer to this question is their race. Despite the jury's decision that the State had not proved Simpson guilty, only 32% of whites in a *Newsweek* poll agreed with the not-guilty verdict (*Newsweek*, 1995). In contrast, 85% of African Americans agreed with the verdict. Similarly, whereas 80% of African Americans thought the jury was fair and impartial, only 50% of whites agreed (see Figure 10–2).

Underlying these figures are deep divisions in attitudes about the U.S. justice system, which many African Americans feel is biased against them. For instance, when a jury made up of 10 whites and no African Americans acquitted the white Los Angeles police officers charged

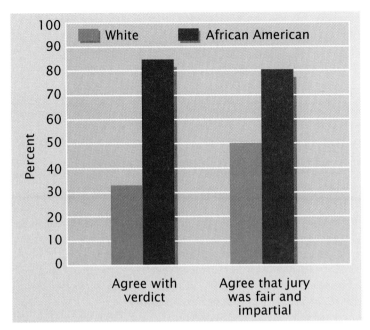

FIGURE 10–2   African American and White Attitudes Toward the Simpson Verdict African Americans were far more likely to look favorably on the O. J. Simpson verdict than whites. (*Source: Newsweek, 1995.*)

in the videotaped beating of Rodney King, many people attributed the acquittal to racism on the part of the jurors. And in many urban areas, in which juries are often made up largely of African Americans, the rate of acquittal for African American defendants is considerably higher than in areas in which juries have few or no African Americans. (We'll talk more about the legal system and ethnicity in Chapter 13.)

It is hardly surprising that people of different ethnicities hold discrepant attitudes. As we first discussed in Chapter 3, the experiences of members of groups who encounter prejudice and discrimination are often quite different from those of majority groups. In turn, these experiences are likely to shape the acquisition of particular kinds of attitudes.

REVIEW AND RETHINK

Review

- Attitudes can be defined as evaluations, as memories, and in terms of the ABC tripartite model. Social learning, a derivative of operant conditioning, also helps explain attitude acquisition.

- The processes of classical and operant conditioning underlie attitude acquisition.

- Attitudes have critical psychological functions, including knowledge functions and self functions.

- Attitude-measurement techniques include direct and indirect, or covert, procedures.

Rethink

- What are the three components in the tripartite model of attitudes? Which component is reflected most strongly in a semantic differential scale measurement?

- How are attitudes formed? Might the ways in which attitudes are formed differ depending on the specific attitude in question?

- What important functions do attitudes serve? What is the nature of these functions? Which function would expedite a shopping trip to the grocery store?

- What are some advantages and disadvantages of direct attitude-measurement techniques? Of covert techniques? What disadvantages of direct techniques do covert techniques attempt to overcome?

THE CONSISTENCY OF ATTITUDES

Put yourself in Marian Keech's living room. It is approaching midnight, December 21, the time when Keech, a self-proclaimed psychic, has predicted the arrival of a group of aliens calling themselves the Guardians. Over the past months, you've become convinced that Keech is able to receive messages from the Guardians, who have warned her that they are going to destroy the earth in a cataclysmic flood.

But you're one of the lucky ones. Because of your association with Keech, you will be picked up by the Guardians and flown away to safety just before the flood is to occur. You've quit your job, packed your bags, discarded the zippers from your clothing (metal and flying saucers do not mix, according to Keech), and you're ready to start your adventure.

Midnight comes and goes with no sign of the Guardians. To your horror, you realize that Keech is wrong, and you are trapped on the soon-to-be-destroyed earth.

Fortunately, Keech was also wrong about something else: No flooding occurred, and the end of the world did not come.

Imagining yourself in that situation, you might think that you would be more than a bit annoyed with Keech. But the true believers who sat in Keech's living room that evening reacted very differently. They saluted Keech as a hero when she announced that, because of the prayers and great faith of her small band of believers, God had decided to spare the earth.

Within the next few days, the people who had waited with Keech in the room became even more convinced of her powers to foresee the future, firmly believing that one day the Guardians would indeed come for them. Their attitudes toward Keech, which were positive to begin with, became even more positive than they had been prior to the night of the 21st (Festinger, Riecken, & Schachter, 1956).

This curious but true scenario, described in the classic book *When Prophecy Fails,* illustrates the importance people place on maintaining consistency. To maintain consistency between their attitudes and behavior, the group members attempted to justify their actions. They could not simply admit they were wrong, thereby making themselves look awfully foolish for quitting their jobs, selling their homes, alarming and estranging their family and friends, and engaging in other irreversible acts that led up to the night of December 21st. Instead, they sought to justify what they had done by intensifying their allegiance to Keech and her prediction. The more committed they became, the more justification they were able to muster for their actions.

COGNITIVE CONSISTENCY AND ATTITUDES

As the case of Marian Keech and her followers illustrates, consistency—at least in attitudes—strongly influences behavior. In fact, the hypothesis that we strive to maintain consistency, both in the individual components of an attitude and between various attitudes, is supported by a great deal of evidence.

Cognitive consistency approaches to attitudes focus on the ways people strive to maintain consistency within and among attitudes, as well as on the ways they manage to reconcile inconsistencies of which they are aware (Spellman, Ullman, & Holyoak, 1993; Millar & Millar, 1998). Such approaches assume that people are reasonably rational and thoughtful and strive to make sense out of what they think, feel, and do. The natural outcome of these cognitive efforts to behave reasonably and rationally, according to consistency theories, is that people actively construct and interpret the world in order to make consistent what is inconsistent (Cialdini & deNicholas, 1989; Beauvois & Joule, 1999).

cognitive consistency: An approach that focuses on the ways people strive to maintain consistency within and between attitudes, as well as on the ways they manage to reconcile inconsistencies of which they are aware.

All cognitive consistency approaches to attitudes share the basic principle that inconsistency is a psychologically uncomfortable state that prompts people to seek ways to reduce it. Several kinds of inconsistencies can trigger such an effort.

For example, inconsistency can exist between the cognitive and affective aspects of an attitude ("Drinking is bad for people, but I sure enjoy doing it"). Or the affect felt toward an individual can be inconsistent with that person's position on a particular issue ("I really like Jake, but he is the worst sexist I know"). Finally, inconsistencies can exist between cognitions and behavioral intentions ("I know that safe sex is important, but I do not need to practice it because I have sex only with safe partners"). Whatever the inconsistency, cognitive consistency approaches suggest that people are motivated to reduce the discrepancy.

Consistency is not just something that is seen between different aspects of attitudes; it is typically a feature of the relationship between behavior and attitudes. But what happens when we carry out behaviors that are incongruent with our attitudes? We'll look at several approaches that help answer this question, starting with research on the effects of role playing.

ROLE PLAYING: FROM BEHAVIOR TO ATTITUDES

"Smile, though your heart is breaking." Such advice, offered in the lyrics of an old song, may be right on target, given the increasing evidence that the behaviors we enact may well induce us to acquire attitudes consistent with the behavior.

According to the *role approach to attitudes,* our behavior often follows prescribed **roles,** the behaviors that are associated with and come to be expected of people in a given position. We are all familiar with the attributes of certain important roles. For instance, the role of student encompasses the behaviors of studying, listening to a teacher, and attending class. The role of employer involves paying employees, holding employee evaluations, and providing direction and advice on how to accomplish particular tasks. Like a theatrical role, then, the roles of everyday social interaction prescribe the routine, appropriate conduct associated with a given position.

But roles do more than just provide direction on how to behave. They actually influence the attitudes that we hold. In fact, carrying out the behaviors associated with a role may actually lead people to adopt attitudes consistent with the role.

Consider, for instance, the results of social psychologist Philip Zimbardo's stunning demonstration of the power of roles. In the study, Zimbardo and colleagues set up a mock prison in the basement of the Stanford University psychology department, complete with cells, solitary confinement cubicles, and a small recreation area. The researchers then advertised for participants who were willing to spend 2 weeks in a study of prison life. Once they identified the study participants, a flip of a coin designated who would be a prisoner and who would be a prison guard. Neither prisoners nor guards were told how to fulfill their roles (Zimbardo, 1973; Haney, Banks, & Zimbardo, 1973; Haney & Zimbardo, 1998).

On the first day of the study, prisoners were picked up unexpectedly at their homes and brought, by police car, to the basement "prison." They were given loose-fitting, baggy prison smocks, and a chain was clamped to their ankle. The guards received uniforms, nightsticks, handcuffs, and whistles. Apart from a few rules, the guards and prisoners were given little direction on what to do; they had only their conception of what the role of guard and prisoner required of them.

After just a few days, it became apparent that no direction was necessary: Both parties had a clear, and ultimately frightening, conception of the behavior and expectations associated with their roles. The guards became abusive to the prisoners, waking them at odd hours and subjecting them to arbitrary punishment. They withheld food from the prisoners and forced them into hard labor. Their attitude toward the prisoners matched their actions: They saw them as unruly, uncooperative, and deserving of the treatment they were receiving.

The prisoners were initially rebellious, but they soon became docile and subservient to the guards. They became extremely demoralized, and one slipped into a depression so severe he was released after just a few days. In fact, after only 6 days of captivity, the remaining prisoners' reactions became so extreme that the study was terminated—to the disappointment

roles: Behaviors that are associated with and come to be expected of people in a given position.

Most smokers are aware that smoking is linked to lung cancer. In the language of cognitive dissonance theory, "I am a smoker" does not fit psychologically with "Smoking causes lung cancer."

of the guards, who were enjoying their taste of power over what they had come to believe were good-for-nothing prisoners.

The experiment (which drew harsh criticism, on both methodological and ethical grounds) provided a clear lesson: Enacting a role can have a powerful consequence on people's attitudes, inducing them to change their attitudes in less than benign ways. What starts off as just a role can become more than a part we play; it can modify our very view of the world and our attitudes toward others and even ourselves. In fact, as we see next, when people's behavior and attitudes clash, they may expend a great deal of cognitive effort to bring them into synch.

COGNITIVE DISSONANCE THEORY

You've just spent an hour as a participant in an experiment, performing the excruciatingly boring task of placing spools on a tray and twisting a series of square pegs around and around. "Why in the world did I ever agree to do this?" you ask yourself as you finally finish. Just as you're about to leave, though, the experimenter, with a sheepish look on his face, makes an unusual request.

The experimenter says that, due to a scheduling problem, he needs the services of a confederate for the next participant, and asks if you might be willing to help out by preparing a participant for the task you just completed. (The experiment you've just done, he explains, actually concerns the effects of motivational preparation on task performance. Although you did the task with no advance preparation, participants in another condition are provided with information about the task before starting.) Further, the experimenter asks if you would consider being "on call" to participate as a confederate to prepare participants in future experiments.

The next participant is due to arrive at any minute. You ask what kind of information you need to provide this person before the experiment. Simple, according to the experimenter: You just say that the task is fun, fascinating, and exciting. For this, you'll be paid $1.

If you agree to the experimenter's request and tell the next participant how interesting the task will be, receiving $1 for your trouble, something you never expected will probably happen: Your attitude toward the initial task will change, and you'll come to feel more positively toward it. Even more surprisingly, your attitude toward the task will undoubtedly be more favorable than if the experimenter had offered you $20 to be his confederate (Festinger & Carlsmith, 1959).

The explanation for this surprising state of affairs is found in one of the most influential theories ever put forward in the field of social psychology—cognitive dissonance theory (Festinger, 1957). According to the theory, **cognitive dissonance**, a state of psychological tension, is aroused when a person simultaneously holds two ideas or thoughts—cognitions— that contradict each other (Johnson, Kelly, & LeBlanc, 1995; Harmon-Jones & Mills, 1999; Sakai, 1999). For example, most smokers know that smoking is linked to lung cancer. In the language of cognitive dissonance theory, the cognition "I am a smoker" does not fit

cognitive dissonance: A state of psychological tension that is aroused when a person simultaneously holds two ideas or thoughts—cognitions— that contradict one another.

psychologically with the cognition "Smoking causes lung cancer," and the lack of fit creates the state of psychological tension referred to as dissonance.

When we experience dissonance, we are motivated to reduce it. We can do this in a variety of ways (Simon, Greenberg, & Brehm, 1995; Joule & Beauvois, 1998; Leippe & Eisenstadt, 1999; Schultz & Lepper, 1999). First, we can modify one (or even both) of the cognitions: "I smoke so little that it hardly counts as smoking." Second, we can change the perceived importance of one of the cognitions: "The evidence that links smoking to lung cancer is weak and inconclusive." Third, we can add new cognitions to the cognitive equation: "Nobody in my family has ever had cancer, and my vegetarian diet compensates for the cigarettes I smoke." Fourth, we can deny that the two cognitions are related to one another: "I don't believe that smoking will lead to lung cancer." No matter what method we use, the result is the same: a reduction in dissonance, illustrated in Figure 10–3 (Simon, Greenberg, & Brehm, 1995; Harmon-Jones & Mills, 1999).

Dissonance theory explains the results of the situation described earlier, in which participants were offered either $20 or $1 to act as confederates. The scenario was employed in an actual experiment conducted in the late 1950s that proved to be a groundbreaking demonstration of the validity of cognitive dissonance theory (Festinger & Carlsmith, 1959).

According to a dissonance theorist's point of view, the $20 that participants were paid to tell people things they did not believe provided ample justification for the deception in which they were engaged. (Taking inflation into account, $20 at the time the experiment was run is the equivalent of close to $100 today.) Little dissonance would be expected to arise.

But consider the participants who were offered only $1 to say something they didn't believe. These individuals experienced **insufficient justification**, a situation in which people perform, for a minimal inducement, a behavior that is discrepant with their true attitudes. Participants in the insufficient-justification condition were left holding two contradictory cognitions:

- Cognition 1: I believe the task is boring.
- Cognition 2: I'm telling others the task is interesting, with little justification.

FIGURE 10–3   Dissonance Produced from Smoking The two contradictory cognitions that (1) I smoke, and (2) Smoking leads to cancer, produce cognitive dissonance, which may be reduced in several ways.

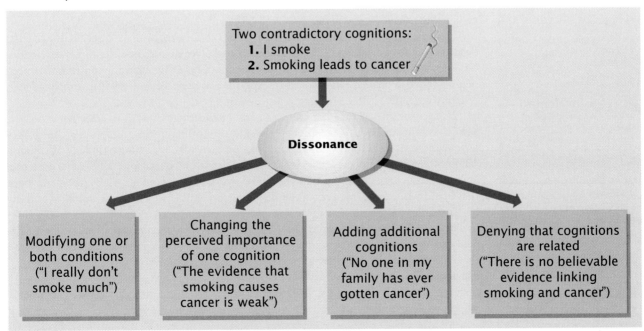

How could these participants reduce their dissonance? It was hard to deny that they had agreed to tell others that the task was interesting (the second cognition), because that denial would fly in the face of reality. It was easier to change the first cognition—the route most participants followed. When asked how much they enjoyed the initial task, participants in the $1 condition stated that they enjoyed the peg turning significantly more than did those who were paid $20.

One of the most striking features of this result is that it disagrees with what other theoretical approaches might predict. If we were to take a strict learning theory approach (or even just rely on common sense), we might well reason that a person who was paid a larger sum would come to hold more positive attitudes than someone who was paid a lower amount. After all, the presumed reinforcement value of the money would be greater when more, rather than less, money was offered. But this was not the case at all, a finding that supports the validity of cognitive dissonance theory.

The initial work on cognitive dissonance theory marked the beginning of a decades-long search for the conditions that arouse dissonance and lead to attitude change. Dissonance, it turns out, is readily aroused and occurs under many different circumstances (Harmon-Jones et al., 1996; Girandola, 1997; Hosseini, 1997; McGregor, Newby-Clark, & Zanna, 1999).

Consider, for instance, something as straightforward as buying a new stereo. You go to the store, and the salesperson shows you two models that fit your needs: Hitech and Goodsound. The Hitech model is state-of-the-art; it has lots of fancy buttons, an obscure feature called parallel sound, and some terrific-looking graphic tone gauges. Goodsound, on the other hand, is a reliable old standard. It's been around for years and has a good reputation. It does not look as sharp or have as many features as the Hitech brand, but it delivers fine sound.

After much anguish, you finally choose Goodsound. As you hand over your credit card, though, and ponder whether you made the right choice, you experience an uneasy feeling: dissonance!

Your discomfort is not surprising: Suddenly you hold two discrepant cognitions. One cognition includes all the positive qualities of the rejected Hitech model (it looks so good) and the negative qualities of the Goodsound model you've chosen (its lack of features). The second cognition is the major, and inescapable, fact that you're in the midst of buying the Goodsound model.

Happily, though, dissonance-reduction processes come to the rescue. You can't very well deny that you've bought the Goodsound model, because the clerk is boxing it up right before your eyes. But you can turn to the other set of cognitions and try to maximize the positive features of your purchase and minimize its negative qualities. You can ask the clerk to describe how some of the features of your model operate, or you can ask how often it needs repair, certain what the answer will be.

Choosing from several alternatives, then, brings about a recasting of attitudes due to postdecision cognitive dissonance. In **postdecision cognitive dissonance**, the chosen alternative becomes more positive, and the unchosen one more negative. This phenomenon has been demonstrated repeatedly in laboratory experiments (e.g., Brehm, 1956; Aronson, 1997; Murphy & Miller, 1997).

Postdecision dissonance has another consequence: It may lead to selective exposure. **Selective exposure** occurs when people seek out information that supports a choice they have made and avoid information that is inconsistent with that choice (Frey & Wicklund, 1978; Sweeney & Gruber, 1984; Frey, 1986; Dietrich & Berkowitz, 1997). For instance, after purchasing the Goodsound model, you may read every word of an advertisement about that brand while avoiding a friend who recently bought a Hitech stereo and likes nothing better than to talk about how great it is.

For a theory that is now approaching the start of its fifth decade, cognitive dissonance has held up surprisingly well. Nevertheless, current dissonance researchers suggest that although the basic tenets of the theory are accurate, dissonance is less universal than originally thought, and that it is aroused only under certain conditions.

For example, Joel Cooper and Russell Fazio (1984) argue that dissonance occurs only when people feel that they have personal responsibility for their actions. In their view, if

postdecision cognitive dissonance:
A situation in which the chosen alternative becomes more positive, and the unchosen one more negative.

selective exposure: A consequence of postdecision dissonance that occurs when people seek out information that supports a choice they have made and avoid information that is inconsistent with that choice.

participants in the Festinger and Carlsmith (1959) study believed they had no choice but to act as the experimenter's confederate (perhaps the experimenter was also their unprincipled introductory psychology professor, and they suspected that their class grade was vulnerable), they would likely experience little or no dissonance. Participants who felt forced to lie to fellow students about the experiment and consequently experienced no remorse would probably have felt little dissonance. (Although in actuality participants in the study *were* induced by the experimenter to agree to act as confederates, at least the illusion existed that the choice to participate was theirs—leading them to experience dissonance.)

Finally, for people to experience dissonance, they must also experience some degree of physiological arousal. Although Festinger was never terribly explicit about the specific underpinnings of the state of dissonance, it has become apparent that the unpleasantness of dissonance is brought about by actual changes in physiological arousal (Croyle & Cooper, 1983; Elkin & Leippe, 1986; Joule, 1987; Etgen & Rosen, 1993). Of course, for the dissonance to have any effect on a person's attitudes, the person must be able to attribute the arousal explicitly to dissonant cognitions. If a student attributes her discomfort to having just jogged 6 miles or to drinking six cups of coffee, it is unlikely that she will be motivated to change her attitudes (Zanna & Cooper, 1974; Frey, Fries, & Osnabrugge, 1983; Cooper, 1999).

"It's probably all for the best. Those meals were awfully rich."

ALTERNATIVES TO COGNITIVE DISSONANCE THEORY: IS DISSONANCE THE RIGHT ROUTE TO ATTITUDE CHANGE?

Although the ravages of time—and experimental investigation—have largely been kind to cognitive dissonance theory, a significant note of dissent exists. Although few social psychologists argue that the experimental findings and results of dissonance experiments are in error, some have developed fundamental misgivings about explanations that rest solely on the phenomenon of cognitive dissonance. Rather than finding flaws in the patterns of results coming from experimental work designed to confirm dissonance theory, they suggest that the findings have very different implications from those arrived at by dissonance theorists. In other words, no one questions the results, but some question the lessons to be learned from them. We turn now to some of the alternatives to cognitive dissonance explanations for these results.

Self-perception: The rational observer looks inward.   Return once again to the Festinger and Carlsmith (1959) study, and put yourself in the place of the participant. You might argue to yourself that $20 is ample justification to say that the experiment is fascinating, regardless of your personal belief. There's clearly no need to look inward and figure out why you're doing what you're doing.

But suppose you agreed to the experimenter's request for a mere $1. Here, as you examine your motivations, things are a bit more puzzling. Why did you agree to his request? To solve this little problem, you try out the perspective of an outside observer who might be watching the experimental scene play out. By taking this approach you are able to come up with a solution: You reason that, from a logical point of view, your agreement to make positive statements for so little material justification must mean that you really did enjoy the task. Consequently, when asked your attitude about the task, you shift to a more positive response.

It's important to recognize that the ultimate result is the same as that suggested by cognitive dissonance theory: Attitudes tend to shift when the justification is low (the $1 condition) and change little when the justification is strong (the $20 condition). What changes, however, is the underlying explanation, which is embodied in an approach known as self-perception theory.

According to *self-perception theory*, championed by social psychologist Daryl Bem (1967, 1972) and first discussed in Chapter 4, people sometimes form and maintain attitudes by observing their own behavior. To the extent that our attitudes are ambiguous or unclear, we look inward at ourselves and our own behavior to understand our attitudes—a process analogous to our use of other people's behavior to infer *their* attitudes. Based on what we encounter within, we rationally determine our attitudes.

In a test of self-perception theory, Bem (1972) carried out what he referred to as an "interpersonal replication" of the Festinger and Carlsmith (1959) experiment in which he presented a detailed description of the original study. He asked participants to predict the attitude that an imaginary participant would hold at the end of the study.

Bem's findings corresponded to those of the original study quite precisely: The observers guessed that the participants in the $1 condition would hold more positive attitudes than those in the $20 condition. Bem reasoned that when the external inducement is low (the $1 condition), the observer takes the behavior as an indication of the true attitude. More crucially, Bem argued that the participants themselves went through the same logical process, inferring their attitude on the basis of their behavior. Consequently, dissonance theory predictions to the contrary, no arousal due to dissonance was necessary to produce a shift in attitude. What produced the change were the participants' rational, logical powers of deduction.

It makes sense. However, you may begin to see a flaw in Bem's reasoning—one that his critics were quick to identify. Despite the fact that the results of an interpersonal simulation match those of an original experiment, no guarantee exists that the underlying psychological processes that produced the two sets of results were identical. Furthermore, because both dissonance and self-perception theories make the same predictions about attitudes, there appears to be no reason to choose one over the other.

Still, the fact that both theories made identical predictions was provocative, and it caused researchers to redouble their efforts to identify which of the two provides the more accurate explanation. The result was basically a draw, although certain situations may favor one theory over the other (Beauvois, Bungert, & Mariette, 1995; Harmon-Jones, Brehm, Greenberg, & Simon, 1996; Harmon-Jones, 1999).

According to a careful review of the literature by Russell Fazio and colleagues (Fazio, Zanna, & Cooper, 1977), cognitive dissonance theory best accounts for situations in which people are induced to behave in ways that strongly contradict their attitudes. For instance, when with little justification you say you love something that you actually hate, you are likely to experience the disagreeable arousal that dissonance theory predicts.

In contrast, mild discrepancies between attitude and behavior are unlikely to produce arousal and dissonance. For instance, unenthusiastically saying that you like something when in fact you're actually unsure about it creates just a minor discrepancy between attitude and behavior ("I'm not sure how I feel about the tie, but I just told Bill it looks fine"). In such low-discrepancy situations, dissonance is unlikely to be aroused, and you will be more likely to act like the rational observer of your own behavior that self-perception theory predicts.

Self-affirmation: Eliminating the sting of dissonance. According to social psychologist Claude Steele (1988), it is not so much the inconsistency between two cognitions that brings about dissonance. Instead, it is the threat that the inconsistency poses to our self-concept (Steele, 1998; Aronson et al., 1999; Spencer, Steele, & Quinn, 1999).

Consider, for instance, how people who smoke are confronted with knowledge that they are engaging in an unhealthy activity. In classic dissonance theory, the means of remediating the inconsistency is to change one (or both) of the cognitions regarding the act of smoking. By altering their cognitions, smokers are able to bring the cognitive situation back into synch.

In Steele's view, however, another process may explain how people resolve the dissonance. According to his **self-affirmation theory**, people who experience dissonance may deal with it by seeking to assert their adequacy as individuals. To affirm their self-worth, they may engage in activities that have little or nothing to do with smoking—such as aiding the homeless, working harder in their academic or occupational pursuits, or trying to be better parents to their children. The dissonance between cognitions still exists; people are well aware that their smoking and the health consequences of their behavior are dissonant. However, what has changed is that with enhanced self-esteem the dissonance has lost its sting.

Several experiments demonstrate the link between dissonant cognitions and self-affirmation (Heine & Lehman, 1997; Beauregard & Dunning, 1998; Aronson, Cohen, & Nail, 1999). In one, for example, Steele identified a group of students at the University of Washington who were strongly opposed to an impending tuition hike (likely not hard to find!) (Steele,

self-affirmation theory: The theory that people who experience dissonance may deal with it by seeking to assert their adequacy as individuals.

1988). When these students came to the laboratory, they were told the experiment in which they were to participate involved writing essays for a "legislative survey" about tuition increases. Because of a supposed oversupply of essays against the tuition rise, they were asked to write one in favor of the hike—an activity designed to arouse dissonance between their cognitions (against the hike) and their behavior (writing an essay in favor of the hike).

To influence the degree of dissonance, the experimenters led the participants to believe they had varying degrees of choice in writing the essay. Participants in one condition were given essentially no choice in the matter and were told they were required to complete the questionnaire—a condition that produced relatively little dissonance. Participants in the other condition, however, were maneuvered into thinking that they had ample choice in writing the essay. These participants, of course, experienced considerable dissonance.

As we would expect, participants in the high-dissonance condition who were asked their attitudes about the tuition hike just after they wrote the essay expressed more favorable attitudes toward the impending hike than those who were in the low-dissonance condition (see the first two bars in Figure 10–4). Such a result is entirely consistent with classic dissonance theory.

Remember, though, that the experiment was designed to test self-affirmation theory. To do this, it was necessary to give participants the opportunity to affirm an important aspect of their self-concepts just before having their attitudes assessed. In so doing, any dissonance produced would potentially be less aversive, consequently producing less of a threat to their self-esteem.

To provide participants with the opportunity to affirm their self-concepts, Steele identified two subgroups of participants opposed to tuition hikes. One group consisted of those who held a set of strong economic–political values; participants in the other group did not. According to self-affirmation theory, if the participants with the strong values were given the opportunity to display or affirm this aspect of themselves, dissonance would be less likely to produce a change in attitudes. But for participants who did not hold such a value orientation, providing them the opportunity to assert their economic–political values would not matter: They would experience dissonance and would be expected to show attitude change.

This is just what happened, as you can see in the third and fourth bars in Figure 10–4. When participants with strong economic–political values were given the opportunity to

FIGURE 10–4   Dissonance as Self-Affirmation Higher numbers indicate more support for the tuition hike, reflecting more dissonance-reducing attitude change. In the first two conditions, the typical dissonance effect was found: Low choice led to low dissonance (and hence no attitude change), while high choice led to high dissonance (and therefore attitude change). In contrast, for participants in the last two conditions, who were given the opportunity to affirm their economic–political values, little dissonance (and consequently little attitude change) occurred for participants who held such values strongly. In contrast, for those who held the values weakly, the lack of opportunity for self-affirmation increased dissonance (and consequent attitude change). (*Source:* Steele, 1988.)

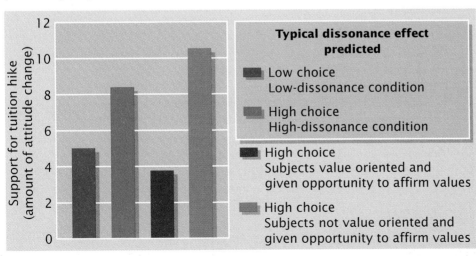

complete a questionnaire about their values just after writing the pro-tuition-hike essay (and therefore were able to assert an important part of their self-concept), they were much less likely to show attitude change. Rather, they remained opposed to the tuition hike. Apparently, dissonance was not aroused. On the other hand, participants who did not hold strong economic–political values showed the typical consequences of dissonance, even when given an opportunity to complete the values questionnaire: They were likely to show more favorable attitudes toward the tuition hike after writing their essays, because the questionnaire did not provide an opportunity to affirm their self-worth.

The three faces of dissonance.   Few theories have spawned as much research and theorizing as cognitive dissonance theory. As we have seen in the three explanations for dissonance-related phenomena, there is little argument regarding the basic tenets of the theory. Holding discrepant or contradictory cognitions often does lead to shifts in attitude. However, it is the specific nature of the underlying phenomenon that remains in question (e.g., Harmon-Jones, Greenberg, Solomon, & Simon, 1996; Devine et al., 1999).

According to classic dissonance theory, dissonance is an unpleasant, aversive state. It leads to actual physiological arousal that people are motivated to eliminate. On the other hand, self-perception theory maintains that attitude change comes about because of the inferences that people make about their own behavior. Finally, self-affirmation theory suggests that dissonance need not be an unpleasant state that motivates people to change their attitudes—*if* the means exist for affirming their self-worth.

The difficulty in choosing among the three explanations is that all of them rely on variants of a similar principle: A discrepancy in cognition leads to efforts to make our attitudes consistent with our behavior. The success of all three approaches suggests that although there may be different routes to dealing with inconsistency, we aspire to a match between attitudes and behavior.

On the other hand, success in attaining consistency sometimes eludes us. Indeed, as we see next, just how closely attitudes and behavior match up has proved to be one of the most important—and sometimes vexing—questions confronting social psychologists who study attitudes.

REVIEW AND RETHINK

Review

- People strive to maintain consistency, both in individual components of attitudes and among attitudes.

- Cognitive dissonance theory proposes that a state of psychological tension is aroused when a person simultaneously holds two cognitions that contradict each other.

- Self-perception theory and self-affirmation theory offer alternatives to cognitive dissonance explanations.

Rethink

- According to *When Prophecy Fails,* what is the typical reaction of cult followers when confronted with evidence suggesting that their leader may be a fraud? Can you use cognitive dissonance theory to explain other possible reactions to this scenario? How?

- According to self-perception theory, would you enjoy a task more if you were paid $10 or $5 for completing it? Compare this prediction with that made by learning theory.

- What would cognitive dissonance theory suggest about the possibility of using operant conditioning with attitudes? Describe an attempt to use operant conditioning on an attitude that would be unlikely to succeed, and one that would be likely to succeed.

- Why are social psychologists unable to ascertain which of the three competing explanations for the dissonance literature is correct? Is it possible that more than one theory is correct? Defend your answer.

ATTITUDES AND BEHAVIOR: WHAT ARE THE LINKS?

It's the 1930s, and prejudice against Asian Americans is widespread and blatant. You're the owner of a small hotel, and one day a well-dressed Asian American couple, accompanied by a Caucasian, asks to spend the night. Despite the strong prejudice against Asian Americans, you say without hesitation, "Of course. We have several rooms available. Just sign the guest register here."

A few months later, you receive a letter requesting a reservation. The letter notes that the people needing a room are Asian American. Without even bothering to extend the courtesy of a reply, you throw the request in the trash.

People observing your behavior in both instances probably would be perplexed. The negative attitudes implied by your failure to reply to the letter hardly seem to fit with your ready acceptance of the Asian American couple when they stood in front of you. The most plausible conclusion: Attitudes and behavior are not linked.

In fact, this was the reasoning used by Richard LaPiere, who in the 1930s conducted a study that has become a classic. LaPiere accompanied a Chinese couple on a 3-month, 10,000-mile trip, stopping at some 250 hotels and restaurants. In every establishment but one, he and the couple received service (LaPiere, 1934).

A few months later, LaPiere sent a letter to every place they had stopped, asking whether the establishment would serve patrons of Asian ancestry. Staff at about 50% of the establishments didn't even bother to respond. Of those establishments whose staff did reply, almost 92% flatly said "No"; the rest said "Maybe."

LaPiere concluded that attitudes and behavior were unrelated. Social psychologists embraced this reasoning for several decades. Still, it seemed puzzling: If one of the components of attitudes was an intention to behave in a particular way, and if people strive to maintain consistency, why weren't attitudes and behavior linked?

Part of the answer, it turns out, comes from the methodological difficulties that were later found to have flawed LaPiere's study. For example, there is no way of ascertaining whether the individuals who answered LaPiere's letter (and remember that only 50% even took the time to reply) were the same ones who actually permitted the Chinese couple to stop at their establishments. Furthermore, the Chinese couple may have received subtle signs of prejudice and disapproval, such as unpleasant service or nonverbal indicators of displeasure, even though they were allowed into an establishment. In sum, the actual *correspondence,* or similarity, between attitude and behavior might have been more apparent if the study had employed a more sensitive measure.

With these serious shortcomings, it is no wonder that the study was incapable of establishing a link between attitudes and behavior. Moreover, had LaPiere's study been the only one unable to find evidence for a link, the idea would have quickly died. Instead, dozens of studies followed, supporting the conclusion that attitudes and behavior are not linked. By 1969, after thoroughly sifting through the existing research literature, social psychologist Allan Wicker found that the average correlation between measures of attitudes and measures of behavior was an extremely modest +.30. Wicker concluded that only a minimal link exists between attitudes and behavior (Wicker, 1969).

THE RIGHT ANSWER TO THE WRONG QUESTION

However, Wicker's review was not to be the last word. In fact, in some ways it provided an answer to the wrong question. Wicker focused on the question of *whether* attitudes are related to behavior. However, a more appropriate question would have been: *Under what circumstances* are attitudes and behavior linked? When social psychologists began to investigate this issue, their understanding of how attitudes and behavior are related took a giant step forward (Petty & Krosnick, 1995).

Why would attitudes be linked to behavior at some times and not others? The answer is that many times our behavior is influenced by factors inherent in the situation, and at such

Although Catholics may subscribe to the general teachings of the Catholic Church and the Pope, their behavior relating to certain issues—such as the use of birth control—may be inconsistent with their overall attitudes.

times our personal attitudes are less influential in governing our behavior. For instance, a teenager may have a positive attitude toward music videos, but she may not watch MTV much because her parents are firmly opposed to it (and are in charge of the television). A bigoted white restaurant owner in San Antonio may hold a negative attitude regarding Latinos, but he still serves them because it is illegal not to do so or because he would be hurt economically if he didn't. You may love to eat red meat, but you order tofu burgers in the presence of your vegetarian friends to avoid offending them.

In sum, holding a particular attitude is no guarantee that that attitude will determine behavior in a given situation (Roche & Ramsbey, 1993; Barker et al., 1994). The question we need to address, then, is this: Under what circumstances are attitudes and behavior related?

WHEN ATTITUDES AND BEHAVIOR ARE LINKED

Imagine an unmarried woman who holds a generally negative attitude about abortion. To her dismay, she learns that she is pregnant, and she tries to decide what to do. After considering the options, she ultimately decides that abortion is her best option. Is her behavior unrelated to her attitude? To answer the question, we must take several factors into account, including the relevance of the attitude to the behavior, the strength and stability of the attitude, and factors relating to the specifics of the situation (Doll & Ajzen, 1992; Kraus, 1995; Reinecke, Schmidt, & Ajzen, 1997a).

Relevance of attitude to behavior.   Before we can expect to find a link between an attitude and a behavior, we need to be certain that the attitude being assessed is one that is relevant, or pertinent, to the specific object of interest (Ajzen & Fishbein, 1977). For instance, when LaPiere asked in his letter whether an Asian American couple would be welcomed at an establishment, he most likely elicited an attitude regarding Asian Americans in general, stereotypical terms—and not one having to do with well-dressed Asian Americans accompanied by a Caucasian.

Similarly, although common sense might suggest that a woman's negative attitude regarding abortion would prevent her from having one, we need to consider whether other attitudes might be more relevant, given the specifics of the situation. For instance, attitudes regarding the difficulties of unwed motherhood or fears of embarrassing her parents may be more relevant in such a situation.

Strength, importance, and stability of attitudes.   Obviously, the stronger and more important the attitude, the more likely that it will influence behavior. For instance, if your attitude about abortion is grounded in strong religious and moral beliefs, you are considerably more likely to act in a manner consistent with the attitude than if your attitude is relatively weak. Similarly, a person with firm attitudinal convictions regarding a political candidate is considerably more likely to vote for the candidate than is someone who is unsure and wavering in attitudinal support for the candidate (Petty & Krosnick, 1995; Zuwerink & Devine, 1996; Liu & Latané, 1998).

Furthermore, attitudes that are relatively stable and enduring are more likely to affect behavior than those that are relatively recent in origin (Doll & Ajzen, 1992; Kraus, 1995). A lifelong Democrat is less likely to be swayed by the rhetoric of a Republican candidate than is someone whose only contact with the Democratic Party was during the previous election (Davidson & Jaccard, 1979; Kallgren & Wood, 1986).

Attitudes, behavior, and the situation.   You know it's important to floss your teeth. You even feel pretty good when you floss, knowing that you've potentially spared yourself a lecture on dental hygiene on your next visit to the dentist. You have good intentions, too; you always aim to floss your teeth. All three components of an attitude are in place: cognition, affect, and behavioral intention. So why do you not floss more often?

The answer to the apparent inconsistency between attitude and behavior rests on the specific aspects of the situation that surround the attitude and require action or behavior of some kind. You may feel too tired to floss. You may have run out of floss. You may think that you've brushed your teeth with such vigor that you don't need to floss. You may decide you have no time to floss.

As this example illustrates, several attributes of a situation may conspire to prevent people from demonstrating behavior consistent with the attitude they hold. Exhibiting behavior consistent with an attitude may entail certain costs, such as effort, time, material, and equipment. The absence of any one or a combination of these may produce a discrepancy between attitude and behavior.

Situational factors play a central role in an influential theory originally proposed by social psychologists Martin Fishbein and Icek Ajzen (pronounced "I-zen") and reformulated by Ajzen in the mid-1980s (Ajzen & Fishbein, 1980; Ajzen, 1985; Madden, Ellen, & Ajzen, 1992; Doll & Ajzen, 1992). The **theory of planned behavior** suggests that the likelihood that a person's behavior will be consistent with his or her attitude depends on a measured, rational decision-making process that considers a combination of several factors (see Figure 10–5).

The most influential and immediate determinant of behavior is, not surprisingly, a person's behavioral intention (Kim & Hunter, 1993; Reinecke, Schmidt, & Ajzen, 1997b; Leone, Perugini, & Ercolani, 1999). A **behavioral intention** reflects a person's plan or resolve—his or her intent—to engage in a behavior that relates to the attitude. For example, you might intend to begin a low-fat diet to lower the risk of heart attack and lose weight.

How do behavioral intentions arise? As you can see in Figure 10–5, an individual's behavioral intentions to do something arise in part from particular attitudes that person holds about the behavior and related topics. In the model, attitudes (for example, feeling positively toward a low-fat diet) are considered primarily in terms of evaluations of particular behaviors.

In addition to attitudes, though, two additional, equally important factors result in behavioral intention: subjective norms and perceived behavioral control. A **subjective norm** is

theory of planned behavior: The notion suggesting the likelihood that someone will behave in a way consistent with an attitude depends on a measured, rational decision-making process that considers a combination of several factors.

behavioral intention: The probability that people place on the likelihood that they will engage in a behavior that is relevant to a held attitude.

subjective norms: The factor in behavioral intention that takes into account the perceived social pressure to carry out the behavior.

FIGURE 10–5   The Theory of Planned Behavior The link between attitudes and behavior is not a direct one. According to the theory of planned behavior, behavior is the result of an intention to behave in a particular way. However, the intention is a result of an attitude, subjective norm, and perceived behavioral control. (*Source:* Based on Ajzen, 1987, p. 46.)

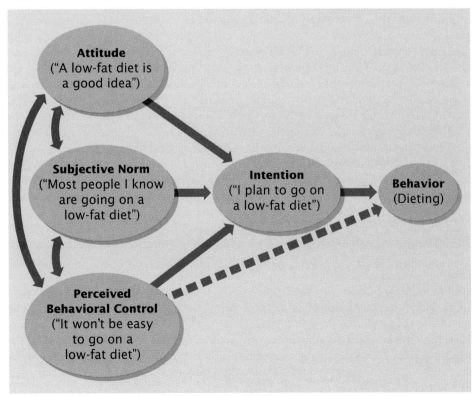

perceived behavioral control: The factor in behavioral intention that takes into account the ease or difficulty of carrying out the behavior, based on prior experience and anticipated barriers to performing it.

accessibility: The degree to which an attitude can be brought to mind.

the perceived social pressure to carry out the behavior, and **perceived behavioral control** is the perceived ease or difficulty of carrying out the behavior, based on prior experience and anticipated barriers to performing it.

For instance, a subjective norm about a low-fat diet may be the fact that many friends are going on similar diets and that dieting is an admirable thing to do. Perceived behavioral control might be manifested in the idea that such a diet would be hard to maintain and that there are many obstacles to staying on such a diet. Subjective norms directly affect behavioral intention, whereas perceived behavioral control has an impact on both behavioral intention and actual behavior (Giles & Cairns, 1995).

In sum, only by jointly considering a person's attitude, subjective norms, and perceived behavioral control relevant to the attitude can we understand behavioral intentions, which in turn lead to actual behavior. The model suggests, then, that attitudes and behavior are related—but the linkage is not direct.

Does the model of planned behavior provide an accurate account of attitude–behavior links? The vast majority of research evidence suggests that the basic model is, in fact, quite precise, although its precision depends on the accuracy with which each component of the model is measured. Furthermore, the model has been applied to a wide variety of settings in such diverse attitudinal arenas as purchasing an automobile, engaging in safer sex, studying, behaving prosocially, speeding, and exercising (e.g., Kerner & Grossman, 1998; Courneya et al., 1999; Leone, Perugini, & Ercolani, 1999; Sutton, McVey, & Glanz, 1999).

ATTITUDES WITHOUT AWARENESS: WHEN RATIONALITY STUMBLES

Although the theory of planned behavior is largely successful in predicting behavior from attitudes, not everyone agrees with its basic presumption that people typically act on a rational basis. On the contrary, some recent approaches reject the notion that people thoughtfully consider behavioral alternatives on the basis of attitudes and then act on the choices they've rationally made. Instead, these approaches suggest that people's behavior is sometimes based on attitudes below conscious awareness—and that in some cases, behavior may be entirely unrelated to attitudes (Verplanken et al., 1994).

Consider smoking, for example. People who smoke may continue to do so long after the attitudes that gave rise to the behavior initially (such as the desire to act cool or to fit in with peers) have completely vanished. Indeed, you may know smokers who readily state that their attitudes toward smoking are entirely negative, that they hate the mess, the cost, and the fact that it offends other people. But nonetheless, they continue to smoke, because the behavior has become habitual and occurs without conscious thought (Ronis, Yates, & Kirscht, 1989). As a result, in "automatic" behaviors such as smoking, attitudes and behavior may be completely independent.

In other cases, attitudes do guide our behavior—but without our awareness. Specifically, attitudes vary in their **accessibility**, the degree to which an attitude can be brought to mind (Fazio, Blascovich, & Driscoll, 1992; Fazio & Powell, 1997; Fazio, 1998). Some attitudes are readily accessible from memory, and just mentioning them immediately brings their evaluative component to mind. ("The president of the United States" and "your mother" are two good examples of highly accessible attitudes for most people.) In contrast, other attitudes are relatively low in accessibility; the evaluative component is not readily triggered, and the memory connections between the object of the attitude and our evaluation not particularly strong. (Consider your attitude toward "toothpicks" as one example of an attitude likely to be low in accessibility.)

The greater the accessibility of an attitude, the more likely it is that our behavior will be affected when the attitude is brought to mind (Bassili, 1995; Posavac, Sanbonmatsu, & Fazio, 1997). Even more important, we need not be aware of this process to be influenced by the attitude—a point brought home by a series of experiments carried out by social psychologist Russell Fazio and colleagues (Fazio, 1990). For instance, in one of these experiments participants were presented with a target object about which they had a positive or negative attitude (Fazio et al., 1986). This initial presentation was meant to prime participants, arousing the memory network that contained the attitude and the particular evaluations associated with its object.

In the next part of the experiment, the experimenter presented the participants with a list of adjectives, some of which were positive and some negative. Asked to indicate as quickly as possible which of the adjectives were positive and which were negative—by pressing a key marked "good" or "bad"—participants answered more quickly when the adjective was consistent with the attitude that had been primed.

For example, participants who had been primed first by seeing the word *cockroach* (about which, like most of us, they held a negative evaluation) were quicker to identify adjectives such as *disgusting* as "bad" adjectives. This effect was most pronounced for attitudes that were highly accessible—those attitudes having strong links between the target of the attitude and the target's evaluation in memory (Fazio et al., 1986).

In summary, it is now clear that our behavior can be influenced by our attitudes in subtle ways, even when we are unaware that the attitude has relevance to the situation or that the attitude has been activated. Although the research demonstrating this phenomenon is not extensive at this point (e.g., Fiske & Taylor, 1991), the implications are profound. For instance, if people hold particular attitudes toward members of minority groups, those attitudes may alter or bias their behavior toward members of the group, even if the people are not aware that their behavior is being affected. Similarly, as we consider in the Applying Social Psychology box, our understanding of our own attitudes can affect us in unexpected ways.

Can attitudes be acquired without our knowing it?   The ability of existing attitudes to subtly influence our behavior raises another possibility: That attitudes may be *acquired* without awareness. Such a notion has been seized on by advertising agencies, who have examined the possibility of *subliminal advertising*. In this type of advertising, commercial messages are presented outside conscious awareness so that people are unaware that they have been exposed to a message. The possibility of subliminal advertising was first raised by a supposed demonstration in a New Jersey drive-in movie in the 1950s, where the words *Drink Coke* and *Eat popcorn* were flashed on a screen for one-third of a millisecond during films. The theater reported that sales of Coke and popcorn soared.

Despite these claims, scientific studies have been unable to demonstrate the efficacy of subliminal advertising. In fact, no reputable study has found evidence that subliminal messages can change attitudes. Moreover, even the Coke-and-popcorn demonstration turned out to be a hoax (Greenwald et al., 1991). Although people are able to perceive and retain at least some kinds of information about which they are not aware, such information is fleeting and has little subsequent effect on their behavior (Greenwald, Draine, & Abrams, 1996; Greenwald & Draine, 1998).

This has not stopped the public from believing that subliminal messages can influence people's conduct. For instance, the parents of two boys who attempted suicide sued the rock band Judas Priest, alleging that subliminal messages saying "Do it!" embedded in a song about the hopelessness of life drove them to kill themselves (Neely, 1990). A judge disagreed, however, throwing the case out of court—as would most social psychologists.

Despite claims for the phenomenon of subliminal advertising, there is no evidence that it is a mechanism by which attitudes are influenced. These people are buying popcorn because they want to, not because they perceived a hidden message flashed across a film screen.

APPLYING SOCIAL PSYCHOLOGY
WHEN IT HELPS TO KNOW YOUR ATTITUDES:
THE LINK BETWEEN ATTITUDES AND STRESS AND HEALTH IN COLLEGE

Can knowing your attitudes bring you better health?

That's one conclusion that can be drawn from a study by social psychologists Russell Fazio and Martha Powell (1997), who examined how the accessibility of attitudes affects college students' stress and health.

In the study, first-year college students were asked a series of questions about their attitudes toward a variety of academic concerns, including possible majors, types of classes, and study habits at the start of the first term of college. In addition, they completed questions about stress in their lives and the state of their physical and mental health. Two months later they completed the measures of stress and health a second time.

The results of the study showed that the ease with which participants could express their attitudes—as measured by the time it took them to register their likes and dislikes when presented with an academically relevant issue—was related to their stress and health. But the relationship was not simple and depended on whether participants entered college in good or bad health. For students in good health at the start of college, those with more accessible attitudes toward academic topics were less affected by the stress they experienced than those with

less accessible attitudes. Being aware of their academic likes and dislikes helped those students experiencing stress to withstand it more effectively.

For students who entered college in poorer health, attitude accessibility also helped, but in a different way. For those students experiencing considerable stress, their health continued to be poor, regardless of attitude accessibility. But for those students who experienced less stress, the greater their attitude accessibility, the more their health improved.

Why should attitude accessibility be related to more effective coping with stress and improvements in health? The answer is that knowing what you believe helps you make decisions more easily. Rather than having to mull over academic concerns—probably the primary source of stress in first-year college students—those with accessible attitudes are able to come to decisions quickly, without the need of continual reflection.

The relationship between attitude accessibility and stress and health is another example of how basic theory and research can be applied to practical issues. Attitudes clearly serve to help us function effectively and manage our lives.

THE INFORMED CONSUMER OF SOCIAL PSYCHOLOGY

EVALUATING ATTITUDE SURVEYS

"The President's popularity rating has fallen to an all-time low."

"Forty-two percent of Americans believe that hunting seals for their skins should be banned."

"Seven in ten college students say that they regularly practice safe sex."

Anyone who reads a newspaper or watches the nightly news is familiar with assertions such as these. The attitudes of the American people are assessed regularly on topics ranging from airline safety to the treatment of zoo animals.

What we typically do not learn from these news stories, however, is just how accurate such survey results are. As pollster Lydia K. Saad's comments in the Speaking of Social Psychology interview suggested, summary statements derived from surveys are only as good as the data on which they are based. To evaluate such survey results, then, we need to consider several questions:

♦ Was a carefully chosen, *representative sample* used? If a survey assesses attitudes only from voters living in Iowa, the results should not be generalized to voters across the country.

♦ What was the specific question asked of survey respondents? Consider, for instance, a question that asks whether a person agrees or disagrees with the following statements:

"Because everyone is entitled to quality health care, a national health care system is necessary."

"Because the quality of health care in the United States is the best in the world, a national health care system is unnecessary."

In both of these sentences, the introductory clause would be expected to move respondents toward agreement. Similarly, use of emotionally loaded phrases such as "police brutality" or "the President's policy" in a survey might unduly influence respondents' answers (Oskamp, 1977).

◆ Did the social desirability needs of the survey respondents bias the results? People who are surveyed often want to be helpful and want to avoid showing their ignorance. Therefore, they may say that they agree with a policy about which they know little or nothing ("I think the government's passport policy is pretty good.")

◆ Finally, are the results statistically meaningful? As we discussed in Chapter 1, in order for differences to be real, they must meet certain statistical criteria that help rule out the possibility that observed differences are due simply to chance. Just knowing that, compared with 47% of Democrats, only 43% of Republicans approve of a given policy is not very informative. To interpret the 4% difference, we need to know whether it represents a *statistically significant* difference—a formal standard that can be determined only through mathematics, and not merely by eyeballing the data.

In sum, be very cautious when considering the results of everyday attitude assessments. Sometimes the results are far less than meets the eye.

REVIEW AND RETHINK

Review

* The relationship between attitudes and behavior depends on several factors, including the degree of correspondence between attitude and behavior; the relevance of an attitude to a behavior; the strength, importance, and stability of an attitude; and the situation.

* According to the theory of planned behavior, the major determinant of behavior is a person's behavioral intention, which is influenced by subjective norms and perceived behavioral control.

* Social cognitive approaches suggest that behavior is sometimes based on attitudes without awareness.

* People must take into account several factors when evaluating a survey, including the nature of the sample and the questions, the potential influence of social desirability on responses, and the statistical significance of the results.

Rethink

* The very definition of an attitude implies that attitudes strongly affect behavior. What evidence led Allan Wicker to conclude in 1969 that attitudes only weakly affected behavior? Was he correct?

* When are attitudes most likely to influence behavior? What characteristics of the attitude affect the attitude–behavior relationship? What characteristics of the situation affect this relationship?

* According to Ajzen, what hypothetical construct is most predictive of future behavior? What factors influence this construct?

LOOKING BACK

What is an attitude?

1. The predominant definition considers attitudes to be learned predispositions to respond in a favorable or unfavorable manner to a particular person, object, or idea. However, two other important approaches exist. A more cognitive approach considers attitudes to be a set of interrelated memories about a particular person, object, or idea. According to the ABC tripartite model, attitudes comprise three components: affective, behavioral, and cognitive. (p. 330)

How are attitudes formed, and what functions do they serve?

2. Several processes help explain the formation of attitudes. Among the basic processes are classical conditioning and operant conditioning, with social learning being of particular importance. (p. 333)

3. Regardless of how they are formed, attitudes serve two main functions. The knowledge function of attitudes refers to those aspects of attitudes that permit people to organize and make sense of the world. In contrast, the self function of attitudes permits people to create and maintain a positive sense of themselves. (p. 335)

4. Attitudes are hypothetical constructs and thus cannot be observed with the senses, but must be measured either directly or covertly. Among the procedures used to measure attitudes directly are Likert scales, the semantic differential, and Guttman scales. Covert measures that are used include gauging facial expressions, changes in facial muscles, and brain wave patterns. (p. 336)

Are our attitudes internally consistent, and how do we strive to maintain consistency?

5. Cognitive consistency approaches to attitudes focus on the ways people strive to maintain consistency within and between attitudes, as well as the ways they manage to reconcile inconsistencies. (p. 342)

6. One of the most influential theories of cognitive consistency is the theory of cognitive dissonance. Cognitive dissonance is a state of psychological tension aroused when a person simultaneously holds two ideas or thoughts—cognitions—that contradict one another. When people experience dissonance, they are motivated to reduce it through several means. (p. 344)

7. Several alternative explanations exist for phenomena explained by cognitive dissonance theory. Self-perception theory suggests that people form and maintain attitudes by observing their own behavior. Self-affirmation theory contends that people who experience dissonance may seek to deal with it by asserting their self-adequacy or worth as individuals. (p. 347)

How is behavior related to attitudes?

8. The extent to which attitudes affect behavior depends on several factors, including the degree of correspondence between attitude and behavior; the relevance of an attitude to a behavior; the strength, importance, and stability of an attitude; and situational factors. (p. 351)

9. The theory of planned behavior proposes that the likelihood that someone will behave consistently with an attitude depends on a measured, rational decision-making process. The major determinant of behavior in this process is an individual's behavioral intention. In turn, behavioral intention is produced by a combination of attitude, subjective norms, and perceived behavioral control. (p. 353)

10. Recent social cognitive approaches to attitude suggest that our behavior is sometimes based on attitudes without our awareness, and that in some cases our behavior is entirely unrelated to our attitudes. One of the most critical factors determining when an attitude will affect behavior is its accessibility. (p. 354)

What factors should we consider in evaluating the results of attitude surveys?

11. To evaluate the results of a survey, we need to consider these questions: Was a carefully chosen, representative sample used? What was the specific question asked of survey respondents? Did the social desirability needs of the survey respondents bias the results? Finally, are the results statistically meaningful? (p. 356)

EPILOGUE

As we've seen throughout this chapter, the concept of attitudes is not a simple one. Social psychologists have yet to agree on a single definition of attitudes, and researchers still struggle to specify the circumstances under which attitudes and behavior are linked.

At the same time, though, the various approaches that seek to explain attitudes have led to significant advances in social psychology. As we'll discuss in the next chapter, social psychologists have developed numerous ways to change people's attitudes. This important field of study is referred to as *persuasion*. The study of persuasion, which has considerable practical value, could not have taken place without the achievements in our theoretical understanding of attitudes that we discussed in this chapter. Once again, social psychologist Kurt Lewin's dictum, first mentioned in Chapter 1, applies: There is nothing so practical as a good theory.

Before we move on to the topic of persuasion, return to the prologue of this chapter, on the murder of Dr. Barnett Slepian by an unknown assailant, presumably because Slepian conducted abortions. Consider these questions:

1. How might the ABC tripartite model of attitudes apply to the attitudes of both Dr. Slepian and his killer regarding abortion?
2. In what ways did social learning apparently operate differently to form Slepian's and his killer's attitudes toward abortion.
3. Using the concept of cognitive dissonance, explain how Slepian's killer might have justified his views on abortion.
4. How might Slepian's killer have reconciled his opposition to abortion, which involves the death of a fetus, with his murder of Slepian?
5. How do the concepts of behavioral intention, subjective norm, and perceived behavioral control apply to Slepian's killer?

KEY TERMS AND CONCEPTS

ABC tripartite model (p. 332)

accessibility (p. 354)

attitudes (p. 330)

behavioral intention (p. 353)

cognitive consistency (p. 342)

cognitive dissonance (p. 344)

covert measure of attitude (p. 340)

Guttman scales (p. 338)

hypothetical constructs (p. 336)

insufficient justification (p. 345)

knowledge function of attitudes (p. 335)

Likert scale (p. 336)

perceived behavioral control (p. 354)

postdecision cognitive dissonance (p. 346)

roles (p. 343)

selective exposure (p. 346)

self function of attitudes (p. 335)

self-affirmation theory (p. 348)

semantic differential (p. 336)

subjective norms (p. 353)

theory of planned behavior (p. 353)

CHAPTER 11

PERSUASION

Changing Attitudes
and Behavior

PROLOGUE

Meet You in Aisle Three

The attitudes of consumers are continually being monitored.

It's a bright winter morning in Buffalo, and Top's supermarket on Erie Road is bustling. Customers snake through the aisles, some stopping to look at special displays while others dart by, en route to the fastest checkout lane. Over in the health and beauty aids section, Jerilyn Schueler waits. A field interviewer for market research firm Elrick & Lavidge, Schueler is scouting for customers buying a [certain] packaged good. The manufacturer wants to know why people buy its brand—or the competition's. Is it the price? The packaging? Promotional displays?

Unfortunately, there's not much aisle traffic, so Schueler keeps herself busy arranging shelves and assisting shoppers. Then she notices a young mother dropping the right item into her cart. Schueler jumps to action, introducing herself and asking the woman if she has time to answer a few questions. The shopper agrees, perhaps swayed by the crisp $5 bill she'll earn. Schueler breathes a quiet sigh of relief and begins the interview. (Lach, 1999, p. 41) ■

LOOKING AHEAD

The motivation behind Schueler's activity is to learn about consumers' attitudes and beliefs about the product—ultimately in order to craft advertisements that will persuade consumers to purchase more of the product. These advertisements will join the enormous number of efforts at persuasion that confront us seemingly incessantly. We are all the recipients of messages designed to make us behave in a particular manner or to change our attitudes about a product, a person, or an idea.

In fact, most of us are exposed to some 50,000 commercials every year, each designed to change or reinforce our attitudes. And it is not just commercials that communicate messages of persuasion. Politicians, teachers, family, friends, and even foes attempt to change our attitudes. The messages come in conversation, through the airwaves, in the mail, on billboards and bumper stickers, and on the Levi's tag on the back of your roommate's jeans. In fact, some economists have argued that persuasion, in one form or another, accounts for *one quarter* of the entire gross national product of the United States (Bennett, 1994; Stiff, 1994).

In this chapter, we consider what social psychologists have learned about **persuasion**, the process by which attitudes are changed. We discuss the ways in which persuasive information is perceived and processed cognitively, and we examine how various types of processing can be primed through the use of particular kinds of persuasive messages.

We also explore the sources of persuasive messages, and we see how characteristics of the person delivering the message affect its reception. Then we consider the message itself,

persuasion: The process by which attitudes are changed.

focusing on such aspects as how much information should be presented and how often it should be repeated for maximum persuasive impact. We also look at personal characteristics of individuals that may predispose them to be susceptible to persuasion.

Finally, we focus on persuasion in the marketplace, examining how advertisers attempt to persuade consumers through their advertising messages, the kinds of appeals that are used in ads, and how advertisers determine who are the most likely targets of persuasion. But we also describe ways to beat persuaders at their own game, focusing on how people can resist persuasion and remain independent.

In sum, after reading this chapter, you'll be able to answer these questions:

◆ What are the cognitive paths to persuasion?

◆ What characteristics of the message source produce the greatest persuasion?

◆ How do messages differ in their ability to elicit persuasion?

◆ What personal characteristics are associated most with persuasion?

◆ How do advertisers devise effective persuasive messages?

CENTRAL OR PERIPHERAL? PURSUING THE ROUTE TO PERSUASION

Who was the most significant figure of the 1988 presidential campaign? In some ways, it was neither of the two candidates, George Bush nor Michael Dukakis. Instead, it was Willie Horton.

Horton was the "star" of what is widely regarded as the most influential political commercial of the campaign. In the ad, the Bush campaign told Horton's story: An African American convicted of murder, Horton was serving a prison term in a Massachusetts jail. At one point, he was released for a weekend on a furlough program. During his furlough, he fled Massachusetts and raped a white woman in another state.

The point of Bush's ad? Dukakis, who was then the governor of Massachusetts, was not only soft on crime in general, but he showed poor judgment in supporting the furlough program. Indeed, the ad implied that Dukakis was somehow responsible for Horton's leaving prison that weekend and committing the rape (Pratkanis & Aronson, 1992).

Why was the advertisement so successful in placing Dukakis in a negative light and persuading the electorate to vote against him? The answer can be found in the discovery that there are two paths to persuasion, according to attitude experts Richard Petty and John Cacioppo (1986a, 1986b).

central route persuasion: The route to persuasion that occurs on the basis of the logic, merit, or strength of the arguments.

peripheral route persuasion: The route to persuasion that occurs when people are persuaded on the basis of factors unrelated to the nature or quality of the content of a persuasive message.

elaboration likelihood model: The theory that suggests that central route persuasion occurs when the recipient carefully considers arguments and expends cognitive effort in elaborating the meaning and implication of a message.

THE ELABORATION LIKELIHOOD MODEL: TWO PATHS TO PERSUASION

Petty and Cacioppo argue that persuasion follows one of two routes: the central route and the peripheral route. In **central route persuasion**, persuasion occurs on the basis of the logic, merit, or strength of the arguments. People are swayed in their judgments because of the soundness and sensibility of the position being put forward.

In contrast, **peripheral route persuasion** occurs when people are persuaded on the basis of factors unrelated to the nature or quality of the content of a persuasive message. Instead, they are influenced by factors that are irrelevant or extraneous to the topic or issue, such as who is providing the message or the length of the arguments.

In a theory summarizing their position, called the **elaboration likelihood model**, Petty and Cacioppo suggest that central route persuasion occurs when the recipient is motivated to pay attention, carefully considers arguments, and expends cognitive effort in elaborating the meaning and implication of a message. When central route persuasion occurs, people

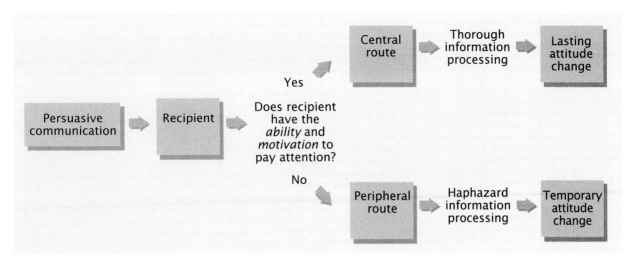

FIGURE 11–1   Central or Peripheral Route Processing When people process information relatively thoroughly, and have the *ability* and *motivation* to pay attention, they think about the topic using central route processing. In contrast, if they lack the ability and motivation, the result is peripheral route processing.

process information relatively thoroughly, considering the content of the message. In short, when people have the *ability* and *motivation,* they think about the topic using central route processing (see Figure 11–1).

In contrast, peripheral route persuasion takes place when people do not have the ability, aren't motivated to pay attention, and don't take the time, or make the effort, to consider the content or meaning of a persuasive message. Instead, they focus on aspects of the message that are immaterial to its content.

The Willie Horton ad is a good example of a persuasive message that was designed to produce attitude change via the peripheral route. The message never considered the value and deficiencies of the furlough system, and it never discussed Bush's merits and how he would solve the problem the furlough program presented. Instead, the message evoked and highlighted raw emotions regarding a killer-turned-rapist. Further, the fact that Horton was an African American who had raped a white woman added racial overtones to the content of the message.

Of course, an advertisement that promoted central route processing could have been produced. The ad might have focused on the role of furloughs in prison reform or on the demographics of prison populations. It is unlikely, however, that most viewers would have paid attention to such an ad, let alone be persuaded by it. Consequently, the makers of the Willie Horton ad—as well as the creators of many other types of advertising—avoided a measured, reasoned discussion of the topic.

Providing a particular type of message, however, does not ensure that a certain kind of cognitive processing will automatically occur. The mere fact that a message emphasizes peripheral concerns (such as racial issues or candidate Dukakis's image as "soft on crime") does not mean that peripheral processing will necessarily take place. A viewer motivated to be critical might well invoke central route processing and see the fallacies of the argument (White & Harkins, 1994). Conversely, the fact that a message emphasizes the merits of an argument does not ensure that central route processing will take place. Instead, an inattentive or bored message recipient might well focus on irrelevant cues—such as the misfit of a speaker's jacket or the good looks of the advocate—and engage in peripheral route processing.

One of the important determinants of whether central or peripheral route processing occurs is the availability of heuristics. **Heuristics** are personal principles or rules of thumb

heuristics: Personal principles or rules of thumb that permit us to make decisions on the basis of limited information and with relatively little cognitive effort.

Concerts like Farm Aid, where well-known performers donate their services to raise money and awareness involving a cause, operate by peripheral route processing.

that permit us to make decisions on the basis of limited information and with relatively little cognitive effort (Chaiken, 1987). Although heuristics permit us to deal effectively with the enormous amount of information we encounter every day, their use may also lead to relatively unreflective attitude change. For example, we might hold the heuristic that "longer arguments are better than shorter ones" or that "people with a Ph.D. know more than people without them." By invoking such heuristics without thinking through their validity, we avoid evaluating arguments on their merits, thereby employing peripheral route processing.

THE IDEAL ROUTE TO ENDURING ATTITUDE CHANGE

Does peripheral route processing or central route processing produce the greatest degree and the greatest persistence of attitude change? The answer is clear and straightforward: The most lasting and persistent attitude change is brought about by central route processing (Heppner et al., 1995; Petty, Heesacker, & Hughes, 1997). If people have the opportunity to consider and elaborate on an argument, they can begin to understand the argument's merits and potentially even come up with a few more supportive arguments of their own. As a result, the greater the intensity of cognitive work, the more likely that attitude change will be enduring.

Peripheral route processing can also sway attitudes, but the degree of change is not likely to be as strong or as lasting as when central route processing is employed. People who do not expend the cognitive effort to consider and cognitively amplify the issues involved in a topic are less likely to experience long-term attitude changes. Clearly, central route persuasion techniques seem preferable to peripheral route techniques. Why, then, do politicians, advertisers, salespeople, and other professional persuaders invariably employ persuasive communications that promote peripheral route processing?

The reason is that central route processing is considerably more difficult to elicit than peripheral route processing. Two conditions must be met if central route processing is to proceed. First, people must be sufficiently *motivated* to expend the cognitive effort to think about the issue (Mitra,1995; Killeya & Johnson, 1998; van Knippenberg, 1999). They need to have sufficient interest in the topic to warrant the effort they must make to elaborate on the message. Unfortunately, most of us do not have the time, energy, or inclination to consider carefully every persuasive message to which we are exposed. Consequently, central route processing may never take place or may readily fall by the wayside if the motivation to think about the issue is not present.

The second key to determining whether central or peripheral route processing is employed relates to a message recipient's *ability* to process it (DeBono & McDermott, 1994; Smith & Shaffer, 1995; Aaker & Williams, 1998). No matter how carefully a concerned party may craft a message about the possibility of a nuclear meltdown, the physics involved may be so mysterious that we might be unable to understand the core of the communication. Similarly, if we are distracted by activities in the midst of the message—as when the dog leaps on the couch while we're watching a television commercial—central route processing is unlikely to occur.

In sum, central route processing promotes longer-lasting attitude change than peripheral route processing, but recipients' motivation and ability to consider a persuasive communication determine whether central or peripheral route processing will occur. The nature of the processing employed by the recipient of a message, however, is only part of the story in determining how attitudes are changed. To get a full picture of the process of persuasion, we also need to consider the origin of a persuasive message and various characteristics of the recipients of that message.

THE MESSAGE SOURCE: THE ROOTS OF PERSUASION

Are you more likely to be persuaded to use a particular toothpaste by the president of the United States or the president of the American Dental Association? No matter how much you like the U.S. president or how appealing his smile, it is highly unlikely that his views on toothpaste will lead you to change your brand. The president of the American Dental Association is another story; the views of that individual are likely to carry some weight.

As this example illustrates, the source of a message can play a major role in determining whether the message is persuasive. Among the most important factors are the expertise (Wilson & Sherrell, 1993) and trustworthiness of communicators and their attractiveness and likability (Roskos-Ewoldsen & Fazio, 1992; DeBono & Klein, 1993; Petty & Wegener, 1998a).

COMMUNICATOR CREDIBILITY: EXPERTISE AND TRUSTWORTHINESS

When a newspaper wishes to identify a source whose name may be unknown to its readership, it often identifies that person as "an expert on. . . ." The source thereby receives instant credibility. People place great stock in the opinions of experts (Maddux & Rogers, 1980; Hass, 1981; Kavanoor, Grewal, & Blodgett, 1997). We are much more likely to be swayed by a theory of why the dinosaurs became extinct when it is presented by an award-winning biologist than when it is put forward by a junior high school student. Furthermore, experts have credibility even in areas in which their expertise is questionable (Aronson & Golden, 1962; Petty, Wegener, & Fabrigar, 1997).

For example, William Shockley, a Nobel-prize-winning physicist, developed a theory that, because of genetic factors, African Americans had lower intelligence than whites. Although his hypothesis had no basis in reality—it was roundly refuted by critics in psychology—it attracted a fair amount of attention, largely because of Shockley's Nobel credentials. The fact that expertise in physics does not translate into expertise in genetics was lost on some recipients of Shockley's message.

This does not imply that experts are invariably credible. If we believe that an expert has an ulterior motive, for instance, we are less prone to be swayed by his or her message (Eagly

sleeper effect: An increase in the degree of persuasiveness of a message that occurs with the passage of time.

& Chaiken, 1998). For instance, a physician in the employ of a drug company who asserts that the company's new drug is entirely safe is considerably less credible than an employee of the U.S. Food and Drug Administration making the same statement.

Experts, then, must be trustworthy to be credible. If we feel they are not completely honest, or that they are simply telling us what we want to hear, we are less apt to be persuaded by their arguments, no matter how compelling and carefully crafted the arguments are (Priester & Petty, 1995; Petty & Wegener, 1998b).

Of course, the opposite is also true: The more it appears that experts are arguing *against* their own best personal interests, the higher their credibility. A politician who makes a pro-environmental speech before the members of a company accused of polluting the atmosphere will be considered to be more credible than one who takes a pro-environmental position in a speech before the Sierra Club.

Even message sources with little credibility, however, are not without their persuasive resources—a point illustrated by a phenomenon called the sleeper effect. The **sleeper effect** is an increase in the degree of persuasiveness of a message that occurs with the passage of time (Hovland & Weiss, 1951; Dukes, Stein, & Ullman, 1997; Underwood & Pezdek, 1998). It was discovered in a study conducted during the 1940s. In the study, a group of American soldiers watched a pro-U.S. film (Hovland, Lumsdaine, & Sheffield, 1949). Five days after viewing the movie, they showed little attitude change. But 9 weeks later, the soldiers were more apt to show more positive attitudes toward the United States than a control group of soldiers who had never viewed the film. Obviously, between day 5 and week 9 something had happened to bring about attitude change, and that something was dubbed the sleeper effect.

To explain the sleeper effect, the investigators turned to the credibility of the message source. Because the soldiers viewed the original message as questionable—they held the U.S. Army in low regard and saw its messages as biased—the message had little initial credibility. Consequently, they tended to discount the message of the film. However, after several weeks had gone by, the source of the information was forgotten, but the content of the message had been retained. This explanation came to be known as the *discounting cue hypothesis,* and it rests on the notion that the way we store information about the message is different from the way we store information about the message source, and we recall these kinds of information with different degrees of success.

Over the years, the sleeper effect has proved to be elusive. Sometimes investigators were able to demonstrate its existence, and other times they were not (Cook et al., 1979; Pratkanis et al., 1988). Frustration reached a peak in the 1970s when attitude researchers Paulette Gillig and Anthony Greenwald (1974) wrote a paper asking, "Is it time to lay the sleeper effect to rest?"

Ultimately, the research community answered the question with a resounding no. In fact, recent studies have not only demonstrated the reality of the sleeper effect but also pinpointed the conditions under which it occurs.

For instance, in one experiment, all participants were exposed to persuasive information arguing against a 4-day workweek, suggesting that it reduced employee satisfaction and created many other difficulties (Pratkanis et al., 1988). In some conditions, participants also received several additional bits of data meant to act as *discounting cues*—messages contradicting the initial message. The discounting cues indicated that new evidence contradicted the conclusion that the 4-day workweek was unsuccessful. However, the timing of the discounting cues differed for different groups of participants. Some participants were exposed to the discounting cues prior to reading the information about the 4-day week; others were exposed to the discounting cues after reading that information; and some did not receive the discounting cues at all. In addition, a control group of participants received no message.

The results of the study showed that participants who received the message against the 4-day workweek alone (without discounting cues) were swayed by the information initially, showing more agreement with the message. However, the attitude change did not last. After 6 weeks had passed, they showed little attitude change. Those who received the discounting cues prior to reading the information showed little attitude change, both just after exposure and 6 weeks later.

If we receive information contradicting an earlier persuasive message, we may experience the sleeper effect. In such a case, the attitude change brought about by the initial persuasive message is ultimately even stronger than if we hadn't received the contradictory information.

In contrast, those participants who received the discounting cues after reading the information displayed the sleeper effect: They showed little attitude change initially, but their agreement with the message against the 4-day workweek actually increased over the 6-week period. For them, attitude change was greatest later, rather than earlier—the sleeper effect (see Figure 11–2).

These results suggest that the sleeper effect is valid, but only under certain conditions. For one thing, discounting cues must follow the persuasive message. If they come before, they influence the way a message is initially evaluated and learned. When this happens, any attitude change is likely to reflect both the discounting cues and the information itself, and both kinds of information are likely to be recalled to the same extent when the attitude is assessed after the passage of time. Hence, there would be little difference between immediate measures of recall and later ones.

In contrast, information that is initially presented by itself might be learned in one way, and the subsequent discounting cue is learned in another way. In this case, the two sets of data would be stored in memory separately and might well be forgotten at separate rates. Although the two kinds of information would be expected to be recalled equally well during immediate measures of attitudes, the information in the message may linger in memory, whereas the discounting cue may be forgotten. When this occurs, the information in the message would be influential after the passage of time.

How might you use this information about the sleeper effect in practice? Suppose you are a politician presenting information about yourself in a magazine ad, trying to convince voters to support your candidacy. Keeping the sleeper effect in mind, you might strive to disguise your message, making it appear to be part of the magazine's text, and not an advertisement.

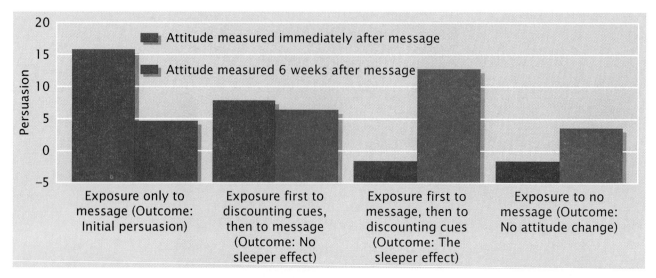

FIGURE 11–2 The Sleeper Effect When a message opposing a 4-day workweek was read alone, it produced some initial attitude change, but 6 weeks later it had little effect. When the initial message was preceded by discounting cues, attitudes changed little over time. But when the message was read first and then followed by the discounting cues, a sleeper effect occurred in which initial attitude change was low but subsequent attitude change was high. (*Source:* Pratkanis et al., 1988.)

Only in the last paragraph of the "article" would you admit that the text was actually an advertisement.

Although the recognition that the "article" was actually an advertisement might cause your readers temporary annoyance (and increase the possibility that they will discount the ad initially), the end result may be in your favor. The sleeper effect suggests that after a certain amount of time has gone by, the discounting information will be forgotten, and only the favorable information about your candidacy may be remembered and accepted by the reader. (Magazines are aware of this phenomenon, by the way, and most require that advertisements be prominently identified as such on each page.)

COMMUNICATOR ATTRACTIVENESS AND LIKABILITY

You'd probably be startled to find an advertising campaign featuring the recommendations of the Unabomber. Instead, commercials tend to feature the likes of entertainment stars and prominent athletes such as Bill Cosby and Michael Jordan (see Table 11–1).

The use of celebrities to pitch products stems from the fact that the attractiveness of a communicator is a key factor in determining how persuasive a message will be (Reingen & Kernan, 1993). For instance, physical attractiveness clearly plays a role in a person's ability to persuade others; people tend to be more persuaded by those who are good-looking than those who are less so (Chaiken, 1979; Guerrero, DeVito, & Hecht, 1999). Furthermore, it is not just physical attractiveness that produces greater persuasion; general social attractiveness—such as that found in famous, but not-necessarily-handsome sports stars—is enough to make a communicator more persuasive (Chaiken, 1980; Roskos-Ewoldson & Fazio, 1992; Sharma, 1999).

Happily, the link between attractiveness and persuasibility is not ironclad; we are not destined to follow slavishly what the attractive wish us to do. Indeed, in some cases the use of celebrity endorsements backfires. For example, O. J. Simpson's value as a spokesperson for Hertz rental cars dropped the moment he was indicted for murder (Lipman, 1991).

Furthermore, communicator attractiveness has considerably less impact in instances when people are led to use central route, as opposed to peripheral route, processing (DeBono,

TABLE 11–1	Top TV Endorsers Ranked by Consumer Appeal

The following sports and entertainment celebrities were judged to be the most credible endorsers of products, according to consumers during 1997.

SPORTS PRESENTERS	ENTERTAINMENT PRESENTERS
1. Michael Jordan	1. Candice Bergen
2. Tiger Woods	2. Jerry Seinfeld
3. Dennis Rodman	3. Paul Reiser
4. Shaquille O'Neal	4. Rosie O'Donnell
5. Scottie Pippen	5. Bill Cosby
6. Grant Hill	6. Cindy Crawford
7. Dan Marino	7. James Earl Jones
8. George Foreman	8. Tim Allen
9. Charles Barkley	9. Elizabeth Taylor
10. Cal Ripken	10. Oprah Winfrey

Source: Video Storyboard Tests, Inc. 1997.

1992). For example, in one experiment participants were presented with a message communicated either by famous and admired sports figures or by anonymous, middle-aged people from Bakersfield, California (Petty, Cacioppo, & Schumann, 1983). When the participants were relatively uninvolved and unmotivated to consider message content (and thereby used peripheral route processing), the celebrity endorsers made a difference, producing greater attitude change. But when the participants were involved and motivated to pay attention to the message—and thereby employed central route processing—the attractiveness of the communicators had no effect (Petty et al., 1983).

REVIEW AND RETHINK

Review

- According to the elaboration likelihood model, persuasion follows either the central or peripheral route.
- A communicator's expertise and trustworthiness, characteristics of message credibility, are a major source of a message's effectiveness.
- The sleeper effect, which occurs under certain specific conditions, is an increase in message persuasiveness as time passes.
- A communicator's attractiveness and likability are related to persuasiveness.

Rethink

- If you were to devise a message designed for peripheral route processing, what characteristics would it have?
- What factors affect perceptions of source credibility? Is the trust afforded experts always logical?
- Aside from credibility, what characteristics of a message source affect persuasiveness? Recall the beautiful-is-good stereotype discussed in Chapter 6. How does this stereotype relate to source persuasiveness?

THE MESSAGE: CRAFTING THE COMMUNICATION

Illinois Power was in trouble. The television program "60 Minutes" had just done a story that charged that the nuclear power company had seriously mismanaged its finances, to the point of running up thousands of dollars in cost overruns. In this age of corporate public relations, the company knew it had to do something. One solution was to write a press release that described all the positive accomplishments the company had made in the areas of nuclear power and financial management. Another possibility was to take on "60 Minutes" directly by developing a message that outlined each of the charges by "60 Minutes" and then explained why each charge was false. If you were working for Illinois Power, which message strategy would you select? (Perloff, 1993, p. 166)

The answer to the question (which we'll come back to a bit later) is provided by years of research on whether one- or two-sided messages are most persuasive. Indeed, issues regarding how best to formulate an argument are central to the study of persuasion.

If an audience is motivated and able to use central route processing, the way in which arguments are crafted and presented plays a primary role in determining how well others are influenced by the message. In following the central route, people consider and pay attention to how big the hole in the ozone layer is, or why one automobile is safer than another, or why they should vote in the primary. In these circumstances, whether they heed a speaker's call, however, depends on the quality of the arguments they hear and how these arguments are presented.

THE AMOUNT AND TYPE OF INFORMATION

In the old fifties television show *Dragnet,* detective Joe Friday was clear in the kind of information he wanted: "The facts, ma'am, just the facts." But how many facts make for a persuasive argument?

In formulating a persuasive message, more is sometimes—but not always—better. If the arguments are equally strong and valid, then the more arguments you present, the more persuasive you will be. This is true regardless of whether recipients employ central or peripheral route processing. If central route processing occurs, the strong arguments provide support for the position that is being promoted. If peripheral route processing occurs, people fall back on the heuristic that "a longer argument must be a better argument" without carefully evaluating the message (Petty & Cacioppo, 1984, 1986a; Stasson & Davis, 1989; Petty, Wegener, & Fabrigar, 1997; Petty & Wegener, 1998a).

However, if additional arguments are relatively weak, they should be used only if peripheral processing is taking place. In the peripheral route, the quality of the arguments doesn't particularly matter, because the message recipient is not paying close attention. But if central route processing is occurring and the arguments are being evaluated on their merits, weak arguments detract from the overall message and may even raise counterarguments in the mind of the listener. A speaker's general point may be diluted if the additional arguments are weak; this suggests that a speaker is better off presenting fewer, but more solid, arguments if central route processing is occurring (Calder, Insko, & Yandell, 1974; Petty & Cacioppo, 1984; Harkins & Petty, 1987).

POINT AND COUNTERPOINT: ONE OR BOTH SIDES OF THE COIN?

During the 1996 Clinton–Dole presidential campaign, critics protested the recurrent use of negative advertising by both candidates. In negative advertising, each candidate not only presented his own side of an argument, but also simultaneously attacked his adversary's position. The widespread use of negative advertising in political campaigns suggests that it is an effective strategy. In fact, negative advertising holds substantial risks. Although it permits a politician to attack an opponent, it also implicitly suggests that the adversary's position has enough merit to warrant a response. Furthermore, it raises the unwelcome possibility that

Despite its popularity, negative campaigning or advertising runs the risk of raising the profile of an opponent or competitor's product, as well as the possibility that members of the audience may actually find the other person's message more attractive.

someone observing the attack will find the opponent's position more convincing. If this occurs, clearly it would have been better not to mention the opponent's position in the first place and merely present one's own.

To social psychologists, this issue has been considered in the more general terms of identifying whether communicators are better off sticking with their own side of an issue, or whether it makes more sense to present as well the other side of the argument and then refute it. The answer is that it depends largely on the target audience of the message.

If the audience is relatively well educated, disagrees with the intended message, is aware that there are many different perspectives on an issue, and is likely to be exposed to subsequent information, a communicator is better off presenting both sides of an issue. Conversely, audiences who are less educated, who are initially favorable to the speaker's point of view, and who themselves see the issue as one-sided are more likely to be influenced by one-sided presentations than by two-sided communications (Hovland et al., 1949; Sudefeld & Borrie, 1978; Petty ,Wegener, & White, 1998).

Given the complexity of these findings, what advice might a social psychologist give to a candidate about to enter a political contest? The best counsel would be to tailor each message to the specific audience that will hear it. When speaking to the party faithful, who are likely to agree already with the broad outlines of the candidate's position, the candidate should stick to a one-sided message in order to reinforce and strengthen the audience's commitment. However, when reaching out to uncommitted voters, a candidate should take a more measured approach, providing both sides of the argument and refuting the opposition's position.

The Illinois Power executives assumed that viewers of "60 Minutes" would be reasonably well educated, would likely agree with the program's charges, but would also be aware that there was more than one perspective on the issue. This set of conditions suggested that a two-sided presentation, in which each allegation was rebutted, would be best.

Was Illinois Power correct in its assessment? Research suggests that it was. The company produced a videotape containing a two-sided message and distributed it across the country. Research on its effectiveness suggested that, compared with individuals who saw only the "60 Minutes" presentation, people exposed to the tape found the "60 Minutes" presentation less believable and the power company more credible (Clavier & Kalupa, 1983; Perloff, 1993).

REPEATING THE MESSAGE

An often-repeated set of commercials involved actress Candice Bergen extolling the virtues of Sprint's one-dime-a-minute long-distance telephone rate. Was there a moment when, after repeatedly seeing the same commercials, people who had initially found them amusing shifted their attitudes, and instead saw them—and the underlying message to use Sprint— irritating?

As we discussed in Chapter 6 when we considered interpersonal attraction, familiarity generally breeds not contempt, but attraction. The greater our acquaintance with persons or objects, the more likely we are to hold positive attitudes toward them. And consistent with these conclusions, the amount and persistence of attitude change increase for at least the first several times we are exposed to a message (Cook & Wadsworth, 1972).

On the other hand, there can be too much of a good thing: Researchers have found that increasing repetitions of a message add little, and may even decrease the effectiveness of the message in producing attitude change (Cacioppo & Petty, 1979; Calder & Sternthal, 1980; Eagley & Chaiken, 1998).

How quickly a message wears out its welcome depends, in part, on its complexity. More complex messages can benefit from increased repetitions, as there is more to learn and retain. Simple messages, such as slogans, can be heard only so many times before they become tedious and unpleasant. Professionals in the advertising field call this "wear-out."

To avoid wear-out, advertisers sometimes resort to repetition-with-variation. In this procedure, the basic message is presented repeatedly, but it undergoes subtle transformations each time it is delivered. For example, advertisements may display a close-up of a bottle of dishwasher detergent from the front, side, or rear; or a driver may be shown sitting behind the wheel of a Honda while driving through the city, country, or suburbs. The message is basically the same, although the context varies slightly.

Repetition-with-variation is effective in promoting positive attitudes—as long as people don't think too much about the message. When people engage in peripheral route processing, they're apt to find that the variations relieve the boredom that might be expected from unvaried repetition. On the other hand, if they are processing along the central route, their increased scrutiny of the message may lead to boredom, even if it is presented with variation, or they may engage in more critical thinking about the content of the message (Schumann, Petty, & Clemons, 1990).

Advertisers, of course, can rest easy: Few people scrutinize advertisements very thoughtfully. The repetition-with-variation strategy that is a mainstay of advertisements, then, is likely to be effective (Haugtvedt et al., 1994).

FEAR APPEALS: STRIKING FEAR IN THE HEART OF ATTITUDES

If you have unprotected sex, you might get AIDS and die.

Few appeals for safer sex make such blatant statements. Why? Not because the statement is untrue. Quite the contrary: It is an accurate prediction in the age of sexual freedom and the AIDS epidemic.

Quite simply, we are unlikely to encounter such statements because of a long history of research on **fear appeals**, messages designed to change attitudes by producing apprehension and anxiety if they are not followed. According to the accumulated research, strong fear appeals—by themselves—do not produce significant attitude change. Instead, they cause so much distress that they are more likely to arouse people's defenses. Instead of accepting and following the message, listeners are more likely to ignore it because it is so unpleasant (Mewborn & Rogers, 1979; Natarajan, 1979; Witte, 1998).

For example, when people see a video that graphically illustrates what happens to the lungs after one contracts lung cancer from smoking, the likely result is not a reduction in smoking but rather a sense of disgust over the film. Similarly, when people are told to wear bicycle safety helmets to protect themselves from horrible brain damage if they are in a crash, they are unlikely to follow the advice, because it may be so threatening that they repress the gist of the message. In some cases, then, milder fear appeals may produce greater attitude change than stronger fear appeals. For instance, a warning may be more reasonable that ineffective flossing will produce bleeding gums (a relatively mild fear appeal) than the more exaggerated warning that one's teeth will fall out (Janis, 1967; Dziokonski & Weber, 1977; Henthorne, LaTour, & Natarajan, 1993).

On the other hand, strong fear appeals can be effective—if they are accompanied by specific, precise recommendations for actions to take if one wants to avoid the danger. For

fear appeals: Messages designed to change attitudes by producing apprehension and anxiety if they are not followed.

instance, rather than simply suggesting that smoking leads to frightful lung cancer, a message needs to communicate specific ways in which a person can stop smoking (Maddux & Rogers, 1983). Similarly, to persuade people to wear bike helmets, it would be useful to pair the fear-evoking message with information on what kinds of helmets work best and where they can be purchased (Leventhal, 1970; Axelrod & Apsche, 1982).

The key to successful fear appeals is to make people feel they are vulnerable to a threat, but that there are actions they can take to overcome the threat, and they have the capability of taking those actions (Rogers, 1983; Struckman-Johnson et al., 1994; Anderson & Guerrero, 1998; Witte et al., 1998).

For instance, suppose your goal were to reduce the incidence of breast and testicular cancer by persuading people to carry out self-examinations to check for lumps—a simple and effective procedure. To do this, you might begin by making people feel vulnerable, perhaps by revealing that each year 40,000 women die of breast cancer and 6,000 men of testicular cancer.

After creating this sense of vulnerability, the message would need to show that corrective actions can be taken to avoid these kinds of cancer, and that any individual is able to carry out those actions. Hence, an effective message would incorporate specific information regarding how to perform a self-examination. (Also see the Speaking of Social Psychology interview.)

THE TARGET OF PERSUASION: RECEIVING THE MESSAGE

When politicians go out on the stump, they do not give the same speech to the National Evangelical Association that they give to a group of rock video producers. When Honda places an ad in *Rolling Stone* magazine, it's not the same advertisement that runs in the *New York Times*.

Even though the goals are similar—vote for me, purchase a Honda—the persuasive approach takes into account the identity and character of the audience. For good reason: Targets of persuasive messages react quite distinctly according to their specific characteristics.

The early research on the relationship between persuasion and receiver attributes sought to identify personal characteristics that consistently led people to be easy or difficult prey for persuasive messages (Hovland & Janis, 1959). Were unintelligent people more easily persuaded than intelligent ones? Were men influenced more readily than women? Did people with low self-esteem respond more readily to persuasive messages than those with high self-esteem?

As it turned out, the exercise was futile. Very few people were invariably easy marks; nor were many people always immune to persuasion. Instead, it turns out that people's reactions to persuasive messages depend on a combination of several factors: the kind of message that is being communicated, its source, their own personal qualities, and even their emotional states (McGuire, 1985). We'll consider how two such factors (a person's characteristic level of thoughtfulness or cognitive activity, and a person's mood) relate to attitude change.

THE NEED FOR COGNITION

Look at the statements presented in Table 11–2. Which ones do you agree with?

People who agree with the first two statements, and disagree with the rest, have a relatively high need for cognition. **Need for cognition** is a person's habitual level of thoughtfulness and cognitive activity. If you enjoy pondering and philosophizing about the world around you, your need for cognition is relatively high. Conversely, if you become impatient when forced to spend too much time thinking about things, your need for cognition probably is relatively low (Cacioppo et al., 1996).

When exposed to a persuasive message, people who are high in the need for cognition tend to produce a greater number of responses to the message—in other words, they think more about it. However, this thinking does not invariably lead to either an acceptance or a rejection of the message. Instead, their reaction depends on the specific content of the message.

need for cognition: A person's habitual level of thoughtfulness and cognitive activity.

SPEAKING OF SOCIAL PSYCHOLOGY

Frank Kaiser

Creative Director

Year of Birth: 1935

Education: B.A., Political Science, DePauw University; M.A., Political Economy, University of Edinburgh, Scotland

Home: Miami, Florida

"You have to look for the inherent drama in a product—to see if there is something that will immediately stand up and say, 'Look at me, this is what you're looking for.'"

To many people, the Internet and World Wide Web offer a way of finding and managing information. To advertising executives such as Frank Kaiser, head of Kaiser Communications, Inc., the Internet is something more: a new medium for advertising.

"Try to think of advertising on the Internet today as the first few seconds of the Big Bang when the universe was created. It's in such a flux," Kaiser asserted. "With the Internet, instead of targeting a group, you're talking to one person at a time. That's what makes is so interesting. But I think at this point it's more of a promise than a reality," he added.

Kaiser, who started as a journalist and then joined the prestigious Leo Burnett agency in Chicago, noted that while the medium may be a new one, the basics of advertising remain much the same.

"Leo Burnett talked about there being no dull products, just dull copy writers, and he was right. You have to look for the inherent drama in a product—to see if there is something that

TABLE 11–2	The Need for Cognition

Which of the following statements apply to you?

1. I really enjoy a task that involves coming up with new solutions to problems.
2. I would prefer a task that is intellectual, difficult, and important to one that is somewhat important but does not require much thought.
3. Learning new ways to think doesn't excite me very much.
4. I think only as hard as I have to.
5. I like tasks that require little thought once I've learned them.
6. I prefer to think about small, daily projects rather than long-term ones.
7. I would rather do something that requires little thought than something that is sure to challenge my thinking abilities.
8. I find little satisfaction in deliberating hard and for long hours.
9. I don't like to be responsible for a situation that requires a lot of thinking.

Scoring: The more you agree with statements 1 and 2 and disagree with the rest, the greater the likelihood that you have a high need for cognition.

Source: Cacioppo & Petty, 1982.

will immediately stand up and say, 'Look at me, this is what you're looking for.' Once you know your product, it's then important to know who your customer is," Kaiser said.

One of the ways a potential customer is found is through focus groups and actually going out into the field and mingling with potential buyers.

"The promise of the Internet for advertisers is the possibility of one-on-one advertising and being interactive. It's a combination of publishing and television."

"A number of years ago, when I was working on Jello, I would spend a whole day standing by the Jello rack in a supermarket. Every time someone would pick up a box of Jello, I would ask him or her why. Sometimes the best advertising comes from what people say.

"Advertising should involve the reader, and have the reader participate somehow," he said. "We try to set up what the product can do for the customer and how it does it better than the competition, and that positions your market. At that point you can get into a creative strategy."

The World Wide Web, according to Kaiser, presents some new factors in how to go about developing a consumer base and making advertising work. Currently, the system of banners on a Web site doesn't seem to be doing the job.

"Most of the ads on the Internet are banner ads, but people just don't see them anymore," he explained. "It's a 'culture of the free' on the Internet, which is one of the things that has made it grow so fast. Advertising, to be successful, has to be presented within that culture, it has to give you something: free information. The promise of the Internet for advertisers is the possibility of one-on-one advertising and being interactive. It's a combination of publishing and television. You can have video, sound, and demos streamed directly to the customer.

"The difference from traditional advertising is that it's one-on-one on the Internet, and in that case you're talking to each customer in a different way. You can talk directly to their concerns," he added.

A high-quality, multiple-argument, detail-laden message is likely to produce attitude change, whereas a weak message, containing relatively few low-quality, undetailed arguments, is likely to produce little attitude change (Cacioppo, Petty, & Morris, 1983; Cacioppo, Petty, Losch, & Kim, 1986; Petty & Wegener, 1998b).

But what of people low in the need for cognition? What kind of arguments are most effective for them? It turns out that for individuals who are low in the need for cognition, the quality of the argument matters very little. The reason is that people low in the need for cognition tend to stick to the peripheral processing route (Haugtvedt, Petty, & Cacioppo, 1992; Shestowsky, Wegener, & Fabrigar, 1998). Relying on heuristics, those handy rules of thumb that make peripheral route processing so effortless, people low in the need for cognition tend to be influenced by factors other than the quality and detail of the message content (Chaiken, 1987; Mantel & Kardes, 1999).

We should not think, however, that people high in the need for cognition are necessarily more adept at evaluating messages to which they are exposed. Both those high and those low in the need for cognition are susceptible to persuasive evidence, but that evidence must be demonstrated in different ways for high-cognition people than for low-cognition people. For example, participants in one experiment read details of a murder case and watched a 45-minute interrogation of a defendant, whose answers were rather ambiguous regarding her guilt or innocence (Kassin, Reddy, & Tulloch, 1990). Participants also heard a summary

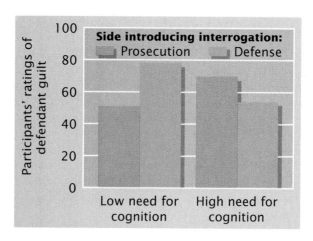

FIGURE 11–3 Guilty or Innocent? When mock jurors were asked to rate the validity of a defendant's story, their ratings of guilt varied according to their need for cognition and whether the prosecution or defense presented arguments first. (*Source:* Kassin, Reddy, & Tulloch, 1990.)

of the case presented by the defendant's attorney and the prosecutor. In some cases, they first heard the defense attorney and then the prosecutor; in others, the order was reversed.

The reactions of the participants, who were asked to judge the validity of the defendant's story, varied according to whether they were high or low in need for cognition, and according to the order of presentation of the attorneys' summaries. Participants high in need for cognition were more swayed by the person they heard first—a phenomenon known as the *primacy effect.* Apparently, they carefully evaluated what the first speaker had to say and found that evidence convincing. The later presentation did not sway them.

The result was different for those participants who were low in cognition. They showed a *recency effect,* being influenced most by whomever they heard last. Having the last word consequently made the greater impact on individuals who were low in need for cognition (see Figure 11–3).

In short, the degree to which we habitually think about the world and process information—our need for cognition—has an important impact on the kind of persuasive material that will influence us most. Remember that it is not people who are either high or low in need for cognition who are invariably more or less easy to influence. Instead, the degree to which we can be persuaded depends on the kind of persuasive message we receive and the circumstances at the time we receive it. To complicate matters more, it turns out that we're more susceptible to persuasion at certain periods of our lives, as we discuss in the Applying Social Psychology box.

MOODS: HAPPY TO BE PERSUADED?

If you'd just won the lottery, you know you'd be in a good mood. Would your mood also make you more easily persuaded by a con man? The answer is that it probably would: Placing

Chances are this couple will be susceptible to persuasion simply because they are in a good mood.

APPLYING SOCIAL PSYCHOLOGY
THE SURGE AND DECLINE OF ATTITUDE STRENGTH:
ARE THE YOUNG OR THE OLD MOST SUSCEPTIBLE TO PERSUASION?

If you were to guess, who would you say would be the most open to change in their attitudes: a younger or an older person?

Most people guess that it would be younger people. Stereotypes of older people suggest that they are resistant to change and more fixed in their attitudes—a stereotype that for many years was consistent with thinking by social psychologists. They reasoned that as people accumulate more experiences across the life span, their attitudes become increasingly stable and more persistent, and therefore less susceptible to persuasion and the influence of others.

However, recent research suggests otherwise. According to social psychologists Penny Visser and Jon Krosnick (1998), there are two periods in which people are most open to change in their attitudes: when they are young, and when they are old. It is in middle age that people are most resistant to change.

In one study supporting the conclusion, participants in a telephone survey were asked to respond to a military conflict involving two fictitious countries. After being given a variety of information about the situation, they were asked whether they thought the United States should use military force or stay out of the conflict. Participants who said the United States should use military force were then asked, "If the United Nations believes that Americans should not use military force in this conflict, would you be willing to change your mind about using our military?" On the other hand, participants who said the United States should stay out were asked, "If the United Nations believes that Americans should use military force in this conflict, would you be willing to change your mind about using our military?"

The results of the survey found that up until about the age of 60, willingness to consider changing one's attitude declined, but then began to increase at that point. Subsequent studies confirmed the initial finding: People are most susceptible to attitude change in the periods of early adulthood and late adulthood.

Several reasons explain why attitudes are most likely to change during early and late adulthood, and they are not necessarily identical during the two periods. People in early adulthood are often in transition between different roles, don't have well-established social networks and the social support that comes with such networks, and may not have thought about many attitudes deeply. As they get older, however, they begin to place more importance on their attitudes, think about them more, and become more confident about them—leading to increased resistance to change.

In contrast, during late adulthood, attitudes may become less important, people may have decreased certainty about their attitudes, and social support may decline. Furthermore, intellectual flexibility may decline, leading to an inability to produce effective counterarguments. All these changes at the end of the life cycle make it more likely that people will be increasingly susceptible to persuasion.

The findings have implications for society, particularly because the number of people in late adulthood will increase disproportionately over the next decades. If the number of older citizens increase, public opinion may become less stable.

---

people in a good mood makes them more susceptible to persuasion. For example, participants in one study were led to believe they had unexpectedly won a prize—a belief that placed them in a good mood. These participants, along with others who were not led to believe they had won and were therefore in a neutral mood, were then exposed to an unrelated persuasive message regarding acid rain. The message was supposedly written by either an expert or a nonexpert and included either nine strong arguments or nine relatively weak arguments (Mackie & Worth, 1991; Schwarz, Bless, & Bohner, 1991; Petty et al., 1993; Rosselli, Skelly, & Mackie, 1995).

As can be seen in Figure 11–4, participants' moods affected their responses. For people in a good mood, it didn't much matter whether the arguments were strong or weak; attitude changes were quite similar. But for people in a neutral mood, the nature of the arguments did make a difference. For them, strong arguments were considerably more persuasive.

Mood also affected responsiveness to expert and nonexpert sources. Here, participants in a positive mood were more apt to change their attitude when the message was written by an expert than by a nonexpert; but for neutral-mood participants, the expertise of the writer had no effect.

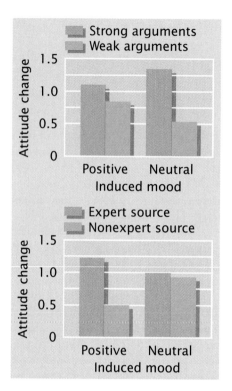

FIGURE 11–4   Mood and Attitude Change
For people in a good mood, it does not matter substantially whether the arguments are strong or weak. But for people in a neutral mood, the nature of the arguments makes a significant difference. Mood also affects responsiveness to the source of a message. People in a positive mood are more apt to change their attitude when the message is communicated by an expert, but the expertise of the communicator has little effect for people in a neutral mood. (*Source:* Adapted from Mackie & Worth, 1991.)

What accounts for these results? If you think back to our earlier discussion of central and peripheral route processing, you'll recall that the quality of the arguments was related to central route processing, whereas speaker expertise was related to peripheral route processing. This distinction may explain these results. What appears to be happening is that placing someone in a good mood is distracting and therefore increases the likelihood of peripheral route processing (van der Pligt et al., 1998). Consequently, factors such as expertise that are associated with peripheral route processing would be expected to have a significant impact on attitude change. In contrast, factors such as argument strength, which relate to central route processing, would be less likely to affect attitude change in people who are feeling good (Bohner & Apostolidou, 1994).

In sum, people in a positive mood are apt to be distracted, perhaps thinking about their good fortune, and therefore more likely to engage in peripheral route processing. As a result, a good mood may lead someone to be happier but also more gullible.

REVIEW AND RETHINK

Review

- The amount and type of information in a message affects persuasion.

- Whether a one-sided or a two-sided message is more appropriate depends on the circumstances.

- Message repetition may be effective, especially for complex messages; however, excessive repetition may cause wear-out.

- Fear appeals may be useful if they are accompanied by specific, precise recommendations.

- Both a message recipient's need for cognition and her or his mood are associated with ease of persuasion.

Rethink

- Under what circumstances are two-sided arguments more effective than one-sided arguments? Would you recommend using a two-sided argument in a television ad for a soft drink? Why or why not?

- During which program would a fear ad be most effective: a situation comedy, a dramatic series, or the nightly news? Explain.

- What target characteristics seem to be most important in connection with persuasion?

- Describe the relationship you would expect to find between need for cognition and the following aspects of persuasion: source credibility, amount of message information, quality of message information, and repetition with variation.

PERSUASION IN THE MARKETPLACE

It's late December, and for the last few weeks you've been subjected to a media blitz by Ed McMahon telling you about the American Family Publishers Sweepstakes. You've seen friendly, trustworthy Ed introducing a past winner of $1 million. You've seen the letter on TV. Finally, it arrives, your "LAST CHANCE! Million Dollar Document" warning you, "Don't Throw Away! This is the letter you just saw on TV!" . . .

You now open the big envelope. On the large, official-looking document, you find your name throughout the text at least 20 times in various sizes of type. The first large print catches your eye: There's your name before ". . . SHALL BE PAID A FULL ONE MILLION DOLLARS." In contrasting color in the upper margin is the constant reminder, "LAST CHANCE!" A little farther down, there's your name again with nine—count 'em—nine Personal Prize Claim Numbers. . . .

The next piece of paper has a color picture of Ed, more instructions, and photos of a Mercedes, a mink coat, a cabin cruiser, and a beautiful home. "Become a Multimillionaire and Treat Yourself to the Things You Want Most!" you're told.

After extensive reading you finally figure out what to paste where to enter the contest. You also have a big page of colorful, perforated, sticky stamps that can be pasted on the entry blank to purchase any of a variety of magazines. Another full-color sheet from Ed tells you, "You can take it from me—THERE ARE NO LOWER PRICES AVAILABLE ANYWHERE TO THE GENERAL PUBLIC. American Family values are GUARANTEED UNBEATABLE!" There is also a list of selected magazines that offer Free Bonus Gifts, such as watches and desk clocks. You decide a Money-Manager Calculator would be useful—so you order Newsweek, *which will keep you better informed for school. Besides the good price, you don't have to pay now, because you'll be billed in the future. Also there's a money-back guarantee if you don't like the subscription—and, as it says, "You risk nothing!" So, you get the calculator,* Newsweek *at a great price, and maybe . . . just maybe . . . BIG, BIG BUCKS!!! (Peter & Olson, 1987, p. 305–306)*

Each year, just after Christmas, the airwaves are saturated with the news that the mail will soon bring you your chance to win millions, while also enjoying the opportunity to purchase subscriptions to your favorite magazines. It is not pure chance that brings these sales pitches out after the Christmas season. Research carried out by advertisers has shown that at this time of year consumers are most receptive to messages that promise the chance to win a big jackpot (Peter & Olson, 1987). After all, the bills for all those expensive holiday presents are coming due, and who could not use a sudden windfall to help pay them off?

Probably the most sophisticated use of the basic principles of persuasion that have been identified by social psychologists is the study of consumer behavior. The exploration of **consumer behavior** focuses on understanding buying habits and the effects of advertising on buyer behavior. Social psychologists specializing in consumer behavior explore how consumers are affected by particular kinds of advertising and how they make decisions to purchase (or forgo) specific products (Clark, Brock, & Stewart, 1994; Kardes, 1999).

consumer behavior: The study of behavior that focuses on understanding buying habits and the effects of advertising on buyer behavior.

You are most likely to get an invitation to enter a sweepstakes after the Christmas holiday season, when the possibility of obtaining quick cash may be particularly appealing.

PERSUASIVE ADVERTISING: CHANGING CONSUMERS' COLLECTIVE MINDS

If you are like the average American, you watch more than 700 advertisements on television each week. In that same week, you may be exposed to several hundred additional commercials on the radio and in newspapers and magazines (Aaker & Myers, 1987).

All those advertisements may seem pretty much alike to you as they pass by in a blur. However, although all advertisements are designed to promote the purchase of some product or service, they actually have several different purposes (Kotler, 1986). For instance, the primary purpose of some advertisements is informative. **Informative advertising** is designed to introduce new products, to suggest new ways of using an existing product, or to correct false impressions about a product. In this sort of advertising, the goal is to generate demand for a class of products. For instance, the insurance industry runs advertisements in which the general objective is to promote the idea that everyone needs some sort of life insurance.

In contrast, **selective demand advertising** is designed to establish or modify attitudes about a particular brand of product or service, compared with other brands of the same kind of product or service. Selective demand ads build preferences for particular products or brands, advocate shifting brands (Wansink, 1994), or attempt to persuade customers to buy a certain product immediately, rather than at a later date (Aaker & Biel, 1993; Abraham-Murali & Littrell, 1995).

Some kinds of selective demand advertising also make straightforward or indirect comparisons between different brands (Barone & Miniard, 1999). For instance, ads for Scope mouthwash state that it fights bad breath without giving purchasers "medicine breath." The message: One acquires objectionable "medicine breath" from the use of Scope's major competitor, Listerine.

Finally, the third major type of advertising is reminder advertising. In **reminder advertising**, the goal is to keep consumers thinking about a product or to reinforce the message that preferring a particular brand is appropriate. For example, when Hallmark sponsors

informative advertising: Advertising that is designed to introduce new products, to suggest new ways of using an existing product, or to correct false impressions about a product.

selective demand advertising: Advertising designed to establish or modify attitudes about a particular brand of product or service, compared with other brands of the same kind of product or service.

reminder advertising: Advertising designed to keep consumers thinking about a product or to reinforce the message that preferring a particular brand is appropriate.

television's "Mobil Masterpiece Theater", its purpose is largely to remind people of the brand name "Mobil." Similarly, some advertisements seek to assure consumers that they have made an appropriate decision in already purchasing a product. Hence, commercials showing satisfied customers are designed not only to persuade potential purchasers to buy the product, but also to assure those who have already made a purchase that they made the right choice (Batra, Lehmann, & Singh, 1993).

ADVERTISING MESSAGES: RELATING CONSUMERS AND PRODUCTS

Regardless of the particular goals of an advertising campaign, the most effective persuasion takes place when the advertisement takes into account the relationship between consumers and products. For instance, one aspect of this relationship is the extent to which consumers understand the product and are involved with it (Berger, 1986; Andrews, Durvasula, & Akhter, 1990; Homer & Kahle, 1990; Hoeffler & Ariely, 1999; Kokkinaki & Lunt, 1999; Yukl, Kim, & Chavez, 1999).

As Figure 11–5 illustrates, involvement is one major dimension relating to consumer attitudes about products. Involvement pertains both to the amount of prior experience the consumer has with a product and the degree of consumer interest in it (Hitchon & Thorson, 1994).

The second major dimension centers on the knowledge, meaning, beliefs, and thoughts that are activated when consumers consider a product. Some products are considered primarily in terms of their cognitive aspects—the rational, thoughtful associations of the product. When we consider a product in cognitive terms, the functions of the product are primary. Consequently, when we think of insecticides or cameras, we consider them primarily in functional, cognitive terms.

In contrast, we consider other products more in emotional and affective terms. Our thoughts about products of this type are primarily nonlinguistic, consisting of visual images or the sensory aspects of the product. For example, most of us conceive of perfume in terms not of its chemical composition but of its fragrance and its potential use in social situations. Similarly, items such as favorite foods or flashy automobiles may evoke primarily emotional reactions and images.

According to social psychologist David Berger, a product's location on the grid shown in Figure 11–5 points to the best way to devise advertising for the product (Berger, 1986). For instance, products that are located toward the emotional end of the cognitive–emotional dimension are advertised in ways that are considerably different from the ways that are used for products that are more cognitive in nature. Consequently, perfume—a product with strong emotional connotations—is best promoted through advertisements that evoke the emotional aspects of the product. In practice, this results in advertisements that emphasize the sexual implications of the use of perfume. Perfume advertising also pioneered the use of "scent strips," which are samples of the products that can be placed in magazine or mail advertisements. By actually incorporating the perfume's fragrance with the written message, ad writers aim to establish a classically conditioned association (Gubernick, 1986).

In some cases, advertising attempts to shift the location of a product on the grid. For example, a South American manufacturer was faced with a problem. It had produced thousands of unattractive green refrigerators that lacked many features. Meanwhile, the manufacturer's competition was promoting refrigerators that contained substantially more features, such as built-in icemakers. The manufacturer's dilemma: Consumers view refrigerators primarily in cognitive terms, and cognitively speaking, these particular refrigerators had relatively little to recommend them.

The solution? The advertising agency devised an ad campaign to shift the refrigerator from the cognitive quadrant of the grid to the emotional–affective quadrant. Their advertisements displayed Venezuelan beauty queens alongside the refrigerators, now identified as "another Venezuelan beauty." All 5,000 refrigerators sold in just 3 months (Berger, 1986).

In sum, by analyzing the way consumers perceive a product, advertisers are able to create ad campaigns tailored to consumers' relationship with the particular product (Putrevu &

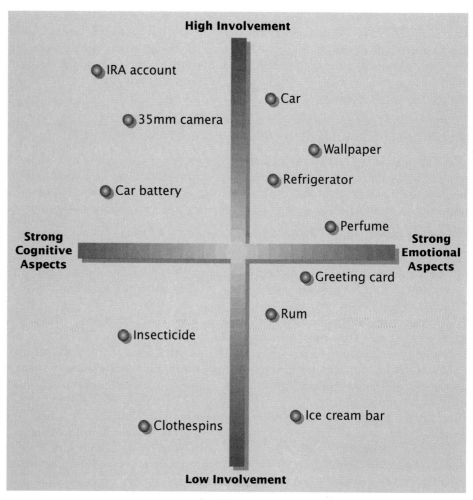

FIGURE 11–5 Consumer Product Characteristics As this graph indicates, consumer products can be placed on a grid with two dimensions. The first dimension is involvement, reflecting prior experience and interest in the product. The second reflects whether a product is strong in cognitive or emotional aspects. For example, a camera is relatively high in involvement and in cognitive aspects. In contrast, an ice cream bar is low in involvement and has strong emotional aspects. (*Source:* Adapted from Berger, 1986, p. 35.)

Lord, 1994; Holyfield, 1999). Furthermore, advertising can not only try to persuade consumers to purchase particular products, but also strive to change the more fundamental nature of the consumer–product relationship.

THE APPEAL OF ADVERTISING: HARD SELL, SOFT SELL

Consider these advertising claims:

> No aspirin cures headaches better.
> This is the best auto on the market.
> The strongest stain remover ever sold.

Now, compare the phrases above to these:

> You'll brighten your day with this coffee.
> People will say you're in love when you use this deodorant.
> You'll say that happy days are here when you eat these hot dogs.

Clearly, these two sets of statements are very different in tone. Those in the first set are more direct, focusing on the qualities of the products. Those in the second set are much more tranquil, evoking positive images about the products but saying relatively little about what they can accomplish.

The two sets of phrases actually exemplify the two major strategies used by advertisers (DeBono & Snyder, 1989; DeBono & Krim, 1997; Jones, 1997). The first strategy is the **hard sell**, an advertising approach that focuses on the qualities of the product itself. When using the hard sell, advertisers focus on the function of the product, how it performs, its taste, or its effect on the life of the consumer. For example, when the electronics manufacturer Zenith claims that "The quality goes in before the name goes on," it is using a hard-sell approach.

In contrast to the hard sell, the **soft sell** strives to link a product with a pleasant image related to the product's use. In using a soft-sell approach, advertisers attempt to suggest that potential product purchasers can project or achieve a desirable image through the use of the product.

Hence, when an ad for Close-up toothpaste reminds you that "Tartar isn't sexy," its goal is to link the use of Close-up (and its destruction of tarter) with the presumably desirable consequence of sexiness. Similarly, advertisers wanted men who saw the Marlboro man, the embodiment of robust masculinity, to feel that they would also personify highly masculine qualities if they merely smoked Marlboros. (Women had their own soft-sell role models: Virginia Slims cigarette advertisements included attractive, slender females projecting a sophisticated, elegant image.)

In some cases, both hard-sell and soft-sell approaches are consolidated into a single advertisement. Consider the BMW automobile advertisement that stated, "BMW meets the demands of the 90s with its spirit intact" and "A safe car needn't be a boring one." By touting the safety benefits of the BMW (a hard-sell approach) while still claiming that its "spirit" is unbroken and that it is not boring (a soft-sell approach), BMW tries to offer the best of both worlds.

PSYCHOGRAPHICS:
THE DEMOGRAPHY OF ADVERTISING

Who are the people most likely to buy Peter Pan Peanut Butter?

Although this question may not seem particularly pressing to you, to the makers of the product it is crucial. Unless they know who the potential customers are, they cannot target their advertising to these people.

Fortunately—at least from the perspective of the makers of Peter Pan Peanut Butter—researchers have been able to identify the buyers rather precisely. For example, in the New York metropolitan area, the heaviest consumers tend to live in suburban and rural households, to have children, and to live in families headed by 18- to 54-year-olds. They tend to rent home videos frequently, go to theme parks, watch television at rates below the national average, and listen to radio at rates above the national average (McCarthy, 1991).

The manufacturers of Peter Pan Peanut Butter have come to their understanding of who their potential purchasers are through the technique of psychographics. **Psychographics** is a method for dividing people into lifestyle profiles that are related to purchasing patterns (Rice, 1988). These profiles group people according to factors such as race and ethnic background, marital status, and educational levels, and also according to the kinds of activities that they participate in. By using psychographics, professional persuaders can analyze consumers' values, needs, attitudes, and motivation to purchase particular items (Heath, 1996; Endler & Rosenstein, 1997; Kahle & Chiagouris, 1997).

Probably the most widely used blueprint for classifying consumers is the "Values and Lifestyles 2" system, or VALS 2 for short. VALS 2, a revision of an earlier model known as VALS 1, stems from psychologist Abraham Maslow's hierarchy of needs, which represents people's progression of motivational needs from the most basic, physiological level to higher-order needs such as esteem and self-actualization (Maslow, 1987; Wells, Burnett, & Moriarty, 1992; Rowan, 1998).

hard sell: An advertising approach that focuses on the qualities of the product itself.

soft sell: An advertising approach that strives to link a product with a pleasant image related to the product's use.

psychographics: A method for dividing people into lifestyle profiles that are related to purchasing patterns.

According to VALS 2, consumers can be divided into eight groups, depending on their position along two independent dimensions: resources and self-orientation. Resources include income, education, self-confidence, intelligence, eagerness to buy, and energy level.

The second dimension, self-orientation, is the pattern of attitudes and behaviors that relate to a person's self-image. There are three types of self-image in VALS 2: principle oriented, status oriented, and action oriented. Principle-oriented consumers make choices based on their beliefs or principles, not on the basis of emotions, events, or the desire for approval. Status-oriented consumers are influenced most by the opinions of others and their need for approval from others. Finally, action-oriented consumers are most influenced by a desire for social or physical activity, variety, and risk taking.

By considering where people lie along the two dimensions of resources and self-orientation, users of VALS 2 can place people into one of eight groups, with the labels actualizers, fulfilleds, achievers, experiencers, believers, strivers, makers, and strugglers (see Figure 11–6). For instance, actualizers are successful, sophisticated, and active consumers with high self-esteem and abundant resources. At the other end of the resources continuum are the strugglers; they have very limited financial resources, live in poverty, are poorly educated, and lack strong social ties.

The largest group, encompassing 16% of consumers, is believers. Believers are conservative, conventional individuals. They have established routines, largely organized around their homes, families, and the social and religious organizations to which they belong. They tend to prefer American products and well-known brands. Their resources are modest but sufficient to meet their needs.

A good deal of research suggests that VALS 2 offers a reliable means of segmenting consumers into reasonable groups. Consumers make purchases in patterns congruent with their VALS categories (Loudon & Della Bitta, 1993; Heath, 1996; Allen & Ng, 1999). For instance, actualizers are likely to be attracted to expensive foreign cars, whereas believers are more likely to own pickup trucks.

Of course, VALS 2 is not the only technique used to assess consumer attitudes and values. For instance, some researchers use perceptual mapping to understand how consumers view

FIGURE 11–6   VALS 2 Lifestyles VALS 2 groups are arranged vertically by their resources and horizontally by their self-orientation.

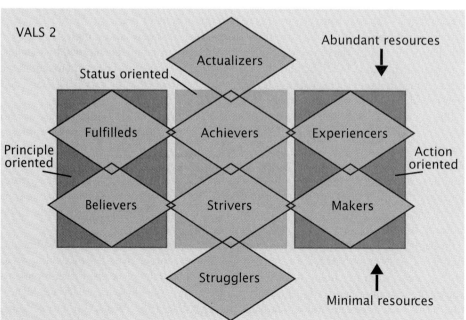

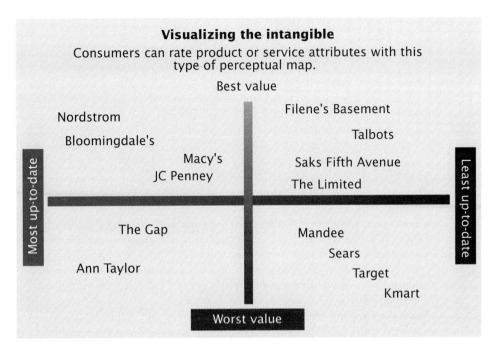

FIGURE 11–7   Consumer Perception of Goods and Retailers Some researchers use perceptual mapping to examine and understand how the average consumer views goods and the retailers that provide them. (*Source:* Sabrena Qualitative Research Service, 1996, p. 42.)

consumer goods and retailers. Figure 11–7 illustrates the grid produced when a group of consumers was asked to rate retailers in terms of value and how up-to-date they were.

CULTURE AND CONSUMERS

Members of various racial and ethnic groups don't respond uniformly to advertising strategies—a fact about which advertisers, as well as social psychologists, are becoming increasing aware (Piirto, 1991a). Research shows that the purchasing decisions of African Americans, Hispanics, and whites differ significantly. For instance, African Americans are more loyal to national brand names than whites, and Hispanics purchase more juice than other groups (Engel & Blackwell, 1982; Boone & Krutz, 1986; Aaker & Biel, 1993).

In some cases, manufacturers of consumer products have attempted to target ads to specific populations—with mixed results. For instance, one ad about telephone service, targeted to Hispanics, involved a Puerto Rican actress telling her husband to "run downstairs and phone Mary. Tell her we'll be a little tardy." Unfortunately, the ad was not successful because it did not take into account two characteristics of most Hispanic cultures. First, because Hispanic cultures tend to be relatively male-oriented, the scenario of a wife telling her husband so directly what he should do is implausible. Furthermore, because most Hispanic cultures have more relaxed, less rigid norms about time, running a little late would not be a cause for concern (McGrath, 1988; Englis, 1993).

In some cases, targeting ads and products to particular populations takes a questionable turn. For instance, the R.J. Reynolds Tobacco Company briefly toyed with the idea of distributing a brand of cigarettes called "Uptown." When it became obvious that the brand was targeted toward African Americans, the product was condemned by the secretary of the U.S. Department of Health and Human Services. Eventually, the brand was discontinued (Quinn, 1990).

EXPLORING DIVERSITY

THE INFORMED CONSUMER OF SOCIAL PSYCHOLOGY

RESISTING THE POWERS OF PERSUASION

We are continually the targets of persuasion. Not only are we bombarded with media communications, but our family, friends, and even foes are constantly presenting information suggesting that their point of view is the correct one.

In this age of omnipresent forces of persuasion, it is not easy to maintain independent decision making. Still, it is possible to retain one's point of view and resist being a pawn of persuaders. Social psychologists have devised several strategies for maintaining independence and considering persuasive messages in a cool and rational manner. Among the most effective:

◆ *Inoculation.* Medical researchers learned long ago that if we expose people to a weakened form of smallpox germs, they will produce antibodies that will later be able to repel a full-scale onslaught of the disease.

Social psychologist William McGuire (1964) suggested that people could similarly be made resistant to persuasive appeals by "inoculating" them with counterattitudinal information *prior* to a full-scale attack on their attitudes. Specifically, McGuire suggested that people's attitudes were especially vulnerable to attack when they had rarely heard contradictory arguments. This is especially the case for widely accepted views and cultural truisms, such as "It is important to brush your teeth after every meal."

Indeed, when faced with arguments contrary to widely accepted views, people tend to change attitudes fairly readily. In contrast, if they previously have been exposed to at least some opposing arguments and also provided the means to refute the opposition (the social psychological equivalent of a shot-in-the-arm), they are considerably more likely to resist the persuasive attack (Burgoon & Miller, 1990).

In short, one way you can counteract persuasive messages is to anticipate and prepare yourself for an upcoming persuasive onslaught. By inoculating yourself before exposure, you'll be able to resist the persuasive efforts of others.

◆ *Taking the role of devil's advocate.* A devil's advocate is someone who takes a certain position not necessarily from conviction but more for the sake of argument. According to social psychologists Anthony Pratkanis and Elliot Aronson, one constructive technique for retaining your independence is to adopt the role of the devil's advocate. Specifically, put yourself into the shoes (and head) of the source of the persuasive message, and ask yourself questions such as:

What does the source of information have to gain?

Why are these choices being presented to me in this manner?

Are there other options and other ways of presenting those options?

What would happen if I chose something other than the recommended option?

What are the arguments for the other side? (Pratkanis & Aronson, 1992, p. 213)

By asking yourself—and answering—questions such as these, you're in a considerably better position to understand the underlying intent of the message. Ultimately, such knowledge will better enable you to make up your own mind, rather than unwittingly being persuaded by the information being communicated to you.

◆ *Forewarning.* Forewarned is forearmed. Consider this warning: "Brace yourself: You're about to be the recipient of a persuasive message." Is a warning such as this—explicitly stating that you will soon encounter a communication intended to influence you—sufficient to allow you to keep your independence?

In many cases, the answer is yes. If the issues at hand are important and you have a reasonable amount of knowledge about them, knowing that you are the target of persuasion will increase the possibility that you can remain independent.

There are two reasons why the forewarning effect occurs. First, the knowledge that you are about to be persuasively attacked permits you to spend some time thinking about supportive arguments for your own position and counterarguments against the persuader's position. And second, such awareness may raise your defenses; you may become obstinate and attempt to resist the persuasive attempt. In some cases, in fact, forewarning produces a boomerang effect: After learning that you may be the target of persuasion, you become even more committed to your initial position (Hass & Grady, 1975; Cialdini & Petty, 1981).

None of these methods is foolproof. All of us, at times, are going to fall prey to the powerful clout of persuasive messages. However, these techniques can give us at least a fighting chance to ward off unwarranted persuasion and maintain our independence.

REVIEW AND RETHINK

Review

* Types of advertisements include informative, selective demand, and reminder advertising.
* Consumer involvement and understanding of a product are associated with advertising effectiveness.
* Hard-sell advertising focuses on product qualities, whereas the soft sell attempts to associate products with positive images and emotions.
* Psychographics is a method for grouping people according to lifestyle profiles.

Rethink

* Define the three broad classes of advertisements. What approach would be most appropriate for a company that enjoys the largest market share within its retail area?
* Would hard-sell or soft-sell tactics be more effective in promoting a brand of cigarettes? Describe both a soft-sell and a hard-sell ad that could be used in an antismoking campaign. Which do you think would be more effective?
* How does VALS 2 enable advertisers to increase the effectiveness of their ads? What type of advertising would you use to persuade principle-oriented consumers? Briefly describe an ad that would appeal to strivers.

LOOKING BACK

What are the cognitive paths to persuasion?

1. Persuasion follows two paths, the central route and the peripheral route. Central route persuasion occurs on the basis of the logic, merit, or strength of the arguments. Peripheral route persuasion occurs when people are persuaded on the basis of factors unrelated to the nature or quality of the content of a persuasive message. Instead, they respond to irrelevant or extraneous factors such as who is providing the message or the length of the arguments. (p. 362)

2. The most lasting and persistent attitude change is brought about by central route processing. Although peripheral route processing can sway attitudes, the degree of change is not likely to be as strong or as lasting as when central route processing is employed. (p. 364)

3. Two conditions must be met if central route processing is to proceed. First, people must be sufficiently motivated to expend the cognitive effort to think about the issue. Second, they must have the ability to process the information. (p. 364)

What characteristics of the message source produce the greatest persuasion?

4. The credibility of the source of a message, relating to the source's expertise and trustworthiness, is a major determinant of persuasibility. Even message sources with little credibility can be persuasive, as illustrated by the sleeper effect. The sleeper effect is an increase in the persuasibility of a message that occurs with the passage of time. (p. 365)

5. Other important factors related to the message source's persuasive abilities are the communicator's attractiveness and likability. Celebrities are often used to persuade consumers to use products, even when the celebrity has no special expertise regarding the product. (p. 368)

How do messages differ in their ability to elicit persuasion?

6. The amount and kind of information contained in a message affect persuasion. If additional arguments are equally strong and valid, then more information results in greater persuasion. If the additional arguments are weak, then their effectiveness depends on the presence of peripheral route processing. (p. 370)

7. Whether the message should present only one side of an issue or both sides depends on the target audience. In addition, repetition of a message, up to a point, produces greater and more persistent attitude change. The success of repetition depends on the message's complexity. (p. 371)

8. The success of fear appeals, messages designed to change attitudes by producing apprehension and anxiety if the messages are not followed, depends on their accompaniment by specific, precise recommendations for actions that will help receivers avoid the danger. If no such information is provided, strong fear appeals may be ignored because they arouse so much anxiety. (p. 372)

What personal characteristics are associated most with persuasion?

9. Early research was unable to identify personal characteristics that consistently lead people to be easy or difficult to persuade. More recent research suggests that people's reactions to persuasive messages depend on a combination of the kind of message that is being communicated, its source, and the specific personal qualities of the target. (p. 373)

10. The need for cognition, a person's habitual level of thoughtfulness and cognitive activity, is associated with persuasibility, although much depends on the specific content of the message. Mood, too, is related to persuasion. For instance, a good mood leads to an increased likelihood of peripheral route processing. (p. 373)

How do advertisers devise effective persuasive messages?

11. Informative advertising is designed to introduce new products, to suggest new ways of using an existing product, or to correct false impressions about a product. In contrast, selective demand advertising is designed to establish or modify attitudes about a particular brand of product or service, compared with other brands of the same kind of product or service. Finally, in reminder advertising, the goal is to keep consumers thinking about a product or to reinforce the message that preferring a brand is appropriate. (p. 380)

12. Consumer involvement with and understanding of a product are associated with the effectiveness of various types of advertising. In addition, ads differ in whether they use a hard-sell approach (focusing on the qualities of the product) or a soft-sell approach (focusing on linking a product's use with pleasant images). (p. 383)

PROLOGUE

Web of Death

While the Heaven's Gate suicides were extreme, the influences on members of the cult to follow orders are not that different from those we encounter in our everyday lives.

They led quiet lives, making little impression on their neighbors in the posh San Diego suburb of Rancho Santa Fe. Although some of them had earlier suffered broken romances, the death of a loved one, or any one of the typical tragedies that are part and parcel of everyday life, most seemed no different from the average person while they were growing up. They came from ordinary backgrounds and could be anyone's parents, friends, or children.

Yet, in the end, they were far from ordinary. They belonged to a group called Heaven's Gate, and they called their leader Do (pronounced "doe"). They dressed similarly, in baggy clothing designed to hide their figures, and had similar short haircuts. They tried to avoid sex and even identification as male or female, and many of the men were castrated.

Their obscurity ended when 39 of the members of Heaven's Gate committed mass suicide. Found with eerie purple shrouds over their faces, each had taken a deadly mixture of barbiturates and alcohol. Packed suitcases lay nearby, and their pockets contained rolls of quarters and $5 bills. All wore new Nike sneakers.

Their suicide, according to accounts left behind on the World Wide Web, was an effort to shed their outer "vehicles" and move to the next evolutionary level, a starry utopia in the heavens. Under the orders of their leader, Do, they killed themselves with the expectation that they would soon be picked up by a spaceship hovering behind the comet Hale-Bopp. ■

LOOKING AHEAD

The perplexing behavior of the Heaven's Gate group raises a variety of puzzling issues, the most central of which is this: Why would a group of people obey the dictates of a leader who ordered them to commit mass suicide?

Although the Heaven's Gate incident is extreme, the forces that led the members of the Heaven's Gate cult to follow their leader's orders are not all that different from those we encounter in our everyday lives. How often do we follow the mandate of an instructor, or employer, or parent—even if we do not agree with it? How often are we influenced by the latest fad in clothing or music? And how often do we go along with other people not because we agree with them but because we want to be accepted by the group?

social influence: The area of social psychology that explores how people are affected by the real or imagined pressure of other individuals or a group.

In this chapter, we consider the topic of social influence. **Social influence** is the area of social psychology that explores how people are affected by the real or imagined pressure of other individuals or a group. The influence may be intentional, as in the case of the Heaven's Gate leader Do, who urged his followers to commit mass suicide. On the other hand, social influence may be unintentional, as when a group's majority induces a minority to adhere to its position because of the fear of potential embarrassment or ridicule. Either way, the outcome is the same: a change in behavior as a result of real or imagined pressure from others.

We will consider a variety of social influences in this chapter—ranging from indirect, implicit social influence to direct, overt pressures (see Figure 12–1). We begin with a discussion of conformity, which occurs when people change their behavior or attitudes out of a desire to follow the beliefs or standards of others. We discuss the underlying reasons why people conform, and the factors that permit some people to maintain independence in the face of group pressures. We also examine the ways in which a group minority can exert social influence on a group majority.

Our discussion then turns to compliance—yielding to direct, explicit appeals to change one's behavior or point of view. A more explicit form of social pressure than conformity, compliance, as we will see, can be sought by means of several distinct strategies.

Finally, we examine obedience—social pressure that is the result of direct commands. We consider historical cases of blind obedience, after which we turn to experimental studies of the phenomenon, which help explain its dynamics.

In sum, after reading this chapter, you'll be able to answer these questions:

- ◆ Why do people conform to the views and behavior of others?

- ◆ What factors promote independence from conformity pressures?

- ◆ What strategies can be employed to make others compliant, and how can such pressures be resisted?

- ◆ Why are people so readily obedient to authority figures?

FIGURE 12–1   The Varieties of Social Influence Social influence varies according to the directness of the request.

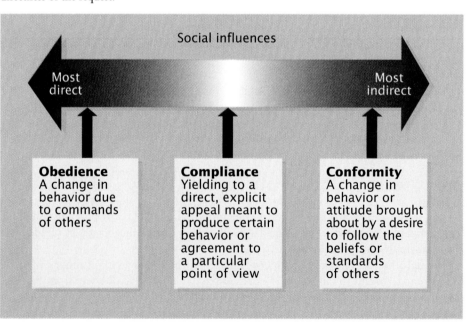

This boy's obvious allegiance to basketball star Michael Jordan is one example of the power of social influence.

CONFORMITY

You are sitting at a table with a group of five fellow students, participating in what seems to be a pretty straightforward experiment. The researcher has explained that he is studying perception, and that he'll be showing you a series of cards on which lines are printed. Your job is simple: Along with the other participants, you are to announce in turn which of three lines is similar in length to a fourth line, which he calls the "standard."

At first, nothing seems amiss. The other participants in the experiments look at the lines and make the obvious response, identical to your own. But on the third set of lines, you are startled when the first participant to respond seems to make a mistake. Even more surprising, the second participant makes the same error. When the third, fourth, and fifth participants make the same mistake, you are in turmoil. How can they all be wrong? Is there something about the lines they see and you don't? Are your eyes failing you? What explains this mysterious coincidence?

At this point, you probably have an inkling about what is happening in this experiment, because by now you are aware of the lengths to which social psychologists will go to study social behavior. The other participants in the study were actually confederates of the experimenter, trained to give unanimous, erroneous responses.

But consider the plight of an individual unschooled in the ways of social psychology. For the average person, the situation is baffling. When others in the study all respond with what seems to be the same wrong response on such an easy task, the participant must make a choice between relying on his or her own sensory judgment versus going along with the group.

This situation, devised by social psychologist Solomon Asch, has become a classic in the investigation of conformity. **Conformity** is a change in behavior or attitudes brought about by a desire to follow the beliefs or standards of others. As we might suspect from the situation above, conformity may involve public acceptance of a group's position, but private disapproval of it—a process known as **public compliance**. Sometimes, however, true persuasion occurs, and a person's private opinion actually changes as well—a phenomenon known as

conformity: A change in behavior or attitudes brought about by a desire to follow the beliefs or standards of others.

public compliance: Public acceptance of a group's position but private disapproval of the same position.

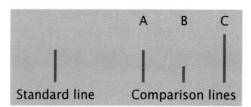

FIGURE 12–2 Asch's Conformity Task
In Solomon Asch's classic study, participants were shown a standard line and asked to state out loud which of the three other lines matched the standard length. This appeared to be an easy task—until confederates began unanimously choosing the wrong answer.

private acceptance (Hall, Varca, & Fisher, 1986; Van Knippenberg & Wilke, 1988; Massey, Freeman, & Zelditch, 1997).

How do participants respond to the plight into which the Asch study casts them (see Figure 12–2)? In many cases, they go along with the group. Specifically, in about one-third of the trials participants conformed to the unanimous but erroneous group decision, choosing an alternative that was clearly in error.

But there are also significant individual differences: Some participants conform all the time, whereas others remain totally independent of the pressure. Nonetheless, more than three-quarters of the participants in the experiment conformed at least once to the others' inaccurate judgments (Asch, 1951).

NORMATIVE AND INFORMATIONAL SOCIAL INFLUENCE

To understand why people conform to group pressure, social psychologists have distinguished between two types of social pressure: normative social influence and informational social influence (Deutsch & Gerard, 1955; Kaplan & Miller, 1987; Campbell & Fairey, 1989; Greenberg, 1997; Cialdini & Trost, 1998; van Knippenberg, 1999). **Normative social influence** is pressure that reflects group norms, which are expectations regarding appropriate behavior held by those belonging to groups. Normative social influence operates because of our desire to meet the expectations of a group.

One reason people conform, then, is because experience has shown that transgressors of group norms are punished in some way by the other members of the group. Consequently, an individual may appear to agree with a majority to avoid the anticipated unpleasant consequences of violating group standards. Hence, in Asch's experiment participants may conform to avoid the presumed retaliation of the other participants for defying the majority response (Neto, 1995).

Another reason we conform is that in many cases we must rely on the perceptions, experience, and knowledge of others because we are unable to experience firsthand certain aspects of the world. How many of us have measured the distance between New York and California, for example? Clearly, we need to rely on other people to provide us with information about the world. **Informational social influence** is pressure to conform that emanates from our assumption that others have knowledge that we lack.

We conform to informational social influence in a particular situation because we think that group members have information about the situation that we do not. Participants in Asch's experiment may be prone to conform if they feel that the other participants have some sort of special insight into the situation. Similarly, we may be influenced by a majority position on an environmental issue such as the necessity of recycling because we feel those in the majority simply know more about the issue than we do.

When we consider why people are influenced by informational social pressure, we realize that conformity is not invariably an objectionable or a morally deficient behavior. Other people do know more about certain things than we do, and we cannot verify every piece of information on our own. Further, even when we try to rely on our own senses to make a judgment, we are not always accurate. For instance, one of the earliest examinations of conformity relied on a visual illusion called the *autokinetic effect,* the illusion that a small, stationary light in a darkened room appears to move.

private acceptance: A phenomenon in which a person's private opinion changes as a result of true persuasion.

normative social influence: Pressure that reflects group norms, which are expectations regarding appropriate behavior held by those belonging to groups.

informational social influence: Pressure to conform that emanates from our assumption that others have knowledge that we lack.

The autokinetic effect is especially susceptible to social influence because it is so ambiguous. When people make judgments without others present, they vary widely in their estimates of how much the stationary pinpoint of light moves, with judgments ranging from less than an inch to more than a foot. Interestingly, though, when the same people are later brought together in groups and asked to announce their judgments aloud, their estimates begin to converge. After a relatively short time, participants in a group end up with similar reports about the extent of the light's movement (Sherif & Sherif, 1969; MacNeil & Sherif, 1976; see Figure 12–3). Even more important, when people are subsequently separated once more and are again asked to make individual judgments, their estimates are similar to those they made while they were part of the group.

In sum, both informational and normative social influence produce conformity. Furthermore, under most circumstances, neither type of influence functions by itself. Instead, informational and normative social influence work in unison in most situations.

For example, participants in the Asch experiment who conformed likely did so out of a desire to avoid contradicting group norms and potentially being laughed at, embarrassed, or punished in some way by the group—a response to normative social influence. At the same time, though, participants may have assumed that the others in the experiment had greater experience in the task or perceived something in the situation that they were missing—a response to informational social influence.

FACTORS PRODUCING CONFORMITY: THE FINE POINTS OF ACCOMMODATING TO A GROUP

Although any group situation holds the potential for normative and informational social pressures to produce conformity, people do not invariably conform to the behavior of others. Why do people submissively conform in some situations and maintain independence in others? To answer that question, we need to take a look at several factors that social psychologists have identified as critical in intensifying or weakening conformity (Allen, 1965;

FIGURE 12–3   The Autokinetic Effect at Work Initially, participants' judgments of the degree of movement of what was actually a stationary light diverged significantly. However, over the course of several group sessions in which they had to announce their judgments aloud, their ratings increasingly converged. (*Source:* Sherif, 1936.)

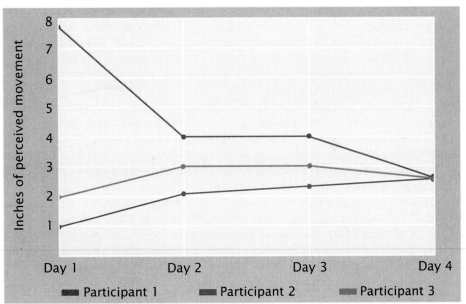

The more a person is attracted to a group and its members, the more likely that person is to conform to the group's standards. The TV show *Friends* not only reflects current fashion, but also helps mold it.

Tanford & Penrod, 1984; Nail, 1986; Kuczynski & Hildebrant, 1997; Avtgis, 1998; Cialdini & Trost, 1998).

The strength of the ties between the individual and the group is one determinant of how likely a person is to conform to the group's position. For instance, the more a person is attracted to a group and its members, the more likely that person is to conform to the group's standards (Brehm & Mann, 1975; Hogg & Hardie, 1992; Bearden, Rose, & Teel, 1994; Pool, Wood, & Leck, 1998). Consequently, members of a popular, high-status sorority are likely to produce high levels of conformity pressure on members who value highly the perceived prestige of the group. At the same time, however, members who find the group unattractive are less likely to yield to the pressure to conform to its standards. If you dislike the sorority and the type of people who populate it, you'll be unlikely to experience much desire to conform to group norms.

Within a group, the status of a person's position also affects his or her susceptibility to conformity pressures. **Status** is the social rank a person holds within a group. In general, lower-status people conform more than higher-status people (Larsen et al., 1979; Williams, 1984). However, in some cases high-status group leaders may conform more to group norms than people in nonleadership roles. Leaders may conform to maintain and bolster their leadership positions by going along with the other group members (Nagata, 1980).

Finally, pressures to conform are greatest in groups whose members are similar to one another. This explanation relates to our earlier discussion in Chapter 4 about people's need for social comparison, by which people compare themselves to others to judge their own abilities, attitudes, and behavior. The more similar others are to ourselves, the more apt we are to use them for comparison purposes. As a consequence, their social influence on our own behavior is likely to be greater (Insko, Sedlak, & Lipsitz, 1982; Pool, Wood, & Leck, 1998).

status: The social rank a person holds within a group.

THE NUMBERS OF CONFORMITY: THE OPPOSITION DOESN'T ALWAYS COUNT

Suppose you find yourself in a meeting whose purpose is to decide whether to offer passenger-side air bags as a standard feature for your company's forthcoming new car model. You strongly favor the option, but everyone else argues that it will be too expensive, that the passenger seat is occupied infrequently, and that safety data do not support the installation of air bags. Will you be more likely to conform to the majority opinion if there are three people opposing you or if there are ten?

It seems reasonable to assume that the more people who are aligned against the position we hold, the more likely we would be to cave in to the majority position. In fact, such an assumption is both right and wrong. Up to a point, the presence of more people leads to greater conformity. After the number in the majority reaches a critical—and, it turns out, surprisingly modest—point, however, conformity levels off. In fact, in some cases conformity may decrease slightly when more people are added to the majority. Specifically, most research has found that conformity increases as the size of a united majority grows to around four or five people; above that size, conformity levels off (Rosenberg, 1961; Gerard, Whilhelmy, & Conolley, 1968; Stang, 1976; Clark, 1998).

According to social psychologists Bibb Latané and Sharon Wolf, the decreasing influence of increasing majorities can be explained by social impact theory (Wolf, 1985; Latané, 1997; Hart, Stasson, & Karau, 1999). **Social impact theory** suggests that the effect of a majority on a minority rests on three basic factors—the majority's strength, immediacy, and number (Latané et al., 1995). The strength of a majority relates to its status, competence, and general relationship to a target of influence. Immediacy refers to the physical proximity of an influence source. And number relates to the quantity of individuals in the majority.

To explain why simply increasing the sheer number of members in the majority does not lead to a corresponding increase in conformity, Latané and Wolf use the analogy of lighting a room. They note that when a room is in total darkness, turning on a light of any brightness appears to make an enormous difference. But once the brightness reaches a level that permits a person to see enough to navigate around the furniture, each subsequent increase in lighting has a successively smaller impact. In a similar fashion, social impact theory suggests that as a unanimous majority increases in size, each additional person provides relatively less influence than the previous person—a prediction that characterizes a good deal of research on the topic (see Figure 12–4).

Although social impact theory provides one explanation for the leveling-off in the impact of increasingly large majorities, it is not the full explanation (e.g., Jackson, 1986; Mullen,

social impact theory: The theory that suggests that the effect of a majority on a minority rests on three basic factors—the majority's strength, immediacy, and number.

FIGURE 12–4   Social Impact Theory As the number of people in a united majority increases, the social impact of each new individual declines. Consequently, conformity increases sharply at first, but it begins to level off as more people join the majority. (*Source:* Latané, 1981, p. 344.)

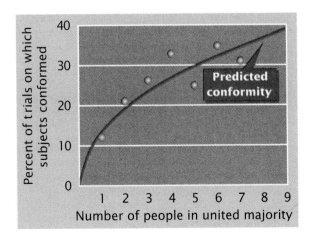

social supporter: A person holding a position similar to one's own.

1986; Clark & Maass, 1990; Crano & Alvaro, 1998). For example, as the size of a majority aligned against us increases, we may come to feel increasingly under siege. We may perceive ourselves as the targets of a concerted effort to get us to conform, and we might feel that members of the majority do not even truly share the view they are expressing. Ironically, we may come to assume that the majority is less unanimous and uniform in its views than it appears to be. As a consequence, we may be able to withstand the influence of a large majority more readily than a small one (Wilder, 1977).

SOCIAL SUPPORT: DISCOVERING A PARTNER IN DISUNITY

Having an ally who shares our views always helps, but never more than when we are facing a majority unanimously aligned against us. In fact, having even a single **social supporter**, a person holding a similar position, typically allows an individual to remain independent of the group (Allen, 1975; Wilder & Allen, 1977; Boyanowsky et al., 1981).

For instance, in Asch's classic studies, when a social supporter was present, conformity was reduced to 15% of what it was when a partner was not present (Asch, 1952, 1955). The effect of having a social supporter is so powerful that the competence of the supporter doesn't even matter much.

In one study, for example, participants were told that the purpose of the experiment was to make visual judgments in a group situation (Allen & Levine, 1971). However, one of the other supposed participants—the person who would later turn out to be the participant's social supporter—appeared to be completely incompetent at the visual task, miserably failing a vision test administered at the start of the experiment. Nonetheless, this same individual later made visual judgments that were surprisingly accurate. These judgments provided the participant with a potential social supporter against the rest of the group's "judgments," which, on most trials, were unanimously incorrect. Even though the social supporter apparently had impaired vision, which meant that his correct answers could be attributed to chance, participants' conformity to the group dropped significantly compared with another experimental condition in which no social supporter was present.

In sum, standing alone in a group and maintaining an unpopular position is decidedly difficult. However, the presence of even one ally who agrees with our stand is enough to allow us to elude the grip of conformity pressures.

GENDER DIFFERENCES IN CONFORMITY: DO WOMEN OR MEN YIELD MORE?

Not too long ago, researchers were convinced that women conform more than men do. For instance, one early, influential review of the literature noted that a ". . . difference in amount of conformity for males and females has been repeatedly demonstrated, with females generally conforming more than males" (Allen, 1965, p. 159). Subsequent research began to chip away at that assertion. Partially as a reaction to the growing women's movement of the 1960s and 1970s, social psychologists began to take a second look at gender differences. They found a picture considerably more complicated than they anticipated.

For example, one major review of the conformity literature, conducted by social psychologists Alice Eagly and Linda Carli (1981), confirmed that in group settings, women generally conformed more than men. However, closer examination revealed a potentially biasing factor: the sex of the researcher. Almost 80% of the studies were carried out by males, and these male researchers tended to obtain greater female conformity than female researchers did. In fact, experiments conducted by female researchers tended to show no gender differences.

Why should this be the case? One possibility is that male and female experimenters make different decisions about which of their findings they seek to publish. Female experimenters may be more likely than male experimenters to choose to publish findings of "no difference" in conformity between men and women. Consequently, given that more studies were conducted by men, the findings of a difference in conformity would be more apt to be reflected in the literature than studies that found no difference.

A more likely explanation may lie in the choice of topics used in the typical conformity experiment. If researchers tend to use topics of a stereotypically "masculine" nature in their studies, such as discussions of football or warfare, women may conform more than men because of their perceived lack of expertise in the subject matter. Conversely, if the topic is more familiar to women than to men, then we might expect greater conformity on the part of men. Because most conformity studies had been conducted by male experimenters, the topics they employed in their studies may have reflected more "masculine" subjects than "feminine" ones—leading to the appearance of greater conformity on the part of female participants (Eagly & Carli, 1981).

The possibility that the topic area used in an experiment affects the experimental outcome is not farfetched. According to one study that directly tested the possibility, the kind of items used to elicit group pressure had a predictable effect, depending on whether the items were more familiar to men, to women, or were neutral (Sistrunk & McDavid, 1971). Males conformed most on the "feminine" items; females most on the "masculine" items; and there was no difference between males and females on the items that were equally familiar to both sexes.

After the publication of Eagly and Carli's review, the prevailing opinion among social psychologists was that the differences in conformity between males and females that had been found in the past might well be largely attributable to research problems and experimental misinterpretations. Gender differences, then, appeared to be minor, unreliable, and not terribly important.

But this conclusion was not to be the last word (Collin, DiSano, & Malik, 1994; Burgoon & Klingle, 1998). Current thinking has come full circle, suggesting that sometimes women do indeed conform more than men—but only under certain circumstances. In public, face-to-face clashes in which they can be observed by others, women are more apt to hide their true feelings and go along with the group than when they are not being observed. Conversely, when men are in similar public situations where their behavior is under the scrutiny of others, they are less likely to conform to the group than when they are alone (Tuthill & Forsyth, 1982; Eagly & Chravala, 1986; Guarino, Fridrich, & Sitton, 1994).

The roots of the differences in conformity between men and women may be traced to differences in the importance of gender roles in public and private situations. When people are in a public, confrontational setting, they are concerned about how well they are representing themselves and how closely their behavior adheres to what people expect of them. The traditional female gender role emphasizes relationship maintenance and getting along with others, whereas the traditional male role is more confrontational and assertive.

As a result, to meet the expectations of others, both males and females are more likely to present their behavior in ways that are consistent with their own traditional gender roles—but only in public settings. In private, they can be themselves. Consequently, in private situations differences between men's and women's conformity behavior diminish (Eagly, Wood, & Fishbaugh, 1981; Eagly, 1987; Wood et al., 1997).

Of course, there are other explanations for gender differences in conformity. For instance, because of societal barriers, women may hold positions of lower status than men in some groups. As we have seen, low-status individuals tend to conform more than high-status individuals. Thus, status factors, and not gender, may lead to public conformity (Unger & Crawford, 1996).

Both the gender role and status explanations of conformity differences in men and women suggest that if changes occur in gender roles and status, the nature of conformity differences may also change. Hence, the ending of the story of gender differences in conformity has yet to be written.

CULTURE AND CONFORMITY

Mahatma Gandhi urged his fellow citizens of India to engage in passive resistance to secure their independence.

When Mahatma Gandhi exhorted citizens of India to conform to his then-radical views of passive resistance, he did so by making an emotional appeal based on the right to "manufacture salt" and "weave one's own cloth" (Sinha, 1990, cited in Moghaddam, Taylor, & Wright, 1993). Although such encouragement sounds rather odd to the ear of residents of North America at the beginning of the 21st century, in fact it was quite effective in rallying supporters to Gandhi's cause.

Clearly, conformity to social norms depends on the content of those norms. Moreover, the degree to which conformity is typical and valued varies from one culture to another. Consider, for instance, one of the primary dimensions on which cultures differ: individualism versus collectivism (Triandis, 1990, 1994). Societies reflecting **individualism** hold that the personal identity, uniqueness, freedom, and worth of the individual person are central. People in individualistic societies emphasize that their own goals should hold greater weight than the goals of the groups to which they belong.

In contrast, other cultures reflect **collectivism**, the notion that the well-being of the group is more important than that of the individual. People in collectivistic cultures emphasize the welfare of the groups to which they belong, sometimes at the expense of their own personal well-being. They also place a high value on harmony in person–group relations.

Given that people in individualistic cultures view the world differently from people in collectivistic cultures, we might expect to find differences in levels of conformity between the two types of cultures. And this is just what psychologists Rod Bond and Peter Smith found in an analysis of over 100 Asch-type conformity studies. Bond and Smith discovered that people in collectivistic countries—who highly value their group membership and seek good relations with other members of their groups—show relatively higher levels of conformity. In contrast, people in more individualistic countries, in which individualism and individual uniqueness are highly valued, are apt to show lower levels of conformity (Bond & Smith, 1996).

In their analysis, Bond and Smith also found changes in conformity over time. Examining studies conducted in the United States, the researchers found a clear decline in the degree of conformity displayed by participants in Asch-type experiments from the early 1950s to the present. The decline suggests that cultural norms promoting greater individuality and the questioning of authority may have emerged over the period, leading to a decrease in conformity.

Although general patterns emerged from Bond and Smith's review of conformity studies, there were many exceptions. For instance, some research finds that people in countries that we might expect to be more conforming, based on the largely collectivistic nature of their society, actually show less conformity than people in the United States. For instance, people in Japan, which is generally considered a collectivistic country, show less conformity in Asch-type experiments than people in the United States, a considerably more individualistic country (Timaeus, 1968; Frager, 1970). Although such findings may be surprising in the light of stereotypes about the high levels of conformity among the Japanese, it might be that the Asch situation, which involves conformity to strangers and not to people of authority or to other group members, might have evoked relatively low conformity among Japanese participants in the laboratory (Moghaddam, Taylor, & Wright, 1993). If such an explanation is valid, it highlights the difficulty involved in drawing conclusions from experimental procedures developed in one culture and imported to others.

Other cross-cultural research has considered how specific facets of society might be related to conformity. For instance, psychologist John Berry hypothesized that the nature of food

individualism: The notion that the personal identity, uniqueness, freedom, and worth of the individual person is central.

collectivism: The notion that the well-being of the group is more important than that of the individual.

accumulation in a society was related to conformity. His explanation goes like this: Societies in which food accumulation depends on hunting and fishing require individual initiative and effort, whereas those that depend more on agriculture require greater cooperation and community activities. We might expect, then, that people in cultures that depend on hunting and fishing would show greater independence and less conformity, whereas people in cultures that rely on agriculture would show greater conformity. To test this hypothesis, Berry compared two societies: the Temne of Sierra Leone in Africa, and the Eskimo of Baffin Island in Canada. The Temne primarily rely on agriculture for food, whereas the Eskimo generally hunt to gather food. As would be predicted, the Temne people showed more conformity than members of the Eskimo culture (Berry, 1966, 1967).

INDIVIDUAL INFLUENCE OVER THE GROUP: WHEN ONE CAN OVERCOME MANY

When Sigmund Freud first developed his psychoanalytic theory in the early 1900s, he was met with skepticism and derision. The concepts of unconscious processes, infant sexuality, and libido were regarded as absurd and even subversive. According to one biographer, Freud and his disciples were thought of "not only as sexual perverts but also as either obsessive or paranoid psychopaths, and the combination was thought to be a real danger to the community" (Jones, 1961, p. 299).

How did Freud respond to this reaction? Never retreating from his lone position of dissent from the majority view of the scientific community, he instead reiterated, refined, and expanded his theory. He unrelentingly advocated for his convictions, and he presented a consistent (and persistent) view to the world.

We all know the outcome: Freud's theories have far outlasted his harshest critics. His work has had enormous influence not only on the treatment of abnormal behavior but on Western intellectual thought in general.

Although in most cases majorities influence minorities, there are many historical examples of single individuals influencing majority thinking. Consider, for instance, such influential figures as Charles Darwin, Susan B. Anthony, and Martin Luther King, Jr., all of whom faced initial skepticism but remained firm in their positions long enough to bring a majority around to their way of thinking. Such examples lead to an important question: What are the circumstances under which a single member or a minority in a group can influence and change the opinions held by the majority?

Freud's technique of remaining persistently unchanged suggests a general strategy of engaging in a consistent demonstration of one's beliefs and behavior. In fact, some social psychologists have suggested that unvarying consistency is the key to minority influence. Others, however, have suggested that a more effective strategy for influencing a majority is for the minority to conform first and only later to deviate from the group. As we will see, each approach has achieved substantial experimental support.

Minority consistency: The no-waffle position.   Social psychologist Serge Moscovici, working in laboratories in Europe, argues that the key to successful minority social influence over a majority is consistency (Moscovici & Faucheaux, 1972; Moscovici & Mugny, 1983; Crano & Chen, 1998). He suggests that a minority's unyielding insistence on its own point of view creates a conflict that prevents the smooth functioning of a group. In turn, this conflict may cause the majority to rethink its position and eventually be swayed by the minority's position.

One of Moscovici's initial experiments illustrates the effect that a consistent minority can have on a majority (Moscovici, Lage, & Naffrechoux, 1969). In the study, groups of six female participants were told that they would be making judgments about the color of a group of 36 slides. Unbeknownst to the participants, all the slides were blue—although they did vary in the intensity of the blue. In addition, the participants did not know that two of

The apparent certainty of a minority may lead a majority to question and rethink its own point of view, a tactic that has been used by minority political parties and minority rights groups for generations.

the group members were confederates who had been instructed to answer on every slide that the color was green (a clearly incorrect response). There was also a control condition, which consisted of groups of six actual participants and no confederates.

After taking a public test for color blindness, the participants were shown the series of 36 slides. For each slide, participants answered sequentially and aloud. The results showed a clear influence of the (erroneous) minority on the majority. In comparison with the control condition, in which less than 1% of the responses were erroneous, more than 8% of the responses in the groups with confederates incorrectly identified the color as green. In fact, about 30% of the experimental participants answered incorrectly at least once.

Equally intriguing is the subsequent finding that the consistent minority influenced the majority even after the experiment had ended. After responding in the group of six, each participant was taken individually to another room and shown a series of 16 disks that this time did vary in color—from very green to blue-green to very blue. Participants were told to categorize each disk as blue or green, and they were not given the opportunity to make compromise judgments such as blue-green.

The most significant finding from this postexperimental task concerned the judgments obtained for the blue-green disks. Participants who had been exposed to the consistent minority in their groups were more likely in the individual task to say "green" than "blue" for the blue-green disks, indicating that the effects of the minority persisted beyond their physical presence. Moreover, those most likely to be affected by the group during the postexperimental phase were those who had been least susceptible to the influence of the consistent minority during the experiment itself. Consequently, even those participants who appeared at first to remain independent of the minority were apparently influenced by the minority's unfluctuating responses.

How does the consistency of the minority influence the majority? We have already considered one possibility: that a consistent minority chips away at the consensus that group members try to maintain. In time, the persistent erosion by the minority may lead the majority to rethink its position.

In addition, Moscovici suggests that the minority, due to its persistence, is likely to be perceived by the majority as holding an intense, strong position. The minority is also likely to be seen as quite confident in its views, as it continues to be unyielding in the face of the implicit group pressure to conform. This apparent certainty of the minority may lead the majority to question and rethink its own point of view, thereby increasing any lack of confidence on the part of the majority. In this way, the consistent minority can exert influence over, and potentially modify, the majority's position. In fact, for generations, such a tactic has been used by minority political parties and religions—with some degree of success (Mugny & Perez, 1991; Wood et al., 1994; Alvaro & Crano, 1996; Martin, 1996; Kaarbo & Beasley, 1998; Levine, 1999).

Conform first, then deviate: A bait-and-switch tactic.   Members who deviate from the group typically face a potential problem. As we mentioned earlier, they are often disliked and are sometimes excluded from future group activities (Levine, 1989; Kruglanski & Webster, 1991; Avaro & Crano, 1997; Marques et al., 1998; Pool, Wood, & Leck, 1998). Given this possibility, Moscovici's unyielding consistency strategy for modifying the majority view places a minority in real peril. Rather than trying to understand the minority's position, the majority may simply reject it and ignore the minority members. In some cases, then, minority consistency may fail.

Social psychologist Edwin Hollander (1980) offers an alternative strategy. He suggests that by initially conforming to the established majority position of the group, a minority establishes its "credentials." Furthermore, initial conformity provides status within the group. Once the minority group member's credentials and status have been proved, the member is able to deviate from the group majority.

The mechanism underlying a person's ability to espouse an unpopular view is referred to as idiosyncrasy credit. **Idiosyncrasy credit** is a psychological "currency" that permits deviation from the group (Estrada, Brown, & Lee, 1995). Like money, idiosyncrasy credit can be earned and later spent (Hollander, 1958; Hollander, Julian, & Haaland, 1965).

A group member can accumulate idiosyncrasy credit by demonstrating competence and fulfilling the group's expectations regarding appropriate behavior. When the person has built up sufficient credit, he or she can make a withdrawal, which occurs when that person deviates from the group's majority position. Through the use of such credit, a deviate is able to dodge the group majority's sanctions or rejection, which might otherwise have occurred. Of course, eventually the idiosyncrasy credit will be depleted, and the person espousing a minority position must resume adherence to the majority position to maintain a firm standing in the group (Lortie-Lussier, 1987).

Clearly, the notion of idiosyncrasy credit suggests a technique for influencing a group majority that is very different from Moscovici's consistency approach (see Table 12–1). For

idiosyncrasy credit: A psychological "currency" that permits deviation from the group.

TABLE 12-1	Comparing Methods of Minority Influence	
THEORY	**PROCESS**	**EXPLANATION**
Moscovici's consistency theory	Minority is consistent in presenting its point of view	Unyielding insistence creates conflict, which may cause majority to rethink its position and eventually be swayed
Hollander's idiosyncrasy theory	Minority accumulates idiosyncrasy credit by initially maintaining majority position, then expends idiosyncrasy credit by deviating from the majority positions	The use of idiosyncrasy credit will allow the minority to avoid the majority's sanctions or rejection, which might otherwise have occurred

example, if Freud had taken the idiosyncrasy credit approach at face value, he would initially have conformed to the predominant views of his era. Then, once he had established his credentials as a follower of the status quo, he would have been free—at least for a time—to present his deviant perspective. (In one sense, Freud followed this scenario, because his early life was somewhat conventional, such as his early acceptance of standard medical practice just after he graduated from medical school.)

Hollander's process for gaining idiosyncrasy credit actually is somewhat similar to the bait-and-switch technique that deceptive advertisers sometimes employ. In bait and switch, potential buyers are lured into a store on the basis of unusually low prices. Then, at the store, salespeople steer them toward a more expensive item that the advertiser was actually trying to sell. Similarly, in the idiosyncrasy approach to individual influence, a minority that at first conforms to the majority's view in order to be in a better position later to make a persuasive case is—in a sense—laying out a lure for the majority, which may later be more willing to bite at the minority's position.

Consistency versus bait and switch: When is one preferable to the other?   Given that Moscovici's consistency approach and Hollander's idiosyncrasy credit perspective suggest quite different tactics on the part of would-be minority influences, under what conditions is each of the two techniques more effective? At this point, the answer is ambiguous.

In a comprehensive review of close to 100 studies of minority influence, social psychologist Wendy Wood and colleagues found strong support for the notion that consistency is a central component of minority influence. Furthermore, Wood and colleagues determined that minority influence was most pronounced in instances where conformity was assessed indirectly, with attitude measures that were taken in private, as opposed to more direct, public measures (Wood et al., 1994).

The studies Wood examined were not entirely consistent, however, and experimental evidence supports both the consistency and idiosyncratic credit approaches. Furthermore, few direct comparative tests of the two theories exist, and those that have been done often show inconsistent results. In sum, experts remain undecided as to which of the two approaches provides the best description of how minorities can influence a majority (Maass & Clark, 1984; Lortie-Lussier, 1987; Clark & Maass, 1988, 1990).

The work on minority influence raises a broader question: Are the processes and principles under which minority influence operates identical to those used by majorities to influence minorities in groups? Two schools of thought provide competing answers to this question. According to the **single-process approach**, both majorities and minorities employ similar influence techniques. In this view, although influence pressures from a minority may differ from the majority in their magnitude, with minority influence typically being less intense, minority and majority influence are qualitatively similar (Tanford & Penrod, 1984; Wolf, 1985; Mackie & Hunter, 1999).

However, a significant number of social psychologists support a dual-process approach. The **dual-process approach** argues that minority influence differs from majority influence not just in degree but also in kind. In arguing for a dual-process approach, social psychologist Charlan Nemeth (1986) contends that people succumb to a majority position because of strong pressure that produces temporary but often superficial conformity. Often, no lasting change in position occurs. In contrast, when a minority is able to alter the majority's position, the change tends to be more genuine and enduring. Minority dissension forces the majority to consider the issue at hand from a variety of perspectives, only one of which may be the view proposed by the minority (Mucchi-Faina, 1994). Because the majority's thinking becomes broader and more complex, the ultimate decision is of a higher quality and is therefore likely to be more lasting (Maass & Clark, 1983; Nemeth, 1986, 1995; Nemeth et al., 1990; Peterson & Nemeth, 1996; Bohner, Frank, & Erb, 1998; Crano & Chen, 1998).

We still do not know for certain whether majority and minority pressures represent single or dual processes (e.g., Nemeth & Kwan, 1985; Mackie, 1987). Probably the truth lies somewhere in between, with single processes operating in some kinds of situations and dual processes operating in others (Chaiken & Stangor, 1987; Kruglanski & Mackie, 1989;

single-process approach (to majority/minority influence): The theory that both majorities and minorities employ similar influence techniques.

dual-process approach (to majority/minority influence): The theory that minority influence differs from majority influence not just in degree but also in kind.

Baker & Petty, 1994). What is clear is that social influence is not a one-way street. Both majorities and minorities can influence each other, making groups a rich tapestry of competing sources and targets of social influence. (See also the Speaking of Social Psychology interview.)

REVIEW AND RETHINK

Review

- Conformity is a change in behavior or attitudes brought about by a desire to follow the beliefs or standards of others.

- Normative and informational social pressures produce conformity, and both situational factors and gender and cultural factors are related to conformity.

- Minorities may use several strategies to remain independent from a majority.

Rethink

- What evidence suggests that participants in Asch's experiments were influenced by normative social pressure? What evidence suggests they were influenced by informational pressure?

- Which type of conformity pressure might be stronger in groups whose members are very similar and in groups whose members are proud of their membership? Why?

- If you were to conduct the Asch study today, would you expect to find gender-related effects in your data? Why?

- Which technique for influencing the majority would be most effective for producing normative pressure and for producing informational pressure?

COMPLIANCE

It's taken days of searching, but you've finally found the new car of your dreams. You've fallen in love with it, and the salesperson informs you that you could be behind the wheel in just 2 days.

Because you think of yourself as a savvy consumer, you took the time to read an article on negotiating before shopping for the car. You're quite pleased with yourself because, after a good deal of dickering, the salesperson has agreed to what looks like a great price.

After you fill out a batch of forms, the deal seems almost complete. The salesperson says the only thing left is the "OK" from his manager. He goes into a back office and is gone for several minutes. However, when he returns, he has a pained expression on his face. "I'm really embarrassed," he says, "but my manager will not approve the deal. He told me that at the price we agreed to, the dealership would actually end up losing money.

"But look," he continues, "Rather than kill the deal, I was able to get him to agree to a price that's just $500 more than the figure we originally agreed to. We're still taking a beating, but I want your business badly. I know it's more than you wanted to pay, but it's the only way he'll OK the deal."

You mull it over a short time, and you come to a decision: You'll take the new deal. After all, $500 more is just a drop in the bucket on a transaction that costs thousands of dollars, and you're still getting a good price on the car. Besides, while the salesperson was talking to his manager you were picturing yourself driving the car and showing it to your friends. You smile and tell the salesperson you agree to the new price.

Your smile might be a little less bright if you realized the truth about the situation: You've been had. As we will discover, you have been the victim of a carefully thought-out procedure

compliance: Yielding to direct, explicit appeals meant to produce certain behavior or agreement with a particular point of view.

designed to nudge you into compliance with a higher price, without your feeling much distress in the process.

We turn now to a consideration of compliance. **Compliance** consists of yielding to direct, explicit appeals meant to produce certain behavior or agreement with a particular point of view. Whereas the pressures on a person to conform are generally implicit and not in the form of direct requests or demands, compliance pressures are more overt. In compliance, there is little ambiguity in the social pressure that is brought to bear—a car salesperson urges you to accept a deal, a jewelry store clerk offers the opinion that the purchase of a bigger diamond is actually a better value, or a store sells compact discs in a 2-for-1 sale. As we will see, social psychologists have identified a variety of strategies that produce compliance.

THE FOOT-IN-THE-DOOR TECHNIQUE: ASKING FOR A LITTLE TO GAIN A LOT

A friend asks to use your computer printer to print out a one-page paper. It's a small request, and you're happy to comply. The next day, though, she asks to print out a draft of her 100-page honors thesis using your printer. Do you agree to her request this time?

SPEAKING OF SOCIAL PSYCHOLOGY

Mariana Shorter

Drill Sergeant

Year of Birth:	1963
Education:	U. S. Army Advanced Individual Training, Track Vehicle Mechanic
Home:	Aberdeen Proving Grounds, Maryland

Although today's army is technologically a far cry from the primitive legions of the Roman Empire, some of the most important factors crucial for an army to function well, such as obedience and conformity, have not changed. Mariana Shorter, a drill sergeant in the United States Army, notes that although individual officers may have their own approach, the bottom line is that soldiers need to obey superior officers.

"Every leader has his or her own style."

"Every leader has his or her own style," said Shorter. "I have a type of leadership style where I listen. I'm not a yeller, but if things get out of hand, I make communication a one-way street: 'I talk, and you listen and perform.' I make it clear to new recruits that I am a drill sergeant 24 hours a day."

Part of Shorter's authority comes from the example she sets for those under her. "I don't have them do anything I can't do myself," she noted.

Shorter, who has served in the army for more than 15 years, is responsible for close to 100 new recruits at a time, of whom most are men but a significant minority are women.

You probably will, because you've been the recipient of the foot-in-the-door technique. In the **foot-in-the-door technique**, a target of social influence is first asked to agree to a small request, but later is asked to comply with a more important one. It turns out that if the person agrees to the first request, compliance with the later, larger request is considerably more likely.

The foot-in-the-door phenomenon was first demonstrated in a study by social psychologists Jonathan Freedman and Scott Fraser, who had experimenters go door-to-door in a neighborhood asking residents to sign a petition in favor of safe driving (Freedman & Fraser, 1966). Almost everyone complied with such a small, mild request.

However, a few weeks later, a different experimenter contacted the residents and asked for a much larger request, bordering on the outrageous—that they erect on their front lawns huge signs that said "Drive Carefully." Surprisingly, more than half of those who had signed the initial petition agreed to the second request. In comparison, only 17% of a group of people who had not been asked to sign the initial petition were willing to place signs on their lawns.

Subsequent research not only has confirmed these initial findings regarding the foot-in-the-door technique but also has added this additional principle: The larger the initial request, the greater the subsequent compliance that can be expected (Beaman et al., 1983;

foot-in-the-door technique:
A technique of social influence in which the target of social influence is first asked to agree to a small request, but later is asked to comply with a larger one.

She noted that she tried to deal with the male and female recruits with equality, stressing conformity in both their treatment and their behavior.

"We instill teamwork, but not to the extent where you are doing the work for some other soldier who is not pulling his or her weight."

"I have seen men offer to carry a heavy tool box for the women, but I tell them that they do not have time to carry it for others. They have to carry it for themselves. This is where you start to get in the habit of toting things alone.

"It used to be that men and women were segregated in their living quarters, but now we require soldiers to sleep together, all wearing physical fitness T-shirts and shorts. This way if we are in a war situation it would not be a shock to the soldiers to have to integrate," Shorter said.

All the hard training has a specific purpose, according to Shorter, and that is to make each soldier self-sufficient and productive in case of war.

"The actual reality sinks in when you are at war. When I was in the Gulf War, part of our job was to pick up damaged vehicles to repair. These are not toys, and if you are not listening or paying attention, you are looking at a potential serious injury.

"You must first get their attention, and if you get it on day one, you've done well. But if you can't control their attention span, they are like children," Shorter explained. "A lot of accidents are due to lack of following orders and lack of respect."

Shorter notes that although each soldier must be responsible for himself or herself, the army functions as a group.

"We instill teamwork, but not to the extent where you are doing the work for some other soldier who is not pulling his or her weight. Before you can perform as a team, you must pull yourself together as an individual," she said. "Out in the field you need a team to survive, but you cannot solely depend on any one person."

That "free gift" may actually have a price attached to it: one's future compliance. In an example of the foot-in-the-door technique, a target of social influence is first asked to agree to a small request, such as accepting a small, but free gift. Later, though, the target is asked to agree to a larger request such as completing an application for a charge card—and is much more likely to comply.

Dillard, Hunter, & Burgoon, 1984; Dillard, 1991; Bell et al., 1994; Dolin & Booth-Butterfield, 1995; Chartrand, Pinckert, & Burger, 1999).

But why is the foot-in-the-door strategy effective? There are several reasons. For one thing, involvement with the small request may result in the development of an explicit interest in an issue. Taking an action, even the most trivial, makes a person more committed to an issue, thereby increasing the likelihood of future compliance.

Another reason for the success of the foot-in-the-door procedure relates to self-perception theory. Agreement to the initial, small request begins a process in which people come to redefine themselves in certain ways that are consistent with their initial behavior. For instance, they may start to see themselves as social activists with an interest in safe driving (as in the Freedman and Fraser experiment), or they may come to view themselves as people who use Fuller brushes. Such a change in self-perception may increase their willingness to comply with later, larger requests.

Finally, some researchers argue that persuasion occurs because the requests provide information about the situation. In particular, compliance is likely to occur if the requests make norms of conduct relevant (Reno, Cialdini, & Kallgren, 1993), and agreement to the requests permits the attainment of significant personal goals (Gorassini & Olson, 1995).

THE DOOR-IN-THE-FACE TECHNIQUE: ASKING FOR A LOT TO GET A LITTLE

You've always had an interest in campaigns to end world hunger, and you've even attended some lectures and occasionally passed out literature on your college campus. So you're not all that surprised when you get a call from the Feed the World's Hungry campaign asking for a donation. You're stunned when you hear the size of the request, though: $100. You immediately refuse, saying that such an amount is out of the question. But when the fund raiser then asks for a $35 donation instead, you think for a minute and then agree. You usually wouldn't donate so much, but, after all, it is an important cause.

You've just encountered the **door-in-the-face technique**, a procedure in which a large request, to which refusal is expected, is followed by a smaller one. By employing a strategy that is virtually the opposite of the foot-in-the-door, requesters expect that the initial, outlandishly large request makes targets of persuasion more receptive to the subsequent smaller request (Dillard, 1991; Reeves et al., 1991; O'Keefe & Figge, 1997; Patch, Hoang, & Stahelski, 1997).

The utility of the door-in-the-face procedure is illustrated by a field study carried out by social psychologist Robert Cialdini (Cialdini et al., 1975). In the study, college students were approached by researchers posing as representatives of a youth counseling program. The students were asked to make a substantial commitment—act as unpaid counselors for juvenile delinquents for 2 hours a week for a minimum of 2 years. Unsurprisingly, no one agreed to such a substantial request.

Later, though, when they were asked to agree to the much smaller (although not insubstantial) favor of taking a group of delinquents on a 2-hour trip to the zoo, about 50% of those approached agreed. In comparison, only 17% of a control group, who had not first been asked the larger favor, agreed to chaperone the delinquents. The door-in-the-face technique is common, and you've probably used it at some time in your life. Perhaps you asked your parents for a giant raise in your allowance, hoping that they would settle for a smaller amount. In the same way, television writers have been known to sprinkle their scripts with obscenities that they know network censors will remove in order to preserve other key phrases that otherwise might be questionable (Cialdini, 1988).

The door-in-the-face procedure is effective largely due to the exchange of reciprocal concessions between the person making the request and the target of persuasion. In **reciprocal concessions**, requesters are seen to make a compromise (by reducing the size of their initial request), thereby inviting a concession on the part of those who initially refused the request. The consequence is that people are more willing to comply with the smaller request. Obviously, the principle of reciprocal concession stems from the norm of reciprocity, which—as we discussed in Chapter 8—asserts that we help those who have helped us in the past.

Other factors besides the principle of reciprocal concessions contribute to the effectiveness of the door-in-the-face technique. For instance, self-presentational factors may be at work (Pendleton & Batson, 1979). People who refuse the first request, even when it is unreasonable, may fear that they will be seen by others as inflexible, inconsiderate, and unhelpful individuals. When the second—and more reasonable request—comes along, they feel compelled to comply in order to avoid being characterized by the unfavorable labels.

Finally, the success of the door-in-the-face tactic may stem from perceptual factors. If you think back to your introductory psychology class, you probably learned about a phenomenon known as perceptual contrast when you studied sensation and perception. Perceptual contrast works like this: After exposure to a very powerful stimulus (say, a bright light), a new stimulus (such as a dimmer light) appears even less potent than it would if presented by itself.

Applying this principle to the door-in-the-face phenomenon, we see that exposure to the initial, large request may make the second request seem more modest in comparison. Consequently, a person's willingness to agree to it will be higher (Shanab & O'Neill, 1979; Cantrill & Seibold, 1986).

THE THAT'S-NOT-ALL TECHNIQUE: DISCOUNTER'S DELIGHT

"The price of this dress is $80. But that's not all: If you buy it *right now*, I'll give it to you for just $70."

You've probably heard similar sales pitches. But did you know that you'll be much more likely to make the purchase than if you were told from the start that the regular price was $70?

door-in-the-face technique: A technique of social influence in which a large request, to which refusal is expected, is followed by a smaller one.

reciprocal concessions: A technique of social influence in which requesters are seen to make a compromise (by reducing the size of their initial request), thereby inviting a concession on the part of those who initially refused the request.

APPLYING SOCIAL PSYCHOLOGY
IT'S ONLY 300 PENNIES—WHAT A BARGAIN!:
USING THE DISRUPT-THEN-REFRAME TECHNIQUE TO OBTAIN COMPLIANCE

What's the difference between 300 pennies and $3.00? The answer is significantly greater compliance.

At least that's the message from research conducted by social psychologists Barbara Davis and Eric Knowles (1999). In their work, the researchers began with the premise that influence attempts create an approach–avoidance motivational conflict in targets. When subjected to social influence requests, people often wish to make a purchase or help out (the approach motivation), but at the same time are not eager to commit time or money (the avoidance motivation). Although most influence strategies focus on the approach motivation, providing additional reasons or incentives for compliance, it is also possible to decrease the strength of avoidance motivation—a strategy called the *disrupt-then-reframe (DTR) technique.*

The DTR technique works by first disrupting resistance by phrasing a request in an out-of-the-ordinary, unusual manner. After the unusual request, which temporarily disrupts a target's thoughts, a more traditional pitch is made. Based in part on action identification theory, which—as we first discussed in Chapter 4—suggests that the level at which people view their own behavior affects subsequent actions, the DTR technique suggests that a disruption makes people more susceptible to influence techniques. Consequently, when the influence attempt is repeated but reframed in a slightly different way, it becomes more effective.

A series of studies demonstrated the effectiveness of the DTR technique. In the studies, experimenters went door-to-door selling note cards for a charity. Because the cards were useful and their purchase helped charity, the experimenters assumed that people would feel approach motivation, wishing to purchase the cards. At the same time, though, it was assumed that they would also experience avoidance motivation, wishing to avoid spending money for the cards or responding to door-to-door sales pitches. The approach–avoidance conflict, it was thought, would make participants ripe for the DTR technique.

To implement the DTR technique, the experimenters initiated a subtle disruption in the sales request, making it seem out of the ordinary, by stating the cost of the cards in pennies ("The price of these note cards is 300 pennies.") But immediately following this slightly odd request, an additional reason for purchasing the cards was added when the experimenter said, "It's a bargain!"

Compared with participants who were not told the price in pennies, but merely were told the cost was $3 and it was a bargain, those who received the initial information about the cost in pennies showed a significantly higher rate of compliance. Specifically, 65% of the participants in the disrupt-then-reframe condition complied, whereas only 35% of those in a reframe-only condition ("They're $3. It's a bargain!") complied.

In short, telling someone that the cost of something is 300 pennies, which is a bargain, differs significantly from telling someone that the cost is $3, which is a bargain—despite the two amounts being identical. It is the unusual nature of the initial request that seems to make the critical difference. By disrupting the typical persuasive "script," the DTR technique reduces the strength of avoidance motivation and permits approach motivation to become more dominant. That the disruption need only be minimal illustrates the power of the DTR technique.

In the **that's-not-all technique**, a customer is offered a deal at an initial, often inflated, price. But just after making the initial offer, the salesperson immediately offers an incentive, discount, or bonus to clinch the deal. Although the technique seems transparent, it is quite effective.

For example, in one experiment, researchers sold cupcakes at a campus fair. In one condition, the cupcakes were peddled at the regular price of 75 cents each. But in another condition, customers were told the price was $1.00, but had been discounted to 75 cents. You guessed it: The discounted cupcakes sold faster than the regularly priced ones, despite their identical prices (Burger, 1986; Pollock et al., 1998).

that's-not-all technique: A technique of social influence in which a customer is offered a deal at an initial, often inflated, price; then immediately after making the initial offer, the salesperson offers an incentive, discount, or bonus to clinch the deal.

THE LOWBALL: START SMALL, FINISH BIG

Think back to the car purchase that we discussed earlier, in which the salesperson suddenly jacks up the price at the last minute by claiming that the original deal was not approved by the sales manager. Similar scenarios are routinely played out every day at car dealerships, and they result in consumers being fleeced out of hundreds of dollars.

The technique is known as lowballing. In **lowballing**, an initial agreement is reached, but then the seller reveals additional costs. Lowballing works because it fits the processes we go through when making a consumer purchase decision. Just prior to committing ourselves to an initial purchase decision, we consider both the advantages and disadvantages of the deal. But when we finally reach a decision, we tend to emphasize the advantages of the deal in order to justify our decision. In fact, we may overemphasize the advantages due to postdecision cognitive dissonance.

Consequently, while the salesperson is off getting final approval, we're cognitively busy, convincing ourselves of the wisdom of the deal. When the salesperson returns with the news that the deal has become unhinged and that the price must go up, we're ready to leap for the bait. The typical reaction is to tell ourselves that despite the higher price, the deal is still so good that we should not refuse it (Cialdini, 1988).

There's another reason that lowballing may be effective. Good salespersons attempt to make you like them, and they try to instill the sense that the two of you are in the early stages of building a personal relationship. If that is the case, you may accept the higher-priced deal because you genuinely feel that it is out of the salesperson's hands and the cost increase is due solely to the sales manager's stubbornness. Your sense of personal commitment to the salesperson, then, may propel you toward accepting the deal (Burger & Petty, 1981). (For another approach to obtaining compliance, see the accompanying Applying Social Psychology feature.)

> **lowballing:** A technique in which an initial agreement is reached, but then the seller reveals additional costs.

AVOIDING COMPLIANCE BY JUST SAYING NO

THE INFORMED CONSUMER OF SOCIAL PSYCHOLOGY

Learning to "just say no" is one of the best ways to deal with requests for compliance with which you are uncomfortable.

By now, you've probably learned enough about compliance tactics to develop a healthy skepticism regarding any salesperson you meet. In fact, you may be discouraged, thinking that the average person has few weapons at his or her disposal with which to defend against attacks by those trying to gain compliance.

Nothing could be further from the truth. Your very awareness of the range of compliance techniques makes you less of a mark. Furthermore, you can employ several countercompliance techniques to avoid becoming a "patsy." Among those techniques suggested by social psychologist Robert Cialdini, an expert in social influence, are the following (Cialdini, 1993, 1996):

◆ *Redefine the situation.* As we all know, "free" gifts often have strings attached. But if you don't consider them as no-strings-attached gifts, their power to evoke the rule of reciprocity or to act as the foot-in-the-door will be greatly diminished. Thus, it is critical to look a gift horse in the mouth and to label freebies for what they are: attempts to make you feel obligated to the giver.

◆ *Avoid consistency for consistency's sake.* Although we have seen in prior chapters that efforts to maintain consistency (in our attitudes, behavior, and so forth) are characteristic of our social lives, it does not have to be that way. By becoming aware of the self-induced pressures to behave consistently, we can avoid situations in which consistency is actually harmful to our better interests. For instance, it is not logical to maintain a consistent commitment after a deal that we have initially struck has changed significantly—such as with the addition of several hundred dollars to an agreed-upon price.

◆ *Avoid mindlessness.* People are sometimes in a state of mindlessness, not thinking about what they are doing. Because a state of mindlessness increases our susceptibility to compliance tactics, we need to be vigilant regarding the underlying message we are receiving. This means looking beyond what people are telling us and trying to determine their underlying motives.

◆ *Just say no.* No law of human conduct requires you to be agreeable to people who seek your compliance with their attempts at social influence. Indeed, a healthy degree of skepticism is in order whenever anyone attempts to influence your behavior. Even if you are dealing with something like a "Save-the-Planet Foundation" (who could be against saving the planet?), you need to be vigilant whenever anyone tries to convince you of anything. Except when you are certain that others' motives are devoid of self-interest, you should assume that their compliance tactics are being employed more for their benefit than for your own.

REVIEW AND RETHINK

Review

* Compliance is yielding to direct, explicit appeals.

* The foot-in-the-door, door-in-the-face, and that's-not-all techniques are intended to lead to compliance.

* Several strategies can reduce compliance.

Rethink

* How does compliance differ from conformity?

* The foot-in-the-door and the door-in-the-face techniques suggest exactly the opposite strategy when trying to persuade someone. How can both be correct?

* Explain how cognitive dissonance might contribute to the effectiveness of lowballing techniques.

* What advice would you give to others to help them avoid being duped into buying something they don't want or paying too much for it?

OBEDIENCE

How would you react if you found yourself in the following situation?

In a shopping mall, you pass by a stranger in a white laboratory jacket standing in front of one of the stores. In the store window is a sign that reads "Research Associates." As you walk by, the man calls out to you, asking for a few minutes of your time. He says he needs your assistance, and he is willing to pay for it.

You ask what he wants, and the stranger tells you that he has devised a new way of improving memory, and he wants your help in testing it. He tells you that he'd like you to teach a person a list of word pairs and then to give the person a test.

The novel part of the procedure, which he wishes to test, is that you must give the learner a shock for each mistake on the test. He shows you a shock generator that you are to use, which contains switches ranging from 30 to 450 volts. The switches are labeled from "slight shock" through "danger: severe shock" at the top level, where there are three red X's.

When you express hesitation about administering the shocks, he tells you not to worry: Although the shocks may be painful to the learner, they will produce no lasting damage.

Would you comply with the stranger's request? You probably are fairly sure that you, like most people, would be quick to balk. Obviously, it is far from a reasonable scenario, and few people would be inclined to go along with such a request.

But let's modify the scenario a bit. Suppose the man, rather than being an unidentified stranger about whom you had no knowledge, was instead identified as a psychologist conducting an experiment. Or assume that it was your employer, or your professor, or your military commander. At this point would you not be more likely to comply with the request for help, despite its improbable, even bizarre, nature?

If you still think it unlikely that you would submit to such a request, you might wish to rethink your response. For as we shall see, a landmark series of studies carried out in the 1960s suggests that you might well be inclined to obey, giving shocks of increasing intensity to a luckless learner.

We turn now to the social psychological phenomenon of obedience. **Obedience** is a change in behavior due to the commands of others in authority. Unlike conformity and compliance, in which people are gently guided or steered toward a particular position, obedience is the result of a more active approach to social influence. In obedience, direct orders are meant to elicit direct submission.

OBEDIENCE TO AUTHORITY: ONLY FOLLOWING ORDERS

For many people, the My Lai massacre in 1968 signified all that was wrong with the Vietnam War. In the massacre, a group of U.S. Army soldiers brutalized, raped, and killed hundreds of civilians in the tiny village of My Lai. Masses of civilians—children, the elderly, women—were herded into drainage ditches and executed. Babies were bayoneted, and one woman was raped just after watching soldiers kill her children. According to one journalist, as soon as they entered the village, troops began to "systematically ransack the hamlet and slaughter the people, kill the livestock, and destroy the crops. Men poured rifle and machine-gun fire into huts without knowing—or seemingly caring—who was inside" (Hersh, 1970, pp. 49–50). The soldiers who participated in the carnage explained that they were only following orders to rid the area of North Vietnamese Communist enemies.

When details of the My Lai massacre came to light during the Vietnam War, many people saw it as an exceptional event, an awful one-time aberration. But the pages of history tell a different story. Events as varied as the Holocaust, torture in South America, and Bosnian Serb "ethnic cleansing" all testify to this darker side of human behavior.

The people involved in events such as these typically share a common excuse: They simply were following the orders of their superiors. And, as far as it goes, such an explanation is often accurate. People in such situations are often behaving in ways that are consistent with what legitimate authority figures tell them to do. For instance, soldiers who participated in the My Lai massacre argued that they were following the orders of their superior, Lt. William Calley. Calley, in turn, argued that he was simply following the orders of his superiors, ridding the village of My Lai of supposed Communist sympathizers.

In an analysis of obedience, social psychologist Herbert Kelman and sociologist Lee Hamilton suggest that obedience to authorities is based on three factors: the legitimacy of the system, the legitimacy of the authorities or power holders within the system, and the legitimacy of their demands (Kelman & Hamilton, 1989). The legitimacy of the system refers to the degree to which an authority group that holds sway over a person is seen as appropriate and rightful. The group may be a government, a unit of government such as an army, a religious organization, or even a family. Whatever the explicit nature of the group,

obedience: A change in behavior due to the commands of others in authority.

it commands obedience due to its position within society and an individual's view of its place in society.

The legitimacy of the authorities or power holders is largely based on the way those individuals come to hold their positions. The winner of a presidential election is a legitimate authority, as is the general who has moved up in the ranks of the army. In contrast, a leader who comes to power through a rigged election or a military revolt may not be seen as having legitimate authority.

Finally, the third factor that affects obedience to authorities is the legitimacy of the authority or power holder's demands. The legitimacy of demands refers to a person's perception that what is being demanded fits within the framework of a valid, justifiable request.

To the extent that a seemingly legitimate demand is seen as emanating from a legitimate authority within a legitimate system, it is likely to be obeyed without question. However, should any one of the three factors (the system, the authority figure, or the demand itself) be seen as less than legitimate, the likelihood of obeying the demand will be diminished.

Kelman and Hamilton's analysis of obedience to authorities is a social psychological one, resting on the impact of an individual's perception of the legitimacy of a particular demand. What the analysis doesn't focus on, however, is personality factors.

The omission is no accident. For example, participants in the My Lai massacre do not seem to have been mentally ill or disturbed or to have had any fundamental personality disorders. Indeed, more than half of a national sample of Americans said in a survey that they would have shot all the inhabitants of a Vietnamese village if so ordered. Such sentiments suggest that the participants in the massacre only did what other Americans think they would do in similar circumstances (Kelman & Lawrence, 1972).

Similarly, people who participated in the German Holocaust during World War II were not out of the ordinary. Even Adolf Eichmann, who committed some of the most heinous crimes, has been described as "an average man of middle-class origins and normal middle-class upbringing, a man without identifiable criminal tendencies" (Von Lang & Sibyll, 1983).

Hence, most evidence suggests that people who participated in the long list of bloodbaths and instances of genocide that punctuate world history differed relatively little from the average person (Staub, 1989). But what leads an ordinary individual to cross the line and commit a deed that in retrospect can only be labeled as abhorrent and repugnant? This is one of the questions that social psychologist Stanley Milgram sought to answer in a pioneering—and controversial—series of studies that he began in the early 1960s.

OBEDIENCE TO AUTHORITY: THE MILGRAM STUDIES

In many respects, Milgram's studies were not too different from the scenario laid out in the opening passage of this section. Participants were recruited to participate in an experiment that ostensibly dealt with the topic of learning. They were told that the experimenter was testing a way to enhance memorization and that the basic procedure required that a learner memorize a list of pairs of words. Following the memorization phase, the participants would test the learners. Each time a learner made an error, a participant administered a shock, using the formidable shock generator pictured in Figure 12–5.

In reality, of course, the real topic of the experiment was obedience to authority. Milgram was seeking to learn the degree to which people would follow the commands of an experimenter, who during the course of the experiment urged that learners be administered shocks of a higher and higher intensity.

On hearing of the study, most people predicted that only a rare, and possibly disturbed, participant would be willing to progress too far in the procedure—a view shared by a group of distinguished psychiatrists. The psychiatrists, who were polled when the experiments were first conducted, surmised that only one in a thousand people would give the highest-level shock. The prevalent opinion was that most people would not go beyond the 150-volt level. Other individuals, without any special training, were even more conservative, with many predicting that none of the participants would administer shocks.

FIGURE 12–5   The Milgram "Shock Generator" and "Victim" This impressive—but bogus—"shock generator" was used to make participants think that they were giving shocks to a supposed victim, who was connected to the generator by electrodes.

The reality was quite different. Neither distinguished psychiatrists nor untrained individuals were able to predict accurately how Milgram's participants would perform. Surprisingly, 65% of the participants who participated in the experiment gave the highest-level shock of 450 volts (Milgram, 1974).

These startling results are tempered by the fact that in all cases the learners were confederates of the experimenter and did not receive any electric shocks. However, this is small solace, because the participants were unaware of this situation. They presumably believed that they were administering painful shocks at the behest of the experimenter.

Over the course of a decade, Milgram tried a number of variants of his original study. For instance, in one experiment he manipulated the physical proximity of the victim to the participants. In one condition (called the "remote condition"), the victims could be neither seen nor heard; in another (the "voice feedback condition"), they could not be seen, but their verbal protestations could be heard from the next room. In the two remaining conditions, the victims were in the same room as the participant. In one case, a learner was positioned just a few feet away (the "proximity condition"). In the final case, the participant actually had to place the victim's hand on a shock plate in order to administer the shock (the "touch proximity" condition).

As you might guess, increasing proximity led to decreasing obedience. Figure 12–6 illustrates the mean maximum shock for each of the four conditions. Similarly, the percentage of participants who were obedient also declined as proximity increased. Still, the absolute level of obedience was high even in the most extreme condition. For instance, even when participants had to take the hand of the victim (who, at the 150-volt level, demanded to be set free and would not voluntarily touch the shock plate), a full 30% of the participants obeyed the experimenter's wishes and gave the maximum shock.

Troubled by his findings, Milgram thought that perhaps his results might be an aberration caused by the location of the original studies, which were held on the campus of prestigious Yale University. Thinking that obedience might be lower elsewhere, he arranged for the same studies to be conducted in an anonymous laboratory, seemingly unaffiliated with a university, in a small, economically downtrodden city. However, the results there were similar with those obtained at the Yale campus.

Further studies investigated whether personality or demographic characteristics differentiated those who gave the highest-level shocks from those who were not obedient. However, he found few distinctions among participants—a finding that has held up to the present. For example, no general personality differences distinguish obedient from disobedient participants. Furthermore, there are no gender differences: Men and women are equally obedient (Blass & Krackow, 1991).

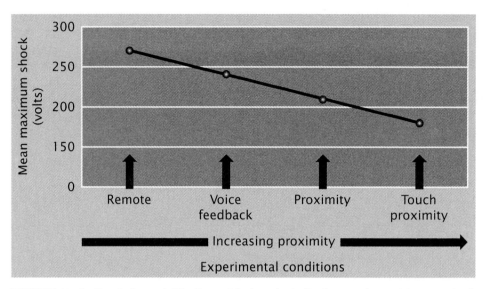

FIGURE 12–6 **Proximity and Obedience** Victims physically closer to the participant received less severe shocks than those who were further away. (*Source:* Milgram, 1974.)

In short, the preponderance of evidence suggests that situational factors play a powerful role in determining obedience. Put any of us in circumstances similar to the one in which Milgram placed his participants, and our behavior probably will be similar to theirs.

The return of the "only following orders" defense. Why were so many participants obedient? Extensive interviews with participants following their participation in the experiment revealed a theme similar to the one referred to by the soldiers in the My Lai massacre: They were only following orders.

In addition, participants in the Milgram study claimed that they had been obedient because they believed that the experimenter would be responsible for any potential ill effects that befell the learner. The primary justification provided by participants for their obedience was that they felt little or no personal responsibility for their actions. They claimed any unfavorable ramifications were the responsibility of the experimenter, whose orders they were simply following and who explicitly had told them that he accepted full responsibility for the situation.

In fact, the experimenter had been explicit in accepting culpability and exonerating the participants. For instance, even participants who ended up totally obedient to the experimenter rarely complied without at least some form of protest. Many expressed concerns, although sometimes tentatively, about the learner's well-being. When that occurred, the experimenter used a series of standardized prods of increasing intensity, designed to secure the participant's obedience.

At the first protest, the experimenter said, "Please continue." If participants continued to object, the experimenter moved through these phrases: "The experiment requires that you continue"; then, "It is absolutely essential that you continue"; and finally, "You have no other choice, you must go on." Such statements reinforced the experimenter's initial assertion that participants should feel no personal responsibility for their actions because he, the experimenter, accepted complete responsibility (Darley, 1995; Avtgis, 1998).

Was obedience illusory? The critics respond. The results of Milgram's studies were startling, and they led to a good deal of controversy. Some of the questions that were raised were methodological (Orne & Holland, 1968). Did participants really believe they were giving shocks to the confederate? Furthermore, could the obedience that was observed in the study be attributable to the fact that participants knew they were in the protected environment of a psychological laboratory?

After all, the experimental situation was, at best, unusual and even strange. A calm, detached experimenter urges a participant to continue giving shocks, even when the learner shouts in protest. In addition, thoughtful participants might wonder, even as they are being asked to increase the intensity of the shocks, why they are needed at all. If the study were actually about understanding the effects of punishment on learning, why couldn't the experimenter act as the teacher? What did the participant's presence add to the study?

Such alternative interpretations cannot be ruled out entirely. However, the behavior of the typical participant in the experiments makes it appear that participants were taken in by the experimenter's cover story. Participants displayed strong emotional reactions while administering the shocks. They sweated; they stuttered; they bit their lips; they broke into nervous laughter. Many reported feeling anxious and upset after the experiment.

If we accept that participants were taken in by the experimental procedure—which most social psychologists do—then another troubling question arises: Were the Milgram experiments ethical? Some observers answer no. For instance, some social psychologists suggest that it was unethical in the first place to put participants in a situation in which they were pressed to carry out acts that normally would be unthinkable to them (Baumrind, 1964; Korn, 1997).

Even worse, according to critics, was the extreme tension participants displayed during the course of the experiment. In their view, some participants might show lasting adverse consequences from their experimental participation (see Table 12–2).

TABLE 12–2 You Be the Judge

Although critics of the Milgram obedience to authority experiment suggest that subjects were placed under undue stress, Milgram responded that there was no evidence of subjects being unduly pressured in the experiment. The following is a transcript of an actual session with one subject, who ended up giving the highest-level shock. What are your reactions?

150 volts delivered. You want me to keep going?

165 volts delivered. That guy is hollering in there. There's a lot of them here. He's liable to have a heart condition. You want me to go?

180 volts delivered. He can't stand it! I'm not going to kill that man in there! You hear him hollering? He's hollering. He can't stand it. What if something happens to him? . . . I'm not going to get that man sick in there. He's hollering in there. You know what I mean? I mean I refuse to take responsibility. He's getting hurt in there. He's in there hollering. Too many left here. Geez, if he gets them wrong. There's too many of them left. I mean who is going to take responsibility if anything happens to the gentleman?

[*The experimenter accepts responsibility.*]

All right.

195 volts delivered. You see he's hollering. Hear that. Gee, I don't know.

[*The experimenter says: "The experiment requires that you go on."*]—I know it does, sir, but I mean—ugh—he don't know what he's in for. He's up to 195 volts.

210 volts delivered.

225 volts delivered.

240 volts delivered. Aw, no. You mean I've got to keep going up with the scale? No sir. I'm not going to kill that man! I'm not going to give him 450 volts!

[*The experimenter says: "The experiment requires that you go on."*]—I know it does, but that man is hollering in there, sir . . .

Source: Milgram, 1965.

In reply to such criticisms, Milgram claimed that a full debriefing of participants after the experiment had eradicated any negative outcomes of participation. Furthermore, long-term follow-ups also indicated no effects due to participation (Milgram, 1977b). Nevertheless, the ethical issue cannot be dismissed. It remains an important, if ultimately unresolvable, footnote to Milgram's work.

Independent of ethical issues, Milgram's studies reveal an important fact: Authority figures can induce people to perform antisocial acts with relative ease. And although it would be comforting to suggest that Milgram's work reflects past senselessness and that people today are less likely to act obediently, this just isn't so. In a recent analysis of experimental replications and extensions that have been carried out in the decades since Milgram's work first began, social psychologist Thomas Blass and colleagues found no systematic shift in the magnitude of obedience shown by participants (Blass & Krackow, 1991; Elms, 1995; Meeus & Raaijmakers, 1995; Miller, Collins, & Brief, 1995).

The real world, too, shows little evidence for a decline in the inclination of people to follow orders, as one can infer from such cases as the Serbian ethnic cleansing that we discussed at the start of the book. Obedience remains a very real phenomenon—but not, as we discuss next, the entire story.

DEFYING SOCIAL PRESSURE: ASSERTING ONE'S HUMANITY

Although it is depressingly easy to think of examples of blind obedience to authority, we should not forget that there are also instances in which people's inherent humanity overcame the strongest of social pressure. For instance, consider the group of people who have come to be known as rescuers. Fighting against the awesome pressures of the Nazi regime, the rescuers risked their own lives to save Jews and other potential victims of the Nazi efforts to exterminate non-Aryans. Some rescuers hid people in their homes; others made arrangements for them to escape, at great risk to themselves (Oliner & Oliner, 1988).

Some researchers have sought to understand the factors that lead people to rebel against authority. For instance, in one experiment, college students were asked to complete a probing, embarrassing, very personal questionnaire with a small group of other students, who were actually confederates (Feldman & Scheibe, 1972). Depending on condition, varying numbers of confederates rebelled against the experimenter, saying (quite reasonably) that they refused to complete the questionnaire, and leaving the experiment. The results showed that the more confederates who rebelled, the more likely it was that the actual participants would dissent.

Such research illustrates that people need not be the pawns of others' attempts at pressure. When the injustice of a situation is made apparent (as by the behavior of dissenters), people are perfectly capable of rebelling against an illegitimate authority. Conformity and obedience to social pressure are not, then, an inevitable part of the human condition.

REVIEW AND RETHINK

Review

- Obedience is a change in behavior due to the commands of others in authority.

- The perceived legitimacy of the system, of authorities or power holders, and of demands are associated with obedience.

- Milgram's studies showed that many people would be surprisingly obedient to the commands of another person.

Rethink

- How does obedience differ from conformity and compliance?

- Consider a soldier at My Lai and a participant in Milgram's original obedience experiment. Identify and compare factors in each situation that affected these individuals' willingness to comply.

- According to Kelman and Hamilton, what three factors determine the likelihood that a request will be obeyed? Discuss the Milgram experiments in terms of these factors.

- Which of the methods to help resist unwanted pressure to comply that were discussed earlier can be helpful in resisting unwanted pressure to be obedient?

L O O K I N G   B A C K

Why do people conform to the views and behavior of others?

1. Conformity is one of the basic responses to social influence, in which people are affected by real or imagined pressure applied by other individuals or a group. Conformity is a change in behavior or attitudes brought about by a desire to follow the beliefs or standards of others. (p. 392)

2. People conform due to normative and informational social influence. Normative social influence is pressure that reflects group norms, which are expectations regarding appropriate behavior held by those belonging to groups. In contrast, informational social influence is pressure to conform that emanates from the assumption that others have knowledge that we lack. (p. 394)

3. Among the factors that promote conformity are the nature of the relationship a person has to a group, the number of people aligned against an individual, and the presence of a social supporter (a person holding a position similar to one's own). Some individual differences, such as gender and cultural background, are related to conformity, although the relationships are complex. (p. 395)

What factors promote independence from conformity pressures?

4. Two strategies may be employed by group minorities who wish to remain independent from the group. One, proposed by Moscovici, suggests that a minority will have maximal influence if it displays unvarying consistency. The second, suggested by Hollander, calls for the accumulation of idiosyncrasy credit by first conforming to the group. When enough credit is amassed, deviation from the majority position is possible. (p. 401)

5. One source of controversy is whether majority and minority social influence operate differently. The single-process approach suggests that both majorities and minorities employ similar influence techniques. In contrast, dual-process approaches suggest that majorities and minorities exert their influence in qualitatively different ways. Neither position has been fully upheld. (p. 403)

What strategies can be employed to make others compliant, and how can such pressures be resisted?

6. Several strategies have been developed to produce compliance, which is defined as yielding to direct, explicit appeals meant to produce a certain behavior or induce agreement with a particular point of view. For instance, in the foot-in-the-door

technique, a target of social influence is first asked to agree to a small request, and then is asked later to comply with a larger one. In contrast, the door-in-the-face technique is a procedure in which a large request, to which refusal is expected, is followed by a smaller one. The door-in-the-face procedure is effective primarily because of the exchange of reciprocal concessions between the person making the request and the target of persuasion. (p. 406)

7. In the that's-not-all technique, a customer is offered a deal at an initial, often inflated, price. But after making the initial offer, the salesperson immediately offers an incentive, discount, or bonus to clinch the deal. In contrast, lowballing occurs when an initial agreement is reached, but then the seller reveals additional costs. (p. 410)

8. Several methods can reduce a person's unwitting compliance. These include redefining the situation, avoiding consistency for consistency's sake, avoiding mindlessness, and just saying no. (p. 411)

Why are people so readily obedient to authority figures?

9. According to Kelman and Hamilton's analysis, obedience, a change in behavior that is due to the commands of others in authority, occurs because of three factors: the perceived legitimacy of the system, of authorities or power holders, and of demands. (p. 413)

10. Milgram's studies of obedience employed a procedure in which participants were asked to administer increasingly intense (but simulated) shocks to a victim. Although experts predicted that almost no participants would give the highest-level shock, 65% of the participants who participated in the basic form of the experiment gave the maximum shock. (p. 414)

11. Participants reported that they were obedient because they were following the experimenter's orders, who they believed would be responsible for any potential ill effects. However, the experiment has been criticized on both methodological and ethical grounds. (p. 416)

EPILOGUE

One can easily focus purely on the negative sides of conformity, compliance, and obedience, looking at how they induce people to do things that they might not necessarily wish to do. However, our social world would not operate very effectively without these phenomena. Indeed, from the moment of birth, caregivers attempt to make children increasingly responsive to social regulation and aware of social norms.

Consequently, in the next chapter, we consider how the law and the political system under which we operate affect our behavior. We look at how we, as citizens, accept that others have legitimate authority over us and what we do, and what effect our acceptance of the law and of our political system has on our everyday social world.

Before we proceed, however, turn back once more to the prologue of this chapter, regarding the case of the Heaven's Gate mass suicide. Consider these questions:

1. Would you classify the mass suicides as conformity, compliance, or obedience? Why?

2. What specific social psychological processes might have been at work in causing the suicides?

3. The people who belonged to the Heaven's Gate group seemed, on the outside, basically ordinary. Do you believe they must have suffered from some hidden,

underlying psychological disorder, or could social pressures alone fully account for their behavior? Why?

4. What strategies, based on social psychological findings, might you employ to persuade members of the group not to take their lives?

5. Based on Milgram's findings, do you think the members of the Heaven's Gate group could have been persuaded to direct their violence toward others, rather than at themselves through suicide? Explain.

—————— KEY TERMS AND CONCEPTS ——————

collectivism (p. 400)

compliance (p. 406)

conformity (p. 393)

door-in-the-face technique (p. 409)

dual-process approach (to majority/minority influence) (p. 404)

foot-in-the-door technique (p. 407)

idiosyncrasy credit (p. 403)

individualism (p. 400)

informational social influence (p. 394)

lowballing (p. 411)

normative social influence (p. 394)

obedience (p. 413)

private acceptance (p. 394)

public compliance (p. 393)

reciprocal concessions (p. 409)

single-process approach (to majority/minority influence) (p. 404)

social impact theory (p. 397)

social influence (p. 392)

social supporter (p. 398)

status (p. 396)

that's-not-all technique (p. 410)

CHAPTER 13

LAW AND ORDER

Applying Social Psychology in the Legal and Political Arenas

PROLOGUE

The Dream Team Finds Its Dream Jurors

In addition to a high-powered legal defense, O. J. Simpson also had the skills of jury profiler Jo-Ellan Dimitrius on his side.

Y ou may not know her name, but Jo-Ellan Dimitrius may have had more influence over the outcome of the O. J. Simpson trial than the "dream team" of lawyers who represented the defendant.

Dimitrius led a team of jury consultants hired by the defense team who sought to identify the type of juror who would be most likely to find Simpson "not guilty" of the charge of murdering his ex-wife, Nicole Brown Simpson, and her friend Ron Goldman. Using a combination of survey techniques and mock juries, Dimitrius concluded that a jury with a preponderance of African American women would be most inclined to believe in Simpson's innocence and consequently most beneficial to the defense. Based on these findings, the defense attorneys did everything they could to ensure that the jury would contain numerous African American women during the jury-selection phase of the trial, and they were largely successful in their efforts.

In retrospect, the consultants' recommendations appear to have been on target. After deliberating for less than four hours, the jury found Simpson not guilty. (Toobin, 1996) ■

LOOKING AHEAD

The ability to understand and even predict how jurors will behave in particular cases is based on social psychological research and theory. In fact, the application of social psychology to the legal system addresses a broad array of issues, including such questions as what factors influence the accuracy of witness's memories, how do juries evaluate evidence, what characteristics of a defendant influence the judicial process, and how do juries decide when a person is guilty "beyond a reasonable doubt."

In this chapter, we examine social psychological approaches to the law and the broader arena of politics. Social psychology has a unique role to play in these domains. Unlike legal and political theoreticians, who view judicial and political issues largely in terms of the formal application of a body of laws and societal rules, social psychologists regard the legal and political realms as social microcosms. They view the people involved in the judicial and political arena in terms of their relationships with one another and as individuals whose social judgments can affect crucial—and sometimes life-and-death—outcomes.

We begin by examining the major players in the criminal justice system: the defendant, the judge, and the jury. We consider how a defendant's characteristics affect assumptions of guilt or innocence; how judges can influence juries regarding matters of the law; and how a jury's size and makeup produce different types of verdicts. We discuss the social psychology of criminal activity and the ways criminals explain their failure to comply with the law.

Finally, we consider several issues of concern to social psychologists interested in the broader political system. We concentrate on leadership, examining the factors behind a person's rise to a leadership position. We also examine manifestations of power, and we suggest that power has several distinct bases.

In sum, after reading this chapter, you'll be able to answer these questions:

◆ What are the social psychological factors that affect defendants and judges in criminal trials?

◆ How do juries reach decisions?

◆ How do social psychological factors affect criminal activity?

◆ What steps can be taken to make trials fairer?

◆ How are political party affiliation and voter choices determined?

◆ What are the major explanations for leadership?

◆ On what basis is power acquired, and what are the consequences of wielding power?

THE LAW AND THE COURTROOM

Crime and suspense thrillers usually present a familiar cast of characters: the tough, disagreeable defendant, in need of a shave; the attractive, modest victim; the honorable, silver-haired judge; the vigorous, self-righteous defense attorney; and the crusading district attorney, eager to add another conviction to a record that is attracting attention in local political circles. And of course, there's also the jury: those 12 upstanding citizens who watch the trial, hear the evidence, and retire to the privacy of the deliberation room to render justice in a fair and impartial way.

Those are the stereotypes. The reality, though, is quite different. In actual courtrooms, the cast of characters is much more varied than the stereotypes suggest, matching the range and variability of humanity. Some defendants are guilty, and some are innocent. Some victims are amiable and evoke compassion, and others are sullen and unpleasant. Some judges are fair, and others are dishonest and corrupt. The attorneys—for the prosecution and for the defense—may all be seeking justice, or they may be working to further their own careers at the expense of others. Some jurors may be conscientiously fulfilling their responsibilities as citizens, whereas others may be biased and unfair.

The diversity among the key players in the legal system limits the precision with which the judicial system operates. Despite carefully thought-out rules and procedures devised over centuries, legal practice is subject to distortions, biases, and errors of judgment. Above all, legal decisions are social decisions, made on the basis of numerous interacting factors of a social psychological nature. We'll consider several of the major players in courtroom settings to illustrate how social psychological factors affect judicial decisions.

THE DEFENDANT

Despite the goal of equal justice for everyone, all defendants are not treated the same. In fact, what should be irrelevant characteristics—such as physical appearance, gender, and race—have a significant influence on jurors' decisions about guilt and innocence.

Physical appearance.   As we first discussed in Chapter 6, physical appearance plays a powerful role in determining interpersonal attraction. It is not surprising, then, that jurors are influenced by a defendant's attractiveness. In most cases, the influence is positive: Both jurors and judges are more lenient when defendants are physically attractive than when they are less attractive (Bagby et al., 1994; Mazzella & Feingold, 1994; Erian et al., 1998). Attractive defendants are not only more likely to be found innocent, but also less likely to be sent to jail if they are found guilty. Moreover, if they do go to prison, they tend to receive shorter sentences (Stewart, 1980; DeSantis & Kayson, 1997). Even the bail set for attractive defendants is apt to be lower than for unattractive defendants (Downs & Lyons, 1991).

However, attractiveness is not always an asset in the courtroom. For example, if the defendant's physical appearance seems to have been used advantageously during a crime, jurors may give harsher sentences to more attractive than to less attractive defendants.

In an experiment that demonstrated the importance of physical attractiveness, social psychologists Harold Sigall and Nancy Ostrove (1975) told participants acting as mock jurors that a female defendant had been involved in one of two kinds of crimes: a burglary in which $2,200 was stolen, or a swindle in which a bachelor was persuaded to invest $2,200 in a nonexistent corporation. One group of participants was told the defendant was attractive; the other group of participants was told the defendant was unattractive.

When the crime was burglary, the mock jurors handed out a more lenient sentence to the attractive burglar than to the unattractive one (Wuensch et al., 1993). But when the crime was a swindle, they gave the attractive defendant a slightly harsher sentence than the unattractive one. The reason: The attractive swindler was seen as using her beauty in the service of her criminal activity.

Race and gender.   Physical attractiveness is not the only characteristic of defendants that affects the judicial process. Another powerful factor is race. As you might expect, members of racial minorities often receive more severe treatment at the hands of the courts than members of the racial majority (Bohm,1994; Dovidio et al., 1997; Dauidistel et al., 1999). If African Americans are accused of committing a crime, they are more likely to be convicted than whites. Furthermore, African Americans receive longer prison terms than whites convicted of similar crimes (DeSantis & Kayson, 1997; Haney & Zimbardo, 1998).

Moreover, the punishment that defendants receive is related to the race of the victim. An African American who kills a white person is significantly more likely to receive the death penalty than an African American who kills another African American (Hymes et al., 1993; Sorenson & Wallace, 1995; Thomson, 1997).

Gender, too, plays a role in defendants' success at clearing their names in the judicial process. Male and female defendants are not treated identically in the judicial arena, depending on the nature of the crime and other specifics of the situation (Mazzella & Feingold, 1994; Salekin et al., 1995; DeSantis & Kayson, 1997). For example, in one experimental simulation, mock jurors heard a case in which the defendant stabbed a victim with a kitchen knife. In one condition the defendant was described as a woman and the victim as a man, and in the other condition the defendant was said to be a man and the victim a woman.

Except for the gender switch, the descriptions of the incident were identical; nevertheless, jurors were significantly more likely to judge the female defendant guilty than the male defendant (see Figure 13–1). Apparently, the woman was more likely to be seen as guilty because her behavior was inconsistent with the traditional female gender role. In the eyes of this simulated jury, then, a woman who was accused of acting like a man was probably guilty (Cruse & Leigh, 1987).

Why should jurors think that a woman who behaves like a man is likely to be guilty? One reason may be that the vast majority of serious crimes are, in fact, committed by men. Close to 90% of all people arrested for murder, rape, robbery, and assault are male (U.S. Department of Justice, 1990). Such statistics are not terribly surprising, given their consistency with the traditional male gender role, which encompasses such characteristics as aggressive, unemotional, and tough.

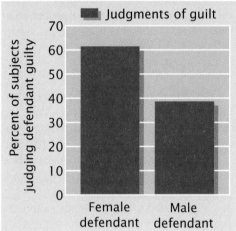

FIGURE 13–1   **Influences on the Processing of Trial Testimony** A female defendant who stabbed a male victim was more likely to be judged guilty than a male defendant who stabbed a female victim, apparently reflecting mock jurors' perception that stabbing is incompatible with the traditional female gender role. (*Source:* Based on data reported in Cruse & Leigh, 1987.)

THE JUDGE

Wise. Uncompromising. Fair.

If these descriptions match your beliefs about trial judges, you may be misguided, for the reality is in many ways inconsistent with this view. Although judges clearly hold the most power in any courtroom drama, like other experts they are susceptible to the same kinds of biases as other people (Slovic, Fischhoff, & Lichenstein, 1977; King, 1998).

One reason for the discrepancy between the "ideal" judge and the reality is that in many respects, judges' backgrounds are not all that different from those of the average person. Although the educational level and socioeconomic status of a judge are often higher than the norm, these differences do not guarantee that judges possess special qualities that distinguish their decision-making abilities from the layperson's. In fact, judges are sometimes elected or appointed for purely political reasons. Consequently, merit may take a back seat to politics or commitment to a particular ideology (such as being pro-choice or pro-life on the abortion issue).

But even the best-qualified judge, being human, may fall into the same attribution and judgmental traps as nonexperts. Because the decision-making processes of human beings are open to many varieties of errors, even the most honest and upright judges may be prone to error.

Consider, for instance, how judges set bail. Judges have wide latitude on the amount of bail that a defendant must pay in order to be free prior to trial, and they are supposed to take into account all relevant information. For instance, a judge typically is supposed to consider such factors as the prosecutor's recommendation, the defense attorney's recommendation, the extent of a defendant's community ties, and the nature of the defendant's prior criminal record.

However, an analysis of actual bail decisions demonstrates that only the prosecutor's and defense attorney's recommendations had a direct, significant effect on judges' decisions (Ebbesen & Konecni, 1982). Community ties and prior criminal record had either an indirect effect or no effect on the decision-making process.

The verbal and nonverbal demeanor of judges also varies significantly and can affect judicial outcomes. For instance, jurors react differently to judges who exude warmth and confidence than those who are colder and appear less confident (Blanck, 1991; Blanck & Rosenthal, 1992). In fact, in some cases, the nonverbal behavior of a judge represents outright bias (Halverson, Hallahan, & Rosenthal, 1997). For example, one burglary conviction was overturned when evidence was presented that the trial judge had expressed disbelief by placing his hands at the sides of his head, shaking his head negatively, leaning back, and swiveling in his chair so his back was facing the jury (*State v. Barron*, 1971). In addition, appeals courts regularly consider the "emphatic or overbearing" nature of a judge's verbal and nonverbal behavior in deciding whether a trial has been conducted properly (Blanck & Rosenthal, 1992).

Judges also vary widely in terms of the sentences they assign to defendants who have been convicted by a jury. Even when judges must follow mandatory sentencing guidelines, they still have wide discretion in sentencing. Consequently, a criminal found guilty in one judge's courtroom may receive a sentence that is literally a lifetime longer than someone found guilty in another judge's courtroom (Provorse & Sarata, 1989; Doob & Beaulieu, 1992).

Discrepancies in sentencing among judges are produced, in part, by differing philosophical orientations judges bring to the courtroom, relating to their general understanding of the causes of crime. One analysis of judges' behavior found two basic types of judges. One type includes judges who emphasize the social factors that lead a person to become involved in crime, such as poverty and a difficult childhood. Such judges emphasize the rehabilitative possibilities of prison. The other type includes judges who focused on criminals' personal responsibility for their crimes and view a prison term as punishment and retribution for the criminals' behavior (Carroll et al., 1987; Davis et al., 1993).

As you might expect, judges with these two very different perspectives tend to deliver very different kinds of sentences. Judges who hold society and circumstances to blame for criminal activity tend to give shorter sentences than those who perceive the criminal as more responsible for the crime.

THE JURY

In most trials, the jury makes the ultimate decision as to the guilt or innocence of a defendant. Is it possible to predict a jury's decision? Increasing evidence from a variety of sources suggests that the answer is a qualified yes, as social psychologists develop increasingly sophisticated and accurate models of the factors that affect jury decision-making processes.

Jury compliance with judges' instructions: Forget it.   Suppose, during the course of a trial, a witness blurts out that she heard that the defendant, now on trial, had several prior convictions. The defendant's attorney immediately jumps up, enters an objection, and asks that the witness's statement be ruled inadmissible. The judge agrees and orders the jury to disregard the information.

Both the verbal and nonverbal demeanor of a judge can affect judicial outcomes. Studies have found that jurors react differently to judges who exude warmth and confidence compared with those who appear colder and less confident.

If you were part of that jury, how successful would you be in following the judge's instructions? Most jurors find it nearly impossible—not due to outright disobedience, but because they simply cannot erase the memory from their deliberations (Wissler & Saks, 1985; Fein, McClosky, & Tomlinson, 1997; Kassin & Studebaker, 1998; Thompson & Fuqua, 1998).

Social psychologist Daniel Wegner (1989) refers to this as the "white bear" phenomenon. According to Wegner, if someone tells us to avoid thinking about a particular topic—such as a white bear—the opposite actually occurs: That topic becomes particularly prominent in our thoughts. In fact, the more we try to suppress a thought, the more likely it is that we will think about it (Wegner et al., 1990; Wegner & Erber, 1992; Gold & Wegner, 1995).

But there are other reasons that jurors might not comply with a judge's instructions. For example, in some cases, jurors may avoid following judges' instructions simply because they feel that by doing so they will reach a more equitable decision—even if they are technically breaking the law by disregarding the instructions. Similarly, jurors may ignore a judges' instructions and disregard a defendant's confession if they feel it has been obtained through coercion (Kassin & Sommers, 1997; Kassin & Sukel, 1997).

Jurors' views about the potential punishment that a defendant may receive can influence their verdicts. For instance, jurors who hold strong views about capital punishment may allow their attitudes to influence their decision-making processes. It is often jurors' sense of justice, then, that leads them to ignore judges' admonitions regarding the use of certain kinds of information—no matter what a judge tells them (Luginbuhl & Burkhead, 1994; Berger, 1997; Paglia & Schuller, 1998).

Does noncompliance with judges' instructions about the use of certain kinds of information actually affect sentencing? Experimental findings suggest that it does. For example, one experiment provided mock jurors certain information about a defendant, which they were later informed should not be considered in their deliberations. Despite these instructions, however, the inadmissible evidence significantly affected the jurors' verdicts and sentences (Sue, Smith, & Caldwell, 1973; Fleming, Wegener, & Petty, 1999).

In addition, jurors may fail to comply with a judge's instructions if they perceive that the instructions are obstructing their independence. Under these circumstances, jurors might experience feelings of reactance. As we discussed first in Chapter 5, *reactance* is an unpleasant emotional and cognitive reaction, often expressed as hostility and anger, that occurs when one's freedom is restricted (Brehm & Brehm, 1981). Reactance may lead to a boomerang effect: Jurors may place particular weight on the inadmissible evidence, producing a decision that runs directly counter to the instructions (Clark, 1994; Seguin & Horowitz, 1984).

In a series of experiments, social psychologist Eugene Borgida (1982) presented mock jurors with a description of a rape case. Some jurors were explicitly instructed that admissions made by the rape victim regarding her prior sexual experiences should be disregarded because they had no bearing on whether she had, as the defendant claimed, consented to having sexual intercourse with him. In fact, jurors who received these instructions were *more* likely to find the accused rapist innocent than those who did not. Apparently, the jurors interpreted the explicit instruction as a threat to their decision-making freedom, and they reacted in a way that directly contradicted the judge's admonitions. Sometimes, then, explicit and precise instructions to a jury may backfire.

Juror comprehension: Understanding the law.   Even when jurors attempt to comply with judges' instructions, they may unwittingly make errors. Although such mistakes can occur at several points in a trial, they most often happen just prior to jury deliberations, when judges typically interpret for jurors the laws that are relevant to the case. The manner in which the judge defines the legal issues has a substantial impact on jury behavior (Nagao & McClain, 1983; Smith, 1991a; Greene & Loftus, 1998).

In certain cases, some jurors are simply unable to comprehend what the judge is talking about. To make their instructions precise, judges may use technical legal terms, or they may provide so much detail that their instructions become incomprehensible to a person unschooled in the nuances of the law (Wiener, Pritchard, & Weston, 1995; English & Sales, 1997; Frank & Applegate, 1998).

Furthermore, even when jurors think they have understood a judge's instructions, they may misinterpret rules of law. For example, one study found that only about half the jurors in a criminal case grasped the fundamental fact that the burden of proof rests on the prosecution and not the defense—even after they had been explicitly informed. Furthermore, jurors' prior knowledge of the law, gleaned in part from such sources as television shows and novels, influences their deliberations (Strawn & Buchanan, 1976; Smith, 1991b; Kuhn, Weinstock, & Flaton, 1994).

Some social psychologists suggest that jurors try to make sense of the evidence they hear during a trial by creating one or more scenarios about what happened. For example, social psychologists Nancy Pennington and Reid Hastie note that as jurors listen to the testimony, they develop a story in which they formulate speculative scenarios that include explanations for why the people involved in the case behaved as they did. Then, when judges provide instructions about the law prior to jury deliberation, jurors evaluate the stories they have constructed to see how well they fit the legal criteria of guilt or innocence (Pennington & Hastie, 1992, 1993; Olsen-Fulero & Fulero, 1997).

Although jurors sometimes have only a limited and biased understanding of the law, they can be helped to make more informed decisions (Penrod & Heuer, 1997; Stallard & Worthington, 1998; Robbennolt, Penrod, & Heuer, 1999). For instance, jurors may be able to make less biased decisions when judges' instructions are free of legal jargon and are expressed in everyday language, as considered in the Applying Social Psychology box.

Even with clear information, however, juror deliberations do not proceed in an unbiased manner. For instance, jurors are subject to a **leniency bias**, the tendency for jury deliberation to lead more often to acquittal than conviction. Generally, if all other factors are equal, jurors are more likely to convict a defendant before they start deliberations than after. Moreover, they are more apt to convict a defendant when asked privately than when they are in a group (MacCoun & Kerr, 1988).

Who counts? Jury math.   In legal theory, a juror is a juror is a juror. Each has an equal voice in determining the guilt or innocence of a defendant.

leniency bias: The tendency for jury deliberation to lead more often to acquittal than conviction.

The reality is different (Pennington & Hastie, 1990). As in any other group situation, some members of a jury emerge as leaders, casting a strong influence on the other members, and others fade into the background. Some jurors enter the jury room partial to conviction, whereas others feel that a defendant is probably innocent. What determines which juror's view prevails in such a situation?

One influential factor appears to be the size of the jury. A traditional jury has 12 members, a number inherited from the British legal tradition. The rationale for this figure was that 12 people somehow better represented a cross-section of the citizenry than a smaller number.

In recent years, however, the number of jurors required for a trial has begun to shrink. Beginning in the 1970s, 6-person juries became permissible in all cases except those involving the death penalty. In ruling on the legality of the 6-person jury in the case of *Williams v. Florida,* the Supreme Court pointed to the findings from Solomon Asch's work on conformity that we discussed in Chapter 12.

Unfortunately, the Court did not do its homework very well (Saks, 1977). Misinterpreting Asch's (1956) work, the Court claimed that Asch's findings suggested that a 1:5 split in a 6-person jury was identical to a 2:10 split in a 12-person jury. To the Court, a single minority juror seemed to be under no more psychological pressure to conform to a 5-person majority than 2 minority jurors would be to conform to a 10-person majority.

The justices erred, though. As you'll recall, Asch found that having a single social supporter allowed a minority group member to remain independent, whereas having no allies led to

APPLYING SOCIAL PSYCHOLOGY
WHEN SIMPLE IS FAIRER: REDUCING THE INFLUENCE OF JUDGES' PRECONCEPTIONS THROUGH BETTER JURY INSTRUCTIONS

Judges are people, too.

And that means that no matter how hard they try to keep their own opinions from biasing a jury, it's difficult for them to completely hide their real feelings. The reason is nonverbal "leakage" (first discussed in Chapter 2), in which a person's true beliefs and emotions are revealed unintentionally through their facial expressions and body movements. If jurors are sensitive to the demeanor of a judge, they may be influenced by the judge's underlying assumptions about the guilt or innocence of a defendant, even if the judge struggles to hide his or her own beliefs (Ekman, 1997; Frank, Ekman, & Friesen, 1997).

However, new research suggests that a simple procedural change in the way judges offer instructions to the jury can reduce the consequences of judges' unintentional revelation of their opinion. Traditionally, jurors receive instructions that are complex and use archaic language, making them hard to understand. In fact, social psychologist Robert Rosenthal and colleagues hypothesized that the complex instructions often were so hard to understand that jurors would rely more heavily on nonverbal information unintentionally supplied by the judge. On the other hand, if the instructions were more understandable, jurors would be more inclined to use them and would pay less attention to judges' demeanor (Halverson et al., 1997).

To test the hypothesis, participants in an experiment initially read either a standard or a simplified set of jury instructions and then watched a videotape of an actual trial. They then watched videotaped jury instructions from an actual judge who either believed the defendant was guilty or one who thought the defendant was not guilty.

Participants who heard the instructions from a judge who thought the defendant was guilty were more inclined to convict the defendant than when they heard instructions from a judge who thought the defendant was innocent. On the other hand, participants who received the more understandable instructions were less affected by the judge's underlying belief about the defendant's guilt.

As expected, then, simplified instructions permitted participants to ignore the judge's nonverbal behavior, making more independent assessments of the defendant's guilt or innocence. The results suggest that simplifying juror instructions would result in more independent jurors, improving the fairness of the judicial system.

While social psychological research has found that a 12-person jury is superior to a smaller one, the evidence is not entirely consistent.

considerable conformity. For a minority juror in a 2:10 split, then, the pressures to conform are relatively weak, given that he or she has another person in the minority. In contrast, a minority juror in a 1:5 split is much more likely to experience intense pressure to conform.

Using conformity research as a guide, then, large juries may be preferable to smaller ones, if the goal is the careful consideration of both minority and majority opinions. Other findings support such a conclusion.

For example, research comparing individual and group decision making suggests that groups may reach better (although more time-consuming) decisions than individuals (Liang, Moreland, & Argote, 1995; Wegner, 1995). Groups tend to remember information better than individuals. Larger juries are also more likely than smaller ones to represent minority segments of the population, providing the potential of more diversity in jurors' points of view (Wrightsman, 1991; Davis et al., 1997; Saks & Marti, 1997).

In sum, social psychological research points to the superiority of 12-person juries to smaller ones. However, the evidence is not entirely consistent. Some research, for instance, suggests that the differences in the ultimate verdicts of 6-person compared with 12-person juries are not substantial (Saks, 1977). On the issue of jury size, then, the final verdict has yet to be rendered.

REVIEW AND RETHINK

Review

- Several characteristics of defendants, including attractiveness, gender, and race, affect judicial outcomes.
- Judges are also susceptible to biases that can introduce error into courtroom proceedings.
- Among the factors affecting jurors' decisions are their difficulty in understanding judges' instructions, their disregard of instructions, and the size of the jury.

Rethink

- How does the beautiful-is-good stereotype affect courtroom proceedings? What other stereotypes may influence the jury decision-making process?
- In some states judges make sentencing decisions, whereas in others separate jury trials are held for sentencing. What are the pros and cons of each system?

- Both prosecuting and defense attorneys generally try to avoid having college students put on juries. Yet, research on juries is conducted on many college campuses using students as participants. Discuss the possible implications of this inconsistency.

- Imagine you are a defense attorney and that your case is going badly. Based on your knowledge of juror comprehension, what kinds of closing arguments might you make to persuade the jury?

JUROR CHARACTERISTICS: PREDICTING JURY DECISIONS

Clarence Darrow, the most famous attorney of his time, had this to say about the characteristics of jurors:

> I try to get a jury with little education but with much human emotion. The Irish are always the best jurymen for the defense. I don't want a Scotchman, for he has too little human feelings; I don't want a Scandinavian, for he has too strong a respect for law as law. In general, I don't want a religious person, for he believes in sin and punishment. The defense should avoid rich men who have a high regard for the law, as they make and use it. The smug and ultra-respectable think they are the guardians of the society, and they believe the law is for them. (Quoted in Sutherland & Cressey, 1974, p. 417)

Although Darrow was obviously wrong in his sweeping generalizations about members of various ethnic and demographic groups—there is little evidence to support the view that members of particular groups behave in characteristic ways on juries—certain juror characteristics do affect decision-making behavior. We'll consider a few of these characteristics, including juror personality traits, exposure to pretrial publicity, and attitudes toward the death penalty.

Personality and juror behavior.   Several personality characteristics are associated with juror behavior. For example, highly dogmatic or closed-minded jurors, who are intolerant of ambiguity and tend to make extreme judgments of people as a way of resolving uncertainty, are more influenced by judges' instructions than are nondogmatic jurors (Kerwin & Shaffer, 1991).

Similarly, juror *authoritarianism* (a complex mix of rigidity, social and political conservatism, conformity to social norms, and submissiveness to authority) is associated with juror behavior (Narby, Cutler, & Moran, 1993; Valliant & Loring, 1998). People high in authoritarianism are more apt not only to convict defendants but also to recommend longer sentences (Bray & Noble, 1978; Moran & Comfort, 1986; Shaffer, Plummer, & Hammock, 1986). There are exceptions to this generalization, however. If the defendant is an authority figure or was following the orders of an authority figure, jurors high in authoritarianism are likely to decide in his or her favor (Hamilton, 1976; Narby, Cutler, & Moran, 1993).

By and large, though, the search for a consistent relationship between personality characteristics and juror conduct has yielded inconsistent and weak results (Matlon et al., 1986; Reskin & Visher, 1986; Hastie, Schkade, & Payne, 1998). No single personality trait or demographic factor is invariably associated with juror behavior.

What does seem to make a difference in juror decisions, however, is the degree of similarity between a juror and the defendant in a trial. The greater the similarity in attitudes and demographic characteristics between a juror and the defendant, the greater the leniency toward the defendant (Monahan & Loftus, 1982; Kerr et al., 1995). It is not surprising, then, that many defense lawyers suggested that the most sympathetic defense juror in the O. J. Simpson murder trial would be male, African American, and a football fan—just like Simpson.

Like many people in the United States, you probably had an opinion about whether O. J. Simpson was innocent or guilty well before his trial had begun.

Exposure to pretrial publicity.   Like most people in the United States, you probably had an opinion about whether O. J. Simpson was innocent or guilty well before his trial started, based on the massive publicity in the case. If you were a juror, could you set aside your beliefs and begin the trial unaffected by your earlier opinion?

Probably not. For one thing, public opinion surveys show that the more people know about a case from pretrial publicity, the more they assume a defendant is guilty. Why is this true? The answer is that far more news about a case typically comes from police and prosecutors' offices, particularly early after an arrest has been made, and consequently it tends to be biased against a defendant. Given the power of first impressions (recall the potency of the primacy effect, which we discussed in Chapter 2), this initial negative information may be difficult for jurors to disregard when they enter the courtroom (Moran & Cutler, 1991; Ogloff & Vidmar, 1994; Studebaker & Penrod, 1997; Wilson & Bornstein, 1998).

Furthermore, even after the initial flurry of information about a case is made public, defendants often have a hard time getting their side of the story out. (The exception is in rare, high-profile cases such as O. J. Simpson, in which prominent defense attorneys are able to generate substantial publicity of their own.) In most cases, then, throughout the entire pretrial period publicity tends to be biased in favor of the prosecution.

Most jurors have difficulty disregarding such information. Even if they do not enter the courtroom having made a decision that a defendant is innocent or guilty, they may interpret what they hear during the trial in terms of their prior impressions of the evidence. In short, even the most conscientious juror may find it difficult to enter the courtroom as a *tabula rasa*, or blank slate, as the law requires.

Death qualification.   We mentioned earlier that jurors who have strong views about capital punishment may sometimes ignore judges' instructions about the issue. However, such jurors often never even make it onto a jury. The reason is a procedure known as death qualification.

Death qualification is a practice in which judges exclude potential jurors from a jury who indicate they could not, because of their prior beliefs, vote for a death penalty. Clearly, this

death qualification: A practice in which judges exclude from a jury potential jurors who indicate they could not, because of their prior beliefs, vote for a death penalty.

voir dire: Proceedings in which prospective jurors can be questioned as to their impartiality and background in order to eliminate those who are biased toward or against a particular side.

is a logical practice: If the law permits a death penalty in a given case, jurors who say they are unwilling to uphold such a law should not be allowed on a jury.

But there's a problem: What if the pool of people that are left after death qualification—a group that states they are willing to vote for death—also differ in their readiness to convict a defendant? In fact, this is the case. Jurors who support the use of the death penalty are also more likely to vote for a conviction of a defendant (Allen, Mabry, & McKelton, 1998; Filkins, Smith, & Tindale, 1998).

The practice of death qualification, then, raises an ethical predicament. Although including jurors who state up front that they would be unable to uphold a key element of the law (the death penalty) does not seem reasonable, stacking the jury with people who are more likely to convict a defendant is also unfair. This issue continues to engage both social psychologists and legal scholars.

Picking among jurors: The search for the sympathetic jury.   The relative weakness of the relationship between personal characteristics and juror behavior has not stopped trial attorneys and prosecutors from searching for a means to choose a group of jurors who will be sympathetic to their side, as we discussed in the chapter prologue. Known as *scientific jury selection*, the pursuit of congenial jurors is accomplished before the start of a trial during *voir dire* proceedings, in which prospective jurors can be questioned as to their impartiality and background in order to eliminate those who are biased toward or against a particular side.

Turning *voir dire* on its head, a whole industry has developed that seeks to help the legal profession identify jurors sympathetic to one side or the other. Typically, experts hired by the defense or prosecution (like that in the O. J. Simpson trial) administer a series of questionnaires to a sample of registered voters in the area in which a trial is being held. By asking pertinent questions about the trial, the defendants, and the prosecution, they hope to identify general attitudinal patterns and demographic factors that relate to a predisposition to favor acquittal or conviction in a particular case (Patterson, 1986; J. Schwartz, 1993).

Subsequently, when a jury is being chosen for the actual trial, attorneys can identify potential jurors who have attitudes and demographic characteristics similar to those of the survey respondents who seem, from the survey results, most prone to acquit or convict the defendant. Using this procedure, defense attorneys can challenge conviction-prone jurors and remove them before they take their places on the jury—yielding a jury that is presumably inclined to vote for acquittal. In the same way, the prosecution may be able to identify and attempt to remove jurors who are prone to be sympathetic to the defense.

Does it work? To some degree. However, "scientific" jury selection procedures are not invariably better at producing a desired result. For the moment, at least, identification of the "perfect" juror remains an unfinished task. (For more on juror selection techniques, see the Speaking of Social Psychology interview.)

THE VALIDITY OF EYEWITNESS TESTIMONY: MEMORY ON TRIAL

In the end, no one was satisfied—not the parents, who suspected that their children had been sexually molested; not the defendants, whose lives were shattered by the accusations; and not the children themselves, who had to testify in court about hazy memories of events that had (or had not) occurred years before.

The source of all this dissatisfaction was the outcome of a 33-week, $15 million trial, one of the longest and most expensive in U.S. history. After 9 weeks of deliberation, the jury acquitted the defendants of 52 counts of child sexual abuse and announced it was deadlocked on 13 other counts.

During the trial, Ray Buckey and his mother, Peggy McMartin Buckey, stood accused of molesting dozens of preschool-age children who attended the exclusive day care center they operated. At the trial, some of the young witnesses—now 10 and 11 years old—recited in detail how the Buckeys had abused them while they attended the school, providing vivid details of events that had occurred years earlier.

At the same time, though, some of the children's recollections seemed suspect, including bizarre tales of jumping out of airplanes and digging up bodies at a cemetery. In the end, the jurors simply could not accept the validity of the children's testimony, and the Buckeys were freed.

The Buckey case illustrates the suggestibility of trial witnesses and the fragility of their memories. Children, in particular, are susceptible to errors. For one thing, their lower level of cognitive sophistication makes them prone to inaccuracy. Furthermore, when they are exposed to information subsequent to an event, young children's memories are especially vulnerable to the influence of others. This vulnerability may be particularly strong when an event is highly emotional or stressful (Ceci & Bruck, 1995; Lewis et al., 1995; Schacter, Kagan, & Leichtman, 1995; Cassel, Roebers, & Bjorklund, 1996).

The amount of pretrial publicity in the Buckey case was huge, and the children who were supposedly molested were repeatedly interviewed. During the trial, then, instead of providing an accurate recollection of events, the children may have responded with information to which they had been exposed during the interviewing process (Loftus & Ketcham, 1991; Loftus, 1992).

Difficulties in assessing the validity of witnesses' memories are not limited to children (Devenport, Penrod, & Cutler, 1997; Brown, Scheflin, & Hammond, 1998). Adults, too, are prone to a considerable degree of error. Consider, for instance, an experiment conducted during a New York City television news program (Buckhout, 1975). Viewers saw a 12-second film of a mugging and then viewed a six-person lineup that included the actual assailant. Members of the audience were invited to call in to identify the actual assailant. Out of more than 2,000 viewers who phoned, about 15% were correct—a figure no different from what would be expected if the viewers had guessed randomly.

So-called repressed memories are even more prone to error. Memory specialist Elizabeth Loftus notes how easily false memories can be implanted in people's minds (Hyman, Husband, & Billings, 1995; Roediger & McDermott, 1995). For instance, she conducted an experiment in which a student named Jack wrote a passage that he gave to his younger brother Chris, who was 14 years old. It described an occurrence that actually never had happened:

> It was 1981 or 1982. I remember that Chris was 5. We had gone shopping at the University City shopping mall in Spokane. After some panic, we found Chris being led down the mall by a tall, oldish man (I think he was wearing a flannel shirt). Chris was crying and holding the man's hand. The man explained that he had found Chris walking around crying his eyes out just a few moments before and was trying to help him find his parents. (Loftus, 1993, p. 352)

A few weeks after reading the story, Chris had become convinced that the event had actually occurred. When asked to recall the event, he vividly described the color of the man's flannel shirt, his bald head, and how he had felt "really scared." He even remembered crying and subsequently discussing the occurrence with his mother. Even after he was told that the event had not happened, Chris maintained that the memory was true.

According to Loftus, people are susceptible to **reconstructive memories**—memories that are altered by exposure to postevent information—for several reasons. One reason is that they may forget the source of a memory, confusing the memory of an actual event with the memory of a story they have been told (Bowers & Farvolden, 1996a). In fact, certain therapists have been accused of promoting the development of false memories by encouraging their patients to delve into their memories, supposedly looking for childhood sexual experiences (Garry, Loftus, & Brown, 1994; Bowers & Farvolden, 1996b; Schacter, 1996).

Another reason for memory failures is related to social expectations and stereotypes (Fyock & Stangor, 1994; Hirt, McDonald, & Erikson, 1995; Leichtman & Ceci, 1995). The expectations a person has about the way in which the world operates influence how he or she perceives and remembers information. If people hold the stereotype that members of certain

reconstructive memories: Memories that are altered by exposure to postevent information.

SPEAKING OF SOCIAL PSYCHOLOGY

Joy Stapp

Trial Consultant

Year of Birth: 1947

Education: B.A., Psychology and Mathematics, University of Texas at Austin; M.A., Social Psychology, University of California at Santa Barbara; Ph.D., Social Psychology, University of Texas at Austin

Home: Houston, Texas

"Most of our time is spent developing an effective trial strategy that shapes juror perceptions of the evidence from beginning to end."

The idea of using a trial consultant to help select a jury is not new: It's been around for at least 20 years. Moreover, the use of trial consultants isn't limited to such high-profile criminal cases as those of O. J. Simpson and the Menendez brothers. In fact, the trial consultant plays a vital role in many types of legal actions, most of them very low profile.

Joy Stapp, a partner in the Houston, Texas–based firm of Stapp Singleton, concentrates on civil cases involving commercial litigation, antitrust suits, intellectual properties disputes, and patent and trademark cases. She points out that the work of trial consultants is hardly confined to jury selection; the range of trial-related services that firms like hers offer is surprisingly large.

"Although we are often involved in jury selection and direct work with witnesses, most of our time is spent developing an effective trial strategy that shapes juror perceptions of the evidence from beginning to end. We try to impart an interpretation through witnesses and exhibits, reinforce it in closing arguments, and see that it leads to a favorable verdict for our clients," she explains.

minority groups are more prone to criminal activity than the white majority, they are going to perceive and remember events within this context (Loftus, 1993; Wells, 1993).

For example, in a set of classic studies, participants were shown a drawing of a subway scene, similar to the one shown in Figure 13–2 (Allport & Postman, 1945). Among the characters in the picture was an empty-handed African American conversing with a white man who was holding a razor. Participants were asked to describe the picture to another person who had not seen it, who in turn recounted it to another person, and so forth. The typical story told by the last person in the chain included, as a major element, an African American holding a razor. Clearly, the communication of the description had altered it to match social expectations and stereotypes.

Another important reason that eyewitnesses are prone to error concerns their motivational and emotional state during a crime. Eyewitnesses may be motivated to remember events in particular ways. For example, the victim of a stabbing may believe that he did not provoke his assailant prior to being stabbed, and as a result he may well forget the angry words that were exchanged before the stabbing.

One of the reasons that Stapp puts less emphasis on jury selection is that the control that can be exercised on the juror is limited. Instead, her focus is on understanding how jurors think.

"We are looking to find out what the jury thinks of the multitude of issues that they will be confronted with," Stapp says. "Do they understand them? Are they for them or against them? Then through testing we determine why they make the decisions they make, what beliefs and values they bring to court, and how they interpret what they hear.

> *"Eighty percent of jurors come to some sort of decision during, or shortly after, the opening statement."*

"We work closely with the trial team to develop a presentation that accurately and fairly represents each side's case. Compared with the typical mock trial, we use a relatively large sample of at least 60 surrogate jurors," she adds. "In some cases, we do just one study; in other cases, we are able to do multiple projects to test trial strategies or particular issues, or to develop juror profiles."

One crucial area of any trial is the opening statement. It is at this point that most jurors come to a conclusion about the case, according to Stapp.

"Eighty percent of jurors come to some sort of decision during, or shortly after, the opening statement," she says. "Humans are active receivers of information, not passive receivers. I'm sure jurors try to keep an open mind and try to listen carefully, but it is a fact of human nature and social psychology that people make up their minds very early on the basis of limited information. First impressions overwhelm the field. The opening statement takes on tremendous importance."

Despite this fact and some recent criticisms of jury trials, Stapp feels the jury system works very well.

"Given the information that a jury gets to hear during a trial, they almost always come to a good decision. Jurors are very conscientious and take their job very seriously," Stapp notes. "When it seems that they have failed, it is more a failure of the case that was presented to them. It may not have been clearly presented, or it may not have addressed the concerns they had."

Similarly, highly aroused, emotional eyewitnesses may be inaccurate in their recollections. For instance, people who witness a mugging are apt to be apprehensive, anxious, and concerned about their own safety; consequently, their ability to observe and recall the facts of the mugging dispassionately may be impaired. However, emotional arousal may not always bring errors in recall: Sometimes heightened arousal may actually cause various details to be stored in memory with greater clarity (Christianson, 1992; Cutler & Penrod, 1995; Lang, Dhillon, & Dong, 1995).

The way in which questions to eyewitnesses are framed and worded can also have a significant impact on the responses they elicit. For instance, in one study, participants viewed a short film of two cars crashing into each other. Some of the participants were asked, "About how fast were the cars going when they *smashed* into each other?," whereas others were asked, "About how fast were the cars going when they *contacted* each other?" When queried about "smashing" cars, the average participant's estimate was 40.8 miles an hours; but when the question was framed in terms of cars "contacting" each other, the average estimate was only 30.8 miles per hour (Loftus & Palmer, 1974). In addition, when the words *collided, bumped,*

FIGURE 13–2   The Fallacies of Memory In a classic study, participants were shown a drawing of a subway scene, similar to this one, in which one of the characters was an empty-handed African American conversing with a white man who was holding a razor. Participants were asked to describe the picture to another person who had not seen the picture, who in turn recounted it to another person, and so forth. The typical story told by the last person in the chain included, as a major element, an African American holding a razor. (*Source:* Allport & Postman, 1945.)

and *hit* were used in the question, participants estimated speeds in between the two extremes of *smashed* and *contacted* (see Figure 13–3).

Unfortunately, no clues exist that can invariably inform us as to when an eyewitness's memory is in error. In fact, sometimes unsure, hesitant witnesses recall details with accuracy, whereas at other times highly confident witnesses make substantial errors (Luus & Wells, 1994; Penrod & Cutler, 1995; Sporer et al., 1995). However, research has found that certain circumstances are likely to reflect errors or distortions in memory (Wall, 1965; Platz & Hosch, 1988; Kassin, Ellsworth, & Smith, 1989; Wrightsman, 1991). Specifically, memory errors in identification are likely if

- Witnesses first say they are unable to identify anyone.

- The defendant was known to the witness before the crime but was not originally identified when the witness was first questioned.

- A major discrepancy exists between the witness's first description of the perpetrator of the crime and the actual appearance of a defendant.

- A witness first identifies someone else and then retracts the identification.

- The witness and the person identified belong to different racial groups.

- A long period has elapsed between the crime and the identification of a perpetrator (Kihlstrom, 1994).

Although not every eyewitness recollection is distorted or in error, juries need to remember these human fallibilities when they consider the fate of a suspect.

THE SOCIAL PSYCHOLOGY OF CRIMINAL BEHAVIOR

Most of us, at one time or another, have broken the law. For most of us, the offenses have been relatively minor, such as jaywalking, parking illegally, underage drinking, and the like. Some people shade the truth when they fill out their tax returns, and others engage in outright fraud, hiding income they have received or taking deductions they have not earned. Still others have committed major crimes, such as theft, embezzlement, and murder.

Although compliance with the law represents a major social issue, the field of social psychology has been relatively silent on the subject. Most of the crime-related research that has been conducted has concentrated on circumstances that occur after a crime has been committed. However, some social psychologists have taken an innovative tack by concentrating on the prevention of crime. Working with the police, they have developed programs, based largely on social psychological principles, to reduce the occurrence of criminal activities (Winkel, 1991; Tolan & Guerra, 1994; Yoshikawa, 1994).

Crime prevention.   One example of the joint efforts of social psychologists and the criminal justice system is a field study conducted in the Asylum Hill section of Hartford, Connecticut, a poor area with a high crime rate. As part of the study, three key changes were introduced in Asylum Hill (Fowler, 1981). First, a police team was assigned permanently to the area. This change permitted the police to develop close social ties with area residents and enabled them to become more familiar with the specific crime problems in the area.

A second major change concerned auto and pedestrian traffic patterns. To emphasize the residential nature of the area and to provide the residents a greater sense of control over their neighborhood, some streets were closed to vehicular traffic altogether, and others were made one-way. Finally, neighborhood organizations were formed to provide citizen input into plans to reduce crime. Through these organizations, the residents' sense of control was further enhanced, making those who lived in the area feel more responsible for what happened there.

The program was a success. Burglary rates in Asylum Hill fell significantly, compared with other parts of the city. Other street crimes also dropped, although to a lesser degree. The psychological consequences were beneficial as well: Residents were less likely to express fears that they would be victims of burglary and to identify burglary as a significant neighborhood problem.

FIGURE 13–3   Stacking the Deck After viewing an accident involving two cars, participants were asked to estimate the speed of the collision. Estimates varied substantially depending on the way the question was worded. (*Source:* Loftus & Palmer, 1974.)

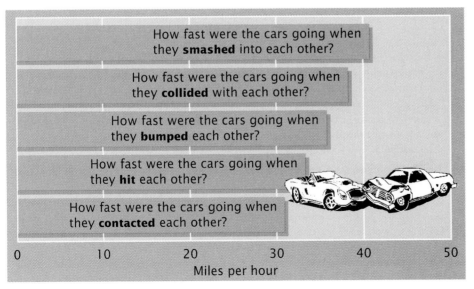

The results of the Asylum Hill program are consistent with other research that shows that making people feel responsible for crime prevention can help reduce criminal activity (Austin, 1979; Klentz & Beaman, 1981). For instance, making people feel that they are personally responsible for helping to stop crime increases their sense of involvement in the situation. It also increases the likelihood that they will actively intercede in situations in which intervention is desirable.

Similarly, Neighborhood Watch programs, in which residents of an area collectively pledge to keep an eye out for possible criminal activity, also help increase the responsibility felt by individuals living in such a neighborhood. Simply erecting signs saying that Neighborhood Watch programs are in effect fulfills two specific goals. First, it provides a warning to potential criminals that the neighborhood is particularly vigilant. Second, it reminds residents of their personal responsibility in fighting neighborhood crime.

Excuses: Justifying criminal activity. "I didn't do it" is often the first excuse offered by people—adults and children—who have been caught performing illicit activities. But it's not the last. Once it becomes clear that a person has in fact committed an offense, the person can offer a variety of excuses. Typically, people use one of five justifications to explain behavior that violates society's standards of conduct. Gresham Sykes and David Matza (1957) describe these justifications collectively as **techniques of neutralization**: (1) denying responsibility, (2) denying harm and injury, (3) blaming the victim, (4) denouncing authorities, and (5) invoking higher principles or authority.

- *Denying responsibility.* Although people may admit to an act, they refuse to accept responsibility for it. They typically deflect blame from themselves to the ills of society—living in a bad neighborhood, poverty, or poor schooling—as well as to being enticed into an illegal act by others. Basically, people using this technique refuse to acknowledge that they are personally responsible. By shifting the responsibility to some external agent, perpetrators feel they deserve no punishment (Tomita, 1990).

- *Denying harm and injury.* Rather than accepting the reports of authorities that they did real damage, perpetrators may try to translate their actions into something more benign (Strutton, Vitell, & Pelton, 1994). Take, for example, a college student who helps knock down the goal posts following a football game. To the university, the student is guilty of damaging expensive university property. To the student, the behavior represents minor mischief, hardly worthy of note (Tomita, 1990).

- *Blaming the victim.* One excuse used by perpetrators of criminal acts is that the victim deserved whatever befell him or her. For instance, rapists may justify their acts by saying that the rape was the fault of the victim—a phenomenon known as **victimization** (Cowan & Curtis, 1994). For instance, a victim may be said to have dressed in such a provocative manner that she was "asking for it."

  In extreme cases, blaming the victim translates into *dehumanization,* a phenomenon in which the victim is perceived as lacking human characteristics and consequently as being unworthy of equitable and considerate treatment. Dehumanization was frequently used by Nazi war criminals who participated in the Holocaust, in which Jews and members of other religious, racial, and ethnic groups were targeted for systematic extermination. The excuse was that because members of these groups were somehow less than human, they did not deserve humane treatment.

- *Denouncing authorities.* Another neutralization strategy used by people who have committed criminal acts is to condemn social institutions or authority figures (Strutton, Vitell, & Pelton, 1994). Saying that the political system is corrupt permits a low-salaried government worker to feel justified in embezzling government money, and it allowed people like Timothy McVeigh, convicted of the Oklahoma City bombing, to justify the killing of innocent individuals. Similarly, if you feel that the police and judicial system are unfair, committing criminal acts may be easier for you because you may feel that no matter what you do, you cannot do anything worse than what they do. In essence, the argument is that two wrongs make a right (Mitchell & Dodder, 1983).

techniques of neutralization: Justifications used to explain behavior that violates society's standards of conduct.

victimization: A justification used by perpetrators of violent actions to claim that the act was the fault of the victim.

Timothy McVeigh, convicted of the Oklahoma City bombing of this federal building, justified his actions as a way of denouncing authority. His behavior was a response to the FBI's aggressive tactics at the Branch Davidian's complex in Waco, Texas.

Condemnation of authorities is a manifestation of the norm of reciprocity, which we first spoke about in Chapter 8. As you may recall, the norm of reciprocity suggests that we should treat others as they have treated us. Criminals may justify their acts because others have treated them in ways that they deem illegal.

◆ *Invoking higher principles or authority.* Some people who act illegally justify their actions because they consider the goal they seek to achieve as more important than the laws they are breaking. Excuses of this type are often given by people who hold illegal demonstrations, for example, or by antiabortion activists who have murdered people who carry out abortions. Likewise, members of the Mafia may refuse to testify against a fellow Mafioso, even at great personal cost. Their refusal is based on the concept of *omerta,* or code of silence, that they pledge to honor when they become members. The maintenance of *omerta* is seen as representing a higher-order authority than the more conventional control of the legal system (Mitchell & Dodder, 1983).

The benefits of neutralization.   These five techniques of neutralization provide a measure of both psychological and legal relief to perpetrators of crimes (Dabney, 1995). By shifting responsibility from themselves, perpetrators can maintain a relatively positive self-image and even cast themselves in the role of the victim. In extreme cases, criminal perpetrators can end up feeling that they are worse off than their alleged victims.

Of course, such attributions make later rehabilitation of criminals a difficult task. If people feel no responsibility for their actions, it is unlikely that they will be receptive to attempts to get them to change their antisocial behavior.

The legal system is something of a coconspirator in the maintenance of harmful, maladaptive attributions of responsibility. For instance, criminal perpetrators may be found innocent if they can prove in court that they were the targets of entrapment. **Entrapment** occurs when a person is lured by a law enforcement agent into committing a crime. However, entrapment ultimately may legitimatize the notion that people are not actually responsible for their criminal activities by arguing that they were enticed into them.

entrapment: A situation in which a person is lured by a law enforcement agent into committing a crime.

MAKING CRIMINAL TRIALS FAIRER

We've seen the biases that tend to color the fair and equitable administration of justice. Based on this work, social psychologists have made several suggestions to improve the quality of justice that is meted out at trials. Among them are the following suggestions by social psychologist Lawrence Wrightsman (1987):

◆ Increase the representativeness of people on juries by ensuring that all citizens have an equal chance to be on a jury and by keeping to an absolute minimum the number of exemptions from jury duty.

◆ Decrease the opportunity for defense attorneys and prosecutors to remove particular potential jurors prior to a trial. Preventing "scientific" selection of juries by either side in a criminal case would reduce potential bias in the outcome.

◆ Videotape trial presentations and edit out unwanted material. Such a procedure would address the difficulty of jurors' not being able to forget inadmissible testimony, even when instructed to do so.

◆ Instruct jurors in simple, clear, and direct language, avoiding legal jargon. For example, employing specific probabilities or percentages about guilt and innocence may make it easier for jurors to understand the concept of "reasonable doubt" (Elwork, Sales, & Alfini, 1982; Kagehiro, 1990; Frank & Applegate, 1998).

◆ Allow jurors access to a videotape of the trial while they deliberate.

REVIEW AND RETHINK

Review

• Although the evidence is weak that juror demographic factors are related to conviction rates, efforts have been made to select conviction- or acquittal-prone juries systematically.

• Eyewitness recollections of criminal activities and perpetrators are often faulty and unreliable.

• Among the most promising strategies for reducing crime are efforts to increase the sense of responsibility for crime prevention felt by residents in neighborhoods.

• Criminals employ five main types of justifications for their conduct, called techniques of neutralization.

Rethink

• What sorts of interviewer questions and nonverbal communications might have induced the children who testified against Peggy and Ray Buckey to believe that they recalled abusive actions committed when they were in preschool?

• Identification of members of different racial groups is more likely to be erroneous than identification of members of one's own racial group. What person perception phenomenon may underlie this bias?

• What techniques can the police use to instill in community members a sense of personal responsibility for crime prevention?

• Discuss the five techniques of neutralization in the context of how (a) convicted rapists and (b) income tax evaders might maintain their moral innocence.

POLITICS, LEADERSHIP, AND POWER

He found it a curious phenomenon. When social psychologist Theodore Newcomb first came to teach at Bennington College, a small, elite institution for women, he was struck by the difference in political views between the first-year students and those in the senior class. The entering students tended to be politically and socially conservative, similar to their wealthy, upper-class, and largely conservative parents. In contrast, the seniors were quite liberal, far more similar to the largely liberal faculty at the school than their parents. What was the reason?

In a classic study, Newcomb concluded that the students' *reference group,* the group to which people compare themselves in terms of important attitudes, opinions, and values, shifted during the course of 4 years of college. Initially, the reference group had been their parents and their parents' friends, but by the time they finished college, it had changed to their professors and fellow students (Newcomb et al., 1967; Alwin, Cohen, & Newcomb, 1991).

Clearly, our political views are shaped to a large extent by such social psychological forces. We turn now to some of the major political factors identified by social psychologists working in the area of **political psychology**, the branch of psychology that examines the psychological aspects of political behavior.

POLITICAL SOCIALIZATION: THE ROOTS OF POLITICAL BELIEF

You probably know who your parents voted for in the last presidential election, as well as whether they are Democrats, Republicans, or independents. Your familiarity with their political views is no accident: Many of our own political beliefs stem from them.

Political socialization, the process by which people develop political attitudes, values, and voting habits, begins when most of us are very young and often has a lasting influence on us. Parents play a particularly important role. One reason is that most children spend more time with their parents than anyone else when they are young, and this exposure has a cumulative effect. Even when people are too young to understand the complexities of politics, they are able to absorb such concrete labels as political affiliation or to remember whom their parents supported.

Not surprisingly, then, people tend to agree with the political views of their parents, unless they are exposed to strong, contrasting views over a long period. This was the situation with the Bennington College students. In the majority of cases, however, most people vote for the same candidate in presidential elections as their parents and have the same party affiliation.

Children do not always grow up mirroring their parents' views, however. In some cases, their mothers and fathers frequently disagree between themselves. It is hardly surprising that a child who is exposed to divergent sets of parental views adopts more mixed views than a child in a household in which mothers and fathers share the same views. Furthermore, households in which the parents show relatively little interest in politics are less likely to have children who share the parents' political affiliation than parents who hold firmer beliefs (Jennings & Niemi, 1974; Dalton, 1980; Barner-Barry & Rosenwein, 1985; Berman, 1997).

In short, parents play a crucial role in producing political socialization. Of course, other factors play a part. For instance, the media are an important influence, particularly in the light of the many hours that the average American household spends watching television.

LEADERSHIP

Julius Caesar, Catherine the Great, Mahatma Gandhi, Martin Luther King, Jr., Simon Bolivar, Elizabeth Cady Stanton, Bill Clinton. All very different people, with distinct skills and personalities. Yet all fall into the same category: leader. Each of these individuals inspired and influenced millions of people, inducing others to accept them as legitimate authority figures, rulers, and advocates for their own interests. All of these leaders inspired others to place their trust in them.

political psychology: The branch of psychology that examines the psychological aspects of political behavior.

political socialization: The process by which people develop political attitudes, values, and voting habits, which begins when most of us are very young and often has a lasting influence on us.

great person theory of leadership: The theory that certain people are born to lead.

transformational leaders: Leaders who spur their followers into behavior that surpasses their personal interests.

What factors led people to perceive these individuals as leaders, capable of influencing and regulating the behavior of others? Are some people "born" leaders with special characteristics that would make them influential under any circumstances? Conversely, is there something about a historical situation or set of circumstances that propels a person toward leadership, relatively independent of the characteristics of that person? Or, does the truth lie somewhere in between? These questions, raised by philosophers, historians, and political scientists, have also been addressed by social psychologists (Bass, 1990). We will examine some of the answers they have found.

Great person approaches to leadership: Leaders are born, not made.   "The history of the world is the history of great men." When the well-known historian Thomas Carlyle wrote these words, he was endorsing an approach to leadership that has come to be called the great person theory. (He was also promoting a somewhat restrictive view of history, given that, at least in recent times, great women as well as great men have risen to positions of leadership.)

According to the **great person theory of leadership**, certain people are born to lead (Bass, 1981). The theory proposes that some features of an individual's personality or character—in other words, certain traits of greatness—lead that individual to rise naturally to a position of leadership.

The great person theory attracted several generations of theoreticians, for on the surface it seems quite reasonable. It certainly is plausible that great leaders such as Martin Luther King, Jr., and George Washington embodied specific characteristics that set them apart from most other people. Similarly, even leaders of local organizations, such as college club presidents and town mayors, appear to have traits that thrust them into leadership roles.

However, despite the commonsense appeal of the theory, the evidence in support of the great person approach has been minimal at best (Hollander, 1985; Dubinsky, Yammarino, & Jolson, 1995; Carless, 1998), and sheds little light on leadership (Hollander, 1985). For instance, some evidence suggests that the typical leader is slightly more intelligent than average. Furthermore, leaders tend to be more extroverted and dominant, slightly better adjusted, more self-confident, possessed of a higher need for power, and taller and heavier than nonleaders (Hollander, 1985; Winter, 1987; Smith & Forti, 1998). (Consider this bit of trivia: Since 1900, in every presidential election except for two, the taller of the two major candidates won. Perhaps Bill Clinton's height advantage over Bob Dole was one factor in Clinton's success in the 1996 presidential election.)

Unfortunately, although some traits appear to be associated with leadership, the relationships are not very strong and do not offer much insight into the causes of leadership. For one thing, they focus on the differences between leaders and followers and do not consider the degree of success ultimately achieved by the leader. Because people who become leaders are not always successful (consider the domestic failings of the Nixon presidency, for example), great person theories need to take account of the distinction between effective and ineffective leaders.

Furthermore, finding that leaders hold particular traits raises a chicken-and-egg question of whether the trait existed prior to the acquisition of leadership or developed as a result of the individual's being thrust into a leadership position. Consider this question: Does the trait of self-confidence lead someone to emerge as a leader, or does self-confidence arise because a person assumes the role of leader? Those who have been elected president of the United States, for instance, find themselves in a world apart from everyday life, with a large, supportive, agreeable, and sometimes subservient staff. Who wouldn't feel more self-confident under these circumstances?

Despite the difficulties with the great person theory, recent evidence suggests that some especially inspiring leaders have characteristics that differentiate them from nonleaders. In particular, Bernard Bass (1985, 1990, 1997) suggests that distinguished, outstanding individuals such as Nelson Mandela and John Kennedy are **transformational leaders**, who spur their followers into behavior that surpasses their own personal interests. Followers of transformational leaders are driven less by the promise of individual gain than by the vision of a

Although the "great person theory" has not been supported, a leader of the magnitude of South Africa's Nelson Mandela has characteristics that spur his followers to behavior that surpasses their own personal interests.

greater good for a greater number of people. Transformational leaders are able to motivate others by inspiring them with a vision for a better future and by prompting them to look beyond their immediate interests. Such leaders have *charisma,* a personal magnetism that produces trust and respect. In addition, they are inspiring and intellectually stimulating. Finally, they have the ability to consider others as individuals, making them feel that the leader has a personal stake in their welfare (Ross & Offerman, 1997; Avolio & Bass, 1998; Yukl, 1999).

Some experts in political psychology have suggested taking another route in the search for the critical characteristics of leadership. Presidential scholar James David Barber (1985, 1992) suggests that the most fruitful approach to understanding leadership, at least on the level of the U.S. presidency, is to examine two primary dimensions: vigor and emotion. By classifying presidential vigor on a passive–active dimension and presidential emotion on a positive–negative dimension, Barber has deciphered and often predicted presidential success.

More specifically, Barber argues that the vigor dimension relates to the degree to which a president either takes a dynamic, energetic role in promoting particular policies (an active president) or is more reactive to others' proposals (a passive president). The emotion dimension relates to a president's prevalent emotional state. For instance, some presidents are relatively positive, enjoying the political arena, whereas others are more negative, behaving out of duty and not appearing to enjoy the political fray.

Because the two dimensions are independent of each other, one can classify U.S. presidents into one of the four combinations shown in Table 13–1. Based on their life histories and experiences, most presidents fall rather neatly into one of the four categories.

For instance, presidents Nixon and Johnson exemplify the active–negative category: hard-driving and energetic, yet at the same time focused on their own personal obsessions and negativity. The active–negative category is thought to produce the most perilous presidencies. The individuals in this category tend to be perfectionists, introspective, and rigid. When they are threatened, their predominant reaction is to lash out at enemies, and they find compromise difficult.

TABLE 13-1	Presidential Personality	
	POSITIVE	**NEGATIVE**
Active	Franklin D. Roosevelt	Woodrow Wilson
	Harry S. Truman	Lyndon Johnson
	John F. Kennedy	Richard M. Nixon
	George Bush	
	Bill Clinton	
Passive	Warren Harding	Calvin Coolidge
	Ronald Reagan	Dwight D. Eisenhower

Source: Barber, 1985, 1992.

In contrast, passive–positive presidents enjoy the affection that the presidency brings to them. However, they are fixed more on themselves than on others, leading them to a passivity in their political behavior. Such presidents, exemplified by Harding and Reagan, are rather easily manipulated by others.

Presidents such as Coolidge and Eisenhower, who typify the passive–negative category, see themselves as disinterested in politics. They feel compelled to enter politics because of their noble, high-minded principles, but they do not enjoy it much. Regarding themselves as above the fray of political life, they don't introduce many new policy initiatives.

Finally, we come to the active–positive category. Exemplified by Truman and Kennedy, the presidents in this category find politics great fun. They enjoy the give-and-take of political action, and they are able to make things happen. Their presidencies are often considered to be particularly effective. However, this is not always true: The dynamism and positive outlook of active–positive presidents may lead them to take unusual risks.

Despite the identification of the transformational leadership pattern and the utility of classifying U.S. presidents along certain dimensions, the great person theory remains largely in disrepute. The central hypothesis of the great person theory—that certain characteristics or personality traits boost persons into positions of leadership—has not been supported. Without considering the specifics of a particular situation, identifying any single trait or set of traits that differentiates leaders from followers has proved difficult. Similarly, no evidence suggests that certain traits differentiate effective leaders from ineffective ones. We need, then, to turn to the characteristics of particular situations to understand the emergence of leadership.

Situational approaches to leadership: Under the right circumstances, anyone can be president. One of the enduring cultural beliefs in the United States is that anyone, regardless of background, can grow up to become president of the country. It is a belief supported by the rise to power of such presidents as Jimmy Carter, Ronald Reagan, and Bill Clinton, all of whose origins were, in fact, truly humble.

The rise to power of such individuals suggests that almost anyone can rise to leadership, independent of personal characteristics, if the situation calls for leadership. For example, Harry Truman was thrust unexpectedly into the U.S. presidency when Franklin Roosevelt died in 1945. Truman became a decisive and, some say, great president. Similarly, Dwight Eisenhower was elected president largely because of his World War II record and not because of inherent leadership skills.

According to the **situational approach to leadership**, people become leaders in response to the characteristics of the situation in which they find themselves. In this view, leaders, in general, do not share any particular personality traits. For instance, the mayor of Peoria, Illinois, the head of the National Rifle Association, and the president of the League of Women Voters would not be assumed to have similar personality traits and characteristics. Instead, the situation requires certain skills in a leader (Wofford, 1994; Vecchio, 1997).

The situational approach, then, suggests that a particular person can be a leader in one setting and not another, because the characteristics of the situation, and not the qualities of

situational approach to leadership:
The theory that people become leaders in response to the characteristics of the situation in which they find themselves.

the person, determine who becomes a leader. In its most extreme form, the situation hypothesis suggests that anyone can become a leader, providing she or he finds the appropriate situation in which to lead.

Despite the romantic appeal of the view that any of us—no matter what our abilities and personality—can rise to a leadership position if the situation is of a certain sort, the research conducted to examine the situational approach has not been supportive. Although studies on leadership in groups have found that certain situations are more likely to produce particular leadership requirements, researchers have been unable to demonstrate that a situation, by itself, determines who becomes a leader (Vroom, 1997; Konst, Vonk, & van der Vlist, 1999).

However, there is a kernel of truth in the situational approach to leadership: Particular kinds of circumstances seem to thrust individuals into leadership positions. For example, a group structure that presents the opportunity to communicate with others increases the likelihood that the person who is an effective communicator will become the group's leader (Guetzkow, 1968; McGill & Slocum, 1998). Specifically, the greater the ability of a person to communicate with others in a group or organization, the more likely it is that that person will become the leader of the group. Still, reliance on the situational approach to leadership has its drawbacks. Most glaringly, little research supports the theory that people ignore personality traits and abilities in determining who becomes and remains a leader.

More fundamentally, the basic premise of the situational approach can be questioned. It seems unlikely, for instance, that anyone can become president of the United States, no matter how favorable the situation is for his or her rise to power. Furthermore, the situational approach ignores the possibility that leaders may modify their behavior to fit a particular situation, or alter the situation to fit their behavior. Because of such objections to the situational model, social psychologists have turned to a consideration of theories of leadership that take both the situation and the leader's characteristics into account—interactional approaches to leadership.

Interactional approaches to leadership: Person + situation = leadership.   According to the interactional approach to leadership, Bill Clinton's victory in the 1996 U.S. presidential race was no accident. Instead, his particular personality traits meshed more closely with voters' perceptions of what the country required than those of the other candidates. Clinton's reelection, then, was the result of a unique combination of his personality and situational requirements.

According to **interactional approaches to leadership**, different situations call for particular kinds of leaders. This view holds that in certain types of situations one kind of leader will be likely to emerge and be most effective, whereas in other circumstances another kind of leader will emerge and be more effective (Chemers, 1997; Vecchio, 1997; Hughes, Ginnett, & Curphy, 1998).

The most influential interactional approach to leadership is social psychologist Fred Fiedler's contingency model (Fiedler & Garcia, 1987; Ayman, Chemers, & Fiedler, 1995, 1997). According to the **contingency model**, leader effectiveness is based on several key situational factors and leaders' particular traits. The model, which has spawned hundreds of studies, is generally quite effective in identifying the particular type of leader that is appropriate for certain situations.

Fiedler argues that three key situational factors are critical. The first situational factor is the *relationship between the leader and group members,* which can range from positive to negative. The second situational characteristic is the *degree of structure* in the task the group is attempting to accomplish; tasks can be clear and unambiguous (high structured), or they can be vague and ambiguous (low structured). The third characteristic in Fiedler's model is the *power* the leader holds over the other group members, which consists of the amount of rewards (and punishments) that the leader is able to control.

By considering jointly these three factors, we can assess the overall favorability of a situation for a leader. In the most favorable situation, the relationship between leader and followers is positive, the task is highly structured, and the leader's power is strong. In contrast,

interactional approaches to leadership: The theory that different situations call for particular kinds of leaders.

contingency model: The model that states that leader effectiveness is based on several key situational factors and leaders' particular traits.

situations most unfavorable to a leader are those in which relations between leader and followers are poor, the task is unstructured, and the leader's power is weak.

However, Fiedler argues that it is not enough to take only situational factors into account; we also need to look at personality characteristics of the leader. Depending on their personality, some leaders are going to be more effective in certain situations than others. To Fiedler, the key personality factor is the motivational style of the leader, which refers to whether the leader is motivated primarily toward accomplishing the group's task or toward maintaining positive group relationships. Hence, leaders tend to be either *task-oriented*—in which the completion of the task is of greatest importance—or *relationship-oriented*—in which the personal relations of the members are weighted more heavily.

The contingency model suggests that task-oriented leaders are most effective in situations that are highly favorable or highly unfavorable for the leader. In highly favorable situations, the group is already task-oriented and ready to be led. In highly unfavorable conditions, task-oriented leaders, who are assertive and directive, can take a more active role, prodding followers. In contrast, relationship-oriented leaders don't do as well under conditions that are highly favorable or unfavorable. In highly favorable conditions, they tend to insert themselves unnecessarily into the situation, when their input really is not necessary. And in highly unfavorable situations, their focus on relationships prevents them from exerting strong leadership and structuring the situation to permit the accomplishment of their goals.

It is in moderately favorable situations that relationship-oriented leaders shine. In such cases, their emphasis on relationships allows them to motivate their followers, and their sensitivity to the needs of group members increases the chances of success.

To what extent has research supported these predictions about which leaders will excel under specific conditions? The answer seems to depend on whether the research was conducted inside or outside the laboratory. Studies conducted in the laboratory show quite consistently that the contingency model predicts leader effectiveness (Peters, Hartke, & Pohlmann, 1985; Fiedler & Garcia, 1987; Hughes, Ginnett, & Curphy, 1998).

Outside the laboratory, however, the picture is more mixed. Some field studies have shown that leadership follows the patterns suggested by the theory. In fact, studies in which leaders are taught techniques for modifying situations to optimize the match with their personality have had impressive results. In one field experiment, for instance, West Point platoon leaders were tutored in the basics of the contingency model and were taught how to alter situations so that an optimal match could exist between their leadership style and the group. The training obviously paid off: The platoon leaders who received instruction in the contingency model were more apt to be ranked first or second in their company than those who had not received training (Csoka & Bons, 1978).

At the same time, however, some field studies have produced results contrary to the predictions of the contingency model, suggesting that the theory is not the last word on leadership. Still, the contingency model of leader effectiveness remains the best articulated, most comprehensive, and best supported of any interactional model of leadership (Schriesheim, Tepper, & Tetrault, 1994; Ayman, Chemers, & Fiedler, 1997).

GENDER AND CULTURAL PATTERNS IN LEADERSHIP

Do males and females lead in similar ways? Are leadership patterns the same in other cultures? To answer these questions, we turn now to a consideration of gender and cultural factors in leadership.

Gender and leadership.   Until the 20th century, the history of world leaders has been almost exclusively the history of male leaders. Even recently, despite some notable exceptions, such as former prime ministers Golda Meir of Israel and Margaret Thatcher of Great Britain, political leaders have typically been men.

The relative lack of women in leadership roles has led some people to presume that certain crucial differences may exist between men and women in terms of leadership styles or capabilities—differences that may prevent women from rising to leadership positions. Others suggest, however, that the relative rarity of female leaders is due primarily to social stereotypes that prevent women from rising to positions of leadership, and that the actual leadership behavior displayed by men and women differs very little. They point to the large increase in the number of women elected to the U.S. Congress in the past few years and to the fact that the number of women in corporate leadership positions continues to rise.

Studies of female leaders, such as former Israeli Prime Minister Golda Meir, find that while men and women have different styles of status and leadership behavior, they tend to be equally effective.

To consider this question, social psychologists Alice Eagly and Blair Johnson carefully reviewed the results of more than 150 separate studies of leadership (Eagly & Johnson, 1990). They found that female and male leaders adopt similar approaches to performing tasks and maintaining interpersonal relationships. They also found a difference in leadership style in work and organizational settings: Female leaders favor a more democratic, participative style, whereas males display a more autocratic, directive style (Brewer, Socha, & Potter, 1996). One possible explanation is that women, who tend to display higher interpersonal skills than men, find it easier than men to work within a democratic framework, which requires a good deal of give-and-take. Men, in contrast, may feel more comfortable leading in a more directive manner, in which it is less necessary to deal with the politics of participative decision making.

The studies also revealed that women who adopt a leadership style more consistent with typical male leadership behavior are often viewed negatively. For instance, female leaders who use the autocratic leadership style typical of males are likely to be underestimated and even belittled. Men, in particular, seem to find a woman in an authority position threatening. For example, when men encounter a woman who has authority over men of the same age and social class as herself, the typical reaction is to downgrade their view of her subordinates ("What kind of man would work for a woman?") rather than to elevate her status ("Isn't it great that she has achieved such a good position?") (Jacobson et al., 1977; Wiley & Eskilson, 1982; Brinkerhoff & Booth, 1984).

Similarly, women who hold leadership positions that are viewed as stereotypically masculine—such as business manager—are stigmatized. When a woman assumes a position that society traditionally views as rightfully male, the view of the woman's femininity may suffer (Eagly, Makhijani, & Klonsky, 1992).

The nonverbal behavior of men and women also relates to perceptions of differential status and accomplishment. For instance, a striking degree of similarity exists between the nonverbal behavior of women and that of low-status men in experiments examining leadership and status. In such research, women often show tense posture, smile relatively often, and avert their eyes and watch others. Surprisingly, low-status men exhibit quite similar behaviors (see Table 13–2). Research examining other types of nonverbal behavior, including eye contact and other signs of visual dominance, supports the notion that women's nonverbal behavior is similar to that of men in low-status, as compared to high-status, positions (Lott, 1987; Dovidio et al., 1988).

Clearly, women and men may have different styles of status and leadership behavior (Druskat, 1994). However, the more important issue may be *effectiveness*. Are there gender differences in leadership effectiveness?

TABLE 13–2	**Powerful Gestures: Examples of Nonverbal Behaviors Related to Power**			
	BETWEEN STATUS NONEQUALS		**BETWEEN MEN AND WOMEN**	
Nonverbal Behavior	**Used by Superior**	**Used by Subordinate**	**Used by Men**	**Used by Women**
Demeanor	Informal	Circumspect	Informal	Circumspect
Posture	Relaxed	Tense	Relaxed	Tense
Personal space	Closeness (option)	Distance	Closeness	Distance
Touching	Touch (option)	Don't touch	Touch	Don't touch
Eye contact	Stare, ignore	Avert eyes, watch	Stare, ignore	Avert eyes, watch
Facial expression	Don't smile	Smile	Don't smile	Smile
Emotional expression	Hide	Show	Hide	Show
Self-disclosure	Don't disclose	Disclose	Don't disclose	Disclose

Source: Adapted from Henley, 1977.

According to Alice Eagly and colleagues, the answer is a qualified no. In an analysis of more than 100 studies of leadership effectiveness, they found that, overall, male and female leaders were equally effective. However, men and women do not do equally well in every situation. Men are more effective in roles seen as traditionally masculine, and women are more effective in roles defined in traditionally feminine terms (Eagly, Karau, & Makhijani, 1995).

Specifically, women were more effective than men in positions requiring considerable interpersonal abilities, such as cooperativeness and getting along with others. In contrast, men were more effective on tasks requiring strong abilities in directing and controlling people. Furthermore, men were more effective in situations in which men held the majority of both leadership and subordinate positions.

In short, the issue of gender differences in leadership is subtle and complex. Although male and female leaders differ in their use of authoritative versus democratic leadership styles, they differ little—if at all—in terms of overall effectiveness. At the same time, women who rise to high-status positions are sometimes devalued by others. Also, the impression that others draw of women in leadership roles may be negative, particularly if these women behave the same way as men in high-status positions.

Given the obstacles that society puts in place for women in high-status, leadership positions, it is not surprising that the number of women leaders is proportionately small. In fact, some 95% of the top positions in the largest corporations in the United States are held by white males. If societal stereotypes hold that males are more appropriate leaders than females, an invisible barrier, sometimes called the "glass ceiling," may continue to prevent the rise of women to high leadership positions (U.S. Department of Labor, 1995).

Culture and leadership.   When we consider leadership in different cultures, we find that several of the factors that theories of leadership in Western cultures have identified as important are not (Maczynski et al., 1994). For example, Fiedler's contingency model is not fully supported by the results of experiments conducted in some other cultures. Specifically, research shows that the ablest leaders in bank organizations in the Philippines are more task-oriented, whereas those in Hong Kong are more relationship-oriented (Bennett, 1977). Although the most obvious explanation is that situational contingencies operate differently in the two cultures (Tannenbaum, 1980), nobody has explained just what those particular contingencies are.

One promising approach to understanding differences in leadership styles comes from work comparing cultures that favor collectivism with cultures that are more individualistic. As we discussed in Chapter 12, cultures reflecting collectivism place greater emphasis on the group's well-being than on that of the individual (Misumi, 1995). In contrast, societies reflecting individualism emphasize personal identity, uniqueness, and individual freedom. In individualistic societies, the emphasis is on accomplishment of one's own goals (Hui, 1988).

Cross-cultural research on leadership suggests that the meanings that followers attribute to the tasks that leaders carry out are relatively different in collectivistic than in individualistic societies. For instance, psychologist Peter Smith and colleagues compared perceptions of leaders in two collectivistic cultures (Hong Kong and Japan) with perceptions in two individualistic societies (the United States and Great Britain). They found that leaders in the collectivistic cultures were perceived as carrying out a broader range of behaviors and appeared to be less specialized in their tasks. In contrast, leaders in the individualistic cultures were more apt to be perceived as specializing in activities primarily oriented either to completing the task or to maintaining good social relations within the group (Smith et al., 1990).

Other research shows that leaders in organizational settings have different preferences regarding the behavior of subordinates. For instance, organizational leaders in highly developed Western countries, such as the United States and Great Britain, prefer subordinates to be relatively more active and involved. In comparison, managers in less developed countries, such as Greece and India, favor more passive subordinates (Barrett & Bass, 1970; Tannenbaum, 1980; Gibson & Marcoulides, 1995).

CHOOSING A LEADER:
THE POLITICS OF VOTER CHOICE

Backers of Dwight D. Eisenhower were right on target when they printed the slogan "I like Ike" on millions of buttons and bumper stickers. Although they may not have known it at the time, the most important dimension in choosing a leader is often the candidate's likability. In fact, even party affiliation is less critical than how much a voter likes and feels comfortable with a candidate. In most instances, people vote for the person with whom they feel most comfortable (Markus, 1982; Kinder & Sears, 1985; Lanoue & Bowler, 1998).

For political figures, the quality of likability is actually grounded in two kinds of information: the traits candidates are seen to hold, and the emotions candidates demonstrate. In terms of traits, competence and integrity are the most important components of liking. For instance, the fact that Eisenhower played a pivotal role in winning World War II was seen by many as an illustration of his competence, making him a popular candidate.

The emotions that politicians project also affect voter preferences. Candidates attempt to produce positive emotions and simultaneously to avoid behavior that might kindle negative emotions. For instance, one of Ronald Reagan's strengths as president was his ability to communicate a "good news" message to voters, as illustrated by an effective advertising campaign during his successful quest for reelection, stressing that it was "morning in America." In contrast, when Jimmy Carter (Reagan's opponent in 1980) talked about a "malaise" affecting the country, his popularity plummeted (Pentony, 1998; Morris, Roberts, & Baker, 1999).

The importance of voter emotions is illustrated by research examining the degree of optimism displayed by candidates. Because an optimistic speech presumably produces positive emotions, we might expect that politicians who behave optimistically would gain the most voter support. In fact, this appears to be true. An analysis of the degree of optimism expressed in presidential candidates' speeches delivered during their nominating conventions shows a clear distinction between winners and losers: Between 1948 and 1984, the more optimistic candidate went on to win in every election except one (Zullow & Seligman, 1990).

THE NATURE OF POWER

◆ A senate staff member laughs uproariously at his boss's joke, despite its lack of humor.

◆ A driver of a powerful Porsche stays within the speed limit to avoid getting a ticket.

◆ A teenager buys Calvin Klein underwear after seeing an ad in which Antonio Sabato Jr. models them.

◆ An incumbent politician loses a bitter election and then dutifully agrees to cooperate with the winner's transition team.

◆ Despite your reservations, you follow the advice of your physician and go on a salt-free diet and begin a vigorous exercise regime to lower your blood pressure.

◆ The president's chief of staff is invited to lunch by a reporter and is pumped for information.

The common thread in all of these situations? Each represents an example of social power. **Social power** consists of one person's ability to control and shape the behavior of others. Although power is most obvious in the political realm, the concept is useful in understanding behavior in a number of situations. In fact, social psychologists have identified six forms of power, corresponding to each of the above examples (French & Raven, 1959; Raven, 1988, 1992, 1993):

Reward power.   One form of power that enables people to influence others is the ability to provide rewards when others comply with their wishes. Employers can give raises, parents can hand out candy bars, teachers can give good grades to those who conform to their standards and directions. Of course, such power is highly situation specific. For example, although a Senate staffer may laugh uproariously at a senator's joke, the senator's constituents may not feel compelled to do so—they have the (reward) power to reelect the senator (Jurma & Wright, 1990; Henry, Peterson, & Wilson, 1997).

Coercive power.   Coercive power refers to a person's ability to deliver punishments. As such, it can be considered the opposite side of the coin from reward power. Coercive power can be an effective technique, as those of us know who carefully monitor our driving speed in order to avoid a ticket. However, coercive control has its drawbacks (Sulzer-Azaroff & Mayer, 1991; Verhoek-Miller & Miller, 1997). For instance, the use of coercive power can lead to reactance if people feel their personal freedom is being restricted. People seem to realize the downside of coercive power, and most of us prefer to use reward power instead, if the choice is available (Molm, 1988, 1997).

Referent power.   For people who find golf pro Tiger Woods engaging and attractive and wish to be like him, he is high in referent power. Referent power is held by those we respect, find attractive, and wish to emulate. Such people act as models whom we want to emulate. To be like them, we mimic their behavior, appearance, dress, language, or mannerisms, hoping that we will take on their characteristics. The source of referent power, then, lies in a powerful person's ability to motivate others to act like him or her. A parent who tries to get a younger child to follow the example of her older sibling, or leaders who act courageously in order to get their followers to make their own sacrifices, are using referent power (Gold & Raven, 1992; Salem, Grant, & Campbell, 1998).

Legitimate power.   One kind of power, called legitimate power, arises from the formal position or role a person occupies. Legitimate power is often couched in terms of "should's" and "ought's." For example, parents tell their children to obey not because of logical arguments but because children are "supposed" to listen to their parents.

One of the unique characteristics of legitimate power is that its holders do not have to rely on rational arguments to convince others of their right to exercise it. Instead, the power flows inherently from the individual's position or role. For example, when a professor announces a long, involved, and difficult assignment, the class dutifully complies, with little

social power: One person's ability to control and shape the behavior of others.

or no argument. Moreover, the specific individual holding legitimate power is less crucial than in the other kinds of power. Presidents of the United States come and go, but the legitimate power of the presidency remains high and relatively independent of who is in office at a given time (Yukl & Falbe, 1991).

Expert power.   The dictum "knowledge is power" refers to the influence that experts exert over our lives. Expert power derives from a power holder's superior knowledge and abilities. For instance, physicians have the ability to effect radical changes in our lifestyles with their advice. In fact, even when physicians make recommendations that raise misgivings, we are likely to defer to their greater knowledge.

Expert power is specific to a person's special area of expertise. Consequently, no matter how willing we are to comply with our physician's medical advice, we would be considerably less willing to comply with that same person's advice on automobile repair (Harrow & Loewenthal, 1992).

Informational power.   The most transitory type of power is informational power. Informational power is power related to the specific content of a person's knowledge. People who hold valuable information are sought out and complied with because of their superior knowledge.

Ironically, once the information they hold is communicated, people with informational power lose their clout. For example, a clerk at a college treasurer's office who can tell a student how to get her student loan check issued loses all power as soon as the information is communicated (Eyuboglu & Atac, 1991).

THE HAZARDS OF POWER

Power has a bad name. In a society that cherishes the concepts of equality and individuality, the notion that some people wield power over others is sometimes looked at with disfavor.

Yet, many of our societal institutions would operate badly or not at all if there were not at least some execution and distribution of power. Politicians could not govern without the power given to them by constitutions and legal systems. Similarly, teachers could not teach without the power to make assignments or to discipline unruly children. Large organizations would break down if clear lines of authority did not exist.

At the same time, power, if abused, can corrupt the power holder. According to social psychologist David Kipnis, power may produce four increasingly excessive results. First, the desire for power becomes a need in and of itself, apart from the larger goals that the power is intended to fulfill, such as accomplishing a task. Second, the ease in using power encourages power holders to use power to benefit themselves, at the expense of those under their power. Next, power holders receive unwarranted positive feedback—even adulation—from others, which produces an inflated sense of self-worth.

Finally, power may lead the power holder to devalue others. For instance, in one simulation experiment, managers with substantial power tended to view their subordinates as working only for money (which could be controlled by the managers). In contrast, managers who had less power attributed their subordinates' efforts to high internal motivation (Kipnis, 1974, 1976). In sum, once people gain meaningful power, they tend to see the worst in others.

Having an inflated view of one's power may also lead power holders to overstep the bounds of appropriateness. For instance, when Franklin D. Roosevelt was elected president by a huge majority, he took several actions that the courts later ruled unconstitutional. Such behavior exemplifies the **mandate phenomenon**, in which a person with strong support exceeds group norms and seeks even more power (Forsyth, 1990; Conger, 1998).

Ultimately, power holders may become absorbed in seeking power and may become motivated by the need for power. In fact, many people who have power have a strong **need for power**, a personality characteristic in which an individual has a tendency to seek impact,

mandate phenomenon: Behavior in which a person with strong support exceeds group norms and seeks even more power.

need for power: A personality characteristic in which an individual has a tendency to seek impact, control, or influence over others, and to be seen as a powerful person.

control, or influence over others, and to be seen as a powerful person (Winter, 1973, 1987; Jenkins, 1994).

Despite this pessimistic view of the corrupting influence of power, the U.S. political system provides voters with the ultimate means to correct the abuse of power—voting an incumbent out of office. Power may corrupt, but corrupt power will not necessarily endure.

REVIEW AND RETHINK

Review

- The great person, situational, and interactional approaches seek to explain leadership emergence and effectiveness.
- Likability is a critical factor in voter choice.
- Social power consists of one person's ability to control and shape the behavior of others.
- Holding power has several drawbacks.

Rethink

- In exploring the question of what separates a person who becomes a leader from a person who does not, which type of explanation has been most successful—personality, situational, or a mix of the two? Why?
- In the question of which leaders will be successful, which type of explanation has been most successful—personality, situational, or a mix of the two? Why?
- Consider Barber's theory of presidential personality in the context of Fiedler's contingency model of leadership. Who would have been a more effective leader during World War II: Lyndon Johnson or Warren Harding? Who would have been a better leader in today's uncertain times?
- Based on your knowledge of stereotype formation, suggest how the stereotype of women's inability to lead might have developed. How might it be changed?
- How does expert power differ from informational power? How does legitimate power differ from coercive power?

LOOKING BACK

What are the social psychological factors that affect defendants and judges in criminal trials?

1. Legal decisions are at least in part social ones, based on factors of a social psychological nature. For example, the physical attractiveness of a defendant typically has a positive influence on judgments of defendant innocence. On the other hand, if the defendant's physical attractiveness seems to have been used profitably during a crime, jurors may give harsher sentences to more attractive than to less attractive defendants. Other defendant characteristics, such as gender and race, also play a role in jurors' perceptions of guilt and innocence. (p. 424)

2. Despite judges' greater knowledge of and experience with the law, they are susceptible to biases. Furthermore, they exhibit dramatic differences in setting bail and sentencing. Such differences may be based on prior attitudes and judicial philosophy. (p. 426)

How do juries reach decisions?

3. Jury decisions can be better understood by considering social psychological factors. For example, jurors have difficulty ignoring evidence that they have heard but have been instructed to disregard. In addition, jurors' sense of justice or reactance to instructions may lead them to ignore a judge's instructions. Finally, a jury may simply misunderstand a judge's instructions. (p. 427)

4. Although it is legal for juries to be smaller than the traditional 12, smaller juries produce different psychological dynamics than larger ones. For example, a 2:10 jury split has different psychological consequences for jurors holding minority positions than a 1:5 split. (p. 430)

5. Although some demographic differences in jury members' willingness to convict have been reported, by and large the results are not compelling. However, some personality factors do seem important, such as dogmatism and authoritarianism. Nonetheless, social psychologists remain skeptical over attempts to choose conviction- or acquittal-prone juries systematically. (p. 432)

6. Eyewitness memories are unreliable for several reasons. For one thing, social expectations and stereotypes affect the ways that people perceive and remember information. In addition, eyewitnesses' motivational and emotional states during crimes affect their recall. Finally, the way in which a question is framed and asked affects witnesses' recollections. (p. 435)

How do social psychological factors affect criminal activity?

7. To reduce crime, law enforcement authorities have attempted to develop closer social ties with residents of crime-ridden areas, to give residents a greater sense of control over their environment, and to form neighborhood organizations. (p. 439)

8. The major justifications for criminal behavior, called techniques of neutralization, include denying responsibility, denying harm and injury, blaming the victim, denouncing authorities, and invoking higher principles or authority. (p. 440)

What steps can be taken to make trials fairer?

9. Possible approaches to making the trial process fairer include increasing the representativeness of people on juries; decreasing the opportunity to remove potential jurors from a jury; videotaping trial presentations and editing out inadmissible material; instructing jurors in simpler language; and allowing jurors access to videotapes of the trial while they are deliberating. (p. 442)

How are political party affiliation and voter choices determined?

10. Political views are shaped to a large extent by social psychological factors. For instance, political socialization, the process by which people develop political attitudes, values, and voting habits, begins with the influence of parents at an early age. (p. 443)

What are the major explanations for leadership?

11. The great person theory of leadership proposes that aspects of a person's personality or character—traits of greatness, in other words—lead that individual to rise naturally to a position of leadership. Although most evidence does not support the theory, some leaders, particularly transformational leaders, fit the great person theory fairly well. (p. 444)

12. According to the situational approach to leadership, people become leaders due to the characteristics of the situation in which they find themselves. As with the great person theory, there is little consistent supportive evidence that situations bring about leadership. (p. 446)

13. According to interactional approaches to leadership, different situations call for particular kinds of leaders. This view holds that in certain types of situations, one kind of leader will be likely to emerge and be most effective, whereas under other circumstances another kind of leader might emerge and be more effective. For instance, Fiedler's contingency model suggests that leader effectiveness is a joint consequence of (1) the overall degree of favorability of the situation to a leader, and (2) the leader's motivational style, which refers to whether the leader is primarily task-oriented or relationship-oriented. (p. 447)

14. Both gender and culture affect leadership. For example, although women and men have been found to be generally similar in terms of the concern they display regarding task accomplishment and the maintenance of personal relationships, female leaders favor a more democratic style, whereas males display a more autocratic style. In addition, there are cultural differences in leadership, such as the difference in perceptions of leaders in collectivistic and individualistic societies. (p. 448)

15. One of the primary factors in determining people's choice of leaders is likability. Likability is based on two types of information: personal traits and the emotions displayed by the leader. (p. 451)

On what basis is power acquired, and what are the consequences of wielding power?

16. An individual's ability to lead often rests on his or her social power, which is a person's ability to control and shape another's behavior. The six major bases on which social power rests are reward power, coercive power, referent power, legitimate power, expert power, and informational power. (p. 452)

17. Power may lead to several negative consequences, such as becoming a need in and of itself, the use of power to benefit the power holder, an inflated sense of self-worth, and the devaluation of others. It can also lead to the mandate phenomenon, in which a person with strong support exceeds group norms and seeks even more power. (p. 453)

EPILOGUE

In the past two chapters, we've considered the conditions under which people are susceptible to the influence of others. Beginning with theoretical approaches to conformity, compliance, and obedience, we saw how people react to implicit and explicit social pressure.

In this chapter, we've discussed social influence in the context of two applied areas: the legal system and politics. We've seen how the rule of law, codified over centuries, is still susceptible to some very real biases. In essence, even the most fundamental of society's institutions—law and politics—are influenced by social psychological factors.

Before we proceed to the next chapter, turn to the prologue of this chapter on the "dream team's" use of jury consultant Jo-Ellan Dimitrius in the O. J. Simpson trial, and consider these questions:

1. If you were asked to use scientific methods to help select jurors systematically, what characteristics would you look for in the "ideal" juror sympathetic to the defense? Why?

2. What if you were advising the prosecution in determining the "ideal" juror? What characteristics would you seek out?

3. Does systematic selection of jurors really work? Is it fair? Does it give the side that uses it an unfair advantage?

4. If you were the judge in the O. J. Simpson trial, do you think you could have remained impartial, despite your own private opinions about his guilt or innocence? What could you have done to try to be impartial?

5. If only one juror believed Simpson to be guilty, what would the chances be of an acquittal or a hung jury (in which a unanimous decision is not reached)? Why? What if two jurors had been convinced of Simpson's guilt?

KEY TERMS AND CONCEPTS

contingency model (p. 447)

death qualification (p. 433)

entrapment (p. 441)

great person theory of leadership (p. 444)

interactional approaches to leadership (p. 447)

leniency bias (p. 429)

mandate phenomenon (p. 453)

need for power (p. 453)

political psychology (p. 443)

political socialization (p. 443)

reconstructive memories (p. 435)

situational approach to leadership (p. 446)

social power (p. 452)

techniques of neutralization (p. 440)

transformational leaders (p. 444)

victimization (p. 440)

voir dire (p. 434)

CHAPTER 14

GROUPS
Joining with Others

PROLOGUE

Challenging the Group

The tragic launch of the shuttle Challenger.

On the Florida coast, the weather, usually balmy, was unseasonably cold, and predictions for the next day were for even colder temperatures. The chilly weather on that January day in 1986 made NASA officials nervous; they had never held a launch in such cold weather. Yet the takeoff of the space shuttle *Challenger* on January 28, 1986, had already been postponed several times, and NASA officials were eager to get the astronauts into space. The presence on the crew of teacher Christa McAuliffe was designed to focus the public's attention on the mission, and as a result the launch was under unusual scrutiny by the press and public.

NASA officials faced a difficult decision: Did the subfreezing temperatures pose a significant risk to the launch—a risk sufficient to postpone it? To make the decision, NASA convened several groups of experts to review the pros and cons. Some cautionary information was already in hand. Several months before, an engineer involved in the manufacture of the shuttle rocket had warned that extreme environmental conditions could make a group of rubber seals so brittle that they could deteriorate. The result, he cautioned, could be a catastrophic failure of the shuttle.

However, NASA officials largely ignored the warning, along with additional reservations that arose from a group of engineers the night before the launch. Consulted about the low temperatures predicted for the next day, these engineers strongly urged a delay in the launch. They told their supervisors that their firm opinion was that the shuttle could fail in such cold temperatures.

However, NASA officials, who were anxious to get the shuttle off the ground, gave little consideration to the engineers' views. In fact, they ordered the engineers to rethink their recommendation. Ultimately, the person who made the final decision never even learned of the engineers' concerns; subordinate members of the launch team "protected" him from the conflicting information.

As we know today, the engineers' warnings were sadly prophetic. The rocket seals did fail on launch. The shuttle rocket exploded, and all seven astronauts on board died. Despite the input of many individuals, the wrong decision was made. ■

LOOKING AHEAD

With 20/20 hindsight, we can see clearly that the people involved in the *Challenger* disaster made the wrong decision. But why? Couldn't groups of knowledgeable people avoid such a calamity by rationally making a decision that properly took into account all relevant factors? Don't group decisions, made by people with differing information, expertise, skills, and personalities, represent an improvement over those made by a solitary individual?

As we'll see in this chapter, the answers to such questions are not simple. For the past century, social psychologists have addressed questions about groups, and one of the first formal social psychological experiments examined the issue of whether individual or group performance is superior. In this chapter, we'll explore the social psychological perspective on groups.

We begin by considering how, in a formal sense, a group differs from a mere aggregation of individuals. After examining the criteria that identify a group, we consider the underlying structure of a group. We examine how people in groups play particular roles and how each individual is associated with a status that determines how he or she is evaluated by others. We also consider the standards, or norms, that groups provide and how groups differ in terms of attractiveness to their members.

In addition, we discuss the benefits and costs of participation in groups. We consider the circumstances under which the presence of others can boost or diminish performance, examine collective behavior, and identify some techniques for optimizing group performance.

We then turn to the ways in which groups solve problems and make decisions, examining the stages that groups follow in approaching challenges, and looking at different frameworks that groups may adopt. Finally, after considering the factors that affect the quality of group problem solving and decision making, we discuss how in certain kinds of groups members may be subject to defective thinking and how to improve decision making in such situations.

In sum, after reading this chapter, you'll be able to answer these questions:

- How can we formally define a group?
- What are the major characteristics of groups?
- How does the presence of others affect performance, for better or worse?
- What are the processes by which groups strive to solve problems and reach decisions?
- What factors affect the quality of problem solving and decision making?

WHAT MAKES A GROUP A GROUP?

You stand at a bus stop, waiting with several others for the next bus to come.

You sing "Happy Birthday" with the other guests at your grandmother's seventy-fifth birthday party.

Along with a troop of teammates, you go door-to-door collecting money to support your intramural hockey team.

You participate unenthusiastically in weekend military exercises with your ROTC unit, which you joined only to get scholarship benefits.

If you keep track of your activities for a few weeks, you'll probably find that you spend relatively little time alone. Instead, you'll most likely learn that a substantial portion of your waking hours is spent in the presence of others, participating with other people in group situations.

It does not seem all that hard to know what a group is, but that hasn't proved to be the case. Partly because the study of groups has played a central role in the development of social psychology, there are almost as many definitions of "group" as there have been social psychologists.

Consider some of the questions that are raised when we contemplate how to define a group: Does a group exist only when members interact? Must people consider themselves to be part of a group in order to be part of one? Do group members need to communicate with one another? Do they need to share attitudes or goals? All these questions, as well as many others, have been addressed and highlighted by particular definitions of groups (Forsyth, 1990).

DEFINING CHARACTERISTICS OF GROUPS

According to many social psychologists, though, the most useful view of groups involves the consideration of several basic criteria that all groups seem to share. In this view, a **group** consists of two or more people who (1) interact with one another; (2) perceive themselves as a group; and (3) are interdependent. Let's consider each of the criteria in turn.

Interaction.   At the most basic level, groups must permit some form of interaction among their members. It need not be physical, face-to-face interaction, however; written interaction may suffice.

Perception of group membership.   To be part of a group, people must view themselves as group members. For example, a random assemblage of people milling about at an airport gate waiting to board a plane would generally not be considered a group because the individuals would perceive themselves as being associated with one another in only the loosest sense.

A corollary to the principle of perception of membership is that persons in groups not only perceive themselves as group members, but usually are perceived as a group by others. Consequently, the implications of group membership can sometimes be forced on people who do not consider themselves as members of a group. Prime examples are the ethnic, racial, and religious groups to which a person belongs. For instance, even if individuals believe they are not affected by being members of a racial minority, their group membership may make a significant difference in how others view them.

Interdependence.   A group exists only when the group members are interdependent. Events that affect one group member affect other members, and the behavior of members has significant consequences for the success of the group in meeting its goals. For instance, if a football team is successful, all members share in the glory; when the team loses, it is a loss for the group as a whole. In sum, each person's outcomes are affected by what others do when members of a group are interdependent.

If we return to the examples described at the beginning of this section and apply these three criteria, it becomes clear that only some of the scenarios represent groups in a social psychological sense. For example, waiting for a bus is hardly a group situation: Interaction is minimal, the perception of group membership is low, and there is little interdependence. In contrast, your grandmother's birthday and fund-raising for the intramural hockey team clearly are group situations, because interaction is high, the perception of being in a group is real, and group members are interdependent.

Finally, your unenthusiastic participation in an Army ROTC unit represents a more difficult definitional problem. Although you obviously engage in interaction, and others may perceive you to be part of the group, the interdependence criterion may or may not be met, depending on the consistency between your goals and motivation and those of the other participants. Whether a congregation of people is a group, then, depends in part on the eye of the beholder.

THE STRUCTURE OF GROUPS

"Felicia, would you mind taking the minutes of the meeting?"

If you are Felicia, you might well object—if you think you were asked to take notes primarily because of your gender as a woman.

However, until the last 2 decades or so, a woman in a group setting would not have found it all that objectionable—or even surprising—to be asked to take minutes at the meeting. Because most secretaries were female, people assumed that women were somehow better suited than men to take notes. As we discussed in Chapter 3, such sexist notions and mistaken assumptions can cause harm as well as errors. What is important for our examination of groups, however, is that they are examples of how people fall into particular patterns of behavior in group situations.

Is this a group? Only if the members meet three criteria: interacting with one another, perceiving themselves as a group, and being interdependent.

group: Two or more people who (1) interact with one another; (2) perceive themselves as a group; and (3) are interdependent.

group structure: Regular, stable patterns of behavior in groups.

The regular, stable patterns of behavior in groups are known collectively as **group structure**, and they have important consequences for the effective operation of groups. In some cases, group structure is explicit. For instance, work groups typically have executives, managers, and workers, and each of these has explicit roles attached to the position. In other cases, however, the structure of a group is more informal. For example, some groups have a person who typically is serious and oriented to accomplishing the group's task, whereas another person may play the role of group clown, constantly cracking jokes but not getting all that much done. We'll consider four major aspects of groups: roles, status, norms, and cohesiveness.

Roles: Playing our part in a group.   A person's typical conduct in a group can be considered a role. As we first discussed in Chapter 10, *roles* are the behaviors that are associated with, and come to be expected of, people in given positions. Sometimes roles evolve during the course of group interaction; in other cases they are assigned to people as they enter the group (Hare, 1994; Rose, 1994; McMahon & Goatley, 1995; Stevenson &

SOCIAL.WEB
FINDING YOUR GROUP ON THE WEB

I just thought, "Oh God. What if they find out that I'm gay?" It was the fear and shame…. I watched the whole Gay Pride march in Washington in 1993, and I wept when I saw that. I mean I cried so hard, thinking "I wish I could be there," because I never felt like I belonged anywhere."—Ellen DeGeneres (Handy, 1997)

Groups provide important benefits to their members, such as a sense of belongingness, self-pride, and information about appropriate behavior. But what if you were a member of a group whose members you could rarely recognize and who in fact often tried to hide their membership?

For members of groups who are *stigmatized*—groups held in low esteem by society—one reaction is often to hide membership. But not all stigmatized group members can do this. For instance, those with conspicuous stigmatized identities, such as obesity or physical handicaps, are easily identified by others. Ironically, though, they may be better off psychologically than those with concealable stigmas, such as incest survivors, people with epilepsy, and gays and lesbians. Unlike those with conspicuous stigmatized identities, those with concealable stigmatized identities are less likely to be aware of being in contact with others who share their stigmas. Furthermore, they may encounter people who offer negative opinions of those with concealable stigmatized identities, being unaware that the person with whom they are sharing their views is a member of the group in question. The result may be that individuals with concealable stigmatized identities may feel isolated, lonely, and alienated.

On the other hand, *virtual groups* may offer an important avenue for those with concealable stigmatized identities to reach out to others. According to social psychologists Katelyn McKenna and John Bargh (1998), individuals with concealable stigmatized identities would be strongly motivated to seek out others who are similar in specialized Internet newsgroups, groups on the Web who share their thoughts anonymously in messages that are read by others. Such newsgroups range from owners of Ford Cameros or exotic pets to groups composed of those with highly specific concealable and conspicuous stigmas.

For those with concealable stigmas, virtual groups offer the opportunity to interact, anonymously, with those who share a similar stigma. Because this may be one of the few ways for interaction—albeit virtual interaction—to occur, the newsgroups may take on unusual significance in members' lives.

To test this hypothesis, McKenna and Bargh carried out a study in which they examined the reactions of people who posted messages on an Internet bulletin board. They reasoned that those with concealable stigmas would be particularly sensitive to the positivity of responses others made to their messages—more so than those with an unconcealable stigma and those without any stigma. To test the hypothesis, they examined a sampling of Internet newsgroups representing concealable stigma (alt.homosexual, alt.drugs, alt.sex.bondage, and alt.sex.spanking), conspicuous stigma (soc.support. fat-acceptance, alt.support.stuttering, alt.support.cerebral-palsy, and alt.baldspot), as well as some mainstream groups (alt.culture.us.1970s, alt.parents-teens, alt.politic.economics, and alt.tv.melrose-place). The researchers examined the frequency with which a poster continued to post messages following positive and negative feedback.

Wright, 1999). In either case, roles have a considerable impact on people's behavior in the group.

The way we play a particular role is a consequence of the culture in which we live (Mudrack & Farrell, 1994; Hubbard, 1999; Thomas, 1999). Although some aspects of roles are universal (there is no culture in which the role of "woman" does not include child care), other components of roles vary drastically. For example, in traditional societies such as many fundamentalist Muslim cultures, the role of women revolves around the home and family. Every other aspect of the role is secondary, particularly those that do not involve the family. In contrast, the current definition of the role of woman in most Western societies reflects the importance of individualism and fulfillment of each person's particular talents and wishes. As a consequence, greater stress is placed on behavior that results in an increase in the equality between the sexes (Moghaddam, Taylor, & Wright, 1993).

Furthermore, as we discuss in the Social Web box, our behavior is also a consequence of the cybergroups to which we belong and those that we seek out.

FIGURE 14–1   Internet Groups Can Provide Important Benefits The results of different kinds of feedback were more pronounced for those with concealable stigma. They also posted more messages per person than members of other groups. (*Source:* McKenna & Bargh, 1998.)

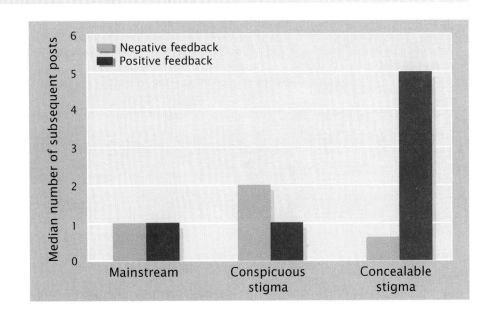

As shown in Figure 14–1, the result of different kinds of feedback was particularly pronounced for those with concealable stigma. Furthermore, members of concealable stigma newsgroups posted more messages per person than members of the other groups—a further indication of the importance of the newsgroup to the people posting messages.

Further studies found that newsgroup participation not only was more significant for those with concealable stigmas, but also grew in importance for those who participated. Furthermore, this participation led to greater self-acceptance, as well as a greater likelihood of coming out to others regarding the concealed stigma.

In short, membership in the virtual group had several positive consequences for those with concealable stigma. Virtual groups, then, may offer the same sort of benefits as membership in actual groups.

SPEAKING OF SOCIAL PSYCHOLOGY

Gloria Balague

Sport Team Specialist

Year of Birth: 1941

Education: Five-year degree in Psychology, University of Barcelona, Spain; M.A., Psychology, University of Illinois at Chicago; Ph.D., Clinical and Social Psychology, University of Illinois at Chicago

Home: Chicago, Illinois

Although teamwork is a foundation for any successful endeavor involving a group of people pursuing a single goal, in the highly competitive area of sports, teamwork makes or breaks the success of the group.

Sports psychologist Gloria Balague, who has worked closely with the 1992 U.S. Olympic track and field team and the 1992 and 1996 U.S. Olympic gymnastics teams, notes that a sports team's success is affected by several factors relating to group performance.

"Spectators can have a major impact on the performance of a team. It often raises the level of motivation, but it also raises the level of anxiety. Depending on the level of the team's experience, this anxiety can affect the outcome," she said.

"For an experienced team, it enhances performance, and consequently the increase in anxiety can increase the intensity of play, which is good," Balague added. "With an inexperienced team, it tends to interfere. Moreover, for those teams that require a lot of precision—such as basketball—the skills are less likely to tolerate anxiety."

According to Balague, pressure becomes exceptionally high when one individual on a team is more clearly defined as responsible, such as goalie in hockey or soccer, a kicker in football, or a basketball player shooting a foul shot.

> *"One of the best skills a team can have is the ability to communicate with each other openly and effectively."*

Status: Evaluating others.   Every member of a group is not held in similar regard. In work groups, for example, people of greater authority have bigger desks, larger offices, and better views from their windows. They may have their own secretaries and assistants, and they may even have separate rest rooms.

Such perks reflect differences in status among group members. As we first discussed in Chapter 12, *status* is the social rank a person holds within a group. People of higher status have greater access to the group's resources, and they have the authority either to tell others what to do directly or to wield influence over them indirectly. In contrast, group members of lower status tend to follow the lead of higher-status members.

What determines the status of a group member? Two factors are central: the magnitude of a person's contribution to the success of the group in achieving its goals, and the degree of power the person wields over others. People who contribute prominently to a group's accomplishments will be viewed as significant participants and will be held in high regard by the other members (Suchner & Jackson, 1976; Kelsey, 1998; Milanovich et al., 1998). (Consider, for example, the accolades accorded to football stars, whose prowess on the field

Two other areas of importance that can affect teamwork are communications and coaching.

"One of the best skills a team can have is the ability to communicate with each other openly and effectively," Balague said. "As soon as the lines of communication break down, a team can start to lose effectiveness, and it can happen quickly.

> *"Ultimately, it is very important to a team's success to have a mixture of athletes with a variety of skills, ranging from physical to social."*

"For instance, if one of the team members gets anxious and makes a mistake, and another team member makes a face, a third member can interpret this as anger. As play continues, communication becomes unchecked," she explained. "Performance can be affected dramatically and confidence is also affected. If they think a particular team member will not pull his or her weight, then they won't pass the ball to that person."

Coaching is also a major factor in determining the success of a team. According to Balague, one of the most common mistakes a coach can make is being too negative when interacting with team members.

"Coaches have a tendency to tell athletes what they do wrong, and that's relatively negative and often not very helpful," said Balague. "What the athletes need to be told is how to do something right. If they are only told what they are doing wrong, you can see the morale of the team sinking. They need to know what they can do right to build confidence."

Finally, players on the bench—teammates who are not actually participating in the competition—can strongly influence a team's performance.

"When the team becomes demoralized and the bench becomes quiet, and they hang their heads, it transmits the sense of loss. Players on the field pick up on that. It does have an impact," she said.

"Ultimately, it is very important to a team's success to have a mixture of athletes with a variety of skills, ranging from physical to social."

translates into team victories.) Similarly, people who control the outcomes of the group—those who hold power—are generally held in high regard, primarily because they are able to control the group's limited resources. For instance, in work groups, the ability of managers to determine the amount of subordinates' salaries lends them considerable status.

Although holding a particular role or position in a group can determine a person's status, an individual's personal characteristics also play a part. A person who is more intelligent, friendlier, and physically more attractive, or who has other positively valued characteristics, will typically be of higher status than someone who has fewer valued attributes (Propp, 1995; Ridgeway, Diekema, & Johnson, 1995; Stormshak et al., 1999). (Also see the Speaking of Social Psychology interview.)

Norms: Following the rules.   In addition to roles and status, norms are a third central facet underlying group members' conduct. As we discussed before, *norms* are the rules that guide people's behavior. Norms may be written (as in a group's constitution or bylaws), or, in less formal groups, unwritten (Miller & Prentice, 1996).

Norms can be prescriptive or proscriptive.   **Prescriptive norms** suggest to people the way they ought to behave; **proscriptive norms** inform people about behaviors they should avoid. When a fraternity member wears a baseball cap because most members of the group do so, he is responding to prescriptive norms; when that same member avoids going to a Barry Manilow concert because of the kidding he'd get if he did, he is responding to proscriptive norms.

Group norms can be so powerful that they override an individual member's self-interest (Kerr, 1997). For example, a classic study conducted in a switchboard manufacturing plant found that there was an informal norm to produce two switchboards per day, in contrast to management's goal, based on time-and-motion studies, of producing two-and-a-half switchboards per day (Roethlisberger & Dickson, 1939). Workers who produced either more or less than the informal goal of two per day were subjected to verbal abuse from their co-workers for their transgression. Underproducers were called "chiselers," and overproducers were called "speed kings" and "rate busters." The overproducers were even punished physically by being punched on the arm by their co-workers. In this way, workers maintained a norm of moderate productivity.

What is most noteworthy about the power of these norms, particularly those that prevented high productivity, is that they conflicted with the workers' self-interest. Because workers' pay was based on their production, their voluntary restriction on productivity resulted in a lower paycheck.

Of course, groups may have multiple norms, not all of which are equally important to their members. For instance, norms relevant to the immediate goals of a group typically exert the greatest influence on a group's activities, although other norms may also come into play (Weldon & Weingart, 1993; Devos, 1998; Wellen, Hogg, & Terry, 1998). There is greater tolerance for deviation from these less central norms than from more important norms. For instance, a person who breaks a norm by drinking tea when most people drink coffee will receive less disapproval than an office worker who wears jeans when the norm is to wear a suit and tie (Rossi & Berk, 1985; Marques et al., 1998).

In some cases, norms condone activities that are blatantly illegal (Harris, 1994). In one recent case, a major airline company had a problem with thefts by company employees from passenger bags and cargo shipments. Despite appeals from company executives for other employees to support solving the problem, employees did not step forward, although it was clear that they had to be fully aware of what was happening. Eventually, the company was forced to offer a large reward—up to $10,000—to overcome employee norms about squealing (Miner, 1992).

Group cohesiveness: Attraction to the group.   Just as individuals vary in their attractiveness, so do groups. The extent to which the members of a group find the group attractive is known as **group cohesiveness**. Groups in which the members are committed to the group and are strongly attracted to it are considered to be high in cohesiveness. Conversely, groups in which there is little attraction on the part of the members are said to be low in cohesiveness.

Group cohesiveness is produced by a variety of factors. For instance, the more a group is able to attain its goals, the greater will be its cohesiveness (Farmer & Roth, 1998; Karau & Hart, 1998; Wech et al., 1998). In some cases, though, even unsuccessful groups are high in cohesiveness (Turner et al., 1984; Langfred, 1998).

You may have experienced belonging to a group that is not particularly successful. For instance, you might have worked on a school newspaper that, because of limited resources, was not widely read or highly respected by the student body. Or you might have been in the cast or crew of a play that few people attended. Yet, despite the fact that the formal goals of such groups went unmet, the group may have been highly attractive to you. Why?

One answer resides in the nature of the other group members and of the group's activities. If we find group members attractive, the inability of the group to meet its formal goals

prescriptive norms: Norms that suggest to people the way they ought to behave.

proscriptive norms: Norms that inform people about behaviors they should avoid.

group cohesiveness: The extent to which members of a group find the group attractive.

Highly cohesive groups can foster self-esteem, but also share basic uniform attitudes and tend to conform to the standards of the group.

becomes less critical. Instead, the social interactions that the group provides may become increasingly central to the group experience. Hence, if we shift what we wish to achieve from group membership away from one outcome (such as creating a newspaper that all students read and enjoy) and toward another (such as enjoying the camaraderie of others), we are more likely to find the group experience a positive one. In these circumstances, group cohesiveness is likely to rise.

High group cohesiveness tends to produce certain results. For example, members of highly cohesive groups tend to maintain their membership longer than members of less cohesive groups (Robinson & Carron, 1982). Furthermore, groups that are high in cohesiveness wield more influence over their membership. Members of religious cults and other highly cohesive groups, for example, often share decidedly uniform attitudes and conform to the standards of the group. One dramatic illustration of this phenomenon is the case of David Koresh and his Branch Davidian cult in Waco, Texas, whose compound was stormed by the FBI and burned to the ground in 1993. Koresh's followers cut their ties to friends and family and accepted Koresh's biblical teachings without question. Members who deviated were placed under intense—and quite effective—social pressure to conform to Koresh's teachings.

Membership in highly cohesive groups yields some personal benefits as well (Hoyle & Crawford, 1994; Fisher & Kent, 1998; Henderson et al., 1998). For instance, members of highly cohesive groups have higher self-esteem and display less anxiety than members of groups with less cohesiveness. Apparently, high cohesiveness leads to greater acceptance and trust of the group's members, which in turn allows each member to feel more secure and develop high self-regard (Julian, Bishop, & Fiedler, 1966; Wheeless, Wheeless, & Dickson-Markman, 1982; Stokes, 1983; Karasawa, 1988; Roark & Sharah, 1989; Kirkcaldy et al., 1998).

Finally, group cohesiveness is related to group productivity, but not in a simple way. We might assume, for example, that cohesive groups, given their tendency to maintain membership and influence members, would represent an ideal means to maintain and even increase productivity in work-related groups. However, it turns out that this is true only in groups in which the norms, or standards, accepted by the group members support high productivity. If the norms favor only minimal productivity (such as doing as little as one can get away with), then high cohesiveness can keep productivity at a minimum (Seashore, 1954; Dorfman & Stephan, 1984; Mullen & Copper, 1994; Langfred, 1998).

The manner in which cohesiveness relates to group productivity illustrates a central principle of group behavior: Groups have neither consistently positive nor consistently negative effects on their members. Instead, membership in groups provides both benefits and costs, as we discuss next.

REVIEW AND RETHINK

Review

- Formal groups consist of two or more people who interact with one another, perceive themselves as a group, and are interdependent.

- Group structure includes roles, status, norms, and cohesiveness.

Rethink

- According to the definition of groups proposed in this section, would a dues-paying member of Amnesty International, a charity that works for social justice, be part of a group? If you had to reduce the definition of groups down one criterion, what would it be? Explain.

- Describe how group roles can influence members' behavior. How is this influence different from that of group norms?

- How does physical attractiveness affect status within a group? How does it affect group cohesiveness?

BEHAVIOR IN GROUPS: THE BENEFITS AND COSTS OF MEMBERSHIP

You wake up with a clear memory of the events of the previous day, although they still do not make too much sense. Why did you get into that stupid argument at the conference? Was it really necessary to get into such a heated debate? Why did your arguments become so extreme that after a while even you had trouble believing what you were saying? When you're in a group, why can't you control your urge to stake out a position and defend it, no matter how persuasive the arguments on the other side? What is it about group situations that prevents you from discussing things in a cool, rational way?

If you've ever found yourself in a similar situation, you know the powerful effect that groups can have on our actions. Sometimes the influence of groups brings out the best in us. At other times, though, when we are in groups we say things and act in ways that reflect poorly on ourselves.

The consequences of group membership, then, are neither invariably positive nor negative. Instead, particular group processes result in very different outcomes. We focus now on some of the benefits—and costs—of group participation.

SOCIAL FACILITATION

When are runners most likely to perform their best—when they are running a track alone, or when they are running in a group, competing with others?

If you're a serious jogger, you probably already know the answer to the question. If not, you'll be able to figure out the answer yourself by examining the results of one of the earliest research studies carried out in social psychology.

The work began when psychologist Norman Triplett became interested in the performance of bicycle racers in the late 1800s. As a bicycling buff, Triplett noticed a clear pattern: Racing times were significantly faster for rides made during competition with other riders than when a lone rider tried to beat the best time established for a track. Triplett theorized that the presence of others acted to release riders' "extra energy" and caused them to pedal faster.

To test this reasoning, Triplett carried out an experiment in which children were asked to turn reels like those on a fishing rod that moved a marker around a four-meter course. The reels were set up so that the children could either work alone or compete with another child. Triplett found that children moved the marker significantly faster when competing with a peer than when operating the reel by themselves, thereby confirming the results of the bicycle racer studies. Subsequent research, conducted early in the history of the field, showed that the phenomenon was not restricted to competitive situations; even the presence of others as noncompeting spectators could lead to improved performance (Dashiell, 1930).

The results of this early research suggested a clear principle: The presence of others leads to improvements in performance. Indeed, the phenomenon was recognized with a name— **social facilitation**—that refers to any change in performance that occurs when others are present. (This is one of those cases where scientific terminology does not match everyday usage; as social psychologists use the term, *facilitation* can mean not only improvements in performance—the more typical usage—but also declines in performance due to the presence of others.)

At first, the principle seemed to have few exceptions. In general, activities (which might range from running to using a computer) tended to be carried out more quickly or effectively in the presence of others than when done alone (e.g., Robinson-Staveley & Cooper, 1990; Seidel, Stasser, & Collier, 1998). However, as more data were collected, many exceptions emerged to the prediction that performance would improve when others are present. In fact, a variety of studies demonstrated that in many cases the presence of others seemed to lead to *reductions* in performance. For instance, although the presence of others produced improved performance of simple multiplication problems, refutations of Greek maxims took a turn for the worse when tried in the presence of others (Allport, 1924; Baron, Kerr, & Miller, 1992).

This puzzling state of affairs went unresolved until the 1960s, when social psychologist Robert Zajonc (pronounced "zi-ence," rhymes with "science") came up with a solution that has proved surprisingly durable. Zajonc (1965) suggested that the presence of other people raises our general level of emotional arousal, as indicated by increases in heart rate, perspiration, and hormonal activity. (Think what it's like to perform a solo at a concert or to make an oral report to a class.) Because work from the field of learning psychology has demonstrated that higher levels of arousal lead to better performance of well-learned behaviors (Parfitt, Hardy, & Pates, 1995), the performance of well-learned behaviors should be enhanced by the presence of others—the social facilitation effect.

At the same time, learning psychologists have also found that higher arousal leads to declines in performance of poorly learned responses. As a result, the higher arousal caused by the presence of others ought to cause poorer performance in responses that are poorly learned. In sum, the *mere presence* of others will cause either increases or decreases in performance, depending on whether the behavior in question is well learned or poorly learned.

Zajonc's simple and elegant solution solved a mystery that had troubled social psychology for decades. But, like a detective who identifies the murderer but not the motive, Zajonc had provided an explanation, focusing on the mere presence of others, that was not fully satisfying, at least in the view of many researchers. Specifically, the reason why the presence of others leads to arousal has remained a matter of some debate. Several possibilities have been put forward.

According to Nicholas Cottrell, it is not the mere presence of others that leads to facilitation effects. Instead, the presence of others produces arousal because we are apprehensive about how they are appraising us (Cottrell, 1972). According to the concept of **evaluation apprehension**, the presence of others leads to the inference that the audience is evaluating us, a circumstance that is definitely physiologically arousing.

If this reasoning is correct, social facilitation should occur only when others are paying attention to us; when others are present but are not paying attention, and are therefore unable to evaluate our performance, social facilitation effects should be reduced. And that seems to be just what happens (Aiello & Svec, 1993; Aiello & Kolb, 1995; Rousseau & Standing, 1995; Aronson, Quinn, & Spencer, 1998). For example, in one experiment, joggers ran in the presence of a spectator, who was actually a confederate (Strube, Miles, & Finch, 1981). In one condition, the spectator was barely attentive to the jogger, but in the other, the spectator kept close tabs, constantly gazing at the jogger and even making eye contact. As an evaluation apprehension explanation would lead us to predict, the attentive spectator led to social facilitation effects: Joggers ran more swiftly than when they were alone. But the inattentive spectator produced speeds no greater than when the joggers were alone.

social facilitation: Any change in performance that occurs when others are present.

evaluation apprehension: The presence of others that leads to the inference that the audience is evaluating us, a circumstance that is definitely physiologically arousing.

The mere presence of others does not foster better performance. It can either increase or decrease performance levels depending on whether the behavior in question is well-learned or not.

Yet, evaluation apprehension is not the full story behind social facilitation, because the phenomenon frequently occurs under circumstances in which evaluation is unlikely to be a factor. For example, even the most committed animal rights advocates would find it implausible that cockroaches feel much in the way of evaluation apprehension. Yet, such creatures clearly demonstrate social facilitation effects.

In one experiment, run-of-the-mill household cockroaches progressed through a simple maze more quickly when they were in the presence of four observer cockroaches than when they were by themselves (Zajonc, Heingartner, & Herman, 1969). Conversely, they performed more slowly in a more complex maze (it required a turn) when observer cockroaches were present. Hence, the classic social facilitation prediction was confirmed: improved performance on simple tasks, and declines in performance on complex ones.

Similar findings have been found with other species, such as armadillos, chickens (Keeling & Hurnik, 1993; Duncan et al., 1998), capuchin monkeys (Visalbergi, Valente, & Fragaszy, 1998), terns (Palestis & Burger, 1998), and opossums, who presumably are as little concerned as cockroaches about the evaluation of them made by others of their species. Consequently, social psychologists have suggested explanations for social facilitation based on psychological mechanisms that are not unique to humans and dependent on their more sophisticated cognitive abilities.

One alternative is distraction-conflict theory (Sanders, 1983; Baron, 1986). According to **distraction-conflict theory**, social facilitation effects occur because the presence of others is distracting, and our attention becomes divided between the task at hand and the others who are present. This divided attention leads to conflict, which in turn leads to higher physiological arousal. When the task is simple, the interference due to the distraction is minimal, and the increased arousal is strong enough to overcome the distraction and produce superior performance. But when the task is difficult, the increase in arousal is not large enough to overcome the distraction caused by the presence of others, and performance declines.

In sum, distraction-conflict theory, like the other explanations of social facilitation, explains why the arousal due to the presence of others leads to better performance on simple tasks and declines in performance on more complex and difficult ones. What makes distraction-conflict theory unique is the source of the arousal: It stems from the fact that people divide their attention between at least two compelling targets of interest.

We've seen that there are several competing explanations for the social facilitation effect (see Figure 14–2 for a summary), no one of which has unquestioned experimental support (Geen, 1989). As a consequence, social psychologists have begun to reject the notion that a single explanation can fully account for all instances of social facilitation. Instead, current research has been designed to test the circumstances under which particular explanations most effectively account for the data.

distraction-conflict theory:
The theory that social facilitation effects occur because the presence of others is distracting, and our attention becomes divided between the task at hand and the others who are present.

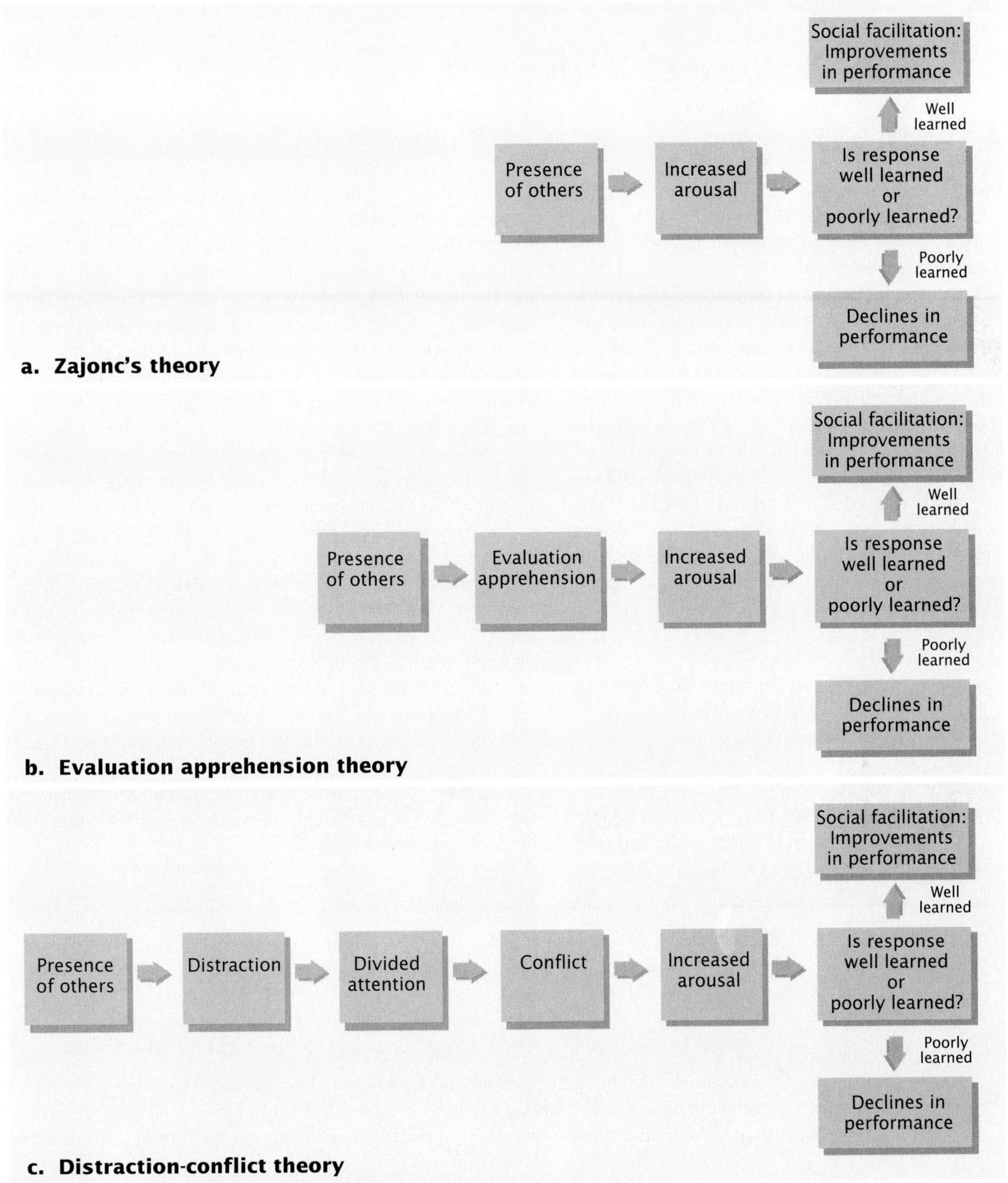

a. Zajonc's theory

b. Evaluation apprehension theory

c. Distraction-conflict theory

FIGURE 14–2   Three Explanations for the Social Facilitation Effect Three prominent explanations for the social facilitation effect are (**a**) Zajonc's theory that the presence of others raises our general arousal level, which in turn improves performance; (**b**) Cottrell's theory of evaluation apprehension, which states that performance improves only when we believe others are paying attention to us; and (**c**) distraction-conflict theory, which states that the presence of others causes distraction, which affects performance. Despite their differences, all three theories agree that the presence of others improves performance of well-learned tasks and impedes performance of poorly learned tasks.

APPLYING SOCIAL PSYCHOLOGY
AVOIDING THE FRIENDLY FACE:
WHY WE DO BETTER WITH AN UNSUPPORTIVE AUDIENCE

If you want to do your best in front of an audience, avoid filling it with friendly supporters. Instead, if you want to perform at peak capacity, keep your friends at home and hope for a nonsupportive audience, because you'll do better.

This surprising conclusion comes from a series of experiments conducted by social psychologists Jennifer Butler and Roy Baumeister (1998). In the studies, they investigated whether the natural inclination that most people have to fill an audience with friends who support them results in better performance.

Several reasons suggest that a supportive audience might be beneficial. Friendly faces in an audience provide emotional support, and feeling positively and more relaxed presumably should transfer to better performance. A supportive audience may also lead to increases in perceived control, self-efficacy, and self-worth. In support of such reasoning, sports psychologists have found that generally a home court advantage exists: teams do better when playing at home than on the road (Schwartz & Barsky, 1977; Cohen & McKay, 1984; Moore & Brylinski, 1995; Steenland & Deddens, 1997).

On the other hand, supportive audiences are not invariably helpful. People may be more motivated to look good in front of people with whom they know they'll be interacting in the future. In addition, an audience with high expectations can increase the pressure to perform well, leading to greater self-scrutiny. Rather than their goal being to do their best, people may adopt the goal of avoiding mistakes—perhaps by reducing their speed—and ultimately performing less well.

To answer whether the consequences of a supportive audience are beneficial or detrimental, Butler and Baumeister asked participants to complete a skilled task in front of a supportive audience composed of a friend or a stranger who would benefit financially from the participant's success. Compared with a neutral or hostile audience—or no audience at all—participants actually did worse in the presence of a supportive audience if the task was hard. On the other hand, if the task was easy, the kind of audience did not matter.

Why did participants perform less well on difficult tasks in the presence of a supportive audience? Although they said they liked having a supportive audience, people performing before a supportive audience engaged in what could be called *futile caution*, in which they worked more slowly to avoid mistakes—but performed no more accurately as a result. Ironically, the strategy of caution may have been adopted in order to avoid failure, but ultimately resulted in performance that was not as good as that used by people whose audience was nonsupportive. On the other hand, when working before an adversarial audience, people may feel they have little to lose, because the audience is not going to like them much anyway. In such a case, they adopt an aggressive strategy and take risks—going more rapidly—and ultimately performing well.

In short, if it's emotional support you're seeking from an audience, invite your friends to watch you perform. But don't expect to do your best.

Although conflicting theories have been proposed to explain social facilitation, the effects of the phenomenon are among the longest-established findings in social psychology, and they have produced some important applications. Drawing on the findings, for example, Robert Zajonc has suggested—only in part facetiously—how a savvy student could prepare for an exam:

> Study all alone, preferably in an isolated cubicle, and arrange to take your examination in the company of many other students, on stage, and in the presence of a large audience. The examination results would be beyond your wildest expectations, provided, of course, you learned the material quite thoroughly. (Zajonc, 1965, p. 274)

(For a discussion of how the presence of supportive audiences affects performance, see the Applying Social Psychology box.)

SOCIAL LOAFING

social loafing: The decrease in individual effort that occurs when people engage in shared group activity.

We all know that "many hands make light work." Or do we? As we've seen several times before, cultural truisms often contain little truth and not infrequently contradict one another. With this maxim, however, the research has securely backed up the contention that having more people work on a problem makes an individual participant's job a little easier.

The issue is not a new one: In the beginning of this century, Max Ringelmann, a French agricultural engineer, provided clear evidence that as more people work on a task, each one expends less effort. Ringelmann asked his participants to pull on a rope as hard as they could. He measured each participant's effort while pulling alone and with one, two, or seven others. The results were clear: The greater the number of people pulling, the less hard the average individual pulled (Ringelmann, 1913; Kravitz & Martin, 1986).

These results exemplify a phenomenon that has come to be known as social loafing. **Social loafing** represents the decrease in individual effort that occurs when people engage in shared group activity (see Figure 14–3; Karau & Williams, 1993, 1995; Comer, 1995; Pettijohn, 1998). Such loafing occurs in a wide variety of situations, ranging from performance on tasks involving physical activity to participation in perceptual and intellectual tasks. Whenever people work together to attain some goal, in tasks as diverse as completing a joint class report or participating in a tug-of-war, social loafing on the part of some group members is possible (e.g., Petty, Harkins, & Williams, 1980; Szymanski & Harkins, 1987; Pratarelli & McIntyre, 1994; Latané, 1997; Hoeksema-van Orden, Gaillard, & Buunk, 1998).

Social loafing has been found in a variety of different cultures, including India (Atoum & Farah, 1993), Japan, and Taiwan. Indeed, one extreme application of this view might be to attribute the fall of communism to the use of collective industrial and agricultural techniques, which emphasized group productivity rather than individual contributions. Collective social

FIGURE 14–3   Social Loafing A collection of 49 studies involving more than 4,000 participants revealed that as the size of the group increases, effort decreases, leading to the phenomenon of social loafing. Each dot represents the combined data from one of the studies. (*Source:* Williams, Jackson, & Karau, 1995).

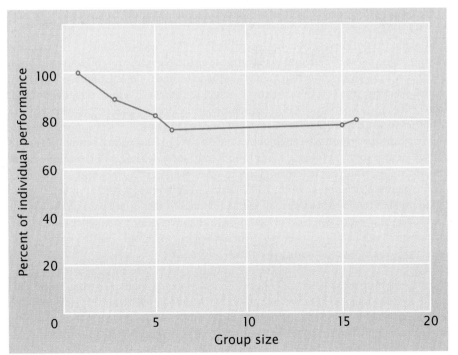

Some observers have suggested that the fall of communism in the former Soviet Union (symbolized by this toppled statue of Lenin) is related in part to pervasive social loafing—the decrease in individual effort that occurs when people engage in shared group activity.

norms may have set the stage for social loafing on a grand scale (Gabrenya, Latané, & Wang, 1983; Williams & Williams, 1984; Heller, 1997).

In sum, social loafing is a pervasive phenomenon (Williams, Jackson, & Karau, 1992; Karau & Williams, 1993; Tinley Smoot, 1998). However, we hardly become lazy in all social situations. For example, if our motivation to succeed is sufficiently great, we may perform at peak levels, regardless of whether we are working with others or alone (Price, 1993; Karau & Hart, 1998). Similarly, if we think that our contribution to the group effort can be individually identified, we're considerably more likely to contribute fully to it (Harkins & Szymanski, 1989; Miles & Greenberg, 1993).

The different circumstances in which social loafing does and does not occur have led researchers to suggest several different explanations for the phenomenon. One possibility is that participants in a group effort may perceive others in the group as being less motivated or less skilled than they are, and this conclusion might lead them to reduce their own output (Chapman et al., 1993; Robbins, 1995; Charbonnier et al., 1998). If the task is relatively trivial, why bother to work hard, if others aren't? On the other hand, if the task is meaningful, group participants may expect that their contributions will make a relatively significant difference when others are not working hard; in this case, social loafing will be minimized as group members engage in social compensation for their weaker coparticipants (Williams & Karau, 1991; Karau & Williams, 1995, 1997; Williams & Sommer, 1997).

A second explanation for the social loafing phenomenon is that group participants choose goals that are less ambitious when others are present than when they are alone. In this case, they may assume that the task will be easier when others are involved. Because of their lowered goals, they may expend less effort (Meyers, 1997).

Social loafing may also be a result of the perception of participants that when they are in a group their own efforts are less closely linked to any potential outcomes than when they are alone. If a group member follows such logic, he or she has less reason to expend much energy on the task.

Cultural factors may also influence social loafing. For instance, people from Eastern cultures are somewhat less susceptible to social loafing than those from Western cultures (Karau

& Williams, 1993; Heller, 1997). Why? The reason may relate to the greater emphasis on group and social orientations common in Eastern cultures and the greater emphasis on individualism found in Western cultures—a phenomenon we'll return to in the Exploring Diversity section (Triandis, 1989).

At this point, there is no single, compelling explanation for the phenomenon of social loafing, and we are left with several alternatives, each of which is plausible. Still, despite our current inability to identify the cause of the phenomenon, there is no escaping its reality. People working together in group situations are susceptible to slacking off, contributing only a fraction of what they would if they were working independently (Karau & Williams, 1993, 1995, 1997; Karau & Hart, 1998).

INDIVIDUALISM VERSUS COLLECTIVISM: DOES THE INDIVIDUAL OR THE GROUP PREVAIL?

EXPLORING DIVERSITY

Are you often influenced by the moods of your neighbors? Do you think people should take their parents' advice in determining their career plans? Would you help a colleague at work if he or she needed money to pay utility bills?

If you answer yes to questions such as these, you may hold a view of the world that is dissimilar from that of most people in the dominant North American culture. Each of these questions, drawn from a questionnaire devised by social psychologist C. Harry Hui, suggests a particular value orientation that is characteristic of many Asian and other non-Western cultures. (More items from the questionnaire are found in Table 14–1.)

As we first discussed in Chapter 12, the differing value orientations are known as individualism and collectivism. *Individualism* holds that the personal identity, uniqueness, freedom, and worth of the individual are more consequential than group membership. People living in individualistic cultures deemphasize the welfare of the groups to which they belong, instead valuing the attainment of personal goals. In contrast, *collectivism* holds that the well-being of the groups to which one belongs is more important than one's own personal welfare (Triandis, 1990, 1994, 1998).

Whether a society predominately supports individualism or collectivism is related to a wide variety of social behaviors. For example, societies with individualistic value systems tend to have strong economic and industrial development. In contrast, industrialization is relatively weaker in more collectivistic societies, such as in India (Hofstede, 1980).

Whether a culture is predominately collectivistic or individualistic influences the kinds of attributions people make of their own and others' behavior (Morris & Peng, 1994). For instance, research comparing attributions made by people living in Japan (a more collectivistic culture) with those living in the more individualistic North American culture have shown pervasive attributional differences (Kawanishi, 1995).

Specifically, as we first noted in Chapter 2, American students are more likely to attribute their performance to stable, internal causes (such as their natural level of intelligence), whereas Japanese students are more apt to emphasize temporary, situational factors such as (lack of) effort. The Japanese view stems in part from Confucian writings about the importance of hard work to the realization of one's goals. Japan's collectivistic orientation minimizes individual differences in ability and accentuates the role of hard work and perseverance.

In contrast, North Americans are more likely to attribute school performance to innate intelligence. If a student does not do well, he or she is seen as lacking the intellectual abilities that would lead to good performance (Holloway et al., 1986; Holloway, 1988).

For example, one cross-cultural study examined attributions made by mothers of fifth-grade children in Japan and the United States. The participants were asked to apportion responsibility for poor performance in mathematics to each of several different potential causes, such as lack of ability, lack of effort, poor training at school, and bad luck. As you can see in Figure 14–4, striking cultural differences emerged. Japanese mothers attributed poor performance in math primarily to a lack of effort. In contrast, mothers in the United States

TABLE 14–1   Assessing Individualism and Collectivism

Agreement with the following items, adapted from a scale devised by C. Harry Hui, suggests whether a person has an individualistic or collectivistic orientation.

Spouse-related

Collectivistic orientation: If I am married, the decision of where to work should be jointly made with my spouse.

Individualistic orientation: If I am interested in a job that my spouse is not very enthusiastic about, I should apply for it anyway.

Parent-related

Collectivistic orientation: It is reasonable for me to continue my father's business.

Individualistic orientation: I would not share my ideas and newly acquired knowledge with my parents.

Kin-related

Collectivistic orientation: If a relative told me that he/she is in financial difficulty, I would help, within my means.

Individualistic orientation: Each family has its own problems unique to itself. It does not help to tell relatives about your problems.

Neighbor-related

Collectivistic orientation: I enjoy meeting and talking to my neighbors every day.

Individualistic orientation: I have never chatted with my neighbors about the political future of this state.

Friend-related

Collectivistic orientation: I like to live close to my good friends.

Individualistic orientation: I would pay absolutely no attention to my close friends' views when deciding what kind of work to do.

Coworker-related

Collectivistic orientation: Classmates' assistance is indispensable to getting a good grade at school.

Individualistic orientation: I have never loaned my camera/coat to any colleagues/classmates.

Source: Hui, 1988.

divided their attributions for poor performance more evenly among several causes and considered a lack of ability to be far more influential than the Japanese did (Hess et al., 1986).

Obviously, such differences in attributions regarding the cause of academic performance influence the general reaction people have to poor performance. For Japanese students, poor performance is seen as a temporary state that hard work will remedy. American students, on the other hand, react to academic failure with discouragement, a loss of self-esteem, and withdrawal from academic endeavors, rather than with a determination to work hard to overcome their difficulty (Stevenson, 1992; Stevenson & Stigler, 1992).

The comparative attributional styles of Japanese and American students may explain the differences in educational performance that are found in the two cultures. Although in first grade there is relatively little difference between Asian and American students in mathematics performance, by fifth grade Asian students consistently outperform American students on standardized tests of mathematics achievement. Results on reading tests are similar: Although Americans actually outperform Asians in reading scores in the first grade, by fifth grade the Asian children have caught up with the Americans (Stevenson & Lee, 1990; Geary et al., 1996).

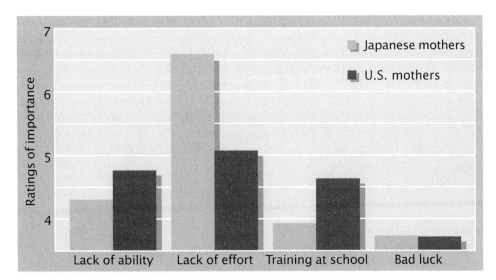

FIGURE 14–4   Mothers' Attributions for Poor Math Performance To Japanese mothers, lack of effort is the most important reason for a child's poor performance in math. In contrast, U.S. mothers saw several causes as equally important. (*Source:* Adapted from Hess et al., 1986, p. 160.)

Differences associated with a collectivistic compared with an individualistic orientation can be seen within other contexts. For instance, the ways people in a given culture distribute scarce resources, and their helpfulness in general, are related to the kind of value orientation predominant in the culture.

For example, when distributing rewards to members of their own group, people in collectivistic cultures tend to focus on the norm of equality (equal rewards for all, regardless of performance) and the neediness of the recipient. In contrast, people in individualistic societies tend to distribute rewards on the basis of a norm of equity, in which rewards are commensurate with the quality of performance. However, cross-cultural differences in distributing resources become less pronounced if the person receiving the reward is not a member of the group to which the allocator belongs. Specifically, distribution norms are considerably less powerful when the person who is in need is not a member of the same cultural group as the help provider, a phenomenon that is particularly true in collectivistic cultures (Leung & Bond, 1984).

LOSING CONTROL IN GROUPS: EMERGENT NORMS, DEINDIVIDUATION, AND COLLECTIVE VIOLENCE

"They're robbing the market!" The news seared along the Block. A hundred manic looters surged past the Vermont Square Shopping Center. Some swung axes, others crowbars; some had lock cutters. They smashed the windows at the ABC Supermarket. They snapped the lock at Sunny Swap Meet. They piled into a pickup and tried to bash through the steel shutter at the Best Discount housewares store. Then they plunged into Tong's Tropical Fish store and ran out with boa constrictors, fish—even the turtles. When it was all over, one observer, eyes glinting, walked up to a Korean merchant studying the ruins. "Get out of here, motherf—," he shouted. "I'll burn your motherf— ass. I'll bring 'em back to burn your ass a second time!" (Hammer, 1992, p. 40)

Pure rage was unleashed in Los Angeles during riots in the early 1990s. Tearing the fabric of the city apart, causing dozens of deaths and hundreds of millions of dollars in property damage, the riots followed the announcement of a "not guilty" verdict for the white police officers accused of brutality in beating African American Rodney King in Los Angeles. A jury's unexpected verdict, which confounded public anticipation of a guilty decision, released a wave of seemingly random violence that enveloped the city for days.

What explains this behavior? Although most research on groups has concentrated on relatively small collectives of individuals, some investigators have focused on larger groups. Starting with the observations of the French theoretician Gustave LeBon (1896)—who argued that large groups produced a collective mindset he called a *group mind*—social psychologists and sociologists have sought to identify the forces that shape collective behavior in large groups. One particular area of focus has been the collective violence found in riots (Reicher, 1996).

Riots are violent public disorders created by groups of people. Although riots initially appear to be composed of chaotic, unrelated acts of violence, their seemingly haphazard nature is only surface deep. The reality is that riots are considerably more organized than they at first appear. According to social psychologists who study large groups, rioting represents an example of **collective behavior** that occurs in groups of people who are relatively unorganized yet who hold a sense of unity and may work toward similar goals.

One leading explanation of such collective behavior, known as the **emergent norm perspective**, suggests that a group definition of appropriate behavior—essentially a new norm—arises in violent mobs (Aguirre, Quarantelli, & Mendoza, 1988). Specifically, this theory suggests that when crowds form they are initially made up of heterogeneous people who do not necessarily share similar motivation and behavior. However, once in the situation, people develop norms regarding appropriate behavior, and these norms are communicated throughout the crowd by observation. Because of implicit pressures to conform to the norm, individual crowd members may behave in ways that are quite at odds with their typical conduct (Killian, 1980).

According to this explanation, rioting crowds in Los Angeles were not uniformly composed of individuals who were habitually aggressive and violent. Instead, rioters may have been everyday citizens who were vulnerable to the apparent emergent norm of violent behavior. How might such a norm emerge? Presumably, it would take only a few conspicuous acts of violence to provide the impression that a norm was developing in which aggressive acts were legitimate and permissible.

The emergent norm perspective helps us understand how antisocial norms emerge in crowd behavior. It does not explain, however, why other norms—such as those supporting prosocial behavior—do not arise or prevail in crowd situations (McPhail, 1991). In fact, a few conspicuous examples of heroism occurred during the Los Angeles riots. In one well-publicized case, several onlookers helped a truck driver who had been pulled from the cab of his truck and beaten senseless by members of an angry mob. Their help enabled the driver to reach the safety of a hospital. It is unclear why these helpful models would not in turn create an emergent norm of helpfulness and nonaggression in the same way that the aggressive behavior triggered the norm of violence.

The shortcomings of the emergent norm perspective suggest that additional factors are at work during situations in which mob violence occurs (Mann, Newton, & Innes, 1982). One explanation focuses on **deindividuation**, the reduction of a person's sense of individuality and a corresponding increase in the person's willingness to engage in deviant behavior. According to the deindividuation approach, participation in crowds reduces individuals' concerns about being evaluated by others and about maintaining a positive social image. Thus, members of large groups feel anonymous and do not think of one another as individuals. Furthermore, their self-awareness becomes reduced as they focus on others and on events occurring around them (Postmes & Spears, 1998, Postmes, Spears, & Lea, 1998).

In a sense, then, people in violent crowds lose a sense of themselves, and their internal norms and values regarding appropriate and nonviolent conduct do not come into play. Because these norms of social control and nonviolence, which would otherwise keep their behavior in check, are not operating, people are more willing to engage in antisocial and violent behavior (Prentice-Dunn, 1990; Wilson & Brewer, 1993; Bovasso, 1997).

When a riot occurs, as in Los Angeles after the police beating of Rodney King was televised, it is the result of multiple factors, including an emergent norm of violent behavior and deindividuation.

Finally, deindividuation predicts a decline in people's sense of accountability for their actions. If many others are engaged in antisocial acts such as looting, any single individual may feel that the probability of getting caught by the authorities is relatively minimal. Therefore, the potential costs of such violent behavior may be viewed as relatively low. Such reasoning can lead to an increase in unrestrained, violent behavior (Prentice-Dunn & Rogers, 1982; Lachman, 1993).

The deindividuation perspective suggests several ways of preventing the violence that may grow out of mob behavior. One method is to attempt to reduce deindividuation by making people feel personally accountable for their actions. For instance, a visible police presence may enhance an individual's self-awareness and also increase the perceived risk of participation in violent, unlawful acts.

Efforts along these lines were made to stave off the Los Angeles riots. A well-publicized church service was held just after the Rodney King verdict was announced, at which community leaders urged citizens to engage in peaceful demonstrations that would show their inner strength and peacefulness. Translated into social psychological terms, the community leaders were encouraging norms of social responsibility and discouraging those relating to violence.

Unfortunately, the rioting began even before the service was over, and calls for calm went unheeded. The ensuing disturbances resulted in death, injury, and property damage on a large scale.

OBTAINING MAXIMUM EFFORT IN GROUPS

We've seen how easy it is for people in groups to engage in social loafing. Fortunately, social psychologists have devised ways to reduce the consequences of social loafing and maximize the output of all group members. The following guidelines suggest several ways to minimize productivity losses in groups and to magnify the benefits of groups (Shepperd, 1995):

THE INFORMED CONSUMER OF SOCIAL PSYCHOLOGY

- ◆ *Increase members' sense of personal responsibility and incentives to contribute.* Groups should be structured so that each group member is made to feel personally responsible for the outcomes of the group as a whole. One of the best ways to do this is to make sure that each person feels that his or her input is personally identifiable and will not be lost among the other members' contributions (Hardy & Latané, 1986). In addition, group output should be evaluated on the basis of individual contributions, not just on the success or failure of the group as a whole. In this way, individuals will have a personal incentive to succeed (Harkins, 1987; Shepperd, 1993).

- ◆ *Increase feelings of individual self-efficacy, and make members feel that their contributions are indispensable.* Group members need to understand that they are capable of making successful contributions to the joint effort. As we have seen, a sense of self-efficacy and the expectation of success enhance performance in groups. Consequently, instilling expectations of success will decrease social loafing and lead to optimal output. Furthermore, members who feel that they are making an indispensable contribution—one that can't be made by anyone else—will be more motivated to contribute to the group (Shepperd, 1993).

◆ *Make the group's activities involving.* When the group's task is involving, interesting, or challenging, social loafing is minimized (Brickner, Harkins, & Ostrom, 1986; Harkins & Petty, 1982; Zaccaro, 1984). Consequently, one way to reduce social loafing is to ensure that whatever the group is trying to accomplish keeps members engaged.

◆ *Optimize trust in the other group members.* If you thought that the other members of a group were not working as hard as they could, what would you do? According to social psychologist Norbert Kerr (1983), you might hold yourself back. After all, why give others a free ride, allowing them to share in the rewards of the group, even though their efforts are minimal? Kerr suggests that the perception that some group members are "free riders," people who put in minimal effort but benefit from the group's rewards, leads other group members to reduce their own efforts. One solution to the free-rider problem is to ensure that group members trust that their fellow members are putting in maximum effort. By making all members feel that everyone is working as hard as possible, group members can reduce the incidence of free riding (Williams & Karau, 1991).

◆ *Make each member's contribution highly visible.* If people's contributions to the group task are noticeable and obvious, social loafing will not occur. Consequently, it is worthwhile to recognize and publicize personal achievement (Matsui, Kakuyama, & Uy Onglatco, 1987; Price, 1987).

REVIEW AND RETHINK

Review

• Social facilitation refers to a change in performance due to the presence of others.

• Social loafing refers to the decrease in individual effort that occurs when people engage in shared group activity.

• Several strategies can be employed to reduce social loafing.

• One basic dimension along which cultures are divided is individualism versus collectivism.

• The emergent norm perspective and deindividuation have been suggested as explanations for collective violence.

Rethink

• What experimental evidence supports the evaluation apprehension explanation of social facilitation? What evidence refutes this hypothesis? How might you resolve this conflicting evidence?

• What aspect of the presence of others determines whether social facilitation or social loafing processes will result?

• Which suggestions for eluding social loafing can also be applied to increasing social facilitation in work settings? Explain your answers.

• What does it mean to say that a culture is collectivistic? How do collectivistic and individualistic cultures differ with respect to helping behavior?

GROUP PROBLEM SOLVING AND DECISION MAKING

When "a hundred clever heads join a group, one big nincompoop is the result."

Was the famous therapist and personality theorist Carl Jung correct when he made this observation, arguing that group solutions are inferior to those made by individuals? Although the issue is a simple one, the answer has proved to be more complex than Jung's tongue-in-cheek statement would imply. In some cases, groups arrive at more and better solutions to problems and make better decisions; in other cases, individuals working alone are more effective problem solvers and decision makers (Parks & Sanna, 1999). The challenge for social psychologists has been to identify the circumstances under which one type of problem solving and decision making—individual or group—is better than the other (Witte & Davis, 1996; Gigone & Hastie, 1997).

THE PROCESSES THAT UNDERLIE PROBLEM SOLVING AND DECISION MAKING: JOINING FORCES IN GROUPS

To address the question of whether individuals or groups are *better* at solving problems and making decisions, we first need to know something about *how* groups solve problems—the processes that describe what a group does when confronting an issue (Castellan, 1993; Witte & Davis, 1996; Ahlawat, 1999).

Tracing the course of group decision making.   When a group must come to a decision, how do the members proceed? Typically, groups move through four stages in their efforts to reach a decision: orientation, discussion, decision, and implementation (Forsyth, 1990; see Figure 14–5).

In the orientation stage, the group seeks to identify the task it is trying to accomplish and the strategy it will use to accomplish it. The task may be to reach a decision about an immediate, specific problem, or it may be to resolve some longstanding conflict that requires a long-term strategy. For instance, a group seeking to determine a new alcohol policy for

FIGURE 14–5   The Stages of Decision Making Groups typically move through four stages in their efforts to reach a decision: orientation, discussion, decision, and implementation. (*Source:* Forsyth, 1990.)

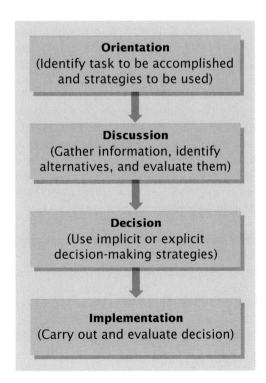

Orientation
(Identify task to be accomplished and strategies to be used)

Discussion
(Gather information, identify alternatives, and evaluate them)

Decision
(Use implicit or explicit decision-making strategies)

Implementation
(Carry out and evaluate decision)

In decision making, two heads are not always better than one.

university functions might decide that it wishes to hold a series of three meetings, one of which will be open to the public.

In most groups, the orientation stage is relatively brief. Most group members typically are motivated to begin immediately on the task itself, rather than spending a great deal of time discussing the process or strategy the group will use to reach a decision (Varela, 1971; Hackman & Morris, 1975).

The second stage marks the beginning of the actual discussion to solve the problem. Here, groups generally gather information about the problem, identify the alternatives, and evaluate each of them. There is a certain amount of verbal hypothesis testing, as group members suggest ideas and consider how the decision might actually play out. For instance, the alcohol policy group might discuss the legal ramifications of unintentionally serving alcohol to minors, as well as the reactions of students if liquor is banned outright.

The actual decision is made in the third stage. Using either implicit or explicit decision-making strategies decided on in the first stage, groups reach a final decision. This stage may include a consolidation period, in which group members try to convince those who harbor doubts about the wisdom of the decision that it is in fact the best one. In our example, for instance, an alcohol policy would actually be adopted by the group during this stage.

The last stage of decision making is implementation. The implementation stage comprises two aspects: carrying out the decision by ensuring that it gets accomplished, and evaluating the decision. Actually, the evaluation of a decision often marks the re-initiation of the four-stage cycle. If evaluation establishes that a mistake was made, the group may seek to come to a better solution, returning to the stages of orientation and discussion. For instance, the alcohol policy group might issue a letter to all members of the campus community, informing them of its decisions and explaining why it adopted the policy. The group might also ask for feedback from those affected by the policy and take steps to monitor the success of its implementation.

The framework for group decision making. In making decisions, groups rely on either explicit or implicit social decision schemes. A **social decision scheme** is the way individual judgments and preferences are combined into a collective decision. Social decision schemes may be explicit: A group's bylaws may stipulate that "the majority rules" or, in the case of juries, a law may require unanimous decisions. In other decision-making groups, however, the social decision scheme is never articulated and may remain obscure and even mystifying to some members (Stasser, Kerr, & Davis, 1989).

Social decision schemes vary in two major ways—strictness and distribution of power (Miller, 1989). The strictness of a scheme pertains to the degree to which group members

social decision scheme: The way individual judgments and preferences are combined into a collective decision.

must hold similar views in order for a group to reach a decision. A scheme that requires unanimity is relatively strict, because every member must agree with the group decision. In contrast, a majority scheme is much less strict, because a minority of members can disagree without preventing the group from reaching a decision.

The second major dimension of social decision schemes relates to power distribution. In some groups, power is spread equally among all the group members. In more authoritarian groups, however, decision-making power resides in a single person.

The strictness and power distribution of social decision schemes together play a central role in determining the outcome of decision making. For example, the stricter the decision scheme, the less likely it is that the group will be able to come to a particular decision. Furthermore, if decisions are reached under strict decision schemes, they are apt to be compromises (Miller, 1985, 1989; Sorkin, West, & Robinson, 1998).

Ironically, stricter schemes and more equal power distributions are more likely to lead to greater conflict during group discussions than schemes that are less strict and power distributions that are less egalitarian. For instance, if all members of a committee must agree on what the theme for a school dance is going to be and each member has equal power to veto the decision, there may be substantial conflict. In contrast, if the officers of the committee have the final say, the amount of conflict may be inconsequential.

In addition, the degree to which a decision is perceived as fair depends on how much the decision reflects the preferences of group members. Even the decisions of a dictatorship may be viewed as equitable if group members perceive that the decision reflects the group's majority view (Miller et al., 1987).

In sum, the decision scheme used by a group has a critical impact on group deliberations and the decision that is ultimately reached (Kameda & Sugimori, 1993). Table 14–2 summarizes the impact of the strictness of a decision scheme on group decision making.

Guidelines for group decision making.   In addition to decision schemes, groups also employ social combination rules in their efforts to make decisions and solve problems. According to social psychologist Ivan Steiner, **social combination rules** are the guidelines used by members of groups to decide what needs to be done and how the task should be divided up among group members (Steiner, 1976). Steiner suggests that social combination rules can be thought of as recipes for group process, analogous to recipes for baking a cake. In fact, he provides several "recipes" for groups, depending on the kind of task that the group is trying to accomplish. Among his favorite recipes are the following, summarized in Table 14–3: additive tasks, disjunctive tasks, compensatory tasks, and conjunctive tasks.

social combination rules: The guidelines used by members of groups to decide what needs to be done and how the task should be divided among group members.

TABLE 14–2	Decision Making in Groups: The Effects of the Strictness of the Social Decision Scheme	
	STRICTER SCHEMES	**MORE LENIENT SCHEMES**
Reaching a decision	Less likely	More likely
Reaching a compromise	More likely	Less likely
Satisfaction with the decision	More likely	Less likely
Duration of discussion	Longer	Shorter
Perception of discussion by members	Uncomfortable, difficult, but thorough and adequate	Comfortable, easier but less thorough and less adequate
Fairness	Seen as more fair	Seen as less fair

Source: Based on Miller, 1989.

TABLE 14-3	Recipes for Group Success		
According to social psychologist Ivan Steiner, different tasks require different "recipes" to ensure that the optimal solution will be found. Among the most popular recipes:			
TASK TYPE	**DESCRIPTION**	**EXAMPLE**	**STRATEGY**
Additive	Individual inputs are added together	Shoveling snow	Each member maximizes output, and everyone attempts to coordinate
Disjunctive	Group selects best solution from pool of individual members' judgments	Either/or, multiple-choice problems with a correct answer	Identify best/smartest member, use his or her response
Compensatory	Group product is average of individual judgments	Averaging estimates or ratings	Calculate the mean response
Conjunctive	All group members must contribute	Rock climbing, relay race, class group projects	All members work their hardest.

Source: Based on Steiner, 1972, 1976.

process loss: Aspects of a group's interaction patterns that hinder performance and prevent the group from operating at 100% proficiency.

- *Additive tasks.* An additive task is one in which each person's contribution is added to everyone else's. For instance, shoveling snow is additive: Each person's accomplishments add to the total group's performance. The more people involved, the more snow shoveled. The recipe here is simple: Each member does as much as he or she can, and all participants attempt to coordinate their activities with the other participants.

- *Disjunctive tasks.* Disjunctive tasks require a single choice among several alternatives, one of which is correct and the others wrong. For instance, a group seeking the answer to a newspaper trivia game would be involved in a disjunctive task. The recipe for disjunctive tasks is to identify the most competent member of the group and present that person's solution to the group for approval. If it is not obvious who the most able person is, then all members should work simultaneously on the solution.

- *Compensatory tasks.* Compensatory tasks require the averaging of individual judgments to produce a group product. Members of college admissions committees often make individual judgments about a candidate and then use an averaging process to determine whether a candidate should be accepted. The recipe here is a mathematical one in which the decision is made by averaging the judgments of individual group members who devise solutions on their own.

- *Conjunctive tasks.* If you've ever tried rock climbing, you know that you are strapped together with the other climbers in your party during your ascent. You can advance only as quickly as the slowest and least skilled member of your group. In dealing with conjunctive problems, then, group members must adjust their performance to fit the least competent individual.

   Despite the potential frustration involved in carrying out a conjunctive task, there is a way to optimize success: Although all members of the group should be encouraged to work their hardest, the weakest members should receive the most support. In addition, the stronger members should be encouraged to follow the pace of these weaker members.

Although groups can benefit from Steiner's "recipes," they do not always reach their potential. Often they suffer from **process loss**, aspects of a group's interaction patterns that hinder performance and prevent the group from operating at 100% proficiency. For example, if certain members of a group simply don't get along with one another, the group may be ineffective in reaching its goal—no matter what kind of social combination rule is being followed. In short, the quality of interactions of the various members with one another and with the

According to Steiner's conceptualization of group tasks, a conjunctive task such as running a relay race means that the group is only as strong as its weakest member.

group as a whole may prevent the group from reaching its potential (Salazar, 1995; Carletta, Garrod, & Fraser-Krauss, 1998).

THE QUALITY OF DECISION MAKING: ARE MANY HEADS BETTER THAN ONE?

We've seen that decision-making groups operate according to regular patterns, moving through a series of stages. But what of the nature and quality of the decisions they make? Are these decisions better than those made by individuals?

Resolving the issue of whether groups solve problems better than individuals do has proved to be a formidable challenge. The reason the issue has proved so troublesome rests in part on the way one phrases the question. For example, if we consider whether groups or individuals arrive at more accurate solutions to problems more quickly, then we come up with the answer that groups are better. Groups typically produce more and higher-quality solutions to problems than the same number of people working alone (e.g., Davis, 1969; Laughlin, 1980; Brown et al., 1998).

However, if we consider whether it is more efficient to use groups or individuals, we find that although groups reach solutions more quickly, the cost in time expended per individual is greater in group situations. In other words, although groups produce a greater number of accurate solutions, they do so at a cost of time, in the form of total person-hours expended. If you happened to be footing the payroll bill, then, your inclination might be to use individuals acting alone to solve problems. The cost to you would be smaller, although the quality of the solutions might not be quite as high.

In sum, the way in which we can answer the question of whether groups or individuals find better solutions and make better decisions depends in part on the particulars of the situation and our goals in asking the question in the first place. Furthermore, several group phenomena can affect the group's functioning. We consider several, including brainstorming, the composition of the group, group polarization, and groupthink.

Brainstorming.   Brainstorming is a procedure designed to generate ideas in groups. In **brainstorming**, group members are asked to produce as many ideas, in as uninhibited a manner, as they possibly can. Initially, other group members are told to withhold criticism, in an attempt to create an atmosphere that overcomes evaluation apprehension and encourages the generation of ideas. Only later are the ideas evaluated. The procedure is widely used in business and industry as a way to optimize creativity (Osborn, 1957; Jung & Avolio, 1998).

Unfortunately, research has never shown brainstorming to be effective. In fact, most research suggests that it is a less effective technique than allowing the same number of group members to generate ideas on their own (Mullen, Johnson, & Salas, 1991; Paulus, Larey, & Ortega, 1995; Nijstad, Stroebe, & Lodewijkx, 1999).

The primary reason for the ineffectiveness of brainstorming lies in process loss due to production blocking. **Production blocking** reflects the strongly held social norm that in a group only one person can speak at a given time. Although most of us do not spend much time thinking about it, we automatically obey our society's implicit rule that it is discourteous, as well as impractical, to speak while another person is speaking.

The rule against simultaneous speaking prevents people from blurting out their ideas the moment that they think of them. When group members restrict the immediate expression of ideas, they may later forget them, or they may decide not to articulate them because the ideas seem irrelevant or less original. Consequently, they ultimately are less likely to express the ideas. This type of production blocking does not occur when people generate ideas by themselves (Camacho & Paulus, 1995; Cooper et al., 1998; Sosik, Avolio, & Kahai, 1998).

Despite the evidence that production blocking makes brainstorming ineffective, brainstorming remains firmly embedded in many institutions. Why is this true? According to social psychologists Michael Diehl and Wolfgang Stroebe, one part of the answer lies in what they call the "illusion of group effectivity" (Stroebe, Diehl, & Abakoumkin, 1992). This

brainstorming: A procedure in which group members are asked to produce as many ideas, in as uninhibited a manner, as they possibly can.

production blocking: The inhibition of group members' expressing their ideas because of the social norm that in a group only one person can speak at a given time.

illusion is produced in part because people enjoy working in groups, and their enjoyment makes group production of ideas seem desirable and motivating. In addition, members of groups perceive that they are producing more ideas than is actually the case—a type of illusory correlational bias of the sort that we first considered in Chapter 3 (Paulus et al., 1993). In sum, although research does not suggest that brainstorming is an optimal procedure, it will probably continue to be employed.

Group membership: Is there an optimal group composition?   Suppose you were establishing a group to address the problem of how to keep people from speeding on a busy road that had been a traditional short-cut from a town's business district to the center of your college campus. Would you be better off if you chose a group of like-minded individuals who saw the world from similar perspectives and had similar levels of expertise and statuses, or would having a heterogeneous group of individuals, with very different views, expertise, and statuses be preferable?

To answer the question, consider a classic problem used in the research on group problem solving:

> A man bought a horse for $60 and sold it for $70. Then he bought it back for $80 and sold it for $90. How much money did he make in the horse business? (Baron, Kerr, & Miller, 1992, p. 39)

The problem is straightforward, and there is only one correct solution.* Presumably, any group that includes at least one person capable of solving it alone can, as a group, come up with the right answer, because all that that one person has to do is explain it to the others. However, this simple scenario doesn't always take place. In fact, in one early study that used the problem, one-fifth of the groups rejected the correct answer and came up with some other, erroneous solution (Maier & Solem, 1952).

The group's rebuff of the correct response underscored the social psychological quality of group behavior. Clearly, group performance depends on more than the ability and skills of the individual (Innami, 1994; Maznevski, 1994; Stewart, 1998). For example, the status of the person who actually has the correct solution influences the degree to which the group will accept the right answer. People in relatively low-status positions in a group are less persuasive than those of higher status. In fact, persons of low status may be unwilling to present their solution to the group in the first place (Torrence, 1954; Tjosvold & Deemer, 1980; Dubrovsky, Kiesler, & Sethna, 1991; Mizruchi & Potts, 1998). Similarly, a person who is low in self-confidence is less likely to be convincing to the group, and the other members may reject the solution of the less confident person due to this lack of persuasiveness (Hinsz, 1990; Littlepage et al., 1995; Peterson, 1999).

Gender factors have also been found to affect group performance, although the differences that have been identified between men's and women's performances have been inconsistent. For example, some studies have found that men's groups outperformed women's groups (e.g., Hoffman & Maier, 1961); others have found that women's groups do better than men's groups (e.g., Kerr, 1983); and still others have found little difference between men's and women's groups (e.g., Shaw & Harkey, 1976; Van Hiel & Schittekatte, 1998).

The contradictory findings about gender differences in group behavior finally were reconciled through a careful meta-analysis of the research literature. According to social psychologist Wendy Wood (1987), a review of more than 50 relevant studies showed that two key factors determined whether male or female groups would be superior: the nature of the group's task and the interaction style of the group. All-male groups tended to accomplish best tasks that were stereotypically male-oriented or that tapped skills with which men were generally more experienced. Similarly, all-female groups were better at tasks that were stereotypically female-oriented or with which women were more apt to have experience. For example, male groups were more likely to excel on tasks involving mathematical skill or

*The answer is $20, in case you're wondering.

Groups of men tend to excel at tasks that are stereotypically male-oriented, such as those involving physical strength. Women tend to excel at stereotypically female-oriented tasks, such as those requiring verbal skills.

physical strength, whereas female groups did better on verbally oriented tasks (Wood, Polek, & Aiken, 1985).

The second factor that explained differences in male and female performance had to do with contrasting interaction styles. Male groups typically use a task-oriented interaction style in which the focus of the interaction is on getting the task accomplished. In contrast, female groups are more interpersonally oriented, tending to be more interested than men in maintaining the social fabric of their interactions. As a consequence, male groups tend to be more efficient at tasks that require high efficiency and productivity, whereas female groups perform better at tasks that require cooperation and other sorts of interpersonal finesse (Wood & Karten, 1986).

In sum, neither male nor female groups are invariably better. Instead, optimal performance occurs when the task is best suited to the particular qualities of the people making up the group.

Group polarization: Going to extremes.   You're a member of a group charged with determining whether student activity fees should be increased, and if so, by how much. The members of the group start their deliberations by expressing a range of views, a few leaning toward keeping the current fees, others suggesting that at least a 5% increase is necessary. As a group, you discuss the issue over the course of several meetings, and finally you vote on the question. To your surprise, the increase to which the members of the committee agree is 7%—higher than even the most extreme person's initial suggestion!

You've experienced the phenomenon of group polarization. According to social psychologists David Myers and Helmut Lamm, **group polarization** is the exaggeration of a group's initial tendencies following group discussion (Myers & Lamm, 1976; Myers, 1982; Liu & Latané, 1998).

The principle that group decisions tend to become more extreme following discussion grew out of a finding that captured the imagination of social psychologists during the 1960s and early 1970s. According to a body of research that blossomed during that time, the commonsense view that group decision making produced more conservative, less extreme decisions (which were therefore more workable) was wrong. Instead, evidence pointed to just the opposite phenomenon: that groups often tend to make riskier decisions than individuals solving the same problems on their own.

The finding of greater riskiness in groups was dubbed the **risky shift**, and the phenomenon spawned literally dozens of experiments designed to explain it. The trouble with all this work was that the risky shift did not always occur. In fact, in some situations the groups behaved in just the opposite way, making decisions that were less risky than their initial positions.

After examining the seeming inconsistency across various studies, social psychologists figured out the solution. The risky shift was seen as just one part of the broader phenomenon of group polarization. The risky shift occurred when the initial positions of the group tended toward the risky; group decisions became riskier as a result. However, when the initial views

group polarization: The exaggeration of a group's initial tendencies following group discussion.

risky shift: The finding that groups often make riskier decisions than individuals alone.

groupthink: A type of thinking in which group members share such strong motivation to achieve consensus that they lose the ability to evaluate alternative points of view critically.

of the group members were on the conservative, less risky side, group discussion resulted in a decision that was ultimately more conservative (BarNir, 1998).

Group polarization has been demonstrated in a variety of contexts, ranging from the military and business to terrorist organizations (McCauley & Segal, 1987). For instance, in one study, groups of army officers, ROTC cadets, and non-military-affiliated university students discussed solutions regarding action following a hypothetical international military crisis threatening U.S. security (Minix & Semmell, cited in Lamm & Myers, 1978). Both student groups were consistently more likely to suggest diplomatic alternatives than the army officers, who tended to recommend military action. More importantly, following discussion with others in their own group category, members of each group showed polarization by becoming more extreme in their attitudes than they had been initially. Hence, polarization had occurred, and the groups' differences had become exaggerated.

Why does polarization occur? There are several reasons. One explanation is informational social influence, which we discussed in Chapter 12 in relation to conformity. You will recall that informational social influence rests on our belief that others may have more information about an issue and consequently know more about it than we do. Relating this to polarization, the arguments made during a group discussion tend to support the position that is generally accepted. Because each person within the group is not likely to have thought of all the previous arguments in support of his or her position, these new arguments—which are, after all, supportive of most people's initial view—are likely to reinforce the initial position. As a result, this new information induces the group, as a whole, to take a more extreme position than the individuals making up the group took initially (Isenberg, 1986; Lamm, 1988; Mongeau & Garlick, 1988; Brauer, Judd, & Gliner, 1995; Oakes, Haslam, & Turner, 1998).

A second explanation rests on the kind of social comparison processes that we considered in Chapter 4. The social comparison view suggests that prior to group discussion, people think the view that they hold is reasonable, appropriate, and perhaps even superior to others' positions. However, when they participate in the group discussion, they may learn that others hold views that are even more extreme—and potentially more "correct"—than their own. To maintain their perception of the appropriateness of their own views, then, they shift to a more extreme position as a way of making their views agree with, and perhaps even one-up, the positions of the others in the group (Goethals & Zanna, 1979; Isenberg, 1986; McGarty et al., 1992; Brauer, Judd, & Gliner, 1995; Raven, 1998).

The precise explanation for group polarization remains elusive. Still, the phenomenon is real, and numerous real-life examples of extreme (and in retrospect poor) decisions probably reflect polarization. For instance, the decision behind the slow but steady escalation of fighting during the Vietnam War holds all the elements that suggest group polarization was at work. Similarly, when opponents and supporters of abortion argue the issue, they often slip into arguments that are increasingly extreme.

Groupthink. If you think back to the *Challenger* disaster described at the beginning of the chapter, it may seem surprising that the combined minds of so many at NASA and at the space shuttle manufacturer could be so wrong in their assessment of the safety of the launch. However, the decision to launch is not all that surprising in the context of a phenomenon called groupthink (Esser & Lindoerfer, 1989; Moorhead, Ference, & Neck, 1991; Esser, 1998; Rosander, Stiwne, & Granstroem, 1998).

According to social psychologist Irving Janis, **groupthink** is a type of thinking in which group members share such strong motivation to achieve consensus that they lose the ability to evaluate alternative points of view critically (Janis, 1972, 1989; 't Hart, 1991; Moorhead, Neck, & West, 1998; Paulus, 1998). Groupthink has several central characteristics (also see Figure 14–6):

- ◆ The group develops the illusion that it is invulnerable and cannot make significant errors.

- ◆ Members of the group—individually and collectively—rationalize and discount information that contradicts the predominant view of the group.

- ◆ The group views other groups stereotypically, enabling it to disregard their opinions.

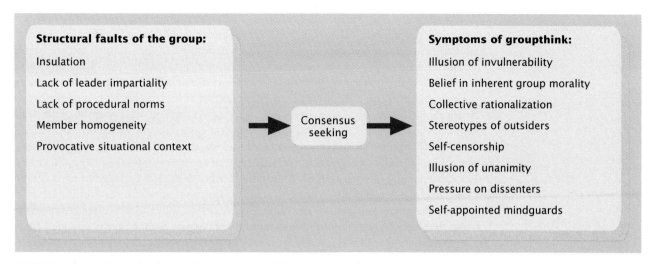

FIGURE 14–6   Groupthink Model Many historical decisions carry the distinct characteristic of groupthink. This model outlines the basic process in which groupthink develops. First, certain characteristics of the group (called "structural faults"), coupled with a provocative situation, lead to consensus seeking among group members. In turn, these factors produce the symptoms of groupthink. (*Source:* Adapted from Janis & Mann, 1977.)

◆ Members with views contrary to those of the majority are pressured to adopt the majority view, thereby stifling minority opinions.

◆ Because group members feel pressure to conform, an illusion of unanimity develops, thereby reinforcing the dominant view.

◆ "Mindguards" emerge, group members who act to protect the group from divergent or contradictory information.

Many major historical decisions bear the hallmarks of groupthink, ranging from Neville Chamberlain's appeasement of Germany before World War II to the Nixon administration's decision to lie about the Watergate break-in.

For instance, when President John F. Kennedy formed a group to evaluate a CIA plan to support an invasion of Cuba in 1961, he chose people with a proven ability to make the right decision. Yet, this group did just the opposite, choosing a course that led to one of the worst foreign policy fiascoes in U.S. history. Planned and executed by Kennedy and his advisors, the abortive invasion was an immediate disaster. The plan called for a force of about 1,400 Cuban exiles to land at the Bay of Pigs in Cuba and, with the help of the general Cuban populace (who were expected to revolt spontaneously at the start of the invasion), to overthrow the Communist government.

In actuality, things went wrong from the beginning. The exile force was poorly equipped, the Cuban air force was able to mount a strong offensive, and within 3 days most of the invasion force had been captured by the vastly larger Cuban militia. Just about everything that could have gone wrong did go wrong. In Kennedy's own words, the question was "How could we have been so stupid?" Social psychologist Irving Janis provided an answer to this question: Kennedy and his advisors had been subject to groupthink.

Although, in retrospect, groupthink seems to explain a variety of improper decisions, critics have complained that it represents 20/20 hindsight. Specifically, they suggest that the reliance on case studies of selected historical events may lead researchers to overlook aspects of the events that don't correspond to the groupthink hypothesis. Furthermore, because analyses of historical events can be made only in retrospect, no way exists of experimentally and unequivocally testing Janis's formulation.

However, a careful analysis of a series of historical events—some of which were hypothesized to show groupthink and others not—supports the basic validity of the groupthink formulation.

Social psychologist Philip Tetlock and colleagues carefully and objectively examined 10 historical decision-making episodes (Tetlock et al., 1992). In their research, trained judges were provided with a series of pairs of statements, such as "The group leader is insulated from criticism" versus "The group leader is exposed to a wide range of views and arguments." By objectively rating the extent to which such statements were characteristic of each historical episode, the researchers were able to identify objectively particular characteristics of historical events.

Tetlock and colleagues found clear support for several critical aspects of the groupthink formulation. For instance, poor group decisions were related to a lack of appropriate procedures for solving problems. However, not all factors presumed to cause groupthink were shown to be critically important. For instance, group cohesiveness was not, by itself, central to the development of symptoms of groupthink (Mullen et al., 1994; Hogg & Hains, 1998).

Not all research examining group decision making has supported the groupthink phenomenon, however (Fuller & Aldag, 1998; Kramer, 1998; Whyte, 1998). In a review of the studies that have examined groupthink, social psychologists Ramon Aldag and Sally Riggs Fuller concluded that the evidence was unconvincing. Furthermore, they pointed to several factors that the groupthink formulation ignores, including the role of norms, leader power, the nature of the task before the group, and the amount of time a group has been in existence (Aldag & Fuller, 1993).

In short, the concept of groupthink is controversial, and research supporting its existence is mixed. Still, under some circumstances groups make shockingly poor decisions, and groupthink does seem to explain some, if not all, instances of defective decision making.

Is there a way to prevent groupthink from occurring? According to Janis, one approach is to increase the quantity and quality of information available to the group. For example, experts who represent a wide divergence of views can be included in the deliberations of the group. The group can encourage members to play the role of devil's advocate (Janis, 1982).

Furthermore, the group leader might encourage criticism and refrain from voicing an opinion early in group discussions. The group can also develop explicit procedures for presenting and dealing with divergent information (Heinemann, Farrell, & Schmitt, 1994; Neck & Manz, 1994). Finally, after a tentative decision has been reached, the group can hold later meetings to air any remaining doubts or to bring up new ideas. By using such techniques, groups can minimize groupthink.

The bottom line on groups.   Potential pitfalls in group decision making, such as group polarization and groupthink, might lead us to presume that decisions made in groups are generally inferior to decisions made by individuals. However, such a conclusion is too narrow and extreme, for several reasons.

For one thing, groups collectively have greater knowledge and more information about a topic than any single individual. Moreover, groups also bring a broader perspective to bear on a topic than individuals. Consequently, group members may produce a greater quantity of solutions as a group than when they act alone.

Groups, then, are often more effective in reaching appropriate decisions than individuals working alone. But no group is inevitably successful. Members of groups must tread a cautious path to avoid the pitfalls that may occur when making decisions with other people.

REVIEW AND RETHINK

Review

- In reaching decisions, groups move through a series of four stages and employ social decision schemes and social combination rules.

- Although groups typically come to more accurate solutions more quickly than individuals, they are less efficient than individuals working alone.

- Group polarization and groupthink affect the quality of decisions.

Rethink

- According to social combination rules theorist Ivan Steiner, what is the first step in deciding how to organize a problem-solving group? In what type of group is social loafing most likely to occur?

- Would group polarization be more or less extreme in groups characterized by a strict social decision scheme? In groups characterized by little distribution of power? Why?

- Why might group polarization based on informational social influence lead to better decisions? Why might it lead to worse decisions?

- Compare group polarization and groupthink. In what way is the latter an example of the former?

LOOKING BACK

How can we formally define a group?

1. For an aggregate of people to be considered a group in a formal sense, several criteria must be met. Specifically, a group consists of two or more people who interact with one another, perceive themselves as a group, and are interdependent. (p. 461)

What are the major characteristics of groups?

2. Group structure comprises the regular, stable patterns of behavior that occur in groups. Among the most important elements of group structure are roles, status, norms, and cohesiveness. (p. 462)

3. Roles are the behaviors associated with and expected of people in a given position. The roles people assume exert a powerful influence on their behavior. (p. 462)

4. Roles differ in status, which refers to the evaluation of a role or of a person holding a role. The two major determinants of status are the magnitude of a person's contribution to the success of a group in achieving its goals, and the degree of power a person wields over others. (p. 464)

5. Norms are the rules that guide people's behavior in groups. Prescriptive norms suggest ways people ought to behave, whereas proscriptive norms inform people about behaviors they should avoid. (p. 465)

6. Group cohesiveness is the extent to which the members of a group find the group attractive. High group cohesiveness results in longer maintenance of membership, greater influence over members, and high self-esteem and lower anxiety among members. Cohesiveness also influences group productivity, depending on the group norms. (p. 466)

How does the presence of others affect performance, for better or worse?

7. Social facilitation refers to the change in performance due to the presence of others. According to one explanation, the mere presence of others raises the general level of emotional arousal, leading to improved performance in well-learned activities but declines in the performance of poorly learned activities. (p. 469)

8. Other explanations for social facilitation effects suggest that the presence of others leads to evaluation apprehension, the perception that the audience is evaluating us. Alternatively, distraction-conflict theory proposes that social facilitation effects occur because the presence of others is distracting, and our attention becomes divided

between the task at hand and the others who are present. This divided attention leads to conflict, which in turn leads to higher physiological arousal. (p. 469)

9. Social loafing represents the decrease in individual effort that occurs when people engage in shared group activity. Among the explanations for social loafing are that group participants perceive that others work less than they do; that group participants choose less ambitious goals; that group participants' efforts are less closely linked to group outcomes; and that social loafing is related to self-efficacy. (p. 473)

10. Collective behavior occurs in groups of people who are relatively unorganized, yet hold a sense of unity and may work toward similar goals. The emergent norm explanation for rioting suggests that a group definition of appropriate behavior—a new norm—arises in violent mobs. In contrast, the deindividuation explanation suggests that participation in a mob reduces a person's sense of individuality and increases the person's willingness to engage in deviant behavior. (p. 478)

11. Among the strategies to reduce social loafing are increasing group members' sense of personal responsibility and incentives to contribute; increasing feelings of individual self-efficacy and making members feel that their contributions are indispensable; making the group's activities involving; optimizing trust in the other group members; and making each member's contribution highly visible. (p. 479)

What are the processes by which groups strive to solve problems and reach decisions?

12. In reaching decisions, groups generally move through a series of four stages: orientation, discussion, decision, and implementation. (p. 481)

13. To come to decisions, groups use social decision schemes, which are the means by which individual judgments and preferences are combined into a collective decision. Social decision schemes may be explicit or implicit, and they may vary in strictness and power distribution. (p. 482)

14. Social combination rules are the guidelines used by members of groups to decide what needs to be done and how the task should be divided among group members. Optimal group performance varies according to whether the task is additive, disjunctive, compensatory, or conjunctive. However, process loss (aspects of interaction patterns that hinder performance) may reduce a group's ability to solve a problem effectively. (p. 483)

What factors affect the quality of problem solving and decision making?

15. Although groups typically arrive at more accurate solutions to problems more quickly than individuals, they do so at the expense of efficiency. Based on total number of person-hours, then, groups expend more time than individuals. (p. 485)

16. Brainstorming, in which group members are asked to produce as many ideas as they can without fear of criticism, is a technique intended to optimize creativity. However, research suggests that the method is not particularly effective, as production blocking may reduce the generation of ideas. (p. 485)

17. The composition of a group affects its problem-solving abilities. For instance, members' status influences the degree to which their solutions are accepted by other members. In addition, men and women differ in their contributions to group performance, depending on the task. (p. 486)

18. Group decisions are often inferior to those made by individuals. One reason is the phenomenon of group polarization, the exaggeration of a group's initial tendencies following group discussion. Group polarization is explained by informational social influence or social comparison processes. (p. 487)

19. Group decisions also may suffer due to groupthink. Groupthink is a type of thinking in which group members share such strong motivation to achieve consensus that they do not critically evaluate alternative points of view. (p. 488)

20. However, group decisions are not invariably inferior. Groups usually have greater knowledge and more information than any one member. In addition, they have a wider perspective. As a consequence, they may produce better solutions than individuals acting alone. (p. 490)

EPILOGUE

In this chapter, we've examined what social psychologists have learned about people's behavior in groups. We've looked at such aspects of groups as their structure, the kinds of behavior that occurs when groups try to solve problems and make decisions, and the quality of the solutions that result.

Throughout this chapter, however, the groups we've considered are fairly small. In fact, the theoretical literature on which our discussions have been based typically employs a relatively narrow range of groups, often consisting of as few as four or five—sometimes even fewer—individuals.

In the next chapter, though, we turn to a different species of group—organizations and culture. Although much of the basic material we've covered applies to these larger groups, the analysis applied to phenomena in these larger arenas is different in focus and type. Still, the basic goals of understanding social behavior remain intact as social psychologists expand the scope of their studies.

At this point, however, turn back to the prologue to this chapter, regarding the group decision making that preceded the *Challenger* disaster, and consider these questions:

1. What were the social pressures that led NASA to ignore the warnings of the engineers who suggested that the launch be delayed?

2. Based on your reading of this and earlier chapters, what strategies could the engineers have employed to make their views more persuasive?

3. Would you assume that the individuals who work in the space program form particularly cohesive bonds? Why?

4. What could NASA do to ensure that the views of all relevant groups are considered more fully in future space missions?

5. Is launching a space vehicle an additive, disjunctive, compensatory, or conjunctive task? Why? What group problem-solving strategy is most appropriate in this case?

KEY TERMS AND CONCEPTS

brainstorming (p. 485)

collective behavior (p. 478)

deindividuation (p. 478)

distraction-conflict theory (p. 470)

emergent norm perspective (p. 478)

evaluation apprehension (p. 469)

group (p. 461)

group cohesiveness (p. 466)

group polarization (p. 487)

group structure (p. 462)

groupthink (p. 488)

prescriptive norms (p. 466)

process loss (p. 484)

production blocking (p. 485)

proscriptive norms (p. 466)

risky shift (p. 487)

social combination rules (p. 483)

social decision scheme (p. 482)

social facilitation (p. 469)

social loafing (p. 473)

CHAPTER 15

BUSINESS, ORGANIZATIONS, AND THE ENVIRONMENT

Applying Social Psychology in a Complex World

PROLOGUE

High-Tech Boot Camp

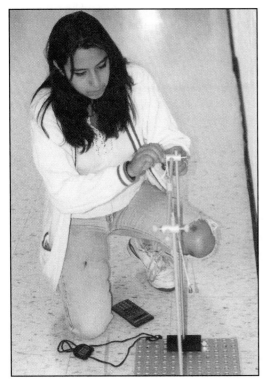

Transformations is a program that provides free high technology training to women.

Juliana Custodio didn't know how to turn on a computer until last fall. Today, she is working as a machinist and will soon be earning $13 an hour. After that, Custodio plans to continue her schooling to become a mechanical engineer. "I want to learn to program so I can get a job anywhere, any place, any time."

Custodio is a graduate of Transformations, a privately funded program that provides free high-tech training to undereducated, underemployed women in the Denver area. Based in a converted military barracks at the former Lowry Air Force base just outside Denver, Transformations has put two dozen women ages 34 to 58 through a 14-week technology "boot camp." The survivors, says program director Mary Hillsman, have emerged to continue their schooling or find a job—at salaries between $18,000 and $35,000.

"The program is geared toward women because women have not historically been encouraged into math and the sciences," Hillsman says. "We're showing women how things work, the kinds of things dads used to show their sons when they were out tinkering in the garage."

For Custodio, learning how things work is a dream she could not have imagined six months ago. It helped her land a job with a living wage and full health benefits for herself and her three children.

"When I was sitting in those Transformation classes, I never thought I'd use any of it," she says, "but I use all of it every day—the math, the schematics, the blueprint reading, all of it. It was hard, I felt like quitting, but I didn't." (Lynch, 1999, p. 1)

LOOKING AHEAD

Transformations doesn't teach just specific technological skills to workers like Juliana Custodio. It also motivates them, gives them self-confidence, and imparts strategies for working successfully with others within organizations—topics that fall within the realm of social psychology.

In this chapter, we focus on several applied areas of social psychology. Moving beyond the discussion of groups that we began in the last chapter, we examine organizations and the processes by which members learn to be functioning, successful members of them. We'll focus on business organizations, because not only do they represent a growing interest to social psychologists, but the majority of us spend some, if not all, of our working lives within such organizations.

Specifically, the chapter begins with a discussion of different models of organizations. We examine how organizations are structured, and how they develop their own cultures.

Next, we turn to the ways business organizations socialize their members and choose new employees. We discuss how communications travel through organizations, and how the communication system affects productivity and member satisfaction. Finally, we consider the effects of leaving the workforce, both because of job loss and downsizing and because of retirement.

We then consider another applied topic with roots in social psychology: how the physical environment shapes our behavior. We consider how the experience of crowding affects us. We also discuss territoriality, in which feelings of ownership develop over a particular geographic area. We end by looking at personal space, which suggests that we try to maintain "bubbles" around our bodies.

In sum, after reading this chapter, you'll be able to answer these questions:

- ◆ What models explain the basic structure of organizations?
- ◆ How do organizations maintain particular cultures and teach them to newcomers?
- ◆ How is information communicated in organizations?
- ◆ What are the consequences of job loss and retirement?
- ◆ In what ways is human behavior affected by the physical and social environment?

ORGANIZATIONS: GROUPS AT WORK

Consider these rules for workers in a Chicago department store in the early 1900s:

1. Store must be open from 6 A.M. to 9 P.M.
2. Store must be swept; counters and base shelves dusted; lamps trimmed, filled, and chimneys cleaned; a pail of water, also a bucket of coal brought in before breakfast; and attend to customers who will call.
3. Store must not be open on the Sabbath day unless necessary and then only for a few minutes.
4. The employee who is in the habit of smoking Spanish cigars, being shaved at the barber shop, and going to dances and other places of amusement will surely give his employer reason to be suspicious of honesty and integrity.
5. Each employee must not pay less than $5 per year to the church and must attend Sunday school regularly.
6. Men employees are given one evening a week for courting and two if they go to prayer meeting.
7. After 14 hours of work in the store, the leisure time should be spent mostly in reading. (Cited in Mitchell, 1982)

If these rules strike you as hopelessly dated and outmoded, consider the plight of workers employed today at a major insurance company. Except for two 15-minute breaks and a lunch hour, workers are tied to computer terminals, processing health claims. Their every keystroke is monitored by both human and electronic supervisors, who tally how rapidly they perform their duties.

Employees never know how big their paychecks will be until they receive their pay envelopes at the end of each week. Wages are based on a formula so complicated that it is

If you've ever had to stand in line then you've probably experienced the bureaucratic model of organization which can often be unproductive.

impossible for employees to keep track of how successful they are. In fact, paychecks may vary by hundreds of dollars from one week to the next (*New York Times,* 1984).

HOW ORGANIZATIONS OPERATE: THE RULES OF THE GAME

Obviously, not all business **organizations** (groups of people working together to attain common goals) employ such unpleasant working conditions. In fact, organizations have wide variations in their underlying philosophies, which are reflected in particular organizational models. Four basic models have been identified: bureaucratic models, human relations models, contingency models, and Japanese models (Taylor, 1984).

Bureaucratic models.   Both the department store and the insurance company described earlier follow what is known as the bureaucratic model of workplace organizations. The **bureaucratic model** represents the attempt to apply rationality and efficiency to the functioning of organizations (Weber, 1952).

According to the bureaucratic model, the ideal organization has explicit rules, regulations, and procedures for every task. There is a rigid division of labor: Employees have well-defined jobs and perform the same task repeatedly for maximum efficiency (Baron & Bielby, 1986).

According to the bureaucratic model, decision making should be centralized and decisions should be passed down along a well-established chain of command. Most typically, communication is rigidly controlled, and messages are communicated only to the position above and below one's own.

Are bureaucratic models effective? Anyone who has stood in line at a university financial aid office to pick up a form or who has waited for an hour at a state motor vehicle registry to renew a driver's license knows the answer. Despite the best of intentions, organizations run on the bureaucratic model are often unproductive, ineffective, and inefficient. As centralization and the number of rules and regulations increase, employees feel alienated from the organization. Worker attitudes contrary to formal management policy often take hold, leading to inefficiency and organizational dysfunction. In response to the emphasis on rules, workers also become quite rigid, a situation that leads to difficulties in solving problems (Magalhaes, 1984; Rojas & Gil, 1989).

organizations: Groups of people working together to attain common goals.

bureaucratic model (of organizations): The organizational model that attempts to apply rationality and efficiency to the functioning of organizations.

Human relations models.   The difficulties with the bureaucratic model led to the development of an alternative framework to shape the workings of organizations: the human relations model. The **human relations model** emphasizes the social psychological nature of organizations. Rather than focusing on the structure of an organization, as the bureaucratic model does, the human relations model emphasizes the social context of the organization. In focusing on the social interactions and the psychological state of members of an organization, the human relations model assumes that a pleasant psychological environment will lead to greater organizational success. A happy worker, in this view, is a more productive worker (Taylor, 1984; Macher, 1986).

However, happy workers are not necessarily more productive workers. Organizations with highly cohesive work groups may have higher productivity only if the work groups' informal norms support higher production—which often is not the case. Furthermore, human relations models of organizations sometimes have focused so heavily on the nature and quality of social interactions that the ultimate goal of the organization—to accomplish some task—is forgotten in the effort to create a pleasant, psychologically supportive environment (Rastogi, 1987).

Contingency models.   A more recent approach to organizations is to consider them in the context of a system. Instead of focusing on organizational structure (as in the bureaucratic model) or on the network of social relations within organizations (as in the human relations model), the **contingency model** of social relations focuses on how specific features of an organization's environment affect its operation (Tosi & Slocum, 1984; Tayeb, 1987; Tosi, 1991).

Contingency models emphasize the means by which organizational change can be accomplished in the face of shifting conditions. Customers may change their preferences, new legislation may be passed, or some dramatic, well-publicized event, such as the Oklahoma City bombing, may occur, modifying the environment in which an organization operates. To adapt to such modifications, the organization must be ready to change and develop. Organizations using contingency models are apt to emphasize problem-solving and analytic skills.

Although the contingency model provides a useful approach to understanding the functioning of organizations, it does not tell the full story. For instance, the model stresses the need for organizations to respond to changing environmental conditions, but it does not identify particular ways in which this can be done. Specifically, the contingency model suggests that there is no single way to structure an organization. Although this suggestion is undoubtedly true, it sidesteps the issue of what course of action one should take in designing the optimal organizational structure.

Japanese models.   The **Japanese model** of organizations emphasizes decision making by group consensus, shared responsibility, and concern for employee welfare, both on and off the job. Although a significant downturn in the Asian economy in the late 1990s made the Japanese model less popular, certain aspects are still regarded as beneficial.

For instance, one typical feature of Japanese models is the regular use of **quality circles**, small groups that meet frequently to solve problems and ensure excellence. The groups contain members from many levels within the organization. By using participative methods of decision making and problem solving, in which unanimity and consensus are sought, workers can gain a sense of responsibility for their work. Production appears to be of higher quality as a result of participation in such circles (Ouchi, 1981; Cotton, 1993; Geehr et al., 1995).

On the other hand, critics of the Japanese approach say its emphasis on teamwork stifles individual creativity. Furthermore, some surveys show that Japanese supervisors have lower satisfaction with their jobs and report more stress than supervisors in the United States (DeFrank et al., 1985). Consequently, most organizational experts now suggest that a combination of Japanese and Western management systems may be most effective—as we discuss in the Exploring Diversity section.

human relations model (of organizations): The organizational model that emphasizes the social psychological nature of organizations.

contingency model (of organizations): The organizational model that focuses on how specific features of an organization's environment affect its operation.

Japanese model (of organizations): The organizational model that emphasizes decision making by group consensus, shared responsibility, and concern for employee welfare, both on and off the job.

quality circles: Small groups within an organization that meet frequently to solve problems and ensure excellence.

WHERE EAST MEETS WEST:
BLENDING JAPANESE AND U.S. APPROACHES TO ORGANIZATIONS

EXPLORING DIVERSITY

> The event begins with a series of vigorous group exercises. Clothed in shorts and T-shirts, the participants start with calisthenics, shouting the cadence in unison. The main event is a series of relay races, tug-of-war games, and similar diversions. People with high-salaried, white-collar jobs team up with blue-collar assembly line workers. During the event, conversation often centers on such topics as *kaizen, muda,* and *nemawashi.*

Although this event may sound like the Japanese equivalent of a Fourth of July observance, that is hardly the case. The locale is Fremont, California, and the occasion is the annual picnic of New United Motor Manufacturing, Inc., or NUMMI for short.

NUMMI is a joint venture by General Motors and Toyota, created to produce Chevrolets and Toyotas. Using a plant abandoned by GM, the NUMMI factory is more efficient than almost any other auto-making facility in the United States.

NUMMI's success emerged not by accident, but because of a conscious decision to adopt a Japanese organizational model. Among the most important features of the model:

◆ Decisions are made by consensus. When a decision is being considered, everyone involved is informed, and a consensus is allowed to emerge. Building a consensus ensures that alternatives will be considered.

◆ Reward and responsibility are shared collectively. If the organization does well, everyone is rewarded; if the company shows poor results, all members of the organization share the blame. Such a philosophy contrasts with many U.S. companies, where employees may be rewarded even if the company has a bad year—and some may receive only minimal salary increases even if the company has done well.

◆ The principle of *kaizen,* the constant search for improvement, underlies organizational activities. The norm of *kaizen* permeates Japanese business organizations, focusing not only on product improvements, but also on employees, who constantly strive to improve themselves.

◆ Job security is strong. Although employees are not guaranteed a job for life, they have contracts that provide for the strongest job security in the auto industry. (Rehder & Smith, 1986; Wood, 1990; NUMMI, 1999).

In the case of NUMMI, these principles were followed in several ways. NUMMI invested in extensive retraining for its employees, sending hundreds to Japan for specialized instruction. Employees became team members who *nemawashi* (discussed) how to eliminate *muda* (waste) and make continual *kaizen* (improvements). Teams of six to eight members periodically exchange jobs, in contrast to the traditional American model in which the same individual always performs the identical job on an assembly line.

On the other hand, some aspects of the Japanese organizational model do not travel well when they meet the realities of the U.S. workplace. For one thing, almost no U.S. business organizations make ironclad promises of lifetime employment. Furthermore, one unintended result of strong job security is that there is little opportunity for employees to change jobs and move to other companies, given the stability of each organization's workforce. Even if someone is hired into a new job, he or she typically must start at an entry-level position (and salary). Consequently, there is little eagerness to change organizations. In sum, there are significant drawbacks to the Japanese organizational model.

Clearly, neither the Japanese nor Western model represents the single best approach to organizations. In fact, according to organizational expert William Ouchi, the optimal perspective may be a combination of the two (Ouchi, 1981). In what he designates as "Theory Z," Ouchi suggests that the most effective organizations have some of the following characteristics, which represent a combination of Japanese and Western approaches:

◆ The promise of employment is fairly long-term, but not for a lifetime.

◆ Promotions are made at a slower rate than in the United States, but more quickly than the very slow pattern typical in Japan.

◆ Decision making is accomplished through participation and consensus. Decisions are not made entirely by a single individual, as is often the case in the United States, nor are they made solely in groups.

◆ Concern over employee welfare extends to aspects beyond the job but does not reach into every aspect of life. In contrast, U.S. approaches largely ignore workers' lives outside the office, whereas Japanese approaches typically encompass all parts of workers' lives, both in and out of the organization.

By combining the Japanese and Western approaches to organizations, businesses may discover the best of both worlds. In fact, Japanese organizations may be becoming more like those in the United States, and those in the United States may be adapting various aspects of the Japanese system (Luthans, 1989).

THE CULTURE OF ORGANIZATIONS

A visitor to the Aetna Insurance Company only a few years ago would be struck by the neat, orderly cubicles filled with desks, inhabited by neatly dressed people in suits, jackets, and ties. The desks were of a uniform size, and in fact a corporate manual provides strict rules as to the size of the desk in relationship to the position held by the desk's occupant. With a promotion came an increase in desk size.

A tour of the Microsoft Corporation, producer of the fabulously successful Windows computer software, would have yielded a very different impression. Coats and ties are rarely seen. You might encounter a group of programmers in bathing suits, playing volleyball. If you listen to the interchanges around you, you might think that you've stumbled onto a set for Star Trek. For instance, you are likely to hear such conversational snippets as "He's very high bandwidth," "Your idea has no granularity," "She's hardcore about spreadsheets," and "He went nonlinear on me." (Rebellow, 1992, p. 63)

The differences between the two companies are not just superficial; rather, they reflect deep differences in organizational culture. **Organizational culture** is the dominant pattern of basic assumptions, perceptions, thoughts, feelings, and attitudes held by members of an organization (Schein, 1990). For instance, organizational psychologist Fred Luthans (1989) gives the example of the U.S. Marine Corps, which strives to teach new recruits the "Marine way." Recruits are taught to think and act as Marines, as they are led to change previous ways of behaving. In a sense, the Marine Corps attempts to modify the very identity of new recruits, indoctrinating them with an entirely new set of values that reflect the corps.

Other organizations have their own cultures, although typically they are not as aggressive as the Marines in teaching them to newcomers. Among the most important features of corporate culture are the following (Luthans, 1989):

◆ *Regularities in behavior.* When people in a particular organization get together, they engage in common rituals and use a similar kind of language and terminology.

◆ *Norms.* As we discussed in Chapter 14, groups within organizations have standards that guide behavior. These norms permeate group life. For instance, some organizations have informal norms regarding when people take coffee breaks, what they eat for lunch, and where they hang out together after work.

◆ *Shared values and philosophy.* Members of an organization are expected to share a set of core values and a philosophy. The philosophy might be something as crass as "make a profit," or it might be more uplifting, such as "improve the quality of life for the most people."

organizational culture:
The dominant pattern of basic assumptions, perceptions, thoughts, feelings, and attitudes held by members of an organization.

"What's amazing to me is that this late in the game we still have to settle our differences with rocks."

© The New Yorker Collection 1993. Jack Ziegler from cartoonbank.com.

◆ *Organizational climate.* Different organizations have very different climates. The climate is the overall perception one gets upon entering the organization. It is based on physical layout, what the members are wearing, how they speak to one another, and how members interact with outsiders.

Although all organizations have cultures, the cultures vary widely in how pervasive they are. In some companies, for example, the culture is strong and uniform. Almost all members share the organization's values, and the culture has a major impact on the day-to-day activities of the members. In other organizations, in contrast, the culture is relatively weak and has little effect on the operation of the organization.

Furthermore, regardless of whether they have strong or weak cultures, organizations can also harbor subcultures. **Organizational subcultures** are the shared assumptions, perceptions, thoughts, feelings, and attitudes that are held by a relatively small minority of members of an organization and that differ from the dominant organizational culture.

Subcultures may develop when a group of workers experience particular difficulties, and they often occur within smaller units of a larger organization. For example, in some companies the computer software development group may have norms and values that are very different from those of the larger corporation. This difference may lead to animosity between those subscribing to the dominant culture and those following the subculture.

The specific nature of an organization's culture varies widely from one organization to another. However, researchers have found that business organizations fall into several broad categories, which are presented in Table 15–1.

A company's organizational culture is connected to the larger cultural context of a given society (Tayeb, 1987; Maczynski et al., 1997). For example, comparisons of French and American supervisors show major differences in attitudes toward employee behaviors, including different assessments of which behaviors are considered appropriate cause for concern, and which permit intervention. Specifically, French supervisors are less likely than American

organizational subcultures:
The shared assumptions, perceptions, thoughts, feelings, and attitudes that are held by a relatively small minority of members of an organization and that differ from the dominant organizational culture.

TABLE 15-1   Organizational Culture Profiles

	Tough-Guy, Macho	Work Hard/Play Hard	Bet Your Company	Process
Name of the Culture				
Type of risks that are assumed	High	Low	High	Low
Type of feedback from decisions	Fast	Fast	Slow	Slow
Typical kinds of organizations that use this culture	Construction, cosmetics, television, radio, venture capitalism, management consulting	Real estate, computer firms, auto distributors, door-to-door sales operations, retail stores, mass consumer sales	Oil, aerospace, capital goods manufacturers, architectural firms, investment banks, mining and smelting firms, military	Banks, insurance companies, utilities, pharmaceuticals, financial-service organizations, many agencies of the government
The ways survivors and/or heroes in this culture behave	They have a tough attitude. They are individualistic. They can tolerate all-or-nothing risks. They are superstitious.	They are super salespeople. They often are friendly, hail-fellow-well-met types. They use a team approach to problem solving. They are nonsuperstitious.	They can endure long-term ambiguity. They always double-check their decisions. They are technically competent. They have a strong respect for authority.	They are very cautious and protective of their own flank. They are orderly and punctual. They are good at attending to detail. They always follow established procedures.
Strengths of the personnel/culture	They can get things done in short order.	They are able to quickly produce a high volume of work.	They can generate high-quality inventions and major scientific breakthroughs.	They bring order and system to the workplace.
Weaknesses of the personnel/culture	They do not learn from past mistakes. Everything tends to be short-term in orientation. The virtues of cooperation are ignored.	They look for quick-fix solutions. They have a short-term perspective. They are more committed to action than to problem solving.	They are extremely slow in getting things done. Their organizations are vulnerable to short-term economic fluctuations. Their organizations often face cash-flow problems.	There is lots of red tape. Initiative is downplayed. They face long hours and boring work.
Habits of the survivors and/or heroes	They dress in fashion. They live in "in" places. They like one-on-one sports such as tennis. They enjoy scoring points off one another in verbal interaction.	They avoid extremes in dress. They live in tract houses. They prefer team sports such as touch football. They like to drink together.	They dress according to their organizational rank. Their housing matches their hierarchical position. They like sports such as golf, in which the outcome is unclear until the end of the game. The older members serve as mentors for the younger ones.	They dress according to hierarchical rank. They live in apartments or no-frills homes. They enjoy process sports like jogging and swimming. They like discussing memos.

Source: Adapted from Deal & Kennedy, 1982.

supervisors to be concerned about the type of clothing an employee wears to work, how much alcohol an employee drinks at lunch, and whether an employee is faithful to his or her spouse. Such organizational differences are likely to reflect broader cultural differences in attitudes.

Whatever the specific nature of an organization's culture, people do not automatically adopt the culture upon joining. As we consider next, there is an initiation period during which newcomers are taught, either explicitly or implicitly, the organizational culture.

REVIEW AND RETHINK

Review

- Organizations are groups of people working together to attain common goals.

- The four basic models of organizations are the bureaucratic, human relations, contingency, and Japanese models.

- Organizations have cultures, which are patterns of assumptions, perceptions, thoughts, feelings, and attitudes shared by their members. Some organizations also harbor subcultures.

Rethink

- Compare the Japanese model of organizations with the three Western models. What cultural factors might work for and against the implementation of the Japanese model in Western society—and vice versa?

- How does organizational "culture" differ from organizational "climate"? What does the "strength" of the culture within an organization refer to?

ORGANIZATIONAL SOCIALIZATION

It's been a curious month. After being hired for what you thought was the job of your dreams at General Construction, you've spent the first month learning the realities of organizational life. Although you knew before you started that working in a large organization would involve dealing with a well-established system, you never expected it would be so different from college. After all, you had mastered the college bureaucracy, and by the time you were a senior you understood the system enough so that you could get done just about anything you wanted.

But General Construction was different. To accomplish the most ordinary task, you spent a good amount of time filling out forms, and as for doing anything innovative, well, forget it. Your fellow employees and even your supervisor discouraged you from making waves. All your confidence in your new ideas and faith that you would be able to bring about innovative change were just about gone—and you'd been working at the job for only a month. How did your attitudes change so quickly?

It usually does not take too long for employees at both large and small organizations to "learn the ropes." In addition to a formal orientation that occurs in most organizations, the informal communication of appropriate conduct is also accomplished early in a job.

Organizational socialization is the process by which an individual comes to adopt behaviors and attitudes similar to those of others in an organization. In an organizational context, the concept of socialization, first used to explain how children learn customary and acceptable behaviors in a particular culture, considers how people "learn the ropes" in group settings. It relates both to the formal indoctrination and training people receive and to the informal communication of norms from older members of the organization.

Formal and informal socialization do not always convey the same messages about the operation of the organization. Although formal socialization may convey management's ideal

organizational socialization:
The process by which an individual comes to adopt behaviors and attitudes similar to those of others in an organization.

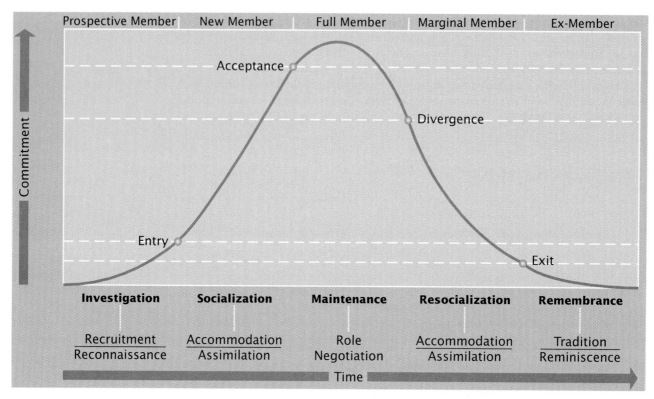

FIGURE 15–1 A Model of Group Socialization Over a period of time, socialization in a group changes in a regular pattern. (*Source:* Moreland & Levine, 1982.)

view of how employees should behave, with the goal of maximizing profit and minimizing expenses, informal socialization may provide a contradictory message. For example, a company's formal rules may state that long-distance phone calls must not be billed to the company. Informally, an employee may learn from a co-worker that phone bills are never checked and that employees can make long-distance calls without fear of discovery. In fact, the employee may learn that most employees regard free telephone calls as a perk of the job—a very contradictory message from the one provided by the formal socialization process.

Socialization in organizations, as well as in groups in general, proceeds through a series of stages. Illustrated in Figure 15–1, the stages are investigation, socialization, maintenance, resocialization, and remembrance (Moreland & Levine, 1982, 1988).

◆ *Investigation.* Before you formally commit yourself to membership in a group or organization, you would likely try to find out as much as you could about it. Social psychologists Richard Moreland and John Levine dub this procedure *reconnaissance,* in which people attempt to compare the benefits and costs of membership. At the same time, the organization engages in *recruitment,* gauging the contributions a potential new member might make. If the individual and the organization agree that membership is appropriate, *entry* takes place.

◆ *Socialization.* Following actual entry, a newcomer enters the formal stage of socialization. During this period, the group or organization attempts to indoctrinate the newcomer into existing norms and attitudes, while the newcomer tries to shed incompatible norms and attitudes. This process is not always a one-way street in which newcomers are forced to modify their views and the organization remains unaltered. Instead, change may occur reciprocally. The organization may be forced to make accommodations to newcomers, particularly when the newcomers enter the organization at higher levels of authority. At the same time, newcomers must formulate changes in their own points of view and positions.

At the point when the socialization phase is complete, a transition point known as *acceptance* marks the time when a newcomer is confirmed and endorsed as a full member of the group or organization. In many cases acceptance occurs fairly rapidly, whereas in other cases it never fully occurs at all. In such cases both the newcomer and the organization are likely to find the situation objectionable, and the new member is likely to leave the organization.

◆ *Maintenance.* Even after someone becomes a full-fledged member of an organization, socialization is not complete. In fact, socialization forces may become even stronger as long-time veterans of the organization seek to make new members adhere to the existing norms. However, veterans also experience socialization pressures. In addition to adjusting to the presence of new members, they may also face changes in organizational goals or changes in their own standing within the group. For instance, veterans may find themselves under the authority of a new boss who may seek to modify established procedures.

The maintenance stage can last indefinitely, although eventually everyone reaches the point of departure from the organization. Employees retire, and members of student organizations graduate.

In some cases, though, maintenance does not proceed smoothly. Organizational changes may become too extreme for a member to accept and tolerate, or a member's interests, goals, and aspirations may change, making membership less attractive. In other cases, the organization becomes dissatisfied with a member's performance or contribution. When such situations occur, another transition point is reached, known as *divergence,* which leads into the next stage, resocialization.

◆ *Resocialization.* If the member or the group (or both) becomes sufficiently dissatisfied with the situation, the resocialization stage begins. In resocialization, the organization attempts to change dissatisfied members in ways that might help them become more accepting of the group as it currently stands. At the same time, members may try to produce changes that will make the group more acceptable.

Resocialization can end in one of two ways. The first way is that resocialization increases a person's commitment to the group (and vice versa), and the person once again is seen as a full member of the organization. In such a case, the person moves back into the earlier stage of maintenance.

The second way is more negative—people terminate their involvement in the group. This point is known as the *exit point.* If the situation reaches this point, people move into the final stage in the process: remembrance.

◆ *Remembrance.* In the final stage, remembrance, both the individual who has left the organization and the remaining members reassess the person's contributions to the organization. Members *reminisce* about their term in the organization, considering how well the group fulfilled their personal needs. Sometimes these reminiscences have a tendency to rewrite history. For instance, attendees at retirement dinners are sometimes astounded to hear the important contributions made by a former co-worker who in reality contributed only marginally to the group.

ORGANIZATIONAL COMMUNICATION: WORKING THROUGH CHANNELS

If you have a gripe with the company you work for, to whom should you communicate your concern?

In many organizations, your complaint must be channeled to one person, and one person only—your immediate supervisor. In such a situation, organizational rules will not permit you to mention your difficulty to the company president, even if you see her eating lunch every day in the employee cafeteria. In contrast, other organizations provide employees with the opportunity to contact their company higher-ups directly. Are employees who can communicate to multiple company executives more satisfied with their jobs than those who can talk to only one supervisor? Some research suggests that the answer is yes.

centralization (of communication network): The degree to which people occupying a position can communicate with others.

information saturation: An overload of communications from the other group members.

Communication channels.   How members of an organization can "work through channels" represents a central feature of organizations. Almost all organizations are structured so that communications follow a specific pattern or arrangement. Furthermore, such patterns can have a direct bearing on the efficiency and satisfaction of the members of the organization.

One of the most critical features bearing on communication is a position's degree of centralization. **Centralization** reflects the degree to which people occupying a position can communicate with others. With greater centralization, certain individuals have considerable opportunities to communicate with others, because information flows through those in the center of the organization. Everyone else has few opportunities, because information passes through the person in the more centralized position.

In more decentralized organizations, however, all members of an organization have a relatively similar opportunity to communicate with others, and everyone has an equal opportunity to have access to information. In a decentralized organization, then, no single individual holds the advantage when it comes to the ability to communicate with others.

In highly centralized organizations, people with the most opportunities and freedom to communicate have a distinct advantage. For instance, they are most likely to take leadership roles and be seen as leaders. They are also more likely to be satisfied than those who have only limited opportunities to communicate with others (Leavitt, 1951; Shaw, 1981).

Why do people in centralized positions have such an advantage? One reason is that, as the old saying goes, knowledge is power. A person occupying a central position knows more about what is happening in the organization, and this knowledge, in turn, may permit such an individual to solve problems more effectively than a person with less information.

People who occupy central positions in highly centralized groups tend to be relatively satisfied, but peripheral members tend to show less satisfaction. As a consequence, if we consider the group as a whole, the overall level of satisfaction in highly centralized groups tends to be lower than in more decentralized ones (Krackhardt & Porter, 1986).

But the advantages of being in central positions do not extend to every domain. People in central positions may experience **information saturation**, an overload of communications from the other group members. When saturation occurs, people in centralized positions receive and produce so many messages that they are unable to perform their jobs effectively or efficiently.

Because saturation is most apt to occur when the organization's tasks are complex, centralized communication patterns may not be appropriate for intricate, difficult, and complicated tasks. For these circumstances, decentralized communication patterns may be more effective. In contrast, centralized patterns seem to work best for more straightforward, simple, and routine jobs.

Electronic mail.   When the chief executive officer of IBM reads his e-mail messages, he may find messages not only from senior managers of the company but also from any one of the tens of thousands of employees who work at all levels of the company. The reason is a deliberate policy that permits any employee to get in touch electronically with top managers.

The use of e-mail has some important consequences for communication. For one thing, e-mail often does not include information about users' social status. Consequently, it may reduce the consequences of status differences between members of the organization, permitting higher-status managers to obtain more information about what is really going on in the organization than they otherwise might (Dubrovsky, Kiesler, & Sethna, 1991).

Furthermore, the ease with which e-mail can be used increases the opportunities for users to communicate with one another. Theoretically, at least, this use ought to break down barriers between organizational employees and increase the amount of information that employees have at their disposal. The increased communications may also lead to saturation, however, as people become inundated with information, some of which may be irrelevant to their jobs.

Research on the social psychological outcomes of using e-mail is in its early stages. We do not know yet whether the ultimate consequences of its use will be largely positive or negative for either employee job performance or job satisfaction (Sproull & Kiesler, 1991; McGrath & Hollingshead, 1994; Anderson, 1995).

In highly centralized organizations, people with the most opportunities and freedom to communicate have a distinct advantage. However, they also run the risk of information saturation.

WHEN JOBS END: WORK STOPPAGES

Drive along the asphalt river of Interstate 95 across the Rhode Island border and into the pristine confines of Connecticut. Stop at that first tourist information center with its sheaves of brochures promising lazy delights. What could anyone possibly guess of Steven A. Holthausen, the portly man behind the counter who dispenses the answers?

Certainly not that for 2 decades he was a $1,000-a-week loan officer. Not that he survived three bank mergers only to be told, upon returning from a family vacation, that he no longer had a job. Not that his wife kicked him out and his children shunned him. Not that he slid to the bottom step of the economic ladder, pumping gas at a station owned by a former bank customer, being a guinea pig in a drug test, and driving a car for a salesman who had lost his license for drunkenness. Not that, at 51, he makes do on $1,000 a month as a tourist guide, a quarter of his earlier salary. And not that he is worried that his modest job is itself fragile and that he may have to work next as a clerk in a brother's liquor store. (Uchitelle & Kleinfield, 1996, p. 1)

Steven Holthausen's situation is all too familiar to many workers in the late 1990s. In one-third of all households, a family member has lost a job, and since 1970 more than 43 million jobs have disappeared. And although far more jobs have been created during the same time period than have been lost, increasingly the jobs that are disappearing are those of higher-paid workers, caught in a web of organizational *downsizing,* the process by which a company shrinks the size of its workforce to increase its profits.

The social psychological consequences of losing one's job are enormous, particularly given the important role that work plays in people's lives. We'll consider two very different forms of stopping work—involuntary termination and retirement—and the consequences of each.

Job loss and downsizing.   Because work plays an important role in people's lives, the loss of one's job goes well beyond financial considerations. People who are unemployed frequently experience a variety of psychological and physical symptoms, including insomnia, anxiety, depression, and irritability. Their self-confidence may decline, and they may find that they cannot concentrate. In fact, statistics show that every time the U.S. unemployment rate increases by 1%, the suicide rate increases 4.7% and admissions to psychiatric facilities go up 4% for men and 2% for women (Walker & Mann, 1987; Kates, Grieff, & Hagen, 1990; Connor, 1992).

Who is worse off: workers who are fired for poor performance, or workers terminated through no fault of their own during organizational downsizing? Although we might expect that workers who are fired for poor performance experience greater psychological distress than those whose employment is terminated through no fault of their own, this may not be the case. In fact, workers who are victims of downsizing face a considerable psychological

TABLE 15–2	Stages of Retirement
STAGE	**CHARACTERISTIC**
Honeymoon	In this period, former workers engage in a variety of activities, such as travel, that were previously hindered by working full time.
Disenchantment	In this stage, retirees feel that retirement is not all that they thought it would be. They may miss the stimulation of a job or may find it difficult to keep busy.
Reorientation	At this point, retirees reconsider their options and become engaged in new, more fulfilling activities. If successful, it leads them to the next stage.
Retirement routine	Here the retiree comes to grips with the realities of retirement and feels fulfilled with this new phase of life. Not all reach this stage; some may feel disenchanted with retirement for years.
Termination	Although some people terminate retirement by going back to work, termination occurs for most people because of major physical deterioration where their health becomes so bad they can no longer function independently.

Source: Atchley, 1982.

challenge. The implicit worker–employer contract, in which good work and loyalty should be rewarded with continued employment, is broken when an organization downsizes. As a consequence, workers may feel abandoned and mistreated (Seppa, 1996).

Retirement.   Retirement is very different from involuntary termination. However, the consequences of retirement depend considerably on why it occurs. Some people retire because they are burned out, and others retire because they feel they are not accomplishing as much as in previous stages of their careers. Finally, some people retire not because they planned to, but because of financial incentives offered by their organizations.

In contrast, some people retire for more positive reasons. They look forward to the added free time that retirement provides, planning to use it for increased travel, visiting friends, studying, or spending more time with family.

Whatever the reason behind retirement, retirees tend to pass through a series of stages (Atchley, 1982, 1985; see Table 15–2). First, in the *honeymoon* period, former workers throw themselves into activities for which they did not have time earlier. Next, they may move into the *disenchantment* period, in which they decide that retirement is not all that it was cracked up to be. They may have trouble keeping busy and miss the stimulation of the job.

The next stage is *reorientation,* in which retirees reconsider their options and become involved in new, more stimulating activities. This can lead to the *retirement routine* stage, in which retirees find fulfillment, falling into patterns in which they feel happy and successful. Not everyone reaches this stage.

The consequences of retirement depend considerably on why it occurs.

Finally, most retirees move into the *termination* stage. In this stage, some event—such as returning to work or physical deterioration—brings the positive period of retirement to an end.

Not everyone proceeds through all the stages or even passes through them in the same order. Nevertheless, retirement from work has important consequences.

mentors: Informal instructors who can act as socialization guides for newcomers.

EASING YOUR PATH INTO A NEW ORGANIZATION

For some people socialization into a new group proceeds relatively smoothly, whereas for others it is a rocky and sometimes ultimately impassable road. How can you make your socialization into an organization more effective? In their discussion of strategies that groups use to produce successful socialization, social psychologists Richard Moreland and John Levine (1989) shed light on ways newcomers to groups can foster their own socialization:

◆ Choose the right organization in the first place. Not everyone belongs in every group or organization. A free-spirited, independent individual might do best in a company with loose regulations and might stumble in an organization with a rigid, hierarchical structure.

◆ Take advantage of initiation opportunities. In some cases, initiations may be informal, as when organization veterans are especially solicitous of new members. In other instances, initiations can be formal and elaborate. For example, new employees of a large bank in Japan go through a set of rigorous activities. During their first 3 months, they have to meditate and fast at a Zen monastery, carry out basic training exercises at a military base, participate in community service activities, take a 25-mile hike, and vacation together at a spartan resort (Rohlen, 1973). Whether informal or formal, initiations serve an important purpose, and newcomers should take advantage of every opportunity to participate.

◆ Identify a mentor. Organizational **mentors** are informal instructors who can act as socialization guides for newcomers. Mentors can describe the unwritten, informal norms of an organization and teach newcomers to avoid possible pitfalls. They can also help newcomers by persuading veterans in groups to be more accepting and helpful to the newcomer.

Although these techniques will not guarantee that newcomers in groups and organizations will fit in smoothly, they do optimize their chances of success.

THE INFORMED CONSUMER OF SOCIAL PSYCHOLOGY

REVIEW AND RETHINK

Review

• Organizations employ both formal and informal socialization processes to indoctrinate new members.

• Organizations differ in their communication patterns, with some being centralized and others decentralized.

• Employees leave work either voluntarily, through retirement, or involuntarily, through job loss and downsizing.

Rethink

• Explain the difference between formal and informal organizational socialization. When the two sources provide contradictory messages, which is more likely to prevail? Why?

• Describe the concepts of "acceptance" and "divergence" in organizational socialization. What is "resocialization"?

- What effect might the phenomenon of information saturation have on a highly centralized organization that happens to have a decentralized e-mail policy?

- According to contemporary organizational communications theories, what level of centralization would be most effective in running the executive branch of a government? Does the United States use such a level of centralization? Explain.

- What process do you think a worker goes through who has been involuntarily discharged from an organization? In what ways is it similar to, or dissimilar from, the process following voluntary retirement?

SOCIAL PSYCHOLOGY AND THE ENVIRONMENT: LIVING IN A COMPLEX WORLD

Where are you at this moment? In your bedroom, with a compact disc playing in the background? In a cafeteria, with people at tables around you chatting? Sitting alone by a campus pond, glancing occasionally at the ducks floating lazily by? Riding a bus crammed with passengers?

Wherever you are, you are doubtless being affected by the environment. The noise level, the other people nearby, the experience of solitude or of being crowded—all these features of the environment are influencing your behavior, as well as that of the people around you.

Social psychologists have become central participants in a relatively new field, environmental psychology, which considers the effects of people's surroundings on their social behavior. **Environmental psychology** examines the interrelationships between the physical and social environment and their impact on behavior (Veitch & Arkkelin, 1995; Gardner & Stern, 1996; Sommer, 1999).

Social psychologists, working with architects, biologists, geographers, economists, and environmental scientists, have sought to answer a variety of questions about the way in which we are affected by our environment, as well as the opposite question concerning the impact of our behavior on the environment. They have investigated a variety of questions: How does the atmospheric environment, including temperature, humidity, wind, and even ion concentration in the air, affect us? How do architectural features of housing and institutions influence behavior, and can buildings be designed more effectively to promote prosocial behavior? How can environmental and technological disasters be prevented? What can be done to influence people to preserve their environment through such measures as recycling and forest preservation?

We'll sample a few of the main areas of environmental psychology. Our focus will be on those topics on which social psychologists have had the greatest impact, including crowding, territoriality, and personal space. But first read the Speaking of Social Psychology interview with environmental psychologist Jennifer Veitch.

THE EXPERIENCE OF CROWDING

With 50% of the U.S. population living on just 1% of the land, the experience of crowding is an important fact in many people's daily lives. When we hear the term *crowding,* certain images probably come to mind: people riding a subway car during rush hour, a tiny apartment that houses a large family, a standing-room-only performance at a theater. However, a precise scientific definition of crowding is considerably more difficult to produce. Amount of space by itself is clearly insufficient: People may feel crowded in a bus but not at a party in someone's living room, even if the square footage is identical. Likewise, the number of people, by itself, is not sufficient to define crowding. For instance, someone in a vast football stadium may not feel crowded, even though the number of people in the stadium is in the tens of thousands.

Clearly, then, definitions of crowding that rely on space and numbers of people alone are insufficient. Most social psychologists feel that a crucial aspect in understanding crowding

environmental psychology:
The discipline that examines the interrelationships between the physical and social environment and their impact on behavior.

is a person's *psychological experience* related to both number of people and available space. **Crowding** refers to the psychological or subjective factors in a multiperson situation—how an individual perceives a given number of people in a particular space. Crowding is viewed as a psychological state that is stressful and that motivates attempts to bring about its cessation or reduction. In contrast, **density** refers to the purely physical and spatial aspects of a situation–the number of people per spatial unit (Jain, 1993; Edwards et al., 1994).

crowding: The psychological or subjective factors in a situation—how an individual perceives a given number of people in a particular place.

density: The purely physical and spatial aspects of a situation—the number of people per spatial unit.

Why People Feel Crowded.   What leads people to experience high density as crowding? Several factors seem to be involved (Evans & Lepore, 1992):

◆ *Stimulus overload.* One reason that high density results in a negative psychological state is that it may overwhelm and, ultimately, overload people's perceptual systems. In this view, the presence of others is not particularly different from any sort of excessive stimulation, be it noise, heat, or light. To reduce this excessive stimulation, people try to escape, either by actually leaving the area or by psychologically "tuning out" the presence of others.

◆ *Loss of control.* A second explanation for the experience of crowding relates to feelings of loss of control that may occur in the presence of others. Excessive numbers of people in a relatively small area can lead individuals to feel that their behavioral control and freedom have been reduced. Although at first these individuals will try to gain command of a situation in which they experience loss of control, ultimately they may experience a sense of learned helplessness, feeling that no matter what actions they take they will be unable to change the situation (Burger, Oakman, & Bullard, 1983; Lepore, Evans, & Schneider, 1992; Davies, 1994a).

◆ *Ecological factors.* High density may be unpleasant because it leads to a scarcity of valued resources, thereby preventing people from accomplishing their intentions and completing what they'd like to do. Resources might be anything from actual materials that are being used to construct something to roles that people play in a given situation. For instance, if too many people are in a group that is constructing a float for a parade, certain people may be left out or have nothing to do. These people may experience a sense of crowding—whereas others, who are able to be more involved in the task, will not have the same unpleasant perception. According to this view, then, the way people define a situation determines whether they will feel crowded.

◆ *Focus of attention.* When people are in high-density situations, their focus of attention may shift. If they focus attention on other people in the situation, they are likely to experience crowding; if they focus attention on some other aspect of the situation, they will not (Worchel & Brown, 1984). For example, we may feel crowded in a noisy subway because there is so little else to attend to that our attention is likely to be focused on the multitude of people who surround us. In contrast, we may feel relatively uncrowded in a situation of equal density, such as a party, in which our attention is focused on a specific conversation with one other person.

The consequences of crowding.   The most common initial reaction to crowding is a change in emotional state: People report feeling unhappy, anxious, fearful, or angry in crowded environments. Just anticipating that an environment will be crowded produces negative emotions. Furthermore, we like others less in crowded environments, and we are less apt to help them (Fuller et al., 1993; Evans, Lepore, & Schroeder, 1996; Gress & Heft, 1998).

However, both gender and cultural differences exist in reactions to crowding. For instance, females react less negatively than males to being crowded. Why is this so? One explanation rests on differing socialization processes in Western cultures for men and women: Women may learn to be more affiliative than males and therefore find crowding less aversive, whereas men are socialized to show greater competitiveness, and crowding may arouse their competitive tendencies (Aiello, Nicosia, & Thompson, 1979; Ruback & Pandey, 1996).

Cross-cultural studies have found that Asians are more tolerant than Westerners of high density. Such differences may be due to different cultural experiences, given that population densities in many urban areas of Asia are considerably higher than those in Western cities (Gillis, Richard, & Hagan, 1986; Ekblad, 1996).

In extreme cases, crowding may be so great that people simply become immobilized.

SPEAKING OF SOCIAL PSYCHOLOGY

Jennifer A. Veitch
Environmental Psychologist

Year of Birth: 1964

Education: BSc, BA (Hons), Psychology, University of Manitoba, Winnipeg, Manitoba, Canada; M.A., Psychology, Queen's University, Kingston, Ontario, Canada; Ph.D., Psychology, University of Victoria, Victoria, British Columbia, Canada

Home: Ottawa, Ontario, Canada

For most of us, the surroundings in which we live and work largely go unnoticed on an everyday basis. But a growing body of research suggests that even the subtlest environmental factors can have a profound effect on our day-to-day lives.

According to Jennifer Veitch, research officer for the Institute for Research in Construction, a part of the National Research Council of Canada, everything from lighting to the presence of plants can influence various behaviors.

"Some of these relationships are familiar to us from everyday experience," she noted. "For example, settings such as living rooms with soft furniture, deep carpets, and paintings on the walls bring about different sorts of social behaviors from classrooms with rows of hard chairs and desks. Similarly, we know that dimming the lights or lighting candles sets the stage for a romantic dinner.

"Research evidence shows that aesthetically pleasing surroundings lead to more favorable judgments about others than do unpleasant surroundings," said Veitch, "In addition, the

> *"Aesthetically pleasing surroundings lead to more favorable judgments about others than do unpleasant surroundings."*

In addition to the psychological consequences that crowding produces, crowding also is associated with declines in physical functioning. For example, crowding results in an increase in heart rate, blood pressure, and the level of adrenaline in the circulatory system. Ultimately, it can even lead to an increase in illness (Baron et al., 1976; Evans et al., 1998).

For example, one of the most striking illustrations of the link between crowding and health was carried out by Paulus, McCain, and Cox (1978), who examined death rates for prison inmates over a 16-year period. In that time the prison population ranged from a low of about 375 to a high of about 650. At the same time, the death rate ranged from 0.7 to about 3.0 per hundred prisoners. What is most interesting about these figures is the close correspondence at any given time between prison population and death rate. As shown in Figure 15–2, as the population rose and fell, so did the death rate.

Although clear links exist among crowding, stress, and illness (e.g., Schaeffer, Baum, & Paulus, 1984; Paulus & McCain, 1983; Freeman & Stansfeld, 1998), results such as these are correlational in nature. We cannot assume that crowding itself *causes* illness, only that there is a relationship, because some other factor associated with crowding may be the underlying cause of poor health. For example, high social density may lead to poor sanitation, which ultimately leads to the higher incidence of illness (Veitch & Arkkelin, 1995).

kind of surroundings affect more subtle factors such as the amount of client disclosure in a therapy setting."

What constitutes an optimum environment? "A healthy environment is one in which the potential for physical stressors is minimized, and conditions are created that allow people to do what they need to in the space," Veitch noted. "But while there are codes and guidelines that are used when specifying proper conditions for an environment, new information is uncovered that requires the guidelines to be revised.

> *"A healthy environment is one in which the potential for physical stressors is minimized, and conditions are created that allow people to do what they need to in the space."*

"A good example of this change is the evolution of lighting standards in North America during this century," she explained. "The earliest codes specified lighting levels that would be considered dark today. But by the 1960s, lighting levels had increased by a factor of 10 in some settings. Today, however, they are back down by about half in those same settings, due to computer screens that became brighter and had higher resolution. In addition, we found that higher levels of lighting did not produce a proportional benefit in visibility or performance, as had been initially thought. And energy awareness made conservation a priority."

Performance can certainly be affected by an environment, but according to Veitch, the way in which it is affected depends on a number of factors. "The effects depend on the task, the particular environmental feature that is in question, and on the individual," she said. "For example, there is evidence that some people are sensitive to the concentration of positive ions in the air. These individuals show slower reaction time in the presence of high positive ion concentrations, in contrast to most people, who are unaffected."

Sometimes the consequences of environmental stressors are not immediately apparent, but become clear later, Veitch explained. "People can sustain performance levels on simple tasks even when exposed to loud, uncontrollable, and unpredictable noise. However, they show negative aftereffects when the noise ends, such as poorer performance and lower tolerance to frustration."

Furthermore, in extreme cases, crowding may be so great that it simply immobilizes people. For instance, although aggression generally increases with crowding, aggression actually drops at very high levels of crowding (Loo, 1978). The explanation is probably similar to what we discussed when we considered the relationship between aggression and heat in Chapter 9. Like high temperatures, high levels of crowding may either discourage people from taking action or may cause them to flee to less crowded surroundings. Consequently, under conditions of extreme crowding, aggression may simply take too much energy to bother with (Baron & Ransberger, 1978; Bell, 1992; Anderson, Deuser, & DeNeve, 1995; Anderson & Anderson, 1998). (For more on the consequences of crowding, see the Applying Social Psychology box.)

TERRITORIALITY

Imagine that you tend to do most of your studying in the library. In fact, you have found a quiet corner of the reserve reading room that you habitually use. Because the room is generally uncrowded, you are able to sit at the same table each time. Over the course of the semester, you come to think of the table and chair as yours, even though you know they are in a public place.

territoriality: The feelings of ownership that develop over a particular geographic area.

However, one day just before final exams, when the whole library is much more crowded, you find someone sitting not just at "your" table but in "your" chair. Feeling angered, you go over to the intruder. You are about to tell her that she ought to move, but you stop, feeling that you really have no right to complain. After all, you don't own that space, do you?

This scenario is played out in one way or another many times in many places. People feel protective of an area that they use habitually, whether it's a library table, a park bench, an office, a parking spot, or a home. These feelings reflect **territoriality**, emotions and behavior associated with the ownership or occupation of a place or area. Territoriality frequently involves personalizing the location and defending it against intrusion.

Several types of territories exit, including primary territories, secondary territories, and public territories (Altman, 1975; Taylor & Stough, 1978).

♦ *Primary territories* are under the complete, long-term control of their users and are perceived as such both by their owners and by others. Intrusions by others are regarded as serious normative errors and may even present threats to a person's well-being. The best examples of a primary territory are a person's home and, to a lesser degree, his or her office.

♦ *Secondary territories* are under less personal control. The use of secondary territories is not permanent, and any one individual is not the only user over the course of a day. The territories may be personalized while being occupied, but the personalization ends when the owner leaves the area. Our earlier description of a particular seat in a library is a good example of a secondary territory. Observers will perceive that a user has temporary ownership. Even if a user leaves the area temporarily, such as to use a restroom or to have lunch, others will view the space as temporarily "reserved" for the user. On the other hand, when the user leaves the area for an extended period of time, the area can legitimately be claimed by others.

♦ *Public territories* are areas that any member of the public has the right to use. Areas such as beaches, parks, telephone booths, and buses all represent public territories. These areas are not owned in either a formal or an informal sense but rather are open to anyone who wants

FIGURE 15–2   The Link Between Crowding and Health A study that examined death rates of inmates in a state psychiatric prison over a 16-year period discovered a close correspondence between prison population and death rate. (*Source:* Paulus, McCain, & Cox, 1978.)

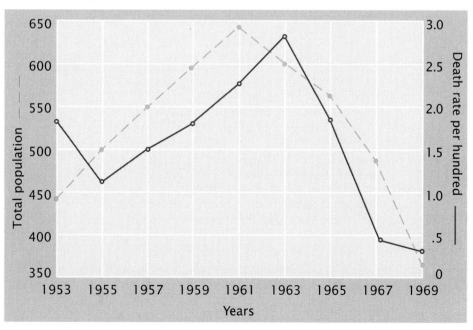

APPLYING SOCIAL PSYCHOLOGY
LIVING IN TOO CLOSE QUARTERS: HOW CROWDING HARMS WELL-BEING

Children face many threats to their well-being living in India, which contains some of the largest—and poorest—urban areas of the world. One of the greatest threats may be that their housing is extremely crowded.

According to research by Gary Evans and colleagues, who studied 10- to 12-year-old children living in Poona, India, chronic residential crowding was associated with a variety of difficulties in social behavior and adjustment. Specifically, children whose homes were more crowded had problems in school adjustment, performed less well in school, and had higher blood pressure. They were also more likely to experience learned helplessness, the belief that one can exert no control over one's environment. As we discussed in Chapter 5, when people hold such beliefs, they feel unable to escape their environment and may simply give up. In some cases, learned helplessness can lead to a profound sense of depression (Evans et al., 1998).

The study also found that boys and girls reacted differently to crowding. Boys living under more crowded conditions were more likely to have higher blood pressure than girls. On the other hand, girls living under more crowded conditions were more likely to experience learned helplessness than boys.

What leads to the negative consequences of crowding? One key factor seems to be that children experience more conflict in their relationships with their parents, and their relationships are consequently less socially supportive. Under conditions of extreme crowding, parents are less responsive to their children, and there are greater levels of conflict and hostility. Children in such homes show greater anger, and they are more likely to be the recipients of punishment. Parents living under such conditions have weaker social ties with each other and other family members.

to use them. As soon as a user leaves a public territory, the territory becomes open to anyone. However, while an individual is using them, they do take on aspects of ownership by the occupant—although on a temporary basis. Thus, a person sitting on a park bench will not be asked to leave by another person; the bench occupant, by his or her mere presence, takes temporary control of the territory. But as soon as the first person leaves, the second is legitimately entitled to claim the space.

People's reactions to violations of territoriality differ markedly according to which type of territory is in question. For example, violations of primary territories may readily produce aggression—sometimes at extreme levels. Indeed, local laws often permit the killing of an intruder in someone's home; people who commit that act are rarely prosecuted. In contrast, violations of secondary and public territories are relatively unlikely to evoke overt aggression.

A field study by social psychologists Stephen Worchel and Margaret Lollis (1982) shows that there are also cultural differences in how various types of territories are defended. The study examined the responses of home dwellers in the United States and Greece to contamination by bags of litter of primary, secondary, and public territories. The investigators hypothesized that litter would be disposed of more rapidly when it was found on primary and secondary territories (areas that the residents controlled most directly) than on public territories (which were not under their personal control).

In the study, an experimenter placed litter on the front yard, on the sidewalk in front of the residence, or on the street curb in front of a home, and measured the speed with which the litter was removed. (If the litter had not been removed within 24 hours, the experimenter picked it up.) As Figure 15–3 shows, there was little difference in speed of removal according to culture when the litter was put in the residents' yards. In contrast, the litter was removed faster from the sidewalk and curb areas in the United States than in Greece.

The results suggest that the different areas may be perceived differently by the members of the two cultures. In Greece, both the sidewalk and the curb are thought of as public territories, whereas in the United States they are more likely to be considered secondary territories.

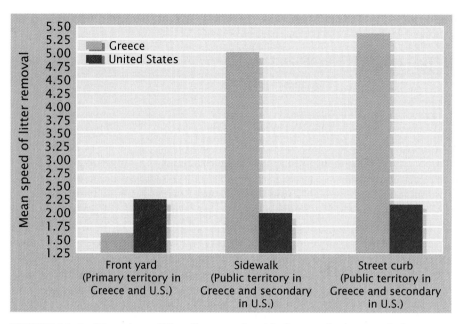

FIGURE 15–3   Litter Away When litter was placed in front yards, there was little difference in the speed of litter removal for people living in Greece compared with the United States; front yards are primary territories in both countries. But cultural differences emerged with litter placed on sidewalks and street curbs, which are public territories in Greece and secondary territories in the United States. (*Source:* Worchel & Lollis, 1982.)

These results also suggest an interesting strategy for increasing public responsibility for litter removal: A change in the perception of territorial control may make individuals come to feel more responsible for the care of particular areas.

Besides evoking attempts at defense, territories also produce positive responses. In a demonstration of what has been called the "home, sweet home effect," people are more at ease and like new acquaintances better when they meet them in their own dormitory rooms than when the first meeting takes place in the acquaintance's room (Edney, 1975; Taylor & Lanni, 1981).

The "home, sweet home" effect may help explain the "home field advantage," the phenomenon in which sports teams frequently perform better during home games than road games (Altman, 1975). It is likely that the home team's knowledge of the idiosyncrasies of its own field, wind patterns, fans, and the like proves advantageous. This awareness may help team members to feel more relaxed or generally more positive about playing at home—ultimately leading to better performance.

Marking a territory: Staking out your turf.   The significance of territories is indicated by the care with which people use markers to delineate the boundaries of the territories that belong to them. Although animals often mark their territories by physiological means, as those of us with male dogs know quite graphically, human beings employ physical markers such as fences, walls, hedges, and No Trespassing signs.

In general, primary territories are the most overtly demarcated, whereas secondary and public territories are demarcated more subtly. When people are unable to use physical markers, they may use bodily markers such as touch to establish a territory and subsequently maintain control over it. For instance, people who had just started playing a game at a new arcade machine spent significantly more time touching the machine when a stranger appeared to be watching them start to play than when a friend was watching. It seems that the stranger's observation led the player to experience feelings of territorial threat, to which he or she responded with the marker of touching. In contrast the presence of the observing friend did not necessitate marking (Werner, Brown, & Damron, 1981).

PERSONAL SPACE:
COME AND GET A LITTLE BIT CLOSER

How would you react if a stranger sat down next to you on a bus and leaned so close that you felt the side of his body pressing against yours?

Most of us would pull away, and our feelings of liking would hover near zero. The reason is that we have a well-defined sense of **personal space**, the area around a person's body into which others may not enter. Like territoriality, personal space is used to regulate the areas around us.

Personal space is like a bubble that surrounds a person, psychologically "protecting" the person from intrusions by others. The bubble analogy is a bit too simple, however. The area that we protect actually extends into three dimensions, taking into account the fact that different areas of the body may have different spatial requirements. According to the model shown in Figure 15–4, personal space is greatest for the top half of the body but tapers below the waist toward the floor. Furthermore, personal space is not rigid; it grows and shrinks according to the situation, the people with whom we are interacting, and our own personality characteristics.

Interpersonal attraction is related to just how much we allow others to invade our personal space. Generally speaking, the more we like someone the closer we permit her or him to come. In fact, there are well-defined standards for spacing, depending on the intimacy of the interaction. According to anthropologist Edward Hall (1966), middle-class Americans tend to interact with one another at a distance of 18 inches or less for the most intimate interactions. Casual interactions with friends are held at distances from 18 inches to 4 feet, and people tend to space themselves from 4 to 12 feet apart when conducting impersonal business. Finally, there is a "public zone," which extends from 12 feet to the limits of hearing, generally about 25 feet. Formal occasions, such as lectures and judicial proceedings, occur at this distance.

People use distance to draw inferences about how much others are attracted to them (Mehrabian, 1968a, 1968b). For instance, one experiment found that people who were asked to imagine that another person was standing 3 feet away thought that they would be liked significantly more than when the other person was imagined to be 7 feet away. Another experiment, in which participants were asked to space themselves as if they liked (or disliked) another person, found that participants chose to stand considerably closer to the person they liked (Mehrabian, 1968a, 1968b). Of course, such data suffer from a methodological drawback: Participants' perceptions of how they space themselves might be quite different from what they would do when interacting with an actual person (Love & Aiello, 1980).

Furthermore, extremes of closeness are not always related positively to interpersonal attraction. If the interaction is basically positive, increased proximity is related to enhanced liking. But if the interaction is initially negative, nearness can lead to increased negativity on the part of the interactants (Schiffenbauer & Schiavo, 1976). Ultimately, then, increased proximity may not lead to enhanced attraction between two people, but to its opposite.

One of the intriguing findings related to interpersonal spacing is that different cultures have very different standards regarding the appropriate distance to maintain when conversing. For instance, when Arabs converse they tend to sit closer to one another than Americans do when conversing (Watson & Graves, 1966). In fact, Arabs tend to converse casually at a distance of just 1 foot, whereas Americans tend to hold conversations with nonintimate friends at distances of 4 to 12 feet, as mentioned earlier. It is not hard to imagine the discomfort that a newly acquainted American and Arab would feel conversing with each other, each trying to maintain an "appropriate" distance. As the Arab tried to edge closer, the American would be likely to try to back away. Unless some equilibrium was reached, interpersonal attraction between the partners would likely suffer.

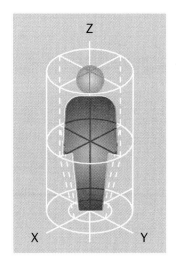

FIGURE 15–4   Personal Space A personal space zone surrounds a person three dimensionally, "protecting" him or her from the intrusion of others. (*Source:* Hayduk, 1978.)

personal space: The area around a person's body into which others may not enter.

The amount of personal space a person prefers depends on the situation, personality characteristics, the nature of the relationship involved, and cultural factors.

REVIEW AND RETHINK

Review

- Environmental psychology studies the interrelationships between the physical and social environment and human behavior.

- Crowding is an emotional and psychological state that arises in multiperson situations and causes stress; it contrasts with density, which is a quantitative physical phenomenon.

- Territoriality is a feeling of ownership or occupation of a place or area. People's territories are divided into primary, secondary, and public territories.

- People define an area of personal space around them, which they protect from intrusion. The amount of personal space a person requires differs depending on the situation, on personality characteristics, on personal attraction and liking, and on culture.

Rethink

- Do the definitions of crowding held by city dwellers differ from those of country dwellers? Why?

- If drivers caught in traffic jams experience crowding, which factors are probably involved: stimulus overload, loss of control, ecological factors, or focus of attention? Why?

- Does research on crowding have implications for policies relating to public housing? Why?

- Why do you think differences were found in perceptions of public and private territories in the United States and Greece? How might apartment or dormitory dwellers differ from homeowners in their perceptions of public and private territories?

- Might different definitions of personal space cause conflict among persons from different cultures? Among persons from different cultures within the United States? If so, how?

LOOKING BACK

What models explain the basic structure of organizations?

1. Organizations, groups of people working together to attain common goals, operate according to four basic models. The bureaucratic model represents the attempt to apply rationality and efficiency to the functioning of organizations. The human relations model emphasizes the social psychological structure of an organization. Contingency models focus on how specific features of an organization's environment affects the way it operates. Japanese models typically include a lifetime employment guarantee, quality circles, shared responsibility, and adherence to the principle of *kaizen,* the constant search for improvement. (p. 497)

2. Attempts to apply Japanese models in the United States have had to face the different realities of the U.S. business and cultural situation. With some modifications, combined Japanese American structures that use many Japanese-style techniques can be made to work in the United States. (p. 499)

How do organizations maintain particular cultures and teach them to newcomers?

3. Organizational culture is the dominant pattern of assumptions, perceptions, thoughts, feelings, and attitudes held by members of an organization. The basic features of an organizational culture include regularities in behavior, norms, shared values and philosophy, and organizational climate. (p. 500)

4. Organizational socialization is the process by which a newcomer to an organization comes to display behavior and attitudes similar to those of others in the organization. Socialization moves through a series of stages: investigation, socialization, maintenance, resocialization, and remembrance. (p. 503)

How is information communicated in organizations?

5. Organizations vary in terms of centralization, the degree to which people occupying any given position can communicate with others. People who occupy central positions in highly centralized groups tend to be relatively satisfied and become leaders, but most members of highly centralized organizations are less satisfied. (p. 506)

6. People in central positions may experience information saturation, an overload of communications from others in the organization. Because communications tend to be greatest around complex tasks, centralized communication patterns may be inappropriate for such tasks. (p. 506)

7. The effects of electronic mail on organizational communication patterns is as yet unknown, but it is possible that e-mail may have a tendency either to break down communication barriers within organizations or to increase information saturation. (p. 506)

What are the consequences of job loss and retirement?

8. Job loss can have serious social psychological consequences, because work plays a very important role in people's lives. Effects can include both physical and psychological symptoms. (p. 507)

9. Workers who retire from their jobs often proceed through a series of stages, including a honeymoon period, disenchantment, reorientation, the retirement routine stage, and the termination stage. (p. 508)

In what ways is human behavior affected by the physical and social environment?

10.   Environmental psychologists study the impact of the physical and social environment on human behavior. Social psychologists have had significant influence in environmental psychology, especially in work on crowding, territoriality, and personal space. (p. 510)

11.   Crowding is the psychological perception of stress in multiperson situations, in contrast with density, which is a purely quantitative measure. High density may be experienced as crowding when any of several factors is present, including stimulus overload, loss of control, certain ecological factors relating to resource availability, and a focus of attention on the number of people in the environment instead of on other environmental features. (p. 511)

12.   Crowding may have serious consequences for health, liking, and helping or aggressive behavior. The perception of crowding shows both cultural and gender influences. (p. 511)

13.   People exhibit territoriality, the sense of ownership or occupation of a particular place. There are several types of territories, including primary territories, secondary territories, and public territories, which evoke different levels of protective response when they are invaded. Definitions of these territories differ across cultures. (p. 514)

14.   People also have a sense of personal space, the area around the person to which access is restricted. Definitions of personal space differ according to the situation, personality characteristics, the degree of liking felt by the person, and cultural factors. (p. 517)

EPILOGUE

Our journey through the field of social psychology has ended with a consideration of groups and organizations. Beginning in the previous chapter, where we discussed how aggregates of people join together to form groups, we moved to the larger arena of organizations. We considered different models of organizations and the basic processes that underlie their functioning. We discussed organizational culture, socialization, and communication, and we touched on the effects of job loss on people's lives. Finally, we discussed interactions between the physical and social environment and human behavior, focusing on those areas in which social psychologists have been particularly influential.

As we've seen throughout this book, social psychological theory and research have made significant contributions to our understanding of how the social world operates. At the same time, such work has led to significant applied contributions, producing real improvement in people's lives.

Yet the story of social psychology remains incomplete. The field is advancing on many fronts, continuing to unfold and grow. New theories are being developed, research continues, and applications continue to be derived. To quote poet Robert Browning, the best is yet to be.

As we finish our consideration of this active and growing field, turn back to the prologue of this chapter, on the experience of Juliana Custodio and Transformations. Consider these questions:

1.   Why might a "boot camp" atmosphere help particular individuals who have little prior professional experience learn job-related skills?

2.   In addition to basic technological skills, what social skills would you try to teach people enrolled in the Transformations program, based on what was discussed in the chapter regarding organizations?

3. What socialization steps will graduates of Transformations likely go through when they take their first job?

4. Will socialization processes differ depending on whether the organizations that the new employees join use bureaucratic, human relations, contingency, or Japanese models? If so, in what ways?

KEY TERMS AND CONCEPTS
---

bureaucratic model (of organizations) (p. 497)

centralization (of communication network) (p. 506)

contingency model (of organizations) (p. 498)

crowding (p. 511)

density (p. 511)

environmental psychology (p. 510)

human relations model (of organizations) (p. 498)

information saturation (p. 506)

Japanese model (of organizations) (p. 498)

mentors (p. 509)

organizational culture (p. 500)

organizational socialization (p. 503)

organizational subcultures (p. 501)

organizations (p. 497)

personal space (p. 517)

quality circles (p. 498)

territoriality (p. 514)

GLOSSARY

ABC tripartite model The notion that attitudes are composed of three components: an affective component, a behavioral component, and a cognitive component. (Ch. 10)

accessibility The degree to which an attitude can be brought to mind. (Ch. 10)

acquired immunodeficiency syndrome (AIDS) A fatal disease caused by a virus that destroys the body's immune system and has no known cure. (Ch. 5)

action identification theory The theory that suggests that people's interpretation of their own behavior varies in terms of whether the behavior is seen at a high or low level. (Ch. 4)

active behavioral coping A behavioral approach in which people mobilize to fight the illness directly, resulting in higher self-esteem, better mood, and increases in perceived social support. (Ch. 5)

actor–observer bias The tendency of people to attribute their behavior to situational factors, whereas people observing the behavior tend to attribute it to the actors' stable, unchanging dispositions. (Ch. 4)

agentic Professions associated with getting things accomplished. (Ch. 3)

aggression Intentional injury or harm to another person. (Ch. 9)

aggressive cues Learned stimuli that have previously been associated with aggression. (Ch. 9)

altruism Helping behavior that is beneficial to others but requires clear self-sacrifice. (Ch. 8)

altruistic personality A concept suggesting that certain individuals have enduring personality characteristics that consistently lead them to help. (Ch. 8)

ambivalent stereotyping Stereotyping combining both hostile and favorable beliefs about outgroup members. (Ch. 3)

androgynous A state in which gender roles encompass characteristics thought typical of both sexes. (Ch. 3)

anxious–ambivalent attachment The style of attachment that is seen in children who show great distress when separated from their caregivers, but who appear angry on their return. (Ch. 6)

archival research Research in which an investigator analyzes existing records or documents in an effort to confirm a hypothesis. (Ch. 1)

attachment The positive emotional bond that develops between a child and a particular individual. (Ch. 6)

attitudes Learned predispositions to respond in a favorable or unfavorable manner to a particular person, object, or idea. (Ch. 10)

attribution The process by which people attempt to identify the causes of others' and their own behavior. (Ch. 2)

attribution approaches Approaches to social cognition that seek to identify how we understand what brings about the behavior—our own and others'—that we observe. (Ch. 2)

attribution training The approach in which inaccurate, harmful attributions are replaced with more accurate, and beneficial, ones. (Ch. 5)

attributional model of helping and emotions A model suggesting that the nature of an attribution for a request for help determines a person's emotional response and the help provided. (Ch. 8)

attributional style A tendency to make certain kinds of causal attributions across different situations. (Ch. 5)

audience pleasing Behavior designed to make an audience feel good. (Ch. 4)

automaticity The processing of social information that requires little or no effort, is routine, and often occurs outside awareness. (Ch. 2)

availability heuristic A rule applied in judging the likelihood of an event by considering the ease with which it can be recalled from memory. (Ch. 2)

avoidant attachment The style of attachment that characterizes relationships in which the child appears relatively indifferent to caregivers and avoids interactions with them. (Ch. 6)

avoidant coping Behavior in which people refuse to think about their illness, and they evade or postpone acting in ways that deal directly with the disease. (Ch. 5)

balance theory The approach in which people strive for consistency, or balance, in their likes and dislikes. (Ch. 6)

base-rate fallacy The tendency to underemphasize base-rate data because of the influence of more prominent, although ultimately less meaningful, information. (Ch. 2)

beautiful-is-good stereotype The belief that physically attractive people possess a wide range of positive characteristics. (Ch. 6)

behavioral intention The probability that people place on the likelihood that they will engage in a behavior that is relevant to a held attitude. (Ch. 10)

brainstorming A procedure in which group members are asked to produce as many ideas, in as uninhibited a manner, as they possibly can. (Ch. 14)

bureaucratic model (of organizations) The organizational model that attempts to apply rationality and efficiency to the functioning of organizations. (Ch. 15)

cataclysmic events Strong stressors that occur suddenly and affect many people simultaneously. (Ch. 5)

catharsis The process of discharging aggressive energy that is continually built up within people. (Ch. 9)

central route persuasion The route to persuasion that occurs on the basis of the logic, merit, or strength of the arguments. (Ch. 11)

central traits Characteristics that serve to organize an impression of another person and provide a framework for interpreting other information about that person. (Ch. 2)

centralization (of communication network) The degree to which people occupying a position can communicate with others. (Ch. 15)

close relationships A relationship characterized by at least one of three factors: emotional attachment, need fulfillment, and interdependence. (Ch. 7)

cognitive algebra approach An explanation for impression formation that suggests that perceivers consider each individual trait; evaluate each trait individually, in isolation

523

from the others; and then combine the evaluations into an overall judgment. (Ch. 2)

cognitive consistency   An approach that focuses on the ways people strive to maintain consistency within and between attitudes, as well as on the ways they manage to reconcile inconsistencies of which they are aware. (Ch. 10)

cognitive dissonance   A state of psychological tension that is aroused when a person simultaneously holds two ideas or thoughts—cognitions—that contradict one another. (Ch. 10)

cognitive neoassociationistic model   Berkowitz's theory that aversive circumstances produce negative affect, in the form of anger, hostility, or irritation. (Ch. 9)

cohabitation   The state in which an unmarried couple choose to live together. (Ch. 7)

collective behavior   Behavior that occurs in groups of people who are relatively unorganized yet who hold a sense of unity and may work toward similar goals. (Ch. 14)

collectivism   The notion that the well-being of the group is more important than that of the individual. (Ch. 12)

collectivistic culture   A culture that emphasizes membership in groups and the group's well-being. (Ch. 2)

communal   Professions associated with relationships. (Ch. 3)

communal relationship   A relationship where the participants feel mutual responsibility, and each provides benefits according to the other's needs or to exhibit concern for the other person. (Ch. 7)

companionate love   The strong affection that we have for those with whom our lives are deeply involved. (Ch. 7)

comparison level theories   Theories that suggest that attraction to others is based on comparison of a relationship to some hypothetical baseline. (Ch. 6)

compliance   Yielding to direct, explicit appeals meant to produce certain behavior or agreement with a particular point of view. (Ch. 12)

conditions   The differing treatments that are given to the different groups in an experiment. (Ch. 1)

confederates   Employees or colleagues of the experimenter who pose as participants in an experiment and who may be used to produce a scene that has impact on subjects, engaging and involving them. (Ch. 1)

confirmation biases   The tendency to seek out, interpret, or formulate information that is consistent with one's current beliefs. (Ch. 2)

conformity   A change in behavior or attitudes brought about by a desire to follow the beliefs or standards of others. (Ch. 12)

confusion of responsibility   A state in which observers assume that a person who is actually aiding a victim is in some way responsible for the emergency situation. (Ch. 8)

consumer behavior   The study of behavior that focuses on understanding buying habits and the effects of advertising on buyer behavior. (Ch. 11)

contact hypothesis   The hypothesis is that direct contact between hostile groups that will reduce prejudice only under certain conditions. (Ch. 3)

contingency model   The model that states that leader effectiveness is based on several key situational factors and leaders' particular traits. (Ch. 13)

contingency model (of organizations)   The organizational model that focuses on how specific features of an organization's environment affect its operation. (Ch. 15)

control   The degree to which an experimenter is able to limit and restrict events within the experiment to those that are intended. (Ch. 1)

control group   The no-treatment or alternative-treatment group in an experiment. (Ch. 1)

convenience samples   Samples chosen more because participants are easily available than for their representativeness. (Ch. 1)

coping   The effort to control, reduce, or learn to tolerate the threats that lead to stress. (Ch. 5)

correlational research   Research that seeks to identify whether an association or relationship between two factors exists, regardless of whether one factor produces changes in the other. (Ch. 1)

correspondent inferences   Observers' notions of how closely an overt behavior or action represents a specific underlying intention, trait, or disposition. (Ch. 2)

counterfactual thinking   Thinking that evaluates an actual event by considering alternative, and often more desirable, hypothetical outcomes. (Ch. 2)

covert measure of attitude   An approach to measuring behavior in which the measurement technique is disguised in some way. (Ch. 10)

creative nonadherence   A situation in which patients adjust or augment a treatment prescribed by a physician, relying on their own medical judgment and experience. (Ch. 5)

crowding   The psychological or subjective factors in a situation—how an individual perceives a given number of people in a particular place. (Ch. 15)

daily hassles (or background stressors)   The minor irritants of life that produce minor stress. (Ch. 5)

death qualification   A practice in which judges exclude from a jury potential jurors who indicate they could not, because of their prior beliefs, vote for a death penalty. (Ch. 13)

debriefing   A full, careful explanation of the procedures used in the study. (Ch. 1)

defense mechanisms   Unconscious reactions to threats that reduce anxiety by distorting or denying the true nature of the situation. (Ch. 5)

defensive attributions   Attributions that enable observers to deal with perceived inequities in others' lives and to maintain the belief that the world is just. (Ch. 2)

deindividuation   The reduction of a person's sense of individuality and a corresponding increase in the person's willingness to engage in deviant behavior. (Ch. 14)

demand characteristics   The cues that participants receive in an experiment that provide information regarding expected or appropriate behavior. (Ch. 1)

density   The purely physical and spatial aspects of a situation—the number of people per spatial unit. (Ch. 15)

dependent variable   The variable that is measured in an experiment and is expected to change as a result of the experimental manipulation. (Ch. 1)

descriptive self-disclosure   Self-disclosure in which people share facts about their lives. (Ch. 7)

diffusion of responsibility   The tendency for people to feel that responsibility for acting is shared, or diffused, among those present. (Ch. 8)

discrimination   Negative (or sometimes positive) actions taken toward members of a particular group because of their membership in the group. (Ch. 3)

display rules   Guidelines that govern the appropriateness of nonverbal shows of emotion. (Ch. 2)

dispositional causes Reasons for behavior that rest on the personality traits and characteristics of the individual carrying out the behavior. (Ch. 2)

distraction-conflict theory The theory that social facilitation effects occur because the presence of others is distracting, and our attention becomes divided between the task at hand and the others who are present. (Ch. 14)

door-in-the-face technique A technique of social influence in which a large request, to which refusal is expected, is followed by a smaller one. (Ch. 12)

double standard The view that premarital sex is permissible for men but not for women. (Ch. 7)

dual-process approach (to majority/ minority influence) The theory that minority influence differs from majority influence not just in degree but also in kind. (Ch. 12)

egoism Behavior motivated by self-benefit. (Ch. 8)

elaboration likelihood model The theory that suggests that central route persuasion occurs when the recipient carefully considers arguments and expends cognitive effort in elaborating the meaning and implication of a message. (Ch. 11)

emergent norm perspective The perspective that suggests a group definition of appropriate behavior—essentially a new norm—arises in violent mobs. (Ch. 14)

emotional aggression Aggression with the explicit goal of hurting a victim. (Ch. 9)

emotional isolation A form of loneliness in which a person feels a lack of deep emotional attachment to one specific person. (Ch. 6)

empathy An emotional response corresponding to the feelings of another person. (Ch. 8)

empathy–altruism hypothesis The theory that empathy lies at the heart of altruistic behavior. (Ch. 8)

entrapment A situation in which a person is lured by a law enforcement agent into committing a crime. (Ch. 13)

environmental psychology The discipline that examines the interrelationships between the physical and social environment and their impact on behavior. (Ch. 15)

equity theory The theory that suggests that people take into account not only their own outcomes, but also the outcomes that are perceived to be attained by others. (Ch. 6)

evaluation apprehension The presence of others that leads to the inference that the audience is evaluating us, a circumstance that is definitely physiologically arousing. (Ch. 14)

evaluation research A technique designed to determine the effects of a research program—specifically, whether it is meeting its goals—and to contribute information to help improve the program in the future. (Ch. 1)

evaluative self-disclosure Self-disclosure in which people communicate information about personal feelings. (Ch. 7)

exchange relationships Associations based on an economic model of interaction, in which people seek to maximize their benefits and minimize their costs. (Ch. 7)

excitation transfer model The theory that states that physiological arousal acts to intensify subsequent emotional experiences, even if they are unrelated to the initial arousal. (Ch. 9)

exemplification A technique in which people attempt to create the impression of moral superiority and integrity. (Ch. 4)

experiment Procedure to test a hypothesis. (Ch. 1)

experimental research Research designed to discover causal relationships between various factors, in which the researcher deliberately introduces a change in a situation in order to observe the effect that change has on the situation. (Ch. 1)

extrinsic motivation Motivation that causes people to participate in activities for tangible rewards. (Ch. 4)

false consensus effect The tendency to overestimate the degree of agreement for our own opinions, beliefs, and attributes. (Ch. 2)

fear appeals Messages designed to change attitudes by producing apprehension and anxiety if they are not followed. (Ch. 11)

field study A research investigation carried out in a naturally occurring setting. (Ch. 1)

foot-in-the-door technique A technique of social influence in which the target of social influence is first asked to agree to a small request, but later is asked to comply with a larger one. (Ch. 12)

frustration The thwarting or blocking of some ongoing behavior directed toward a desired goal. (Ch. 9)

frustration–aggression hypothesis The theory that frustration always leads to aggression of some sort, and that aggression is *always* the result of some form of frustration. (Ch. 9)

fundamental attribution error The tendency to overattribute others' behavior to dispositional causes and the corresponding failure to recognize the importance of situational causes. (Ch. 2)

gender roles The set of expectations, defined by society, that indicate what is appropriate behavior for males and females. (Ch. 3)

gender schema The cognitive framework that organizes information relevant to gender. (Ch. 3)

great person theory of leadership The theory that certain people are born to lead. (Ch. 13)

group Two or more people who (1) interact with one another; (2) perceive themselves as a group; and (3) are interdependent. (Ch. 14)

group cohesiveness The extent to which members of a group find the group attractive. (Ch. 14)

group polarization The exaggeration of a group's initial tendencies following group discussion. (Ch. 14)

group structure Regular, stable patterns of behavior in groups. (Ch. 14)

groupthink A type of thinking in which group members share such strong motivation to achieve consensus that they lose the ability to evaluate alternative points of view critically. (Ch. 14)

Guttman scales A measurement that presents a gradation of attitudes, ranging from the least extreme to the most extreme. (Ch. 10)

hard sell An advertising approach that focuses on the qualities of the product itself. (Ch. 11)

hardiness A personality characteristic associated with a lower rate of stress-related illness. (Ch. 5)

health psychology The specialty area that focuses on physical health, illness, and wellness. (Ch. 5)

heuristics Personal principles or rules of thumb that permit us to make decisions on the basis of limited information and with relatively little cognitive effort. (Ch. 11)

homogamy The tendency to marry someone who is similar in age, race, education, religion, and other basic demographic characteristics. (Ch. 7)

human relations model (of organizations) The organizational model that emphasizes the social psychological nature of organizations. (Ch. 15)

hypothesis A prediction stated in a way that permits it to be tested. (Ch. 1)

hypothetical constructs Abstract concepts that cannot be directly observed. (Ch. 10)

identity The combination of roles and group categories to which a person belongs, along with the set of personal meanings and experiences related to the roles and categories. (Ch. 4)

idiosyncrasy credit A psychological "currency" that permits deviation from the group. (Ch. 12)

illusory correlation The result of people overestimating the strength of a relationship between two distinctive or unusual events. (Ch. 3)

independent variable The variable that is manipulated in the experiment by the researchers. (Ch. 1)

individualism The notion that the personal identity, uniqueness, freedom, and worth of the individual person is central. (Ch. 12)

individualistic culture A culture that emphasizes personal identity, individual uniqueness, and individual freedom. (Ch. 2)

information saturation An overload of communications from the other group members. (Ch. 15)

informational social influence Pressure to conform that emanates from our assumption that others have knowledge that we lack. (Ch. 12)

informative advertising Advertising that is designed to introduce new products, to suggest new ways of using an existing product, or to correct false impressions about a product. (Ch. 11)

ingratiation A deliberate effort to make a favorable impression. (Ch. 4)

ingroup A group to which a person feels that he or she belongs. (Ch. 3)

ingroup–outgroup bias The tendency to hold less favorable views about groups to which we do not belong, while holding more favorable opinions about groups to which we do belong. (Ch. 3)

instrumental aggression Aggression in which the goal is to obtain something of value. (Ch. 9)

insufficient justification A situation in which people perform, for a minimal inducement, a behavior that is discrepant with their true attitudes. (Ch. 10)

interactional approaches to leadership The theory that different situations call for particular kinds of leaders. (Ch. 13)

interdependence The degree of influence two people have over each other and the quantity of activities in which they jointly engage. (Ch. 7)

interpersonal attraction The degree of liking that people have for one another. (Ch. 6)

interpersonal repulsion The desire to escape from another's presence; it is the opposite of interpersonal attraction. (Ch. 6)

intimacy The status in which a person communicates important feelings and information to another through a process of self-disclosure. (Ch. 7)

intimidation A self-presentation strategy in which people communicate an ability and inclination to produce negative outcomes for other people. (Ch. 4)

intrinsic motivation Motivation that causes people to participate in activities for their own enjoyment, not for the reward the activities bring them. (Ch. 4)

Japanese model (of organizations) The organizational model that emphasizes decision making by group consensus, shared responsibility, and concern for employee welfare, both on and off the job. (Ch. 15)

jigsaw technique A classroom procedure for increasing intergroup interaction based on the way one constructs a jigsaw puzzle. (Ch. 3)

knowledge function of attitudes The aspect of attitudes that permits us to organize and make sense of the world. (Ch. 10)

labeling theory of passionate love The theory that suggests that people experience romantic love when intense physiological arousal and situational cues occur together. (Ch. 7)

laboratory study A research investigation conducted in a controlled setting explicitly designed to hold events constant. (Ch. 1)

learned helplessness The belief that one can exert no control over one's environment. (Ch. 5)

learning approaches to aggression The theory suggesting that aggression is based on prior learning. (Ch. 9)

leniency bias The tendency for jury deliberation to lead more often to acquittal than conviction. (Ch. 13)

Likert scale An approach to the measurement of attitudes in which objects are rated on the basis of a numbered evaluative response scale. (Ch. 10)

loneliness The inability to maintain the level of affiliation one desires. (Ch. 6)

lowballing A technique in which an initial agreement is reached, but then the seller reveals additional costs. (Ch. 12)

mandate phenomenon Behavior in which a person with strong support exceeds group norms and seeks even more power. (Ch. 13)

marriage gradient The tendency for men to marry women who are slightly younger, smaller, and lower in status, and women to marry men who are slightly older, larger, and higher in status. (Ch. 7)

matching hypothesis The theory that suggests that people are attracted to those whose level of physical attractiveness is similar to their own. (Ch. 6)

mentors Informal instructors who can act as socialization guides for newcomers. (Ch. 15)

mere exposure effect The phenomenon that repeated exposure to any stimulus increases the positivity of its evaluation. (Ch. 6)

minority group A group whose members have significantly less power, control, and influence over their own lives than do members of a dominant group. (Ch. 3)

models People whose behavior can be imitated and who provide a guide to appropriate behavior. (Ch. 9)

modern racism A subtle form of prejudice in which people appear, on the surface, not to harbor prejudice, but actually do hold racist attitudes. (Ch. 3)

motivated tactician model The approach to social cognition in which the way people view the world depends on their goals, motivations, and needs. (Ch. 2)

motivational biases Sources of error that stem from a need to present oneself well, either to impress others or to maintain one's self-esteem. (Ch. 2)

naturalistic observation A process in which investigators observe some naturally occurring behavior but do not intervene in the situation. (Ch. 1)

need complementarity hypothesis The notion that individuals are attracted to others who have significantly different personalities, but whose needs complement their own. (Ch. 6)

need for affiliation The desire to seek relationships with other people. (Ch. 6)

need for belongingness The need to establish and maintain at least a minimum number of interpersonal relationships. (Ch. 6)

need for cognition A person's habitual level of thoughtfulness and cognitive activity. (Ch. 11)

need for power A personality characteristic in which an individual has a tendency to seek impact, control, or influence over others, and to be seen as a powerful person. (Ch. 13)

negative affect model of aggression The theory that high temperatures, as well as other aversive stimuli in the physical environment, can lead to higher aggression—but only to a point. (Ch. 9)

negative state relief (NSR) model The model that seeks to explain the relationship between bad mood and helping behavior by focusing on the consequences of prosocial behavior for the help *provider*. (Ch. 8)

nonparticipant observation The type of naturalistic observation in which the researcher records people's behavior in a given setting but does not actually enter into it. (Ch. 1)

nonverbal behavior People's actions separate from speech that are used as indications of their inner feelings. (Ch. 2)

norm of noninvolvement A standard of behavior that causes people to avoid becoming psychologically (and physically) entangled with others. (Ch. 8)

norm of reciprocity The norm asserting that we should help others because they have helped us in the past or may help us in the future. (Ch. 8)

norm of social responsibility The norm suggesting that people should respond to the reasonable needs of others, and that all people have a societal obligation to aid those in need. (Ch. 8)

normative social influence Pressure that reflects group norms, which are expectations regarding appropriate behavior held by those belonging to groups. (Ch. 12)

norms General standards or expectations regarding appropriate behavior. (Ch. 8)

obedience A change in behavior due to the commands of others in authority. (Ch. 12)

operationalization The process of translating a hypothesis into specific testable procedures that can be measured and observed. (Ch. 1)

organizational culture The dominant pattern of basic assumptions, perceptions, thoughts, feelings, and attitudes held by members of an organization. (Ch. 15)

organizational socialization The process by which an individual comes to adopt behaviors and attitudes similar to those of others in an organization. (Ch. 15)

organizational subcultures The shared assumptions, perceptions, thoughts, feelings, and attitudes that are held by a relatively small minority of members of an organization and that differ from the dominant organizational culture. (Ch. 15)

organizations Groups of people working together to attain common goals. (Ch. 15)

outgroup A group to which a person feels that he or she does not belong. (Ch. 3)

outgroup homogeneity bias The perception that there is less variability among the members of outgroups than within one's own ingroup. (Ch. 3)

overhelping The offering of help in a way that makes the recipient seem incapable, inept, and generally incompetent. (Ch. 8)

overjustification A phenomenon that occurs when incentives are used to bring about behavior that would have been done voluntarily, without any incentive. (Ch. 4)

participant observation The type of naturalistic observation in which the researcher actually engages in the activities of the people being observed. (Ch. 1)

passionate (or romantic) love A state of intense absorption in someone. (Ch. 7)

perceived behavioral control The factor in behavioral intention that takes into account the ease or difficulty of carrying out the behavior, based on prior experience and anticipated barriers to performing it. (Ch. 10)

peripheral route persuasion The route to persuasion that occurs when people are persuaded on the basis of factors unrelated to the nature or quality of the content of a persuasive message. (Ch. 11)

permissiveness with affection standard The view that premarital intercourse is permissible for both men and women if it occurs within a long-term, committed, or loving relationship. (Ch. 7)

person perception approaches Approaches to social cognition that consider the ways

people assess and combine the traits of other persons to form overall impressions. (Ch. 2)

person positivity bias ("Pollyanna effect") The tendency to see the world (and other people) in positive terms. (Ch. 2)

personal norms Our own personal sense of obligation to help a specific person in a specific situation. (Ch. 8)

personal space The area around a person's body into which others may not enter. (Ch. 15)

personal stressors Major life events that have immediate negative consequences. (Ch. 5)

persuasion The process by which attitudes are changed. (Ch. 11)

pluralistic ignorance A state that occurs when bystanders in an emergency or ambiguous situation use the behavior of others to determine whether help is actually required. (Ch. 8)

political psychology The branch of psychology that examines the psychological aspects of political behavior. (Ch. 13)

political socialization The process by which people develop political attitudes, values, and voting habits, which begins when most of us are very young and often has a lasting influence on us. (Ch. 13)

possible selves Those aspects of the self that relate to the future. (Ch. 4)

POSSLQs Persons of the opposite sex sharing living quarters—the term given by the U.S. Department of the Census to couples who cohabitate. (Ch. 7)

postdecision cognitive dissonance A situation in which the chosen alternative becomes more positive, and the unchosen one more negative. (Ch. 10)

power semantic The power or status level that a conversant holds. (Ch. 4)

prejudice The negative (or positive) evaluations or judgments of members of a group that are based primarily on membership in the group and not necessarily on the particular characteristics of individuals. (Ch. 3)

prescriptive norms Norms that suggest to people the way they ought to behave. (Ch. 14)

priming The process by which recent exposure to stimuli such as people, ideas, or even mere words influences the interpretation of new information. (Ch. 2)

private acceptance A phenomenon in which a person's private opinion changes as a result of true persuasion. (Ch. 12)

private self-consciousness   One's awareness of inner thoughts, feelings, and self-evaluations. (Ch. 4)

process loss   Aspects of a group's interaction patterns that hinder performance and prevent the group from operating at 100% proficiency. (Ch. 14)

production blocking   The inhibition of group members' expressing their ideas because of the social norm that in a group only one person can speak at a given time. (Ch. 14)

proscriptive norms   Norms that inform people about behaviors they should avoid. (Ch. 14)

prosocial behavior   Helping behavior that benefits others. (Ch. 8)

prosocial collectivism   Motivation with the goal of increasing the welfare of a group or collective. (Ch. 8)

prosocial principlism   Motivation with the goal of upholding some moral principle. (Ch. 8)

psychographics   A method for dividing people into lifestyle profiles that are related to purchasing patterns. (Ch. 11)

psychoneuroimmunology (PNI)   The study of the relationship between psychological factors and the immune system. (Ch. 5)

psychophysiological conditions   Medical problems related to the interaction of psychological, emotional, and physical difficulties. (Ch. 5)

public compliance   Public acceptance of a group's position but private disapproval of the same position. (Ch. 12)

public self-consciousness   A focus on one's outward behavior and on appearances that are visible to others. (Ch. 4)

quality circles   Small groups within an organization that meet frequently to solve problems and ensure excellence. (Ch. 15)

racism   Prejudice directed at people because of their race. (Ch. 3)

random assignment   In an experiment, the method of assigning subjects to particular groups on the basis of chance. (Ch. 1)

rape   The act of one person forcing another to submit to sexual activity. (Ch. 7)

reactance   A disagreeable emotional and cognitive reaction that results from the restriction of one's freedom that can be associated with medical regimens. (Ch. 5)

realistic conflict theory   The theory that argues that prejudice is the outcome of direct competition over valued, but limited, resources. (Ch. 3)

reciprocal concessions   A technique of social influence in which requesters are seen to make a compromise (by reducing the size of their initial request), thereby inviting a concession on the part of those who initially refused the request. (Ch. 12)

reciprocity of liking   The social psychological finding which states that you like those who like you. (Ch. 6)

reciprocity of self-disclosure   The theory that as intimacy between two people deepens the recipients of intimate information respond in kind. (Ch. 7)

reconstructive memories   Memories that are altered by exposure to postevent information. (Ch. 13)

reinforcement-affect model   The theory that liking follows the basic principles of learning embodied in classical and operant conditioning. (Ch. 6)

Relationship Closeness Inventory   A method used to measure the strength of relationships objectively. (Ch. 7)

relative deprivation   The sense that one lacks a desired resource in comparison to another group, which is perceived to have more. (Ch. 3)

reminder advertising   Advertising designed to keep consumers thinking about a product or to reinforce the message that preferring a particular brand is appropriate. (Ch. 11)

representativeness heuristic   The rule that is applied when judging people by the degree to which they represent a certain category. (Ch. 2)

risky shift   The finding that groups often make riskier decisions than individuals alone. (Ch. 14)

roles   Behaviors that are associated with and come to be expected of people in a given position. (Ch. 10)

Romeo and Juliet effect   The phenomenon in which couples who experience strong parental interference in their relationships report greater love for one another than those who receive little interference. (Ch. 7)

schema approaches   Approaches to social cognition that consider how people organize information and store it in memory, and how this information is used to understand behavior. (Ch. 2)

schemas   Organized bodies of information stored in memory. (Ch. 2)

secure attachment   The style of attachment that characterizes a positive, healthy relationship between a child and an adult, based primarily on trust in the adult's comfort and love. (Ch. 6)

selective demand advertising   Advertising designed to establish or modify attitudes about a particular brand of product or service, compared with other brands of the same kind of product or service. (Ch. 11)

selective exposure   A consequence of postdecision dissonance that occurs when people seek out information that supports a choice they have made and avoid information that is inconsistent with that choice. (Ch. 10)

self function of attitudes   The aspect of attitudes that enables people to create and maintain a positive sense of oneself. (Ch. 10)

self-affirmation theory   The theory that people who experience dissonance may deal with it by seeking to assert their adequacy as individuals. (Ch. 10)

self-awareness   A state in which attention is focused on the self. (Ch. 4)

self-complexity   The phenomenon of viewing oneself as having many distinct facets. (Ch. 5)

self-concept   An individual's sense of identity; the set of beliefs he or she is like as an individual. (Ch. 4)

self-construction   Self-presentation meant to corroborate our own view of ourselves. (Ch. 4)

self-disclosure   A situation in which information about the self is exchanged with others. (Ch. 5)

self-discrepancy theory   The theory that states that the discrepancy between self-concept and self-guides leads to negative emotions and ultimately to lower psychological well-being. (Ch. 5)

self-efficacy   Learned expectations that one is capable of carrying out a behavior or producing a desired outcome in a particular situation. (Ch. 4)

self-esteem   The affective component of self, a person's general and specific positive and negative self-evaluations. (Ch. 4)

self-evaluation maintenance theory   The theory that people will react to the accomplishments of important people in their lives by showing either jealousy or pride. (Ch. 4)

self-fulfilling prophecy The tendency for people to act in a way that is consistent with their expectation, belief, or cognition about an event or behavior, thereby increasing the likelihood that the event or behavior will occur. (Ch. 2)

self-handicapping A tactic in which people set up circumstances that allow them to avoid attributing poor performance to low ability and instead permit them to attribute failure to less threatening causes. (Ch. 4)

self-monitoring The regulation of one's behavior to meet the demands of a situation or the expectations of others. (Ch. 4)

self-perception theory The theory that suggests that people come to be aware of their own dispositions, emotions, attitudes, and other internal states in the same way they learn about other people—through observation of behavior. (Ch. 4)

self-presentation The process by which people attempt to create specific, generally positive impressions regarding themselves. (Ch. 4)

self-promotion An action designed to make a person seem more competent. (Ch. 4)

self-reference effect The phenomenon in which information is recalled better when it is related to the self. (Ch. 4)

self-regulation failure Inadequacies in the control of one's behavior. (Ch. 5)

self-schema The organized body of information that relates to a person's self. (Ch. 4)

self-serving bias A general tendency to attribute one's own success to internal factors—skill, ability, or effort—and to attribute failure to external factors, such as chance or a particular situation. (Ch. 2)

self-verification The desire to be perceived by others in a way that is consistent with our self-concept. (Ch. 4)

semantic differential An approach to the measurement of attitudes in which objects are rated on the basis of a pair of adjectives that are opposites, such as, good–bad, attractive–unattractive. (Ch. 10)

sexism Prejudice directed at women or men because of their gender. (Ch. 3)

single-process approach (to majority/ minority influence) The theory that both majorities and minorities employ similar influence techniques. (Ch. 12)

situational approach to leadership The theory that people become leaders in response to the characteristics of the situation in which they find themselves. (Ch. 13)

situational causes Reasons for behavior that rest on the demands or constraints of a given social setting; most situations call for certain kinds of behavior. (Ch. 2)

sleeper effect An increase in the degree of persuasiveness of a message that occurs with the passage of time. (Ch. 11)

social anxiety The experience of negative emotions revolving around interactions with others. (Ch. 6)

social categorization The process of classifying people according to particular social characteristics. (Ch. 3)

social cognition The study of how people understand and make sense of others and themselves. (Ch. 2)

social combination rules The guidelines used by members of groups to decide what needs to be done and how the task should be divided up among group members. (Ch. 14)

social comparison The need to evaluate one's opinions and abilities by comparing them to those of other people. (Ch. 4)

social decision scheme The way individual judgments and preferences are combined into a collective decision. (Ch. 14)

social facilitation Any change in performance that occurs when others are present. (Ch. 14)

social identity theory The theory that suggests people use group membership as a source of pride and self-worth. (Ch. 3)

social impact theory The theory that suggests that the effect of a majority on a minority rests on three basic factors—the majority's strength, immediacy, and number. (Ch. 12)

social influence The area of social psychology that explores how people are affected by the real or imagined pressure of other individuals or a group. (Ch. 12)

social isolation A form of loneliness in which people suffer from a lack of friends, associates, or relatives. (Ch. 6)

social learning theory The theory that emphasizes how social and environmental conditions teach individuals to be aggressive. (Ch. 9)

social loafing The decrease in individual effort that occurs when people engage in shared group activity. (Ch. 14)

social perception The task of making sense of people by going beyond appearance and behavior to what lies beneath the surface. (Ch. 2)

social power One person's ability to control and shape the behavior of others. (Ch. 13)

social psychology The scientific study of how people's thoughts, feelings, and actions are affected by others. (Ch. 1)

social support Assistance and comfort supplied by a network of caring, interested people, which is a boon to people living under stressful circumstances. (Ch. 5)

social supporter A person holding a position similar to one's own. (Ch. 12)

soft sell An advertising approach that strives to link a product with a pleasant image related to the product's use. (Ch. 11)

solidarity semantic The degree of shared social experience that exists between two people. (Ch. 4)

status The social rank a person holds within a group. (Ch. 12)

stereotype A set of beliefs and expectations about members of a group that are held simply because of their membership in the group. (Ch. 3)

stereotype vulnerability Obstacles to performance that come from awareness of the stereotypes held by society about minority student performance. (Ch. 4)

stimulus-value-role (SVR) theory The theory that relationships proceed in a fixed order through a series of three stages: stimulus stage, value stage, and role stage. (Ch. 7)

stress The response to events that threaten or challenge us. (Ch. 5)

stressors Circumstances that produce threats to our well-being. (Ch. 5)

subjective norms The factor in behavioral intention that takes into account the perceived social pressure to carry out the behavior. (Ch. 10)

supplication A means of self-presentation which consists of creating the impression that one is needy, weak, and dependent. (Ch. 4)

survey research Research in which an investigator chooses people to represent some larger population and asks them a series of questions about their behavior, thoughts, or attitudes. (Ch. 1)

techniques of neutralization Justifications used to explain behavior that violates society's standards of conduct. (Ch. 13)

territoriality The feelings of ownership that develop over a particular geographic area. (Ch. 15)

that's-not-all technique A technique of social influence in which a customer is offered a deal at an initial, often inflated, price; then immediately after making the initial offer, the salesperson offers an incentive, discount, or bonus to clinch the deal. (Ch. 12)

theory of planned behavior The notion suggesting the likelihood that someone will behave in a way consistent with an attitude depends on a measured, rational decision-making process that considers a combination of several factors. (Ch. 10)

theory of social penetration The theory that suggests that relationships gradually progress through increasingly deeper intimacy. (Ch. 7)

threat to self-esteem model The model that argues that the way in which help is offered influences whether the help is viewed as positive or negative. (Ch. 8)

transformational leaders Leaders who spur their followers into behavior that surpasses their personal interests. (Ch. 13)

treatment The procedure in an experiment provided by an investigator. (Ch. 1)

treatment group The group that receives the treatment in an experiment. (Ch. 1)

two-factor theory of emotion The theory that states that emotions are a joint result of (1) nonspecific physiological arousal and (2) the interpretation of the arousal. (Ch. 4)

Type A behavior pattern Behavior that is characterized by competitiveness, impatience, and a tendency toward frustration and hostility. (Ch. 5)

Type B behavior pattern Behavior that is characterized by noncompetitiveness, patience, and a lack of aggression. (Ch. 5)

ultimate attribution error The tendency among people holding strong stereotypes to attribute negative behavior on the part of a minority group member to dispositional characteristics, and correspondingly, to attribute positive behavior on the part of a minority group member to situational factors. (Ch. 3)

unilateral awareness The level at which individuals view the outward characteristics of others. (Ch. 7)

uplifts Minor positive events that make people feel good, even if only temporarily. (Ch. 5)

victimization A justification used by perpetrators of violent actions to claim that the act was the fault of the victim. (Ch. 13)

violence A deliberate attempt to carry out serious physical—but not psychological—injury. (Ch. 9)

voir dire Proceedings in which prospective jurors can be questioned as to their impartiality and background in order to eliminate those who are biased toward or against a particular side. (Ch. 13)

REFERENCES

Aaker, D. A., & Biel, A. L. (1993). *Brand equity and advertising: Advertising's role in building strong brands.* Hillsdale, NJ: Erlbaum.

Aaker, D. A., & Myers, J. G. (1987). *Advertising management.* Englewood Cliffs, NJ: Prentice-Hall.

Aaker, J. L., & Williams, P. (1998). Empathy versus pride: The influence of emotional appeals across cultures. *Journal of Consumer Research, 25* (3), 241–261.

Abelson, R. P. (1981). The psychological status of the script concept. *American Psychologist, 36,* 715–729.

Abraham-Murali, L., & Littrell, M. A. (1995). Consumers' perceptions of apparel quality over time: An exploratory study. *Clothing & Textiles Research Journal, 13,* 149–158.

Abrams, D., & Hogg, M. A. (Eds.). (1999). *Social identity and social cognition* (pp. 315–331). Malden, MA: Blackwell.

Abramson, L. Y., Alloy, L. B., & Metalsky, G. I. (1995). Hopelessness depression. In G. M. Buchanan & M. E. Seligman (Eds.), *Explanatory style.* Hillsdale, NJ: Erlbaum.

Abramson, L. Y., Metalsky, G. I., & Alloy, L. B. (1989). Hopelessness depression: A theory-based subtype. *Psychological Review, 96,* 358–372.

Achee, J., Tesser, A., & Pilkington, C. (1994). Social perception: A test of the role of arousal in self-evaluation maintenance processes. Special Issue: Affect in social judgments and cognition. *European Journal of Social Psychology, 24,* 147–159.

Adams, G. R., & Crane, P. (1980). An assessment of parents' and teachers' expectations of preschool children's social preference for attractive or unattractive children and adults. *Child Development, 51,* 224–231.

Aderman, D., & Berkowitz, L. (1983). Self-concern and the unwillingness to be helpful. *Social Psychology Quarterly, 46,* 293–301.

Adorno, T. W., Frenkel-Brunswik, E., Levinson, R. N., & Sanford, R. N. (1950). *The authoritarian personality.* New York: Harper & Row.

Agnew, C. R., & Thompson, V. D. (1994). Causal inferences and responsibility attributions concerning an HIV-positive target: The double-edged sword of physical attractiveness. *Journal of Social Behavior & Personality, 9,* 181–190.

Agnew, C. R., Van Lange, P. A. M., Rusbult, C. E., & Langston, C. A. (1998). Cognitive interdependence: Commitment and the mental representation of close relationships. *Journal of Personality & Social Psychology, 74,* 939–954.

Agnostinelli, G., Sherman, S. J., Presson, C. C., & Chassin, L. (1992). Self-protection and self-enhancement biases in estimates of population prevalence. *Personality and Social Psychology Bulletin, 18,* 631–642.

Aguirre, B. E., Quarantelli, E. L., & Mendoza, J. L. (1988). The collective behavior of fads: The characteristics, effects, and career of streaking. *American Sociological Review, 53,* 569–584.

Ahlawat, S. S. (1999). Order effects and memory for evidence in individual versus group decision making in auditing. *Journal of Behavioral Decision Making, 12* (1), 71–88.

Aiello, J. R., & Kolb, K. J. (1995). Electronic performance monitoring and social context: Impact on productivity and stress. *Journal of Applied Psychology, 80,* 339–353.

Aiello, J. R., Nicosia, G., & Thompson, D. E. (1979). Physiological, social, and behavioral consequences of crowding on children and adolescents. *Child Development, 50,* 195–202.

Aiello, J. R., & Svec, C. M. (1993). Computer monitoring of work performance: Extending the social facilitation framework to electronic presence. Special Issue: Computer monitoring. *Journal of Applied Social Psychology, 23,* 537–548.

Ainsworth, M. D. S., Blehar, M. C., Waters, E., & Wall, S. (1978). *Patterns of attachment: A psychological study of the strange situation.* Hillsdale, NJ: Erlbaum.

Ainsworth, M. S. (1979). Infant-mother attachment. *American Psychologist, 34,* 932–937.

Ajzen, I. (1985). From intentions to actions: A theory of planned behavior. In J. Kuhland & J. Beckman (Eds.), *Action-control: From cognitions to behavior.* Heidelberg: Springer.

Ajzen, I. (1987). Attitudes, traits, and actions: Dispositional prediction of behavior in personality and social psychology. In L. Berkowitz (Ed.), *Advances in experimental social psychology* (Vol. 20). San Diego: Academic Press.

Ajzen, I., & Fishbein, M. (1977). Attitude-behavior relations: A theoretical analysis and review of empirical research. *Psychological Bulletin, 84,* 888–918.

Ajzen, I., & Fishbein, M. (1980). *Understanding attitudes and predicting social behavior.* Englewood Cliffs, NJ: Prentice-Hall.

Ajzen, I., Timko, C., & White, J. B. (1982). Self-monitoring and the attitude-behavior relation. *Journal of Personality and Social Psychology, 42,* 426–435.

Albright, J. S., Alloy, L. B., Barch, D., & Dykman, B. M. (1993). Social comparison by dysphoric and nondysphoric college students: The grass isn't always greener on the other side. *Cognitive Therapy & Research, 17,* 485–509.

Aldag, R. J., & Fuller, S. R. (1993). Beyond fiasco: A reappraisal of the groupthink phenomenon and a new model of group decision processes. *Psychological Bulletin, 113,* 533–552.

Aldana, S. G., Sutton, L. D., Jacobson, B. H., & Quirk, M. G. (1996). Relationships between leisure time physical activity and perceived stress. *Perceptual & Motor Skill, 82,* 315–321.

Alexander, M. J., & Higgins, E. T. (1993). Emotional trade-offs of becoming a parent: How social roles influence self-discrepancy effects. *Journal of Personality & Social Psychology, 65,* 1259–1269.

Alicke, M. D., LoSchiavo, F. M., Zerbst, J., & Zhang, S. (1998). The person who out performs me is a genius: Maintaining perceived competence in upward social comparison. *Journal of Personality & Social Psychology, 73,* 781–789.

Allen, M., D'Alessio, D., & Brezgel, K. (1995). A meta-analysis summarizing the effects of pornography: II. Aggression after exposure. *Human Communication Research, 22,* 258–283.

Allen, M., Emmers, T., Gebhardt, L., & Giery, M. A. (1995). Exposure to pornography and acceptance of rape myths. *Journal of Communication, 45,* 5–26.

Allen, M., Mabry, E., & McKelton, D. (1998). Impact of juror attitudes about the death penalty on juror evaluations of guilt and punishment: A meta-analysis. *Law & Human Behavior, 22* (6), 715–731.

Allen, M. W., & Ng, S. H. (1999). The direct and indirect influences of human values on product ownership. *Journal of Economic Psychology, 20* (1), 5–39.

Allen, V. L. (1965). Situational factors in conformity. In L. Berkowitz (Ed.), *Advances in experimental social psychology* (Vol. 2). New York: Academic Press.

Allen, V. L. (1975). Social support for nonconformity. In L. Berkowitz (Ed.), *Advances in experimental social psychology* (Vol. 8). New York: Academic Press.

Allen, V. L., & Levine, J. M. (1971). Social support and conformity: The role of independent assessment of reality. *Journal of Experimental Social Psychology, 7,* 48–58.

Alley, T. R. (1988). *Social and applied aspects of perceiving faces.* Hillsdale, NJ: Erlbaum.

Alley, T. R., & Cunningham, M. R. (1991). Averaged faces are attractive, but very attractive faces are not average. *Psychological Science, 2,* 123–125.

Alloy, L. B., Lipman, A. J., & Abramson, L. Y. (1992). Attributional style as a vulnerability factor for depression: Validation by past history of mood disorders. Special Issue: Cognitive vulnerability to psychological dysfunction. *Cognitive Therapy & Research, 16,* 391–407.

Allport, F. H. (1924). *Social psychology.* Boston: Houghton Mifflin.

Allport, G. W. (1954). *The nature of prejudice.* Cambridge, MA: Addison-Wesley.

Allport, G. W., & Postman, L. J. (1945). The basic psychology of rumor. *Transactions of the New York Academy of Sciences, 8* (Series II), 61–81.

Alpert, J. J. (1964). Broken appointments. *Pediatrics, 34,* 127–132.

Altman, I. (1975). *The environment and social behavior.* Monterey, CA: Brooks/Cole.

Altman, I., & Taylor, D. A. (1973). *Social penetration: The development of interpersonal relationships.* New York: Holt, Rinehart & Winston.

Alvaro, E. M., & Crano, W. D. (1996). Cognitive responses to minority- or majority-based communications: Factors that underlie minority influence. *British Journal of Social Psychology, 35,* 105–121.

Alvaro, E. M., & Crano, W. D. (1997). Indirect minority influence: Evidence for leniency in source evaluation and counterargumentation. *Journal of Personality & Social Psychology, 72* (5), 949–964.

Alwin, D. F., Cohen, R. L., & Newcomb, T. M. (1991). *Political attitudes over the life span: The Bennington women after fifty years.* Madison: University of Wisconsin Press.

Amabile, T. M. (1983). *The social psychology of creativity.* New York: Springer-Verlag.

Amabile, T. M., Hennessey, B. A., & Grossman, B. S. (1986). Social influences on creativity: The effects of contracted-for reward. *Journal of Personality and Social Psychology, 50,* 14–23.

Ambady, N., & Rosenthal, R. (1992). Thin slices of expressive behavior as predictors of interpersonal consequences: A meta-analysis. *Psychological Bulletin, 111,* 256–274.

Ambady, N., & Rosenthal, R. (1993). Half a minute: Predicting teacher evaluations from thin slices of nonverbal behavior and physical attractiveness. *Journal of Personality and Social psychology, 64,* 431–441.

American College Health Association. (1989). *Guidelines on acquaintance rape.* Washington, DC: Author.

American Psychological Association. (1990). *Guidelines for ethical conduct in the care and use of animals.* Washington, DC: Author.

American Psychological Association. (1993a). *APA personnel survey.* Washington, DC: Author.

American Psychological Association. (1996). Ethical rules and procedures. *American Psychologist, 51,* 221–247.

American Psychological Association, Research Office. (1999). *Ph.D. recipients in psychology from U.S. universities by sex and subfield: 1920–1998.* Washington, DC: Author.

Anastasio, P., Bachman, B., Gaertner, S., & Dovidio, J. (1997). Categorization, recategorization and common ingroup identity. In R. Spears & P. J. Oakes (Eds.), *The social psychology of stereotyping and group life.* Oxford, England: Blackwell.

Andersen, P. A., & Guerrero, L. K. (Eds.). (1998). *Handbook of communication and emotion: Research, theory, applications, and contexts.* San Diego: Academic Press.

Anderson, C. A. (1989). Temperature and aggression: Ubiquitous effects of heat on occurrence of human violence. *Psychological Bulletin, 106,* 74–96.

Anderson, C. A., & Anderson, D. C. (1984). Ambient temperature and violent crime: Tests of the linear and curvilinear hypotheses. *Journal of Personality and Social Psychology, 46,* 91–97.

Anderson, C. A., & Anderson, K. B. (1996). Violent crime rate studies in philosophical context: A destructive testing approach to heat and southern culture of violence effects. *Journal of Personality and Social Psychology, 70,* 740–756.

Anderson, C. A., & Anderson, K. B. (1998). Temperature and aggression: Paradox, controversy, and a (fairly) clear picture. In R. G. Geen & E. Donnerstein (Eds.), *Human aggression: Theories, research, and implications for social policy* (pp. 247–298). San Diego: Academic Press.

Anderson, C. A., & DeNeve, K. M. (1992). Temperature, aggression, and the negative affect escape model. *Psychological Bulletin, 111,* 347–351.

Anderson, C. A., Deuser, W. E., & DeNeve, K. M. (1995). Hot temperatures, hostile affect, hostile cognition, and arousal: Tests of a general model of affective aggression. *Personality & Social Psychology Bulletin, 21,* 434–448.

Anderson, C. A., & Lindsay, J. J. (1998). The development, perseverance, and change of naive theories. *Social Cognition, 16,* 8–30.

Anderson, D. F., & Cychosz, C. M. (1995). Exploration of the relationship between exercise behavior and exercise identity. *Journal of Sport Behavior, 18,* 159–166.

Anderson, E. H. (1995). Personality, appraisal, and adaptational outcomes in HIV seropositive men and women. *Research in Nursing & Health, 18,* 303–312.

Anderson, L. R., & Randlet, L. (1994). Self-monitoring, perceived control and satisfaction with self-disclosure of sexual orientation. *Journal of Social Behavior & Personality, 9,* 789–800.

Anderson, N. H. (1965). Averaging versus adding as a stimulus-combination rule in impression formation. *Journal of Experimental Psychology, 70,* 394–400.

Anderson, N. H. (1981). *Foundations of information integration theory.* New York: Academic Press.

Anderson, T. A. (1992, March 15). Terry Anderson looks back: Blindfold and chains. *New York Times,* p. A10.

Anderson, V. L. (1993). Gender differences in altruism among Holocaust rescuers. *Journal of Social Behavior & Personality, 8,* 43–58.

Andersson, L. (1998). Loneliness research and interventions: A review of the literature. *Aging & Mental Health, 2,* 264–274.

Andrews, J. C., Durvasula, S., & Akhter, S. H. (1990). A framework for conceptualizing and measuring the involvement construct in advertising research. *Journal of Advertising, 19* (4), 27–40.

Antonak, R. F., & Livneh, H. (1995). Direct and indirect methods to measure attitudes toward persons with disabilities, with an exegesis of the error-choice test method. *Rehabilitation Psychology, 40,* 3–24.

Archer, D., Iritani, B., Kimes, D. D., & Barrios, M. (1983). Five studies of sex differences in facial prominence. *Journal of Personality and Social Psychology, 45,* 725–735.

Archer, D., Pettigrew, T. F., & Aronson, E. (1992). Making research apply: High stakes public policy in a regulatory environment. *American Psychologist, 47,* 1233–1236.

Archer, J. (1994). Testosterone and aggression. *Journal of Offender Rehabilitation, 21,* 3–39.

Archibald, F. S., Bartholomew, K., & Marx, R. (1995). Loneliness in early adolescence: A test of the cognitive discrepancy model of loneliness. *Personality & Social Psychology Bulletin, 21,* 296–301.

Arkin, R. M., & Baumgardner, A. H. (1985). Self-handicapping. In J. H. Harvey & G. Weary (Eds.), *Attribution: Basic issues and applications* (pp. 169–202). New York: Academic Press.

Arkin, R. M., Oleson, K. C., Shaver, K. G., & Schneider, D. J. (1998). Self-handicapping. In J. M. Darley & J. Cooper (Eds.), *Attribution and social interaction: The legacy of Edward E. Jones.* Washington, DC: American Psychological Association.

Arms, R. L., Russell, G. W., & Sandiland, M. L. (1979). Effects of viewing aggressive sports on the hostility of spectators. *Social Psychology Quarterly, 42,* 275–279.

Aron, A., Dutton, D. G., Aron, E. N., & Iverson, A. (1989). Experiences of falling in love. *Journal of Social and Personal Relationships, 6,* 243–257.

Aronson, E. (1988). *The social animal* (3rd ed.). San Francisco: W. H. Freeman.

Aronson, E. (1997). The theory of cognitive dissonance: The evolution and vicissitudes of an idea. In C. McGarty & S. A. Haslam (Eds.), *The message of social psychology: Perspectives on mind in society* (pp. 20–35). Oxford: Blackwell.

Aronson, E., Ellsworth, P. C., Carlsmith, J. M., & Gonzales, M. H. (1990). *Methods of research in social psychology* (2nd ed.). New York: McGraw-Hill.

Aronson, E., & Golden, B. W. (1962). The effect of relevant and irrelevant aspects of communicator credibility on attitude change. *Journal of Personality, 30,* 135–146.

Aronson, E., & Mills, J. (1959). The effect of severity of initiation on liking for a group. *Journal of Abnormal and Social Psychology, 59,* 177–181.

Aronson, E., Stephan, W., Sikes, J., Blaney, N., & Snapp, M. (1978). *Cooperation in the classroom.* Beverly Hills, CA: Sage.

Aronson, E., Willerman, B., & Floyd, J. (1966). The effect of a pratfall on increasing interpersonal attractiveness. *Psychonomic Science, 4,* 227–228.

Aronson, E., Wilson, T. D., & Brewer, M. B. (1998). Experimentation in social psychology. In D. T. Gilbert, S. T. Fiske, & G. Lindzey (Eds.), *Handbook of social psychology* (4th ed.). New York: McGraw-Hill.

Aronson, J., Cohen, G., Nail, P. R. (1999). Self-affirmation theory: An update and appraisal. In E. Harmon-Jones & J. Mills (Eds.), *Cognitive dissonance: Progress on a pivotal theory in social psychology.* (pp. 127–147). Washington, DC: American Psychological Association.

Aronson, J., Lustina, M. J., Good, C., Keough, K., Steele, C. M., & Brown, J. (1999). When white men can't do math: Necessary and sufficient factors in stereotype threat. *Journal of Experimental Social Psychology, 35* (1), 29–46.

Aronson, J., Quinn, D. M., & Spencer, S. J. (1998). Stereotype threat and the academic underperformance of minorities and women. In J. K. Swim & C. Stangor (Eds.), *Prejudice: The target's perspective* (pp. 83–103). San Diego: Academic Press.

Asch, S. E. (1946). Forming impressions of personality. *Journal of Abnormal and Social Psychology, 41,* 258–290.

Asch, S. E. (1951). Effects of group pressure upon the modification and distortion of judgments. In H. Guetzkow (Ed.), *Groups, leadership, and men.* Pittsburgh, PA: Carnegie Press.

Asch, S. E. (1952). *Social psychology.* Englewood Cliffs, NJ: Prentice-Hall.

Asch, S. E. (1955). Opinions and social pressure. *Scientific American, 193,* 31–55.

Asch, S. E. (1956). Studies of independence and conformity: A minority of one against a unanimous majority. *Psychological Monographs, 70,* 416.

Asch, S. E., & Zukier, H. (1984). Thinking about persons. *Journal of Personality and Social Psychology, 46,* 1230–1240.

Asendorpf, J. B., Warkentin, V., & Baudonniere, P. (1996). Self-awareness and other-awareness. II: Mirror self-recognition, social contingency awareness, and synchronic imitation. *Developmental Psychology, 32,* 313–321.

Ashton, M. C., Paunonen, S. V., Helmes, E., & Jackson, D. N. (1998). Kin altruism, reciprocal altruism, and the Big Five personality factors. *Evolution & Human Behavior, 19,* 243–255.

Aspinwall, L. G., & Taylor, S. E. (1993). Effects of social comparison direction, threat, and self-esteem on affect, self-evaluation, and expected

success. *Journal of Personality & Social Psychology, 64,* 708–722.

Atchley, R. C. (1982). Retirement: Leaving the world of work. *Annals of the American Academy of Political and Social Science, 464,* 120–131.

Atchley, R. C. (1985). *Social forces and aging: An introduction to social gerontology.* Belmont, CA: Wadsworth.

Atoum, A. O., & Farah, A. M. (1993). Social loafing and personal involvement among Jordanian college students. *Journal of Social Psychology, 133,* 785–789.

Aune, R. K. (1999). The effects of perfume use on perceptions of attractiveness and competence. In L. K. Guerrero, J. A. DeVito, & M. L. Hecht (Eds.), *The nonverbal communication reader: Classic and contemporary readings* (2nd ed.). Prospect Heights, IL: Waveland Press.

Austin, W. (1979). Justice, freedom, and self-interest in intergroup conflict. In W. G. Austin & S. Worchel (Eds.), *The social psychology of intergroup relations.* Monterey, CA: Brooks/Cole.

Avolio, B. J., & Bass, B. M. (1995). Individual consideration viewed at multiple levels of analysis: A multi-level framework for examining the diffusion of transformational leadership. Special Issue: Leadership: The multiple-level approaches (Part I). *Leadership Quarterly, 6,* 199–218.

Avtgis, T. A. (1998). Locus of control and persuasion, social influence, and conformity: A meta-analytic review. *Psychological Reports, 83* (3), 899–903.

Axelrod, S., & Apsche, J. (1982). *The effects of punishment on human behavior.* New York: Academic Press.

Ayman, R., Chemers, M. M., & Fiedler, F. (1995). The contingency model of leadership effectiveness: Its level of analysis. Special Issue: Leadership: The multiple-level approaches (Part I). *Leadership Quarterly, 6,* 147–167.

Ayman, R., Chemers, M. M., & Fiedler, F. (1997). The contingency model of leadership effectiveness: Its levels of analysis. In R. P. Vecchio (Ed.), *Leadership: Understanding the dynamics of power and influence in organizations* (pp. 351–377). Notre Dame, IN: University of Notre Dame Press.

Bach, G., & Wyden, P. (1968). *The intimate enemy: How to fight fair in love and marriage.* New York: Avon.

Bagby, R. M., Parker, J. D., Rector, N. A., & Kalemba, V. (1994). Racial prejudice in the Canadian legal system: Juror decisions in a simulated rape trial. Special Issue: Race, ethnicity, and the law. *Law & Human Behavior, 18,* 339–350.

Bagby, R. M., & Rector, N. A. (1992). Self-criticism, dependency and the Five Factor Model of personality in depression: Assessing construct overlap. *Personality & Individual Differences, 24,* 895–897.

Baker, S. M., & Petty, R. E. (1994). Majority and minority influence: Source-position imbalance as

a determinant of message scrutiny. *Journal of Personality & Social Psychology, 67,* 5–19.

Bakhurst, D., & Sypnowich, C. (1995). *The social self.* Newbury Park, CA: Sage.

Banaji, M. R., & Hardin, C. D. (1996). Automatic stereotyping. *Psychological Science, 7,* 136–141.

Bandura, A. (1973). *Aggression: A social learning analysis.* Englewood Cliffs, NJ: Prentice-Hall.

Bandura, A. (1974). Behavior theory and the models of man. *American Psychologist, 29,* 859–869.

Bandura, A. (1977). *Social learning theory.* Englewood Cliffs, NJ: Prentice-Hall.

Bandura, A. (1978). Social learning theory of aggression. *Journal of Communication, 28,* 12–29.

Bandura, A. (1982). Self-efficacy mechanisms in human agency. *American Psychologist, 37,* 122–147.

Bandura, A. (1983). Psychological mechanisms of aggression. In R. G. Geen & E. I. Donnerstein (Eds.), *Aggression: Theoretical and empirical reviews, Vol. 1: Theoretical and methodological issues.* New York: Academic Press.

Bandura, A. (1988). Perceived self-efficacy: Exercise of control through self-belief. In J. P. Dauwalder, M. Perez, & V. Hobbi (Eds.), *Annual series of European research in behavior therapy* (Vol. 2). Lisse, The Netherlands: Swets & Zietlinger.

Bandura, A. (1993). Perceived self-efficacy in cognitive development and functioning. *Educational Psychologist, 28,* 117–148.

Bandura, A. (Ed.). (1995). *Self-efficacy in changing societies.* New York: Cambridge University Press.

Bandura, A., Grusec, J. E., & Menlove, F. L. (1967). Vicarious extinction of avoidance behavior. *Journal of Personality and Social Psychology, 5,* 16–23.

Bandura, A., Ross, D., & Ross, S. (1963). Vicarious reinforcement and imitative learning. *Journal of Abnormal and Social Psychology, 67,* 601–607.

Banerjee, M. (1997). Hidden emotions: Preschoolers' knowledge of appearance-reality and emotion display rules. *Social Cognition, 15,* 107–132.

Banks, R. R., & Eberhardt, J. L. (1998). Social psychological processes and the legal bases of racial categorization. In J. L. Eberhardt & S. T. Fiske (Eds.), *Confronting racism: The problem and the response.* Thousand Oaks, CA: Sage.

Barber, J. D. (1985). *The presidential character: Predicting performance in the White House* (3rd ed.). Englewood Cliffs, NJ: Prentice-Hall.

Barber, J. D. (1992). Prediction as a test for hypothesis: Application to the psychology of presidents. *Political Psychology, 13,* 543–552.

Barber, N. (1994). Machiavellianism and altruism: Effect of relatedness of target person on Machiavellian and helping attitudes. *Psychological Reports, 75,* 403–422.

Bargh, J. A. (1989a). Conditional automaticity: Varieties of automatic influence in social perception and cognition. In J. S. Uleman & J. A. Bargh (Eds.), *Unintended thought: Causes and consequences for judgment, emotion, and behavior.* New York: Guilford.

Bargh, J. A. (1989b). Auto-Motives: Preconscious determinants of social interaction. In J. A. Bargh (Ed.), *Unintended thought* (pp. 93–130). New York: Guilford.

Bargh, J. A., & Pietromonaco, P. (1982). Automatic information processing and social perception: The influence of trait information presented outside of conscious awareness on impression formation. *Journal of Personality and Social Psychology, 43,* 437–449.

Bargh, J. A., Raymond, P., Pryor, J. B., & Strack, F. (1995). Attractiveness of the underling: An automatic power-sex association and its consequences for sexual harassment and aggression. *Journal of Personality and Social Psychology, 68,* 768–781.

Bar-Hillel, M. (1980). The base-rate fallacy in probability judgments. *Acta Pscyhologica, 44,* 211–233.

Barker, K., Fong, L., Grossman, S., & Quin, C. (1994). Comparison of self-reported recycling attitudes and behaviors with actual behavior. *Psychological Reports, 75,* 571–577.

Barner-Barry, C., & Rosenwein, R. (1985). *Psychological perspectives on politics.* Englewood Cliffs, NJ: Prentice-Hall.

Barnes, M. L., & Sternberg, R. J. (1997). A hierarchical model of love and its prediction of satisfaction in close relationships. In R. J. Sternberg & M. Hojjat (Eds.), *Satisfaction in close relationships.* New York: Guilford.

BarNir, A. (1998). Can group- and issue-related factors predict choice shift? A meta-analysis of group decisions on life dilemmas. *Small Group Research, 29* (3), 308–338.

Baron, J. (1997). The illusion of morality as self-interest: A reason to cooperate in social dilemmas. *Psychological Science, 8,* 330–335.

Baron, J. N., & Bielby, W. T. (1986). The proliferation of job titles in organizations. *Administrative Science Quarterly, 31,* 561–586.

Baron, R. A. (1983). The control of human aggression: An optimistic perspective. *Journal of Social and Clinical Psychology, 1,* 97–119.

Baron, R. A. (1997). The sweet smell of . . . helping: Effects of pleasant ambient fragrance on prosocial behavior in shopping malls. *Personality & Social Psychology Bulletin, 23,* 498–503.

Baron, R. A., & Kepner, C. R. (1970). Model's behavior and attraction toward the model as determinants of adult aggressive behavior. *Journal of Personality and Social Personality, 14,* 335–344.

Baron, R. A., & Ransberger, V. M. (1978). Ambient temperature and the occurrence of collective violence: The "long, hot summer" revisited. *Journal of Personality and Social Psychology, 36,* 351–360.

Baron, R. A., & Richardson, D. R. (1994). *Human aggression* (2nd ed.). New York: Plenum.

Baron, R. A., Russell, G. W., & Arms, R. L. (1984). Negative ions and behavior. *Journal of Personality and Social Psychology, 48,* 746–754.

Baron, R. M., Mandel, D. R., Adams, C. A., & Griffen, L. M. (1976). Effects of social density in university residential environments. *Journal of Personality and Social Psychology, 34,* 434–446.

Baron, R. S. (1986). Distraction-conflict theory: Progress and problems. In L. Berkowitz (Ed.), *Advances in experimental social psychology* (Vol. 20). New York: Academic Press.

Baron, R. S., Kerr, N. L., & Miller, N. (1992). *Group process, group decision, group action.* Pacific Grove, CA: Brooks/Cole.

Barone, M. J., & Miniard, P. W. (1999). How and when factual ad claims mislead consumers: Examining the deceptive consequences of copy interactions for partial comparative advertisements. *Journal of Marketing Research, 36* (1), 58–74.

Barrett, G. V., & Bass, B. M. (1970). Comparative surveys of managerial attitudes and behavior. In J. Bradburn (Ed.), *Comparative management: Teaching, training and research.* New York: Graduate School of Business Administration, New York University.

Barry, H., III, Josephson, L., Lauer, E., & Marshall, C. (1976). Traits inculcated in childhood: Cross-cultural codes V. *Ethnology, 15,* 83–114.

Bass, A. (1996, April 21). Is anger good for you? *Boston Globe Magazine,* pp. 20–41.

Bass, B. M. (1981). From leaderless group discussions to the cross-national assessment of managers. *Journal of Management, 7,* 63–76.

Bass, B. M. (1985). *Leadership and performance beyond expectations.* New York: Free Press.

Bass, B. M. (1990). *Bass & Stogdill's handbook of leadership: Theory, research, & managerial applications* (3rd ed.). New York: Free Press.

Bass, B. M. (1997). From transactional to transformational leadership: Learning to share the vision. In R. P. Vecchio (Ed.), *Leadership: Understanding the dynamics of power and influence in organizations* (pp. 318–333). Notre Dame, IN: University of Notre Dame Press.

Bassili, J. (1995). Response latency and the accessibility of voting intentions: What contributes to accessibility and how it affects voter choice. *Personality & Social Psychology Bulletin, 21,* 686–695.

Bassili, J. N., & Roy, J. (1998). On the representation of strong and weak attitudes about policy in memory. *Political Psychology, 19* (4), 669–681.

Batra, R., Lehmann, D. R., & Singh, D. (1993). The brand personality component of brand goodwill: Some antecedents and consequences. In D. A. Aaker & A. L. Biel (Eds.), *Brand equity and advertising: Advertising's role in building strong brands.* Hillsdale, NJ: Erlbaum.

Batson, C. D. (1990a). Good Samaritans—or priests and Levites? Using William James as a guide in the study of religious prosocial motivation. Special Issue: Centennial celebration of the Principles of Psychology. *Personality and Social Psychology Bulletin, 16,* 758–768.

Batson, C.D. (1990b). How social an animal? The human capacity for caring. *American Psychologist, 45,* 336–346.

Batson, C. D. (1991). *The altruism question: Toward a social-psychological answer.* Hillsdale, NJ: Erlbaum.

Batson, C. D. (1993). Communal and exchange relationships: What is the difference? *Personality and Social Psychology Bulletin, 19,* 677–683.

Batson, C. D. (1994). Why act for the public good? Four answers. Special Issue: The self and the collective. *Personality & Social Psychology Bulletin, 20,* 603–610.

Batson, C. D. (1998). Altruism and prosocial behavior. In D. T. Gilbert and S. T. Fiske (Eds.), *The handbook of social psychology* (Vol. 2, 4th ed., pp. 282–316). Boston, MA: McGraw-Hill.

Batson, C. D., Ahmad, N., Yin, J., Bedell, S. J., Johnson, J. W., Templin, C. M., & Whiteside, A. (1999). Two threats to the common good: Self-interested egoism and empathy and empathy-induced altruism. *Personality & Social Psychology Bulletin, 25,* 3–16.

Batson, C. D., Cochran, P. J., Biederman, M. F., Bloser, J. L., Ryan, M. J., & Vogt, B. (1978). Failure to help when in a hurry: Callousness or conflict? *Personality and Social Psychology Bulletin, 4,* 97–101.

Batson, C. D., Klein, T. R., Highberger, L., & Shaw, L. L. (1995). Immorality from empathy-induced altruism: When compassion and justice conflict. *Journal of Personality & Social Psychology, 68,* 1042–1054.

Batson, C. D., & Oleson, K. C. (1991). Current status of the empathy-altruism hypothesis. *Review of Personality and Social Psychology, 12,* 62–85.

Batson, C. D., & Weeks, J. L. (1996). Mood effects of unsuccessful helping: Another test of the empathy-altruism hypothesis. *Personality and Social Psychology Bulletin, 22,* 148–157.

Baum, A. (1994). Behavioral, biological, and environmental interactions in disease processes. In S. Blumenthal, K. Matthews, & S. Weiss (Eds.), *New research frontiers in behavioral medicine: Proceedings of the National Conference.* Washington, DC: NIH Publications.

Baumeister, R. F. (1982). A self-presentational view of social phenomena. *Psychological Bulletin, 91,* 3–26.

Baumeister, R. F. (1991). *Escaping the self.* New York: Basic Books.

Baumeister, R. F. (Ed.). (1993). *Self-esteem: The puzzle of low self-regard.* New York: Plenum.

Baumeister, R. F. (1997a). The enigmatic appeal of sexual masochism: Why people desire pain, bondage, and humiliation in sex. *Journal of Social & Clinical Psychology, 16,* 133–150.

Baumeister, R. F. (1997b). Identity, self-concept, and self-esteem: The self lost and found. In R. Hogan & J. A. Johnson (Eds.), *Handbook of personality psychology.* San Diego, CA: Academic Press.

Baumeister, R. F. (1998). The self. In D. T. Gilbert & S. T. Fiske (Eds,), *The handbook of social psychology* (4th ed.). Boston, MA: McGraw-Hill.

Baumeister, R. F., Dori, G. A., & Hastings, S. (1998). Belongingness and temporal bracketing in personal accounts of changes in self-esteem. *Journal of Research in Personality, 32,* 222–235.

Baumeister, R. F., & Heatherton, T. F. (1996). Self-regulation failure: An overview. *Psychological Inquiry, 7,* 1–15.

Baumeister, R. F., Heatherton, T. F., & Tice, D. M. (1993). When ego threats lead to self-regulation failure: Negative consequences of high self-esteem. *Journal of Personality & Social Psychology, 64,* 141–156.

Baumeister, R. F., Heatherton, T. F., & Tice, D. (1994). *Losing control: How and why people fail at self-regulation.* San Diego: Academic Press.

Baumeister, R. F., & Hutton, D. G. (1987). A self-presentational perspective on group processes. In B. Mullen & G. R. Goethals (Eds.), *Theories of group behavior.* New York: Springer-Verlag.

Baumeister, R. F., Hutton, D. G., & Tice, D. M. (1989). Cognitive processes during deliberate self-presentation: How self-presenters alter and misinterpret the behavior of their interaction partners. *Journal of Experimental Social Psychology, 25,* 59–78.

Baumeister, R. F., & Jones, E. E. (1978). When self-presentation is constrained by the target's knowledge: Consistency and compensation. *Journal of Personality and Social Psychology, 36,* 608–618.

Baumeister, R. F., & Leary, M. R. (1995). The need to belong: Desire for interpersonal attachments as a fundamental human motivation. *Psychological Bulletin, 117,* 497–529.

Baumeister, R. F., Leith, K. P., Muraven, M., & Bratslavsky, E. (1998). Self-regulation as a key to success in life. In D. Pushkar & W. M. Bukowski (Eds.), *Improving competence across the lifespan: Building interventions based on theory and research.* New York: Plenum.

Baumgardner, A. H. (1991). Claiming depressive symptoms as a self-handicap: A protective self-presentation strategy. *Basic and Applied Social Psychology, 12,* 97–113.

Baumgardner, A., Lake, A. E., & Arkin, R. M. (1985). Claiming mood as a self-handicap: The influence of spoiled and unspoiled public identities. *Personality and Social Psychology Bulletin, 11,* 349–357.

Baumrind, D. (1964). Some thoughts on the ethics of reading Milgram's "Behavioral study of obedience." *American Psychologist, 19,* 421–423.

Beach, S. H., & Tesser, A. (1993). Decision-making power and marital satisfaction: A self-evaluation maintenance perspective. *Journal of Social & Clinical Psychology, 12,* 471–494.

Beach, S. R. H., Tesser, A., Fincham, F. D., Jones, D. J., Johnson, D., & Whitaker, D. J. (1998). Pleasure and pain in doing well, together: An investigation of performance-related affect in close relationships. *Journal of Personality & Social Psychology, 74,* 923–938.

Beall, A. E., & Sternberg, R. J. (1995). The social construction of love. *Journal of Social & Personal Relationships, 12,* 417–438.

Beaman, A. L., Cole, C. M., Preston, M., Klentz, B., & Steblay, N. M. (1983). Fifteen years of foot-in-the-door research: A meta-analysis. *Personality and Social Psychology Bulletin, 9,* 181–196.

Bearden, W. O., Rose, R. L., & Teel, J. E. (1994). Correlates of conformity in the consumption of illicit drugs and alcohol. Special Issue: Linking theory to policy. *Journal of Business Research, 30,* 25–31.

Beauregard, K. S., & Dunning, D. (1998). Turning up the contrast: Self-enhancement motives prompt egocentric contrast effects in social judgments. *Journal of Personality & Social Psychology, 74* (3), 606–621.

Beauvois, J., & Joule, R. (1999). A radical point of view on dissonance theory. In E. Harmon-Jones & J. Mills (Eds.), *Cognitive dissonance: Progress on a pivotal theory in social psychology,* Science conference series (pp. 43–70). Washington, DC: American Psychological Association.

Beauvois, J. L., Bungert, M., & Mariette, P. (1995). Forced compliance: Commitment to compliance and commitment to activity. *European Journal of Social Psychology, 25,* 17–26.

Beck, A. T. (1991). Cognitive therapy: A 30-year perspective. *American Psychologist, 46,* 368–375.

Beck, A. T., Rush, A. J., Shaw, B. F., & Emery, G. (1979). *Cognition therapy of depression.* New York: Guilford.

Becker, M. H. (1985). Patient adherence to prescribed therapies. *Medical Care, 23,* 539–555.

Beckman, H. B., & Frankel, R. M. (1984). The effect of physician behavior on the collection of data. *Annals of Internal Medicine, 101,* 692–696.

Beckman, L. (1970). Effects of students' performance on teachers' and observers' attributions of causality. *Journal of Educational Psychology, 61,* 76–82.

Beena, C., & Poduval, P. R. (1992). Gender differences in work stress of executives. *Psychological Studies, 37,* 109–113.

Begley, S. (1998, July 13). You're OK, I'm terrific: 'Self-esteem' backfires. *Newsweek,* p. 69.

Belansky, E. S., & Boggiano, A. K. (1994). Predicting helping behaviors: The role of gender and instrumental/expressive self-schemata. *Sex Roles, 30,* 647–661.

Belgrave, F. Z., & Lewis, D. M. (1994). The role of social support in compliance and other health behaviors for African Americans with chronic illnesses. Special Issue: Psychosocial aspects of sickle cell disease: Past, present, and future directions of research. *Journal of Health & Social Policy, 5,* 55–68.

Bell, B. (1993). Emotional loneliness and the perceived similarity of one's ideas and interests. *Journal of Social Behavior & Personality, 8,* 273–280.

Bell, J., Grekul, J., Lamba, N., & Minas, C. (1995). The impact of cost on student helping behavior. *Journal of Social Psychology, 135,* 49–56.

Bell, J. L. (1995). Traumatic event debriefing: Service delivery designs and the role of social work. *Social Work, 40,* 36–43.

Bell, P. A. (1992). In defense of the negative affect escape model of heat and aggression. *Psychological Bulletin, 111,* 342–346.

Bell, R. A., Cholerton, M., Fraczek, K. E., & Rohlfs, G. S. (1994). Encouraging donations to charity: A field study of competing and complementary factors in tactic sequencing. *Western Journal of Communication, 58,* 98–115.

Bell, S. T., Kuriloff, P. J., & Lottes, I. (1994). Understanding attributions of blame in stranger rape and date rape situations: An examination of gender, race, identification, and students' social perceptions of rape victims. *Journal of Applied Social Psychology, 24,* 1719–1734.

Belmore, S. M. (1987). Determinants of attention during impression formation. *Journal of Experimental Psychology: Learning, Memory, and Cognition, 13,* 480–489.

Belsky, J., Garduque, L., & Hrncir, E. (1984). Assessing performance, competence, and executive capacity in infant play: Relations to home environment and security of attachment. *Developmental Psychology, 20,* 406–417.

Belsky, J., Rovine, M., & Fish, M. (1989). The developing family system. In M. Gunnar (Ed.), *Systems and development: Minnesota symposium on child psychology, Vol. 22.* Hillsdale, NJ: Erlbaum.

Bem, D. J. (1967). Self-perception: An alternative interpretation of cognitive dissonance phenomena. *Psychological Review, 74,* 183–200.

Bem, D. J. (1972). Self-perception theory. In L. Berkowitz (Ed.), *Advances in experimental and social psychology* (Vol. 6, pp. 1–62). New York: Academic Press.

Bem, D. J., & McConnell, H. K. (1970). Testing the self-perception explanation of dissonance phenomena: On the salience of premanipulation attitudes. *Journal of Personality and Social Psychology, 14,* 23–31.

Bem, S. L. (1982). Gender schema theory and self-schema theory compared: A comment on Markus, Crane, Bernstein, and Siladi's "Self-schemas and gender." *Journal of Personality and Social Psychology, 43,* 1192–1194.

Bem, S. L. (1983). Gender schema theory and its implications for child development: Raising gender-aschematic children in a gender-schematic society. *Signs, 8,* 598–616.

Bem, S. L. (1984). Androgyny and gender schema theory: A conceptual and empirical integration. *Nebraska Symposium on Motivation, 32,* 179–226.

Bem, S. L. (1987). Gender schema theory and its implications for child development: Raising gender-aschematic children in a gender-schematic society. In R. M. Walsh (Ed.), *The psychology of women: Ongoing debates.* New Haven: Yale University Press.

Bem, S. L. (1993). *Lenses of gender.* New Haven, CT: Yale University Press.

Bem, S. L. (1998). *An unconventional family.* New Haven, CT: Yale University Press.

Ben-Ari, A. T. (1995). Coming out: A dialectic of intimacy and privacy. *Families in Society, 76,* 306–314.

Bennett, A. (1994, January 10). Economists + Meeting = A zillion causes and effects. *Wall Street Journal,* p. B1.

Bennett, M. (1977). Testing management theories cross-culturally. *Journal of Applied Psychology, 62,* 578–581.

Benson, H. (1993). The relaxation response. In D. Goleman & J. Gurin (Eds.), *Mind-body medicine.* Yonkers, NY: Consumer Reports Books.

Bentler, P. M., & Newcomb, M. D. (1978). Longitudinal study of marital success and failure. *Journal of Consulting and Clinical Psychology, 46,* 1053–1070.

Berg, J. H., & Archer, R. L. (1982). Responses of self-disclosure and interaction goals. *Journal of Experimental Social Psychology, 18,* 501–512.

Berger, D. (1986, January). Theory into practice: The FCB grid. *European Research,* 35–46.

Berger, S. H. (1997). Do juries listen to jury instructions? *Bulletin of the American Academy of Psychiatry & the Law, 25* (4), 565–570.

Berglas, S., & Jones, E. E. (1978). Drug choice as a self-handicapping strategy in response to noncontingent success. *Journal of Personality and Social Psychology, 36,* 405–417.

Berkowitz, L. (1972). Social norms, feelings, and other factors affecting helping and altruism. In L. Berkowitz (Ed.), *Advances in experimental social psychology* (Vol. 6). New York: Academic Press.

Berkowitz, L. (1974). Some determinants of impulsive aggression: The role of mediated associations with reinforcements for aggression. *Psychological Review, 81,* 165–176.

Berkowitz, L. (1984). Some effects of thoughts on anti- and prosocial influences of media events: A cognitive-neoassociation analysis. *Psychological Bulletin, 95,* 410–427.

Berkowitz, L. (1989). Frustration-aggression hypothesis: Examination and reformulation. *Psychological Bulletin, 106,* 59–73.

Berkowitz, L. (1990). On the formation and regulation of anger and aggression: A cognitive-neoassociationistic analysis. *American Psychologist, 45,* 494–503.

Berkowitz, L. (1993a). *Aggression: Its causes, consequences, and control.* New York: McGraw-Hill.

Berkowitz, L. (1993b). Pain and aggression: Some findings and implications. Special Issue: The pain system: A multilevel model for the study of motivation and emotion. *Motivation & Emotion, 17,* 277–293.

Berkowitz, L. (1998). Affective aggression: The role of stress, pain, and negative affect. In R. G. Geen & E. Donnerstein (Eds.), *Human aggression:*

Theories, research, and implications for social policy (pp. 23–48). San Diego, CA: Academic Press.

Berkowitz, L., & Geen, R. G. (1966). Film violence and the cue properties of available targets. *Journal of Personality and Social Psychology, 3,* 525–530.

Berkowitz, L., & LePage, A. (1967). Weapons as aggression-eliciting stimuli. *Journal of Personality and Social Psychology, 7,* 202–207.

Berkowitz, L., & Powers, P. C. (1979). Effects of timing and justification of witnessed aggression on the observers' punitiveness. *Journal of Research in Personality, 13,* 71–80.

Berlyne, D. E. (1970). Novelty, complexity, and hedonic value. *Perception and Psychophysics, 8,* 279–286.

Berman, S. (1997). *Children's social consciousness and the development of social responsibility.* Albany: State University of New York Press.

Bernard, J. (1982). *The future of marriage.* New Haven, CT: Yale University Press.

Bernieri, F. J., & Rosenthal, R. (1991). Interpersonal coordination: Behavior matching and interactional synchrony. In R. S. Feldman & B. Rimé (Eds.), *Fundamentals of Nonverbal Behavior.* Cambridge, England: Cambridge University Press.

Berry, D. S. (1990). Taking people at face value: Evidence for the kernel of truth hypothesis. *Social Cognition, 8,* 343–361.

Berry, D. S. (1991). Attractive faces are not all created equal: Joint effects of facial babyishness and attractiveness on social perception. *Personality & Social Psychology Bulletin, 17,* 523–531.

Berry, J. W. (1966). Temne and Eskimo perceptual skills. *International Journal of Psychology, 1,* 207–229.

Berry, J. W. (1967). Independence and conformity in subsistence-level societies. *Journal of Personality and Social Psychology, 7,* 415–418.

Berscheid, E. (1985). Interpersonal attraction. In G. Lindzey & E. Aronson (Eds.), *Handbook of social psychology* (Vol. 2). New York: Random House.

Berscheid, E., Graziano, W., Monson, T., & Dermer, M. (1976). Outcome dependency: Attention, attribution, and attraction. *Journal of Personality and Social Psychology, 34,* 978–989.

Berscheid, E., & Reis, H. T. (1998). Attraction and close relationships. In D. T. Gilbert & S. T. Fiske (Eds.), *The handbook of social psychology* (4th ed.). Boston, MA: McGraw-Hill.

Berscheid, E., Snyder, M., & Omoto, A. M. (1989a). The Relationship Closeness Inventory: Assessing the closeness of interpersonal relationships. *Journal of Personality and Social Psychology, 57,* 792–807.

Berscheid, E., Snyder, M., & Omoto, A. M. (1989b). Issues in studying close relationships: Conceptualizing and measuring closeness. In C. Hendrick (Ed.), *Review of personality and social psychology: Vol. 10. Close relationships.* Newbury Park, CA: Sage.

Berscheid, E., & Walster, E. (1974). Physical attractiveness. In L. Berkowitz (Ed.), *Advances in experimental social psychology* (Vol. 7, pp. 157–215). New York: Academic Press.

Berscheid, E., Walster, E., & Campbell, R. (1974). Grow old with me. Cited in E. Berscheid & E. Walster, Physical attractiveness. In L. Berkowitz (Ed.), *Advances in experimental social psychology* (Vol. 7). New York: Academic Press.

Best, C., Dansky, B. S., & Kilpatrick, D. G. (1992). Medical students' attitudes about female rape victims. *Journal of Interpersonal Violence, 7,* 175–188.

Bettencourt, B. A., & Kernahan, C. (1997). A meta-analysis of aggression in the presence of violent cues: Effects of gender differences and aversive provocation. *Aggressive Behavior, 23,* 447–456.

Bettencourt, B. A., & Miller, N. (1996). Gender differences in aggression as a function of provocation: A meta-analysis. *Psychological Bulletin, 119,* 422–447.

Betancourt, H., & Lopez, S. R. (1993). The study of culture, ethnicity, and race in American Psychology. *American Psychologist, 48,* 1586–1596.

Betz, A. L., Gannon, K. M., & Skowronski, J. J. (1992). The moment of tenure and the moment of truth: When it pays to be aware of recency effects in social judgments. *Social Cognition, 10,* 397–413.

Biaggio, M. K. (1980). Anger arousal and personality characteristics. *Journal of Personality and Social Psychology, 39,* 352–356.

Bianchi, S. M., & Spain, D. (1986). *American women in transition.* New York: Russell Sage Foundation.

Bickman, L. (1971). The effect of another bystander's ability to help on bystander intervention in an emergency. *Journal of Experimental Social Psychology, 7,* 367–379.

Bickman, L. (1994). Social influence and diffusion of responsibility in an emergency. In B. Puka (Ed.), *Reaching out: Caring, altruism, and prosocial behavior. Vol. 7: Moral development: A compendium* (pp. 42–49). New York: Garland.

Bierhoff, H. W., Klein, R., & Kramp, P. (1991). Evidence for the altruistic personality from data on accident research. *Journal of Personality, 59,* 263–280.

Biernat, M., Manis, M., & Nelson, T. E. (1991). Stereotypes and standards of judgment. *Journal of Personality and Social Psychology, 60,* 485–499.

Biernat, M., Vescio, T. K., Theno, S. A., & Crandall, C. (1996). Values and prejudice: Toward understanding the impact of American values on outgroup attitudes. In C. Seligman & J. M. Olson (Eds.), *The psychology of values: The Ontario symposium on personality and social psychology* (Vol. 8.), Mahwah, NJ: Erlbaum.

Biernat, M., & Wortman, C. B. (1991). Sharing of home responsibilities between professionally employed women and their husbands. *Journal of Personality and Social Psychology, 60,* 844–860.

Bird, G., & Melville, K. (1994). *Families and intimate relationships.* New York: McGraw-Hill.

Birnbaum, M. H., & Mellers, B. A. (1979). Stimulus recognition may mediate exposure effects. *Journal of Personality and Social Psychology, 37,* 391–394.

Birnbaum, M. H., & Sotoodeh, Y. (1991). Measurement of stress: Scaling magnitudes of life changes. *Psychological Science, 2,* 236–243.

Bjarnadottir, A. (1998). *Individual performance in customer service roles.* Dissertation Abstracts International: Section B: The Sciences & Engineering, 58, (10–B).

Black, L. E., Eastwood, M. M., Sprenkle, D. H., & Smith, E. (1991). An exploratory analysis of the construct of leavers versus left as it relates to Levinger's social exchange theory of attractions, barriers, and alternative attractions. Special Issue: Marital instability and divorce outcomes: Issues for therapists and educators. *Journal of Divorce and Remarriage, 15* (1–2), 127–139.

Blackwell, D. L. (1998). Marital homogamy in the United States: The influence of individual and paternal education. *Social Science Research, 27,* 159–188.

Blair, I. V., & Banaji, M. R. (1996). Automatic and controlled processes in stereotype priming. *Journal of Personality & Social Psychology, 70,* 1142–1163.

Blanchard, F. A., Lilly, R., & Vaughn, L. A. (1991). Reducing the expression of racial prejudice. *Psychological Science, 2,* 101–105.

Blanck, P. D. (1991). What empirical research tells us: Studying judges' and juries' behavior. *American University Law Review, 40,* 775–804.

Blanck, P. D., & Rosenthal, R. (1992). Nonverbal behavior in the courtroom. In R. S. Feldman (Ed.), *Applications of nonverbal behavioral theory and research.* Hillsdale, NJ: Erlbaum.

Blanton, H., Buunk, B. P., Gibbons, F. X., & Kuyper, H. (1999). When better-than-others compare upward: Choice of comparison and comparative evaluation as independent predictors of academic performance. *Journal of Personality & Social Psychology, 76,* 420–430.

Blass, T., & Krackow, A. (1991, June). *The Milgram obedience experiments: Students' views vs. scholarly perspectives and actual findings.* Paper presented at the annual meeting of the American Psychological Society, Washington, D.C.

Blumstein, P., & Schwartz, P. (1983). *American couples.* New York: William Morrow.

Bobocel, D. R., Son Hing, L. S., Davey, L. M., Stanley, D. J., & Zanna, M. P. (1998). Justice-based opposition to social policies: Is it genuine? *Journal of Personality & Social Psychology, 75,* 653–669.

Bodenmann, G. (1995). A systemic-transactional conceptualization of stress and coping in couples. *Schweizerische Zeitschrift fur Psychologie, 54,* 34–49.

Boeringer, S. B. (1994). Pornography and sexual aggression: Associations of violent and nonviolent depictions with rape and rape proclivity. *Deviant Behavior, 15,* 289–304.

Bohm, R. M. (1994). Capital punishment in two judicial circuits in Georgia: A description of the key actors and the decision-making process. Special Issue: Race, ethnicity, and the law. *Law & Human Behavior, 18,* 319–338.

Bohner, G., & Apostolidou, W. (1994). Mood and persuasion: Independent effects of affect before and after message processing. *Journal of Social Psychology, 134,* 707–709.

Bohner, G., Bless, H., Schwarz, N., & Strack, H. (1988). What triggers causal attributions? The impact of valence and subjective probability. *European Journal of Social Psychology, 18,* 335–348.

Bohner, G., Frank, E., & Erb, H. (1998). Heuristic processing of distinctiveness information in minority and majority influence. *European Journal of Social Psychology, 28* (5), 855–860.

Bond, R., & Smith, P. B. (1996). Culture and conformity: A meta-analysis of studies using Asch's (1952b, 1956) line judgment task. *Psychological Bulletin, 119,* 111–137.

Boone, L. E., & Krutz, D. L. (1986). *Contemporary marketing* (5th ed.). Chicago: Dryden.

Borden, V. M. H., & Levinger, G. (1991). Interpersonal transformations in intimate relationships. In W. H. Jones & D. Perlman (Eds.), *Advances in personal relationships* (Vol. 2). London: Jessica Kingsley.

Borgida, E. (1982). Legal reform of rape laws: Social psychological and constitutional considerations. In L. Bickman (Ed.), *Applied social psychology* (Vol. 2).

Bornstein, M. H. (1989). Sensitive periods in development: Structured characteristics and causal interpretations. *Psychological Bulletin, 105,* 179–197.

Bornstein, R. F. (1994). Dependency as a social cue: A meta-analytic review of research on the dependency-helping relationship. *Journal of Research in Personality, 28,* 182–213.

Bornstein, R. F., & D'Agostino, P. R. (1992). Stimulus recognition and the mere exposure effect. *Journal of Personality and Social Psychology, 63,* 545–552.

Bornstein, R. F., Riggs, J. M., Hill, E. L., & Calabrese, C. (1996). Activity, passivity, self-denigration, and self-promotion: Toward an interactionist model of interpersonal dependency. *Journal of Personality, 64,* 637–673.

Borrello, G. M., & Thompson, B. (1990). An hierarchical analysis of the Hendrick-Hendrick measure of Lee's typology of love. *Journal of Social Behavior and Personality, 5,* 327–342.

Bossard, J. H. S. (1932). Residential proinquity as a factor in mate selection. *American Journal of Sociology, 38,* 219–224.

Bosveld, W., Koomen, W., & Vogelaar, R. (1997). Construing a social issue: Effects on attitudes and the false consensus effects. *British Journal of Social Psychology, 36,* 263–272.

Bovasso, G. (1997). The interaction of depersonalization and deindividuation. *Journal of Social Distress & the Homeless, 6* (3), 213–228.

Bower, G. H. (1986). Prime time in cognitive psychology. In P. Eelen (Ed.), *Cognitive research behavior therapy: Beyond the conditioning paradigm.* Amsterdam: North Holland Publishers.

Bowers, K. S., & Farvolden, P. (1996a). Revisiting a century-old Freudian slip—From suggestion disavowed to the truth repressed. *Psychological Bulletin, 119,* 355–380.

Bowers, K. S., & Farvolden, P. (1996b). The search for the canonical experience: Reply to Pennebaker and Memon (1996). *Psychological Bulletin, 119,* 386–389.

Bowlby, J. (1969). *Attachment and loss.* New York: Basic books.

Bowman, G. D., & Stern, M. (1995). Adjustment to occupational stress: The relationship of perceived control to effectiveness of coping strategies. *Journal of Counseling Psychology, 42,* 294–303.

Boyanowsky, E. O., Allen, V. L., Bragg, B. W., & Lepinski, J. (1981). Generalization of independence created by social support. *Psychological Record, 31,* 475–488.

Boyd, J. R., Covington, T. R., Stanaszek, W. F., & Coussons, R. T. (1974). Drug defaulting, II. Analysis of noncompliance patterns. *American Journal of Hospital Pharmacy, 31,* 485–491.

Bradbury, T. N., Beach, S. R. H., Fincham, F. D., & Nelson, G. M. (1996). Attributions and behavior in functional and dysfunctional marriages. *Journal of Consulting & Clinical Psychology, 64,* 569–576.

Bradbury, T. N., & Fincham, F. D. (1990). Attributions in marriage: Review and critique. *Psychological Bulletin, 107,* 3–33.

Bradbury, T. N., & Fincham, F. D. (1992). Attributions and behavior in marital interaction. *Journal of Personality and Social Psychology, 63,* 613–628.

Branscombe, N. R., Ellemers, N., Spears, R., & Doosje, B. (1999). The context and content of social identity threat. In N. Ellemers & R. Spears, (Eds.), *Social identity: Context, commitment, content.* Oxford, England: Blackwell.

Brauer, M., Judd, C. M., & Gliner, M. D. (1995). The effects of repeated expressions on attitude polarization during group discussions. *Journal of Personality & Social Psychology, 68,* 1014–1029.

Braun, N. A., Kirchner, L. A., Hartman, M. S., Overton, K. J., & Caldwell, T. E. (1998). Establishing a descriptive database for teachers with aggressive students. *Journal of Behavioral Education, 8,* 457–470.

Bray, R. M., & Noble, A. M. (1978). Authoritarianism and decisions of mock juries: Evidence of jury bias and group polarization. *Journal of Personality and Social Psychology, 36,* 1424–1430.

Breay, E., & Gentry, M. (1990, April). *Perceptions of a sexual double standard.* Paper presented at the

Eastern Psychological Association annual meeting, Philadelphia.

Breckler, S. J. (1984). Empirical validation of affect, behavior, and cognition as distinct components of attitude. *Journal of Personality and Social Psychology, 47,* 1191–1205.

Brehm, J. W. (1956). Post-decision changes in desirability of alternatives. *Journal of Abnormal and Social Psychology, 52,* 384–389.

Brehm, J. W., & Mann, M. (1975). Effect of importance of freedom and attraction to group members on influence produced by group pressure. *Journal of Personality and Social Psychology, 31,* 816–824.

Brehm, S. S. (1988). Passionate love. In R. J. Sternberg & M. L. Barnes (Eds.), *The psychology of love* (pp. 232–263). New Haven: Yale University Press.

Brehm, S. S. (1992). *Intimate relationships* (2nd ed.). New York: McGraw-Hill.

Brehm, S. S., & Brehm, J. W. (1981). *Psychological reactance.* New York: Academic Press.

Bretherton, I. (1992). The origins of attachment theory: John Bowlby and Mary Ainsworth. *Developmental Psychology, 28,* 759–775.

Brewer, M. B. (1988). A dual process model of impression formation. In T. K. Srull & R. S. Wyer, Jr. (Eds.), *Advances in social cognition* (Vol. 1, pp. 1–36). Hillsdale, NJ: Erlbaum.

Brewer, M. B. (1996). When contact is not enough: Social identity and intergroup cooperation. *International Journal of Intercultural Relations, 20,* 291–303.

Brewer, M. B., & Kramer, R. M. (1985). The psychology of intergroup attitudes and behavior. *Annual Review of Psychology, 36,* 219–243.

Brewer, M. B., & Lui, L. L. (1989). The primacy of age and sex in the structure of person categories. *Social Cognition, 7,* 262–274.

Brewer, M. B., Weber, J. G., & Carini, B. (1995). Person memory in intergroup contexts: Categorization versus individuation. *Journal of Personality & Social Psychology, 69,* 29–40.

Brewer, N., Socha, L., & Potter, R. (1996). Gender differences in supervisors' use of performance feedback. *Journal of Applied Social Psychology, 26,* 786–803.

Brewin, C. (1998). Intrusive memories, depression and PTSD. *Psychologist, 11,* 281–283.

Brickner, M. A., Harkins, S. G., & Ostrom, T. M. (1986). Effects of personal involvement: Thought-provoking implications for social loafing. *Journal of Personality and Social Psychology, 51,* 763–770.

Bridges, F., & Coady, N. P. (1996). Affiliation, urban size, urgency, and cost of responses to lost letters. *Psychological Reports, 79,* 775–780.

Bridges, J. S. (1988). Sex differences in occupational performance expectations. *Psychology of Women Quarterly, 12,* 75–90.

Brinkerhoff, D. B., & Booth, A. (1984). Gender, dominance, and stress. *Journal of Social and Biological Structures, 7,* 159–177.

Broadstock, M., & Borland, R. (1998). Using information for emotion-focused coping: Cancer patients' use of a cancer helpline. *British Journal of Health Psychology, 3,* 319–332.

Brockner, J., & Swap, W. C. (1983). Resolving the relationships between placebos, misattribution, and insomnia: An individual-differences perspective. *Journal of Personality and Social Psychology, 45,* 32–42.

Brodsky, S. L., & Scogin, F. R. (1988). Inmates in protective custody: First data on emotional effects. *Forensic Reports, 1,* 267–280.

Brooks, L., Cornelius, A., Greenfield, E., & Joseph, R. (1995). The relation of career-related work or internship experiences to the career development of college seniors. *Journal of Vocational Behavior, 46,* 332–349.

Broverman, I. K., Vogel, S. R., Broverman, D. M., Clarkson, F. E., & Rosenkrantz, P. S. (1972). Sex-role stereotypes: A current appraisal. *Journal of Social Issues, 28,* 59–78.

Brown, D., Scheflin, A. W., & Hammond, D. C. (1998). *Memory, trauma treatment, and the law.* New York: Norton.

Brown, J. D. (1991). Staying fit and staying well: Physical fitness as a moderator of life stress. *Journal of Personality and Social Psychology, 60,* 368–375.

Brown, J. D., & Dutton, K. A. (1995). Truth and consequences: The costs and benefits of accurate self-knowledge. *Personality and Social Psychology Bulletin, 21,* 1288–1296.

Brown, J. D., & McGill, K. L. (1989). The cost of good fortune: When positive life events produce negative health consequences. *Journal of Personality and Social psychology, 54,* 321–329.

Brown, R. (1996). The language of social relationship. In D. I. Slobin & J. Gerhardt (Eds.), *Social interaction, social context, and language: Essays in honor of Susan Ervin-Tripp.* Mahwah, NJ: Erlbaum.

Brown, R., Condor, S., Matthews, A., & Wade, G. (1986). Explaining intergroup differentiation in an industrial organization. *Journal of Occupational Psychology, 59,* 273–286.

Brown, R., & Gilman, A. (1960). The pronouns of power and solidarity. In T. A. Sebok (Ed.), *Style in language* (pp. 253–276). Cambridge, MA: M.I.T. Press.

Brown, R. J., & Williams, J. (1984). Group identification: The same thing to all people? *Human Relations, 37,* 547–564.

Brown, V., Tumeo, M., Larey, T. S., & Paulus, P. B. (1998). Modeling cognitive interactions during group brainstorming. *Small Group Research, 29* (4), 495–526.

Browne, A., & Williams, K. R. (1993). Gender, intimacy, and lethal violence: Trends from 1976–1987. *Gender & Society, 7,* 78–98.

Brownell, K. D. (1991). Dieting and the search for the perfect body: Where physiology and culture collide. *Behavior Therapy, 22,* 1–12.

Bryan, J. H., & Test, M. A. (1967). Models and helping: Naturalistic studies in aiding behavior. *Journal of Personality and Social Psychology, 6,* 400–407.

Buckalew, L. W., & Buckalew, N. M. (1995). Survey of the nature and prevalence of patients' noncompliance and implications for intervention. *Psychological Reports, 76,* 315–321.

Buckalew, L. W., & Sallis, R. E. (1986). Patient compliance and medication perception. *Journal of Clinical Psychology, 42,* 49–53.

Buckhout, R. (1975). Nearly 2000 witnesses can be wrong. *Social Action and the Law, 2,* 7.

Bull, R., & Rumsey, N. (1988). *The social psychology of facial appearance.* New York: Springer-Verlag.

Buller, D. B., & Street, R. L., Jr. (1992). Physician-patient relationships. In R. S. Feldman (Ed.), *Applications of nonverbal behavioral theories and research.* Hillsdale, NJ: Erlbaum.

Bumpass, L., Martin, T., & Sweet, J. (1991). The impact of family background and early marital factors on marital disruption. *Journal of Family Issues, 12,* 22–42.

Burger, J. M. (1986). Increasing compliance by improving the deal: The that's-not-all technique. *Journal of Personality and Social Psychology, 51,* 277–283.

Burger, J. M. (1992). *Desire for control: Personality, social, and clinical perspectives.* New York: Plenum.

Burger, J. M., Horita, M., Kinoshita, L., Roberts, K., et al. (1997). Effects of time on the norm of reciprocity. *Basic & Applied Social Psychology, 19,* 91–100.

Burger, J. M., Oakman, J. A., & Bullard, N. G. (1983). Desire for control and the perception of crowding. *Personality and Social Psychology Bulletin, 9,* 475–479.

Burger, J. M., & Petty, R. E. (1981). The low-ball compliance technique: Task or person commitment? *Journal of Personality and Social Psychology, 40,* 492–500.

Burgess, E. W., & Wallin, P. (1953). *Engagement and marriage.* Philadelphia: Lippincott.

Burgoon, M., & Klingle, R. S. (1998). Gender differences in being influential and/or influenced: A challenge to prior explanations. In D. J. Canary & K. Dindia (Eds.), *Sex differences and similarities in communication: Critical essays and empirical investigations of sex and gender in interaction. LEA's communication series* (pp. 257–285). Mahwah, NJ: Erlbaum.

Burgoon, M., & Miller, M. D. (1990). Overcoming resistance to persuasion via contiguous reinforcement and repetition of message. *Psychological Reports, 66,* 1011–1022.

Burleson, B. R., Kunkel, A. W., & Szolwinski, J. B. (1997). Similarity in cognitive complexity and attraction to friends and lovers: Experimental and correlational studies. *Journal of Constructivist Psychology, 10,* 221–248.

Burleson, B. R., & Samter, W. (1996). Similarity in the communication skills of young adults:

Foundations of attraction, friendship, and relationship satisfaction. *Communication Reports, 9,* 127–139.

Burn, S. M. (1992). Loss of control, attributions, and helplessness in the homeless. *Journal of Applied Social Psychology, 22,* 1161–1174.

Burnstein, E., Crandall, C., & Kitayama, S. (1994). Some neo-Darwinian decision rules for altruism: Weighing cues for inclusive fitness as a function of the biological importance of the decision. *Journal of Personality and Social Psychology, 67,* 773–789.

Bush, P. J., & Osterweis, M. (1978). Pathways to medicine use. *Journal of Health and Social Behavior, 19,* 179–189.

Bushman, B. J. (1995). Moderating role of trait aggressiveness in the effects of violent media on aggression. *Journal of Personality and Social Psychology, 69,* 950–960.

Bushman, B. J. (1998). Priming effects of media violence on the accessibility of aggressive constructs in memory. *Personality & Social Psychology Bulletin, 24,* 537–545.

Bushman, B. J., & Anderson, C. A. (1998). Methodology in the study of aggression: Integrating experimental and nonexperimental findings. In R. G. Geen & E. Donnerstein (Eds.), *Human aggression: Theories, research, and implications for social policy* (pp. 23–48). San Diego, CA: Academic Press.

Bushman, B. J., & Baumeister, R. F. (1998). Threatened egotism, narcissism, self-esteem, and direct and displaced aggression: Does self-love or self-hate lead to violence? *Journal of Personality and Social Psychology, 75,* 219–229.

Bushman, B. J., Baumeister, R. F., & Stack, A. D. (1999). Catharsis, aggression, and persuasive influence: Self-fulfilling or self-defeating prophecies? *Journal of Personality & Social Psychology, 76,* 367–376.

Bushman, B. J., & Geen, R. G. (1990). Role of cognitive-emotional mediators and individual differences in the effects of media violence on aggression. *Journal of Personality and Social Psychology, 58,* 156–163.

Buss, A. H. (1961). *The psychology of aggression.* New York: Wiley.

Buss, A. H., & Durkee, A. (1957). An inventory for assessing different kinds of hostility. *Journal of Consulting Psychology, 21,* 343–349.

Buss, D. M. (1991). Conflict in married couples: Personality predictors of anger and upset. *Journal of Personality, 59,* 663–688.

Buss, D. M., & Kenrick, D. T. (1998). Evolutionary social psychology. In D. T. Gilbert, S. T. Fiske, & G. Lindzey (Eds.), *Handbook of social Psychology* (4th ed.). New York: McGraw-Hill.

Buss, D. M., & Shackelford, T. K . (1997). Human aggression in evolutionary psychological perspective. *Clinical Psychology Review, 17,* 605–619.

Buss, D. M., et al. (1990). International preferences in selecting mates: A study of 37 cultures. *Journal of Cross-Cultural Psychology 21,* 5–47.

Butler, J. L., & Baumeister, R. F. (1998). The trouble with friendly faces: Skilled performance with a supportive audience. *Journal of Personality & Social Psychology, 75,* 1213–1230.

Buunk, B. P. (1995). Comparison direction and comparison dimension among disabled individuals: Toward a refined conceptualization of social comparison under stress. *Personality & Social Psychology Bulletin, 21,* 316–330.

Buunk, B. P., Schaufeli, W. B., & Ybema, J. F. (1994). Burnout, uncertainty, and the desire for social comparison among nurses. *Journal of Applied Social Psychology, 24,* 1701–1718.

Byrne, D. (1971). *The attraction paradigm.* New York: Academic Press.

Byrne, D., & Clore, G. L. (1966). Predicting interpersonal attraction toward strangers presented in three different stimulus modes. *Psychonomic Science, 4,* 87–93.

Byrne, D., & Clore, G. L. (1970). A reinforcement model of evaluative responses. *Personality: An International Journal, 1,* 103–128.

Byrne, D., Clore, G. L., & Smeaton, G. (1986). The attraction hypothesis: Do similar attitudes affect anything? *Journal of Personality and Social Psychology, 51,* 1167–1170.

Byrne, D., & Murnen, S. K. (1988). Maintaining loving relationships. In R. J. Sternberg & M. L. Barnes (Eds.), *The psychology of love.* New Haven, CT: Yale University Press.

Cacioppo, J. T. (1994). Social neuroscience: Autonomic, neuroendocrine, and immune responses to stress. *Psychophysiology, 31,* 113–128.

Cacioppo, J. T., & Berntson, G. G. (1994). Relationship between attitudes and evaluative space: A critical review, with emphasis on the separability of positive and negative substrates. *Psychological Bulletin, 115,* 401–423.

Cacioppo, J. T., Berntson, G. G., & Crites, S. L., Jr. (1996). Social neuroscience: Principles of psychophysiological arousal and response. In E. T. Higgins & A. W. Kruglanski (Eds.), *Social psychology: Handbook of basic principles.* New York: Guilford Press.

Cacioppo, J. T., Crites, S. L., Berntson, G. G., & Coles, M. G. (1993). If attitudes affect how stimuli are processed, should they not affect the event-related brain potential? *Psychological Science, 4,* 108–112.

Cacioppo, J. T., & Gardner, W. L. (1999). Emotions. *Annual Review of Psychology, 50,* 191–214.

Cacioppo, J. T., Malarkey, W. B., Kiecolt-Glaser, J. K., & Uchino, B. N. (1995). Heterogeneity in neuroendocrine and immune responses to brief psychological stressors as a function of autonomic cardiac activation. *Psychosomatic Medicine, 57,* 154–164.

Cacioppo, J. T., Marshall-Goodell, B. S., Tassinary, L. G., & Petty, R. E. (1992). Rudimentary determinants of attitudes: Classical conditioning is more effective when prior knowledge about the attitude stimulus is low than high. *Journal of Experimental Social Psychology, 28,* 207–233.

Cacioppo, J. T., & Petty, R. E. (1979). Effects of message repetition and position on cognitive response, recall, and persuasion. *Journal of Personality and Social Psychology, 37,* 97–109.

Cacioppo, J. T., & Petty, R. E. (1982). The need for cognition. *Journal of Personality and Social Psychology, 42,* 116–131.

Cacioppo, J. T., Petty, R. E., Kao, C. F., & Rodriguez, R. (1986). Central and peripheral routes to persuasion: An individual difference perspective. *Journal of Personality and Social Psychology, 51,* 1032–1043.

Cacioppo, J. T., Petty, R. E., & Losch, M. E. (1986). Attributions of responsibility for helping and doing harm: Evidence for confusion of responsibility. *Journal of Personality and Social Psychology, 50,* 100–105.

Cacioppo, J. T., Petty, R. E., Losch, M. E., & Kim, H. S. (1986). Electromyographic activity over facial muscle regions can differentiate the valence and intensity of affective reactions. *Journal of Personality and Social Psychology, 50,* 260–268.

Cacioppo, J. T., Petty, R. E., & Morris, K. J. (1983). Effects of need for cognition on message evaluation, recall, and persuasion. *Journal of Personality and Social Psychology, 45,* 805–818.

Calder, B. J., Insko, C. A., & Yandell, B. (1974). The relation of cognitive and memorial processes to persuasion on a simulated jury trial. *Journal of Applied Social Psychology, 4,* 62–93.

Calder, B. J., & Sternthal, B. (1980). Television commercial wear-out: An information-processing view. *Journal of Marketing Research, 17,* 173–186.

Caldwell, M. A., & Peplau, L. A. (1984). The balance of power in lesbian relationships. *Sex Roles, 23,* 713–725.

Camacho, L. M., & Paulus, P. B. (1995). The role of social anxiousness in group brainstorming. *Journal of Personality & Social Psychology, 68,* 1071–1080.

Camarena, P. M., Sarigiani, P. A., & Petersen, A. C. (1990). Gender-specific pathways to intimacy in early adolescence. *Journal of Youth and Adolescence, 19,* 19–32.

Campbell, J. D., & Fairey, P. J. (1989). Informational and normative routes to conformity: The effect of faction size as a function of norm extremity and attention to the stimulus. *Journal of Personality and Social Psychology, 57,* 457–468.

Campbell, W. K., & Sedikides, C. (1999). Self-threat magnifies the self-serving bias: A meta-analytic integration. *Review of General Psychology, 3,* 23–43.

Canary, D. J., Cupach, W. R., & Messman, S. J. (1995). *Relationship conflict.* Newbury Park, CA: Sage.

Canary, D. J., & Dindia, K. (Eds.). (1998). *Sex differences and similarities in communication: Critical essays and empirical investigations of sex and gender in interaction.* Mahwah, NJ: Erlbaum.

Canary, D. J., & Stafford, L. (1994). *Maintaining relationships through strategic and routine interaction.* San Diego, CA: Academic Press.

Canary, D. J., Weger, H., & Stafford, L. (1991). Couples' argument sequences and their associations with relational characteristics. *Western Journal of Speech Communication, 55,* 159–179.

Candee, D., & Kohlberg, L. (1987). Moral judgment and moral action: A reanalysis of Haan, Smith, and Block's (1986) free-speech data. *Journal of Personality and Social Psychology, 52,* 554–564.

Cantor, N., & Mischel, W. (1979). Prototypes in person perception. In L. Berkowitz (Ed.), *Advances in experimental social psychology* (Vol. 12). New York: Academic Press.

Cantrill, J. G., & Seibold, D. R. (1986). The perceptual contrast explanation of sequential request strategy effectiveness. *Human Communication Research, 13,* 253–267.

Carless, S. A. (1998). Assessing the discriminant validity of transformational leader behaviour as measured by the MLQ. *Journal of Occupational & Organizational Psychology, 71* (4), 353–358.

Carletta, J., Garrod, S., & Fraser-Krauss, H. (1998). Placement of authority and communication patterns in workplace groups: The consequences for innovation. *Small Group Research, 29* (5), 531–559.

Carll, E. K. (1999). *Violence in our lives: Impact on workplace, home, and community.* Boston: Allyn & Bacon, Inc.

Carlo, G., Eisenberg, N., Troyer, D., Switzer, G., & Speer, A. L. (1991). The altruistic personality: In what contexts is it apparent? *Journal of Personality and Social Psychology, 61,* 450–458.

Carlson, M., Charlin, V., & Miller, N. (1988). Positive mood and helping behavior: A test of six hypotheses. *Psychological Bulletin, 102,* 91–108.

Carlson, M., Charlin, V., & Miller, N. (1994). Positive mood and helping behavior: A test of six hypotheses. In B. Puka (Ed.), *Reaching out: Caring, altruism, and prosocial behavior. Moral development: A compendium* (Vol. 7, pp. 111–129). New York: Garland.

Carlson, M., Marcus-Newhall, A., & Miller, N. (1989). Evidence for a general construct of aggression. *Personality and Social Psychology Bulletin, 15,* 377–389.

Carlson, M., Marcus-Newhall, A., & Miller, N. (1990). Effects of situational aggression cues: A quantitative review. *Journal of Personality and Social Psychology, 58,* 622–633.

Carrere, S., & Gottman, J. M. (1999). Predicting the future of marriages. In E. M. Hetherington (Ed.), *Coping with divorce, single parenting, and remarriage: A risk and resiliency perspective.* Mahwah, NJ: Erlbaum.

Carroll, S. J., Perkowitz, W. T., Lurigio, A. J., & Waver, F. M. (1987). Sentencing goals, causal

attributions, ideology, and personality. *Journal of Personality and Social Psychology, 50,* 107–118.

Carson, R. C., Butcher, J. N., & Coleman, J. C. (1992). *Abnormal psychology and modern life* (9th ed.). New York: HarperCollins.

Carstensen, L. L., Gottman, J. M., & Levenson, R. W. (1995). Emotional behavior in long-term marriage. *Psychology & Aging, 10,* 140–149.

Carver, C. S., Pozo, C., Harris, S. D., & Noriega, V. (1993). How coping mediates the effect of optimism on distress: A study of women with early stage breast cancer. *Journal of Personality & Social Psychology, 65,* 375–390.

Carver, C. S., & Scheier, M. F. (1993). Vigilant and avoidant coping in two patient samples. In H. W. Krohne (Ed.), *Attention and avoidance: Strategies in coping with aversiveness.* Goettingen, Germany: Hogrefe & Huber.

Cassel, W. S., Roebers, C. E., & Bjorklund, D. F. (1996). Developmental patterns of eyewitness responses to repeated and increasingly suggestive questions. *Journal of Experimental Child Psychology, 61,* 116–133.

Castellan, N. J., Jr. (Ed.). (1993). *Individual and group decision making.* Hillsdale, NJ: Erlbaum.

Ceci, S. J., & Bruck, M. (1995). *Jeopardy in the courtroom.* Washington, DC: American Psychological Association.

Chaiken, S. (1979). Communicator physical attractiveness and persuasion. *Journal of Personality and Social Psychology, 37,* 1387–1397.

Chaiken, S. (1980). Heuristic versus systematic information processing and the use of source versus message cues in persuasion. *Journal of Personality and Social Psychology, 39,* 752–766.

Chaiken, S. (1987). The heuristic model of persuasion. In M. P. Zanna, J. M. Olson, & C. P. Herman (Eds.), *Social influence: The Ontario symposium* (Vol. 5). Hillsdale, NJ: Erlbaum.

Chaiken, S., & Stangor, S. (1987). Attitudes and attitude change. *Annual Review of Psychology, 38,* 575–630.

Chaiken, S., Wood, W., & Eagly, A. H. (1996). Principles of persuasion. In E. T. Higgins & A. W. Kruglanski (Eds.), *Social psychology: Handbook of basic principles.* New York: Guilford.

Chamberlain, K., & Zika, S. (1990). The minor events approach to stress: Support for the use of daily hassles. *British Journal of Psychology, 81,* 469–481.

Chambers, J. W., Clark, T., Dantzler, L., & Baldwin, J. A. (1994). Perceived attractiveness, facial features, and African self-consciousness. *Journal of Black Psychology, 20,* 305–324.

Chang, E. C. (1998). Dispositional optimism and primary and secondary appraisal of a stressor: Controlling for confounding influences and relations to coping and psychological and physical adjustment. *Journal of Personality & Social Psychology, 74,* 1109–1120.

Chapdelaine, A., Kenny, D. A., & LaFontana, K. M. (1994). Matchmaker, matchmaker, can you

make me a match? Predicting liking between two unacquainted persons. *Journal of Personality and Social Psychology, 67,* 83–91.

Chapkis, W. (1986). *Beauty secrets: Women and the politics of appearance.* Boston: South End Press.

Chapman, J. G., Arenson, S., Carrigan, M. H., & Gryckiewicz, J. (1993). Motivational loss in small task groups: Free riding on a cognitive task. *Genetic, Social, & General Psychology Monographs, 119* (1), 57–73.

Charbonnier, E., Huguet, P., Brauer, M., & Monteil, J. (1998). Social loafing and self-beliefs: People's collective effort depends on the extent to which they distinguish themselves as better than others. *Social Behavior & Personality, 26* (4), 329–340.

Chartrand, T., Pinckert, S., & Burger, J. M. (1999). When manipulation backfires: The effects of time delay and requester on the foot-in-the-door technique. *Journal of Applied Social Psychology, 29* (1), 211–221.

Chastain, G. D., & Landrum, R. E. (Eds.). (1999). *Protecting human subjects: Departmental subject pools and institutional review boards.* Washington, DC: American Psychological Association.

Chemers, M. M. (1997). *An integrative theory of leadership.* Mahwah, NJ: Erlbaum.

Chen, Y., Brockner, J., & Katz, T. (1998). Toward an explanation of cultural differences in in-group favoritism: The role of individual versus collective primacy. *Journal of Personality & Social Psychology, 75,* 1490–1502.

Cheng, P. W., & Novick, L. R. (1990). A probalistic contrast model of causal induction. *Journal of Personality and Social Psychology, 58,* 545–567.

Cherlin, A. J., Furstenberg, F. F., Jr., Chase-Lansdale, P. L., Kiernan, K. E., Robins, P. K., Morrison, D. R., & Teitler, J. O. (1991, June 7). Longitudinal studies of effects of divorce on children in Great Britain and the United States. *Science, 252,* 1386–1389.

Cho, W., & Cross, S. E. (1995). Taiwanese love styles and their association with self-esteem and relationship quality. *Genetic, Social, & General Psychology Monographs, 121,* 283–309.

Choi, I., Nisbett, R. E., & Norenzayan, A. (1999). Causal attribution across cultures: Variation and universality. *Psychological Bulletin, 125,* 47–63.

Chrisler, J. C., & Levy, K. B. (1990). The media construct a menstrual monster: A content analysis of PMS articles in the popular press. *Women & Health, 16,* 89–104.

Christianson, S. (1992). Emotional stress and eyewitness memory: A critical review. *Psychological Bulletin, 112,* 284–309.

Chwalisz, K., Diener, E., & Gallagher, D. (1988). Autonomic arousal feedback and emotional experience: Evidence from the spinal-cord injured. *Journal of Personality and Social Psychology, 54,* 820–828.

Cialdini, R. B. (1988). *Influence: Science and practice* (2nd ed.). Glenview, IL: Scott, Foresman.

Cialdini, R. (1993). *Influence: Science and practice* (3rd ed.). New York: HarperCollins.

Cialdini, R. B. (1991). Altruism or egoism? That is (still) the question. *Psychological Inquiry, 2,* 124–126.

Cialdini, R. B. (1996). *Influence: Science and Practice* (3rd ed.). New York: Talman.

Cialdini, R. B., Brown, S. L., Lewis, B. P., Luce, C., et al. (1997). Reinterpreting the empathy-altruism relationship: When one into one equals oneness. *Journal of Personality & Social Psychology, 73,* 481-494.

Cialdini, R. B., & deNicholas, M. E. (1989). Self-presentation by association. *Journal of Personality and Social Psychology, 57,* 626–631.

Cialdini, R. B., & Fultz, J. (1990). Interpreting the negative mood-helping literature via "mega"-analysis: A contrary view. *Psychological Bulletin, 107,* 210–214.

Cialdini, R. B., & Kenrick, D. T. (1976). Altruism as hedonism: A social development perspective on the relationship of negative mood state and helping. *Journal of Personality and Social Psychology, 34,* 907–914.

Cialdini, R. B., Kenrick, D. T., & Baumann, D. J. (1982). Effects of mood on prosocial behavior in children and adults. In N. Eisenberg (Ed.), *The development of prosocial behavior.* Orlando, FL: Academic Press.

Cialdini, R. B., & Petty, R. E. (1981). Anticipatory opinion effects. In R. E. Petty, T. M. Ostrom, & T. C. Brock (Eds.), *Cognitive responses in persuasion.* Hillsdale, NJ: Erlbaum.

Cialdini, R. B., Schaller, M., Houlihan, D., Arps, K., Fultz, J., & Beaman, A. L. (1987). Empathy-based helping: Is it selflessly or selfishly motivated? *Journal of Personality and Social Psychology, 52,* 749–758.

Cialdini, R. B., & Trost, M. R. (1998). Social influence: Social norms, conformity and compliance. In D. T. Gilbert, S. T. Fiske, & G. Lindzey (Eds.), *The handbook of social psychology, Vol. 2* (4th ed., pp. 151–192). Boston, MA: McGraw-Hill.

Cialdini, R. B., Vincent, J. E., Lewis, S. K., Catalan, J., Wheeler, D., & Darby, B. L. (1975). Reciprocal concessions procedure for inducing compliance: The door-in-the-face technique. *Journal of Personality and Social Psychology, 31,* 206–215.

CIRE (Cooperative Institutional Research Program of the American Council on Education). (1990). *The American freshman: national norms for fall 1990.* Los Angeles: American Council on Education.

Clark, E. M., Brock, T. C., & Stewart, D. W. (Eds.). (1994). *Attention, attitude, and affect in response to advertising.* Hillsdale, NJ: Erlbaum.

Clark, H. H. (1985). Language use and language users. In G. Lindzey & E. Aronson (Eds.), *Handbook of social psychology* (Vol. 2, 3rd ed.). New York: Random House.

Clark, M. L., & Ayers, M. (1992). Friendship similarity during early adolescence: Gender and racial patterns. *Journal of Psychology, 126,* 393–405.

Clark, M. L., & Ayers, M. (1993). Friendship expectations and friendship evaluations: Reciprocity and gender effects. *Youth & Society, 24,* 299–313.

Clark, M. S. (1984). Record keeping in two types of relationships. *Journal of Personality and Social Psychology, 47,* 549–557.

Clark, M. S., & Mills, J. (1979). Interpersonal attraction in exchange and communal relationships. *Journal of Personality and Social Psychology, 37,* 12–24.

Clark, M. S., & Mills, J. (1993). The difference between communal and exchange relationships: What it is and is not. *Personality and Social Psychology Bulletin, 19,* 684–691.

Clark, M. S., Mills, J. R., & Corcoran, D. M. (1989). Keeping track of needs and inputs of friends and strangers. *Personality and Social Psychology Bulletin, 15,* 533–542.

Clark, M. S., & Reis, H. T. (1988). Interpersonal processes in close relationships. *Annual Review of Psychology, 39,* 609–672.

Clark, R. D. (1994). The role of censorship in minority influence. *European Journal of Social Psychology, 24,* 331–338.

Clark, R. D., III. (1998). Minority influence: The role of the rate of majority defection and persuasive arguments. *European Journal of Social Psychology, 28* (5), 787–796.

Clark, R. D., III, & Maass, A. (1988). Social categorization in minority influence. *European Journal of Social Psychology, 18,* 347–364.

Clark, R. D., III, & Maass, A. (1990). The effects of majority size on minority influence. *European Journal of Social Psychology, 20,* 99–117.

Clavier, D. W., & Kalupa, F. B. (1983). Public rebuttals to "trial by television." *Public Relations Review, 9,* 24–36.

Clement, U., & Schoennesson, L. N. (1998). Subjective HIV attribution theories, coping and psychological functioning among homosexual men with HIV. *AIDS Care, 10,* 355–363.

Clinton, A. M., & Anderson, L. R. (1999). Social and emotional loneliness: Gender differences and relationships with self-monitoring and perceived control. *Journal of Black Psychology, 25,* 61–77.

Coates, J. (1997). Women's friendships, women's talk. In R. Wodak (Ed.), *Gender and discourse. Sage studies in discourse.* London: Sage.

Coats, E. J., Feldman, R. S., & Schwartzberg, S. (1994). *Critical thinking: General principles and case studies.* New York: McGraw-Hill.

Cohen, C. E. (1981). Person categories and social perception: Testing some boundaries of the processing effects of prior knowledge. *Journal of Personality and Social Psychology, 40,* 441–452.

Cohen, D., & Nisbett, R. E. (1994). Self-protection and the culture of honor: Explaining southern violence. Special Issue: The self and the collective. *Personality & Social Psychology Bulletin, 20,* 551–567.

Cohen, D., & Nisbett, R. E. (1997). Field experiments examining the culture of honor: The role of institutions in perpetuating norms about violence. *Personality & Social Psychology Bulletin, 23,* 1188–1199.

Cohen, D., Nisbett, R. E., Bowdle, B. F., & Schwarz, N. (1996). Insult, aggression, and the southern culture of honor: An "experimental ethnography." *Journal of Personality and Social Psychology, 70,* 945–960.

Cohen, G., Stanhope, N., & Conway, M. A. (1992). Age differences in the retention of knowledge by young and elderly students. *British Journal of Developmental Psychology, 10,* 153–164.

Cohen, S. (1996). Psychological stress, immunity, and upper respiratory infections. *Current Directions in Psychological Science, 5,* 86–90.

Cohen, S., & McKay, G. (1984). Social support, stress, and the buffering hypothesis: A theoretical analysis. In A. Baum, J. E. Singer, & S. E. Taylor (Eds.), *Handbook of psychology and health* (Vol. 4). Hillsdale, NJ: Erlbaum.

Cohen, S., Tyrrell, D. A., & Smith, A. P. (1993). Negative life events, perceived stress, negative affect, and susceptibility to the common cold. *Journal of Personality and Social Psychology, 64,* 131–140.

Cohn, L. B. (1996, August). Violent video games: Aggression, arousal, and desensitization in young adolescent boys. *Dissertation Abstracts International, 57,* 2B.

Collin, C. A., Di Sano, F., & Malik, R. (1994). Effects of confederate and subject gender on conformity in a color classification task. *Social Behavior & Personality, 22,* 355–364.

Collins, L. H. (1998). Competition and contact: The dynamics behind resistance to affirmative action in academe. In L. H. Collins & J. C. Chrisler (Eds.), *Career strategies for women in academe: Arming Athena.* Thousand Oaks, CA: Sage.

Collins, M. A., & Zebrowitz, L. A. (1995). The contributions of appearance to occupational outcomes in civilian and military settings. *Journal of Applied Social Psychology, 25,* 129–163.

Collins, N. L., & Miller, L. C. (1994). Self-disclosure and liking: A meta-analytic review. *Psychological Bulletin, 116,* 457–475.

Colon, H. M., Sahai, H., Robles, R. R., & Matos, T. D. (1995). Effects of a community outreach program in HIV risk behaviors among injection drug users in San Juan, Puerto Rico: An analysis of trends. *AIDS Education & Prevention, 7,* 195–209.

Colvin, C. R., & Block, J. (1994). Do positive illusions foster mental health? An examination of the Taylor and Brown formulation. *Psycholgocial Bulletin, 116,* 3–20.

Colvin, C. R., Block, J., & Funder, D. C. (1995). Overly positive self-evaluations and personality:

Negative implications for mental health. *Journal of Personality and Social Psychology, 68,* 1152–1162.

Colvin, C. R., & Funder, D. C. (1991). Predicting personality and behavior: A boundary on the acquaintanceship effect. *Journal of Personality and Social Psychology, 60,* 884–894.

Comer, D. R. (1995). A model of social loafing in real work groups. *Human Relations, 48,* 647–667.

Commerford, M. C., Gular, E., Orr, D. A., & Reznikoff, M. (1994). Coping and psychological distress in women with HIV/AIDS. *Journal of Community Psychology, 22,* 224–230.

Compton, W. M., Cottler, L. D., Decker, S. H., Meager, D., & Stringfellow, R. (1992). Legal needle buying in St. Louis. *American Journal of Public Health, 82,* 595–596.

Condon, J. W., & Crano, W. D. (1988). Inferred evaluation and the relation between attitude similarity and interpersonal attraction. *Journal of Personality and Social Psychology, 54,* 789–797.

Conduit, E. (1995). *The body under stress: Developing skills for keeping healthy.* Mahwah, NJ: Erlbaum.

Conger, J. A. (1998). The dark side of leadership. In G. R. Hickman (Ed.), *Leading organizations: Perspectives for a new era* (pp. 250–260). Thousand Oaks, CA: Sage.

Conger, R. D., Rueter, M. A., & Elder, G. H., Jr. (1999). Couple resilience to economic pressure. *Journal of Personality & Social Psychology, 76,* 54–71.

Connor, R. (1992). *Cracking the over-50 job market.* New York: Penguin Books.

Conway, M. A., & Dewhurst, S. A. (1995). The self and recollective experience. *Applied Cognitive Psychology, 9,* 1–19.

Cook, P. W. (1997). *Abused men: The hidden side of domestic violence.* Westport, CT: Praeger.

Cook, T. D., Gruder, C. L., Hennigan, K. M., & Flay, B. R. (1979). History of the sleeper effect: Some logical pitfalls in accepting the null hypothesis. *Psychological Bulletin, 86,* 662–679.

Cook, T. D., & Wadsworth, A. (1972). Attitude change and the paired-associate learning of minimal cognitive elements. *Journal of Personality, 40,* 50–61.

Cooley, C. H. (1902). *Human nature and the social order.* New York: Scribners.

Coons, C. J., Howard-Hamilton, M., & Waryold, D. (1995). College sports and fan aggression: Implications for residence hall discipline. *Journal of College Student Development, 36,* 587–593.

Cooper, A., Sportolari, L. (1997). Romance in cyberspace: Understanding online attraction. *Journal of Sex Education & Therapy, 22,* 7–14.

Cooper, J. (1999). Unwanted consequences and the self: In search of the motivation for dissonance reduction. In E. Harmon-Jones & J. Mills (Eds.), *Cognitive dissonance: Progress on a pivotal theory in social psychology. Science conference series* (pp. 149–173). Washington, DC: American Psychological Association.

Cooper, J., & Fazio, R. (1984). A new look at dissonance theory. In L. Berkowitz (Ed.), *Advances in experimental social psychology* (Vol. 17). New York: Academic Press.

Cooper, J., & Mackie, D. (1986). Video games and aggression in children. *Journal of Applied Social Psychology, 16,* 726–744.

Cooper, W. H., Gallupe, R. B., Pollard, S., & Cadsby, J. (1998). Some liberating effects of anonymous electronic brainstorming. *Small Group Research, 29* (2), 147–178.

Corneil, W., Beaton, R., Murphy, S., Johnson, C., & Pike, K. (1999). Exposure to traumatic incidents and prevalence of posttraumatic stress symptomatology in urban firefighters in two countries. *Journal of Occupational Health Psychology, 4,* 131–141.

Cotton, J. L. (1993). *Employee involvement.* Newbury Park, CA: Sage.

Cottrell, N. B. (1972). Social facilitation. In C. G. McClintock (Ed.), *Experimental social psychology* (pp. 185–236). New York: Holt.

Courneya, K. S., Friedenreich, C. M., Arthur, K., & Bobick, T. M. (1999). Understanding exercise motivation in colorectal cancer patients: A prospective study using the theory of planned behavior. *Rehabilitation Psychology, 44* (1), 68–84.

Cowan, G., & Curtis, S. R. (1994). Predictors of rape occurrence and victim blame in the William Kennedy Smith case. *Journal of Applied Social Psychology, 24,* 12–20.

Cowan, N. (1992). Verbal memory span and the timing of spoken recall. *Journal of Memory and Language, 31,* 668–684.

Cowan, P. A., & Cowan, C. P. (1988). Changes in marriage during the transition to parenthood: Must we blame the baby? In G. Y. Michaels & W. A. Goldberg (Eds.), *The transition to parenthood: Current theory and research.* Cambridge, England: Cambridge University Press.

Cramer, J. A. (1995). Optimizing long-term patient compliance. *Neurology, 45,* S25–S28.

Crandall, R. (1972). Field extension of the frequency-affect findings. *Psychological Reports, 31,* 371–374.

Crano, W. D., & Alvaro, E. M. (1998). The context/comparison model of social influence: Mechanisms, structure, and linkages that underlie indirect attitude change. In W. Stroebe & M. Hewstone (Eds.), *European Review of Social Psychology* (Vol. 8, pp. 175–202). Chichester, England: Wiley.

Crano, W. D., & Chen, X. (1998). The leniency contract and persistence of majority and minority influence. *Journal of Personality & Social Psychology, 74* (6), 1437–1450.

Crites, S. L., Cacioppo, J. T., Gardner, W. L., & Berntson, G. G. (1995). Bioelectrical echoes from evaluative categorization: II. A late positive brain potential that varies as a function of attitude registration rather than attitude report. *Journal of Personality & Social Psychology, 68,* 997–1013.

Crosby, F. J. (1991). *Juggling: The unexpected advantages of balancing career and home for women, their families, and society.* New York: Free Press.

Cross, H. A., Halcomb, C. G., & Matter, W. W. (1967). Imprinting and exposure learning in rats given early auditory stimulation. *Psychonomic Science, 10,* 223–234.

Cross, S. E., & Markus, H. R. (1994). Self-schemas, possible selves, and competent performance. *Journal of Educational Psychology, 86,* 423–438.

Crossette, B. (1995, December 10). Female genital mutilation by immigrants is becoming cause of concern in the U.S. *New York Times,* p. 18.

Croyle, R. T., & Cooper, J. (1983). Dissonance arousal: Physiological evidence. *Journal of Personality and Social Psychology, 45,* 782–791.

Croyle, R. T., & Hunt, J. R. (1991). Coping with health threat: Social influence processes in reactions to medical test results. *Journal of Personality and Social Psychology, 60,* 382–389.

Cruse, D., & Leigh, B. C. (1987). 'Adam's Rib' revisited: Legal and non-legal influences on the processing of trial testimony. *Social Behavior, 2,* 221–230.

Csoka, L. S., & Bons, P. M. (1978). Manipulating the situation to fit the leader's style—two validation studies of Leader Match. *Journal of Applied Psychology, 63,* 295–300.

Cummings, J. (1987, October 6). An earthquake aftershock: Calls to mental health triple. *The New York Times,* p. A1.

Cunningham, M. R. (1986). Measuring the physical in physical attractiveness: Quasi-experiments on the sociobiology of female facial beauty. *Journal of Personality and Social Psychology, 50,* 925–935.

Cunningham, M. R., Barbee, A. P., & Pike, C. L. (1990). What do women want? Facialmetric assessment of multiple motives in the perception of male facial physical attractiveness. *Journal of Personality and Social Psychology, 59,* 61–72.

Cunningham, M. R., Roberts, A. R., Barbee, A. P., & Druen, P. B. (1995). "Their ideas of beauty are, on the whole, the same as ours": Consistency and variability in the cross-cultural perception of female physical attractiveness. *Journal of Personality & Social Psychology, 68,* 261–279.

Curtis, R. C., & Miller, K. (1986). Believing another likes or dislikes you: Behavior making the beliefs come true. *Journal of Personality and Social Psychology, 51,* 284–290.

Cutler, B. L., & Penrod, S. D. (1995). *Mistaken identification: The eyewitness, psychology and the law.* Cambridge: Cambridge University Press.

Cutrona, C. (1982). Transition to college: Loneliness and the process of social adjustment. In L. A. Peplau & D. Perlman (Eds.), *Loneliness: A sourcebook of current theory, research, and therapy.* New York: Wiley.

D'Antoni, T. (1999, February 21). Stop the clock. *New York Times Magazine,* p. 26.

da Gloria, J., Duda, D., Pahlavan, F., & Bonnet, P. (1989). "Weapons effect" revisited: Motor effects of the reception of aversive stimulation and exposure to pictures of firearms. *Aggressive Behavior, 15,* 265–271.

Dabney, D. (1995). Neutralization and deviance in the workplace: Theft of supplies and medicines by hospital nurses. *Deviant Behavior, 16,* 311–313.

Dalton, R. J. (1980). Reassessing parental socialization: Indicator unreliability versus generational transfer. *American Political Science Review, 74,* 421–431.

Damon, W. (Ed.). (1989). *Child development today and tomorrow.* San Francisco: Jossey-Bass.

Danziger, S., & Wheeler, D. (1975). Economics of crime: Punishment or income redistribution. *Review of Social Economy, 33,* 113–131.

Darley, J. M. (1995). Constructive and destructive obedience: A taxonomy of principal-agent relationships. *Journal of Social Issues, 51,* 125–154.

Darley, J. M., & Batson, C. D. (1973). "From Jerusalem to Jericho": A study of situational and dispositional variables in helping behavior. *Journal of Personality and Social Psychology, 27,* 100–108.

Darley, J. M., Fleming, J. H., Hilton, J. L., & Swan, W. B. (1988). Dispelling negative expectancies: The impact of interaction goals and target characteristics on the expectancy confirmation process. *Journal of Experimental Social Psychology, 24,* 19–36.

Darley, J. M., & Latané, B. (1968). Bystanders intervention in emergencies: Diffusion of responsibility. *Journal of Personality and Social Psychology, 8,* 377–383.

Darley, J. M., & Schultz, T. R. (1990). Moral rules: Their content and acquisition. *Annual Review of Psychology, 25,* 525–556.

Dashiell, J. F. (1930). An experimental analysis of some group effects. *Journal of Abnormal and Social Psychology, 25,* 190–199.

Daudistel, H. C., Hosch, H. M., Holmes, M. D., & Graves, J. B. (1999). Effects of defendant ethnicity on juries' dispositions of felony cases. *Journal of Applied Social Psychology, 29* (2), 317–336.

David, D., Kutcher, G. S., Jackson, E. I., & Mellman, T. A. (1999). Psychotic symptoms in combat-related posttraumatic stress disorder. *Journal of Clinical Psychiatry, 60,* 29–32.

Davidson, A. R., & Jaccard, J. J. (1979). Variables that moderate the attitude-behavior relation: Results of a longitudinal survey. *Journal of Personality and Social Psychology, 45,* 997–1009.

Davidson, D., & Hirtle, S. C. (1990). Effects of nondiscrepant and discrepant information on the use of base rates. *American Journal of Pscyhology, 103,* 343–357.

Davies, M. F. (1994a). The physical situation. In P. Alexander Hare & H. H. Blumberg (Eds.), *Small group research: A handbook* (pp. 11–39). Norwood, NJ: Ablex.

Davies, M. F. (1994b). Private self-consciousness and the perceived accuracy of true and false personality feedback. *Personality & Individual Differences, 17,* 697–701.

Davies, M. F. (1997). Private self-consciousness and the acceptance of personality feedback: Confirmatory processing in the evaluation of general vs. specific self-information. *Journal of Research in Personality, 31,* 78–92.

Davis, B. P., & Knowles, E. S. (1999). A disrupt-then-reframe technique of social influence. *Journal of Personality & Social Psychology, 76,* 192–199.

Davis, J. H. (1969). *Group performance.* Reading, MA: Addison-Wesley.

Davis, J. H., Hulbert, L., Au, W. T., Chen, X., & Zarnoth, P. (1997). Effects of group size and procedural influence on consensual judgments of quantity: The examples of damage awards and mock civil juries. *Journal of Personality & Social Psychology, 73* (4), 703–718.

Davis, M. H. (1994). *Empathy: A social psychological approach.* Madison, WI: Brown & Benchmark.

Davis, M. H., Luce, C., & Kraus, S. J. (1994). The heritability of characteristics associated with dispositional empathy. *Journal of Personality, 62,* 369–391.

Davis, M. S. (1968). Variations in patients' compliance with doctors' advice: An empirical analysis of patterns of communication. *American Journal of Public Health, 58,* 274–288.

Davis, T. L., Severy, L. J., Kraus, S. J., Whitaker, J. M. (1993). Predictors of sentencing decisions: The beliefs, personality variables, and demographic factors of juvenile justice personnel. *Journal of Applied Social Psychology, 23,* 451–477.

Davison, K. P., & Pennebaker, J. W. (1997). Virtual narratives: Illness representations in online support groups. In K. J. Petrie & J. A. Weinman (Eds.), *Perceptions of health and illness: Current research and applications.* Singapore: Harwood Academic Publishers.

Dawes, R. M. (1998). Behavioral decision making and judgment. In D. T. Gilbert & S. T. Fiske (Eds.), *The handbook of social psychology* (Vol. 2, 4th ed.). Boston, MA: McGraw-Hill.

Dawes, R. M., van de Kragt, A. J. C., & Orbell, J. M. (1988). Not me or thee but we: The importance of group identity in eliciting cooperation in dilemma situations: Experimental manipulations. *Acta Psychologica, 68,* 83–97.

Deal, T. E., & Kennedy, A. A. (1982). *Corporate cultures: The rites and rituals of corporate life.* Reading, MA: Addison-Wesley.

Deater-Deckard, K., & Dodge, K. A. (1997). Externalizing behavior problems and discipline revisited: Nonlinear effects and variation by culture, context, and gender. *Psychological Inquiry, 8,* 161–175.

Deaton, A. V. (1985). Adaptive noncompliance in pediatric asthma: The parent as expert. *Journal of Pediatric Psychology, 10,* 1–14.

Deaux, K. (1992). Personalizing identity and socializing self. In G. Breakwell (Ed.), *Social psychology of identity and the self-concept.* London: Academic Press.

Deaux, K. (1993). Reconstructing social identity. *Personality and Social Psychology Bulletin, 19,* 4–12.

Deaux, K. (1995). How basic can you be? The evolution of research on gender stereotypes. Special Issue: Gender stereotyping, sexual harassment, and the law. *Journal of Social Issues, 51,* 11–20.

Deaux, K., & Ethier, K. A. (1998). Negotiating social identity. In J. K. Swim & C. Stangor (Eds.), *Prejudice: The target's perspective.* San Diego, CA: Academic Press.

Deaux, K., & LaFrance, M. (1998). Gender. In D. T. Gilbert & S. T. Fiske (Eds.), *The handbook of social psychology* (4th ed.). Boston, MA: McGraw-Hill.

Deaux, K., Reid, A., Mizrahi, K., & Cotting, D. (1999). Connecting the person to the social: The functions of social identification. In T. R. Tyler & R. M. Kramer (Eds.), *The psychology of the social self. Applied social research.* Mahwah, NJ: Erlbaum.

Deaux, K., Reid, A., Mizrahi, K., & Ethier, K. A. (1995). Parameters of social identity. *Journal of Personality & Social Psychology, 68,* 280–291.

DeBono, K. G. (1992). Pleasant scents and persuasion: An information processing approach. *Journal of Applied Social Psychology, 22,* 910–919.

DeBono, K. G., & Klein, C. (1993). Source expertise and persuasion: The moderating role of recipient dogmatism. *Personality & Social Psychology Bulletin, 19,* 167–173.

DeBono, K. G., & Krim, S. (1997). Compliments and perceptions of product quality: An individual difference perspective. *Journal of Applied Social Psychology, 27* (15), 1359–1366.

DeBono, K. G., & McDermott, J. B. (1994). Trait anxiety and persuasion: Individual differences in information processing strategies. *Journal of Research in Personality, 28,* 395–407.

DeBono, K. G., & Omoto, A. M. (1993). Individual differences in predicting behavioral intentions from attitude and subjective norm. *Journal of Social Psychology, 133,* 825–831.

DeBono, K. G., & Snyder, M. (1989). Understanding consumer decision-making processes: The role of form and function in product evaluation. *Journal of Applied Social Psychology, 19,* 416–424.

Deci, E. L., & Ryan, R. M. (1985). *Intrinsic motivation and self-determination in human behavior.* New York: Plenum.

DeFrank, R. S., Matteson, M. T., Schweiger, D. M., & Ivancevich, J. M. (1985). The impact of culture on the management practices of Japanese and American CEOs. *Organizational Dynamics, 13,* 62–70.

Deluga, R., & Perry, J. T. (1994). The role of subordinate performance and ingratiation in leader-member exchanges. *Group & Organization Management, 19,* 67–86.

De Michele, P. E., Gansneder, B., & Solomon, G. B. (1998). Success and failure attributions of wrestlers: Further evidence of the self-serving bias. *Journal of Sport Behavior, 21,* 242–255.

deMunck, V. C. (1998). *Romantic love and sexual behavior: Perspectives from the social sciences.* Westport, CT: Praeger.

Dengerink, H. A., & Covey, M. K. (1983). Implications of an escape-avoidance theory of aggressive response to attack. In R. G. Geen & E. I. Donnerstein (Eds.), *Aggression: Theoretical and empirical reviews. Vol. 1: Theoretical and methodological issues.* New York: Academic Press.

DeParle, J. (1993, March 19). Sharp criticism for Head Start, even by friends. *New York Times,* p. A1.

DePaulo, B. M. (1991). Nonverbal behavior and self-presentation. *Psychological Bulletin, 105,* 122–131.

Derlega, V. J. (1988). Self-disclosure: Inside or outside the mainstream of social psychological research? Special Issue: The state of social psychology: Issues, themes, and controversies. *Journal of Social Behavior and Personality, 3,* 27–34.

Derlega, V. J., Metts, S., Petronio, S., & Margulis, S. T. (1993). *Self-disclosure.* Newbury Park, CA: Sage.

DeSantis, A., & Kayson, W. A. (1997). Defendants' characteristics of attractiveness, race, and sex and sentencing decisions. *Psychological Reports, 81* (2), 679–683.

Desforges, D. M., Lord, C. G., Ramsey, S. L., Mason, J. A., VanLeeuwen, M. D., West, S. C., & Lepper, M. R. (1991). Effects of structured cooperative contact on changing negative attitudes toward stigmatized social groups. *Journal of Personality and Social Psychology, 60,* 531–544.

Deutsch, F. M., Lussier, J. B., & Servis, L. J. (1993). Husbands at home: Predcitors of paternal participation in childcare and housework. *Journal of Personality and Social Psychology, 65,* 1154–1166.

Deutsch, M., & Gerard, H. B. (1955). A study of normative and informational social influence upon individual judgment. *Journal of Abnormal and Social Psychology, 51,* 629–636.

Devenport, J. L., Penrod, S. D., & Cutler, B. L. (1997). Eyewitness identification evidence: Commonsense evaluations. *Psychology, Public Policy, & Law, 3* (2–3), 338–361.

Devine, P. G. (1989). Stereotypes and prejudice: Their automatic and controlled components. *Journal of Personality and Social Psychology, 56,* 5–18.

Devine, P. G. (1996, January/February). Breaking the prejudice habit. *Psychological Science Agenda,* p. 10–11.

Devine, P. G., Monteith, M. J., Zuwerink, J. R., & Elliot, A. J. (1991). Prejudice with and without compunction. *Journal of Personality and Social Psychology, 60,* 817–830.

Devine, P. G., & Sherman, S. J. (1992). Intuitive versus rational judgment and the role of stereotyping the human condition: Kirk or Spock? *Psychological Inquiry, 3,* 153–159.

Devine, P. G, Tauer, J. M., Barron, K. E., Elliot, A. J., & Vance, K. M. (1999). Moving beyond attitude change in the study of dissonance-related processes. In E. Harmon-Jones & J. Mills (Eds.), *Cognitive dissonance: Progress on a pivotal theory in social psychology. Science conference series* (pp. 297–323). Washington, DC: American Psychological Association.

Devos, T. (1998). Ingroup bias and dimensional relevance. *Schweizerische Zeitschrift Fuer Psychologie—Revue Suisse de Psychologie, 57* (3), 153–162.

Dewsbury, D. A. (1981). Effects of novelty on copulatory behavior: The Coolidge effect and related phenomena. *Psychological Bulletin, 89,* 464–482.

Dickerson, A. E. (1995). Action identification may explain why the doing of activities in occupational therapy effects positive changes in clients. *British Journal of Occupational Therapy, 58,* 461–464.

Diener, E., & Diener, C. (1996). Most people are happy. *Psychological Science, 7,* 181–185.

Diener, E., Suh, E. M., Lucas, R. E., & Smith, H. L. (1999). Subjective well-being: Three decades of progress. *Psychological Bulletin, 125,* 276–302.

Diener, E., Wolsic, B., & Fujita, F. (1995). Physical attractiveness and subjective well-being. *Journal of Personality and Social Psychology, 69,* 120–129.

Dietrich, D. M., & Berkowitz, L. (1997). Alleviation of dissonance by engaging in prosocial behavior or receiving ego-enhancing feedback. *Journal of Social Behavior & Personality, 12* (2), 557–566.

Dill, J. C., & Anderson, C. A. (1999). Loneliness, shyness, and depression: The etiology and interrelationships of everyday problems in living. In T. Joiner & J. C. Coyne (Eds.), *The interactional nature of depression: Advances in interpersonal approaches.* Washington, DC: American Psychological Association.

Dillard, J. P. (1991). The current status of research on sequential-request compliance techniques. Special Issue: Meta-analysis in personality and social psychology. *Personality and Social Psychology Bulletin, 17,* 283–288.

Dillard, J. P., Hunter, J. E., & Burgoon, M. (1984). Sequential-request persuasive strategies: Meta-analysis of foot-in-the-door and door-in-the-face. *Human Communication Research, 10,* 461–488.

DiMatteo, M. R., & DiNicola, D. D. (1982). *Achieving patient compliance: The psychology of the medical practitioner's role.* New York: Pergamon.

DiMatteo, M. R., Reiter, R. C., & Gambone, J. C. (1994). Enhancing medication adherence through communication and informed collaborative choice. Special Issue: Communicating with patients about their medications. *Health Communication, 6,* 253–265.

Dimberg, U. (1997). Facial reactions: Rapidly evoked emotional responses. *Journal of Psychophysiology, 11* (2), 115–123.

Dimberg, U., & Karlsson, B. (1997). Facial reactions to different emotionally relevant stimuli. *Scandinavian Journal of Psychology, 38,* 297–303.

Dindia, K., & Allen, M. (1992). Sex differences in self-disclosure: A meta-analysis. *Psychological Bulletin, 112,* 106–124.

Dion, K. K. (1972). Physical attractiveness and evaluations of children's transgressions. *Journal of Personality and Social Psychology, 24,* 207–213.

Dion, K. K., & Dion, K. L. (1996). Cultural perspectives on romantic love. *Personal Relationships, 3,* 5–17.

Dion, K. L., & Dion, K. K. (1988). Romantic love: Individual and cultural perspectives. In R. J. Sternberg & M. L. Barnes (Eds.), *The psychology of love.* New Haven, CT: Yale University Press.

Dodge, K. A., Bates, J. E., & Petit, G. S. (1990, December 20). Mechanisms in the cycle of violence. *Science, 250,* 1678–1683.

Dodgson, P. G., & Wood, J. V. (1998). Self-esteem and the cognitive accessibility of strengths and weaknesses after failure. *Journal of Personality & Social Psychology, 75,* 178–197.

Doherty, K., & Schlenker, B. R. (1995). Excuses as mood protection: The impact of supportive and challenging feedback from others. *Journal of Social & Clinical Psychology, 14,* 147–164.

Dohrenwend, B. S., Dohrenwend, B. P., Dodson, M., & Shrout, P. E. (1984). Symptoms, hassles, social supports, and life events: The problem of confounded measures. *Journal of Abnormal Psychology, 93,* 222–230.

Dolgin, K. G., & Kim, S. (1994). Adolescents' disclosure to best and good friends: The effects of gender and topic intimacy. *Social Development, 3,* 146–157.

Dolgin, K. G., Meyer, L., & Schwartz, J. (1991). Effects of gender, target's gender, topic, and self-esteem on disclosure to best and middling friends. *Sex Roles, 25,* 311–329.

Dolgin, K. G., & Minowa, N. (1997). Gender differences in self-presentation: A comparison of the roles of flatteringness and intimacy in self-disclosure to friends. *Sex Roles, 36,* 371–380.

Dolin, D. J., & Booth-Butterfield, S. (1995). Foot-in-the-door and cancer prevention. *Health Communication, 7,* 55–66.

Doll, J., & Ajzen, I. (1992). Accessibility and stability of predictors in the theory of planned behavior. *Journal of Personality and Social Psychology, 63,* 754–765.

Dollard, J., Doob, L. W., Miller, N. E., Mowrer, O. H., & Sears, R. R. (1939). *Frustration and aggression.* New Haven, CT: Yale University Press.

Domjan, M. (1998). *The principles of learning and behavior* (4th ed.). Pacific Grove, CA: Brooks/Cole.

Donnerstein, E., & Linz, D. (1998). Mass media, sexual violence, and male viewers. In M. E. Odem & J. Clay-Warner (Eds.), *Confronting rape and sexual assault. Worlds of women, No. 3,* (pp. 181–198). Wilmington, DE: SR Books/Scholarly Resources.

Donnerstein, E., & Malamuth, N. (1997). Pornography: Its consequences on the observer. In L. B. Schlesinger & E. Revitch (Eds.), *Sexual dynamics of anti-social behavior* (2nd ed., pp. 30–49). Springfield, IL: Charles C Thomas.

Donnerstein, M., & Donnerstein, E. (1977). Modeling in the control of interracial aggression: The problem of generality. *Journal of Personality, 45,* 100–116.

Donnerstein, M., & Donnerstein, E. (1978). Direct and vicarious censure in the control of interracial aggression. *Journal of Personality, 46,* 162–175.

Donovan, R. J., & Leivers, S. (1993). Using paid advertising to modify racial stereotype beliefs. *Public Opinion Quarterly, 57,* 205–218.

Doob, A. N., & Beaulieu, L. A. (1992). Variation in the exercise of judicial discretion with young offenders. *Canadian Journal of Criminology, 34,* 35–50.

Dooley, P. A. (1995). Perceptions of the onset controllability of AIDS and helping judgments: An attributional analysis. *Journal of Applied Social Psychology, 25,* 858–869.

Dorfman, P. W., & Stephan, W. G. (1984). The effects of group performance on cognitions, satisfaction, and behavior: A process model. *Journal of Management, 10,* 173–192.

Dovidio, J. F., Allen, J. L., & Schroeder, D. A. (1990). Specificity of empathy-induced helping: Evidence for altruistic motivation. *Journal of Personality and Social Psychology, 59,* 249–260.

Dovidio, J. F., Ellyson, S. L., Keating, C. F., Heltman, K., & Brown, C. E. (1988). The relationship of social power to visual displays of dominance between men and women. *Journal of Personality and Social Psychology, 54,* 233–242.

Dovidio, J. F., & Gaertner, S. L. (1986). *Prejudice, discrimination, and racism: Theory and research.* Orlando, FL: Academic Press.

Dovidio, J. F., & Gaertner, S. L. (1991). Changes in the expression of racial prejudice. In H. Knopke, J. Norrell, & R. Rogers (Eds.), *Opening doors: An appraisal of race relations in contemporary America.* Tuscaloosa: University of Alabama Press.

Dovidio, J. F., Gaertner, S. L., Isen, A. M., & Lowrance, R. (1995). Group representations and intergroup bias: Positive affect, similarity, and group size. *Personality & Social Psychology Bulletin, 21,* 856–865.

Dovidio, J. F., Gaertner, S. L., & Validzic, A. (1998). Intergroup bias: Status, differentiation, and a common in-group identity. *Journal of Personality & Social Psychology, 75,* 109–120.

Dovidio, J. F., Kawakami, K., Johnson, C., Johnson, B., & Howard, A. (1997). On the nature of prejudice: Automatic and controlled processes. *Journal of Experimental Social Psychology, 33,* 510–540.

Dovidio, J. F., Smith, J. K., Donnella, A. G., & Gaertner, S. L. (1997). Racial attitudes and the death penalty. *Journal of Applied Social Psychology, 27* (16), 1468–1487.

Downs, A. C., & Lyons, P. M. (1991). Natural observations of the links between attractiveness and initial legal judgments. *Personality and Social Psychology Bulletin, 17,* 541–547.

Drabman, R. S., & Thomas, M. H. (1974). Exposure to filmed violence and children's tolerance of real life aggression. *Personality and Social Psychology Bulletin, 1,* 198–199.

Drieschner, K., & Lange, A. (1999). A review of cognitive factors in the etiology of rape: Theories, empirical studies, and implications. *Clinical Psychology Review, 19,* 57–77.

Driscoll, R., Davis, K. W., & Lipitz, M. E. (1972). Parental interference and romantic love. *Journal of Personality and Social Psychology, 24,* 1–10.

Druskat, V. U. (1994). Gender and leadership style: Transformational and transactional leadership in the Roman Catholic Church. *Leadership Quarterly, 5,* 99–119.

Dubinsky, A. J., Yammarino, F. J., & Jolson, M. A. (1995). An examination of linkages between personal characteristics and dimensions of transformational leadership. *Journal of Business & Psychology, 9,* 315–335.

DuBois, D. L., & Hirsch, B. J. (1990). School and neighborhood friendship patterns of blacks and whites in early adolescence. *Child Development, 61,* 524–536.

Dubrovsky, V. J., Kiesler, S., & Sethna, B. N. (1991). The equalization phenomenon: Status effects in computer-mediated and face-to-face decision-making groups. *Human Computer Interacton, 6,* 119–146.

Duck, S. W. (Ed.). (1982). *Personal relationships: Vol. 4. Dissolving personal relationships.* New York: Academic.

Duck, S. W. (1984). *Personal relationships 4: Dissolving personal relationships.* Duluth, MN: Academic Press.

Duck, S. (1988). *Relating to others.* Chicago: Dorsey.

Duck, S., & Wood, J. T. (Eds.). (1995). *Confronting relationship challenges.* Thousand Oaks, CA: Sage.

Duckitt, J. (1993). Right-wing authoritarianism among white South African students: Its measurement and correlates. *Journal of Social Psychology, 133,* 553–563.

Duckitt, J. (1994a). *The social psychology of prejudice.* New York: Praeger.

Duckitt, J., & Mphuthing, T. (1998). Group identification and intergroup attitudes: A longitudinal analysis in South Africa. *Journal of Personality & Social Psychology, 74,* 80–85.

Duckitt, J. H. (1992). Patterns of prejudice: Group interests and intergroup attitudes. *South African Journal of Psychology, 22,* 147–156.

Dugan, E., & Kivett, V. R. (1994). The importance of emotional and social isolation to loneliness among very old rural adults. *Gerontologist, 34,* 340–346.

Dukes, R. L., Stein, J. A., & Ullman, J. B. (1997). Long-term impact of Drug Abuse Resistance Education (D. A. R. E.): Results of a 6–year follow-up. *Evaluation Review, 21* (4), 483–500.

Duncan, I. J. H, Widowski, T. M., Malleau, A. E., Lindberg, A. C., & Petherick, J. C. (1998). External factors and causation of dustbathing in domestic hens. *Behavioural Processes, 43* (2), 219–228.

Dunkel-Schetter, C., Folkman, S., & Lazarus, R. S. (1987). Correlates of social support receipt. *Journal of Personality and Social Psychology, 53,* 71–80.

Duranti, A. (1992). Language and bodies in social space: Samoan ceremonial greetings. *American Anthropologist, 94,* 657–691.

Durkin, K., & Nugent, B. (1998). Kindergarten children's gender-role expectations for television actors. *Sex Roles, 38,* 387–402.

Dutton, D. G., & Aron, A. P. (1974). Some evidence for heightened sexual attraction under conditions of high anxiety. *Journal of Personality and Social Psychology, 30,* 510–517.

Duval, T. S., Duval, V. H., & Mulilis, J. P. (1992). Effects of self-focus, discrepancy between self and standard, and outcome expectancy favorability on the tendency to match self to standard or to withdraw. *Journal of Personality and Social Psychology, 62,* 340–348.

Duxbury, L. E., & Higgins, C. A. (1991). Gender differences in work-family conflict. *Journal of Applied Psychology, 76,* 60–73.

Duxbury, L., Higgins, C., & Lee, C. (1994). Work-family conflict: A comparison by gender, family type, and perceived control. *Journal of Family Issues, 15,* 449–466.

Dykstra, P. A. (1995). Loneliness among the never and formerly married: The importance of supportive friendships and a desire for independence. *Journals of Gerontology: Series B: Psychological Sciences & Social Sciences, 50B,* S321–S329.

Dziokonski, W., & Weber, S. J. (1977). Repression-sensitization, perceived vulnerability, and the fear appeal communication. *Journal of Social Psychology, 102,* 105–112.

Eagly, A. H. (1987). *Sex differences in social behavior: A social role interpretation.* Hillsdale, NJ: Erlbaum.

Eagly, A. H., & Carli, L. L. (1981). Sex of researchers and sex-typed communications as determinants of sex differences in influenceability: A meta-analysis of social influence studies. *Psychological Bulletin, 90,* 1–20.

Eagly, A. H., & Chaiken, S. (1993). *The psychology of attitudes.* Fort Worth: Harcourt Brace Jovanovich.

Eagly, A. H., & Chaiken, S. (1998). Attitude structure and function. In D. T. Gilbert, S. T. Fiske, & G. Lindzey (Eds.), *The handbook of social psychology* (Vol. 2, 4th ed., pp. 269–322). Boston: McGraw-Hill.

Eagly, A. H., Chen, S., Chaiken, S., & Shaw-Barnes, K. (1999). The impact of attitudes on memory: An affair to remember. *Psychological Bulletin, 125* (1), 64–89.

Eagly, A. H., & Chravala, C. (1986). Sex differences in conformity: Status and gender-role interpretations. *Psychology of Women Quarterly, 10,* 203–220.

Eagly, A., & Crowley, M. (1986). Gender and helping behavior: A meta-analytic review of the social psychological literature. *Psychological Bulletin, 100,* 283–308.

Eagly, A. H., & Johnson, B. T. (1990). Gender and leadership style: A meta-analysis. *Psychological Bulletin, 108,* 233–256.

Eagly, A. H., Karau, S. J., & Makhijani, M. G. (1995). Gender and the effectiveness of leaders: A meta-analysis. *Psychological Bulletin, 117,* 125–145.

Eagly, A. H., Makhijani, M. G., & Klonsky, B. G. (1992). Gender and the evaluation of leaders: A meta-analysis. *Psychological Bulletin, 111,* 3–22.

Eagly, A., & Mladinic, A. (1989). Gender stereotypes and attitudes toward women and men. *Personality and Social Psychology Bulletin, 15,* 543–558.

Eagly, A. H., & Steffen, V. J. (1984). Gender stereotypes stem from the distribution of women and men into social roles. *Journal of Personality and Social Psychology, 46,* 735–754.

Eagly, A. H., & Steffen, V. J. (1986a). Gender and aggressive behavior: A meta-analytic review of the social psychological literature. *Psychological Bulletin, 100,* 309–330.

Eagly, A. H., & Steffen, V. J. (1986b). Gender stereotypes, occupational roles, and beliefs about part-time employees. *Psychology of Women Quarterly, 10,* 252–262.

Eagly, A. H., & Wood, W. (1999). The origins of sex differences in human behavior: Evolved dispositions versus social roles. *American Psychologist, 54,* 408–423.

Eagly, A. H., Wood, W., & Fishbaugh, L. (1981). Sex differences in conformity: Surveillance by the group as a determinant of male nonconformity. *Journal of Personality and Social Psychology, 40,* 384–394.

Ebbesen, E. B., Kjos, G. L., & Konecni, V. J. (1976). Spatial ecology: Its effects on the choice of friends and enemies. *Journal of Experimental Social Psychology, 12,* 505–518.

Ebbesen, E. B., & Konecni, V. J. (1982). An analysis of the bail system. In. V. J. Konecni & E. B. Ebbesen (Eds.), *A social-psychological analysis* (pp. 191–229). San Francisco: Freeman.

Eccles, J. S., Barber, B., & Jozefowicz, D. (1999). Linking gender to educational, occupational, and recreational choices: Applying the Eccles et al. model of achievement-related choices. In W. B. Swann & J. H. Langlois (Eds.), *Sexism and stereotypes in modern society: The gender science of Janet Taylor Spence.* Washington, DC: American Psychological Association.

Eccles, J. S., Jacobs, J. E., & Harold, R. D. (1990). Gender role stereotypes, expectancy effects and parents' socialization of gender differences. *Journal of Social Issues, 46,* 183–201.

Eccles, J. S., Wigfield, A., Flanagan, C. A., Miller, C., Reuman, D. A., & Yee, D. (1989). Self-concepts, domain values, and self-esteem: Relations and changes at early adolescence. *Journal of Personality, 57,* 283–310.

Eden, D. (1990). Pygmalion without interpersonal contrast effects: Whole groups gain from raising manager expectations. *Journal of Applied Psychology, 75,* 394–398.

Eden, D., & Zuk, Y. (1995). Seasickness as a self-fulfilling prophecy: Raising self-efficacy to boost performance at sea. *Journal of Applied Psychology, 80,* 628–635.

Edney, J. J. (1975). Territoriality and control: A field experiment. *Journal of Personality and Social Psychology, 31,* 1108–1115.

Edwards, J. N., Fuller, T. D., Sermsri, S., & Vorakitphokatorn, S. (1994). Why people feel crowded: An examination of objective and subjective crowding. *Population & Environment: A Journal of Interdisciplinary Studies, 16,* 149–173.

Edwards, J. N., Fuller, T. D., Vorakitphokatorn, S., & Sermsri, S. (1994). *Household crowding and its consequences.* Boulder, CO: Westview Press.

Edwards, R. (1995, February). New tools help gauge marital success. *APA Monitor,* p. 6.

Egeland, J. A., Gerhard, D. S., Pauls, D. L., Sussex, J. N., Kidd, K. K., Allen, C. R., Hostetter, A. M., & Housman, D. E. (1987). Bipolar effective disorders linked to DNA markers on chromosome 11. *Nature, 325,* 783–787.

Eisenberg, N. (1986). *Altruistic emotion, cognition, and behavior.* Hillsdale, NJ: Erlbaum.

Eisenberg, N. (1991). Meta-analytic contributions to the literature on prosocial behavior. *Personality and Social Psychology Bulletin, 17,* 273–282.

Eisenberg, N., Futhrie, I. K., Fabes, R. A., Reiser, M., Murphy, B. C., Holglrlen, R., Maszk, P., & Losoya, S. (1997). The relations of regulations and emotionality to resiliency and competent social functioning in elementary school children. *Child Development, 68,* 295–311.

Ekblad, S. (1996). Ecological psychology in Chinese societies. In M. H. Bond (Ed.), *The handbook of Chinese psychology* (pp. 379–392). Hong Kong: Oxford University Press.

Ekman, P. (1997). Deception, lying, and demeanor. In D. F. Halpern, A. E. Voiskounsky, et al. (Eds.), *States of mind: American and post-Soviet perspectives on contemporary issues in psychology.* New York: Oxford University Press.

Ekman, P., & Friesen, W. V. (1975). *Unmasking the face.* Englewood Cliffs, NJ: Prentice-Hall.

Ekman, P., & Friesen, W. V. (1999). Hand movements. In L. K. Guerrero, J. A. DeVito, & M. L. Hecht (Eds.), *The nonverbal communication reader: Classic and contemporary readings* (2nd ed.). Prospect Heights, IL: Waveland Press.

Ekman, P., Friesen, W. V., & Ellsworth, P. (1972). *Emotion in the human face.* Elmsford, NY: Pergamon Press.

Ekman, P., Friesen, W., & O'Sullivan, M. (1988). Smiles when lying. *Journal of Personality and Social Psychology, 54,* 414–420.

Ekman, P., & O'Sullivan, M. (1991). Facial expression: Methods, means, and moues. In R. S. Feldman & B. Rime (Eds.), *Fundamentals of nonverbal*

behavior. Cambridge, England: Cambridge University Press.

Elkin, R. A., & Leippe, M. R. (1986). Physiological arousal, dissonance, and attitude change: Evidence for a dissonance-arousal link and a "Don't remind me" effect. *Journal of Personality and Social Psychology, 51,* 55–65.

Ellemers, N., & Bos, A. E. R. (1998). Social identity, relative deprivation, and coping with the threat of position loss: A field study among native shopkeepers in Amsterdam. *Journal of Applied Social Psychology, 28,* 1987–2006.

Ellison, R. (1952). *Invisible man.* New York: Random House.

Elms, A. C. (1995). Obedience in retrospect. *Journal of Social Issues, 51,* 21–31.

Elwork, A., Sales, B. D., & Alfini, J. J. (1982). *Making jury instructions understandable.* Charlottesville, VA: Miche.

Emmons, R. A., & Colby, P. M. (1995). Emotional conflict and well-being: Relation to perceived availability, daily utilization, and observer reports of social support. *Journal of Personality & Social Psychology, 68,* 947–959.

Endler, N. S., & Rosenstein, A. J. (1997). Evolution of the personality construct in marketing and its applicability to contemporary personality research. *Journal of Consumer Psychology, 6* (1), 55–66.

Engel, J. F., & Blackwell, R. D. (1982). *Consumer behavior* (4th ed.). Hillsdale, NJ: Erlbaum.

Englis, B. G. (Ed.). (1993). *Global and multinational advertising.* Hillsdale, NJ: Erlbaum.

English, P. W., & Sales, B. D. (1997). A ceiling or consistency effect for the comprehension of jury instructions. *Psychology, Public Policy, & Law, 3* (2–3), 381–401.

Epley, N., & Huff, C. (1998). Suspicion, affective response, and educational benefit as a result of deception in psychology research. *Personality & Social Psychology Bulletin, 24,* 759–768.

Erdle, S., Sansom, M., Cole, M. R., & Heapy, N. (1992). Sex differences in personality correlates of helping behavior. *Personality & Individual Differences, 13,* 931–936.

Erdley, C. A., & Asher, S. R. (1998). Linkages between children's beliefs about the legitimacy of aggression and their behavior. *Social Development, 7* (3), 321–339.

Erian, M., Lin, C., Patel, N., Neal, A., & Geiselman, R. E. (1998). Juror verdicts as a function of victim and defendant attractiveness in sexual assault cases. *American Journal of Forensic Psychology, 16* (3), 25–40.

Eron, L. D., Gentry, J. H., & Schlegel, P. (1994). *Reason to hope: A psychosocial perspective on violence and youth.* Washington, DC: American Psychological Association.

Eron, L. D., & Huesmann, L. R. (1984). The control of aggressive behavior by changes in attitudes, values, and the conditions of learning. In R. J. Blanchard & D. C. Blanchard (Eds.), *Advances in the study of aggression* (Vol. 1). New York: Academic Press.

Eron, L. D., Huesmann, L. R., Lefkowitz, M. M., & Walder, L. O. (1972). Does television violence cause aggression? *American Psychologist, 27,* 253–263.

Esser, J. K. (1998). Alive and well after 25 years: A review of groupthink research. *Organizational Behavior & Human Decision Processes, 73* (2–3), 116–141.

Esser, J. K., & Lindoerfer, J. S. (1989). Groupthink and the space shuttle Challenger accident: Toward a quantitative case analysis. *Journal of Behavioral Decision Making, 2,* 167–177.

Esses, V. M., & Zanna, M. P. (1995). Mood and the expression of ethnic stereotypes. *Journal of Personality and Social Psychology, 69,* 1052–1068.

Esterberg, K. G., Moen, P., & Dempster-McCain, D. (1994). Transition to divorce: A life-course approach to women's marital duration and dissolution. *Sociological Quarterly, 35,* 289–307.

Estrada, M., Brown, J., & Lee, F. (1995). Who gets the credit? Perceptions of idiosyncrasy credit in work groups. *Small Group Research, 26,* 56–76.

Etgen, M. P., & Rosen, E. F. (1993). Cognitive dissonance: Physiological arousal in the performance expectancy paradigm. *Bulletin of the Psychonomic Society, 31,* 229–231.

Ethier, K., & Deaux, K. (1990). Hispanics in ivy: Assessing identity and perceived threat. Special Issue: Gender and ethnicity: Perspectives on dual status. *Sex Roles, 22,* 427–440.

Ethier, K. A., & Deaux, K. (1994). Negotiating social identity when contexts change: Maintaining identification and responding to threat. *Journal of Personality & Social Psychology, 67,* 243–251.

Evans, D. L. (1993, March 1). The wrong examples. *Newsweek,* p. 10.

Evans, D. W. (1994). Self-complexity and its relation to development, symptomatology and self-perception during adolescence. *Child Psychiatry & Human Development, 24,* 173–182.

Evans, G. W., Hygge, S., & Bullinger, M. (1995). Chronic noise and psychological stress. *Psychological Science, 6,* 333–338.

Evans, G. W., & Lepore, S. J. (1992). Conceptual and analytic issues in crowding research. *Journal of Environmental Psychology, 12,* 163–173.

Evans, G. W., Lepore, S. J., & Schroeder, A. (1996). The role of interior design elements in human responses to crowding. *Journal of Personality & Social Psychology, 70,* 41–46.

Evans, G. W., Lepore, S. J., Shejwal, B. R., & Palsane, M. N. (1998). Chronic residential crowding and children's well-being: An ecological perspective. *Child Development, 69,* 1514–1523.

Everly, G. S., Jr., & Lating, J. M. (Eds.). (1995). *Psychotraumatology.* New York: Plenum.

Evinger, S. (1996). How to read race (Categories of race and ethnicity and the 2000 Census). *American Demographics, 18,* 36–42.

Evuleocha, S. U., & Ugbah, S. D. (1989). Stereotypes, counter-stereotypes, and Black television images in the 1990s. *Western Journal of Black Studies, 13,* 197–205.

Eyuboglu, N., & Atac, O. A. (1991). Informational power: A means for increased control in channels of distribution. *Psychology and Marketing, 8,* 197–213.

Fabrigar, L. R., & Petty, R. E. (1999). The role of the affective and cognitive bases of attitudes in susceptibility to affectively and cognitively based persuasion. *Personality & Social Psychology Bulletin, 25* (3), 363–381.

Fabrikant, G. (1996, April 8). The young and restless audience. *New York Times,* pp. D1, D8.

Farmer, S. M., & Roth, J. (1998). Conflict-handling behavior in work groups: Effects of group structure, decision processes, and time. *Small Group Research, 29* (6), 669–713.

Fazio, R. H. (1990). Multiple processes by which attitudes guide behavior: The MODE model as an integrative framework. In M. Zanna (Ed.), *Advances in experimental social psychology.* San Diego, CA: Academic Press.

Fazio, R. H. (1995). Attitudes as object-evaluation associations: Determinants, consequences, and correlates of attitude accessibility. In R. E. Petty & J. A. Krosnick (Eds.), *Attitude strength: Antecedents and consequences.* Mahwah, NJ: Erlbaum.

Fazio, R. H. (1998). Further evidence regarding the multiple category problem: The roles of attitude accessibility and hierarchical control. In R. S. Wyer, Jr. (Ed.), *Stereotype activation and inhibition. Vol. 11: Advances in social cognition* (pp. 97–108). Mahwah, NJ: Erlbaum.

Fazio, R. H., Blascovich, J., & Driscoll, D. M. (1992). On the functional value of attitudes: The influence of accessible attitudes on the ease and quality of decision making. *Personality and Social Psychology Bulletin, 18,* 388–401.

Fazio, R. H., Jackson, J. R., Dunton, B. C., & Williams, C. J. (1995). Variability in automatic activation as an unobtrusive measure of racial attitudes: A bona fide pipeline? *Journal of Personality and Social Psychology, 69,* 1013–1027.

Fazio, R. H., & Powell, M. C. (1997). On the value of knowing one's likes and dislikes: Attitude accessibility, stress, and health in college. *Psychological Science, 8* (6), 430–436.

Fazio, R. H., Sanbonmatsu, D. M., Powell, M. C., & Kardes, F. R. (1986). On the automatic activation of attitudes. *Journal of Personality and Social Psychology, 50,* 229–238.

Fazio, R. H., Zanna, M. P., & Cooper, J. (1977). Dissonance and self-perception: An integrative view of each theory's proper domain of application. *Journal of Experimental Social Psychology, 13,* 464–479.

Fehr, B. (1994). Prototype-based assessment of laypeople's views of love. *Personal Relationships, 1,* 309–331.

Fehr, B. (1995). *Friendship processes.* New York: Sage.

Fehr, B., Baldwin, M., Collins, L., Patterson, S., & Benditt, R. (1999). Anger in close relationships: An interpersonal script analysis. *Personality & Social Psychology Bulletin, 25,* 299–312.

Fehr, B., & Russell, J. A. (1991). The concept of love viewed from a prototype perspective. *Journal of Personality and Social Psychology, 60,* 425–438.

Feick, D. L., & Rhodewalt, F. (1997). The double-edged sword of self-handicapping: Discounting, augmentation, and the protection and enhancement of self-esteem. *Motivation & Emotion, 21,* 147–163.

Fein, S., McCloskey, A. L., & Tomlinson, T. M. (1997). Can the jury disregard that information? The use of suspicion to reduce the prejudicial effects of pretrial publicity and inadmissible testimony. *Personality & Social Psychology Bulletin, 23* (11), 1215–1226.

Feingold, A. (1988). Matching for attractiveness in romantic partners and same-sex friends: A meta-analysis and theoretical critique. *Psychological Bulletin, 104,* 226–235.

Feingold, A. (1992a). Gender differences in mate selection preferences: A test of the parental investment model. *Psychological Bulletin, 112,* 125–139.

Feingold, A. (1992b). Good-looking people are not what we think. *Psychological Bulletin, 111,* 304–341.

Feldman, R. S. (1976). Nonverbal disclosure of deception and interpersonal affect. *Journal of Educational Psychology, 68,* 807–816.

Feldman, R. S. (Ed.). (1982). *Development of nonverbal behavior in children.* New York: Springer-Verlag.

Feldman, R. S. (Ed.). (1990). *The social psychology of education: Current research and theory.* Cambridge, England: Cambridge University Press.

Feldman, R. S. (Ed.). (1992). *Applications of nonverbal behavioral theories and research.* Hillsdale, NJ: Erlbaum.

Feldman, R. S., & Rimé, B. (Eds.). (1991). *Fundamentals of nonverbal behavior.* Cambridge, England: Cambridge University Press.

Feldman, R. S., & Scheibe, K. E. (1972). Determinants of dissent in a psychological experiment. *Journal of Personality, 40,* 331–348.

Feldman, R. S., & Theiss, A. J. (1982). The teacher and student as Pygmalions: The joint effects of teacher and student expectation. *Journal of Educational Psychology, 74,* 217–223.

Feldt, R. C., Jagodzinski, M., & McKinley, K. (1997). Examination-related feedback, mood, and helping: A correlational study. *Psychological Reports, 80,* 239–242.

Fenigstein, A., Scheier, M. F., & Buss, A. H. (1975). Public and private self-consciousness: Assessment and theory. *Journal of Consulting and Clinical Psychology, 43,* 522–527.

Ferguson, T. (1993). Working with your doctor. In D. Goleman & J. Gurin (Eds.), *Mind-body medicine.* Yonkers, NY: Consumer Reports Books.

Fernandez, E., & Sheffield, J. (1996). Relative contributions of life events versus daily hassles to the frequency and intensity of headaches. *Headache, 36,* 595–602.

Ferrari, J. R. (1991a). Compulsive procrastination: Some self-reported characteristics. Annual Meeting of the Eastern Psychological Association (1990, Philadelphia, Pennsylvania). *Psychological Reports, 68,* 455–458.

Ferrari, J. R. (1991b). Self-handicapping by procrastinators: Protecting self-esteem, social-esteem, or both? *Journal of Research in Personality, 25,* 245–261.

Ferrari, M. D., & Sternberg, R. J. (Eds.). (1998). *Self-awareness: Its nature and development.* New York: Guilford.

Feshbach, N. D., & Feshbach, S. (1982). Empathy training and the regulation of aggression: Potentialities and limitations. *Academic Psychology Bulletin, 4,* 399–413.

Feshbach, S. (1984). The catharsis hypothesis, aggressive drive, and the reduction of aggression. *Aggressive Behavior, 10,* 91–101.

Festinger, L. (1954). A theory of social comparison processes. *Human Relations, 7,* 117–140.

Festinger, L. (1957). *A theory of cognitive dissonance.* Stanford, CA: Stanford University Press.

Festinger, L., & Carlsmith, J. M. (1959). Cognitive consequences of forced compliance. *Journal of Abnormal and Social Psychology, 58,* 203–210.

Festinger, L., Riecken, H. W., & Schachter, S. (1956). *When prophecy fails.* Minneapolis: University of Minnesota Press.

Festinger, L., Schachter, S., & Back, K. (1950). *Social pressures in informal groups: A study of a housing community.* New York: Harper.

Fiedler, F. E., & Garcia, J. E. (1987). *Leadership: Cognitive resources and performance.* New York: Wiley.

Figley, C. R. (1973). Child density and the marital relationship. *Journal of Marriage and the Family, 35,* 272–282.

Filkins, J. W., Smith, C. M., & Tindale, R. S. (1998). An evaluation of the biasing effects of death qualification: A meta-analytic/computer simulation approach. In R. S. Tindale, L. Heath, J. Edwards, E. J. Posavac, F. B. Bryant, Y. Suarez-Balcazar, E. Henderson-King, & J. Myers (Eds.), *Theory and research on small groups: Social psychological applications to social issues* (Vol. 4, pp. 153–175). New York: Plenum.

Fincham, F. D., & Bradbury, T. N. (1992). Assessing attributions in marriage: The relationship attribution measure. *Journal of Personality and Social Psychology 62,* 457–468.

Finck, H. T. (1902). *Romantic love and personal beauty: Their development, causal relations, historic and national peculiarities.* London: Macmillan.

Fine, L. M., & Schumann, D. W. (1992). The nature and role of salesperson perceptions: The interactive effects of salesperson/customer personalities. *Journal of Consumer Psychology, 1,* 285–296.

Fingerhut, L. A., & Kleinman, J. C. (1990). International and interstate comparisons of homicide among young males. *Journal of the American Medical Association, 263,* 3292–3295.

Fischer, C. S. (1976). *The urban experience.* San Diego, CA: Harcourt Brace Jovanovich.

Fischer, K., Schoeneman, T. J., & Rubanowitz, D. E. (1987). Attributions in the advice columns: II. The dimensionality of actors' and observers' explanations for interpersonal problems. *Personality and Social Psychology Bulletin, 13,* 458–466.

Fischer, W. F. (1963). Sharing in preschool children as a function of amount and type of reinforcement. *Genetic Psychology Monographs, 68,* 215–245.

Fischman, J. (1987). Type A on trial. *Psychology Today, 21,* 42–50.

Fishbein, H. D., & Imai, S. (1993). Preschoolers select playmates on the basis of gender and race. *Journal of Applied Developmental Psychology, 14,* 303–316.

Fisher, D. L., & Kent, H. B. (1998). Associations between teacher personality and classroom environment. *Journal of Classroom Interaction, 33* (1), 5–13.

Fisher, J. D., Bell, P. A., & Baum, A. (1984). *Environmental psychology* (2nd ed.). New York: Holt, Rinehart & Winston.

Fisher, J. D., Nadler, A., & DePaulo, B. M. (Eds.). (1983). *New directions in helping: Recipient reactions to aid.* New York: Academic Press.

Fisher, J. D., Nadler, A., & Whitcher-Alagna, S. (1982). Recipient reactions to aid. *Psycholgical Bulletin, 81,* 27–54.

Fiske, A. P. (1991a). *Structures of social life: The four elementary forms of human relations.* New York: Free Press.

Fiske, A. P. (1991b). The cultural relativity of selfish indvidualism. In M. S. Clark (Ed.), *Prosocial behavior.* Newbury Park, CA: Sage.

Fiske, A. P., Kitayama, S., Markus, H. R., & Nisbett, R. E. (1998). The cultural matrix of social psychology. In D. T. Gilbert & S. T. Fiske (Eds.), *The handbook of social psychology* (4th ed.). Boston, MA: McGraw-Hill.

Fiske, S. T. (1992). Thinking is for doing: Portraits of social cognition from daguerreotype to laserphoto. *Journal of Personality and Social Psychology, 63,* 877–889.

Fiske, S. T. (1993). Controlling other people: The impact of power on stereotyping. *American Psychologist, 48,* 621–628.

Fiske, S. T. (1997). Stereotyping, prejudice, and discrimination. In D. T. Gilbert, St. T. Fiske, & G. Lindzey (Eds.), *The handbook of motivation and cognition.* New York: McGraw-Hill.

Fiske, S. T., & Neuberg, S. L. (1990). A continuum of impression formation, from category-based to individuating processes: Influences of information and motivation on attention and interpretation. In M. P. Zanna (Ed.), *Advances in experimental social psychology* (Vol. 23, pp. 1–74). New York: Academic Press.

Fiske, S. T., & Pavelchak, M. A. (1986). Category-based versus piecemeal-based affective responses: Developments in schema-triggered affect. In R. M. Sorrentino & E. T. Higgins (Eds.), *Handbook of motivation and cognition: Foundations of social behavior* (pp. 167–203). New York: Guilford Press.

Fiske, S. T., & Taylor, S. E. (1991). *Social cognition* (2nd ed.). New York: McGraw-Hill.

Fiske, S. T., & Von Hendy, H. M. (1992). Personality feedback and situational norms can control stereotyping processes. *Journal of Personality and Social Psychology, 62,* 577–596.

Fitness, J., & Fletcher, G. J. (1993). Love, hate, anger, and jealousy in close relationships: A prototype and cognitive appraisal analysis. *Journal of Personality & Social Psychology, 65,* 942–958.

Flaks, D. K., Ficher, I., Masterpasqua, F., & Joseph, G. (1995). Lesbians choosing motherhood: A comparative study of lesbian and heterosexual parents and their children. Special Issue: Sexual orientation and human development. *Developmental Psychology, 31,* 105–114.

Fleishman, J. A., & Fogel, B. (1994). Coping and depressive symptoms among young people with AIDS. *Health Psychology, 13,* 156–169.

Fleming, M. A., Wegener, D. T., & Petty, R. E. (1999). Procedural and legal motivations to correct for perceived judicial biases. *Journal of Experimental Social Psychology, 35* (2), 186–203.

Fletcher, G. J. O., Simpson, J. A., Thomas, G., & Giles, L. (1999). Ideals in intimate relationships. *Journal of Personality & Social Psychology, 76,* 72–89.

Flippen, A. R., Hornstein, H. A., Siegal, W. E., & Weitzman, E. A. (1996). A comparison of similarity and interdependence as triggers for in-group formation. *Personality & Social Psychology Bulletin, 22,* 882–893.

Florian, V., Mikulincer, M., & Taubman, O. (1995). Does hardiness contribute to mental health during a stressful real-life situation? The roles of appraisal and coping. *Journal of Personality and Social Psychology, 68,* 687–695.

Floyd, F. J., & Wasner, G. H. (1994). Social exchange, equity, and commitment: Structural equation modeling of dating relationships. *Journal of Family Psychology, 8,* 55–73.

Foa, E. B., & Riggs, D. S. (1995). Posttraumatic stress disorder following assault: Theoretical considerations and empirical findings. *Current Directions in Psychological Science, 4,* 61–65.

Foddy, M., & Crundall, I. (1993). A field study of social comparison processes in ability evaluation. *British Journal of Social Psychology, 32,* 287–305.

Fogel, A., Toda, S., & Kawai, M. (1988). Mother–infant face-to-face interaction in Japan and the United States: A laboratory comparison using 3-month-old infants. *Developmental Psychology, 24,* 398–406.

Folkman, S., & Lazarus, R. S. (1988). Coping as a mediator of emotion. *Journal of Personality and Social Psychology, 54,* 466–475.

Forgas, J. P. (1993). On making sense of odd couples: Mood effects on the perception of mismatched relationships. *Personality and Social Psychology Bulletin, 19,* 59–70.

Forgas, J. P., & Fiedler, K. (1996). Us and them: Mood effects on intergroup discrimination. *Journal of Personality and Social Psychology, 70,* 28–40.

Försterling, F. (1985). Attributional retraining: A review. *Psychological Bulletin, 98,* 468–495.

Försterling, F. (1989). Models of covariation and attribution: How do they relate to the analogy of analysis of variance? *Journal of Personality and Social Psychology, 57,* 615–625.

Forsyth, D. (1990). *Group dynamics.* Pacific Grove, CA: Brooks/Cole.

Forsyth, D. R., & Kelley, K. N. (1996). Heuristic-based biases in estimations of personal contributions to collective endeavors. In J. L. Nye & A. M. Brower (Eds.), *What's social about social cognition? Research on socially shared cognition in small groups.* Thousand Oaks, CA: Sage.

Forsyth, D. R., & Wibberly, K. H. (1993). The self-reference effect: Demonstrating schematic processing in the classroom. *Teaching of Psychology, 20,* 237–238.

Forward, J., Canter, R., & Krisch, N. (1976). Role-enactment and deception: Alternative paradigms? *American Psychologist, 31,* 595–604.

Fowler, F. J. (1981). Evaluating a complex crime control experiment. *Applied Social Psychology Annual, 2,* 165–187.

Fowler, F. J., Jr. (1993). *Survey research methods.* Newbury Park, CA: Sage.

Frable, D. E., & Bem, S. L. (1985). If you're gender-schematic, all members of the opposite sex look alike. *Journal of Personality and Social Psychology, 49,* 459–468.

Frager, R. (1970). Conformity and anti-conformity in Japan. *Journal of Personality and Social Psychology, 15,* 203–310.

Fraley, R. C., & Shaver, P. R. (1998). Airport separations: A naturalistic study of adult attachment dynamics in separating couples. *Journal of Personality & Social Psychology, 75,* 1198–1212.

Frank, J., & Applegate, B. K. (1998). Assessing juror understanding of capital-sentencing instructions. *Crime & Delinquency, 44* (3), 412–433.

Frank, M. G., Ekman, P., & Friesen, W. V. (1997). Behavioral markers and recognizability of the smile of enjoyment. In P. Ekman & E. L. Rosenberg (Eds.), *What the face reveals: Basic and applied studies of spontaneous expression using the Facial Action Coding System (FACS). Series in affective science.* New York: Oxford University Press.

Freedman, J. (1996, May). *Harvard Mental Health Letter,* pp. 4–6.

Freedman, J. L., & Fraser, S. C. (1966). Compliance without pressure: The foot-in-the-door technique. *Journal of Personality and Social Psychology, 8,* 528–548.

Freedman, R. (1986). *Beauty bound.* Lexington, MA: D. C. Heath.

Freedy, J. R., & Hobfoll, S. E. (1995). *Traumatic stress: From theory to pracitce.* New York: Plenum.

Freeman, H. L., & Stansfeld, S. A. (1998). Psychosocial effects of urban environments, noise, and crowding. In A. Lundberg (Ed.), *The environment and mental health: A guide for clinicians* (pp. 147–173). Mahwah, NJ: Erlbaum.

French, J. R. P., Jr., & Raven, B. H. (1959). The bases of social power. In D. Cartwright (Ed.), *Studies in social power.* Ann Arbor: University of Michigan Press.

Freud, S. (1920). *A general introduction to psychoanalysis.* New York: Boni & Liveright.

Frey, D. (1986). Recent research on selective exposure to information. In L. Berkowitz (Ed.), *Advances in experimental social psychology* (Vol. 19). New York: Academic Press.

Frey, D., Fries, A., & Osnabrugge, G. (1983). Reactions to failure after taking a placebo: A study of dissonance reduction. *Personality and Social Psychology Bulletin, 9,* 481–488.

Frey, D., & Wicklund, R. A. (1978). A clarification of selective exposure: The impact of choice. *Journal of Experimental Social Psychology, 14,* 132–139.

Friedman, L. C., Nelson, D. V., Baer, P. E., & Lane, M. (1992). The relationship of dispositional optimism, daily life stress, and domestic environment to coping methods used by cancer patients. *Journal of Behavioral Medicine, 15,* 127–141.

Fry, D. P. (1992). "Respect for the rights of others is peace": Learning aggression versus nonaggression among the Zapotec. *American Anthropologist, 94,* 621–639.

Fuchs, I., Eisenberg, N., Hertz-Lazarowitz, R., & Sharabany, R. (1986). Kibbutz, Israeli city and American children's moral reasoning about prosocial moral conflicts. *Merrill-Palmer Quarterly, 32,* 37–50.

Fulk, B. M. (1996). The effects of combined strategy and attribution training on LD adolescents' spelling performance. *Exceptionality, 6,* 13–27.

Fuller, S. R., & Aldag, R. J. (1998). Organizational Tonypandy: Lessons from a quarter century of groupthink phenomenon. *Organizational Behavior & Human Decision Processes, 73* (2–3), 163–184.

Fuller, T. D., Edwards, J. N., Sermsri, S., & Vorakitphokatorn, S. (1993). Housing, stress, and physical well-being: Evidence from Thailand. *Social Science & Medicine, 36,* 1417–1428.

Funder, D. C. (1987). Errors and mistakes: Evaluating the accuracy of social judgment. *Psychological Bulletin, 101,* 75–90.

Fyock, J., & Stangor, C. (1994). The role of memory biases in stereotype maintenance. *British Journal of Social Psychology, 33,* 331–343.

Gabrenya, W. K., Latané, B., & Wang, Y. (1983). Social loafing in cross-cultural perspective: Chinese on Taiwan. *Journal of Cross-Cultural Psychology, 14,* 368–384.

Gadzella, B. M. (1994). Student-Life Stress Inventory: Identification of and reactions to stressors. *Psychological Reports, 74,* 395–402.

Gaertner, S. L., & Dovidio, J. F. (1986). The aversive form of racism. In J. F. Dovidio & S. L. Gaertner (Eds.), *Prejudice, discrimination, and racism: Theory and research* (pp. 61–89). Orlando, FL: Academic Press.

Gaertner, S. L., Dovidio, J. F., Rust, M. C., Nier, J. A., Banker, B. S., Ward, C. M., Mottola, G. R., & Houlette, M. (1999). Reducing intergroup bias: Elements of intergroup cooperation. *Journal of Personality & Social Psychology, 76,* 388–402.

Gaertner, S. L., Mann, J., Murrell, A., & Dovidio, J. F. (1989). Reducing intergroup bias: The benefits of recategorization. *Journal of Personality and Social Psychology, 57,* 239–249.

Gaertner, S. L., Rust, M. C., Dovidio, J. F., Bachman, B. A., et al. (1994). The contact hypothesis: The role of a common ingroup identity on reducing intergroup bias. Special Issue: Social cognition in small groups. *Small Group Research, 25,* 224–249.

Gage, A. J., & Meekers, D. (1994). Sexual activity before marriage in sub-Saharan Africa. *Social Biology, 41,* 44–60.

Gahr, E. (1999, April 30). Gore for sale; computer games at a store near you . . . be afraid. Be very afraid. *The Wall Street Journal,* p. W13.

Gaines, S. O., Jr., & Reed, E. S. (1995). Prejudice: From Allport to duBois. *American Psychologist, 50,* 96–103.

Gallup, G. G., Jr. (1977). Self-recognition in primates: A comparative approach to the bidirectional properties of consciousness. *American Psychologist, 32,* 329–337.

Gallup, G. G. (1995). Mirrors, minds, and cetaceans. *Consciousness & Cognition: An International Journal, 4,* 226–228.

Gardner, G. T., & Stern, P. C. (1996). *Environmental problems and human behavior.* Boston: Allyn & Bacon.

Gardner, W. L. (1992). Lessons in organizational dramaturgy: The art of impression management. *Organizational Dynamics, 21,* 33–46.

Garry, M., Loftus, E. F., & Brown, S. W. (1994). Memory: A river runs through it. Special Issue: The recovered memory/false memory debate. *Consciousness & Cognition: An International Journal, 3,* 438–451.

Gatchel, R. J., & Baum, A. (1983). *An introduction to health psychology.* Reading, MA: Addison-Wesley.

Gavrilova, E. A., & Shabanova, L. F. (1998). Stress-induced disorders of immune function and their psychocorrection. *Human Physiology, 24,* 114–121.

Geary, D. C. (1998). Sexual selection, the division of labor, and the evolution of sex differences. *Behavioral & Brain Sciences, 21,* 444–448.

Geary, D. C., Salthouse, T. A., Chen, G., & Fan, L. (1996). Are East Asian versus American differences in arithmetical ability a recent phenomenon? *Developmental Psychology, 32,* 254–262.

Geehr, J. L., Burke, M. J., Sulzer, J. L., & Jefferson, L. (1995). Quality circles: The effects of varying degrees of voluntary participation on employee attitudes and program efficacy. *Educational and Psychological Measurement, 55,* 124–134.

Geen, R. G. (1989). Alternative conceptions of social facilitation. In P. Paulus (Ed.), *Psychology of group influence* (2nd ed.) Hillsdale, NJ: Erlbaum.

Gelles, R. J., & Cornell, C. P. (1990). *Intimate violence in families* (2nd ed.). Newbury Park, CA: Sage.

Gelman, D. (1990, July 23). The mind of the rapist. *Newsweek,* pp. 46–52.

Gentry, M. (1998). The sexual double standard: The influence of number of relationships and level of sexual activity on judgments of women and men. *Psychology of Women Quarterly, 22,* 505–511.

George, D. M., Carroll, P., Kersnick, R., & Calderon, K. (1998). Gender-related patterns of helping among friends. *Psychology of Women Quarterly, 22,* 685–704.

George, T. R. (1994). Self-confidence and baseball performance: A causal examination of self-efficacy theory. *Journal of Sport & Exercise Psychology, 16,* 381–399.

Gerard, H. B. (1988). School desegregation: The social science role. In P. A. Katz & K. A. Taylor (Eds.), *Eliminating racism: Profiles in controversy.* New York: Plenum.

Gerard, H. B., Whilhelmy, R. A., & Conolley, E. S. (1968). Conformity and group size. *Journal of Personality and Social Psychology, 8,* 79–82.

Gerbner, G. (1996). *Violence in cable-originated television programs: A report to the National Cable Television Association.* Philadelphia: Annenberg School for Communication, University of Pennsylvania.

Gerbner, G., Morgan, M., & Signorelli, N. (1993). [Television violence]. Unpublished study. Philadelphia: University of Pennsylvania.

Gergen, K. J. (1967). Social psychology as history. *Journal of Personality and Social Psychology, 26,* 309–320.

Gergen, K. J. (1973). Social psychology as history. *Journal of Personality and Social Psychology, 26,* 309–320.

Giacalone, R. A., & Rosenfeld, P. (1986). Self-presentation and self-promotion in an organizational setting. *Journal of Social Psychology, 126,* 321–326.

Gibbons, F. X. (1990). Sexual standards and reactions to pornography: Enhancing behavioral consistency through self-focused attention. *Journal of Personality and Social Psychology, 36,* 976–987.

Gibbons, F. X., Benbow, C. P., & Gerrard, M. (1994). From top dog to bottom half: Social comparison strategies in response to poor performance. *Journal of Personality and Social Psychology, 67,* 638–652.

Gibbons, F. X., & Wicklund, R. A. (1982). Self-focused attention and helping behavior. *Journal of Personality and Social Psychology, 43,* 462–474.

Gibbons, F. X., & Wright, R. A. (1983). Self-focused attention and reactions to conflicting standards. *Journal of Research in Personality, 17,* 263–273.

Gibson, C. B., & Marcoulides, G. A. (1995). The invariance of leadership styles across four countries. *Journal of Managerial Issues, 7,* 176–192.

Gifford, R., & Hine, D. W. (1997). "I'm cooperative, but you're greedy": Some cognitive tendencies in a common dilemma. *Canadian Journal of Behavioural Science, 29,* 257–265.

Gigone, D., & Hastie, R. (1997). The impact of information on small group choice. *Journal of Personality & Social Psychology, 72,* 132–140.

Gilbert, D. T. (1989). Thinking lightly about others: Automatic components of the social inference process. In J. S. Uleman & J. A. Bargh (Eds.), *Unintended thought: Causes and consequences for judgment, emotion, and behavior.* New York: Guilford.

Gilbert, D. T., & Hixon, J. G. (1991). The trouble thinking: Activation and application of stereotypic beliefs. *Journal of Personality and Social Psychology, 60,* 509–517.

Gilbert, D. T., Krull, D. S., & Pelham, B. W. (1988). Of thoughts unspoken: Social inference and the self-regulation of behavior. *Journal of Personality and Social Psychology, 55,* 685–694.

Gilbert, D. T., & Malone, P. S. (1995). The correspondence bias. *Psychological Bulletin, 117,* 21–38.

Gilbert, D. T., McNulty, S. E., Giuliano, T. A., & Benson, J. E. (1992). Blurry words and fuzzy deeds: The attribution of obscure behavior. *Journal of Personality and Social Psychology, 62,* 18–25.

Gilbert, D. T., Miller, A. G., & Ross, L. (1998). Speeding with Ned: A personal view of the correspondence bias. In J. M. Darley & J. Cooper (Eds.), *Attribution and social interaction: The legacy of Edward E. Jones.* Washington, DC: American Psychological Association.

Gilbert, D. T., & Osborne, R. E. (1989). Thinking backward: Some curable and incurable consequences of cognitive busyness. *Journal of Personality and Social Psychology, 54,* 940–949.

Gilbert, D. T., Pelham, B. W., & Krull, D. S. (1988). Of thoughts unspoken: Social inference and the self-regulation of behavior. *Journal of Personality and Social Psychology, 55,* 685–694.

Gilbert, D. T. , & Silvera, D. H. (1996). Overhelping. *Journal of Personality and Social Psychology, 70,* 678–690.

Giles, M., & Cairns, E. (1995). Blood donation and Ajzen's theory of planned behaviour: An examination of perceived behavioural control. *British Journal of Social Psychology, 34,* 173–188.

Gillig, P. M., & Greenwald, A. G. (1974). Is it time to lay the sleeper effect to rest? *Journal of Personality and Social Psychology, 29,* 132–139.

Gillis, A. R., Richard, M. A., & Hagan, J. (1986). Ethnic susceptibility to crowding: An empirical analysis. *Environment and Behavior, 18,* 683–706.

Gioia, D. A., & Sims, H. P. (1985). Self-serving bias and actor-observer differences in organizations: An empirical analysis. *Journal of Applied Social Psychology, 15,* 547–563.

Girandola, F. (1997). Double forced compliance and cognitive dissonance theory. *Journal of Social Psychology, 137* (5), 594–605.

Gladstone, T. R., & Kaslow, N. J. (1995). Depression and attributions in children and adolescents: A meta-analytic review. *Journal of Abnormal Child Psychology, 23,* 597–606.

Gladue, B. A., & Bailey, J. M. (1995). Aggressiveness, competitiveness, and human sexual orientation. *Psychoneuroendocrinology, 20,* 475–485.

Glaser, R., Rice, J., Speicher, C. E., Stout, J. C., & Kiecolt-Glaser, J. K. (1986). Stress depresses interferon production by leukocytes and concomitant with a decrease in natural killer cell activity. *Behavioral Neuroscience, 100,* 675–678.

Glenn, N. (1991). The recent trend in marital success in the United States. *Jounral of Marriage and the Family, 43,* 409–421.

Glenn, N. D. (1990). Quantitative research on marital quality in the 1980s: A critical review. *Journal of Marriage and the Family, 52,* 818–831.

Glenn, N. D., & Weaver, C. N. (1988). The changing relationship of marital status to reported happiness. *Journal of Marriage and the Family, 50,* 317–324.

Glick, P., & Fiske, S. T. (1999). Sexism and other "isms": Independence, status, and the ambivalent content of stereotypes. In W. B. Swann, Jr. & J. H. Langlois (Eds.), *Sexism and stereotypes in modern society: The gender science of Janet Taylor Spence.* Washington, DC: American Psychological Association.

Glick, P., Zion, C., & Nelson, C. (1988). What mediates sex discrimination in hiring decisions? *Journal of Personality and Social Psychology, 55,* 178–186.

Goethals, G. R., & Darley, J. (1977). Social comparison theory: An attributional approach. In J. M. Suls & R. L. Miller (Eds.), *Social comparison processes: Theoretical and empirical perspectives* (pp. 259–278). Washington, DC: Hemisphere.

Goethals, G. R., & Zanna, M. P. (1979). The role of social comparison in choice of shifts. *Journal of Personality and Social Psychology, 37,* 1469–1476.

Gold, D. B., & Wegner, D. M. (1995). Origins of ruminative thought: Trauma, incompleteness, nondisclosure, and suppression. Special Issue: Rumination and intrusive thoughts. *Journal of Applied Social Psychology, 25,* 1245–1261.

Gold, G. J., & Raven, B. H. (1992). Interpersonal influence strategies in the Churchill-Roosevelt bases-for-destroyers exchange. *Journal of Social Behavior and Personality, 7,* 245–272.

Goleman, D. (1988, January 21). Physicians may bungle key part of treatment: The medical interview. *The New York Times*, p. B16.

Goleman, D. (1989, February 21). Want a happy marriage? Learn to fight a good fight. *The New York Times*, pp. C1, C6.

Gonzales, M. H. (1992). A thousand pardons: The effectiveness of verbal remedial tactics during account episodes. *Journal of Language & Social Psychology, 11,* 133–151.

Gonzalez-Intal, A. M. (1991). Relative deprivation theory and collective political violence in the Philippines. *Philippine Journal of Psychology, 24,* 22–38.

Googans, B., & Burden, D. (1987). Vulnerability of working parents: Balancing work and home roles. *Social Work, 32,* 295–300.

Gorassini, D. R., & Olson, J. M . (1995). Does self-perception change explain the foot-in-the-door effect? *Journal of Personality & Social Psychology, 69,* 91–105.

Gordon, R. A., & Vicari, P. J. (1992). Eminence in social psychology: A comparison of textbook citation, Social Sciences Citation Index, and research productivity rankings. *Personality and Social Psychology Bulletin, 18,* 26–38.

Gottman, J. G. (1999, April 19). Know your spouse. *Newsweek*.

Gottman, J. M., & Krokoff, L J. (1989). Marital interaction and satisfaction: A longitudinal view. *Journal of Consulting and Clinical Psychology, 57* (1), 47–52.

Gottman, J. M., & Silver, N. (1999). *The seven principles for making marriage work*. New York: Crown Publishing.

Gouldner, A. W. (1960). The notion of reciprocity: A preliminary statement. *American Sociological Review, 25,* 161–178.

Gow, J. (1996). Reconsidering gender roles on MTV: Depictions in the most popular music videos of the early 1990s. *Communication Reports, 9,* 151–161.

Graham, S. (1992). "Most of the subjects were white and middle class": Trends in published research on African Americans in selected APA journals, 1970–1989. *American Psychologist, 47,* 629–639.

Granberg, D. (1987). Candidate preference, membership group, and estimates of voting behavior. *Social Cognition, 5,* 323–335.

Granot, H. (1995). Israeli emergency social and mental health services in the Gulf War: Observations and experiences of a mental health professional. Special Issue: Disasters and crises: A mental health counseling perspective. *Journal of Mental Health Counseling, 17,* 336–346.

Graziano, A. M., Lindquist, C. M., Kunce, L. J., & Munjal, K. (1992). Physical punishment in childhood and current attitudes: An exploratory comparison of college students in the United States and India. *Journal of Interpersonal Violence, 7,* 147–155.

Graziano, W. G., & Bryant, W. H. M. (1998). Self-monitoring and the self-attribution of positive emotions. *Journal of Personality & Social Psychology, 74,* 250–261.

Green, D. P., Glaser, J., & Rich, A. (1998). From lynching to gay bashing: The elusive connection between economic conditions and hate crime. *Journal of Personality & Social Psychology, 75,* 82–92.

Green, S. K., Lightfoot, M. A., Bandy, C., & Buchanan, D. R. (1985). A general model of the attribution process. *Basic and Applied Social Psychology, 6,* 159–179.

Greenberg, J. (1997). A social influence model of employee theft: Beyond the fraud triangle. In R. J. Lewicki, R. J. Bies, & B. H. Sheppard (Eds.), *Research on negotiation in organizations,* (Vol. 6, pp. 29–51). Greenwich, CT: Jai Press.

Greenberg, J., & Folger, R. (1988). *Controversial issues in social research methods.* New York: Springer-Verlag.

Greenberg, M. S., Westcott, D. R., & Bailey, S. E. (1998). When believing is seeing: The effect of scripts on eyewitness memory. *Law & Human Behavior, 22,* 685–694.

Greene, E., & Loftus, E. F. (1998). Psycholegal research on jury damage awards. *Current Directions in Psychological Science, 7* (2), 50–54.

Greenwald, A. G., & Banaji, M. R. (1995). Implicit social cognition: Attitudes, self-esteem, and stereotypes. *Psychological Review, 102,* 4–27.

Greenwald, A. G., & Draine, S. C. (1998). Distinguishing unconscious from conscious cognition—Reasonable assumptions and replicable findings: Reply to Merikle and Reingold (1998) and Dosher (1998). *Journal of Experimental Psychology: General, 127* (3), 320–324.

Greenwald, A. G., Draine, S. C., & Abrams, R. L. (1996). Three cognitive markers of unconscious semantic activation. *Science, 273,* 1699–1702.

Greenwald, A. G., Spangenberg, E. R., Pratkanis, A. R., & Eskenazi, J. (1991). Double-blind tests of subliminal self-help audiotapes. *Psychological Science, 2,* 119–122.

Greenwell, J., & Dengerink, H. A. (1973). The role of perceived versus actual attack in human physical aggression. *Journal of Personality and Social Psychology, 26,* 66–71.

Gress, J. E., & Heft, H. (1998). Do territorial actions attenuate the effects of high density? A field study. In J. Sanford & B. R. Connell (Eds.), *People, places and public policy* (pp. 47–52). Edmond, OK: Environmental Design Research Association.

Grieshaber, S. (1998). Constructing the gendered infant. In N. Yelland (Ed.), *Gender in early childhood.* New York: Routledge.

Griffiths, M. (1997). Video games and aggression. *Psychologist, 10,* 397–401.

Grigoroiu-Serbanescu, M. (1994). Current genetic models of primary affective disorders. *Revue Roumaine de Neurologie et Psychiatrie, 32,* 29–41.

Grossman, R. P., & Till, B. D. (1998). The persistence of classically conditioned brand attitudes. *Journal of Advertising, 27* (1), 23–31.

Grote, N. K., & Clark, M. S. (1998). Distributive justice norms and family work: What is perceived as ideal, what is applied and what predicts perceived fairness? *Social Justice Research, 11,* 243–269.

Grunbaum, J. A., Vernon, S. W., & Clasen, C. M. (1997). The association between anger and hostility and risk factors for coronary heart disease in children and adolescents: A review. *Annals of Behavioral Medicine, 19,* 179–189.

Grusec, J. E. (1982). Socialization processes and the development of altruism. In J. P. Rushton & R. M. Sorrentino (Eds.), *Altruism and helping behavior.* Hillsdale, NJ: Erlbaum.

Grusec, J. E. (1991). The socialization of altruism. In M. S. Clark (Ed.), *Prosocial behavior.* Newbury Park, CA: Sage.

Grusec, J. E., & Dix, T. (1986). The socialization of prosocial behavior: Theory and reality. In C. Zahn-Waxler, E. M. Cummings, & R. Iannotti (Eds.), *Altruism and aggression: Biological and social origins.* New York: Cambridge University Press.

Grusec, J. E., & Kuczynski, L. (Eds.). (1997). *Parenting and children's internalization of values: A handbook of contemporary theory.* New York: Wiley.

Grusec, J. E., & Skubiski, S. L. (1970). Model nurturance, demand characteristics of the modeling experiment, and altruism. *Journal of Personality and Social Psychology, 14,* 352–359.

Grusec, J. E., Rudy, D., & Martini, T. (1997). Parenting cognitions and child outcomes: An overview and implications for children's internalization of values. In J. E. Grusec & L. Kuczynski (Eds.), *Parenting and children's internalization of values: A handbook of contemporary theory* (pp. 259–282). New York: Wiley.

Grush, J. E. (1980). Impact of candidate expenditures, regionality, and prior outcomes on the 1976 Democratic presidential primaries. *Journal of Personality and Social Psychology, 38,* 337–347.

Gruzelier, J., Clow, A., Evans, P., Lazar, I., & Walker, L. (1998). Mind-body influences on immunity: Lateralized control, stress, individual difference predictors, and prophylaxis. In P. Csermely (Ed.), *Stress of life: From molecules to man. Annals of the New York Academy of Sciences* (Vol. 851). New York: New York Academy of Sciences.

GSS News. (1998, August). No. 12. Chicago: National Opinion Research at the University of Chicago.

Guarino, A., Michael, W. B., & Hocevar, D. (1998). Self-monitoring and student integration of community college students. *Journal of Social Psychology, 138,* 754–757.

Guarino, M., Fridrich, P., & Sitton, S. (1994). Male and female conformity in eating behavior. *Psychological Reports, 75,* 603–609.

Gubernick, L. (1986). The nose knows. *Forbes,* pp. 280–281.

Guerin, B. (1994). Attitudes and beliefs as verbal behavior. Special Section: Attitudes and behavior in social psychology. *Behavior Analyst, 17,* 155–163.

Guerrero, L. K., DeVito, J. A., & Hecht, M. L. (Eds.). (1999). *The nonverbal communication reader: Classic and contemporary readings* (2nd ed.). Prospect Heights, IL: Waveland.

Guetzkow, H. (1968). Differentiation of roles in task-oriented groups. In D. Cartwright & A. Zander (Eds.), *Group dynamics: Research and theory* (3rd ed.). New York: Harper & Row.

Guisinger, S., & Blatt, S. J. (1994). Individuality and relatedness: Evolution of a fundamental dialectic. *American Psychologist, 49,* 104–111.

Gump, B. B., & Kulik, J. A. (1997). Stress, affiliation, and emotional contagion. *Journal of Personality & Social Psychology, 72,* 305–319.

Gunter, B. (1988). The importance of studying viewers' perceptions of television violence. Special Issue: Violence on television. *Current Psychology Research and Reviews, 7,* 26–42.

Gunter, B., & Furnham, A. (1986). Sex and personality differences in recall of violent and nonviolent news from three presentation modalities. *Personality and Individual Differences, 7,* 829–837.

Gupta, U., & Singh, P. (1982). An exploratory study of love and liking and type of marriages. *Indian Journal of Applied Psychology, 19,* 92–97.

Guttman, L. (1944). A basis for scaling qualitative data. *American Sociological Review, 9,* 139–150.

Guydish, J., Clark, G., Garcia, D., & Bucardo, J. (1995). Evaluation of needle exchange using street-based survey methods. *Journal of Drug Issues, 25,* 33–41.

Haack, L. J., Metalsky, G. I., Dykman, B. M., & Abramson, L. Y. (1996). Use of current situational information and causal inference: Do dysphoric individuals make "unwarranted" causal inferences? *Cognitive Therapy & Research, 20,* 309–331.

Haaga, D. A., & Beck, A. T. (1995). Perspectives on depressive realism: Implications for cognitive theory of depression. *Behaviour Research & Therapy, 33,* 41–48.

Hackel, L. S., & Ruble, D. N. (1992). Changes in the marital relationship after the first baby is born: Predicting the impact of expectancy disconfirmation. *Journal of Personality and Social Psychology, 62,* 944–957.

Hackman, J. R., & Morris, C. G. (1975). Group tasks, group interaction process, and group performance effectiveness: A review and proposed integration. In L. Berkowitz (Ed.), *Advances in experimental social psychology* (Vol. 8). New York: Academic Press.

Hadlow, J., & Pitts, M. (1991). The understanding of common health terms by doctors, nurses and patients. *Social Science & Medicine, 32,* 193–196.

Hahn, J., & Blass, T. (1997). Dating partner preferences: A function of similarity of love styles. *Journal of Social Behavior & Personality, 12,* 595–610.

Halberstadt, A. G. (1991). Toward an ecology of expressiveness: Family socialization in particular and a model in general. In R. S. Feldman & B. Rimé (Eds.), *Fundamentals of nonverbal behavior.* Cambridge, England: Cambridge University Press.

Halberstadt, A. G., Grotjohn, D. K., Johnson, C. A., & Furth, M. S. (1992). Children's abilities and strategies in managing the facial display of affect. *Journal of Nonverbal Behavior, 16,* 215–230.

Hall, E. T. (1966). *The hidden dimension.* Garden City, NY: Doubleday.

Hall, J. A., Roter, D. L., & Rand, C. S. (1981). Communication of affect between patient and physician. *Journal of Health and Social Behavior, 22,* 18–30.

Hall, R. G., Varca, P. E., & Fisher, T. D. (1986). The effect of reference groups, opinion polls, and attitude polarization on attitude formation and change. *Political Psychology, 7,* 309–321.

Hallinan, M. T., & Williams, R. A. (1989). Interracial friendship choices in secondary schools. *American Sociological Review, 54,* 67–78.

Halloran, E. C., Doumas, D. M., John, R. S., & Margolin, G. (1999). The relationship between aggression in children and locus of control beliefs. *Journal of Genetic Psychology, 160,* 5–21.

Halverson, A. M., Hallahan, M., Hart, A. J., & Rosenthal, R. (1997). Reducing the biasing effects of judges' nonverbal behavior with simplified jury instruction. *Journal of Applied Psychology, 82,* 590–598.

Hamill, R., Wilson, T. D., & Nisbett, R. E. (1980). Insensitivity to sample bias: Generalizing from atypical cases. *Journal of Personality and Social Psychology, 39,* 578–589.

Hamilton, D. L. (1979). A cognitive-attributional analysis of stereotyping. In L. Berkowitz (Ed.), *Advances in experimental social psychology* (Vol. 12, pp. 53–84). New York: Academic Press.

Hamilton, D. L., & Gifford, R. K. (1976). Illusory correlation in interpersonal perception: A cognitive basis of stereotypic judgments. *Journal of Experimental Social Psychology, 12,* 393–407.

Hamilton, D. L., Sherman, S. J., & Ruvolo, C. M. (1990). Stereotype-based expectancies: Effects on information processing and social behavior. *Journal of Social Issues, 46,* 35–60.

Hamilton, D. L., & Trolier, T. K. (1986). Stereotypes and stereotyping: An overview of the cognitive approach. In J. F. Dovidio & S. L. Gaertner (Eds.), *Prejudice, discrimination, and racism* (pp. 127–163). Orlando, FL: Academic Press.

Hamilton, M., & Yee, J. (1990). Rape knowledge and propensity to rape. *Journal of Research in Personality, 24,* 111–122.

Hamilton, V. L. (1976). Individual differences in ascriptions of responsibility, guilt, and appropriate judgment. In G. Berman, C. Nemeth, & N. Vidmar (Eds.), *Psychology and the law.* Lexington, MA: Heath.

Hamilton, V. L., & Hagiwara, S. (1998). Roles, responsibility, and accounts across cultures. Special Issue: Social psychological approaches to responsibility and justice. The view across cultures. *International Journal of Psychology, 27,* 157–179.

Hammelman, T. L. (1995). The Persian Gulf conflict: The impact of stressors as perceived by Army Reservists. *Health & Social Work, 20,* 140–145.

Hammer, J. (1992, October 26). Must Blacks be buffoons? *Newsweek,* pp. 70–71.

Handy, B. (1997, April 14). He called me Degenerate? *Time, 149,* p. 86.

Haney, C., Banks, C., & Zimbardo, P. (1973). Interpersonal dynamics in a simulated prison. *International Journal of Criminology and Penology, 1,* 69–97.

Haney, C., & Zimbardo, P. (1998). The past and future of U.S. prison policy: Twenty-five years after the Stanford Prison Experiment. *American Psychologist, 53,* 709–727.

Hanna, J. L. (1984). Black/white nonverbal differences, dance, and dissonance: Implications for desegregation. In A. Wolfgang (Ed.), *Nonverbal behavior: Perspectives, applications, intercultural insights.* Lewiston, NY: Hogrefe.

Hansen, C. H. (1989). Priming sex-role stereotypic even schemas with rock music videos: Effects on impression favorability, trait inferences, and recall of subsequent male-female interaction. *Basic and Applied Social Psychology, 10,* 371–391.

Hardy, C., & Latané, B. (1986). Social loafing on a cheering task. *Social Science, 71,* 165–172.

Hare, A. P. (1994). Types of roles in small groups: A bit of history and a current perspective. *Small Group Research, 25,* 433–448.

Harkins, S. G. (1987). Social loafing and social facilitation. *Journal of Experimental Social Psychology, 23,* 1–18.

Harkins, S. G., & Petty, R. E. (1982). Effects of task difficulty and task uniqueness on social loafing. *Journal of Personality & Social Psychology, 43,* 1214–1229.

Harkins, S. G., & Petty, R. E. (1987). Information utility and the multiple source effect. *Journal of Personality and Social Psychology, 52,* 260–268.

Harkins, S. G., & Szymanski, K. (1989). Social loafing and group evaluation. *Journal of Personality and Social Psychology, 56,* 934–941.

Harmon, A. (1999, February 20). Internet changes language for :-) & :-(. *New York Times,* p. B7.

Harmon-Jones, E. (1999). Toward an understanding of the motivation underlying dissonance effects: Is the production of aversive consequences necessary? In E. Harmon-Jones & J. Mills (Eds.), *Cognitive dissonance: Progress on a pivotal theory in social psychology. Science conference series.* Washington, DC: American Psychological Association.

Harmon-Jones, E., Brehm, J. W., Greenberg, J., & Simon, L. (1996). Evidence that the production of aversive consequences is not necessary to create cognitive dissonance. *Journal of Personality & Social Psychology, 70,* 5–16.

Harmon-Jones, E., Greenberg, J., Solomon, S., & Simon, L. (1996). The effects of mortality salience on intergroup bias between minimal groups. *European Journal of Social Psychology, 26,* 677–681.

Harmon-Jones, E., & Mills, J. (Ed.). (1999). *Cognitive dissonance: Progress on a pivotal theory in social psychology.* Washington, DC: American Psychological Association.

Harrell, W. A. (1994). Effects of blind pedestrians on motorists. *Journal of Social Psychology, 134,* 529–539.

Harris Poll. (1984). Patients changing physicians. Washington, DC: Harris Poll.

Harris, M. J. (1991). Controversy and cumulation: Meta-analysis and research on interpersonal expectancy effects. *Personality and Social Psychology Bulletin, 17,* 316–322.

Harris, M. B. (1994). Gender of subject and target as mediators of aggression. *Journal of Applied Social Psychology, 24,* 453–471.

Harris, M. J., Milich, R., Corbitt, E. M., Hoover, D. W., et al. (1992). Self-fulfilling effects of stigmatizing information on children's social interactions. *Journal of Personality and Social Psychology, 63,* 41–50.

Harrison, A. A. (1977). Mere exposure. In L. Berkowitz (Ed.), *Advances in experimental social psychology* (Vol. 10). New York: Academic Press.

Harrison, J. A., & Wells, R. B. (1991). Bystander effects on male helping behavior: Social comparison and diffusion of responsibility. *Representative Research in Social Psychology, 19,* 53–63.

Harrow, J., & Loewenthal, D. E. (1992). Management research supervision: Some users' perspectives on roles, interventions and power. *Management Education and Development, 23,* 54–64.

Hart, J. W., Stasson, M. F., & Karau, S. J. (1999). Effects of source expertise and physical distance on minority influence. *Group Dynamics, 3* (1), 81–92.

Hart, P. M., Wearing, A. J., & Headey, B. (1994). Perceived quality of life, personality, and work experiences: Construct validation of the Police Daily Hassles and Uplifts Scales. *Criminal Justice & Behavior, 21,* 283–311.

Hartstone, M., & Augoustinos, M. (1995). The minimal group paradigm: Categorization into two versus three groups. *European Journal of Psychology, 25,* 179–193.

Harvey, J. H. (1989). People's naive understandings of their close relationships: Attributional and personal construct perspectives. *International Journal of Personal Construct Psychology, 2,* 37–48.

Harvey, J. H., & Weary, G. (Eds.). (1984). *Attribution: Basic issues and applications.* New York: Academic Press.

Harway, M., & Evans, K. (1996). Working in groups with men who batter. In M. P. Andronico (Ed.), *Men in groups: Insights, interventions, and psychoeducational work.* Washington, DC: American Psychological Association.

Haslam, S. A., Oakes, P. J., & Turner, J. C. (1996). Social identity, self-categorization, and the perceived homogeneity of ingroups and outgroups: The interaction between social motivation and cognition. In R. M. Sorrentino & E. T. Higgins (Eds.), *Handbook of motivation and cognition* (Vol. 3). New York: Guilford Press.

Hass, R. G. (1981). Effects of source characteristics on the cognitive processing of persuasive messages and attitude change. In R. Petty, T. Ostrom, & T. Brock (Eds.), *Cognitive response in persuasion.* Hillsdale, NJ: Erlbaum.

Hass, R. G., & Grady, K. (1975). Temporal delay, type of forewarning, and resistance to influence. *Journal of Experimental Social Psychology, 11,* 459–469.

Hastie, R., Schkade, D. A., & Payne, J. W. (1998). A study of juror and jury judgments in civil cases: Deciding liability for punitive damages. *Law & Human Behavior, 22* (3), 287–314.

Hatfield, E. (1988). Passionate and companionate love. In R. J. Sternberg & M. L. Barnes (Eds.), *The psychology of love* (pp. 191–217). New Haven: Yale University Press.

Hatfield, E., & Sprecher, S. (1986). *Mirror, mirror . . . The importance of looks in everyday life.* Albany, NY: SUNY Press.

Haugtvedt, C. P., Petty, R. E., & Cacioppo, J. T. (1992). Need for cognition and advertising: Understanding the role of personality variables in consumer behavior. *Journal of Consumer Psychology, 1,* 239–260.

Haugtvedt, C. P., Schumann, D. W., Schneier, W. L., & Warren, W. L. (1994). Advertising repetition and variation strategies: Implications for understanding attitude strength. *Journal of Consumer Research, 21,* 176–189.

Haverkamp, B. E. (1993). Confirmatory bias in hypothesis testing for client-identified and counselor self-generated hypotheses. *Journal of Counseling Psychology, 40,* 303–315.

Hayduk, L. A. (1978). Personal space: An evaluative and orienting overview. *Psychological Bulletin, 85,* 117–134.

Hayes, A. F. (1995). Age preferences for same- and opposite-sex partners. *Journal of Social Psychology, 135,* 125–133.

Haynes, R. B., Wang, E., & da-Mota-Gomes, M. (1987). A critical view of interventions to improve compliance with prescribed medications. *Patient Education and Counseling, 10,* 155–166.

Hays, R. B. (1984). The development and maintenance of friendship. *Journal of Personality and Social Relationships, 1,* 75–98.

Hays, R. B. (1985). A longitudinal study of friendship development. *Journal of Personality and Social Psychology 48,* 909–924.

Hazan, C., & Shaver, P. R. (1994). Attachment as an organizational framework for research on close relationships. *Psychological Inquiry, 5,* 1–22.

Hazan, C., & Shaver, P. R. (1994). Deeper into attachment theory. *Psychological Inquiry, 5,* 68–79.

Heath, R. P. (1996, July). The frontiers of psychographics. *American Demographics,* pp. 38–43.

Heatherton, T. F., & Baumeister, R. F. (1996). Self-regulation failure: Past, present, and future. *Psychological Inquiry, 7,* 90–98.

Heatherton, T. F., Kiwan, D., & Hebl, M. R. (1995, August). *The stigma of obesity in women: The difference is black and white.* Paper presented at the annual meeting of the American Psychological Association, New York.

Heatherton, T. F., & Polivy, J. (1991). Development and validation of a scale for measuring state self-esteem. *Journal of Personality and Social Psychology, 60,* 895–910.

Heaven, P. C. L., Connors, J., & Pretorius, A. (1998). Victim characteristics and attribution of rape blame in Australia and South Africa. *Journal of Social Psychology, 138,* 131–133.

Hebl, M. R., & Heatherton, T. F. (1998). The stigma of obesity in women: The difference is black and white. *Personality & Social Psychology Bulletin, 24,* 417–426.

Hecht, M. L., Marston, P. J., & Larkey, L. K. (1994). Love ways and relationship quality in heterosexual relationships. *Journal of Social & Personal Relationships, 11,* 25–43.

Hedge, A., & Yousif, Y. H. (1992). Effects of urban size, urgency, and cost on helpfulness: A cross-cultural comparison between the United Kingdom and the Sudan. *Journal of Cross-Cultural Psychology, 23,* 107–115.

Hedrick, T. E., Bickman, L., & Rog, D. J. (1993). *Planning applied research design.* Newbury Park, CA: Sage.

Heider, F. (1958). *The psychology of interpersonal relations.* New York: Wiley.

Heilman, M. E., & Stopeck, M. H. (1985). Attractiveness and corporate success: Different causal attributions for men and women. *Journal of Applied Psychology, 70,* 379–388.

Heiman, G. W. (1999). *Research methods in psychology* (2nd ed.). Boston, MA: Houghton Mifflin.

Heine, S. J., & Lehman, D. R. (1997). Culture, dissonance, and self-affirmation. *Personality & Social Psychology Bulletin, 23,* 389–400.

Heinemann, G. D., Farrell, M. P., & Schmitt, M. H. (1994). Groupthink theory and research: Implications for decision making in geriatric health care teams. Special Issue: Conceptual foundations for interdisciplinary education in gerontology and geriatrics. *Educational Gerontology, 20,* 71–85.

Heller, D. M. (1997). Cultural diversity and team performance: Testing for social loafing effects. *Dissertation Abstracts International Section A: Humanities & Social Sciences, 58* (3–A), 0978.

Heller, R. F., Saltzstein, H. D., & Caspe, W. B. (1992). Heuristics in medical and non-medical decision-making. *Quarterly Journal of Experimental*

Psychology: Human Experimental Psychology, 44A, 211–235.

Henderson, J., Bourgeois, A. E., LeUnes, A., & Meyers, M. C. (1998). Group cohesiveness, mood disturbance, and stress in female basketball players. *Small Group Research, 29* (2), 212–225.

Hendrick, C., & Hendrick, S. (1986). A theory and method of love. *Journal of Personality and Social Psychology, 50,* 392–402.

Hendrick, C., & Hendrick, S. (1989). Research on love: Does it measure up? *Journal of Personality and Social Psychology, 56,* 784–794.

Hendrick, C., & Seyfried, B. A. (1974). Salience of similarity awareness and attraction: A comparison of balance vs. reinforcement predictions. *Memory and Cognition, 2,* 1–4.

Hendrick, S. S., & Hendrick, C. (1997). Love and satisfaction. In R. J. Sternberg & M. Hojjat (Eds.), *Satisfaction in close relationships.* New York: Guilford.

Henley, N. (1977). *Body politics: Power, sex, and nonverbal communication.* Englewood Cliffs, NJ: Prentice-Hall.

Henry, C. S., Peterson, G. W., & Wilson, S. M. (1997). Adolescent social competence and parental satisfaction. *Journal of Adolescent Research, 12* (3), 389–409.

Hensel, N. H. (1991). Social leadership skills in young children. *Roeper Review, 14,* 4–6.

Henthorne, T. L., LaTour, M. S., & Nataraajan, R. (1993). Fear appeals in print advertising: An analysis of arousal and ad response. *Journal of Advertising, 22,* 59–69.

Heppner, M. J., Good, G. E., Hillenbrand-Gunn, T. L., & Hawkins, A. K. (1995). Examining sex differences in altering attitudes about rape: A test of the Elaboration Likelihood Model. *Journal of Counseling & Development, 73,* 640–647.

Herek, G. M., Kimmel, D. C., Amaro, H., & Melton, G. B. (1991). Avoiding heterosexist bias in psychological research. *American Psychologist, 46,* 957–963.

Herr, P. M. (1986). Consequences of priming: Judgment and behavior. *Journal of Personality and Social Psychology, 51,* 1106–1115.

Herringer, L. G., & Garza, R. T. (1987). Perceptual accentuation in minimal groups. *European Journal of Social Psychology, 17,* 347–352.

Hersh, S. (1970). *My Lai 4: A report on the massacre and its aftermath.* New York: Vintage Books.

Hess, R. D., Azuma, H., Kashiwagi, K., Dickson, W. P., Nagano, S., Holloway, S., Miyake, K., Price, G., Hatano, G., & McDevitt, T. (1986). Family influences on school readiness and achievement in Japan and the United States: An overview of longitudinal study. In H. Stevenson, H. Azuma, & K. Hakuta (Eds.), *Child development and education in Japan.* New York: W. H. Freeman.

Hewston, M., Stroebe, W., Codol, J. P., & Stephenson, G. M. (1988). *Introduction to social psychology: A European perspective.* New York: Academic Press.

Higgins, E. T. (1989). Self-discrepancy theory: What patterns of self-beliefs cause people to suffer? In L. Berkowitz (Ed.), *Advances in experimental and social psychology* (Vol. 22, pp. 93–136). New York: Academic Press.

Higgins, E. T. (1997). Biases in social cognition: "Aboutness" as a general principle. In C. McGarty & S. A. Haslam (Eds.), *The message of social psychology: Perspectives on mind in society.* Oxford, England: Blackwell.

Higgins, E. T., & Brendl, C. M. (1995). Accessibility and applicability: Some "activation rules" influencing judgment. *Journal of Experimental Social Psychology, 31,* 218–243.

Higgins, E. T., Rholes, C. R., & Jones, C. R. (1977). Category accessibility and impression formation. *Journal of Experimental Social Psychology, 13,* 141–154.

Higgins, E. T., Strauman, T., & Klein, R. (1986). Standards and the process of self-evaluation: Multiple effects from multiple stages. In R. M. Sorrentino & E. T. Higgins (Eds.), *Handbook of motivation and cognition: Foundations of social behavior* (pp. 23–63). New York: Guilford Press.

Higgins, R. L., & Snyder, C. R. (1989). Excuses gone awry: An analysis of self-defeating excuses. In R. C. Curtis (Ed.), *Self-defeating behaviors: Experimental research, clinical impressions, and practical implications.* New York: Plenum.

Higgins, R. L., Snyder, C. R., & Berglas, S. (1990). *Self-handicapping: The paradox that isn't.* New York: Plenum.

Higher Education Research Institute. (1996). *The American freshman: National norms for Fall, 1995.* Los Angeles: Higher Education Research Institute, UCLA.

Hill, C. T., & Stull, D. E. (1981). Sex differences in effects of social and value similarity in same-sex friendship. *Journal of Personality and Social Psychology, 41,* 488–502.

Hill, W. F. (1978). Effects of mere exposure on preferences in nonhuman mammals. *Psychological Bulletin, 85,* 1177–1198.

Hilsman, R., & Garber, J. (1995). A test of the cognitive diathesis-stress model of depression in children: Academic stressors, attributional style, perceived competence, and control. *Journal of Personality & Social Psychology, 69,* 370–380.

Hilton, A., Potvin, L., & Sachdev, I. (1989). Ethnic relations in rental housing: A social psychological approach. *Canadian Journal of Behavioural Science, 21,* 121–131.

Hilton, J. L., & Darley, J. M. (1991). The effects of interaction goals on person perception. In M. P. Zanna (Ed.), *Advances in experimental social psychology* (Vol. 24). San Diego, CA: Academic Press.

Hilton, J. L., Miller, D. T., Fein, S., & Darley, J. M. (1990). When dispositional inferences are suspended: Diagnosing and calibrating traits. *Revue Internationale de Psychologie Sociale, 3,* 519–537.

Hinsz, V. (1990). Cognitive and consensus processes in group recognition memory performance. *Journal of Personality and Social Psychology, 54,* 237–246.

Hiroto, D. S., & Seligman, M. E. P. (1975). Generality of learned helplessness in man. *Journal of Personality and Social Psychology, 31,* 311–327.

Hirt, E. R., Deppe, R. K., & Gordon, L. J. (1991). Self-reported versus behavioral self-handicapping: Empirical evidence for a theoretical distinction. *Journal of Personality and Social Psychology, 61,* 981–991.

Hirt, E. R., McDonald, H. E., & Erikson, G. A. (1995). How do I remember thee? The role of encoding set and delay in reconstructive memory processes. *Journal of Experimental Social Psychology, 31,* 379–409.

Hitchon, J. C., & Thorson, E. (1994). Effects of emotion and product involvement on the experience of repeated commercial viewing. *Journal of Broadcasting & Electronic Media, 39,* 376–389.

Hoberman, H. M. (1990). Study group report on the impact of television violence on adolescents. Conference: Teens and television (1988, Los Angeles, California). *Journal of Adolescent Health Care, 11,* 45–49.

Hobfoll, S. E., Spielberger, C. D., Breznitz, S., Figley, C., Folkman, S., Lepper-Green, B., Meichenbaum, D., Milgram, N. A., Sandler, I., Sarason, I., & van der Kolk, B. (1991). War-related stress: Addressing the stress of war and other traumatic events. *American Psychologist, 46,* 848–855.

Hochwaelder, J. (1996). Effects of self-schema on assumptions about and processing of schema-consistent traits of other persons. *Perceptual & Motor Skills, 82,* 1267–1278.

Hoeffler, S., & Ariely, D. (1999). Constructing stable preferences: A look into dimensions of experience and their impact on preference stability. *Journal of Consumer Psychology, 8* (2), 113–139.

Hoeksema-van Orden, C. Y. D., Gaillard, A. W. K., & Buunk, B. P. (1998). Social loafing under fatigue. *Journal of Personality & Social Psychology, 75* (5), 1179–1190.

Hoffman, L. R., & Maier, N. R. F. (1961). Sex differences, sex composition, and group problem solving. *Journal of Abnormal and Social Psychology, 63,* 454–456.

Hoffman, L. W. (1989). Effects of maternal employment in the two-parent family. *American Psychologist, 44,* 283–292.

Hofstede, G. (1980). *Culture's consequences.* Beverly Hills, CA: Sage.

Hogg, M. A., & Hains, S. C. (1998). Friendship and group identification: A new look at the role of cohesiveness in groupthink. *European Journal of Social Psychology, 128* (3), 323–341.

Hogg, M. A., & Hardie, E. A. (1992). Prototypicality, conformity and depersonalized attraction: A self-categorization analysis of group cohesiveness. *British Journal of Social Psychology, 31,* 41–56.

Holahan, C. J., & Moos, R. H. (1987). Personal and contextual determinants of coping strategies.

Journal of Personality and Social Psychology, 52, 946–955.

Holahan, C. J., & Moos, R. H. (1990). Life stressors, resistance factors, and improved psychological functioning: An extension of the stress resistance paradigm. *Journal of Personality and Social Psychology, 58,* 909–917.

Holden, G. W., Coleman, S. M., & Schmidt, K. L. (1995). Why 3-year-old children get spanked: Parent and child determinants as reported by college-educated mothers. *Merrill-Palmer Quarterly, 41,* 431–452.

Holden, G. W., Geffner, R., & Jouriles, E. N. (Eds.). (1998). *Children exposed to marital violence: Theory, research, and applied issues.* Washington, DC: American Psychological Association.

Holden, G. W., & Miller, P. C. (1999). Enduring and different: A meta-analysis of the similarity in parents' child rearing. *Psychological Bulletin, 125,* 223–254.

Holland, J. C., & Lewis, S. (1993). Emotions and cancer: What do we really know? In D. Goleman & J. Gurin (Eds.), *Mind-body medicine.* Yonkers, NY: Consumer Reports Books.

Hollander, E. P. (1958). Conformity, status, and idiosyncrasy credit. *Psychological Review, 65,* 117–127.

Hollander, E. P. (1980). Leadership and social exchange processes. In K. J. Gergen, M. Greenberg, & R. Willis (Eds.), *Social exchange: Advances in theory and research.* New York: Plenum.

Hollander, E. P. (1985). Leadership and power. In G. Lindzey & E. Aronson (Eds.), *Handbook of social psychology* (3rd ed., Vol. 2, pp. 485–537). New York: Random House.

Hollander, E. P., Julian, J. W., & Haaland, G. (1965). Conformity process and prior group support. *Journal of Personality and Social Psychology, 2,* 850–852.

Holloway, S. D. (1988). Concepts of ability and effort in Japan and the United States. *A Review of Educational Research, 58,* 327–345.

Holloway, S. D., Kashiwagi, K., Hess, R. D., & Azuuma, H. (1986). Causal attributions by Japanese and American mothers and children about performance in mathematics. *International Journal of Psychology, 21,* 269–286.

Holmes, J. G., & Boon, S. D. (1990). Developments in the field of close relationships: Creating foundations for intervention strategies. *Personality and Social Psychology Bulletin, 16,* 23–41.

Holmes, T. H., & Rahe, R. H. (1967). The social readjustment scale. *Journal of Psychosomatic Research, 11,* 42–51.

Holtgraves, T. (1997). Styles of language use: Individual and cultural variability in conversational indirectness. *Journal of Personality & Social Psychology, 73,* 624–637.

Holtgraves, T., Srull, T. K., & Socall, D. (1989). Conversation memory: The effects of speaker status on memory for the assertiveness of conversation remarks. *Journal of Personality and Social Psychology, 56,* 149–160.

Holyfield, L. (1999). Manufacturing adventure: The buying and selling of emotions. *Journal of Contemporary Ethnography, 28* (1), 3–32.

Homer, P. M., & Kahle, L. R. (1990). Source expertise, time of source identification, and involvement in persuasion: An elaborative processing perspective. *Journal of Advertising, 19* (1), 30–39.

Hooker, K., & Kaus, C. R. (1995). Health-related possible selves in young and middle adulthood. *Psychology & Aging, 9,* 126–133.

Horner, K. L. (1998). Individuality in vulnerability: Influences on physical health. *Journal of Health Psychology, 3,* 71–85.

Hornstein, G. A., & Truesdell, S. E. (1988). Development of intimate conversation in close relationships. *Journal of Social and Clinical Psychology, 7,* 49–64.

Hosch, H. M., & Platz, S. J. (1984). Self-monitoring and eyewitness accuracy. *Personality and Social Psychology Bulletin, 10,* 289–292.

Hosseini, H. (1997). Cognitive dissonance as a means of explaining economics of irrationality and uncertainty. *Journal of Socio-Economics, 26* (2), 181–189.

Houston, B. K. (1983). Psychophysiological responsibilities and the Type A behavior patter. *Journal of Research in Personality, 17,* 22–39.

Houston, D. A., Doan, K., & Roskos-Ewoldsen, D. (1999). Negative political advertising and choice conflict. *Journal of Experimental Psychology: Applied, 5,* 3–16.

Houston, D. M. (1995). Surviving a failure: Efficacy and a laboratory-based test of the hopelessness model of depression. *European Journal of Social Psychology, 25,* 545–558.

Hovland, C. I., Janis, I. L. (Eds.). (1959). *Personality and persuadability.* New Haven, CT: Yale University Press.

Hovland, C. I., Lumsdaine, A. A., & Sheffield, F. D. (1949). *Experiments in mass communication.* Princeton, NJ: Princeton University Press.

Hovland, C. I., & Weiss, W. (1951). The influence of source credibility on communication effectiveness. *Public Opinion Quarterly, 15,* 635–650.

Hoyle, R. H., & Crawford, A. M. (1994). Use of individual-level data to investigate group phenomena: Issues and strategies. Special Issue: Research problems and methodology. *Small Group Research, 25,* 464–485.

Hubbard, A. S. (1999). Cultural and status differences in intergroup conflict resolution: A longitudinal study of a Middle East dialogue group in the United States. *Human Relations, 52* (3), 303–325.

Huddy, L., & Sears, D. O. (1995). Opposition to bilingual education: Prejudice or the defense of realistic interests? *Social Psychology Quarterly, 58,* 133–143.

Huesmann, L. R. (1986). Psychological processes promoting the relation between exposure to media violence and aggressive behavior by the viewer. *Journal of Social Issues, 42,* 125–139.

Huesmann, L. R. (1998). The role of social information processing and cognitive schema in the acquisition and maintenance of habitual aggressive behavior. In R. G. Geen, G. Russell, & E. Donnerstein (Eds.), *Human aggression: Theories, research, and implications for social policy* (pp. 73–109). San Diego, CA: Academic Press.

Huesmann, L. R., Eron, L. D., Klein, R., Brice, P., & Fischer, P. (1983). Mitigating the imitation of aggressive behaviors by changing children's attitudes about media violence. *Journal of Personality and Social Psychology, 45,* 899–910.

Huesmann, L. R., Lagerspetz, K., & Eron, L. D. (1984). Intervening variables in the TV violence-aggression relation: Evidence from two countries. *Developmental Psychology, 20,* 746–775.

Huesmann, L. R., Maxwell, C. D., Eron, L., Dalhberg, L. L., Guerra, N. G., Tolan, P. H., VanAcker, R., & Henry, D. (1996). Evaluating a cognitive/ecological program for the prevention of aggression among urban children. *American Journal of Preventive Medicine, 12* (Suppl), 120–128.

Huesmann, L. R., & Moise, J. (1996, June). Media violence: A demonstrated public health threat to children. *Harvard Mental Health Letter,* pp. 5–7.

Hughes, J. O., & Sandler, B. R. (1987). *"Friends" raping friends: Could it happen to you?* Washington, DC: Association of American Colleges.

Hughes, R. L., Ginnett, R. C., & Curphy, G. J. (1998). Contingency theories of leadership. In G. R. Hickman (Ed.), *Leading organizations: Perspectives for a new era* (pp. 141–157). Thousand Oaks, CA: Sage.

Hui, C. H. (1988). Measurement of individualism-collectivism. *Journal of Research in Personality, 22,* 17–36.

Hunter, C. E., & Ross, M. W. (1991). Determinants of health-care workers' attitudes toward people with AIDS. *Journal of Applied Social Psychology, 21,* 947–956.

Huston, A. C., Donnerstein, E., Fairchild, H., Feshbach, N. D., Katz, P. A., Murray, J. P., Rubinstein, E. A., Wilcox, B. L., & Zuckerman, D. (1992). *Big world, small screen: The role of television in American society.* Lincoln: Univeristy of Nebrakska Press.

Huston, T., & Levinger, G. (1978). Interpersonal attraction and relationships. *Annual Review of Psychology, 29,* 115–156.

Huston, T. L., & Vangelisti, A. L. (1991). Socioemotional behavior and satisfaction in marital relationships: A longitudinal study. *Journal of Personality and Social Psychology, 61,* 721–733.

Hutton, D. G., & Baumeister, R. F. (1992). Self-awareness and attitude change: Seeing oneself on the central route to persuasion. *Personality and Social Psychology Bulletin, 18,* 68–75.

Hyde, J. S. (1990). *Understanding human sexuality.* New York: McGraw-Hill.

Hyde, J. S. (1994). Should psychologists study gender differences? Yes, with some guidelines. *Feminism & Psychology, 4,* 507–512.

Hyman, I. E., Husband, T. H., & Billings, F. J. (1995). False memories of childhood experiences. *Applied Cognitive Psychology, 9,* 181–197.

Hymes, R. W., Leinart, M., Rowe, S., & Rogers, W. (1993). Acquaintance rape: The effect of race of defendant and race of victim on white juror decisions. *Journal of Social Psychology, 133,* 627–634.

Iacobucci, D., & McGill, A. L. (1990). Analysis of attribution data: Theory testing and effects estimation. *Journal of Personality and Social Psychology, 59,* 426–441.

Ickes, W. (1993). Traditional gender roles: Do they make, and then break, our relationships? *Journal of Social Issues, 49,* 71–86.

Iedema, J., & Poppe, M. (1994). The effect of self-presentation on social value orientation. *Journal of Social Psychology, 134,* 771–782.

Ingledew, D. K., & McDonagh, G. (1998). What coping functions are served when health behaviours are used as coping strategies? *Journal of Health Psychology, 3,* 195–213.

Innami, I. (1994). The quality of group decisions, group verbal behavior, and intervention. *Organizational Behavior & Human Decision Processes, 60,* 409–430.

Insko, C. A. (1965). Verbal reinforcement of attitude. *Journal of Personality and Social Psychology, 2,* 621–623.

Insko, C. A., Sedlak, A. J., & Lipsitz, A. (1982). A two-valued logic or two-valued balance resolution of the challenge of agreement and attraction effects in p-o-x triads, and a theoretical perspective on conformity and hedonism. *European Journal of Social Psychology, 12,* 143–167.

Ironson, G. (1993, April). National Institutes of Health symposium on gender and stress. Bethesda, Maryland.

Isen, A. M., Clark, M., & Schwartz, M. F. (1976). Duration of the effect of good mood on helping: "Footprints on the sands of time." *Journal of Personality and Social Psychology, 34,* 385–393.

Isen, A. M., & Levin, P. F. (1972). Effect of feeling good on helping: Cookies and kindness. *Journal of Personality and Social Psychology, 21,* 384–388.

Isenberg, D. J. (1986). Group polarization: A critical review and meta-analysis. *Journal of Personality and Social Psychology, 58,* 487–498.

Ito, T. A., Larsen, J. T., Smith, N. K., & Cacioppo, J. T. (1998). Negative information weighs more heavily on the brain: The negativity bias in evaluative categorizations. *Journal of Personality & Social Psychology, 75* (4), 887–900.

Jackson, J. M. (1986). In defense of social impact theory: Comment on Mullen. *Journal of Personality and Social Psychology, 50,* 511–513.

Jacobson, M. B., Antonelli, J., Winning, P. U., & Opeil, D. (1977). Women as authority figures: The use and nonuse of authority. *Sex Roles, 4,* 43–50.

Jaffe, Y., & Yinon, Y. (1979). Retaliatory aggression in individuals and groups. *European Journal of Social Psychology, 9,* 177–186.

Jahoda, G. (1986). Nature, culture and social psychology. *European Journal of Social Psychology, 16,* 17–30.

Jain, U. (1993). Effects of density: The role of moderators for the consequences of crowding. *Psychologia: An International Journal of Psychology in the Orient, 36,* 133–139.

James, W. (1890). *Principles of psychology.* New York: Holt.

Jamieson, D. W., Lydon, J. E., Stewart, G., & Zanna, M. P. (1987). Pygmalion revisited: New evidence for student expectancy effects in the classroom. *Journal of Educational Psychology, 79,* 461–466.

Janda, L. H., & Klenke-Hamel, K. E. (1980). *Human sexuality.* New York: Van Nostrand.

Janis, I. L. (1967). Effects of fear arousal on attitude change: Recent developments in theory and experimental research. In L. Berkowitz (Ed.), *Advances in experimental social psychology* (Vol. 3). New York: Academic Press.

Janis, I. L. (1972). *Victims of groupthink: A psychological study of foreign-policy decisions and fiascoes.* Boston: Houghton-Mifflin.

Janis, I. L. (1982). Counteracting the adverse effects of concurrence-seeking in policy-planning groups: Theory and research perspectives. In H. Brandstatter, J. H. Davis, & G. Stocker-Kreichgauer (Eds.), *Group decision making.* New York: Academic Press.

Janis, I. L. (1989). *Crucial decisions: Leadership in policy-making management.* New York: Free Press.

Janis, I. L., & Mann, L. (1977). Emergency decision making: A theoretical analysis of responses to disaster warnings. *Journal of Human Stress, 3,* 35–48.

Jankowiak, W. R., & Fischer, E. F. (1992). A cross-cultural perspective on romantic love. *Ethnology, 31,* 149–155.

Jankowiak, W. R., & Fischer, E. F. (1998). A cross-cultural perspective on romantic love. In J. M. Jenkins & K. Oatley (Eds.), *Human emotions: A reader.* Malden, MA: Blackwell.

Janoff-Bulman, R. (1992). *Shattered assumptions: Towards a new psychology of trauma.* New York: Free Press.

Janoski, T., & Wilson, J. (1995). Pathways to voluntarism: Family socialization and status transmission models. *Social Forces, 74,* 271–292.

Janssens, J. M. A. M., & Dekovic, M. (1997). Child rearing, prosocial moral reasoning, and prosocial behaviour. *International Journal of Behavioral Development, 20,* 509–527.

Javier, R. A., Herron, W. G., & Bergman, A. (1995). A psychosocial view of mental illness: An introduction. Special Issue: A psychosocial view of mental illness. *Journal of Social Distress & the Homeless, 4,* 73–78.

Jemmott, J. B., III, Pettigrew, T. F., & Johnson, J. T. (1983, August). *The effects of in-group versus out-group membership in social perception.* Paper presented at the 91st Annual Convention of the American Psychological Association, Anaheim, CA.

Jenkins, L. S., & Gortner, S. R. (1998). Correlates of self-efficacy expectation and prediction of walking behavior in cardiac surgery elders. *Annals of Behavioral Medicine, 20,* 99–103.

Jenkins, S. R. (1994). Need for power and women's careers over 14 years: Structural power, job satisfaction, and motive change. *Journal of Personality & Social Psychology, 66,* 155–165.

Jenner, H. (1990). The Pygmalion effect: The importance of expectancies. *Alcoholism Treatment Quarterly, 7,* 127–133.

Jennings, M. K., & Niemi, R. G. (1974). *The political character of adolescence.* Princeton, NJ: Princeton University Press.

Johnson, C., & Mullen, B. (1994). Evidence for the accessibility of paired distinctiveness in distinctiveness-based illusory correlation in stereotyping. *Personality & Social Psychology Bulletin, 20,* 65–70.

Johnson, M. P., Huston, T. L., Gaines, S. O., & Levinger, G. (1992). Patterns of married life among young couples. Special Issue: Social networks. *Journal of Social and Personal Relationships, 9,* 343–364.

Johnson, R., Hobfoll, S. E., & Zalberg-Linetzy, A. (1993). Social support knowledge and behavior and relational intimacy: A dyadic study. *Journal of Family Psychology, 6,* 266–277.

Johnson, R. W., Kelly, R. J., & LeBlanc, B. A. (1995). Motivational basis of dissonance: Aversive consequences of inconsistency. *Personality & Social Psychology Bulletin, 21,* 850–855.

Johnson-George, C., & Swap, W. (1982). Measurment of specific interpersonal trust: Construction and validation of a scale to assess trust in a specific other. *Journal of Personality and Social Psychology, 43,* 1306–1317.

Joiner, T. E., Metalsky, G. I., & Wonderlich, S. A. (1995). Bulimic symptoms and the development of depressive symptoms: The moderating role of attributional style. *Cognitive Therapy & Research, 19,* 651–666.

Jones, B. (1997). Age differences in response to high- and low-threat driver improvement warning letters. *Journal of Safety Research, 28* (1), 15–28.

Jones, D. C. (1991). Friendship satisfaction and gender: An examination of sex differences in contributors to friendship satisfaction. *Journal of Social and Personal Relationships, 8,* 167–185.

Jones, E. (1961). *The life and work of Sigmund Freud.* New York: Basic Books.

Jones, E. E. (1964). *Ingratiation: A social psychological analysis.* New York: Appleton-Century-Crofts.

Jones, E. E. (1979). The rocky road from acts to dispositions. *American Psychologist, 34,* 107–117.

Jones, E. E. (1990). *Interpersonal perception.* New York: Freeman.

Jones, E. E. (1998). Major developments in five decades of social psychology. In D. T. Gilbert, S. T. Fiske, & G. Lindzey (Eds.), *Handbook of social psychology* (4th ed.). New York: McGraw-Hill.

Jones, E. E., & Berglas, S. (1978). Control of attributions about the self through self-handicapping strategies: The appeal of alcohol and the role of under-achievement. *Personality and Social Psychology Bulletin, 4,* 200–206.

Jones, E. E., & Davis, K. E. (1965). A theory of correspondent inferences: From acts to dispositions. In L. Berkowitz (Ed.), *Advances in experimental social psychology* (Vol. 2). New York: Academic Press.

Jones, E. E., Gergen, K. J., & Davis, K. E. (1961). Role playing variations and their informational value on person perception. *Journal of Abnormal and Social Psychology, 63,* 302–310.

Jones, E. E., & Goethals, G. R. (1972). *Order effects in impression formation: Attribution context and the nature of the entity.* Morristown, NJ: General Learning Press.

Jones, E. E., & Harris, V. A. (1967). The attribution of attitudes. *Journal of Experimental and Social Psychology, 3,* 1–24.

Jones, E. E., & Nisbett, R. E. (1972). The actor and the observer: Divergent perceptions of the causes of behavior. In E. E. Jones, D. E. Kanouse, H. H. Kelley, R. E. Nisbett, S. Valins, & B. Weiner (Eds.), *Attribution: Perceiving the causes of behavior* (pp. 79–94). Morristown, NJ: General Learning Press.

Jones, E. E., & Pittman, T. S. (1982). Toward a general theory of strategic self-presentation. In J. Suls (Ed.), *Psychological perspectives on the self.* Hillsdale, NJ: Erlbaum.

Jones, J. M. (1994). Our similiarities are different: Toward a psychology of affirmative diversity. In E. J. Trickett, R. J. Watts, & D. Birman (Eds.), *Human diversity: Perspectives on people in context.* The Jossey-Bass social and behavioral science series. San Francisco: Jossey-Bass.

Jones, J. P. (1997). Is advertising still salesmanship? *Journal of Advertising Research, 37,* 9–15.

Jones, M. (1993). Influence of self-monitoring on dating motivations. *Journal of Research in Personality, 27,* 197–206.

Jones, R. A. (1985). *Research methods in the social and behavioral sciences.* Sunderland, MA: Sinauer.

Jones, R. W., & Bates, J. E. (1978). Satisfaction in male homosexual couples. *Journal of Homosexuality, 3,* 217–224.

Joule, R. V. (1987). La dissonance cognitive: un etat de motivation? / Arousal properties of dissonance. *Annee Psychologique, 87,* 273–290.

Joule, R., & Beauvois, J. (1998). Cognitive dissonance theory: A radical view. In W. Stroebe & M. Hewstone (Eds.), *European Review of Social Psychology* (Vol. 8, pp. 1–32). Chichester, England: Wiley.

Jourard, S. M. (1971). *The transparent self.* New York: Van Nostrand Reinhold.

Judd, C. M., & Park, B. (1988). Out-group homogeneity: Judgments of variability at the individual and group levels. *Journal of Personality and Social Psychology, 54,* 778–788.

Judd, C. M., Ryan, C. S., & Park, B. (1991). Accuracy in the judgment of in-group and out-group variability. *Journal of Personality and Social Psychology, 61,* 366–379.

Julian, J. W., Bishop, D. W., & Fiedler, F. E. (1966). Quasitherapeutic effects of intergroup competition. *Journal of Personality and Social Psychology, 5,* 321–327.

Julius, M. (1990). *Women who supress their anger.* Paper presented at the Gerontological Society of America. Washington, DC.

Jung, D. I., & Avolio, B. J. (1998). Examination of transformational leadership and group process among Caucasian- and Asian-Americans: Are they different? In T. A. Scandura & M. G. Serapio (Eds.), *Research in international business and international relations: Leadership and innovation in emerging markets* (Vol. 7, pp. 29–66). Stamford, CT: Jai Press.

Jurma, W. E., & Wright, B. C. (1990). Follower reactions to male and female leaders who maintain or lose reward power. *Small Group Research, 21,* 97–112.

Jussim, L., & Eccles, J. S. (1992). Teacher expectations: II. Construction and reflection of student achievement. *Journal of Personality and Social Psychology, 63,* 947–961.

Jussim, L., Milburn, M., & Nelson, W. (1991). Emotional openness: Sex-role stereotypes and self-perceptions. *Representative Research in Social Psychology, 19,* 35–52.

Jussim, L., Nelson, T. E., Manis, M., & Soffin, S. (1995). Prejudice, stereotypes, and labeling effects: Sources of bias in person perception. *Journal of Personality and Social Psychology, 68,* 228–246.

Kaarbo, J., & Beasley, R. K. (1998). A political perspective on minority influence and strategic group composition. In D. H. Gruenfeld (Ed.), *Composition research on managing groups and teams* (Vol. 1, pp. 125–147). Stamford, CT: Jai Press.

Kagehiro, D. K. (1990). Defining the standards of proof in jury instructions. *Psychological Science, 1,* 194–200.

Kahle, L. R., & Chiagouris, L. (Eds.). (1997). *Values, lifestyles, and psychographics.* Mahwah, NJ: Erlbaum.

Kahneman, D., & Tversky, A. (1973). On the psychology of prediction. *Psychological Review, 80,* 237–251.

Kahneman, D., & Tversky, A. (1982). The simulation heuristic. In D. Kahneman, P. Slovic, & A. Tversky (Eds.), *Judgment under uncertainty: Heuristics and biases.* New York: Cambridge University Press.

Kaiser, S. B. (1999). Women's appearance and clothing within organizations. In L. K. Guerrero & J. A. DeVito (Eds.), *The nonverbal communication reader: Classic and contemporary readings* (2nd ed.). Prospect Heights, IL: Waveland Press.

Kalafat, J., Elias, M., & Gara, M. A. (1993). The relationship of bystander intervention variables to adolescents' responses to suicidal peers. *Journal of Primary Prevention, 13,* 231–244.

Kalb, M. (1983). The conception of the alternative and the decision to divorce. *American Journal of Psychotherapy, 37,* 346–356.

Kalichman, S. C., Somlai, A., Adair, V., & Weir, S. S. (1996). Psychological factors in HIV testing among sexually transmitted disease clinic patients: An exploratory study. *Psychology & Health, 11,* 593–604.

Kalick, S. M., Zebrowitz, L. A., Langlois, J. H., & Johnson, R. M. (1998). Does human facial attractiveness honestly advertise health? Longitudinal data on an evolutionary question. *Psychological Science, 9,* 8–13.

Kallgren, C. A., & Wood, W. (1986). Access to attitude-relevant information in memory as a determinant of attitude-behavior consistency. *Journal of Experimental Social Psychology, 22,* 328–338.

Kalmijn, M. (1998). Intermarriage and homogamy: Causes, patterns, trends. *Annual Review of Sociology, 24,* 395–421.

Kalthoff, R. A., & Neimeyer, R. A. (1993). Self-complexity and psychological distress: A test of the buffering model. *International Journal of Personal Construct Psychology, 6,* 327–349.

Kameda, T., & Sugimori, S. (1993). Psychological entrapment in group decision making: An assigned decision rule and a groupthink phenomenon. *Journal of Personality and Social Psychology, 65,* 282–292.

Kaniasty, K., & Norris, F. H. (1995). Mobilization and deterioration of social support following natural disasters. *Current Directions in Psychological Science, 4,* 94–98.

Kanner, A. D., Coyne, J. C., Schaefer, L., & Lazarus, R. (1981). Comparison of two modes of stress measurement: Daily hassles and uplifts versus major life events. *Journal of Behavioral Medicine, 4,* 14.

Kaplan, M. F. (1975). Information integration in social judgment: Interaction of judge and informational components. In M. F. Kaplan & S. Schwartz (Eds.), *Human judgment and decision processes.* New York: Academic Press.

Kaplan, M. F., & Miller, C. E. (1987). Group decision making and normative versus informational influence: Effects of type of issue and assigned decision rule. *Journal of Personality and Social Psychology, 53,* 306–313.

Kaplan, R. M., Sallis, J. F., Jr., & Patterson, T. L. (1993). *Health and human behavior.* New York: McGraw-Hill.

Karasawa, M. (1988). Effects of cohesiveness and inferiority upon ingroup favoritism. *Japanese Psychological Research, 30,* 49–59.

Karau, S. J., & Hart, J. W. (1998). Group cohesiveness and social loafing: Effects of a social interaction manipulation on individual motivation within groups. *Group Dynamics, 2* (3), 185–191.

Karau, S. J., & Williams, K. D. (1993). Social loafing: A meta-analytic review and theoretical integration. *Journal of Personality and Social Psychology, 65,* 681–706.

Karau, S. J., & Williams, K. D. (1995). Social loafing: Research findings, implications, and future directions. *Current Directions in Psychological Science, 4,* 134–140.

Karau, S. J., & Williams, K. D. (1997). The effects of group cohesiveness on social loafing and social compensation. *Group Dynamics, 1* (2), 156–168.

Kardes, F. R. (1999). Psychology applied to consumer behavior. In A. M. Stec & D. A. Bernstein (Eds.), *Psychology: Fields of application* (pp. 82–97). Boston: Houghton Mifflin.

Karlins, M., Coffman, T. L., & Walters, G. (1969). On the fading of social stereotypes: Studies in three generations of college students. *Journal of Personality and Social Psychology, 13,* 1–16.

Kassin, S. M., Ellsworth, P. C., & Smith, V. L. (1989). The "general acceptance" of psychological research on eyewitness testimony: A survey of the experts. *American Psychologist, 44,* 1089–1098.

Kassin, S. M., Reddy, M. E., & Tulloch, W. F. (1990). Juror interpretations of ambiguous evidence: The need for cognition, presentation, order, persuasion. *Law and Human Behavior, 14,* 43–55.

Kassin, S. M., & Sommers, S. R. (1997). Inadmissible testimony, instructions to disregard, and the jury: Substantive versus procedural considerations. *Personality & Social Psychology Bulletin, 23,* 1046–1054.

Kassin, S. M., & Studebaker, C. A. (1998). Instructions to disregard and the jury: Curative and paradoxical effects. In J. M. Golding & C. M. MacLeod (Eds.), *Intentional forgetting: Interdisciplinary approaches* (pp. 413–434). Mahwah, NJ: Erlbaum.

Kassin, S. M., & Sukel, H. (1997). Coerced confessions and the jury: An experimental test of the "harmless error" rule. *Law & Human Behavior, 21* (1), 27–46.

Kates, N., Grieff, B., & Hagen, D. (1990). *The psychosocial impact of job loss.* Washington, DC: American Psychiatric Press.

Katz, D., & Braly, K. (1933). Racial stereotypes of one hundred college students. *Journal of Abnormal and Social Psychology, 28,* 280–290.

Katz, I., & Hass, R. G. (1988). Racial ambivalence and American Value Conflict: Correlational and priming studies of dual cognitive structures. *Journal of Personality and Social Psychology, 55,* 893–905.

Katz, P. A. (Ed.). (1976). *Towards the elimination of racism.* New York: Pergamon.

Kaufman, J., & Zigler, E. (1987). Do abused children become abusive parents? *American Journal of Orthopsychiatry, 57,* 186–192.

Kavanoor, S., Grewal, D., & Blodgett, J. (1997). Ads promoting OTC medications: The effect of ad format and credibility on beliefs, attitudes, and purchase intentions. *Journal of Business Research, 40* (3), 219–227.

Kawanishi, Y. (1995). The effects of culture on beliefs about stress and coping: Causal attribution of Anglo-American and Japanese persons. *Journal of Contemporary Psychotherapy, 25,* 49–60.

Kay, S. (1999, May 10). Violence / threats by U. S. students in the wake of Columbine shootings. *Newsweek,* pp. 32–33.

Keane, A., Pickett, M., Jepson, C., & McCorkle, R. (1994). Psychological distress in survivors of residential fires. *Social Science & Medicine, 38,* 1055–1060.

Keating, C. F. (1985). Human dominance signals: The primate in us. In S. L. Ellyson & J. F. Dovidio (Eds.), *Power, dominance, and nonverbal behavior.* New York: Springer-Verlag.

Keeling, L. J., & Hurnik, J. F. (1993). Chickens show socially facilitated feeding behaviour in response to a video image of a conspecific. *Applied Animal Behaviour Science, 36,* 223–231.

Kelley, H. H. (1950). The warm-cold variable in first impressions of persons. *Journal of Personality, 18,* 431–439.

Kelley, H. H. (1967). Attribution theory in social psychology. *Nebraska Symposium on Motivation, 15,* 192–238.

Kelley, H. H. (1972). Attribution in social interaction. In E. E. Jones (Ed.), *Attribution: Perceiving the causes of behavior.* Morristown, NJ: General Learning Press.

Kelley, H. H., Berscheid, E., Christensen, A., Harvey, J. H., Huston, T. L., Levinger, G., McClintock, E., Peplau, L. A., & Peterson, D. R. (1983). *Close relationships.* New York: Freeman.

Kelley, H. H., & Michela, J. L. (1980). Attribution theory and research. *Annual Review of Psychology, 31,* 457–501.

Kelly, E. L., & Conley, J. J. (1987). Personality and compatibility: A prospective analysis of marital stability and marital satisfaction. *Journal of Personality and Social Psychology, 52,* 27–40.

Kelman, H. C. (1967). Human use of human subjects: The problem of deception in social psychological experiments. *Psychological Bulletin, 67,* 1–11.

Kelman, H. C. (1968). *A time to speak: On human values and social research.* San Francisco: Jossey-Bass.

Kelman, H. C., & Hamilton, V. L. (1989). *Crimes of obedience.* New Haven, CT: Yale University Press.

Kelman, H. C., & Lawrence, L. (1972). Assignment of responsibility in the case of Lt. Calley: Preliminary report on a national survey. *Journal of Social Issues, 28,* 177–212.

Kelsey, B. L. (1998). The dynamics of multicultural groups: Ethnicity as a determinant of leadership. *Small Group Research, 29* (5), 602–623.

Kenny, D. A. (1994). *Interpersonal perception.* New York: Guilford.

Kenrick, D. T., Groth, G. E., Trost, M. R., & Sadalla, E. K. (1993). Integrating evolutionary and social exchange perspectives on relationships: Effects of gender, self-appraisal, and involvement level on mate selection criteria. *Journal of Personality & Social Psychology, 64,* 951–969.

Kenrick, D. T., & Keefe, R. C. (1992). Age preferences in mates reflect sex differences in human reproductive strategies. *Behavioral & Brain Sciences, 15,* 75–133.

Kerckhoff, A. C., & Davis, K. E. (1962). Value consensus and need complementarity in mate selection. *American Sociological Review, 27,* 295–303.

Kerner, M. S., & Grossman, A. H. (1998). Attitudinal, social, and practical correlates to fitness behavior: A test of the theory of planned behavior. *Perceptual & Motor Skills, 87* (3, Pt 2), 1139–1154.

Kerr, N. L. (1983). Motivation losses in small groups: A social dilemma analysis. *Journal of Personality and Social Psychology, 45,* 819–828.

Kerr, N. L. (1997). Norms in social dilemmas. In D. Schroeder (Ed.), *Social dilemmas: Social psychological perspectives.* New York: Praeger.

Kerr, N. L., Garst, J., Lewandowski, D. A., & Harris, S. E. (1997). That still, small voice: Commitment to cooperate as an internalized versus a social norm. *Personality & Social Psychology Bulletin, 23,* 1300–1311.

Kerr, N. L., Hymes, R. W., Anderson, A. B., & Weathers, J. E. (1995). Defendant-juror similarity and mock juror judgments. *Law & Human Behavior, 19,* 545–567.

Kerwin, J., & Shaffer, D. R. (1991). The effects of jury dogmatism on reactions to jury nullification instructions. *Personality and Social Psychology Bulletin, 17,* 140–146.

Kiecolt-Glaser, J. K., & Glaser, R. (1991). Psychosocial factors, stress, disease, and immunity. In R. Ader, D. L. Felten, & N. Cohen (Eds.), *Psychoneuroimmunology.* San Diego, CA: Academic Press.

Kiecolt-Glaser, J. K., & Glaser, R. (1995). Psychoneuroimmunology and health consequences: Data and shared mechanisms. *Psychosomatic Medicine, 57,* 269–274.

Kiecolt-Glaser, J. K., Glaser, R., Cacioppo, J. T., Malarkey, W. B. (1998). Marital stress: Immunologic, neuroendocrine, and autonomic correlates. In S. M. McCann & J. M. Lipton (Eds.), *Neuroimmunomodulation: Molecular aspects, integrative systems, and clinical advances.* Annals of the New York Academy of Sciences (Vol. 840). New York: New York Academy of Sciences.

Kiecolt-Glaser, J. K., Page, G. G., Marucha, P. T., MacCallum, R. C., & Glaser, R. (1998). Psychological influences on surgical recovery: Perspectives from psychoneuroimmunology. *American Psychologis, 53,* 1209–1218.

Kiecolt-Glaser, R., & Kiecolt-Glaser, J. K. (1993). Mind and immunity. In D. Goleman & J. Gurin, (Eds.), *Mind-body medicine.* Yonkers, NY: Consumer Reports Books.

Kiehl, S. (1998, August 12). Living a lesson in friendship: As college roomate, teen will be disabled friend's attendant. *The Boston Globe,* p. C1.

Kiesler, S., Siegel, J., & McGuire, T. (1984). Social psychological aspects of computer-mediated communication. *American Psychologist, 39,* 1123–1134.

Kihlstrom, J. F. (1994). Hypnosis, delayed recall, and the principles of memory. Special Issue: Hypnosis and delayed recall. *International Journal of Clinical & Experimental Hypnosis, 42,* 337–345.

Kikendall, K. A. (1994). Self-discrepancy as an important factor in addressing women's emotional reactions to infertility. *Professional Psychology: Research & Practice, 25,* 214–220.

Kilduff, M., & Day, D. V. (1994). Do chameleons get ahead? The effects of self-monitoring on managerial careers. *Academy of Management Journal, 37,* 1047–1060.

Killeya, L. A., & Johnson, B. T. (1998). Experimental induction of biased systematic processing: The directed-thought technique. *Personality & Social Psychology Bulletin, 24* (1), 17–33.

Killian, L. M. (1980). Theory of collective behavior: The mainstream revisited. In H. M. Blalock, Jr. (Ed.), *Sociological theory and research.* New York: Free Press.

Kim, J., Lim, J., & Bhargava, M. (1998). The role of affect in attitude formation: A classical conditioning approach. *Journal of the Academy of Marketing Science, 26* (2), 143–152.

Kim, M., & Hunter, J. E. (1993). Relationships among attitudes, behavioral intentions, and behavior: A meta-analysis of past research. *Communication Research, 20,* 331–364.

Kinder, D. R., & Sears, D. O. (1985). Public opinion and political action. In G. Lindzey & E. Aronson (Eds.), *Handbook of social psychology* (3rd ed.). New York: Random House.

King, K. L. (1998). Does the law matter? Federal district court decision-making in fair housing cases, 1968–89. *Social Science Research, 27* (4), 388–409.

Kipnis, D. (1976). *The powerholders.* Chicago: University of Chicago Press.

Kipnis, D. M. (1974). Inner direction, other direction and achievement motivation. *Human Development, 17,* 321–343.

Kirkcaldy, B. D., Eysenck, M., Furnham, A. F., & Siefen, G. (1998). Gender, anxiety and self-image. *Personality & Individual Differences, 24* (5), 677–684.

Klein, J. G. (1991). Negativity effects in impression formation: A test in the political arena. *Personality and Social Psychology Bulletin, 17,* 412–418.

Klein, S. B., & Loftus, J. (1988). The nature of self-referent encoding: The contributions of elaborative and organizational processess. *Journal of Personality and Social Psychology, 55,* 5–11.

Klein, S. B., Loftus, J., & Burton, H. A. (1989). Two self-reference effects: The importance of distinguishing between self-descriptiveness judgments and autobiographical retrieval in self-referent encoding. *Journal of Personality and Social Psychology, 56,* 853–865.

Kleinke, C. L. (1986). *Meeting and understanding people.* New York: Freeman.

Kleinman, A. (1991, July). The psychiatry of culture and the culture of psychiatry. *Harvard Mental Health Letter.*

Klentz, B., & Beaman, A. L. (1981). The effects of type of information and method of dissemination on the reporting of a shoplifter. *Journal of Applied Social Psychology, 11,* 64–82.

Klineberg, O. (1990). A personal perspective on the development of social psychology. *Annals of the New York Academy of Sciences, 602,* 35–50.

Knight, G. P., Fabes, R. A., & Higgins, D. A. (1996). Concerns about drawing causal inferences from meta-analyses: An example in the study of gender differences in aggression. *Psychological Bulletin, 119,* 410–421.

Knight, G. P., Jonson, L. G., Carlo, G., & Eisenberg, N. (1994). A multiplicative model of the dispositional antecedents of a prosocial behavior: Predicting more of the people more of the time. *Journal of Personality and Social Psychology, 66,* 178–183.

Kohn, A. (1988, October). Beyond selfishness. *Psychology Today,* pp. 34–38.

Kokkinaki, F., & Lunt, P. (1999). The effect of advertising message involvement on brand attitude accessibility. *Journal of Economic Psychology, 20* (1), 41–51.

Kolb, K. J., & Jussim, L. (1994). Teacher expectations and underachieving gifted children. *Roeper Review, 17,* 26–30.

Kollock, P., Blumstein, P., & Schwartz, P. (1994). The judgment of equity in intimate relationships. *Social Psychology Quarterly, 57,* 340–351.

Konst, D., Vonk, R., & van der Vlist, R. (1999). Inferences about causes and consequences of behavior of leaders and subordinates. *Journal of Organizational Behavior, 20,* 261–271.

Korn, J. H. (1997). *Illusions of reality: A history of deception in social psychology.* Albany: State University of New York Press.

Koski, L. R., & Shaver, P. R. (1997). Attachment and relationship satisfaction across the lifespan. In R. J. Sternberg & M. Hojjat (Eds.), *Satisfaction in close relationships.* New York: Guilford.

Koss, M. P., Dinero, T. E., Siebel, C. A., & Cox, S. L. (1988). Stranger and acquaintance rape: Are there differences in the victim's experience? *Psychology of Women Quarterly, 12,* 1–24.

Kotler, P. (1986). *Principles of marketing* (3rd ed.). Englewood Cliffs, NJ: Prentice-Hall.

Kotre, J., & Hall, E. (1990). *Seasons of life.* Boston: Little, Brown.

Krackhardt, D., & Porter, L. W. (1986). The snowball effect: Turnover embedded in communication networks. *Journal of Applied Psychology, 71,* 50–55.

Kramer, R. M. (1998). Revisiting the Bay of Pigs and Vietnam decisions 25 years later: How well has the groupthink hypothesis stood the test of time? *Organizational Behavior & Human Decision Processes, 73* (2–3), 236–271.

Kraus, S. J. (1995). Attitudes and the prediction of behavior: A meta-analysis of the empirical literature. *Personality & Social Psychology Bulletin, 21,* 58–75.

Kravitz, D. A., & Martin, B. (1986). Ringelmann rediscovered: The original article. *Journal of Personality and Social Psychology, 50,* 936–941.

Kristiansen, C. M., & Giulietti, R. (1990). Perceptions of wife abuse: Effects of gender attitudes toward women, and just-world beliefs among college students. *Psychology of Women Quarterly, 14,* 177–189.

Kristof, N. (1996, February 11). Who needs love? In Japan many couples don't. *The New York Times,* p. A1.

Krueger, J., & Clement, R. W. (1994). The truly false consensus effect: An ineradicable and egocentric bias in social perception. *Journal of Personality and Social Psychology, 67,* 596–610.

Krueger, R. F., & Caspi, A. (1993). Personality, arousal, and pleasure: A test of competing models of interpersonal attraction. *Personality & Individual Differences, 14,* 105–111.

Kruglanski, A., & Mackie, D. M. (1989). Majority and minority influence: A judgmental process analysis. In W. Stroebe & M. Hewstone (Eds.), *Advances in European social psychology.* London: Wiley.

Kruglanski, A. E., & Mayseless, O. (1987). Motivational effects in the social comparison opinions. *Journal of Personality and Social Psychology, 53,* 834–842.

Kruglanski, A. W. (1989). The psychology of being "right": The problem of accuracy in social perception and cognition. *Psychological Bulletin, 106,* 395–409.

Kruglanski, A. W. (1990). Lay epistemic theory in social cognitive psychology. *Psychological Inquiry, 1,* 181–197.

Kruglanski, A. W., & Freund, T. (1983). The freezing and unfreezing of lay-inferences: Effects of impressional primacy, ethnic stereotyping, and numerical anchoring. *Journal of Experimental Social Psychology, 19,* 448–468.

Kruglanski, A. W., & Webster, D. M. (1991). Group members' reactions to opinion deviates and conformists at varying degrees of proximity to decision deadline and of environmental noise. *Journal of Personality and Social Psychology, 61,* 212–225.

Krull, D. S., & Erickson, D. J. (1995). Inferential hopscotch: How people draw social inferences from behavior. *Current Directions in Psychological Science, 4,* 35–38.

Krysan, M. (1998). Privacy and the expression of White racial attitudes: A comparison across three contexts. *Public Opinion Quarterly, 62* (4), 506–544.

Kryzanowski, E., & Stewin, L. (1985). Developmental implications in youth counseling: Gender socialization. *International Journal for the Advancement of Counseling, 8,* 265–278.

Kubota, K. (1997). Intergroup discrimination and illusory correlation induced by social category: Minority, majority, and outsider. *Japanese Journal of Psychology, 68,* 120–128.

Kuczynski, L., & Hildebrandt, N. (1997). Models of conformity and resistance in socialization theory. In J. E. Grusec & L. Kuczynski (Eds.), *Parenting and children's internalization of values: A handbook of contemporary theory* (pp. 227–256). New York: Wiley.

Kuhn, D., Weinstock, M., & Flaton, R. (1994). How well do jurors reason? Competence dimensions of individual variation in a juror reasoning task. *Psychological Science, 5,* 289–294.

Kulik, J. A., & Mahler, H. I. M. (1997). Social comparison, affiliation, and coping with acute medical threats. In B. P. Buunk & F. X. Gibbons (Eds.), *Health, coping, and well-being: Perspectives from social comparison theory.* Mahwah, NJ: Erlbaum.

Kulik, J. A., Mahler, H. I. M., & Earnest, A. (1994). Social comparison and affiliation under threat: Going beyond the affiliate-choice paradigm. *Journal of Personality and Social Psychology, 66,* 301–309.

Kulik, J. A., Mahler, H. I. M., & Moore, P. J. (1996). Social comparison and affiliation under threat: Effects on recovery from major surgery. *Journal of Personality & Social Psychology, 71,* 967–979.

Kulik, L. (1998). Occupational sex-typing and occupational prestige: A comparative study of adolescents and adults in Israel. *Youth & Society, 30,* 164–181.

Kunkel, D., Wilson, B., Donnerstein, E., & Blumenthal, E. (1995). Measuring television violence: The importance of context. *Journal of Broadcasting & Electronic Media, 39,* 284–291.

Kurdek, L. A. (1991). Correlates of relationship satisfaction in cohabiting gay and lesbian couples: Integration of contextual, investment, and problem-solving models. *Journal of Personality and Social Psychology, 61,* 910–922.

Kurdek, L. A. (1992). Relationship stability and relationship satisfaction in cohabiting gay and lesbian couples: A prospective longitudinal test of the contextual and interdependence models. *Journal of Social & Personal Relationships, 9,* 125–142.

Kurdek, L. A. (1993). The allocation of household labor in gay, lesbian, and heterosexual married children. *Journal of Social Issues, 49,* 127–139.

Kurdek, L. A. (1994). Lesbian and gay couples. In A. R. D'Augelli & C. J. Patterson (Eds.), *Lesbian and gay identities over the lifespan: Psychological perspectives on personal, relational, and community processes.* New York: Oxford University Press.

Kurdek, L. A. (1995). Developmental changes in relationship quality in gay and lesbian cohabiting couples. *Developmental Psychology, 31,* 86–94.

Kurdek, L. A. (1998). Relationship outcomes and their predictors: Longitudinal evidence from heterosexual married, gay cohabiting, and lesbian cohabiting couples. *Journal of Marriage & the Family, 60,* 553–568.

Kwan, V. S. Y., Bond, M. H., & Singelis, T. M. (1997). Pancultural explanations for life satisfaction: Adding relationship harmony to self-esteem. *Journal of Personality & Social Psychology, 73,* 1038–1051.

Kwok, D. C. (1995). The self-perception of competence by Canadian and Chinese children. *Psychologia: An International Journal of Psychology in the Orient, 38,* 9–16.

Kwon, S., & Oei, T. P. (1994). The roles of two levels of cognitions in the development, maintenance, and treatment of depression. *Clinical Psychology Review, 14,* 331–358.

Lach, J. (1999, April). Meet you in aisle three. *American Demographics,* pp. 41–42.

Lachman, S. J. (1993). Psychology and riots. *Psychology: A Journal of Human Behavior, 30,* 16–23.

Lahno, B. (1995). Trust, reputation, and exit in exchange relationships. *Journal of Conflict Resolution, 39,* 495–510.

Laine, K. (1998). Finnish students' attributions for school-based loneliness. *Scandinavian Journal of Educational Research, 42,* 401–413.

Lakey, B., & Heller, K. (1985). Response biases and the relation between negative life events and psychological symptoms. *Journal of Personality and Social Psychology, 49,* 1662–1668.

Lamb, M. E. (1982). The bonding phenomenon: Misinterpretations and their implications. *Journal of Pediatrics, 101,* 555–557.

Lambert, W. W. (1971). Cross-cultural backgrounds to personality development and the socialization of aggression: Findings from the Six Culture study. In W. W. Lambert & R. Weisbrod (Eds.), *Comparative perspectives in social psychology.* Boston: Little Brown.

Lamm, H. (1988). A review of our research on group polarization: Eleven experiments on the effects of group discussion on risk acceptance, probability estimation, and negotiation positions. ONR Conference: The psychology of the social group (1987, London, England). *Psychological Reports, 62,* 807–813.

Lamm, H., & Myers, D. G. (1978). Group-induced polarization of attitudes and behavior. In L. Berkowitz (Ed.), *Advances in experimental social psychology* (Vol. 2, pp. 145–195). New York: Academic Press.

Lamm, H., & Wiesmann, U. (1997). Subjective attributes of attraction: How people characterize their liking, their love, and their being in love. *Personal Relationships, 4,* 271–284.

Lane, J. D., & Wegner, D. M. (1995). The cognitive consequences of secrecy. *Journal of Personality & Social Psychology, 69,* 237–253.

Lang, A., Dhillon, K., & Dong, Q. (1995). The effects of emotional arousal and valence on television viewers' cognitive capacity and memory. *Journal of Broadcasting & Electronic Media, 39,* 313–327.

Langford, T., & Ponting, J. R. (1992). Canadians' responses to aboriginal issues: The roles of prejudice, perceived group conflict and economic conservatism. Special Issue: Social inequality. *Canadian Review of Sociology & Anthropology, 29,* 140–166.

Langfred, C. W. (1998). Is group cohesiveness a double-edged sword? An investigation of the effects of cohesiveness on performance. *Small Group Research, 29* (1), 124–143.

Langlois, J. H., Ritter, J. M., Casey, R. J., & Sawin, D. B. (1995). Infant attractiveness predicts maternal behaviors and attitudes. *Developmental Psychology, 31,* 464–472.

Langlois, J. H., Roggman, L. A., Casey, R. J., Ritter, J. M., Rieser-Danner, L. A., & Jenkins, V. Y. (1987). Infant preferences for attractive faces: Rudiments of a stereotype? *Developmental Psychology, 23,* 363–369.

Langlois, J. H., Roggman, L. A., & Rieser-Danner, L. A. (1990). Infants' differential social responses to attractive and unattractive faces. *Developmental Psychology, 26,* 153–159.

Lanoue, D. J., & Bowler, S. (1998). Picking the winners: Perceptions of party viability and their impact on voting behavior. *Social Science Quarterly, 79* (2), 361–377.

LaPiere, R. T. (1934). Attitudes vs. action. *Social Forces, 13,* 230–237.

Larose, H., Tracy, J., & McKelvie, S. J. (1993). Effects of gender on the physical attractiveness stereotype. *Journal of Psychology, 127,* 677–680.

Larsen, K. S., Triplett, J. S., Brant, W. D., & Langenberg, D. (1979). Collaborator status, subject characteristics, and conformity in the Asch paradigm. *Journal of Social Psychology, 108,* 259–263.

Lash, S. J., Eisler, R. M., & Southard, D. R. (1995). Sex differences in cardiovascular reactivity as a function of the appraised gender relevance of the stressor. *Behavioral Medicine, 21,* 86–94.

Lassiter, G. D., Stone, J. I., & Weigold, M. F. (1988). Effect of leading questions on the self-monitoring correlation. *Personality and Social Psychology Bulletin, 13,* 537–545.

Laszlo, J. (1986). Scripts for interpersonal situations. *Studia Psychologica, 28,* 125–135.

Latané, B. (1981). The psychology of social impact. *American Psychologist, 36,* 343–356.

Latané, B. (1997). Dynamic social impact: The societal consequences of human interaction. In C. McGarty & S. A. Haslam (Eds.), *The message of social psychology: Perspectives on mind in society* (pp. 200–220). Oxford, England: Blackwell.

Latané, B., & Darley, J. M. (1968). Group inhibition of bystander intervention. *Journal of Personality and Social Psychology, 10,* 215–221.

Latané, B., & Darley, J. M. (1970). *The unresponsive bystander: Why doesn't he help?* New York: Appleton Century Crofts.

Latané, B., Liu, J. H., Nowak, A., & Bonevento, M. (1995). Distance matters: Physical space and social impact. *Personality & Social Psychology Bulletin, 21,* 795–805.

Latané, B., & Nida, S. (1981). Ten years of research on group size and helping. *Psychological Bulletin, 89,* 308–324.

Laughlin, P. R. (1980). Social combination process of cooperative, problem-solving groups at verbal intellective tasks. In M. Fishbein (Ed.), *Progress in social psychology* (Vol. 1). Hillsdale, NJ: Erlbaum.

Laurenceau, J., Barrett, L. F., & Pietromonaco, P. R. (1998). Intimacy as an interpersonal process: The importance of self-disclosure, partner disclosure, and perceived partner responsiveness in interpersonal exchanges. *Journal of Personality & Social Psychology, 74,* 1238–1251.

Laursen, B., & Williams, V. A. (1997). Perceptions of interdependence and closeness in family and peer relationships among adolescents with and without romantic partners. In S. Shulman & W. A. Collins (Eds.), *Romantic relationships in adolescence: Developmental perspectives. New directions for child development, No. 78.* San Francisco, CA: Jossey-Bass.

Lavee, Y., Sharlin, S., & Katz, R. (1996). The effect of parenting stress on marital quality: An integrated mother-father model. *Journal of Family Issues, 17,* 114–135.

Lavine, H., Burgess, D., Snyder, M., Transue, J., Sullivan, J. L., Haney, B., & Wagner, S. H. (1999). Threat, authoritarianism, and voting: An investigation of personality and persuasion. *Personality & Social Psychology Bulletin, 25,* 337–347.

Lazar, B. A. (1994). Why social work should care: Television violence and children. *Child and Adolescent Social Work Journal, 11,* 3–19.

Lazarus, A. A., & Abramovitz, A. (1962). The use of "emotive imagery" in the treatment of children's phobias. *Journal of Mental Science, 108,* 191–195.

Lazarus, R. S. (1993). From psychological stress to the emotions: A history of changing outlooks. *Annual Review of Psychology, 44,* 1–21.

Lazarus, R. S. (1999). *Stress and emotion: A new synthesis.* New York: Springer.

Lazarus, R. S., & Cohen, J. B. (1977). Environmental stress. In I. Altman & J. F. Wohlwill (Eds.), *Human behavior and the environment: Current theory and research* (Vol. 2). New York: Plenum Press.

Lazarus, R., DeLongis, A., Folkman, S., & Gruen, R. (1985). Stress and adaptation outcomes: The problem of confounded measures. *American Psychologist, 40,* 770–779.

Lazarus, R. S., & Folkman, S. (1984). *Stress, appraisal, and coping.* New York: Springer.

Leary, M. R., & Shepperd, J. A. (1986). Behavioral self-handicaps versus self-reported handicaps: A conceptual note. *Journal of Personality and Social Psychology, 51,* 1265–1268.

Leavitt, H. J. (1951). Some effects of certain communication patterns on group performance. *Journal of Abnormal and Social Psychology, 46,* 38–50.

LeBon, G. (1896). *The crowd: A study of the popular mind.* London: Ernest Benn.

Lee, J. A. (1974). The styles of loving. *Psychology Today, 8,* pp. 43–50.

Lee, J. A. (1977). A typology of styles of loving. *Personality and Social Psychology Bulletin, 3,* 173–182.

Lee, M. E., Matsumoto, D., Kobayashi, M., Krupp, D., Maniatis, E. F., & Roberts, W. (1992). Cultural influences on nonverbal behavior in applied settings. In R. S. Feldman (Ed.), *Applications of nonverbal behavioral theories and research.* Hillsdale, NJ: Erlbaum.

Lee, Y., Jussim, L. J., & McCauley, C. R. (Eds.). (1995). *Stereotype accuracy: Toward appreciating group differences.* Washington, DC: American Psychological Association.

Lee, Y. T., McCauley, C. R., & Draguns, J. G. (Eds.). (1999). *Personality and person perception across cultures.* Mahwah, NJ: Erlbaum.

Lehman, D. R., & Taylor, S. E. (1988). Date with an earthquake: Coping with a probable, unpredictable disaster. *Personality and Social Psychology Bulletin, 13,* 546–555.

Leichtman, M. D., & Ceci, S. J. (1995). The effects of stereotypes and suggestions on preschoolers' reports. *Developmental Psychology, 31,* 568–578.

Leigh, H., & Reiser, M. F. (1980). *The patient.* New York: Plenum.

Leippe, M. R., & Eisenstadt, D. (1999). A self-accountability model of dissonance reduction: Multiple modes on a continuum of elaboration. In E. Harmon-Jones & J. Mills (Eds.), *Cognitive dissonance: Progress on a pivotal theory in social psychology. Science conference series* (pp. 201–232). Washington, DC: American Psychological Association.

Lemoine, J., & Mougne, C. (1983). Why has death stalked the refugees? *Natural History, 92,* 6–19.

Leone, C., & Corte, V. (1994). Concern for self-presentation and self-congruence: Self-monitoring, Machiavellianism, and social contacts. *Social Behavior & Personality, 22,* 305–312.

Leone, L., Perugini, M., & Ercolani, A. P. (1999). A comparison of three models of attitude-behavior relationships in the studying behavior domain. *European Journal of Social Psychology, 29* (2–3), 161–189.

Lepore, L., & Brown, R. (1999). Exploring automatic stereotype activation: A challenge to the inevitability of prejudice. In D. Abrams & M. Hogg (Eds.), *Social identity and social cognition.* Malden, MA: Blackwell.

Lepore, S. J., Evans, G. W., & Schneider, M. L. (1992). Role of control and social support in explaining the stress of hassles and crowding. *Environment and Behavior, 24,* 795–811.

Lepper, H. S., Martin, L. R., & DiMatteo, M. R. (1995). A model of nonverbal exchange in physician–patient expectations for patient involvement. *Journal of Nonverbal Behavior, 19,* 207–222.

Lepper, M. R. (1983). Extrinsic reward and intrinsic motivation: Implications for the classroom. In J. M. Levine & M. C. Wung (Eds.), *Teacher and student perceptions: Implications for learning* (pp. 281–317). Hillsdale, NJ: Erlbaum.

Lepper, M. R., & Greene, D. (1978). *The hidden costs of reward.* Hillsdale, NJ: Erlbaum.

Lepper, M. R., Greene, D., & Nisbett, R. E. (1996). Undermining children's intrinsic interest with extrinsic reward: A test of the "overjustification" hypothesis. In S. Fein & S. Spencer (Eds.), *Readings in social psychology: The art and science of research.* Boston, MA: Houghton Mifflin.

Lerner, M. J. (1980). *The belief in a just world: A fundamental delusion.* New York: Plenum.

Lerner, M. J., & Meindl, J. R. (1981). Justice and altruism. In J. P. Rushton & R. M. Sorrentino (Eds.), *Altruism and helping behavior: Social, personality, and developmental perspectives.* Hillsdale, NJ: Erlbaum.

Leung, K., & Bond, M. H. (1984). The impact of cultural collectivism on reward allocation. *Journal of Personality and Social Psychology, 47,* 793–804.

Leventhal, H. (1970). Findings and theory in the study of fear communications. In L. Berkowitz (Ed.), *Advances in experimental social psychology* (Vol. 5, pp. 119–186). New York: Academic Press.

Leventhal, H., Nerenz, D., & Leventhal, E. (1985). Feelings of threat and private views of illness: Factors in dehumanization in the medical care system. In R. Baum and J. E. Singer (Eds.), *Advances in environmental psychology* (Vol. 4). Hillsdale, NJ: Erlbaum.

Levine, J. (1999, May). *Minority influence.* Paper presented at the annual University of Massachusetts Adversity Conference, Amherst, MA.

Levine, J. M. (1989). Reaction to opinion deviance in small groups. In P. B. Paulhus (Ed.), *Psychology of group influence* (2nd ed.). Hillsdale, NJ: Erlbaum.

LeVine, R. A., & Campbell, D. T. (1972). *Ethnocentrism: Theories of conflict, ethnic attitudes and group behavior.* New York: Wiley.

Levine, R. V. (1993, February). Is love a luxury? *American Demographics,* pp. 27–29.

Levine, R. V., Martinez, T. S., Brase, G., & Sorenson, K. (1994). Helping in 36 U.S. cities. *Journal of Personality and Social Psychology, 67,* 69–82.

Levinger, G. A. (1974). A three-level approach to attraction: Toward an understanding of pair relatedness. In T. L. Huston (Ed.), *Foundations of interpersonal attraction.* New York: Academic Press.

Levinger, G. A. (1983). Development and change. In H. H. Kelley (Ed.), *Close relationships.* San Francisco: Freeman.

Levinger, G. A., Senn, D. J., & Jorgensen, B. W. (1970). Progress toward permanence in courtship: A test of the Kerckhoff-David hypothesis. *Sociometry, 33,* 427–443.

Levinson, S. C. (1980). Speech act theory: The state of the art. *Language and Linguistics Teaching: Abstracts, 1,* 5–24.

Levy, E. (1990). Stage, sex and suffering of women in American films. *Empirical Studies of the Arts, 8,* 53–76.

Levy, S. M., Lee, J., Bagley, C., & Lippman, M. (1988). Survival hazard analysis in first recurrent breast cancer patients. Seven-year follow-up. *Psychosomatic Medicine, 50,* 520–528.

Levy, S. M., & Roberts, D. C. (1992). Clinical significance of psychoneuroimmunology: Prediction of cancer outcomes. In N. Schneiderman, P. McCabe, & A. Baum (Eds.), *Stress and disease processes.* Hillsdale, NJ: Erlbaum.

Lewin, K. (1931). *Die psychologische Situation bein Lohn und Strafe.* Leipzig: S. Hirzel.

Lewin, K. (1935). *A dynamic theory of personality.* New York: McGraw-Hill.

Lewin, K. (1936). *Principles of topological psychology.* New York: McGraw-Hill.

Lewin, K. (1943). Forces behind food habits and methods of change. *Bulletin of the National Research Council, 108,* 35–65.

Lewin, K. (1951). *Field theory in social science.* New York: Harper.

Lewin, K., Lippitt, R., & White, R. K. (1939). Patterns of aggressive behavior in experimentally created "social climates." *Journal of Social Psychology, 10,* 271–299.

Lewis, M., & Brooks-Gunn, J. (1979). *Social cognition and the acquisition of self.* New York: Plenum.

Lewis, C., Wilkins, R., Baker, L., & Woobey, A. (1995). "Is this man your daddy?" Suggestibility in children's eyewitness identification of a family member. *Child Abuse & Neglect, 19,* 739–744.

Lewis, C. S. (1958). *The allegory of love: A study in medieval traditions.* New York: Oxford University Press.

Ley, P. (1982). Giving information to patients. In J. R. Eiser (Ed.), *Social psychology and behavioral medicine.* New York: Wiley.

Ley, R. (1977). Encoding specificity and unidirectional associates in cued recall. *Memory and Cognition, 5,* 523–528.

Liang, D. W., Moreland, R., & Argote, L. (1995). Group versus individual training and group performance: The mediating factor of transactive memory. *Personality & Social Psychology Bulletin, 21,* 384–393.

Liebert, R. M. (1975). Modeling and the media. *School Psychology Digest, 4,* 22–29.

Liebert, R. M., & Sprafkin, J. (1988). *The early window: Effects of television on children and youth* (3rd ed.). New York: Pergamon.

Lightdale, J. R., & Prentice, D. A. (1994). Rethinking sex differences in aggression: Aggressive behavior in the absence of social roles. *Personality & Social Psychology Bulletin, 20,* 34–44.

Likert, R. (1932). A technique for the measurement of attitudes [Special issue]. *Archives of Psychology* (140).

Lin, E. H., Von Korff, M., Katon, W., & Bush, T. (1995). The role of the primary care physician in patients' adherence to antidepressant therapy. *Medical Care, 33,* 67–74.

Linneweber, V., Mummendey, A., Bornewasser, M., & Loschper, G. (1984). Classification of situations specific to field and behaviour: The context of aggressive interactions in schools. *European Journal of Social Psychology, 14,* 281–295.

Linville, P. W. (1982). The complexity-extremity effect and age-based stereotyping. *Journal of Personality and Social Psychology, 42,* 193–211.

Linville, P. W. (1987). Self-complexity as a cognitive buffer against stress-related illness and depression. *Journal of Personality and Social Psychology, 52,* 663–676.

Linville, P. W., & Carlston, D. E. (1994). Social cognition of the self. In P. G. Devine & D. L. Hamilton (Eds.), *Social cognition: Impact on social psychology.* San Diego, CA: Academic Press.

Linville, P. W., & Fischer, G. W. (1993). Exemplar and abstraction models of perceived group variability and stereotypicality. *Social Cognition, 11,* 92–125.

Linville, P. W., & Fischer, G. W. (1998). Group variability and covariation: Effects on intergroup judgment and behavior. In C. Sedikides & J. Schopler (Eds.), *Intergroup cognition and intergroup behavior* (pp. 123–150). Mahwah, NJ: Erlbaum.

Linville, P. W., Fischer, G. W., & Yoon, C. (1996). Perceived covariation among the features of ingroup and outgroup members: The outgroup covariation effect. *Journal of Personality and Social Psychology, 70,* 421–436.

Linz, D. G., Donnerstein, E., & Adams, S. M. (1989). Physiological desenitization and judgments about female victims of violence. *Human Communication Research, 5.*

Lipman, J. (1991, September 4). Celebrity pitchmen are popular again. *Wall Street Journal,* p. B1.

Lippa, R. (1976). Expressive control and the leakage of dispositional introversion-extroversion during role-playing teaching. *Journal of Personality, 44,* 541–559.

Lippa, R., & Donaldson, S. I. (1990). Self-monitoring and idiographic measures of behavioral variability across interpersonal relationships. *Journal of Personality, 58,* 465–479.

Lisak, D., & Roth, S. (1988). Motivational factors in nonincarcerated sexually aggressive men. *Journal of Personality and Social Psychology, 55,* 795–802.

Liskin, L. (1985, November–December). Youth in the 1980s: Social and health concerns 4. *Population Reports, 8.*

Littlepage, G. E., Schmidt, G. W., Whisler, E. W., & Frost, A. G. (1995). An input-process-output analysis of influence and performance in problem-solving groups. *Journal of Personality and Social Psychology, 69,* 877–889.

Liu, J. H., & Latané, B. (1998). The catastrophic link between the importance and extremity of political attitudes. *Political Behavior, 20* (2), 105–126.

Liu, J., Zhang, W., & Tang, R. (1993). Research on the occurrence of self-awareness in infants. *Psychological Science (China), 16,* 355–358.

Locher, P., Unger, G., Sociedade, P., & Wahl, J. (1993). At first glance: Accessibility of the physical attractiveness stereotype. *Sex Roles, 28,* 729–743.

Loftus, E. F. (1992). When lie becomes memory's truth: Memory distortion after exposure to misinformation. *Current Directions in Psychological Science, 1,* 121–123.

Loftus, E. F. (1993). Psychologists in the eyewitness world. *American Psychologist, 48,* 550–552.

Loftus, E. F., & Ketcham, K. (1991). *Witness for the defense: The accused, the eyewitness who puts memory on trial.* New York: St. Martin's Press.

Loftus, E. F., & Palmer, J. C. (1974). Reconstruction of automobile destruction: An example of the interface between language and memory. *Journal of Verbal Learning and Verbal Behavior, 13,* 585–589.

Logan, G. D., & Cowan, W. B. (1984). On the ability to inhibit thought and action: A theory of an act of control. *Psychological Review, 91,* 295–327.

Loo, C. M. (1978). Density, crowding and preschool children. In A. Baum & Y. Epstein (Eds.), *Human response to crowding.* Hillsdale, NJ: Erlbaum.

Lorenz, K. (1966). *On aggression.* New York: Harcourt, Brace, Jovanovich.

Lorenz, K. (1974). *Civilized man's eight deadly sins.* New York: Harcourt, Brace, Jovanovich.

Lorenzi-Cioldi, F. (1993). They all look alike, but so do we . . . sometimes: Perceptions of in-group and out-group homogeneity as a function of sex and context. Special Issue: Social processes in small groups: II. Studying social processes in small groups. *British Journal of Social Psychology, 32,* 111–124.

Lortie-Lussier, M. (1987). Minority influence and idiosyncrasy credit: A new comparison of the Moscovici and Hollander theories of innovation. *European Journal of Social Psychology, 17,* 431–446.

Lott, A. J., & Lott, B. E. (1974). The role of reward in the formation of positive interpersonal attitudes. In T. L. Huston (Ed.), *Foundations of interpersonal attraction* (pp. 171–189). New York: Academic Press.

Lott, B. (1987). Sexist discrimination as distancing behavior: I. A laboratory demonstration. *Psychology of Women Quarterly, 11,* 47–58.

Lott, B., & Maluso, D. (Eds.). (1995). *The social psychology of interpersonal discrimination.* New York: Guilford.

Loudon, D. L., & Della Bitta, A. J. (1993). *Consumer behavior: Concepts and applications* (4th ed.). New York: McGraw-Hill.

Lovas, L. (1997). Influence of aggression on the perception of behaviour of the incident participants from the perspective of the victim. *Ceskoslovenska Psychologie, 41,* 399–409.

Love, K. D., & Aiello, J. R. (1980). Using projective techniques to measure interaction distance: A methodological note. *Personality and Social Psychology Bulletin, 6,* 102–104.

Love, P., & Brown, J. T. (1999). Creating passion and intimacy. In J. Carlson & L. Sperry (Eds.), *The intimate couple.* Philadelphia, PA: Brunner/Mazel.

Luckey, E. B., & Bain, J. K. (1970). Children: A factor in marital satisfaction. *Journal of Marriage and the Family, 32,* 43–44.

Luginbuhl, J., & Burkhead, M. (1994). Sources of bias and arbitrariness in the capital trial. *Journal of Social Issues, 50,* 103–124.

Luginbuhl, J., & Palmer, R. (1991). Impression management aspects of self-handicapping: Positive and negative effects. *Personality and Social Psychology Bulletin, 17,* 655–662.

Luks, A. (1988, October). Helper's high. *Psychology Today,* pp. 39–42.

Lundin, T. (1995). Transportation disasters: A review. Special Section: Transportation disasters. *Journal of Traumatic Stress, 8,* 381–389.

Luthans, F. (1989). *Organizational behavior* (5th ed.). New York: McGraw-Hill.

Luus, C. A., & Wells, G. L. (1994). The malleability of eyewitness confidence: Co-witness and perseverance effects. *Journal of Applied Psychology, 79,* 714–723.

Lykken, D., & Tellegen, A. (1996). Happiness is a stochastic phenomenon. *Psychological Science, 7,* 186–189.

Lynch, D. (1999, June 10). High-tech transformations. Available: *http://abcnews.go.com/sections/tech/ WiredWomen/wiredwomen990421.html*

Lyness, S. A. (1993). Predictors of differences between Type A and B individuals in heart rate and blood pressure reactivity. *Psychological Bulletin, 114,* 266–295.

Lysak, H., Rule, B. G., & Dobbs, A. R. (1989). Conceptions of aggression: Prototype or defining features? *Personality and Social Psychology Bulletin, 15,* 233–243.

Lytton, H., & Romney, D. M. (1991). Parents' differential socialization of boys and girls: A meta-analysis. *Psychological Bulletin, 109,* 267–296.

Maass, A., & Clark, R. D. (1983). Internalization versus compliance: Differential processes underlying minority influence and conformity. *European Journal of Social Psychology, 13,* 197–215.

Maass, A., & Clark, R. D. (1984). Hidden impact of minorities: Fifteen years of minority influence research. *Psychological Bulletin, 95,* 428–450.

Maccoby, E. E., & Jacklin, C. N. (1974). *The psychology of sex differences.* Stanford, CA: Stanford University Press.

MacCoun, R. J., & Kerr, N. L. (1988). Asymmetric influence in mock jury deliberation: Jurors' bias for leniency. *Journal of Personality and Social Psychology, 54,* 21–33.

MacDermid, S. M., Huston, T. L., & McHale, S. M. (1990). Changes in marriage associated with the transition to parenthood: Individual differences as a function of sex-role attitudes and changes in division of labor. *Journal of Marriage and the Family, 52,* 475–486.

MacEwen, K. E. (1994). Refining the intergenerational transmission hypothesis. *Journal of Interpersonal Violence, 9,* 350–365.

Macher, K. (1986). The politics of organizations. *Personnel Journal, 65,* 80–84.

Mackie, D. M. (1987). Systematic and nonsystematic processing of majority and minority persuasive communications. *Journal of Personality and Social Psychology, 53,* 41–52.

Mackie, D. M., & Worth, L. T. (1991). Feeling good, but not thinking straight: The impact of positive mood on persuasion. In J. Forgas (Ed.), *Emotion and social judgments.* Oxford, England: Pergamon Press.

Mackie, D. M., & Hunter, S. B. (1999). Majority and minority influence: The interactions of social identity and social cognition mediators. In D. Abrams & M. A. Hogg (Eds.), *Social identity and social cognition* (pp. 332–353). Malden, MA: Blackwell.

MacLean, A. P., & Peters, R. D. (1995). Graduate student couples: Dyadic satisfaction in relation to type of partnership and demographic characteristics. *Canadian Journal of Behavioural Science, 27,* 120–124.

MacNeil, M. K., & Sherif, M. (1976). Norm change over subject generations as a function of arbitrariness of prescribed norms. *Journal of Personality and Social Psychology, 34,* 762–773.

Macrae, C. N., Hewstone, M., & Griffiths, R. J. (1993). Processing load and memory for stereotype-based information. *European Journal of Social Psychology, 23,* 77–87.

Macrae, C. N., Stangor, C., & Milne, A. B. (1994). Activating social stereotypes: A functional analysis. *Journal of Experimental Social Psychology, 30,* 370–389.

Maczynski, J., Jago, A. G., Reber, G., & Bohnisch, W. (1994). Culture and leadership styles: A comparison of Polish, Austrian, and U.S. managers. *Polish Psychological Bulletin, 25,* 303–315.

Maczynski, J., Lindell, M., Motowidlo, S. J., Sigfrids, C., & Jarmuz, S. (1997). A comparison of organizational and societal culture in Finland and Poland. *Polish Psychological Bulletin, 28,* 269–278.

Madden, T. J., Ellen, P. S., & Ajzen, I. (1992). A comparison of the theory of planned behavior and the theory of reasoned action. *Personality and Social Psychology Bulletin, 18,* 3–9.

Maddie, S. R., Barone, P. T., & Puccetti, M. C. (1987). Stressful events are indeed a factor in physical illness: Reply to Schroeder and Costa (1984). *Journal of Personality and Social Psychology, 52,* 833–843.

Maddux, C. D., Stoltenberg, & J. H. Harvey (Eds.). (1990). *Interfaces in psychology: Social perception in clinical and counseling psychology.* Lubbock, TX: Texas Tech Press.

Maddux, J. E., & Rogers, R. W. (1980). Effects of source expertness, physical attractiveness, and supporting arguments on persuasion: A case of brains over beauty. *Journal of Personality and Social Psychology, 39,* 833–843.

Maddux, J. E., & Rogers, R. W. (1983). Protection motivation and self-efficacy: A revised theory of fear appeals and attitude change. *Journal of Experimental Social Psychology, 19,* 469–479.

Magalhaes, R. (1984). Organization development in Latin countries: Fact or fiction? *Leadership and Organization Development Journal, 5,* 17–21.

Mahler, M. S., Pine, F., & Bergman, A. (1975). *The psychological birth of the human infant.* New York: Basic Books.

Mahoney, E. R. (1983). *Human sexuality.* New York: McGraw-Hill.

Maier, N. R. F., & Solem, A. R. (1952). The contribution of a discussion leader to the quality of group thinking: The effective use of minority opinions. *Human Relations, 5,* 277–288.

Mak, M., & de Koning, P. (1995). Clinical research in aggressive patients, pitfalls in study design and measurement of aggression. *Progress in Neuro-Psychopharmacology & Biological Psychiatry, 19,* 993–1017.

Malamuth, N. M. (1998). The confluence model as an organizing framework for research on sexually aggressive men: Risk moderators, imagined aggression, and pornography consumption. In R. G. Geen, G. Russell, & E. Donnerstein (Eds.), *Human aggression: Theories, research, and implications for social policy* (pp. 229–245). San Diego, CA: Academic Press.

Malamuth, N. M., & Check, J. V. P. (1985). The effects of aggressive pornography on beliefs in rape myths: Individual differences. *Journal of Research in Personality, 15,* 436–446.

Malatesta, C. Z., & Lamb, C. (1987, August). *Emotion socialization during the second year.* Paper presented at the Annual Meeting of the American Psychological Association, New York City.

Mancuso, R. A., & Pennebaker, J. W. (1994, August). *Resolving vs. dredging up past traumas: The effects of writing.* Paper presented at the Annual Meeting of the American Psycholgoical Association, Los Angeles.

Mann, L. (1980). Cross-cultural studies in small groups. In H. C. Triandis & R. W. Brislin (Eds.), *Handbook of cross-cultural psychology* (Vol. 5). Boston: Allyn & Bacon.

Mann, L., Newton, J. W., & Innes, J. M. (1982). A test between deindividuation and emergent norm theories of crowd aggression. *Journal of Personality and Social Psychology, 42,* 260–272.

Manstead, A. S. R. (1991). Expressiveness as an individual difference. In R. S. Feldman & B. Rimé (Eds.), *Fundamentals of nonverbal behavior.* Cambridge, England: Cambridge University Press.

Manstead, A. S. R. (1997). Situations, belongingness, attitudes, and culture: Four lessons learned from social psychology. In C. McGarty & S. A. Haslam (Eds.), *The message of social psychology: Perspectives on mind in society.* Oxford, England: Blackwell.

Mantel, S. P., & Kardes, F. R. (1999). The role of direction of comparison, attribute-based processing, and attitude-based processing in consumer preference. *Journal of Consumer Research, 25* (4), 335–352.

Manucia, G. K., Baumann, D. J., & Cialdini, R. B. (1984). Mood influences on helping: Direct effects or side effects? *Journal of Personality and Social Psychology, 46,* 357–364.

Margolin, L. (1989). Gender and the prerogatives of dating and marriage: An experimental assessment of a sample of college students. *Sex Roles, 20,* 91–102.

Marino, R. V., Rosenfeld, W., Narula, P., & Karakurum, M. (1991). Impact of pediatricians' attire on children and parents. *Journal of Developmental and Behavioral Pediatrics, 12,* 98–101.

Markman, H. J. (1981). Prediction of marital distress: A 5-year follow-up. *Journal of Consulting and Clinical Psychology, 49,* 760–762.

Marks, G., & Miller, N. (1987). Ten years of research on the false-consensus effect: An empirical and theoretical review. *Psychological Bulletin, 102,* 72–90.

Markus, G. B. (1982). Political attitudes during an election year: A report of the 1980 NES Panel Study. *American Political Science Review, 76,* 538–560.

Markus, H. (1977). Self-schemata and processing information about the self. *Journal of Personality and Social Psychology, 35,* 63–78.

Markus, H. R., & Kitayama, S. (1991). Culture and the self: Implications for cognition, emotion, and motivation. *Psychological Review, 98,* 224–253.

Markus, H. R., & Kitayama, S. (1994). A collective fear of the collective: Implications for selves and theories of selves. Special Issue: The self and the collective. *Personality and Social Psychology Bulletin, 20,* 568–579.

Markus, H. R., & Kitayama, S. (1998). The cultural psychology of personality. *Journal of Cross-Cultural Psychology, 29,* 63–87.

Markus, H., & Nurius, P. (1986). Possible selves. *American Psychologist, 41,* 954–969.

Markus, H., & Sentis, K. P. (1982). The self in social information processing. In J. Suls (Ed.), *Psychological perspectives on the self* (Vol. 1, pp. 41–70). Hillsdale, NJ: Erlbaum.

Markus, H. R., Smith, J., & Moreland, R. L. (1985). Role of the self-rconcept in the perception of others. *Journal of Personality and Social Psychology, 49,* 1494–1512.

Marques, J., Abrams, D., Paez, D., & Martinez-Taboada, C. (1998). The role of categorization and in-group norms in judgments of groups and their members. *Journal of Personality & Social Psychology, 75* (4), 976–988.

Mars, D. (1981). Creativity and urban policy leadership. *Journal of Creative Behavior, 15,* 199–204.

Marsh, H. W. (1986). Global self-esteem: Its relation to specific facets of self-concept and their

importance. *Journal of Personality and Social Psychology, 51,* 1224–1236.

Marshall, G. D., & Zimbardo, P. G. (1979). Affective consequences of inadequately explained physiological arousal. *Journal of Personality and Social Psychology, 37,* 970–988.

Marten, K., & Psarakos, S. (1995). Using self-view television to distinguish between self-examination and social behavior in the bottlenose dolphin (Tursiops truncatus). *Consciousness & Cognition: An International Journal, 4,* 205–225.

Martin, A. J. (1975). *One man, hurt.* New York: Macmillan.

Martin, B. A. (1989). Gender differences in salary expectations. Current salary information is provided. *Psychology of Women Quarterly, 13,* 87–96.

Martin, R. (1996). Minority influence and argument generation. *British Journal of Social Psychology, 35,* 91–103.

Marucha, P. T., Kiecolt-Glaser, J. K., & Favagehi, M. (1998). Mucosal wound healing is impaired by examination stress. *Psychosomatic Medicine, 60,* 362–365.

Marx, M. B., Garrity, T. F., & Bowers, F. R. (1975). The influence of recent life experience on the health of college freshmen. *Journal of Psychosomatic Research, 19,* 87–98.

Maslow, A. H. (1987). *Motivation and personality* (3rd ed.). New York: Harper & Row.

Massey, K., Freeman, S., & Zelditch, M. (1997). Status, power, and accounts. *Social Psychology Quarterly, 60* (3), 238–251.

Mathis, J. O., & Lampe, R. E. (1991). Corporal punishment: A TACD issue. *TACD Journal, 19,* 27–32.

Matlon, R. J., Davis, J. W., Catchings, B. W., & Derr, W. R. (1986). Factors affecting jury decision-making. *Social Action and the Law, 12,* 41–48.

Matsui, T., Kakuyama, T., & UyOnglatco, M. (1987). Effects of goals and feedback on performance in groups. *Journal of Applied Psychology, 72,* 407–415.

Matsui, Y. (1981). A structural analysis of helping. *Japanese Journal of Psychology, 52,* 226–232.

Matsumoto, D. (1990). Cultural similarities and differences in display rules. *Motivation and Emotion, 14,* 195–214.

Matsumoto, D. (1992). American-Japanese cultural differences in the recognition of universal facial expressions. *Journal of Cross-Cultural Psychology, 23,* 72–84.

Matsumoto, D. (1993). Ethnic differences in affect intensity, emotion judgments, display rule attitudes, and self-reported emotional expression in an American sample. *Motivation and Emotion, 17,* 107–123.

Matsumoto, D. (1996). *Unmasking Japan: Myths and realities about the emotions of the Japanese.* Stanford, CA: Stanford University Press.

Matsumoto, D., & Ekman, P. (1989). American-Japanese cultural differences in intensity ratings

of facial expressions of emotion. *Motivation and Emotion, 13,* 80–87.

Matsuo, M. (1994). Effort reduction and task choice as self-handicapping strategies. *Japanese Journal of Experimental Social Psychology, 34,* 10–20.

Matthews, K. A. (1982). Psychological perspectives on the Type A behavior pattern. *Psychological Bulletin, 91,* 293–323.

Maxson, S. C. (1998). Homologoous genes, aggression, and animal models. *Developmental Neuropsychology, 14,* 143–156.

Mayo, C., & LaFrance, M. (1978). On the acquisition of nonverbal communication: A review. *Merrill-Palmer Quarterly, 24,* 213–228.

Maznevski, M. L. (1994). Understanding our differences: Performance in decision-making groups with diverse members. *Human Relations, 47,* 531–552.

Mazzella, R., & Feingold, A. (1994). The effects of physical attractiveness, race, socioeconomic status, and gender of defendants and victims on judgments of mock jurors: A meta-analysis. *Journal of Applied Social Psychology, 24,* 1315–1344.

McArthur, L. A. (1972). The how and what of why: Some determinants and consequences of causal attribution. *Journal of Personality and Social Psychology, 22,* 171–193.

McArthur, L. Z., & Berry, D. S. (1987). Cross-cultural agreement in perceptions of babyfaced adults. *Journal of Cross-Cultural Psychology, 18,* 165–192.

McCann, C. D., Higgins, E. T., & Fondacaro, R. A. (1991). Primacy and recency in communication and self-persuasion: How successive audiences and multiple encodings influence subsequent evaluative judgments. Special Issue: Social cognition and communication: Human judgment in its social context. *Social Cognition, 9,* 47–66.

McCarthy, M. J. (1991, March 18). Marketers zero in on their customers. *Wall Street Journal,* p. B1.

McCaul, K. D., Ployhart, R. E., Hinsz, V. B., & McCaul, H. S. (1995). Appraisals of a consistent versus a similar politician: Voter preferences and intuitive judgments. *Journal of Personality and Social Psychology, 68,* 292–299.

McCaul, K. D., Veltum, L. G., Boyechko, V., & Crawford, J. J. (1990). Understanding attributions of victim blame for rape: Sex, violence, and foreseeability. *Journal of Applied Social Psychology, 20,* 1–26.

McCauley, C. R., & Segal, M. E. (1987). Social psychology of terrorist groups. In C. Hendrick (Ed.), *Group processes and intergroup relations: Review of personality and social psychology* (Vol. 9). Newbury Park, CA: Sage.

McConahay, J. B. (1986). Modern racism, ambivalence and the modern racism scale. In J. F. Dovidio & S. L. Gaertner (Eds.), *Prejudice, discrimination, and racism: Theory and research* (pp. 91–125). Orlando, FL: Academic Press.

McConahay, J. B., Hardee, B. B., & Batts, V. (1981). Has racism declined in America? It depends on who is asking and what is asked. *Journal of Conflict Resolution, 25,* 563–579.

McConnell, A. R., Leibold, J. M., & Sherman, S. J. (1997). Within-target illusory correlations and the formation of context-dependent attitudes. *Journal of Personality & Social Psychology, 73,* 675–686.

McConnell, A. R., Sherman, S. J., & Hamilton, D. L. (1994). Illusory correlation in the perception of groups: An extension of the distinctiveness-based account. *Journal of Personality and Social Psychology, 67,* 414–429.

McDougall, W. (1908). *An introduction to social psychology.* Boston: Luce.

McGarty, C., Turner, J. C., Hogg, M. A., & David, B., et al. (1992). Group polarization as conformity to the prototypical group member. *British Journal of Social Psychology, 31,* 1–19.

McGill, M. E., & Slocum, J. W., Jr. (1998). A little leadership, please? *Organizational Dynamics, 26* (3), 39–49.

McGrath, J. E. (Ed.). (1988). *The social psychology of time: New perspectives.* Newbury Park, CA: Sage.

McGrath, J. E., & Hollingshead, A. B. (1994). *Groups interacting with technology.* Thousand Oaks, CA: Sage.

McGregor, I., Newby-Clark, I. R., & Zanna, M. P. (1999). "Remembering" dissonance: Simultaneous accessibility of inconsistent cognitive elements moderates epistemic discomfort. In E. Harmon-Jones & J. Mills (Eds.), *Cognitive dissonance: Progress on a pivotal theory in social psychology. Science conference series* (pp. 325–353). Washington, DC: American Psychological Association.

McGuire, W. J. (1964). Inducing resistance to persuasion. In L. Berkowitz (Ed.), *Advances in experimental and social psychology* (Vol. 1). New York: Academic Press.

McGuire, W. J. (1985). Attitudes and attitude change. In G. Lindzey & E. Aronson (Eds.), *Handbook of social psychology* (3rd ed., Vol. 2). New York: Random House.

McKean, K. J. (1994). Academic helplessness: Applying learned helplessness theory to undergraduates who give up when faced with academic setbacks. *College Student Journal, 28,* 456–462.

McKelvie, S. J. (1990). The Asch primacy effect: Robust but not infallible. *Journal of Social Behavior and Personality, 5,* 135–150.

McKenna, J. J. (1983). Primate aggression and evolution: An overview of sociobiological and anthropological perspectives. *Bulletin of the American Academy of Psychiatry and the Law, 11,* 105–130.

McKenna, K. Y. A., & Bargh, J. A. (1998). Coming out in the age of the Internet: Identity "demarginalization" through virtual group participation. *Journal of Personality and Social Psychology, 75,* 681–694.

McKillip, J., & Riedel, S. L. (1983). External validity of matching on physical attractiveness for same and opposite sex couples. *Journal of Applied Social Psychology, 13,* 328–337.

McKinlay, J. B. (1975). Who is really ignorant—physician or patient? *Journal of Health and Social Behavior, 16,* 3–11.

McLean, H. M., & Kalin, R. (1994). Congruence between self-image and occupational stereotypes in students entering gender-dominated occupations. *Canadian Journal of Behavioural Science, 26,* 142–162.

McMahon, S. I., & Goatley, V. J. (1995). Fifth graders helping peers discuss texts in student-led groups. *Journal of Educational Research, 89,* 23–34.

McNulty, S. E., & Swann, W. B. (1994). Identity negotiation in roommate relationships: The self as architect and consequence of social reality. *Journal of Personality and Social Psychology, 67,* 1012–1023.

McPhail, P. (1991). *The myth of the madding crowd.* New York: de Gruyther.

McQueen, M. (1991, May 17). Voters' responses to poll disclose huge chasm between social attitudes of blacks and whites. *Wall Street Journal,* p. A16.

Medvec, V. H., & Savitsky, K. (1997). When doing better means feeling worse: The effects of categorical cutoff points on counterfactual thinking and satisfaction. *Journal of Personality and Social Psychology, 72,* 1284–1296.

Meeus, W. H., & Raaijmakers, Q. A. (1995). Obedience in modern society: The Utrecht studies. *Journal of Social Issues, 51,* 155–175.

Mehrabian, A. (1968a). Inference of attitude from the posture orientation and distance of a communicator. *Journal of Consulting and Clinical Psychology, 32,* 296–308.

Mehrabian, A. (1968b). Relationship of attitude to seated posture, orientation, and distance. *Journal of Personality and Social Psychology, 10,* 26–30.

Meleshko, K. G. A., & Alden, L. E. (1993). Anxiety and self-disclosure: Toward a motivational model. *Journal of Personality and Social Psychology, 64,* 1000–1009.

Menec, V. H., & Perry, R. P. (1998). Reactions to stigmas among Canadian students: Testing attribution-affect-help judgment model. *Journal of Social Psychology, 138,* 443–453.

Mentzer, S. J., & Snyder, M. L. (1982). The doctor and the patient: A psychological perspective. In G. S. Sanders & J. Suls (Eds.), *Social psychology of health and illness* (pp. 161–181). Hillsdale, NJ: Erlbaum.

Metee, D. R., & Aronson, E. (1974). Affective reactions to appraisal from others. In T. L. Huston (Ed.), *Foundations of interpersonal attraction* (pp. 235–283). New York: Academic Press.

Metts, S., Cupach, W. R., & Bejlovec, R. A. (1989). "I love you too much to ever start liking you": Redefining romantic relationships. *Journal of Personality and Social Psychology, 37,* 602–607.

Mewborn, C. R., & Rogers, R. W. (1979). Effects of threatening and reassuring components of fear appeals on physiological and verbal measures of emotion and attitudes. *Journal of Experimental Social Psychology, 15,* 242–253.

Meyer, J. P., & Mulherin, A. (1980). From attribution to helping: An analysis of the mediating effects of affect and expectancy. *Journal of Personality and Social Psychology, 39,* 201–210.

Meyer, J. P., & Pepper, S. (1977). Need compatibility and marital adjustment in young married couples. *Journal of Personality and Social Psychology, 35,* 331–342.

Meyer, T. P. (1972). The effects of sexually arousing violent films on aggressive behavior. *Journal of Sex Research, 8,* 324–331.

Meyers, S. A. (1997). Increasing student participation and productivity in small-group activities for psychology classes. *Teaching of Psychology, 24* (2), 105–115.

Michael, M. (1996). *Constructing identities.* Newbury Park, CA: Sage.

Midlarsky, E., Bryan, J. H., & Brickman, P. (1973). Aversive approval: Interactive effects of modeling and reinforcement on altruistic behavior. *Child Development, 44,* 321–328.

Miell, D. E., & Duck, S. W. (1986). Strategies in developing friendship. In V. J. Derlega & B. A. Winstead (Eds.), *Friendship and social interaction.* New York: Springer-Verlag.

Mikulincer, M., & Florian, V. (1996). Emotional reactions to interpersonal losses over the life span: An attachment theoretical perspective. In C. Magai & S. H. McFadden (Eds.), *Handbook of emotion, adult development, and aging.* San Diego, CA: Academic Press.

Milanovich, D. M., Driskell, J. E., Stout, R. J., & Salas, E. (1998). Status and cockpit dynamics: A review and empirical study. *Group Dynamics, 2* (3), 155–167.

Miles, J. A., & Greenberg, J. (1993). Using punishment threats to attenuate social loafing effects among swimmers. *Organizational Behavior & Human Decision Processes, 56,* 246–265.

Milgram, S. (1974). *Obedience to authority.* New York: Harper & Row.

Milgram, S. (1977a, October). Subject reaction: The neglected factor in the ethics of experimentation. *Hastings Center Report,* 19–23.

Milgram, S. (1977b). *The individual in a social world: Essays and experiments.* Reading, MA: Addison-Wesley.

Millar, M. G., & Millar, K. U. (1998). The effects of prior experience and thought on the attitude-behavior relation. *Social Behavior & Personality, 26* (2), 105–114.

Miller, A. G., Collins, B. E., & Brief, D. E. (1995). Perspectives on obedience to authority: The legacy of the Milgram experiments. *Journal of Social Issues, 51,* 1–19.

Miller, A. H. (1998). Neuroendocrine and immune system interactions in stress and depression. *Psychiatric Clinics of North America, 21,* 443–463.

Miller, C. E. (1985). Group decision making under majority and unanimity decision rules. *Social Psychology Quarterly, 48,* 354–363.

Miller, C. E. (1989). The social psychological effects of group decision rules. In P. B. Paulhus (Ed.), *Psychology of group influence.* Hillsdale, NJ: Erlbaum.

Miller, C. E., Jackson, P., Mueller, J., & Schersching, C. (1987). Some social psychological effects of group decision rules. *Journal of Personality and Social Psychology, 52,* 325–332.

Miller, C. T., & Felicio, D. M. (1990). Person positivity bias: Are individuals liked better than groups? *Journal of Experimental Social Psychology, 26,* 408–420.

Miller, D. T., & McFarland, C. (1987). Pluralistic ignorance: When similarity is interpreted as dissimilarity. *Journal of Personality and Social Psychology, 53,* 298–305.

Miller, D. T., & Prentice, D. A. (1994). Collective errors and errors about the collective. Special Issue: The self and the collective. *Personality & Social Psychology Bulletin, 20,* 541–550.

Miller, D. T., & Prentice, D. A. (1996). The construction of social norms and standards. In E. T. Higgins & A. W. Kruglanski (Eds.), *Social psychology: Handbook of basic principles.* New York: Guilford.

Miller, G. R., & Stiff, J. B. (1992). Applied issues in studying deceptive communication. In R. S. Feldman (Ed.), *Applications of nonverbal behavioral theories and research.* Hillsdale, NJ: Erlbaum.

Miller, G. R., & Stiff, J. B. (1992). Applied issues in studying deceptive communication. In R. S. Feldman & B. Rimé (Eds.), *Fundamentals of nonverbal behavior.* Cambridge, England: Cambridge University Press.

Miller, J. G. (1997). Culture and self: Uncovering the cultural grounding of psychological theory. In J. G. Snodgrass & R. L. Thompson (Eds.), The self across psychology: Self-recognition, self-awareness, and the self concept. *Annals of the New York Academy of Sciences,* (Vol. 818, pp. 217–231). New York: New York Academy of Sciences.

Miller, J. G., & Bersoff, D. M. (1994). Cultural influences on the moral status of reciprocity and the discounting of endogenous motivation. Special Issue: The self and the collective. *Personality and Social Psychology Bulletin, 20,* 592–602.

Miller, L. C. (1990). Intimacy and liking: Mutual influence and the role of unique relationships. *Journal of Personality and Social Psychology, 59,* 50–60.

Miller, L. C., & Kenny, D. A. (1986). Reciprocity of self-disclosure at the individual and dyadic levels: A social relationship analysis. *Journal of Personality and Social Psychology, 50,* 713–719.

Miller, N., & Brewer, M. B. (1984). *Groups in contact: The psychology of desegregation.* New York: Academic Press.

Miller, R. L. (1995). Assisting gay men to maintain safer sex: An evaluation of an AIDS service organization's safer sex maintenance program. *AIDS Education & Prevention, 7,* 48–63.

Miller, T. Q., Smith, T. W., Turner, C. W., Guijarro, M. L., & Hallet, A. J. (1996). A meta-analytic review of research on hostility and physical health. *Psychological Bulletin, 119,* 322–348.

Mills, P. J., & Dimsdale, J. E. (1993). Anger suppression: Its relationship to b-adrenergic receptor sensitivity and stress-induced changes in blood pressure. *Psychological Medicine, 23,* 673–678.

Mineka, S., & Henderson, R. W. (1985). Controllability and predictability in acquired motivation. *Annual Review of Psychology, 36,* 495–529.

Miner, J. B. (1992). *Industrial-organizational psychology.* New York: McGraw-Hill.

Mishra, A. K., & Spreitzer, G. M. (1998). Explaining how survivors respond to downsizing: The roles of trust, empowerment, justice, and work redesign. *Academy of Management Review, 23,* 567–588.

Misumi, J. (1995). The development in Japan of the Performance-Maintenance (PM) Theory of Leadership. Special Issue: Gender stereotyping, sexual harassment, and the law. *Journal of Social Issues, 51,* 213–228.

Mitchell, J., & Dodder, R. A. (1983). Types of neutralization and types of delinquency. *Journal of Youth and Adolescence, 12,* 307–318.

Mitchell, P. (1997, February 28). Opposites connect. *Daily Hampshire Gazette, Hampshire Life,* p. 11.

Mitchell, T. R. (1982). *People in organizations: An introduction to organizational behavior* (2nd ed.). New York: McGraw-Hill.

Mitra, A. (1995). Price cue utilization in produce evaluations: The moderating role of motivation and attribute information. Special Issue: Pricing strategy and the marketing mix. *Journal of Business Research, 33,* 187–195.

Mizruchi, M. S., & Potts, B. B. (1998). Centrality and power revisited: Actor success in group decision making. *Social Networks, 20* (4), 353–387.

Moffat, M. (1989). *Coming of age in New Jersey.* New Brunswick, NJ: Rutgers University Press.

Moghaddam, F. M., Taylor, D. M., & Wright, S. C. (1993). *Social psychology in cross-cultural perspective.* New York: Freeman.

Mok, T. A. (1998). Getting the message: Media images and stereotypes and their effect on Asian Americans. *Cultural Diversity & Ethnic Minority Psychology, 4,* 185–202.

Molitor, F., & Hirsch, K. W. (1994). Children's toleration of real-life aggression after exposure to media violence: A replication of the Drabman and Thomas studies. *Child Study Journal, 24,* 191–207.

Molm, L. D. (1988). The structure and use of power: A comparison of reward and punishment power. *Social Psychology Quarterly, 51,* 108–122.

Molm, L. D. (1997). Risk and power use: Constraints on the use of coercion in exchange. *American Sociological Review, 62* (1), 113–133.

Monahan, J., & Loftus, E. F. (1982). The psychology of law. *Annual Reviews, 33,* 441–475.

Mone, M. A., Baker, D. D., & Jeffries, F. (1995). Predictive validity and time dependency of self-efficacy, self-esteem, personal goals, and academic performance. *Educational & Psychological Measurement, 55,* 716–727.

Mongeau, P. A., & Garlick, R. (1988). Social comparison and persuasive arguments as determinants of group polarization. *Communication Research Reports, 5,* 120–125.

Moore, D. S., & Erickson, P. O. (1985). Age, gender, and ethnic differences in sexual and contraceptive knowledge, attitude, and behavior. *Family and Community Health, 8,* 38–51.

Moore, J. C., & Brylinski, J. (1995). Facility familiarity and the home advantage. *Journal of Sport Behavior, 18,* 302–310.

Moorhead, G., Ference, R., & Neck, C. P. (1991). Group decision fiascoes continue: Space shuttle Challenger and a revised groupthink framework. *Human Relations, 44,* 539–550.

Moorhead, G., Neck, C. P., & West, M. S. (1998). The tendency toward defective decision making within self-managing teams: The relevance of groupthink for the 21st century. *Organizational Behavior & Human Decision Processes, 73* (2–3), 327–351.

Moran, G., & Comfort, J. C. (1986). Neither "tentative" nor "fragmentary": Verdict preference of impaneled felony jurors as a function of attitude toward capital punishment. *Journal of Applied Psychology, 71,* 146–155.

Moran, G., & Cutler, B. L. (1991). The prejudicial impact of pretrial publicity. *Journal of Applied Social Psychology, 21,* 345–367.

Moreland, R. L., & Beach, S. R. (1992). Exposure effects in the classroom: The development of affinity among students. *Journal of Experimental Social Psychology, 28,* 255–276.

Moreland, R. L., & Levine, J. M. (1982). Socialization in small groups: Temporal changes in individual-group relations. In L. Berkowitz (Ed.), *Advances in experimental social psychology* (Vol. 15). New York: Academic Press.

Moreland, R. L., & Levine, J. M. (1988). Group dynamics over time: Development and socialization in small groups. In J. E. McGrath (Ed.), *The social psychology of time: New perspectives.* Newbury Park, CA: Sage.

Moreland, R. L., & Levine, J. M. (1989). Newcomers and oldtimers in small groups. In P. B. Paulhus (Ed.), *Psychology of group influence* (2nd ed.). Hillsdale, NJ: Erlbaum.

Morell, V. (1993, June 18). Evidence found for a possible 'aggression gene' [news; published erratum appears in *Science* 1993 Oct 15;262(5132):321]. *Science, 260,* 1722–1723.

Moretti, M. M., & Higgins, E. T. (1990). Relating self-discrepancy to self-esteem: The contribution of discrepancy beyond actual-self ratings. *Journal of Experimental and Social Psychology, 26,* 108–123.

Morgan, M. (1983). Symbolic victimization and real world fear. *Human Communication Research, 9,* 146–157.

Morris, G. H., & Chenail, R. J. (1995). *The talk of the clinic.* Hillsdale, NJ: Erlbaum.

Morris, J. D., Roberts, M. S., & Baker, G. F. (1999). Emotional responses of African American voters to ad messages. In L. L. Kaid & D. G. Bystrom (Eds.), *The electronic election: Perspectives on the 1996 campaign communication* (pp. 257–274). Mahwah, NJ: Erlbaum.

Morris, M. W., & Peng, K. (1994). Culture and cause: American and Chinese attributions for social and physical events. *Journal of Personality and Social Psychology, 67,* 949–971.

Morris, W. N., Bois, J. L., Pearson, J. A., Rountree, C. A., Samaha, G. M., Wachtler, J., & Wright, S. L. (1976). Collective coping with stress: Group reactions to fear, anxiety, and ambiguity. *Journal of Personality and Social Psychology, 33,* 674–679.

Morrow, G. D., Clark, E. M., & Brock, K. F. (1995). Individual and partner love styles: Implications for the quality of romantic involvements. *Journal of Social & Personal Relationships, 12,* 363–387.

Morrow, G. D., & O'Sullivan, C. (1998). Romantic ideals as comparison levels: Implications for satisfaction and commitment in romantic involvements. In V. C. de Munck (Ed.), *Romantic love and sexual behavior: Perspectives from the social sciences.* Westport, CT: Praeger.

Morton, T. L. (1978). Intimacy and reciprocity of exchange: A comparison of spouses and strangers. *Journal of Personality and Social Psychology, 36,* 72–81.

Moscovici, S., & Faucheaux, C. (1972). Social influence, conformity bias, and the study of active minorities. In L. Berkowitz (Ed.), *Advances in experimental social psychology* (Vol. 6). New York: Academic Press.

Moscovici, S., Lage, E., & Naffrechoux, M. (1969). Influence of a consistent minority on the responses of a majority in a color perception task. *Sociometry, 32,* 365–380.

Moscovici, S., & Mugny, G. (1983). Minority influence. II: Minority influence. In C. Nemeth (Ed.), *Social psychology: Classic and contemporary integrations.* Chicago: Rand McNally.

Mosher, D. L., & Anderson, R. D. (1986). Macho personality, sexual aggression, and reactions to guided imagery of realistic rape. *Journal of Research in Personality, 20,* 77–94.

Moskowitz, G. B. (1993). Individual differences in social categorization: The influence of personal need for structure on spontaneous trait inferences. *Journal of Personality and Social Psychology, 65,* 132–142.

Moss, M. K., & Page, R. A. (1972). Reinforcement and helping behavior. *Journal of Applied Social Psychology, 2,* 360–371.

Mroczek, D. K., & Kolarz, C. M. (1998). The effect of age on positive and negative affect: A developmental perspective on happiness. *Journal of Personality & Social Psychology, 75,* 1333–1349.

Mucchi-Faina, A. (1994). Minority influence: The effects of social status of an inclusive versus exclusive group. *European Journal of Social Psychology, 24,* 679–692.

Mudrack, P. E., & Farrell, G. M. (1994). The need for dominance scale of the Manifest Needs Questionnaire and role behaviour in groups. *Applied Psychology: An International Review, 43,* 399–413.

Muehlenhard, C. L., & Hollabaugh, L. C. (1988). Do women sometimes say no when they mean yes? The prevalence and correlates of women's token resistance to sex. *Journal of Personality and Social Psychology, 54,* 872–879.

Mugny, G., & Perez, J. A. (1991). *The social psychology of minority influence.* Hillsdale, NJ: Erlbaum.

Mullen, B. (1986). Strength and immediacy of sources: A meta-analytic evaluation of the forgotten elements of social impact theory. *Journal of Personality and Social Psychology, 48,* 1458–1466.

Mullen, B., Anthony, T., Salas, E., & Driskell, J. E. (1994). Group cohesiveness and quality of decision making: An integration of tests of the groupthink hypothesis. Special Issue: Social cognition in small groups. *Small Group Research, 25,* 267–283.

Mullen, B., Brown, R., & Smith, C. (1992). Ingroup bias as a function of salience, relevance, and status: An integration. *European Journal of Social Psychology, 22,* 103–122.

Mullen, B., & Copper, C. (1994). The relation between group cohesiveness and performance: An integration. *Psychological Bulletin, 115,* 210–227.

Mullen, B., & Johnson, C. (1995). Cognitive representation in ethnophaulisms and illusory correlation in stereotyping. *Personality & Social Psychology Bulletin, 21,* 420–433.

Mullen, B., Johnson, C., & Anthony, T. (1994). Relative group size and cognitive representations of ingroup and outgroup: The phenomenology of being in a group. Special Issues: Social cognition in small groups. *Small Group Research, 25,* 250–266.

Mullen, B., Johnson, C., & Salas, E. (1991). Productivity loss in brainstorming groups: A meta-analytic integration. *Basic and Applied Social Psychology, 12,* 3–23.

Muller, R. T., Hunter, J. E., & Stollak, G. (1995). The intergenerational transmission of corporal punishment: A comparison of social learning and temperament models. *Child Abuse & Neglect, 19,* 1323–1335.

Mullin, C. R., & Linz, D. (1995). Desensitization and resensitization to violence against women: Effects of exposure to sexually violent films on judgments of domestic violence victims. *Journal of Personality and Social Psychology, 69,* 449–459.

Mummendey, A., Kessler, T., Klink, A., & Mielke, R. (1999). Strategies to cope with negative social identity: Predictions by social identity theory and relative deprivation theory. *Journal of Personality & Social Psychology, 76,* 229–245.

Murdaugh, C. L. (1998). Problems with adherence in the elderly. In S. A. Shumaker & E. B. Schron (Eds.), *The handbook of health behavior change* (2nd ed.). New York: Springer.

Murphy, P. L., & Miller, C. T. (1997). Postdecisional dissonance and the commodified self-concept: A cross-cultural examination. *Personality & Social Psychology Bulletin, 23* (1), 50–62.

Murphy, S. A., Beaton, R. D., Cain, K., & Pike, K. (1994). Gender differences in fire fighter job stressors and symptoms of stress. *Women & Health, 22,* 55–69.

Murray, S. L., & Holmes, J. G. (1997). A leap of faith? Positive illusions in romantic relationships. *Personality & Social Psychology Bulletin, 23,* 586–604.

Murray, S. L., Holmes, J. G., & Griffin, D. W. (1996). The benefits of positive illusions: Idealization and the construction of satisfaction in close relationships. *Journal of Personality and Social Psychology, 70,* 79–98.

Murstein, B. I. (1976). *Who will marry whom? Theories and research in marital choice.* New York: Springer.

Murstein, B. I. (1986). *Paths to marriage.* Beverly Hills, CA: Sage.

Murstein, B. I. (1987). A clarification and extension of the SVR theory of dyadic pairing. *Journal of Marriage and the Family, 49,* 929–933.

Myers, D. G. (1982). Polarizing effects of social interaction. In H. Brandstatter, J. H. Davis, & G. Stocker-Kreichgauer (Eds.), *Group decision making.* New York: Academic Press.

Myers, D. G., & Diener, E. (1996, May). The pursuit of happiness. *Scientific American,* pp. 70–72.

Myers, D. G., & Lamm, H. (1976). The group polarization phenomenon. *Psychological Bulletin, 83,* 602–627.

Nagao, D. H., & McClain, L. (1983, May). *The effects of judge's instructions concerning reasonable doubt on mock juror's verdicts.* Paper presented at the annual meeting of the Midwestern Psychological Association, Chicago, Illinois.

Nagata, Y. (1980). Status as a determinant of conformity to and deviation from the group norm. *Japanese Journal of Psychology, 51,* 152–159.

Nagel, J. (1995). Resource competition theories. *American Behavioral Scientist, 38,* 442–458.

Nail, P. R. (1986). Toward an integration of some models and theories of social response. *Psychological Bulletin, 100,* 190–206.

Narby, D. J., Cutler, B. L., & Moran, G. (1993). A meta-analysis of the association between authoritarianism and jurors' perceptions of defendant culpability. *Journal of Applied Psychology, 78,* 34–42.

Nasby, W. (1996). Private and public self-consciousness and articulation of the ought self from private and public vantages. *Journal of Personality, 64,* 131–156.

Nass, G. D. (1978). *Marriage and the family.* Reading, MA: Addison-Wesley.

Natarajan, V. (1979). Defensive avoidance hypothesis in ear arousal research. *Indian Journal of Clinical Psychology, 6,* 21–26.

Nathawat, S. S., & Joshi, U. (1997). The effect of hardiness and Type A behavior pattern on the perception of life events and their relationship to psychological well-being. *Indian Journal of Clinical Psychology, 24,* 52–57.

National Institute of Mental Health (NIMH). (1993). *Application for intramural support.* Bethesda, MD: National Institute of Mental Health.

Neck, C. P., & Manz, C. C. (1994). From groupthink to teamthink: Toward the creation of constructive thought patterns in self-managing work teams. *Human Relations, 47,* 929–952.

Neely, K. (1990, October 4). Judas Priest gets off the hook. *Rolling Stone, 588,* p. 39.

Neimeyer, R. A., & Mitchell, K. A. (1988). Similarity and attraction: A longitudinal study. *Journal of Social and Personal Relationships, 5,* 131–148.

Nemeth, C. (1986). Differential contributions of majority and minority influence. *Psychological Review, 93,* 1–10.

Nemeth, C. J. (1995). Dissent as driving cognition, attitudes, and judgments. *Social Cognition, 13,* 273–291.

Nemeth, C., & Kwan, J. L. (1985). Originality of word associations as a function of majority vs. minority influence. *Social Psychology Quarterly, 48,* 277–282.

Nemeth, C., Mayseless, O., Sherman, J., & Brown, Y. (1990). Exposure to dissent and recall of information. *Journal of Personality and Social Psychology, 58,* 429–437.

Neto, F. (1995). Conformity and independence revisited. *Social Behavior and Personality, 23,* 217–222.

Neubauer, A. C., & Malle, B. F. (1997). Questionnaire response latencies: Implications for personality assessment and self-schema theory. *European Journal of Psychological Assessment, 13,* 109–117.

Neuberg, S. L. (1989). The goal of forming accurate impressions during social interactions: Attenuating the impact of negative expectancies. *Journal of Personality and Social Psychology 56,* 374–386.

Neuberg, S. L., Cialdini, R. B., Brown, S. L., & Luce, C., et al. (1997). Does empathy lead to anything more than superficial helping? Comment on Batson et al. (1997). *Journal of Personality & Social Psychology, 73,* 510–516.

Newcomb, T. M. (1961). *The acquaintance process.* New York: Holt, Rinehart & Winston.

Newcomb, T. M., Koenig, K. E., Flacks, R., & Warwick, D. P. (1967). *Persistence and change: Bennington College and its students after 25 years.* New York: Wiley.

Ng, S. H., & Bradac, J. J. (1993). *Power in language.* Thousand Oaks, CA: Sage.

Nicholson, W. D., & Long, B. C. (1990). Self-esteem, social support, internalized homophobia, and coping strategies of HIV+ gay men. *Journal of Consulting and Clinical Psychology, 58,* 873–876.

Niedenthal, P. M., & Cantor, N. (1986). Affective responses as guides to category-based inferences. *Motivation and Emotion, 10,* 217–232.

Niedenthal, P. M., Setterlund, M. B., & Wherry, M. B. (1992). Possible self-complexity and affective reactions to goal-relevant evaluation. *Journal of Personality and Social Psychology, 63,* 5–16.

Niemann, Y. F., Jennings, L., Rozelle, R. M., Baxter, J. C., & Suillivan, E. (1994). Use of free responses and cluster analysis to determine stereotypes of eight groups. *Personality and Social Psychology Bulletin, 20,* 379–390.

Nijstad, B. A., Stroebe, W., & Lodewijkx, H. F. M. (1999). Persistence of brainstorming groups: How do people know when to stop? *Journal of Experimental Social Psychology, 35* (2), 165–185.

Nisbett, R. E. (1993). Violence and U.S. regional culture. *American Psychologist, 48,* 441–449.

Nisbett, R. E., & Cohen, D. (1996). *Culture of honor: The psychology of violence in the South.* Boulder, CO: Westview Press.

Nisbett, R. E., & Ross, L. (1980). *Human inference: Strategies and shortcomings of social judgment.* Englewood Cliffs, NJ: Prentice-Hall.

Nock, S. L. (1995). A comparison of marriages and cohabiting relationships. *Journal of Family Issues, 16,* 53–76.

Noller, P. (1992). Nonverbal communication in marriage. In R. S. Feldman (Ed.), *Applications of nonverbal behavioral theories and research.* Hillsdale, NJ: Erlbaum.

Noller, P., & Feeney, J. A. (1998). Communication in early marriage: Responses to conflict, nonverbal accuracy, and conversational patterns. In T. N. Bradbury (Ed.), *The developmental course of marital dysfunction.* New York: Cambridge University Press.

Noller, P., Feeney, J. A., & Ward, C. M. (1997). Determinants of marital quality: A partial test of Lewis and Spanier's model. *Journal of Family Studies, 3,* 226–251.

Norem, J. K. (1998). Why should we lower our defenses about defense mechanisms? *Journal of Personality, 66,* 895–917.

Norman, P., Collins, S., Conner, M., & Martin, R. (1995). Attributions, cognitions, and coping styles: Teleworkers' reactions to work-related problems. *Journal of Applied Social Psychology, 25,* 117–128.

Northrop, C. E. (1990, February). How Good Samaritan laws do and don't protect you. *Nursing, 20* (2), 50–51.

Nowak, M. A., May, R. M., & Sigmund, K. (1995, June). The arithmetics of mutual help. *Scientific American,* pp. 76–81.

NUMMI (New United Motor Manufacturing, Inc.). (1999). Corporate Web site. Available: *http://www.nummi.com*

Nurmi, J. (1993). Self-handicapping and a failure-trap strategy: A cognitive approach to problem behavior and delinquency. *Psychiatria Fennica, 24,* 75–85.

Nye, J. L., & Brower, A. M. (1996). *What's social about social cognition?: Social cognition in small groups.* New York: Sage.

Nyklicek, I., Vingerhoets, A. J., Van Heck, G. L., & Van Limpt, M. C. A. M. (1998). Defensive coping in relation to causal blood pressure and self-reported daily hassles and life events. *Journal of Behavioral Medicine, 21,* 145–161.

Oakes, P., Haslam, S. A., & Turner, J. C. (1998). The role of prototypicality in group influence and cohesion: Contextual variation in the graded structure of social categories. In S. Worchel, J. F. Morales, D. Paez, & J. Deschamps (Eds.), *Social identity: International perspectives* (pp. 75–92). London, England: Sage.

Ofosu, H. B., Lafreniere, K. D., & Senn, C. Y. (1998). Body image perception among women of African descent: A normative context? *Feminism & Psychology, 8,* 303–323.

Ogloff, J. R. P., & Vidmar, N. (1994). The impact of pretrial publicity on jurors: A study to compare the relative effects of televion and print media in a child sex abuse case. *Law and Human Behavior, 18,* 507–525.

O'Keefe, D. J., & Figge, M. (1997). A guilt-based explanation of the door-in-the-face influence strategy. *Human Communication Research, 24* (1), 64–81.

Oliner, S. P., & Oliner, P. M. (1988). *The altruistic personality: Rescuers of Jews in Nazi Europe.* New York: Free Press.

Oliver, M. B. (1994). Portrayals of crime, race, and aggression in "reality-based" police shows: A content analysis. *Journal of Broadcasting & Electronic Media, 38,* 179–192.

Oliver, M. B., & Hyde, J. S. (1993). Gender differences in sexuality: A meta-analysis. *Psychological Bulletin, 114,* 29–51.

Olsen-Fulero, L., & Fulero, S. M. (1997). Commonsense rape judgments: An empathy-complexity theory of rape juror story making. *Psychology, Public Policy, & Law, 3* (2–3), 402–427.

Olson, D. A., & Shultz, K. S. (1994). Gender differences in the dimensionality of social support. *Journal of Applied Social Psychology, 24,* 1221–1232.

Olson, J. M., Herman, C. P., & Zanna, M. P. (Eds.). (1986). *Relative deprivation and social comparison: The Ontario Symposium* (Vol. 4). Hillsdale, NJ: Erlbaum.

Olson, J. M., & Ross, M. (1988). False feedback about placebo effectiveness: Consequences for the misattribution of speech anxiety. *Journal of Experimental Social Psychology, 24,* 275–281.

O'Neal, M. R., & Chissom, B. S. (1994). Comparison of three methods for assessing attitudes. *Perceptual and Motor Skills, 78,* 1251–1258.

Ono, K. O. (1998). Communicating prejudice in the media: Upending racial categories in doubles.

In M. L. Hecht (Ed.), *Communicating prejudice.* Thousand Oaks, CA: Sage.

Orbach, I., Singer, R. N., & Murphey, M. (1997). Changing attributions with an attribution training technique related to basketball dribbling. *Sport Psychologist, 11,* 294–304.

Orne, M. T., & Holland, C. C. (1968). On the ecological validity of laboratory deceptions. *International Journal of Psychiatry, 6,* 282–293.

Orpen, C. (1995). Self-efficacy beliefs and job performance among Black managers in South Africa. *Psychological Reports, 76,* 649–650.

Orpen, C. (1996). The effects of ingratiation and self-promotion tactics on employee career success. *Social Behavior & Personality, 24,* 213–214.

Orth-Gomer, K., Chesney, M. A., & Wenger, N. K. (Eds.). (1996). *Women, stress, and heart disease.* Mahwah, NJ: Erlbaum.

Orth-Gomer, K., & Schneiderman, N. (1995). *Behavioral medicine approaches to cardiovascular disease prevention.* Hillsdale, NJ: Erlbaum.

Orth-Gomer, K., & Schneiderman, N. (Eds.). (1996). *Behavioral medicine approaches to cardiovascular disease prevention.* Mahwah, NJ: Erlbaum.

Orvis, B. R., Cunningham, J. D., & Kelley, H. H. (1975). A closer examination of causal inference: The role of consensus, distinctiveness and consistency information. *Journal of Personality and Social Psychology, 32,* 605–616.

Osberg, T. M., & Shrauger, J. S. (1986). Retrospective versus prospective causal judgments of self and others' behavior. *Journal of Social Psychology, 126,* 169–178.

Osborn, A. F. (1957). *Applied imagination.* New York: Scribners.

Osborne, J. W. (1995). Academics, self-esteem, and race: A look at the underlying assumptions of the disidentification hypothesis. *Personality and Social Psychology Bulletin, 21,* 449–455.

Osgood, C. E., Suci, G. J., & Tannenbaum, P. H. (1957). *The measurement of meaning.* Urbana: University of Illinois Press.

Oskamp, S. (1977). *Attitudes and opinions.* Englewood Cliffs, NJ: Prentice-Hall.

Ostrom, T. M., Carpenter, S. L., Sedikdes, C., & Li, F. (1993). Differential processing of in-group and out-group information. *Journal of Personality and Social Psychology, 64,* 21–34.

O'Sullivan, L. F. (1995). Less is more: The effects of sexual experience on judgments of men's and women's personality characteristics and relationship desirability. *Sex Roles, 33,* 159–181.

Ouchi, W. G. (1981). *Theory Z: How American business can meet the Japanese challenge.* Reading, MA: Addison-Wesley.

Oyserman, D. (1993). The lens of personhood: Viewing the self and others in a multicultural society. *Journal of Personality and Social Psychology, 65,* 993–1009.

Oyserman, D., Gant, L., & Ager, J. (1995). A socially contextualized model of African-American identity: Possible selves and school persistence.

Journal of Personality & Social Psychology, 69, 1216–1232.

Oyserman, D., & Markus, H. R. (1998). Self as social representation. In U. Flick (Ed.), *The psychology of the social.* New York: Cambridge University Press.

Pace, T. M. (1988). Schema theory: A framework for research and practice in psychotherapy. *Journal of Cognitive Psychotherapy, 2,* 147–163.

Paglia, A., & Schuller, R. A. (1998). Jurors' use of hearsay evidence: The effects of type and timing of instructions. *Law & Human Behavior, 22* (5), 501–518.

Paik, H., & Comstock, G. (1994). The effects of television violence on antisocial behavior: A meta-analysis. *Communication Research, 21,* 516–546.

Pajares, F., & Miller, M. D. (1995). Mathematics self-efficacy and mathematics performances: The need for specificity of assessment. *Journal of Counseling Psychology, 42,* 190–198.

Palestis, B. G., & Burger, J. (1998). Evidence for social facilitation of preening in the common tern. *Animal Behaviour, 56* (5), 1107–1111.

Palinkas, L. A., & Browner, D. (1995). Effects of prolonged isolation in extreme environments on stress, coping, and depression. *Journal of Applied Social Psychology, 25,* 557–576.

Palmero, F., Codina, V., & Rosel, J. (1993). Psychophysiological activation, reactivity, and recovery in Type A and Type B scorers when in a stressful laboratory situation. *Psychological Reports, 73,* 803–811.

Papsdorf, M., & Alden, L. (1998). Mediators of social rejection in social anxiety: Similarity, self-disclosure, and overt signs of anxiety. *Journal of Research in Personality, 32,* 351–369.

Parfitt, G., Hardy, L., & Pates, J. (1995). Somatic anxiety and physiological arousal: Their effects upon a high anaerobic, low memory demand task. *International Journal of Sport Psychology, 26,* 196–213.

Paris, J. (1994). Evolutionary social science and transcultural psychiatry. *Transcultural Psychiatric Research Review, 31,* 339–367.

Parker, B. L., & Drummond-Reeves, S. J. (1993). The death of a dyad: Relational autopsy, analysis, and aftermath. *Journal of Divorce and Remarriage, 21,* 95–119.

Parker, G. (1994). Depression research: Now and the future. *Mental Health in Australia, 6,* 41–45.

Parker, S. T. (1996). Apprenticeship in tool-mediated extractive foraging: The origins of imitation, teaching, and self-awareness in great apes. In A. E. Russon & K. A. Bard (Eds.), *Reaching into thought: The minds of the great apes.* Cambridge, England: Cambridge University Press.

Parker, S., Nichter, M., Nichter, M., & Vuckovic, N. (1995). Body image and weight concerns among African American and White adolescent females: Differences that make a difference. *Human Organization, 54,* 103–114.

Parks, C. D., & Sanna, L. J. (1999). *Group performance and interaction.* Boulder, CO: Westview Press.

Parlee, M. B. (1979, October). The friendship bond. *Psychology Today, 13,* pp. 43–45.

Parrott, R. (1994). Exploring family practitioners' and patients' information exchange about prescribed medications: Implications for practitioners' interviewing and patients' understanding. Special Issue: Communicating with patients about their medications. *Health Communication, 6,* 267–280.

Patch, M. E., Hoang, V. R., & Stahelski, A. J. (1997). The use of metacommunication in compliance: Door-in-the-face and single-request strategies. *Journal of Social Psychology, 137* (1), 88–94.

Patterson, A. H. (1986). Scientific jury selection: The need for a case specific approach. *Social Action and the Law, 11,* 105–109.

Patterson, C. J. (1992). Children of lesbian and gay parents. *Child Development, 63,* 1025–1042.

Patterson, C. J. (1994). Lesbians and gay families. *Current Directions in Psychological Science, 3,* 62–64.

Paulus, P. B. (1998). Developing consensus about groupthink after all these years. *Organizational Behavior & Human Decision Processes, 73* (2–3), 362–374.

Paulus, P. B., Dzindolet, M. T., Poletes, G., & Camacho, L. M. (1993). Perception of performance in group brainstorming: The illusion of group productivity. *Personality and Social Psychology Bulletin, 19,* 78–89.

Paulus, P. B., Larey, T. S., & Ortega, A. H. (1995). Performance and perceptions of brainstormer in an organizational setting. *Basic and Applied Social Psychology, 17,* 249–265.

Paulus, P. B., & McCain, G. (1983). Crowding in jails. *Basic and Applied Social Psychology, 4,* 89–107.

Paulus, P. B., McCain, G., & Cox, V. C. (1978). Death rates, psychiatric commitments, blood pressure, and perceived crowding as a function of institutional crowding. *Environmental Psychology and Nonverbal Behavior, 3,* 107–116.

Pavlov, I. (1927). *Conditioned reflexes.* Oxford: Oxford University Press.

Peck, C. L., & King, N. J. (1982). Increasing patient compliance with prescriptions. *Journal of the American Medical Association, 248,* 2874–2877.

Pelham, B. W., & Swann, W. B., Jr. (1989). From self-conceptions to self-worth: The sources and structure of self-esteem. *Journal of Personality and Social Psychology, 57,* 672–680.

Pendleton, M. G., & Batson, C. D. (1979). Self-presentation and the door-in-the-face technique for inducing compliance. *Personality and Social Psychology Bulletin, 5,* 77–81.

Pennebaker, J. W. (1990). *Opening up; The healing power of confiding in others.* New York: Morrow.

Pennebaker, J. W. (1993). Putting stress into words: Health, linguistic, and therapeutic implications.

American Psychological Association (1992, Washington, DC). *Behaviour Research & Therapy, 31*, 539–548.

Pennebaker, J. W. (1998). Conflict and canned meat. *Psychological Inquiry, 9*, 219–220.

Pennebaker, J. W., & Beall, S. (1986). Confronting a traumatic event: Toward an understanding of inhibition and disease. *Journal of Abnormal Psychology, 95*, 274–281.

Pennebaker, J. W., Rimé, B., & Blankenship, V. E. (1996). Stereotypes of emotional expressiveness of northerners and southerners: A cross-cultural test of Montesquieu's hypotheses. *Journal of Personality and Social Psychology, 70*, 372–380.

Pennington, N., & Hastie, R. (1990). Practical implications of psychological research on juror and jury decision making. *Personality and Social Psychology Bulletin, 16*, 90–105.

Pennington, N., & Hastie, R. (1992). Explaining the evidence: Tests of the story model for juror decision making. *Journal of Personality and Social Psychology, 62*, 189–206.

Pennington, N., & Hastie, R. (1993). Reasoning in explanation-based decision making. Special Issue: Reasoning and decision making. *Cognition, 49*, 123–163.

Penrod, S., & Cutler, B. (1995). Witness confidence and witness accuracy: Assessing their forensic relation. Special Issue: Witness memory and law. *Psychology, Public Policy, & Law, 1*, 817–845.

Penrod, S. D., & Heuer, L. (1997). Tweaking commonsense: Assessing aids to jury decision making. *Psychology, Public Policy, & Law, 3*, 259–284.

Pentony, J. F. (1998). Effects of negative campaigning on vote, semantic differential, and thought listing. *Journal of Applied Social Psychology, 28* (23), 2131–2149.

Peplau, L. A., & Cochran, S. D. (1990). A relationship perspective on homosexuality. In D. P. McWhirter, S. A. Sanders, & J. M. Reinisch (Eds.), *Homosexuality / heterosexuality: The Kinsey scale and current research*. New York: Oxford University Press.

Peplau, L. A., Micelli, M., & Morasch, B. (1982). Loneliness and self-evaluation. In L. A. Peplau & D. Perlman (Eds.), *Loneliness: A sourcebook of current theory, research, and therapy*. New York: Wiley.

Peplau, L. A., Padesky, C., & Hamilton, M. (1982). Satisfaction in lesbian relationships. *Journal of Homosexuality, 8*, 23–25.

Peplau, L. A., & Perlman, D. (Eds.). (1982). *Loneliness: A sourcebook of current theory, research and therapy*. New York: Wiley.

Perez-Pena, R. (1996, June 11). Police offer knew sketch in park attack. *New York Times*, p. B3.

Perloff, R. M. (1993). *The dynamics of persuasion*. Hillsdale, NJ: Erlbaum.

Perrett, D. I., Lee, K. J., Penton-Voak, I., Rowland, D., Yoshikawa, S., Burt, D. M., Henzi, S. P., Castles, D. L., & Akamatsu, S. (1998, August 27). Effects of sexual dimorphism on facial attractiveness. *Nature, 394*, pp. 884–887.

Peter, J. P., & Olson, J. C. (1987). *Consumer behavior: Marketing strategy perspectives*. Homewood, IL: Irwin.

Peters, L. H., Hartke, D. D., & Pohlmann, J. T. (1985). Fiedler's contingency theory of leadership: An application of the meta-analysis procedures of Schmidt and Hunter. *Psychological Bulletin, 97*, 274–285.

Peterson, C., & Barrett, L. C. (1987). Explanatory style and academic performance among university freshmen. *Journal of Personality and Social Psychology, 53*, 603–607.

Peterson, B. E., Doty, R. M., & Winter, D. G. (1993). Authoritarianism and attidues toward contemporary social issues. *Personality and Social Psychology Bulletin, 19*, 174–184.

Peterson, R. S. (1999). Can you have too much of a good thing? The limits of voice for improving satisfaction with leaders. *Personality & Social Psychology Bulletin, 25* (3), 313–324.

Peterson, R. S., & Nemeth, C. J. (1996). Focus versus flexibility: Majority and minority influence can both improve performance. *Personality and Social Psychology Bulletin, 22*, 14–23.

Petrie, K. J., Booth, R. J., & Pennebaker, J. W. (1998). The immunological effects of thought suppression. *Journal of Personality & Social Psychology, 75*, 1264–1272.

Petrie, K. J., Booth, R. J., Pennebaker, J. W., & Davison, K. P. (1995). Disclosure of trauma and immune response to a hepatitus B vaccination program. *Journal of Consulting and Clinical Psychology, 63*, 787–792.

Pettigrew, T. F. (1979). The ultimate attribution error: Extending Allport's cognitive analysis of prejudice. *Personality and Social Psychology Bulletin, 5*, 461–476.

Pettigrew, T. F. (1989). The nature of modern racism in the United States. *Revue Internationale de Psychologie Sociale, 2*, 291–303.

Pettigrew, T. F. (1997). Generalized intergroup contact effects on prejudice. *Personality & Social Psychology Bulletin, 23*, 173–185.

Pettijohn, T. F. (Ed.). (1998). *Sources: Notable selections in social psychology* (2nd ed.). Guilford, CT: Dushkin/McGraw-Hill.

Pettingale, K. W., Morris, T., Greer, S., & Haybittle, J. L. (1985). Mental attitudes to cancer: An additional prognostic factor. *Lancet*, p. 750.

Petty, R., Harkins, S., & Williams, K. (1980). The effects of diffusion of cognitive effort on attitudes: An information processing view. *Journal of Personality and Social Psychology, 38*, 81–92.

Petty, R. E., & Cacioppo, J. T. (1984). The effects of involvement on response to argument quantity and quality: Central and peripheral routes to persuasion. *Journal of Personality and Social Psychology, 46*, 69–81.

Petty, R. E., & Cacioppo, J. T. (1986a). The elaboration likelihood model of persuasion. In L. Berkowitz (Ed.), *Advances in experimental social psychology* (Vol. 19). New York: Academic Press.

Petty, R. E., & Cacioppo, J. T. (1986b). *Communication and persuasion: Central and peripheral routes to attitude change*. New York: Springer-Verlag.

Petty, R. E., Cacioppo, J. T., & Schumann, D. (1983). Central and peripheral routes to advertising effectiveness: The moderating role of involvement. *Journal of Consumer Research, 10*, 134–148.

Petty, R. E., Heesacker, M., & Hughes, J. N. (1997). The elaboration likelihood model: Implications for the practice of school psychology. *Journal of School Psychology, 35* (2), 107–136.

Petty, R. E., & Krosnick, J. A. (Eds.). (1995). *Attitude strength: Antecedents and consequences*. Mahwah, NJ: Erlbaum.

Petty, R. E., Schumann, D. W., Richman, S. A., & Strathman, A. J. (1993). Positive mood and persuasion: Different roles for affect under high- and low-elaboration conditions. *Journal of Personality and Social Psychology, 64*, 5–20.

Petty, R. T., & Wegener, D. T. (1998a). Attitude change: Multiple roles for persuasion variables. In D. T. Gilbert, S. T. Fiske, & G. Lindzey (Eds.), *The handbook of social psychology* (Vol. 2, 4th ed., pp. 323–390). Boston: McGraw-Hill.

Petty, R. T., & Wegener, D. T. (1998b). Matching versus mismatching attitude functions: Implications for scrutiny of persuasive messages. *Personality & Social Psychology Bulletin, 24* (3), 227–240.

Petty, R. E., Wegener, D. T., & Fabrigar, L. R. (1997). Attitudes and attitude change. *Annual Review of Psychology, 48*, 609–647.

Petty, R. E., Wegener, D. T., & White, P. H. (1998). Flexible correction processes in social judgment: Implications for persuasion. *Social Cognition, 16* (1), 93–113.

Peven, D. E., & Shulman, B. H. (1999). The issue of intimacy in marriage. In J. Carlson & L. Sperry (Eds.), *The intimate couple*. Philadelphia, PA: Brunner/Mazel.

Pfeifer, J. E. (1992). The psychological framing of cults: Schematic representations and cult evaluations. *Journal of Applied Social Psychology, 22*, 531–544.

Pfeifer, J. E., & Ogloff, J. R. (1991). Ambiguity and guilt determinations: A modern racism perspective. *Journal of Applied Social Psychology, 21*, 1713–1725.

Philippot, P., Feldman, R. S., & Coats, E. J. (Eds.). (1999). *Social determinants of nonverbal behavior*. Cambridge, England: Cambridge University Press.

Philippot, P., Schwarz, N., Carrera, P., DeVries, N., & VanYperen, N. W. (1991). Differential effects of priming at the encoding and judgment stage. *European Journal of Social Psychology, 21*, 293–302.

Phillips, D. P. (1982). The impact of fictional television stories on U.S. adult fatalities: New evidence on the effect of the mass media on violence. *American Journal of Sociology, 87*, 1340–1359.

Phillips, D. P. (1986). Natural experiments on the effects of mass media violence on fatal aggression: Strengths and weaknesses of a new approach. In L.

Berkowitz (Ed.), *Advances in experimental social psychology* (Vol. 19). Orlando, FL: Academic Press.

Phillips, L. E. (1999, February). Love, American style. *American Demographics,* pp. 56–57.

Piattelli-Palmarini, M. (1994). *Inevitable illusions: How the mistakes of reason rule our minds.* New York: Wiley.

Pierce, G. R., Sarason, B. R., & Sarason, I. G. (Eds.). (1996). *Handbook of social support and the family.* New York: Plenum.

Pierce, W. D., & Epling, W. F. (1999). *Behavior analysis and learning* (2nd ed.). Upper Saddle River, NJ: Prentice-Hall.

Pietromonaco, P. R., & Markus, H. (1985). The nature of negative thoughts in depression. *Journal of Personality and Social Psychology, 48,* 799–807.

Piirto, R. (1991a). *Beyond mind games: The marketing power of psychographics.* Ithaca, NY: American Demographics.

Piirto, R. (1991b, July). VALS the second time. *American Demographics,* p. 6.

Piliavin, J. A., & Callero, P. L. (1991). *Giving blood: The development of an altruistic identity.* Baltimore: Johns Hopkins University Press.

Piliavin, J. A., Evans, D. E., & Callero, P. (1984). Learning to "give unnamed strangers": The process of commitment to regular blood donation. In E. Staub, D. Bar-Tal, J. Karylowski, & J. Reykowski (Eds.), *The development and maintenance of prosocial behavior: International perspectives.* New York: Plenum.

Piliavin, J. A., & Piliavin, I. M. (1972). Effect of blood on reactions to a victim. *Journal of Personality and Social Psychology, 23,* 353–361.

Pilkington, C. J., Tesser, A., & Stephens, D. (1991). Complementarity in romantic relationships: A self-evaluation maintenance perspective. *Journal of Social & Personal Relationships, 8,* 481–504.

Pilkington, N. W., & Lydon, J. E. (1997). The relative effect of attitude similarity and attitude dissimilarity on interpersonal attraction: Investigating the moderating roles of prejudice and group membership. *Personality & Social Psychology Bulletin, 23,* 107–122.

Pinto, A., & Francis, G. (1993). Cognitive correlates of depressive symptoms in hospitalized adolescents. *Adolescence, 28,* 661–672.

Pizzagalli, D., Koenig, T., Regard, M., & Lehmann, D. (1998). Faces and emotions: Brain electric field sources during covert emotional processing. *Neuropsychologia, 36* (4), 323–332.

Platz, S. J., & Hosch, H. M. (1988). Cross-racial/ethnic eyewitness identification: A field study. *Journal of Applied Social Psychology, 18,* 972–984.

Plichta, S. B., Duncan, M. M., & Plichta, L. (1996). Spouse abuse, patient-physician communication, and patient satisfaction. *American Journal of Preventive Medicine, 12,* 297–303.

Polasky, L. J., & Holahan, C. K. (1998). Maternal self-discrepancies, interrole conflict, and negative affect among married professional women with children. *Journal of Family Psychology, 12,* 388–401.

Pollock, C. L., Smith, S. D., Knowles, E. S., & Bruce, H. J. (1998). Mindfulness limits compliance with the that's-not-all technique. *Personality & Social Psychology Bulletin, 24,* 1153–1157.

Pomerleau, A., Bolduc, D., Malcuit, G., & Cossette, L. (1990). Pink or blue: Environmental gender stereotypes in the first two years of life. *Sex Roles, 22,* 359–367.

Pool, G. J., Wood, W., & Leck, K. (1998). The self-esteem motive in social influence: Agreement with valued majorities and disagreement with derogated minorities. *Journal of Personality & Social Psychology, 75* (4) 967–975.

Popenoe, D. (1987). Beyond the nuclear family: A statistical portrait of the changing family in Sweden. *Journal of Marriage and the Family, 49,* 173–183.

Posavac, S. S., Sanbonmatsu, D. M., & Fazio, R. H. (1997). Considering the best choice: Effects of the salience and accessibility of alternatives on attitude-decision consistency. *Journal of Personality & Social Psychology, 72* (2), 253–261.

Postmes, T., & Spears, R. (1998) Deindividuation and antinormative behavior: A meta-analysis. *Psychological Bulletin, 123* (3), 238–259.

Postmes, T., Spears, R., & Lea, M. (1998). Breaching or building social boundaries? Side-effects of computer-mediated communication. *Communication Research, 25* (6), 689–715.

Post-White, J. (1998). The role of sense of coherence in mediating the effects of mental imagery on immune function, cancer outcome, and quality of life. In H. I. McCubbin & E. A. Thompson (Eds.), *Stress, coping, and health in families: Sense of coherence and resiliency. Resiliency in families series* (Vol. 1). Thousand Oaks, CA: Sage.

Prager, K. J. (1995). *The psychology of intimacy.* New York: Guilford.

Pratarelli, M. E., & McIntyre, J. A. (1994). Effects of social loafing on word recognition. *Perceptual & Motor Skills, 78,* 455–464.

Pratkanis, A. R., & Aronson, E. (1992). *The age of propaganda: The everyday use and abuse of persuasion.* New York: Freeman.

Pratkanis, A. R., & Greenwald, A. G. (1989). A sociocognitive model of attitude structure and function. In L. Berkowitz (Ed.), *Advances in experimental social psychology* (Vol. 22). New York: Academic Press.

Pratkanis, A. R., Greenwald, A. G., Leippe, M. R., & Baumgardner, M. H. (1988). In search of reliable persuasion effects: III. The sleeper effect is dead: Long live the sleeper effect. *Journal of Personality and Social Psychology, 54,* 203–218.

Pratto, F., & Bargh, J. A. (1991). Stereotyping based on apparently individuating information: Trait and global components of sex stereotypes under attention overload. *Journal of Experimental Social Psychology 27,* 26–47.

Prentice-Dunn, S. (1990). Perspectives on research classics: Two routes to collective violence. *Contemporary Social Psychology, 14,* 217–218.

Prentice-Dunn, S., & Rogers, R. W. (1982). Effects of public and private self-awareness on deindividuation and aggression. *Journal of Personality and Social Psychology, 43,* 503–513.

Price, D. W., & Goodman, G. S. (1990). Visiting the wizard: Children's memory for a recurring event. *Child Development, 61,* 664–680.

Price, K. H. (1987). Decision responsibility, task responsibility, identifiability, and social loafing. *Organizational Behavior and Human Decision Processes, 40,* 330–345.

Price, K. H. (1993). Working hard to get people to loaf. *Basic and Applied Social Psychology, 14,* 329–344.

Priester, J. R., & Petty, R. E. (1995). Source attributions and persuasion: Perceived honesty as a determinant of message scrutiny. *Personality and Social Psychology Bulletin, 21,* 637–654.

Prislin, R., Akrap, L., & Sprah, B. (1987). Self-monitoring and attitude-behaviour relationship. *Revija za Psihologiju, 17,* 37–45.

Propp, K. M. (1995). An experimental examination of biological sex as a status cue in decision-making groups and its influence on information use. *Small Group Research, 26,* 451–474.

Provorse, D., & Sarata, B. (1989). The social psychology of juvenile court judges in rural communities. *Journal of Rural Community Psychology, 10,* 3–15.

Proxmire, W. (1975). Press release, U.S. Senate Office. Washington, DC.

PsychINFO. (1998). *Distribution of serial, book & chapter records by classification category.* Washington, DC: American Psychological Association.

Ptacek, J. T., Smith, R. E., & Dodge, K. L. (1994). Gender differences in coping with stress: When stressor and appraisals do not differ. *Personality and Social Psychology Bulletin, 20,* 421–430.

Putrevu, S., & Lord, K. R. (1994). Comparative and noncomparative advertising: Attitudinal effects under cognitive and affective involvement conditions. *Journal of Advertising, 23,* 77–91.

Pyszczynski, T., & Greenberg, J. (1987). Self-regulatory perseveration and the depressive self-focusing style: A self-awareness theory of depression. *Psychological Bulletin, 102,* 122–138.

Qian, Z., & Preston, S. H. (1993). Changes in American marriage, 1972 to 1987: Availability and forces of attraction by age and education. *American Sociological Review, 58,* 482–495.

Quattrone, G. A. (1986). On the perception of a group's variability. In S. Worchel & W. G. Austin (Eds.), *Psychology of intergroup relations* (2nd ed.). Chicago: Nelson Hall.

Quick, R. (1995, September 11). Betty Crocker plans to mix ethnic looks for her new face. *Wall Street Journal,* pp. A1, A9.

Quinn, M. (1990, January 29). Don't aim that pack at us. *Time,* p. 60.

Raag, T., & Rackliff, C. L. (1998). Preschoolers' awareness of social expectations of gender: Relationships to toy choices. *Sex Roles, 38,* 685–700.

Ragland, D. R., & Brand, R. J. (1988). Type A behavior and mortality from coronary heart disease. *New England Journal of Medicine, 313,* 65–69.

Rahe, R. H., & Arthur, R. J. (1978). Life change and illness studies: Past history and future directions. *Human Stress, 4,* 3–15.

Rapoff, M. A., & Christophersen, E. R. (1982). Improving compliance in pediatric practice. *Pediatric Clinics of North America, 29,* 339–357.

Rastogi, P. N. (1987). Essence of leadership. *Vikalpa, 12,* 37–41.

Raven, B. H. (1988, August). *French and Raven 30 years later: Power, interaction and personal influence.* Paper presented at the International Congress of Psychology, Sydney, Australia.

Raven, B. H. (1992). A power/interaction model of interpersonal influence: French and Raven thirty years later. *Journal of Social Behavior and Personality, 7,* 217–244.

Raven, B. H. (1993). The bases of power: Origins and recent developments. *Journal of Social Issues, 49,* 227–251.

Raven, B. H. (1998). Groupthink, Bay of Pigs, and Watergate reconsidered. *Organizational Behavior & Human Decision Processes, 73* (2–3), 352–361.

Rawson, H. E., Bloomer, K., & Kendall, A. (1994). Stress, anxiety, depression, and physical illness in college students. *Journal of Genetic Psychology, 155,* 321–330.

Rebellow, K. (1992, February 24). Microsoft: Bill Gates's baby is on top of the world. Can it stay there? *Business Week,* pp. 60–64.

Redmond, R., & Redmond, X. (1994). *Anger kills.* New York: Harper Perrenial.

Reeve, H. K. (1998). Acting for the good of others: Kinship and reciprocity with some new twists. In C. B. Crawford & D. L. Krebs (Eds.), *Handbook of evolutionary psychology: Ideas, issues, and applications* (pp. 43–85). Mahwah, NJ: Erlbaum.

Reeves, R. A., Baker, G. A., Boyd, J. G., & Cialdini, R. B. (1991). The door-in-the-face technique: Reciprocal concessions vs. self-presentational explanations. *Journal of Social Behavior and Personality, 6,* 545–558.

Regan, P. C., Kocan, E. R., & Whitlock, T. (1998). Ain't love grand! A prototype analysis of the concept of romantic love. *Journal of Social & Personal Relationships, 15,* 411–420.

"Reggie White's Address to the State Assembly." (1998, April 4). *The Post Crescent,* Appleton, WI, p. A9. Reported in Glick, P., & Fiske, S. (in press). Ambivalent stereotypes as legitimizing ideologies: Differentiating paternalistic and envious prejudice.

Rehder, R. R., & Smith, M. M. (1986). KAIZEN and the art of labor relations. *Personnel Journal, 65,* 82–93.

Reicher, S. D. (1996). The Battle of Westminster: Developing the social identity model of crowd behaviour in order to explain the initiation and development of collective conflict. *European Journal of Social Psychology, 26,* 115–134.

Reichl, A. J. (1997). Ingroup favouritism and outgroup favouritism in low status minimal groups: Differential responses to status-related and status-unrelated measures. *European Journal of Social Psychology, 27,* 617–633.

Reifman, A., Klein, J. G., & Murphy, S. T. (1989). Self-monitoring and age. *Psychology and Aging, 4,* 245–246.

Reifman, A. S., Larrick, R. P., & Fein, S. (1991). Temper and temperature on the diamond: The heat-aggression relationship in major league baseball. *Personality and Social Psychology Bulletin, 17,* 580–585.

Reimer, J., Paolitto, D. P., & Hersch, R. H. (1983). *Promoting moral growth: From Piaget to Kohlberg* (2nd ed.). New York: Longman.

Reinecke, J., Schmidt, P., & Ajzen, I. (1997a). Condom or no condom in new sexual contacts? Explanation and prediction with the Theory of Planned Behavior in a longitudinal study. *Zeitschrift Fuer Sozialpsychologie, 28* (3), 210–222.

Reinecke, J., Schmidt, P., & Ajzen, I. (1997b). Birth control versus AIDS prevention: A hierarchical model of condom use among young people. *Journal of Applied Social Psychology, 27* (9), 743–759.

Reingen, P. H., & Kernan, J. B. (1993). Social perception and interpersonal influence: Some consequences of the physical attractiveness stereotype in a personal selling setting. *Journal of Consumer Psychology, 2,* 25–38.

Reis, H. T., & Shaver, P. (1988). Intimacy as an interpersonal process. In S. Duck (Ed.), *Handbook of personal relationships: Theory, relationships and interventions.* Chichester, England: Wiley.

Reis, H. T., Wilson, I. M., Monestere, C., Bernstein, S., Clark, K., Seidl, E., Franco, M., Gioioso, E., Freeman, L., & Radoane, K. (1990). What is smiling is beautiful and good. *European Journal of Social Psychology, 20,* 259–267.

Reisenzein, R. (1983). The Schachter theory of emotion: Two decades later. *Psychological Bulletin, 94,* 239–264.

Reiss, I. L. (1960). *Premarital sexual standards in America.* New York: Free Press.

Reiss, M. J. (1984). Human sociobiology. *Zygon Journal of Religion and Science, 19,* 117–140.

Reno, R. R., Cialdini, R. B., & Kallgren, C. A. (1993). The transsituational influence of social norms. *Journal of Personality and Social Psychology, 64,* 104–112.

Reskin, B. F., & Visher, C. A. (1986). The impacts of evidence and extralegal factors in jurors' decisions. *Law and Society Review, 20,* 423–438.

Reynolds, K. D., & West, S. G. (1989). Attributional constructs: Their role in the organization of social information memory. *Basic and Applied Social Psychology, 10,* 119–130.

Rhodes, G., Sumich, A., & Byatt, G. (1999). Are average facial configurations attractive only because of their symmetry? *Psychological Science, 10,* 52–58.

Rhodewalt, F., Sanbonmatsu, D. M., Tschanz, B., Feick, D. L., & Waller, A. (1995). Self-handicapping and interpersonal trade-offs: The effects of claimed self-handicaps on observers' performance evaluations and feedback. *Personality and Social Psychology Bulletin, 32,* 1042–1050.

Ricci Bitti, P. E., & Poggi, I. (1991). Symbolic nonverbal behavior: Talking through gestures. In R. S. Feldman & B. Rimé (Eds.), *Fundamentals of nonverbal behavior.* Cambridge, England: Cambridge University Press.

Rice, B. (1988). The selling of life-styles. *Psychology Today, 22,* pp. 46–50.

Rice, F. P. (1999). *Intimate relationships, marriages, & families* (4th ed.). Mountain View, CA: Mayfield.

Richardson, D. R., Hammock, G. S., Smith, S. M., & Gardner, W. (1994). Empathy as a cognitive inhibitor of interpersonal aggression. *Aggressive Behavior, 20,* 275–289.

Rickert, E. J. (1998). Authoritarianism and economic threat: Implications for political behavior. *Political Psychology, 19,* 707–720.

Ridgeway, C. L., Diekema, D., & Johnson, C. (1995). Legitimacy, compliance, and gender in peer groups. *Social Psychology Quarterly, 58,* 298–311.

Rimé, B., & Schiaratura, L. (1991). Gesture and speech. In R. S. Feldman & B. Rimé (Eds.), *Fundamentals of nonverbal behavior.* Cambridge, England: Cambridge University Press.

Ringelmann, M. (1913). Research on animate sources of power: The work of man. *Annales de l'Institut National Agronomique, 2e serietome XII,* 1–40.

Riordan, C. A., & Tedeschi, J. T. (1983). Attraction in aversive environments: Some evidence for classical conditioning and negative reinforcement. *Journal of Personality and Social Psychology, 44,* 683–692.

Ritts, V., Patterson, M. L., & Tubbs, M. E. (1992). Expectations, impressions, and judgments of physically attractive students: A review. *Review of Educational Research, 62,* 413–426.

Ritts, V., & Stein, J. R. (1995). Verification and commitment in marital relationships: An exploration of self-verification theory in community college students. *Psychological Reports, 76,* 383–386.

Roark, A. E., & Sharah, H. S. (1989). Factors related to group cohesiveness. *Small Group Behavior, 20,* 62–69.

Robbennolt, J. K., Penrod, S., & Heuer, L. (1999). Assessing and aiding civil jury competence. In A. K. Hess & I. B. Weiner (Eds.), *The handbook of forensic psychology* (2nd ed., pp. 273–302). New York: Wiley.

Robbins, T. L. (1995). Social loafing on cognitive tasks: An examination of the "sucker effect." *Journal of Business & Psychology, 9,* 337–342.

Roberts, W., & Strayer, J. (1996). Empathy, emotional expressiveness, and prosocial behavior. *Child Development, 67,* 449–470.

Robins, C. J. (1988). Attributions and depression: Why is the literature so inconsistent? *Journal of Personality and Social Psychology, 54,* 236–247.

Robinson, M. D., Johnson, J. T., & Shields, S. A. (1995). On the advantages of modesty: The benefits of a balanced self-presentation. *Communication Research, 22,* 575–591.

Robinson, T. T., & Carron, A. V. (1982). Personal and situational factors associated with dropping out versus maintaining participation in competitive sport. *Journal of Sport Psychology, 4,* 364–378.

Robinson-Staveley, K., & Cooper, J. (1990). Mere presence, gender, and reactions to computers: Studying human-computer interaction in the social context. *Journal of Experimental Social Psychology, 26,* 168–183.

Roche, J. P., & Ramsbey, T. W. (1993). Premarital sexuality: A five-year follow-up study of attitudes and behavior by dating stage. *Adolescence, 28,* 67–80.

Rockman, H. (1994). Matchmaker matchmaker make me a match: The art and conventions of Jewish arranged marriages. *Sexual and Marital Therapy, 9,* 277–284.

Rodriguez, C. M., & Pehi, P. (1998). Depression, anxiety and attributional style in a New Zealand sample of children. *New Zealand Journal of Psychology, 27,* 28–34.

Rodriguez, M. A., Bauer, H. M., Flores-Ortiz, Y., & Szkupinski-Quiroga, S. (1998). Factors affecting patient-physician communication for abused Latina and Asian immigrant women. *Journal of Family Practice, 47,* 309–311.

Roediger, H. L., & McDermott, K. B. (1995). Creating false memories: Remembering words not presented in lists. *Journal of Experimental Psychology: Learning, Memory, & Cognition, 21,* 803–814.

Roese, N. J. (1994). The functional basis of counterfactual thinking. *Journal of Personality and Social Psychology, 66,* 805–818.

Roese, N. J., & Olson, J. M. (1996). Counterfactuals, causal attributions, and the hindsight bias: A conceptual integration. *Journal of Experimental Social Psychology, 32,* 197–227.

Roese, N. J., & Olson, J. M. (1998). *What might have been: The social psychology of counterfactual thinking.* Hillsdale, NJ: Erlbaum.

Roethlisberger, F. J., & Dickson, W. V. (1939). *Management and the worker.* Cambridge, MA: Harvard University Press.

Rogelberg, S. G., & Luong, A. (1998). Nonresponse to mailed surveys: A review and guide. *Current Directions in Psychological Science, 7,* 60–65.

Rogers, M., Miller, N., Mayer, F. S., & Duval, S. (1982). Personal responsibility and salience of the request for help: Determinants of the relation between negative affect and helping behavior.

Journal of Personality and Social Psychology, 43, 956–970.

Rogers, R. W. (1983). Cognitive and physiological processes in fear appeals and attitude change: A revised theory of protection motivation. In J. T. Cacioppo & R. E. Petty (Eds.), *Social psychophysiology.* New York: Guilford.

Rohlen, T. P. (1973). "Spiritual education" in a Japanese bank. *American Anthropologist, 75,* 1542–1562.

Rojahn, K., & Pettigrew, T. F. (1992). Memory for schema-relevant information: A meta-analytic resolution. *British Journal of Social Psychology, 31,* 81–109.

Rojas, L., & Gil, R. M. (1989). The diagnosis of public mental health care bureaucracies. Second World Basque Congress: Diagnosis in psychiatry, (1987, Bilbao, Spain). *British Journal of Psychiatry, 154* (Suppl), 96–100.

Rokeach, M. (1971). Long-range experimental modification of values, attitudes, and behavior. *American Psychologist, 26,* 453–459.

Rollins, B. C., & Cannon, K. L. (1974). Marital satisfaction over the family life cycle. *Journal of Marriage and the Family, 36,* 271–282.

Romano, S. T., & Bordieri, J. E. (1989). Physical attractiveness stereotypes and students' perceptions of college professors. *Psychological Reports, 64,* 1099–1102.

Romero, A. J., & Roberts, R. E. (1998). Perception of discrimination and ethnocultural variables in a diverse group of adolescents. *Journal of Adolescence, 21* (6), 641–656.

Ronis, D. L., Yates, J. F., & Kirscht, J. P. (1989). Attitudes, decisions, and habits as determinants of repeated behavior. In A. R. Pratkanis, S. J. Breckler, & A. G. Greenwald (Eds.), *Attitude structure and function.* Hillsdale, NJ: Erlbaum.

Rosander, M., Stiwne, D., & Granstroem, K. (1998). "Bipolar groupthink": Assessing groupthink tendencies in authentic work groups. *Scandinavian Journal of Psychology, 39* (2), 81–92.

Rose, J. (1994). Communication challenges and role functions of performing groups. *Small Group Research, 25,* 411–432.

Rosenbaum, M. E. (1986). The repulsion hypothesis: On the nondevelopment of relationships. *Journal of Personality and Social Psychology, 51,* 1156–1166.

Rosenbaum, M., & Cohen, E. (1999). Equalitarian marriages, spousal support, resourcefulness, and psychological distress among Israeli working women. *Journal of Vocational Behavior, 54,* 102–113.

Rosenberg, D. (1992, October). Good Samaritan engineers. *Technology Review, 95* (7), 18.

Rosenberg, L. A. (1961). Group size, prior experience, and conformity. *Journal of Abnormal and Social Psychology, 63,* 436–437.

Rosenblatt, P. C., & Anderson, R. M. (1981). Human sexuality in cross-cultural perspective. In M. Cook (Ed.), *The bases of human sexual attraction.* London and New York: Academic Press.

Rosenhan, D. L. (1970). The natural socialization of altruistic autonomy. In J. R. Macaulay & L. Berkowitz (Eds.), *Altruism and helping behavior.* New York: Academic Press.

Rosenman, R. H. (1990). Type A behavior pattern: A personal overview. *Journal of Social Behavior and Personality, 5,* 1–24.

Rosenman, R. H., Brand, R. J., Sholtz, R. I., & Friedman, M. (1976). Multivariate prediction of coronary heart disease during 8.5 year follow-up in the Western collaborative group study. *American Journal of Cardiology, 37,* 903–910.

Rosenthal, R. (1976). *Experimenter effects in behavioral research.* New York: Irvington.

Rosenthal, R. (1991). Teacher expectancy effects: A brief update 25 years after the Pygmalions experiment. *Journal of Research in Education, 1,* 3–12.

Rosenthal, R., & Jacobson, L. (1968). *Pygmalion in the classroom: Teacher expectation and pupils' intellectual development.* New York: Holt, Rinehart and Winston.

Roskos-Ewoldsen, D. R., & Fazio, R. H. (1992). The accessibility of source likability as a determinant of persuasion. *Personality and Social Psychology Bulletin, 18,* 19–25.

Ross, D., Greene, D., & House, P. (1977). The false consensus phenomenon: An attributional bias in self-perception and social-perception processes. *Journal of Experimental Social Psychology, 13,* 279–301.

Ross, E. A. (1908). *Social psychology, an outline and source book.* New York: Macmillan.

Ross, L. (1977). The intuitive psychologist and his shortcomings. Distortions in the attribution process. In L. Berkowitz (Ed.), *Advances in experimental social psychology* (Vol. 10, pp. 174–221). New York: Academic Press.

Ross, L., & Nisbett, R. E. (1991). *The person and the situation.* New York: McGraw-Hill

Ross, S. M., & Offermann, L. R. (1997). Transformational leaders: Measurement of personality attributes and work group performance. *Personality & Social Psychology Bulletin, 23,* 1078–1086.

Rosselli, F., Skelly, J. J., & Mackie, D. M. (1995). Processing rational and emotional messages: The cognitive and affective mediation of persuasion. *Journal of Experimental Social Psychology, 31,* 163–190.

Rossen, E. K., & Buschmann, M. T. (1995). Mental illness in late life: The neurobiology of depression. *Archives of Psychiatric Nursing, 9,* 130–136.

Rossi, P. H., & Berk, R. A. (1985). Varieties of normative consensus. *American Sociological Review, 50,* 333–347.

Rotenberg, K. J., & Chase, N. (1992). Development of the reciprocity of self-disclosure. *Journal of Genetic Psychology, 153,* 75–86.

Rotenberg, K. J., & Korol, S. (1995). The role of loneliness and gender in individuals' love styles. *Journal of Social Behavior and Personality, 10,* 537–546.

Rothbart, M., & John, O. P. (1985). Social categorization and behavioral episodes: A cognitive analysis of the effects of intergroup contact. *Journal of Social Issues, 41,* 81–104.

Rotton, J. (1993). Geophysical variables and behavior: LXXIII. Ubiquitous errors: A reanalysis of Anderson's (1987) "temperature and aggression." *Psychological Reports, 73,* 259–271.

Rotton, J., & Frey, J. (1985). Air pollution, weather, and violent crimes: Concomitant time-series analysis of archival data. *Journal of Personality and Social Psychology, 49,* 1207–1220.

Rousseau, A., & de Man, A. F. (1998). Authoritarian and socially restrictive attitudes toward mental patients in mental health volunteers and nonvolunteers. *Psychological Reports, 83,* 803–806.

Rousseau, F., & Standing, L. (1995). Zero effect of crowding on arousal and performance: On "proving" the null hypothesis. *Perceptual & Motor Skills, 81,* 72–74.

Rowan, J. (1998). Maslow amended. *Journal of Humanistic Psychology, 38* (1), 81–92.

Roy, A. (1993). Genetic and biologic risk factors for suicide in depressive disorders. Special Issue: Fifth Annual New York State Office of Mental Health Research Conference. *Psychiatric Quarterly, 64,* 345–358.

Ruback, R. B., & Pandey, J. (1996). Gender differences in perceptions of household crowding: Stress, affiliation, and role obligations in rural India. *Journal of Applied Social Psychology, 26,* 417–436.

Ruback, R. B., & Weiner, N. A. (Eds.). (1995). *Interpersonal violent behaviors: Social and cultural aspects.* New York: Springer.

Rubenstein, C. (1982, July). Psychology's fruit flies. *Psychology Today,* pp. 83–84.

Rubin, L. B. (1985). *Just friends: The role of friendship in our lives.* New York: Harper & Row.

Rubin, Z. (1973). *Liking and loving.* New York: Holt.

Rubin, Z. (1988). Preface. In R. J. Sternberg & M. L. Barnes (Eds.), *The psychology of love.* New Haven: Yale University Press.

Rubin, Z., Hill, C. T., Peplau, L. A., & Dunkel-Schetter, C. (1980). Self-disclosure in dating couples: Sex roles and the ethic of openness. *Journal of Marriage and the Family, 42,* 305–317.

Rudolph, U. (1993). The self-reference effect: Methodological issues and implications from a schema-theoretical perspective. *European Journal of Social Psychology, 23,* 331–354.

Ruganci, R. N. (1995). Private and public self-consciousness subscales of the Fenigstein, Scheier and Buss self-consciousness scale: A Turkish translation. *Personality and Individual Differences, 18,* 279–282.

Rusbult, C. E., Bissonnette, V. L., Arriaga, X. B., & Cox, C. L. (1998). Accommodation processes during the early years of marriage. In T. N. Bradbury (Ed.), *The developmental course of marital dysfunction.* New York: Cambridge University Press.

Russell, D., Cutrona, C. E., Rose, J., & Yurko, K. (1984). Social and emotional loneliness: An examination of Weiss's typology of loneliness. *Journal of Personality and Social Psychology, 46,* 1313–1321.

Russell, D. E. H., & Howell, N. (1983). The prevalence of rape in the United States revisited. *Signs, 8,* 688–695.

Russell, G. W. (1983). Psychological issues in sports aggression. In H. H. Goldstein (Ed.), *Sports violence.* New York: Springer-Verlag.

Russell, G. W. (1985). Spectator moods at an aggressive sports event. *Journal of Sport Psychology, 3,* 217–227.

Russell, J. A. (1992). Brief comments on the study of emotion concepts. *Revista de Psicologia Social, 7,* 259–263.

Rutkowski, G. K., Gruder, C. L., & Romer, D. (1983). Group cohesiveness, social norms, and bystander intervention. *Journal of Personality and Social Psychology, 44,* 545–552.

Ruvolo, A., & Markus, H. (1992). Possible selves and performance power: The power of self-relevant imagery. *Social Cognition, 9,* 95–124.

Sabrena Qualitative Research Service. (1996). *Consumer perception of goods and retailers.* Westport, CT: Sabrena Qualitative Research Service.

Sacks, M. H. (1993). Exercise for stress control. In D. Goleman & J. Gurin (Eds.), *Mind-body medicine.* Yonkers, NY: Consumer Reports Books.

Sagatun, I. J., & Knudsen, J. H. (1982). Attributional self-presentation for actors and observers in success and failure situations. *Scandinavian Journal of Psychology, 23,* 243–252.

Sakai, H. (1999). A multiplicative power-function model of cognitive dissonance: Toward an integrated theory of cognition, emotion, and behavior after Leon Festinger. In E. Harmon-Jones & J. Mills (Eds.), *Cognitive dissonance: Progress on a pivotal theory in social psychology. Science conference series* (pp. 267–294). Washington, DC: American Psychological Association.

Saks, M. J. (1977). *Jury verdicts: The role of group size and social decision rule.* Lexington, MA: Lexington.

Saks, M. J., & Marti, M. W. (1997). A meta-analysis of the effects of jury size. *Law & Human Behavior, 21* (5), 451–467.

Salazar, A. J. (1995). Understanding the synergistic effects of communication in small groups: Making the most out of group member abilities. *Small Group Research, 26,* 169–199.

Salekin, R. T., Ogloff, J. R., McFarland, C., Rogers, R. (1995). Influencing jurors' perceptions of guilt: Expression of emotionality during testimony. *Behavioral Sciences and the Law, 13,* 293–305.

Salem, D. A., Gant, L., & Campbell, R. (1998). The initiation of mutual-help groups within residential treatment settings. *Community Mental Health Journal, 34* (4), 419–429.

Salovey, P., Mayer, J. D., & Rosenhan, D. L. (1991). Mood and helping: Mood as a motivator of helping and helping as a regulator of mood. *Review of Personality and Social Psychology, 12,* 215–237.

Salovey, P., & Rodin, J. (1985). Cognitions about the self: Connecting feeling states and social behavior. In P. Shaver (Ed.), *Self, situations, and social behavior: Review of personality and social psychology* (Vol. 6). Beverly Hills, CA: Sage.

Salovey, P., & Rosenhan, D. L. (1989). Mood states and prosocial behavior. In H. L. Wagner & A. S. R. Manstead (Eds.), *Handbook of psychophysiology: Emotion and social behavior.* Chichester, England: Wiley.

Salovey, P., Rothman, A. J., & Rodin, J. (1998). Health behavior. In D. T. Gilbert & S. T. Fiske (Eds.), *The handbook of social psychology* (4th ed.). Boston: McGraw-Hill.

Samora, J., Saunders, L., & Larson, R. F. (1961). Medical vocabulary knowledge among hospital patients. *Journal of Health and Social Behavior, 2,* 83–89.

Sampson, R. J., & Laub, J. H. (1993). *Crime in the making: Pathways and turning points through life.* Cambridge, MA: Harvard University Press.

Sanbonmatsu, D. M., Harpster, L. L., Akimoto, S. A., & Moulin, J. B. (1994). Selectivity in generalizations about self and others from performance. *Personality and Social Psychology Bulletin, 20,* 358–366.

Sanders, G. S. (1983). An attentional process model of social facilitation. In A. Hare, H. Bumberg, V. Kent, & M. Davies (Eds.), *Small groups.* London: Wiley.

Sanitioso, R., & Kunda, Z. (1991). Ducking the collection of costly evidence: Motivated use of statistical heuristics. *Journal of Behavioral Decision Making, 4,* 161–178.

Sanoff, A. P., & Minerbrook, S. (1993, April 19). Race on campus. *U.S. News and World Report,* pp. 52–64.

Sanson, A., Montgomery, B., Gault, U., Gridley, H., & Thomson, D. (1996). Punishment and behaviour change: An Australian Psychological Society position paper. *Australian Psychologist, 21,* 157–165.

Scarr, S. (1992). Developmental theories for the 1990s: Development and individual differences. *Child Development, 63,* 1–19.

Scarr, S. (1993). Biological and cultural diversity: The legacy of Darwin for development. *Child Development, 64,* 1333–1353.

Schacter, D. L. (1996). *Searching for memory: The brain, the mind, and the past.* New York: Basic Books.

Schacter, D. L., Kagan, J., & Leichtman, M. D. (1995). True and false memories in children and adults: A cognitive neuroscience perspective. Special Theme: Suggestibility of child witnesses: The social science amicus brief in *State of New Jersey v. Margaret Kelly Michaels. Psychology, Public Policy, & Law, 1,* 411–428.

Schachter, S. (1959). *The psychology of affiliation.* Stanford, CA: Stanford University Press.

Schachter, S., & Singer, J. (1962). Cognitive, social, and physiological determinants of the emotional state. *Psychological Review, 69,* 379–399.

Schaefer, R. T., & Lamm, R. P. (1992). *Sociology* (4th ed.). New York: McGraw-Hill.

Schaeffer, M. A., Baum, A., & Paulus, P. B. (1984, April). *Hormonal effects of crowding in prison.* Paper presented at the annual meeting of the Eastern Psychological Association, Baltimore, MD.

Schaller, M. (1991). Social categorization and the formation of group stereotypes: Further evidence for biased information processing in the perception of group-behavior correlations. *European Journal of Social Psychology, 21,* 25–35.

Schaller, M., & Cialdini, R. B. (1990). Happiness, sadness, and helping: A motivational integration. In R. M. Sorrentino & E. T. Higgins (Eds.), *Handbook of motivation and cognition: Foundations of social behavior* (Vol. 2). New York: Guilford.

Scheier, M. F., & Carver, C. S. (1992). Effects of optimism on psychological and physical well-being: Theoretical overview and empirical update. *Cognitive Therapy and Research, 16,* 201–228.

Schein, E. H. (1990). Organizational culture. *American Psychologist, 45,* 109–119.

Schellhardt, T. D. (1991, October 18). Attractiveness aids men more than women. *Wall Street Journal,* p. B1.

Schiffenbauer, A., & Schiavo, R. S. (1976). Physical distance and attraction: An intensification effect. *Journal of Experimental Social Psychology, 12,* 274–282.

Schkade, D. A., & Kahneman, D. (1998). Does living in California make people happy? A focusing illusion in judgments of life satisfaction. *Psychological Science, 9,* 340–346.

Schlenker, B. (1980). *Impression management: The self-concept, social identity, and interpersonal relations.* Monterey, CA: Brooks/Cole.

Schlenker, B. R. (1982). Translating actions into attitudes: An identity-analytic approach to the explanation of social conduct. In L. Berkowitz (Ed.), *Advances in experimental social psychology* (Vol. 15, pp. 193–247). New York: Academic Press.

Schlenker, B. R., & Weigold, M. F. (1992). Interpersonal processes involving impression regulation and management. *Annual Review of Psychology, 43,* 133–168.

Schlenker, B. R., Weigold, M. F., & Hallam, J. R. (1990). Self-serving attributions in social context: Effects of self-esteem and social pressure. *Journal of Personality and Social Psychology, 58,* 855–863.

Schnake, S. B., & Ruscher, J. B. (1998). Modern racism as a predictor of the linguistic intergroup bias. *Journal of Language & Social Psychology, 17,* 484–491.

Schoeneman, T. J., & Rubanowitz, D. E. (1985). Attributions in the advice columns: Actors observers, causes and reasons. *Personality and Social Psychology Bulletin, 11,* 315–325.

Schouten, P. G. W., & Handelsman, M. M. (1987). Social basis of self-handicapping: The case of depression. *Personality and Social Psychology Bulletin, 13,* 103–110.

Schriesheim, C. A., Tepper, B. J., & Tetrault, L. A. (1994). Least preferred co-worker score, situational control, and leadership effectiveness: A meta-analysis of contingency model performance predictions. *Journal of Applied Psychology, 79,* 561–573.

Schroeder, C. M., & Prentice, D. A. (1998). Exposing pluralistic ignorance to reduce alcohol use among college students. *Journal of Applied Social Psychology, 28,* 2150–2180.

Schruijer, S. L., Blanz, M., Mummendey, A., & Tedeschi, J. (1994). The group-serving bias in evaluating and explaining harmful behavior. *Journal of Social Psychology, 134,* 47–53.

Schultz, N. R., Jr., & Moore, D. (1984). Loneliness: Correlates, attributions, and coping among older adults. *Personality and Social Psychology Bulletin, 10,* 67–77.

Schultz, T. R., & Lepper, M. R. (1999). Computer simulation of cognitive dissonance reduction. In E. Harmon-Jones & J. Mills (Eds.), *Cognitive dissonance: Progress on a pivotal theory in social psychology. Science conference series* (pp. 235–265). Washington, DC: American Psychological Association.

Schuman, H., & Presser, S. (1995). *Questions and answers in attitude surveys.* New York: Sage.

Schumann, D. W., Petty, R. E., & Clemons, D. S. (1990). Predicting the effectiveness of different strategies of advertising variation: A test of the repetition-variation hypotheses. *Journal of Consumer Research, 17,* 192–202.

Schunk, D. H. (1991). Self-efficacy and academic motivation. Special Issue: Current issues and new directions in motivational theory and research. *Educational Psychologist, 26,* 207–231.

Schuster, E., & Eldeston, E. M. (1907). *The inheritance of ability.* London: Dulave.

Schwartz, B., & Barsky, S. F. (1977). The home advantage. *Social Forces, 55,* 641–661.

Schwartz, J. (1993). Marketing the verdict. *American Demographics,* pp. 52–55.

Schwarz, N., Bless, H., & Bohner, G. (1991). Mood and persuasion: Affective states influence the processing of persuasive communications. In M. P. Zanna (Ed.), *Advances in experimental social psychology* (Vol. 24). San Diego, CA: Academic Press.

Schwarz, N., Bless, H., Strack, F., Klumpp, G., Rittenauer-Schatka, H., & Simons, A. (1991). Ease of retrieval as information: Another look at the availability heuristic. *Journal of Personality and Social Psychology, 61,* 195–202.

Scott, C. R. (1990, November 7). As baby boomers age, fewer couples untie the knot. *Wall Street Journal,* pp. B1, B8.

Scott, L., & O'Hara, M. W. (1993). Self-discrepancies in clinically anxious and depressed university students. *Journal of Abnormal Psychology, 102,* 282–287.

Searcy, E., & Eisenberg, N. (1992). Defensiveness in response to aid from a sibling. *Journal of Personality and Social Psychology, 62,* 422–433.

Sears, D. O. (1982). The person-positivity bias. *Journal of Personality and Social Psychology, 44,* 233–250.

Sears, D. O. (1986). College sophomores in the laboratory: Influences of a narrow data base on social psychology's view of human nature. *Journal of Personality and Social Psychology, 51,* 515–530.

Sears, D. O., & Funk, C. L. (1991). The role of self-interest in social and political attitudes. In M. P. Zanna (Ed.), *Advances in experimental social psychology* (Vol. 24). San Diego: Academic Press.

Sears, D. O., & Kinder, D. R. (1985). Whites' opposition to busing: On conceptualizing and operationalizing group conflict. *Journal of Personality and Social Psychology, 48,* 1141–1147.

Sears, D. O., & McConahay, J. B. (1981). *The politics of violence: The new urban Blacks and the Watts riot.* New York: University Press of America.

Seashore, S. E. (1954). *Group cohesiveness in the industrial work group.* Ann Arbor, MI: Institute for Social Research.

Segal, M. W. (1974). Alphabet and attraction: An unobtrusive measure of the effect of propinquity in a field setting. *Journal of Personality and Social Psychology, 30,* 654–657.

Segall, M. H., Lonner, W. J., & Berry, J. W. (1998). Cross-cultural psychology as a scholarly discipline: On the flowering of culture in behavioral research. *American Psychologist, 53,* 1101–1110.

Segerstrom, S. C., Taylor, S. E., Kemeny, M. E., & Fahey, J. L. (1998). Optimism is associated with mood, coping and immune change in response to stress. *Journal of Personality & Social Psychology, 74,* 1646–1655.

Seguin, D. G., & Horowitz, I. A. (1984). The effects of "death qualification" on juror and jury decisioning: An analysis from three perspectives. *Law and Psychology Review, 8,* 49–81.

Seidel, S. D., Stasser, G. L., & Collier, S. A. (1998). Action identification theory as an explanation of social performance. *Group Dynamics, 2* (3), 147–154.

Seligman, L. (1995). *Promoting a fighting spirit.* San Francisco: Jossey-Bass.

Seligman, M. E. P. (1975). *Helplessness: On depression, development, and death.* San Francisco: Freeman.

Sellers, R. M., Rowley, S. A. J., Chavous, T. M., Shelton, J. N., & Smith, M. A. (1997). Multidimensional inventory of black identity: A preliminary investigation of reliability and construct validity. *Journal of Personality & Social Psychology, 73,* 805–815.

Selye, H. (1976). *The stress of life.* New York: McGraw-Hill.

Semin, G. R., & Fiedler, K. (Eds.). (1996). *Applied social psychology.* London: Sage.

Seppa, N. (1996, May). Downsizing: A new form of abandonment. *APA Monitor,* pp. 1, 38.

Serow, R. C. (1993). Why teach? Altruism and career choice among nontraditional recruits to teaching. *Journal of Research & Development in Education, 26,* 197–204.

Seta, J. J., & Seta, C. E. (1987). Payment and value: The generation of an evaluation standard and its effect on value. *Journal of Experimental Social Psychology, 23,* 285–301.

Shaffer, D. R., Pegalis, L. J., & Cornell, D. P. (1991). Interactive effects of social context and sex role identity on female self-disclosure during the acquaintance process. *Sex Roles, 24,* 1–19.

Shaffer, D. R., Pegalis, L. J., & Cornell, D. P. (1992). Gender and self-disclosure revisited: Personal and contextual variations in self-disclosure to same-sex acquaintances. *Journal of Social Psychology, 132,* 307–315.

Shaffer, D. R., Plummer, D., & Hammock, G. (1986). Hath he suffered enough? Effects of jury dogmatism, defendant similarity, and defendant's pretrial suffering on juridic decisions. *Journal of Personality and Social Psychology, 50,* 1059–1067.

Shaffer, D. R., Smith, J. E., & Tomarelli, M. (1982). Self-monitoring as a determinant of self-disclosure reciprocity during the acquaintance process. *Journal of Personality and Social Psychology, 43,* 163–175.

Shaikh, T., & Kanekar, S. (1994). Attitudinal similarity and affiliation need as determinants of interpersonal attraction. *Journal of Social Psychology, 134,* 257–259.

Shanab, M. E., & O'Neill, P. (1979). The effects of contrast upon compliance with socially undesirable requests in the door-in-the-face paradigm. *Canadian Journal of Behavioural Science, 11,* 236–244.

Shapiro, P. A. (1996). Psychiatric aspects of cardiovascular disease. *Psychiatric Clinics of North America, 19,* 613–629.

Shapiro, Y., & Gabbard, G. O. (1994). A reconsideration of altruism from an evolutionary and psychodynamic perspective. *Ethics & Behavior, 4,* 23–42.

Sharma, A. (1999). Does the salesperson like customers? A conceptual and empirical examination of the persuasive effect of perceptions of the salesperson's affect toward customers. *Psychology & Marketing, 16* (2), 141–162.

Sharpe, D., Adair, G. J., & Roese, N. J. (1992). Twenty years of deception research: A decline in subjects' trust? *Personality and Social Psychology Bulletin, 18,* 585–590.

Shaver, P., Hazan, C., & Bradshaw, D. (1988). Love as attachment: The integration of three behavioral systems. In R. J. Sternberg & M. L. Barnes (Eds.), *The psychology of love.* New Haven, CT: Yale University Press.

Shaver, P., & Klinnert, M. (1982). Schachter's theory of affiliation and emotion: Implications of developmental research. In L. Wheeler (Ed.), *Review of personality and social psychology* (Vol. 3). Beverly Hills, CA: Sage.

Shaw, L. L., Batson, C. D., & Todd, R. M. (1994). Empathy avoidance: Forestalling feeling for another in order to escape the motivational consequences. *Journal of Personality and Social Psychology, 67,* 879–887.

Shaw, M. E. (1981). *Group dynamics: The psychology of small group behavior.* New York: McGraw-Hill.

Shaw, M. E., & Harkey, B. (1976). Some effects of conguency of member characteristics and group structure upon group behavior. *Journal of Personality and Social Psychology, 34,* 412–418.

Sheatsley, P. B., & Feldman, J. J. (1964). The assassination of President Kennedy: A preliminary report on public attitude and behavior. *Public Opinion Quarterly, 28,* 189–215.

Sheeran, P., Abraham, C., & Orbell, S. (1999). Psychosocial correlates of heterosexual condom use: A meta-analysis. *Psychological Bulletin, 125,* 90–132.

Sheeran, P., Spears, R., Abraham, S. C. S., & Abrams, D. (1996). Religiosity, gender, and the double standard. *Journal of Psychology, 130,* 23–33.

Shell, R. M., & Eisenberg, N. (1992). A developmental model of recipients' reactions to aid. *Psychological Bulletin, 111,* 413–433.

Shell, R. M., & Eisenberg, N. (1996). Children's reactions to the receipt of direct and indirect help. *Child Development, 67,* 1391–1405.

Shepard, B., & Marshall, A. (1999). Possible selves mapping: Life-career exploration with young adolescents. *Canadian Journal of Counselling, 33,* 37–54.

Shepperd, J. A. (1993). Productivity loss in performance groups: A motivation analysis. *Psychological Bulletin, 11,* 67–81.

Shepperd, J. A. (1995). Remedying motivation and productivity loss in collective settings. *Current Directions in Psychological Science, 4,*131–134.

Shepperd, J. A., & Arkin, R. M. (1989). Determinants of self-handicapping: Task importance and the effects of preexisting handicaps on self-generated handicaps. *Personality and Social Psychology Bulletin, 15,* 101–112.

Sherif, M. (1935). A study of some social factors in perception. *Archives of Psychology,* No. 187.

Sherif, M. (1936). *The psychology of social norms.* New York: Harper.

Sherif, M. (1966). *In common predicament: Social psychology of intergroup conflict and cooperation.* Boston: Houghton-Mifflin.

Sherif, M., & Sherif, C. W. (1969). *Social psychology* (rev. ed.). New York: Harper & Row.

Sherman, S. J., Hamilton, D. L., & Lewis, A. C. (1999). Perceived entitativity and the social identity value of group memberships. In D. Abrams & M. A. Hogg (Eds.), *Social identity and social cognition.* Malden, MA: Blackwell.

Shestowsky, D., Wegener, D. T., & Fabrigar, L. R. (1998). Need for cognition and interpersonal influence: Individual differences in impact on dyadic decisions. *Journal of Personality & Social Psychology, 74* (5), 1317–1328.

Shiffrin, R. M., & Dumais, S. T. (1981). The development of automatism. In J. R. Anderson (Ed.), *Cognitive skills and their acquisition.* Hillsdale, NJ: Erlbaum.

Shiffrin, R. M., & Schneider, W. (1977). Controlled and automatic human information processing: II. Perceptual learning, automatic attending, and a general theory. *Psychological Review, 84,* 127–190.

Shotland, R. L. (1985, June). When bystanders just stand by. *Psychology Today, 19,* 50–55.

Showers, C. J., Abramson, L. Y., & Hogan, M. E. (1998). The dynamic self: How the content and structure of the self-concept change with mood. *Journal of Personality & Social Psychology, 75,* 478–493.

Shrauger, J. S. (1975). Responses to evaluation as a function of initial self-perceptions. *Psychological Bulletin, 82,* 581–596.

Sibicky, M. E., Schroeder, D. A., & Dovidio, J. F. (1995). Empathy and helping: Considering the consequences of intervention. *Basic and Applied Social Psychology, 16,* 435–453.

Sieber, J. E. (1996). Typically unexamined communication processes in research. In B. H. Stanley & J. E. Sieber (Eds.), *Research ethics: A psychological approach.* Lincoln: University of Nebraska Press.

Siebert, A. (1998). *The survivor personality.* New York: Perigee.

Siegert, J. R., & Stamp, G. H. (1994). "Our first big fight" as a milestone in the development of close relationships. *Communication Monographs, 61,* 345–360.

Siegman, A. W., Townsend, S. T., Blumenthal, R. S., Sorkin, J. D., & Civelek, A. C. (1998). Dimensions of anger and CHD in men and women: Self-ratings versus spouse ratings. *Journal of Behavioral Medicine, 21,* 315–336.

Sigall, H., & Ostrove, N. (1975). Beautiful but dangerous: Effects of offender attractiveness and nature of the crime on juridic judgment. *Journal of Personality and Social Psychology, 31,* 410–444.

Sigmund, K. (1995). *Games of life: Explorations in ecology, evolution, and behaviour.* New York: Penguin.

Sikes, S. K. (1971). *The natural history of the African elephant.* New York: American Elsevier Publications.

Silver, R. L., & Wortman, C. B. (1980). Coping with undesirable life events. In J. Barber & M. E. P. Seligman (Eds.), *Human helplessness: Theory and application.* New York: Academic Press.

Silverstein, B., Perdue, L., Peterson, B., & Kelly, E. (1986). The role of the mass media in promoting a thin standard of bodily attractiveness for women. *Sex Roles, 14,* 519–532.

Simon, L., Greenberg, J., & Brehm, J. (1995). Trivialization: The forgotten mode of dissonance reduction. *Journal of Personality and Social Psychology, 68,* 247–260.

Simon, S. B., Howe, L. V., & Kirschenbaum, H. (1972). *Values clarification: A handbook of practi-*

cal strategies for teachers and students. New York: Hart.

Simpson, G. E., & Yinger, J. M. (1985). *Racial and cultural minorities: An analysis of prejudice and discrimination* (5th ed.). New York: Harper & Row.

Simpson, J. A. (1987). The dissolution of romantic relationships: Factors involved in relationship stability and emotional distress. *Journal of Personality and Social Psychology, 53*, 683–692.

Sims, L. (1994). Drawing the boundaries: Exploring gender issues in young children's classifications of work using visual representations. *Early Child Development and Care, 98*, 79–96.

Sinclair, R. C., Lee, T., & Johnson, T. E. (1995). The effect of social-comparison feedback on aggressive responses to erotic and aggressive films. *Journal of Applied Social Psychology, 25*, 818–837.

Singelis, T. M. (1994). The measurement of independent and interdependent self-construals. Special Issue: The self and the collective. *Personality and Social Psychology Bulletin, 20*, 580–591.

Singelis, T., Choo, P., & Hatfield, E. (1995). Love schemas and romantic love. *Journal of Social Behavior & Personality, 10*, 15–36.

Singh, B. R. (1991). Teaching methods for reducing prejudice and enhancing academic achievement for all children. *Educational Studies, 17*, 157–171.

Singh, D. (1995). Female judgment of male attractiveness and desirability for relationships: Role of waist-to-hip ratio and financial status. *Journal of Personality and Social Psychology, 69*, 1089–1101.

Singh, R., Onglatco, M. L. U., Sriram, N., & Tay, A. B. G. (1997). The warm-cold variable in impression formation: Evidence for the positive-negative asymmetry. *British Journal of Social Psychology, 36*, 457–477.

Sinha, J. B. P. (1990). Role of psychology in national development. In G. Misra (Ed.), *Applied social psychology in India.* New Delhi: Sage.

Sistrunk, F., & McDavid, J. W. (1971). Sex variable in conformity behavior. *Journal of Personality and Social Psychology, 17*, 200–207.

Skinner, B. F. (1957). *Verbal behavior.* New York: Macmillan.

Skinner, B. F. (1983). *A matter of consequences.* New York: Knopf.

Skowronski, J. J., & Carlston, D. E. (1989). Negativity and extremity biases in impression formation: A review of explanations. *Psychological Bulletin, 105*, 131–142.

Slade, M. (1995, February 15). We forgot to write a headline. But it's not our fault. *The New York Times,* p. 5.

Sleek, S. (1998, September). Isolation increases with Internet use. *APA Monitor,* p. 29.

Slovic, P., Fischhoff, B., & Lichtenstein, S. (1976). Cognitive processes and societal risk taking. In J. S. Carroll & J. W. Payne (Eds.), *Cognition and social behavior* (pp. 165–184). Hillsdale, NJ: Erlbaum.

Slovic, P., Fischhoff, B., & Lichtenstein, S. (1977). Behavioral decision theory. *Annual Review of Psychology, 28*, 1–39.

Slowiaczek, L. M., Klayman, J., Sherman, S. J., & Skov, B. (1989). *Information selection and use in hypothesis testing: What is a good question, what is a good answer.* Unpublished manuscript.

Smadi, A. A. (1991). Dynamics of marriage as interpreted through control theory. *Journal of Reality Therapy, 10*, 44–50.

Smari, J., Bjarnadottir, A., & Bragadottir, B. (1998). Social anxiety, social skills and expectancy/cost of negative social events. *Scandinavian Journal of Behaviour Therapy, 27*, 149–155.

Smeaton, G., Byrne, D., & Murnen, S. K. (1989). The repulsion hypothesis revisited: Similarity irrelevance or assimilarity bias? *Journal of Personality and Social Psychology, 56*, 54–59.

Smith, C. A., & Ellsworth, P. C. (1987). Patterns of appraisal and emotion related to taking an exam. *Journal of Personality and Social Psychology, 52*, 475–488.

Smith, E. R. (1998). Mental representation and memory. In D. T. Gilbert & S. T. Fiske (Eds.), *The handbook of social psychology* (Vol. 2, 4th ed.). Boston: McGraw-Hill.

Smith, E. R., Becker, M. A., Byrne, D., Przybyla, D. P. (1993). Sexual attitudes of males and females as predictors of interpersonal attraction and marital compatibility. *Journal of Applied Social Psychology, 23*, 1011–1034.

Smith, H. S., & Cohen, L. H. (1993). Self-complexity and reactions to a relationship breakup. *Journal of Social and Clinical Psychology, 12*, 367–384.

Smith, J. A., & Forti, R. J. (1998). A pattern approach to the study of leader emergence. *Leadership Quarterly, 9* (2), 147–160.

Smith, K. D., Keating, J. P., & Stotland, E. (1989). Altruism reconsidered: The effect of denying feedback on a victim's status to empathic witnesses. *Journal of Personality and Social Psychology, 57*, 641–650.

Smith, M. B. (1990). Psychology in the public interest: What have we done? What can we do? *American Psychologist, 45*, 530–536.

Smith, P. B., Peterson, M. F., Bond, M., & Misumi, J. (1990). Leader style and leader behaviour in individualistic and collectivistic cultures. In S. Iwawaki, Y. Kashima, & K. Leung (Eds.), *Innovations in cross-cultural psychology.* Amsterdam, The Netherlands: Swets & Zeitlinger.

Smith, S. L., & Donnerstein, E. (1998). Harmful effects of exposure to media violence: Learning of aggression, emotional desensitization, and fear. In R. G. Geen, G. Russell, & E. Donnerstein (Eds.), *Human aggression: Theories, research, and implications for social policy* (pp. 167–202). San Diego, CA: Academic Press.

Smith, S. M., & Shaffer, D. R. (1995). Speed of speech and persuasion: Evidence for multiple effects. *Personality & Social Psychology Bulletin, 21*, 1051–1060.

Smith, V. L. (1991a). Impact of pretrial instructions on jurors' information processing and decision

making. *Journal of Applied Psychology, 76*, 220–228.

Smith, V. L. (1991b). Prototypes in the courtroom: Lay representations of legal concepts. *Journal of Personality and Social Psychology, 61*, 857–872

Smyth, J. M., Stone, A. A., Hurewitz, A., & Kaell, A. (1999). Writing about stressful experiences on symptom reduction in patients with asthma or rheumatoid arthritis. *Journal of the American Medical Association, 281*, 1304–1309.

Snyder, C. R., & Higgins, R. L. (1988). Excuses: Their effective role in the negotiation of reality. *Psychological Bulletin, 104*, 23–35.

Snyder, M. (1974). The self-monitoring of expressive behavior. *Journal of Personality and Social Psychology, 30*, 526–537.

Snyder, M. (1977). Impression management. In L. S. Wrightsman (Ed.), *Social psychology in the seventies* (pp. 115–145). New York: Wiley.

Snyder, M. (1987). *Public appearances/Private realities: The psychology of self-monitoring.* New York: W. H. Freeman.

Snyder, M. (1992). Motivational foundations of behavioral confirmation. In M. P. Zanna (Ed.), *Advances in experimental social psychology* (Vol. 25). San Diego, CA: Academic Press.

Snyder, M. (1993). Basic research and practical problems: The promise of a "functional" personality and social psychology. *Personality and Social Psychology Bulletin, 19*, 251–264.

Snyder, M. (1995). Self-monitoring: Public appearances versus private realities. In G. G. Brannigan & R. Merrens (Eds.), *The social psychologists: Research adventures. McGraw-Hill series in social psychology.* New York: McGraw-Hill.

Snyder, M., Campbell, B. H., & Preston, E. (1982). Testing hypotheses about human nature: Assessing the accuracy of social stereotypes. *Social Cognition, 1*, 256–272.

Snyder, M., & Cantor, N. (1979). Testing hypotheses about other people: The use of historical knowledge. *Journal of Experimental Social Psychology, 15*, 330–343.

Snyder, M., & DeBono, K. G. (1989). Dopamine and schizophrenia. In A. R. Pratkanis, S. J. Breckler, & A. G. Greenwald (Eds.), *Attitude structure and function.* Hillsdale, NJ: Erlbaum.

Snyder, M., & Gangestad, S. (1986). On the nature of self-monitoring: Matters of assessment, matters of validity. *Journal of Personality and Social Psychology, 51*, 125–139.

Snyder, M., Gangestad, S., & Simpson, J. A. (1983). Choosing friends as activity partners: The role of self-monitoring. *Journal of Personality and Social Psychology, 45*, 1061–1072.

Snyder, M., & Simpson, J. A. (1984). Self-monitoring and dating relationships. *Journal of Personality and Social Psychology, 47*, 1281–1291.

Snyder, M., & Swann, W. B., Jr. (1978). Hypothesis-testing processes in social interaction. *Journal of Personality and Social Psychology, 36*, 1202–1212.

Sober, E., & Wilson, D. S. (1998). *Unto others: The evolution and psychology of unselfish behavior.* Cambridge, MA: Harvard University Press.

Solomon, Z. (1993). *Combat stress reaction: The enduring toll of war.* New York: Plenum.

Solomon, Z. (1994). *Coping with war-induced stress.* New York: Plenum.

Sommer, R. (1999). Psychology applied to the environment. In A. M. Stec & A. Douglas (Eds.), *Psychology: Fields of application* (pp. 148–164). Boston, MA: Houghton Mifflin.

Song, J. A., Bergen, M. B., & Schumm, W. R. (1995). Sexual satisfaction among Korean-American couples in the midwestern United States. *Journal of Sex and Marital Therapy, 21,* 147–158.

Sorensen, J. R., & Wallace, D. H. (1995). Capital punishment in Missouri: Examining the issue of racial disparity. *Behavioral Sciences and the Law, 13,* 61–80.

Sorenson, S. B., & Siegel, J. M. (1992). Gender, ethnicity, and sexual assault: Findings from the Los Angeles epidemiological catchment area study. *Journal of Social Issues, 48,* 93–104.

Sorkin, R. D., West, R., & Robinson, D. E. (1998). Group performance depends on the majority rule. *Psychological Science, 9* (6), 456–463.

Sosik, J. J., Avolio, B. J., & Kahai, S. S. (1998). Inspiring group creativity: Comparing anonymous and identified electronic brainstorming. *Small Group Research, 29* (1), 3–31.

Spanier, G. B. (1983). Married and unmarried cohabitation in the United States: 1980. *Journal of Marriage and the Family, 45,* 277–288.

Spears, R., & Haslam, S. A. (1997). Stereotyping and the burden of cognitive load. In R. Spears & P. J. Oakes (Eds.), *The social psychology of stereotyping and group life.* Oxford, England: Blackwell.

Spellman, B. A., Ullman, J. B., & Holyoak, K. J. (1993). A coherence model of cognitive consistency: Dynamics of attitude change during the Persian Gulf War. *Journal of Social Issues, 49,* 147–165.

Spence, J. T., Helmreich, R., & Stapp, J. (1973). A short version of the Attitude toward Women Scale (AWS). *Bulletin of the Psychonomic Society, 2,* 219–220.

Spencer, S. J., Steele, C. M., & Quinn, D. M. (1999). Stereotype threat and women's math performance. *Journal of Experimental Social Psychology, 35* (1), 4–28.

Spivey, C. B., & Prentice-Dunn, S. (1990). Assessing the directionality of deindividuated behavior: Effects of deindividuation, modeling, and private self-consciousness on aggressive and prosocial responses. *Basic and Applied Social Psychology, 11,* 387–403.

Sporer, S. L., Penrod, S., Read, D., & Cutler, B. (1995). Choosing, confidence, and accuracy: A meta-analysis of the confidence-accuracy relation in eyewitness identification studies. *Psychological Bulletin, 118,* 315–327.

Sprecher, S. (1992). How men and women expect to feel and behave in response to inequity in close relationships. *Social Psychology Quarterly, 55,* 57–69.

Sprecher, S. (1999). "I love you more today than yesterday": Romantic partners' perceptions of changes in love and related affect over time. *Journal of Personality & Social Psychology, 76,* 46–53.

Sprecher, S., & Hatfield, E. (1996). Premarital sexual standards among U.S. college students: Comparison with Russian and Japanese students. *Archives of Sexual Behavior, 25,* 261–288.

Sprecher, S., Sullivan, Q., & Hatfield, E. (1994). Mate selection preferences: Gender differences examined in a national sample. *Journal of Personality and Social Psychology, 66,* 1074–1080.

Sproull, L., & Kiesler, S. (1991). *Connections: New ways of working in the networked organization.* Cambridge, MA: MIT Press.

St. Pierre, R., Herendeen, N. M., Moore, D. S., & Nagle, A. M. (1994). Does occupational stereotyping still exist? *Journal of Psychology, 128,* 589–598.

Staats, A. W., & Staats, C. K. (1958). Attitudes established by classical conditioning. *Journal of Abnormal and Social Psychology, 57,* 37–40.

Stajkovic, A. D., & Luthans, F. (1998). Self-efficacy and work-related performance: A meta-analysis. *Psychological Bulletin, 124,* 240–261.

Stallard, M. J., & Worthington, D. L. (1998). Reducing the hindsight bias utilizing attorney closing arguments. *Law & Human Behavior, 22* (6), 671–683.

Staner, L., Linkowski, P., & Mendlewicz, J. (1994). Biological markers as classifiers for depression: A multivariate study. *Progress in Neuro-Psychopharmacology & Biological Psychiatry, 18,* 899–914.

Stang, D. J. (1973). Six theories of repeated exposure and affect. *Catalog of Selected Documents in Psychology, 126.*

Stang, D. J. (1976). Group size effects on conformity. *Journal of Social Psychology, 98,* 175–181.

Stangor, C., Lynch, L., Changming, D., & Glass, B. (1992). Categorization of individuals on the basis of multiple social features. *Journal of Personality and Social Psychology, 62,* 207–218.

Stanley, B. H., Sieber, J. E., & Melton, G. B., (Eds.). (1996). *Research ethics: A psychological approach.* Lincoln, NE: University of Nebraska Press.

Stanton, A. L., Danoff-Burg, S., Cameron, C. L., Cameron, M., Snider, P. R., & Kirk, S. B. (1999). Social comparison and adjustment to breast cancer: An experimental examination of upward affiliation and downward evaluation. *Health Psychology, 18,* 151–158.

Stapinski, H. (1999, February). Y Not Love? *American Demographics,* pp. 63–68.

Stasser, G., Kerr, N. L., & Davis, J. H. (1989). Influence processes and consensus models in decision-making groups. In P. B. Paulus (Ed.), *Psy-*

chology of group influence (2nd ed.). Hillsdale, NJ: Erlbaum.

Stasson, M. F., & Davis, J. H. (1989). The relative effects of the number of arguments, number of argument sources and number of opinion positions in group-mediated opinion change. *British Journal of Social Psychology, 28,* 251–262.

State vs. Barron, 465 S. W. 2d 523, 527–78 (no. Ct. App. 1971).

Staub, E. (1989). *The roots of evil: The origins of genocide and other group violence.* Cambridge, England: Cambridge University Press.

Staudinger, U. M., Fleeson, W., & Baltes, P. B. (1999). Predictors of subjective physical health and global well-being: Similarities and differences between the United States and Germany. *Journal of Personality & Social Psychology, 76,* 305–319.

Staudinger, U. M., Freund, A. M., Linden, M., & Maas, I. (1999). Self, personality, and life regulation: Facets of psychological resilience in old age. In P. B. Baltes & K. U. Mayer (Eds.), *The Berlin Aging Study: Aging from 70 to 100.* New York: Cambridge University Press.

Steele, C. M. (1988). The psychology of self-affirmation: Sustaining the integrity of the self. In L. Berkowitz (Ed.), *Social psychological studies of the self: Perspectives and programs* (pp. 261–302). San Diego, CA: Academic Press.

Steele, C. M. (1992, April). Race and the schooling of Black Americans. *Atlantic, 269,* pp. 68–78.

Steele, C. M. (1998). Stereotyping and its threat are real. *American Psychologist, 53* (6), 680–681.

Steele, C. M., & Aronson, J. (1995). Stereotype threat and the intellectual test performance of African Americans. *Journal of Personality and Social Psychology, 69,* 797–811.

Steele, C. M., & Aronson, J. (1998). Stereotype threat and the test performance of academically successful African Americans. In C. Jencks & M. Phillips (Eds.), *The Black-White test score gap.* Washington, DC: Brookings Institution.

Steenland, K., & Deddens, J. A. (1997). Effect of travel and rest on performance of professional basketball players. *Sleep, 20,* 366–369.

Stein, J. A., & Nyamathi, A. (1999). Gender differences in relationships among stress, coping, and health risk behaviors in impoverished, minority populations. *Personality & Individual Differences, 26,* 141–157.

Stein, L. B., & Brodsky, S. L. (1995). When infants wail: Frustration and gender as variables in distress disclosure. *Journal of General Psychology, 122,* 19–27.

Stein, M., & Baum, A. S. (Eds.). (1995). *Chronic diseases: Perspectives in behavioral medicine.* Mahwah, NJ: Erlbaum.

Steinberg, L., & Silverberg, S. B. (1987). Influences on marital satisfaction during the middle stages of the family life cycle. *Journal of Marriage and the Family, 49,* 751–760.

Steiner, I. (1972). *Group process and productivity.* New York: Academic.

Steiner, I. (1976). Task-performing groups. In J. W. Thibaut, J. T. Spence, & R. C. Carson (Eds.), *Contemporary topics in social psychology.* Morristown, NJ: General Learning Press.

Stephan, W. G. (1985). Intergroup relations. In G. Lindzey & E. Aronson (Eds.), *Handbook of social psychology* (Vol. 2, pp. 599–658). New York: Random House.

Stephan, W. G. (1986). The effects of school desegregation: An evaluation 30 years after *Brown.* In M. J. Saks & L. Saxe (Eds.), *Advances in applied social psychology* (Vol. 3, pp. 181–206). Hillsdale, NJ: Erlbaum.

Sternberg, R. J. (1985). Implicit theories of intelligence, creativity, and wisdom. *Journal of Personality and Social Psychology, 49,* 607–627.

Sternberg, R. J. (1986). A triangular theory of love. *Psychological Review, 93,* 119–135.

Sternberg, R. J. (1987). Liking versus loving: A comparative evaluation of theories. *Psychological Bulletin, 102,* 331–345.

Sternberg, R. J. (1988). Triangulating love. In R. J. Sternberg & M. J. Barnes (Eds.), *The psychology of love.* New Haven, CT: Yale University Press.

Sternberg, R. J. (1997). Construct validation of a triangular love scale. *European Journal of Social Psychology, 27,* 313–335.

Stevens, C. K., & Kristof, A. L. (1995). Making the right impression: A field study of applicant impression management during job interviews. *Journal of Applied Psychology, 80,* 587–606.

Stevens, R. (1996). *Understanding the self.* Newbury Park, CA: Sage.

Stevenson, H. W. (1992, December). Learning from Asian schools. *Scientific American,* pp. 70–75.

Stevenson, H. W., & Lee, S. Y. (1990). Contexts of achievement: A study of American, Chinese, and Japanese children. *Monographs of the Society for Research in Child Development, No. 221, 55,* Nos. 1–2.

Stevenson, H. W., & Stigler, J. W. (1992). *The learning gap: Why our schools are failing and what we can learn from Japanese and Chinese education.* New York: Summit.

Stevenson, J. L., & Wright, P. S. (1999). Chapter 11: Group Dynamics. *Activities, Adaptation & Aging, 23* (3), 139–173.

Stewart, D. D. (1998). Stereotypes, negativity bias, and the discussion of unshared information in decision-making groups. *Small Group Research, 29,* 643–668.

Stewart, D. W., & Kamins, M. A. (1993). *Secondary research: Information sources and methods.* Newbury Park, CA: Sage.

Stewart, J. E., II. (1980). Defendant's attractiveness as a factor in the outcome of criminal trials: An observational study. *Journal of Applied Psychology, 10,* 348–361.

Stewart, R. H. (1965). Effect of continuous responding on the order effect in personality impression formation. *Journal of Personality and Social Psychology, 1,* 161–165.

Stice, E., & Shaw, H. E. (1994). Adverse effects of the media-portrayed thin-ideal on women and linkages to bulimic symptomatology. *Journal of social and Clinical Psychology, 13,* 288–308.

Stiff, J. B. (1994). *Persuasive communication.* New York: Guilford.

Stokes, J. P. (1983). Components of group cohesion: Intermember attraction, instrumental value, and risk taking. *Small Group Behavior, 14,* 163–173.

Stone, A. A., Neale, J. M., Cox, D. S., Napoli, A., et al. (1994). Daily events are associated with a secretory immune response to an oral antigen in me. *Health Psychology, 13,* 440–446.

Stone, G. C. (1979). Patient compliance and the role of the expert. *Journal of Social Issues, 35,* 34–59.

Storms, M. D. (1973). Videotape and the attribution process: Reversing actors' and observers' points of view. *Journal of Personality and Social Psychology, 27,* 165–175.

Storms, M. D., & McCaul, K. (1976). Attribution processes and emotional exacerbation of dysfunctional behavior. In J. H. Harvey, W. J. Ickes, & R. F. Kidd (Eds.), *New directions in attribution research* (Vol. 1, pp. 143–169). Hillsdale, NJ: Erlbaum.

Storms, M. D., & Nisbett, R. E. (1970). Insomnia and the attribution process. *Journal of Personality and Social Psychology, 16,* 219–328.

Stormshak, E. A., Bierman, K. L., Bruschi, C., Dodge, K. A., & Coie, J. D. (1999). The relation between behavior problems and peer preference in different classroom contexts. *Child Development, 70* (1), 169–182.

Strassberg, Z., Dodge, K. A., Pettit, G. S., & Bates, J. E. (1994). Spanking in the home and children's subsequent aggression toward kindergarten peers. *Development and Psychopathology, 6,* 445–461.

Straus, M. A., & Gelles, R. J. (Eds.). (1990). *Physical violence in American families.* New Brunswick, NJ: Transaction.

Strawn, D. V., & Buchanan, R. W. (1976). Jury confusion: A threat to justice. *Judicature, 59,* 478–483.

Striacker, L. J., Messick, S., & Jackson, D. N. (1969). Dimensionality of social influence. *Proceedings of the 76th annual convention of the American Psychological Association, 1968, 3,* 189–190.

Stroebe, W., Diehl, M., Abakoumkin, G. (1992). The illusion of group effectivity. *Personality and Social Psychology Bulletin, 18,* 643–650.

Stroh, P. K. (1995).Voters as pragmatic cognitive misers: The accuracy-effort trade-off in the candidate evaluation process. In M. Lodge & K. M. McGraw (Eds.), *Political judgment: Structure and process.* Ann Arbor: University of Michigan Press.

Strube, M. (Ed.). (1990). Type A behavior [Special Issue]. *Journal of Social Behavior and Personality, 5,* 101–110.

Strube, M. J., Miles, M. E., & Finch, W. H. (1981). The social facilitation of a simple task: Field tests

of alternative explanations. *Personality and Social Psychology Bulletin, 7,* 701–707.

Struckman-Johnson, C., Struckman-Johnson, D., Gilliland, R. C., & Ausman, A. (1994). Effect of persuasive appeals in AIDS PSAs and condom commercials on intentions to use condoms. *Journal of Applied Social Psychology, 24,* 2223–2244.

Strutton, D., Vitell, S. J., & Pelton, L. E. (1994). How consumers may justify inappropriate behavior in market settings: An application on the techniques of neutralization. *Journal of Business Research, 30,* 253–260.

Studebaker, C. A., & Penrod, S. D. (1997). Pretrial publicity: The media, the law, and common sense. *Psychology, Public Policy, & Law, 3* (2–3), 428–460.

Stukas, A., Snyder, M., & Clary, G. (1999). The effects of "mandatory volunteerism" on intentions to volunteer. *Psychological Science, 10,* 59–64.

Suchner, R. W., & Jackson, D. (1976). Responsibility and status: A causal or only a spurios relationship? *Sociometry, 39,* 243–256.

Sudefeld, P., & Borrie, R. A. (1978). Sensory deprivation, attitude change, and defense against persuasion. *Canadian Journal of Behavioural Science, 10,* 16–27.

Sue, S., Smith, S. E., & Caldwell, C. (1973). Effects of inadmissible evidence on the decisions of simulated jurors: A moral dilemma. *Journal of Applied Social Psychology, 3,* 345–353.

Suls, J., & Rosnow, J. (1988). Concerns about artifacts in behavioral research. In M. Morawski (Ed.), *The rise of experimentation in American psychology* (pp. 163–187). New Haven, CT: Yale University Press.

Suls, J., & Wills, T. A. (Eds.). (1991). *Social comparison: Contemporary theory and research.* Hillsdale, NJ: Erlbaum.

Sulzer-Azaroff, B., & Mayer, G. R. (1991). *Behavior analysis for lasting change.* Fort Worth, TX: Holt.

Surra, C. A. (1991). Mate selection and premarital relationships. In A. Booth (Ed.), *Contemporary families* (pp. 54–57). Minneapolis, MN: National Council on Family Relations.

Sutherland, E. H., & Cressey, D. R. (1974). *Principles of criminology* (9th ed.). New York: Lippincott.

Sutton, S., McVey, D., & Glanz, A. (1999). A comparative test of the theory of reasoned action and the theory of planned behavior in the prediction of condom use intentions in a national sample of English young people. *Health Psychology, 18* (1), 72–81.

Swan, S., & Wyer, R. S., Jr. (1997). Gender stereotypes and social identity: How being in the minority affects judgment of self and others. *Personality & Social Psychology Bulletin, 23,* 1265–1276.

Swann, W. B., Jr. (1987). Identity negotiation: Where two roads meet. *Journal of Personality and Social Psychology, 53,* 1038–1051.

Swann, W. B. (1992). Seeking "truth," finding despair: Some unhappy consequences of a negative self-concept. *Current Directions in Psychological Science, 1,* 15–18.

Swann, W. B. (1997). The trouble with change: Self-verification and allegiance to the self. *Psychological Science, 8,* 177–180.

Swann, W. B., Jr., Hixon, J. G., & DeLaRonde, C. (1992). Embracing the bitter "truth": Negative self-concepts and marital commitment. *Psychological Science, 3,* 118–121.

Swann, W. B., Jr., Langlois, J. H., & Gilbert, L. A. (Eds.). (1999). *Sexism and stereotypes in modern society: The gender science of Janet Taylor Spence.* Washington, DC: American Psychological Association.

Swann, W. B., Jr., Stein-Seroussi, A., & Giesler, B. J. (1992). Why people self-verify. *Journal of Personality and Social Psychology, 62,* 392–401.

Sweeney, P. D., & Gruber, K. L. (1984). Selective exposure: Voter information preferences and the Watergate affair. *Journal of Personality and Social Psychology, 46,* 1208–1221.

Sweet, E. (1985, October). Date rape: The story of an epidemic and those who deny it. *Ms/Campus Times,* pp. 56–59.

Swim, J. (1993). In search of gender bias in evaluations and trait inferences: The role of diagnosticity and gender stereotypicality of behavioral information. *Sex Roles, 29,* 213–237.

Swim, J. K., & Hyers, L. L. (1999). Excuse me—What did you just say?!: Women's public and private responses to sexist remarks. *Journal of Experimental Social Psychology, 35,* 68–88.

Sykes, G., & Matza, D. (1957). Techniques of neutralization: A theory of delinquency. *American Sociological Review, 22,* 664–670.

Symons, C. S., & Johnson, B. T. (1997). The self-reference effect in memory: A meta-analysis. *Psychological Bulletin, 121,* 371–394.

Syvalahti, E. K. (1994). Biological aspects of depression. Yrjo Jahnsson Foundation VIII Medical Symposium: Depression: Preventive and risk factors (1992, Porvoo, Finland). *Acta Psychiatrica Scandinavica, 89,* 11–15.

Szymanski, K., & Harkins, S. (1987). Social loafing and self-evaluation with a social standard. *Journal of Personality and Social Psychology, 53,* 891–897.

Tachibana, Y., Ohgishi, M., & Monden, K. (1984). Experimental study of aggression and catharsis in Japanese. *Perceptual and Motor Skills, 58,* 207–212.

Tajfel, H. (1982). *Social identity and intergroup relations.* London: Cambridge University Press.

Tajfel, H., & Turner, J. C. (1986). The social identity theory of intergroup behavior. In S. Worchel & W. G. Austin (Eds.), *Psychology of intergroup relations.* Chicago: Nelson Hall.

Tandon, K., Ansari, M. A., Kapoor, A. (1991). Attributing upward influence attempts in organizations. *Journal of Psychology, 125,* 59–63.

Tanford, S., & Penrod, S. (1984). Social interference processes in juror judgments of multiple-offense trials. *Journal of Personality and Social Psychology,, 47,* 749–765.

Tang, S., & Hall, V. C. (1995). The overjustification effect: A meta-analysis. *Applied Cognitive Psychology, 9,* 365–404.

Tangney, J. P., Hill-Barlow, D., Wagner, P. E., Marschall, D. E., Borenstein, J. K., Sanftner, J., Mohr, T., & Gramzow, R. (1996). Assessing individual differences in constructive versus destructive responses to anger across the lifespan. *Journal of Personality and Social Psychology, 70,* 780–796.

Tannen, D. (1991). *You just don't understand.* New York: Ballantine.

Tannen, D. (Ed.). (1993). *Gender and conversational interaction.* New York: Oxford University Press.

Tannenbaum, A. S. (1980). Organizational psychology. In H. C. Triandis & R. W. Brislin (Eds.), *Handbook of cross-cultural psychology: Social psychology* (Vol. 5). Boston: Allyn & Bacon.

Tanner, J. E., & Byrne, R. W. (1993). Concealing facial evidence of mood: Perspective-taking in a captive gorilla? *Primates, 34,* 451–457.

Taraban, C. B., & Hendrick, C. (1995). Personality perceptions associated with six styles of love. *Journal of Social and Personal Relationships, 12,* 453–461.

Tayeb, M. (1987). Contingency theory and culture: A study of matched English and the Indian manufacturing firms. *Organization Studies, 8,* 241–261.

Taylor, D. G. (1982). Pluralistic ignorance and the spiral of silence: A formal analysis. *Public Opinion Quarterly, 46,* 311–335.

Taylor, D. M., & Jaggi, V. (1974). Ethnocentrism and causal attribution in a south Indian context. *Journal of Cross-Cultural Psychology, 5,* 162–171.

Taylor, G. (1990, July 9). Good Samaritans kick. *The National Law Journal, 12 (*44), 2.

Taylor, R., & Stough, R. R. (1978). Territorial cognition: Assessing Altman's typology. *Journal of Personality and Social Psychology, 36,* 418–423.

Taylor, R. B., & Lanni, J. C. (1981). Territorial dominance: The influence of the resident advantage in triadic decision-making. *Journal of Personality and Social Psychology, 41,* 909–915.

Taylor, R. G. (1984). The potential impact of humanistic psychology on modern administrative style: II. Administrative models and psychological variants. *Psychology: A Quarterly Journal of Human Behavior, 21,* 1–9.

Taylor, S. E. (1991). *Health psychology.* New York: McGraw-Hill.

Taylor, S. E. (1995). *Health psychology* (3rd ed.). New York: McGraw-Hill.

Taylor, S. E., & Armor, D. A. (1996). Positive illusions and coping with adversity. *Journal of Personality, 64,* 873–898.

Taylor, S. E., & Brown, J. D. (1988). Illusion and well-being: A social psychological perspective on mental health. *Psychological Bulletin, 103,* 193–210.

Taylor, S. E., & Brown, J. D. (1994). Positive illusions and well-being revisited: Separating fact from fiction. *Psychological Bulletin, 116,* 21–27.

Taylor, S. E., Buunk, B. P., & Aspinwall, L. G. (1990). Social comparison, stress, and coping. *Personality and Social Psychology Bulletin, 16,* 74–89.

Taylor, S. E., & Fiske, S. T. (1978). Salience, attention, and attribution: Top of the head phenomena. In L. Berkowitz (Ed.), *Advances in experimental social psychology* (Vol. 11, pp. 249–288). New York: Academic Press.

Taylor, S. E., Helgeson, V. S., Reed, G. M., & Skokan, L. A. (1991). Self-generated feelings of control and adjustment to physical illness. *Journal of Social Issues, 47,* 91–109.

Taylor, S. E., Kemeny, M. E., Aspinwall, L. G., & Schneider, S. G. (1992). Optimism, coping, psychological distress, and high-risk sexual behavior among men at risk for acquired immunodeficiency syndrome (AIDS). *Journal of Personality & Social Psychology, 63,* 460–473.

Taylor, S. E., Kemeny, M. E., Schneider, S. G., & Aspinwall, L. G. (1993). Coping with the threat of AIDS. In J. B. Pryor & G. D. Reeder (Eds.), *The social psychology of HIV infection.* Hillsdale, NJ: Erlbaum.

Taylor, S. P., & Pisano, R. (1971). Physical aggression as a function of frustration and physical attachment. *Journal of Social Psychology, 84,* 261–267.

Taylor, S. E., & Thompson, S. C. (1982). Stalking the elusive "vividness" effect. *Psychological Review, 89,* 155–181.

Teigen, K. H. (1995). How good is good luck? The role of counterfactual thinking in the perception of lucky and unlucky events. *European Journal of Social Psychology, 25,* 281–302.

Teixeira, M. P., & Gomes, W. B. (1995). Self-consciousness scale: A Brazilian version. *Psychological Reports, 77,* 423–427.

Tennen, H., & Affleck, G. (1998). Personality and transformation in the face of adversity. In R. G. Tedeschi & C. L. Park (Eds.), *Posttraumatic growth: Positive changes in the aftermath of crisis. The LEA series in personality and clinical psychology.* Mahwah, NJ: Erlbaum.

Terborg, J. R. (1977). Women in management: A research review. *Journal of Applied Psychology, 62,* 647–664.

Teske, R. H., & Hazlett, M. H. (1985). A scale for measurement of attitudes toward handgun control. *Journal of Criminal Justice, 13,* 373–379.

Tesser, A. (1993). The importance of heritability in psychological research: The case of attitudes. *Psycholigcal Review, 100,* 129–142.

Tesser, A., & Brodie, M. (1971). A note on the evaluation of a computer date. *Psychonomic Science, 23,* 300.

Tessor, A. (1988). Toward a self-evaluation maintenance model of social behavior. In L. Berkowitz

(Ed.), *Advances in experimental and social psychology* (Vol. 21, pp. 181–227). New York: Academic Press.

Tetlock, P. E., Peterson, R. S., McGuire, C., Chang, S., & Feld, P. (1992). Assessing political group dynamics: A test of the groupthink model. *Journal of Personality and Social Psychology, 63*, 403–425.

t'Hart, P. (1991). Irving L. Janis' victims of groupthink. *Political Psychology, 12*, 247–278.

The new addicts. (1984, May 20). *The New York Times*, p. 50.

They've got love. (1999, February 15). *People Weekly*, pp. 46–51.

Thibaut, J. W., & Kelley, H. H. (1959). *The social psychology of groups*. New York: Wiley.

Thomas, D. C. (1999). Cultural diversity and work group effectiveness: An experimental study. *Journal of Cross-Cultural Psychology, 30* (2), 242–263.

Thompson, E. P., Roman, R. J., Moskowitz, G. B., Chaiken, S., et al. (1994). Accuracy motivation attenuates covert priming: The systematic processing of social information. *Journal of Personality and Social Psychology, 66*, 474–489.

Thompson, L. (1998). A new look at social cognition in groups. *Basic & Applied Social Psychology, 20*, 3–5.

Thompson, M. G., & Heller, K. (1990). Facets of support related to well-being: Quantitative social isolation and perceived family support in a sample of elderly women. *Psychology and Aging, 5*, 535–544.

Thompson, S. C. (1988, August). *An intervention to increase physician-patient communication*. Paper presented at the annual meeting of the American Psychological Association, Atlanta.

Thompson, S. C., Nanni, C., & Schwankovsky, L. (1990). Patient-oriented interventions to improve communication in a medical office visit. *Health Psychology, 9*, 390–404.

Thompson, S. H., Corwin, S. J., Rogan, T. J., & Sargent, R. G. (1999). Body size beliefs and weight concerns among mothers and their adolescent children. *Journal of Child & Family Studies, 8*, 91–108.

Thompson, W. C., & Fuqua, J. (1998). "The jury will disregard . . .": A brief guide to inadmissible evidence. In J. M. Golding & C. M. MacLeod (Eds.), *Intentional forgetting: Interdisciplinary approaches* (pp. 435–452). Mahwah, NJ: Erlbaum.

Thomson, E. (1997). Discrimination and the death penalty in Arizona. *Criminal Justice Review, 22* (1), 65–76.

Thoresen, C. E., & Low, K. G. (1990). Women and the Type A behavior pattern: Review and commentary. *Journal of Social Behavior and Personality, 5*, 117–133.

Thornton, B. (1992). Repression and its mediating influence on the defensive attribution of responsibility. *Journal of Research in Personality, 26*, 44–57.

Thornton, B., Hogate, L., Moirs, K., Pinette, M., & Presby, W. (1986). Physiological evidence for an arousal-based motivational bias in the defensive attribution of responsibility. *Journal of Experimental Social Psychology, 22*, 148–162.

Tice, D. M. (1991). Esteem protection or enhancement? Self-handicapping motives and attributions differ by trait self-esteem. *Journal of Personality and Social Psychology, 60*, 711–725.

Tice, D. M., Butler, J. L., Muraven, M. B., & Stillwell, A. M. (1995). When modesty prevails: Differential favorability of self-presentation to friends and strangers. *Journal of Personality and Social Psychology, 69*, 1120–1138.

Timaeus, E. (1968). Untersuchungen zum sogenannten konformen Verhatten. *Zeitschrfit fur experimentelle und angewandte psychologie, 15*, 176–194.

Tindale, R. S. (1993). Decision errors made by individuals and groups. In N. J. Castellan (Ed.), *Individual and group decision making: Current issues*. Hillsdale, NJ: Erlbaum.

Tinley Smoot, D. A. (1998). Effects of linear and non-linear incentive pay systems with individual and group payouts on the social psychology phenomenon of social loafing. *Dissertation Abstracts International: Section B: The Sciences & Engineering, 58* (8-B), 4434.

Titus, T. G. (1991). Effects of rehearsal instructions on the primacy effect in free recall. *Psychological Reports, 68*, 1371–1377.

Tjosvold, D., & Deemer, D. K. (1980). Effects of controversy within a cooperative or competitive context on organizational decision making. *Journal of Applied Psychology, 65*, 590–595.

Tolan, P. H., & Guerra, N. G. (1994). Prevention of delinquency: Current status and issues. *Applied & Preventive Psychology, 3*, 251–273.

Tolstedt, B. E., & Stokes, J. P. (1984). Self-disclosure, intimacy, and the depenetration process. *Journal of Personality and Social Psychology, 46*, 84–90.

Tomita, S. K. (1990). The denial of elder mistreatment by victims and abusers: The application of neutralization theory. *Violence and Victims, 5*, 171–184.

Toobin, J. (1996). *The run of his life: The People vs. O.J. Simpson*. New York: Random House.

Tornstam, L. (1992). Loneliness in marriage. *Journal of Social and Perosnal Relationships, 9*, 197–217.

Torrence, E. P. (1954). Some consequences of power differences on decision making in permanent and temporary three-man groups. *Research Studies, State College of Washington, 22*, 130–140.

Tosi, H. L. (1991). The organization as a context for leadership theory: A multilevel approach. *Leadership Quarterly, 2*, 205–228.

Tosi, H. L., & Slocum, J. W. (1984). Contingency theory: Some suggested directions. *Journal of Management, 10*, 9–26.

Toynbee, P. (1977). *Patients*. New York: Harcourt Brace Jovanovich.

Traugott, M. W., & Price, V. E. (1991, November). *Exit polls in the 1989 Virginia gubernatorial race: Where did they go wrong?* Paper presented at the annual meeting of the Midwest Association for Public Opinion Research, Chicago.

Tremblay, R. E., Schaal, B., Boulerice, B., Arseneault, L., Soussignan, R., & Perusse, D. (1997). Male physical aggression, social dominance, and testosterone levels at puberty: A developmental perspective. In A. Raine & P. Brennan (Eds.), *Biosocial bases of violence. NATO ASI series: Series A: Life sciences* (Vol. 292, pp. 271–291). New York: Plenum.

Triandis, H. C. (1989). The self and social behavior in differing cultural contexts. *Psychological Review, 96*, 506–520.

Triandis, H. C. (1990). Cross-cultural studies of individualism and collectivism. In J. Berman (Ed.), *Nebraska symposium on motivation, 1989*. Lincoln: University of Nebraska.

Triandis, H. C. (1994). *Culture and social behavior*. New York: McGraw-Hill.

Triandis, H. C. (1998). Vertical and horizontal individualism and collectivism: Theory and research implications for international comparative management. In J. L. C. Cheng & R. B. Peterson (Eds.), *Advances in international comparative management* (Vol. 12, pp. 7–35). Stamford, CT: Jai Press.

Triplett, N. (1897). The dynamogenic factors in pacemaking and competition. *American Journal of Psychology, 9*, 507–533.

Trivers, R. L. (1971). The evolution of reciprocal altruism. *Quarterly Review of Biology, 46*, 35–57.

Trobst, K. K., Collins, R. L., & Embree, J. M. (1994). The role of emotion in social support provision: Gender, empathy and expressions of distress. *Journal of Social and Personal Relationships, 11*, 45–62.

Truss, C., Goffee, R., & Jones, G. (1995). Segregated occupations and gender stereotyping: A study of secretarial work in Europe. *Human Relations, 48*, 1331–1354.

Tucker, M. B., & Mitchell-Kernan, C. (1995). *The decline in marriage among African Americans*. New York: Russell Sage Foundation.

Tulving, E., & Schacter, D. L. (1990, January 19). Priming and human memory systems. *Science, 247*, 301–306.

Tur-Kaspa, H., Weisel, A., & Segev, L. (1998). Attributions for feelings of loneliness of students with learning disabilities. *Learning Disabilities Research & Practice, 13*, 89–94.

Turkle, S. (1997). *Life on the screen: Identity in the age of the Internet*. New York: Touchstone Books.

Turner, J. C. (1987). *Rediscovering the social group: A self-categorization theory*. New York: Basil Blackwell.

Turner, J. C., Oakes, P. J., Haslam, S. A., & McGarty, C. (1984). Self and collective: Cognition and social context. Special Issue: The self and the collective. *Personality and Social Psychology Bulletin, 20*, 454–463.

Turner, J. C., & Onorato, R. S. (1999). Social identity, personality, and the self-concept: A self-categorizing perspective. In T. R. Tyler & R. M. Kramer (Eds.), *The psychology of the social self. Applied social research.* Mahwah, NJ: Erlbaum.

Turner, M. E., Pratkanis, A. R., Probasco, P., & Leve, C. (1992). Threat, cohesion, and group effectiveness: Testing a social identity maintenance perspective on groupthink. *Journal of Personality and Social Psychology, 63,* 781–796.

Tuthill, D. M., & Forsyth, D. R. (1982). Sex differences in opinion conformity and dissent. *Journal of Social Psychology, 116,* 205–210.

TV Week. (1992, May 31). Boston, MA: Boston Sunday Globe.

Tzeng, O. C. S., & Gomez, M. (1992). Behavioral reinforcement paradigm of love. In O. C. S. Tzeng (Ed.), *Theories of love development, maintenance, and dissolution: Octagonal cycle and differential perspectives.* New York: Praeger.

U. S. Bureau of the Census. (1990). *Statistical abstract of the United States.* Washington, DC: U.S. Government Printing Office.

U. S. Bureau of Census. (1996). *Current projections of the population makeup of the U. S.* Washington, DC: U. S. Bureau of Census.

U. S. Bureau of the Census. (1998). *Unmarried-couple households.* Washington, DC: U. S. Bureaus of the Census.

U. S. Bureau of Census. (1999). *Cohabitation in the United States.* Washington, DC: U. S. Bureau of Census.

U. S. Bureau of Labor Statistics. (1993). *Average wages earned by women compared to men.* Washington, DC: U. S. Bureau of Labor Statistics.

U. S. Commission on Civil Rights. (1990). *Intimidation and violence: Racial and religious bigotry in the United States.* Washington, DC: U.S. Commission on Civil Rights.

U. S. Department of Education. (1999). *Minority population projections.* Washington, DC: U.S. Department of Education.

U. S. Department of Justice. (1990). *Sourcebook of criminal justice statistics.* Washington, DC: U.S. Department of Justice.

U.S. Department of Labor. (1995). *Good for business: Making full use of the nation's human capital. Report of the Federal Glass Ceiling Commission.* Washington, DC: U.S. Department of Labor.

U.S. Department of Labor. (1999). Women's bureau Web page. Available: *http://www.dol.gov/dol/wb/*

U.S. News & World Report. (1991, May 6), p. 91.

Uchino, B. N., Cacioppo, J. T., Malarkey, W., & Glaser, R. (1995). Individual differences in cardiac sympathetic control predict endocrine and immune responses to acute psychological stress. *Journal of Personality & Social Psychology, 69,* 736–743.

Uchitelle, L., & Kleinfield, N. R. (1996, March 3). On the battlefields of business, millions of casualties. *New York Times,* pp. 1, 26.

Udo, T. (1993, January). *A study of moral judgment and moral action: A case of adolescent girls in residential treatment.* Dissertation Abstracts International, 53 (7–B), 3798–3799.

Uehara, E. S. (1995). Reciprocity reconsidered: Gouldner's "moral norm of reciprocity" and social support. *Journal of Social & Personal Relationships, 12,* 483–502.

Uleman, J. S., & Moskowitz, G. B. (1994). Unintended effects of foals on unintended inferences. *Journal of Personality and Social Psychology, 66,* 490–501.

Underwood, J., & Pezdek, K. (1998). Memory suggestibility as an example of the sleeper effect. *Psychonomic Bulletin & Review, 5* (3), 449–453.

Unger, L. S., & Thumuluri, L. K. (1997). Trait empathy and continuous helping: The case of voluntarism. *Journal of Social Behavior & Personality, 12,* 785–800.

Unger, R. K., & Crawford, M. E. (1992). *Women and gender: A feminist psychology.* Philadelphia, PA: Temple University Press.

Unger, R., & Crawford, M. (1996). *Women and gender: A feminist psychology* (2nd ed.). New York: McGraw-Hill.

Urban, L. M., & Miller, N. (1998). A theoretical analysis of crossed categorization effects: A meta-analysis. *Journal of Personality & Social Psychology, 74,* 894–908.

Urbanska, M. L. (1992, July 17). Wedded to the single life: Attitudes, economy delaying marriages. *USA Today,* p. A8.

Vakratsas, D., & Ambler, T. (1999). How advertising works: What do we really know? *Journal of Marketing, 63,* 26–43.

Valins, S. (1966). Cognitive effects of false heart rate feedback. *Journal of Personality and Social Psychology, 4,* 400–408.

Vallacher, R. R., & Wegner, D. M. (1985). *A theory of action identification.* Hillsdale, NJ: Erlbaum.

Vallacher, R. R., & Wegner, D. M. (1989). Levels of personal agency: Individual variation in action identification. *Journal of Personality and Social Psychology, 57,* 660–671.

Valliant, P. M., & Loring, J. E. (1998). Leadership style and personality of mock jurors and the effect on sentencing decisions. *Social Behavior & Personality, 26* (4), 421–424.

van der Pligt, J., Zeelenberg, M., van Dijk, W. W., de Vries, N. K., & Richard, R. (1998). Affect, attitudes and decisions: Let's be more specific. In W. Stroebe & M. Hewstone (Eds.), *European Review of Social Psychology* (Vol. 8., pp. 33–66). Chichester, England: Wiley.

van Eck, M., Nicolson, N. A., & Berkhof, J. (1998). Effects of stressful daily events on mood states: Relationship to global perceived stress. *Journal of Personality & Social Psychology, 75,* 1572–1585.

Van Hiel, A., & Schittekatte, M. (1998). Information exchange in context: Effects of gender composition of group, accountability, and intergroup perception on group decision making. *Journal of Applied Social Psychology, 28* (22), 2049–2067.

Van Hightower, N. R., & Gorton, J. (1998). Domestic violence among patients at two rural health care clinics: Prevalence and social correlates. *Public Health Nursing, 15,* 355–362.

Van Knippenberg, A., & Wilke, H. (1988). Social categorization and attitude change. *European Journal of Social Psychology, 18,* 395–406.

Van Knippenberg, D. (1999). Social identity and persuasion: Reconsidering the role of group membership. In D. Abrams & M. A. Hogg (Eds.), *Social identity and social cognition* (pp. 315–331). Malden, MA: Blackwell.

Van Manen, S., & Pietromonaco, P. (1994). *Acquaintance and consistency influence memory from interpersonal information.* Unpublished manuscript, University of Massachusetts at Amherst.

Van Vugt, M., Howard, C., & Moss, S. (1998). Being better than some but not better than average: Self-enhancing comparisons in aerobics. *British Journal of Social Psychology, 37,* 185–201.

van Wel, F., & Knobbout, J. (1998). Adolescents and fear appeals. *International Journal of Adolescence & Youth, 7,* 121–135.

Van Yperen, N. W., & Buunk, B. P. (1991). Sex-role attitudes, social comparison, and satisfaciton with relationships. *Social Psychology Quarterly, 54,* 169–180.

Vanbeselaere, N. (1993). Ingroup bias in the minimal group situation: An experimental test of the inequity prevention hypothesis. *Basic & Applied Social Psychology, 14,* 385–400.

Van Boven, S., & Gesalman, A. B. (1998, June 22). A fatal ride in the night. *Newsweek,* p. 33.

VanWinkle, D. L., Calhoun, L. G., Cann, A., & Tedeschi, R. (1998). Social reactions to attempted suicide: The effects of gender and physical attractiveness. *Omega-Journal of Death & Dying, 37,* 89–100.

Vanzetti, N., & Duck, S. (Eds). (1996). *A lifetime of relationships.* Pacific Grove, CA: Brooks/Cole.

Varela, J. A. (1971). *Psychological solutions to social problems.* New York: Academic Press.

Vecchio, R. P. (Ed). (1997). *Leadership: Understanding the dynamics of power and influence in organizations.* Notre Dame, IN: University of Notre Dame Press.

Veeninga, A., & Kraaimaat, F. W. (1995). Causal attributions in premenstrual syndrome. *Psychology & Health, 10,* 219–228.

Veitch, R., & Arkkelin, D. (1995). *Environmental psychology: An interdisciplinary perspective.* Englewood Cliffs, NJ: Prentice-Hall.

Velicer, W. F., Redding, C. A., Richmond, R. L., Greeley, J., et al. (1992). A time series investigation of three nicotine regulation models. *Addictive Behavior, 17,* 325–345.

Verhoek-Miller, N., & Miller, D. I. (1997). Teacher power style and student satisfaction. *Psychology: A Quarterly Journal of Human Behavior, 34* (1), 48–51.

Verkuyten, M. (1995). Self-esteem, self-concept stability, and aspects of ethnic identity among minority and majority youth in the Netherlands. *Journal of Youth & Adolescence, 24,* 155–175.

Verplanck, W. S. (1955). People processing: Strategies of organizational socialization. *Organizational Dynamics, 15,* 26–27.

Verplanken, B., Aarts, H., van Knippenberg, A., & van Knippenberg, C. (1994). Attitude versus general habit: Antecedents of travel mode choice. *Journal of Applied Social Psychology, 24,* 285–300.

Visalberghi, E., Valente, M., & Fragaszy, D. (1998). Social context and consumption of unfamiliar foods by Capuchin monkeys (Cebus apella) over repeated encounters. *American Journal of Primatology, 45* (4), 367–380.

Visser, P. S., & Krosnick, J. A. (1998). Development of attitude strength over the life cycle: Surge and decline. *Journal of Personality & Social Psychology, 75,* 1389–1410.

Von Lang, J., & Sibyll, C. (Eds.). (1983). *Eichmann interrogated.* (Ralph Manheim, Trans.). New York: Farrar, Straus & Giroux.

Vonk, R. (1993). The negativity effect in trait ratings and in open-ended descriptions of persons. *Personality and Social Psychology Bulletin, 19,* 269–278.

Vonk, R. (1996). The slime effect: Ruthless judgments about people licking upward and kicking downward. *Gedrag en Organisatie, 9,* 29–37.

Vonk, R. (1998). The slime effect: Suspicion and dislike of likeable behavior toward superiors. *Journal of Personality & Social Psychology, 74,* 849–864.

Vorauer, J. D., & Ross, M. (1993). Making mountains out of molehills: An informational goals analysis of self- and social perception. Special Issue: On inferring personal dispositions from behavior. *Personality and Social Psychology Bulletin, 19,* 620–632.

Vrij, A., van der Steen, J., & Koppelaar, L. (1994). Aggression of police officers as a function of temperature: An experiment with the Fire Arms Training System. *Journal of Community and Applied Social Psychology, 4,* 365–370.

Vroom, V. H. (1997). Can leaders learn to lead? In R. P. Vecchio (Ed.), *Leadership: Understanding the dynamics of power and influence in organizations* (pp. 278–291). Notre Dame, IN: University of Notre Dame Press.

Wadden, T. A., Stunkard, A. J., Rich, L., Rubin, C. J., Sweidel, G., & McKinney, S. (1990). Obesity in Black adolescent girls: A controlled clinical trial of treatment by diet, behavior, modification, and parental support. *Pediatrics, 85,* 345–352.

Wagner, M., Schuetze, Y., & Lang, F. R. (1999). Social relationships in old age. In P. B. Baltes & K. U. Mayer (Eds.), *The Berlin aging study: Aging from 70 to 100.* New York: Cambridge University Press.

Wahl, O. F. (1995). *Media madness: Public images of mental illness.* New Brunswick, NJ: Rutgers University Press.

Waitzkin, H. (1985). Information giving in medical care. *Journal of Health and Social Behavior, 26,* 81–101.

Waitzkin, H., & Stoeckle, J. D. (1976). Information control and the micropolitics of health care. *Journal of Social Issues, 10,* 263–276.

Walker, I., & Crogan, M. (1998). Academic performance, prejudice, and the Jigsaw classroom: New pieces to the puzzle. *Journal of Community & Applied Social Psychology, 8,* 381–393.

Walker, I., & Mann, L. (1987). Unemployment, relative deprivation and social protest. *Personality and Social Psychology Bulletin, 13,* 275–283.

Walker, L. E. (1984). *The battered woman syndrome.* New York: Springer.

Walker, L. E. (1989). Psychology and violence against women. *Amerian Psychologist, 44,* 695–702.

Wall, P. M. (1965). *Eyewitness identification in criminal cases.* Springfield, IL: Charles C Thomas.

Wallach, L., & Wallach, M. A. (1994). Gergen versus the mainstream: Are hypotheses in social psychology subject to empirical test? *Journal of Personality and Social Psychology, 67,* 233–242.

Waller, N. G., Koietin, B. A., Bouchard, T. J., Jr., Lykken, D. T., & Tellegen, A. (1990). Genetic and environmental influences on religious interests, attitudes, and values: A study of twins reared apart and together. *Psychological Science, 1,* 138–142.

Walsh, N. A., Meister, L. A., & Kleinke, C. L. (1977). Interpersonal attraction and visual behavior as a function of perceived arousal and evaluation by an opposite sex person. *Journal of Social Psychology, 103,* 65–74.

Walster, (Hatfield) E., Aronson, V., Abrahams, D., & Rottman, L. (1966). Importance of physical attractiveness in dating behavior. *Journal of Personality and Social Psychology, 4,* 508–516.

Walster, (Hatfield) E., & Walster, G. W. (1978). *Love.* Reading, MA: Addison-Wesley.

Walster, (Hatfield) E., Walster, G. W., & Berscheid, E. (1978). *Equity: Theory and research.* Boston: Allyn & Bacon.

Walster, E., Walster, G. W., & Traupmann, J. (1978). Equity and premarital sex. *Journal of Personality and Social Psychology, 36,* 82–92.

Wansink, B. (1994). Advertising's impact on category substitution. *Journal of Marketing Research, 31,* 505–515.

Waring, E. M., Schaefer, B., & Fry, R. (1994). The influence of therapeutic self-disclosure on perceived marital intimacy. *Journal of Sex and Marital Therapy, 20,* 135–146.

Warren, P. E., & Walker, I. (1991). Empathy, effectiveness and donations to charity: Social psychology's contribution. *British Journal of Social Psychology, 30,* 325–337.

Warren, R., & Kurlychek, R. T. (1981). Treatment of maladaptive anger and aggression: Catharsis vs. behavior therapy. *Corrective and Social Psychiatry and Journal of Behavior Technology, Methods and Therapy, 27,* 135–139.

Warshaw, R. (1988). *I never called it rape: The "Ms." report on recognizing, fighting, and surviving date rape and acquaintance rape.* New York: Harper & Row.

Waters, H. F. (1993, July 12). Networks under the gun. *Newsweek,* pp. 64–66.

Watkins, M. J., & Peynircioglu, Z. F. (1984). Determining perceived meaning during impression formation: Another look at the meaning change hypothesis. *Journal of Personality and Social Psychology, 46,* 1005–1016.

Watson, M., & Greer, S. (1998). Personality and coping. In J. C. Holland (Ed.), *Psycho-oncology.* New York: Oxford University Press.

Watson, O. M., & Graves, T. D. (1966). Quantitative research in proxemic behavior. *American Anthropologist, 68,* 971–985.

Webb, E. J., Campbell, D. T., Schwartz, D., & Sechrest, L. (1966). *Unobtrusive measures: Nonreactive research in the social sciences.* Chicago: Rand McNally.

Weber, M. (1952). The essentials of bureaucratic organization: An ideal-type construction. In R. K. Merton (Ed.), *A reader in bureaucracy.* Glencoe, Ill: Free Press.

Wech, B. A., Mossholder, K. W., Steel, R. P., & Bennett, N. (1998). Does work group cohesiveness affect individuals' performance and organizational commitment? A cross-level examination. *Small Group Research, 29* (4), 472–494.

Wegner, D. M. (1989). *White bears and other unwanted thoughts: Suppression, obsession, and the psychology of mental control.* New York: Viking.

Wegner, D. M. (1994). Ironic processes of mental control. *Psychological Review, 101,* 34–52.

Wegner, D. M. (1995). A computer network model of human transactive memory. *Social Cognition, 13,* 319–339.

Wegner, D. M., & Bargh, J. A. (1998). Control and automaticity in social life. In D. T. Gilbert & S. T. Fiske (Eds.), *The handbook of social psychology* (4th ed.). Boston, MA: McGraw-Hill.

Wegner, D. M., & Erber, R. (1992). The hyperaccessibility of suppressed thoughts. *Journal of Personality and Social Psychology, 63,* 903–912.

Wegner, D. M., Shortt, J. W., Blake, A. W., & Page, M. S. (1990). The suppression of exciting thoughts. *Journal of Personality and Social Psychology, 58,* 409–418.

Wegner, D. M., Vallacher, R. R., & Dizadji, D. (1989). Do alcoholics know what they're doing? Identifications of the act of drinking. *Basic and Applied Social Psychology, 10,* 197–210.

Wegener, D. T., & Petty, R. E. (1994). Mood management across affective states: The hedonic contingency hypothesis. *Journal of Personality and Social Psychology, 66,* 1034–1048.

Weiner, B. (1980). A cognitive (attribution) emotion-action model of motivated behavior: An analysis of judgments of helpgiving. *Journal of Personality and Social Psychology, 39,* 186–200.

Weiner, B. (1996). Searching for order in social motivation. *Psychological Inquiry, 7,* 199–216.

Weintraub, M. (1976). Intelligent noncompliance and capricious compliance. In L. Lasagna (Ed.), *Patient compliance.* Mt. Kisco, NY: Futura.

Weisberg, H. F., Krosnick, J. A., & Bowen, B. D. (1996). *An introduction to survey research and data analysis* (3rd ed.). Newbury Park, CA: Sage.

Weiss, R. S. (1973). *Loneliness: The experience of emotional and social isolation.* Cambridge, MA: M.I.T. Press.

Weldon, E., & Weingart, L. R. (1993). Group goals and group performance. *British Journal of Social Psychology, 32,* 307–334.

Wellen, J. M., Hogg, M. A., & Terry, D. J. (1998). Group norms and attitude-behavior consistency: The role of group salience and mood. *Group Dynamics, 2* (1), 48–56.

Wells, G. L. (1993). What do we know about eyewitness identification? *American Psychologist, 48,* 553–571.

Wells, W., Burnett, J., & Moriarty, S. (1992). *Advertising: Principles and practice.* Englewood Cliffs, NJ: Prentice-Hall.

Werner, C. M., Brown, B. B., & Damron, G. (1981). Territorial marking in a game arcade. *Journal of Personality and Social Psychology, 41,* 1094–1104.

Werner, E. E. (1993). Risk, resilience, and recovery: Perspectives from the Kauai Longitudinal Study. *Development and Psychopathology, 5,* 503–515.

Werner, E. E. (1995). Resilience in development. *Current Directions in Psychological Science, 4,* 81–85.

Wetzel, C. G., & Walton, M. D. (1985). Developing biased social judgments: The false-consensus effect. *Journal of Personality and Social Psychology, 49,* 1352–1359.

Wheeler, L. (1974). Social comparison and selective affiliation. In T. L. Huston (Ed.), *Foundations of interpersonal attraction* (pp. 309–328). New York: Academic Press.

Wheeler, L., & Kim, Y. (1997). What is beautiful is culturally good: The physical attractiveness stereotype has different content in collectivistic cultures. *Personality & Social Psychology Bulletin, 23,* 795–800.

Wheeless, L. R., Wheeless, V. E., & Dickson-Markman, F. (1982). A research note: The relations among social and task perceptions in small groups. *Small Group Behavior, 13,* 373–384.

Whitbeck, L. B., & Hoyt, D. R. (1994). Social prestige and assortive mating: A comparison of students from 1956 and 1988. *Journal of Social and Personal Relationships, 11,* 137–145.

White, G. (1989). Media and violence: The case of professional football championship games. *Aggressive Behavior, 15,* 423–433.

White, J. W., & Humphrey, J. A. (1991). Young people's attitudes toward rape. In A. Parrot & L. Bechhofer (Eds.), *Acquaintance rape: The hidden crime.* New York: Wiley.

White, P. A. (1992). The anthropomorphic machine: Causal order in nature and the world view of common sense. *British Journal of Psychology, 83,* 61–96.

White, P. H., & Harkins, S. G. (1994). Race of source effects in the Elaboration Likelihood Model. *Journal of Personality and Social Psychology, 67,* 790–807.

Whites v. blacks. (1995, October 16). *Newsweek,* pp. 28–35.

Whiting, B. B. (1965). Sex identity conflict and physical violence: A comparative study. *American Anthropologist, 67,* 123–140.

Whiting, B. B., & Edwards, C. P. (1988). *Children of different worlds: The foundation of social behavior.* Cambridge, MA: Harvard University Press.

Whiting, B. M., & Whiting, J. W. (1975). *Children of six countries: A psychological analysis.* Cambridge, MA: Harvard University Press.

Whyte, G. (1998). Recasting Janis's groupthink model: The key role of collective efficacy in decision fiascoes. *Organizational Behavior & Human Decision Processes, 73* (2–3), 185–209.

Whyte, W. F. (1981). *Street corner society: The social structure of an Italian slum* (3rd ed.). Chicago: University of Chicago Press.

Wicker, A. W. (1969). Attitudes versus actions: The relationship of verbal and overt behavioral responses to attitude objects. *Journal of Social Issues, 25,* 41–78.

Wicklund, R. A. (1975). Objective self awareness. In L. Berkowitz (Ed.), *Advances in experimental social psychology* (Vol. 8). New York: Academic Press.

Wicklund, R. A., & Frey, D. (1980). Self awareness theory: When the self makes a difference. In D. M. Wegner & R. R. Vallacher (Eds.), *The self in social psychology* (pp. 31–54). New York: Oxford University Press.

Wiebe, D. J., & Williams, P. G. (1992). Hardiness and health: A social psychophysiological perspective on stress and adaptation. Special Issue: Social psychophysiology. *Journal of Social and Clinical Psychology, 11,* 238–262.

Wiener, R. L., Pritchard, C. C., Weston, M. (1995). Comprehensibility of approved jury instructions in capital murder cases. *Journal of Applied Psychology, 80,* 455–467.

Wilder, D. A. (1977). Perception of groups, size of opposition, and social influence. *Journal of Experimental Social Psychology, 19,* 173–177.

Wilder, D. A. (1986). Social categorization: Implications for creation and reduction of intergroup bias. In L. Berkowitz (Ed.), *Advances in experimental social psychology* (Vol. 19). San Diego, CA: Academic.

Wilder, D. A. (1990). Some determinants of the persuasive power of in-groups and the out-groups: Organization of information and attribution of independence. *Journal of Personality and Social Psychology, 59,* 1202–1213.

Wilder, D. A., & Allen, V. L. (1977). Veridical social support, extreme social support, and conformity. *Representative Research in Social Psychology, 8,* 33–41.

Wiley, M. G., & Eskilson, A. (1982). Coping in the corporation: Sex role constraints. *Journal of Applied Social Psychology, 12,* 1–11.

Williams, J. E., & Best, D. L. (1990). *Measuring sex stereotypes: A multination study.* Newbury Park, CA: Sage.

Williams, J. M. (1984). Assertiveness as a mediating variable in conformity to confederates of high and low status. *Psychological Reports, 55,* 415–418.

Williams, K. D., Jackson, J. M., & Karau, S. J. (1992). Collective hedonism: A social loafing analysis of social dilemmas. In D. A. Schroeder (Ed.), *Social dilemmas: Social psychological perspectives.* New York: Praeger.

Williams, K. D., & Karau, S. J. (1991). Social loafing and social compensation: The effects of expectations of co-worker performance. *Journal of Personality and Social Psychology, 61,* 570–581.

Williams, K. D., & Sommer, K. L. (1997). Social ostracism by coworkers: Does rejection lead to loafing or compensation? *Personality & Social Psychology Bulletin, 23* (7), 693–706.

Williams, K. D., & Williams, K. B. (1984). *Social loafing in Japan: A Cross-Cultural Development Study.* Paper presented at the Midwestern Psychological Association, Chicago.

Williams, M. B., Zinner, E. S., & Ellis, R. R. (1999). The connection between grief and trauma: An overview. In E. S. Zinner & M. B. Williams (Eds.), *When a community weeps: Case studies in group survivorship. Series in trauma and loss.* Philadelphia, PA: Brunner/Mazel.

Williams, R. B., Jr. (1993). Hostility and the heart. In D. Goleman & J. Gurin (Eds.), *Mind-body medicine.* Yonkers, NY: Consumer Reports Books.

Williams, R. B., Jr., Barefoot, J. C., Haney, T. L., Harrell, F. E., Jr., Blumenthal, J. A., Pryor, D. B., & Peterson, B. (1988). Type A behavior and angiographically documented coronary atherscerosis in a sample of 2,289 patients. *Psychosomatic Medicine, 50,* 139–152.

Williamson, G. M., & Clark, M. S. (1996). Impact of desired relationship type on affective reactions to choosing and being required to help. In S. Fein & S. Spencer (Eds.), *Readings in social psychology: The art and science of research.* Boston: Houghton Mifflin.

Williamson, G. M., & Schulz, R. (1995). Caring for a family member with cancer: Past communal behavior and affective reactions. *Journal of Applied Social Psychology, 25,* 93–116.

Wills, T. A. (1981). Downward comparison principles in social psychology. *Psychological Bulletin, 90,* 245–271.

Wilson, B. J., & Smith, S. L. (1998). Children's responses to emotional portrayals on television. In P. A. Andersen & L. K. Guerrero (Eds.), *Handbook of communication and emotion: Research, theory, applications, and contexts* (pp. 533–569). San Diego, CA: Academic Press.

Wilson, C., & Brewer, N. (1993). Individuals and groups dealing with conflict: Findings from police on patrol. *Basic and Applied Social Psychology, 14,* 55–67.

Wilson, D. S., & Sober, E. (1994). Reintroducing group selection to the human behavioral sciences. *Behavioral and Brain Sciences, 17,* 585–564.

Wilson, E. J., & Sherrell, D. L. (1993). Source effects in communication and persuasion research: A meta-analysis of effect size. *Journal of the Academy of Marketing Science, 21,* 101–112.

Wilson, E. O. (1975). *Sociobiology: The new synthesis.* Cambridge, MA: Belkap Press of Harvard University Press.

Wilson, G., & Nias, D. (1999). Beauty can't be beat. In L. K. Guerrero & J. A. DeVito (Eds.), *The nonverbal communication reader: Classic and contemporary readings* (2nd ed.). Prospect Heights, IL: Waveland Press.

Wilson, J. P., & Petruska, R. (1984). Motivation, model attributes, and prosocial behavior. *Journal of Personality and Social Psychology, 46,* 458–468.

Wilson, J. P., & Raphael, B. (Eds.). (1993). *International handbook of traumatic stress syndromes.* New York: Plenum.

Wilson, J. R., & Bornstein, B. H. (1998). Methodological considerations in pretrial publicity research: Is the medium the message? *Law & Human Behavior, 22* (5), 585–597.

Wilson, T., & Linville, P. (1982). Improving academic performance of college freshmen: Attribution therapy revisited. *Journal of Personality and Social Psychology, 42,* 367–376.

Wilson, T., & Linville, P. (1985). Improving the performance of college freshmen with attributional techniques. *Journal of Personality and Social Psychology, 49,* 287–293.

Winch, R. F. (1958). *Mate selection: A study of complementary needs.* New York: Harper & Row.

Winge, D., & Ulvik, A. (1995). Confrontations with reality: Crisis intervention services for traumatized families after a school bus accident in Norway. Special Section: Transportation disasters. *Journal of Traumatic Stress, 8,* 429–444.

Winkel, F. W. (1991). Police communication programs aimed at burglary victims: A review of studies and an experimental evaluation. *Journal of Community and Applied Social Psychology, 1,* 275–289.

Winter, D. G. (1973). *The power motive.* New York: Free Press.

Winter, D. G. (1987). Leader appeal, leader performance, and the motive profile of leaders and followers: A study of American presidents and elections. *Journal of Personality and Social Psychology, 52,* 196–202.

Wissler, R. L., & Saks, M. J. (1985). On the inefficacy of limiting instructions: When jurors use prior conviction evidence to decide on guilt. *Law and Human Behavior, 9,* 37–48.

Witt, G. E. (1999). Say What You Mean. *American Demographics, 21,* p. 23.

Witte, E. H., & Davis, J. H. (Eds.). (1996). *Understanding group behavior* (Vol. 1). Mahwah, NJ: Erlbaum.

Witte, K. (1998). Fear as motivator, fear as inhibitor: Using the extended parallel process model to explain fear appeal successes and failures. In P. A. Andersen & L. K. Guerrero (Eds.), *Handbook of communication and emotion: Research, theory, applications, and contexts* (pp. 423–450). San Diego: Academic Press.

Witte, K., Berkowitz, J. M., Cameron, K. A., & McKeon, J. K. (1998). Preventing the spread of genital warts: Using fear appeals to promote self-protective behaviors. *Health Education & Behavior, 25* (5), 571–585.

Wittenbrink, B., Hilton, J. L., & Gist, P. L. (1998). In search of similarity: Stereotypes as naive theories in social categorization. *Social Cognition, 16,* 31–55.

Wofford, J. C. (1994). Effects of situational variables on leader's choice of behavior. *Psychological Reports, 75,* 1289–1290.

Wolf, S. (1985). Manifest and latent influence of majorities and minorities. *Journal of Personality and Social Psychology, 48,* 899–908.

Wolf, T. M., Dralle, P. W., Morse, E. V., Simon, P. M., Balson, P. M., Gaumer, R. H., & Williams, M. H. (1991). A biopsychosocial examination of symptomatic and asymptomatic HIV-infected patients. *International Journal of Psychiatry and Medicine, 21,* 263–279.

Wood, J. V., Saltzberg, J. A., & Goldsamt, L. A. (1990). Does affect induce self-focused attention? *Journal of Personality and Social Psychology, 5,* 899–908.

Wood, S. (1990). Tacit skills, the Japanese management model and new technology. Special Issue: Skills, qualifications, employment. *Applied Psychology: An International Review, 39,* 169–190.

Wood, W. (1987). A meta-analytic review of sex differences in group performance. *Psychological Bulletin, 102,* 53–71.

Wood, W., Christensen, P. N., Hebl, M. R., & Rothgerber, H. (1997). Conformity to sex-typed norms, affect, and the self-concept. *Journal of Personality & Social Psychology, 73* (3), 523–535.

Wood, W., & Karten, S. J. (1986). Sex differences in interaction style as a product of perceived sex differences in competence. *Journal of Personality and Social Psychology, 50,* 341–347.

Wood, W., Lundgren, S., Ouellette, J., Busceme, S., & Blackston, T. (1994). Minority influence: A meta-analytic review of social influence processes. *Psychological Bulletin, 115,* 323–345.

Wood, W., Polek, D., & Aiken, C. (1985). Sex differences in group task performance. *Journal of Personality and Social Psychology, 48,* 63–71.

Wood, W., Wong, F. Y., & Chachere, J. G. (1991). Effects of media violence on viewers' aggression in unconstrained social interaction. *Psychological Bulletin, 109,* 371–383.

Worchel, S., & Brown, E. H. (1984). The role of plausibility in influencing environmental attributions. *Journal of Experimental Social Psychology, 13,* 131–140.

Worchel, S., & Lollis, M. (1982). Reactions to territorial contamination as a function of culture. *Personality and Social Psychology Bulletin, 20,* 86–96.

Word, C. O., Zanna, M. P., & Cooper, J. (1974). The nonverbal mediation of self-fulfilling prophecies in interracial interaction. *Journal of Experimental Social Psychology, 10,* 109–120.

Workman, J. E., & Johnson, K. K. (1991). The role of cosmetics in impression formation. *Clothing and Textiles Research Journal, 10,* 63–67.

Worth, L. T., Smith, J., & Mackie, D. M. (1992). Gender schematicity and preference for gender-typed products. *Psychology and Marketing, 9,* 17–30.

Wright, T. (1999, January 22). A one-number census: Some related history (U.S. Census Bureau plans for year 2000). *Science, 283,* 491.

Wrightsman, L. S. (1987). *Psychology and the legal system.* Monterey, CA: Brooks/Cole Publishing.

Wrightsman, L. S. (1991). *Psychology and the legal system* (2nd ed.). Belmont, CA: Brooks/Cole.

Wuensch, K. L., Chia, R. C., Castellow, W. A., & Chuang, C. (1993). Effects of physical attractiveness, sex, and type of crime on mock juror decisions: A replication with Chinese students. *Journal of Cross-Cultural Psychology, 24,* 414–427.

Wyatt, G. E. (1992). Sociocultural context of African-American and White American women's rape. *Journal of Social Issues, 48,* 77–91.

Wyer, R. S., Jr. (1988). Social memory and social judgment. In P. R. Solomon, G. R. Goethals, C. M. Kelley, & B. R. Stephens (Eds.), *Perspectives in memory research.* New York: Springer-Verlag.

Xiaohe, X., & Whyte, M. K. (1990). Love matches and arranged marriages: A Chinese replication. *Journal of Marriage and the Family, 52,* 709–722.

Yancey, G. B., & Eastman, R. L. (1995). Comparison of undergraduates with older adults on love styles and life satisfaction. *Psychological Reports, 76,* 1211–1218.

Yang, K. S., & Ho, D. Y. F. (1988). The role of yuan in Chinese social life: A conceptual and empirical analysis. In A. C. Paranjpe, D. Y. F. Ho, & R. W. Rieber (Eds.), *Asian contributions to psychology.* New York: Praeger.

Yasutake, D., Bryan, T., & Dohrn, E. (1996). The effects of combining peer tutoring and attribution training on students' perceived self-competence. *RASE: Remedial & Special Education, 17,* 83–91.

Yee, J. L., & Greenberg, M. S. (1998). Reactions to crime victims: Effects of victims' emotional state and type of relationship. *Journal of Social & Clinical Psychology, 17,* 209–226.

Yinon, Y., Mayraz, A., & Fox, S. (1994). Age and the false-consensus effect. *Journal of Social Psychology, 134,* 717–725.

Yoshikawa, H. (1994). Prevention as cumulative protection: Effects of early family support and education on chronic delinquency and its risks. *Psychological Bulletin, 115,* 28–54.

Young, M., Denny, G., Luquis, R., & Young, T. (1998). Correlates of sexual satisfaction in marriage. *The Canadian Journal of Human Sexuality, 7,* 115–127.

Young, T. J., & French, L. A. (1998). Heights of U.S. presidents: A trend analysis for 1948–1996. *Perceptual & Motor Skills, 87,* 321–322.

Ystgaard, M., Tambs, K., & Dalgard, O. S. (1999). Life stress, social support and psychological distress in late adolescence: A longitudinal study. *Social Psychiatry & Psychiatric Epidemiology, 34,* 12–19.

Yukl, G. (1999). Leadership competencies required for the new army and approaches for developing them. In J. G. Hunt, G. E. Dodge, & L. Wong (Eds.), *Out-of-the-box leadership: Transforming the twenty-first-century army and other top-performing organizations. Monographs in leadership and management* (Vol. 1, pp. 255–276). Stamford, CT: Jai Press.

Yukl, G., & Falbe, C. M. (1991). Importance of different power sources in downward and lateral relations. *Journal of Applied Psychology, 76,* 416–423.

Yukl, G., Kim, H., & Chavez, C. (1999). Task importance, feasibility, and agent influence behavior as determinants of target commitment. *Journal of Applied Psychology, 84* (1), 137–143.

Yzerbyt, V. Y., Leyens, J. P., & Schadron, G. (1997). Social judgeability and the dilution of stereotypes: The impact of the nature and sequence of information. *Personality & Social Psychology Bulletin, 23,* 1312–1322.

Zaccaro, S. J. (1984). Social loafing: The role of task attractiveness. *Personality and Social Psychology Bulletin, 10,* 99–106.

Zajonc, R. B. (1965). Social facilitation. *Science, 149,* 269–274.

Zajonc, R. B. (1968). The attitudinal effects of mere exposure. *Journal of Personality and Social Psychology, 9,* 1–27.

Zajonc, R. B., Adelmann, P. K., Murphy, S. T., & Niedenthal, P. M. (1987). Convergence in the physical appearance of spouses. *Motivation and Emotion, 11,* 335–346.

Zajonc, R. B., Heingartner, A., & Herman, E. M. (1969). Social enhancement and impairment of performance in the cockroach. *Journal of Personality and Social Psychology, 13,* 83–92.

Zaleski, E. H., Levey-Thors, C., & Schiaffino, K. M. (1998). Coping mechanisms, stress, social support, and health problems in college students. *Applied Developmental Science, 2,* 127–137.

Zanna, M. P., & Cooper, J. (1974). Dissonance and the pill: An attribution approach to studying the arousal properties of dissonance. *Journal of Personality and Social Psychology, 29,* 703–709.

Zarate, M. A., & Smith, E. R. (1990). Person categorization and stereotyping. *Social Cognition, 8,* 161–185.

Zebrowitz, L. A. (1997). *Reading faces: Window to the soul?* Boulder, CO: Westview Press.

Zebrowitz, L. A., Brownlow, S., & Olson, K. (1992). Baby talk to the babyfaced. *Journal of Nonverbal Behavior, 16,* 143–158.

Zebrowitz, L., & Montepare, J. M. (1990). *Impressions of babyfaced and mater-faced individuals across the lifespan.* Manuscript in preparation, cited in Zebrowitz, 1990.

Zebrowitz-McArthur, L. (1988). Person perception in cross-cultural perspective. In M. H. Bond (Ed.), *The cross-cultural challenge to social psychology.* Newbury Park, CA: Sage.

Zeidner, M., & Ben-Zur, H. (1993). Coping with a national crisis: The Israeli experience with the threat of missile attacks. *Personality & Individual Differences, 14,* 209–224.

Zelen, S. L. (Ed.). (1991). *New models, new extensions of attribution theory.* New York: Springer-Verlag.

Zielenziger, M. (1998, April 16). Education and social pressures are taking their toll on Japan's youth. *Knight-Ridder/Tribune News Service.*

Zillman, D. (1983). Transfer of excitation in emotional behavior. In J. T. Cacioppo & R. E. Petty (Eds.), *Social psychophysiology.* New York: Academic Press.

Zillman, D. (1984). *Connections between sex and aggression.* Hillsdale, NJ: Erlbaum.

Zillman, D. (1988). Cognition-excitation interdependencies in aggressive behavior. *Aggressive behavior, 14,* 51–64.

Zillmann, D. (1994). Cognition-excitation interdependencies in the escalation of anger and angry aggression. In M. Potegal & J. F. Knutson (Eds.), *The dynamics of aggression: Biological and social processes in dyads and groups* (pp. 45–71). Hillsdale, NJ: Erlbaum.

Zillman, D., Hoyt, J. L., & Day, K. D. (1974). Strength and duration of the effect of aggressive, violent, and erotic communications on subsequent aggressive behavior. *Communication Research, 1,* 286–306.

Zillman, D., Katcher, A., & Milavsky, B. (1972). Excitation transfer from physical exercise to subsequent aggressive behavior. *Journal of Experimental Social Psychology, 8,* 247–259.

Zillman, D., & Weaver, J. B., III. (1999). Effects of prolonged exposure to gratuitous media violence on provoked and unprovoked hostile behavior. *Journal of Applied Social Psychology, 29,* 145–165.

Zimbardo, P. G. (1973). On the ethics of intervention in human psychological research: With special reference to the Stanford prison experiment. *Cognition, 2,* 243–256.

Zinberg, N. E. (1976). Normal psychology of the aging process, revisited (I): Social learning and self-image in aging. *Journal of Geriatric Psychiatry, 9,* 131–150.

Zuckerman, M., Knee, C. R., Hodgins, H. S., & Miyake, K. (1995). Hypothesis confirmation: The joint effect of positive test strategy and acquiescence response set. *Journal of Personality and Social Psychology, 68,* 52–60.

Zuckerman, M., Miyake, K., & Elkin, C. S. (1995). Effects of attractiveness and maturity of face and voice on interpersonal impressions. *Journal of Research in Personality, 29,* 253–272.

Zuckerman, M., Kieffer, S. C., & Knee, C. R. (1998). Consequences of self-handicapping: Effects on coping, academic performance, and adjustment. *Journal of Personality & Social Psychology, 74,* 1619–1628.

Zullow, H. M., & Seligman, M. E. P. (1990). "Pessimistic rumination predicts defeat of presidential candidates, 1900 to 1984": Response. *Psychological Inquiry, 1,* 80–85.

Zuwerink, J. R., & Devine, P. G. (1996). Attitude importance and resistance to persuasion: It's not just the thought that counts. *Journal of Personality and Social Psychology, 70,* 931–944.

CREDITS

PHOTOGRAPHS

Chapter 1 Opener A. Ramey, PhotoEdit; p. 3 Darko Bandic, AP/Wide World Photos; p. 6 Rhoda Sidney, Stock Boston; p. 8 Yvonne Hemsey, Liaison Agency, Inc.; p. 12 Elie Bernager, Stone; p. 16 Robert Feldman; p. 19 Tony Freeman, PhotoEdit; p. 23 John G. Graiff; p. 28 Byron, Monkmeyer Press; p. 31 Rhoda Sidney.

Chapter 2 Opener Robert Landau, Corbis; p. 41 Bill Pugliano, Liaison Agency, Inc.; p. 45 (a–g) Paul Ekman, Ph.D., Professor of Psychology; p. 48 Groves, Robert Feldman; p. 52 Elena Rooraid, PhotoEdit; p. 58 Bob Daemmrich, Stock Boston; p. 59 Francene Keery, Stock Boston; p. 63 Ellis Herwig, Stock Boston; p. 67 McCarten, PhotoEdit; p. 68 Amy Sancetta, AP/World Wide Photos; p. 73 Rhoda Sidney, Stock Boston.

Chapter 3 Opener David Young-Wolff, PhotoEdit; p. 79 Liaison Agency, Inc.; p. 82 Bob Daemmrich, The Image Works; p. 86 Bob Daemmrich, Stock Boston; p. 90 David Ulmer, Stock Boston; p. 94 Alain Le Bot, Liaison Agency, Inc.; p. 99 Elsa Peterson, Stock Boston; p. 102 (left) Bob Daemmrich, Stock Boston; p. 102 (right) J. Kramer, The Image Works; p. 108 Robert Feldman.

Chapter 4 Opener Joseph Nettis, Stock Boston; p. 113 Dirck Halstead, Liaison Agency, Inc.; p. 117 Richard Hutchings, PhotoEdit; p. 121 Zillioux, Liaison Agency, Inc.; p. 129 Lawrence Migdale, Stock Boston; p. 134 Bob Daemmrich, Stock Boston; p. 139 Stephen Agricola, Stock Boston; p. 143 (a–c) Paul Ekman, Ph.D., Professor of Psychology; p. 144 Robert Feldman.

Chapter 5 Opener Bruce Ayres, Stone; p. 151 Corbis; p. 158 Bill Aron, PhotoEdit; p. 162 Lien/Nibauer Photography, Liaison Agency, Inc.; p. 166 Kevin Horan, Stock Boston; p. 172 Roger W. Vargo/L.A. Daily News, Corbis Sygma Photo News; p. 176 Robert Feldman; p. 178 Mark Richards, PhotoEdit; p. 182 Stevie Grand/Science Photo Library, Photo Researchers, Inc.

Chapter 6 Opener Tony Freeman, PhotoEdit; p. 191 Myrleen, PhotoEdit; p. 192 Corbis Sygma Photo News; p. 195 Robert Brenner, Photo-Edit; p. 198 Richard Pasley, Stock Boston; p. 200 Robert Feldman; p. 205 Mark Antman, The Image Works; p. 209 Mike Okoniewski, The Image Works; p. 212 Laurie Sparham, AP/Wide World Photos; p. 217 Willie L. Hill, Jr., Stock Boston.

Chapter 7 Opener David Young-Wolff, PhotoEdit; p. 223 David Young-Wolff, PhotoEdit; p. 227 Jerry Irwin, Photo Researchers, Inc.; p. 231 David Young-Wolff, PhotoEdit; p. 235 Butch Martin, The Image

Bank; p. 240 Susan Greenwood, Liaison Agency, Inc.; p. 242 Scott Thompson, Ph.D.; p. 246 Bachmann, PhotoEdit; p. 250 Arlene Collins, Monkmeyer Press; p. 254 Carol Halebian, Liaison Agency, Inc.; p. 260 Bob Daemmrich, Stock Boston.

Chapter 8 Opener Wesley Bocxe, Photo Researchers, Inc.; p. 265 Mark Wilson, The Boston Globe; p. 269 Robert Brenner, PhotoEdit; p. 272 A. Ramey, Stock Boston; p. 277 Laima Druskis, Stock Boston; p. 283 Trevor, Inc., Monkmeyer Press; p. 287 Gary Wagner, Stock Boston; p. 290 Robert Feldman.

Chapter 9 Opener Tom Prettyman, PhotoEdit; p. 297 Kevin Higley, AP/Wide World Photos; p. 300 Mark Burnett, Stock Boston; p. 302 (left) Topham, The Image Works; p. 302 (right) George H. Harrison, Grant Heilman Photography, Inc.; p. 305 Bob Daemmrich, Stock Boston; p. 309 Jerry Wachter, Photo Researchers, Inc.; p. 312 Steven Dearinger, Kansas State University "Collegian"; p. 317 Robert Brenner, PhotoEdit; p. 320 David Young-Wolff, PhotoEdit.

Chapter 10 Opener Reuters, Corbis; p. 329 David Duprey, AP/Wide World Photos; p. 334 AP/Wide World Photos; p. 338 Pryde Brown Photographs, Robert Feldman; p. 340 Larry Fisher/Quad–City Times, AP/Wide World Photos; p. 344 Bob Daemmrich, Stock Boston; p. 352 UPI, Corbis; p. 355 Rhoda Sidney, PhotoEdit.

Chapter 11 Opener John Marchael, Jenny Holzer; p. 361 Michael Newman, PhotoEdit; p. 364 Copyright © Neal Preston, Corbis; p. 367 Elena Houghton, AP/Wide World Photos; p. 371 Larry Downing, AP/Wide World Photos; p. 374 Kaiser Communications, Inc.; p. 378 Harry Cabluck, AP/Wide World Photos; p. 382 Reader's Digest.

Chapter 12 Opener Robert McElroy, Woodfin Camp & Associates; p. 391 David Young-Wolff, PhotoEdit; p. 393 Jonathan Ferrey, Allsport Photography (USA), Inc.; p. 396 Lynne Sladky, AP/Wide World Photos; p. 400 AP/Wide World Photos; p. 402 Bettman, Corbis/Copyright © Bettmann/Corbis; p. 406 Robert Feldman; p. 408 Robert Brenner, PhotoEdit; p. 411 Myrleen Ferguson, PhotoEdit; p. 415 (left and right) Alexandra Milgram. From the film *Obedience*. Copyright © 1965 by Stanley Milgram and distributed by Penn State Media Sales. Permission granted from Alexandra Milgram.

Chapter 13 Opener Jean Marc Giboux, Liaison Agency, Inc.; p. 423 Dana Fisher, AP/Wide World Photos; p. 426 David R. Frazier, Photo Researchers, Inc.; p. 428 Photo by Philip Kamrass © Albany Times Union, The Image Works; p. 431 Billy

Barnes, Stock Boston; p. 433 SIPA Press; p. 436 Robert Feldman; p. 441 Dale Lightfoot, SIPA Press; p. 445 De Keerle-UK Press, Liaison Agency, Inc.; p. 449 Corbis.

Chapter 14 Opener Lawrence Migdale/Pix; p. 459 NASA Headquarters; p. 461 Okoniewski, The Image Works; p. 464 Robert Feldman; p. 467 Robert M. Garcia, SIPA Press; p. 470 A. Ramey, PhotoEdit; p. 474 AP/Wide World Photos; p. 479 Sylvie Kreiss, Liaison Agency, Inc.; p. 484 Bob Daemmrich, Stock Boston; p. 487 Robert Brenner, PhotoEdit.

Chapter 15 Opener Bruce Ayres, Stone; p. 495 Colorado Community College and Occupational Education System; p. 497 David Young-Wolff, PhotoEdit; p. 507 Michael Newman, PhotoEdit; p. 508 Alan Oddie, PhotoEdit; p. 511 Robert Brenner, PhotoEdit; p. 512 Jennifer A. Veitch, Research Officer; p. 518 W. Hill, Jr., The Image Works.

CARTOONS, TABLES, AND FIGURES

Chapter 1 **Figure 1–2** Adapted material from Summary Report Doctorate Recipients from United States Universities (selected years). Table compiled by Research Office, APA, Washington, DC. Copyright © 1996 by the American Psychological Association. Adapted with permission of APA; **Figure 1–3** Chronicle of Higher Education, 1999; **Figure 1–7** Higher Education Research Institute (1996). Freshman ambivalence about affirmative action. Los Angeles: Higher Education Research Institute, Graduate School of Education, UCLA; **Figure 1–8** Graham, S. (1992). Most of the subjects were white and middle class: Trends in published research on African Americans in selected APA journals 1970–1989. *American Psychologist, 47,* 629–639. Copyright © 1992 by the American Psychological Association. Adapted with permission.

Chapter 2 **Figure 2–5** Gilbert, D. T., & Pelham, B. W., & Krull, D. S. (1988). Of thoughts unspoken: Social inference and the self-regulation of behavior. *Journal of Personality and Social Psychology, 55,* 685–694. Copyright © 1988 by the American Psychological Association. Adapted with permission; **Figure 2–6** Morris, M. W., & Peng, K. (1994). Culture and cause: American and Chinese attributions for social and physical events. *Journal of Personality and Social Psychology, 67,* 949–971. Copyright © 1994 by the American Psychological Association. Adapted with permission; **Figure 2–7** Cantor, N., & Mischel, W. (1979). Prototypes in person perception. In L. Berkowitz (Ed.), Advances in experimental social psychology (Vol. 12). New York: Academic Press. Reprinted with permission. Academic Press, Inc.; **Figure 2–8** Holtgraves, T., Srull, T. K., & Socall, D. (1989). Conversation memory: The effects or speaker status on memory for the assertiveness of conversation remarks. *Journal of Personality and Social Psychology, 56,* 149–160, Table 3. Copyright © 1989 by the American Psychological Association. Adapted with permission; **Figure 2–9** Medvec, V. H., & Savitsky, K. (1997). When doing better means feeling worse: The effects of categorical cutoff points on counterfactual thinking and satisfaction. *Journal of Personality and Social Psychology, 72,* 1284–1296. Copyright © 1997 by the American Psychological Association. Reprinted with permission.

Chapter 3 Figure 3–2 Taylor, D. M., & Jaggi, V. (1974). Ethnocentrism and causal attribution in a south Indian context. *Journal of Cross Cultural Psychology, 5,* 162–171, Table 2. Copyright © 1974 by Sage Publications. Reprinted by Permission of Sage Publications, Inc.; **Figure 3–4** *The Wall Street Journal*/NBC News Poll reported in McQueen, 1991; **Figure 3–5** Smith, M. B. (1990). "Ethnic Images" in *GSS Topical Report,* No. 19. By permission of National Opinion Research Center; **Figure 3–6** Devine, P. G., Monteith, M. J., Zuwerink, J. R., & Elliot, A. J. (1991). Prejudice with and without compunction. *Journal of Personality and Social Psychology, 60,* 817–830. Copyright © 1991 by the American Psychological Association. Adapted with permission; **Figure 3–8** Frable, D. E., & Bem, S. L. (1985). If you're gender-schematic, all members of the opposite sex look alike. *Journal of Personality and Social Psychology, 49,* 459–468. Copyright © 1985 by the American Psychological Association. Adapted with permission.**Table 3–1** Levy, E. (1990). Stage, sex and suffering of women in American films. *Empirical Studies of the Arts, 8,* 53–76. Reprinted by permission of Baywood Publishing Company, Inc., and the author; **Table 3–2** Adapted from GSS News, No. 12, August 1998. By permission of the National Opinion Research Center; **Table 3–3** Williams, J. E., & Best, D. L. (1990). Measuring sex stereotypes: A multi-nation study. Newbury Park, CA: Sage. Adapted from Table 3.5, p. 77. Copyright © 1990 by the authors. Reprinted by Permission of Sage Publications, Inc.

Chapter 4 Figure 4–1 (cartoon) Drawing by Skalisky © 1991 The New Yorker Magazine, Inc.; **Figure 4–2** Markus, H. R., Smith, J., & Moreland, R. L. (1985). Role of the self-concept in the perception of others. *Journal of Personality and Social Psychology, 49,* 1494–1512. Copyright © 1985 by the American Psychological Association. Adapted with permission; **Figure 4–3** Deaux, K. (1992). Personalizing identity and socializing self. In G. Breakwell (Ed.), *Social psychology of identity and the self-concept.* London: Academic Press. Copyright © 1992 by Academic Press, Ltd. Reprinted by permission; **Figure 4–4** Markus, H. R., & Kitayama, S. (1991). Culture and the self: Implications for cognition, emotion, and motivation. *Psychological*

Review, 98, 224–253. Copyright © 1991 by the American Psychological Association. Adapted with permission; **Figure 4–6** Bushman, B. J., & Baumeister, R. F. (1998). Threatened egotism, narcissism, self-esteem, and direct and displaced aggression: Does self-love or self-hate lead to violence? *Journal of Personality and Social Psychology, 75,* 219–229. Copyright © 1998 by the American Psychological Association. Reprinted with permission; **Figure 4–7** From p. 800 of Steele, C. M., & Aronson, J. (1995). Stereotype threat and the intellectual test performance of African Americans. *Journal of Personality and Social Psychology, 69,* 797–811. Copyright © 1995 by the American Psychological Association. Adapted with permission; **Figure 4–8** Arkin, R. M., & Baumgardner, A. H. (1985). Self-handicapping. In J. H. Harvey & G. Weary (Eds.), *Attribution: Basic issues and applications* (pp. 169–202). New York: Academic Press. Reprinted with permission. Academic Press, Inc.; **Figure 4–9** Snyder, C. R., & Higgins, R. L. (1988). Excuses: Their effective role in the negotiation of reality. *Psychological Bulletin, 104,* 23–35. Copyright © 1988 by the American Psychological Association. Adapted with permission; **Table 4–1** Ethier, K.A., & Deaux, K. (1990). Hispanics in ivy: Assessing identity and perceived threat. *Sex Roles, 22,* 427–440. Used by permission of Plenum Publishing Corporation; **Table 4–2** Fenigstein, A., Scheier, M. F., & Buss, A. H. (1975). Public and private self-consciousness: Assessment and theory. *Journal of Consulting and Clinical Psychology, 43,* 522–527. Copyright © 1975 by the American Psychological Association. Adapted with permission; **Table 4–3** Snyder, M., & Gangestad, S. (1986). On the nature of self-monitoring: Matters of assessment, matters of validity. *Journal of Personality and Social Psychology, 51,* 125–139. Copyright © 1986 by the American Psychological Association. Adapted with permission; **Table 4–4** Jones, E. E. (1990). *Intepersonal perception.* Copyright ©1990 by W. H. Freeman and Company. Used with permission.

Chapter 5 Figure 5–1 Petrie, K. J., Booth, R. J., & Pennebaker, J. W. (1998). The immunological effects of thought suppression. *Journal of Personality and Social Psychology, 75,* 1264–1272. Copyright © 1998 by the American Psychological Association. Reprinted with permission; **Figure 5–2** Abramson, L. Y., Metalsky, G. I., & Alloy, L. B. (1989). Hopelessness depression: A theory-based subtype. *Psychological Review, 96,* 358–372. Copyright © 1989 by the American Psychological Association. Adapted with permission; **Figure 5–3** Diener, E., Suh, E. M., Lucas, R. E., & Smith, H. L. (1999). Subjective well-being: Three decades of progress. *Psychological Bulletin, 125,* 276–302. Copyright © 1999 by the American Psychological Association. Reprinted with permission; **Figure 5–4** Kaplan, R. M., Sallis, J. F., Jr., & Patterson, T. L. (1993*). Health and human behavior.* NY: McGraw-Hill. Reproduced with permission of The McGraw-Hill Companies. **Figure 5–5** HASSLES—From Chamberlain, K., & Zika, S. (1990). The minor events approach to stress: Support for the use of daily hassles. *British Journal of Psychology, 81,*

469–481; **Figure 5–5** UPLIFTS—Kanner, A. D., Coyne, J. C., Schaefer, & Lazarus, R. (1981). Comparison of two modes of stress measurement: Daily hassles and uplifts versus major life events. *Journal of Behavioral Medicine, 4,* 14. Used by permission of Plenum Publishing Co.; **Figure 5–6** The National Institute of Health; **Figure 5–7** Petting, K. W., Morris, T., Greer, S., & Haybittle, J. L. (1985). Mental attitudes to cancer: An additional prognostic factor. *Lancet, p. 750.* Copyright © 1985 by The Lancet Ltd. Reprinted by permission of the publisher; **Table 5–1** Murphy, S. A., Beaton, R. D., Cain, K., & Pike, K. (1994). Gender differences in fire fighter job stressors and symptoms of stress. *Women & Health, 22,* 55–69. Haworth Press; **Table 5–2** Holmes, T. H., & Rahe, R. H. (1967). The social readjustment scale. *Journal of Psychosomatic Research, 11,* 213–218. Reprinted by permission of Elsevier Science, UK; **Table 5–3** Adapted from Siebert, A. (1998). The survivor personality. New York: Perigee; **Table 5–4** Benson, H. (1993). The relaxation response. In D. Goleman & J. Gurin (Eds.) *Mind-body medicine.* Yonkers, NY: Consumer Reports Books. Reprinted with permission of Dr. Herbert Benson; **Table 5–6** Taylor, S. E. (1991). Health psychology. NY: McGraw-Hill. (pg. 324). Reproduced with the permission of The McGraw-Hill Companies; **Table 5–6** From Ley, P., Bradshaw, P. W., Kincey, J. A., & Atherton, S. T. (1977). Increasing patients' satisfaction with communications. *British Journal of Social and Clinical Psychology, 15,* 403–413; **Cartoon** (p. 155) Copyright © 2000 Mike Twohy from cartoonbank.com. All rights reserved.

Chapter 6 Figure 6–2 Byrne, D., & Clore, G. L. (1966). Predicting interpersonal attraction toward strangers presented in three different stimulus modes. *Psychonomic Science, 4.* Reprinted by permission of Psychonomic Society, Inc.; **Figure 6–3** Byrne, D., Clore, G. L., & Smeaton, G. (1986). The attraction hypothesis: Do similar attitudes affect anything? *Journal of Personality and Social Psychology, 51,* 1167–1170. Copyright © 1986 by the American Psychological Association. Adapted with permission; **Figure 6–4** Parlee, M. B. (1979, October). The friendship bond. *Psychology Today, 13,* 43–45. Reprinted with permission from *Psychology Today* Magazine, Copyright © 1979 by Sussex Publishers, Inc.; **Figure 6–5** Langlois, J. H., Ritter, J. M., Casey, R. J., & Sawin, D. B. (1995). Infant attractiveness predicts maternal behaviors and attitudes. *Developmental Psychology, 31,* 464–472. Copyright © 1995 by the American Psychological Association. Adapted with permission; **Figure 6–6** Cunningham, M. R. (1986). Measuring the physical in physical attractiveness: Quasi-experiments on interpersonal relationships. *Journal of Personality and Social Psychology, 50,* 925–935. Copyright © 1986 by the American Psychological Association. Adapted with permission; **Figure 6–7** Silverstein, B., Perdue, L., Peterson, B., & Kelly, E. (1986). The role of the mass media in promoting a thin standard of bodily attractiveness for women. *Sex Roles, 14,* 519–532. Reprinted by permission of Plenum Publishing Corporation; **Table 6–1** Shaver, P., Hazan, C., &

Bradshaw, D. (1988). Love as attachment: The integration of three behavioral systems. In R. J. Sternberg & M. L. Barnes (Eds.), *The Psychology of Love.* (p. 80). New Haven, CT: Yale University Press. Copyright © 1988 by Yale University Press. Reprinted by permission of the publisher.

Chapter 7 Figure 7–1 Levinger, G. A. (1974). A three-level approach to attraction: Toward an understanding of pair relatedness. In T. L. Huston (Ed.*),* *Foundations of interpersonal attraction.* New York: Academic Press; **Figure 7–2** Murstein, B. I. (1987). A clarification and extension of the SVR theory of dyadic pairing. *Journal of Marriage and the Family, 49,* 929–947. Copyright © 1987 by the National Council on Family Relations, 3989 Central Ave., NE, Suite 550, Minneapolis, MN 55421. Reprinted by permission; **Figure 7–3** Reprinted by permission of the Gallup Poll News Service; **Figure 7–4** Sternberg, R. J. (1986). A triangular theory of love. *Psychological Review, 93,* 119–135. Based on Table 2. Copyright © 1986 by the American Psychological Association. Adapted with permission; **Figure 7–5** Sternberg, R. J. (1986). A triangular theory of love. *Psychological Review, 93,* 119–135. Copyright © 1986 by the American Psychological Association. Adapted with permission; **Figure 7–6** Janda, L. H. & Klenke-Hamel, K. E. (1980). *Human Sexuality.* New York: Van Nostrand Reinhold. Copyright © 1980 by the authors. Reprinted by permission of L. H. Janda; **Figure 7–7** Levine, R. V. (1993, February). Is love a luxury? *American Demographics,* 27–29. Reprinted with permission Copyright © 1993 American Demographics; **Figure 7–8** Rollins, B. C., & Cannon, K. L. (1974). Marital Satisfaction over the family life cycle. *Journal of Marriage and the Family, 36,* 271–282 Copyright © 1974 by the National Council on Family Relations, 3989 Cental Ave., NE, Suite 550, Minneapolis, MN 55421. Reprinted by permission; **Figure 7–10** The Population Council (1995). *Divorce rates around the world.* New York: The Population Council; **Figure 7–11** Duck, S. W. (Ed.). (1982). Based on *Personal relationships: Vol. 4. Dissolving personal relationships.* New York: Academic Press. Used by permission of Academic Press; **Table 7–1** Berscheid, E., Snyder, M., & Omoto, A. M. (1989). The Relationship Closeness Inventory: Assessing the closeness of interpersonal relationships. *Journal of Personality and Social Psychology, 57,* 792–807. Copyright © 1989 by the American Psychological Association. Adapted with permission; **Table 7–2** Rubin, Z., Hill, C. T., Peplau, L. A., & Dunkel-Schetter, C. (1980). Self-disclosure in dating couples: Sex roles and the ethic of openness. *Journal of Marriage and the Family, 42,* 305–317. Copyright © 1974 by National Council on Family Relations, 389 Cental Ave., NE, Suite 550, Minneapolis, MN 55421. Reprinted by permission; **Table 7–3** Fehr, B., & Russell, J. A. (1991). The concept of love viewed from a prototype perspective. *Journal of Personality and Social Psychology, 60,* 425–438. Copyright © 1991 by the American Psychological Association. Adapted with permission; **Table 7–4** Buss, D. M., Abbott, M., Angleitner, A., Asherian, A., et al. (1990).

International preferences in selecting mates: A study of 37 cultures. *Journal of Cross-Cultural Psychology, 21,* 5–47. Copyright © 1990 by Sage Publications. Reprinted by permission of Sage Publications, Inc.; **Table 7–5** Gottman, J. (1999, April 19). Know your spouse. *Newsweek.* Copyright © 1999 by Newsweek, Inc. All rights reserved. Reprinted by permission.

Chapter 8 Figure 8–1 Latané, B., & Darley, J. M. (1970). The unresponsive bystander: Why doesn't he help? New York: Appleton Century Crofts. Copyright © 1970 by the authors. Adapted by permission of Prentice Hall, Inc., Upper Saddle River, NJ; **Figure 8–2** Batson, C. D. (1991). *The altruism question: Toward a social-psychological answer.* Hillsdale, NJ: Erlbaum. Reprinted by permission of Lawrence Erlbaum Associates, Inc.; **Figure 8–3** Dovidio, J. F., Allen, J. L., & Schroeder, D. A. (1990). Specificity of empathy-induced helping: Evidence for altruistic motivation. *Journal of Personality and Social Psychology, 59,* 249–260. Copyright © 1990 by the American Psychological Association. Adapted with permission; **Figure 8–4** Meyer, J. P., & Mulherin, A. (1980). From attribution to helping: An analysis of the mediating effects of effect and expectancy. *Journal of Personality and Social Psychology, 39,* 201–210. Copyright © 1980 by the American Psychological Association. Adapted with permission; **Figure 8–4** Weiner, B. (1980). A cognitive (attribution) emotion-action model of motivated behavior: An analysis of judgments of helpgiving. *Journal of Personality and Social Psychology, 39,* 186–200. Copyright © 1980 by the American Psychological Association. Adapted with permission; **Figure 8–5** Gilbert, D. T., & Silvera, D.H. (1996). Overhelping. Journal of *Personality and Social Psychology, 70,* 678–690. Copyright © 1996 by the American Psychological Association. Reprinted with permission; **Figure 8–6** Luks, A. (1988, October). Helper's high. *Psychology Today,* 39–42. Copyright © 1988 by Sussex Publishers, Inc. Reprinted with permission from *Psychology Today* Magazine; **Table 8–1** Whiting, B. M., & Whiting, J. W. (1975). *Children of six countries: A psychological analysis.* Cambridge, MA: Harvard University Press. Copyright © the President and Fellows of Harvard College; **Table 8–3** Levine, R. V., Martinez, T. S., Brase, G., & Sorenson, K. (1994). Helping in 36 U.S. cities. *Journal of Personality and Social Psychology, 67,* 69–82. Copyright © 1994 by the American Psychological Association. Adapted with permission; **Cartoon** (p. 270) Copyright © 2000 Robert Mankoff cartoonbank.com. All rights reserved.

Chapter 9 Figure 9–1 Kay, S (1999, May 10). Violence/threats by U.S. students in the wake of the Columbine shootings. *Newsweek.* Copyright © 1999 by Newsweek, Inc. All rights reserved. Reprinted by permission; **Figure 9–2** Zillman, D. (1983). Transfer of excitation in emotional behavior. In J.T. Cacioppo & R.E. Petty (Eds.*),* *Social psychophysiology.* New York: Academic Press; **Figure 9–3 (a)** Reifman, A.S., Larrick, R.P., & Fein, S. (1991). Temper and temperature on the diamond:

The heat-aggression relationship in major league baseball. *Personality and Social Psychology Bulletin, 17,* 580–585. Copyright © 1991 by Sage Publications. Reprinted by permission of Sage Publications, Inc.; **Figure 9–3 (b)** Anderson, C. A., & Anderson, D. C. (1984). Ambient temperature and violent crime: Tests of the linear and curvilinear hypotheses. *Journal of Personality and Social Psychology, 46,* 91–97. Copyright © 1984 by the American Psychological Association. Adapted with permission; **Figure 9–4** Cohen, D., Nisbett, R. E., Bowdle, B. F., & Schwarz, N. (1996). Insult, aggression, and the southern culture of honor: An "experimental ethnography." *Journal of Personality and Social Psychology, 70,* 945–960. Copyright © 1996 by the American Psychological Association. Adapted with permission; **Figure 9–5** Used by permission from George Gerbner; **Figure 9–6** Fingerhut, L. A., & Kleinman, J. C. (1990). International and interstate comparisons of homicide among young males. *Journal of the American Medical Association, 263,* 3292–3295; **Table 9–1** Buss, A. H., & Durkee, A. (1957). An inventory for assessing different kinds of hostility. *Journal of Consulting Psychology, 21,* 343–349. Copyright © 1996 by the American Psychological Association. Adapted with permission.

Chapter 10 Figure 10–2 Newsweek-Princeton Survey Research. Copyright © 1995 by Newsweek, Inc. All rights reserved. Reprinted by permission; **Figure 10–4** Steele, C. M. (1988). The psychology of self-affirmation: Sustaining the integrity of the self. In L. Berkowitz (Ed.), *Social psychological studies of the self: Perspectives and programs* (pp. 261–302). San Diego, CA: Academic Press. Reprinted with permission. Academic Press, Inc.; **Figure 10–5** Ajzen, I. (1987). Attitudes, traits, and actions: Dispositional prediction of behavior in personality and social psychology. In L. Berkowitz (Ed.*),* *Advances in experimental social psychology.* (Vol. 20). San Diego: Academic Press. Reprinted with permission. Academic Press, Inc.; **Table 10–1** From Spence, J. T., Helmreich, R., & Stapp, J. (1973). A short version of the Attitude toward Women Scale (AWS). *Bulletin of the Psychonomic Society, 2,* 219–220. Reprinted by permission of Psychonomic Society, Inc. and *Journal of Criminal Justice, 13,* 373–379; **Table 10–1** Teske, R. H., & Hazlett, M. H (1985). *A scale for measurement of attitudes toward handgun control.* Copyright © 1985 with kind permission from Elsevier Science Ltd, The Boulevard, Langford Lane, Kidlington OX5 1GB, UK; **Cartoon** (p. 347) Copyright The New Yorker Collection © 1995. Edward Sorel from cartoonbank.com. All rights reserved.

Chapter 11 Figure 11–2 Pratkanis, A. R., Greenwald, A. G., Leippe, M. R., & Baumgardner, M. H. (1988). In search of reliable persuasion effects: III. The sleeper effect is dead: Long live the sleeper effect. *Journal of Personality and Social Psychology, 54,* 203–218. Copyright © 1988 by the American Psychological Association. Adapted with permission; **Figure 11–3** Kassin, S. M., Reddy,

M.E., & Tulloch, W. F. (1990). Juror interpretations of ambiguous evidence: The need for cognition, presentation, order, persuasion. *Law and Human Behavior, 14,* 43–55. Reprinted with permission of Plenum Publishing Corporation; **Figure 11–4** Mackie, D. M., & Worth, L. T. (1991). Feeling good, but not thinking straight: The impact of positive mood on persuasion. In J. Forgas (Ed.), *Emotion and social judgments.* Oxford, England: Pergamon Press; **Figure 11–5** Berger, D. (1986, January). Theory into practice: The FCB grid. *European Research,* 35–46. European Society for Opinion & Marketing Research; **Figure 11–6** Values and Lifestyles 2 system, VALS 2. SRI International, Menlo Park, California; **Figure 11–7** *American Demographics* (1996). Sabrena Qualitative Research Service (1996). Westport, CT; **Table 11–1** Video Storyboard Tests, Inc., 1997; **Table 11–2** Cacioppo, J. T., & Petty, R .E. (1982). The need for cognition. *Journal of Personality and Social Psychology, 42,* 116–131.

Chapter 12 Figure 12–3 Sherif, M. (1936). *The psychology of social norms.* New York: Harper; **Figure 12–4** Latané, B. (1981). The psychology of social impact. *American Psychologist, 36,* 343–356. Copyright © 1981 by the American Psychological Association. Adapted with permission; **Figure 12–6** Milgram, S. (1974*). Obedience to authority.* New York: Harper & Row; **Table 12–2** From Milgram, S. (1965). Some conditions of Obedience and Disobedience to Authority. *Human Relations, Vol. 18, No. 1,* p. 67. Permission granted by Alexandra Milgram.

Chapter 13 Figure 13–1 Cruse, D., & Leigh, B. C. (1987). 'Adam's Rib' revisited: Legal and non-legal influences on the processing of trial testimony. *Social Behavior, 2,* 221–230. Society for Personality Research; **Figure 13–2** Allport, G. W., & Postman, L. J. (1945). The basic psychology of rumor. *Transactions of the New York Academy of Sciences, 8* (Series II), 61–81; **Figure 13–3** Loftus, E. F., & Palmer, J. C. (1974). Reconstruction of automobile destruction: An example of the interface between language and memory. *Journal of Verbal Learning and Verbal Behavior, 13,* 585–589; **Table 13–1** Barber, J. D. (1992). Prediction as a test for hypothesis: Application to the psychology of presidents. *Political Psychology, 13,* 543–552. Reprinted by permission of Blackwell Publishers, Inc.; **Table 13–2** Henley, N. (1977). *Body politics: power, sex, and nonverbal communication.* Englewood Cliffs, NJ: Prentice-Hall.

Chapter 14 Figure 14–1 McKenna, K. Y. A., & Bargh, J. A. (1998). Coming out in the age of the Internet: Identity "demarginalization" through virtual group participation. *Journal of Personality and Social Psychology, 75,* 681–694. Copyright © 1998 by the American Psychological Association. Reprinted with permission; **Figure 14–3** Williams, K. D., Jackson, J. M., & Karau, S. J. (1995) In D. A. Schroeder (Ed*.), Social dilemmas: Perspectives on individuals and groups.* Praeger Publishers, an imprint of Greenwood Publishing Group, Inc., Westport, CT, 1995. Copyright © 1995 by D. A. Schroeder Reprinted with permission; **Figure 14–4** Hess, R. D., et al. (1986). Maternal expectations for mastery of developmental tasks in Japan and the United States. *International Journal of Psychology, 15,* 259–271. Reprinted by permission of the International Union of Psychological Science; **Figure 14–5** Forsyth, D. R. (Ed.) (1990). *Group Dynamics.* Copyright © 1990 by D. R. Forsyth. Reprinted by permission of Wadsworth, a division of Thomson Learning, fax 800-730-2215; **Figure 14–6** Janis, I. L., & Mann, L. (1977). Emergency decision making: A theoretical analysis of responses to disaster warnings. *Journal of Human Stress, 3,* 35–48. Published by Heldref Publications, 1319 Eighteenth St., N.W., Washington, DC 20036–1802.

Copyright © 1977; **Table 14–1** Hui, C. H. (1988). Measurement of individualism-collectivism. *Journal of Research in Personality, 22,* 17–36. Reprinted with permission of Academic Press, Inc.; **Table 14–2** Miller, C. E. (1989). The social psychological effects of group decision rules. In P.B. Paulhus (Ed.), *Psychology of group influence.* Hillsdale, NJ: Erlbaum; **Cartoon** (p. 482) Copyright © 2000 Charles Barsotti from cartoonbank.com. All rights reserved.

Chapter 15 Figure 15–1 Moreland, R. L., & Levine, J. M. (1982). Socialization in small groups: Temporal changes in individual-group relations. In L. Berkowitz (Ed*.), Advances in experimental social psychology.* (Vol. 15). NY: Academic Press. Reprinted with permission. Academic Press, Inc; **Figure 15–2** Paulus, P. B., McCain, G., & Cox, V. C. (1978). Death rates, psychiatric commitments, blood pressure, and perceived crowding as a function of institutional crowding. *Environmental Psychology and Nonverbal Behavior, 3,* 107–116. **Figure 15–3** Worchel, S., & Lollis, M. (1982). Reactions to territorial contamination as a function of culture. *Personality and Social Psychology Bulletin, 20,* 86–96. Copyright © 1982 by Sage Publications. Reprinted by permission of Sage Publications, Inc.; **Figure 15–4** Hayduk, L. A. (1978). Personal space: An evaluative and orienting overview. *Psychological Bulletin, 85,* 117–134. Copyright © 1978 by the American Psychological Association. Adapted with permission; **Table 15–1** Deal, T., & Kennedy, A. (1992). *Corporate Cultures.* Copyright © 1982 by Perseus Books. Reprinted by permission of Perseus Books. Table adapted from pages 107–127; **Table 15–2** Atchley, R. C. (1982). Retirement: Leaving the world of work. *Annals of the American Academy of Political and Social Science, 464,* 120–131. Copyright © 1982 by Sage Publications. Reprinted by permission of Sage Publications, Inc.; **Cartoon** (p. 501) Copyright © The New Yorker Collection 1993. Jack Ziegler from cartoonbank.com.

NAME INDEX

SUBJECT INDEX

$$
\begin{array}{r}
3 \\
4\,)\,128 \\
108 \\
42 \\
92 \\
40 \\
50 \\
48 \\
93 \\
86 \\
\hline
687
\end{array}
$$